P9-CLS-319

GREAT BRITAIN

36th Edition

Where to Stay and Eat
for All Budgets

Must-See Sights
and Local Secrets

Ratings You Can Trust

Fodor's Travel Publications   New York, Toronto, London, Sydney, Auckland
www.fodors.com

FODOR'S GREAT BRITAIN

Editor: Linda Cabasin

Editorial Production: Eric B. Wechter
Editorial Contributors: Robert Andrews, Ferne Arfin, Nick Bruno, Christi Daugherty, Adam Gold, Julius Honnor, Kate Hughes, Shona Main, Fiona Parrott, Roger Thomas, Alex Wijeratna
Maps: David Lindroth, *cartographer;* Rebecca Baer and Bob Blake, *map editors*
Design: Fabrizio La Rocca, *creative director;* Guido Caroti, *art director;* Melanie Marin, *senior picture editor*
Production/Manufacturing: Colleen Ziemba
Cover Photo (Punters along the Backs of the River Cam): Nik Wheeler

Thirty-sixth Edition

ISBN 978–1–4000–1688–4

ISSN 0071–6405

SPECIAL SALES

This book is available for special discounts for bulk purchases for sales promotions or premiums. Special editions, including personalized covers, excerpts of existing books, and corporate imprints, can be created in large quantities for special needs. For more information, write to Special Markets/Premium Sales, 1745 Broadway, MD 6-2, New York, NY 10019, or e-mail specialmarkets@randomhouse.com.

AN IMPORTANT TIP & AN INVITATION

Although all prices, opening times, and other details in this book are based on information supplied to us at press time, changes occur all the time in the travel world, and Fodor's cannot accept responsibility for facts that become outdated or for inadvertent errors or omissions. So **always confirm information when it matters,** especially if you're making a detour to visit a specific place. Your experiences—positive and negative—matter to us. If we have missed or misstated something, **please write to us.** We follow up on all suggestions. Contact the Great Britain editor at editors@fodors.com or c/o Fodor's at 1745 Broadway, New York, NY 10019.

PRINTED IN THE UNITED STATES OF AMERICA

10 9 8 7 6 5 4 3 2

Be a Fodor's Correspondent

Your opinion matters. It matters to us. It matters to your fellow Fodor's travelers, too. And we'd like to hear it. In fact, we *need* to hear it.

When you share your experiences and opinions, you become an active member of the Fodor's community. That means we'll not only use your feedback to make our books better, but we'll publish your names and comments whenever possible. Throughout our guides, look for "Word of Mouth," excerpts of your unvarnished feedback.

Here's how you can help improve Fodor's for all of us.

Tell us when we're right. We rely on local writers to give you an insider's perspective. But our writers and staff editors—who are the best in the business—depend on you. Your positive feedback is a vote to renew our recommendations for the next edition.

Tell us when we're wrong. We're proud that we update most of our guides every year. But we're not perfect. Things change. Hotels cut services. Museums change hours. Charming cafés lose charm. If our writer didn't quite capture the essence of a place, tell us how you'd do it differently. If any of our descriptions are inaccurate or inadequate, we'll incorporate your changes in the next edition and will correct factual errors at fodors.com *immediately.*

Tell us what to include. You probably have had fantastic travel experiences that aren't yet in Fodor's. Why not share them with a community of like-minded travelers? Maybe you chanced upon a pub or B&B that you don't want to keep to yourself. Tell us why we should include it. And share your discoveries and experiences with everyone directly at fodors.com. Your input may lead us to add a new listing or highlight a place we cover with a "Highly Recommended" star or with our highest rating, "Fodor's Choice."

Give us your opinion instantly at our feedback center at www.fodors.com/feedback. You may also e-mail editors@fodors.com with the subject line "Great Britain Editor." Or send your nominations, comments, and complaints by mail to Great Britain Editor, Fodor's, 1745 Broadway, New York, NY 10019.

You and travelers like you are the heart of the Fodor's community. Make our community richer by sharing your experiences. Be a Fodor's correspondent.

Happy traveling!

Tim Jarrell, Publisher

CONTENTS

CONTENTS

ABOUT THIS BOOK

Our Ratings

Sometimes you find terrific travel experiences and sometimes they just find you. But usually the burden is on you to select the right combination of experiences. That's where our ratings come in.

As travelers we've all discovered a place so wonderful that its worthiness is obvious. And sometimes superlatives don't do that place justice: you just have to be there to know. These sights, properties, and experiences get our highest rating, **Fodor's Choice**, indicated by orange stars throughout this book.

Black stars highlight sights and properties we deem **Highly Recommended**, places that our writers, editors, and readers praise again and again for consistency and excellence.

There's another category: any place we include in this book is by definition worth your time, unless we say otherwise. And we will.

Disagree with any of our choices? Care to nominate a place or suggest that we rate one more highly? Visit our feedback center at www.fodors.com/feedback.

Budget Well

Hotel and restaurant price categories from £ to £££££ are defined in the opening pages of each chapter. For attractions, we always give standard adult admission fees; reductions are usually available for children, students, and senior citizens. Want to pay with plastic? **AE, DC, MC, V** following restaurant and hotel listings indicate if American Express, Diner's Club, MasterCard, and Visa are accepted.

Restaurants

Unless we state otherwise, restaurants are open for lunch and dinner daily. We mention dress only when there's a specific requirement and reservations only when they're essential or not accepted—it's always best to book ahead.

Hotels

Hotels have private bath, phone, TV, and air-conditioning and operate on the European Plan (aka EP, meaning without meals), unless we specify that they use the Continental Plan (CP, with a continental breakfast), Breakfast Plan (BP, with a full breakfast), or Modified American Plan (MAP, with breakfast and dinner). We always list fa-

cilities but not whether you'll be charged an extra fee to use them, so when pricing accommodations, find out what's included.

Many Listings
- ★ Fodor's Choice
- ★ Highly recommended
- ⊠ Physical address
- ✛ Directions
- ⌀ Mailing address
- ☎ Telephone
- 🖷 Fax
- ⊕ On the Web
- ✉ E-mail
- 🎫 Admission fee
- ☉ Open/closed times
- Ⓤ Underground (Tube)
- ▭ Credit cards

Hotels & Restaurants
- 🏨 Hotel
- 🛏 Number of rooms
- ♨ Facilities
- 🍽 Meal plans
- ✕ Restaurant
- ⌢ Reservations
- 🏛 Dress code
- ↘ Smoking
- ⸮ BYOB
- ✕🏨 Hotel with restaurant that warrants a visit

Outdoors
- ⛳ Golf

Other
- ℭ Family-friendly
- 🛈 Contact information
- ⇨ See also
- ⊠ Branch address
- ☞ Take note

WHEN TO GO

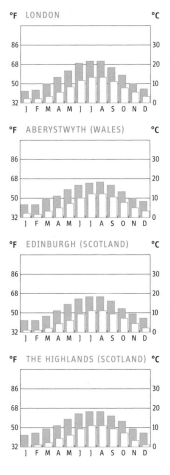

The British tourist season is year-round—with short lulls. It peaks from mid-April to mid-October, with another burst at Christmas (although many historic houses close from October to Easter). The countryside is greenest in spring, whereas in fall the northern moorlands and Scottish Highlands are at their most colorful. June is a good month to visit Wales and the Lake District. During July and August, when most of the British take vacations, accommodations in popular resorts and areas are in high demand and at their most expensive. The shoulder seasons of May and June, and September and October, can be less crowded, though more people seem to be traveling during these months. This said, Edinburgh festival time in August, when up to six major arts festivals are under way, is thrilling—the highlight of many a trip. The winter cultural season in London is lively, with opera, ballet, and theater among the prime attractions. Hotel rates are lower in winter, too, making up for the often gray skies. Museums and sights can be busy during school vacations called half-terms: these are generally the third week in October, the last week of December and first week of January, the third week of February, the last week of March, and the first week of June.

Climate

Generally, the climate in England and Wales is mild, though the weather has been volatile in recent years. Summer temperatures can reach the 90s and the atmosphere can be humid. In winter there can be heavy frost, snow, thick fog, and, of course, plenty of the rain for which Britain is well known. In Scotland, you can be unlucky and spend a summer week under low clouds and drizzle. Generally Scotland is three or four degrees cooler than southern England, and the east is drier and colder than the west. Winter days in Scotland are very short; they can be cold and dreary or filled with brilliant light.

🔝 Forecasts **Weather Channel** (⊕ www.weather.com).

WHAT'S WHERE

Great Britain and the United Kingdom—what's the difference? Great Britain includes England, Wales, and Scotland. In fact these are three countries; Wales and Scotland have their own parliaments, with different degrees of self-government. Add Northern Ireland, and you have the political entity known as the United Kingdom, with London as its capital.

LONDON

The heart and soul of modern Britain, London is not just the nation's financial and governmental center but one of the world's great capitals. Because of that, you already know some of what to expect—mammoth museums, posh palaces, double-decker buses, iconic sights such as Big Ben and Westminster Abbey—and you won't be disappointed. But it's impossible to overlook the modern city melded with the historic one, and there are more harried commuters, noisy traffic, endless litter, and petty crime than you might expect. This is a great, rambling metropolis, and for all London's faults and high costs, the atmosphere is undeniably exhilarating, created by the presence of so many theaters, universities, powerhouse corporations, and a vast multinational population in excess of 8 million people, all scattered among villagelike neighborhoods with distinct personalities. Leicester Square is packed with tourists; Knightsbridge is populated by millionaires; Bloomsbury is filled with intellectuals, and on Fleet Street you can't swing a briefcase without hitting a lawyer. London is big, overwhelming, and cacophonous—just as it should be.

THE SOUTHEAST

The place where William the Conqueror first set foot when he arrived from France to claim the nation and build strongholds all over England, this compact green and pleasant region southeast of London stretches out to the coast. For Londoners, the area can seem like one big suburb, but for you it's much more than that. There's funky Brighton by the sea, with its artsy vibe, good dining, and legendary nightlife scene, all of which are largely incongruous for an area that otherwise too often languishes in the grip of chain restaurants and small, rural pubs. Still, who needs to eat when there's so much to do? You could be wandering through the medieval castles of Bodiam, Leeds, and Hever; pondering the fate of Thomas à Becket at Canterbury Cathedral; or getting gardening tips at Sissinghurst and other noted beauty spots. Around

Tunbridge Wells is a cluster of historic homes, from medieval Ightham Mote to Elizabethan Penshurst Place. It's so close to London that much of the area is day-trip material.

THE SOUTH

Here, in the counties of Hampshire, Dorset, and Wiltshire, begins the quintessential English countryside of gentle hills, green pastures, small towns, and peace and quiet. Jane Austen and Thomas Hardy are among the writers who found inspiration here, and literary pilgrims follow in their footsteps. Portsmouth, one of the few cities of any size, is largely uninspiring except for some great museums such as the Portsmouth Historic Dockyard; don't come to the South if you're looking for an urban scene. Instead, wonder at the mysterious stone circles of Avebury and Stonehenge, and take in the bustling towns of Winchester and Salisbury, with their imposing cathedrals. Out in the countryside, grand manors—such as Stourhead, Wilton House, and Longleat with its safari park—offer imposing evidence of the ambitions of their builders. At the area's southernmost edge, the rolling hills turn into the flat seaside landscape of Dorset, packed with Britons on holiday in the summertime, and the fossil-rich Jurassic Coast.

THE WEST COUNTRY

In poll after poll, the southwestern peninsula counties of Somerset, Devon, and Cornwall are where most Britons say they would like to live. It's easy to see why: ocean currents keep the area sunnier and warmer than the rest of the country (the Eden Project and other gardens take advantage of this climate), and many of the beaches are sandy, rather than rocky. The waves bring in the surfers, and with them comes a distinctly un-English, no-worries lifestyle, particularly in Cornwall, with its artsy coastal villages. Miles of quiet countryside are dotted with only a few pretty towns, including Wells, Exeter, and Bath, one of the most popular towns for travelers. Bath is actually a grand Georgian town, with visible Roman history in the ruins of the mineral-spring baths, glorious 18th- and 19th-century architecture created with the local stone, and some good places to eat. The vibrant city of Bristol has modern restaurants and exciting nightlife, which much of the rest of the region lacks. Beyond the towns, the green hills and the brooding heaths and moors of Exmoor and Dartmoor, punctuated with enigmatic stone circles and rocky outcroppings, attract hikers and horseback riders.

WHAT'S WHERE

OXFORD & THE THAMES VALLEY	The Thames Valley is bedroom-community central for Londoners, with the home-improvement stores, giant supermarkets, and real-estate agencies that come with that territory, but this is England, so the suburbs include medieval towns like Windsor, where, alongside hordes of commoners, the Queen also spends most of her time (she doesn't much like Buckingham Palace, they say). Then there are the soaring golden spires of Oxford, which can be seen for miles in the flat countryside around that busy but lovely university town with its small rivers, excellent pubs, and bookish locals. Given the beauty of the landscape and its proximity to London, the area is a popular weekend escape, with good restaurants and prices to match. It's unsurprising, too, that there are plenty of stately homes, so you can explore the lives of the rich and famous at places like the over-the-top baroque Blenheim Palace.
THE COTSWOLDS & SHAKESPEARE COUNTRY	Pretty as a picture, the famous Cotswolds region is a small gem filled with tranquil villages, adorable golden stone cottages with neat-as-a-pin gardens, dignified churches, posh antiques shops, and salt-of-the-earth country folk keeping it all preserved in aspic. It's beautiful, but it may come to look somewhat the same: the perfect villages—Chipping Campden, Upper Slaughter, Bourton-on-the-Water—can blur together once you've soaked up all the tea and scones you've ever wanted. Beyond the obvious sights are treasures including Hidcote Manor Gardens, Snowshill Manor, and Chastleton House. Just north of the Cotswolds (and about 100 mi from London) is Stratford-upon-Avon, a leafy, literary, theatrical town. It's worth braving the tour groups and souvenir shops, particularly for anyone who loves Shakespeare. You can wander through Shakespeare's birthplace, catch his plays at the Royal Shakespeare Theatre, drink in Shakespeare-theme pubs . . . it never seems to end. Escape, after a while, to Warwickshire, to see gentle landscape and battlemented Warwick Castle.
THE NORTHWEST	Here are two of England's biggest, grittiest cities, which have fans as well as detractors, but are not at the top of many visitors' lists. The Northwest also has some glorious, well-known countryside and stately homes, making for two very different experiences. Liverpool still rides the coattails of the Beatles but may be breaking free a bit, since, like nearby Manchester, it has transformed some of its old docks and warehouses into interesting museums, modern malls, sleek hotels, restaurants,

and condominiums. Both cities are known for buzzing nightlife, and their restaurant scenes are steadily improving, although this is still not a culinary center. In contrast, to the east are the vistas, both gentle and rugged, of the Peak District. Walkers and hikers can spend days going from village to village; Chatsworth and Haddon Hall, famous houses but very different from each other, are an additional draw. Also in the region are Chester (close to Liverpool), with its medieval walls and black-and-white half-timber buildings and the the worthwhile Industrial Revolution museums of Ironbridge Gorge.

THE LAKE DISTRICT

Bordered by Scotland and the waters of Solway Firth, Morecambe Bay, and the Irish Sea, this is a startlingly beautiful area of craggy hills, wild moorland, stone cottages, and glittering silvery lakes. As you go north, the scenery becomes even more dramatic, so pick your route accordingly. The Lake District, now a national park, has drawn seekers of beauty since 19th-century poets and writers including William Wordsworth first made it famous. The area's enormous popularity with nature lovers and hikers means that you must head off the map to avoid crowds in summer; Windermere in particular can be overly busy. Still, it's the kind of place where you will chase sheep out of the road at some point, and that's part of its draw, along with literary links. High points are Wordsworth's homes at Rydal and Grasmere, John Ruskin's abode at Coniston, and Beatrix Potter's tiny house near Hawkshead. Just don't expect sunshine—on average it rains 250 days each year.

CAMBRIDGE & EAST ANGLIA

Parts of this rural, generally flat region (some find it boring) are becoming far-flung outposts of London, as city types head north to Suffolk and Norfolk for homes and weekend retreats. For visitors, the biggest lure remains Cambridge, a possible daytrip from London. You can hire a boat and go punting on the River Cam—the students will tease you if you struggle—after you explore the medieval halls of learning and such marvels as King's College Chapel. Out in the countryside are Ely's glorious cathedral and time-warp towns such as Bury St. Edmunds and Tudor Lavenham. For something different, check out Orford and Aldeburgh on the coast. Visiting Londoners have encouraged the growth of quality gastro-pubs and restaurants, so you can feed your stomach as well as your eyes when you explore the peaceful Suffolk vistas immortalized by Gainsborough and Constable.

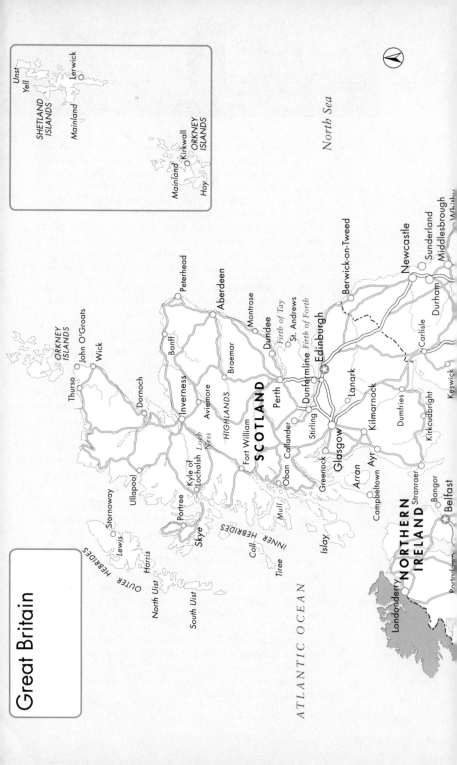

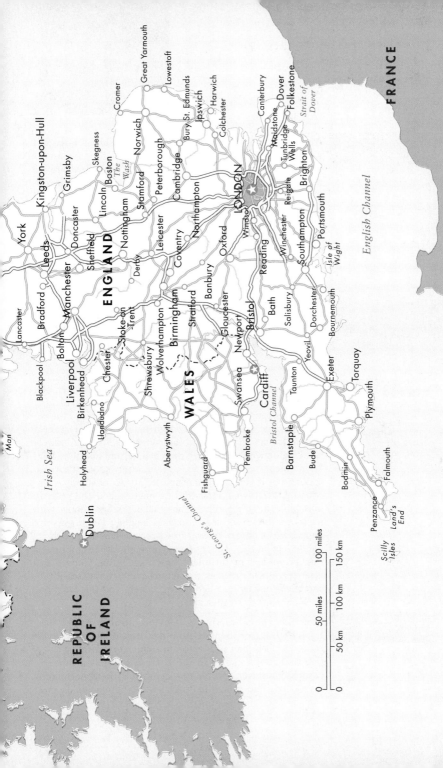

WHAT'S WHERE

YORKSHIRE & THE NORTHEAST	A wilder part of England in the north, Yorkshire is large and varied, with more appeal for lovers of the outdoors than for urban sophisticates. On the landlocked side of Yorkshire are the moors and dales that inspired the Brontë sisters and continue to delight walkers. The ancient walled city of York, with magnificent Gothic York Minster, is deservedly prime tourist territory; don't miss nearby Castle Howard, one of Britain's finest stately homes. Rievaulx Abbey (Yorkshire has superb monastic remains) is also worth seeing. The Northeast region that borders Scotland is wild and empty, with spectacular countryside. This is relatively unvisited country, except for a few key sites, but some people find the remoteness appealing. With its stone cathedral, Durham is a popular, perfectly preserved medieval city. You can walk or bike in the footsteps of Roman soldiers along the sturdy length of Hadrian's Wall. Slightly younger, but still old and awesome, are the castles that stand guard on the stark Northumberland coastline, including Bamburgh and Dunstanburgh.
WALES	Clinging to the western edge of England, Wales is green and ruggedly beautiful, with mountainous inland scenery reaching out to a magnificent coastline. With the exception of the engaging capital, Cardiff, and the tough, industrial city of Swansea (where Dylan Thomas lived and wrote), this is an entirely rural region with more sheep than people, and one more low-key and less visited except for certain beauty spots. It's worth seeking out if you appreciate subtler attractions such as bucolic market towns, industrial heritage sights, and country inns. Wales has three stunning national parks: Snowdonia, with its footpath-beribboned mountain heights; Pembrokeshire Coast, with ocean views; and Brecon Beacons, with its windswept heights. The country is properly famous for its castles, reminders of turbulent times, including Conwy and Caernarfon. On the coast are picturesque Victorian seaside resort towns including Aberystwyth, where you can catch one of Wales's noted steam trains.
EDINBURGH & THE LOTHIANS	Scotland's capital captivates many people at first sight, with Edinburgh Castle looming from the crags of an ancient volcano, and Georgian and Victorian architecture forming a skyline that looks locked in the past. But this is a modern, cosmopolitan city, and the new Scottish Parliament Building says so loud and clear. Edinburgh has everything you'd expect

from a capital and should not be missed: numerous iconic sights (even more than Glasgow, its rival 50 miles to the west, offers), lovely cobbled streets, and plenty of first-class restaurants. However, lodging, food, and even pub prices are high; there's a lot of traffic and too many tourists, particularly in August during the Edinburgh International Festival. The Lothians—West Lothian, East Lothian, and Midlothian—beckon Edinburghers as well as visitors with quick getaways to coastal towns, quiet beaches, ancient chapels (including Rosslyn Chapel, mentioned in *The Da Vinci Code*), and castles.

GLASGOW

In Gaelic, Glasgow means "the Dear Green Place," a fitting title for the city with more parks per square mile than any other in Europe. The city has changed dramatically over the years, from prosperous Victorian hub to depressed urban area. Today a re-energized Glasgow is thriving, famous for its passion for football (soccer) and stylish shops that beat those in Edinburgh hands-down. Its distinguished university is over 500 years old and worth a visit, as are Kelvingrove Park and the stunning Kelvingrove Art Gallery. Glasgow is proud of its buildings by two great homegrown architects, Charles Rennie Mackintosh and Alexander Thomson. Trendy cafés and well-preserved pubs, some with live music, are a refuge for those interested in more local, thirst-quenching activities. Yes, the city has some rough patches, but major cleanup efforts have been made. True, you're guaranteed rain, but you don't have to worry about armies of tourists in Scotland's largest and friendliest city.

THE BORDERS & THE SOUTHWEST

Gateway to Scotland, the Borders and Southwest are rustic; not a lot happens here, and they aren't the top tourist destinations—but that's not necessarily a bad thing. The Borders, site of past conflict between Scotland and England, is known for being the home of Sir Walter Scott, the 19th-century author of *Ivanhoe*. It's also Scotland's main woolen-goods district; if you want a warm sweater or scarf, this is the place to come. The countryside is made up of great rolling fields, wooded river valleys, and farmland running south from Lothian to England. People interested in walking, stately homes, and magnificent, ruined abbeys tend to spend their vacations here. The Southwest, or Dumfries and Galloway region, is perfect for scenic drives and castles. It's on the shores of the Solway Firth where palm trees and other exotic fauna thrive due to the North Atlantic Drift (Scotland's Gulf Stream). Inland

WHAT'S WHERE

the landscape transforms to a darker scene where moorlands lie blanketed in thick forests.

THE CENTRAL HIGHLANDS, FIFE & ANGUS

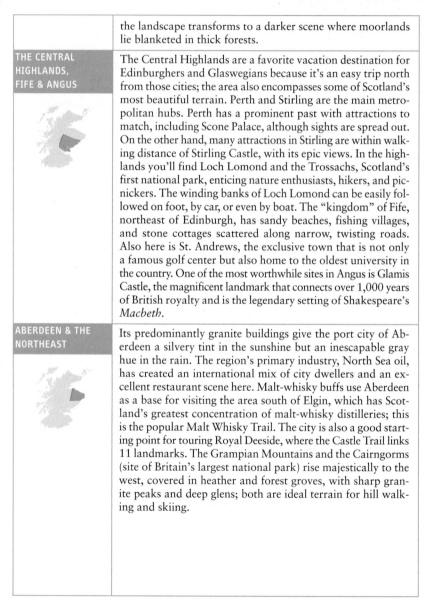

The Central Highlands are a favorite vacation destination for Edinburghers and Glaswegians because it's an easy trip north from those cities; the area also encompasses some of Scotland's most beautiful terrain. Perth and Stirling are the main metropolitan hubs. Perth has a prominent past with attractions to match, including Scone Palace, although sights are spread out. On the other hand, many attractions in Stirling are within walking distance of Stirling Castle, with its epic views. In the highlands you'll find Loch Lomond and the Trossachs, Scotland's first national park, enticing nature enthusiasts, hikers, and picnickers. The winding banks of Loch Lomond can be easily followed on foot, by car, or even by boat. The "kingdom" of Fife, northeast of Edinburgh, has sandy beaches, fishing villages, and stone cottages scattered along narrow, twisting roads. Also here is St. Andrews, the exclusive town that is not only a famous golf center but also home to the oldest university in the country. One of the most worthwhile sites in Angus is Glamis Castle, the magnificent landmark that connects over 1,000 years of British royalty and is the legendary setting of Shakespeare's *Macbeth*.

ABERDEEN & THE NORTHEAST

Its predominantly granite buildings give the port city of Aberdeen a silvery tint in the sunshine but an inescapable gray hue in the rain. The region's primary industry, North Sea oil, has created an international mix of city dwellers and an excellent restaurant scene here. Malt-whisky buffs use Aberdeen as a base for visiting the area south of Elgin, which has Scotland's greatest concentration of malt-whisky distilleries; this is the popular Malt Whisky Trail. The city is also a good starting point for touring Royal Deeside, where the Castle Trail links 11 landmarks. The Grampian Mountains and the Cairngorms (site of Britain's largest national park) rise majestically to the west, covered in heather and forest groves, with sharp granite peaks and deep glens; both are ideal terrain for hill walking and skiing.

ARGYLL & THE ISLES	Although this fractured southwestern coastline is one of Scotland's less-visited areas, it has an excellent selection of gardens and religious sites to choose from. To experience the region in full, you need to catch a ferry to Mull and the southern isles; the adorable town of Oban, a great place for a fish-and-chips supper, is where you catch these ferries. If you like whisky, go to Islay; if it's mountains your after, then Jura is a better bet; if the most important Christian site in the country strikes a chord, make Iona your destination. If you want to see all of Scotland's diversity shrunk down to a smaller, more manageable size, Arran is the place to go. The area does catch rain from Atlantic weather systems, but its beauty makes the wetness worthwhile.
THE GREAT GLEN, NORTHERN HIGHLANDS & SKYE	An awe-inspiring valley laced with rivers and streams defines the Great Glen, which is ringed by Scotland's tallest mountains. It also contains, perhaps, the monster Nessie, who resides in murky Loch Ness. Nearby Inverness—a town useful mostly as a base for exploring the area—encourages the hype. There are prettier lochs in Scotland, but Loch Ness draws the crowds. Mountaineers and naturalists are drawn to the Great Glen because of Ben Nevis, Britain's tallest mountain. It deserves some of your time, even if you don't plan on climbing it. At its base is Fort William, a town worth stopping in only for supplies. Those interested in Scottish history should head to Glencoe, the haunting location where in 1692 MacDonald clan members were massacred by the Campbell clan, or to Culloden, where Bonnie Prince Charlie's forces were destroyed in 1746. To many Scots, the Northern Highlands are the real Scotland—the land of the lore of clans, big moody skies, and wild rolling moors. It's home to one of Scotland's most picturesque castles, Eilean Donan, which you pass on the way to the Isle of Skye. Don't let the tour buses stop you; the castle deserves a visit. Skye is ideal for moderate walks and has remote beaches and misty mountains.

QUINTESSENTIAL GREAT BRITAIN

Pints & Pubs

Pop in for a pint at a pub to encounter what has been the center—literally the "public house"—of British social life for centuries. The basic pub recipe calls for a variety of beers on draft—dark creamy stouts like Guinness; bitter, including brews such as Tetley's and Bass; and lager, the blondest and blandest of the trio—a dart board, oak paneling, and paisley carpets. Throw in a bunch of young suits in the big cities, a generous dash of undergrads in places such as Oxford or Cambridge, and, in rural areas, a healthy helping of blokes around the television and ladies in the corner sipping their *halves* (half pints) and having a *natter* (gossip). In smaller pubs, listen in and enjoy the banter among the regulars—you may even be privy to the occasional *barney* (harmless argument). Join in if you care to, but remember not to take anything too seriously—a severe breach of pub etiquette. Make your visit soon: the encroachment of gastro-pubs (an ever-expanding variety of bar-restaurant hybrids) is just one of the forces challenging traditional pub culture.

Daily Rags

To blend in with the British, stash your street map, slide a folded newspaper under your arm, and head for the nearest park bench or café. Lose yourself in any one of the 11 national dailies, some now being published in tabloid size, for often well-written insight into Britain's worldview. For a dose of tabloid melodrama, choose the *Sun,* the country's most popular newspaper. The sensational headlines are hard to miss— "Prince's Cheating Scandal" and "Empire Strikes Bark: Dogs Dress Up as Vader"— and you can safely assume that the topless model on Page 3 has helped rather than hindered the paper's success. The biweekly *Private Eye* offers British wit at its best, specializing in political cartoons, punchy parodies, and satirical reporting.

If you want to get a sense of contemporary British culture, and indulge in some of its pleasures, start by familiarizing yourself with the rituals of daily life. Here are a few highlights—things you can take part in with relative ease.

A Lovely Cuppa

For almost four centuries, the British and tea have been immersed in a love affair passionate enough to survive revolutions, rations, tariffs, and lattes, but also soothing, as whistling kettles across the nation mark moments of quiet comfort in public places and in homes and offices. The ritual known as "afternoon tea" had its beginnings in the early 19th century, in the private chambers of the duchess of Bedford, where she and her "ladies of leisure" indulged in afternoons of pastries and fragrant blends. But you don't need to dress up to lift your pinky to sip the steamy brew. Department stores and tearooms across the nation offer everything from simple tea and biscuits to shockingly overpriced spreads with sandwiches and cakes that would impress even the duchess herself. And if tea is not your cup of tea, don't worry; there's no shame for those who prefer coffee with their scones and clotted cream.

Sports Fever

Whoever says Britain is not an overtly religious country has failed to consider the cult of sports mania that has descended on the land. Whether water events (such as Henley and the Head of the River Race) or a land competition (a soccer game anywhere, the Flora London Marathon), most bring people to the edge of their seats—or more often the living room couch, thanks to satellite television. To partake in the rite, you'll need Pimm's (*the* drink for swank spectators of the Henley Royal Regatta) or beer (*the* drink for most everything else). You may experience the exhilaration yourself—which, you'll probably sense, is not for the love of a sport, but for the love of *sport* itself.

IF YOU LIKE

Castles & Stately Homes

Exploring the diversity and magnificence of Britain's castles and stately homes, from Norman towers to Palladian palaces, can occupy most of a blissful vacation. Whether world-famous or less-visited, owned by royalty, aristocratic families, or the National Trust, each abode has tales to tell about history or domestic life. Castles and houses are spread around the nation (with fewer stately homes in Cornwall, the Lake District, and Wales), but certain clusters may help your planning. Note that most stately homes are open only from spring through fall. England's southeastern coast is lined with sturdy castles; nearby but inland, around Royal Tunbridge Wells, are treasure-stuffed piles (as stately homes are known) such as Hever Castle and Knole. West of Salisbury are Wilton House, Stourhead, and Longleat, and the Cotswolds have a rich assortment. Wales, unmissable for castle lovers, has Edward I's "iron ring," including Harlech and Conwy. Scotland has Georgian and Victorian masterpieces, and famous fortresses in areas such as the Borders and Royal Deeside. London visitors won't miss out, either: Buckingham and Kensington palaces, the Tower of London, Hampton Court Palace, and Windsor Castle lie within easy reach.

- **Blenheim Palace, Thames Valley.** A baroque extravaganza touted as England's only rival to Versailles, this pile is the home of the 11th duke of Marlborough.

- **Edinburgh Castle, Scotland.** This commanding stone fortification is Scotland's symbolic heart.

- **Petworth House, the Southeast.** One of the National Trust's greatest treasure houses shows off magnificent art from Gainsborough and J. M. W. Turner.

Charming Villages

Year after year, armies of tourists with images of green meadows, thatched or tile roofs, and colorful flowerbeds flock to Britain's countryside, for good reason. Most will find their way to famously adorable towns along the Thames, magical seaside resorts in the West Country, and a smattering of fairy-tale hamlets in the Cotswolds—a hilly area in west-central England renowned for its golden and gray stone cottages. However, torrential tourist traffic has made these once-quintessentially quaint areas a little *too* accessible for some. Steer clear of busy Cotswolds towns such as Broadway in summer (especially on weekends); Snowshill is a more unspoiled option. Choose a weekday to visit the Thames Valley towns, which attract Londoners. To avoid some crowds, consider the pastoral flatlands of East Anglia beyond Cambridge, where historic villages remain relatively undiscovered. Wales, with its mountainside hamlets and sleepy seaside resorts, is another option. In Scotland, you can unwind in the Borders towns or seek quieter havens on islands such as Arran and Islay.

- **Crail, Central Highlands, Fife & Angus.** Set on the North Sea, this village has distinctive, Dutch-influenced architecture.

- **Lavenham, East Anglia.** This village is full of perfectly preserved Tudor buildings, the former houses of wool merchants and weavers.

- **Portmeirion, Wales.** A fantasy-Italianate village, complete with town hall and grand hotel, is quite un-Welsh but totally charming.

Glorious Gardens

Despite being cursed with impertinent weather and short summers, British gardeners will gladly grab a gardening tool and attack a misbehaving rose garden for just a few short months of enjoyment. The Tudors were the first to produce gardens that were more than strictly utilitarian, and since then French, Italian, Dutch, and even Japanese ideas have been imported and adapted to suit the national aesthetic. A pilgrimage to a garden is an essential part of any spring or summer trip, whether you visit a large educational garden such as Kew Gardens near London; a period gem such as Arts-and-Crafts Hidcote Manor in the Cotswolds; or gardens that are part of a stately home and as lovely as the house. Green havens thrive all over the country, but perhaps the most fertile hunting grounds are in Oxfordshire, Gloucestershire (including the Cotswolds), and Kent (the "Garden of England"). Some of these visions of paradise have limited hours, and most close in winter; they're all worth the trip.

- **Sissinghurst Castle Garden, Southeast.** Vita Sackville-West's masterpiece, set within the remains of a Tudor castle, is busy in summer but also spectacular in autumn.

- **Stourhead, South.** One of the country's most impressive house-and-garden combinations is an artful 18th-century sanctuary with a tranquil lake, colorful shrubs, and grottoes.

- **Eden Project, West Country.** A former china pit now showcases spectacular conservatories in geodesic domes as well as sprawling outdoor gardens that emphasize conservation; the result is inspirational.

Urban Action

London has everything a world capital should have—rich culture and history, thrilling art and theater scenes, world-class restaurants, and sensational shopping—along with crowds, traffic, and high prices. Edinburgh, with its old castle and new Parliament, is very popular but can get packed in summer. These two shouldn't be missed, but if you appreciate modern cities, fall out of the tourist trap and spend time in some of Britain's reviving urban centers, including those in its former industrial heartland, where blossoming multiculturalism has paved the way for a unique vibe. Football (soccer) fans might take in a match in Manchester or Liverpool, two bitter sporting rivals in the Northwest, or join hordes of fans to watch the game at a local pub. Manchester's museums are excellent, and its downtown is worth a look, as are its famous clubs. Liverpool claims the Beatles sites but also the stellar museums of the Albert Dock; it's transforming itself for a stint as the European Union's Capital of Culture in 2008. In Wales, see what's gentrifying in Cardiff and the reborn Cardiff Bay area.

- **Brighton, Southeast.** Bold, bright, and boisterous are the words to describe a seaside charmer that has everything from the dazzling Royal Pavilion to the trendy shops of the Lanes.

- **Bristol, West Country.** With its lively waterfront and homegrown music talent, this youthful city has vibrant nightlife as well as a long history.

- **Glasgow, Scotland.** Another former industrial city is polishing its Victorian buildings and artistic treasures; the shopping and nightlife scenes really buzz.

Ancient Mysteries

Stone circles as well as ancient stone and earthen forts and mounds offer tantalizing hints about Britain's mysterious prehistoric inhabitants. England's southwestern landscape, particularly the Salisbury Plain, Dorset, and the eastern side of Cornwall, has a notably rich concentration of these sites, perplexing mysteries that human nature compels us to try to solve. Stonehenge, the stone circle begun 5,000 years ago, stands on the wide Salisbury Plain; crowds detract from the magic, so arrive early or late to appreciate the monument's timeless power. Hypotheses about its purpose range from the scientific (ancient calendar) to the fantastic (a gift from extinct giants). Other relics dot the Avebury area to the north. These include, beside the Avebury Stone Circles, the West Kennett Long Barrow, a chambered tomb, and Silbury Hill, a 130-foot man-made mound. Equally enigmatic are Maiden Castle, a colossal prehistoric hill fort near Dorchester, and the nearby figure of a giant carved into the hillside overlooking Cerne Abbas. The most impressive of the many ancient sites in Scotland are on its far-flung islands; Arran is one of the more accessible.

- **Avebury Stone Circles, South.** Large and marvelously evocative, these circles surround part of the village of Avebury; stop at the Alexander Keiller Museum to learn about the site.

- **Castlerigg Stone Circle, Lake District.** Ringed by mountains, these stones have a setting that is as awesome as the surviving remains.

- **Machrie Moor Stone Circles, Argyll & the Isles.** The isle of Arran has the marvelous Machrie Moor Stone Circles, with granite boulders and red sandstone circles.

Wonderful Walks

Britain seems to be designed with walking in mind—footpaths wind through the contours of the landscape, and popular routes are well-endowed with cozy bed-and-breakfasts and pubs. Your decisions will be what kind of landscape you prefer (coast or countryside, flat or mountainous) and how long a hike you want, though you can often do just part of a long-distance trail such as the Thames Path. Ramble through one of the country's national parks (which are sprinkled with towns), and you'll generally find well-maintained trails and handy maps at local tourist information centers. Some of England's most famous walking spots are in the Lake District, from a short meander to a major mountain trek—but beware of summer congestion. Yorkshire's dales and moors are also popular. Cross the border to Wales, where the ferocious peaks in Snowdonia National Park promise challenging hikes. Scotland has everything from low-lying glens to huge mountains; the Borders area has some easier hikes, but long-distance Highland walks are always demanding. Wherever you hike, always be prepared for storms or fogs.

- **Brecon Beacons National Park, Wales.** A short drive north of Cardiff, this park has high, grassy mountains, lakes, and craggy limestone gorges; there are both easy and challenging paths.

- **Glen Nevis, Great Glen, Northern Highlands & Skye.** Here some lovely but moderate hikes lead past waterfalls, croft ruins, and forested gorges.

- **South West Coast Path, West Country.** Spectacular is the word for the 630-mi trail that winds from Minehead in Somerset to Poole Harbour in Dorset.

Theater

There's no better antidote to an overdose of castles, museums, and gardens than a face-to-face encounter with another British specialty, the theater. London is the heart and soul of the action: here, companies famous and lesser-known consistently churn out superb productions, from musicals and monologues to comedies and avant-garde dramas. Be sure to sample theater outside London, wherever you travel. Stratford-upon-Avon may be the Bard's hometown, but festivals all over the country celebrate Shakespeare's work; one of the best is London's Shakespeare Under the Stars in Regent's Park. Around Christmas, Windsor's Theatre Royal specializes in pantomime—theatrical entertainment with puppetry, slapstick, and music. Glasgow is Scotland's major arts center, with many excellent choices: the Tron Theatre focuses on contemporary plays, and the Citizens' Theatre likes to push the edge. Theatrical arts are often a major component of British festivals: you can see musicals at the Exeter Festival (West Country) and street theater at the Edinburgh Finge. Try a university production; you may see the next big star.

- **Edinburgh International Festival, Edinburgh & the Lothians.** Watch stellar dramatic performances at this summer arts festival, or take in some shows at the more adventurous Fringe festival.

- **Minack Theatre, West Country.** This open-air theater in coastal Cornwall, near Land's End and Penzance, nuzzles the slope of a sandy cliff against the backdrop of the sparkling blue sea.

- **Royal Shakespeare Theatre, Shakespeare Country.** Seeing any play by the Bard performed in his hometown is an unforgettable theatrical experience.

Country-House Hotels

In all their luxurious glory, country-house hotels are an essential part of the British landscape, particularly in the southern part of the country. Whether you choose a converted castle, a baronial manor, or an neoclassical retreat, these are places to indulge yourself and escape, however briefly (many are pricey), most realities of modern life. Some hotels are traditional in style, with flowery fabrics; a newer breed juxtaposes modern design with the traditional architecture. At some hotels, spas and sports—and even meeting facilities—are becoming more elaborate, but service is less stuffy. Consider just having dinner; notable chefs are turning up in more hotel kitchens. The West Country's concentration includes Bovey Castle and Gidleigh Park in Dartmoor, and the Cotswolds are prime ground for these retreats. Also consider the smaller hotels in Wales, where pampering often comes with a lower price tag and a more intimate atmosphere. ■ TIP➔ **Before you reserve, ask if a wedding party will be using the hotel during your stay; these can take over a smaller establishment.**

- **Ballachulish House, Great Glen, Northern Highlands & Skye.** The lakeside setting and golf course are pluses, but it's the food that makes this retreat near Glencoe truly special.

- **Bodysgallen Hall, Wales.** Walled gardens and the option of private cottage suites around the grounds create privacy at this hotel near the resort of Llandudno; antiques and polished wood set the tone.

- **Middlethorpe Hall, Yorkshire.** This handsome, superbly restored 18th-century mansion near York looks like a Gainsborough painting come to life.

GREAT ITINERARY

BEST OF BRITAIN: UNFORGETTABLE IMAGES, 14 DAYS

Day 1: London

The capital is just the jumping-off point for this trip, so choose a few highlights that grab your interest. If it's the Changing of the Guard at Buckingham Palace, check the time to be sure you catch the pageantry. If Westminster Abbey appeals to your sense of history, arrive as early as you can. Pick a museum (many are free, so you needn't linger), whether it's the National Gallery on Trafalgar Square, the British Museum in Bloomsbury, or a smaller gem like the Queen's Gallery. Stroll Hyde Park or take a boat ride on the Thames before you find a pub or Indian restaurant for dinner. End with a play; the experience of theatergoing may be as interesting as whatever work you see.

Day 2: Salisbury & Stonehenge

Visible for miles around, Salisbury Cathedral's soaring spire is an unforgettable image of rural England. See the Magna Carta in the cathedral's Chapter House as you explore this marvel of medieval engineering (prebook a roof tour if you can), and walk the town path to get the view John Constable painted. Go early or late in the day to avoid the largest crowds at Stonehenge; you can also prebook an after-hours tour. Use your imagination to appreciate these enigmatic stone circles, set in isolation on wide-open Salisbury Plain.

Day 3: Bath

Bath's immaculately preserved, golden-stone Georgian architecture helps you recapture the late 18th century and the town's heyday as a fashionable spa, complete with England's only true hot springs. Take time to stroll; don't miss the Royal Crescent (No.

1 may be open, allowing you to view a period interior), and sip the Pump Room's vile-tasting water as Jane Austen's characters might have. The Roman Baths, a must-see, is an amazing relic of the ancient empire, complete with curses left by soldiers. You may want to make time for a spa treatment at Thermae.

Day 4: Oxford & Blenheim Palace

Join a two-hour guided tour of Oxford's glorious quadrangles, chapels, and gardens to get the best access to these centuries-old academic treasures. This leaves time for a jaunt to magnificent Blenheim Palace, a unique combination of baroque opulence (inside and out) and gorgeous parkland. Be sure to stroll the grounds for the full experience. For a classic Oxford experience, join students in pub crawling around Jericho, the hopping nightlife district.

Days 5–6: Stratford-upon-Avon & the Cotswolds

Take a pass on Stratford if you don't care about you-know-who. Fans of Shakespeare can see his birthplace and Anne Hathaway's Cottage (walking there is a delight) here, then top it all off with a performance at the Royal Shakespeare Theatre. Start the day early and be prepared for crowds. Use Stratford as a base to explore the Cotswolds. Explore beautiful Chipping Campden, with its lost-in-time streets; gardens lovers may want to visit nearby Hidcote Manor Garden. Antique-shop in fairy-tale Stow-on-the-Wold and feed the ducks at the brook in Lower Slaughter for further tastes of the mellow stone villages and dreamy green landscapes for which the area is beloved.

are Victorian rather than Tudor), and the Rows, a series of two-story shops with medieval crypts beneath, and the fine City Walls are sights you can't pass by.

Days 9–10: The Lake District

In the area extending north beyond Windermere, explore the English lakes on foot; a gentle walk or a more vigorous hike is the best way to appreciate the jagged, majestic mountains that surround the lakes. Hikers pack the area in summer and on weekends, so rent a car to seek out the more isolated routes. Take a cruise on Windermere or Coniston Water, or rent a boat, for another way to see the mountains. If you have time for one Wordsworth-linked site, head to Dove Cottage in Grasmere; you can even have afternoon tea there. To escape the crowds, head north to the green valley of Borrowdale, encompassed by craggy peaks.

Day 11: Glasgow & Loch Lomond

Scotland has astonishing variety, even within a small area. Glasgow, its largest city, hums with fresh creative energy today. Check out its striking Victorian architecture (including buildings by Charles Rennie Mackintosh) and take in the treasures at the Kelvingrove Art Gallery and Museum, set in sprawling Kelvingrove Park. Leave the city for Loch Lomond, Scotland's largest loch in terms of surface area; it's less than an hour's drive north of Glasgow. The hard rocks to the north confine the loch there to a long, thin ribbon,

Days 7–8: North Wales & Chester

Head to Wales and the pleasantly old-fashioned Victorian resort town of Llandudno for a classic seaside stay, and take the cable car up Great Orme for great views. Gain perspective on North Wales from the top of Conwy's medieval city walls, and buy a guidebook or take a tour to appreciate its ruined castle, built by Edward I to intimidate the Welsh. Peruse the delights of nearby Bodnant Garden, set against the backdrop of the mountains of Snowdonia. Castle lovers may want to make an excursion to Caernarfon Castle, another of Edward's fortresses. Chester, back in England, has plenty of half-timber buildings (some

GREAT
ITINERARY

and the more yielding Lowlands allow it to spread out and assume a softer, wider form. Around the loch, the Lowlands' fields and lush hedgerows quickly give way to dark woods and crags. Visit Loch Lomond Shores at Balloch on the loch's southern tip, with the Loch Lomond and Trossachs National Park Gateway Centre. The winding banks of Loch Lomond can be easily followed on foot, by car, or even by boat.

Day 12: Loch Ness & Inverness

Inverness, about 175 miles north Glasgow, may be known as the capital of the Highlands, but it's more a base for exploring nearby sights than a place to tour. Here you are in the Great Glen, a valley crisscrossed by sparkling rivers and streams and ringed by brooding mountains. This is castle country, and rich in history; possible excursions near Inverness are Culloden Moor, site of a major defeat for Bonnie Prince Charlie in 1746, as well as Cawdor Castle, still lived in by the family. Urquhart Castle, near Drumnadrochit, is a favorite Loch Ness monster–watching spot. Whether or not you believe in Nessie, you can take in the beauty of the loch by driving along its shore. At the southern tip, at Fort Augustus, you can see the locks of the Caledonian Canal in action. The canal, which links the lochs of the Great Glen—Loch Lochy, Loch Oich, and Loch Ness—has awesome vistas of lochs, mountains, and glens in all directions.

Days 13–14: Edinburgh

Finish your trip in grand style in Scotland's capital; you'll most likely need to transfer to Glasgow Airport for your flight home. Three sights are really critical to understanding the city and Scotland: ancient Edinburgh Castle (touring it can take half a day), the Palace of Holyroodhouse, and the new Scottish Parliament, housed in a strikingly modern building. But you needn't let sightseeing exhaust you. Just take a stroll among the ancient buildings along the Royal Mile in Old Town or explore the neoclassical grandeur of New Town to appreciate the lasting legacies of the city's influence and prosperity. And be sure to stop in one of the city's pubs for a well-deserved beer or a wee dram, and perhaps to hear some music.

TIPS

❶ Train travelers should keep in mind that regional "Rovers" and "Rangers" offer unlimited train travel in 1-day, 3-day or weeklong increments. See www.nationalrail.co.uk/promotions/ for details. Also check out BritRail passes, which must be purchased before your trip.

❷ Buses are time-consuming, but more scenic and cheaper than train travel. National Express offers funfares—fares to and from London to 31 cities as low as £1 if booked more than 24 hrs in advance. Or check out low-cost Megabus.

❸ You can adjust this itinerary to suit your interests. If Scotland is important, consider skipping Wales and proceeding to the Lake District from Stratford. Likewise, you can forgo a visit to Glasgow if you opt for more time to make trips from Inverness. You could also add time to your London stay.

❹ It's easy to visit Stonehenge from Bath, as well as from Salisbury, if you choose to pass up Salisbury.

❺ Buy theater tickets well in advance for Stratford.

ON THE CALENDAR

	Britain's top seasonal events are listed below, and any one of them could provide the stuff of lasting memories. Tickets for popular sporting events must be obtained months in advance. VisitBritain's Web site, ⊕ www.visitbritain.com, also has information about events.
ONGOING 2007	**Highland 2007** (⊕ www.highland2007.com) is a year-long celebration of Highland culture with a broad focus on the art, history, environment, scientific contributions, and sports of this Scottish region. Events are varied—everything from a six-city Festival of Design to orienteering and curling championships. Existing events and festivals will have special features.
Mid-July– mid-Sept.	**Henry Wood Promenade Concerts,** known universally in England as "the Proms," is a celebrated series of classical-music concerts. ⊠ *Royal Albert Hall, Kensington Gore, London SW7* ☎ *020/ 7589–8212* ⊕ *www.bbc.co.uk/proms.*
WINTER Dec. 27– Jan. 2	**Hogmanay,** an energetic, Scottish-style celebration of the new year in Edinburgh, includes candlelight processions, concerts, and fireworks. Cities throughout Scotland have gotten into the act with similar festivities. ☎ *0131/529–3914* ⊕ *www.edinburghshogmanay.org.*
Dec. 31	**New Year's Eve at Trafalgar Square** in London is a huge, freezing, sometimes drunken slosh through the fountains to celebrate the new year. Not organized by any official body, it is held in the ceremonial heart of London under an enormous Christmas tree.
Jan. 25	**Burns Night** dinners and other events are held throughout Scotland in memory of Robert Burns on his birthday.
Mid-Jan.–Early Feb.	**Celtic Connections** (⊠ Glasgow Royal Concert Hall, 2 Sauchiehall St., Glasgow ☎ 0141/353–8000 ⊕ www.celticconnections.com), an annual homage to Celtic music, hosts hands-on workshops and musicians from all over the world.
SPRING Late Mar.	The **Head of the River Boat Race** offers the spectacle of up to 420 eight-man crews dipping their 6,720 oars in the Thames as they race from Mortlake to Putney. The best view is from Surrey Bank above Chiswick Bridge (Tube to Chiswick); check *Time Out* for the starting time, which depends on the tide. The **Oxford versus Cambridge University Boat Race** takes place a week or two later, in the opposite direction but over the same 4½-mi course, carrying on a tradition going back to 1829. Around a quarter of a million people watch from the banks of the river.

ON THE CALENDAR

Mid-Apr.	**Flora London Marathon** runners start in Greenwich and Blackheath at 9–9:30 AM and run via the Docklands, the Tower of London, and Parliament Square to the Mall. ⊕ *www.london-marathon.co.uk.*
Apr. 21	The **Queen's Birthday** earns a showy 41-gun salute at Hyde Park in London. In June, Elizabeth II's ceremonial birthday is celebrated by Trooping the Colour.
April 30	The **Beltane Fire Festival** (☎ 0131/228–5353 ⊕ www.beltane.org) celebrates the rites of spring according to the traditional Celtic calendar. You can witness displays of pyrotechnics and elaborately-costumed mythological creatures at Calton Hill in Edinburgh.
Mid–late May	The **Chelsea Flower Show,** a prestigious four-day floral extravaganza, covers 22 acres on the Royal Hospital grounds in London's Chelsea neighborhood. Tickets can sell out well in advance of the event. ✉ *Royal Horticultural Society, Royal Hospital Rd., London SW3* ☎ *0870/906–3781* ⊕ *www.rhs.org.uk/chelsea.*
Late May	The **Hay Festival** in the Welsh border town of Hay-on-Wye gathers authors and readers from all over the world for a weeklong celebration of the town's status as the used-book capital of the world. ✉ *Hay-on-Wye* ☎ *01497/821–299* ⊕ *www.hayfestival.co.uk.*
Late May	The **Perth Festival of the Arts** (☎ 01738/472706 ⊕ www.perthfestival.co.uk) offers orchestral and choral concerts, drama, opera, and ballet throughout Perth.
SUMMER June–Aug.	**Highland Games,** held annually in many Highland towns, include athletic and cultural events such as hammer throwing, caber tossing, Highland dancing, and pipe-band performances.
Early June	**Trooping the Colour** is Queen Elizabeth's official birthday show at Horse Guards Parade, Whitehall, London. (Her actual birthday is in April.) Note that on the two previous Saturdays, there are Queenless rehearsals—the Colonel's Review and the Major General's Review. *Write for tickets from January 1 to February 28 (enclose SASE or International Reply Coupon):* ⌨ *Ticket Office, Headquarters Household Division, Horse Guards, London SW1 2AX* ☎ *020/7414–2479.*
Mid-June	**Royal Ascot** is the most glamorous date in British horse racing. Usually held during the third week of June, the four-day event is graced by the Queen and other celebrities. Reserve months in advance for tickets. ✉ *Ascot Racecourse, Ascot, Berkshire* ☎ *01344/876876* ⊕ *www.ascot.co.uk.*

Late June	**Glastonbury Festival,** the biggest musical event in England, sprawls across Somerset farmland, where hundreds of bands (rock, pop, folk, and world music) perform on a half-dozen stages for three days and nights. Tickets may sell out in three hours. ☎ *0870/165–2005* ⊕ *www.glastonburyfestivals.co.uk.*
Late June–early July	**Wimbledon Lawn Tennis Championships** get bigger every year. Applications for the ticket lottery for the two-week tournament are available October through December of the preceding year. ⌂ *All-England Lawn Tennis & Croquet Club, Church Rd., Wimbledon, London SW19 5AE* ☎ *020/8946–2244* ⊕ *www.wimbledon.org.*
Late June–early July	**Royal Henley Regatta** attracts premier rowers from around the world on the first weekend in July. High society lines the banks of the Thames during this four-day event. ✉ *Henley-on-Thames, Oxfordshire* ☎ *01491/572153* ⊕ *www.hrr.co.uk.*
Late June–late July	**City of London Festival** fills the City with theater, poetry, classical music, and dance performed by international artists. ☎ *020/7377–0540* ⊕ *www.colf.org.*
Early July	**Hampton Court Palace Flower Show,** a five-day event on the grounds of the palace, nearly rivals the Chelsea Flower Show for glamour. ✉ *Hampton Court Palace, East Molesey, Surrey* ☎ *0870/906–3791* ⊕ *www.rhs.org.uk/hamptoncourt.*
Early–mid-July	**Llangollen International Musical Eisteddfod** sees the little Welsh town of Llangollen overflow with music, including concerts and competitions. Participants come from more than 40 nations. ✉ *Musical Eisteddfod Office, Llangollen* ☎ *01978/860000* ⊕ *www. international-eisteddfod.co.uk.*
Late July–early Aug.	The **National Eisteddfod** of Wales, a weeklong celebration of Welsh language and culture, is held in different Welsh cities each year. The festival features musical and literary performances. ☎ *029/2076–3777* ⊕ *www.eisteddfod.org.uk.*
Mid-Aug.–early Sept.	**Edinburgh International Festival,** a massive three-week-long event turns all of Edinburgh into a stage for musical, theatrical, and comedic acts from around the world. ✉ *Castlehill, EH1 2NE* ☎ *0131/473–2000 tickets* ⊕ *www.eif.co.uk.*
Mid-Aug.–early Sept.	**Edinburgh Festival Fringe,** literally and figuratively at the edges of the Edinburgh International Festival, the Fringe offers a showcase to new and rising theatrical and comedic talent. ☎ *0131/226–0026* ⊕ *www.edfringe.com.*

ON THE CALENDAR

Late Aug.	**International Beatles Festival** sees hundreds of Beatles tribute bands descend on Liverpool for a week to play to fans. ✉ *Liverpool* ☎ *0151/236–9091* ⊕ *www.visitliverpool.com.*
Late Aug.	**Notting Hill Carnival,** one of the liveliest street festivals in London, includes Caribbean foods, reggae music, and street parades. ✉ *Notting Hill, London* ☎ *020/8964–0544.*
FALL Early Sept.	The **Braemar Royal Highland Gathering** (☎ 013397/55377 ⊕ www.braemargathering.org) hosts kilted clansmen from all over Scotland.
Sept.	**London Open House** is a rare one-day chance to view historic London interiors of buildings usually closed to the public. ☎ *020/7267–7644* ⊕ *www.londonopenhouse.org.*
Mid-Oct.	**Cheltenham Festival of Literature** draws world-renowned authors, actors, and critics to the elegant, Regency-era town. ☎ *01242/227979* ⊕ *www.cheltenhamfestivals.co.uk.*
Mid-Oct.	The **Royal National Mod** (☎ 01463/709705 ⊕ www.the-mod.co.uk) is a Gaelic festival with speech competitions and plays (in Gaelic), in addition to piping, choir, and highland dancing performances. The location in Scotland changes each year.
Early Nov.	**Glasgay** (☎ 0141/552–7575 ⊕ www.glasgay.co.uk) is a celebration of gay comedy, music, film, theater, visual art, performance art, and literature taking place in and around Glasgow.
Nov. 5	**Guy Fawkes Day** commemorates a foiled 1605 attempt to blow up Parliament. Fireworks shows and bonfires are held all over the country, with the biggest celebrations in Lewes in Sussex.

London

WORD OF MOUTH

"We took the tube to Victoria and walked to the Queen's Gallery at Buckingham Palace. Loads of important paintings, jewels, Fabergé eggs, Sèvres, gold and china dinner pieces. . . I'm sure the Queen throws very nice parties."

—Kayb95

"Kensington Gardens and Hyde Park are great people-watching places, and they have lovely flower plantings, the Serpentine, Princess Di play area—lots going on."

—carefreecelt

Updated by
Ferne Arfin,
Christi
Daugherty,
Julius Honnor,
and Alex
Wijeratna

LONDON IS AN ANCIENT CITY whose history greets you at every turn. To gain a sense of its continuity, stand on Waterloo Bridge at sunset. To the east, the great globe of St. Paul's Cathedral glows golden in the fading sunlight as it has since the 17th century, still majestic amid the modern towers of glass and steel that hem it in. To the west stand the mock-medieval ramparts of Westminster, home to the "Mother of Parliaments," which has met here or hereabouts since the 1250s. Past them both snakes the swift, dark Thames, following the same course as when it flowed past the Roman settlement of Londinium nearly 2,000 years ago. If the city contained only its famous landmarks—the Tower of London, Big Ben, Westminster Abbey, Buckingham Palace—it would still rank as one of the world's top cities. But London is so much more.

A city that loves to be explored, London beckons with great museums, royal pageantry, and history-steeped houses. There's no other place like it in its agglomeration of architectural sins and sudden intervention of almost rural sights, in its medley of styles, in its mixture of the green loveliness of parks and the modern gleam of neon. Discovering it takes a bit of work, however. Modern-day London largely reflects its medieval layout, a willfully difficult tangle of streets. Even Londoners, most of whom own a dog-eared copy of an indispensable A–Z street finder, get lost in their own city. But the bewildering street patterns will be a plus for anyone who likes to get lost in atmosphere. London is a walker's city and will repay every moment you spend exploring on foot.

You should not only visit St. Paul's Cathedral and the Tower of London but also set aside some time for random wandering. Walk in the city's backstreets and mews, around Park Lane and Kensington. Pass up Buckingham Palace for Kensington Palace. Take in the National Gallery, but don't forget London's "time-machine" museums, such as the 19th-century home of Sir John Soane. Abandon the city's standard-issue chain stores for its wonderful markets.

Today London is one of the coolest cities in the world. Millennium fever left its trophies, with the opening of buildings and bridges and revamped museums, and the city's art, style, fashion, and dining scenes make headlines around the world. London's chefs have become superstars. Its fashion designers have conquered Paris, avant-garde artists have caused waves at the august Royal Academy of Arts, the raging after-hours scene is packed with music mavens ready to catch the Next Big Thing, and the theater continues its tradition of radical, shocking productions. In 2005, the city won the bid to host the 2012 Olympics.

Although the outward shapes may alter and the inner spirit may be warmer, the base-rocks of London's character and tradition remain the same. The British bobby is alive and well. The tall, red, double-decker buses (in an updated model) still lumber from stop to stop, although their aesthetic match at street level, the glossy red telephone booth, has been replaced by glass and steel boxes. Then there's that greatest living link with the past—the Royal Family. Don't let the tag of "typical tourist destination" stop you from enjoying the pageantry of the Windsors: the Changing of the Guard, at Buckingham Palace and at Whitehall, is one of the greatest free shows in the world.

GREAT DAYS OUT

London overflows with choices: from exploring local pubs and tea rooms to taking in great theater and concerts, it's easy to fill a day. A stroll through a quiet neighborhood or a ride on the Thames may be as satisfying as seeing a world-famous museum. Below are suggestions for different experiences. Mix and match them to suit your taste.

CROWNING GLORIES

This regal runaround packs more into a day than most cities can offer in a week. Hit Westminster Abbey early to avoid the crowds, then cut through St. James's Park to catch the Changing of the Guard at 11:20 at Buckingham Palace. Take a quick detour to the Tudor delights of St. James's Palace, before a promenade down the Mall and Carlton House Terrace, and through Admiralty Arch to Trafalgar Square. Choose from the treasures of the National Gallery, the Who's Who of the National Portrait Gallery, or a brass rubbing in the crypt of St. Martin's-in-the-Fields. This leaves a stroll down Whitehall—past Downing Street, Horse Guards Parade, and Banqueting House—to the Houses of Parliament, where you have the option of prebooking a tour, or trying to get in to see a debate. If you have any time or energy left, stroll through Green and Hyde Parks to Kensington Palace, childhood home of Queen Victoria, and (for aspiring princesses everywhere) the Royal Dress Collection.

MUSEUM MAGIC

London has one of the finest collections of museums in the world, and many are free. Some resemble hands-on playgrounds that will keep children and adults amused for hours; others take a more classical approach. One of the latter is the British Museum in Bloomsbury, an Aladdin's cave of treasures from across the world. While in the area, pop into the nearby museum of architect Sir John Soane or the Theatre Museum.

Alternatively, South Kensington's "Museum Mile" on Cromwell Road houses a triple-whammy that makes for a substantial day's-worth of diversion: the Victoria & Albert Museum, the Natural History Museum, and the Science Museum.

RETAIL THERAPY

It's not hard to shop 'til you drop in London's West End. Start with the upscale on New Bond Street, an awesome sweep of expense and elegance. In the afternoon, head to Oxford Street, which encompasses four tube stations and is unbeatable for mass-market shopping. Run the gauntlet of designers, cheap odds and ends, department stores, and ferocious pedestrians: it's seriously busy.

A more sedate but utterly fashionable experience can be found in Knightsbridge, wandering between Harvey Nichols and Harrods department stores. Head south down Sloane Street to Sloane Square and head out along King's Road, with boutiques galore. To dip into the ever-expanding world of urban chic, try an afternoon in the lively Portobello street market in Notting Hill, where you can pick up remnants of various bygone ages: glassware, furniture, art, and clothes.

EXPLORING LONDON

London grew from a wooden bridge built over the Thames in the year AD 43 to its current 600 square mi and 7 million souls in haphazard fashion, meandering from its two official centers: Westminster, seat of government and royalty, to the west, and the City, site of finance and commerce, to the east. In these two areas are most of the grand buildings that have played a central role in British history: the Tower of London and St. Paul's Cathedral, Westminster Abbey and the Houses of Parliament, Buckingham Palace, and the older royal palace of St. James's.

London's *un*official centers multiply and mutate year after year, and it would be a shame to stop only at the postcard views. Life is not lived in monuments, as the patrician patrons of the great Georgian architects understood when they commissioned the city's elegant squares and town houses. Within a few minutes' walk of Buckingham Palace, for instance, lie St. James's and Mayfair, neighboring quarters of elegant town houses built for the nobility during the 17th and early 18th centuries and now notable for shopping opportunities. Westminster Abbey's original vegetable patch (or convent garden), which became the site of London's first square, Covent Garden, is now a popular stop.

Hyde Park and Kensington Gardens, preserved by past kings and queens for their own hunting and relaxation, create a swath of parkland across the city center. A walk across Hyde Park brings you to the museum district of South Kensington, with the Natural History Museum, the Science Museum, and the Victoria & Albert Museum. If the great parks such as Hyde Park are, in Lord Chatham's phrase, "the lungs of London," then the River Thames is its backbone. The South Bank has many cultural highlights: the theaters of the South Bank Centre, the Hayward Gallery, Tate Modern, and the reconstruction of Shakespeare's Globe theater. The London Eye observation wheel here gives stunning city views, or you can walk across the Millennium or Hungerford bridges. Farther downstream is the gorgeous 17th- and 18th-century symmetry of Greenwich, and its maritime attractions.

Westminster & Royal London

If you have time to visit only one part of London, this is it. Westminster and Royal London might be called "London for Beginners." If you went no farther than these few acres, you would have seen many of the famous sights, from the Houses of Parliament, Big Ben, Westminster Abbey, and Buckingham Palace, to two of the world's greatest art collections, in the National and Tate Britain galleries. You can truly call this area Royal London, since it is bounded by the triangle of streets that make up the route that the Queen usually takes when journeying from Buckingham Palace to Westminster Abbey or to the Houses of Parliament on state occasions. The three points on this royal triangle are Trafalgar Square, Westminster, and Buckingham Palace. Naturally, in an area that regularly sees the pomp and pageantry of royal occasions, the streets are wide and the vistas long. St. James's Park lies at the heart

TOP REASONS TO GO

Westminster Abbey: The most exciting church in the land is the final resting place for the men and women who built Britain.

Buckingham Palace: Not the prettiest royal palace, but a must-see for the glimpse it affords of modern royal life. Don't forget the collection of art and china at the Queen's Gallery next door.

St. Paul's Cathedral: No matter how many times you have been here, the scale and elegance of Sir Christopher Wren's masterpiece take the breath away. Climb the enormous dome for fantastic views across London.

Tower of London: The Tower is London at its majestic, idiosyncratic best. This is the heart of the kingdom, with foundations dating back nine centuries.

British Museum: If you want to journey through time and space without leaving Bloomsbury, a visit to the British Museum has hours of eye-catching artifacts from civilizations around the world.

Shakespeare's Globe Theatre: You can catch a Shakespeare play almost every night of the year in London. But watching an offering from the Bard in a re-created

version of the galleried Tudor theater for which he wrote is a special thrill.

Hampton Court Palace: These buildings won over Henry VIII and became his favorite royal residence. Tudor charm, grand gardens, a wing designed by Christopher Wren, and a picturesque upstream Thames location make Hampton Court a great day out.

Tate Modern: A visit here is more of an event than the average museum stop. Tate Modern, inside a striking 1930s power station, is a hip, immensely successful addition to the London gallery landscape.

National Gallery: Whatever the collective noun is for a set of Old Masters—a palette? a canvas?—there are enough here to have the most casual art enthusiast purring with admiration. Enjoy Trafalgar Square on the doorstep.

London's central parks: It seems churlish to pick out only one. The four central parks are all within walking distance: pick St. James's Park for fairy-tale views; Green Park for hillocks and wide boulevards; Regent's Park for its open-air theater and the London Zoo; and Hyde Park for rowing on the Serpentine Lido.

of the triangle, which has a feeling of timeless dignity. This is concentrated sightseeing, so pace yourself. For a large part of the year, much of Royal London is floodlighted at night, adding to the theatricality of the experience.

TIMING It's easy to spend a few days in this area, so plan carefully. Allow as much time as you can for the three great museums—the National Gallery and the Tate Britain require *at least* two hours each, the National Portrait Gallery one to two. Westminster Abbey can take a half day—especially in summer when lines are long. In summer, you can get inside Bucking-

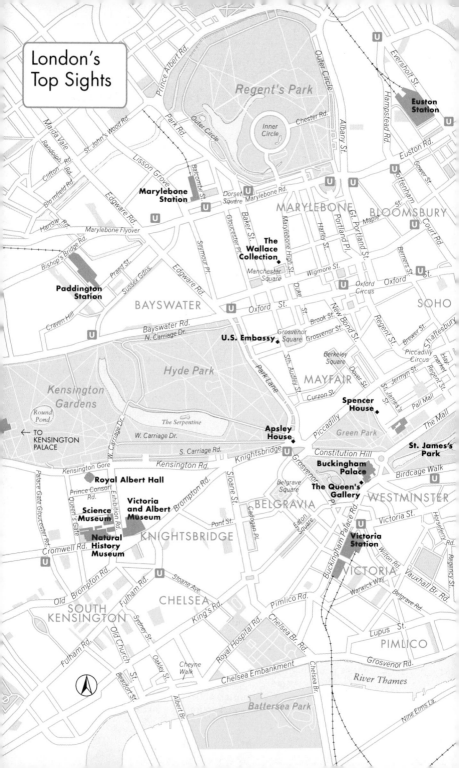

London's Top Sights

Regent's Park

Inner Circle

Euston Station

Maida Vale

Randolph Rd.
Clifton
Blomfield Rd.

Prince Albert Rd.

St. John's Wood Rd.

Park Rd.

Outer Circle

Lisson Grove

Eversholt St.

Hampstead Rd.

Chester Rd.

Albany St.

Euston Rd.

Gower St.

Tottenham

MARYLEBONE

BLOOMSBURY

Marylebone Station

Harrow Rd.

Edgware Rd.

Marylebone Flyover

Bishop's Bridge Rd.

Praed St.

Sussex Gdns.

Paddington Station

Craven Hill

BAYSWATER

Bayswater Rd.
N. Carriage Dr.

Dorset
Square

Balcombe St.

Gloucester Pl.

Baker St.

Seymour Pl.

Edgware Rd.

Marylebone Rd.

The Wallace Collection

Manchester
Square

Harley St.

Portland Pl.

Gt. Portland St.

Maple
St.

Court Rd.

Berners St.

SOHO

Wigmore St.

Oxford
Circus

Oxford

Oxford St.

U.S. Embassy

Brook St.

Grosvenor
Square

Grosvenor St.

New Bond St.

Regent St.

Brewer St.

Shaftesbury

Piccadilly
Circus

Haymarket

Regent St.

Hyde Park

Kensington Gardens

Round
Pond

← TO
KENSINGTON
PALACE

The Serpentine

W. Carriage Dr.

S. Carriage Dr.

Kensington Gore

Kensington Rd.

Knightsbridge

Park Lane

MAYFAIR

Berkeley
Square

Curzon St.

S. Audley St.

Dover St.

Spencer House

Apsley House

Piccadilly

Constitution Hill

Berkeley
Square

Jermyn St.

St. James's St.

Pall Mall

Green Park

The Mall

St. James's Park

Birdcage Walk

WESTMINSTER

Buckingham Palace

The Queen's Gallery

Royal Albert Hall

Prince Consort
Rd.

Exhibition Rd.

Queen's Gate

Science Museum

Victoria and Albert Museum

Natural History Museum

Palace Gate

Gloucester Rd.

Cromwell Rd.

Brompton Rd.

Sloane St.

Cadogan Pl.

Pont St.

KNIGHTSBRIDGE

Eaton
Square

BELGRAVIA

Belgrave
Square

Grosvenor Pl.

Buckingham Palace Rd.

Victoria St.

Victoria St.

Horseferry Rd.

Victoria Station

VICTORIA

Wilton Rd.

Warwick Way

Belgrave Rd.

Old Brompton Rd.

Fulham Rd.

Sydney St.

Sloane Ave.

CHELSEA

King's Rd.

Royal Hospital Rd.

Chelsea Br. Rd.

Pimlico Rd.

Lupus St.

PIMLICO

Grosvenor Rd.

SOUTH KENSINGTON

Fulham Rd.

Old Church St.

Oakley St.

Beaufort St.

Cheyne
Walk

Chelsea Embankment

Albert Br.

Chelsea Br.

River Thames

Nine Elms La.

Battersea Park

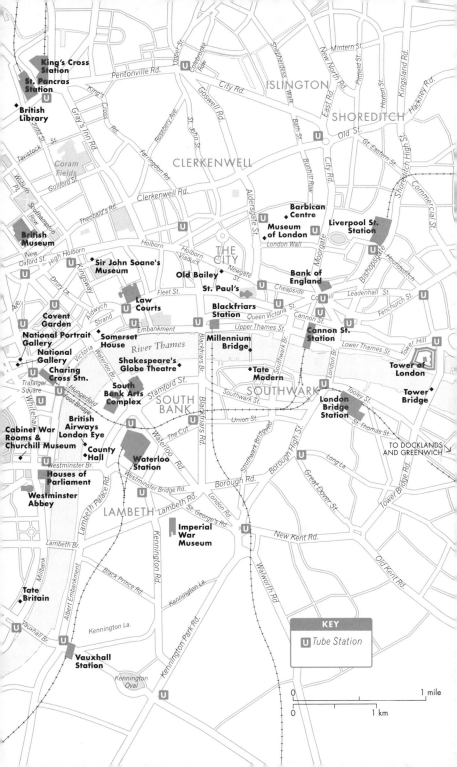

King's Cross
Station

St. Pancras
Station

◆ British
Library

Pentonville Rd.

ISLINGTON

Mintern St.

SHOREDITCH

Tavistock St.

Coram
Fields

Guilford St.

CLERKENWELL

Clerkenwell Rd.

Old St.

Barbican
• Centre

Liverpool St.
Station

Theobald's Rd.

British
Museum

New
Oxford St.

High Holborn

Museum
of London

London Wall

THE
CITY

Holborn
Viaduct

Newgate St.

Bank of
England

Holborn

■ Sir John Soane's
Museum

Old Bailey

St. Paul's

Cheapside

Leadenhall St.

Covent
Garden

National Portrait
Gallery

National
Gallery

Law
Courts

Somerset
House

Strand

Embankment

Blackfriars
Station

Queen Victoria St.

Upper Thames St.

Cannon St.
Station

Lower Thames St.

Tower of
London

Charing
Cross Stn.

Trafalgar
Square

Whitehall

River Thames

Shakespeare's
Globe Theatre

South
Bank Arts
Complex

SOUTH
BANK

Millennium
Bridge

Tate
Modern

Southwark St.

SOUTHWARK

London
Bridge
Station

Tower
Bridge

Cabinet War
Rooms &
Churchill Museum

British
Airways
London Eye

County
Hall

Waterloo
Station

Union St.

St. Thomas St.

TO DOCKLANDS
AND GREENWICH

Houses of
Parliament

Westminster
Abbey

LAMBETH

Lambeth Rd.

Borough Rd.

New Kent Rd.

Imperial
War
Museum

St. George's Rd.

Tate
Britain

Black Prince Rd.

Kennington La.

Walworth Rd.

Old Kent Rd.

Vauxhall
Station

Kennington
Oval

0   1 mile

0   1 km

London
Postal Districts

ham Palace and Clarence House; a half-day's operation will be increased to a whole day if you see Spencer House (open Sunday only), the Royal Mews, or the Queen's Gallery. If the Changing of the Guard is a priority, time yourself accordingly.

GETTING HERE   Trafalgar Square—easy to access and in the center of the action—is a good place to start. Take the tube to Embankment (District and Circle lines) and walk north until you cross the Strand, or get out at Charing Cross (Bakerloo, Jubilee, and Northern lines), where the Northumberland Avenue exit deposits you on the southeast corner of the square. Practically all buses stop around here, including buses 3, 9, 11, 12, 16, 24, 29, 53, 88, 139, and 159. Alternative tube stations on the south side are St. James's Park (on the District and Circle lines), which is the best for Buckingham Palace, or the next stop, Westminster, which deposits you in the shadow of Big Ben.

Numbers in the margin correspond to numbers on the Westminster & Royal London map.

Main Attractions

❽ Buckingham Palace. Supreme among the symbols of London—indeed of
Fodor'sChoice   Britain generally and of the Royal Family in particular—Buckingham Palace
★   tops many must-see lists, although the building itself is no masterpiece and has housed the monarch only since Victoria (1819–1901) moved here from Kensington Palace on her accession in 1837. Its great gray bulk sums up the imperious splendor of so much of the city: stately, magnificent, and ponderous. In 1824 the palace was substantially rebuilt by John Nash, that tireless architect, for George IV, that tireless spendthrift. Compared with other great London residences, it is a fairly recent affair: the Portland-stone facade dates from 1913, and the interior was renovated and redecorated after World War II bombs damaged it. The palace contains some 600 rooms, including the Ballroom and the Throne Room. The state rooms are where much of the business of royalty is played out—investitures, state banquets, and receptions for the great and good—and are only open to the public while the Royal Family is away during the summer. The royal apartments are in the north wing; when the Queen is in, the royal standard is raised. The **Changing of the Guard**—which, with all the pomp and ceremony monarchists and children adore, remains one of London's best free shows—culminates in front of the palace. Marching to live music, the guards proceed up the Mall from St. James's Palace to Buckingham Palace. Shortly afterward, the replacement guard approaches from Wellington Barracks via Birdcage Walk. Once the old and new guards are in the forecourt, the old guard symbolically hands over the keys to the palace. ■ TIP➜ **Get there by 10:30 AM to grab a spot in the best viewing section at the gate facing the palace, since most of the hoopla takes place behind the railings in the forecourt.** ⊠ *Buckingham Palace Rd., St. James's, SW1* ☎ *020/7766–7300* ⊕ *www.royal.gov.uk* £14, includes audio tour, credit-card reservations subject to booking charge; prebooking recommended ⊙ Late July–late Sept., daily 9:45–6, last admission 3:45; confirm dates, which are subject to Queen's mandate. Changing of the Guard Apr.–July, daily 11:30 AM; Aug.–Mar., alternating days only 11:30 AM ☐ AE, MC, V Ⓤ Victoria, St. James's Park.*

★ ☽ ⑬ **Cabinet War Rooms & Churchill Museum.** From this small maze of bombproof underground rooms—in the back of the hulking Foreign Office—Britain's World War II fortunes were directed. During air raids, the cabinet met here, and the Cabinet Room is still arranged as if a meeting were about to convene. In the Map Room, the Allied campaign is charted. The Prime Minister's Room holds the desk from which Winston Churchill made his morale-boosting broadcasts, and the Telephone Room has his hotline to FDR. The rest of the rooms have been preserved as they were at the end of the war. The PM's "suite" of rooms for dining, cooking, and sleeping have been restored, too. By far the most exciting addition is the **Churchill Museum,** which opened in 2005 on the 40th anniversary of the great man's death. Different interactive zones explore his life and achievements—and failures, too—through objects and documents, many of which, such as his personal papers, had not been revealed to the public. ⊠ *Clive Steps, King Charles St., Westminster, SW1A* ☎ *020/7930–6961* ⊕ *www.iwm.org.uk* ⊠ *£11, includes audio tour* ☉ *Daily 9:30–6; last admission 5* Ⓤ *Westminster.*

⑯ **Horse Guards Parade.** Once the tiltyard of Whitehall Palace, where jousting tournaments were held, the Horse Guards Parade is now notable mainly for the annual Trooping the Colour ceremony, in which the Queen takes the Royal Salute, her official birthday gift, on the second Saturday in June. (Like Paddington Bear, the Queen has two birthdays; her real one is on April 21.) There is pageantry galore, with marching bands and throngs of onlookers. At the Whitehall facade of Horse Guards, the changing of two mounted sentries known as the **mounted guard** provides what may be London's most frequently exercised photo opportunity. ⊠ *Whitehall, Westminster, SW1* ☉ *Queen's mounted-guard ceremony Mon.–Sat. 11 AM, Sun. 10 AM* Ⓤ *Westminster.*

⑪ **Houses of Parliament.** Seat of Great Britain's government, the Houses of
Fodor'sChoice Parliament are, arguably, the city's most famous and photogenic sight.
★ Facing them you see, from left to right, Big Ben—keeping watch on the corner—the Houses of Parliament themselves, Westminster Hall (the oldest part of the complex), and the Victoria Tower. The most romantic view of the complex is from the opposite, south side of the river, a vista especially dramatic at night when the spires, pinnacles, and towers of the great building are floodlighted green and gold. After a catastrophic fire in 1834, these buildings arose, designed in glorious, mock-medieval style by two Victorian-era architects, Sir Charles Barry and Augustus Pugin. The Palace of Westminster, as the complex is still properly called, was established by Edward the Confessor in the 11th century. It has served as the seat of English administrative power, on and off, ever since. Now virtually the symbol of London, the 1858 **Clock Tower** designed by Pugin contains the bell known as **Big Ben** that chimes on the hour (and the quarters). Weighing a mighty 13 tons, the bell takes its name from Sir Benjamin Hall, the far-from-slim Westminster building-works commissioner. At the other end of Parliament is the 336-foot-high **Victoria Tower.** There are two houses, the Lords and the Commons. You can see democracy in action in the Visitors' Galleries—if, that is, you're patient enough to wait in line for hours (the Lords line is shorter) or have applied in advance for the special "line of route" tour for overseas visitors in sum-

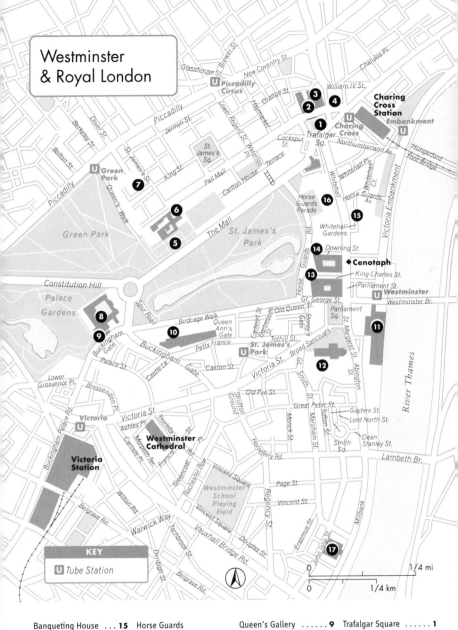

Westminster & Royal London

mer (late July through August and mid-September through early October). Tickets can be prebooked by phone or on the Web site; alternatively, you can take a chance and buy same-day tickets from the ticket office opposite the Houses of Parliament. The time to catch the action is Question Time—when the prime minister defends himself against the attacks of his "right honorable friends" on Wednesday between noon and 2:30 PM. For a special exhibition devoted to the

> ## A VIEW TO REMEMBER
>
> The most romantic view of Parliament is from the opposite (south) side of the river, especially dramatic at night when the spires, pinnacles, and towers are floodlighted green and gold—a fairytale vision only missing the presence of Peter Pan and Wendy on their way to Never-Never Land.

history of Parliament, head to the **Jewel Tower,** across the street from Victoria Tower, on Abingdon Street. Be sure to have your name placed in advance on the waiting list for the twice-weekly tours of the **Lord Chancellor's Residence,** a popular attraction since its renovation. ⊠ *St. Stephen's Entrance, St. Margaret St., Westminster, SW1* ☎ *020/ 7219–4272 Commons information, 020/7219–3107 Lords information, 020/7222–2219 Jewel Tower, 020/7219–2184 Lord Chancellor's Residence, 0870/906–3773 summer tours* ⊕ *www.parliament.uk* ▥ *Free, £7 summer tours* ☉ *Commons Mon. 2:30–10:30, Tues. and Wed. 11:30–7:30, Thurs. 11:30–6:30, Fri. 9:30–3 although not every Fri.; Lords Mon.–Thurs. 2:30–10; Lord Chancellor's Residence Tues. and Thurs. 10:30–12:30. Closed Easter wk, late July–early Sept., 3 wks for party conference recess mid-Sept.–early Oct., and 3 wks at Christmas* Ⓤ *Westminster.*

❷ National Gallery. Jan Van Eyck's *Arnolfini Marriage,* Leonardo da Vinci's *Virgin and Child,* Diego Velázquez's *Rokeby Venus,* John Constable's *Hay Wain* . . . you get the picture. There are approximately 2,200 other paintings in this museum, many of them among the most treasured works of art anywhere. The museum's low, gray, colonnaded, neoclassical facade fills the north side of Trafalgar Square. The gallery's east wing in sleek black and white marble has cafés and improved visitor information, such as boards with a color code for different eras of paintings. The National's collection includes paintings of the early Renaissance— in the modern Sainsbury Wing—the Flemish and Dutch masters, the Spanish school, and the English tradition (notably William Hogarth, Thomas Gainsborough, George Stubbs, and Constable).

FodorśChoice
★

The **Micro Gallery,** a computer information center in the Sainsbury Wing, is a great place to start. You can access information on any work, choose your favorites, and print out a free personal tour map. There's another computer center in the espresso bar in the lower hall. In addition to the four mentioned above, the museum's top 10 includes Paolo Uccello's *Battle of San Romano* (children love its knights on horseback), Giovanni Bellini's *Doge Leonardo Loredan* (notice the snail-shell buttons), Sandro Botticelli's *Venus and Mars,* Caravaggio's *Supper at Emmaus* (almost cinematically lit), J. M. W. Turner's *Fighting Téméraire* (one of the artist's greatest sunsets), and Georges Seurat's *Bathers at Asnières*. The museum is too overwhelming to absorb in a single viewing, but the free admission encourages repeat visits. For a great time-out, head for the brasserie, Crivelli's Garden, in the Sainsbury Wing. The ultracool National Gallery Café in the east wing makes a fun stop even if you're not visiting the gallery. ⊠ *Trafalgar Sq., Westminster, WC2* ☎ *020/7747–2885* ⊕ *www.nationalgallery.org.uk* ▣ *Free, charge for special exhibitions* ☉ *Daily 10–6, Wed. until 9; 1-hr free guided tour starts at Sainsbury Wing daily at 11:30 and 2:30, and additionally Wed. 6 and 6:30, Sat. 12:30 and 3:30* Ⓤ *Charing Cross, Leicester Sq.*

★ ❸ **National Portrait Gallery.** An idiosyncratic collection that presents a potted history of Britain through its people, past and present, this museum is an essential stop for all history and literature buffs. As an art collection it is eccentric, because the subject, not the artist, is the point. Many of the faces are obscure, because the portraits outlasted their sitters' fame—not so surprising when the portraitists are such greats as Sir Joshua Reynolds, Gainsborough, Sir Thomas Lawrence, and George Romney. But the annotation is comprehensive, the layout is easy to negotiate—chronological, with the oldest at the top—and there's a separate research center for those who get hooked on particular personages. The spacious, bright galleries are accessible via a state-of-the-art escalator, which lets you view the paintings as you ascend to a skylighted space displaying the oldest works in the Tudor Gallery. At the summit, a sleek restaurant, open beyond gallery hours, will satiate skyline droolers. ⊠ *St. Martin's Pl., Covent Garden, WC2* ☎ *020/7312–2463 recorded information* ⊕ *www.npg.org.uk* ▣ *Free, charge for special exhibitions* ☉ *Mon.–Wed. and weekends 10–6, Thurs. and Fri. 10–9* Ⓤ *Charing Cross, Leicester Sq.*

★ ❾ **Queen's Gallery.** The former chapel at the south side of Buckingham Palace is now a temple of art and rare objects, acquired by kings and queens over the centuries. The Pennethorne Gallery is dominated by the larger-than-life portrait of Charles I (Van Dyck) in equestrian mode, which almost overshadows works by Holbein, Frans Hals, Jan Vermeer, and Rubens. These contrast starkly with the frank portrait of Queen Elizabeth II by Lucian Freud in the Nash Gallery. Between and beneath the paintings are cabinets, tables, and silverwork. ■ TIP➔ **The E-gallery reveals hidden details of some artworks, allowing you to open lockets and remove a sword from its scabbard.** Admission is by timed ticket. ⊠ *Buckingham Palace, Buckingham Palace Rd., St. James's, SW1* ☎ *020/7766–7301* ⊕ *www.royal.gov.uk* ▣ *£7.50* ☉ *Daily 10–5:30; last admission 4:30* Ⓤ *Victoria, St. James's Park.*

☘ **St. James's Park.** With three palaces at its borders, St. James's Park is the most royal of the royal parks. It's also London's smallest, most ornamental park, as well as the oldest; it was acquired by Henry VIII in 1532 for a deer park. About 17 species of birds—including pelicans, geese, ducks, and swans (which belong to the Queen)—now breed around the lake, attracting ornithologists at dawn. Later on summer days the deck chairs (which you must pay to use) are crammed with office workers lunching while being serenaded by music from the bandstands. One of the best times to stroll the leafy walkways is after dark, with Westminster Abbey and the Houses of Parliament rising above the floodlighted lake. ⊠ *The Mall or Horse Guards approach, or Birdcage Walk, St. James's, SW1* Ⓤ *St. James's Park, Westminster.*

★ ⑰ **Tate Britain.** This museum, funded by the sugar magnate Sir Henry Tate, is a brilliant celebration of great British artists from the 16th century to the present day. Each room has a theme and includes key works by major British artists: Van Dyck, Hogarth, and Reynolds rub shoulders with Rossetti, Sickert, Hockney, and Bacon, for example. Not to be missed is the generous selection of Constable landscapes. The collection's crowning glory is the Turner Bequest, consisting of Romantic painter J. M. W. Turner's personal collection. He left it to the nation on condition that the works be displayed together. The James Stirling–designed Clore Gallery (to the right of the main gallery) opened in 1987 to fulfill his wish, and it should not be missed. You can rent an audio guide with commentaries by curators, experts, and some of the artists themselves. ⊠ *Millbank, Westminster, SW1* ☎ *020/7887–800, 020/7887–8008 recorded information* ⊕ *www.tate.org.uk* ✆ *Free, exhibitions £3–£10* ☉ *Daily 10–5:50* Ⓤ *Pimlico (signposted 5-min walk).*

❶ **Trafalgar Square.** This is the center of London, by dint of a plaque on the corner of the Strand and Charing Cross Road from which distances on U.K. signposts are measured. Great events, such as royal weddings, political protests, and sporting triumphs, always draw crowds to the city's most famous square. The commanding open space is built on the grand scale demanded by its central position in the capital of an empire that once reached to the farthest corners of the globe. Trafalgar Square takes its name from the Battle of Trafalgar, Admiral Lord Horatio Nelson's great naval victory over the French, in 1805. Appropriately, the dominant landmark here is **Nelson's Column,** a 145-foot-high granite perch from which E. H. Baily's 1843 statue of Nelson keeps watch. The **equestrian statue of Charles I,** looking south toward the Banqueting House, receives a wreath on the anniversary of his execution, January 30. ⊠ *Trafalgar Sq., Westminster SW1* Ⓤ *Charing Cross, Leicester Sq.*

⑫ **Westminster Abbey.** A monument to the nation's rich—and often bloody and scandalous—history, the abbey rises on the Thames skyline as one of London's most iconic sites. Nearly all of Britain's monarchs have been crowned here since the coronation of William the Conqueror on Christmas Day 1066—and most are buried here, too. The abbey's majestic main nave is packed with memories (and, often, crowds), as it has witnessed many splendid royal events. Other than the mysterious gloom of the vast interior, the first thing that strikes most people is the proliferation of statues, tombs, and commemorative tablets. In parts, the building seems more like a stonemason's yard than a place of worship. But in its latter capacity, this landmark truly comes into its own. Although attending a service is not something to undertake purely for sightseeing reasons, it provides a glimpse of the abbey in its full majesty, with the service accompanied by music from the Westminster choristers and the organ that composer Henry Purcell once played.

Fodor'sChoice
★

The current abbey is a largely 13th- and 14th-century rebuilding of the 11th-century church founded by Edward the Confessor, with one no-

Where to See the Royals

1

THE QUEEN AND THE ROYAL FAMILY attend some 400 functions a year, and if you want to know what they are doing on any given date, turn to the *Court Circular* printed in the major London dailies. But most people want to see the Royals in all their dazzling pomp and circumstance. For this, the best bet is the second Saturday in June, when Trooping the Colour is usually held to celebrate the Queen's official birthday. This spectacular parade begins when she leaves Buckingham Palace in her carriage and rides down the Mall to arrive at Horse Guards Parade at 11 AM exactly.

If you wish to obtain one of the 7,000 seats (no more than two per request, distributed by ballot), enclose a letter and self-addressed, stamped envelope or International Reply Coupon—January to February 28 only—to Ticket Office, Headquarters

Household Division, Horse Guards, London SW1A 2AX, ☎ 020/7414–2479. You can also just line up along the Mall with your binoculars.

Another time you can catch the Queen in all her regalia is when she and the Duke of Edinburgh ride in state to Westminster to open the Houses of Parliament. In late October or early November, the famous gilded coach is escorted by the Household Cavalry. As the Queen enters the building, the air shakes with the booming of heavy guns, and all London knows that the democratic processes have once again been renewed with all their age-old ceremony.

Should you miss seeing the Queen, or if you just want to read about the Royals, visit ⊕ www.royal.gov.uk, the official Web site of the British monarchy.

---

table addition being the 18th-century twin towers over the west entrance, designed by Sir Christopher Wren and completed by Nicholas Hawksmoor. Entering by the north door to follow the one-way route through the abbey, what you see first on your left are the extravagant 18th-century monuments of statesmen in the north transept, as well as the north-transept chapels. Look up to your right to see the painted-glass rose window, the largest of its kind. At many points the view of the abbey is crowded by the many statues and screens; to your right is the mostly 19th-century choir screen (part is 13th-century), and to the left is the sacrarium, containing the medieval kings' tombs that screen the **Chapel of St. Edward** (because of its fragility the shrine is closed off, unless you take a tour with the verger—ask at the admission desk when you enter). Continuing to the foot of the Henry VII Chapel steps, you can still see the hot seat of power, the **Coronation Chair,** which has been graced by nearly every royal posterior. Then proceed into one of the architectural glories of Britain, the **Henry VII Chapel** (also known as the Lady Chapel), passing the huge white marble tomb of Elizabeth I, buried with her half-sister, "Bloody" Mary I, whose death she ordered. All around the chapel are magnificent sculptures of saints, philosophers, and kings, with mermaids and monsters carved on the choir-stall misericords (undersides), and exquisite fan vaulting above (binoculars will help you spot the statues high on the walls)—the last riot of medieval design in England and one of the miracles of Western architecture.

Continue to **Poets' Corner;** in 1400 Geoffrey Chaucer became the first poet to be buried here. There are memorials to William Shakespeare, William Blake, and Charles Dickens (who is also buried here). Outside the west front is an archway into the quiet, green **Dean's Yard** and the entrance to the **Cloisters.** If time allows, visit the **Chapter House,** a stunning octagonal room, adorned with 14th-century frescoes, where the King's Council met between 1257 and 1547. The **Abbey Museum** is in the **Undercroft,** which survives from Edward the Confessor's original church. The museum includes effigies made from the death masks and actual clothing of Charles II and Admiral Lord Nelson, among other fascinating relics. Adjoining these rooms, the **Little Cloister** is a quiet haven. Just beyond, the **College Garden,** under cultivation for more than 900 years, is planted with medicinal herbs. As you return to the abbey, look again at the truly awe-inspiring nave. Pause for the **Tomb of the Unknown Warrior,** an anonymous World War I martyr who lies buried here in memory of the soldiers fallen in both world wars.

Arrive early if possible, but be prepared to wait in line to tour the abbey. You can rent an audio guide (£3) or ask the information desk about 90-minute verger-led tours (£4). Photography is not permitted. ⊠ *Broad Sanctuary, Westminster, SW1* ☎ *020/7222–5152* ⊕ *www. westminster-abbey.org* 🖭 *Abbey and museum £10* ⊘ *Abbey Mon., Tues., Thurs., and Fri. 9:30–3:45, Wed. 9:30–6, Sat. 9–1:45 (closes 1 hr after last admission). Museum daily 10:30–4. Cloisters daily 8–6. College Garden Tues.–Thurs. Apr.–Sept. 10–6, Oct.–Mar. 10–4. Separate admission for Chapter House daily 10–4. Abbey closed to visitors during weekday and Sun. services* Ⓤ *Westminster.*

Also Worth Seeing

⓯ **Banqueting House.** Commissioned by James I, Inigo Jones (1573–1652), one of England's great architects, created this banqueting hall in 1619–22 out of an old remnant of the Tudor Palace of Whitehall. Influenced by Andrea Palladio's work, which he saw during a sojourn in Tuscany, Jones remade the palace with Palladian sophistication and purity. James I's son, Charles I, enhanced the interior by employing the Flemish painter Peter Paul Rubens to glorify his father all over the ceiling. These allegorical paintings, depicting a wise monarch being received into heaven, were the last thing Charles saw before he was beheaded on a scaffold outside in 1649. Phone or check the Web site for information about lunchtime concerts. ⊠ *Whitehall, Westminster, SW1A* ☎ *020/ 7930–4179, 0870/751–5178 recorded information, 0870/751– 5187 concert tickets* ⊕ *www.hrp. org.uk* 🖭 *£4.50, includes free audio*

IN A HURRY?

If you're pressed for time, concentrate on these four Abbey highlights: the Coronation Chair; tombs of Elizabeth I and Mary, Queen of Scots, in the Chapel of Henry VII; Poets' Corner; and Tomb of the Unknown Warrior.

guide ⊙ *Mon.–Sat. 10–5, last admission 4:30. Closed Christmas wk* Ⓤ *Charing Cross, Embankment, Westminster.*

❺ **Clarence House.** The London home of the late Queen Elizabeth the Queen Mother for nearly 50 years, this Regency mansion is the Prince of Wales's residence. Built by John Nash for the duke of Clarence, it has remained a royal home—the present monarch, Queen Elizabeth, lived here after her marriage. The rooms have been sensitively preserved as the Queen Mother chose, with works of art from the Royal Collection. It is less palace, and more home (for Prince Charles, his wife Camilla, and his sons William and Harry), with informal family pictures and comfortable sofas. The tour (by timed-ticket entry only) is of the ground-floor rooms. ⊠ *The Mall, St. James's SW1* ☎ *020/7766–7303* ⊕ *www. royal.gov.uk* ⊠ *£6* ⊙ *Aug.–mid-Oct.; call for hrs* Ⓤ *Green Park.*

⓮ **Downing Street.** The British version of the White House occupies three unassuming 18th-century houses. No. 10 has been the official residence of the prime minister since 1732. The cabinet office, hub of the British system of government, is on the ground floor; the prime minister's private apartment is on the top floor. The chancellor of the exchequer traditionally occupies No. 11. Downing Street is cordoned off, but you should be able to catch a glimpse of it from Whitehall. Just south of Downing Street, in the middle of Whitehall, is the **Cenotaph,** a stark white monolith designed in 1920 by Edward Lutyens to commemorate the 1918 Armistice. ⊠ *Whitehall, Westminster, SW1* Ⓤ *Westminster.*

❻ **St. James's Palace.** With its scarlet-coated guard posted at the gate, this small palace of Tudor brick was a home for many British sovereigns, including the Elizabeth I and Charles I, who spent his last night here before his execution. Today it is the working office of another Charles—the Prince of Wales. Something to ponder as you look (you can't go in): foreign ambassadors to Britain are still accredited to the Court of St. James's even though it has rarely been a primary royal residence. ⊠ *Friary Court, St. James's, SW1* ⊕ *www.royal.gov.uk* Ⓤ *Green Park.*

⟲ ❹ **St. Martin-in-the-Fields.** One of Britain's best-loved churches, St. Martin's was completed in 1726; James Gibbs's classical temple-with-spire design became a familiar pattern for churches in colonial America. The church is a haven for music lovers; the Academy of St. Martin-in-the-Fields, an internationally known orchestra, was founded here, and popular lunchtime and evening concerts (free or reasonably priced) continue today. ■ TIP➡ **You can pop in and attend rehearsals for free, a tranquil break from the city's bustle.** The church's fusty interior is wonderful for music making, but the wooden benches make hard seats. The Crypt is a hive of lively activity, with an excellent café and bookshop, plus the **London Brass-Rubbing Centre,** where you can make your own life-size souvenir knight, lady, or monarch from replica tomb brasses. ⊠ *Trafalgar Sq., Covent Garden, WC2* ☎ *020/7766–1100, 020/7839–8362 evening-concert credit-card bookings* ⊕ *www.stmartin-in-the-fields.org* ⊙ *Church daily 8–8; crypt Mon.–Sat. 10–8 (brass-rubbing center until 6), Sun. noon–6; box office Mon.–Sat. 10–5* Ⓤ *Charing Cross, Leicester Sq.*

❼ Spencer House. Ancestral abode of the Spencers, the family of Princess Diana, this great mansion is perhaps the finest London example of 18th-century elegance on a domestic scale. The house was built in 1766 for the first earl Spencer, heir to the first duchess of Marlborough; the family hasn't lived here since 1926. The most ostentatious part of the house is the florid bow window of the Palm Room: covered with stucco palm trees, it conjures up both ancient Palmyra and modern Miami Beach. The garden, of Henry Holland design, has plantings of his era. Both the house and garden can be seen only by guided tour, so book in advance. ✉ *27 St. James's Pl., St. James's, SW1* ☎ *020/7499–8620* ⊕ *www. spencerhouse.co.uk* 🎟 *£9* ⊙ *House: Feb.–July and Sept.–Dec., Sun. 10:45–4:45; 1-hr guided tour leaves about every 25 mins (tickets on sale Sun. at 10:30). Garden: late May–July* Ⓤ *Green Park.*

❿ Wellington Barracks. These are the headquarters of the Queen's five regiments of foot guards, who protect the sovereign and patrol her palace dressed in tunics of gold-purled scarlet and tall busbies of black bearskin. The entrance to the **Guards Museum** is next to the Guards Chapel. ✉ *Wellington Barracks, Birdcage Walk, Westminster, SW1* ☎ *020/ 7414–3428* 🎟 *£2* ⊙ *Daily 10–4; last admission 3:30* Ⓤ *St. James's Park.*

Soho & Covent Garden

Once a red-light district, the Soho of today delivers more "grown-up" than "adult" entertainment. Its theaters, restaurants, pubs, and clubs merge with the first-run cinemas of Leicester Square and the venerable venues (Royal and English National Operas) of Covent Garden to create the mega-entertainment district known as the West End. During the day, Covent Garden's historic piazza is packed with shoppers and sightseers, whereas Soho reverts to the business side of its lively, late-night scene—ad agencies, media, film distributors, actors, agents and casting agents, all looking for one another.

A quadrilateral bounded by Regent Street, Coventry and Cranbourn streets, Charing Cross Road, and the eastern half of Oxford Street encloses Soho. For many years Soho was London's peep show–sex shop–brothel center. Legislation in the mid-1980s granted expensive licenses to a few such establishments and closed down the rest. Today Soho remains the address of wonderful ethnic restaurants, including those of London's Chinatown.

The Covent Garden Market became the Covent Garden Piazza in 1980. It was originally the "convent garden" belonging to the Abbey of St. Peter at Westminster (later Westminster Abbey), and still functions as the center of a neighborhood—one that has always been alluded to as "colorful." After centuries of magnificence and misery, Covent Garden became London's vegetable and flower market in the 19th century. When the produce moved to the Nine Elms Market in Vauxhall in 1974, the glass-covered market halls took on new life with stores and entertainment. Today it bustles with tourists and shoppers.

TIMING   Although you may well get lost in the area's winding streets, you can whiz around both neighborhoods in an hour or you can spend all day—

for shopping, lunch, and Somerset House. You might stop by Leicester Square and visit tkts, the Society of London Theatre (SOLT) half-price ticket kiosk (opens at 10 Monday through Saturday, noon Sunday), pick up tickets for later, and walk, shop, and eat in between.

GETTING HERE   Take any train to the Piccadilly Circus station (on the Piccadilly and Bakerloo lines or Leicester Square and Northern lines for Soho). Get off at Covent Garden on the Piccadilly Line for Covent Garden and Embankment (Bakerloo, Northern, District and Circle lines) or Charing Cross (Northern, Bakerloo and main railway lines) for the area south of the Strand. Bus numbers 14, 19, and 38 run along Shaftesbury Avenue; 24, 29, and 176 run along Charing Cross Road; and 6, 9, 11, 13, 15, 23, 77A, 91, 139, and 176 run along the Strand.

Numbers in the margin correspond to numbers on the Soho & Covent Garden map.

Main Attractions

Courtauld Institute Gallery. One of London's most beloved art collections, the Courtauld is in the grounds of the 18th-century **Somerset House.** Founded in 1931 by textile magnate Samuel Courtauld to house his private collection, this is one of the world's finest impressionist and postimpressionist galleries, with works by masters from Bonnard to Van Gogh. A déja vu moment with Cézanne, Degas, Seurat, or Monet awaits on every wall (Manet's *Bar at the Folies-Bergère* is the star), with bonus post-Renaissance works thrown in. ⊠ *The Strand, Covent Garden, WC2* ☎ *020/7848–2526* ⊕ *www.courtauld.ac.uk* ⊠ *£5, free Mon. 10–2, except bank holidays;* ⊙ *Daily 10–6; last admission at 5:15* Ⓤ *Covent Garden, Holborn, Temple.*

☁ ❷ **Covent Garden Piazza.** The restored 1840 market building around which Covent Garden pivots is known as the Piazza. Inigo Jones, the King's Surveyor of Works, designed the entire area in the 1630s, including **St. Paul's Church** (known as the actors' church). Buskers perform under the church's portico, where the first scene of the play *Pygmalion* (and the musical *My Fair Lady*) take place. Inside the Piazza, the shops are mostly higher-class clothing chains, plus a couple of cafés and some knickknack stores that are good for gifts. There's the superior **Apple Market** for crafts on most days, too. If you turn right, you'll reach the indoor **Jubilee Market,** which, with its stalls of clothing, army-surplus gear, and more crafts and knickknacks, is disappointingly ordinary. In summer it may seem that everyone you see around the Piazza (and the crowds are legion) is a fellow tourist, but there's still plenty of office life in the area. Londoners who shop in the area tend to head for Neal Street and the area to the left of the subway entrance rather than the touristy market itself. By

FEELING PECKISH?

Although they may set out a few tables, the coffee shops and snack bars along the Covent Garden market buildings are better for takeout than for comfortable coffee breaks or lunches. They can be overpriced and of iffy quality. Head for Soho when the munchies strike.

the church in the square, street performers—from global musicians to jugglers and mimes—play to the crowds, as they have done since the first English Punch and Judy Show, staged here in the 17th century. ✉ *Bordered by Henrietta St., King St., Russell St., and Bedford St., Covent Garden, WC2* Ⓤ *Covent Garden.*

★ ❺ **Somerset House.** This grand 18th-century pile, constructed during the reign of George III, was designed to house government offices, principally those of the navy. The gracious rooms on the south side of the building, by the river, are free, including the Seamen's Waiting Hall and the Nelson Stair. The **Courtauld Institute Gallery** occupies most of the north building, facing the busy Strand. Cafés and a river terrace adjoin the property, and a footbridge leads on to Waterloo Bridge. In the vaults of the house is the **Gilbert Collection,** a museum with intricate works of silver, gold snuffboxes, and Italian mosaics. **The Hermitage Rooms** have treasures from the State Hermitage Museum in Russia. ✉ *The Strand, Covent Garden, WC2* ☎ *020/7845–4600, 020/7485–4630 Hermitage information* ⊕ *www.somerset-house.org.uk* ✉ *Somerset House free; galleries £5 each* ⊙ *Daily 10–6; last admission at 5:15* Ⓤ *Charing Cross.*

Also Worth Seeing

❶ **Leicester Square.** Looking at the neon of the major movie houses, the fast-food outlets (plus a useful Häagen-Dazs café), and the disco entrances, you'd never guess the square was laid out around 1630. By the 19th century it was already bustling and disreputable, and now it's usually one of the few places crowded after midnight—with suburban teenagers, backpackers, and London's swelling ranks of the homeless. That said, it's not a threatening place, and the liveliness can be quite cheering. But be on your guard—any place so full of tourists and people a little the worse for wear is bound to attract pickpockets and Leicester Square certainly does. In the middle is a statue of a sulking Shakespeare, clearly wishing he were somewhere else and perhaps remembering the days when the cinemas were live theaters—burlesque houses, but live all the same. Here, too, are figures of Hogarth, Reynolds, and Charlie Chaplin. ■ TIP→ **One landmark worth visiting is tkts,** the Society of London Theatre ticket kiosk, which sells half-price tickets for many of that evening's performances. It's open Monday through Saturday from 10 AM to 7 PM, and Sunday from noon to 3 PM. ✉ *Leicester Sq., Covent Garden, WC2* Ⓤ *Covent Garden.*

☯ **London's Transport Museum.** Normally housed in the old Flower Market at the southeast corner of the Covent Garden Piazza, the museum is closed for redevelopment and not scheduled to reopen until late 2007. Most exhibits have been moved to a temporary location, the Museum Depot in the West London suburbs. The Depot is occasionally open for guided tours and open weekends. Visit the museum's Web site for access information. ⊕ *www.ltmuseum.co.uk.*

❸ **Royal Opera House.** London's premier opera and ballet venue was designed in 1858 by E. M. Barry, son of Sir Charles, the architect of the House of Commons building. Without doubt, the glass-and-steel Floral Hall is the most jaw-dropping feature, and you can wander in during the day, when there may be free lunchtime concerts and events. The

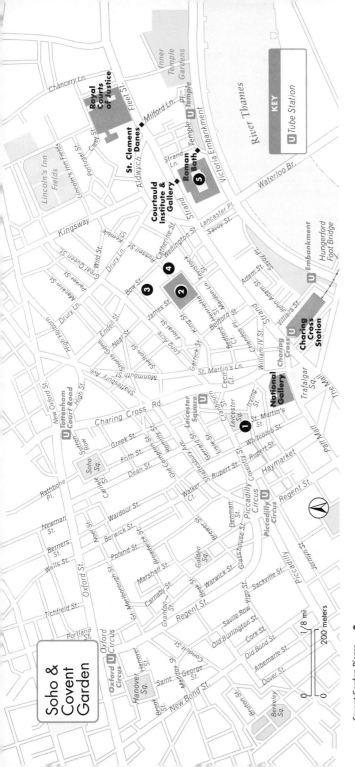

Soho &
Covent
Garden

River Thames

Covent Garden Piazza . . **2**
Leicester Square **1**
Royal Opera House **3**
Somerset House **5**
Theatre Museum **4**

Amphitheatre Bar and Piazza concourse give a splendid panorama across the city. ✉ *Bow St., Covent Garden, WC2* ☏ *020/7304–4000* ⊕ *www.royaloperahouse.org* Ⓤ *Covent Garden.*

☺ ❹ **Theatre Museum.** This mostly below-ground museum aims to re-create the excitement of theater itself. There are usually programs in progress allowing children to have a giant dressing-up session. Permanent exhibits paint a history of the English stage from the 16th century to Mick Jagger's jumpsuit, with tens of thousands of theater playbills and sections on such topics as pantomime—the peculiar British theatrical tradition when men dress as ugly women, known as Panto Dames, and girls wear tights and play princes. There's a ticket desk for "real" theaters around town, plus an archive holding video recordings and audiotapes of significant British theatrical productions. ✉ *7 Russell St., Covent Garden, WC2* ☏ *020/7943–4700* ⊕ *www.theatremuseum.org* ✑ *Free* ⊙ *Tues.–Sun. 10–6; last admission 5:30* Ⓤ *Covent Garden.*

Bloomsbury & Legal London

The hub of intellectual London, Bloomsbury is anchored by the British Museum and the University of London, which houses—among other institutions—the internationally ranked London School of Economics and the School of Oriental and African Studies. As a result, the streets and cafés around Bloomsbury's Russell Square are often crawling with students and professors engaged in heated conversation, and literary agents and academics surf the shelves of the antiquarian bookstores nearby.

The character of an area of London can change visibly from one street to the next. Nowhere is this so clear as in the contrast between fun-loving Soho and intellectual Bloomsbury, a mere 100 yards to the northeast, or between arty, trendy Covent Garden and—on the other side of Kingsway—sober Holborn (pronounced *hoe*-bun). Bloomsbury is known for its famous flowering of literary-arty bohemia, personified during the first three decades of the 20th century by the clique known as the Bloomsbury Group, including Virginia Woolf, E. M. Forster, Vanessa Bell, and Lytton Strachey. Holborn, filled with ancient buildings of the legal profession, is more interesting and beautiful than you might suppose. The Great Fire of 1666 razed most of the city but spared the buildings of legal London, and all of Holborn oozes history. Leading landmarks here are the Inns of Court, where the country's top solicitors and barristers have had their chambers for centuries.

TIMING Both Bloomsbury and Holborn are almost purely residential and should be seen by day. Bloomsbury includes the British Museum, where you could spend two hours—or two days. The Charles Dickens Museum is also worth a stop. In legal London, most of the highlights are in the architecture, with the exception of Sir John Soane's Museum. Avoid the area around King's Cross Station at night.

GETTING HERE You can walk easily around Bloomsbury, and the Russell Square tube stop on the Piccadilly Line leaves you right at the corner of Russell Square. The best tube stops for the Inns of Court are Holborn on the Central and Piccadilly lines or Chancery Lane on the Central Line. Tottenham

Court Road on the Northern and Central lines or Russell Square (Piccadilly Line) are best for the British Museum. You can often find taxis near the British Museum or by the entrance to the hotels off Russell Square. Bus 7 is the best bus for the British Museum; for Inns of Court, take Bus 8, 17, 25, 45, 46, or 242 to High Holborn or Bus 17, 19, 38, 45, 46, 55, or 243 to Theobalds Road.

Numbers in the margin correspond to numbers on the Bloomsbury & Legal London map.

Main Attractions

FodorsChoice
★

① **British Museum.** With a facade like a great temple, this celebrated treasure house, filled with plunder of incalculable value and beauty from around the globe, occupies a ponderous Greco-Victorian building that makes a suitably grand impression. Inside are some of the greatest relics of humankind: the Elgin Marbles, the Rosetta Stone, the Sutton Hoo Treasure—almost everything, it seems, but the Ark of the Covenant. Many sections have been updated, particularly in ethnography, including the impressive **Sainsbury African Galleries.** The focal point is the **Great Court,** a brilliant techno-classical design with a vast glass roof that highlights and reveals the museum's most well-kept secret—an inner courtyard. The revered **Reading Room** has a blue-and-gold dome, ancient tomes, and computer screens. If you want to navigate the highlights of the almost 100 galleries, join at least one of the free **Eyeopener** 50-minute tours by museum guides (details at the information desk).

The collection began in 1753 and grew quickly, thanks to enthusiastic kleptomaniacs during the Napoléonic Wars—most notoriously the seventh earl of Elgin, who acquired the marbles from the Parthenon and Erechtheum in Athens during his term as British ambassador in Constantinople. Here follows a highly edited résumé (in order of encounter) of the British Museum's greatest hits: close to the entrance hall, in Room 4, is the **Rosetta Stone,** found by French soldiers in 1799, and carved in 196 BC with a decree of Ptolemy V in Egyptian hieroglyphics, demotic (a cursive script developed in Egypt), and Greek. This inscription provided the French Egyptologist Jean-François Champollion with the key to deciphering hieroglyphics. Maybe the **Parthenon Marbles** ought to be back in Greece, but since these graceful sculptures are here, make a beeline for them in Room 18, west of the entrance in the Parthenon Galleries. These galleries include the spectacular remains of the Parthenon frieze that girdled the cella of Athena's temple on the Acropolis, carved around 440 BC. Also in the West Wing is one of the Seven Wonders of the Ancient World—in fragment form—in Room 21: the **Mausoleum of Halikarnassos.** The **JP Morgan Chase North American Gallery** (Room 26) has one of the largest collections of native culture outside the North American continent, going back to the earliest hunters 10,000 years ago.

Upstairs are some of the most popular galleries, especially beloved by children: Rooms 62 and 63, where the **Egyptian mummies** live. Nearby are the glittering 4th-century **Mildenhall Treasure** and the equally splendid 8th-century Anglo-Saxon **Sutton Hoo Treasure** (with a magnificent helmet and jewelry). A more prosaic exhibit is that of Pete Marsh, sen-

timentally named by the archaeologists who unearthed the **Lindow
Man** from a Cheshire peat marsh;
poor Pete was ritually slain in the
1st century, probably as a human
sacrifice. The **Korean Gallery** (Room
67) delves into the art and archaeology of the country, including precious porcelain and colorful screens.
⊠ *Great Russell St., Bloomsbury,
WC1* ☎ *020/7636–1555* ⊕ *www.
thebritishmuseum.ac.uk* ⊠ *Free,
suggested donation £2* ☉ *Museum
Sat.–Wed. 10–5:30, Thurs. and Fri.
10–8:30. Great Court Sun.–Wed.
9–6, Thurs.–Sat. 9 AM–11 PM*
Ⓤ *Holborn, Russell Sq., Tottenham
Court Rd.*

ⓒ ❹ **Dickens House Museum.** This is the only one of the many London houses
Charles Dickens (1812–70) inhabited that's still standing. The great novelist wrote *Oliver Twist* and *Nicholas Nickleby* and finished *The Pickwick Papers* here between 1837 and 1839. The house looks exactly as
it would have in Dickens's day, complete with first editions, letters, and
tall clerk's desk, plus a treat for Lionel Bart fans—his score for the musical *Oliver!* Christmas is a memorable time to visit, as the rooms are
decorated in traditional style. ⊠ *48 Doughty St., Bloomsbury, WC1*
☎ *020/7405–2127* ⊕ *www.dickensmuseum.com* ⊠ *£5* ☉ *Mon.–Sat.
10–5, Sun. 11–5; last admission at 4:30* Ⓤ *Chancery La., Russell Sq.*

★ ❻ **Lincoln's Inn.** There's plenty to see at one of the oldest and most comely
of the Inns of Court—from the Chancery Lane Tudor brick gatehouse
to the wide-open, tree-lined Lincoln's Inn Fields and the 15th-century
chapel. The wisteria-clad New Square is the city's only complete 17th-
century square. ⊠ *Chancery La., Bloomsbury, WC2* ☎ *020/7405–1393*
⊠ *Free* ☉ *Gardens weekdays 7–7; chapel weekdays noon–2:30; public may also attend Sun. service at 11:30 in chapel during legal terms*
Ⓤ *Chancery La.*

★ ❺ **Sir John Soane's Museum.** Guaranteed to raise a smile from the most blasé
traveler, this collection hardly deserves the burden of its dry name. Sir
John, architect of the Bank of England, who lived here from 1790 to
1831, created one of London's most idiosyncratic and fascinating houses.
He obviously had enormous fun with his home, having had the means
to finance great experiments in perspective and scale and to fill the space
with some wonderful pieces. Everywhere mirrors and colors play tricks
with light and space, and split-level floors worthy of a fairground fun
house disorient you. In a basement chamber sits the vast 1300 BC sar-
cophagus of Seti I, lighted by a skylight two stories above. ⊠ *13 Lincoln's Inn Fields, Bloomsbury, WC2* ☎ *020/7405–2107* ⊕ *www.soane.
org* ⊠ *Free, Sat. tour £3* ☉ *Tues.–Sat. 10–5; also 6–9 PM on 1st Tues.
of every month; tours Sat. at 2:30* Ⓤ *Holborn.*

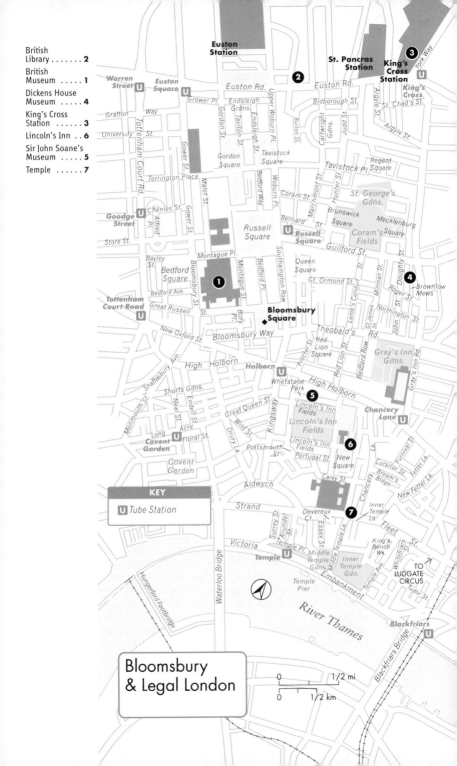

Euston
Station

St. Pancras
Station

King's
Cross
Station

②

③

York Way

King's
Cross

Warren
Street

Euston
Square

Euston Rd.

Euston Rd.

St. Chad's St.

Argyle St.

Grafton
Way

Grower Pl.

Endsleigh
Grdns.

Upper Woburn Pl.

Burton St.

Bidborough St.

Cartwright
Gdns.

Judd St.

Argyle St.

University
Street

Gordon St.

Tavistock St.

Endsleigh St.

Gordon
Square

Tavistock
Square

Regent
Square

Tottenham Court Rd.

Gower St.

Torrington Place

Malet St.

Bedford Way

Woburn Pl.

Coram St.

Marchmont St.

Tavistock Pl.

Hunter St.

St. George's
Gdns.

Goodge
Street

Chenies St.

Alfred Pl.

Gower St.

Bedford Way

Bernard St.

Brunswick
Square

Mecklenburg
Square

Store St.

Russell
Square

Russell
Square

Coram's
Fields

Bayley
St.

Bloomsbury St.

Montague Pl.

Montague St.

Bedford Pl.

Southampton Row

Guilford St.

Doughty St.

Bedford
Square

Queen
Square

Gt. Ormond St.

Lamb's Conduit St.

Millman St.

Roger St.

④

Brownlow
Mews

Tottenham
Court Road

Bedford Ave.

Great Russell
St.

Bury Pl.

①

◆ **Bloomsbury
Square**

Theobald's

John St.

Northington St.

New Oxford St.

Bloomsbury Way

Red
Lion Square

Red Lion St.

Bedford Row

James St.

Rd.

Gray's Inn
Gdns.

Shaftesbury Ave.

High Holborn

Holborn

Procter St.

High Holborn

Gray's Inn Rd.

Shorts Gdns.

Neal St.

Endell St.

Whetstone
Park

Chancery
Lane

Monmouth St.

Great Queen St.

Kingsway

⑤

Lincoln's Inn
Fields

Lincoln's Inn
Fields

New Fetter La.

Long
Acre

Floral St.

Drury La.

Wild St.

Cursitor St.

Bream's
Bldgs.

Furnival St.

Fetter La.

Covent
Garden

Portsmouth
St.

Portugal St.

New
Square

⑥

Chancery La.

Covent
Garden

Carey St.

Aldwych

KEY

U *Tube Station*

Strand

Surrey St.

Arundel St.

Devereux
Ct.

Essex St.

⑦

Inner
Temple
La.

Fleet St.

King's
Bench Wk.

Whitefriars St.

TO
LUDGATE
CIRCUS

Victoria

Temple

Temple Pl.

Middle
Temple
Gdns.

Middle Temple La.

Inner
Temple Gdn.

Temple Ave.

Tudor St.

Waterloo Bridge

Hungerford Footbridge

Temple
Pier

Embankment

River Thames

Blackfriars

Blackfriars
Bridge

**Bloomsbury
& Legal London**

0   1/2 mi

0   1/2 km

Also Worth Seeing

② **British Library.** Since 1759, the British Library had been housed in the British Museum—but space ran out in the 1990s, necessitating this grand edifice, a few blocks north of the museum, between Euston and St. Pancras stations. The collection includes 18 million volumes, and the library's treasures are on public view. ■ TIP→ **Don't miss the fine John Ritblat Gallery,** which displays the Magna Carta, the Gutenberg Bible, Jane Austen's manuscripts, Shakespeare's First Folio, and musical manuscripts by George Frideric Handel and Sir Paul McCartney. Use the headphones to listen to some interesting snippets in a small showcase of the **National Sound Archive,** such as the voice of Florence Nightingale and an extract from the Beatles' last tour interview. ⊠ *96 Euston Rd., Bloomsbury, NW1* ☎ *020/7412–7332* ⊕ *www.bl.uk* ☞ *Free; charge for special exhibitions* ⊙ *Mon. and Wed.–Fri. 9:30–6, Tues. 9:30–8, Sat. 9:30–5, Sun. and bank holiday Mon. 11–5* Ⓤ *Euston or King's Cross.*

Ⓒ **❸** **King's Cross Station.** Known for its 120-foot-tall clock tower, this yellow-brick Italianate building with large, arched windows was constructed in 1851–52 as the London terminus for the Great Northern Railway. Harry Potter took the Hogwarts Express to school from the imaginary platform 9¾ (platforms 4 and 5 were the actual shooting site) in the movies based on J. K. Rowling's popular novels. The station has put up a sign for platform 9¾; you can snap a picture there. ⊠ *Euston Rd. and York Way, Euston, NW1* ☎ *0845/748–4950* Ⓤ *King's Cross.*

❼ **Temple.** This is the collective name for the **Inner Temple** and **Middle Temple,** and its entrance, the point of entry into the City, is marked by a young (1880) bronze griffin, the **Temple Bar Memorial,** which makes a splendidly heraldic snapshot and marks the symbolic City Border. In the buildings opposite is an elaborate stone arch through which you pass into Middle Temple Lane, past a row of 17th-century timber-frame houses, and on into Fountain Court. If the Elizabethan **Middle Temple Hall** is open, don't miss its hammer-beam roof—among the finest in the land. ⊠ *Middle Temple La., Bloomsbury, EC4* ☎ *020/7427–4800* ⊙ *Weekdays 10–11 and, when not in use, 2–4* Ⓤ *Temple.*

The City

The City, as opposed to the city, is the capital's fast-beating financial heart. Behind a host of imposing neoclassical facades lie the banks and exchanges whose frantic trade determines the fortunes that underpin London—and the country. But the "Square Mile" is much more than London's Wall Street—the capital's economic-engine room also has currency as a religious and political center. St. Paul's Cathedral has looked after Londoners' souls since the 7th century, and the Tower of London—that moat-surrounded royal fortress, prison, and jewel house—has taken care of beheading them. The City's maze of backstreets is also home to a host of old churches, marketplaces, and cozy pubs.

The City extends eastward from Temple Bar to the Tower of London, and north from the Thames to Chiswell Street. The pedestrian-only Millennium Bridge connects the area with the South Bank; it's well worth the walk. Twice, the City has been nearly wiped off the face of the earth. The Great Fire of 1666 necessitated a total reconstruction, in which Sir Christopher Wren had a big hand, contributing not only his masterpiece, St. Paul's Cathedral, but 49 additional parish churches. The second wave of destruction was dealt by the German bombers of World War II. The ruins were rebuilt, but slowly, and with no overall plan, leaving the City a patchwork of the old and the new, the interesting and the flagrantly awful. Since a mere 8,000 or so people call it home, the nation's financial center is deserted on weekends, with restaurants shuttered.

TIMING   The "Square Mile" is as compact as the nickname suggests, with very little distance between points of interest, making it easy to dip into the City in short bursts. For full immersion in the Tower of London, set aside half a day. Allow an hour minimum for the Museum of London, St. Paul's Cathedral, and the Tower Bridge each. On weekends, without the scurrying suits, the City is nearly empty, yet this is when the major attractions are at their busiest. So if you can manage to come on a weekday, do so.

GETTING HERE   The City is well-served by tube stops. St. Paul's and Bank, on the Central Line, and Mansion House, Cannon Street, and Monument, on the District and Circle lines, deliver visitors to the heart of the City. Liverpool Street and Aldgate border the City's eastern edge, whereas Chancery Lane and Farringdon lie to the west. Barbican and Moorgate provide easy access to the theaters and galleries of the Barbican, whereas Blackfriars, to the south, leads to Ludgate Circus and Fleet Street.

Numbers in the margin correspond to numbers on the City map.

Main Attractions

❻ Millennium Bridge. Norman Foster and sculptor Anthony Caro designed this strikingly modern, pedestrian-only bridge of aluminum and steel. The bridge connects the City—the St. Paul's Cathedral area—with the Tate Modern art gallery. On the South Bank side, the bridge marks the middle of the **Millennium Mile,** a walkway taking in a clutch of popular sights. The views from the bridge are breathtaking, with perhaps the best-ever view of St. Paul's. ✉ *Peters Hill to Bankside, The City, South Bank, EC4, SE1* Ⓤ *Mansion House, Blackfriars, or Southwark.*

⓫ Monument. Commemorating the "dreadful visitation" of the Great Fire of 1666, the world's tallest isolated stone column is the work of Christopher Wren. The viewing gallery is 311 steps up the 202-foot-high structure. ✉ *Monument St., The City, EC3* ☎ *020/7626–2717* ⊕ *www. towerbridge.org.uk* 💷 *£2, combination ticket gives £1 discount off entry to Tower Bridge* ☉ *Daily 10–5:40; hrs subject to change, phone before visiting* Ⓤ *Monument.*

★ ☺ ❺ Museum of London. If there's one place to get the history of London sorted out, right from 450,000 BC to the present day, it's here—although there's a great deal to sort out: Oliver Cromwell's death mask, Queen Victoria's crinolined gowns, Selfridges' art-deco elevators, and the Lord Mayor's coach are just some of the goodies. The displays—like one of the Great Fire, a 1940s air-raid shelter, a Georgian prison cell, a Roman living room, and a Victorian street complete with fully stocked shops—

are complemented by rich soundscapes that atmospherically re-create London life through the ages. ⊠ *London Wall, The City, EC2* ☎ *020/ 7600–0807* ⊕ *www.museumoflondon.org.uk* ☒ *Free* ☉ *Mon.–Sat. 10–5:50, Sun. noon–5:50, last admission 5:30* Ⓤ *Barbican.*

❷ St. Bride's. The distinctively tiered steeple of this Christopher Wren–designed church gave rise to the shape of the traditional wedding cake. As St. Paul's (in Covent Garden) is the actors' church, so St. Bride's belongs to journalists. The crypts house a museum of the church's rich history, and a bit of Roman sidewalk. ⊠ *Fleet St., The City, EC4* ☎ *020/7427–0133* ⊕ *www.stbrides.com* ☒ *Free* ☉ *Weekdays 8–6, Sat. 11–3, Sun. for services only 10–1 and 5–7:30; crypt closed Sun.* Ⓤ *Chancery La.*

❼ St. Mary-le-Bow. Christopher Wren's 1673 church has one of the most famous sets of bells—a Londoner must be born within the sound of Bow Bells to be a true cockney. The origin of that idea was probably the curfew rung on the Bow Bells during the 14th century. The name comes from the bow-shape arches in the Norman crypt, which now holds a popular vegetarian café open for breakfast and lunch. ⊠ *Cheapside, The City, EC2* ☎ *020/7248–5139* ⊕ *www.stmarylebow.co.uk* ☉ *Mon.–Thurs. 6:30–5:45, Fri. 6:30–4* Ⓤ *Mansion House.*

❹ St. Paul's Cathedral. The symbolic heart of London, St. Paul's may take your breath away, even more so now that it's been spruced up for its 300th anniversary. The dome—the world's third largest—peeps through the skyline from many an angle around London. The structure is Sir Christopher Wren's masterpiece, completed in 1710 after 35 years of building, and, much later, miraculously spared (mostly) by World War II bombs. Wren's first plan, known as the New Model, did not make it past the drawing board. The second, known as the Great Model, got as far as the 20-foot oak rendering you can see here before it also was rejected. The third was accepted, with the fortunate coda that the architect be allowed to make changes as he saw fit. Without that, there would be no dome, since the approved design had a steeple. When you enter and see the dome from the inside, it may seem smaller than you expected. It *is* smaller, and 60 feet lower than the lead-covered outer dome. Beneath the lantern is Wren's famous epitaph, which his son composed and had set into the pavement, and which reads succinctly: LECTOR, SI MONUMENTUM REQUIRIS, CIRCUMSPICE—"Reader, if you seek his monument, look around you." The epitaph also appears on Wren's memorial in the Crypt. Up 259 spiral steps is the **Whispering Gallery,** an acoustic phenomenon; you whisper something to the wall on one side, and a second later it transmits clearly to the other side, 107 feet away. Ascend to the **Stone Gallery,** which encircles the base of the dome. Farther up (280 feet from ground level) is the small **Golden Gallery,** around the dome's highest point. From both these galleries (if you have a head for heights) you can walk outside for a spectacular panorama of London. The climb up the spiraling steps can be fun for older kids.

The remains of the poet John Donne, who was dean of St. Paul's for his final 10 years (he died in 1631), are in the south choir aisle. The vivacious choir-stall carvings nearby are the work of Grinling Gibbons, as

The City

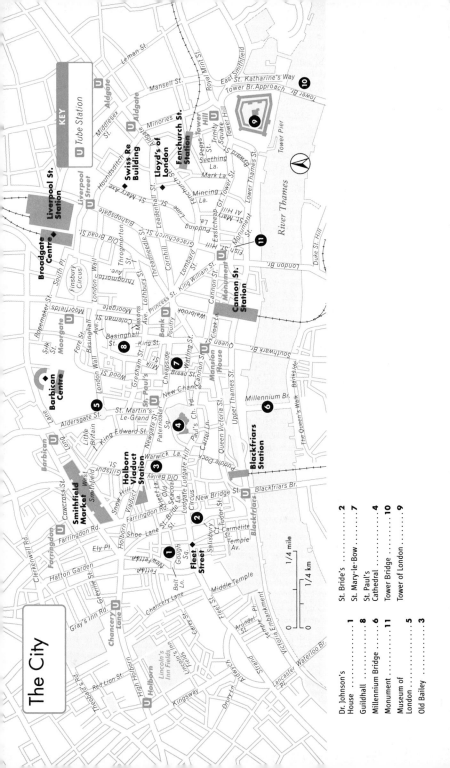

KEY

U Tube Station

are those on the organ, which Wren designed and Handel played. Behind the high altar is the **American Memorial Chapel,** dedicated in 1958 to the 28,000 GIs stationed in the United Kingdom who lost their lives in World War II. Among the famous whose remains lie in the **Crypt** are the duke of Wellington and Admiral Lord Nelson. The Crypt also has a gift shop and a café. ⊠ *St. Paul's Churchyard, The City, EC4* ☎ *020/7236–4128* ⊕ *www.stpauls.co.uk* ⊠ *£9, audio tour £3.50, guided tour £3* ☉ *Cathedral Mon.–Sat. 8:30–4, closed occasionally for special services; ambulatory, Crypt, and galleries Mon.–Sat. 9–5:15. Shop and Crypt Café also open Sun. 10:30–5* Ⓤ *St. Paul's.*

★ ☺ ❿ **Tower Bridge.** Despite its appearance, this Victorian youngster dates from 1894. Constructed of steel, then clothed in Portland stone, the bridge was built in the Gothic style to complement the Tower of London next door. It's famous for the enormous bascules, the "arms" that open to allow large ships through. The **Tower Bridge Experience** exhibition is a fun tour inside the structure to discover how one of the world's most famous bridges actually works. One highlight is the glorious view from up high on the covered walkway between the turrets. ☎ *020/7403–3761* ⊕ *www.towerbridge.org.uk* ⊠ *£5.50, joint ticket available for Monument* ☉ *Daily 9:30–5:30; last admission 5* Ⓤ *Tower Hill.*

★ ☺ ❾ **Tower of London.** Nowhere else does London's history come to life so vividly as in this minicity of 20 towers filled with heraldry and treasure, the intimate details of lords and dukes and princes and sovereigns etched in the walls (literally, in some places), and quite a few pints of royal blood spilled on the stones. ■ **TIP→ This is one of Britain's most popular sights—the Crown Jewels are here—and you can avoid lines by buying a ticket in advance on the Web site, by phone, or at any tube station; arriving before 11 can also help at busy times.** The visitor center provides an introduction to the Tower. Allow at least three hours for exploring, and take time to stroll along the battlements for a wonderful overview.

The Tower holds the royal gems because it's still one of the royal palaces, although no monarch since Henry VII has called it home. It has also housed the Royal Mint, the Public Records, the Royal Menagerie (which formed the basis of the London Zoo), and the Royal Observatory, although its most renowned and titillating function has been as a jail and place of torture and execution.

A person was mighty privileged to be beheaded in the peace and seclusion of **Tower Green** instead of before the mob at Tower Hill. In fact, only seven people were ever important enough—among them Anne Boleyn and Catherine Howard, wives two and five of Henry VIII's six; Elizabeth I's friend Robert Devereux, earl of Essex; and the nine-day queen, Lady Jane Grey, age 17.

Free tours depart every half hour or so from the Middle Tower. They are conducted by the 39 Yeoman Warders, better known as Beefeaters—ex-servicemen dressed in resplendent navy-and-red (scarlet-and-gold on special occasions) Tudor outfits. Beefeaters have been guarding the Tower since Henry VII appointed them in 1485. One of them, the Yeoman Ravenmaster, is responsible for making life comfortable for the Tower ravens (six birds plus reserves)—an important duty, because if the ravens were to desert the Tower, goes the legend, the kingdom would fall. Today, the Tower takes no chances: the ravens' wings are clipped.

In prime position stands the oldest part of the Tower and the most conspicuous of its buildings, the **White Tower;** the other towers were built in the next few centuries. This central keep was begun in 1078 by William the Conqueror; Henry III (1207–72) had it whitewashed, which is where the name comes from. The spiral staircase is the only way up, and here are the **Royal Armouries,** with a collection of arms and armor. Most of the interior of the White Tower has been altered over the centuries, but the **Chapel of St. John the Evangelist,** downstairs from the armories, is a pure example of 11th-century Norman style—very rare, very simple, and very beautiful. Across the moat, **Traitors' Gate** lies to the right. Opposite Traitors' Gate is the former Garden Tower, better known since about 1570 as the **Bloody Tower.** Its name comes from one of the most famous unsolved murders in history, the saga of the "little princes in the Tower." In 1483 the uncrowned boy king, Edward V, and his brother Richard were left here by their uncle, Richard of Gloucester, after the death of their father, Edward IV. They were never seen again, Gloucester was crowned Richard III, and in 1674 two little skeletons were found under the stairs to the White Tower. The obvious conclusions have always been drawn—and were, in fact, even before the skeletons were discovered. The **New Armouries** have become a restaurant.

The most famous exhibits are the **Crown Jewels,** in the Jewel House, Waterloo Block. Moving walkways on either side of the jewels hasten progress at the busiest times. You get so close to the fabled gems you feel you could polish them (there are, however, wafers of bulletproof glass), if your eyes weren't so dazzled by the sparkle of the gems, enhanced with special lighting. Before you see them, you view a short film that includes scenes from Elizabeth's 1953 coronation. However, they are polished every January by the crown jewelers. A brief résumé of the top jewels: finest of all is the Royal Sceptre, containing the earth's largest cut diamond, the 530-carat Star of Africa. This is also known as Cullinan I, having been cut from the South African Cullinan, which weighed 20 ounces when dug up from a De Beers mine at the beginning of the 20th century. Another chip off the block, Cullinan II, lives on the Imperial State Crown (made for Queen Victoria's coronation in 1838 and adapted to hold the large diamond); Elizabeth II wore this crown at her coronation and wears it annually for the State Opening of Parliament. Another famous gem is the Koh-i-noor, or "Mountain of Light." The legendary diamond, which was supposed to bring luck to women, came from India, and was given to the Queen in 1850. You can see it, in cut-down shape, in the late Queen Mother's Crown.

The little chapel of **St. Peter ad Vincula** is the second church on the site, and it conceals the remains of some 2,000 people executed at the Tower, Anne Boleyn and Catherine Howard among them.

Evocative **Beauchamp Tower** was built west of Tower Green by Edward I (1272–1307). It was soon designated as a jail for the higher class of miscreant, including Lady Jane Grey, who is thought to have added her Latin graffiti to the many inscriptions carved by prisoners here.

For tickets to the Ceremony of the Keys (locking of main gates, nightly between 9:30 and 10), write well in advance to the Resident Governor and Keeper of the Jewel House (at the Queen's House, address below). Give your name, the date you wish to attend (include alternate dates), and number of people (up to seven) in your party, and enclose a self-addressed, stamped envelope. ⊠ *H. M. Tower of London, Tower Hill, The City, EC3N* ☎ *0870/756–6060 recorded information and advance booking* ⊕ *www.hrp.org.uk* ✎ *£15; joint tickets available with Kensington Palace and Hampton Court Palace* ☉ *Mar.–Oct., Tues.–Sat. 9–6, Sun. and Mon. 10–6; Nov.–Feb., Tues.–Sat. 9–5, Sun. and Mon. 10–5. Tower closes 1 hr after last admission time and all internal bldgs. close 30 mins after last admission. Free Yeoman Warder guided tours leave daily from Middle Tower (subject to weather and availability) about every 30 mins until 3:30 Mar.–Oct., 2:30 Nov.–Feb.* Ⓤ *Tower Hill.*

Also Worth Seeing

❶ **Dr. Johnson's House.** This is where Samuel Johnson lived between 1746 and 1759, compiling his famous *Dictionary of the English Language* in the attic as his health deteriorated. The only one of Johnson's residences remaining today, its elegant Georgian lines make it exactly the kind of place you would expect the Great Bear, as Johnson was nicknamed, to live. It's a shrine to a most literary man who was passionate about London, and it includes a first edition of his dictionary among the mementos of Johnson and his friend and diarist James Boswell. ⊠ *17 Gough Sq., The City, EC4* ☎ *020/7353–3745* ⊕ *www.drjohnsonshouse. org* ✎ *£4* ☉ *May–Sept., Mon.–Sat. 11–5:30; Oct.–Apr., Mon.–Sat. 11–5; closed bank holidays* Ⓤ *Blackfriars, Chancery La.*

❽ **Guildhall.** In the symbolic center of the City, the Corporation of London ceremonially elects and installs its Lord Mayor, as it has done for 800 years. The Guildhall was built in 1411, and although it failed to escape either the 1666 or 1940 flames, its core survived. The fabulous Great Hall is a patchwork of coats of arms. To the right of Guildhall Yard is the **Guildhall Art Gallery,** which includes portraits of the great and the good, cityscapes, famous battles, and a slightly cloying Pre-Raphaelite section. The construction of the gallery led to the discovery of London's only Roman amphitheater, which had lain underneath for more than 1,800 years. The 1970s west wing houses the the **Clockmakers' Company Museum,** with more than 600 timepieces. ⊠ *Gresham St., The City, EC2* ☎ *020/7606–3030, 020/7332–3700 gallery* ⊕ *www. guildhall-art-gallery.org.uk* ✎ *Free, gallery and amphitheater £2.50* ☉ *Mon.–Sat. 9:30–5; museum weekdays 9:30–4:45; gallery Mon.–Sat. 10–5, Sun. noon–4* Ⓤ *St. Paul's, Moorgate, Bank, Mansion House.*

┃ OFF THE
BEATEN
PATH

JACK THE RIPPER'S LONDON – *Cor blimey, guv'nor, Jack the Ripper woz here!* Several organizations offer tours of "Jack's London"—the (still) mean streets of the East End, the working-class neighborhood directly to the east of the City. Here, in 1888, the Whitechapel murders traumatized Victorian London. At the haunting hour, tour groups head out to Bucks Row and other crime scenes. Even with a large group, this can be a spooky experience. **Original London Walks** (☎ 020/7624–3978 ⊕ www.walks.com) has frequent tours leaving at 7 PM from the Tower Hill tube stop. The **Blood and Tears Walk: London's Horrible Past** (☎ 020/ 7625–5155) goes beyond Jack the Ripper and describes other murderers, as well. Tours depart from the Barbican tube; phone for times.

❸ Old Bailey. The present-day Central Criminal Court is where legendary Newgate Prison stood from the 12th century until the early 20th century. Ask the doorman which current trial is likely to prove juicy, if you're that kind of ghoul—you may catch the conviction of the next Crippen or Christie (England's most notorious wife murderers, both tried here). The day's hearings are posted on the sign outside, but there are security restrictions, and children under 14 are not allowed in; call the information line first. ⊠ *Newgate St., The City, EC4* ☎ *020/7248–3277* ⊕ *www.cityoflondon.gov.uk* ⊗ *Public Gallery weekdays 10:30–1 and 2–5 (approx.); line forms at Newgate St. entrance* Ⓤ *St. Paul's.*

The South Bank

Culture, history, sights: the South Bank has it all. Stretching from the Imperial War Museum in the southwest as far as the Design Museum in the east, high-caliber art, music, film, and theater venues sit alongside the likes of an aquarium, historic warships, and Borough Market, a foodie favorite. Pedestrians cross between the north and south banks using the futuristic Hungerford Bridge and the curvaceous Millennium Bridge, as they take in the compelling views of the Thames.

There's an old North London quip about needing a passport to cross the Thames, but times have changed dramatically. The Tate Modern is the star attraction, installed in a 1930s power station, with the eye-catching Millennium Bridge linking its main door across the river to the City. Near the theaters of the South Bank Centre, the British Airways London Eye observation wheel gives you a flight over the city. The South Bank of the Thames isn't beautiful, but this area of theaters and museums has Culture with a capital C. The '80s brought renovations and innovations such as Hay's Galleria and Butler's Wharf. In the '90s came the OXO Tower, the London Aquarium, and the reconstruction of Shakespeare's Globe. With the new century came the massive mushroom-like building designed by Norman Foster, which sits by the Thames near Tower Bridge; it is City Hall, which houses the London Assembly.

It's fitting that so much of London's artistic life should once again be centered on the South Bank—in the past, Southwark was the location of theaters, taverns, and cockfighting arenas. The Globe Theatre, in which Shakespeare acted and held shares, was one of several here. In truth the Globe was as likely to stage bear-baiting as Shakespeare, but today, at the reconstructed "Wooden O," you can see only the latter. Be sure to take a walk along Bankside, the embankment along the Thames from Southwark to Blackfriars Bridge.

TIMING The South Bank sprawls; block out visiting times based on locations and your interests. The Imperial War Museum demands a couple of hours, and the Tate Modern deserves a whole morning or afternoon to do justice to temporary exhibitions and the permanent collection. A lovely way to spend a half day is a flight on the London Eye (allow two hours), followed by a concert at the Royal Festival Hall or a performance at the National Theatre. An hour spent in the Design Museum is easily combined with a visit to HMS *Belfast,* afterward stopping by to admire the *Golden Hinde* and, farther along, City Hall. The Globe Theatre requires about two hours for the exhibition and two to three hours for a performance. Although this area is liveliest during the week, on Friday or Saturday you can stop by the Borough Market (⇨ Shopping, *below).*

GETTING HERE For the South Bank use Westminster station on the Jubilee or Northern Line, from where you can walk across Westminster Bridge; Embankment on District, Circle, Northern, and Bakerloo lines, where you can walk across Hungerford Bridge; or Waterloo on the Jubilee, Northern, and Bakerloo lines, where it's a five-minute walk to the Royal Festival Hall.In the east, Tower Hill Underground on the District Line can be reached by crossing Tower Bridge; alternatively, use Tower Gateway on the Docklands Light Railway (DLR). London Bridge on the Northern and Jubilee lines is at least 20 minutes on foot from the Design Museum, but a five-minute stroll to Borough Market.

Buses that take you across Westminster Bridge toward the Imperial War Museum include 12 and 159 from Oxford Circus, and 77 from Aldwych to Lambeth Palace. For buses behind the South Bank Centre: 1 from Aldwych and Waterloo to the Imperial War Museum, 68 from Euston and Holborn, 76 from St. Paul's and Moorgate, 168 from Euston and Holborn, 171 from Holborn, 176 from Oxford Circus, and 188 from Russell Square.

To go farther downstream, near Shakespeare's Globe and the OXO Tower, take the 381 from Waterloo to Tooley Street. The new RV1 bus service links Covent Garden, South Bank, Waterloo, Bankside, London Bridge, and Tower Gateway.

For a beautiful view, commuter river services are a more leisurely way to go: the route runs from Savoy Pier to Greenland, and for the South Bank hop off at Bankside or London Bridge City. The Tate Boat service links Tate Modern with Tate Britain.

Numbers in the margin correspond to numbers on the South Bank map.

Main Attractions

★ ☾ ❸ **British Airways London Eye.** If you want a pigeon's-eye view of London, this is the place. The highest observation wheel in the world, at 500 feet, towers over the South Bank from the Jubilee Gardens next to County Hall. For 25 minutes, passengers hover over the city in a slow-motion flight. On a clear day you can take in a range of up to 25 mi, viewing London's most famous landmarks. ■ TIP➜ Buy your ticket online, over the phone, or at the ticket office in advance to avoid the long lines. ⊠ *Jubilee Gardens, South Bank, SE1* ☎ *0870/500–0600* ⊕ *www.ba-londoneye.com* ✉ *£12.50* ☾ *June–Sept., daily 9:30 AM–10 PM; Oct.–May, daily 9:30–8* Ⓤ *Waterloo.*

⓮ Design Museum. This was the first museum in the world to elevate every-day design and design classics to the status of art by placing them in their social and cultural context. Fashion, creative technology, and architecture are explored in thematic displays, and temporary exhibitions provide an in-depth focus. Take a break at the trendsetting Blueprint Café, with its own river terrace. ✉ *28 Shad Thames, South Bank, SE1* ☎ *0870/833–9955* ⊕ *www.designmuseum.org* 🎫 *£7* ☉ *Mon.–Thurs. and weekends 10–5:45, last admission at 5:15; Fri. 10–10, last admission at 9:45* Ⓤ *London Bridge; DLR: Tower Gateway.*

★ ☕ ❶ **Imperial War Museum.** This museum of 20th-century warfare does not glorify bloodshed but attempts to evoke what it was like to live through the two world wars. There's hardware—a Battle of Britain Spitfire, a German V2 rocket—but also an equal amount of war art (John Singer Sargent to Henry Moore) and interactive material. One affecting exhibit, "The Blitz Experience," provides a 10-minute taste of an air raid in a street of acrid smoke, sirens, and searchlights. There's also a Holocaust exhibition. The museum is in an elegantly colonnaded 19th-century building that was once the home of the infamous insane asylum called Bedlam. ✉ *Lambeth Rd., South Bank, SE1* ☎ *020/7416–5320* ⊕ *www.iwm.org.uk* 🎫 *Free* ☉ *Daily 10–6* Ⓤ *Lambeth North.*

❹ **OXO Tower.** This art-deco tower has graduated from its former incarnations as power-generating station and warehouse into a vibrant community with artists' and designers' workshops, restaurants, and cafés. There's an observation deck for a super river vista (St. Paul's to the east, and Somerset House to the west). The biggest draw is martinis at the OXO Tower Restaurant. ✉ *Barge House St., South Bank, SE1* ☎ *020/7401–3610* ⊕ *www.oxotower.co.uk* 🎫 *Free* ☉ *Studios and shops Tues.–Sun. 11–6* Ⓤ *Blackfriars, Waterloo.*

★ ☕ ❻ **Shakespeare's Globe Theatre.** A spectacular theater, this is a replica of Shakespeare's open-roof, wood-and-thatch Globe Playhouse (built in 1599 and burned down in 1613), where most of the Bard's great plays premiered. For several decades, American actor and director Sam Wanamaker worked ceaselessly to raise funds for the theater's reconstruction, 200 yards from its original site, with authentic materials and techniques; his dream was realized in 1996. The "pit," or orchestra level, can take 500 standees—or "groundlings," to use the historical term—in front of the high stage, and 1,000 can sit in the covered wooden bays. A repertory season of three or four plays is presented in summer, in daylight—and sometimes rain. Throughout the year, you can tour the theater as part of the **Shakespeare's Globe Exhibition,** an adjacent museum that provides background material on the Elizabethan theater and the construction of the modern-day Globe. There's also an exhibition at the Globe's near neighbor, the **Rose Theatre,** at 56 Park Street, which was built even earlier, in 1587. ✉ *New Globe Walk, Bankside, South Bank, SE1* ☎ *020/7401–9919 box office, 020/7902–1400 New Shakespeare's Globe Exhibition* ⊕ *www.shakespeares-globe.org* 🎫 *£9 for exhibition and tour; joint ticket available with Rose Theatre* ☉ *Exhibition daily 10–5, plays May–early Oct.; call for schedule* Ⓤ *Mansion House, then* *walk across Southwark Bridge; Blackfriars, then walk across Blackfriars Bridge; or Southwark, then walk down to river.*

⑨ Southwark Cathedral. This cathedral (pronounced *suth*-uck) is the second-oldest Gothic church in London, next to Westminster Abbey. Look for the gaudily renovated 1408 tomb of the poet John Gower, friend of Chaucer, and for the Harvard Chapel, named after John Harvard, founder of the U.S. college, who was baptized here in 1608. Also buried here is Edmund Shakespeare, brother of William. ⊠ *Montague Close, South Bank, SE1* ☎ *020/7367–6700* ⊕ *www.southwark.anglican.org* ✉ *Free, suggested donation £4* ⊘ *Daily 8–6* Ⓤ *London Bridge.*

⑤ Tate Modern. This former power station has glowered on the banks on
FodorśChoice the Thames since the 1930s, and after a dazzling renovation by Herzog
★ de Meuron, provides a grand space for a massive collection of international modern art. The vast Turbine Hall is a dramatic entrance point.

On permanent display in the galleries are classic works from 1900 to the present day, by Matisse, Picasso, Dalí, Francis Bacon, Andy Warhol, and the most-talked-about upstarts. They are arranged in themes that mix the historic with the contemporary—Landscape, Still Life, and the Nude—on different levels, reached by a moving staircase. This is a good museum for kids, who respond to the unusual

> **WHEN TO GO**
>
> Avoid going to the Tate Modern on weekends, when visitor numbers are at their greatest. Visit during the week or join the cool crowd on Friday evenings, when it's open until 10.

space as well as the art; there are kids' programs, too. The changing exhibitions, for which there are often long lines, are always the talking point of Londoners who have their fingers on the pulse. ⊠ *Bankside, South Bank, SE1* ☎ *020/7887–8888* ⊕ *www.tate.org.uk* ✉ *Free* ⊘ *Sun.–Thurs. 10–6, Fri. and Sat. 10–10* Ⓤ *Blackfriars, Southwark.*

Also Worth Seeing

⑬ Butlers Wharf. An '80s warehouse conversion of deluxe loft apartments, restaurants, and galleries, people now flock here thanks partly to London's saint of the stomach, Sir Terence Conran (also responsible for restaurants Bibendum, Mezzo, and Quaglino's). He has given it his "Gastrodrome" of four restaurants (including the fabulous Pont de la Tour), a vintner's, a deli, and a bakery. ⊠ *South Bank, SE1* Ⓤ *London Bridge or Tower Hill, then walk over bridge.*

⑦ The Clink Prison. Giving rise to the term "the clink," which still refers to a jail, this institution was originally the prison attached to Winchester House, palace of the bishops of Winchester until 1626. It was one of the first prisons to detain women, most of whom were called "Winchester Geese"—a euphemism meaning prostitutes. You'll discover, in graphic detail, how a grisly Tudor prison would operate on a code of cruelty and corruption. ⊠ *1 Clink St., South Bank, SE1* ☎ *020/7403–0900* ⊕ *www.clink.co.uk* ✉ *£5* ⊘ *Weekdays 10–6, weekends 10–9; last admission 1 hr before closing* Ⓤ *London Bridge.*

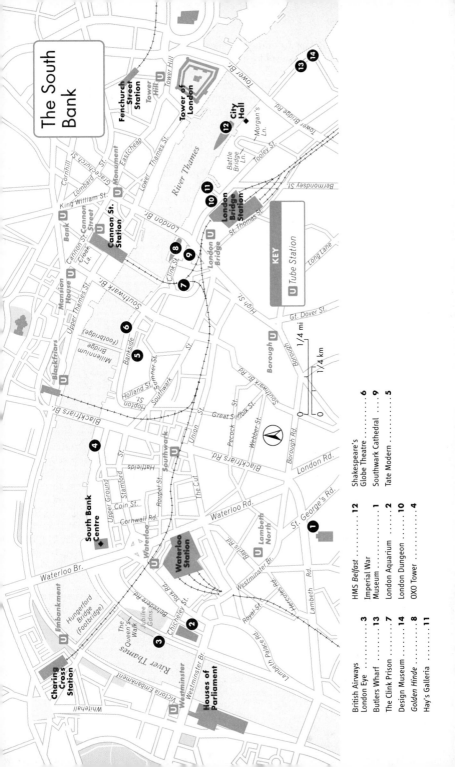

The South Bank

KEY
U Tube Station

British Airways
London Eye **3**
Butlers Wharf **13**
The Clink Prison **7**
Design Museum **14**
Golden Hinde **8**
Hay's Galleria **11**

HMS *Belfast* **12**
Imperial War
Museum **1**
London Aquarium **2**
London Dungeon **10**
OXO Tower **4**

Shakespeare's
Globe Theatre **6**
Southwark Cathedral . . . **9**
Tate Modern **5**

🕐 **⑧** *Golden Hinde.* Sir Francis Drake circumnavigated the globe in this little galleon, or one just like it. This exact replica made a 23-year round-the-world voyage—much of it spent along U.S. coasts, both Pacific and Atlantic—and has settled here to continue its educational purpose. ⊠ *St. Mary Overie Dock, Cathedral St., South Bank, SE1* ☎ *08700/11–8700* ⊕ *www.goldenhinde.co.uk* ⊠ *£3.50, £4.50 for prebooked guided tour* ☉ *Times vary; call ahead* Ⓤ *London Bridge.*

⑪ **Hay's Galleria.** Once known as "London's larder" because of the edibles sold here, Hay's Galleria was reborn in 1987 as a Covent Garden–esque parade of bars and restaurants, offices, and shops, all weatherproofed by a glass atrium roof supported by iron columns. Jugglers, string quartets, and crafts stalls abound. ⊠ *Battle Bridge La., South Bank, SE1* ☎ *020/7940–7770* ⊕ *www.haysgalleria.co.uk* Ⓤ *London Bridge.*

🕐 **⑫** **HMS Belfast.** At 613 feet, this is one of the largest cruisers the Royal Navy ever had. It played an important role in the D-Day landings off Normandy. On board is a riveting outpost of the **Imperial War Museum.** ⊠ *Morgan's La., Tooley St., South Bank, SE1* ☎ *020/7940–6300* ⊕ *www.iwm.org.uk* ⊠ *£8* ☉ *Mar.–Oct., daily 10–6; Nov.–Feb., daily 10–5; last admission 45 mins before closing* Ⓤ *London Bridge.*

🕐 **②** **London Aquarium.** Here's a dark and thrilling glimpse into the waters of the world, focused around a superb three-level aquarium full of sharks and stingrays, among other common and more rare breeds. There are also educational exhibits, hands-on displays, feeding displays, and piscine sights previously unseen on these shores. ⊠ *County Hall, Riverside Bldg., Westminster Bridge Rd., South Bank, SE1* ☎ *020/7967–8000* ⊕ *www.londonaquarium.co.uk* ⊠ *£9.75* ☉ *Daily 10–6; last admission at 5* Ⓤ *Westminster, Waterloo.*

🕐 **⑩** **London Dungeon.** Here's the goriest, grisliest, most gruesome attraction in town, where realistic waxwork people are subjected in graphic detail to all the historical horrors the Tower of London merely tells you about. Tableaux depict famous bloody moments—like Anne Boleyn's decapitation and the martyrdom of St. George—alongside the torture, murder, and ritual slaughter of lesser-known victims, all to a sound track of screaming, wailing, and agonized moaning. There are displays on the Great Fire of London and Jack the Ripper. ⊠ *28–34 Tooley St., South Bank, SE1* ☎ *020/7403–7221* ⊕ *www.thedungeons.com* ⊠ *£14.50* ☉ *Mid-Apr.–mid-July, daily 10–5:30; mid-July–mid-Sept., daily 10–7.30; mid-Sept.–mid-Nov., daily 10–5.30; mid-Nov.–mid-Apr. daily 10:30–5; phone to confirm dates* Ⓤ *London Bridge.*

Kensington, Knightsbridge & Mayfair

Splendid houses with pillared porches, as well as fascinating museums, stylish squares, and glittering antiques shops, line the streets of this elegant area of the Royal Borough of Kensington. Also here is Kensington Palace (the former home of both Diana, Princess of Wales, and Queen Victoria), which put the district literally on the map back in the 17th century. To Kensington's east is one of the highest concentrations of important artifacts anywhere, the "museum mile" of South Kensington, with the rest of Kensington offering peaceful strolls and a noisy main street.

Hyde Park and Kensington Gardens together form by far the biggest of central London's royal parks. It's probably been centuries since any major royal had a casual stroll here, but the parks remain the property of the Crown, and it was the Crown that saved them from being devoured by the city's late-18th-century growth spurt.

Around the borders of Hyde Park are several of London's most beautiful and posh neighborhoods. To the south of the park and a short carriage ride from Buckingham Palace is the splendidly aristocratic enclave of Belgravia. Its white-stucco buildings and grand squares—particularly Belgrave Square—are Regency-era jewels. On the eastern border of Hyde Park is Mayfair, which gives Belgravia a run for its money as London's wealthiest district. Two mansions here allow you to get a peek into the lifestyles of London's rich and famous: Apsley House, the home of the duke of Wellington, and the Wallace Collection, a mansion on Manchester Square stuffed with great art treasures.

TIMING   The best way to approach these neighborhoods is to treat Knightsbridge shopping and the South Kensington museums as separate days out, although the three vast museums may be too much to take in at once. The parks are best in the growing seasons and during fall, when the foliage is turning; the summer roses in Regent's Park are stunning. On Sunday, the Hyde Park and Kensington Gardens railings all along the Bayswater Road are hung with mediocre art, which may slow your progress; this is prime perambulation day for locals.

GETTING HERE   There's good tube service to these areas. On the Central Line, Marble Arch and Bond Street (also Jubilee Line) take you to the heart of Mayfair; the Hyde Park Corner stop on the Piccadilly Line is at the southeast corner of the park, near Apsley House. South Kensington and Gloucester Road on the District, Circle, and Piccadilly lines are convenient stops for the South Kensington museums; Knightsbridge on the Piccadilly Line leaves you close to Harrods and many retail temptations.

Numbers in the margin correspond to numbers on the Kensington, Knightsbridge & Mayfair map.

Main Attractions

★ ❾ **Apsley House (Wellington Museum).** Once known, quite simply, as Number 1, London, this was celebrated as the best address in town. Built by Robert Adam in the 1770s, the mansion was the home of the celebrated conqueror of Napoléon, the duke of Wellington, who lived here from the 1820s until his death in 1852. The great Waterloo Gallery—scene of legendary dinners—is an orgy of opulence. Not to be missed, in every sense, is the gigantic Antonio Canova statue of a nude (but fig-leafed) Bonaparte in the entry stairwell. The free audio guide highlights the most noted works and the superb decor. The house is flanked by imposing statues: opposite is the 1828 Decimus Burton **Wellington Arch** with the four-horse chariot of peace as its pinnacle (open to the public as an exhibition area and viewing platform). Just behind Wellington Arch, and cast from captured French guns, the legendary **Achilles** statue points the way with thrusting shield to the ducal mansion from the tip of Hyde Park. ☒ *Hyde Park Corner* ☎ *020/7499–5676* ⊕ *www.english-heritage. org.uk* ☜ *£4.95* ⊙ *Apr.–Nov., Tues.–Sun. 10–5; Dec.–Mar., Tues.–Sun. 10–4. Also open bank holiday Mon.* Ⓤ *Hyde Park Corner.*

❻ Harrods. Just in case you hadn't noticed it, this well-known shopping destination outlines its domed terra-cotta Edwardian bulk in thousands of white lights at night. Owned by Mohamed Al Fayed, whose son Dodi was killed in the car crash that also claimed Princess Diana's life in 1997, the 15-acre store has wonderful, frenetic sale weeks. Don't miss the extravagant **Food Hall,** with its art-nouveau tiling. ☒ *87–135 Brompton Rd., Knightsbridge, SW1* ☎ *020/7730–1234* ⊕ *www.harrods.com* ⊙ *Mon.–Sat. 10–7, Sun. noon–6* Ⓤ *Knightsbridge.*

☽ Hyde Park. Along with the smaller St. James's and Green parks to the east, Hyde Park started as Henry VIII's hunting grounds. Along its south side runs **Rotten Row,** once Henry's royal path to the hunt—the name is a corruption of *route du roi* (route of the king). It's still used by the Household Cavalry, who live at the **Knightsbridge Barracks**—a high-rise and a low, ugly, red block to the left. This brigade mounts the guard at the palace, and you can see them leave to perform this duty, in full regalia, at about 10:30, or await the return of the ex-guard about noon. Hyde Park is wonderful for strolling, watching the locals, or just relaxing by the **Serpentine,** the long body of water near its southern border. On the south side of the Serpentine, by the Lido, is the site of the **Diana Princess of Wales Memorial Fountain.** On Sunday, **Speakers' Corner,** in the park near Marble Arch, is an unmissable spectacle of vehement, sometimes comical, and always entertaining orators. ☎ *020/ 7298–2000* ⊕ *www.royalparks.gov.uk* ⊙ *Daily 5 AM–midnight* Ⓤ *Hyde Park Corner, Lancaster Gate, Marble Arch.*

☽ Kensington Gardens. More formal than neighboring Hyde Park, Kensington Gardens was first laid out as palace grounds. The paved Italian garden at the top of the Long Water, **The Fountains,** is a reminder of this, although **Kensington Palace** itself is the main clue to its royal status, with the early-19th-century Sunken Garden north of it. Nearby is George Frampton's beloved 1912 *Peter Pan,* a bronze of the boy who lived on an island in the Serpentine and never grew up, and whose creator, J. M. Barrie, lived at 100 Bayswater Road, not 500 yards from here. The **Round Pond** is a magnet for model-boat enthusiasts and duck feeders. The fabulous **Princess Diana Memorial Playground** has specially designed structures and areas on the theme of Barrie's Neverland. ⊕ *www. royalparks.gov.uk* ⊙ *Daily dawn–dusk* Ⓤ *Lancaster Gate, Queensway.*

★ ❺ Kensington Palace. Royals have lived here in grand style for more than 300 years, even though the palace's history has been eclipsed in the near past by the late Princess Diana, a famous resident. A walk through the State Apartments (with an excellent audio-guide device as your companion) puts in perspective the protocol-filled royal lifestyle of the past. When King William III decided in the late 17th century to make his palace at Kensington, 12 years of renovation to the original building were needed by Wren and Hawksmoor before the king and Queen Mary could move in. The palace continued to undergo refurbishment during the reigns of Queen Anne and George I and II. Kensington Palace was home to the young princess Victoria until she succeeded to the throne.

The visitor entrance to the palace is on the Garden Floor and takes you into the Red Saloon and Teck Saloon (after the Kents, the Duke and Duchess of Teck lived here), which display the **Royal Ceremonial Dress Collection** with garments dating to the 18th century. State and occasional dresses, hats, shoes, and gloves from the present Queen's wardrobe are displayed, along with some of Princess Diana's gorgeous evening gowns. Other displays interpret the symbolism of court dress and show the labor that went into producing this attire.

The King's Grand Staircase is the impressive starting point of the tour of the State Apartments; the trompe l'oeil paintings by William Kent on the walls show courtiers looking down. The Presence Chamber (used for formal receptions) is painted in Italian "grotesque" style with mythical gods. The Privy Chamber next to it received more intimate visitors. In this room, the Mortlake tapestries commissioned by Charles I represent the seasons, and the lavish painted ceiling alludes to the godlike status of monarchs. Gilt and Roman columns in the Cupola Room reminded the royal visitor that being admitted beyond the Presence Room was a mark of status. Next come the rooms where Victoria had an ultrastrict upbringing with her parents, the Duke and Duchess of Kent. Originally part of the King's Apartments, these bedrooms and dressing rooms create a pleasantly domestic scene. The King's Gallery returns to the gilded theme; here, copies of Van Dyck's Charles I portraits (the originals are at the Queen's Gallery, Buckingham Palace) dominate the scene, along with two works by Tintoretto. The tour exits via the Queen's Staircase, which leads into the garden.

The Duke and Duchess of Gloucester and Prince and Princess Michael of Kent have apartments here, as did the late Princess Margaret. A photographic exhibition, "Number 1A Kensington Palace: From Courtiers' Lodgings to Royal Home," has opened in her former apartments. ⊠ *The Broad Walk, Kensington Gardens, Kensington, W8* ☎ *0870/751–5170 advance booking and information* ⊕ *www.hrp.org.uk* ✉ *£11.50* ☉ *Mar.–Oct., daily 10–6; Nov.–Feb., daily 10–5; last admission 1 hr before closing* Ⓤ *High St. Kensington.*

NEED A BREAK?

A separate building from the rest of Kensington Palace, the **Orangery** (⊠ The Broad Walk, Kensington Gardens, Kensington, W8 ☎ 020/7376–0239) was built for Queen Anne in 1704–05. The setting, beneath the white-and-gold arches, is perfect for tea, light lunches, and coffee offered daily from 10 to 6.

★ ☾ ❶ **Natural History Museum.** When you want to heed the call of the wild, explore this fun place. Don't be surprised when the dinos notice you— the fierce, animatronic Tyrannosaurus Rex senses when human prey is near and "responds" in character. Don't miss the ambitious Earth Galleries or the Creepy Crawlies Gallery, which includes a nightmarish, super-enlarged scorpion. In the basement, hands-on activities can be experienced in Investigate, which allows you to do just that, with actual objects, from old bones to bugs. The Darwin Centre showcases the museum's entire collection—all 22 million creatures—from a tiny Seychellian frog to the Komodo dragon lizard. Daily Explore tours leave from the museum's main information desk. ⊠ *Cromwell Rd., South Kensington, SW7* ☏ *020/7942–5000* ⊕ *www.nhm.ac.uk* ✉ *Free* ☉ *Mon.–Sat. 10–5:50, Sun. 11–5:50* Ⓤ *South Kensington.*

★ ☙ **Regent's Park.** Laid out in 1812 by John Nash for the Prince Regent (hence the name), who was crowned George IV in 1820, the park was designed to re-create the atmosphere of a grand country residence close to the center of town. A walk around the Outer Circle, taking in the white-stucco terraces of grand houses facing the park, including the famous **Cumberland Terrace**, shows that it succeeds magnificently. The Inner Circle has many garden themes, the most impressive being **Queen Mary's Gardens**, a scented riot of roses in summer. From June through August, the **Regent's Park Open-Air Theatre** (☏ 0870/060–1811 ⊕ www. openairtheatre.org) mounts Shakespeare productions. The park is north of Mayfair. ☏ *020/7486–7905* ⊕ *www.royalparks.gov.uk* Ⓤ *Baker St. or Regent's Park.*

★ ☙ ❷ **Science Museum.** Hands-on exhibits make this museum enormously popular with children and adults. Highlights include *Puffing Billy* (the oldest steam locomotive in the world), and the actual *Apollo 10* capsule. A must-do attraction is the spectacular **Wellcome Wing**, devoted to contemporary science, medicine, and technology, which also has a 450-seat IMAX cinema. Special exhibitions can be great, too. ⊠ *Exhibition Rd., South Kensington, SW7* ☏ *0870/870–4868* ⊕ *www.sciencemuseum. org.uk* ✉ *Free* ☉ *Daily 10–6* Ⓤ *South Kensington.*

★ ☙ ❸ **Victoria & Albert Museum.** Recognizable by the copy of Victoria's Imperial Crown on the lantern above the central cupola, this huge museum showcases the decorative arts of all disciplines, periods, nationalities, and tastes. Prince Albert was responsible for the genesis of this permanent version of the 1851 Great Exhibition, and Victoria laid its foundation stone in her final public London appearance in 1899. The collections of the V&A, as it's always called, are *so* all-encompassing that confusion is a hazard; select a few galleries to focus on. One minute you're gazing on the Jacobean oak, 12-foot-square four-poster Great Bed of Ware (one of the V&A's most prized possessions, given that Shakespeare immortalized it in *Twelfth Night*), and the next, you're in the 20th-century end of the equally celebrated Dress Collection, coveting a Jean Muir frock. The British Galleries provide a social context for British art and design from 1500 to 1900 (from Henry VIII through Victoria), with displays such as George Gilbert Scott's model of the Albert Memorial and the first English fork ever made (1632). Throughout the galleries are interactive corners, where you can discover, design, and build things. Free one-hour tours whirl you by some of the museum's prized treasures. The shop is the museum in microcosm, and quite the best place to buy art-nouveau or arts-and-crafts gifts. ⊠ *Cromwell Rd., South Kensington, SW7* ☏ *020/7942–2000* ⊕ *www.vam.ac.uk* ✉ *Free* ☉ *Thurs.–Tues. 10–5:45; Wed. and last Fri. of month 10–10; tours daily at 10:30, 11:30, 1:30, 3:30 and Wed. at 7:30 PM* Ⓤ *South Kensington.*

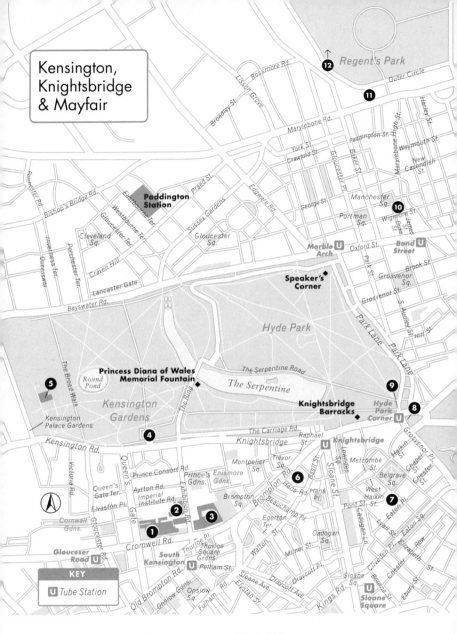

Kensington, Knightsbridge & Mayfair

Regent's Park
Outer Circle
Rossmore Rd.
Lisson Grove
Broadley St.
Marylebone Rd.
York St.
Crawford St.
Gloucester St.
Baker St.
Paddington St.
Marylebone High St.
Harley St.
Weymouth St.
New Cavendish St.

Rochester Rd.
Bishop's Bridge Rd.
Eastbourne Ter.
Westbourne Ter.
Gloucester Ter.
Praed St.
Paddington Station
Sussex Gardens
Edgware Rd.
George St.
Portman Sq.
Manchester Sq.
Wigmore St.
James St.

Cleveland Sq.
Gloucester Sq.
Marble Arch Ⓤ
Oxford St.
Bond Street Ⓤ
Brook St.

Inverness Ter.
Porchester Ter.
Craven Hill
Lancaster Gate
Queensway
Craven Hill
Bayswater Rd.
Speaker's Corner
Grosvenor Sq.
Grosvenor St.
S. Audley St.
Hill St.

The Broad Walk
Round Pond
Princess Diana of Wales Memorial Fountain
Hyde Park
Park Lane
Park Lane

⑤
Kensington Gardens
The Ring
The Serpentine Road
The Serpentine
⑨
Hyde Park Corner Ⓤ
⑧

Kensington Palace Gardens
④
Kensington Rd.
The Carriage Rd.
Knightsbridge
Knightsbridge Barracks
Grosvenor Cres.
Halkin St.

Victoria Rd.
Queen's Gate
Prince Consort Rd.
Prince's Gdns.
Ensmore Gdns
Montpelier Sq.
Trevor Sq.
Raphael St.
Knightsbridge Ⓤ
Lowndes St.
Metcombe St.
Belgrave Sq.
Chapel St.
Chester St.

Queen's Gate Ter.
Ayrton Rd.
Imperial Institute Rd.
Exhibition Rd.
②
Brompton Rd.
Brompton Sq.
⑥
Hans Rd.
Basil St.
Hans Pl.
Sloane St.
West Halkin St.
Eaton Sq.
Eaton Pl.
⑦

Cornwall Gdns.
Elvaston Pl.
③
Beauchamp Pl.
Egerton Ter.
Cadogan Sq.
Walton St.
Cadogan La.
Eaton Ter.
Lyall St.
Cliveden Pl.
Elizabeth St.
Chester Row

Gloucester Road Ⓤ
①
Cromwell Rd.
Thurloe Pl.
South Kensington Ⓤ
Thurloe Square Gdns.
Pelham St.
Milner St.
Draycott Pl.
Sloane Sq. Ⓤ
Bourne St.
Ebury St.

Gloucester Rd.
Old Brompton Rd.
Onslow Gdns.
Onslow Sq.
Fulham Rd.
Sloane Ave.
Draycott Ave.
Elystan St.
Kings Rd.
Sloane Square

KEY
Ⓤ Tube Station

Wallace Collection. Assembled by four generations of marquesses of Hertford, the Wallace Collection is important, exciting, undervisited— and free. Hertford House itself, a fine late-18th-century mansion, is part of the show. The eccentric fourth marquess really built the collection, snapping up paintings by François Boucher, Jean-Honoré Fragonard, Antoine Watteau, and Nicolas Lancret for a song after the French Revolution rendered this art dangerously unfashionable. A highlight among the Gainsborough and Romney portraits is Fragonard's *The Swing,* which conjures up the 18th-century's let-them-eat-cake frivolity. Don't forget to smile back at Frans Hals's *Laughing Cavalier* in the Big Gallery. ⊠ *Hertford House, Manchester Sq., Mayfair, W1* ☎ *020/7563–9500* ⊕ *www.wallacecollection.org* ⊠ *Free, charge for special exhibitions* ☉ *Daily 10–5* Ⓤ *Bond St.*

Also Worth Seeing

OFF THE BEATEN PATH

ABBEY ROAD STUDIOS – Strawberry Fields Forever. Here, outside the Abbey Road Studios, is the world's most famous zebra crossing. Immortalized on the Beatles' *Abbey Road* album of 1969, this footpath is a spot beloved by Beatlemaniacs and baby boomers. The studios (closed to the public) are where the Beatles recorded their entire output from "Love Me Do" on, including *Sgt. Pepper's Lonely Hearts Club Band* (1967). To see Fab Four sites, **Original London Walks** (☎ 020/7624–3978 ⊕ www.walks.com) offers two Beatles tours: The Beatles In-My-Life Walk (11:20 AM at the Baker Street Underground on Saturday and Tuesday) and the Beatles Magical Mystery Tour (10:55 AM at Underground Exit 3, Tottenham Court Road, on Sunday and Thursday), which cover nostalgic landmark Beatles spots in the city. Abbey Road is a 10-minute ride on the Jubilee Line from central London. After you exit, head southwest three blocks down Grove End Road. ⊠ *3 Abbey Rd., Hampstead, NW8* ⊕ *www. abbeyroad.co.uk* Ⓤ *St. John's Wood.*

❹ **Albert Memorial.** This gleaming, neo-Gothic shrine to Prince Albert created by George Gilbert Scott epitomizes the Victorian era. Albert's grieving widow, Queen Victoria, had this elaborate confection (including a 14-foot bronze statue of the prince) erected on the spot where his Great Exhibition had stood a decade before his early death, from typhoid, in 1861. ⊠ *Kensington Gore, opposite Royal Albert Hall, Hyde Park, Kensington, SW7* Ⓤ *Knightsbridge.*

❼ **Belgrave Square.** The square, as well as the streets leading off it, are genuine elite territory and have been since they were built in the mid-1800s. Walk down Belgrave Place toward Eaton Place and you pass two of Belgravia's most beautiful mews: Eaton Mews North and Eccleston Mews, both fronted by grand Westminster-white rusticated entrances right out of a 19th-century engraving.

⓬ **London Zoo.** Opened in 1828 and now housing animals from all over the world, this zoo has long been a local favorite. A modernization program focusing on conservation and education is under way. One highlight is the Web of Life, a conservation and education center. Recent additions include a desert swarming with locusts, meerkats perching on termite mounds, bats and hummingbirds, and an otter exhibit with underwater viewing. In a walk-through forest, you can come face-to-face with a group of black-capped squirrel monkeys. ⊠ *Regent's Park, NW1* ☎ *020/7722–3333* ⊕ *www.londonzoo.co.uk* 🖃 *£13.50* ⊗ *Daily 10–4; last admission 1 hr before closing* Ⓤ *Camden Town, then Bus 274.*

☾ ⓫ **Madame Tussaud's.** This is nothing more, nothing less, than the world's premier exhibition of lifelike waxwork models of celebrities. Madame T. learned her craft while making death masks of French Revolution victims and in 1835 set up her first show of the famous ones near this spot. You can see everyone from Shakespeare to Benny Hill here, but top billing still goes to the murderers in the Chamber of Horrors, who stare glassy-eyed at you—one from the electric chair. ■ TIP➡ **Booking online saves you time and money.** ⊠ *Marylebone Rd., Regent's Park, NW1* ☎ *0870/ 400–3000 for timed entry tickets* ⊕ *www.madame-tussauds.com* 🖃 *From £14.99; prices vary according to day and season, call for details, or check Web site* ⊗ *Sept.–June, weekdays 10–5:30, weekends 9:30–5:30; July and Aug., daily 9:30–5:30* Ⓤ *Baker St.*

Notting Hill. Centered on the famous Portobello Road market (⇨ Shopping, *below*), this district is bordered to the west by Lansdowne Crescent—lined by "the hill's" poshest 19th-century terraced row houses—and to the east by Chepstow Road, with Notting Hill Gate and Westbourne Grove Road marking south and north boundaries. In between, the cool crowd, fashion set, and A- to B-list celebs can be spotted at the chic shops on Westbourne Grove and in the lively bars and cafés on Kensington Park Road. Ⓤ *Notting Hill Gate, Ladbroke Grove.*

❽ **Wellington Arch.** Opposite the duke of Wellington's mansion, Apsley House, this majestic stone arch dominates the busy traffic intersection that is Hyde Park Corner. Designed by Decimus Burton and built in 1828, it was created as a grand entrance to the west side of London and echoes the design of that other landmark gate, Marble Arch, at the north end of Hyde Park. Atop the arch, the Angel of Peace descends on the chariot of war. The arch has a viewing platform with panoramas over the park. ⊠ *Hyde Park Corner, Mayfair, SW1* ☎ *020/7930–2726* ⊕ *www. english-heritage.org.uk* 🖃 *£3* ⊗ *Apr.–Oct., Wed.–Sun. 10–5; Nov.–Mar., Wed.–Sun. 10–4* Ⓤ *Hyde Park Corner.*

Up & Down the Thames

Greenwich
8 mi east of central London.

Greenwich makes an ideal day out from central London, thanks to its historic and maritime attractions. Sir Christopher Wren's Royal Naval College and Inigo Jones's Queen's House reach architectural heights; the Old Royal Observatory measured time for the entire planet; and the Greenwich Meridian divides the world in two. You can stand astride it with one foot in either hemisphere. The National Maritime Museum and the clipper ship *Cutty Sark* will appeal to seafaring types, and landlubbers can stroll the parkland that surround the buildings, the pretty 19th-century houses, and the weekend crafts and antiques markets.

Once, Greenwich was considered remote by Londoners, with only the river as a direct route. With transportation links in the form of the Docklands Light Railway (DLR) and the tube's Jubilee Line, getting here is easy and inexpensive. The quickest route to maritime Greenwich is the tube to Canary Wharf and the Docklands Light Rail to the Greenwich stop. However, river connections to Greenwich make the journey memorable. On the way, the boat glides past famous London sights and the ever-changing Docklands. **Ferries** (☎ 020/7987–1185 from Embankment and Tower piers, ☎ 020/7930–4097 from Westminster Pier, ☎ 020/7740–0400 from Barrier Gardens Pier, ☎ 020/7930–2062 upriver from Westminster Pier) down river from central London to Greenwich take 30 to 55 minutes and leave from different piers. You don't need to reserve.

Cutty Sark. This sleek, romantic clipper was built in 1869, one of fleets and fleets of similar tall-masted wooden ships that plied oceanic highways of the 19th century, trading in exotic commodities—tea, in this case. The *Cutty Sark,* the only surviving clipper, was also the fastest, sailing the China–London route in 1871 in only 107 days. Now the photogenic vessel lies in dry dock, a museum of one kind of seafaring life—and not a comfortable kind for the 28-strong crew, as you'll see. The collection of figureheads is amusing, too. ⊠ *King William Walk, Greenwich, SE10* ☎ *020/8858–3445* ⊕ *www.cuttysark.org.uk* ⊡ *£4.50* ⊙ *Daily 10–5; last admission at 4:30* Ⓤ *DLR: Cutty Sark.*

★ **National Maritime Museum.** One of Greenwich's outstanding attractions contains everything to do with the British at sea, including models, maps, globes, sextants, and uniforms (including the one Nelson died in at the 1805 Battle of Trafalgar, complete with bloodstained bullet hole). Explorers such as Captain James Cook and Robert F. Scott are celebrated, along with the valuable research gleaned from their grueling voyages. The **Queen's House,** the first Palladian building in England (1635), is home to the largest collection of maritime art in the world, including works by William Hogarth, Canaletto, and Joshua Reynolds. ⊠ *Romney Rd., Greenwich, SE10* ☎ *020/8858–4422* ⊕ *www.nmm.ac.uk* ⊡ *Free* ⊙ *Apr.–Sept., daily 10–6; Oct.–Mar., daily 10–5; last admission 4:30* Ⓤ *DLR: Greenwich.*

Old Royal Naval College. Designed by Christopher Wren in 1694 as a home for ancient mariners, these buildings became a school for young ones in 1873; today the University of Greenwich and Trinity College of Music hold classes here. The **Painted Hall,** the college's dining hall, derives its name from the baroque murals of William and Mary. In the opposite building stands the **College Chapel,** which is in a more restrained neo-Grecian style. ⊠ *King William Walk, Greenwich, SE10* ☎ *020/ 8269–4747* ⊕ *www.greenwichfoundation.org.uk* ⊡ *Free, guided tours £4* ⊙ *Painted Hall and College Chapel Mon.–Sat. 10–5, Sun. 12:30–5, last admission 4:15; grounds 8–6* Ⓤ *DLR: Greenwich.*

★ **Ranger's House.** This handsome, early-18th-century villa, which was the Greenwich Park Ranger's official residence during the 19th century, is hung with Stuart and Jacobean portraits. The most interesting diversion is the Wernher Collection, more than 650 works of medieval and Renaissance art (and splendid jewelry) with a north European flavor, amassed by millionaire Julius Wernher at the turn of the 20th century. ⊠ *Chesterfield Walk, Blackheath, Greenwich, SE10* ☎ *020/8853–0035* ⊕ *www.english-heritage.org.uk* 🖃 *£5:30* ⊙ *Apr.–Sept., Wed.–Sun. 10–6; Oct.–Mar., by appointment only* ⊙ *Closed Jan. and Feb.* Ⓤ *DLR: Greenwich; no direct bus access, only to Vanbrugh Hill (from east) and Blackheath Hill (from west).*

★ ⓒ **Royal Observatory.** Founded in 1675 by Charles II, this imposing institution was designed by Christopher Wren for John Flamsteed, the first Astronomer Royal. The red ball you see on its roof has been there since 1833. It drops every day at 1 PM, and you can set your watch by it, as the sailors on the Thames always have. Everyone comes here to be photographed astride the **Prime Meridian,** a brass line laid on the cobblestones at zero-degrees longitude, one side being the eastern, one the western, hemisphere. An exhibit on the solution to the problem of measuring longitude includes John Harrison's famous clocks, H1–H4. ⊠ *Greenwich Park, Greenwich, SE10* ☎ *020/8858–4422* ⊕ *www.rog. nmm.ac.uk* 🖃 *Free* ⊙ *Apr.–Sept., daily 10–6; Oct.–Mar., daily 10–5; last admission 4:30* Ⓤ *DLR: Greenwich.*

Hampton Court Palace

ⓒ *20 mi southwest of central London.*

Fodor's Choice
★

On a loop of the Thames lies Hampton Court, one of London's oldest royal palaces and more like a small town in size; you need a day to do it justice. It's actually two palaces in one—a Tudor residence and a late-17th-century baroque one—as well as a renowned garden. The magnificent Tudor brick house, with its cobbled courtyards and cavernous kitchens, was begun in 1514 by Cardinal Wolsey, the ambitious lord chancellor (roughly, prime minister) of England and archbishop of York. He wanted it to be the best palace in the land, and succeeded so well that Henry VIII grew envious, whereupon Wolsey gave Hampton Court to the king. Henry moved in during 1525, added a great hall and chapel, and proceeded to live much of his astonishing life here. Later, during the reign of William and Mary, Christopher Wren expanded the palace substantially, adding the graceful baroque south and east fronts that are highlights of the palace. Six themed routes, including Henry VIII's State Apartments and the King William III's Apartments, help you plan your visit; special guides in period costume add to the fun.

The site beside the slow-moving Thames is idyllic, with 60 acres of ornamental gardens, lakes, and ponds, including William III's Privy Garden on the palace's south side. Its parterres, sculpted turf, and

> **WORD OF MOUTH**
>
> "[Hampton Court Palace is] a must-see part of your trip to London. You get to experience the feel of life in the castle more than in other royal palaces. You can take the tour at your own pace and there are all sorts of activities to keep you busy."
>
> –Kim from Tennessee

clipped yews and hollies brilliantly set off Wren's addition. Other horticultural highlights are Henry VIII's Pond Garden and the enormous conical yews around the Fountain Garden. On the east side of the house, 544 lime trees were replanted in 2004 along the Long Water, a canal built during the time of Charles II. Perhaps best of all is the almost half-mile of paths in the fiendish maze, planted in 1714. ⊠ *East Molesey on A308* ☎ *0870/752-7777* ⊕ *www.hrp.org.uk* ⊠ *Palace, gardens, and maze £12.30, gardens only £4, maze only £3.50, park grounds free. Joint tickets available with Kensington Palace and Tower of London* ☉ *State apartments Apr.–Oct., daily 10–6, last admission at 5; Nov.–Mar., daily 10–4:30; grounds daily 7–dusk* Ⓤ *Richmond, then Bus R68; National Rail, South West: Hampton Court Station, 35 mins from Waterloo.*

Kew Gardens

Fodor$Choice ★ *6 mi southwest of central London.*

Kew Gardens, or more formally the Royal Botanic Gardens at Kew, is the headquarters of the country's leading botanical institute as well as a spectacular public garden of 300 acres and more than 30,000 species of plants. The highlights of a visit to this UNESCO World Heritage Site are the two great 19th-century greenhouses filled with tropical plants, many of which have been there as long as their housing. The bold glass roofs of the ultramodern Princess of Wales Conservatory shelter no fewer than 10 climatic zones. Two 18th-century royal ladies, Queen Caroline and Princess Augusta, were responsible for the garden's founding. The tube ride to Kew is about 40 minutes, but the gardens are very close to the stop. ⊠ *Kew Rd., Kew* ☎ *020/8332-5655* ⊕ *www.kew.org* ⊠ *£11.75* ☉ *Gardens Apr.–Oct., weekdays 9:30–6:30, weekends 9:30–7:30; Nov.–Mar., daily 9:30–4:30* Ⓤ *Kew Gardens.*

Kew Palace and Queen Charlotte's Cottage. To this day quietly domestic Kew Palace, in Kew Gardens, remains the smallest royal palace in the land. The house offers a glimpse into the 18th century and the life of George III and his family; on display is the royal princesses' dollhouse. Originally known as the Dutch House, it was bought by King George II to provide more room for the extended Royal Family. In spring there's a romantic haze of bluebells. Note: you must purchase admission to Kew Gardens to access the palace. ⊠ *Kew Gardens, Kew* ☎ *0870/751-5179* ⊕ *www.hrp.org.uk* ⊠ *£5* ☉ *May–Sept., daily* Ⓤ *Kew Gardens.*

WHERE TO EAT

No longer would novelist Somerset Maugham be justified in warning, "To eat well in England, you should have breakfast three times a day." England is now one of the hottest places around for restaurants of every culinary flavor, with London at its epicenter. Among the city's 6,700 restaurants are "be-there" eateries, tiny neighborhood joints, gastro-pubs where young-gun foodniks find their feet, and swanky pacesetters frequent, and where celebrity chefs launch their ego flights. Nearly everyone in town is passionate about food and will love telling you where they've eaten recently or where they'd like to go. You, too, will be smitten, since you will spend, on average, 25% of your travel budget on eating out. After feasting on modern British cuisine, visit one (or two) of London's fabulous pubs for a nightcap. Hit the right one on the right night and watch that legendary British reserve melt away.

This restaurant renaissance is due to talented entrepreneurs and chefs: Sir Terence Conran, Marco Pierre White, Gordon Ramsay, Jamie Oliver, and Oliver Peyton lead the list. To keep up with the whirl, each newspaper has reviewers aplenty. Read up on the top tips in the London *Evening Standard* (daily), *Time Out* magazine (weekly), or the food pages of the national newspapers, especially the weekend editions.

The thriving dining scene rests on ethnic cuisines. Thousands of Indian restaurants ensure that Londoners view access to a tasty curry as a birthright. Chinese restaurants in tiny Chinatown and beyond have been around a long time, as have Greek tavernas, and there are even more Italian restaurants than Indian. Now add Thai, Malaysian, Spanish, and Japanese cuisines to those easily found in England's capital. After all this, traditional English food appears as one more exotic cuisine.

Luckily, London also does a good job of catering to people more interested in satisfying their appetites without breaking the bank than in following the latest food fashions. The listings here strike a balance between these extremes and include hip-and-happening places, neighborhood spots, ethnic alternatives, and old favorites.

Two caveats: first, the "no-smoking" trend is sweeping the London dining scene. An outright ban on smoking in public places—such as restaurants—is imminent for 2007. Second, beware of Sunday. Many restaurants are closed, especially in the evening; likewise public holidays. Over the Christmas period, London virtually shuts down—it seems only hotels are prepared to feed travelers. When in doubt, call ahead. It's a good idea to book a table at all times.

Prices & Saving Money

London is not an inexpensive city. A modest meal for two can cost £35 (about $65) and the £100-a-head meal is not so taboo. Damage-control strategies include making lunch your main meal—the top places have bargain lunch menus, halving the price of evening à la carte—and ordering a second appetizer instead of an entrée, to which few places object. Note that an appetizer, usually known as a "starter" or "first course," is sometimes called an "entrée," as it is in France, and an entrée in England is dubbed the "main course" or simply "mains."

Ethnic restaurants have always been a good money-saving bet here, especially the thousands of Indian restaurants (curry is almost the national dish). Sandwich shops and chains proliferate: *see* Where to Refuel Around Town box, *below,* for the best bets. Seek out fixed-price menus, and watch for hidden extras on the check: cover, bread, or vegetables charged separately, and service. Many restaurants exclude service charges from the menu (which the law obliges them to display outside), then add 10% to 15% to the check, or else stamp SERVICE NOT INCLUDED along the bottom, in which case you should add the 10% to 15% yourself. Don't pay twice for service.

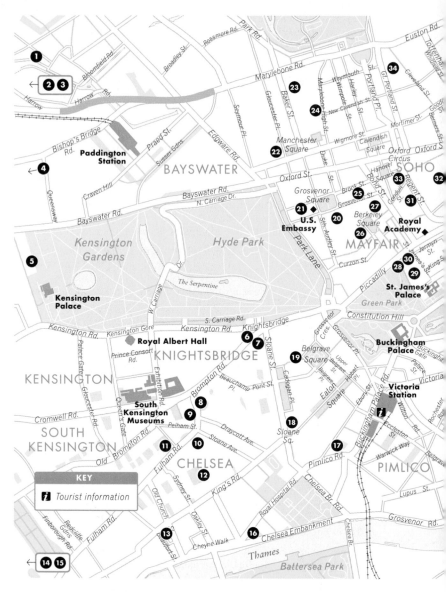

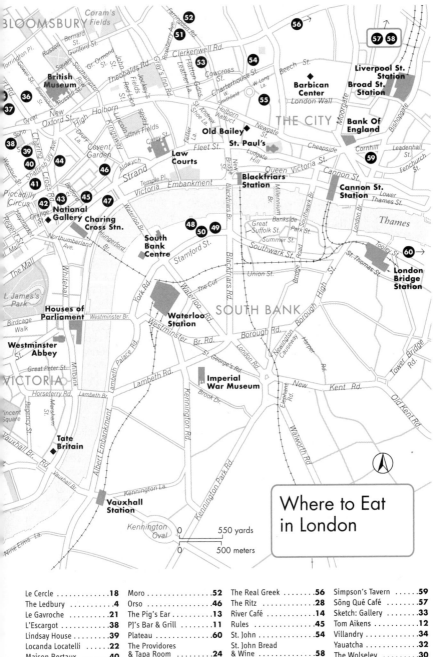

Where to Eat in London

	WHAT IT COSTS In pounds				
	£££££	**££££**	**£££**	**££**	**£**
AT DINNER	over £23	£20–£23	£14–£19	£10–£13	under £10

Prices are per person for a main course, excluding drinks, service, and V.A.T.

Bloomsbury

CHINESE
££–£££££

✕**Hakkasan.** It's *Crouching Tiger* territory at this lauded Cantonese basement restaurant off Tottenham Court Road. Ultrastylish and dimly lighted, Hakkasan is ideal for special occasions, with exquisite dim sum (lunch only), and a cracking cocktail scene. The à la carte is pricey. Its late-night days are Wednesday through Saturday (until 12:30 AM) and there's a two-hour time limit on tables. ⊠ *8 Hanway Pl., Bloomsbury, W1* ☎ *020/7907–7000* ▤ *AE, MC, V* Ⓤ *Tottenham Court Rd.*

ECLECTIC
★ **£££–££££**

✕**The Providores & Tapa Room.** Inventive Kiwi (New Zealand) chef Peter Gordon scores high with his Pacific Rim fusion cuisine in foodie-ville Marylebone. Have a sophisticated meal in the formal restaurant upstairs, or try the more relaxed ground-floor Tapa Room. On the menu you'll find venison and coriander, kangaroo loin, guava sorbet, and roast *chioca* (similar to Jerusalem artichoke). ⊠ *109 Marylebone High St., Bloomsbury, W1* ☎ *020/7935–6175* ▤ *AE, MC, V* Ⓤ *Baker St.*

FRENCH
££–££££
Fodor'sChoice
★

✕**Galvin.** London's lucky to have the Galvin brothers blazing a trail for the bistro de luxe concept on Baker Street. The feted chefs, Chris and Jeff, forsake Michelin stars and cut loose under the brasserie banner. An older crowd enjoys impeccable service in a handsome salon. There's no better crab lasagna in town, and daube of venison, pork with Agen prunes, and halibut with brown shrimp are excellent. ⊠ *66 Baker St., Bloomsbury, W1* ☎ *020/7935–4007* ▤ *AE, DC, MC, V* Ⓤ *Baker Street.*

££–££££

✕**Villandry.** Heaven for food lovers, this posh gourmet deli is crammed with fancy French pâtés, Continental cheeses, fruit tarts, biscuits, organic vegetables, and obscure breads galore. There's a bar, charcuterie, and fashionable dining room frequented by the extended New Labour gang. Breakfast is served from 8 AM. ⊠ *170 Great Portland St., Bloomsbury, W1* ☎ *020/7631–3131* ▤ *AE, MC, V* Ⓤ *Great Portland St.*

THAI
£–£££

✕**Crazy Bear.** Art-deco styling is the draw at this glamour zone in Fitzrovia, ideal for cocktails in the basement lounge, and a Thai- and Asian-influenced meal upstairs. Head for the snapper with lemon zest, and end with cheesecake. ■ TIP➔ **Admire the Murano chandelier, leather booths, ostrich-hide chairs, and the amazing mirrored loos.** ⊠ *26–28 Whitfield St., Bloomsbury, W1* ☎ *020/7631–0088* ⌕ *Reservations essential* ▤ *AE, MC, V* ☉ *Closed Sun.* Ⓤ *Goodge St., Tottenham Court Rd.*

★ **£**

✕**Busabe Eathai.** It's top value for money at this superior high-turnover Thai canteen. It's fitted with bench seats and hardwood tables but is no less seductive for the communal dining. The menu includes noodles, curries, and stir-fries; try chicken with butternut squash, cuttlefish curry, or seafood vermicelli (prawn, squid, and scallops). There are busier branches near Selfridges (8–13 Bird Street) or in Soho (106–110 Wardour Street). ✉ *22 Store St., Bloomsbury, WC1* ☎ *020/7299–7900* ⌦ *Reservations not accepted* ▭ *AE, MC, V* Ⓤ *Tottenham Court Rd.*

Chelsea

AMERICAN-CASUAL
££–££££

✗ **PJ's Bar & Grill.** Enter PJ's and adopt the Polo Joe lifestyle: wooden floors and stained glass, a slowly revolving propeller from a 1911 Vickers Vimy flying boat, and polo memorabilia. The place is relaxed and efficient, and the menu, which includes all-American staples like steaks, salads, and brownies, will please everyone except vegetarians. PJ's is open late and the bartenders can mix it all. Weekend brunch is popular with the beautiful Chelsea set. ✉ *52 Fulham Rd., Chelsea, SW3* ☎ *020/ 7581–0025* ▭ *AE, DC, MC, V* Ⓤ *South Kensington.*

CONTEMPORARY
★ **£–£££**

✗ **The Pig's Ear.** Royal heir Prince William came with friends and split the bill in the 1st-floor dining room at this inventive gastro-pub, off the King's Road. Elbow in at the boisterous ground-floor pub area, or choose a restaurant vibe in the wood-panel salon upstairs. You'll find creative dishes on the short menu: shallot and cider soup, roast bone marrow, or skate wing and leaks are all typical, and executed . . . royally. ✉ *35 Old Church St., Chelsea, SW3* ☎ *020/7352–2908* ⌦ *Reservations essential* ▭ *AE, DC, MC, V* Ⓤ *Sloane Sq.*

FRENCH
£££££
Fodor's Choice
★

✗ **Gordon Ramsay at Royal Hospital Road.** The famous Mr. Ramsay whips up a storm with white beans, lobster, foie gras, and shaved truffles. He's one of Britain's finest chefs, and wins the highest accolades here, where tables are booked months in advance. For £90, splurge on seven courses for £70, dance through a three-course dinner; or try lunch (£40 for three courses) for a gentler check—but watch the wine and those extras. ✉ *68–69 Royal Hospital Rd., Chelsea, SW3* ☎ *020/7352–4441 or 020/ 7352–3334* ⌦ *Reservations essential* ▭ *AE, DC, MC, V* ⊘ *Closed weekends* Ⓤ *Sloane Sq.*

£££££
Fodor's Choice
★

✗ **Tom Aikens.** Wonder chef Tom Aikens trained under French legend Joël Robuchon and excels at his slick modern restaurant. His constructions are intricate: many find delight with his pig's head with pork belly, poached oysters, and "piglet." There's a friendly sommelier to help navigate the hefty wine list. ✉ *43 Elystan St., Chelsea, SW3* ☎ *020/7584–2003* ⌦ *Reservations essential* ▭ *AE, MC, V* Ⓤ *South Kensington.*

££–£££££

✗ **Racine.** There's an upscale buzz at this star of the Brompton Road dining scene. Henry Harris's chic French brasserie excels because he does the simple things well—and

TOP 5

- **Anchor & Hope.** London's leading gastro-pub.

- **Le Gavroche.** Clubby haute cuisine rated London's finest dining experience.

- **St. John.** Adventurous eaters savor the challenge of Fergus Henderson's ultra-British cooking.

- **The Wolseley.** Viennese elegance for any budget at this grand, all-day café.

- **Yauatcha.** Get your dim sum whenever you want it in this ultra *Sex and the City* setting.

doesn't over charge. Classics like smoked duck with French beans or mussels with saffron mousse hit the spot. Desserts and wines by the glass are fairly priced. ✉ *239 Brompton Rd., Chelsea, SW3* ☎ *020/7584–4477* ▤ *AE, MC, V* ⓤ *South Kensington.*

The City

CONTEMPORARY
££–££££
Fodor'sChoice
★

✕ **St. John.** Most people love chef Fergus Henderson's ultra-British cooking at this converted smokehouse in Clerkenwell. His chutzpah is scary: one appetizer is pig skin, and others (calf brain or pig nose and tail) are marginally less extreme. Entrées like bone marrow and parsley salad can appear stark on the plate but arrive with style. Expect an all-French wine list, plus malmseys and port. Try rice pudding with plums, or traditional English Eccles cakes. ✉ *26 St. John St., The City, EC1* ☎ *020/7251–0848 or 020/7251–4998* ⚞ *Reservations essential* ▤ *AE, DC, MC, V* ☾ *Closed Sun. No lunch Sat.* ⓤ *Farringdon.*

££–£££

✕ **St. John Bread & Wine.** The canteen version of St. John in Clerkenwell is a winner no matter what meal of the day: have porridge and prunes for breakfast, seed cake and a glass of Madeira for "elevenses," oxtail and horseradish for lunch, and Gloucester Old Spot ham for dinner. The scrumptious bread is baked on-site, and the wine is mainly French. ■ TIP➔ **It's good before or after a stroll around nearby Old Spitalfields or Brick Lane markets.** ✉ *94–96 Commercial St., The City, E1* ☎ *020/7247–8724* ▤ *AE, MC, V* ⓤ *Aldgate East, Liverpool St.*

ENGLISH
★ **££–£££**

✕ **Coach & Horses.** Farringdon's award-winning rare-breed gastro-pub gets it right on all levels. The inside feels like a proper English pub—retaining original wooden screens and etched glass—and there are quality ales, earnest service, and the kitchen excels through invention. You might find smoked mackerel, crispy pork belly, or Old Spot ham with fava beans and parsley sauce. ■ TIP➔ **Dine in the bar if you want that real English pub sensation.** ✉ *26–28 Ray St., The City, EC1* ☎ *020/7278–8990* ▤ *AE, MC, V* ⓤ *Farringdon.*

£–££

✕ **Simpson's Tavern.** A bastion of tradition, this back-alley chophouse was founded in 1757 and is as "rum and raucous" as ever. It's popular with ruddy-faced City folk, who come for old-school fare: steak-and-kidney pie, liver and bacon, chump chops, potted shrimps (served in small pots with butter), or the house specialty, "stewed cheese" (cheese on toast with béchamel and Worcestershire sauce). Its shared seating and service is "idiosyncratic"—one of its charms. ✉ *38½ Cornhill, at Ball Ct., The City, EC3* ☎ *020/7626–9985* ⚞ *Reservations not accepted* ▤ *AE, DC, MC, V* ☾ *Closed weekends. No dinner* ⓤ *Bank.*

FRENCH
£££££

✕ **Plateau.** Sir Terence Conran's Plateau is an excellent choice for a Canary Wharf business meal, or for something more relaxed. In a slick all-white space, with tulip-shape chairs and floor-to-ceiling plate-glass windows overlooking Canada Square, Plateau has something for everyone; a bar, rotisserie, terrace, smoking room, and main restaurant. Mains like monkfish and leaks and sea bass and parsnip puree are mighty expensive, but this is Canary Wharf where money, it seems, is no object. ✉ *Canada Place, Canary Wharf, The City, E14* ☎ *020/7715–7100* ⚞ *Reservations essential* ▤ *AE, MC, V* ⓤ *Canary Wharf.*

££££–£££££ ✗ **Club Gascon.** It's hard to find a sexier place than this in London. Maybe it's the leather-wall interior, the cut flowers, cute service, or the way the tapas-style, modern, southwestern French cuisine is served (on a rock rather than on a plate). It must be the quality of the foie gras, which you could enjoy from start to finish: feast on duck foie-gras "popcorn," and then have it for pudding with grapes and gingerbread. ⊠ *57 W. Smithfield, The City, EC1* ☎ *020/7796–0600* ⚖ *Reservations essential* ⊟ *AE, MC, V* ⊘ *Closed Sun. No lunch Sat.* Ⓤ *Barbican.*

GREEK ✗ **The Real Greek.** Theodore Kyriakou lifts Greek cuisine up several notches
££–£££ at this Shoreditch favorite. Push costs down with a spread of *meze* (small appetizers) and *fagakia* (mid-size dishes). Lamb sweatbreads, grilled octopus, and Ismir squid with prunes recall a real taste of the mainland, and the all-Greek wine list is worth a sniff. ⊠ *15 Hoxton Market, The City, N1* ☎ *020/7739–8212* ⚖ *Reservations essential* ⊟ *MC, V* ⊘ *Closed Sun.* Ⓤ *Old St.*

MEDITERRANEAN ✗ **Moro.** Up the road from the City, near Clerkenwell and Sadler's Wells
★ **££–£££** dance theater, is Exmouth Market, a cluster of cute shops, an Italian church, and fine restaurants like Moro. The menu includes a mélange of Spanish and North African flavors. Spiced meats, Serrano hams, salt cod, and wood-fired and char-grilled offerings are the secret to Moro's success. There's a long zinc bar, the tables are small, and the only downside is the persistent noise. But then again, that's part of the buzz. ⊠ *34–36 Exmouth Market, The City, EC1* ☎ *020/7833–8336* ⚖ *Reservations essential* ⊟ *AE, DC, MC, V* ⊘ *Closed Sun.* Ⓤ *Farringdon.*

£–£££ ✗ **The Eagle.** The Eagle spearheaded the welcome trend toward pubs serving good meals. As *the* original '90s gastro-pub, it belongs in the "Restaurants" section by virtue of its good-value Portuguese–Spanish food. You'll find about nine dishes on the blackboard menu daily—a pasta, three vegetarian choices, and a risotto usually among them. Many places in London charge twice the price for similar food. ⊠ *159 Farringdon Rd., The City, EC1* ☎ *020/7837–1353* ⚖ *Reservations not accepted* ⊟ *MC, V* Ⓤ *Farringdon.*

VIETNAMESE ✗ **Sông Qué Café.** If you're in Hoxton and looking for an unpretentious
£ place to eat, this Vietnamese canteen offers outstanding value for money. Block out the scruffy Kingsland Road location and tacky decor and instead dig into papaya salad, chili squid, Vietnamese pancakes, and *pho* (beef broth with rice noodles and rare steak). ⊠ *134 Kingsland Rd., The City, E2* ☎ *020/7613–3222* ⊟ *AE, MC, V* Ⓤ *Old St.*

Covent Garden

CONTEMPORARY ✗ **The Ivy.** Though pushed from the highest reaches of London's restau-
★ **£–£££££** rant heirarchy, Ivy is still hard to get into. In a wood-panel room with stained glass, a curious mix of celebs and out-of-towners dine on Caesar salad, salmon cakes, and English classics like shepherd's pie and rhubarb fool (stewed rhubarb and cream). For star-trekking ("Don't look now, dear, but there's Hugh Grant") this is the prime spot in London. The weekend-set lunch is a bargain at £22.50. ■ TIP→ **Try walking in off the street for a table on short notice—it's known to work.** ⊠ *1 West St.,*

Eating English

IN LONDON, LOCAL COULD MEAN any global flavor, but for pure Englishness, roast beef probably tops the list. If you want the best-value traditional Sunday lunch, go to a pub. Gastro-pubs, where Sunday roasts are generally made with top-quality ingredients, are a good bet. The meat is usually served with crisp roast potatoes and carrots, and with the traditional Yorkshire pudding, a savory batter baked in the oven until crisp. A rich, dark gravy is poured on top.

Other tummy liners include shepherd's pie, made with stewed minced lamb and a mashed potato topping and baked until lightly browned on top; cottage pie is a similar dish, but made with minced beef instead of lamb. Steak-and-kidney pie is a delight when done

properly: with chunks of lean beef and ox kidneys, braised with onions and mushrooms in a thick gravy, and topped with a light puff-pastry crust.

Fish-and-chips, usually cod or haddock, comes with thick french fries. A ploughman's lunch in a pub is crusty bread, a strong flavored English cheese with bite (cheddar, blue Stilton, crumbly white Cheshire, or smooth red Leicester), and tangy pickles with a side-salad garnish. As for puddings, seek out a sweet bread-and-butter pudding, served hot with layers of bread and dried fruit baked in a creamy custard until lightly crisp. And we musn't forget the English cream tea, which consists of scones served with strawberry jam and clotted cream, and sandwiches made with wafer-thin slices of cucumber—and, of course, plenty of tea.

Covent Garden, WC2 ☎ *020/7836–4751* ⟋ *Reservations essential* ⊟ *AE, DC, MC, V* Ⓤ *Covent Garden.*

CONTINENTAL
£££££
✕ **Savoy Grill.** Ambitious chef Marcus Wareing triumphs at this bastion of power dining. Kind lighting, wood paneling, and silver-plated pillars mark the art-deco interior, and assembled CEOs, press barons, and politicians have warmed to Wareing's menu. On it are braised pork belly, calves' sweetbread, an "Arnold Bennett" omelet (with smoked haddock and Gruyère béchamel sauce), and chateaubriand. ⊠ *The Savoy, Strand, Covent Garden, WC2* ☎ *020/7592–1600* ⟋ *Reservations essential* 🏛 *Jacket required* ⊟ *AE, MC, V* Ⓤ *Covent Garden.*

ENGLISH
★ £££
✕ **Rules.** Come, escape from the 21st century. Opened in 1798, London's oldest restaurant—and gorgeous institution—has welcomed everyone from Charles Dickens to the current Prince of Wales. It's one of the single most beautiful dining salons in London: plush red banquettes and lacquered Regency yellow walls crammed with oil paintings, engravings, and Victorian cartoons. The menu includes fine historic dishes—try roast beef and Yorkshire pudding or the steak-and-kidney pudding for a taste of the 18th century. Daily specials will, in season, include game from Rules' Teesdale estate. ⊠ *35 Maiden La., Covent Garden, WC2* ☎ *020/7836–5314* ⊟ *AE, DC, MC, V* Ⓤ *Covent Garden.*

ITALIAN
£–£££

✕ **Orso.** Showbiz people gravitate to the midrange Tuscan-inspired food here in Covent Garden. It's not surprising that Orso shares the same snappy attitude as its sister restaurant, Joe Allen. The menu changes daily but always includes excellent pizza and pasta dishes plus entrées based, perhaps, on zucchini and mascarpone or roast sea bass. ⊠ *27 Wellington St., Covent Garden, WC2* ☎ *020/7240–5269* ⌕ *Reservations essential* ⊟ *AE, MC, V* Ⓤ *Covent Garden.*

PAN-ASIAN
£££–£££££

✕ **Asia de Cuba.** Like the trendy St. Martins Lane hotel it resides in, funky Asia de Cuba is designed by Philippe Starck. It's bold and loud—check out the dangling light bulbs, Latino music, library books, mini-TVs, and satin-clad pillars. The food is pan-Asian fusion and you're encouraged to share the family portions. The miso black cod is delicious, as is the calamari salad. Cheap, it ain't, but it's certainly disco. ⊠ *45 St. Martin's La., Covent Garden, WC2* ☎ *020/7300–5588* ⊟ *AE, DC, MC, V* Ⓤ *Leicester Sq.*

SEAFOOD
££–£££££
Fodor'sChoice
★

✕ **J Sheekey.** The A-list go here as an alternative to the Ivy. Sleek and discreet, and linked with Theaterland, J Sheekey is one of Londoners' favorite finds. It charms with wood paneling, alcove tables, cracked tiles, and lava-rock bar tops. Opt for jellied eels, Dover sole, fish stew, cod tongue, and famous Sheekey fish pie. ■ TIP➜ **Save money with the weekend three-course lunch for £21.50; dining at the bar is romantic, too.** ⊠ *28–32 St. Martin's Ct., Covent Garden, WC2* ☎ *020/7240–2565* ⊟ *AE, DC, MC, V* Ⓤ *Leicester Sq.*

Hammersmith

FRENCH
£–£££

✕ **Chez Kristof.** Chez Kristof cleans ups in Brackenbury village with this perfect neighborhood pitch on Hammersmith Grove. The space has a spare look—muted greys, whites, and browns—and attracts swarms of locals. The modern French brasserie food can be salty, but it's more hit than miss—razor clam stew, ox cheek, pig's head or veal trotters all sing for their supper. Go for the buzz, the terrace tables in summer, or the relaxed but glamorous West End vibe. ⊠ *111 Hammersmith Grove, Hammersmith, W6* ☎ *020/741–1177* ⌕ *Reservations essential* ⊟ *AE, DC, MC, V* Ⓤ *Hammersmith.*

ITALIAN
£££££

✕ **River Café.** This canteen-style destination Italian spot started a trend with its single-estate olive oils, simple roasts, and impeccably sourced ingredients. Chefs Rose Gray and Ruth Rogers use ultrafresh, seasonal ingredients, so expect salmon with Sicilian lemons, calamari with red-pepper salsa, and pork and pancetta—plus one of London's highest checks. But remember: if you snag an evening table, this is in distant Hammersmith, and you may be stranded if you haven't booked a cab. Note that tables must be cleared by 11 PM. ⊠ *Thames Wharf, Rainville Rd., Hammersmith, W6* ☎ *020/7386–4200* ⌕ *Reservations essential* ⊟ *AE, DC, MC, V* Ⓤ *Hammersmith.*

Knightsbridge

FRENCH ✕ **The Capital.** The haute cuisine is nearly peerless at this clublike din-
£££££ ing room that retains a grown-up atmosphere and formal service. Chef
Eric Chavot conjures up superb and classic French dishes. Try frogs' legs
with veal sweetbreads, foie gras with pumpkin risotto, roast pigeon and
bacon, or crab lasagna. Desserts follow the same exceptional route.
■ TIP➡ Bargain set-price lunch menus (£29.50) are more affordable than dinner (£48–£68). ⊠ *22–24 Basil St., Knightsbridge, SW3* ☎ *020/7589–5171*
⌂ *Reservations essential* ▤ *AE, DC, MC, V* ⓤ *Knightsbridge.*

★ ££££ ✕ **Le Cercle.** Prepare to be wowed by knockout new French cuisine at
this groundbreaking restaurant and bar, set in a steep, slick basement
off Sloane Square. The tapas-style portions of steak tartare, foie gras,
pigs trotters, quails eggs, and wild mushrooms cry out to be shared.
■ TIP➡ Four to six dishes generally suffice; try wines by the glass for each
round of surprises. ⊠ *1 Wilbraham Pl., Knightsbridge, SW1* ☎ *020/
7901–9999* ⌂ *Reservations essential* ▤ *AE, MC, V* ☽ *Closed Sun. and
Mon.* ⓤ *Sloane Sq.*

££–££££ ✕ **La Poule au Pot.** Americans and the Chelsea set swoon over this candlelight corner of France in Belgravia, where exposed walls, rustic furniture, and potted roses make for romantic meals. Though not spectacular,
the country cooking is decent and rustic. The *poule au pot* (stewed chicken)
and goose with butterbeans are hearty, and there are fine classics, such
as beef bourguignonne and French onion soup, all served by a cheerful
staff. ⊠ *231 Ebury St., Knightsbridge, SW1* ☎ *020/7730–7763* ⌂ *Reservations essential* ▤ *AE, DC, MC, V* ⓤ *Sloane Sq.*

INDIAN ✕ **Amaya.** The demanding and hard-to-fool denizens of Knightsbridge
£–£££££ (and beyond) have anointed Amaya the new posh Indian kid on the block.
The dark-wood paneling, terra-cotta statues, rosewood candles, and
sparkly chandelier set an upscale tone, but it's the spicy grilled fish and
meats from the open show-kitchen that get the juices flowing. Watch
the chefs produce goodies from the tandoor oven, *sigri* (a charcoal grill)
and *tawa* iron skillet, but mind those prices—they're dangerously high.
⊠ *Halkin Archade, 19 Motcomb St., Knightsbridge, SW1* ☎ *0870/
780–8174* ⌂ *Reservations essential* ▤*AE, DC, MC, V* ⓤ*Knightsbridge.*

JAPANESE ✕ **Zuma.** Hats off to this fashionable, Tokyo-style Japanese restaurant.
£££££ Superbly lighted and designed, with polished granite, blond wood, and
exposed pipes, it includes a bar, robata grill, and sushi counter, which
takes no reservations. Try the succulent soft-shell crab, black cod
wrapped in papery hoba leaf, and *wagyuu* beef. A "sake sommelier" is
on hand to help navigate their 30 varieties of rice wine. ⊠ *5 Raphael
St., Knightsbridge, SW7* ☎ *020/7584–1010* ⌂ *Reservations essential*
▤ *AE, DC, MC, V* ⓤ *Knightsbridge.*

Mayfair

CONTEMPORARY ✕ **Angela Hartnett's Menu.** The old-world atmosphere at these mahogany-
£££££ panel dining rooms in the English Connaught hotel is refreshed, thanks
to chef Hartnett's cuisine. The modern European menu (with homage
to Italy, the Mediterranean, Pays Basque, and Spain) is a far cry from

the steak-and-kidney pudding and carved beef-of-old-England days of yore—although some interpretations of die-hard Connaught classics remain. Enjoy tortelli (stuffed pasta) with Swiss chard and sea bream. ⊠ *The Connaught, Carlos Pl., Mayfair, W1* ☎ *020/7592–1222* ⌃ *Reservations essential* ⊟ *AE, DC, MC, V* Ⓤ *Green Park.*

£££££
Fodor'sChoice
★
✕ **Greenhouse.** Hidden behind Mayfair mansions and approached via a spot-lighted garden, this elegant salon is for aficionados of top-class and inventive French cuisine at any price. Sit by the garden windows and feast on foie gras with espresso syrup and Amaretto foam, sea urchin panna cotta, or Limousin veal sweetbreads. The epic 90-odd page wine book spans 2,000 bins, including Château d'Yquem (1887–1990). ⊠ *27A Hay's Mews, Mayfair, W1* ☎ *020/7499–3331* ⌃ *Reservations essential* ⊟ *AE, DC, MC, V* ☻ *Closed Sun. No lunch Sat.* Ⓤ *Green Park.*

FRENCH
£££££
✕ **Gordon Ramsay at Claridge's.** There's a grand and gracious atmosphere at one of London's favorite celebration restaurants (Prime Minister Tony Blair had his 50th here). Consider the three-course lunches (£30), or the opulent set dinners (£60 and £70). Try Gloucester Old Spot pork belly or foie gras and goose breast with Périgord truffle. Book months ahead—choosing a Sunday evening is more likely to yield success. Arrive early for drinks at Claridge's art-deco cocktail bar, one of the sassiest in town. ⊠ *Claridge's, Brook St., Mayfair, W1* ☎ *020/7499–0099* ⌃ *Reservations essential* 🏛 *Jacket required* ⊟ *AE, MC, V* Ⓤ *Bond St.*

£££££
Fodor'sChoice
★
✕ **Le Gavroche.** Chef Michel Roux Jr. inherits the family culinary gene and outperforms at this clubby haven, which some critics rate the best dining in London. His mastery of classic French cuisine—formal, flowery, decorated—makes the fixed-price lunch seem relatively affordable at £44 (with a half bottle of wine, water, and coffee included). In fact, lunch may be the best way to eat here if you don't have an expense account, which most patrons clearly do. Book at least a week in advance. ⊠ *43 Upper Brook St., Mayfair, W1* ☎ *020/7408–0881* ⌃ *Reservations essential* ⊟ *AE, DC, MC, V* ☻ *Closed 10 days at Christmas. No lunch weekends* Ⓤ *Marble Arch.*

★ ££–££££
✕ **Bellamy's.** The Mayfair society crowd loves this uppercrust French brasserie for simple reasons: the discreet front of house, reassuring menu, classy-but-restrained decor, and the fabulously priced all-French wine list. The menu weaves from scrambled eggs with Perigord truffles, through whitebait, coquilles St. Jacques, to entrecôte of beef, rillettes of duck, and *iles flottantes* ("floating islands"—egg custard topped with egg whites). ■ TIP→ **The entrance is through a posh delicatessen next to the restaurant.** ⊠ *18–18a Bruton Pl., Mayfair, W1* ☎ *020/7491–2727* ⊟ *AE, DC, MC, V* Ⓤ *Green Park.*

ITALIAN
★
£££–£££££
✕ **Locanda Locatelli.** Chef Giorgio Locatelli has the golden touch—hence the mile-long waiting list at this sexy Italian restaurant, replete with convex mirrors and cherry-wood dividers. The food is accomplished—superb risottos, handmade pastas, gorgeous fish, beautiful desserts. Be bold and try the nettle risotto or calves' kidney, and lose yourself in the all-Italian wine list. ⊠ *8 Seymour St., Mayfair, W1* ☎ *020/7935–9088* ⌃ *Reservations essential* ⊟ *AE, MC, V* Ⓤ *Marble Arch.*

Notting Hill

CONTEMPORARY ✗ **Cow Dining Room.** The faux-Dublin 1950s backroom bar at this chic
£££ gastro-pub serves rock oysters, salmon cakes, baked brill, and Cornish
crab. Upstairs the chef whips up Brit specialties—roast chicken, ox
tongue, lambs' kidneys, and black pudding are typical temptations. Notting Hill locals love the house special in the bar area: draft Guinness with
a pint of prawns. ✉ *89 Westbourne Park Rd., Notting Hill, W2* ☎ *020/
7221–0021* ⚐ *Reservations essential* ⊟ *MC, V* Ⓤ *Westbourne Park.*

£–£££ ✗ **Electric Brasserie.** There's nowhere better for people-watching than the
Fodor'sChoice Electric on Portobello Road's market day. Go for the bustle of the interior, too—zinc fittings, mirrors, and flattering lighting—and expect oysters, steaks, chunky sandwiches, and seafood platters. Or just settle in
at the bar with a long drink. ✉ *191 Portobello Rd., Notting Hill, W11*
☎ *020/7908–9696* ⊟ *AE, DC, MC, V* Ⓤ *Notting Hill.*

FRENCH ✗ **The Ledbury.** Top-bracket fine dining has arrived at the doorstep of
££££–£££££ Notting Hill's ultra-high-net-worth citizens. Run by the team behind Chez
Bruce in Wandsworth, Ledbury is where to go for highly refined cuisine. It's not cheap—£45 for a three-course dinner—but it's super smart
and professional. There's a short list of fine wines, including 20 half bottles, and seven sherries by the glass. ✉ *127 Ledbury Rd., Notting Hill,
W11* ☎ *0207/7792–9090* ⊟ *AE, MC, V* Ⓤ *Westbourne Park.*

PAN-ASIAN ✗ **E&O.** If you like star-spotting, you'll enjoy E&O, one of London's
£–££££ hippest scene bars and restaurants. E&O means Eastern and Oriental,
and the intelligent mix of Chinese, Japanese, Vietnamese, and Thai
cuisines includes *beaucoup* vegetarian options. Don't skip the dumplings,
black cod, Thai rare-beef, or mango and papaya salads. ✉ *14 Blenheim
Crescent, Notting Hill, W11* ☎ *020/7229–5454* ⚐ *Reservations essential* ⊟ *AE, DC, MC, V* Ⓤ *Ladbroke Grove.*

THAI ✗ **Churchill Thai Kitchen.** There's a cult appeal to this super-value Thai
£ kitchen attached to a traditional English pub. With big portions of all
dishes priced at £5.85, it's a bargain for this high-end district, and full
most nights. The pad thai noodles are a good bet, as are the red-and-
green curries. Mind the abundant foliage in the conservatory. ✉ *Churchill
Arms, 119 Kensington Church St., Notting Hill, W8* ☎ *020/7792–1246*
⊟ *MC, V* Ⓤ *Notting Hill Gate, High St. Kensington.*

St. James's

AUSTRIAN ✗ **The Wolseley.** Enjoy grand elegance at this classic run by Messrs.
£–££££ Corbin and King, London's top restaurateurs. Framed with black lac-
Fodor'sChoice querware, the Viennese-style café begins its long, decadent days with
★ breakfast at 7 AM and is open until midnight. Linger morning, noon,
and night for Nurnberger bratwurst, Wiener schnitzel, Hungarian
goulash, and, for dessert, strudel and *kaiserschmarren* (pancake with
stewed fruit). It's particularly ideal for sinful pastries and weekend afternoon tea. ✉ *160 Piccadilly, St. James's, W1* ☎ *020/7499–6996*
⊟ *AE, DC, MC, V.*

WHERE TO REFUEL AROUND TOWN

When you're on the go or don't have time for a leisurely meal—and Starbucks simply won't cut it—you might want to try a local chain restaurant or sandwich bar. The ones listed below are fairly priced and committed to quality and using fresh ingredients.

Café Rouge: A classic 30-strong French bistro chain that's been around for eons—so "uncool" that it's now almost fashionable. ⊕ www.caferouge.co.uk

Carluccio's Caffé: Affable TV chef Antonio Carluccio's chain of 12 all-day traditional Italian café/bar/food shops are freshly sourced and make brilliant stops on a shopping spree. ⊕ www.carluccios.com

Ed's Easy Diner: Overdose on made-to-order hamburgers at this chain of shiny, retro '50s-theme American diners. ⊕ www.edseasydiner.co.uk

Gourmet Burger Kitchen (aka GBK): Peter Gordon's burger joints are wholesome and handy, with Aberdeen Angus beef, lamb, or venison burgers. ⊕ www.gbkinfo.co.uk

Pizza Express: Serving tasty but utterly predictable pizzas, Pizza Express seems to be everywhere

(there are 95 in London). Soho's branch has a cool live jazz program. ⊕ www.pizzaexpress.com

Pret a Manger: London's take-out supremo isn't just for sandwiches: there are wraps, noodles, sushi, salads, and tea cakes as well. ⊕ www.pretamanger.com

Ranoush Juice Bar: Chewy shwarmas proliferate at these late-night kebab café and juice bars (open until 3 AM daily), which serve kebabs, falafal, and tabbouleh. There are three branches in Kensington and one on Edgware Road. ⊕ www.maroush.com

Strada: Stop here for authentic pizzas baked over a wood fire, plus simple pastas and risottos. It's stylish, cheap, and packed. ⊕ www.strada.co.uk

Tootsies Grill: This superior burger joint does yummy grilled burgers, fries, salads, steaks, BLTs, and chicken spreads. There's a children's meal for £4.95. ⊕ www.tootsiesrestaurants.co.uk

Wagamama: Londoners drain endless bowls of noodles at this chain of high-tech, high-turnover, high-volume Japanese canteens. ⊕ www.wagamama.com

CONTEMPORARY ✕ **Le Caprice.** The glossy '80s Eva Jiricna interior; the perfect service; the
£££–£££££ menu, halfway between Euro-peasant and fashion plate—Le Caprice commands the deepest loyalty of almost any restaurant in London because it gets everything right. From monkfish to forest berries and white-chocolate sauce, the food has no business being so good. Frequented by the older variety of celebrity, it's also some of the best people-watching in town. ⊠ *Arlington House, Arlington St., St. James's, SW1* ☎ *020/7629–2239* ⬥ *Reservations essential* ▤ *AE, DC, MC, V* Ⓤ *Green Park.*

£££–£££££ ✗ **Sketch: Gallery.** The global fashion crowd totally *gets* the unusual design aesthetic at Mourad Mazouz's gastro-emporium. "Momo's" madcap gamble is all about extremes. The lavish Gallery dining room (a true art-gallery space by day) serves carbo-light contemporary cuisine to a funky beat and video projections, and turns into a club Friday and Saturday nights, as soon as staff clear the floor. There's also a bar, cakes in the Parlour Room, lunch in the Glade area, and a lauded "molecular gastronomy" (science-based cuisine) menu in the fine dining, 1st-floor Lecture Room, overseen by French legend Pierre Gagnaire. ⊠ *9 Conduit St., St. James's, W1* ☏ *0870/777–4488* ⌕ *Reservations essential* ▭ *AE, DC, MC, V* ⊗ *Closed Sun.* Ⓤ *Oxford Circus.*

CONTINENTAL
£££££ ✗ **The Ritz.** This palace of gilt, marble, mirror, and trompe l'oeil would moisten Marie Antoinette's eye. Add the view over Green Park and the Ritz's sunken garden, and it seems beside the point to eat. But the cuisine stands up to the visuals, with super-rich morsels—foie gras, lobster, truffles, caviar—all served with a flourish. Englishness is wrested from Louis XVI by a daily roast from the trolley. A three-course lunch at £45 makes the check more bearable than the £75 you would pay for the Friday and Saturday cha-cha-cha dinner–dance (a dying tradition). ⊠ *150 Piccadilly, St. James's, W1* ☏ *020/7493–8181* ⌕ *Reservations essential* ⌂ *Jacket and tie* ▭ *AE, DC, MC, V* Ⓤ *Green Park.*

NORTH AFRICAN
★ **£££** ✗ **Momo.** It's a fun ticket, so go if you can. Mourad Mazouz—"Momo" to friends—rocks beau London with his Casbah-like restaurant off Regent Street. There are Moroccan rugs, fur-skin seats, plus a DJ and often live North African music. Downstairs is the members-only Kemia Bar, and next door is Mô—a cozy Moroccan tearoom, open to all. The cuisine, although good, doesn't *quite* live up to the eclectic atmosphere, but that doesn't stop everyone having a good time. ⊠ *25 Heddon St., St. James's, W1* ☏ *020/7434–4040* ⌕ *Reservations essential* ▭ *AE, DC, MC, V* Ⓤ *Piccadilly Circus.*

Soho

CAFÉS
£ ✗ **Maison Bertaux.** Romantics cherish this tiny, two-story '50s French patisserie because nothing's changed in decades. The pastries and gooey cakes are to die for and are baked on-site; the éclairs are stuffed with light cream and the Black Forrest gâteau is studded with Morello cherries. There are savories, and cute tea services; try not to drool on the window display on the way in or out. ⊠ *28 Greek St., Soho, W1* ☏ *020/7437–6007* ▭ *No credit cards* Ⓤ *Leicester Sq.*

CHINESE
£–£££££ ✗ **Fung Shing.** In terms of service and food, this cool-green restaurant is a cut above the other Lisle–Wardour Street Chinese restaurants. Especially fine and exciting dishes are the crispy baby squid, steamed scallops, and salt-baked chicken, served on or off the bone with a bowl of broth. Reserve a table in the airy backroom conservatory. ⊠ *15 Lisle St., Soho, WC2* ☏ *020/7437–1539* ▭ *AE, DC, MC, V* Ⓤ *Leicester Sq.*

£–£££££
Fodor'sChoice
★ ✗ **Yauatcha.** It's all-day dim sum at this superbly lighted slinky Soho classic. Expertly designed by Christian Liaigre—with a bar-length aquarium, candles, and starry ceiling—the food's a match for the *Sex and the City*

setting. There are wicked dim sum (try prawn and scallops), dumplings, and cocktails, and upstairs is a modern pastry shop. ■ TIP→ **Note the 90-minute turnaround on tables, and ask to dine in the more romantic basement at night.** ✉ *15 Broadwick St., Soho, W1* ☎ *020/7494–8888* ⌆ *Reservations essential* ▤ *AE, MC, V* Ⓤ *Oxford Circus.*

CONTINENTAL ✕ **L'Escargot.** Everyone feels classy at this old-time Soho haunt that
★ **££–£££** serves French food in a sassy art-deco ground-floor salon (there's also the Picasso Room, a 1st-floor formal dining area, replete with Picasso artwork). The fine wines go well with the wood-pigeon *pithiviers* (filled puff pastry), roast pheasant with juniper, or any of the grilled fish. Owned by restaurateur Marco Pierre White, L'Escargot is relaxed, reliable, grown-up, and glamorous. ✉ *48 Greek St., Soho, W1* ☎ *020/7437–2679* ▤ *AE, DC, MC, V* ☾ *Closed Sun.* Ⓤ *Leicester Sq.*

IRISH ✕ **Lindsay House.** Irish chef Richard Corrigan fills up this creaky 1740s
★ Georgian Soho town house with his personality and some of the finest
£££–£££££ food in town. He's known for his invention—combining scallops with pork belly and veal sweetbreads with cauliflower. He excels with Irish beef and mash, and his white asparagus and langoustine can't be bettered. Petits fours with coffee will send you home oh-so-happy. ✉ *21 Romilly St., Soho, W1* ☎ *020/7439–0450* ▤ *AE, DC, MC, V* ☾ *Closed Sun.* Ⓤ *Leicester Sq.*

South Bank

EASTERN ✕ **Baltic.** To dine well in Southwark, come to this vodka-party playground.
EUROPEAN Slick white walls, wooden beams, exposed walls, and an amber chan-
£–£££ delier make this converted coach house a sexy spot for drinks or a decent east European meal. Under the same ownership as Chez Kristof in Hammersmith, Baltic serves fine blinis (with caviar or smoked salmon) and tasty gravlax. Siberian, rye, and rose petal are but a few of the killer vodkas on offer. ✉ *74 Blackfriars Rd., South Bank, SE1* ☎ *020/7928–1111* ▤ *AE, DC, MC, V* Ⓤ *Southwark.*

ENGLISH ✕ **Anchor & Hope.** Great things at reasonable prices come from the open
££–£££ kitchen at this permanently packed, no-reservations gastro-pub on the
Fodor'sChoice Cut: smoked sprats, and crab on toast are two standouts. It's informal,
★ cramped, and highly original, and there are often dishes for groups (whole shoulder of lamb is a good'un). Expect to share a table, too. ✉ *36 The Cut, South Bank, SE1* ☎ *020/7928–9898* ⌆ *Reservations not accepted* ▤ *MC, V* ☾ *Closed Sun.* Ⓤ *Waterloo, Southwark.*

FRENCH ✕ **Chez Bruce.** It's a feat to wrest the title of London's favorite restau-
★ **£££££** rant from the Ivy, and even more so for a neighborhood joint south of the river on Wandsworth Common. Expect peerless yet relaxed service—and wonders from chef-proprietor Bruce Poole. Dive into the lamb's tongue, or experiment with veal, liver, and kidney, and head out with rum baba. The wines are great, the sommelier's superb, and overall it's all rather lovely. ✉ *2 Bellevue Rd., Wandsworth, SW17* ☎ *020/8672–0114* ⌆ *Reservations essential* ▤ *AE, MC, V* Ⓤ *Wandsworth Common rail.*

South Kensington

CONTEMPORARY **ᢦ Bibendum.** This converted 1911 Michelin-tire showroom, adorned with
£££–£££££ awesome stained glass and art-deco prints, remains a smooth-running,
London showpiece. Chef Matthew Harris cooks with Euro-Brit flair. Try
calves' brains, any risotto, Pyrenean lamb with garlic and gravy, or tripe
(just as it ought to be cooked). The £28.50 fixed-price lunch menu is
money well spent, especially on Sunday. ⊠ *Michelin House, 81 Fulham
Rd., South Kensington, SW3* ☎ *020/7581–5817* ᢦ *Reservations essential* ⊟ *AE, DC, MC, V* Ⓤ *South Kensington.*

MEDITERRANEAN **ᢦ The Collection.** Enter through a spotlighted tunnel over a glass draw-
££–£££ bridge, make your way past the style police, and find yourself engulfed
by a fashionable crowd. The huge warehouse setting, with industrial wood
beams and steel cables, a vast bar, and a suspended gallery, makes for
great people-watching. Well-dressed wannabes peck at Mediterranean
food with Japanese and Thai accents. ⊠ *264 Brompton Rd., South Kensington, SW3* ☎ *020/7225–1212* ⊟ *AE, MC, V* Ⓤ *South Kensington.*

PUBS & AFTERNOON TEA

Pubs

The city's pubs, public houses, or "locals" dispense beer, good cheer,
and casual grub in settings that range from ancient wood-beam rooms
to ornate Victorian interiors to utilitarian modern rooms. London's culinary fever has not passed pubs by, however, and gastro-pub fever is still
sweeping the city. At many places, char-grills are being installed in the
kitchen out back, and up front the faded wallpapers are being replaced
by abstract paintings. The best of these luxe pubs are reviewed above.
Some of the following also showcase nouveau pub grub, but whether
you have Moroccan chicken or the usually dismal ploughman's special,
do order a pint. Note that American-style beer is called "lager" in
Britain, whereas the real British brew is "bitter" (usually served warm).
Order up your choice in two sizes—pints or half pints. Some London
pubs also sell "real ale," which is less gassy than bitters and, many would
argue, has a better flavor.

In 2005, England and Wales relaxed their licensing laws and as many
as 5,200 drinking establishments in London extended their opening hours
(the old laws required most pubs to close at 11 PM). And although it's
controversial, the new development only translates into a modest increase
in overall licensing hours.

The list below offers a few pubs selected for central location, historical
interest, a pleasant garden, music, or good food, but you might just as
happily adopt your own temporary local.

ᢦ Black Friar. A step from Blackfriars tube stop, this spectacular pub has
an Arts and Crafts interior that is entertainingly, satirically ecclesiastical, with inlaid mother-of-pearl, wood carvings, stained glass, and marble pillars all over the place. In spite of the finely lettered temperance

tracts on view just below the reliefs of monks, fairies, and friars, there is a favorable group of beers on tap from independent brewers. ✉ *174 Queen Victoria St., The City, EC4* ☎ *020/7236–5474* Ⓤ *Blackfriars.*

✕ **George Inn.** The inn overlooks a courtyard where Shakespeare's plays were once staged. The present building dates from the late 17th century and is central London's last galleried inn. Dickens was a regular, and the George is featured in *Little Dorrit.* Entertainments include Shakespeare performances, medieval jousts, and morris dancing. ✉ *77 Borough High St., South Bank, SE1* ☎ *020/7407–2056* Ⓤ *London Bridge.*

★ ✕ **Lamb & Flag.** This 17th-century pub was once known as the Bucket of Blood because the upstairs room was used as a ring for bare-knuckle boxing. Now it's a trendy, friendly, and bloodless pub, serving food (lunchtime only) and real ale. It's on the edge of Covent Garden, off Garrick Street. ✉ *33 Rose St., Covent Garden, WC2* ☎ *020/7497–9504* Ⓤ *Covent Garden.*

✕ **Museum Tavern.** Across the street from the British Museum, this Victorian pub makes an ideal resting place after the rigors of the culture trail. This heavily restored hostelry once helped Karl Marx unwind after a hard day in the Library. He could have spent his *Kapital* on any of six beers available on tap. ✉ *49 Great Russell St., Bloomsbury, WC1* ☎ *020/7242–8987* Ⓤ *Tottenham Court Rd.*

★ ✕ **Porterhouse.** With arguably the capital's best selection of beers, this oft-crammed pub is a true institution. In the enormous, brewerylike space, you can choose from the 172 international bottles or 9 draft beers brewed by Porterhouse itself in Ireland. Irish dishes include Carlingford mussels and the "Great Craic" burger—made with Irish Angus beef and Irish cheddar. International sports on TV and live music five nights a week provide entertainment. ✉ *21–22 Maiden La., Covent Garden, WC2* ☎ *020/7379–7917* Ⓤ *Covent Garden.*

FodorśChoice ✕ **Prospect of Whitby.** Named after a ship, this is London's oldest riverside pub, dating from 1520. Once upon a time it was called the Devil's Tavern because of the lowlife criminals—thieves and smugglers—who congregated here. Ornamented with pewter ware and nautical objects, this much-loved boozer is often pointed out from boat trips up the Thames. ✉ *57 Wapping Wall, East End, E1* ☎ *020/7481–1095* Ⓤ *Wapping.*

✕ **Sherlock Holmes.** This pub used to be known as the Northumberland Arms, and Arthur Conan Doyle popped in regularly for a pint. It figures in *The Hound of the Baskervilles,* and you can see the hound's head and plaster casts of its huge paws among other Holmes memorabilia in the bar. ✉ *10 Northumberland St., Trafalgar Square, WC2* ☎ *020/ 7930–2644* Ⓤ *Charing Cross.*

FodorśChoice ✕ **Spaniards Inn.** An ideal refueling point when you're on a Hampstead Heath hike, this historic, oak-beam pub has a gorgeous garden, scene of the tea party in Dickens's *Pickwick Papers.* Dick Turpin, the highwayman, frequented the inn; you can see his pistols on display. Shelley, Keats, and Byron hung out here, as did Dickens. It's extremely popular, especially on Sunday, when Londoners roll up for the tasty dishes and amusing dog-washing machine in the parking lot. ⊠ *Spaniards Rd., Hampstead, NW3* ☎ *020/8731–6571* Ⓤ *Hampstead.*

✕ **Star Tavern.** In the heart of elegant Belgravia, this pub has a Georgian-era facade straight off a postcard. The inside is charming, too: Victorian furnishings and two roaring fireplaces make this a popular spot to flop down with an armload of Knightsbridge shopping bags. ⊠ *6 Belgrave Mews W, Belgravia, SW1* ☎ *020/7235–3019* Ⓤ *Knightsbridge.*

Fodor'sChoice ✕ **White Hart.** The drinking destination of the theater community, this
★ elegant, family-owned pub on Drury Lane is one of the best places to mix with cast and crew of the stage. A female-friendly environment, a cheery skylight above the lounge area, and well-above-average pub fare make the White Hart one of the most sociable pubs in London. ⊠ *191 Drury La., Covent Garden, WC2* ☎ *020/7242–2317* Ⓤ *Holborn.*

★ ✕ **White Horse.** This pub in well-to-do Parson's Green has a superb menu with a beer or wine chosen to match each dish. Open early for weekend brunch, too, the "Sloaney Pony" (named for its wealthy Sloane Square clientele) is enormously popular and a place to find many a Hugh Grant and Liz Hurley lookalike. The owner is an expert on cask-conditioned ale, and there are more than 100 wines to choose from. ⊠ *1–3 Parson's Green, Parson's Green, SW6* ☎ *020/7736–2115* Ⓤ *Parsons Green.*

✕ **Ye Olde Cheshire Cheese.** It's a tourist trap, but it's also the most historic of all London pubs (from 1667), and it deserves a visit for its sawdust-covered floors, low wood-beam ceilings, and the 14th-century crypt of Whitefriars' monastery under the cellar bar. This was the most regular of Dr. Johnson's and Dickens's *many* locals (neighborhood pubs). ⊠*145 Fleet St., The City, EC4* ☎ *020/7353–6170* Ⓤ *Blackfriars.*

Afternoon Tea

The English afternoon-tea ritual has been quietly brewing among London polite society. Perhaps it's an anti-Starbucks thing, but nevertheless, it is now ever *so* fashionable to take afternoon tea.

So, what is afternoon tea, exactly? Well, it means real tea (English Breakfast, Ceylon, Indian, or Chinese—and preferably loose leaf) brewed in a china pot, and usually served with china cups and saucers and silver spoons any time between 3 and 5:30 PM daily. In particularly grand places—such as some bigger hotels—there should be elegant finger foods on a three-tier silver tea stand: bread and butter, and crustless cucumber, watercress, and egg sandwiches on the bottom; scones with clotted cream and strawberry preserve in the middle; and rich fruitcake and fancies on top.

Dress is smart casual in posh hotels. Make reservations for all these below.

✕ **Claridge's.** This is the real McCoy, with liveried footmen proffering sandwiches, scones, and superior patisseries (£31.50 for traditional tea, £40 for champagne tea) in the palatial yet genteel foyer, to the sound of the "Hungarian orchestra." ⊠ *Brook St., Mayfair, W1* ☎ *020/7629–8860* ▤ *AE, DC, MC, V* ☯ *Tea served daily at 3, 5, 5:30* Ⓤ *Bond St.*

✕ **Fortnum & Mason.** Upstairs at the Queen's grocers, three set teas are ceremoniously served: standard afternoon tea (sandwiches, scones, and cakes: £22.50), old-fashioned high tea (the traditional nursery meal, adding something more robust and savory: £24.50), and champagne tea (£27.50). ✉ *St. James's Restaurant, 4th fl., 181 Piccadilly, St. James's, W1* ☎ *020/ 7734–8040 Ext. 2241* ▤ *AE, DC, MC, V* ☺ *Tea Mon.–Sat. 3–5:30* Ⓤ *Green Park.*

✕ **Harrods.** For sweet-tooths, the 4th-floor Georgian Restaurant at this well-known department store has a high tea that will give you a sugar rush for a week. ✉ *87–135 Brompton Rd., Knightsbridge, SW3* ☎ *020/ 7730–1234* ▤ *AE, DC, MC, V* ☺ *Tea weekdays 3:30–5:30, Sat. 4–5:30* Ⓤ *Knightsbridge.*

✕ **Kandy Tea House.** This Sri Lankan–run tiny tearoom, off Kensington Church Street, specializes in Ceylon tea. There's delightful cream tea (£8 per person) with homemade scones, clotted cream, and jam, or afternoon tea with cucumber sandwiches. ✉ *4 Holland St., Kensington, W8* ☎ *020/7937–3001* ▤ *MC, V* ☺ *Wed.–Fri. noon–5 PM, weekends noon–6 PM* Ⓤ *High St. Kensington.*

✕ **Patisserie Valerie at Sagne.** Scoff decadent patisseries with afternoon tea at this ever-reliable, reasonably priced, and stylish café. It's a perfect Marylebone High Street resting point, and you'll adore the towering cakes, chandelier, and murals on the walls. ✉ *105 Marylebone High St., Marylebone, W1* ☎ *020/7935–6240* ▤ *AE, MC, V* ☺ *Weekdays 7:30 AM–7 PM, Sat. 8 AM–7 PM, Sun. 9 AM–6 PM* Ⓤ *Marylebone.*

✕ **The Ritz.** The Ritz's huge, stagy, sometimes cold and overly formal Palm Court orchestrates cake stands, silver pots, a harpist, and Louis XVI chaises, plus a great deal of rococo gilt and glitz, all for £34. Reserve four weeks ahead, more for weekends. ✉ *150 Piccadilly, St. James's, W1* ☎ *020/7493–8181* ▤ *AE, DC, MC, V* ☺ *Tea daily 11:30, 1:30, 3:30, and 5:30* Ⓤ *Green Park.*

✕ **The Savoy.** The glamorous Thames-side hotel does one of the most pleasant teas (£28 or £35.50). Its triple-tier cake stands are packed with goodies, and its tailcoated waiters are wonderfully polite. ✉ *Strand, Covent Garden, WC2* ☎ *020/7836–4343* ▤ *AE, DC, MC, V* ☺ *Tea daily 2–4, 4–6* Ⓤ *Charing Cross.*

WHERE TO STAY

It's hard to get a bargain on a London hotel. That is simply a fact of travel life. The dismal exchange rate isn't helping matters. If money is no object, though, you can have the most indulgent luxury imaginable: when it comes to pampering, few do it better than the British. Who wouldn't want to relax in a brocade armchair while a frock-coated retainer serves you scones? No matter what you pay, keep in mind that rooms here tend to be much smaller than in U.S. hotels.

London has yet to get the knack of moderately priced hostelries that offer a high level of quality. Two newer hotels—Zetter Rooms and

Guesthouse West—represent moves in that direction. At the budget level, B&Bs still dominate the category, and most are filled with chintz and traditional furnishings. There are also ultramodern "pod hotels," an Asian concept, such as easyHotel. These offer tiny rooms with just the basics—bed, shower, toilet—for low prices. Slightly less drastic are the chain hotels that have opened in the center of town.

If you can spend a bit of money, London is the place to do it. Prices can soar into the empyrean, but many of the best hotels are worth it. The Pelham and Covent Garden Hotel—both renovated town houses—glitter with Regency-style interiors, proving that the best hoteliers can do a great deal with even the smallest of spaces. Meanwhile, many of the grand, big-name classics have indulged in gorgeous renovations. Paying top dollar does not mean you'll get stately English grandeur—some newer places and renovations reflect neo-Bauhaus minimalism. But that's London for you—always looking for the next new thing.

Which Neighborhood?

Where you stay can affect your experience. The West End is equivalent to downtown, but there's a big difference between, say, posh Park Lane and bustling, touristy Leicester Square. Hotels in Mayfair and St. James's are central and yet distant in both mileage and sensibility from funky, youthful neighborhoods such as Notting Hill and from major tourist sights such as the Tower of London, St. Paul's Cathedral, and the Kensington museums. On the edges of the West End, Soho and Covent Garden are crammed with eateries and entertainment options. South Kensington, Kensington, Chelsea, and Knightsbridge are patrician and peaceful, which will give you a more homey feeling than anything in the West End; Belgravia is super elegant. From Bloomsbury it's a stroll to the shops and restaurants of Covent Garden, to Theatreland, and to the British Museum; Hampstead and Islington are close enough to explore easily, too. Bayswater is an affordable haven north of Hyde Park. The South Bank, with all its cultural attractions, is another option.

Reservations

Wherever you decide to stay, do reserve in advance. London is popular, and special events can fill hotels suddenly. If you arrive without a room, the **London Tourist Board Information Centres** at Heathrow, Victoria Station Forecourt, and Waterloo International Terminal can help. The **VisitLondon Accommodation Booking Service** (☎ 020/7932–2020 ⊕ www. visitlondon.com) is open weekdays 9 to 6, Saturday 10 to 2; it offers a best-price guarantee.

Prices & Money-Saving Options

London is expensive, and in the £££££ category, you can often pay considerably more than £250 per room. Finding a cheap but tolerable double room is a real coup. Look around Russell Square in Bloomsbury, around Victoria and King's Cross stations, on the South Bank, in Bayswater or Earl's Court, or farther out in Shepherd's Bush. Your cheapest option is a B&B (⇨ Bed-and-Breakfasts & Apartment Agencies, *below*) or a dorm bed in a hostel; apartments are an increasing popular choice. For other suggestions, *see* Accommodations *in* Booking Your Trip *in* Essentials.

1

University residence halls offer a cheap alternative during university vacation periods. Whatever the price, *don't* expect a room that's large by American standards. **City University Hall of Residence: Walter Sickert Hall** (⊠ Graham St., N1 8LA ☎ 020/7040–8822 🖨 020/7040–8825 ⊕ www.city.ac.uk/ems) costs £60 for a double year-round and includes continental breakfast. **London School of Economics Vacations** (☎ 020/7955–7575 🖨 0207/955–7676 ⊕ www.lsevacations.co.uk) costs £38 for a double without a toilet to £62 for a double with a toilet. You can choose from a variety of rooms in their five halls of residence around London. **University College London** (⊠ Residence Manager, Campbell House, 5–10 Taviton St., WC1H 0BX ☎ 020/7679–1479 🖨 020/7388–0060) costs £35 to £40 for a double and is open from mid-June to mid-September.

In any event, you should confirm *exactly* what your room costs before checking in. British hotels are obliged by law to display a price chart at the reception desk; study it carefully. In January and February you can often find reduced rates, and large hotels with a business clientele have frequent weekend packages. The usual practice these days in all but the cheaper hotels is for quoted prices to cover room alone; breakfast, whether continental or "full English," costs extra. V.A.T. (Value Added Tax—sales tax) follows the same rule, with the most expensive hotels excluding a hefty 17.5%; middle-of-the-range and budget places include it in the initial quote.

WHAT IT COSTS In pounds				
	£££££	**££££**	**£££**	**££**	**£**
FOR 2 PEOPLE	over £250	£180–£250	£120–£179	£70–£119	under £70

Prices are for a standard double room in high season, including V.A.T., with no meals or, if indicated, CP (with continental breakfast), BP (Breakfast Plan, with full breakfast), or MAP (Modified American Plan, with breakfast and dinner).

Bayswater, Notting Hill & Shepherd's Bush

£££–£££££ 🏨 **The Portobello.** One of London's most famous hotels, the little Portobello (formed from two adjoining Victorian houses) is seriously hip, attracting as many celebrities as ordinary folk, and garnering a stellar reputation in the process. It's certainly a quirky place, with each room individually decorated with random antiques, odd-but-luscious fabrics, statuary, and heaven-knows-what thrown in with a kind of designer abandon here and there. What you'll get for your money cannot be predicted— some rooms have balconies and claw-foot bathtubs; Room 16 has a round bed and an extraordinary Victorian "bathing machine" that actor Johnny Depp is said to have once filled with champagne for his then-girlfriend Kate Moss. ⊠ *22 Stanley Gardens, Notting Hill, W11 2NG ☎ 020/7727–2777 🖨 020/7792–9641 ⊕ www.portobello-hotel.co.uk 🛏 24 rooms ⌂ Restaurant, dining room, room service, fans, in-room safes, some in-room hot tubs, minibars, cable TV, in-room VCRs, in-room data ports, bar, lounge, babysitting, dry cleaning, laundry service, concierge, Internet, business services, car rental, no-smoking rooms; no a/c in*

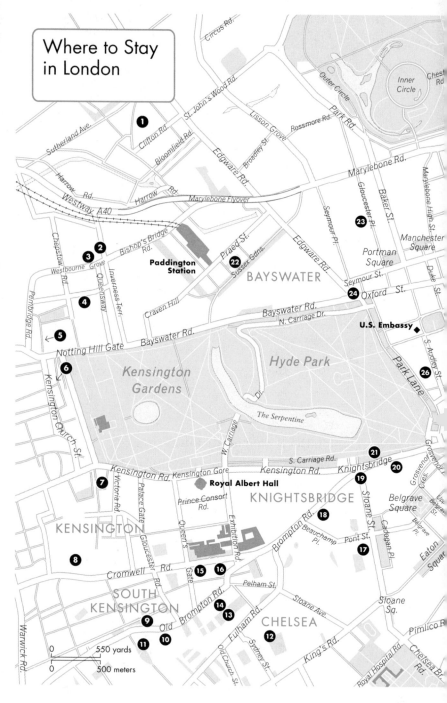

Where to Stay in London

Circus Rd.

Inner Circle

Chest Rd

St. John's Wood Rd.

Outer Circle

Park Rd.

Sutherland Ave.

Clifton Rd.

Bloomfield Rd.

Lisson Grove

Rossmore Rd.

Broadley St.

Edgware Rd.

Marylebone Rd.

Harrow Rd.

Westway A40

Harrow Rd.

Marylebone Flyover

Gloucester Pl.

Baker St.

Marylebone High St.

Chepstow Rd.

Bishop's Bridge Rd.

Westbourne Grove

Queensway

Inverness Terr.

Pembridge Rd.

Praed St.

Sussex Gdns.

Edgware Rd.

Seymour Pl.

Manchester Square

Portman Square

Paddington Station

BAYSWATER

Craven Hill

Seymour St.

Oxford St.

Duke St.

Bayswater Rd.

N. Carriage Dr.

U.S. Embassy ◆

S. Audley St.

Notting Hill Gate

Bayswater Rd.

Kensington Church St.

Kensington Gardens

Hyde Park

Park Lane

Dr.

The Serpentine

W. Carriage

S. Carriage Rd.

Grosvenor Cres.

Victoria Rd.

Palace Gate

Kensington Rd.

Kensington Gore

Kensington Rd.

Knightsbridge

Belgrave Square

Upp. Belgrave St.

Belgrave Pl.

Royal Albert Hall ◆

Prince Consort Rd.

KNIGHTSBRIDGE

Queen's Gate

Exhibition Rd.

Brompton Rd.

Beauchamp Pl.

Pont St.

Cadogan Pl.

Eaton Square

KENSINGTON

Gloucester Rd.

Cromwell Rd.

Pelham St.

Sloane St.

Brompton Rd.

Sloane Ave.

SOUTH KENSINGTON

Old Brompton Rd.

Fulham Rd.

Sloane Ave.

Sloane Sq.

CHELSEA

Warwick Rd.

Sydney St.

King's Rd.

Old Church St.

Royal Hospital Rd.

Pimlico Rd.

Chelsea Br. Rd.

0 ——— 550 yards

0 ——— 500 meters

❶ ❷ ❸ ❹ ❺ ❻ ❼ ❽ ❾ ❿ ⓫ ⓬ ⓭ ⓮ ⓯ ⓰ ⓱ ⓲ ⓳ ⓴ ㉑ ㉒ ㉓ ㉔ ㉖

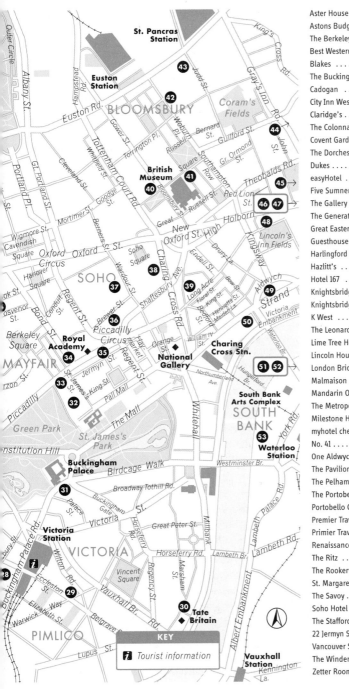

some rooms ⃝I *CP* ⊟ *AE, MC, V* ⊘ *Closed 10 days at Christmas* Ⓤ *Notting Hill Gate.*

££££ 🏨 **K West.** Proud to be coolly modern, K West is hidden away inside an undistinguished glass-and-steel building in the bustling Shepherds Bush. The place can be a bit over-the-top and is probably unsuitable for children. The busy lobby houses the all-white K Lounge, and the minimalist approach continues in the bedrooms where dark wood, soft suede, and sleek beige walls and floors create a designer look; high-grade audiovisual equipment replaces the stimuli of the lounge. Suites have two-person baths and drawers labeled "smut," where you'll find "adult-entertainment" supplies. ⊠ *Richmond Way, Shepherd's Bush, W14 OAX* ☎ *020/7674–1000* 🖷 *020/7674–1050* ⊕ *www.k-west.co. uk* 🛏 *216 rooms, 6 suites* ⤷ *Restaurant, room service, in-room safes, minibars, cable TV with video games, in-room DVDs, in-room data ports, gym, hot tub, massage, sauna, spa, steam room, bar, dry cleaning, laundry service, Internet, meeting rooms, parking (fee), no-smoking rooms* ⊟ *AE, DC, MC, V* ⃝I *CP* Ⓤ *Shepherd's Bush (Central).*

★ ££–££££ 🏨 **Guesthouse West.** The idea behind this hip hotel is to offer high-class chic at moderate prices, and to a certain extent, it succeeds. The minimalist decor and technology—cool black-and-white photos and flat-screen TVs—are very stylish. Rooms, however, are truly tiny, and there's no room service. Nevermind, though, as the restaurant is handy and packed with locals, and the bar is a beautiful homage to the 1930s. ■ TIP→ **The hotel's relationship with a local spa and restaurant provides guests with discounts, and there are guaranteed seats for shows at the small Gate Theatre.** ⊠ *163–165 Westbourne Grove, Notting Hill, W11 2RS* ☎ *020/7792–9800* 🖷 *020/7792–9797* ⊕ *www.guesthousewest.com* 🛏 *20 rooms* ⤷ *Restaurant, cable TV, in-room DVDs, in-room data ports, Wi-Fi, bar, parking (fee), no-smoking rooms* ⊟ *AE, MC, V* Ⓤ *Notting Hill Gate.*

££–£££ 🏨 **Colonnade.** Near a canal filled with colorful narrow boats, this lovely town house rests beautifully in a quiet, residential area known as "Little Venice." From the Freud suite (Sigmund visited regularly in 1938) to the rooms with four-poster beds or balconies, you'll find rich brocades, velvets, and antiques. It's a former home, so each room is different; some are split-level. Extra touches in each are the bathrobe and slippers, bowl of apples, and CD player. The 1920s elevator and Wedgwood lobby fireplace add to the historic style of the place, but the new tapas bar is pleasantly modern. ⊠ *2 Warrington Crescent, Bayswater, W9 1ER* ☎ *020/7286–1052* 🖷 *020/7286–1057* ⊕ *www. theetoncollection.com* 🛏 *15 rooms, 28 suites* ⤷ *Restaurant, dining room, room service, in-room safes, minibars, cable TV, in-room data ports, lobby lounge, wine bar, babysitting, dry cleaning, laundry service, business services, parking (fee), some pets allowed, no-smoking rooms* ⊟ *AE, DC, MC, V* Ⓤ *Warwick Ave.*

££–£££ 🏨 **Portobello Gold.** This no-frills B&B in the heart of the Portobello Road antiques area occupies the floor above the pub and restaurant of the same name. Flat-screen TVs are mounted on the wall, and the beds take up almost the entire room in the doubles, which have their own tiny showers and basins. The best of the bunch is the split-level apartment (£££) with roof terrace, small kitchen, and soothing aquarium. The casual restaurant serves international food at reasonable prices, and there's an Internet café that charges £1 per half hour. ✉ *95–97 Portobello Rd., Notting Hill, W11 2QB* ☎ *020/7460–4910* ⊕ *www.portobellogold.com* ⟿ *7 rooms, 1 apartment* ♿ *Restaurant, room service, cable TV, bar, laundry service* ⊟ *MC, V* |◎| *CP* Ⓤ *Notting Hill Gate.*

££ 🖼 **The Pavilion.** This eccentric town house is a trendy address for fashionistas, actors, and musicians. Often used for fashion shoots, the kitsch bedrooms veer wildly from Moroccan fantasy (the "Casablanca Nights" room) to acres of plaid ("Highland Fling") and satin ("Enter the Dragon"); you'll probably want to take some photos of your own.
■ TIP→ **Triples and family rooms are ideal for groups looking for space *and* style.** ✉ *34–36 Sussex Gardens, Bayswater, W2 1UL* ☎ *020/7262–0905* 🖷 *020/7262–1324* ⊕ *www.pavilionhoteluk.com* ⟿ *30 rooms* ♿ *Room service, fans, cable TV, some in-room DVDs, in-room data ports, lounge, dry cleaning, laundry service, parking (fee), no-smoking rooms; no a/c* ⊟ *AE, D, MC, V* |◎| *CP* Ⓤ *Paddington, Edgware Rd.*

££ 🖼 **Vancouver Studios.** This little hotel in a Victorian town house is perfect for those wanting a home away from home. Rooms come with minikitchens, and you can even pre-order groceries to stock your minirefrigerator on arrival. Each studio has daily maid service as well as room service. Some rooms have working fireplaces, and one opens onto the leafy, paved garden. ✉ *30 Prince's Sq., Bayswater, W2 4NJ* ☎ *020/7243–1270* 🖷 *020/7221–8678* ⊕ *www.vancouverstudios.co.uk* ⟿ *45 studios* ♿ *Room service, kitchens, microwaves, refrigerators, in-room data ports, lounge, dry cleaning, laundry facilities, parking (fee); no a/c* ⊟ *AE, DC, MC, V* Ⓤ *Bayswater, Queensway.*

Bloomsbury, Covent Garden & Soho

★ **£££££** 🖼 **Covent Garden Hotel.** In the midst boisterous Covent Garden, this hotel is now the London home-away-from-home for a mélange of off-duty celebrities, actors, and style mavens. The public salons keep even the most picky happy: with painted silks, style *anglais* ottomans, and 19th-century Romantic oils, they're perfect places to decompress over a glass of sherry. Guest rooms are *World of Interiors* stylish, each showcasing matching-but-mixed couture fabrics to stunning effect. ■ TIP→ **For £30 the popular Saturday-night film club includes dinner in the brasserie and a film in the deluxe in-house cinema.** ✉ *10 Monmouth St., Covent Garden, WC2H 9HB* ☎ *020/7806–1000, 800/553–6674 in U.S.* 🖷 *020/*

TOP 5

- **Hazlitt's.** Theater and literary types favor this 18th-century Soho retreat in prime restaurant territory.

- **Mandarin Oriental.** This exotic hotel never fails to amaze with its miles of marble and gorgeous park views.

- **Milestone.** Laid-back luxury: the fire-lighted lounge is open for drinks all night long.

- **The Rookery.** A gem amid the brash, businesslike hotels of the financial district, the Rookery charms with imported antiques.

- **Zetter Rooms.** This converted warehouse in Holborn dazzles with sleek modern style.

7806–1100 ⊕ *www.firmdale.com* ⟿ *55 rooms, 3 suites* ⚫ *Restaurant, room service, some in-room faxes, in-room safes, minibars, cable TV, in-room VCRs, in-room data ports, gym, spa, cinema, library, babysitting, dry cleaning, laundry service, concierge, Internet, business services, meeting rooms, car rental* ▤ *AE, MC, V* Ⓤ *Covent Garden.*

£££££ 🖼 **One Aldwych.** An understated blend of contemporary and classic results in pure, modern luxury here. Flawlessly designed inside an Edwardian building, One Aldwych is coolly eclectic, with an artsy lobby, feather duvets, Italian linen sheets, and quirky touches (a TV in every bathroom, all-natural toiletries). It's the ultimate in 21st-century style, down to the awesome health club. Suites have amenities such as a private gym, a kitchen, and a terrace. Breakfast is made with organic ingredients. ■ TIP→ **The pool at One Aldwych has speakers under water that play music you can hear when you dive in.** ✉ *1 Aldwych, Covent Garden, WC2 4BZ* ☎ *020/7300–1000* 🖷 *020/7300–1001* ⊕ *www.onealdwych. co.uk* ⟿ *93 rooms, 12 suites* ⚫ *2 restaurants, room service, in-room safes, some kitchens, minibars, cable TV with movies, in-room data ports, indoor pool, health club, spa, 3 bars, cinema, shop, dry cleaning, laundry service, concierge, business services, meeting rooms, parking (fee), no-smoking floors* ▤ *AE, MC, V* Ⓤ *Charing Cross, Covent Garden.*

★ £££££ 🖼 **The Savoy.** Does this grand hotel still measure up to the history? Absolutely. The art-deco rooms are especially fabulous, but all rooms are impeccably maintained, spacious, elegant, and comfortable. A room facing the Thames costs a fortune and requires an early booking, but it's worth it. If in doubt, consider that Monet painted the view of the river from such a room. Bathrooms have sunflower-size showerheads. Top-floor rooms are newer and less charming. ✉ *Strand, Covent Garden, WC2R 0EU* ☎ *020/7836–4343* 🖷 *020/7240–6040* ⊕ *www.savoy-group.com* ⟿ *263 rooms, 19 suites* ⚫ *3 restaurants, room service, in-room fax, in-room safes, minibars, cable TV with movies, in-room VCRs, in-room data ports, indoor pool, gym, hair salon, sauna, spa, steam room, 2 bars, lobby lounge, theater, shop, babysitting, dry cleaning, laundry service, concierge, Internet, business services, meeting rooms, parking (fee), no-smoking rooms* ▤ *AE, DC, MC, V* Ⓤ *Charing Cross.*

££££–£££££ 🖼 **Soho Hotel.** This redbrick, loftlike building opened its doors in 2004, making it the first upscale hotel in gritty Soho. The sleek boutique hotel's public rooms are boldly designed with bright fuschia and acid green, but the large bedrooms are much more calm, most with neutral, beige-and-cream tones, or subtle, sophisticated pinstripes, all offset by modern furniture. The bar and restaurant, Refuel, is one of the city's hot spots, and there are movie-screening rooms downstairs, in case the wide-screen TVs in the rooms aren't big enough. ✉ *4 Richmond Mews, off Dean St., Soho, W1D 3DH* ☎ *020/7559–3000* 🖷 *020/*

WORD OF MOUTH

"I think Bloomsbury's the better location. You can hoof it to the theaters and not have to rely on the Tube, as you do from Kensington. We usually tried to fit in full days before the theater, and yet we liked to go back to the hotel to clean up and change before going out."   –Penny

7559–3003 ⊕ *www.sohohotel.com* ⤴ *85 rooms, 6 apartments* ♿ *Room service, in-room DVDs, in-room broadband, gym, concierge, no-smoking rooms* ☰ *AE, MC, V* Ⓤ *Tottenham Court Rd.*

££££ 🏨 **Hazlitt's.** Three connected, early-18th-century houses, one of which
Fodor's Choice was the last home of essayist William Hazlitt (1778–1830), make up
★ this charming Soho hotel. It's a disarmingly friendly place, full of personality but devoid of elevators. Robust antiques are everywhere, most beds are four-posters, and every room has a Victorian claw-foot tub in its bathroom. There are tiny sitting rooms, wooden staircases, and more restaurants within strolling distance than you could patronize in a year. ■ **TIP**➡ This is *the* London address of visiting antiques dealers and theater and literary types. ✉ *6 Frith St., Soho, W1V 5TZ* ☎ *020/7434–1771* 📠 *020/ 7439–1524* ⊕ *www.hazlittshotel.com* ⤴ *20 rooms, 3 suites* ♿ *Room service, fans, minibars, cable TV, in-room VCRs, in-room data ports, dry cleaning, laundry service, concierge, Internet, meeting rooms, parking (fee), some pets allowed, no-smoking floors; no a/c in some rooms* ☰ *AE, DC, MC, V* Ⓤ *Tottenham Court Rd.*

£££–££££ 🏨 **Zetter Rooms.** By day, the area between Holborn and Clerkenwell is
Fodor's Choice all about business, and rare is the person not wrapped head-to-toe in
★ dark wool-blend, secured neatly with a silk tie. By night, though, those binds are loosened and it's all oh-so-trendy. London's latest "it" hotel reflects both personalities. The dizzying five-story atrium, art-deco staircase, and slick restaurant are your first indications of what to expect at this converted warehouse: a breath of fresh air (and a little space) in London's mostly Victorian hotel scene. Rooms are smoothly done up in soft, dove grey and vanilla fabrics, and the views from the higher floors are wonderful. It's all lovely to look at, and a bargain by London standards. ✉ *86–88 Clerkenwell Rd., Holborn, EC1M 5RJ* ☎ *020/7324–4444* 📠 *020/7324–4445* ⊕ *www.thezetter.com* ⤴ *59 rooms* ♿ *Restaurant, room service, in-room safes, minibars, cable TV, in-room DVDs, in-room data ports, bar, lobby lounge, laundry service, concierge, Internet, business services, no-smoking floors* ☰ *AE, MC, V* Ⓤ *Farringdon.*

£££ 🏨 **Best Western Shaftesbury.** When the Best Western chain set-up house in the midst of historic London, it did an admirable job of fitting in, certainly using as much chrome and frosted glass as anybody could ask for. Complimentary newspapers are scattered about, and bedrooms are ultramodern, with neutral rugs, white walls, dark curtains, and sleek furniture. The price reflects all of this effort, so it's not the typical Best Western bargain, but it's pleasant and ideally situated in the heart of Theaterland. ✉ *65–73 Shaftesbury Ave., Piccadilly, W1D 6EX* ☎ *020/ 7871–6000* 📠 *020/7745–1207* ⊕ *www.bestwestern.com* ⤴ *69 rooms* ♿ *Cable TV, in-room DVDs, in-room broadband, business services, no-smoking rooms* ☰ *AE, MC, V* Ⓤ *Piccadilly Circus.*

££–£££ 🏨 **The Buckingham.** This Georgian town house hotel near Russell Square is a great bargain for the money. Its spacious, attractively designed rooms are all studios and suites. Each has its own bijoux kitchenette, giving you an alternative to eating in restaurants every night. All have marble-and-granite bathrooms and plenty of amenities. Staff are friendly, and the location is an easy walk from the British Museum and Covent Garden. ✉ *11–13 Bayley St., Bedford Sq., Bloomsbury, WC1B 3HD*

☎ 020/7636–2474 🖷 020/7580–4527 ⊕ www.grangehotels.com 📨 17
rooms ♨ Lounge, cable TV with movies, in-room broadband, no-smoking rooms ⊟ MC, V Ⓤ Tottenham Court Rd.

££ 🔲 **Harlingford Hotel.** The Harlingford is by far the sleekest and most contemporary of the Cartwright Gardens hotels. Bold color schemes and beautifully tile bathrooms enliven the family-run place. ■ TIP→ The quad rooms are an excellent choice for traveling families. ⊠ 61–63 Cartwright Gardens, Bloomsbury, WC1H 9EL ☎ 020/7387–1551 🖷 020/7383–4616 ⊕ www.harlingfordhotel.com 📨 43 rooms ♨ In-room data ports, tennis court, lounge; no a/c ⊟ AE, DC, MC, V ⑩ BP Ⓤ Russell Sq.

£–££ 🔲 **St. Margaret's.** A popular hotel near the British Museum and on a street full of budget hotels, St. Margaret's has well-lighted rooms with high ceilings in a Georgian-era building. The friendly family that runs the hotel is sure to welcome you by name if you stay long enough. Rooms are decorated with tasteful wallpaper and a light floral touch, as well as Georgian touches such as a fireplace and beautiful cornice moldings. All have huge windows, and views of the leafy neighborhood. Internet access is free. ⊠ 26 Bedford Pl., Bloomsbury, WC1B 5JL ☎ 020/7636–4277 🖷 020/7323–3066 ⊕ www.stmargaretshotel.co.uk 📨 64 rooms, 12 with bath ♨ Dining room, fans, cable TV, lounge, Internet, no-smoking rooms; no a/c ⊟ MC, V ⑩ BP Ⓤ Russell Sq.

£ 🔲 **The Generator.** This is where the young, enthusiastic traveler comes to find fellow partiers. It's also the cleverest youth hostel in town: set in a former police barracks, its rooms are designed like prison cells, making the most of the bunk beds and dim views. The Internet café provides handy maps and leaflets. The Generator Bar has cheap drinks and a rowdy crowd, and the Fuel Stop cafeteria provides inexpensive meals. There are singles, twins, and dormitory rooms, each with a washbasin, locker, and free bed linens. Prices run from £23 per person for a double room to £17 per person for a 14-bed dorm room. ⊠ MacNaghten House, Compton Pl. off 37 Tavistock Pl., Bloomsbury, WC1H 9SE ☎ 020/7388–7666 🖷 020/7388–7644 ⊕ www.generatorhostels.com 📨 215 beds ♨ Restaurant, fans, lobby lounge, pub, sports bar, recreation room, shop, concierge, Internet, meeting rooms, airport shuttle, travel services, parking (fee), no-smoking floors; no a/c, no room phones, no room TVs ⊟ MC, V ⑩ CP Ⓤ Russell Sq.

The City

£££££ 🔲 **Great Eastern.** This grand old Victorian railway hotel looks lavish and over-the-top on the outside, but inside it's all about modernity, with polished wood, neutral colors, and contemporary art. You'll want for little—there are five restaurants (serving sushi, seafood, brasserie fare, pub food, and haute cuisine), a popular bar, a gorgeous spa, and a boutique selling the covetable Ren bath products with which all the hotel's bathrooms are stocked. Rooms on the 5th and 6th floors are modern lofts, with lots of light. With all the restaurants and bars, also used by locals, this is not a retreat from bustling London life. ⊠ Liverpool St. at Bishopsgate, The City, E2M 7QN ☎ 020/7618–5010 🖷 020/7618–5011 ⊕ www.great-eastern-hotel.co.uk 📨 246 rooms, 21 suites ♨ 5 restaurants, 12 dining rooms, room service, some in-room faxes, in-room safes, minibars, cable TV with video games, in-room VCRs, in-room data ports, gym, spa, 2 bars, pub, library, shop, babysitting, dry cleaning, laundry service, concierge, Internet, business services, meeting rooms, car rental, no-smoking rooms ⊟ AE, DC, MC, V Ⓤ Liverpool St.

££££–£££££   🏨 **The Rookery.** This is an extraordinary hotel, where each beautiful dou-
Fodor'sChoice   ble room is decorated with a lavish, theatrical flair and an eye for his-
★   tory. Many have four-poster beds, each has a claw-foot bathtub, antique carved wooden headboard, and period furnishings, including exquisite salvaged pieces. In the Rook's Nest, the hotel's duplex suite, you can relax in an antique bath in the corner of the bedroom or enjoy a magnificent view of the City's historic buildings. The conservatory, with its small patio garden, is a relaxing place to unwind. ⊠ *12 Peter's La. at Cowcross St., The City, EC1M 6DS* ☎ *020/7336–0931* 🖷 *020/ 7336–0932* ⊕ *www.rookeryhotel.com* ⇖ *30 rooms, 3 suites* ⚏ *Room service, fans, in-room safes, minibars, cable TV, in-room data ports, bar, lobby lounge, library, babysitting, dry cleaning, laundry service, concierge, meeting rooms, airport shuttle, car rental, parking (fee), no-smoking floors; no a/c* ⊟ *AE, DC, MC, V* Ⓤ *Farringdon.*

££££   🏨 **Malmaison.** Part of a small chain of well-regarded U.K. boutique hotels, this Clerkenwell address is very trendy, with contemporary furnishings, clean lines, and all the extras. Stylish rooms are well-decorated in neutral cream and beige, have huge beds and CD systems with a library of music on demand, as well as satellite TVs and free broadband. It prides itself on fast, quality room service, so breakfast in bed can be a pleasure. The whole package is a business traveler's dream. ⊠ *Charterhouse Sq., The City, EC1M 6AH* ☎ *020/7012–3700* 🖷 *020/7012–3702* ⊕ *www. malmaison.com* ⇖ *95 rooms, 2 suites* ⚏ *Restaurant, room service, in-room safes, minibars, cable TV, in-room broadband, gym, bar, babysitting, dry cleaning, laundry service, concierge, meeting room, no-smoking rooms* ⊟ *AE, MC, V* ⦿|*CP* Ⓤ *Barbican, Farringdon.*

£££–££££   🏨 **Renaissance Chancery Court.** This landmark structure, built by the Pearl Assurance Company in 1914, has been transformed into a beautiful Marriott hotel. So striking is the architecture that the building was featured in the film *Howard's End.* The spacious bedrooms are popular with business travelers and the decor has a masculine edge—lots of leather and dark red fabrics. The day spa in the basement is a cocoon of peacefulness. There's marble everywhere, from the floors in public spaces to the bathrooms. The restaurant, Pearl, is known for its modern European cuisine, and the bar, in an old banking hall, has elegant soaring ceilings. ⊠ *252 High Holborn, Holborn, WC1V 7EN* ☎ *020/7829–9888* 🖷 *0207/829–9889* ⊕ *www.renaissancehotels.com/loncc* ⇖ *343 rooms, 14 suites* ⚏ *Restaurant, room service, in-room safes, minibars, cable TV with video games, in-room data ports, gym, sauna, spa, steam room, bar, lobby lounge, shop, babysitting, laundry service, concierge, business services, meeting rooms, no-smoking rooms* ⊟ *AE, MC, V* Ⓤ *Holborn.*

Kensington & South Kensington

£££££   🏨 **Blakes.** Designed by owner Anouska Hempel, Blakes is a fantasy packed with precious Biedermeier, Murano glass, and modern pieces from around the world. Rooms hark back to the days of the British empire, and include Chinese opium dens draped in lush red fabrics, as well as bright spaces with classic colonial furnishings. The foyer sets the tone with piles of cushions, black walls, rattan, and bamboo. The exotic Thai restaurant is a trendy delight. ⊠ *33 Roland Gardens, South Kensington, SW7 3PF* ☎ *020/7370–6701* 🖷 *020/7373–0442* ⊕ *www.blakeshotels. com* ↪ *38 rooms, 11 suites* ⌂ *Restaurant, room service, some in-room faxes, in-room safes, minibars, cable TV, in-room VCRs, in-room data ports, Wi-Fi, gym, bar, babysitting, dry cleaning, laundry service, concierge, Internet, business services, meeting rooms, car rental, parking (fee); no a/c in some rooms* ▭ *AE, DC, MC, V* Ⓤ *South Kensington.*

£££££

Fodor'sChoice

★

🏨 **Milestone Hotel & Apartments.** This pair of intricately decorated Victorian town houses overlooking Kensington Palace and Gardens is an intimate, luxurious alternative to the city's more famous five-star hotels. Great thoughtfulness goes into the hospitality and everything is possible in this special place. You'll be offered a welcome drink upon arrival and, if you so desire, you can return to a post-theater midnight snack in your room or leave with a picnic for the park across the street. The staff is friendly and efficient, but never obsequious. Each sumptuous room is full of antiques; many have canopied beds. Our favorite is the Ascot Room, which is filled with elegant hats of the kind worn at the famous races. ⊠ *1 Kensington Ct., Kensington, W8 5DL* ☎ *020/7917–1000* 🖷 *020/7917–1010* ⊕ *www.milestonehotel.com* ↪ *45 rooms, 12 suites, 6 apartments* ⌂ *2 restaurants, room service, in-room fax, in-room safes, some kitchens, minibars, cable TV with movies, in-room VCRs, gym, hot tub, sauna, bar, lounge, babysitting, dry cleaning, laundry service, concierge, Internet, business services, meeting rooms, some pets allowed (fee); no smoking* ▭ *AE, DC, MC, V* Ⓤ *High St. Kensington.*

££££–£££££

🏨 **The Pelham.** Museum lovers flock to this sweet hotel across the street from the South Kensington tube station. The Natural History, Science, and Victoria & Albert museums are all a short stroll away, as is King's Road. At the end of a day's sightseeing, settle down in front of the fireplace in one of the two snug drawing rooms with their honor bars. The stylish, contemporary rooms by designer Kit Kemp have sash windows and marble bathrooms. Some top-floor rooms have sloping ceilings and casement windows. ⊠ *15 Cromwell Pl., South Kensington, SW7 2LA* ☎ *020/7589–8288, 800/553–6674 in U.S.* 🖷 *020/7584–8444* ⊕ *www.firmdale.com* ↪ *47 rooms, 4 suites* ⌂ *Restaurant, room service, some in-room safes, minibars, cable TV, in-room VCRs, in-room data ports, bar, concierge, business services, meeting rooms, parking (fee)* ▭ *AE, MC, V* Ⓤ *South Kensington.*

★ £££

🏨 **Five Sumner Place.** Once you've checked into this tall Victorian town house on a quiet residential street, you get your own key to the front door and make yourself at home. If the weather is pleasant, you can enjoy the small garden. In the morning, take breakfast in the conservatory. Guest rooms are simply decorated with pleasant Victorian detail and reproduction furniture. ⊠ *5 Sumner Pl., South Kensington, SW7 3EE* ☎ *020/7584–7586* 🖷 *020/7823–9962* ⊕ *www.sumnerplace.com* ↪ *17 rooms* ⌂ *Room service, minibars, in-room broadband, in-room data ports, parking (fee); no a/c, no smoking* ▭ *AE, MC, V* ⑩ *BP* Ⓤ *South Kensington.*

£££ 🏠 **The Gallery.** It's a small, Edwardian world apart from the bustling city, but it's a little pricey for what it has to offer. The Arts and Crafts–style living room has a piano, lush carpets, and cozy fires in the winter. Decor in the guest rooms is slightly dated, the floral fabric a bit old-fashioned, but rooms are pleasant, with solid, comfortable beds, and the bathrooms have London's ubiquitous polished granite. ⊠ *10 Queensberry Pl., South Kensington, SW7 2E8* ☎ *020/7915–0000, 800/270–9206 in U.S.* 🖷 *020/7915–4400* ⊕ *www.eeh.co.uk* 🛏 *34 rooms, 2 suites* ⚒ *Room service, some in-room faxes, in-room safes, some in-room hot tubs, some minibars, cable TV, in-room data ports, bar, dry cleaning, laundry service, concierge, Internet, meeting rooms, airport shuttle; no a/c in some rooms* ⊟ *AE, DC, MC, V* ⍾⊙⍾ *BP* Ⓤ *South Kensington.*

££–£££ 🏠 **Aster House.** Country-casual rooms fill this delightful guesthouse. ■ TIP→ The friendly owners go out of their way to make you feel at home and answer questions, even loaning guests a free cell phone to use while in town. The conservatory where breakfast is served is an airy, light place, and the small garden at the back has a charming pond. Note that this is a five-story building with no elevator. ⊠ *3 Sumner Pl., South Kensington, SW7 3EE* ☎ *020/7581–5888* 🖷 *020/7584–4925* ⊕ *www. welcome2london.com/asterhouse* 🛏 *14 rooms* ⚒ *Dining room, in-room safes, cable TV, lounge, Internet; no smoking* ⊟ *MC, V* ⍾⊙⍾ *BP* Ⓤ *South Kensington.*

££–£££ 🏠 **Astons Budget Studios.** These three redbrick Victorian town houses on a residential street hold studios and apartments. All accommodations have concealed kitchenettes, and the apartments (£££) have marble bathrooms and trouser presses as well. The decor is a bit Scandinavian. ⊠*31 Rosary Gardens, South Kensington, SW7 4NH* ☎*020/7590–6000, 800/525–2810 in U.S.* 🖷 *020/7590–6060* ⊕ *www.astons-apartments. com* 🛏 *43 rooms, 12 suites* ⚒ *Dining room, fans, in-room safes, kitchenettes, microwaves, refrigerators, cable TV, in-room data ports, concierge, Internet, business services, airport shuttle, car rental, parking (fee), some pets allowed, no-smoking floors; no a/c* ⊟ *AE, MC, V* Ⓤ *Gloucester Rd.*

££ 🏠 **Hotel 167.** This white-stucco, Victorian corner house just a two-minute walk from the V&A is no traditional old hostelry. With its strong abstract art pieces and black-and-white tiled floor, the lobby is unique, and the bedrooms are an unpredictable mélange of new and old furniture and colorful fabrics. The breakfast room–lounge is charming, with wrought-iron furniture and sunny yellow walls. Its creative approach has been the subject of a novel (*Hotel 167,* by Jane Solomon) and a song by the rock band Manic Street Preachers. ⊠ *167 Old Brompton Rd., South Kensington, SW5 0AN* ☎ *020/ 7373–3221* 🖷 *020/7373–3360* ⊕ *www.hotel167.com* 🛏 *18 rooms* ⚒ *Dining room, minibars, cable TV; no a/c* ⊟ *AE, DC, MC, V* ⍾⊙⍾ *CP* Ⓤ *Gloucester Rd.*

> **WORD OF MOUTH**
>
> "I prefer South [Kensington] to Bloomsbury for several reasons, one of which is that it has great Tube connections, which will get you anywhere you want to go quickly, and because it's a lovely, quiet, upscale area to come home to each evening."   –Mel]

£ ⊞ **easyHotel.** No London hotel received more attention in 2005 than budget easyHotel. Crammed into a big white town house are 34 tiny rooms, all with double bed and private bathroom, brightly decorated in the trademark orange-and-white of the Easy chain (which includes the Internet cafés "easyeverything" and the budget airline easyJet). The idea behind the hotel is to provide quality basics (bed, sink, shower, toilet) for little money. The tiny reception desk with one staff member can't offer much in terms of service and if you want your room cleaned, it's an additional £10 a day. The concept is a huge hit—easyHotel is fully booked months in advance. ⊠ *14 Lexham Gardens, Kensington, W8 5JE* ☎ *020/7216–1717* ⊕ *www.easyhotel.com* ⇘ *34 rooms* ⌂ *Cable TV; no a/c, no room phones, no smoking* ⊟ *MC, V* Ⓜ *Gloucester Rd.*

Knightsbridge, Chelsea & Belgravia

£££££ ⊞ **The Berkeley.** The elegant Berkeley successfully mixes the old and the new in a luxurious, modern building with a splendid penthouse swimming pool. The bedrooms either have swags of William Morris prints or are art deco. All have sitting areas, CD players, and big bathrooms with bidets. There are spectacular penthouse suites with their own conservatory terraces, and others with saunas or balconies. Dining venues include Marcus Wareing's high-class Pétrus restaurant, Gordon Ramsay's excellent and extremely popular Boxwood café, the eclectic and sumptuous Blue Bar, and the whimsical Caramel Room where morning coffee and decadent doughnuts are served. ⊠ *Wilton Pl., Belgravia, SW1X 7RL* ☎ *020/7235–6000, 800/637–2869 in U.S.* 🖷 *020/7235–4330* ⊕ *www.the-berkeley.com* ⇘ *103 rooms, 55 suites* ⌂ *Restaurant, room service, in-room fax, in-room safes, some kitchens, minibars, cable TV, in-room VCRs, indoor-outdoor pool, gym, hair salon, sauna, spa, Turkish bath, bar, cinema, babysitting, dry cleaning, laundry service, concierge, Internet, business services, meeting rooms, airport shuttle, car rental, parking (fee), no-smoking floors* ⊟ *AE, DC, MC, V* Ⓤ *Knightsbridge.*

★ £££££ ⊞ **Cadogan.** This is both one of London's most beautiful hotels and one of its most historically naughty. A recent overhaul means much of its old stuffiness is gone—elegant golds and creams have replaced fussy florals. The drawing room has rich, wood paneling and deep, comfortable armchairs, and is an excellent place for tea and people-watching. The sophisticated bar urges you to have a martini and a cigar. Breakfast offers the best healthy cereals and fruits alongside decadent pastries. ⊠ *75 Sloane St., Chelsea, SW1X 9SG* ☎ *020/7235–7141* 🖷 *020/7245–0994* ⊕ *www.cadogan.com* ⇘ *65* ⌂ *Restaurant, room service, minibars, cable TV, in-room VCR, in-room data ports, Wi-Fi, tennis courts, bar, lounge, babysitting, dry cleaning, laundry facilities, concierge, no-smoking rooms* ⊟ *AE, MC, V.*

£££££
Fodor'sChoice
★

⊞ **Mandarin Oriental Hyde Park.** Stay here, and the three greats of Knightsbridge—Hyde Park, Harrods, and Harvey Nichols—are on your doorstep. Built in 1880, the Mandarin Oriental is one London's most elegant hotels. Bedrooms are traditional Victorian with hidden high-tech gadgets (Wi-Fi is expected in late 2006) and luxurious touches—potted orchids, delicate chocolates, and fresh fruit. The service here is legendary and includes a butler on every floor. ⊠ *66 Knightsbridge,*

Knightsbridge, SW1X 7LA ☎ *020/7235–2000* 🖷 *020/7235–2001*
⊕ *www.mandarinoriental.com* ➴ *177 rooms, 23 suites* ⚐ *2 restaurants,*
room service, some in-room faxes, in-room safes, minibars, cable TV,
in-room VCRs, in-room data ports, gym, hot tub, sauna, spa, steam room,
bar, babysitting, dry cleaning, laundry service, concierge, Internet, busi-
ness services, meeting rooms, airport shuttle, car rental, parking (fee),
no-smoking rooms ▤ *AE, DC, MC, V* Ⓤ *Knightsbridge.*

£££££   🏨 **No. 41.** This luxurious abode is not a formulaic, paint-by-numbers
hotel. Its designer credentials are clear everywhere, from the unusual tiled
floors to the extraordinary furnishings, which seem to have been drawn
from every corner of the globe. The staff cocoons and pampers its
guests—sit for a second and someone will offer you tea, cocktails,
water—anything that crosses your mind can be yours in a second.
Rooms, some of them split-level, are filled with high-tech gadgets to keep
you in touch with the office back home. When you're not working, you
can relax on the butter-soft leather sofa in front of the fireplace, recline
on the exquisite bed linens and feather duvets, or luxuriate in the marble bath. A "whatever, whenever" button on the telephone connects you
with the helpful, amiable staff. ✉ *41 Buckingham Palace Rd., Victo-*
ria, SW1W 0PS ☎ *020/7300–0041* 🖷 *020/7300–0141* ⊕ *www.41hotel.*
com ➴ *14 rooms, 4 suites* ⚐ *Room service, in-room fax, in-room*
safes, some in-room hot tubs, minibars, cable TV with movies and
video games, in-room broadband, in-room VCRs, in-room data ports,
lounge, babysitting, dry cleaning, laundry service, concierge, Internet,
business services, meeting rooms, car rental, parking (fee), no-smoking
rooms ▤ *AE, DC, MC, V* ⦿l *CP* Ⓤ *Victoria.*

££££–£££££   🏨 **Knightsbridge Hotel.** Just off glamorous Knightsbridge near Harrods
and Harvey Nichols in quiet Beaufort Gardens, this chic hotel is well
placed for shoppers. The balconied suites and regular rooms are wrapped
in bold fabrics, with the beds piled high with warm duvets. All rooms
have CD players, writing desks, and large granite-and-oak bathrooms.
The fully loaded honor bar in the drawing room is an excellent place
to unwind amid African sculptures and modern art. ✉ *10 Beaufort Gar-*
dens, Knightsbridge, SW3 1PT ☎ *020/7584–6300, 800/553–6674 in*
U.S. 🖷 *020/7584–6355* ⊕ *www.knightsbridgehotel.co.uk* ➴ *42 rooms,*
2 suites ⚐ *Room service, in-room safes, minibars, cable TV, some in-*
room VCRs, in-room data ports, gym, bar, library, babysitting, dry
cleaning, laundry service, concierge, Internet, meeting rooms, parking
(fee) ▤ *AE, MC, V* Ⓤ *Knightsbridge.*

£££–£££££   🏨 **myhotel chelsea.** This small, chic hotel tucked away down a Chelsea
side street is a charmer. Rooms are bijoux small, but sophisticated, with
mauve satin throws atop crisp white down comforters. Tiny bathrooms
are made cheery with pale pink granite countertops. Flat-screen TVs,
DVD players, and in-room Wi-Fi all set the place electronically ahead
of many top-level London hotels. The beauty is in the details here—there's
no restaurant, but the fire-warmed bar serves light meals and tea. There's
no pool, but there's an excellent spa. The guest library has DVDs and
books on loan, and offers a quiet place to relax. Best of all, you can get
a good deal if you book in advance via the Web site. ✉ *35 Ixworth Pl.,*
Chelsea, SW3 3QZ ☎ *020/7225–7500* 🖷 *020/7225–7555* ⊕ *www.*

myhotels.com ⤳ *45 rooms, 9 suites* ⟁ *Room service, fans, in-room safes, minibars, cable TV, in-room DVDs, Wi-Fi, gym, massage, spa, bar, library, lounge, babysitting, laundry service, some pets allowed, no-smoking floors* ⊟ *AE, D, MC, V* Ⓤ *South Kensington.*

£££ ▦ **Knightsbridge Green.** Near Harrods and Hyde Park, this modern hotel has affordable triples and quads with sofa beds that are good for families. Rooms are rather plain and could use an update, but they have double-glaze windows that help muffle the sound of traffic on busy Knightsbridge. Breakfast can be delivered to your room, or you could linger in the lounge over complimentary tea and coffee. ⊠ *159 Knightsbridge, Knightsbridge, SW1X 7PD* ☏ *020/7584–6274* 🖷 *020/7225–1635* ⊕ *www.thekghotel.co.uk* ⤳ *28 rooms, 12 suites* ⟁ *In-room safes, cable TV, in-room data ports, babysitting, dry cleaning, concierge, Internet; no smoking* ⊟ *AE, DC, MC, V* Ⓤ *Knightsbridge.*

Mayfair, Marylebone & St. James's

£££££ ▦ **The Dorchester.** Few hotels this opulent manage to be quite so charming. The glamour level is off the scale: 1,500 square yards of gold leaf and 1,100 square yards of marble. Bedrooms (some not as spacious as you might expect) have Irish-linen sheets on canopied beds, brocades and velvets, and Italian marble and etched-glass bathrooms with Floris toiletries. Furnishings throughout are opulent English country-house style, with more than a hint of art deco, in keeping with the original 1930s building. The hotel has embraced modern technology, though, and "e-butlers" help guests figure out the Web TVs in the rooms. ⊠ *Park La., Mayfair, W1A 2HJ* ☏ *020/7629–8888* 🖷 *020/7409–0114* ⊕ *www. dorchesterhotel.com* ⤳ *195 rooms, 55 suites* ⟁ *3 restaurants, in-room safes, minibars, cable TV with movies, in-room VCRs, in-room data ports, gym, health club, hair salon, spa, bar, lobby lounge, nightclub, shop, babysitting, dry cleaning, laundry service, concierge, Internet, business services, meeting rooms, car rental, parking (fee), no-smoking rooms* ⊟ *AE, DC, MC, V* Ⓤ *Marble Arch, Hyde Park Corner.*

£££££ ▦ **Dukes.** This small, exclusive, Edwardian-style hotel with a gas lantern–lighted courtyard entrance is in a discreet cul-de-sac. Overstuffed sofas, oil paintings of assorted dukes, and muted, rich colors create the perfect setting for sipping the finest dry martinis in town. ◼ TIP→ **The hotel's trump card is that, for such a central location, it's peaceful and quiet.** The rooms are cozy with floral prints and wood everywhere. ⊠ *35 St. James's Pl., St. James's, SW1A 1NY* ☏ *020/7491–4840, 800/ 381–4702 in U.S.* 🖷 *020/7493–1264* ⊕ *www.dukeshotel.co.uk* ⤳ *80 rooms, 9 suites* ⟁ *Restaurant, dining room, some in-room faxes, in-room safes, minibars, cable TV, some in-room VCRs, in-room data ports, gym, sauna, spa, steam room, bar, lobby lounge, dry cleaning, laundry service, concierge, business services, meeting rooms, parking (fee)* ⊟ *AE, DC, MC, V* Ⓤ *Green Park.*

£££££ ▦ **The Metropolitan.** This supertrendy hotel is one of the few addresses for visiting fashion, music, and media folk in London. Its Met bar has an exclusive guest list, and the restaurant is the famed Nobu, leased by Japanese wonder-chef Nobu Matsuhisa. The lobby is sleek and postmodern, as are the bedrooms, which have identical minimalist taupe-

and-white furnishings. The best rooms overlook Hyde Park, but all have a groovy minibar hiding the latest alcoholic and health-boosting beverages. ✉ *Old Park La., Mayfair, W1K 1LB* ☎ *020/7447–1000, 800/ 337–4685 in U.S.* 🖷 *020/7447–1100* ⊕ *www.metropolitan.co.uk* 🛏 *137 rooms, 18 suites* ♻ *Restaurant, room service, in-room broadband, in-room fax, in-room safes, minibars, cable TV with movies and video games, some in-room VCRs, in-room data ports, gym, massage, bar, shop, babysitting, dry cleaning, laundry service, concierge, Internet, business services, meeting room, parking (fee), no-smoking floors* ▭ *AE, DC, MC, V* Ⓤ *Hyde Park Corner.*

fffff 🏨 **The Ritz.** Uncapitalized, the word *ritz* has come to mean "posh" or "classy," and this is where the word originated. Memorialized in song by Irving Berlin, this hotel's very name conjures the kind of luxury associated with swagged curtains, handwoven carpets, and the smell of cigars, polish, and fresh lilies. The only thing that has been lost is a certain vein of moneyed naughtiness that someone like F. Scott Fitzgerald, at least, would have banked on. The bedrooms are bastions of pastel Louis XVI style, with gilded furniture and crystal chandeliers. With a ratio of two staff members to every bedroom, you're guaranteed personal service despite the hotel's massive size. ■ TIP→ Formal dress is encouraged, and jeans are not allowed in public areas. ✉ *150 Piccadilly, St. James's, W1J 9BR* ☎ *020/7493–8181* 🖷 *020/7493–2687* ⊕ *www. theritzhotel.co.uk* 🛏 *133 rooms* ♻ *2 restaurants, room service, some in-room faxes, in-room safes, cable TV, some in-room VCRs, in-room data ports, gym, hair salon, bar, babysitting, dry cleaning, laundry service, concierge, Internet, business services, meeting rooms, car rental, parking (fee), no-smoking rooms* ▭ *AE, DC, MC, V* Ⓤ *Piccadilly Circus.*

★ **fffff** 🏨 **The Stafford.** This is a rare find: a posh hotel that offers equal parts elegance and friendliness. It's hard to check-in without meeting the gregarious manager, and his unshakable cheeriness must be infectious, for the staff are also upbeat and helpful. The location is one of the few peaceful spots in the area, down a small lane behind Piccadilly. Its 13 adorable carriage-house rooms, installed in the 18th-century stable block, are relative bargains; each individually decorated room has a cobbled mews entrance and gas-fueled fireplace, exposed beams, and CD player. The popular little American Bar has ties, baseball caps, and toy planes hanging from a ceiling modeled, presumably, on New York's 21 Club. ✉ *St. James's Pl., St. James's, SW1A 1NJ* ☎ *020/7493–0111* 🖷 *020/ 7493–7121* ⊕ *www.thestaffordhotel.co.uk* 🛏 *81 rooms* ♻ *Restaurant, dining room, cable TV, in-room data ports, bar* ▭ *AE, DC, MC, V* Ⓤ *Green Park.*

ffff–fffff 🏨 **Claridge's.** Stay here, and you're staying at a hotel legend (founded **Fodor'sChoice** in 1812), with one of the world's classiest guest lists. The friendly, liv- ★ eried staff is not in the least condescending, and the rooms are luxurious. Enjoy a cup of tea in the lounge, or retreat to the stylish bar for cocktails—or, better, to Gordon Ramsay's inimitable restaurant. The bathrooms are spacious (with enormous showerheads), as are the bedrooms (Victorian or art deco). The grand staircase and magnificent elevator complete with sofa and driver are equally glamorous. Perhaps Spencer Tracy said it best when he remarked that, when he died, he wanted to go not to heaven, but to Claridge's. ⊠ *Brook St., St. James's, W1A 2JQ* ☎ *020/7629–8860, 800/637–2869 in U.S.* 🖷 *020/7499–2210* ⊕ *www.claridges.co.uk* ⟳ *203 rooms* ⟳ *Restaurant, in-room fax, in-room safes, some in-room hot tubs, minibars, cable TV with movies, in-room VCRs, in-room data ports, gym, hair salon, spa, bar, lobby lounge, shop, babysitting, dry cleaning, laundry service, concierge, Internet, business services, meeting rooms, airport shuttle, car rental, parking (fee), no-smoking rooms* ⊟ *AE, DC, MC, V* Ⓤ *Bond St.*

££££–£££££ 🖫 **The Leonard.** Four 18th-century buildings make up a stunning, relaxed, and friendly boutique hotel. Shoppers will appreciate the location, just around the corner from Oxford Street. Rooms are decorated with a judicious mix of lived-in antiques and comfortable reproductions. For more elbow room, try one of the aptly named grand suites, with their palatial sitting rooms and tall windows. The roof garden is great for warm weather, and the welcoming lobby is stocked with complimentary newspapers to read by the fire. ⊠ *15 Seymour St., Mayfair, W1H 5AA* ☎ *020/7935–2010* 🖷 *020/7935–6700* ⊕ *www.theleonard.com* ⟳ *22 rooms, 21 suites* ⟳ *Café, dining room, room service, in-room safes, some kitchens, minibars, cable TV, in-room VCRs, in-room data ports, gym, bar, lounge, babysitting, dry cleaning, laundry service, concierge, Internet, business services, meeting rooms, no-smoking rooms* ⊟ *AE, DC, MC, V* Ⓤ *Marble Arch.*

🐚 ££££ 🖫 **22 Jermyn Street.** This guesthouse is on a fashionable shopping street near Fortnum & Mason. Flexible room configurations, including sitting rooms that convert to bedrooms, mean families have plenty of space. In fact, the hotel rolls out the red carpet for children, providing anything from high chairs and coloring books to nannies and kids' bathrobes. For grown-ups, there are access to a nearby gym, complimentary newspapers, and a shoe shine. ⊠ *22 Jermyn St., St. James's, SW1Y 6HL* ☎ *020/7734–2353, 800/682–7808 in U.S.* 🖷 *020/7734–0750* ⊕ *www.22jermyn.com* ⟳ *5 rooms, 13 suites* ⟳ *Room service, in-room safes, minibars, cable TV with movies, in-room VCRs, in-room data ports, babysitting, dry cleaning, laundry service, concierge, Internet, business services, airport shuttle, car rental, parking (fee)* ⊟ *AE, DC, MC, V* Ⓤ *Piccadilly Circus.*

££ 🖫 **Lincoln House Hotel.** Just north of Oxford Street and Marble Arch, this family-run Georgian town house is done up with lots of wood and plaid. The rooms with three or four beds are more spacious and only slightly more expensive. Rooms have a slightly dated look, but are well equipped. The longer you stay, the cheaper the price. ⊠ *33 Gloucester Pl., Mayfair, W1U 8HY* ☎ *020/7486–7630* 🖷 *020/7486–0166* ⊕ *www.lincoln-house-hotel.co.uk* ⟳ *24 rooms* ⟳ *Some refrigerators, cable TV, in-room data ports, lounge, babysitting, laundry service, parking (fee); no a/c* ⦿ *BP* ⊟ *AE, D, MC, V* Ⓤ *Marble Arch.*

South Bank

££££ 🖫 **London Bridge Hotel.** Steps away from the London Bridge rail and tube station, this thoroughly modern, stylish hotel is popular with business travelers. Most of the South Bank's attractions are within walking distance. Each sleek room is understated and contemporary. Three spacious two-bedroom apartments (£££££) come with kitchen, living room, and

1

dining room. ⊠ *8–18 London Bridge St., South Bank, SE1 9SG* ☎ *020/ 7855–2200* 🖷 *020/7855–2233* 🌐 *www.london-bridge-hotel.co.uk* ⤷ *138 rooms, 3 apartments* ⚒ *Restaurant, room service, in-room safes, some kitchens, minibars, cable TV with movies, in-room broadband, gym, sauna, bar, lobby lounge, dry cleaning, laundry service, concierge, meeting rooms, parking (fee), no-smoking floors* ═ *AE, DC, MC, V* Ⓤ *London Bridge.*

££ 🏨 **Premier Travel Inn County Hall.** Don't get too excited—this neighbor of the riverfront Marriott, is not next to it, but behind it, giving you a window onto the Marriott, not the Thames. Still, you get an incredible value, with the standard facilities of the cookie-cutter rooms of this chain. Best of all for families on a budget are the foldout beds that let you accommodate two kids at no extra charge. *That's* a bargain. ⊠ *Belvedere Rd., South Bank, SE1 7PB* ☎ *0870/238–3300* 🖷 *020/7902–1619* 🌐 *www.premiertravelinn.com* ⤷ *313 rooms* ⚒ *Restaurant, fans, in-room data ports, bar, business services, meeting rooms, parking (fee), no-smoking floors; no a/c* ═ *AE, DC, MC, V* Ⓤ *Westminster.*

££ 🏨 **Premier Travel Inn Southwark.** Practically riverside, this branch of the Premier Travel Inn chain has an excellent location across the cobbled road from Vinopolis, where you can do extensive wine-tastings. Rooms have desks, tea/coffeemakers, and the chain's signature 6-foot-wide beds (really two zipped together). Family rooms can accommodate four people. The nautical Anchor restaurant and pub is adjacent to the hotel. ⊠ *34 Park St., South Bank, SE1 9EF* ☎ *020/7089–2580 or 0870/990– 6402* 🖷 *0870/990–6403* 🌐 *www.premiertravelinn.com* ⤷ *56 rooms* ⚒ *Cable TV, in-room data ports, parking (fee), no-smoking rooms* ═ *AE, DC, MC, V* Ⓤ *London Bridge.*

Westminster & Victoria

🕲 ££££ 🏨 **City Inn Westminster.** In a rather stark steel-and-glass building steps from the Tate Britain, this member of a small U.K. chain has some rooms with spectacular views of Big Ben and the London Eye. Extras like floor-to-ceiling windows, CD players, and flat-screen TVs complement the contemporary, monochrome guest rooms. Cots, baby baths, Nickelodeon, special menus, and baby food are all on tap for kids. The restaurant and bar serve modern British cooking. ⊠ *30 John Islip St., Westminster, SW1P 4DD* ☎ *020/7630–1000* 🖷 *020/7233–7575* 🌐 *www. cityinn.com* ⤷ *444 rooms, 16 suites* ⚒ *Restaurant, room service, in-room safes, minibars, cable TV, in-room DVDs, in-room data ports, gym, bar, lobby lounge, babysitting, dry cleaning, laundry service, concierge, Internet, business services, meeting rooms, parking (fee), no-smoking rooms* ═ *AE, MC, V* Ⓤ *Pimlico.*

££–£££ 🏨 **Lime Tree Hotel.** On a street filled with budget hotels, the Lime Tree stands out for its gracious proprietors, the Davies family, who endeavor to provide a homey atmosphere as well as act as concierges. The flowery rooms include tea/coffeemakers. The triples and quads are suitable for families, but children under five are not allowed. The simple breakfast room covered with notes and gifts from former guests opens onto a garden. ⊠ *135–137 Ebury St., Victoria, SW1W 9RA* ☎ *020/7730–8191*

🖰 *020/7730–7865* ⊕ *www.limetreehotel.co.uk* ➥ *25 rooms* ♨ *Fans, in-room safes; no a/c, no kids under 5* ⦿ *BP* ⊟ *MC, V* Ⓤ *Victoria.*

£–££ ⛺ **Windermere Hotel.** This sweet, inexpensive hotel will not let you forget that it stands on the site of London's first B&B, which opened here in 1881. It's draped in charmingly sunny floral fabrics, kept in good taste by the antique beds and faux-antique fans in the rooms. Bathrooms are thoroughly modern, and the attached restaurant, small though it may be, is actually quite good. The Windermere is an excellent budget option. ✉ *142–144 Warwick Way, Victoria, SW1V 4JE* ☎ *020/7834–4163* 🖰 *020/7630–8831* ➥ *22 rooms* ⊕ *www.windermere-hotel.co.uk* ♨ *Room service, cable TV, in-room data ports, bar, no-smoking floors* ⊟ *MC, V* Ⓤ *Victoria.*

Bed-and-Breakfasts & Apartment Agencies

You can stay with London families in small, homey B&Bs for an up-close-and-personal brush with city life, relax in a pied-à-terre, or rent an entire house. The benefits of using a B&B agency are substantial—the price is cheaper than a hotel room of comparable quality, you have access to the kitchen, and yet you can usually arrange to have your breakfast prepared for you every day. The limitations are fairly minimal—there is no staff at your beck and call should you want something at odd hours, and most are not located in the very center of the city (although many are in lovely and convenient neighborhoods like Notting Hill and Kensington). Prices for attractive rooms in privately owned homes start as low as £60 a night, and go up for more central neighborhoods and larger and more luxurious homes.

££–££££ ⛺ **Coach House London Vacation Rentals.** Stay in the properties of Londoners who are temporarily away. Apartments and houses are primarily in Notting Hill, Kensington, and Chelsea. The extra touches—airport pickup, complimentary starter breakfast provisions, and a welcome drink with a representative—make this service personal. Homes also come with a phone number to call for help in planning your stay. ✉ *2 Tunley Rd., Balham, SW17 7QJ* ☎ *020/8772–1939* 🖰 *0870/133–4957* ⊕ *www.chslondon.com* ⊟ *AE, MC, V* ➣ *Payment by credit card only; 10% deposit required.*

££ ⛺ **Bulldog Club.** This reservation service offers delightful little London flats in sought-after neighborhoods. A three-year membership is about £25, with most properties available for about £105 per night. Full English breakfasts as well as other goodies are often provided. Most of the properties are in Knightsbridge, Kensington, and Chelsea. ✉ *14 Dewhurst Rd., Kensington, W14 0ET* ☎ *020/7371–3202, 877/727–3004 in U.S.* 🖰 *020/7371–2015* ⊕ *www.bulldogclub.com* ⊟ *AE, MC, V.*

££ ⛺ **London B&B.** This long-established family-run agency has some truly spectacular—and some more modest—homes in central London. Check many of them out via its Web site before making a commitment. The staff here is most personable and helpful. ✉ *437 J St., Suite 210, San Diego, CA 92101* ☎ *800/872–2632* 🖰 *619/531–1686* ⊕ *www.londonbandb.com* ➣ *30% deposit required.*

££ ⛺ **Primrose Hill B&B.** This is a small, friendly B&B agency genuinely "committed to the idea that traveling shouldn't be a rip-off." Expatriate

American Gail O'Farrell has family homes (to which you get your own latchkey) in or near village-y Hampstead, all of which are comfortable. So far this has been one of those word-of-mouth secrets, but now that everyone knows, book well ahead. ⊠ *14 Edis St., Regent's Park, NW1 8LG* ☎ *020/7722–6869* ⊟ *No credit cards.*

£–££ 🖼 **At Home in London.** This service offers rooms in private homes in Knightsbridge, Kensington, Mayfair, Chelsea, and West London. Prices are very competitive and include breakfast, and rooms are all approved by the agency. Prices start at £28 a night per room, making this a great alternative to budget hotels. ⊠ *70 Black Lion La., Hammersmith, W6 9BE* ☎ *020/8748–1943* 🖷 *020/8748–2700* ⊕ *www.athomeinlondon. co.uk* ⊟ *MC, V* ✆ *£7.50 per person booking fee.*

£ 🖼 **Host & Guest Service.** In business for 40 years, this service can find you a room based on a huge selection of B&Bs in London as well as the rest of the United Kingdom, even in rural areas. It's a great way to find excellent bargains in small hotels and guesthouses, knowing that all have been vetted by the agency. ⊠ *103 Dawes Rd., Fulham, SW6 7DU* ☎ *020/7385–9922* 🖷 *020/7386–7575* ⊕ *www.host-guest.co.uk* ⊟ *MC, V* ✆ *Full payment in advance.*

NIGHTLIFE & THE ARTS

Whether you prefer a romantic evening at the opera, rhythm and blues with fine French food, the gritty guitar riffs of east London, a pint and gourmet pizza at a local gastro-pub, or swanky cocktails and sushi at London's sexiest lair, the U.K. capital is sure to feed your fancy. Admission prices are not always bargain basement, but when you consider how much a London hotel room costs, the city's arts and nightlife diversions are a bargain.

Nightlife

As with nearly all cosmopolitan centers, the pace with which bars and clubs go in and out of fashion is mind-boggling. The phenomenon of absinthe has been replaced by bourbon's bite and the frenzy for the perfect cocktail recipe, and the dreaded velvet rope has been usurped by the doorbell-ringing mystique of members-only drinking clubs. The understated glamour of North London's Primrose Hill, which makes movie stars feel so at ease, might be considered dull by the über-trendy clubgoers of London's West End, whereas the price of a pint in Chelsea would be dubbed blasphemous by the musicians and poets of racially diverse Brixton. Meanwhile, some of the city's most talked-about nightlife spots are turning out to be those attached to some of its best restaurants and hotels—no wonder when you consider the increased popularity of London cuisine in international circles.

Bars

Time was, bars were just a stopover in an evening full of fun—perhaps the pub first, then a bar, and then it's off to boogie the night away at the nearest dance club. These days, however, bars have become less pit stops and more destinations in themselves. With the addition of dinner menus, DJs, dance floors, and the still-new later opening hours, people now stay into the wee hours of the morning at many fashionable bars.

American Bar. Festooned with a chin-dropping array of club ties, signed celebrity photographs, sporting mementos, and baseball caps, this sensational cocktail bar has superb martinis. A jacket is required after 5 PM. ⊠ *Stafford Hotel, 16–18 St. James's Pl., St. James's, SW1A* ☎ *020/ 7493–0111* ⊘ *Weekdays 11:30 AM–11 PM, Sat. noon–3 PM and 5:30–11 PM, Sun. noon–2:30 PM and 6:30–10:30* Ⓤ *Green Park.*

★ **Annex 3.** The set behind the London-based Les Trois Garcons and Loungelover (three antique dealers) now have this richly decorated den of cocktail inventions. Infused with purple-and-red decor, crystal chandeliers, and walls that resemble the side of a giant Rubik's cube, the très chic Annex 3 just off Regents Street serves traditional and fruity drinks that will please most palettes (as well as Japanese-influenced modern European fare). ⊠ *6 Little Portland St., Fitzrovia, W1W* ☎ *020/ 7631–0700* ⊘ *Mon.–Sat. noon–11 PM* Ⓤ *Oxford Circus.*

Cafe des Amis. This relaxed brasserie–wine bar near the Royal Opera House is the perfect pre- or post-theater spot—and a friendly enough place to go to on your own. More than 30 wines are served by the glass along with a good selection of cheeses. Opera buffs will enjoy the performance and production prints on the walls. ⊠ *11–14 Hanover Pl., Covent Garden, WC2* ☎ *020/7379–3444* ⊘ *Mon.–Sat. 11:30 AM–11:30 PM* Ⓤ *Covent Garden.*

★ **Crazy Bear.** This sexy basement bar with cowhide stools and croc-skin tables feels like Casablanca in Fitzrovia. As you enter Crazy Bear, a spiral staircase leads to a mirrored parlor over which presides a 1947 Murano chandelier; indeed, a suitably smoky, dimly lighted backdrop for Bogey and Bergman. But don't let the opulence fool you: waitresses here are warm and welcoming to an all-ages international crowd abuzz with chatter. ⊠ *26–28 Whitfield St., Fitzrovia, W1T* ☎ *020/7631–0088* ⊘ *Mon.–Sat. noon–11* Ⓤ *Goodge St.*

Dogstar. This popular South London hangout is frequented by local hipsters and counterculture types. The vibe is unpretentious but hip, and the modern Caribbean cuisine is a treat. Visual projections light up the interior and top-name DJs play cutting-edge sounds free on weekdays. Move on to the nearby dance club, Mass, and your sampling of local Brixton life will be complete. ⊠ *389 Coldharbour La., Brixton, SW9* ☎ *020/7733–7515* ⊠ *Free–£5* ⊘ *Mon.–Thurs. and Sun. noon–2 AM, Fri. and Sat. noon–4 AM* Ⓤ *Brixton.*

★ **Late Lounge @ Cocoon.** The "it" place of the moment, the pan-Asian restaurant Cocoon transforms itself into a sophisticated lounge (with DJ) Thursday through Saturday until 3 AM. Smack in the center of the West End on a landmark site, the Late Lounge with its soft peach decor and sanctuarylike setting serves caviar, oysters, a selection of appetizers, and desserts as well as champagne, sake, and cocktails with an Eastern twist. ⊠ *65 Regent St., St. James, W1B* ☎ *087/1332–6347* ⊘ *Thurs.–Sat. 11 PM–3 AM* Ⓤ *Piccadilly Circus.*

Nordic. With Red Erik and Faxe draft beers, shooters called "Husky Poo" and "Danish Bacon Surprise," and crayfish tails and meatballs on the smorgasbord menu, Nordic takes its Scandinavian feel the whole way.

This secluded, shabby-chic bar serves many couples cozied up among travel brochures promoting the Viking lands. The sassy, sweet Longberry is quite possibly the most perfect cocktail ever made. ⊠ *25 Newman St., Soho, W1* ☎ *020/7631–3174* ⊕ *www.nordicbar.com* ⊘ *Weekdays noon–11 PM, Sat. 6 PM–11 PM* Ⓤ *Tottenham Court Rd.*

Comedy

Amused Moose. This dark Soho basement is widely considered the best place to see breaking talent as well as household names doing "secret" shows. Ricky Gervais and Eddie Izzard are among those who have graced this stage and every summer a handful of the Edinburgh Fringe comedians preview here. The bar is open late and there's a DJ and dancing until 5 AM after the show. ⊠ *Moonlighting, 17 Greek St., Soho, W1* ☎ *020/8341–1341* ▭ *£10.50* ⊘ *Showtimes vary, call for details* Ⓤ *Tottenham Court Rd.*

★ **Comedy Store.** Known as the birthplace of alternative comedy, the country's funniest stand-ups have cut their teeth here before being launched onto prime-time TV. Comedy Store Players entertain audiences on Wednesday and Sunday; the Cutting Edge team steps in every Tuesday; and weekends have up-and-coming comedians performing on the same stage as established talent. There's a bar with food also available. ■ TIP➡ Tickets can be booked through Ticketmaster or over the phone. Note that children under 18 are not admitted to this venue. ⊠ *1A Oxendon St., Soho, SW1* ☎ *0870/060–2340* ▭ *£13–£15* ⊘ *Shows Tues.–Thurs. and Sun. 8 PM–10:15 PM, Fri. and Sat. 8 PM–10:15 PM and midnight–2:30 AM* Ⓤ *Piccadilly Circus, Leicester Sq.*

Dance Clubs

The club scene ranges from mammoth-size playgrounds to more intimate venues where you can actually hear your friends talk. Check the daily listings in *Time Out* for "club nights," which are theme nights that take place the same night every week. Another good way to learn about club nights is by picking up fliers in your favorite bar.

FodorśChoice ★ **Cargo.** Housed under a series of old railway arches, this vast brick-wall bar, restaurant, dance floor, and live-music venue pulls an international crowd with its hip vibe and diverse music. Long tables bring people together, as does the food, which draws on global influences and is served tapas-style. ⊠ *83 Rivington St., Shoreditch, EC2* ☎ *0871/075–1741* ⊘ *Mon.–Thurs. noon–1 AM, Fri.–Sun. noon–3 AM* Ⓤ *Old St.*

The End. Co-owned by Mr. C (ex-MC of cult band the Shamen) and tech-house producer Layo, this intimate club was designed by clubbers for clubbers. Top-name DJs, a state-of-the-art sound system, and minimalist steel-and-glass decor—clubbing doesn't get much better than this. Next door, the AKA Bar (owned by same) is a stylish split-level Manhattan-esque cocktail bar with excellent food. ⊠ *18 West Central St., Holborn, WC1* ☎ *020/7419–9199* ⊕ *www.endclub.com* ▭ *£6–£15* ⊘ *Mon. 10 PM–3 AM, Wed. 10:30 PM–3 AM, Thurs. 10 PM–4 AM, Fri. 10 PM–5 AM, and Sat. 10 PM–7 AM. Also some Sun.* Ⓤ *Tottenham Court Rd.*

Fabric. This sprawling subterranean club has been *the* place to be for the past few years. *Fabric Live* hosts drum 'n' bass and hip-hop crews and live acts on Friday; international big-name DJs play slow sexy bass lines and cutting-edge music on Saturday. Sunday is "Polysexual Night." The devastating sound system and bodysonic dance floor ensure that bass riffs vibrate through your entire body. Get there early to avoid a lengthy queue, and don't wear a suit. ⊠ *77A Charterhouse St., East End, EC1* ☎ *020/7336–8898* ⊕ *www.fabriclondon.com* ⊠ *£12–£15* ☉ *Fri. and Sun. 9:30 PM–5 AM, Sat. 10 PM–7 AM* Ⓤ *Farringdon.*

Pacha. London's version of the Ibizan superclub is in a restored 1920s dancehall next to Victoria bus station. The classic surroundings—all wood and chandeliers—don't stop the sounds from being eminently up-to-date. The crowd is slightly older than average and stylish, but not necessarily as monied as you might expect. ⊠ *Terminus Pl., Victoria, SW1* ☎ *020/7833–3139* ⊠ *£15–£20* ☉ *Fri. 10 PM–4 AM, Sat. 10 PM–6 AM* Ⓤ *Victoria.*

Eclectic Music

The Borderline. This important small venue has a solid reputation for booking everything from metal to country and beyond. Oasis, Pearl Jam, Blur, Sheryl Crow, PJ Harvey, Ben Harper, Jeff Buckley, and Counting Crows have all played live here. ⊠ *Orange Yard off Manette St., Soho, W1* ☎ *020/7434–9592* ⊠ *£6–£15* ☉ *Mon.–Sat. 7 PM–3 AM, Sun. 7 PM–11 PM* Ⓤ *Tottenham Court Rd.*

★ **Carling Academy Brixton.** This legendary Brixton venue has seen it all—mods and rockers, hippies and punks. Despite a capacity of almost 5,000 people, this refurbished Victorian hall with original art-deco fixtures retains a clublike charm; it has plenty of bars and upstairs seating. ⊠ *211 Stockwell Rd., Brixton, SW9* ☎ *0870/771–2000* ⊠ *£10–£30* ☉ *Opening hrs vary* Ⓤ *Brixton.*

★ **Union Chapel.** This old chapel has excellent acoustics and sublime architecture. The beauty of the space and its impressive multicultural programming have made it one of London's best musical venues. Performers have included Ravi Shankar, Björk, Beck, Beth Orton, and Bob Geldof, though nowadays you're more likely to hear lower-key alternative country, world music, and jazz. ⊠ *Compton Terr., Islington, N1* ☎ *020/ 7226–1686 or 0870/120–1349* ⊕ *www.unionchapel.org.uk* ⊠ *Free–£25* ☉ *Opening hrs vary* Ⓤ *Highbury & Islington.*

Jazz

Dover Street Restaurant & Jazz Bar. Put on your blue-suede shoes and prepare to dance the night away—that is, after you've feasted from an excellent French–Mediterranean menu. Fun for dates as well as groups, Dover Street Restaurant offers three bars, a DJ, and a stage with the latest live bands performing everything from Jazz to Soul to R&B, all this encircling linen-covered tables with a friendly waitstaff catering to your every whim. ⊠ *8–10 Dover St., Mayfair, W1X* ☎ *0871/332– 4946* ⊠ *£45* ☉ *Weekdays noon–3:30 PM and 7 PM–3 AM, weekends 7 PM–3 AM* Ⓤ *Green Park.*

★ **Jazz Café.** A palace of high-tech cool in bohemian Camden—it remains an essential hangout for fans of both the mainstream end of the repertoire and hip-hop, funk, rap, and Latin fusion. Book ahead if you want a prime table overlooking the stage, in the balcony restaurant. ⊠ *5 Pkwy., Camden Town, NW1* ☎ *020/7916–6060 restaurant reservations, 0870/ 150–0044 standing tickets* ⊠ *£10–£25* ☉ *Mon.–Thurs. 7 PM–1 AM, Fri. and Sat. 7 PM–2 AM, Sun. 7 PM–midnight* Ⓤ *Camden Town.*

Pizza Express. One of the capital's most ubiquitous pizza chains also runs a great Soho jazz venue. The darkly lighted restaurant hosts top-quality international jazz acts every night. The Italian-style thin-crust pizzas are good, too, though on the small side. The Hyde Park branch has a spacious jazz club in the basement that hosts mainstream acts. ⊠ *10 Dean St., Soho, W1* ☎ *020/7439–8722* Ⓤ *Tottenham Court Rd.* ⊠ *11 Knightsbridge, Hyde Park Corner, Knightsbridge, W1* ☎ *020/7235–5273* Ⓤ *Hyde Park Corner* 🗊 *£10–£25* ⊗ *Daily from 11:30 AM for food; music Sun.–Thurs. 9 PM–midnight, Fri. and Sat. 7:30 PM–midnight.*

★ **Ronnie Scott's.** Since the '60s, this legendary jazz club has attracted big names. It's usually crowded and hot, the food isn't great, and service is slow—but the mood can't be beat, even since the sad departure of its eponymous founder and saxophonist. Reservations are recommended. ⊠ *47 Frith St., Soho, W1* ☎ *020/7439–0747* 🗊 *£15–£25 nonmembers, £5–£15 members, annual membership £100* ⊗ *Mon.–Sat. 8:30 PM–3 AM, Sun. 7:30 PM–11 PM* Ⓤ *Leicester Sq.*

Rock

The Astoria. This balconied theater hosts cutting-edge alternative bands (punk, metal, indie guitar). Shows start early, at 7 PM most nights; the building is often cleared, following gigs, for club events. ■ TIP→ **Note that it's closed on some Tuesdays and Wednesdays.** ⊠ *157 Charing Cross Rd., West End, W1* ☎ *020/7434–9592* 🗊 *£8–£25* ⊗ *Mon., Thurs., and Fri. 7 PM–4 AM, Tues., Wed., and Sun. 7 PM–midnight, Sat. 6 PM–4:30 AM* Ⓤ *Tottenham Court Rd.*

★ **Barfly Club.** At one of the finest small clubs in the capital, punk, indie guitar bands, and new metal rock attract a nonmainstream crowd. Weekend club nights upstairs host DJs who rock the decks. ⊠ *49 Chalk Farm Rd., Camden Town, NW1* ☎ *020/7691–4244* 🗊 *£5–£8* ⊗ *Mon.–Thurs. 7:30 PM–midnight, Fri. and Sat. 8 PM–3 AM, Sun. 7:30 PM–11 PM* Ⓤ *Camden Town, Chalk Farm.*

Forum. The best medium- to big-name rock performers consistently play at the 2,000-capacity club. It's a converted 1920 art-deco cinema, with a balcony overlooking the dance floor. Consult the Web site for current listings. ⊠ *9–17 Highgate Rd., Kentish Town, NW5* ☎ *020/7284–1001* ⊕ *www.meanfiddler.com* 🗊 *£12–£25* ⊗ *Opening hrs vary depending on concert schedule* Ⓤ *Kentish Town.*

The Arts

London's arts scene pushes the boundaries, whether you prefer your art classical or modern, or as a contemporary twist on a time-honored classic. Celebrity divas sing original-language librettos at the Royal Opera House; the Almeida Opera focuses on radical productions of new opera and musical theater. Shakespeare's plays are brought to life at the reconstructed Globe Theatre, and challenging new writing is produced at the Royal Court.

To find out what's showing during your stay, the weekly magazine *Time Out* (it comes out every Tuesday) is an invaluable resource. The *Evening Standard,* especially the Thursday edition, also carries listings, as do the "quality" Sunday papers and the Saturday *Independent, Guardian,* and *Times.* Leaflets and fliers are found in most cinema and theater foyers, and you can pick up the free bimonthly *London Theatre Guide* leaflet from most hotels and tourist information centers.

Classical Music

Whether it's cellist Yo-Yo Ma at the Barbican or a Mozart requiem by candlelight, you can hear first-rate musicians in world-class venues almost every day of the year. The London Symphony Orchestra is in residence at the Barbican Centre, although other top orchestras—including the Philharmonia and the Royal Philharmonic—also perform here. Wigmore Hall, a lovely venue for chamber music, is renowned for its song recitals by up-and-coming young instrumentalists. The South Bank Centre has an impressive international-music season, held in the Queen Elizabeth Hall and the small Purcell Room, however refurbishments, due for completion in spring 2007, close the Royal Festival Hall. Full houses are rare, so even at the biggest concert halls you should be able to get a ticket for £12. If you can't book in advance, arrive at the hall an hour before the performance for a chance at returns.

■ TIP➔ Lunchtime concerts take place all over the city in smaller concert halls, the big arts-center foyers, and churches; they usually cost less than £5 or are free, and will feature string quartets, singers, jazz ensembles, or gospel choirs. St. John's, Smith Square, and St. Martin-in-the-Fields are popular locations. Performances usually begin about 1 PM and last one hour.

A great British tradition since 1895, the **Henry Wood Promenade Concerts,** more commonly known as the "Proms" (⊕ www.bbc.co.uk/proms), lasts eight weeks, from July to September, at the Royal Albert Hall. Demand for tickets is so high you must enter a lottery. For regular Proms, tickets run £4 to £80, with hundreds of standing tickets for £4, available at the hall on the night of the concert. ■ TIP➔ The last night is broadcast in Hyde Park on a jumbo-screen, but even here a seat on the grass requires a paid ticket that can set you back around £20.

Barbican Centre. Home to the London Symphony Orchestra (www.lso.co.uk) and frequent host of the English Chamber Orchestra and the BBC Symphony Orchestra, the Barbican has an excellent season of big-name virtuosos. ⊠ *Silk St., East End, EC2* ☎ *0845/120–7518 box office, 020/7638–4141* ⊕ *www.barbican.org.uk* Ⓤ *Barbican.*

Kenwood House. Outdoor concerts are held in the grassy amphitheater in front of Kenwood House on Saturday evenings from July to late August. ⊠ *Hampstead Heath, Hampstead, NW3 7JR* ☎ *0870/333–6206* ⊕ *www.picnicconcerts.com* Ⓤ *Hampstead.*

★ **Royal Albert Hall.** Built in 1871 this splendid iron-and-glass-dome auditorium hosts a varied music program, including Europe's most democratic music festival, the Henry Wood Promenade Concerts—the Proms. The Hall is also open for daily daytime guided tours (£6). ⊠ *Kensington Gore, Kensington, SW7* ☎ *020/7589–8212* ⊕ *www.royalalberthall.com* Ⓤ *South Kensington.*

St. John's, Smith Square. This baroque church behind Westminster Abbey offers chamber-music and organ recitals as well as orchestral concerts September through July. There are occasional lunchtime recitals for £7. ⊠ *Smith Sq., Westminster, W1* ☎ *020/7222–1061* ⊕ *www.sjss.org.uk* Ⓤ *Westminster.*

★ **St. Martin-in-the-Fields.** Popular lunchtime concerts (£3.50 donation suggested) are held in this lovely 1726 church, as are regular evening concerts. ■ TIP→ Stop for a snack at the Café in the Crypt. ⊠ *Trafalgar Sq., Covent Garden, WC2* ☎ *020/7839–8362* ⊕ *www.smitf.org* ⓤ *Charing Cross.*

South Bank Centre. Due to two years' renovation work begun in 2005 (due for completion spring 2007), the Royal Festival Hall's large-scale choral and orchestral works—including its housing of both the Philharmonia and the London Philharmonic orchestras—will be taken on by the other South Bank Centre venues such as the Queen Elizabeth Hall, which hosts chamber orchestras and A-team soloists, and the intimate Purcell Room, where you can listen to chamber music and solo recitals. ⊠ *Belvedere Rd., South Bank, SE1* ☎ *020/7960–4242* ⊕ *www.sbc.org.uk* ⓤ *Waterloo.*

Fodor'sChoice **Wigmore Hall.** Hear chamber-music and song recitals in this charming
★ hall with near-perfect acoustics. Don't miss the mid-morning Sunday concerts. ⊠ *36 Wigmore St., Marylebone, W1* ☎ *020/7935–2141* ⊕ *www.wigmore-hall.org.uk* ⓤ *Bond St.*

Contemporary Art

In the 21st century, the focus of the city's art scene has shifted from west to east, and from the past to the future. Helped by the prominence of the Tate Modern, London's contemporary art scene has never been so high profile. Young British Artists (YBAs, though no longer as young as they once were)—Damien Hirst, Tracey Emin, Gary Hume, Rachel Whiteread, Jake and Dinos Chapman, Sarah Lucas, Gavin Turk, Steve McQueen, and others—are firmly planted in the public imagination. The celebrity status of British artists is in part thanks to the annual Turner Prize, which always stirs up controversy in the media during a month-long display of the work at Tate Britain.

The South Bank, with the Tate Modern and the Hayward Gallery, may house the giants of modern art, but the East End is where the innovative action is. There are dozens of galleries in the fashionable spaces around Old Street. The Whitechapel Art Gallery continues to flourish, exhibiting exciting new British artists and, together with Jay Jopling's influential White Cube in Hoxton Square, is the new East End–art establishment.

Barbican Centre. Innovative exhibitions of 20th-century and current art and design are shown in the Barbican Gallery and **The Curve** (⊠ Free ☉ Mon.–Sat. 11–8). ⊠ *Silk St., East End, EC2* ☎ *020/7638–8891* ⊕ *www.barbican.org.uk* ⊠ *£6–£8, tickets cheaper if booked online in advance* ☉ *Mon., Wed., Fri., and Sat. 11–8, Tues. and Thurs. 11–6, Sun. noon–6* ⓤ *Barbican.*

★ **Hayward Gallery.** This modern-art gallery, a classic example of 1960s Brutalist architecture, is one of London's major venues for important touring exhibitions. ⊠ *Belvedere Rd., South Bank Centre, South Bank, SE1* ☎ *0870/165–6000* ⊕ *www.hayward.org.uk* ⊠ *£7.50, Mon. half-price* ☉ *Thurs. and Sat.–Mon. 10–6, Tues. and Wed. 10–8, Fri. 10–9* ⓤ *Waterloo.*

Institute of Contemporary Arts. Housed in an elegant John Nash–designed Regency terrace, the three galleries have changing exhibitions of contemporary visual art. The ICA also programs contemporary drama, film, new media, literature, and photography. To visit you must be a member; a day membership costs £1.50. ✉ *Nash House, The Mall, St. James's, SW1* ☎ *020/7930–3647 or 020/7930–0493* ⊕ *www.ica.org.uk* 🖭 *Weekdays £1.50, weekends £2.50* ⊙ *Daily noon–7:30* Ⓤ *Charing Cross.*

★ **Lisson.** Owner Nicholas Logsdail represents about 40 blue-chip artists, including minimalist Sol Lewitt and Dan Graham. A new branch, Lisson New Space, down the road at 29 Bell Street features work by younger up-and-coming artists. ✉ *52–54 Bell St., Marylebone, NW1* ☎ *020/7724–2739* ⊕ *www.lissongallery.com* 🖭 *Free* ⊙ *Weekdays 10–6, Sat. 11–5* Ⓤ *Edgware Rd. or Marylebone.*

Photographer's Gallery. Britain's first photography gallery continues to program cutting-edge and provocative photography. ✉ *5 and 8 Great Newport St., Covent Garden, WC2* ☎ *020/7831–1772* ⊕ *www.photonet. org.uk* 🖭 *Free* ⊙ *Mon.–Wed., Fri., and Sat. 11–6, Thurs. 11–8, Sun. noon–6* Ⓤ *Leicester Sq.*

Royal Academy. Housed in an aristocratic mansion and home to Britain's first art school (founded in 1768), the Academy is best known for its blockbuster special exhibitions. ✉ *Burlington House, Soho, W1* ☎ *020/7300–8000* ⊕ *www.royalacademy.org.uk* 🖭 *From £9, prices vary with exhibition* ⊙ *Sun.–Thurs. 10–6, Fri. and Sat. 10 AM–10 PM* Ⓤ *Piccadilly Circus.*

Saatchi Gallery. At this writing, Charles Saatchi's ultramodern gallery was set to reopen in the Duke of York's HQ building in Chelsea in summer 2007; its short-lived tenancy on the South Bank ended acrimoniously in 2005. For more information, visit the Web site. ✉ *Duke of York's HQ, King's Rd., Chelsea SW3 4RY* ☎ *020/7823–2332* ⊕ *www.saatchigallery.co.uk* Ⓤ *Sloane Sq.*

Serpentine Gallery. In a classical 1930 tea pavilion in Kensington Gardens, the Serpentine has an international reputation for exhibitions of modern and contemporary art. ✉ *Kensington Gardens, South Kensington, W2* ☎ *020/7402–6075* ⊕ *www.serpentinegallery.org* 🖭 *Donation* ⊙ *Daily 10–6* Ⓤ *South Kensington.*

Fodor'sChoice **Tate Modern.** This converted power station is the largest modern-art gallery
★ in the world. ■ **TIP→** **The café on the top floor has gorgeous views overlooking the Thames and St. Paul's Cathedral.** ✉ *Bankside, South Bank, SE1* ☎ *020/7887–8008* ⊕ *www.tate.org.uk* 🖭 *Free–£8.50* ⊙ *Daily 10–6, Fri. and Sat. until 10 PM* Ⓤ *Southwark.*

Victoria Miro Gallery. This important commercial gallery has exhibited some of the biggest names on the British contemporary art scene— Chris Ofili, the Chapman brothers, Peter Doig, to name a few. ✉ *16 Wharf Rd., Islington, N1* ☎ *020/7336–8109* ⊕ *www.victoria-miro. com* 🖭 *Free* ⊙ *Tues.–Sat. 10–6* Ⓤ *Old St., Angel.*

★ **Whitechapel Art Gallery.** Established in 1897, this independent East End gallery is one of London's most innovative. ✉ *80–82 Whitechapel High St., East End, E1* ☎ *020/7522–7888* ⊕ *www.whitechapel.org* 🖭 *Free–£8* ⊙ *Tues.–Sun. 11–6, Thurs. 11–9* Ⓤ *Aldgate East.*

★ **White Cube.** Jay Joplin's influential gallery is in a 1920s light-industrial building on Hoxton Square. Many of its artists are Turner Prize stars. ✉ *48 Hoxton Sq., East End, N1* ☎ *020/7749–7450* ⊕ *www.whitecube. com* 🖭 *Free* ⊙ *Tues.–Sat. 10–6* Ⓤ *Old St.*

Dance

The **English National Ballet** and visiting international companies usually perform at the London Coliseum and at Sadler's Wells. The **Royal Ballet,** world renowned for its classical excellence, as well as innovative contemporary dance from several companies and scores of independent choreographers, can be seen at the Royal Opera House. **Royal Festival Hall** (closed for renovations until 2007) in the South Bank Centre has a fine contemporary-dance program that hosts top international companies and British choreographers. **The Place** presents the most daring, cutting-edge dance performances. **Sadler's Wells** hosts ballet companies and regional and international modern-dance troupes. The city's biggest annual event, **Dance Umbrella** (☎ 020/8741–5881 ⊕ www.danceumbrella. co.uk), a six-week season in October and November, showcases international and British-based artists at venues across the city.

DANCE BOX OFFICES **London Coliseum** (✉ St. Martin's La., Covent Garden, WC2N ☎ 020/ 7632–8300 Ⓤ Leicester Sq.).

The Place (✉ 17 Duke's Rd., Bloomsbury, WC1 ☎ 020/7121–1100 Ⓤ Euston).

Royal Opera House (✉ Bow St., Covent Garden, WC2 ☎ 020/7304–4000 Ⓤ Covent Garden).

Sadler's Wells (✉ Rosebery Ave., Islington, EC1 ☎ 020/7863–8000 Ⓤ Angel).

South Bank Centre (✉ Belvedere Rd., South Bank, SE1 ☎ 020/7960–4242 or 0870/380–0400 Ⓤ Embankment, Waterloo).

Film

There are many lovely movie theaters in London and several that are committed to nonmainstream cinema, notably the National Film Theatre. Most of the major houses (Odeon Leicester Square and UCI Empire) are in the Leicester Square–Piccadilly Circus area, where tickets average £10. Monday and matinees are often cheaper, at around £5 to £7, and crowds are smaller.

Curzon Soho. This comfortable cinema runs an artsy program of mixed rep and mainstream films. There's also a Mayfair branch. ✉ *99 Shaftesbury Ave., Soho, W1* ☎ *0871/871–0022* Ⓤ *Piccadilly Circus, Leicester Sq.* ✉ *38 Curzon St., Mayfair, W1* ☎ *020/7495–0500* ⊕ *www. curzoncinemas.com* Ⓤ *Green Park.*

The Electric Cinema. This refurbished Portobello Road art house screens mainstream and international movies. The emphasis is on comfort, with leather sofas, armchairs, footstools, and mini coffee tables for your popcorn. ✉ *191 Portobello Rd., Notting Hill, W11* ☎ *020/7727–9958 information, 020/7908–9696 box office* ⊕ *www.electriccinema.co.uk* Ⓤ *Ladbroke Grove, Notting Hill Gate.*

National Film Theatre (NFT). With easily the best repertory programming in London, the NFT's three cinemas show more than 1,000 titles each year, favoring obscure, foreign, silent, classic, and short films over blockbusters. ■ TIP→ **The** *London Film Festival* **is based here at the NFT; throughout the year there are minifestivals, seminars, and guest speakers.** ✉ *Belvedere Rd., South Bank, SE1* ☎ *020/7633–0274 information, 020/ 7928–3232 box office* ⊕ *www.bfi.org.uk/incinemas/nft/* Ⓤ *Waterloo.*

Opera

The two key players in London's opera scene are the Royal Opera (which ranks with the Metropolitan Opera in New York) and the more innovative English National Opera (ENO), which presents English-language productions at the London Coliseum. Only the Theatre Royal, Drury Lane, has a longer theatrical history than the Royal Opera House, and the current theater—the third to be built on the site since 1858—has a wonderfully restored Victorian auditorium and the Floral Hall foyer, which beautifully integrate with the Covent Garden Piazza.

The Royal Opera House struggles to shrug off its reputation for elitism and mismanagement. Ticket prices go up to £180. It has, however, made good on its promise to be more accessible—the cheapest tickets are just £4. Conditions of purchase vary; call for information. Prices for ENO are generally lower, ranging from £8 to £80. ENO sells same-day balcony seats for as little as £5.

Almeida Opera and BAC Opera (at the Battersea Arts Centre) produce festivals that showcase new opera and cutting-edge music theater. During the summer months, Holland Park Opera presents the usual chestnuts in the open-air theater of leafy Holland Park.

OPERA BOX OFFICES **Almeida Theatre** (✉ Almeida St., Islington, N1 ☎ 020/7359–4404 Ⓤ Angel, Highbury, Islington).
BAC Opera (✉ Lavender Hill, Battersea, SW11 ☎ 020/7223–2223 Ⓤ Clapham Junction).
English National Opera (✉ London Coliseum, St. Martin's La., Covent Garden, WC2 ☎ 0870/145–0200 Ⓤ Leicester Sq.).
Holland Park Opera (✉ Holland Park, Kensington High St., Kensington, W8 ☎ 020/7602–7856 Ⓤ Covent Garden).
★ **Royal Opera House** (✉ Bow St., Covent Garden, WC2 ☎ 020/7304–4000 Ⓤ Covent Garden).

Theater

One of the special experiences the city has to offer is great theater. London's theater scene consists, broadly, of the state-subsidized companies, the Royal National Theatre and the Royal Shakespeare Company; the commercial West End, equivalent to Broadway; and the Fringe—small, experimental companies. Another category could be added: known in the weekly listings magazine *Time Out* as Off-West End, these are shows staged at the longer-established fringe theaters. Most of the West End theaters are in the neighborhood nicknamed Theatreland, around the Strand and Shaftesbury Avenue.

The Royal Shakespeare Company and the Royal National Theatre Company often stage contemporary versions of the classics. The Almeida, Battersea Arts Centre (BAC), Donmar Warehouse, Royal Court Theatre, and the Soho Theatre attract famous actors and have excellent reputations for new writing and innovative theater. These are the places that shape the theater of the future, the venues where you can see an original production before it becomes a (more expensive) hit in the West End. From mid-May through mid-September you can see the Bard served up at the open-air reconstruction of Shakespeare's Globe Theatre on the South Bank.

Theatergoing isn't cheap. Tickets under £10 are a rarity; in the West End you should expect to pay from £15 for a seat in the upper balcony to at least £25 for a good one in the stalls (orchestra) or dress circle (mezzanine). However, as the vast majority of theaters have some tickets (returns and house seats) available on the night of performance, you may find some good deals at box offices as well as at tkts, the Society of London Theatre's discount-ticket booth. Tickets may be booked through ticket agents (extra charges may be high), at theater box offices, or over the phone by credit card; be sure to inquire about any extra fees. All the larger hotels offer theater bookings, but they tack on a hefty service charge. Fringe tickets are always considerably less expensive than tickets for West End productions.

Be *very* careful of scalpers (known locally as "ticket touts") and unscrupulous ticket agents outside theaters and in the line at tkts. They will try to sell tickets at five times the price of the ticket at legitimate box offices, and you pay a stiff fine if caught buying a scalped ticket.

Ticketmaster (☎ 0870/060–0800, 161/385–3211 from U.S. ⊕ www. ticketmaster.co.uk) sells tickets to a number of different theaters, although they charge a booking fee. You can book tickets in the United States through **Keith Prowse** (✉ 234 W. 44th St., Suite 1000, New York, NY 10036 ☎ 800/669–8687 ⊕ www.keithprowse.com).

The **Society of London Theatre** (✉ 32 Rose St., Covent Garden, London WC2 E9E5 ☎ 020/7557–6700 ⊕ www.officiallondontheatre.co.uk) operates tkts, the half-price ticket booth (no phone) on the southwest corner of Leicester Square, and sells the best available seats to performances at nearly all major theaters. It's open Monday through Saturday 10 AM to 7 PM, Sunday noon to 2 PM; there's a £2 service charge. All major credit cards are accepted. The society has good information about theatrical events.

SELECTED
THEATERS
★

Below are some theaters known for excellent or innovative work.

Almeida Theatre. This Off-West End venue premieres excellent new plays and exciting twists on the classics. Hollywood stars often perform here. ✉ *Almeida St., Islington, N1* ☎ *020/7359–4404* ⊕ *www.almeida.co. uk* Ⓤ *Angel, Highbury & Islington.*

BAC. Battersea Arts Centre has an excellent reputation for producing innovative new work. Check out Scratch, a monthly, pay-what-you-can night of low-tech cabaret theater by emerging artists. Tuesday shows also have pay-what-you-can entry. ✉ *176 Lavender Hill, Battersea, SW11* ☎ *020/ 7223–2223* ⊕ *www.bac.org.uk* Ⓤ *British Rail: Clapham Junction.*

Barbican Centre. B.I.T.E. (Barbican International Theatre Events) features groundbreaking dance, drama, and music theater. ✉ *Silk St., East End, EC2* ☎ *020/7638–8891* ⊕ *www.barbican.org.uk* Ⓤ *Barbican.*

Fodor'sChoice
★

Donmar Warehouse. Hollywood stars often perform here in diverse and daring new works, bold interpretations of the classics, and small-scale musicals. ✉ *41 Earlham St., Covent Garden, WC2* ☎ *0870/060–6624* ⊕ *www.donmar-warehouse.com* Ⓤ *Covent Garden.*

The Old Vic. American actor Kevin Spacey is the artistic director of this grand 1818 Victorian theater, one of London's oldest. Laurence Olivier called it his favorite theater. ✉ *The Cut, Southwark, SE1* ☎ *0870/ 060–6628* ⊕ *www.oldvictheatre.com* Ⓤ *Waterloo.*

FodorśChoice ★ **Open Air Theatre.** On a warm summer evening, classical theater in the pastoral, and royal Regent's Park is hard to beat for magical adventure. Enjoy supper before the performance or during intermission on the picnic lawn, and drinks in the spacious bar. ✉ *Inner Circle, Regent's Park, NW1* ☎ *0870/060–1811* ⊕ *www.openairtheatre.org* Ⓤ *Baker St., Regent's Park.*

★ **Royal Court Theatre.** Britain's undisputed epicenter of new writing, the RCT has produced gritty British and international drama since the middle of the 20th century, much of which gets produced in the West End. ■ TIP➡ Don't miss the best deal in town–£7.50 tickets on Monday. ✉ *Sloane Sq., Chelsea, SW1* ☎ *020/7565–5000* ⊕ *www.royalcourttheatre.com* Ⓤ *Sloane Sq.*

★ **Royal National Theatre.** Opened in 1976, the RNT has three theaters: the 1,120-seat Olivier, the 890-seat Lyttelton, and the 300-seat Cottesloe. Musicals, classics, and new plays are in repertoire. ■ TIP➡ An adventurous new ticketing scheme means some Royal National Theatre performances can be seen for as little as £10. It's closed Sunday. ✉ *South Bank Arts Centre, Belvedere Rd., South Bank, SE1* ☎ *020/7452–3000* ⊕ *www.nt-online. org* Ⓤ *Waterloo.*

FodorśChoice ★ **Shakespeare's Globe Theatre.** This faithful reconstruction of the open-air playhouse where Shakespeare worked and wrote many of his greatest plays re-creates the 16th-century theater-going experience. Standing room costs £5. The season runs May through September. ✉ *New Globe Walk, Bankside, South Bank, SE1* ☎ *020/7401–9919* ⊕ *www. shakespeares-globe.org* Ⓤ *Southwark, Mansion House, walk across Southwark Bridge; Blackfriars, walk across Blackfriars Bridge.*

Soho Theatre + Writers' Centre. This sleek theater in the heart of Soho is devoted to fostering new writing and is a prolific presenter of work by emerging writers. ✉ *21 Dean St., Soho, W1* ☎ *020/7478–0100* ⊕ *www. sohotheatre.com* Ⓤ *Tottenham Court Rd.*

Tricycle Theatre. The Tricycle is committed to the best in Irish, African-Caribbean, Asian, and political drama, and the promotion of new plays. ✉ *269 Kilburn High Rd., Kilburn, NW6 7JR* ☎ *020/7328–1000* ⊕ *www.tricycle.co.uk* Ⓤ *Kilburn.*

SPORTS

Cricket

★ **Lord's** (✉ St. John's Wood Rd., St. John's Wood, NW8 ☎ 020/7432–1000) has been hallowed turf for worshippers of England's summer game since 1811, a sport which has enjoyed a renaissance since England beat Australia in 2005. Tickets (by application and lottery) can be hard to procure for the five-day Test Matches (full internationals) and one-day internationals played here. Forms are sent out from mid-November. Standard Test Match tickets cost between £26 and £48. County matches (Middlesex plays here) can usually be seen by lining up on the day of the match.

1

Football

Three of London's football (soccer) clubs competing in the **Premier League** and the Football Association's FA Cup are particularly popular, though not always correspondingly successful: **Arsenal** (✉ Highbury, Avenell Rd., Islington, N5 ☎ 020/7704–4040), **Chelsea** (✉ Stamford Bridge, Fulham Rd., Fulham, SW6 ☎ 0870/300–2322), and **Tottenham Hotspur** ("Spurs"; ✉ White Hart La., 748 High Rd., Tottenham, N17 ☎ 0870/420–5000). Try to buy tickets in advance, and don't get too carried away by the excitement a vast football crowd can generate.

Ice-Skating

★ ☾ It's hard to beat the skating experience at **Somerset House** (✉ The Strand, Covent Garden, WC2 ☎ 020/7845–4670). During December and January a rink is set up in the spectacular courtyard of this central London palace. Its popularity is enormous; if you can't get a ticket, other venues such as Hampton Court Palace and the Natural History Museum also have temporary winter rinks. Adults pay £9.50 to £12, children £6.

Tennis

The **Wimbledon Lawn Tennis Championships,** the most prestigious of the four Grand Slam tournaments, is also one of London's most eagerly awaited annual events. To enter the lottery for show-court tickets, send a self-addressed, stamped envelope (or an international reply coupon) after August 1 and return the application form before December 31 to **All England Lawn Tennis & Croquet Club** (✐ Ticket Office, All England Lawn Tennis & Croquet Club, Box 98, Church Rd., Wimbledon, SW19 5AE ☎ 020/8946–2244). Alternatively, during the last-week-of-June, first-week-of-July tournament, tickets collected from early-departing spectators are resold (profits go to charity). These can provide grandstand seats with plenty to see: play continues until dusk. You can also line up (start as early as possible) for tickets for the outside courts.

SHOPPING

Napoléon was being scornful when he called Britain a nation of shopkeepers, but Londoners have had the last laugh. The finest emporiums are in London, still. You can shop like royalty at Her Majesty's glove maker, discover an uncommon Toby jug in a Kensington antiques shop, or find a leather-bound edition of *Wuthering Heights* on Charing Cross Road. If you have a yen to keep up with the Windsors, head for stores proclaiming they are "By Appointment" to H. M. the Queen—or to Prince Philip or the Prince of Wales. The fashion-forward crowd favors places such as Harvey Nichols or Browns of South Molton Street, whereas the most ardent fashion victims will shoot to Notting Hill, London's prime fashion location. If you have limited time, zoom in on one of the city's grand department stores, such as Harrods, Marks & Spencer, or Selfridges, where you can find enough booty for your entire gift list. Below is a brief introduction to the major shopping areas.

Apart from bankrupting yourself, the only problem you may encounter is exhaustion. London is a town of many far-flung shopping areas.

■ TIP→ Real shophounds plan their excursions with military precision, taking in only one or two shopping districts in a day, with fortifying stops for lunch, tea, and a pint or glass of wine in the pub.

CHELSEA   Chelsea centers on King's Road, once synonymous with ultra-high fashion; it still harbors some designer boutiques, plus antiques and home furnishings stores.

COVENT GARDEN   This neighborhood has chain clothing stores and top designers, stalls selling crafts, and shops selling gifts of every type—bikes, kites, tea, herbs, beads, hats—you name it.

FULHAM   Newly popular, Fulham is divided into two postal districts, SW6 (farther away from the center of town) and SW10 (which is the closer, beyond Chelsea) on the high-fashion King's Road.

KENSINGTON   Kensington's main drag, Kensington High Street, houses some small, classy shops, with a few larger stores at the eastern end. Try Kensington Church Street for expensive antiques, plus a little fashion.

KNIGHTSBRIDGE   Knightsbridge, east of Kensington, has Harrods but also Harvey Nichols, the top clothes stop, and many expensive designers' boutiques along Sloane Street, Walton Street, and Beauchamp Place.

MARYLEBONE   Behind Oxford Street lies this quiet backwater, with Marylebone High Street as its main artery. There are restaurants, upscale delis, and designer furniture stores; chic boutiques spill over onto satellite streets.

MAYFAIR   In Mayfair are the two Bond streets, Old and New, with desirable dress designers, jewelers, and fine art. South Molton Street has high-price, high-style fashion, and the tailors of Savile Row have worldwide reputations.

NOTTING HILL   Go westward from the famous Portobello Road market and explore the Ledbury Road–Westbourne Grove axis, Clarendon Cross, and Kensington Park Road for a mix of antiques and up-to-the-minute must-haves for body and lifestyle. Toward the more bohemian foot of Portobello are Ladbroke Grove and Golborne Road, where, in among the tatty stores, Portuguese cafés, and patisseries, you can bag bargains.

REGENT STREET   At right angles to Oxford Street is Regent Street, with possibly London's most pleasant department store, Liberty, plus Hamleys, the capital's favorite toy store. Shops around once-famous Carnaby Street stock designer youth paraphernalia and 57 varieties of the T-shirt.

ST. JAMES'S   Here the English gentleman buys everything but the suit (which is from Savile Row): handmade hats, shirts and shoes, silver shaving kits, and hip flasks. Nothing in this neighborhood is cheap, in any sense.

Department Stores

Debenhams (⊠ 334–348 Oxford St., Mayfair, W1 ☎ 0844/561–6161 Ⓤ Oxford Circus) has moved up the fashion stakes with the pretty, affordable, Jasper Conran collection for women. Other creations—for men, too—by in-house designers are desirable. **Harrods** (⊠ 87 Brompton Rd., Knightsbridge, SW1 ☎ 020/7730–1234 Ⓤ Knightsbridge), one of the world's most famous department stores, can be forgiven its immodest

FodorśChoice
★

motto, *Omnia, omnibus, ubique* ("everything, for everyone, everywhere"), because it has more than 230 well-stocked departments. The food halls are stunning—so are the crowds, especially during the sales that usually run during the last three weeks of January. **Harvey Nichols** (⊠ 109 Knightsbridge, Knightsbridge, SW1 ☎ 020/7235–5000 Ⓤ Knightsbridge) is famed for five floors of ultimate fashion; every label any chic, well-bred London lady covets is here, as well as a home-furnishings department. It's also known for the restaurant, Fifth Floor. **John Lewis** (⊠ 278 Oxford St., Mayfair, W1 ☎ 020/7629–7711 Ⓤ Oxford Circus) claims as its motto "Never knowingly undersold." This traditional department store carries a good selection of dress fabrics and curtain and

★ upholstery materials. **Liberty** (⊠ 200 Regent St., Mayfair, W1 ☎ 020/ 7734–1234 Ⓤ Oxford Circus), full of nooks and crannies, is famous principally for its fabulous fabrics. It also carries Eastern and exotic goods, menswear, womenswear, fragrances, soaps, and accessories. **Marks & Spencer** (⊠ 458 Oxford St., Mayfair, W1 ☎ 020/7935–7954 Ⓤ Marble Arch) is a major chain that's an integral part of the British way of life—sturdy, practical clothes and good materials. What it *is* renowned

★ for is underwear; the English all buy theirs here. **Selfridges** (⊠ 400 Oxford St., Mayfair, W1 ☎ 0870/837–7377 Ⓤ Bond St.), huge and hip, is giving Harvey Nicks a run as London's leading fashion department store. It's packed with high-profile, popular designer clothes for everyone in the family. There's a theater ticket counter and a British Airways travel shop in the basement.

Specialty Stores

Antiques

★ **Alfie's Antique Market** (⊠ 13–25 Church St., Regent's Park, NW8 ☎ 020/ 7723–6066 Ⓤ Edgware Rd.), a huge labyrinth on several floors, has dealers specializing in anything and everything but particularly in textiles, furniture, and theater memorabilia. Closed Sunday and Monday. **Antiquarius** (⊠ 131–145 King's Rd., Chelsea, SW3 ☎ 020/7351–5353 Ⓤ Sloane Sq.), near Sloane Square, is an indoor antiques market with more than 200 stalls offering collectibles, art-deco brooches, meerschaum pipes, and silver salt cellars. It's closed Sunday. **Grays Antique Market** (⊠ 58 Davies St., Mayfair, W1 ☎ 020/7629–7034 Ⓤ Bond St.) assembles dealers specializing in everything from Sheffield plates to Chippendale furniture. Bargains are not impossible, and proper pedigrees are guaranteed.

★ It's closed Saturday (except December) and Sunday. **London Silver Vaults** (⊠ 53–64 Chancery La., Holborn, WC2 ☎ 020/7242–3844 Ⓤ Chancery La.) has about 40 dealers specializing in antique silver and jewelry. It's closed Saturday afternoon and Sunday.

Books, CDs & Records

BOOKS Charing Cross Road is London's "booksville," with a couple dozen antiquarian booksellers, and many mainstream bookshops, too. **Cecil Court,** off Charing Cross Road, is a pedestrian-only lane filled with specialty bookstores. **Forbidden Planet** (⊠ 179 Shaftesbury Ave., Covent Garden, WC2 ☎ 020/7420–3666 Ⓤ Tottenham Court Rd.) is the place for sci-fi,

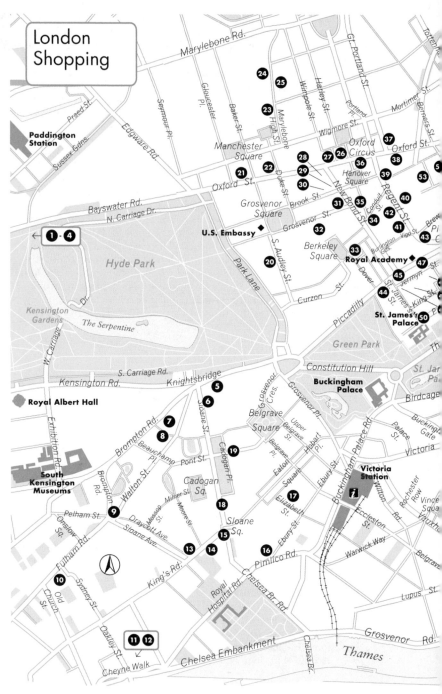

London
Shopping

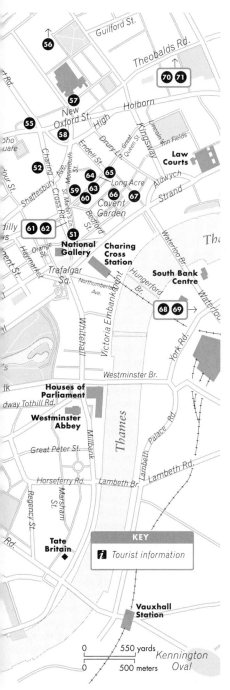

Fodor'sChoice
★ fantasy, horror, and comic books. **Foyles** (⊠ 113–119 Charing Cross Rd., Soho, WC2 ☎ 020/7437–5660 Ⓤ Tottenham Court Rd.) is so vast, you can find almost anything. There are two great, unique concessions: the Silver Moon for women and Ray's Jazz for music. **Gosh!** (⊠ 39 Great Russell St., Bloomsbury, WC1 ☎ 020/7636–1011 Ⓤ Tottenham Court Rd.) stocks classic comics, graphic novels, manga, and independent

Fodor'sChoice
★ minicomics. **Hatchards** (⊠ 187 Piccadilly, St. James's, W1 ☎ 020/ 7439–9921 Ⓤ Piccadilly Circus) has a huge stock and a well-informed staff. **John Sandoe Books, Ltd.** (⊠10 Blacklands Terr., Chelsea, SW3 ☎020/ 7589–9473 Ⓤ Sloane Sq.) has more than 25,000 titles that fill three dollhouse-size floors of an 18th-century house. **Marchpane** (⊠ 16 Cecil Ct., Charing Cross Rd., Covent Garden, WC2 ☎ 020/7836–8661 Ⓤ Leicester Sq.) stocks rare and antique illustrated children's books with many first editions, from 18th-century volumes to Harry Potter. **Stanfords** (⊠ 12 Long Acre, Covent Garden, WC2 ☎ 020/7836–1321 Ⓤ Covent Garden) specializes in travel books and maps. **Tindley & Chapman** (⊠ 4 Cecil Ct., Charing Cross Rd., Covent Garden, WC2 ☎ 020/7240–2161 Ⓤ Leicester Sq.), previously Bell, Book & Radmall, still offers quality antiquarian tomes and specializes in modern first editions. **Waterstone's** (⊠ 203–206 Piccadilly, St. James's, W1 ☎ 020/7851–2400 Ⓤ Piccadilly Circus) is part of an admirable chain with long hours and a program of author readings and signings. Their most upscale branch is book buying as hedonistic leisure activity, with five floors, a studio cocktail lounge with a view, and a café in the basement.

CDS & RECORDS London created the great music megastores that have taken over the globe, but don't forget to check out the many independents for a more eclectic selection. **Blackmarket** (⊠ 25 D'Arblay St., Soho, W1 ☎ 020/ 7437–0478 Ⓤ Oxford Circus), a shop for vinyl lovers, stocks the hottest club music around. **HMV** (⊠ 360 Oxford St., Mayfair, W1 ☎ 020/ 7514–3600 Ⓤ Bond St.), with stores all over London, tends to always be busy. Unless you know exactly what you want, the staff may seem
★ too busy grooving to be of much help. **MDC Opera Shop** (⊠ 31 St. Martins La., Covent Garden, WC2 ☎ 020/7240–0270 Ⓤ Covent Garden) has staff that will guide you to the best performances of the best divas with the best conductors. **Mr CD** (⊠ 80 Berwick St., Soho, W1 ☎ 020/ 7439–1097 Ⓤ Oxford Circus) stocks a wide selection for all tastes in a tiny shop where you must delve to find the bargains. **Virgin Megastore** (⊠ 14–16 Oxford St., Soho, W1 ☎ 020/7631–1234 Ⓤ Tottenham Court Rd.), Richard Branson's pride and joy, carries music of all kinds, books, magazines, and computer games under one roof.

China & Glass

Emma Bridgewater (⊠ 81A Marylebone High St., Marylebone, W1 ☎ 020/7486–6897 Ⓤ Baker St. or Regents Park) is the home of fun and funky plates, mugs, and breakfast tableware for country-style designer
★ kitchens. **David Mellor** (⊠ 4 Sloane Sq., Chelsea, SW1 ☎ 020/7730–4259 Ⓤ Sloane Sq.) sells practical Dartington crystal along with more unique
★ porcelain and pottery pieces by British craftspeople. **Divertimenti** (⊠33–34 Marylebone High St., Marylebone, W1 ☎ 020/7935–0689 Ⓤ Baker St. or Regents Park) specializes in beautiful kitchenware and French pot-
★ tery from Provence. **Summerill & Bishop** (⊠ 100 Portland Rd., Notting

Hill, W11 ☎ 020/7221–4566 ⓤ Holland Park), a little piece of French country, supplies French embroidered linen, Portuguese and Tuscan stoneware, and designer culinary ware. **Thomas Goode** (✉ 19 S. Audley St., Mayfair, W1 ☎ 020/7499–2823 ⓤ Green Park) stocks formal china and lead crystal, including English Wedgwood and Minton, and is one of the world's top shops for these items.

Clothing

★ **Agent Provocateur** (✉ 16 Pont St., Knightsbridge, SW1 ☎ 020/7235–0229 ⓤ Knightsbridge, Sloane Sq.) is the place to go for sexy, naughty-but-nice lingerie in gorgeous fabrics and lace. **Aquascutum** (✉ 100 Regent St., Soho, W1 ☎ 020/7675–8200 ⓤ Piccadilly Circus) is known for its classic raincoats but also stocks expensive garments to wear underneath, for both men and women. Styles keep up

★ with the times but are firmly on the safe side. **Bershka** (✉ 221–223 Oxford St., Marylebone, W1 ☎ 020/7025–6160 ⓤ Oxford Circus) aims to please younger, more street-savvy shoppers than its sister Zara, owned by the same Spanish company. **Burberry** (✉ 21–23 New Bond St., Mayfair, W1 ☎ 020/7839–5222 ⓤ Piccadilly Circus) tries to evoke English tradition, with mahogany closets and merchandise with the trademark "Burberry Check" tartan—scarves, umbrellas, shortbread tins, and those famous raincoat linings. **Daisy & Tom** (✉ 181–183 King's Rd., Chelsea, SW3 ☎ 020/7352–5000 ⓤ Sloane Sq.) is for cool kids and smart parents. On one floor are high-fashion junior clothes (Kenzo, IKKS, and Polo), shoes aplenty (for newborns to 10-year-olds), a bookshop, and a soda-fountain café. **James Lock & Co. Ltd.** (✉ 6 St. James's St., St. James, SW1 ☎ 020/7930–5849 ⓤ Green Park, Piccadilly Circus) is a cozy shop with a full selection of classic and traditional hats. **Nicole Farhi** (✉ 158 New Bond St., Mayfair, W1 ☎ 020/7499–8368 ⓤ Bond St.) makes contemporary yet timeless quality clothes that are standbys in many a working-woman's wardrobe; the men's collection is available

★ at a branch in Covent Garden. **River Island** (✉ 301–306 Oxford St., Soho, W1 ☎ 020/7799–4018 ⓤ Oxford Circus) targets young and dedicated fashion followers. Prices are low and commitment to fast fashion is high.

★ There are branches throughout town. **Topshop** (✉ 214 Oxford St., Soho, W1 ☎ 020/7636–7700 ⓤ Oxford Circus), one of the niftiest retail fashion operations for teens and women, favors top young designers. Topman is the male version of the chain.

TOP 5

- **Portobello Market.** This popular market is still the best for size, variety, and sheer street theater.

- **Harrods Food Halls.** Noisy, colorful, and tempting, the food halls have long been a favorite.

- **Liberty.** The store's historic connection with William Morris and the Arts and Crafts movement is maintained in a focus on design.

- **Selfridges.** The best department store in London has an astonishing selection of goods for the whole family.

- **Hamleys.** With floor after floor of treasures for every child on your shopping list, this is *the* London toy shop.

MENSWEAR **Favourbrook** (⊠ 55 Jermyn St., St. James's, W1 ☎ 020/7491–2337 Ⓤ Piccadilly Circus) tailors exquisite handmade vests, jackets, ties, and cummerbunds. **Ozwald Boateng** (⊠ 12A Savile Row, Mayfair, W1 ☎ 020/ 7437–0620 Ⓤ Piccadilly Circus) is one of the modern breed of bespoke tailors not on Savile Row. His made-to-measure suits are sought after by rock luminaries for their shock-color linings as well as great classic

★ cuts. **Paul Smith** (⊠ 40–44 Floral St., Covent Garden, WC2 ☎ 020/ 7379–7133 Ⓤ Covent Garden) can do the job if you don't want to look

★ outlandish but you're bored with plain pants and sober jackets. **Turnbull & Asser** (⊠ 71–72 Jermyn St., St. James's W1 ☎ 020/7808–3000 Ⓤ Piccadilly Circus) is *the* custom shirtmaker. Alas, the first order must be for a minimum of six shirts, from about £140 each. There are less expensive, still exquisite ready-to-wear shirts, too.

WOMENSWEAR **Agnès B** (⊠ 111 Fulham Rd., South Kensington, SW3 ☎ 020/7225–3477

★ Ⓤ South Kensington) has oh-so-pretty, timeless, understated French clothing. Prices are midrange and worthy for the quality. There are branches in Marylebone High Street (W1) and Heath Street, Hampstead

★ (NW3); Floral Street (WC2) has elegant men's suits. **Browns** (⊠ 23–27 South Molton St., Mayfair, W1 ☎ 020/7491–7833 Ⓤ Bond St.), the first notable store to populate the South Molton Street pedestrian mall, seems to sprout offshoots every time you visit. Well-established designers (Donna Karan, Romeo Gigli, Jasper Conran) rub shoulder pads here with funkier names (Dries van Noten, Jean Paul Gaultier, Hussein Chalayan). The July and January sales are famous. **Jigsaw** (⊠ 126–127 New Bond St., Mayfair, W1 ☎ 020/7491–4484 Ⓤ Bond St.) wins points for its reasonably priced separates, which don't sacrifice quality for fashion and suit women in their twenties to forties. **Jimmy Choo** (⊠ 32 Sloane St., Knightsbridge, SW1 ☎ 020/7823–1051 Ⓤ Knightsbridge), the name on every supermodel's and fashion editor's feet, creates exquisite, elegant shoes; nothing is less than £100.

★ **Koh Samui** (⊠ 65 Monmouth St., Covent Garden, WC2 ☎ 020/ 7240–4280 Ⓤ Covent Garden) stocks the clothing of about 40 hot young designers. Discover the next fashion wave before *Vogue* gets there. **Vivienne Westwood** (⊠ 6 Davies St., Mayfair, W1 ☎ 020/7629–3757 Ⓤ Bond St.), one of the top British designers, produces Pompadour-punk ball gowns, Lady Hamilton vest coats, and foppish getups that still represent the apex of high-style British couture. **Zara** (⊠ 65 Duke of York's Sq., King's Rd., Chelsea, SW3 ☎ 020/7901–8700 Ⓤ Sloane Sq.) has swept Europe. The style is young and snappy, and the prices are low. Don't expect durability—these are fun pieces, for men and kids, too. There are branches around town.

Crafts

Crafts Council Gallery Shop (⊠ 44A Pentonville Rd., Islington, N1 ☎ 020/ 7806–2559 Ⓤ Angel) showcases a microcosm of British crafts—jewelry, glass, ceramics, and toys. A gallery at the V&A Museum has a selec-

★ tion of offerings. The **Lesley Craze Gallery** (⊠ 33–35 Clerkenwell Green, East End, EC1 ☎ 020/7251–9200 Ⓤ Farringdon) carries exquisite jewelry by some 100 young British designers. The adjacent Two gallery specializes in nonprecious metals and sumptuous scarves and textiles. **Linley**

(✉ 60 Pimlico Rd., Chelsea, SW1 ☎ 020/7730–7300 Ⓤ Sloane Sq.) is the outpost for Viscount Linley—the Queen's nephew and one of the finest furniture designers today. The large pieces are expensive, but small desk accessories and objets d'art are available. **London Glassblowing Workshop** (✉ 7 The Leathermarket, Weston St., South Bank, SE1 ☎ 020/7403–2800 Ⓤ London Bridge) showcases glassblowers and designers who make decorative and practical pieces on-site. On weekdays you can see them at work, and buy or commission your own variation. In the Leathermarket are other craftspeople, most notably a silversmith and papermaker. **OXO Tower** (✉ Bargehouse St., South Bank, SE1 ☎ 020/7401–2255 Ⓤ Southwark) holds shops and studios, open Tuesday through Sunday 11 to 6, that sell excellent handmade goods. At Gabriel's Wharf, a few steps farther west along the river, a collection of craftspeople sell porcelain, jewelry, clothes, and more.

Gifts

Cath Kidston (✉ 8 Clarendon Cross, Notting Hill, W11 ☎ 020/7221–4000 Ⓤ Notting Hill Gate) translates fresh ginghams and flower-sprig cotton prints into nightclothes, bed linens, and bath wear. There are also cozy hand-knit sweaters, skirts in flouncy wools, and a children's-wear line. **The Cross** (✉ 141 Portland Rd., Notting Hill, W11 ☎ 020/7727–6760 Ⓤ Notting Hill Gate), is big with the high-style crowd, thanks to its hedonistic, beautiful things: silk scarves, brocade bags, and jeweled baubles. *Fodor'sChoice* ★ **Floris** (✉ 89 Jermyn St., St. James's, W1 ☎ 020/7930–2885 Ⓤ Piccadilly Circus) is one of London's most beautiful shops, with 19th-century glass and mahogany showcases filled with swan's-down powder puffs, cutglass bottles, and faux tortoiseshell combs. *Fodor'sChoice* ★ **Fortnum & Mason** (✉ 181 Piccadilly, St. James's, W1 ☎ 020/7734–8040 Ⓤ Piccadilly Circus), the Queen's grocer, is, paradoxically, the most egalitarian of gift stores, with plenty of luxury foods, stamped with the gold "By Appointment" crest, for less than £5. Try the teas, preserves, tins of pâté, or turtle soup. **General Trading Company** (✉ 2 Symons St., Sloane Sq., Chelsea, SW3 ☎ 020/7730–0411 Ⓤ Sloane Sq.) "does" just about every upper-class wedding gift list, but caters also to slimmer pockets with its merchandise shipped *Fodor'sChoice* ★ from far shores but moored securely to English taste. **Hamleys** (✉ 188–196 Regent St., Soho, W1 ☎ 0870/333–2455 Ⓤ Oxford Circus) is at the top of every London childs' wish list. A Regent Street institution, the shop has demonstrations, a play area, a café, and every cool toy on the planet. **Les Senteurs** (✉ 71 Elizabeth St., Belgravia, SW1 ☎ 020/7730–2322 Ⓤ Sloane Sq.), an intimate, unglossy gem of a perfumery, sells little-known yet timeless fragrances, such as Creed, worn by Eugenie, wife of Emperor Napoléon III. **Lush** (✉ Unit 11, the Piazza, Covent Garden, WC2 ☎ 020/7240–4570 Ⓤ Covent Garden) is crammed with fresh, very ★ wacky, handmade cosmetics. **Penhaligon's** (✉ 41 Wellington St., Covent Garden, WC2 ☎ 020/7836–2150 Ⓤ Covent Garden), established by William Penhaligon, court barber to Queen Victoria, was perfumer to Lord Rothschild and Winston Churchill. The **Tea House** (✉ 15A Neal St., Covent Garden, WC2 ☎ 020/7240–7539 Ⓤ Covent Garden) purveys everything to do with the British national drink. Dispatch your gift list here with "teaphernalia"—strainers, trivets, infusers, and such.

Jewelry

★ **Asprey** (⊠ 167 New Bond St., Mayfair, W1 ☎ 020/7493–6767 Ⓤ Bond St.), described as the "classiest and most luxurious shop in the world,"

Fodor'sChoice offers exquisite jewelry and gifts, both antique and modern. **Butler & Wil-**
★ **son** (⊠ 189 Fulham Rd., Chelsea, SW3 ☎ 020/7352–3045 Ⓤ South Kensington) has irresistible retro costume jewelry and is strong on diamanté, jet, and French gilt. You can also find nostalgic gowns here. There's another branch at 189 Fulham Road, South Kensington, SW3. **Dinny Hall** (⊠ 200 Westbourne Grove, Notting Hill, W11 ☎ 020/7792–3913 Ⓤ Notting Hill Gate) sells simple designs in gold and silver, including dainty gold and diamond earrings or chokers with delicate curls. There's another branch at 54 Fulham Road, SW3. **Garrard** (⊠ 24 Albemarle St., Mayfair, W1 ☎ 020/7758–8520 Ⓤ Bond St.), after sharing premises with Asprey, has returned to its original site; Jade Jagger is the designer employed by the company to draw in the younger market. Garrard is the royal jeweler, in charge of the upkeep of the Crown Jewels.

Prints

Besides print stores, browse around the gallery shops, such as those at the Tate Britain and Tate Modern. In the open air, try hunting around Waterloo Bridge along the Riverside Walk Market, at St. James's Craft Market at St. James's Church in Piccadilly, and at the Apple Market near
★ the Piazza, Covent Garden. **Grosvenor Prints** (⊠ 19 Shelton St., Covent Garden, WC2 ☎ 020/7836–1979 Ⓤ Covent Garden) sells antiquarian prints, with an emphasis on views and architecture of London—and dogs. The **Map House** (⊠ 54 Beauchamp Pl., Knightsbridge, SW3 ☎ 020/ 7589–4325 Ⓤ Knightsbridge) has antique maps in all price ranges, and fine reproductions of maps and prints, especially of botanical subjects and cityscapes.

Street Markets

★ **Bermondsey** is the market the dealers frequent for small antiques, which gives you an idea of its scope. The real bargains start going at 4 AM, but there'll be a few left if you arrive later. Take Bus 15 or 25 to Aldgate, then Bus 42 over Tower Bridge to Bermondsey Square; or take the tube to London Bridge and walk. ⊠ *Long La. and Bermondsey Sq., South Bank, SE1* ⊙ *Fri. 4 AM–noon* Ⓤ *London Bridge.*

★ **Borough Market,** a foodie's delight, carries whole-grain, organic everything, mainly from Britain but with an international flavor. ⊠ *Borough High St., South Bank, SE1* ⊙ *Fri. noon–4:30, Sat. 9–4* Ⓤ *London Bridge, Borough.*

Camden Passage is hugged by curio stores and is dripping with jewelry, silverware, and other antiques. Saturday and Wednesday are when the stalls go up; the rest of the week, only the stores are open. Bus 19 or 38 or the tube will get you there. Despite the name, it's not in Camden but a couple of miles away in Islington. ⊠ *Off Upper St., Islington, N1* ⊙ *Wed. 10–2, Sat. 10–5* Ⓤ *Angel.*

Covent Garden has craft stalls, jewelry designers, clothes makers, potters, and other artisans, who congregate in the undercover central area known as the Apple Market. The Jubilee Market, toward Southampton Street, is less classy (printed T-shirts and the like), but on Monday the selection of vintage collectibles is worthwhile. This is more of a tourist magnet than other markets, and prices may reflect this. ⊠ *The Piazza, Covent Garden, WC2* ⊗ *Daily 9–5* Ⓤ *Covent Garden.*

Fodor'sChoice **Portobello Market,** London's most famous market, still wins the prize for
★ the all-round best. There are 1,500 antiques dealers here, so bargains are still possible. Nearer Notting Hill Gate, prices and quality are highest; the middle is where locals buy fruit and vegetables and hang out in trendy restaurants. Under the Westway elevated highway is a great flea market, and more bric-a-brac and bargains appear as you walk toward Golborne Road. Take Bus 52 or the tube here. ⊠ *Portobello Rd., Notting Hill, W11* ⊗ *Fruit and vegetables Mon.–Wed. and Fri. 8–5, Thurs. 8–1; antiques Fri. 8–3; food market and antiques Sat. 6–4:30* Ⓤ *Ladbroke Grove, Notting Hill Gate.*

Spitalfields, an old 3-acre indoor fruit market near Petticoat Lane, has turned into Trendsville, with crafts and design shops. It also has food and clothes stalls, cafés, and performance areas. On Sunday the place comes alive, with stalls selling antique clothing, handmade rugs, and cookware. The resident stores have lovely things for body and home. For refreshment, you can eat anything from tapas to Thai. ⊠ *Brushfield St., East End, E1* ⊗ *Organic market Fri. and Sun. 10–5; general market weekdays 11–3, Sun. 10–5* Ⓤ *Liverpool St., Aldgate, Aldgate East.*

LONDON ESSENTIALS

Transportation

BY AIR

AIRPORTS & TRANSFERS London has excellent bus and train connections between its airports and downtown. For information about Heathrow, Gatwick, Stansted, and Luton airports, *see* Airports *in* Essentials. Airport Travel Line has information on transfers between Heathrow and Gatwick and into London by bus. However, you may be directed to the numbers listed below. The Transport for London Web site has helpful information.

HEATHROW From Heathrow, the cheapest route into London is via the Piccadilly Line of the Underground. Trains on the tube run every 4 to 8 minutes from all four terminals; the 50-minute trip costs £4.30 one-way and connects with London's extensive tube system. The first train departs at around 5:13 AM (Sunday 5:57 AM) from Terminals 1, 2, 3, and 4; the last train departs from the airport at 11:49 PM (11:30 PM Sunday). The quickest way into London is the Heathrow Express train, which takes 15 minutes to and from Paddington Station in the city center; it's a main hub on the Underground. One-way tickets cost £15 for standard-express class (£26 round-trip). Daily service departs every 15 minutes from Terminals 1, 2, and 3 from around 5:12 AM (Sunday 5:08 AM), and from Terminal 4 from 5:07 AM (5:03 AM Sunday) to 12:06 AM for Terminals 1, 2, and 3, and 12:01 AM for Terminal 4.

Bus service to London is available from the Heathrow Central Bus Station. National Express A2 service costs £8 one-way, £15 round-trip; travel time is about one hour and 40 minutes. Buses leave for King's Cross and Euston, with stops at Marble Arch and Russell Square, every 30 minutes 5:30 AM to 9:45 PM from Terminal 4, 5:45 AM to 10:08 PM from Terminal 3, but can be tedious because there are more than a dozen stops en route. National Express buses leave every 30 minutes 5:40 AM to 9:35 PM to Victoria Coach Station from Heathrow Central Bus Station—connected to arrival terminals by a pedestrian underpass, and next to Heathrow Underground Station for Terminals 1–3: cost is £8 one-way.

GATWICK The Underground does not reach all the way to Gatwick, 27 mi south of the city, so your options there are slightly more limited. You can take regular commuter train service to London Bridge and Victoria stations (approximately £11 one way), or in the opposite direction to Brighton, but it can be crowded. At the best of times there is little room for baggage. During rush hour harried commuters can be impatient with weary air travelers, and you can find yourself standing up all the way. The better option is the fast, nonstop Gatwick Express train that leaves the airport approximately every 15 minutes from 4:35 AM to 1:35 AM. The 30-minute trip costs £13 one-way standard express, £24.50 round-trip. Hourly bus service runs from Gatwick's south terminal to Victoria Station in the city center, with stops along the way at Hooley, Coulsdon, Mitcham, Streatham, Stockwell, and Pimlico. The journey takes 90 minutes and costs £11 one-way. Make sure you get on a direct bus not requiring a change—otherwise the journey could take hours.

STANSTED Stansted, 35 mi northeast of London, serves mainly European destinations. The 45-minute journey on Stansted Express to Liverpool Street Station (with a stop at Tottenham Hale) runs every 15 minutes 8 AM to 5 PM weekdays, and every 30 minutes 5 PM to midnight and 6 AM to 8 AM weekdays, and all day on weekends. The trip costs £14.50 one-way, £24 round-trip. By bus, there's hourly service on National Express Airport bus A6 (24 hours a day) to Victoria Coach Station. The journey costs £10 one-way, £15 round-trip, and takes about 1 hour and 40 minutes. Stops include Golders Green, Finchley Road, St. John's Wood, Baker Street, Marble Arch, and Hyde Park Corner.

LUTON From Luton (30 mi north of London), which, like Stansted, serves mainly British and European airlines, you can take a free shuttle to the nearby Luton Airport Parkway Station, from which you can take a train or bus into London. The Thameslink train service runs to several London stations, terminating at King's Cross Thameslink—an adjunct station about six blocks from the main King's Cross station. It's not the ideal station to arrive in if you're unfamiliar with London, as virtually no signs direct you to the main King's Cross station, and the neighborhood is not good. However, if you're continuing to your hotel by tube, you can walk through a connecting underground tunnel from the platforms. This is the better option. If you're going to walk to the main King's

1

Cross Station, or if you need a taxi, ask one of the station guards for help. Do not strike out blindly on foot—the neighborhood is notorious for muggings and other petty crimes. The journey from Luton to King's Cross Thameslink Station takes about 35 minutes. Trains leave every 10 minutes or so 24 hours a day and cost £10.70 one-way, £19 round-trip. For a cheaper journey, take the Green Line 757 bus service from Luton to Victoria Station. It runs three times an hour, takes about 90 minutes, and costs around £8.

TAXIS If you are thinking of taking a taxi from Heathrow and Gatwick, remember that they can get caught in traffic; the trip from Heathrow, for example, can take more than an hour and costs about £35. From Gatwick, the taxi fare is about £75; the ride takes about an hour and 20 minutes. From Stansted, the £75 journey takes a little over an hour. From Luton, the approximately one-hour journey should cost around £65. Your hotel may be able to recommend a car service for airport transfers; charges are usually about £35 to any of the airports. Add a tip of 10% to 15% to the basic fare.

BETWEEN For transfers between airports, allow at least two to three hours. The
AIRPORTS cheapest option is public transportation: from Gatwick to Stansted, for instance, you can catch the nonexpress commuter train from Gatwick to Victoria Station in London, take the tube to Liverpool Street Station, then catch the train to Stansted from there. To get from Heathrow to Gatwick by public transport, take the tube to King's Cross, then change to the Victoria Line, get to Victoria Station, and take the commuter train to Gatwick. Both of these trips would take about two hours.

The National Express Airport bus is the most direct option between Gatwick and Heathrow. Buses pick up passengers every 15 minutes from 5 AM to 10 PM from both airports. The trip takes 1½ to 2 hours, and the fare is £17.50 one-way, £35 round-trip. It's advisable to book tickets in advance via National Express, especially during peak travel seasons, but you can buy also tickets in the terminals. National Express also runs shuttles between all the other airports, except between Luton and Stansted. Finally, some airlines may offer shuttle services as well—check with your travel agent in advance of your journey.

TICKETS & You can get discounts on many tickets if you book on the Internet. The
INFORMATION Web site for British Airports Authority has links to all the previously mentioned services, with fare details and timetables.

🚩 **Taxis & Shuttles Airport Travel Line** ☎ 0870/574-7777. **British Airports Authority** ⊕ www.baa.co.uk. **Gatwick Express** ☎ 0845/850-1530 ⊕ www.gatwickexpress. co.uk. **Heathrow Express** ☎ 0845/600-1515 ⊕ www.heathrowexpress.co.uk. **National Express** ☎ 0870/580-8080 ⊕ www.nationalexpress.com. **Stansted Express** ☎ 0845/ 850-0150 ⊕ www.stanstedexpress.co.uk. **Transport for London** ☎ 020/7222-1234 ⊕ www.tfl.gov.uk.

BY BUS

Buses, or "coaches," as long-distance services are known, operate mainly from London's Victoria Coach Station to more than 1,200 major towns and cities. Buses are about half as expensive as the train, but trips can take twice as long. For information, *see* By Bus *in* Essentials.

BUS TRAVEL
WITHIN LONDON
In central London, Transport for London (TfL) buses are traditionally bright red double- and single-deckers, although there are now many privately owned buses of different colors. Not all buses run the full length of their route at all times, so check with the driver (ask as you board whether the bus travels to your destination). In central London you must purchase tickets from machines at bus stops along the routes before you board. Bus stops are clearly indicated: the main stops have a red TfL symbol on a white background. When the word REQUEST is written across the sign, you must flag the bus down. Buses are a good way to see the town, but don't take one if you're in a hurry.

London is divided into six concentric zones for tube fares: the more zones you cross, the higher the fare. The same is not true for buses, as a flat-rate fare of £1.50 applies for all bus fares. If you have a prepaid Oystercard (purchase at any tube station) the fare is only 80p. A One-Day Bus Pass for zones one through four is £3.50 (a seven-day pass is £13) but must be bought before boarding the bus, from one of the machines at bus stops, most newsstands, or Underground stations.

If you're traveling on the tube as well as the bus, consider acquiring an Oystercard (an electronic smart card that you can load with as much money as you like; money is then deducted each time you use the card) or getting an off-peak one-day Travelcard (£5.30), which allows unrestricted travel on buses *and* tubes after 9:30 AM and all day on weekends and national holidays. "Peak" travelcards—those for use before 9:30 AM—are more expensive (£7.20). Kids travel free on weekends and public holidays but may be required to show proof of age for 14 to 15 years. If you're planning in advance, you can get a Visitor Travelcard— these are similar to Day Travelcards with the bonus of a booklet of money-off vouchers to major attractions (available only in the United States and Canada, for three, four, and seven days). Visitor Travelcards are available from BritRail or Rail Europe.

Traveling without a valid ticket makes you liable for an on-the-spot fine (£10 at the time of this writing), so always pay your fare before you travel. For more information, there are Transport for London Travel Information Centres at the following tube stations: Euston, Liverpool Street, Piccadilly Circus, Victoria, and Heathrow. Most are open in daytime only; call for hours.

Night Buses can prove helpful when traveling in London from 11 PM to 5 AM—these buses add the prefix "N" to their route numbers and don't run as frequently or operate on quite as many routes as day buses. You may have to transfer at one of the Night Bus nexuses: Victoria, Westminster, and either Piccadilly Circus or Trafalgar Square. For safety reasons, avoid sitting alone on the top deck of a Night Bus.

FARES &
SCHEDULES
🚆 **BritRail** ☎ 877/677–1066 in U.S. ⊕ www.britrail.net. **Rail Europe** ☎ 888/274–8724 ⊕ www.raileurope.com. **Transport for London** ☎ 020/7222–1234 ⊕ www.tfl.gov.uk.

BY CAR
The major approach roads to London are motorways (six-lane highways; look for an "M" followed by a number) or "A" roads; the latter may

be "dual carriageways" (divided highways), or two-lane highways. Motorways (from Heathrow, M4; from Gatwick, M23 to M25, then M3; Stansted, M11) are usually the faster option for getting in and out of town, although rush-hour traffic is horrendous. Stay tuned to local radio stations for regular traffic updates.

The simple advice about driving in London is: don't. Because the city grew as a series of villages, there was never a central street plan, and the result is a chaotic winding mass, made no easier by the one-way street systems. If you must drive in London, remember to drive on the left and stick to the speed limit (30 mph on most city streets).

An £8 "congestion charge" is levied on all vehicles entering central London (bounded by the Inner Ring Road; street signs and "C" road markings note the area) on weekdays from 7 AM to 6:30 PM, excluding bank holidays. Pay in advance or on that day until 10 PM if you're entering the central zone. You can pay by phone, mail, or Internet, or at retail outlets (look for signs indicating how and where you can pay). There are no tollbooths; cameras monitor the area. The penalty for not paying is stiff: £80 (£40 for prompt payment). For current information, check ⊕ www.cclondon.com.

BY TAXI

Taxis are expensive, but if you're with several people, they can be practical. Hotels and main tourist areas have taxi ranks; you can also hail taxis on the street. If the yellow FOR HIRE sign is lighted on top, the taxi is available. Drivers often cruise at night with their signs unlighted, so if you see an unlighted cab, keep your hand up. The fare structure is complicated, but generally fares start at £2.20 and increase by units of 20p (per 125 to 191 yards or 24.5 to 37.6 seconds) after a certain initial distance, which ranges from about 250 yards (late nights) to 381 yards (6 AM to 8 PM on weekdays). Surcharges are added around Christmas and New Year's days. Tips are extra, usually 10% to 15% per ride.

BY TRAIN

London has 15 major train stations, each serving a different area of the country, all accessible by Underground or bus. The once-national British Rail is now private companies, under National Rail, but there is a central rail information number. For further information on train travel, *see* By Train *in* Essentials.

🚆 **National Rail Enquiries** ☎ 0845/748-4950 ⊕ www.nationalrail.co.uk.

BY UNDERGROUND (TUBE)

London's extensive Underground (tube) system has color-coded routes, clear signage, and extensive connections. Trains run out into the suburbs, and all stations are marked with the London Underground circular symbol. (In Britain, the word "subway" means "pedestrian underpass.") Trains are all one class; smoking is *not* allowed on board or in the stations. Some lines have branches (Central, District, Northern, Metropolitan, and Piccadilly), so be sure to note which branch is needed for your destination. Electronic platform signs tell you the final stop and route of the next train and how many minutes until it arrives. The zippy Docklands Light Railway runs through the Docklands with an extension to Greenwich.

London is divided into six concentric zones (ask at Underground ticket booths for a map and booklet, which give details of the ticket options). Most tourist sights are within zone 1, but some are not—Kew Gardens, for example, is in zone 4. If you inadvertently travel into a zone for which you do not have the right ticket, you can purchase an "extension" to your own ticket at the ticket office by the barriers. This usually costs less than a pound, and merely equalizes your fare. As with buses, the cheapest way to travel is to register for an Oystercard (the city's electronic transport smart card) at any tube station. You then pay in as much as you want (usually £20), and your transport fees are deducted each time you use the card on a bus or tube. Your charges are capped at the amount of a one-day travelcard for the zones in which you've traveled. Alternatively, you can buy a travelcard (one-day or weekly) at any tube station. These allow unlimited travel on tubes, commuter trains, and buses within the zones you choose (1–2, or 1–4 usually). The most expensive way to travel is by buying single fares for each leg of the journey. A single journey by tube costs £3 within zone 1 without an Oystercard, and £1.50 with an Oystercard. Note: all these fares increase regularly. For more information, including discount passes, *see By Bus, above.*

The tube begins running just after 5 AM Monday through Saturday; the last services leave central London between midnight and 12:30 AM. On Sunday, trains start two hours later and finish about an hour earlier. Frequency of trains depends on the route and the time of day, but normally you should not have to wait more than 10 minutes in central areas. Most tube stations are not accessible for people with disabilities. Travelers with disabilities should get the free leaflet "Access to the Underground," which lists the stations that are.

🚇 **Transport for London** ☎ 020/7222-1234 ⊕ www.tfl.gov.uk.

Contacts & Resources

ADDRESSES
Central London and its surrounding districts are divided into 32 boroughs—33, counting the City of London. More useful for finding your way around, however, are the subdivisions of London into postal districts. The first one or two letters give the location: N means north, NW means northwest, etc. The numbers aren't quite as helpful—you won't, for example, find W2 next to W3, but the general rule is that the lower numbers, such as W1 or SW1, are closest to the city center. Abbreviated (for general location) or full (for mailing information) postal codes are given for many listings in this chapter. Neighborhood names are also provided.

DISCOUNTS & DEALS
All national collections (such as the Natural History Museum, Science Museum, Victoria & Albert Museum) are free, a real bargain for museumgoers. The London Pass, a smart card, offers entry to more than 50 top attractions, such as museums and tours on boats and buses. The

1

charge is £29 for one day, which can be reduced to £12 per day if a weekly pass is bought. There are optional discounts on travel and restaurants for a higher daily charge. London Pass is available by phone, online, or from the Britain Visitor Centre and Tourist Information Centre branches. For other discounts, *see* Resources *in* Getting Started *in* Essentials.

🗗 **London Pass** ☎ 0870/242-9988 ⊕ www.londonpass.com.

EMERGENCIES

For hospitals in London that provide free 24-hour accident and emergency facilities, the following are listed: in the west of London is Charing Cross Hospital; in the city center is University College Hospital; to the north of the center is the Royal Free Hospital; and on the South Bank of the city center is St. Thomas's Hospital. Bliss Chemist is open daily 9 AM to midnight. NHS Direct offers 24-hour general expert medical advice from the National Health Service. In addition, many main-street branches of Boots, a pharmacy chain, stay open late in rotation.

🗗 **Emergency Services Ambulance, fire, police** ☎ **999. NHS Direct** ☎ 0845/4647.
🗗 **Hospitals Charing Cross Hospital** ⊠ Fulham Palace Rd., Hammersmith, W6 ☎ 020/8846-1234. **Royal Free Hospital** ⊠ Pond St., Hampstead Hampstead, NW3 ☎ 020/7794-0500. **St. Thomas's Hospital** ⊠ Lambeth Palace Rd., South Bank, SE1 ☎ 020/7928-9292. **University College Hospital** ⊠ Grafton Way, Bloomsbury, WC1 ☎ 020/7387-9300.
🗗 **Late-Night Pharmacies Bliss Chemist** ⊠ 5 Marble Arch, Bayswater, W1 ☎ 020/7723-6116.

TOUR OPTIONS

BOAT TOURS In summer, narrow boats and barges cruise London's two canals, the Grand Union and Regent's Canal. Most vessels operate on the latter, which runs between Little Venice in the west (the nearest tube is Warwick Avenue on the Bakerloo Line) and Camden Lock (about 200 yards north of Camden Town tube station). Jason's Trip operates one-way and round-trip narrow-boat cruises on this route. The London Waterbus Company operates this route year-round with a stop at London Zoo: trips run daily April through October and weekends only November through March. Canal Cruises offers three or four cruises daily March through October on the *Jenny Wren* and all year on the cruising restaurant *My Fair Lady* from Walker's Quay, Camden.

Boats cruise the Thames throughout the year, with services for both commuters and tourists; it's a great way to see the city. Most leave from Westminster Pier, Charing Cross Pier, and Tower Pier. Downstream routes go to the Tower of London, Greenwich, and the Thames Barrier; upstream destinations include Kew, Richmond, and Hampton Court. Depending on the destination, river trips may last from 30 minutes to 4 hours. For trips downriver from Charing Cross to Greenwich Pier and historic Greenwich, call Catamaran Cruisers or Westminster Passenger Services (which runs the same route from Westminster Pier). Thames Cruises goes to Greenwich and onward to the Thames Barrier. Westminster Passenger Service (Upriver) runs through summer to Kew and Hampton Court from Westminster Pier. A Rail and River Rover ticket combines the modern wonders of Canary Wharf and Docklands development by Docklands Light Railway with the historic riverside by boat. Tickets are available year-round from Westminster, Tower, and Greenwich piers, and Dockland Light Railway stations. Transport for London (⇨ Bus Travel, *above*) should be able to give information on all companies.

🛈 **Canal Cruises** ☎ 020/7485-4433 ⊕ www.walkersquay.com. **Catamaran Cruisers** ☎ 020/7987-1185 ⊕ www.catamarancruisers.co.uk. **Jason's Trip** ☎ 020/7286-3428 ⊕ www.jasons.co.uk. **DLR Rail and River Rover** ☎ 020/7363-9700 ⊕ www.tfl.gov.uk. **Thames Cruises** ☎ 020/7930-3373. **Westminster Passenger Services** ☎ 020/7930-4097. **Westminster Passenger Service (Upriver)** ☎ 020/7930-2062 ⊕ www.wpsa.co.uk.

BUS TOURS Guided sightseeing tours provide a good introduction to the city from double-decker buses, which are open-top in summer. Tours run daily and depart from Haymarket, Baker Street, Grosvenor Gardens, Marble Arch, and Victoria. You may board or get off at any of about 21 stops to view the sights, and then get back on the next bus. Tickets (£16 to £20) may be bought from the driver; several companies run tours. The Original London Sightseeing Tour also offers frequent daily tours and has informative staff on easily recognizable double-decker buses. Tours depart from 8:30 AM from Baker Street (Madame Tussaud's), Marble Arch (Speakers' Corner), Piccadilly (Haymarket), or Victoria (Victoria Street) around every 12 minutes (less often outside peak summer season). The Big Bus Company runs a similar operation with a Red and Blue tour. The Red is a two-hour tour with 18 stops, and the Blue, one hour with 13. Both start from Marble Arch, Speakers' Corner. Evan Evans offers good bus tours that also visit major sights just outside the city. Another reputable agency for bus tours is Golden Tours/Frames Rickards.

Green Line, Evan Evans, and Frames Rickards offer day excursions by bus to places within easy reach of London, such as Hampton Court, Oxford, Stratford, and Bath.

🛈 **Big Bus Company** ☎ 020/7233-9533 ⊕ www.bigbustours.com. **Evan Evans** ☎ 020/7950-1777 ⊕ www.evanevans.co.uk. **Golden Tours/Frames Rickards** ☎ 020/7233-7030, 800/548-7083 in U.S. ⊕ www.goldentours.co.uk. **Green Line** ☎ 0870/608-7261 ⊕ www.greenline.co.uk. **Original London Sightseeing Tour** ☎ 020/8877-1722 ⊕ www.theoriginaltour.com.

PRIVATE GUIDES Black Taxi Tour of London is a personal tour by cab direct from your hotel. The price is per cab, so the fare can be shared among as many as five people. An introductory two-hour tour is £80 by day, £85 by night. You can hire a Blue Badge–accredited guide (trained by the tourist board) for walking or driving tours.

🛈 **Black Taxi Tour of London** ☎ 020/7935-9363 ⊕ www.blacktaxitours.co.uk. **Blue Badge tour guides** ☎ 020/7403-1115 ⊕ www.blue-badge-guides.com.

WALKING TOURS One of the best ways to get to know London is on foot. Original London Walks has theme tours devoted to the Beatles, Sherlock Holmes, Dickens, Jack the Ripper—you name it (yes, the *Da Vinci Code,* too). If horror and mystery are your interest, then the City holds plenty of that, as you may discover on a Blood and Tears tour (not suitable for younger children). Tour Guides provides themed historic walks led by accredited Blue Badge guides. Peruse the leaflets at a London Tourist Information Centre for special-interest walks.

🚶 **Blood and Tears Walk** ☎ 020/7625-5155. **Original London Walks** ☎ 020/7624-3978 ⊕ www.walks.com. **Tour Guides/Blue Badge** ☎ 020/7495-5504 ⊕ www.tourguides.co.uk.

VISITOR INFORMATION

The main London Tourist Information Centre at Victoria Station Forecourt is open in summer, Monday through Saturday 8 to 7 and Sunday 8 to 5; winter, Monday through Saturday 8 to 6 and Sunday 8:30 to 4; also at Heathrow Airport (Terminals 1, 2, and 3). Britain and London Visitor Centre, open weekdays 9:30 to 6:30, weekends 10 to 4, provides details about travel, accommodations, and entertainment for the whole of Britain, but you need to visit the center in person. VisitLondon, the city's tourist board, has a helpful Web site with links to other sites; you can also book a hotel on the site, with a best-price guarantee.

🚶 **Britain and London Visitor Centre** ✉ 1 Regent St., Piccadilly Circus, St. James's, SW1Y 4NX ☎ No phone ⊕ www.visitbritain.com. **London Tourist Information Centre** ✉ Victoria Station Forecourt, Victoria ☎ No phone. **VisitLondon** ⊕ www.visitlondon.com.

The Southeast

CANTERBURY, DOVER, BRIGHTON, TUNBRIDGE WELLS

WORD OF MOUTH

"One terrific day would be Dover/Walmer/Deal. Dover Castle takes at least half a day but Walmer and Deal Castles are very close, so you can easily do all three in one day—and all are covered by the Great British Heritage Pass. Walmer and Deal were both built by Henry VIII. Deal is a fascinating round defensive castle. Walmer . . . was converted to a grand family home with gorgeous gardens."

—janis

"I'm in the camp of those who really enjoy Brighton—the pier, beach, Lanes, and especially the Royal Pavilion. In the summer the waterfront is kitschy and fun, in the winter melancholy and atmospheric."

—John

Updated by
Christi
Daugherty

IN AN ERA WHEN EVERYTHING SMALL IS FASHIONABLE, from cell phones to digital cameras, the Southeast will inevitably have great appeal. Where ancient hedgerows have been allowed to stand, this is still a landscape of small-scale features and pleasant hills. Viewed from the air, the tiny fields, neatly hedged, form a patchwork quilt. On the ground, once away from the motorways and London commuter tract housing, the Southeast, including Surrey, Kent, and Sussex, East and West, reveals some of England's loveliest countryside. Gentle hills and woodlands are punctuated with farms and storybook villages rooted in history and with cathedral cities waiting to be explored. Rivers wind down to a coast that is alternately sweeping chalk cliff and seaside resort. This area, farthest from the unpredictable influences of the Atlantic, is England at its warmest. Fruit trees and even vineyards flourish in archetypal English landscapes and, often, atypical English sunshine.

Although it is close to London and is one of the most densely populated areas of Britain, the Southeast includes Kent, the "Garden of England." Fields of hops and acre upon acre of orchards burst into a mass of pink and white blossoms in spring and stretch away into the distance, though even here large-scale modern farming has done much to homogenize the landscape. In the Southeast, too, are ancient Canterbury, site of the mother cathedral of England, and Dover, whose chalky white cliffs and brooding castle have become symbols of Britain. Castles and stately homes, such as Petworth House and Knole, are found throughout the region.

Famous seaside towns and resorts dot the coasts of Sussex and Kent, the most famous being that eccentric combination of carnival and culture, Brighton, site of 19th-century England's own Xanadu, the Royal Pavilion. Also on the coast, the busy ports of Newhaven, Folkestone, Dover, and Ramsgate have served for centuries as gateways to continental Europe. The Channel Tunnel, linking Britain to France by rail, runs from near Folkestone.

Indeed, because the English Channel is at its narrowest here, a great deal of British history has been forged in the Southeast. The Romans landed in this area and stayed to rule Britain for four centuries. So did the Saxons—Sussex means "the land of the South Saxons." William ("the Conqueror") of Normandy defeated the Saxons at a battle near Hastings in 1066. Canterbury has been the seat of the Primate of All England, the Archbishop of Canterbury, since Pope Gregory the Great dispatched St. Augustine to convert the heathen hordes of Britain in 597. And long before any of these invaders, the ancient Britons blazed trails that formed the routes for today's modern highways.

Exploring the Southeast

For sightseeing purposes, the Southeast can be divided into four sections. The eastern part of the region takes in the cathedral town of Canterbury, as well as the port city of Dover. The next section stretches along the southern coast from Rye to Lewes. A third area reaches from the coastal city of Brighton west to Chichester. The fourth section takes in the spa town of Royal Tunbridge Wells and western Kent, where the farmland is dotted with stately homes and castles. The larger towns can be easily reached by train or bus from London for a day trip. To visit most castles, grand country homes or quiet villages, though, you will need a car.

About the Restaurants

If you're in a seaside town, look for that great British staple, fish-and-chips. Perhaps "look" isn't the word—just follow your nose. In all the coastal areas, seafood, much of it locally caught, is a specialty. You can try local smoked fish (haddock and mackerel), or the succulent local oysters. Inland, sample fresh local lamb and beef. In cities such as Brighton and Tunbridge Wells, there are numerous restaurants and cafés to choose from, but out in the countryside your options will be more limited.

About the Hotels

All around the coast, resort towns stretch along beaches, their hotels standing cheek by jowl. Of the smaller hotels and guesthouses, only a few remain open year-round; most do business only from mid-April to September or October. Some hotels have all-inclusive rates for a week's stay, which is cheaper than taking room and meals by the day.

WHAT IT COSTS In pounds				
£££££	**££££**	**£££**	**££**	**£**
RESTAURANTS over £22	£18–£22	£13–£17	£7–£12	under £7
HOTELS over £160	£120–£160	£90–£119	£60–£89	under £60

Restaurant prices are for a main course at dinner. Hotel prices are for two people in a standard double room in high season, including V.A.T., with no meals or, if indicated, CP (with continental breakfast), BP (Breakfast Plan, with full breakfast), or MAP (Modified American Plan, with breakfast and dinner).

Timing

Because the counties of Kent, Surrey, and Sussex offer marvelous scenic landscapes, lovers of the open air will want to get their fill of the many outdoor attractions here. Most privately owned castles and mansions are open only between April and September or October, so it's best to tour the Southeast in the spring, summer, or early fall. Failing that, the great parks surrounding the stately houses are often open all year. If crowds tend to spoil your fun, avoid August, Sunday, and national holidays, particularly in Canterbury and the seaside towns.

CANTERBURY TO DOVER

The cathedral city of Canterbury is an ancient place that has attracted travelers since the 12th century. The city's magnificent cathedral, the Mother Church of England, remains a powerful draw. Even in prehistoric times, this part of England was relatively well settled. Saxon settlers, Norman conquerors, and the folk who lived here in late-medieval times all left their mark. From Canterbury, there's rewarding wandering to be done in the gentle Kentish countryside between the city and the busy port of Dover. It is a county of orchards, market gardens, and round oasthouses with their tilted, pointed roofs, once used for drying hops (many have been converted into pricey homes).

TOP REASONS TO GO

Bodiam, Dover, Hever, and Herstmonceux castles: Take your pick: the most evocative castles in a region filled with them dazzle you with their fortitude and fascinate you with their histories.

Brighton: With its nightclubs, sunbathing, and funky, relaxed atmosphere, this is the quintessential English seaside city. From Brighton Pier to the Royal Pavilion, there's something for everyone.

Canterbury Cathedral: This massive building, a textbook of medieval architecture, inspires awe with its soaring towers and flagstone corridors. The past seems very near in such places as Trinity Chapel, where ancient stained-glass windows celebrate Thomas à Becket's miracles.

Rye: Wandering the cobbled streets of this medieval town is a pleasure, and rummaging through its antiques stores is an adventure in itself. Reward yourself afterward as the English do, with tea and scones.

Treasure houses: Here is one of England's richest concentrations of historic homes: among the superlatives are Petworth House, with its luminous paintings by Turner; sprawling Knole, with its set of silver furniture; Ightham Mote, with its Tudor chapel; and Chartwell, home of Winston Churchill.

Canterbury

56 mi southeast of London.

Just mention Canterbury, and many people are taken back to memories of high-school English classes and Geoffrey Chaucer's *Canterbury Tales*, about medieval pilgrims making their way to Canterbury Cathedral. Judging from the tales, however, in those days Canterbury was as much a party for people on horses as it was a spiritual center. The height of Canterbury's popularity came in the 12th century, when thousands of pilgrims flocked here to see the shrine of the murdered Archbishop St. Thomas à Becket, making this southeastern town one of the most visited in England, if not Europe. Buildings that served as pilgrims' inns (and which survived World War II bombing of the city) still dominate the streets of Canterbury's center.

An important Roman city, an Anglo-Saxon center in the Kingdom of Kent, and currently headquarters of the Anglican Church, Canterbury remains a lively place, a fact that has impressed visitors since 1388, when Chaucer wrote his stories. Today, most pilgrims come in search of history and picture-perfect moments rather than spiritual enlightenment, and magnificently medieval Canterbury, with its ancient city walls, leaning Tudor buildings, and remnants of its Roman past, obliges.

The absence of cars in the center brings some tranquillity to its streets, but to see Canterbury at its best, walk around early, before the tourist buses arrive, or wait until after they depart. Most major tourist sites are

The Southeast

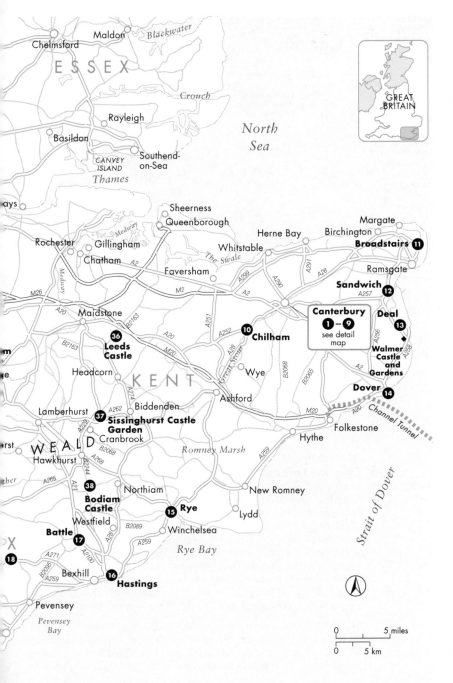

Chelmsford

Maldon *Blackwater*

E S S E X

Crouch

Rayleigh

Basildon

CANVEY ISLAND

Southend-on-Sea

Thames

ays

North Sea

Sheerness

Queenborough

Herne Bay

Margate

Birchington

Broadstairs ⑪

Ramsgate

Whitstable

The Swale

Faversham

Rochester

Gillingham

Chatham

The Medway

Sandwich ⑫

A257

Canterbury
❶–❾
see detail
map

Deal ⑬

A256

Walmer Castle and Gardens

M26

Maidstone

A20

B2163

⑯ ❸❻

Leeds Castle

B2163

Headcorn

K E N T

A20

M20

A251

A252

⑩ **Chilham**

A28

Wye

Great Stour

Ashford

B2068

B2065

Dover ⑭

Channel Tunnel

Lamberhurst

Biddenden

A262

❸❼ **Sissinghurst Castle Garden**

Cranbrook

A229

B2068

Hawkhurst

W E A L D

A265

A21

A229

A274

M20

A20

A2

Folkestone

Hythe

Romney Marsh

A259

New Romney

⑯ ❸❽

Bodiam Castle

Northiam

Westfield

Battle

⑯ ⑰

A271

A21

A2100

A28

B2089

⑮ **Rye**

Winchelsea

Lydd

Rye Bay

A259

⑱

B2096

A259

Bexhill

⑯ **Hastings**

Pevensey

Pevensey Bay

0   5 miles

0   5 km

GREAT BRITAIN

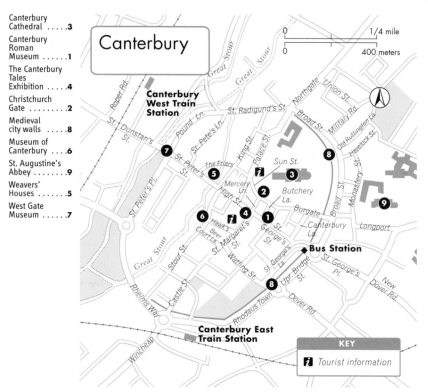

Canterbury

on one street, which crosses a branch of the River Stour in the city. The street changes name three times—beginning as St. George's Street and then becoming High Street and, finally, St. Peter's Street.

Main Attractions

3 Canterbury Cathedral. The focal point of the city was the first of England's great Norman cathedrals. Nucleus of worldwide Anglicanism, the Cathedral Church of Christ Canterbury (its formal name) is a living textbook of medieval architecture. The building was begun in 1070, demolished, begun anew in 1096, and then systematically expanded over the next three centuries. When the original choir section burned to the ground in 1174, another replaced it, designed in the new Gothic style, with tall, pointed arches. Don't miss the *North Choir* aisle, which holds two windows that show Jesus in the Temple, the three kings asleep, and Lot's wife turned to a pillar of salt. The windows are among the earliest parts of the cathedral, but only 33 of the original 208 survive.

Fodor'sChoice
★

The cathedral was only a century old, and still relatively small, when Thomas à Becket, the archbishop of Canterbury, was murdered here in 1170. Becket, a defender of ecclesiastical interests, had angered his friend Henry II, who was heard to exclaim, "Who will rid me of this

2

troublesome priest?" Thinking they were carrying out the king's wishes, four knights burst in on Becket in one of the side chapels and killed him. Two years later Becket was canonized, and Henry II's subsequent submission to the authority of the Church and his penitence helped establish the cathedral as the undisputed center of English Christianity. Becket's tomb, destroyed by Henry VIII in 1538 as part of his campaign to reduce the power of the Church and confiscate its treasures, was one of the most extravagant shrines in Christendom. In **Trinity Chapel,** which held the shrine, you can still see a series of 13th-century stained-glass windows illustrating Becket's miracles. So hallowed was this spot that in 1376, Edward, the Black Prince, warrior son of Edward III and a national hero, was buried near it. The actual site of Becket's murder is down a flight of steps just to the left of the nave. In the corner, a second flight of steps leads down to the enormous Norman **undercroft,** or vaulted cellarage, built in the early 12th century. A row of squat pillars whose capitals dance with animals and monsters supports the roof.

If time permits, be sure to explore the **cloisters** and other small monastic buildings to the north of the cathedral. The 12th-century octagonal water tower is still part of the cathedral's water supply. The Norman staircase in the northwest corner of the Green Court dates from 1167 and is a unique example of the domestic architecture of the times. The cathedral is very popular, so arrive early or late in the day to avoid the worst crowds. ■ TIP➔ You get a map and an overview of the building's history when you enter; audio guides have the most detail, or take a tour for the personal touch. ✉ *Cathedral Precincts* ☎ *01227/762862* ⊕ *www. canterbury-cathedral.org* 🖅 *£5, free for services and ½ hr before closing; £3.50 for tour, £2.95 for audio guide* ☉ *Easter–Sept., Mon.–Sat. 9–6:30, Sun. 12:30–2:30 and 4:30–5:30; Oct.–Easter, Mon.–Sat. 9–5, Sun. 12:30–2:30 and 4:30–5:30. Restricted access during services.*

NEED A BREAK?	**The Custard Tart** (✉ **35A St. Margaret's St.** ☎ **01227/785178**), a short walk from the cathedral, serves freshly made sandwiches, pies, tarts, and cakes. You can take your choice upstairs to the seating area. It's not open for dinner.

❶ **Canterbury Roman Museum.** Below ground, at the level of the remnants of Roman Canterbury, this museum features colorful mosaic Roman pavement and a hypocaust—the Roman version of central heating. Displays of excavated objects (some of which you can hold in the Touch the Past area) and computer-generated reconstructions of Roman buildings and the marketplace help re-create the past. ✉ *Butchery La.* ☎ *01227/ 785575* ⊕ *www.canterbury-museums.co.uk* 🖅 *£2.90* ☉ *June–Oct., Mon.–Sat. 10–5, Sun. 1:30–5; Nov.–May, Mon.–Sat. 10–5; last admission at 4. Closed last wk in Dec.*

❽ **Medieval city walls.** For an essential Canterbury experience, follow the circuit of the 13th- and 14th-century walls, built on the line of the Roman walls. Those to the east survive intact, towering some 20 feet high and offering a sweeping view of the town. You can access these from a number of places, including Castle Street and Broad Street.

Also Worth Seeing

❹ The Canterbury Tales. This kitschy audiovisual (and occasionally olfactory) dramatization of 14th-century English life is popular but touristy. You'll "meet" Chaucer's pilgrims at the Tabard Inn near London and view tableaus illustrating five tales. An actor in period costume often performs a charade as part of the scene. ✉ *St. Margaret's St.* ☎ *01227/479227* ⊕ *www.canterburytales.org.uk* ▭ *£7.25* ⊘ *Nov.–Feb., daily 10–4:30; Mar.–June, Sept. and Oct, daily 10–5; July and Aug., daily 9:30–5.*

❷ Christchurch Gate. This immense gate, built in 1517, leads into the cathedral close. As you pass through, look up at the sculpted heads of two young figures: Prince Arthur, elder brother of Henry VIII, and the young Catherine of Aragon, to whom Arthur was betrothed. After Arthur's death, Catherine married Henry. Her failure to produce a male heir after 25 years of marriage led to Henry's decision to divorce her, creating an irrevocable breach with the Roman Catholic Church and altering the course of English history.

Ⓒ ❻ Museum of Canterbury. The medieval Poor Priests' Hospital is the site of this local museum, where exhibits provide an overview of the city's history and architecture from Roman times to World War II. It's a quirky place that covers everything and everyone associated with the town, including the Blitz, the mysterious death of the 16th-century writer Christopher Marlowe, and the British cartoon characters Bagpuss and Rupert Bear. A renovation and expansion is under way, but the display subjects should not change. ✉ *20 Stour St.* ☎ *01227/475202* ⊕ *www.canterbury-museums.co.uk* ▭ *£3.30* ⊘ *Jan.–May and Oct.–Dec., Mon.–Sat. 10:30–5; June–Sept., Mon.–Sat. 10:30–5, Sun. 1:30–5; last admission at 4.*

❾ St. Augustine's Abbey. Augustine, England's first Christian missionary, was buried here in 597, at one of the oldest monastic sites in the country. The site remained intact for nearly 1,000 years, until Henry VIII seized the abbey in the 16th century, destroying some of the original buildings and converting others into a royal manor for his fourth wife, Anne of Cleves. A free interactive audio tour vividly puts events into context. Contemporary sculpture is placed in the grounds, and in other locations in the city, May through August. ✉ *Longport* ☎ *01227/767345* ⊕ *www.english-heritage.org.uk* ▭ *£3.70* ⊘ *Apr.–Sept., daily 10–6; Oct.–Mar., Wed.–Sun. 10–4.*

❺ Weavers' Houses. Huguenot weavers who settled here after fleeing from religious persecution in France occupied this lopsided group of 16th-century, half-timber buildings. The houses are just past where St. Peter's Street crosses a branch of the River Stour. ✉ *St. Peter's St.*

Ⓒ ❼ West Gate Museum. Only one of the city's seven medieval gatehouses survives, complete with twin castellated towers; it now contains this museum. Inside are medieval bric-a-brac and armaments used by the city guard, as well as more contemporary weaponry. The building became a jail in the 14th century, and you can view the prison cells. ■ **TIP→ Climb to the roof for a panoramic view of the city.** ✉ *St. Peter's St.* ☎ *01227/789576* ⊕ *www.canterbury-museums.co.uk* ▭ *£1.15* ⊘ *Mon.–Sat. 11–12:30 and 1:30–3:30; last admission 1 hr before closing; closed Christmas wk and Good Fri.*

Where to Stay & Eat

★ **££–£££** ✕ **Lloyds.** The magnificent beamed barn roof of this older building remains, but the interior—stripped wooden floor, white walls enlivened by contemporary paintings—and the cooking are definitely up-to-the-minute. A crew of young chefs creates such dishes as roasted pumpkin and amaretto ravioli with Parmesan, and pheasant with kumquats and juniper berries. The ice creams are homemade. ✉ *89–90 St. Dunstan's St.* ☎ *01227/768222* ▭ *AE, MC, V.*

££–£££ ✕ **Weavers.** In the Old Weavers House, one of the Weavers' Houses on the River Stour, this popular restaurant in the center of town is an ideal place to feast in a Tudor setting. The menu lists traditional English, seafood, and pasta dishes, and a good choice of wines. ✉ *1 St. Peter's St.* ☎ *01227/464660* ▭ *AE, MC, V.*

£–£££ ✕ **The Goods Shed.** Next to Canterbury West station, this vaulted wooden space with exposed brick and stone walls was a storage shed in Victorian times. Now it's a farmers' market and restaurant offering a foodie's feast of the best Kentish food—from freshly caught fish and smoked meats to local cider and bread baked on the premises. The menu varies with the availability of the local produce, and food is served at wooden tables on a raised platform. ✉ *Station Rd. W* ☎ *01227/459153* ▭ *MC, V* ☺ *Closed Mon. No dinner Sun.*

£–££ ✕ **Marlowe's.** For lunch or a late-afternoon snack, lively Marlowe's is a worthwhile alternative to the café franchises that populate Canterbury's pedestrian center. The staff is friendly and welcoming, as is the setting—walls are brightly colored and plastered with posters of old-time movie stars. The menu is eclectic: expect lunchtime standards (soup, sandwiches, baked potatoes), Tex-Mex dishes, and daily specials, such as lemon-dill chicken. ✉ *55 St. Peter's St.* ☎ *01227/462194* ⊕ *www.marlowesrestaurant.co.uk* ▭ *AE, DC, MC, V.*

£ ✕ **City Fish Bar.** Long lines and lots of satisfied finger-licking attest to the deserved popularity of this excellent fish-and-chips outlet in the center of town. Everything is freshly fried, the batter crisp and the fish tasty; the fried mushrooms are also surprisingly good. It closes at 7. ✉ *30 St. Margarets St.* ☎ *01227/760873* ▭ *No credit cards.*

££–£££ ✕▥ **Falstaff Hotel.** This old coaching inn with a courtyard sits right outside Westgate. Some of the beamed and oak-furnished bedrooms overlook the River Stour; rooms have a mix of old features and new, and three have four-posters. Classic English fare at the restaurant (£££) includes grilled mackerel with cucumber and beet salad. The central location is a big plus: reserve well in advance. ✉ *8 St. Dunstan's St., CT2 8AF* ☎ *01227/462138* 🖷 *01227/463525* ⊕ *www.english-inns.co.uk* ⇥ *47 rooms* ⌂ *Restaurant, cable TV, in-room broadband, bar, laundry service, Internet room, no-smoking rooms; no a/c* ▭ *AE, DC, MC, V.*

££–££££ ▥ **Magnolia House.** Kept in apple-pie order, this Georgian house, a 10-minute walk from the center of town, is charmingly elegant, with a lovely walled garden. Bedrooms have floral motifs and traditional furnishings; one has a four-poster. Evening meals are available from November to February by prior arrangement. To get here, follow St. Dunstan's Street until London Road and take a left; it will be three blocks on the right side. ✉ *36 St. Dunstan's Terr., CT2 8AX* 🖷 *01227/765121* ⊕ *www.*

magnoliahousecanterbury.co.uk ✏ *7 rooms* ♿ *No a/c, no room phones,
no kids under 12, no smoking* ⊟ *AE, DC, MC, V* ¶⊙¶ *BP.*

££–£££ ⬚ **Ebury Hotel.** Friendly and family-run, this hotel earns raves for its laid-
back attitude and comfortable rooms. Made up of two big Victorian
buildings a 10-minute walk from central Canterbury, it has been sympathetically converted. Rooms are simply decorated but good-size (bathrooms can be a bit tiny), and beds are firm. The cozy lounge has a
wood-burning fireplace, and an attractive indoor pool is perfect for hot
days. The hotel's slightly old-fashioned look is not for everyone, but if
you like the kind of inn that has a house labradoodle, it's perfect.
There's no elevator; ask for a room on the lower floors if you have mobility problems. ⊠ *65–67 New Dover Rd. CT1 3DX* ☎ *01227/768433*
🖷 *01227/459187* ⊕ *www.ebury-hotel.co.uk* ✏ *15 rooms* ♿ *Restaurant, indoor pool, lounge; no a/c* ⊟ *MC, V* ¶⊙¶ *BP.*

££ ⬚ **Cathedral Gate Hotel.** Older even than the adjoining cathedral gateway, this hotel was built as a hostelry for pilgrims in 1438. The large
beams, sloping floors, and twisting corridors are evidence of its medieval
origins; the plainly furnished rooms, however, have been sympathetically modernized. The bow-window restaurant looks out over the But-
termarket. A full English breakfast costs an extra £7. ⊠ *36 Burgate,
CT1 2HA* ☎ *01227/464381* 🖷 *01227/462800* ⊕ *www.cathgate.co.
uk* ✏ *27 rooms* ♿ *Restaurant, bar, some pets allowed; no a/c* ⊟ *AE,
DC, MC, V* ¶⊙¶ *CP.*

££ ⬚ **The White House.** Reputed to have been the house in which Queen
Victoria's head coachman came to live upon retirement, the White
House is a handsome Regency building on a quiet road off St. Peter's
Street, between the city center and Canterbury West train station. Rooms
are decorated in pastel shades with an abundance of floral patterns, and
a few rooms can accommodate up to four people. ⊠ *6 St Peter's La.,
CT1 2BP* ☎ *01227/761836* 🖷 *01227/478622* ⊕ *www.canterburybreaks.
co.uk* ✏ *9 rooms* ♿ *Lounge, no-smoking rooms; no room phones*
⊟ *No credit cards* ¶⊙¶ *BP.*

Nightlife & the Arts

NIGHTLIFE Canterbury is home to a popular university, and the town's many pubs
and bars are busy, often crowded with college-age folks. **Alberry's Wine
Bar** (⊠ St. Margaret's St. ☎ 01227/452378), with late-night jazz and
hip-hop and a trendy crowd, is the coolest place in town. **Simple Simons**
(⊠ 3–9 Church La. ☎ 01227/762355) is known for its real ales–at
least six kinds are available at any time—and its convivial setting in a
wood-paneled building. **Thomas Becket** (⊠ 21 Best La. ☎ 01227/464384),
a marvelous English pub, has a fire crackling in the winter, copper pots
hanging from the ceiling, and a friendly crowd.

THE ARTS The two-week-long, mixed-arts **Canterbury Festival** (☎ 01227/452853
⊕ www.canterburyfestival.co.uk) is held every October.

Shopping

Hawkin's Bazaar (⊠ 34 Burgate ☎ 01227/785809) carries an exceptional
selection of traditional and modern toys and games. The **National Trust
Shop** (⊠ 24 Burgate ☎ 01227/457120) stocks the National Trust line
of household items, ideal for gifts.

2

Chilham

🔟 *5 mi southwest of Canterbury.*

The village square is filled with textbook examples of English rural architecture, with gabled windows beneath undulating roofs. The church dates from the 14th century. From this hilltop village, midway between Canterbury and Ashford on the A252 (off the A28), you can walk the last few miles of the traditional Pilgrim's Way back to Canterbury.

Where to Eat

££ ✕ **White Horse.** This 15th-century inn shadowed by Chilham's church has a pleasant beer garden and provides lunchtime and evening meals superior to the usual pub grub, with many good pasta dishes. The pub used to be a vicarage, and the ghost of a 17th-century vicar is said to regularly appear in front of the large fireplace. ⊠ *The Square* 🕾 *01227/ 730355* 🖃 *MC, V.*

Broadstairs

🔟 *17 mi east of Canterbury.*

Like other Victorian seaside towns such as Margate and Ramsgate on this stretch of coast, Broadstairs was once the playground of vacationing Londoners. Charles Dickens spent many summers here between 1837 and 1851 and wrote glowingly of its bracing freshness. Today grand 19th-century houses line the waterfront. In the off-season Broadstairs is a peaceful retreat, but day-trippers pack the town in July and August.

One of Dickens's favorite abodes was **Bleak House,** perched on a cliff overlooking Viking Bay, where he wrote much of *David Copperfield* and drafted *Bleak House,* after which the building was later renamed. His study and other rooms have been preserved. Displays explore local history, including the wrecks at nearby Goodwin Sands, and the cellars have exhibits about smuggling, a longtime local activity. ⊠ *Fort Rd.* 🕾 *01843/ 862224* 🖾 *£3* 🕘 *Late Feb.–June and Sept.–mid-Dec., daily 10–6; July and Aug., daily 10–9.*

What is now the **Dickens House Museum** was originally the home of Mary Pearson Strong, on whom Dickens based the character of Betsey Trotwood, David Copperfield's aunt. There's a reconstruction of Miss Trotwood's room, a few objects that once belonged to the Dickens family, and prints and photographs commemorating Dickens's association with Broadstairs. ⊠ *2 Victoria Parade* 🕾 *01843/863453* ⊕ *www. dickenshouse.co.uk* 🖾 *£2.30* 🕘 *Apr.–Oct., daily 2–5.*

Where to Stay

£ 🏨 **Admiral Dundonald Hotel.** An ivy-covered Georgian building, the Admiral has just the right Olde English look. Inside the decor is a good mix of antiques and modern pieces, and the mood is both friendly and, in the lounge, a bit formal. Rooms are neat and simply decorated, and the location at the edge of the town center is handy. ⊠ *43 Belvedere Rd., CT10 1PF* 🕾 *01843/862236* 🛏 *12 rooms* ♨ *No a/c, no room phones* 🖃 *MC, V* 🍴 *BP.*

Nightlife & the Arts

Each June, Broadstairs holds a **Dickens Festival** (☎ 01843/865265), last-ing about a week, with readings, people in Dickensian costume, a Dick-ensian cricket match, a Victorian bathing party, and Victorian vaudeville, among other entertainments.

Sandwich

12 *11 mi south of Broadstairs, 12 mi east of Canterbury.*

The coast near Canterbury holds three of the ancient **Cinque Ports** (pronounced sink ports), a confederacy of ports along the southeast seaboard whose heyday lasted from the 12th through the 14th centuries. These towns, originally five in number (hence *cinque,* from the Norman French for "five")—Sandwich, Dover, Hythe, Romney, and Hastings—are rich in history and are generally less crowded than the other resorts of Kent's northeast coast.

In Saxon times Sandwich stood in a sheltered bay; it became the most important of the Cinque Ports in the Middle Ages and later England's chief naval base. From 1500 the port began to silt up, however, and the town is now 2 mi inland, though the River Stour still flows through it. The 16th-century checkerboard barbican (gatehouse) by the toll bridge is one of many medieval and Tudor buildings here; Strand Street has many half-timber structures.

Deal

13 *7 mi south of Sandwich, 8 mi northeast of Dover.*

The large seaside town of Deal is famous in history books as the place where Caesar's legions landed in 55 BC, and it was from here that William Penn set sail in 1682 on his first journey to the American colony he founded, Pennsylvania.

Deal Castle, erected in 1540 and intricately built to the shape of a Tudor rose, is the largest of the coastal defenses constructed by Henry VIII. A moat surrounds its gloomy pas-sages and austere walls. The castle museum has exhibits about prehis-toric, Roman, and Saxon Britain. ⊠ *Victoria Rd.* ☎ *01304/372762* ⊕ *www.english-heritage.org.uk* 🎫 *£3.90* ⊙ *Apr.–Sept., daily 10–6.*

Walmer Castle and Gardens, one of Henry VIII's fortifications, was con-verted in 1708 into the official res-idence of the lord warden of the Cinque Ports, and it now resem-bles a cozy country house. Among the famous lord wardens were

HENRY'S CASTLES

Why did Henry VIII rapidly (1539–1542) build sturdy forts along the southern coast? After enraging the Pope and Europe's Catholic monarchs with his marriages and by seizing control of the wealthy monasteries, he prepared for a possible invasion. It did not come. Today you can bike or walk along the beachfront between Deal and Walmer Castles.

William Pitt the Younger; the duke of Wellington, hero of the Battle of Waterloo, also lived here from 1829 until his death here in 1852 (a small museum contains memorabilia); and Sir Winston Churchill. Except for when the lord warden is in residence, the drawing and dining rooms are open to the public, and attractive gardens and a grassy walk fill what was the moat. ⊠ *A258, 1 mi south of Deal* ☎ *01304/364288* ⊕ *www. english-heritage.org.uk* 🎫 *£6.20* ⊙ *Mar., daily 10–4; Apr.–Sept., daily 10–6; Oct., Wed.–Sun. 10–4.*

Dover

🔞 *8 mi south of Deal, 78 mi east of London.*

The busy passenger port of Dover has for centuries been Britain's gateway to Europe. Its chalk **White Cliffs** are a famous and inspirational sight, though you may find the town itself a bit disappointing; the savage bombardments of World War II and the shortsightedness of postwar developers left the city center an unattractive place. Roman legacies include a lighthouse, adjoining a stout Anglo-Saxon church. The **Roman Painted House,** believed to have been a hotel, includes some wall paintings, along with the remnants of an ingenious heating system. ⊠ *New St.* ☎ *01304/203279* 🎫 *£2* ⊙ *Apr.–Sept., Tues.–Sat. 10–5, Sun. 2–5.*

★ ☺ Spectacular **Dover Castle,** towering high above the ramparts of the White Cliffs, was a mighty medieval castle, and it has served as an important strategic center over the centuries, even in World War II. Most of the castle, including the keep, dates to Norman times. It was begun by Henry II in 1181 but incorporates additions from almost every succeeding century. There's a lot to see here besides the castle rooms: exhibits, many of which will appeal to kids, include the Siege of 1216, the Princess of Wales Regimental Museum, and Castle Fit for a King. ■ TIP➡ **Take time to tour the secret wartime tunnels,** a medieval and Napoléonic-era system that was used as a World War II command center during the evacuation of Dunkirk in 1940. ⊠ *Castle Rd.* ☎ *01304/211067* ⊕ *www. english-heritage.org.uk* 🎫 *£9.50* ⊙ *Feb. and Mar., daily 10–4; Apr.–Sept., daily 10–6; Oct., daily 10–5; Nov.–Jan., Thurs.–Mon. 10–4.*

Where to Stay

£ 🏠 **Number One Guest House.** This popular, family-run guesthouse with garage parking is a great bargain. Wallpapers and porcelain collections decorate the cozy corner terrace home built in the early 19th century, and you can even have breakfast in your room. The walled garden has a fine view of the castle. ⊠ *1 Castle St., CT16 1QH* ☎ *01304/202007* 🖨 *01304/214078* ⊕ *www.number1guesthouse.co.uk* 📠 *4 rooms* ⚲ *No a/c, no room phones* ▭ *No credit cards* ⏏ *BP.*

RYE TO LEWES

From Dover, the coast road winds west through Folkestone (a genteel resort, small port, and Channel Tunnel terminal), across Romney Marsh (reclaimed from the sea and famous for its sheep and, at one time, its ruthless smugglers), to the delightful medieval town of Rye. The region along the coast is noted for the history-rich sites of Hastings and Herstmonceux, as well as for the Glyndebourne Opera House festival, based outside Lewes, a town celebrated for its architectural heritage.

Rye

★ ⑮ *68 mi southeast of London, 34 mi southwest of Dover.*

With cobbled streets and ancient timbered dwellings, Rye is an artist's dream. Once a port (the water retreated, and the harbor is now 2 mi away), the town starts where the sea once lapped at its ankles and then winds its way to the top of a low hill that overlooks the Romney Marshes. Virtually every building in the little town center is intriguingly old; some places were smugglers' retreats. Rye is known for its many antiques stores and antiquarian bookstores, and also for its sheer pleasantness. This place can be easily walked without a map, but if you prefer guidance, the local tourist office has an interesting audio tour of the town as well as maps.

The diminutive **Rye Castle Museum,** below the remains of the castle wall, displays watercolors and examples of Rye pottery, for which the town was famous. ⊠ *3 East St.* ☎ *01797/226728* ⊕ *www.rye.org.uk* ⊠ *£1.90, £2.90 including Ypres Tower* ☉ *Apr.–Oct., Mon., Thurs., Fri. 2–5, weekends 10:30–1; last admission 30 mins before closing.*

At the top of the hill at the center of Rye, the **Church of St. Mary the Virgin** is a classic English village church in a number of architectural styles. ■ TIP→ **You can climb the tower to see amazing views.** The turret clock dates to 1561 and still keeps excellent time. ⊠ *Church Sq.* ☉ *Daily 10–4.*

Down the hill past Church Square, **Ypres Tower** was originally built as part of the town's fortifications (now largely gone) in 1249; it later served as a prison. The stone chambers hold a rather random collection of local items, such as smuggling bric-a-brac and shipbuilding mementos. ⊠ *Gungarden* ☎ *01797/226728* ⊠ *£1.90, £2.90 including Rye Castle* ☉ *Apr.–Oct., Thurs.–Mon. 10–1 and 2–5; Nov.–Mar., weekends 10:30–3:30; last admission 30 mins before closing.*

Something about **Lamb House,** an early 18th-century house, attracts writers. The novelist Henry James lived here from 1898 to 1916. E. F.

> ### MERMAID CALLING
>
> Mermaid Street in Rye is one of the original cobbled streets that heads steeply from the top of the hill to the former harbor. Its name, according to local lore, came from the night a sailor who had sipped a few too many walked down it. He swore he heard a mermaid call him down to the sea.

Benson, onetime mayor of Rye and author of the witty *Lucia* novels (written in the 1920s and 1930s, with some set in a town based on Rye), was a later resident. The ground-floor rooms contain some of James's furniture and personal belongings. ⊠ *West St.* ☎ *01892/890651* ⊕ *www.nationaltrust.org.uk* ⊠ *£3* ☉ *Apr.–Oct., Thurs. and Sat. 2–6; last admission at 5:30.*

Several miles outside Rye, **Tenterden Vineyard** is one of Britain's leading wine producers. The Chapel Down wines have won awards, including one for a sparkling wine. You must join a one-hour guided tour to view the grounds, after which you are free to peruse the herb garden, plant center, shop, and the restaurant, the Grapevine Bistro. ⊠ *Small Hythe* ☎ *01580/763033* ⊕ *www.newwavewines.co.uk* ⌂ *£4.30* ⊙ *June–Sept., daily 10–5; May and Oct., weekends 10–5.*

Where to Stay & Eat

££–£££ ✕ **Landgate Bistro.** Although definitely a bistro, this restaurant in a small shop unit near one of the ancient gateways is serious about its food. Fish is always a good choice, or you can opt for the duck soaked in a tangy port sauce or griddle-cooked cutlets of venison with winter vegetables. A fixed-price menu (£18 for three courses) is available Tuesday through Thursday. ⊠ *5–6 Landgate* ☎ *01797/222829* ⊟ *DC, MC, V* ⊙ *Closed Sun. and Mon., last wk in Dec., and 1st wk in Jan. No lunch.*

£££££ ✕▥ **The Mermaid.** Once the headquarters of a smuggling gang, this classic half-timber inn has served Rye for nearly six centuries. Sloping floors, oak beams, low ceilings, and a huge open hearth in the bar testify to great age: the inn was rebuilt in 1420, though it dates from 1156. Rooms vary in size; some have four-posters. The decor is a bit dated for the price, but the history keeps the crowds coming in. The main restaurant (*££££–£££££*) allows you to soak up the period details while choosing from an extensive English menu. In summer you can have tea in the Tudor Tearoom for a rather steep price. ⊠ *Mermaid St., TN31 7EY* ☎ *01797/223065* ⊟ *01797/225069* ⊕ *www.mermaidinn.com* ⌂ *31 rooms* ⌂ *Restaurant, bar, meeting room; no a/c* ⊟ *AE, MC, V* ▯ *BP.*

£££–££££ ▥ **Jeake's House.** Antiques and books fill the cozy bedrooms of this rambling 1689 house, and print fabrics and brass or mahogany beds add charm. The snug, painted-and-paneled parlor has a wood-burning stove for cold days. Breakfast, which might include deviled kidneys, kippers, or vegetarian nuggets, is served in a galleried room formerly used for Quaker meetings. Book well in advance. ⊠ *Mermaid St., TN31 7ET* ☎ *01797/222828* ⊟ *01797/222623* ⊕ *www.jeakeshouse. com* ⌂ *11 rooms, 10 with bath* ⌂ *Bar, some pets allowed (fee); no a/c, no kids under 8* ⊟ *MC, V* ▯ *BP.*

££–£££ ▥ **The Old Vicarage.** Roses frame the door of this bayfront Georgian house in a peaceful location close to the church in the center of town. The sunny rooms combine Victorian, Edwardian, and French furniture. You can breakfast on homemade bread, scones, and locally produced eggs and bacon in a dining room that overlooks a garden. ⊠ *66 Church Sq., TN31 7HF* ☎ *01797/222119* ⊟ *01797/227466* ⊕ *www.oldvicaragerye.co.uk* ⌂ *4 rooms* ⌂ *No a/c, no room phones, no kids under 8, no smoking* ⊟ *No credit cards* ⊙ *Closed last wk in Dec.* ▯ *BP.*

Shopping

Rye has great antiques shops, perfect for an afternoon of rummaging, with the biggest cluster at the foot of the hill near the tourist information center. The English can find bargains; it's harder for Americans, given the exchange rate. The town still has a number of potteries. **Black Sheep Antiques** (⊠ 72 The Mint ☎ 01797/224508) has a superior selection of antique crystal and silver. **Collectors Corner** (⊠ 2 Market Rd. ☎ 01797/225796) sells a good mix of furniture, art, and silver.

Of Rye's working potteries, **Cinque Ports Pottery** (⊠ The Monastery, Conduit Hill ☎ 01797/222033) is one of the best. **David Sharp Pottery** (⊠ 55 The Mint ☎ 01797/222620) specializes in the ceramic name plaques that are a feature of the town.

Hastings

16 *11 mi southwest of Rye, 68 mi southeast of London.*

This big, sprawling Victorian seaside town will always be associated with the 1066 Norman invasion, when William, duke of Normandy, landed his troops at Pevensey Bay, a few miles west of town, and was met by King Harold's army. A vicious battle ensued. Though it was called the Battle of Hastings, it actually took place 6 mi away at a town now called, well, Battle. Harold's troops had just fought Vikings near York and marched across the country to take on the Normans. Utterly exhausted, Harold never stood a chance, and William became known as William the Conquerer.

Hastings later flourished as a Cinque Port and in the 19th century became one of England's many popular resorts. This is when it got its current looks, which are, particularly from a distance, lovely. Tall row houses painted in lemony hues cover the cliffs around the deep blue sea, and the views from the hilltops are extraordinary. The old town, east of the pier, offers a glimpse into the city's 16th-century past. It has been through difficult times in recent decades, as have many English seaside resorts, and the town developed a reputation as a rough place. However, a gentrification movement has encouraged a slow climb back to respectability. All visitors may notice, though, is that it's a handsome place, and the seafront has all the usual English accoutrements—fish-and-chips shops, candy stores, shops selling junk, miniature golf, and rocky beaches that stretch for miles. ■ TIP→ **Walk to the edge of town away from the castle, and you can often have the beach all to yourself.** Below the East Cliff, tall, black wooden towers called **net shops,** unique to the town, are still used for drying fishermen's nets, and selling fresh seafood.

You can take the West Hill Cliff Railway from George Street precinct to the atmospheric ruins of the Norman **Hastings Castle,** built by

BEACH HUTS

As English as clotted cream, rows of tiny, cheerfully painted, one-room wooden huts brighten the shoreline in Sussex (look for them at the edges of Hastings and Brighton) and elsewhere. The huts originated in the Victorian wheeled bathing machines that were rolled into the water so that women could swim modestly behind them. Eventually the wheels came off, and they and similar structures became favored for storage and as a windbreak. Many huts lack electricity or plumbing but are beloved for their adorableness. Some are rented; others are owned, and prices can be high.

William the Conqueror in 1069. All that remains are fragments of the fortifications, some ancient walls, and a number of gloomy dungeons. Nevertheless, you get an excellent view of the chalky cliffs, the coast, and the town below. "The 1066 Story" retells the Norman invasion using audiovisual technology. ✉ *West Hill* ☎ *01424/781112* ⊕ *www. discoverhastings.co.uk* 🎫*£3.40* ☉ *Easter–Sept., daily 10–5; Oct.–Easter, daily 11–3; last admission 30 mins before closing.*

Waxworks and exhibits recall the history of smuggling at **Smuggler's Adventure,** in a labyrinth of caves and passages a 5- or 10-minute walk above Hastings Castle. ✉ *St. Clement Caves* ☎ *01424/422964* ⊕ *www. smugglersadventure.co.uk* 🎫 *£6.40* ☉ *Easter–Sept., daily 10–5:30; Oct.–Easter, daily 11–4:30; last admission 30 mins before closing.*

Carr Taylor Vineyards are well-known locally for their traditional methods of bottled fermentation, also known as *Méthode Champenoise*. The store also stocks fruit wines, ranging from strawberry to apricot, and mead—a wine of medieval origin—made following the *very* sweet Carr Taylor recipe with fermented grapes, apple juice, and honey. Take the A21 north from Hastings for 3 mi, turn onto the A28, and follow the signs. ✉ *Westfield, Hastings* ☎ *01424/752501* ⊕ *www.carr-taylor. com* 🎫 *Free* ☉ *Daily 10–5; closed last wk of Dec.*

Where to Stay & Eat

££–££££ ✕ **Bonaparte's.** A hands-on approach to food distinguishes this slightly haughty seafront restaurant, which has dark walls and booths for dining. Owner Bob Bone shoots his own game and buys fish fresh from the market to create dishes such as game pie in beer and wine sauce and halibut steak with crayfish tails. His inventive vegetarian choices include a Tibetan roast with buckwheat, spinach, mushrooms, and walnuts. ✉ *64 Eversfield Pl., St. Leonards* ☎ *01424/712218* 🖃 *AE, DC, MC, V* ☉ *Closed Mon. No lunch Sun.*

£ 🏠 **Eagle House.** This guesthouse in St. Leonards, just west of Hastings's city center, is in a large Victorian building with a lovely garden. It's a quirky place with somewhat dated decor, but the guest rooms have Victorian touches. The restaurant uses fresh produce from local farms. ✉ *12 Pevensey Rd., St. Leonards TN38 0JZ* ☎ *01424/430535* 🖶 *01424/ 437771* ⊕ *www.eaglehousehotel.co.uk* 🛏 *18 rooms* ♿ *Restaurant; no a/c* 🖃 *AE, DC, MC, V* �|○| *BP.*

Battle

17 *7 mi northwest of Hastings, 61 mi southeast of London.*

Battle is the actual site of the crucial Battle of Hastings, at which, on October 14, 1066, William of Normandy and his army trounced King Harold's Anglo-Saxon army. Today it's a sweet, quiet town, and a favorite of history buffs.

The ruins of **Battle Abbey,** the great Benedictine abbey William the Conqueror erected after his victory, still convey the sense of past conflict. A memorial stone marks the high altar, which stood on the spot where Harold II was killed. Despite its historical significance, this abbey was

CLOSE UP

Vin Anglais

ENGLISH WINE? Indeed, the English wine industry, ridiculed for years, is beginning to be taken more seriously. English vineyards, mostly in Surrey, Sussex, and Kent, have seen boom years, boosted by the changing climate. The summer of 2003 yielded a particularly good vintage in Southeast England; although the Mediterranean grape harvest was damaged by drought, the weather in England was almost perfect for wine production. Chalky soils in the region are similar to those in the Champagne region of France, and with the success of English sparkling wines, vineyards like Biddenden (near Sissinghurst), Tenterden (next to Rye), and Carr Taylor (Hastings) have attracted the attention of French wine houses. Many vineyards turn out decent whites, often using frost-resistant German grape varieties; some have even produced good wines based on Pinot Noir and Chardonnay grapes. So go ahead: ask for local wines as you're dining in the region.

not spared Henry VIII's wrath, and it was largely destroyed during his dissolution of the monasteries. A visitor center (set to open in fall 2006) has an audiovisual presentation about the battle and its impact on England. You can still take the 1-mi-long walk around the edge of the battlefield and see the remains of many of the abbey's buildings. The **Abbot's House** (closed to the public) is now a girls' school. ⊠ *High St.* ☎ *01424/773792* ⊕ *www.english-heritage.org.uk* ⊠ *£5.50* ◷ *Apr.–Oct. daily 10–6; Nov.–Mar., daily 10–4.*

Where to Stay & Eat

£££ ✕⊡ **Little Hemingfold Hotel.** Forty acres of fields and woodland, including a trout lake and a grass tennis court, provide the main enticement of this informal, early-Victorian-farmhouse hotel. Guest rooms, done in simple country style, are bright and serene, and there's a piano in one of the sitting rooms. The fixed-price dinner in the candlelighted restaurant (££££–£££££) uses homegrown fruit and vegetables; the menu changes daily. The hotel is 2 mi south of Battle off the A2100. ⊠ *Hastings Rd., Telham TN33 0TT* ☎ *01424/774338* ⊟ *01424/775351* ⊕ *www.littlehemingfoldhotel.co.uk* ⊃ *12 rooms* ♧ *Restaurant, tennis court, lake, boating, fishing, croquet, bar, lounge, some pets allowed; no a/c, no kids under 7* ◷ *Closed Jan.–mid-Feb.* ⊟ *AE, MC, V* ⊚ *BP.*

Herstmonceux Castle

★ **⑱** *11 mi southwest of Battle, 61 mi southeast of London.*

At last, a proper fairy-tale castle, with a banner waving from one tower and a glassy moat crossed by what was, surely, once a drawbridge—everything, in fact, except knights in armor. For true castle lovers, Herstmonceux is a fabled name. The redbrick structure was originally built by Sir Roger Fiennes (ancestor of actor Ralph Fiennes) in 1444, although it was altered in the Elizabethan age and again early in the 20th century, after it had largely fallen to ruin. Canada's Queen's University owns the castle, so only part of it is open for guided tours. Highlights include the magnificent ballroom, a medieval room, and the stunning Elizabethan-era staircase. ■ TIP→ **Take time to explore the grounds,** including the formal walled garden, lily-covered lakes, follies, and miles of woodland—the perfect place for a picnic on a sunny afternoon. Or you can try the scones in the castle's tea shop and watch the outside from within. ⊠ *Hailsham* ☏ *01323/834481* ⊕ *www.herstmonceux-castle.com* ⊠ *Castle tours £2.50, grounds £5* ⊙ *Mid-Apr.–Oct., daily 10–6; Oct., daily 10–5; last admission 1 hr before closing.*

Where to Eat

£££–££££   ✕ **The Sundial.** This 17th-century brick farmhouse holds a popular French restaurant run by chef Vincent Rongier and his wife, Mary. The extensive, frequently changing menu lists imaginative choices: foie gras and truffles vie with smoked salmon from the Shetland Isles. The fixed-price options are a good value. ⊠ *Gardner St., Herstmonceux* ☏ *01323/ 832217* ⊟ *DC, MC, V* ⊙ *Closed Mon. No dinner Sun.*

Lewes

★ ⑲   *8 mi northeast of Brighton, 54 mi south of London.*

The town nearest to the celebrated Glyndebourne Opera House, Lewes is so rich in architectural history that the Council for British Archaeology has named it one of the 50 most important English towns. A walk is the best way to appreciate its appealing jumble of building styles and materials—flint, stone, brick, tile—and the secret lanes (called "twittens") behind the castle, with their huge beeches. Here and there are smart antiques shops and secondhand-book dealers. Most of the buildings in the center date to the 18th and 19th centuries.

Something about this town has always attracted rebels. It was once the home of Thomas Paine (1737–1809), whose pamphlet *Common Sense* advocated that the American colonies break with Britain, and was also favored by Virginia Woolf and the Bloomsbury Group, the early-20th-century group of countercultural artistic innovators.

Today Lewes' beauty and proximity to London mean that the counterculture crew can't really afford to live here anymore, but its rebel soul still peeks through from time to time, particularly on Guy Fawkes Night (November 5), the anniversary of Fawkes's attempt to blow up the Houses of Parliament in 1605. The celebration is known countrywide for its massive bonfires and drunken enthusiasm. Guy Fawkes Night here is enthusiastically anti-Catholic (Fawkes was a Catholic fanatic), if tongue-in-cheek. Although the Pope is burned in effigy, he is not alone; figures from popular culture and politics are also burned, in the spirit of (dark-humored) fun.

High above the valley of the River Ouse stand the majestic ruins of **Lewes Castle,** begun in 1100. For a panoramic view of the surrounding region, climb the keep. The **Barbican House Museum** inside the castle includes a sound-and-light show and the Town Model, a re-creation of Lewes in the 19th century. ⊠ *169 High St.* ☏ *01273/486290* ⊕ *www.sussexpast.*

co.uk ⬛ *£4.60, £6 includes Anne of Cleves House* ⊙ *Tues.–Sat. 10–5:30 or dusk; Sun., Mon., and holidays 11–5:30 or dusk; last admission 30 mins before closing; closed Mon. in Jan.*

The 16th-century **Anne of Cleves House,** a fragile, timber-frame building, holds a notable collection of Sussex ironwork and other items of local interest, such as Sussex pottery. A famous painting of the local Guy Fawkes procession is also here. The house was part of Anne of Cleves's divorce settlement from Henry VIII, but she did not live in it. To get to the house, walk down steep, cobbled Keere Street, past lovely Grange Gardens, to Southover High Street. ⊠ *52 Southover High St.* ☎ *01273/ 474610* ⊕ *www.sussexpast.co.uk* ⬛ *£3.10, £6 includes Lewes Castle* ⊙ *Mar.–Oct., Tues.–Sat. 10–5, Sun., Mon., and holidays 11–5; Nov.–Feb., Tues.–Sat. 10–5; last admission at 4.*

Of interest to Bloomsbury fans, **Monk's House** was the home of novelist Virginia Woolf and her husband, Leonard Woolf, who purchased it in 1919. Leonard lived here until his death in 1969. Rooms in the small cottage include Virginia's study and her bedroom. Artists Vanessa Bell (Virginia's sister) and Duncan Grant helped decorate the house. ⊠ *C7, off A27, 3 mi south of Lewes, Rodmell* ☎ *01892/890651* ⊕ *www. nationaltrust.org.uk* ⬛ *£2.90* ⊙ *Apr.–Oct., Wed. and Sat. 2–5:30.*

Art and life mixed at **Charleston,** the farmhouse Vanessa Bell bought in 1916 and decorated with Duncan Grant (who resided here until 1978), fancifully painting the walls, doors, and furniture. The house became a refuge for writers and artists of the Bloomsbury Group and displays ceramics and textiles of the Omega Workshop—in which Bell and Grant participated—and paintings by Picasso and Renoir as well as by Bell and Grant. ⊠ *Off A27, 7 mi east of Lewes, Firle* ☎ *01323/811265* ⊕ *www. charleston.org.uk* ⬛ *£6.50, gardens only £2.50* ⊙ *Mar.–June, Sept., and Oct., Wed. and Sat. 11:30–6, Thurs., Fri., Sun., and national holidays 2–6; July and Aug., Wed.–Sat. 11:30–6, Sun. and national holidays 2–6; last admission at 5.*

Where to Stay & Eat

£££££   ✕ **Circa.** Fascinatingly different food without pretentiousness is the attraction at this ambitious restaurant. Global-fusion dishes such as six-mushroom tortellini with yam crunch and seared blue-fin tuna with *yuzu* (a Japanese citrus fruit) dressing are presented by helpful staff in modern surroundings. The marginally simpler lunch menu is a good value at £13 for two courses. ⊠ *145 High St.* ☎ *01273/471777* ▤ *MC, V* ⊙ *Closed Sun. and Mon.*

££££–£££££   ✕▥ **Horsted Place.** This luxurious manor-house hotel sits on 1,100 acres, a few minutes' drive from Glyndebourne. Built as a private home in 1850 with Gothic Revival elements by Augustus-Charles Pugin, it was owned by a friend of the Queen's until the 1980s, and Elizabeth was a regular visitor. Today it is richly furnished in country-house style and has a magnificent Victorian staircase and a Gothic library with a secret door that leads to a courtyard. The dining room (£££–££££), also Gothic, prepares such elegant fare as roasted quail cutlet. ⊠ *Little*

Horsted TN22 5TS, 2½ mi south of Uckfield, 6 mi north of Lewes
☎ *01825/750581* 🖷 *01825/750459* ⊕ *www.horstedplace.co.uk* ⇗ *15
rooms, 5 suites* ⚙ *Restaurant, cable TV with movies, golf privileges, tennis court, croquet, library, business services, meeting rooms; no a/c*
▭ *AE, DC, MC, V* ⦿ *BP.*

£££££   ⊡ **Shelleys.** A 17th-century building, this hotel on the hilly main road
is a traditional overnight stop for Glyndebourne operagoers. Public
rooms are on the grand scale, lavishly furnished with antiques, and the
garden is a joy. The hotel is known for its old-fashioned but friendly
service. ⊠ *High St., BN7 1XS* ☎ *01273/472361* 🖷 *01273/483152*
⊕ *www.shelleys-hotel.com* ⇗ *19 rooms* ⚙ *Restaurant, bar, meeting
rooms, some pets allowed; no a/c* ▭ *AE, DC, MC, V* ⦿ *BP.*

££   ⊡ **Berkeley House.** In a smart town house in one of Lewes's Georgian
terraces, Berkeley House is a small, welcoming B&B. Rooms are spacious and homey, if somewhat beige, and full English breakfasts are made
using free-range eggs from a local farmer. ⊠ *2 Albion St., BN7 2ND*
☎ *01273/476057* 🖷 *01273/479575* ⊕ *www.berkeleyhousehotel.co.
uk* ⇗ *3 rooms* ⚙ *No a/c* ▭ *AE, DC, MC, V* ⦿ *BP.*

Nightlife & the Arts

NIGHTLIFE   Lewes has a relatively young population and a nightlife scene to match;
there are also many lovely old pubs. It's the home of the excellent Harveys Brewery, and most local pubs serve its concoctions. Try the **Brewers' Arms** (⊠ 91 High St. ☎ 01273/475524), a good pub with a friendly
crowd. **The King's Head** (⊠ 9 Southover High St. ☎ 01273/474628), a
traditional pub, has a good menu with game and fish dishes.

THE ARTS   **Glyndebourne Opera House** (⊠ Glyndebourne, near Lewes ☎ 01273/
813813 ⊕ www.glyndebourne.com) is one of the world's leading opera
venues. Nestled beneath the downs, Glyndebourne combines first-class
productions, a state-of-the-art auditorium, and a beautiful setting. Seats
are *very* expensive (£25–£140) and often difficult to acquire, but they're
worth every penny to aficionados, some of whom wear evening dress
and bring a hamper for a picnic in the gardens. The main season runs
from mid-May to the end of August. The Glyndebourne Touring Company performs here in October, when seats are cheaper and slightly easier to obtain.

Shopping

Antiques shops offer temptation along the busy High Street. Lewes also
has plenty of tiny boutiques and independent clothing stores vying for
your pounds. **Adamczewski** (⊠ 88 High St. ☎ 01273/470105) is a marvelous throwback to the days when everything was made by hand. Its
homemade soaps, scents, and even hand-hewn brooms are works of art.
Cliffe Antiques Centre (⊠ 47 Cliffe High St. ☎ 01273/473266) is a great
place for one-stop antiques shopping, with a fine mix of vintage English prints, estate jewelry, and art at reasonable prices. Classic bone china
and antique glass are the center of attention at **Loius Potts & Co.** (⊠ 43
Cliffe High St. ☎ 01273/472240).

BRIGHTON TO PETWORTH

The self-proclaimed belle of the coast, Brighton is colorful, a bit hippy-ish, young, and endlessly entertaining—a mix of pop culture and carnival. It has been dubbed "London-by-Sea" because so many Londoners have moved here since the 1990s. Their presence gives the city character: there's much more to this place than its sights and the sea.

Outside of town, the soft green downs of Sussex hold stately homes you can visit, including Arundel Castle and Petworth House. Along the way, you'll discover the largest Roman villa in Britain and Chichester, whose cathedral is a poem in stone.

Brighton

9 mi southwest of Lewes, 54 mi south of London.

For more than 200 years, Brighton has been England's most interesting seaside city, and today it is more vibrant, eccentric, and cosmopolitan than ever. A rich cultural mix—Regency architecture, specialty shops, sidewalk cafés, lively arts, and a flourishing gay scene—makes it unique and always unpredictable.

It could be said that Brighton owes its fame and fortune to seawater. In 1750 physician Richard Russell published a book recommending seawater treatment for glandular diseases. The fashionable world flocked to Brighton to take Dr. Russell's "cure," and sea bathing became a popular pastime. Few places in the south of England were better for it, since Brighton's broad beach of smooth pebbles stretches as far as the eye can see. It has been popular with sunbathers ever since. The next windfall for the town was the arrival of the Prince of Wales (later George IV). "Prinny," as he was called, created the Royal Pavilion, a mock-Asian pleasure palace that attracted London society. The visitors triggered a wave of villa-building. Today the elegant terraces of Regency houses are today among the town's greatest attractions.

Londoners are still and flocking to Brighton in ever-growing numbers. Combined with the presence of local university students, the effect is to make this a trendy, young, laid-back city that does, occasionally, burst at its own seams. Property values have skyrocketed in recent years, but all visitors are likely to notice is the good shopping, excellent restaurants, and wild nightlife.

Main Attractions

Beach. The foundation of everything in Brighton is its broad beach, which spreads smoothly from one end of town to the other. In the summer sunbathers, swimmers, and hawkers selling ice cream and toys pack the shore; in the winter people stroll at the water's stormy edge, walking their dogs and searching for seashells. It's a stone beach—covered in a thick blanket of large, smooth pebbles. ■ TIP→ **If you plan on swimming, bring a pair of rubber swimming shoes, as the stones are hard on bare feet.**

23 Brighton Museum and Art Gallery. The grounds of the Royal Pavilion contain this museum, whose buildings were designed as a stable block for the prince regent's horses. The museum includes especially interesting art-nouveau and art-deco collections. Look out for Salvador Dalí's famous sofa in the shape of Mae West's lips, and pause at the Balcony Café for its bird's-eye view over the 20th-century Art and Design Gallery. ✉ *Church St.* ☎ *01273/290900* ⊕ *www.brighton.virtualmuseum.info* 🎟 *Free* ⏲ *Tues. 10–7, Wed.–Sat. 10–5, Sun. 2–5.*

★ **20 Brighton Pier.** Opened in 1899, the pier is an amusement park set above the sea. In the early 20th century it had a music hall and entertainment; today it has carnival rides and game arcades, along with clairvoyants, henna tattoo artists, and greasy food stalls. In the summer, it is always packed with children by day, and teenagers by night. ☎ *01273/609361* ⊕ *www.brightonpier.co.uk* ⏲ *Mid-Sept.–June, daily 10 AM–midnight; July–mid-Sept., daily 9 AM–2 AM.*

24 The Lanes. This maze of alleys and passageways was once the home of fishermen and their families. Closed to vehicular traffic, the area's cobbled streets are filled with interesting restaurants, boutiques, and antiques shops. Fish and seafood restaurants line the heart of the Lanes, at Market Street and Market Square. ✉ *Bordered by West, North, East, and Prince Albert Sts.*

NEED A BREAK? On the street adjacent to the bus stop, and less than a five-minute walk from the Royal Pavilion, the **Mock Turtle** (✉ 4 Pool Valley ☎ 01273/328380) is a great old-fashioned, homey café. Alongside a decent selection of teas and coffees are four types of rarebit, homemade soup, and scones. It's closed Monday.

★ **22 Royal Pavilion.** The most remarkable building on the Steine is this domed and pinnacled fantasy. Planned as a simple seaside villa and built in the fashionable classical style of 1787 by architect Henry Holland, the Pavilion was rebuilt between 1815 and 1822 by John Nash for the prince regent (later George IV), who wanted an exotic, Eastern design with opulent Chinese interiors. Today period furniture and ornaments, some given or lent by the current Royal Family, fill the interior. The two great set pieces are the **Music Room,** styled in the form of a Chinese pavilion, and the **Banqueting Room,** with its enormous flying-dragon "gasolier," or gaslight chandelier, a revolutionary invention in the early 19th century. In the kitchens, palm-tree columns support the ceilings. The upstairs bedrooms contain a selection of cruel caricatures of the prince regent, most produced during his lifetime. The gardens, too, have been restored to Regency splendor, following John Nash's naturalistic design of 1826. ■ **TIP➜** For an elegant time-out, retire to one of the Pavilion's bedrooms, where a tearoom serves snacks and light meals. ✉ *Old Steine* ☎ *01273/290900* ⊕ *www.royalpavilion.org.uk* 🎟 *£7.50* ⏲ *Oct.–Mar., daily 10–5:15; Apr.–Sept., daily 9:30–5:45; last admission 45 mins before closing.*

21 Steine. One of the centers of Brighton's action is the Steine (pronounced steen), a large open area close to the seafront. This was a river mouth until the Prince of Wales had it drained in 1793.

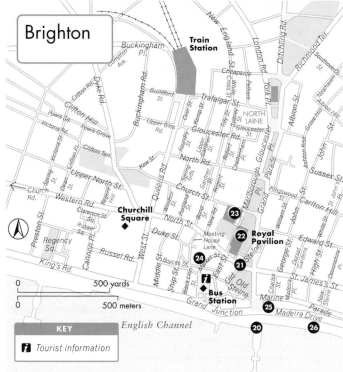

Also Worth Seeing

✋ **㉕** **Sea Life Centre.** Near Brighton Pier, this aquarium has a large number of sea-dwelling creatures—from sharks to sea horses—in more than 30 marine habitats. It also has a giant-turtle convalescence center. Allow two hours to see it. ✉ *Marine Parade* ☎ *01273/604234* ⊕ *www. sealifeeurope.com* 🎫 *£9.50* ⊙ *Apr.–Oct., daily 10–5; Nov.–Mar., daily 10–4.*

✋ **㉖** **Volk's Electric Railway.** Built by inventor Magnus Volk in 1883, this was the first public electric railroad in Britain. In summer you can take the 1¼-mi trip along Marine Parade. ✉ *Marine Parade* ☎ *01273/292718* 🎫 *£1.40 one-way, £2.40 round-trip* ⊙ *Late Mar.–Sept., weekdays 10:30–5, weekends 10:30–6.*

Where to Stay & Eat

££££–£££££ ✕ **One Paston Place.** One of Brighton's best restaurants, this elegant but unstuffy place offers fine French food in a small but uncrowded room, elegantly decorated with cream linens and gilded mirrors. The fixed-price lunch (£16–£19) is the best bargain, although dinner is more leisurely. Main courses of locally raised lamb and freshly caught seafood come with creative but unfussy sauces. Dining here is an event, so jacket and

All Hail the Regent

THE TERM "REGENCY" comes from the last 10 years of the reign of George III (1811–20), who was deemed unfit to rule because of his mental problems. Real power was officially given to the prince of Wales, also known as the prince regent, who became King George IV and ruled until his death in 1830. Throughout his regency, George spent grand sums indulging his flamboyant tastes in architecture and interior decorating—while failing in affairs of state. The distinctive architecture of the Royal Pavilion is a prime, if extreme, example of the Regency style, popularized by architect John Nash (1752–1835) in the early part of the 19th century.

The style is characterized by a diversity of influences—French, Greek, Italian, Persian, Japanese, Chinese, Roman, Indian—you name it. Nash was George IV's favorite architect, beloved for his interest in Indian and Asian designs and for his neoclassical designs, as evidenced in his plans for Regent's Park and its terraces in London.

tie are recommended. ⊠ *1 Paston Pl.* ☎ *01273/606933* 🖃 *AE, MC, V* ☻ *Closed Sun. and Mon.*

£££–££££ ✕ **Nounou.** Inspired by contemporary Moroccan and French cuisine, this polished, romantic restaurant has made headlines in Brighton for its delightful, unique fare. Dishes combine the best French techniques with Moroccan specialties such as tagine of lamb with *merquez* (a spicy lamb sausage) and couscous. Grilled scallops on lemongrass risotto make a great starter. ⊠ *St. George's Rd.* ☎ *01273/682200* 🖃 *AE, MC, V* ☻ *Closed Sun. and Mon.*

£££–££££ ✕ **Seven Dials.** A former bank houses a restaurant that's both striking and surprisingly laid-back. Sophisticated modern English cuisine rules the menu, with choices such as roasted rump of lamb given a new look when served with eggplant caviar and an olive and rosemary sauce. It's worth blowing your diet for the desserts. Business groups and couples gravitate to this place. ⊠ *1 Buckingham Pl.* ☎ *01273/885555* 🖎 *Reservations essential* 🖃 *AE, MC, V.*

££–£££ ✕ **Brighton Rock Beach House.** Come here for a tongue-in-cheek take on a classic New England–beach bar that could have been lifted whole off Cape Cod and dropped in central Brighton. The menu is just as American, with Maine crab cakes, New England clam chowder, and irresistible lobster cheesecake. The mood is pure beach: some tables are outside, surrounded by driftwood (although this is Brighton, so there's no sand). Cool jazz plays as you eat. ⊠ *6 Rock Pl.* ☎ *01273/601139* 🖃 *MC, V.*

£–£££ ✕ **Nia Café.** In the funky North Laine area, Nia has views down Trafalgar Street from its pavement tables. Besides good coffees and leaf teas, excellent café food is available all day, from simple (but freshly made) sandwiches to fillets of cod stuffed with wild mushrooms served with a lemony spinach salad. The decor is basic, but large windows and fresh flowers make it friendly. Nia is also near the station, which is handy if you have time to kill before a train or you need to reenergize before sightseeing. ⊠ *87–88 Trafalgar St.* ☎ *01273/671371* 🖃 *MC, V.*

££££–£££££ ✕🖾 **Drakes.** It's easy to miss the low-key sign for this elegant, modern hotel, tucked away amid the frilly houses on Marine Parade on the seafront. Inside, everything is cool, calm, and sleekly designed. The lobby is dark and sophisticated, and each guest room has its own style, with handmade wallpaper, firm beds covered in luxurious linens, well-designed bathrooms, and art everywhere. Some "feature" rooms have quirky touches, including claw-foot tubs in front of the bedroom windows. Gingerman, the hotel restaurant, has a huge local following for its modern British cuisine (£27 and £32 for two or three courses). ✉ *43–44 Marine Parade* ☎ *01273/696934* ⊕ *www.drakesofbrighton.com* ⇨ *20 rooms* ⚿ *Restaurant, cable TV with movies, in-room data ports, lounge, bar, business services* ▭ *AE, DC, MC, V.*

WORD OF MOUTH

"Brighton is a real city. [It has] a good range of pubs and restaurants, tons of quirky shops . . . Rye will confirm Masterpiece Theatre cliches of England. Brighton will show you what nonsense they are."   –flanneruk

££££ ✕🖾 **Hotel du Vin.** At this outpost of a stylish minichain near the seafront, rooms are crisply modern, with pampering touches such as Egyptian linens and large "monsoon" showers. The bistro restaurant (£££–££££) offers classic fare that makes use of local seafood, and the extensive wine list includes many good values. The wine bar will satisfy connoisseurs (special events take place throughout the year), and you can have a cigar from the cigar gallery before you play billiards. ✉ *Ship St., BN1 1AD* ☎ *01273/718588* ⎙ *01273/718599* ⊕ *www.hotelduvin.com* ⇨ *34 rooms, 3 suites* ⚿ *Restaurant, billiards, wine bar, meeting rooms; no a/c* ▭ *AE, DC, MC, V.*

★ £££££ 🖾 **Grand Hotel.** The city's most famous hotel and a Brighton landmark, the Grand sits on the seafront, a huge, creamy Victorian wedding cake of a building dating from 1864. It's both imposing and elegant, with high-ceiling public rooms richly decorated with enormous chandeliers and plenty of marble. The spacious bedrooms are traditional in style, with luxurious drapes and large bathrooms. It's famous in Britain for having survived an IRA bombing attack in 1984 that targeted Prime Minister Margaret Thatcher and killed five people, although Thatcher survived unscathed. Having tea at the Grand is a Brighton tradition, and highly recommended. ✉ *King's Rd., BN1 2FW* ☎ *01273/224300* ⎙ *01273/224321* ⊕ *www.grandbrighton.co.uk* ⇨ *200 rooms, 3 suites* ⚿ *Restaurant, minibars, cable TV with movies, in-room data ports, indoor pool, gym, massage, sauna, steam room, lounge, nightclub, business services, meeting rooms, some pets allowed (fee); no a/c in some rooms* ▭ *AE, DC, MC, V* ⧨ *BP.*

££££–£££££ 🖾 **Nineteen.** A calm oasis of white, this guesthouse is filled with contemporary art and chic designer accessories. Beds are supported on platforms of glass bricks that filter an ocean-blue light. Massages, yoga sessions, and manicures are pampering amenities. There's a basement kitchen with snacks for guests. ✉ *19 Broad St., BN2 1TJ* ☎ *01273/675529* ⎙ *01273/675531* ⊕ *www.hotelnineteen.co.uk* ⇨ *8 rooms* ⚿ *In-room VCRs, massage, some pets allowed; no a/c, no kids, no smoking* ▭ *MC, V* ⧨ *BP.*

£££–££££ 🏨 **Pelirocco.** Here the imaginations of designers have been given free rein, and the result is a vicarious romp through pop art and rock and roll. Rooms have themes: there's the leopard-print pin-up parlor (Betty's Boudoir), a boxing ring (Ali's Room), and the futuristic Bubble Suite with a plunge bath and mirrored ceiling. It's all way over the top, so you'll either love this place or hate it. ⊠ *10 Regency Sq., BN1 2FG* ☎ *01273/327055* 🖨 *01273/733845* ⊕ *www.hotelpelirocco.co.uk* ⇔ *18 rooms, 1 suite* ⟳ *Room TVs with video games, in-room broadband, in-room data ports, bar, no-smoking rooms; no a/c, no kids under 12 on weekends* ⊟ *AE, MC, V* ⦿ *BP.*

££–££££ 🏨 **Brighton Wave.** This sleekly designed hotel is all about relaxation. Beds are big and covered in soft, white linens; rooms are painted in restful pale shades of blue and white; and breakfast is served in bed. The look is minimal without being cold, and service hits just the right note of friendliness and helpfulness. ⊠ *10 Madeira Pl., BN2 1TN* ☎ *01273/676794* ⊕ *www.brightonwave.com* ⇔ *8 rooms* ⟳ *Cable TV, in-room DVD, Wi-Fi* ⊟ *AE, DC, MC, V* ⦿ *BP.*

££–£££ 🏨 **The Dove.** Washes of light and an uncluttered look are the keynotes of this immaculate Regency house. Rooms at the front have enormous bay-window views across the square, and you can see the sea from the narrow balconies. There's no elevator, and the stairs to the attic rooms are steep. Breakfast includes vegetarian options. ⊠ *18 Regency Sq., BN1 2FG* ☎ *01273/779222* 🖨 *01273/746912* ⊕ *www.thedovehotel.co.uk* ⇔ *9 rooms* ⟳ *Dining room; no a/c* ⊟ *AE, DC, MC, V* ⦿ *BP.*

££–£££ 🏨 **Granville Hotel.** Three grand Victorian buildings facing the sea make up this hotel. Guest rooms, heavily decorated with a theme (themed rooms are a Brighton fad), include the pink-and-white Brighton Rock and the art-deco Noel Coward rooms. Dadu, the hotel's restaurant, is worth a stop. ⊠ *124 King's Rd., BN1 2FY* ☎ *01273/326302* 🖨 *01273/728294* ⊕ *www.granvillehotel.co.uk* ⇔ *24 rooms* ⟳ *Restaurant, coffee shop, some in-room hot tubs, in-room broadband, bar, meeting rooms, some pets allowed; no a/c, no smoking* ⊟ *AE, DC, MC, V* ⦿ *BP.*

Nightlife & the Arts

NIGHTLIFE Brighton is a techno hub, largely because so many DJs have moved here from London. Clubs and bars present live music most nights, and on weekends the entire town can be a bit too raucous for some tastes. This is not a quiet seaside town; it's a seafront city. Try the popular **Above Audio** (⊠ 10 Marine Parade ☎ 01273/606906) in an art-deco building east of Brighton Pier. Specialty nights at the **Funky Buddha Lounge** (⊠ 169 Kings Rd., Arches ☎ 01273/725541) are at the forefront of Brighton's underground, with funk and acid disco blasting out to a fairly sophisticated crowd. Small, friendly, and unfailingly funky, the **Jazz Place** (⊠ 10 Ship St. ☎ 01273/328439) can get a little cramped but makes up for it with cool, jazzy attitude. **The Zap Club** (⊠ 189–192 King's Rd., Arches ☎ 01273/202407), under the arches right on the beach, is Brighton's most well-established club, but no longer as trendy as it once was.

THE ARTS The three-week-long **Brighton Festival** (☎ 01273/706771 ⊕ www.
★ brighton-festival.org.uk), one of England's biggest and liveliest arts festivals, takes place every May in venues around town. The more than 600 events include drama, music, dance, and visual arts.

The **Theatre Royal** (✉ New Rd. ☎ 01273/328488), close to the Royal Pavilion, has a gem of an auditorium that is a favorite venue for shows on their way to or fresh from London's West End.

Shopping

The main shopping area to head for is **the Lanes,** especially for antiques or jewelry. It also has clothing boutiques, coffee shops, and pubs. Across North Street from the Lanes lies the **North Laine,** a network of narrow streets full of little stores, less glossy than those in the Lanes, but fun, funky, and exotic.

Colin Page (✉ 36 Duke St. ☎ 01273/325954), at the western edge of the Lanes, stocks a wealth of antiquarian and secondhand books at all prices. The **Pavilion Shop** (✉ 4–5 Pavilion Bldgs. ☎ 01273/292798), next door to the Royal Pavilion, carries well-designed toys, trinkets, books, and cards—all with a loose Regency theme—and high-quality fabrics, wallpapers, and ceramics based on material in the Pavilion itself. **Oliviers and Co.** (✉ 23A East St. ☎ 01273/739840) sells beautiful, if expensive, tapenades, flavored oils, soaps, candles, and pots—all with an olive content or theme. The old-fashioned **Pecksniff's Bespoke Perfumery** (✉ 45–46 Meeting House La. ☎ 01273/723292) mixes and matches ingredients to suit your wishes. **Simultane** (✉ 52 Ship St. ☎ 01273/777535), a boutique near the waterfront, displays women's fashions from its own label—contemporary looks inspired by the styles of the 1940s and '50s—and clothing from other designers. **Souk Trading** (✉ 4 Little East St. ☎ 01273/776477) supplies an authentic taste of Marrakech for reasonable prices; check out superb lamps, candlesticks, pots, and mirrors.

Arundel

㉗ *23 mi west of Brighton, 60 mi south of London.*

The little hilltop town of Arundel is dominated by its great castle, the much-restored home of the dukes of Norfolk for more than 700 years, and an imposing neo-Gothic Roman Catholic cathedral—the duke is Britain's leading Catholic peer. The town itself is full of interesting old buildings and well worth a stroll.

Begun in the 11th century, vast **Arundel Castle** remains rich with the history of the Fitzalan and Howard families and with paintings by Van Dyck, Gainsborough, and Reynolds. It suffered destruction during the Civil War and was remodeled during the 18th century and the Victorian era. The keep, rising from its conical mound, is as old as the original castle, whereas the barbican and the Barons' Hall date from the 13th century. The castle interior was reconstructed in the fashionable Gothic style of the 19th century. Among the treasures are the rosary beads and prayer book used by Mary, Queen of Scots, in preparing for her execution. The castle's ceremonial entrance is at the top of High Street, but you enter at the bottom, close to the parking lot. ✉ *Mill Rd.* ☎ *01903/882173* ⊕ *www.arundelcastle.org* 💷 *£12, grounds only £6.50* ☉ *Apr.–Oct., Sun.–Fri. noon–5 (grounds open 1 hr earlier); last admission at 4.*

2

Where to Stay & Eat

£–££ ✕ **Black Rabbit.** This renovated 18th-century pub is a find, and you must persevere along Mill Road to find it. Its location by the River Arun, with views of the castle and a bird sanctuary, makes it ideal for a summer lunch. There's a good selection of real ales and an all-day restaurant. ⊠ *Mill Rd., Offham* ☎ *01903/882828* ▭ *DC, MC, V.*

★ ▦ **Amberley Castle.** The lowering of the portcullis every night at mid-

££££–£££££ night is a sure sign that you're in a genuine medieval castle, one that celebrated its 900th birthday in 2003. Across the dry moat, present-day luxury dominates. Antiques and rich drapery furnish the individually designed bedrooms, and many have lattice windows, beamed ceilings, and curtained four-posters. You can dine in either the Queens restaurant, beneath a 12th-century barrel-vaulted ceiling, or amid suits of armor in the Great Room. ⊠ *5 mi north of Arundel, off B2139, Amberley BN18 9LT* ☎ *01798/831992* ▤ *01798/831998* ⊕ *www.amberleycastle.co.uk* ⊋ *20 rooms* ⌂ *Restaurant, in-room hot tubs, in-room VCRs, putting green, tennis court, bar, meeting rooms; no a/c, no kids under 12* ▭ *AE, DC, MC, V* ❙⊙❙ *CP.*

£££–££££ ▦ **Norfolk Arms Hotel.** Like the cathedral and the castle in Arundel, this 18th-century coaching inn on the main street was built by one of the dukes of Norfolk. Some rooms are small (the hotel dubs them "cozy"), but those in an annex in the courtyard block hold bigger, modern rooms. Many are decorated in a frilly style. ⊠ *22 High St., BN18 9AD* ☎ *01903/ 882101* ▤ *01903/884275* ⊕ *www.norfolkarmshotel.com* ⊋ *34 rooms* ⌂ *Restaurant, 2 bars, business services, meeting rooms, some pets allowed (fee); no a/c* ▭ *AE, DC, MC, V* ❙⊙❙ *BP.*

Chichester

28 *10 mi west of Arundel, 66 mi southwest of London.*

The Romans founded Chichester, the capital city of West Sussex, on the low-lying plains between the wooded South Downs and the sea. The city walls and major streets follow the original Roman plan. This cathedral town, a good base for exploring the area, is a well-respected theatrical hub, with a reputation for attracting good acting talent during its summer repertory season.

Norman **Chichester Cathedral,** near the corner of West and South streets, stands on Roman foundations and includes sections from later periods, such as a freestanding bell tower from the 15th century. Inside, a glass panel reveals Roman mosaics uncovered during restoration. Other treasures are the wonderful Saxon limestone reliefs of the raising of Lazarus and Christ arriving in Bethany, both in the choir area. Among the outstanding contemporary artworks are a stained-glass window by Marc Chagall, a colorful tapestry by John Piper, and a painting by Graham Sutherland. ⊠ *West St.* ☎ *01243/782595* ⊕ *www.chichestercathedral. org.uk* ▱ *£3 suggested donation* ⊙ *Easter–Sept., daily 7:15–7; Oct.–Easter, daily 7:15–6. Tours Mon.–Sat. at 11:15 and 2:30.*

Chichester's architecture is mainly Georgian, and its 18th-century stone houses give it a wonderful period appearance. One of the best is **Pallant**

TAKE A HIKE

For those who prefer to travel on their own two feet, the Southeast offers long sweeps of open terrain that makes walking a pleasure. Ardent walkers can explore all or part of the North Downs Way (153 mi) and the South Downs Way (106 mi), following ancient paths along the tops of the downs—the undulating treeless uplands typical of the area. Both trails give you wide views over the countryside. The North Downs Way follows part of the old Pilgrim's Way to Canterbury that so fascinated Chaucer. The South Downs Way crosses the chalk landscape of Sussex Downs, with parts of the route going through deep woodland. Along the way, charming little villages serve the walkers cool ale in inns that have been doing precisely that for centuries. The 30-mi (north–south) Downs Link joins the two routes. Along the Kent coast, the Saxon Shore Way, 143 mi from Gravesend to Rye, passes four Roman forts along its way. Guides to these walks are available from the Southeast England Tourist Board (⊕ www.visitsoutheastengland.com); also check the National Trails Web site (⊕ www.nationaltrail.co.uk).

House, built in 1712 as a wine merchant's mansion. At that time, its state-of-the-art design showed the latest in complicated brickwork and superb wood carving. Appropriate antiques and porcelains furnish the faithfully restored rooms. The **Pallant House Gallery,** attached to the house, showcases a small but important collection of mainly modern British art. Admission includes entry to the **Hans Fiebusch Studio,** nearby in St. Martin's Square, with an exact re-creation of the St. John's Wood (London) studio of this exiled German artist (1898–1998) who was the last member of the so-called degenerate art group. ⊠ 9 N. Pallant ☎ 01243/774557 ⊕ www.pallant.org.uk ☑ £4 ⊙ Tues.–Sat. 10–5, Sun. and national holidays 12:30–5.

In 1960, workers digging a water-main ditch uncovered a Roman wall; so began nine years of archaeological excavation of the **Fishbourne Roman Palace,** the remains of the largest, grandest Roman villa in Britain. Intricate mosaics (including Cupid riding a dolphin) and painted walls lavishly decorate what is left of many of the 100 rooms of the palace, built in the 1st century AD, possibly for local chieftain Tiberius Claudius Togidubnus. It's a glimpse of high living, Roman-leader style. You can explore the sophisticated bathing and heating systems, and the only example of a Roman garden in northern Europe. A good on-site museum displays artifacts from the site and puts the building into historical perspective. The palace is ½ mi west of Chichester. ⊠ Salthill Rd., Fishbourne ☎ 01243/785859 ⊕ www.sussexpast.co.uk ☑ £5.20 ⊙ Mar.–July, Sept., and Oct., daily 10–5; Aug., daily 10–6; Nov.–mid-Dec. and Feb., daily 10–4; mid-Dec.–Jan., weekends 10–4.

★ Twenty acres of woodland provide a backdrop for **Sculpture at Goodwood,** a collection of contemporary British sculpture specially commis-

2

sioned by the Hat Hill Sculpture Foundation. A third of the approximately 40 exhibits change annually, and walks through green fields connect the pieces, sited to maximize their effect. The park is 3 mi north of Chichester, signposted on the right off A286. ☒ *Hat Hill Copse, Goodwood* ☎*01243/538449* ⊕*www.sculpture.org.uk* ☒*£10* ☺*Easter–Oct., Tues.–Sun. and national holidays 10:30–5.*

It's worth a stop in Singleton, a secluded village 5 mi north of Chichester, to see the excellent **Weald and Downland Open Air Museum,** a sanctuary for historical buildings. Among the 45 structures moved to 50 acres of wooded meadows are a cluster of medieval houses, a working water mill, a Tudor market hall, and an ancient blacksmith's shop. ☒ *A286* ☎ *01243/811363* ⊕ *www.wealddown.co.uk* ☒ *£8* ☺ *Apr.–Oct., daily 10:30–6; Nov., Dec., mid-Feb.–Mar., daily 10:30–4; Jan.–mid-Feb., weekends and Wed. 10:30–4:30; last admission 1 hr before closing.*

Where to Stay & Eat

£££ ✕**Comme Ça.** Its location, about a five-minute walk across the park from the Chichester Festival Theatre, makes this attractively converted pub a pleasant spot for a meal before a performance. Bunches of dried hops, suspended from the ceiling, and antique children's toys decorate the dining room. The owner, Michel Navet, is French, and his chef produces authentic French dishes. The fixed-price lunch menu offers two courses for £18 or three for £21. ☒ *67 Broyle Rd.* ☎ *01243/788724* ▭ *AE, DC, MC, V* ☺ *Closed Mon. No dinner Sun. No lunch Tues.*

£££ ▥ **Ship Hotel.** Built in 1790, this architecturally interesting hotel near the Chichester Festival Theatre was originally the home of Admiral Sir George Murray, one of Admiral Nelson's right-hand men. Among the outstanding elements are the flying (partially freestanding) staircase and colonnade. The house has been carefully restored to its 18th-century elegance after spending time as a dental clinic and then an antiques shop, before World War II. Reproduction period furniture fills the pastel guest rooms, which are simpler than the public areas. Prices rise steeply during the Glorious Goodwood horse race in July. ☒ *North St., PO19 1NH* ☎ *01243/778000* ▤ *01243/788000* ⊕ *www.shiphotel.com* ➥ *36 rooms* ☍ *Restaurant, cable TV, bar, meeting rooms, some pets allowed; no a/c* ▭ *AE, DC, MC, V* ▥◎▯ *BP.*

Nightlife & the Arts

The **Chichester Festival Theatre** (☒ Oaklands Park ☎ 01243/781312 ⊕ www.cft.org.uk) presents classics and modern plays from May through September and is a venue for touring companies the rest of the year. Built in 1962, it has an international reputation for innovative performances and attracts theatergoers from across the country, including London.

Petworth House

❷❾ *13 mi northeast of Chichester, 12 mi northwest of Arundel, 54 mi south*
FodorśChoice *of London.*
★

One of the National Trust's greatest treasures, the imposing 17th-century home of Lord and Lady Egremont holds an outstanding collection of

English paintings by Gainsborough, Reynolds, and Van Dyck, as well as 19 oil paintings by the great proponent of Romanticism J. M. W. Turner, who often visited Petworth and immortalized it in luminous drawings. A 13th-century chapel is all that remains of the original manor house. The celebrated landscape architect Capability Brown (1716–83) added a 700-acre deer park. Other highlights include Greek and Roman sculpture and Grinling Gibbons wood carvings, such as those in the spectacular Carved Room. Six rooms in the servants' quarters, among them the old kitchen, are open to the public, and the Servants Block serves light lunches. You can reach the house off A272 and A283 (parking lots are off the latter). Between 11 and 1 visits are by guided tour only. ✉ *Petworth* ☎ *01798/ 342207* ⊕ *www.nationaltrust.org.uk* 🎟 *£8, gardens only £3* ⊙ *House Apr.–late Oct., Sat.–Wed. 11–5; last admission at 4:30. Gardens late Mar.–late Oct., Sat.–Wed. 11–6; Nov.–mid-Dec., Wed.–Sat. 10–3:30. Park daily 8–dusk.*

> ### A TEMPTING TOWN
>
> After you visit Petworth House, take time to explore the small town of Petworth, a jewel studded with narrow old streets and timbered houses. Temptation awaits, too: this is a center for fine antiques and collectibles, with many excellent shops.

MASTERPIECES NEAR TUNBRIDGE WELLS

England is famous for its magnificent stately homes and castles, but many of them are scattered across the country. Within a 15-mi radius of Tunbridge Wells, however, in that area of hills and hidden dells known as the Weald, lies a wealth of architectural wonder in historic homes, castles, and gardens: Penshurst Place, Hever Castle, Chartwell, Knole, Ightham Mote, Leeds Castle, Sissinghurst Castle Garden, and Bodiam Castle.

Royal Tunbridge Wells

30 *39 mi southeast of London.*

Nobody much bothers with the "Royal" anymore, but Tunbridge Wells is no less regal because of it. For whatever reason, this historic bedroom community has been the butt of jokes for years. "Disgusted of Tunbridge Wells" was the national name for anybody who complained at length about small problems. It's seen as conservative and upper-middle class—and so it is. But that doesn't make the town any less attractive and handy as a base for exploring nearby gardens and historic buildings.

The city owes its prosperity to the 17th- and 18th-century passion for spas and mineral baths. In 1606 a mineral-water spring was discovered here, drawing legions of royal visitors looking for eternal health. Tunbridge Wells reached its zenith in the mid-18th century, when Richard "Beau" Nash presided over its social life. The buildings at the lower end of High Street are mostly 18th century, but as the street climbs the hill north, changing its name to Mount Pleasant Road, structures become more modern.

A good place to begin a visit is at the **Pantiles,** a famous promenade with colonnaded shops near the spring on one side of town. Its odd name derives from the Dutch "pan tiles" that originally paved the area. Now bordered on two sides by busy main roads, the Pantiles remains an elegant, tranquil oasis, and the site of the actual well. ■ TIP→ You can still drink the waters when a "dipper" (the traditional water dispenser) is in attendance, from Easter through September.

The **Church of King Charles the Martyr** (⊠ Chapel Pl.), across the road from the Pantiles, dates from 1678, when it was dedicated to Charles I, who had been executed by Parliament in 1649. Its plain exterior belies its splendid interior; take special note of the beautifully plastered baroque ceiling.

Tunbridge Wells Museum and Art Gallery, at the northern end of Mount Pleasant Road, contains a rather scattered but interesting jumble of local artifacts, prehistoric relics, and Victorian toys, as well as an exhibition of Tunbridge Ware pieces: small, wooden items inlaid with tiny pieces of colored woods. ⊠ *Civic Centre, Mount Pleasant Rd.* ☎ *01892/554171* ⊕ *www.visittunbridgewells.com* ⊟ *Free* ☽ *Mon.–Sat. 9:30–5, Sun. 10–4.*

Where to Stay & Eat

★ ✕ **Thackeray's House.** This mid-17th-century tile-hung house, once the **£££–£££££** home of Victorian novelist William Makepeace Thackeray, is now an elegant restaurant known for creative French cuisine. Specialties include honey-and-dill-glazed duck and roasted salmon with herb crust and calamari noodles. The lunchtime menu du jour is a very good value at £13.95 for two courses. ⊠ *85 London Rd.* ☎ *01892/511921* ⊟ *AE, MC, V* ☽ *Closed Mon. and last wk in Dec. No dinner Sun.*

£££–££££ ✕ **Gracelands Palace.** This weird and wonderful place is a temple to Chinese food and, well, Elvis. Owner Paul Chan is famous in the region for his cabaret of Elvis songs and a fixed-price menu (£15–£19) of Szechuan and Cantonese fare. Pictures of Chan and Elvis decorate the building; it's packed most nights with cheerful fans. ⊠ *3 Cumberland Walk* ☎ *01892/540754* ⊟ *AE, MC, V* ☽ *Closed Sun. No lunch Mon.*

£–££ ✕ **Himalayan Gurkha Restaurant.** It's not what you might expect to find in the cozy confines of Tunbridge Wells, but the Nepalese cuisine of this friendly spot is popular with locals. Spicy mountain dishes are cooked with care in traditional clay ovens or barbecued on flaming charcoal. Vegetarian options are appealing, too. ⊠ *31 Church Rd.* ☎ *01892/ 527834* ⊟ *MC, V.*

£–££ ✕ **Mount Edgcumbe Restaurant and Bar.** To some degree, the attraction of this creative restaurant above the old town center is the fact that it's in a candlelighted cave. The fact that it's carved out of the limestone foundation of the Mount Edgcumbe Hotel means that it's a very nice cave indeed. On the menu are Southeast Asian dishes such as chicken *satay* and *beef randang* (beef simmered in spices and coconut milk). ⊠ *The Common, TN4 8BX* ☎ *01892/526823* ⊟ *MC, V.*

£££–£££££ ✕⬚ **Hotel du Vin.** Formerly a private house, this elegant sandstone building dating from 1762 has been transformed into a chic boutique hotel with polished wood floors and luxurious armchairs and sofas. Oriental rugs give public rooms an air of warmth that is both intimate and grand, and guest rooms are modern, with pampering bathrooms. The Burgundy Bar stocks a fine selection of wines from the eponymous region of France. The contemporary menu in the bistro (£££) changes daily but is strong on creamy soups and crisp salads. ⊠ *Crescent Rd., near Mount Pleasant Rd., TN1 2LY* ☎ *01892/526455* 🖷 *01892/512044* ⊕ *www.hotelduvin.com* 🖘 *36 rooms* ⌂ *Restaurant, cable TV, billiards, 2 bars, meeting rooms; no a/c* ⊟ *AE, DC, MC, V.*

£££–££££   🏨 **Spa Hotel.** The Goring family, which also runs the noted Goring Hotel in London, owns this plush hotel. Carefully chosen traditional furnishings and details help maintain the country-house flavor of the 1766 Georgian mansion, although guest rooms come with many modern extras. There are superb views from the 15-acre grounds across the town and into the Weald of Kent. The traditional English fare of the Chandelier Restaurant is popular with locals. ⊠ *Mount Ephraim, TN4 8XJ* ☎ *01892/520331* 🖷 *01892/510575* ⊕ *www.spahotel.co.uk* 🖘 *69 rooms* ⌂ *Restaurant, cable TV, Wi-Fi, tennis court, indoor pool, 2 gyms, hair salon, sauna, spa, croquet, bar, meeting rooms, some pets allowed; no a/c in some rooms* ⊟ *AE, DC, MC, V.*

££–£££   🏨 **Old Parsonage.** This friendly guesthouse, 2 mi south of Tunbridge Wells via A267, stands at the top of a quiet lane beside the village church. Built in 1820, the Georgian manor has lovely antique furniture, a dining room with oak refectory table, and a big conservatory for afternoon tea. Two pubs and a restaurant lie within a short walk of the house. ⊠ *Church La., Frant TN3 9DX* ☎ *01892/750773* ⊕ *www.theoldparsonagehotel. co.uk* 🖘 *3 rooms* ⌂ *Croquet, some pets allowed; no a/c, no room phones, no kids under 7* ⊟ *MC, V* ⎜○⎜ *BP.*

Penshurst Place

★ ③ *7 mi northwest of Royal Tunbridge Wells, 33 mi southeast of London.*

At the center of the adorable hamlet of Penshurst stands one of England's finest medieval manor houses, hidden behind tall trees and walls. Although it has a 14th-century hall, Penshurst is mainly Elizabethan and has been the family home of the Sidneys since 1552, giving it particular historical interest. The most famous Sidney is the Elizabethan poet, Sir Philip, author of *Arcadia.* The **Baron's Hall,** topped with a chestnut roof, is the oldest and one of the grandest halls to survive from the early Middle Ages. Family portraits, furniture, tapestries, and armor help tell the story of this house that was first inhabited in 1341 by Sir John de Pulteney, the very wealthy four-times London mayor. The grounds include a toy museum, gift shop, and the 11-acre walled Italian Garden, which displays tulips and daffodils in spring, roses in July, and mistletoe during the winter months. The house is off Leicester Square, which has late-15th-century half-timber structures adorned with soaring brick chimneys. ⊠ *Off B2188; from Tunbridge Wells, follow A26 and B2176* ☎ *01892/870307* ⊕ *www.penshurstplace.com* 🎟 *£7.50 for house tour, grounds only £6* ⊙ *Mar., weekends noon–5:30; Apr.–Oct., daily noon–5. Grounds daily 10:30–6. Last admission 30 mins before closing.*

Where to Stay & Eat

££–££££ ✕ **Spotted Dog.** This pub first opened its doors in 1520 and hardly appears to have changed. Its big inglenook fireplace and heavy beams give it character, and the good food and friendly crowd make it a pleasure to visit. ✉ *Smarts Hill* ☎ *01892/870253* ▭ *MC, V.*

£££–££££ ▦ **Rose and Crown.** Originally a 16th-century inn, this hotel on the main street in Tonbridge (5 mi east of Penshurst, 5 mi north of Tunbridge Wells) has low-beam ceilings and good Jacobean woodwork in the snug, inviting bar and the restaurant. Guest rooms in the main building are traditionally furnished, whereas rooms in the newer annex are more modern in style. ✉ *125 High St., Tonbridge TN9 1DD* ☎ *01732/357966* 📠 *01732/357194* ⊕ *www.rose-andcrownhotel.co.uk* 🛏 *50 rooms* ☖ *Restaurant, café, cable TV, bar, laundry service, concierge, meeting rooms, free parking; no a/c* ▭ *AE, MC, V* ⊙ *BP.*

Hever Castle

32

Fodor's Choice
★

3 mi west of Penshurst, 10 mi northwest of Royal Tunbridge Wells, 30 mi southeast of London.

For some, 13th-century Hever fits the stereotype of what a castle should look like: all turrets and battlements, the whole encircled by a water lily–bound moat. For others, it's too squat in structure (and perhaps too renovated). Here, at her childhood home, the unfortunate Anne Boleyn, second wife of Henry VIII and mother of Elizabeth I, was courted and won by Henry. He loved her dearly for a time but had her beheaded in 1536 after she failed to give birth to a son. He then gave Boleyn's home to his fourth wife, Anne of Cleves, as a present. Famous though it was, the castle fell into disrepair in the 19th century. American millionaire William Waldorf Astor acquired Hever in 1903, and the Astor family owned it until 1983. Astor built a Tudor village to house his staff (it's now a hotel for corporate functions) and created the stunning gardens, which include an excellent maze, a water maze, ponds, playgrounds, tea shops, gift shops, plant shops—you get the picture. In summer activities are non-stop here, with jousting, falconry exhibitions, country fairs, making this one of southern England's most rewarding castles to visit. ✉ *Off B2026, Hever* ☎ *01732/865224* ⊕ *www.hevercastle.co.uk* 🎟 *£9.80, grounds only £7.80* ⊙ *Castle Apr.–Oct., daily noon–6; Mar. and Nov., daily noon–4. Grounds Apr.–Oct., daily 11–6; Mar. and Nov., daily 11–4. Last admission 1 hr before closing.*

> **WORD OF MOUTH**
>
> "Knole is huge and takes several hours to see. Hever isn't as large a house, but the grounds are enormous and the gardens alone take at least 1.5 to 2 hours. By the way, also very near Hever are Chartwell and Penshurst Place—both of which are much more interesting than Leeds Castle."
>
> –janisj

Chartwell

③ *9 mi north of Hever Castle, 12 mi northwest of Tunbridge Wells, 28 mi southeast of London.*

This grand Victorian mansion with views over the Weald was the home of Sir Winston Churchill from 1924 until his death in 1965. Virtually everything has been kept as it was when he lived here, with his pictures, books, photos, and maps. There's even a half-smoked cigar that the World War II prime minister never finished. Churchill was an amateur artist, and his paintings show a different side of the crusty politician. ■ TIP→ **Be sure to explore Chartwell's rose gardens and take one of the country walks.** ⊠ *Off B2026, Westerham* ☎ *01732/866368* ⊕ *www.nationaltrust. org.uk* ⊠ *£7.50, garden and studio only £4* ☉ *Late Mar.–June and Sept.–early Nov., Wed.–Sun. 11–5; July and Aug., Tues.–Sun. 11–5. Last admission at 4:15.*

Knole

③ *8 mi east of Chartwell, 11 mi north of Royal Tunbridge Wells, 27 mi southeast of London.*

Fodor'sChoice
★

The town of Sevenoaks lies in London's commuter belt, a world away from the baronial air of its premier attraction, Knole, the grand, beloved home of the Sackville family since the 16th century. Begun in the 15th century and enlarged in 1603 by Thomas Sackville, Knole, with its complex of courtyards and buildings, resembles a small town. You'll need most of an afternoon to explore it thoroughly. The house is noted for its tapestries, embroidered furnishings, and the most famous set of 17th-century silver furniture to survive. Most of the salons are in the pre-baroque mode, rather dark and armorial. Paintings on display include family portraits by 18th-century artists Thomas Gainsborough and Sir Joshua Reynolds. The magnificently florid staircase was a novelty in its Elizabethan heyday. Vita Sackville-West grew up at Knole and set her novel *The Edwardians*, a witty account of life among the gilded set, here. Encompassed by a 1,000-acre deer park, the house lies in the center of Sevenoaks, opposite St. Nicholas Church. To get there from Chartwell, drive north to Westerham, then pick up A25 and head east for 8 mi. ⊠ *Off A225* ☎ *01732/450608* ⊕ *www.nationaltrust.org.uk* ⊠ *House £6.80, gardens £2.50* ☉ *Late Mar.–early Nov., Wed.–Sun. and national holidays 11–4, last admission at 3:30; gardens May–Sept., 1st Wed. of each month 11–4, last admission at 3.*

Ightham Mote

★ **③** *7 mi southeast of Knole, 10 mi north of Royal Tunbridge Wells, 31 mi southeast of London.*

Finding Ightham Mote requires careful navigation, but it's worth the effort to see a vision right out of the Middle Ages. To enter this outstanding example of a small manor house, you cross a stone bridge over one of the dreamiest moats in England. This moat, however, does not

CLOSE UP

Tips for Treasure Houses

THROUGHOUT THE SOUTHEAST you can wander through the gorgeous homes of the wealthy and the formerly wealthy. Some are privately owned; hundreds of other homes and castles are owned by the National Trust or English Heritage, organizations that raise part of the money needed to maintain them through entrance fees. Here are some things to keep in mind when you visit:

Houses and castles are unique. You may be free to wander at will, or you may be organized into groups like prisoners behind enemy lines. Sometimes the exterior of a building may be spectacular, but the interior dull. It's also true that the gardens and grounds may be as interesting as the house. Our individual reviews alert you to these instances.

Passes may save you money. If you plan to see lots of houses and castles, buy a pass, such as Visit Britain's Great British Heritage Pass, or to join an organization such as the National Trust (⇨ Resources *in* Getting Started *in* Essentials) and thus get free entry. Check entrance fees against your itinerary to be sure what you will save.

Opening hours are seasonal and change. Hours can change abruptly, so call the day before. Many houses are open only from April to October, and they may have extremely limited hours. In other cases the houses have celebrated parks and gardens that are open much of the year. Consider a trip in shoulder seasons if you can't take the crowds that inevitably pack the most popular houses; or explore lesser-known abodes.

Transportation can be a challenge. If you don't have a car, plan transportation in advance. Some places are deep in the countryside; others are more accessible.

Consider a stay at a property. To get even more up close and personal, you can rent a cottage from the National Trust (⊕ www.nationaltrustcottages. co.uk) or English Heritage (⊕ www. english-heritage.org.uk/ holidaycottages). You could stay in the servants' quarters, a lodge, or even a lighthouse. Some privately owned houses have cottages for rent on their estates; their Web sites generally have this information. Also ⇨ Accommodations *in* Booking Your Trip *in* Essentials.

relate to the "mote" in the name, which refers to the role of the house as a meeting place, or "moot." Ightham (pronounced *i*-tem) Mote's magical exterior has changed little since the 14th century, but within you'll find that it encompasses styles of several periods, Tudor to Victorian. The Great Hall is an antiquarian's delight, both comfy and grand, and the Tudor chapel, drawing room, and billiards room in the northwest quarter are highlights. Take time to explore the 14-acre garden and the woodland walks or to eat at the restaurant. To reach the house from Sevenoaks, follow A25 east to A227 (8 mi) and follow the signs. ⊠ *Off A227, Ivy Hatch, Sevenoaks* ☎ *01732/810378* ⊕ *www.nationaltrust. org.uk* ⊠ *£8.50* ⊙ *Mid-Mar.–Oct., Mon., Wed.–Fri., and Sun.: house 10:30–5:30, garden 10–5:30. Estate daily year-round, dawn–dusk.*

Leeds Castle

36 *19 mi northwest of Royal Tunbridge Wells, 40 mi southeast of London.*

The bubbling River Medway runs through Maidstone, Kent's county seat, with its backdrop of chalky downs. Nearby, the fairy-tale stronghold of Leeds Castle commands two small islands on a peaceful lake. Dating to the 9th century and rebuilt by the Normans in 1119, Leeds (not to be confused with the city of Leeds in the north of England; this one is named after a local village) became a favorite home of many medieval English queens. Henry VIII liked it so much he had it converted from a fortress into a grand palace. The interior doesn't match the glories of the much-photographed exterior, although there are fine paintings and furniture, plus a curious dog-collar museum. The outside attractions are more impressive and include a maze, a grotto, an aviary of native and exotic birds, and woodland gardens. The castle is 5 mi east of Maidstone. ⊠ *A20* ☎ *01622/765400* ⊕ *www.leedscastle.org. uk* 🎫 *13; grounds only £10.50* ☉ *Apr.–Oct., daily 10–5; Nov.–Mar., daily 10–3. Castle closed last Sat. in June and 1st Sat. in July.*

Sissinghurst Castle Garden

37 *10 mi south of Leeds Castle, 53 mi southeast of London.*

Fodor's Choice
★

One of the most famous gardens in the world, Sissinghurst rests deep in the Kentish countryside around the remains of a moated Tudor castle. Unpretentiously beautiful, quintessentially English, the gardens were laid out in the 1930s around the remains of part of the castle by writer Vita Sackville-West (one of the Sackvilles of Knole) and her husband, the diplomat Harold Nicolson. Sackville-West's study and library are open limited hours. ■ TIP➔ **Good times to visit the grounds are June and July, when the roses are in bloom.** The White Garden, with its white flowers and silver-gray foliage, is a classic, and the herb garden and cottage garden show Sackville-West's knowledge of plants. Children may feel restricted in the gardens, and strollers (push chairs, in Britain) are not allowed. From Leeds Castle, make your way south on B2163 and A274 through Headcorn, then follow signs. For those without a car, take a train from London's Charing Cross station and transfer to a bus in Staplehurst. Direct buses operate on Tuesday and Sunday between May and August; at other times, take the bus to Sissinghurst village and walk the remaining 1¼ mi. ⊠ *A262, Cranbrook* ☎ *01580/710701* ⊕ *www.nationaltrust.org.uk* 🎫 *£8.50* ☉ *Mar.–Nov., Mon., Tues., and Fri. 11–6:30, weekends 10–6:30; last admission at 5:30. Admission often restricted because of limited space; a timed ticket system may be in effect, usually May–July.*

Where to Stay & Eat

£ ✕ **Claris's Tea Shop.** Claris's, near Sissinghurst Castle Garden, serves traditional English teas in a half-timber room and displays attractive English crafts items. The Cream Tea set includes scones with butter, fresh cream, preserves, and a pot of tea for £4. There's a garden for summer, and a gift shop stocks china and glass. ⊠ *1–3 High St., Biddenden* ☎ *01580/291025* ▤ *No credit cards* ☉ *Closed Mon. No dinner.*

£ ⊞ **Frogshole Oast.** This converted 18th-century rural oasthouse has three kilns that were once used for drying hops. The house still has many period features, and the rooms and sitting area have some antiques. There's a garden and a natural duck pond. ⊠ *Sissinghurst Rd., 2 mi east of Sissinghurst Castle Garden, Biddenden TN27 8HB* ☎☎ *01580/291935* ✎ *hartley@frogsholeoast.freeserve.co.uk* ⤙ *3 rooms* ⚭ *No a/c, no room TVs* ¶⊙¶ *BP.*

Bodiam Castle

★ ☾ **38** *15 mi southeast of Royal Tunbridge Wells, 57 mi southeast of London.*

Immortalized in paintings, postcards, and photographs, the ruins of Bodiam Castle rise out of the distance like a piece of medieval legend. Its turrets, battlements, wooden portcullis, glassy moat, and 2-feet-thick walls survive, but all that was within them is long gone. Built in 1385 to withstand a threatened French invasion, it was "slighted" (partly demolished) during the English Civil War of 1642–46 and has been uninhabited ever since. Still, you can climb the towers to take in sweeping countryside views, and kids can run around in and around the castle. The castle schedules organized activities for kids during school holidays. ⊠ *Off B2244, Bodiam* ☎ *01580/830436* ⊕ *www.nationaltrust.org.uk* ⤳ *£4.60* ☉ *Mid-Feb.–Oct., daily 10–5 or dusk; Nov.–mid-Feb., weekends 10–4 or dusk; last admission 1 hr before closing.*

SOUTHEAST ESSENTIALS

Transportation

BY AIR

Gatwick Airport, 27 mi south of London, has direct flights from many U.S. cities and is more convenient for this region than Heathrow. The terminal for the British Rail line is in the airport buildings, and there are connections to major towns in the region. *See* London Essentials *in* Chapter 1 for information about transfers from Gatwick to London.

🛦 **Gatwick Airport** ⊠ M23, Junction 9, Crawley ☎ 0870/000–2468 ⊕ www.baa.co.uk.

BY BUS

National Express serves the region from London's Victoria Coach Station. Trips to Brighton and Canterbury take two hours; to Chichester, about three hours. For regional bus transport inquiries, contact Traveline. Maps and timetables are available at bus depots, train stations, local libraries, and tourist information centers.

FARES & SCHEDULES 🚌 **National Express** ☎ 0870/580–8080 ⊕ www.nationalexpress.com. **Traveline** ☎ 0870/608–2608 ⊕ www.traveline.org.uk.

BY CAR

Major routes radiating outward from London to the Southeast are, from west to east, M23/A23 to Brighton (52 mi); A21, passing by Royal Tunbridge Wells to Hastings (65 mi); A20/M20 to Folkestone; and A2/M2 via Canterbury (56 mi) to Dover (71 mi).

A car is the easiest way to get to the stately homes and castles in the region. A good link route for traveling through the region, from Hampshire across the border into Sussex and Kent, is A272 (which becomes A265). It runs through the Weald, which separates the North Downs from the more inviting South Downs. Although smaller roads forge deeper into the downs, even the main roads take you through lovely countryside. The main route east from the downs to the Channel ports and resorts of Kent is A27. To get to Romney Marsh (across the Sussex border in Kent), take A259 from Rye. Be warned that more traffic tickets are issued per traffic warden in Brighton than anywhere else in the country.

BY TRAIN

South Eastern trains serve the area from London's Victoria and Charing Cross (for all areas) and Waterloo (for the west). From London, the trip to Brighton takes about one hour by the fast train, and to Dover, almost two hours. The line running west from Dover passes through Ashford, where you can change trains for Hastings and Eastbourne. There are connections from Eastbourne for Lewes, and from Brighton for Chichester. For all information, call National Rail Enquiries. For railway nostalgia, Steam Dreams runs the *Cathedrals Express* steam train several times a year from London Victoria to Canterbury. Round-trip tickets start at £45.

CUTTING COSTS A Network Railcard costing £20, valid throughout the southern and southeastern regions for a year, entitles you and three companions to one-third off many off-peak fares.

FARES & SCHEDULES ⓘ**National Rail Enquiries** ☎0845/748-4950 ⊕ www.nationalrail.co.uk. **National Railcard** ⊕ www.railcard.co.uk.

South Eastern Trains ☎08706/030405 ⊕ www.setrains.co.uk. **Steam Dreams** ☎01483/209888 ⊕ www.steamdreams.co.uk.

Contacts & Resources

EMERGENCIES

ⓘ **Ambulance, fire, police** ☎ 999. **Royal Sussex County Hospital** ⊠ Eastern Rd., Brighton ☎ 01273/696955. **Canterbury Hospital** ⊠ Ethelbert Rd., Canterbury ☎ 01227/766877.

INTERNET

Internet cafés are easy to find in the bigger towns but are rare in the countryside. Similarly, hotels in towns are more likely to have broadband than those in rural areas. Throughout the region Wi-Fi is not common, although Brighton has a few hot spots.

ⓘ Internet Cafés **Brighton Internet** ⊠ 54 Elm Grove, Brighton ☎ 01273/691688. **Curve Internet** ⊠ 44–47 Gardner St., Brighton ☎ 01273/603031. **Canterbury Library** ⊠ High St., Canterbury ☎ 01227/452747.

2

TOUR OPTIONS

BUS TOURS   City Sightseeing's hop-on, hop-off bus tour of Brighton leaves Brighton Pier on Grand Junction Road every 20 to 30 minutes and lasts about an hour. It operates mid-June through August; the cost is £6.50.

🚌 **City Sightseeing** ☎ 01789/294466 ⊕ www.city-sightseeing.com.

PRIVATE GUIDES   The Southeast England Tourist Board (⇨ Visitor Information) arranges private tours with qualified Blue Badge guides. The Canterbury Guild of Guides provides walking guides who know the city and surrounding area. Tours are at 2 PM every day between Easter and October, with an additional tour at 11:30 AM from Monday to Saturday, during July and August. Tour tickets cost £4.50 and are sold at the Information Center, where the walks begin.

🚌 **Canterbury Guild of Guides** ⊠ Arnett House, Hawks La. ☎ 01227/459779 ⊕ www.canterbury-walks.co.uk.

VISITOR INFORMATION

Tourism Southeast can give you information on tours and excursions. The office is open Monday through Thursday 9 to 5:30 and Friday 9 to 5. Local tourist information centers (TICs) are normally open Monday through Saturday 9:30 to 5:30, but hours vary seasonally; offices are listed below by town.

🚌 **Southeast England Tourist Board** ⊠ The Old Brew House, 1 Warwick Park, Royal Tunbridge Wells TN2 5TU ☎01892/540766 🖷01892/511008 ⊕www.visitsoutheastengland.com. **Arundel** ⊠ 61 High St., BN18 9AJ ☎ 01903/882268 ⊕ www.sussex-by-the-sea.co.uk. **Brighton** ⊠10 Bartholomew Sq., BN1 1JS ☎ 0906/7112255 ⊕ www.visitbrighton.com. **Canterbury** ⊠ 12–13 Sun St., CT1 2HX ☎ 01227/378100 ⊕ www.canterbury.co.uk. **Chichester** ⊠29A South St., PO19 1AH ☎01243/775888 ⊕www.chichester.gov.uk. **Dover** ⊠ The Old Town Gaol, Biggin St., CT16 1DL ☎ 01304/205108. **Hastings** ⊠ Queens Sq., Priory Meadow, TN34 1TL ☎ 01424/781111 ⊠ 2 The Stade ☎ 01424/781111 ⊕ www.visithastings.com. **Lewes** ⊠ 187 High St., BN7 2DE ☎ 01273/483448 ⊕ www.lewes.gov.uk. **Maidstone** ⊠ Town Hall, Middle Row, High St., ME14 1TF ☎ 01622/602169 ⊕ www.tour-maidstone.com. **Royal Tunbridge Wells** ⊠ The Old Fish Market, the Pantiles, TN2 5TN ☎01892/515675 ⊕www.visittunbridgewells.com. **Rye** ⊠ The Heritage Centre, Strand Quay, TN31 7AY ☎ 01797/226696 ⊕ www.rye-tourism.co.uk.

The South

WINCHESTER, SALISBURY & STONEHENGE

WORD OF MOUTH

"People often combine Stonehenge with Salisbury . . . I was just in Salisbury again a couple of weeks ago. Salisbury is a lovely town with a beautiful cathedral. I took the tour of the cathedral's tower; it was fantastic."

—P_M

"Don't pass on Stonehenge! For me, Stonehenge has been the highlight of four visits to England and it is not at all 'disappointing' or 'overcommercialized,' nor is it accessible 'only by guided tour' . . . Even if you go during regular hours, you are not really kept that far away—you can still see the stones well."

—Daisy54

Updated by
Robert
Andrews

CATHEDRALS, STATELY HOMES, STONE CIRCLES—the South, made up of Hampshire, Dorset, and Wiltshire counties, holds all kinds of attractions, and not a few quiet pleasures. Two important cathedrals, Winchester and Salisbury (pronounced *sawls*-bree), are here, as are stately homes—Longleat, Stourhead, and Wilton House, among them—intriguing market towns, and hundreds of haunting prehistoric remains, two of which, Avebury and Stonehenge, should not be missed. These are just the tourist-brochure superlatives. Like those who migrate here from every corner of the country in search of upward mobility, anyone spending time in these parts should rent a bike or a car and set out to discover the back-road villages—*not* found in those brochures. After a drink in the village pub and a look at the cricket game on the village green, stretch out in a field for a nap.

Close to London, the green fields of Hampshire divide the cliffs and coves of Devon and Cornwall to the west from the hustle and bustle of the big city. If you have a coastal destination in mind, you may see this as farmland to rush through, but hit the brakes—there's plenty to see.

One of the area's many historical highlights was when Alfred the Great, teaching religion and letters, made Winchester the capital of 9th-century England and helped lay plans for Britain's first navy, sowing the seeds of the Commonwealth. This well-preserved market town is dominated by its cathedral, an imposing edifice dotted with the Gothic tombs of 15th-century bishops. Winchester is a good center from which to visit quiet villages where so many of England's once great personages, from Florence Nightingale to Lord Mountbatten, lived or died. Jane Austen and her works are enduringly popular, and the road to her home at Chawton has become a much-trodden path.

Beyond the gentle, gardenlike landscape of Hampshire, you can explore the somewhat harsher terrain of Salisbury Plain. Two monuments, millennia apart, stand sentinel over the plain. One is the 404-foot-tall stone spire of Salisbury Cathedral, which dominates the entire Salisbury valley and has been immortalized in oil by John Constable. Not far away is the most imposing and dramatic prehistoric structure in Europe: Stonehenge. The many theories about its construction and purpose only add to its attraction, which endures despite the hordes of visitors.

Other districts have their own pleasures, and many have literary or historical associations. Turn your sights to the Dorset heathland, the countryside explored in the novels of Thomas Hardy. This district is spanned by grass-covered chalk hills—the downs—wooded valleys, and meadows through which course meandering rivers. Along the coastline, Lyme Regis also has literary associations; it was favored by Jane Austen and John Fowles, among others.

The South has been quietly central to England's history for well over 4,000 years, occupied successively by prehistoric man, the Celts, the Romans, the Saxons, and the modern British. History continues to be made here. On D-Day, Allied forces sailed for Normandy this coast; nearly 40 years later, British forces set out to recover the Falklands.

Exploring the South

The wide-open, wind-blown inland county of Wiltshire offers a sharp contrast to the tame, sequestered villages of Hampshire and Dorset and the bustle of Portsmouth. This important naval port has much to see, though you may prefer to overnight in the more compelling towns of Salisbury and Winchester.

The obvious draw outside Salisbury is Stonehenge, but you're also within reach of an equally interesting prehistoric monument, Avebury. From there, you can swing south to the cultivated woodlands of the New Forest. The southern coast of Dorset has a string of holiday resorts interspersed with the ancient sites of Corfe Castle, Maiden Castle, and Cerne Abbas. Lyme Regis, on the Devon border at the center of the wide arc of Lyme Bay, provides a gateway to the World Heritage Site called the Jurassic Coast, with its fossil-rich cliffs from Swanage in the east to Exmouth in the west.

About the Restaurants

In summer, and especially on summer weekends, visitors can overrun the restaurants in small villages, so either book a table in advance or be prepared to wait. The more popular or upscale the restaurant, the more critical a reservation is. For local specialties, try fresh-grilled river trout or sea bass poached in brine, or dine like a king on the New Forest's renowned venison. Hampshire is noted for its pig and sheep farming, and you might zero in on pork and lamb dishes on local restaurant menus.

About the Hotels

Modern hotel chains are well represented, and in rural areas you can choose among elegant country-house hotels, traditional coaching inns (updated to different degrees), and modest guesthouses. Some seaside hotels do not accept one-night bookings in summer.

	WHAT IT COSTS In pounds				
	£££££	**££££**	**£££**	**££**	**£**
RESTAURANTS	over £22	£18–£22	£13–£17	£7–£12	under £7
HOTELS	over £160	£120–£160	£90–£119	£60–£89	under £60

Restaurant prices are for a main course at dinner. Hotel prices are for two people in a standard double room in high season, including V.A.T., with no meals or, if indicated, CP (with continental breakfast), BP (Breakfast Plan, with full breakfast), or MAP (Modified American Plan, with breakfast and dinner).

Timing

Don't plan to visit the cathedrals of Salisbury and Winchester on a Sunday, when your visit will be restricted, or during services, when it won't be appreciated by worshippers. Places such as Stonehenge and Longleat House attract plenty of people at all times; bypass such sights on weekends or public holidays. In summer the coastal resorts are crowded; and it may be difficult to find the accommodations you want. The New Forest is most alluring in spring and early summer (for the foaling season)

TOP REASONS TO GO

Salisbury Cathedral: You may be stunned by the sight of one of England's most spectacular cathedrals; try a tour around the roof and spire for a fascinating angle on this must-see monument.

Stonehenge: Despite mixed reports of just how impressive this greatest of all prehistoric stone circles actually is, don't put off a visit. At the right time of day (early or late is best), this mystical ring can still cast a memorable spell against the backdrop of Salisbury Plain.

House and garden at Stourhead: It's the perfect combination. Acres of parkland, landscaped in the 18th century, induce feelings of Arcadian bliss. There are classical temples, a folly, and gorgeous vistas over the lake, as well as a Palladian mansion to explore.

The New Forest: Get away from it all in the South's most extensive wilderness—crisscrossed by myriad trails that are ideal for horseback riding, hiking, and biking.

Historic Dockyard, Portsmouth: Rule, Britannia! Immerse yourself in the country's seafaring history, including an informative and fascinating tour around Nelson's flagship, HMS *Victory*, conducted by naval personnel.

Literary trails: Jane Austen, Thomas Hardy, and John Fowles have all made this part of Britain a happy stomping ground for book buffs, with a concentration of sights in Chawton, Dorchester, and Lyme Regis.

and fall (for the colorful foliage), whereas summer can be busy with walkers and campers. In fall, take waterproof boots for the puddles.

FROM WINCHESTER TO PORTSMOUTH

From the cathedral city of Winchester, 70 mi southwest of London, you can meander southward to the coast, stopping at the bustling port of Portsmouth to explore its maritime heritage.

Winchester

70 mi southwest of London, 14 mi north of Southampton.

Winchester is among the most historic of English cities, and as you walk the graceful streets and wander the many gardens, a sense of the past envelops you. Although it is now merely the county seat of Hampshire, for more than four centuries Winchester served as England's capital. Here, in AD 827, Egbert was crowned first king of England, and his successor, Alfred the Great, held court until his death in 899. After the Norman Conquest in 1066, William I ("the Conqueror") had himself crowned in London, but took the precaution of repeating the ceremony in Winchester. William also commissioned the local monastery to produce the Domesday Book, a record of the general census begun in 1085.

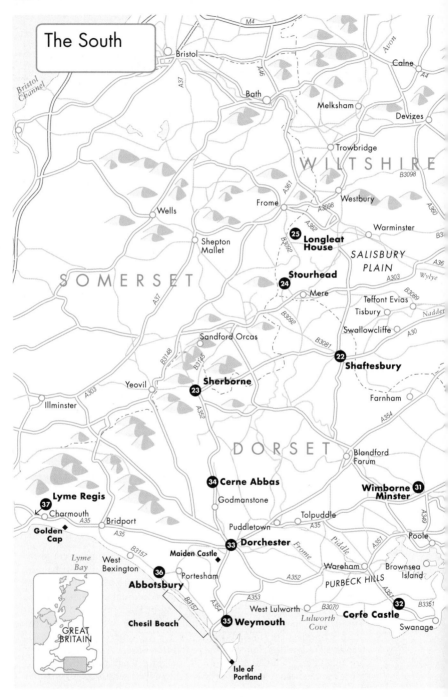

The South

Bristol
Calne
Bristol Channel
Bath
Melksham
Devizes
Trowbridge
WILTSHIRE
Frome
Westbury
Warminster
Wells
25 **Longleat House**
SALISBURY PLAIN
Shepton Mallet
24 **Stourhead**
Mere
Teffont Evias
Tisbury
SOMERSET
Swallowcliffe
Sandford Orcas
22 **Shaftesbury**
Yeovil
23 **Sherborne**
Farnham
Illminster
DORSET
Blandford Forum
34 **Cerne Abbas**
Godmanstone
Wimborne Minster 31
Lyme Regis
Charmouth
Tolpuddle
Poole
107 37
Bridport
Puddletown
Golden Cap
33 **Dorchester**
Frome
Wareham
Brownsea Island
Lyme Bay
West Bexington
Maiden Castle
Piddle
PURBECK HILLS
36 **Abbotsbury**
Portesham
Chesil Beach
West Lulworth
Corfe Castle 32
GREAT BRITAIN
35 **Weymouth**
Lulworth Cove
Swanage
Isle of Portland

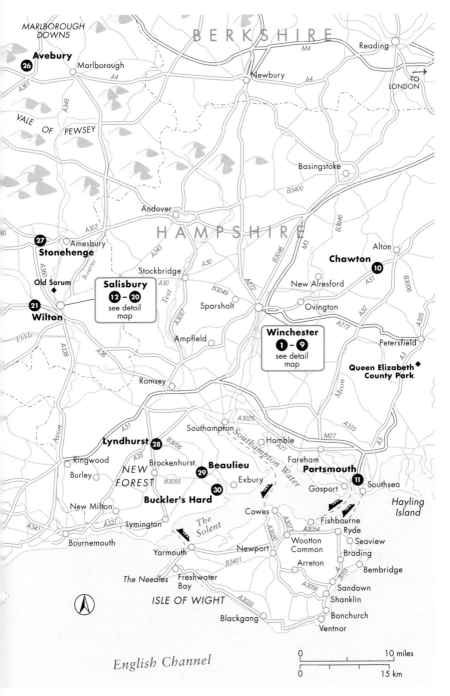

MARLBOROUGH
DOWNS

B E R K S H I R E

M4

Reading

Avebury 26

Marlborough

A4

Newbury

A4

TO
LONDON

A361

A345

VALE OF PEWSEY

Basingstoke

B3400

Andover

H A M P S H I R E

A303

Stonehenge 27

Amesbury

Alton

Chawton 10

A343

Stockbridge

A30

New Alresford

A31

B3006

Old Sarum

Bourne

A30

B3049

Sparsholt

Ovington

A32

A325

Wilton 21

Salisbury
12 – 20
see detail
map

Test

A3057

Ampfield

Winchester
1 – 9
see detail
map

A272

Petersfield

A3

Ebble

A338

A36

Romsey

**Queen Elizabeth
County Park** ◆

Avon

A31

A3025

Southampton

Meon

M27

A333

A3

Lyndhurst 28

B3056

Hamble

Fareham

Ringwood

A35

Brockenhurst

Beaulieu 29

Southampton Water

Portsmouth

Burley

NEW
FOREST

B3055

Exbury

Gosport

11 Southsea

New Milton

Buckler's Hard 30

Cowes

Hayling
Island

A3417

A337

Lymington

The
Solent

Fishbourne

A3054

Ryde

Bournemouth

Yarmouth

Newport

A3020

Wootton
Common

Seaview

Brading

The Needles

Freshwater
Bay

B3401

Arreton

A3055

Bembridge

ISLE OF WIGHT

A3056

Sandown

Shanklin

Blackgang

Bonchurch

Ventnor

English Channel

0 ——————— 10 miles

0 ——————— 15 km

The city remained the center of ecclesiastical, commercial, and political power until the 13th century, when that power shifted to London. Winchester still preserves some of its past glory even if some fast-food outlets and retail chains have moved onto High Street.

Main Attractions

❼ **City Museum.** Across from the cathedral, the museum interprets Winchester's past through displays of Celtic pottery, Roman mosaics, Saxon jewelry and coins, and reconstructed Victorian shops. ⊠ *The Sq.* ☎ *01962/ 848269* 🖾 *Free* ☉ *Apr.–Oct., Mon.–Sat. 10–5, Sun. noon–5; Nov.–Mar., Tues.–Sat. 10–4, Sun. noon–4.*

❷ **Close.** Nearly enveloping the cathedral, this area contains neat lawns and the Deanery, Dome Alley, and Cheyney Court.

❻ **Great Hall.** A few blocks west of the cathedral, this hall is all that remains of the city's Norman castle. Here the English Parliament met for the first time in 1246; Sir Walter Raleigh was tried for conspiracy against King James I and condemned to death in 1603 (although he wasn't beheaded until 1618); and Dame Alice Lisle was sentenced to death by the brutal Judge Jeffreys for sheltering fugitives, after Monmouth's Rebellion in 1685. Occupying one corner of the Great Hall is a huge and gaudy sculpture of Victoria, carved by Sir Alfred Gilbert (responsible for *Eros* in Piccadilly Circus) to mark the Queen's Golden Jubilee in 1887. But the hall's greatest relic hangs on its west wall: King Arthur's Round Table has places for 24 knights and a portrait of Arthur bearing a remarkable resemblance to King Henry VIII. In fact, the table dates back no further than the 13th century and was repainted by order of Henry on the occasion of a visit by the Holy Roman Emperor Charles V; the real Arthur was probably a Celtic cavalry general who held off the invading Saxons after the fall of the Roman Empire in the 5th or 6th century. The Tudor monarchs revived the Arthurian legend for political purposes. Take time to wander through Queen Eleanor's Medieval Garden—a re-creation of a noblewoman's shady retreat. ⊠ *Castle Hill* ☎ *01962/846476* 💷 *Free* ⊙ *Mar.–Oct., daily 10–5; Nov.–Feb., daily 10–4.*

③ King's Gate. On St. Swithun Street on the south side of the Close, this structure was built in the 13th century and is one of two gates remaining from the original city wall. **St. Swithun's Church** is built over King's Gate.

★ ❶ Winchester Cathedral. The city's greatest monument, begun in 1079 and consecrated in 1093, presents a sturdy, chunky appearance in keeping with its Norman construction, so that the Gothic lightness within is even more breathtaking. Its tower, transepts, and crypt, and the inside core of the great Perpendicular nave, reveal some of the world's best surviving examples of Norman architecture. Other features, such as the arcades, the presbytery (behind the choir, holding the high altar), and the windows, are Gothic alterations carried out between the 12th and 14th centuries. Little of the original stained glass has survived, however, thanks to Cromwell's Puritan troops, who ransacked the cathedral in the 17th century during the English Civil War, but you can still see the sumptuously illuminated 12th-century Winchester Bible in the Library and Triforium Gallery.

Among the many well-known people buried in the cathedral are William the Conqueror's son, William II ("Rufus"), mysteriously murdered in the New Forest in 1100; Izaak Walton (1593–1683), author of *The Compleat Angler,* whose memorial window in Silkestede's Chapel was paid for by "the fishermen of England and America"; and Jane Austen, whose grave lies in the north aisle of the nave. Firmly in the 20th century, Antony Gormley's evocative statue, *Sound II* (1986), looms in the crypt, as often as not standing in water (as it was designed to do), because of seasonal flooding. You can also ex-

> **ST. SWITHUN WEATHER**
>
> St. Swithun (died AD 862) is interred in Winchester Cathedral, although he requested outdoor burial. Legend says that when his body was transferred inside from the cathedral's churchyard, it rained for 40 days. Since then, folk wisdom says that rain on St. Swithun's Day (July 15) means 40 more days of wet weather. (Elsewhere in England the name is spelled "Swithin.") Near St. Swithun's Church at King's Gate, at 8 College Street, is the house where Jane Austen died on July 18, 1817, three days after writing a comic poem about the legend of St. Swithun's Day (copies are usually available in the cathedral).

plore the bell tower—with views as far as the Isle of Wight in fair weather—and other recesses of the building on a tour. Special services or ceremonies may mean the cathedral is closed to visits, so telephone first to avoid disappointment. ⊠ *The Close, Cathedral Precincts* ☎ *01962/857200* ⊕ *www.winchester-cathedral.org.uk* 🔊 *£4; Library and Triforium Gallery £1, bell-tower tour £4* ☉ *Mon.–Sat. 8:30–6, Sun. 12:30–3:30, longer for services. Free tours on the hr Mon.–Sat. 10–3, bell-tower tours May–Sept., weekdays 2:15, Sat. 11:30 and 2:15; Oct.–Apr., Wed. 2:15, Sat. 11:30 and 2:15.*

Also Worth Seeing

8 **City Mill.** This working 18th-century water mill, complete with small island garden, is at the east end of High Street. Part of the premises is a National Trust gift shop open year-round, and part is a hostel. ⊠ *Bridge St.* ☎ *01962/870057* ⊕ *www.nationaltrust.org.uk* 🔊 *£3.20* ☉ *Mar., weekends 11–5; Apr. and July–Dec., daily 11–5; May and June, Wed.–Sun. 11–5. Call for milling schedule.*

9 **St. Giles's Hill.** To top off a tour of Winchester, you can climb this hill for a panoramic view of the city. A walk down High Street and Broadway will bring you to the hill.

5 **Westgate.** At the top of High Street, this fortified medieval structure was a debtor's prison for 150 years, and now holds a motley assortment of items relating to Tudor and Stuart times. Suits of armor—examples can be tried on—and the opportunity to make brass rubbings make it popular with kids, and you can take in a view of Winchester from the roof. ⊠ *High St.* ☎ *01962/848269* 🔊 *Free* ☉ *Apr.–Oct., Mon.–Sat. 10–5, Sun. noon–5; Feb. and Mar., Tues.–Sat. 10–4, Sun. noon–4.*

4 **Winchester College.** One of England's oldest "public" (i.e., private) schools was founded in 1382 by Bishop William of Wykeham, who has his own chapel in Winchester Cathedral. The school chapel is notable for its delicately vaulted ceiling. Among the original buildings still in use is Chamber Court, center of college life for six centuries. Notice the "scholars"—students holding academic scholarships—clad in their traditional gowns. ⊠ *College St.* ☎ *01962/621209* ⊕ *www. winchestercollege.co.uk* 🔊 *£3.50* ☉ *1-hr tours Mon., Wed., Fri., and Sat. 10:45, noon, 2:15, and 3:30; Tues. and Thurs. 10:45 and noon; Sun. 2:15 and 3:30.*

Where to Stay & Eat

£££££ ✕ **Chesil Rectory.** The timbered and gabled building may be old English—15th- or 16th-century—but the cuisine is essentially French, mixing classic recipes with local ingredients. On the fixed-price menu, starters such as Jerusalem artichoke soup elegantly complement such main courses as fillet of Hampshire beef Rossini with white truffle pomme puree and Madeira sauce. Service and the antique charm of the surroundings match the quality of the food. ⊠ *1 Chesil St.* ☎ *01962/851555* ☰ *AE, DC, MC, V* ☉ *Closed Sun. and Mon. No lunch Tues.*

££–£££ ✕ **Loch Fyne.** This excellent, fairly priced seafood restaurant, part of a small chain in England and Scotland, has a modern interior behind the 15th-century facade. Inside, the floor-to-ceiling windows create an airy space for dining, and the cheerful service is relaxing. Fish is the center of attention, from peppered mackerel pâté with oatcakes to solid main courses including perfectly poached haddock atop creamed spinach. ⊠ *18 Jewry St.* ☎ *01962/872930* ⌕ *Reservations essential* ▭ *AE, MC, V.*

£–££ ✕ **The Royal Oak.** Try a half pint of draft bitters or dry cider at this lively traditional pub, which claims to have Britain's oldest bar (it has a Saxon wall). The two no-smoking areas—a rarity in British pubs—are in the cellar and on the upper level. Bar meals are served until 9 PM. ⊠ *Royal Oak Passage, off High St.* ☎ *01962/842701* ▭ *AE, MC, V.*

£ ✕ **Cathedral Refectory.** The bold, modern style of this self-service eatery next to the cathedral helps make it a refreshing lunch or snack stop. The menu ranges from traditional soups to cottage pie and fish dishes, but do sample the local "trenchers." This thick bread was used in medieval times as a plate from which to eat meat; once soaked in the meat juices, the bread was passed down to the poor. Today the trenchers, soaked in toppings such as pesto or ham and goat's cheese, are grilled. ⊠ *Inner Close* ☎ *01962/857200* ▭ *MC, V* ⊙ *No dinner.*

££££ ✕⌂ **Hotel du Vin.** Rooms in this elegant redbrick Georgian town house are richly furnished in crisp modern style, with Oriental rugs enhancing the polished wooden floors. Egyptian-cotton bed linens, huge baths, and power showers make for a luxurious stay. The many eclectic wine selections in the stylish bistro (£££–££££) complement traditional French and English fare such as poached fillet of sole and chargrilled rib-eye steak with french fries. Call to arrange a private wine-tasting session. In summer, food is served in the walled garden. ⊠ *14 Southgate St., SO23 9EF* ☎ *01962/841414* ▤ *01962/842458* ⊕ *www.hotelduvin.com* ⇱ *24 rooms* ⌕ *Restaurant, cable TV, in-room data ports, bar, meeting rooms; no a/c* ▭ *AE, DC, MC, V.*

★ £££ ✕⌂ **Wykeham Arms.** This old place is conveniently central, near the cathedral and the college. Bedrooms at the inn itself are cozy and full of quirky knickknacks, with period touches; those across the road in the St. George annex are slightly larger. The bars, happily cluttered with prints and pewter, make use of old school desks for tables. A good wine list sets off the French and English dishes at the restaurant (££–££££), which is popular with locals. ⊠ *75 Kingsgate St., SO23 9PE* ☎ *01962/ 853834* ▤ *01962/854411* ✐ *wykehamarms@accommodating-inns. co.uk* ⇱ *14 rooms* ⌕ *Restaurant, 2 bars, some pets allowed, no-smoking rooms; no a/c, no kids under 14* ▭ *AE, DC, MC, V* ⦿❘ *BP.*

£££££ ⌂ **Lainston House.** Dating from 1668, this elegant country-house hotel in a 63-acre park is discreetly secluded, an obvious attraction for such eminent guests as Margaret Thatcher, who stayed here to write her memoirs. Inside, cedar and oak paneling and other restored 17th-century details adorn the public rooms. Bedrooms, many of which are beamed, are done in warm colors and rich fabrics. Ground-floor suites have access to the gardens, and a converted stable holds luxury rooms. The hotel is 2½ mi northwest of Winchester. ⊠ *Off B3049, Sparsholt SO21 2LT* ☎ *01962/863588* ▤ *01962/776672* ⊕ *www.exclusivehotels. co.uk* ⇱ *50 rooms* ⌕ *Restaurant, some in-room hot tubs, 2 tennis courts, gym, croquet, meeting rooms, helipad, some pets allowed; no a/c in some rooms* ▭ *AE, DC, MC, V* ⦿❘ *BP.*

££££ ⊞ **Winchester Royal.** Formerly a bishop's house and then a convent, this classy hotel lies within easy reach of the cathedral on a quiet side street. Bedrooms, decorated with floral fabrics and dark wood, surround a large inner garden; rooms in the main building have more period features. You can have a good lunch in the bar or a fuller meal in the Conservatory Restaurant. ⊠ *St. Peter St. near High St., SO23 8BS* ☎ *01962/840840* 🖷 *01962/841582* ⊕ *www.forestdale.com* ⟿ *75 rooms* ⚇ *Restaurant, cable TV, Wi-Fi, bar, business services, meeting rooms, some pets allowed (fee); no a/c* ⊟ *AE, DC, MC, V* ¶⊙¶ *BP.*

££ ⊞ **Enmill Lane.** As B&Bs go, this one is first class, with historic character and a modern ethos. The big, converted barn in the peaceful countryside 3 mi west of the center of Winchester makes a good base for exploring nearby villages and the South Downs. The rooms are freshly decorated in neutral tones and filled with personality—not to mention refrigerators stocked with drinks and nibbles—and breakfast includes fresh fruit and such delicacies as fresh duck eggs. ⊠ *Enmill La., Pitt SO22 5QR* ☎ *01962/856740* 🖷 *01962/854219* ⊕ *www.enmill-barn.co.uk* ⟿ *2 rooms* ⚇ *Refrigerator, tennis court, billiards, no-smoking rooms; no a/c, no room phones* ⊟ *No credit cards* ¶⊙¶ *BP.*

Shopping

A complete list of local antiques stores is available from the **Winchester Tourist Information Centre** (⊠ The Guildhall, Broadway ☎ 01962/840500). **King's Walk,** off Friarsgate, has a number of stalls selling antiques, crafts, gift items, and bric-a-brac. **The Jays' Nest** (⊠ King's Walk ☎ 01962/865650) specializes in silver and china. **P&G Wells** (⊠ 11 College St. ☎ 01962/852016), the oldest bookshop in town, stocks new titles and carries a small selection of secondhand books and prints in an annex in nearby Kingsgate Street.

Britain's largest **farmers' market** (☎ 01420/588671 ⊕ www.hampshirefarmersmarkets.co.uk), held in Middle Brook Street on the second and the last Sunday of each month, specializes in local produce and goods that are grown, reared, baked, or caught in Hampshire or within 10 mi of its borders. Look for Dexter beef, the products of water buffalo and Manx Loughton sheep, and walking sticks made from local wood. In September the market is the focal point of Hampshire Hog Day, the hog being the symbol of Hampshire.

OPEN-AIR MARKETS

Exploring a local market can provide a unique sense of place; for a complete list of those in the South, ask Tourism South East (⇨ Visitor Information *in* South Essentials, *below*). Among the best are Winchester's, Salisbury's traditional city market (Tuesday and Saturday), Kingsland Market in Southampton for bric-a-brac (Thursday), and a general country market (Wednesday) at Ringwood, near Bournemouth.

Chawton

⑩ *16 mi east of Winchester.*

Jane Austen (1775–1817) lived the last eight years of her life in the village of Chawton; she moved to Winchester only during her final illness. The site has always drawn literary pilgrims, but with the ongoing release of successful films based on her novels, the popularity of the town among visitors has grown enormously. Here, in an unassuming redbrick house, Austen revised *Sense and Sensibility,* created *Pride and Prejudice,* and worked on *Emma, Persuasion,* and *Mansfield Park.*

★ Now a museum, the rooms of **Jane Austen's House** retain the atmosphere of restricted gentility suitable to the unmarried daughter of a clergyman. In the left-hand parlor, Jane would play her piano every morning, then repair to her mahogany writing desk in the family sitting room—leaving her sister Cassandra to do the household chores ("I find composition impossible with my head full of joints of mutton and doses of rhubarb," Jane wrote). In the early 19th century, the road near the house was a bustling thoroughfare, and one traveler reported that a window view proved that the Misses Austen were "looking very comfortable at breakfast." Jane was famous for working through interruptions, but one protection against the outside world was the famous door that creaked. She asked that its hinges remain unattended to because they gave her warning that someone was coming. ⊠ *Signed off A31/A32 roundabout* ☎ *01420/83262* ⊕ *www.janeaustenmuseum.org.uk* 💷 *£4.50* ☉ *Mar.–Dec., daily 11–4:30; Jan. and Feb., weekends 11–4:30; last admission 30 mins before closing.*

Portsmouth

⑪ *24 mi south of Chawton, 77 mi southwest of London.*

This industrial, largely charmless city was England's naval capital and principal port of departure for centuries. It still has a substantial shipping industry, but the main attraction for travelers are the ferries that set off from here for Europe and the Isle of Wight. Portsmouth also has an extraordinary collection of maritime memorabilia, including well-preserved warships that date back to medieval times. Much of the city is not particularly pleasant, so use common sense before venturing on foot into parts of town that look questionable. Still, the newly developed Gunwharf Quays and the soaring Spinnaker Tower are indications that better days may lie ahead for this weary old coastal town.

Fodor'sChoice ★ The city's most impressive attraction, the **Portsmouth Historic Dockyard,** includes an unrivaled collection of historic ships and the comprehensive Royal Naval Museum (a great place to learn about British naval hero Admiral Lord Horatio Nelson). The dockyard's youngest ship, **HMS *Warrior 1860,*** was England's first ironclad battleship. Admiral Nelson's flagship, **HMS *Victory,*** has been painstakingly restored to appear as she did at the battle at Trafalgar (1805). You can inspect the cramped gun decks, visit

In Search of Jane Austen

A TOUR OF "JANE AUSTEN COUNTRY" in the South of England and beyond can enhance the experience of reading Austen's novels. Thanks to recent film adaptations of *Sense and Sensibility, Emma, Persuasion,* and *Pride and Prejudice,* the great author has captured another audience eager to peer into her decorous 18th- and early-19th-century world. By visiting one or two main locales—such as Chawton and Winchester—it is possible to imagine hearing the tinkle of teacups raised by the likes of Elinor Dashwood and Mr. Darcy. Serious Janeites will want to retrace her life—starting out in the hamlet of Steventon, southwest of Basingstoke, where she spent her first 25 years, then moving on to Bath, Southampton, Chawton, and Winchester.

Jane Austen country—a pleasant landscape filled with intimately scaled villages—is a perfectly civilized stage on which her characters organized visits to stately homes and husband-hunting expeditions. Entering that world, you find that its heart is the tiny Hampshire village of Chawton. Here, at a former bailiff's cottage on her brother's estate—now a museum—Austen produced three of her greatest novels. Her daily 6-mi walks often took her to Chawton Manor—her brother's regal Jacobean mansion, now Chawton House Library, a center for the study of 16th- to 18th-century women's literature (for a consultation, call ☎ 01420/541010 or see ⊕ www.chawton.org)—or to nearby Lyards Farm, where her favorite niece, Anna Lefroy (thought to be the model for Emma Woodhouse), came to live in 1815.

Driving southwest from Chawton, take A31 for about 15 mi to Winchester, where you can visit Austen's austere grave within the cathedral; then take in No. 8 College Street, where her battle with Addison's disease ended with her death on July 18, 1817. Heading 110 mi southwest you can visit Lyme Regis, the 18th-century seaside resort on the Devon border where Austen spent the summers of 1804–05. Here, at the Cobb, the stone jetty that juts into Lyme Bay, Louisa Musgrove jumps off the steps known as Granny's Teeth—a turning point in Chapter 12 of *Persuasion.* Northwest of Winchester by some 60 mi is Bath, the elegant setting that served as the backdrop for some of Austen's razor-sharp observations. The Jane Austen Centre explores the relationship between Bath and the writer.

the cabin where Nelson entertained his officers, and stand on the spot where he was mortally wounded by a French sniper. Visits aboard the *Victory* are by guided tour only and may entail a long wait. The **Mary Rose,** former flagship of the Tudor navy, which capsized and sank in the harbor in 1545, was raised in 1982. Described in the 16th century as "the flower of all the ships that ever sailed," the *Mary Rose* is now housed in a special enclosure, where water continuously sprays her timbers to prevent them from drying out and breaking up. Exhibits in the intriguing *Mary Rose* Museum display more than 1,200 artifacts from the ship. The **Royal Naval Museum** has a fine collection of painted figureheads, extensive exhibits about Nelson and the battle of Trafalgar, and galleries of paintings and mementos recalling naval history from King Alfred to the present. **Action Stations,** an interactive attraction, gives you insight into life in the modern Royal Navy and tests your sea legs with tasks such as piloting boats through gales. **Dockyard Apprentice** showcases the skills of the shipbuilders and craftsmen who constructed and maintained the naval vessels, with illustrations of rope-making, sail-making, caulking, signals, and knots. ⊠ *Historic Dockyard, Portsmouth Naval Base* ☎ *023/9286–1512* ⊕ *www. historicdockyard.co.uk* 🖅 *£16 includes harbor tour; valid for return visits* ⊗ *Apr.–Oct., daily 10–5:30; Nov.–Mar., daily 10–5; last admission 1 hr before closing.*

> ## RULING THE SEAS
>
> Island that it is, Great Britain invested heavily in its Royal Navy, to defend its shores and, eventually, to access its far-flung empire. The first dry dock in Europe was built in 1495 in Portsmouth, by order of Henry VII. His son, Henry VIII, greatly built up the navy early in his reign, but it was still a smaller force than the Spanish Armada, whose attack the English beat back famously in 1588, during the reign of Elizabeth I. It would take another century for England to make its navy the largest, and the world's most powerful, a rank it held up to World War II.

NEED A BREAK? After a slog around the Historic Dockyard you can find rest and replenishment, including seafood, at the harborside **Still & West Country House** (⊠ Bath Sq. ☎ 023/9282–1567), a pub with outdoor seating. It faces the Spice Island Inn, another pub.

Newly erected on the lively Gunwharf Quays development of shops and bars, **Spinnaker Tower** provides a striking visual focus on Portsmouth's skyline. The slender structure, with the form of a mast and billowing sail, rises to a height of 541 feet. An elevator whisks you to three viewing platforms 330 feet high, for thrilling all-around views over the harbor and up to 20 mi beyond. ⊠ *Gunwharf Quays* ☎ *023/9285–7520* ⊕ *www.spinnakertower.co.uk* 🖅 *£4.95* ⊗ *Sun.–Fri. 10–5, Sat. 10–10.*

In the popular **D-Day Museum,** in nearby Southsea, exhibits reconstruct the planning and logistics involved in the D-Day landings, as well as the actual invasion on June 6, 1944. The museum's centerpiece is the Overlord Embroidery ("Overlord" was the code name for the invasion), a 272-foot-long tapestry with 34 panels illustrating the history of World War II, from the Battle of Britain in 1940 to D-Day and the first days of the liberation. ⊠ *Clarence Esplanade, Southsea* ☎ *023/9282–7261* ⊕ *www.ddaymuseum.co.uk* 🖅 *£5.50* ⊗ *Apr.–Oct., daily 10–5:30; Nov.–Mar., daily 10–5; last admission 30 mins before closing.*

Portchester Castle incorporates the walls of a Roman fort built more than 1,600 years ago; these are the most complete set of Roman walls in northern Europe. In the 12th century the castle (now in ruins) was built inside the impressive fortifications. From the keep's central tower you can take in a sweeping view of the harbor and coastline. ⊠ *Off A27, near*

Fareham ☎ *023/9237–8291* ⊕ *www.english-heritage.org.uk* ▣ *£3.70* ⊙ *Apr.–Sept., daily 10–6; Oct.–Mar., daily 10–4.*

Where to Stay & Eat

£££££ ✕ **Bistro Montparnasse.** Modern paintings on terra-cotta walls add a contemporary touch to this bustling restaurant. The reasonable, fixed-price menu may include prawn and lentil bisque, or roasted rump of lamb with caramelized parsnip and garlic puree. ✉ *103 Palmerston Rd., Southsea* ☎ *023/9281–6754* ▭ *AE, MC, V* ⊙ *Closed Sun. and Mon.*

££–£££ ✕ **Lemon Sole.** Seafood doesn't get much fresher than this. After ordering your appetizer and bread from the waiter, you head over to the amply stocked fish bar to choose your main course, which will be priced by its weight. You also select a cooking method, sauces such as citrus or mushroom and fennel, and side dishes. Ask for the sauce on the side, as it can overpower the dish. Fish, meat, and vegetarian options also appear on a menu. This place is better for grown-ups than for kids. ✉ *123 High St.* ☎ *023/9281–1303* ▭ *AE, DC, MC, V* ⊙ *Closed Sun.*

££ ✕▥ **Sally Port.** This timber-frame old tavern opposite the cathedral in Old Portsmouth has subtle nautical associations, such as the top spar around which the Georgian staircase is built; the 40-foot mast is said to have come from a frigate. Sloping floors and marine pictures are additional details. The street-level bar and 1st-floor restaurant (open Friday and Saturday; £–£££) provide good light meals or fuller fare, such as sea bass, Dover sole, steaks, and lamb fillets. Rooms are comfortable and equipped with washbasins and showers; toilets are shared. ✉ *57–58 High St., PO1 2LU* ☎ *023/9282–1860* ▤ *023/9282–1293* ⌤ *10 rooms without bath* ⚲ *Restaurant, bar; no a/c* ▭ *AE, DC, MC, V* ¶⊙¶ *BP.*

£££ ▥ **Westfield Hall.** Portsmouth is well supplied with chain offerings, but this pleasant smaller establishment has personal service and character. It occupies two converted early-20th-century houses close to the water in the resort of Southsea. Rooms (seven are on the ground floor) have large bay windows and are restfully furnished in greens and creams; three sitting rooms provide a place to relax. ✉ *65 Festing Rd., off Eastern Parade, PO4 0NQ* ☎ *023/9282–6971* ▤ *023/9287–0200* ⊕ *www.whhotel.info* ⌤ *26 rooms* ⚲ *Dining room, cable TV, in-room data ports, Wi-Fi, no-smoking rooms; no a/c* ▭ *AE, DC, MC, V* ¶⊙¶ *BP.*

£ ▥ **Sailmaker's Loft.** This low-key bed-and-breakfast in Portsmouth's old town makes a handy option, not least because it's close to the water and some rooms have excellent sea views. It's also convenient to many sights. Rooms are simply decorated but pleasant and full of light; doubles have private bathrooms (singles share a bath), and the owners are friendly. ✉ *5 Bath Sq., PO1 2JL* ☎ *023/9282–3045* ▤ *023/9229–5961* ✉ *sailmakersloft@aol.com* ⌤ *4 rooms, 2 with bath* ⚲ *No a/c* ▭ *No credit cards* ¶⊙¶ *BP.*

The Outdoors

Queen Elizabeth Country Park, part of an Area of Outstanding Beauty in the South Downs, has 1,400 acres of chalk hills and shady beeches with scenic hiking trails. You can climb to the top of Butser Hill (888 feet) to take in a splendid view of the coast. The park lies 12 mi north of Portsmouth, and 4 mi south of the Georgian market town of Petersfield, in a wide valley between wooded hills and open downs. Check the Web site for guided walks and programs. ⊠ *A3* ☎ *023/9259–5040* ⊕ *www. hants.gov.uk/countryside/qecp* 🏷 *Free; car park £1, Sun. £1.50* ⊗ *Park open 24 hrs; visitor center (including café and shop) Apr.–Oct., daily 10–5:30; Nov.–Mar. daily 10–4:30. Closed early to mid-Jan.*

SALISBURY TO STONEHENGE

The roster of famous sights in this area begins in the attractive city of Salisbury, renowned for its glorious cathedral, then loops west around Salisbury Plain, up to the stone circles at Avebury, and back to Stonehenge. A trio of stately homes reveals the ambitions and wealth of the builders—Wilton House with its Inigo Jones–designed state rooms, Stourhead and its exquisite gardens, and the Italian Renaissance pile of Longleat. Your own transportation is essential to see some sites beyond Salisbury, but organized tours leaving from the city will take you to key places such as Stonehenge.

Salisbury

25 mi northwest of Southampton, 55 mi southeast of Bristol, 90 mi southwest of London.

The silhouette of Salisbury Cathedral's majestic spire signals your approach to this historic city long before you arrive. Although the cathedral is the principal interest in the town, and the Cathedral Close one of the country's most atmospheric spots (best experienced on a foggy night), Salisbury has much more to see, not least its largely unspoiled—and relatively traffic-free—old center. Here are stone shops and houses that grew up in the shadow of the great church over the centuries. You're never far from any of the three rivers that meet here, or from the bucolic water meadows that stretch out to the west of the cathedral and provide the best views of it.

Salisbury did not become important until the early 13th century, when the seat of the diocese was transferred here from Old Sarum, the original settlement 2 mi to the north, of which only ruins remain. In the 19th century, novelist Anthony Trollope based his tales of ecclesiastical life, notably *Barchester Towers,* on life here, although his fictional city of Barchester is really an amalgam of Salisbury and Winchester. The local tourist office organizes walks—of differing lengths for varying stamina—to lead you to the treasures.

Main Attractions

Cathedral Close. Salisbury's close forms probably the finest backdrop of any British cathedral, with its smooth lawns and splendid examples of architecture from many periods (except modern) creating a harmonious background. Some of the historic houses are open to the public.

⓮ Mompesson House. One of Britain's most appealing Queen Anne houses, dating from 1701, sits on the north side of Cathedral Close. There are no treasures per se, but some fine original paneling and plasterwork, as well as a fascinating collection of 18th-century drinking glasses, are high-

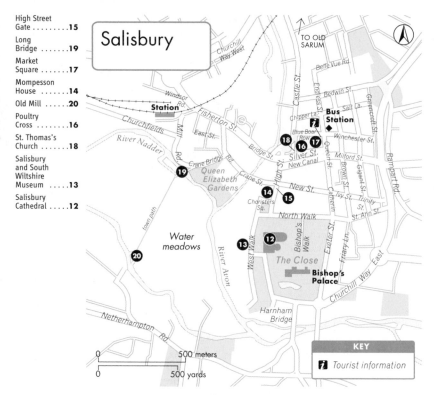

Salisbury

lights. Tea and refreshments are served in a walled garden. ⊠ *The Close* ☎ *01722/335659* ⊕ *www.nationaltrust.org.uk* 🎫 *£4.40* ⊙ *Apr.–Oct., Sat.–Wed. 11–5; last admission 4:30.*

Old Sarum. Massive earthwork ramparts in a bare sweep of Wiltshire countryside are all that remain of the impressive Iron Age hill fort, which was successively taken over by Romans, Saxons, and Normans (who built a castle and cathedral within the earthworks). The site was still fortified in Tudor times, though the population had mostly decamped in the 13th century for the more amenable site of New Sarum, or Salisbury. You can clamber over the huge banks and ditches and take in the bracing views over the chalk downland. ⊠ *Off A345, 2 mi north of Salisbury* ☎ *01722/335398* ⊕ *www.english-heritage.org.uk* 🎫 *£2.90* ⊙ *Apr.–June and Sept., daily 10–5; July and Aug., daily 9–6; Oct., daily 10–4; Nov.–Mar., daily 10–3.*

⑬ Salisbury and South Wiltshire Museum. Models and exhibits at the Stonehenge Gallery of this museum arm you with helpful background information for a visit to the famous stones. Also on view are collections of costumes, lace, embroidery, and Wedgwood, all dwarfed by the medieval pageant figure of St. Christopher, a 14-foot-tall, red-cloaked giant and his companion hobbyhorse, Hob Nob. ⊠ *The King's House, 65 The*

Close ☎ *01722/332151* ⊕ *www.salisburymuseum.org.uk* ☝ *£4* ☾ *July and Aug., Mon.–Sat. 10–5, Sun. 2–5; Sept.–June, Mon.–Sat. 10–5.*

⑫ **Salisbury Cathedral.** Salisbury is dominated by the towering cathedral, a soaring hymn in stone. It is unique among cathedrals in that it was

Fodor's Choice

★ conceived and built as a whole, in the amazingly short span of 38 years (1220–58). The spire, added in 1320, is the tallest in England and a miraculous feat of medieval engineering—even though the point, 404 feet above the ground, is 2½ feet off vertical. For a fictional, keenly imaginative reconstruction of the drama underlying such an achievement, read William Golding's novel *The Spire.* The excellent model of the cathedral in the north transept, the "arm" of the church to your left as you look toward the altar, shows the building about 20 years into construction, and makes clear the ambition of Salisbury's medieval builders. For all their sophistication, the height and immense weight of the great spire have always posed structural problems. In the late 17th century Sir Christopher Wren was summoned from London to strengthen the spire, and in the mid-19th century Sir George Gilbert Scott, a leading Victorian Gothicist, undertook a major program of restoration. He also initiated a clearing out of the interior and removed some less-than-sympathetic 18th-century alterations. Despite this, the interior seems spartan and a little gloomy, but check out the remarkable lancet windows and sculpted tombs of crusaders and other medieval heroes. The clock in the north aisle—probably the oldest working mechanism in Europe, if not the world—was made in 1386. ■ TIP→ **You can join a free 45-minute tour of the church leaving two or more times a day, and there are tours to the roof and spire at least once a day.** The **cloisters** are the largest in England, and the octagonal **Chapter House** contains a marvelous 13th-century frieze showing scenes from the Old Testament. In the Chapter House you can also see one of the four original copies of the **Magna Carta,** the charter of rights the English barons forced King John to accept in 1215; it was sent here for safekeeping in the 13th century. ⊠ *Cathedral Close* ☎ *01722/555120* ⊕ *www.salisburycathedral.org.uk* ☝ *Cathedral £4 requested donation, roof tour £4.50, Chapter House free* ☾ *Cathedral mid-June–Aug., Mon.–Sat. 7:15–7:15, Sun. 7:15–6:15; Sept.–mid-June, daily 7:15–6:15. Chapter House mid-June–Aug., Mon.–Sat. 9:30–6:45, Sun. noon–5:30; Sept.–Oct. and Mar.–mid-June, Mon.–Sat. 9:30–5:30, Sun. noon–5:30; Nov.–Feb., Mon.–Sat. 10–4:30, Sun. noon–4:30. Access to cathedral restricted during services.*

Also Worth Seeing

⑮ **High Street Gate.** On the north side of the Cathedral Close is one of the four castellated stone gateways built to separate the close from the rest of the city. Passing through it, you enter into the heart of the modern town.

⑲ **Long Bridge.** For a classic view of Salisbury, head to the Long Bridge and the town path. From High Street walk west to Mill Road, which leads you across Queen Elizabeth Gardens. Cross the bridge and continue on the town path through the water meadows along here you can find the very spot where John Constable set down his easel to create that 19th-century icon, *Salisbury Cathedral,* now hung in the Constable Room of London's National Gallery.

⑰ Market Square. One of southern England's most popular markets fills this square on Tuesday and Saturday. Permission to hold an annual fair here was granted in 1221, and that right is still exercised for four days every October, when the Charter Fair takes place. A narrow side street links Poultry Cross to Market Square.

⑳ Old Mill. Reached via a 20-minute walk along the town path southwest of the town center, this mill, dating from the 12th century, makes a pleasant destination. It is now a restaurant and coffee shop under the same management as the Old Mill Hotel next door. ⊠ *Town Path, West Harnham.*

⑯ Poultry Cross. One of Salisbury's best-known landmarks, the hexagonal Poultry Cross is the last remaining of the four original medieval market crosses, and dealers still set up their stalls beside it. ⊠ *Silver St.*

⑱ St. Thomas's Church. This church contains a rare medieval doom painting of Judgment Day, the best-preserved and most complete of the few such works left in Britain. Created around 1470 and covering the chancel arch, the scenes of heaven and hell served to instill the fear of damnation into the congregation. ■ **TIP→** It's best seen on a spring or summer evening when the light through the west window illuminates the details. ⊠ *Silver St.* ☎ *01722/322537* ⊠ *Free* ☉ *Apr.–Oct., Mon.–Sat. 9:30–6, Sun. noon–6; Nov.–Mar., Mon.–Sat. 9:30–3:30, Sun. noon–6.*

NEED A BREAK?	In a lively, central location but away from traffic, **Polly Tearooms** (⊠ 8 St. Thomas's Sq. ☎ 01722/336037) provides relief from sightseeing fatigue in the form of lemon curd gâteaux (cakes), Wiltshire cream teas, and freshly ground coffee. It's closed Sunday.

Where to Stay & Eat

££–£££ ✗ **Haunch of Venison.** This wood-panel tavern opposite the Poultry Cross has been going strong for more than six centuries, and brims with period details, such as the mummified hand of an 18th-century card player still clutching his cards, found by workmen in 1903. You can fortify yourself with any of 40-odd malt whiskies, and choose between simple bar food or more substantial meals in its stylish upstairs restaurant **One Minster Street,** where the menu includes pave of beef with seared foie gras and truffle-scented jus. ⊠ *1 Minster St.* ☎ *01722/411313* ⊟ *MC, V.*

££–£££ ✗ **LXIX Bar and Bistro.** A stone's throw from the cathedral, this convivial and relaxed bistro has a cool, modern style, making it an ideal spot for a light lunch or dinner. The menu lists everything from fish cakes and pastas to sea bass and steaks. ⊠ *69 New St.* ☎ *01722/340000* ⊟ *AE, DC, MC, V* ☉ *Closed Sun. and last wk in Dec.*

££ ✗ **Harper's.** Always buzzing, this 2nd-floor restaurant overlooking Market Square has a friendly, neighborhood feel. The mainly English and French dishes include Scotch salmon and New Forest venison casserole with mustard mash, and there are good-value lunches and early-bird dinners. ⊠ *7 Ox Row* ☎ *01722/333118* ⊟ *AE, DC, MC, V* ☉ *Closed Sun. Oct.–May. No lunch Sun. June–Sept.*

££ ✗ **Lemon Tree.** It's just a few steps from Cathedral Close and the High Street Gate to this light, airy bistro. Dishes range from spinach and ricotta pancakes to pork fillets panfried with apricots and pine nuts. You can sit in the small, busy conservatory or in the garden. ⊠ *90–92 Crane St.* ☎ *01722/333471* ▤ *AE, MC, V* ⊘ *Closed Sun.*

★ ££££   ✕▣ **Howard's House.** If you're after complete tranquillity, head for this early-17th-century house 10 mi west of Salisbury, set on 2 acres of grounds in the Nadder valley. French windows lead from the tidy lawns into the restaurant (£££££), which lists sophisticated contemporary fare on its set-price menus, for example Cornish scallop risotto, and desserts include passion fruit curd soufflé. The inviting sitting room mixes pastels and bright fabrics, and the soothing bedrooms use subtle colors. ⊠ *Off B3089, Teffont Evias SP3 5RJ* ☎ *01722/716392* 🖷 *01722/716820* ⊕ *www.howardshousehotel.co.uk* ↝ *9 rooms* ♨ *Restaurant, meeting rooms, some pets allowed (fee); no a/c* ▤ *AE, DC, MC, V* ¶◯¶ *BP.*

££££   ✕▣ **Red Lion Hotel.** A former coaching inn—parts of the building date from 1220—this centrally located hotel in the Best Western consortium makes a good base for exploring the city on foot. It's packed with old clocks and other relics from its long past. Rooms are in either modern or antique style, with an abundance of drapery and rich red, gold, and blue colors. Room 22 has a restored fireplace dating from the inn's original construction. The Vine restaurant (£££££; reservations essential) serves mainly modern British dishes such as roast pork with mustard sauce. ⊠ *Milford St., SP1 2AN* ☎ *01722/323334* 🖷 *01722/325756* ⊕ *www.the-redlion.co.uk* ↝ *51 rooms* ♨ *Restaurant, cable TV, Wi-Fi, business services, meeting rooms; no a/c* ▤ *AE, DC, MC, V.*

£££   ▣ **White Hart.** Behind the pillared portico and imposing classical facade of this 17th-century hotel very near the cathedral lie cozily old-fashioned yet spacious public rooms. The muted cream-and-brown color scheme complements the unhurried pace, and the functional bedrooms (of various sizes) are grouped around the inner courtyard. ⊠ *1 St. John St., SP1 2SD* ☎ *0870/400–8125 or 01722/327476* 🖷 *01722/412761* ⊕ *www.macdonaldhotels.co.uk* ↝ *68 rooms* ♨ *Restaurant, bar, business services, meeting rooms, some pets allowed (fee); no a/c* ▤ *AE, DC, MC, V* ¶◯¶ *BP.*

££   ▣ **Cricket Field House Hotel.** As the name suggests, this modernized gamekeeper's cottage overlooks a cricket ground, allowing you to puzzle over the intricacies of the game at leisure. Some rooms are in the main house and others in the pavilion annex, but all are individually furnished in soft shades. The hotel is on the main A36 road, a mile or so west of Salisbury's center. ⊠ *Wilton Rd., SP2 9NS* ☎🖷 *01722/322595* ⊕ *www.cricketfieldhousehotel.co.uk* ↝ *14 rooms* ♨ *Dining room; no a/c, no kids under 14, no smoking* ▤ *AE, MC, V* ¶◯¶ *BP.*

£   ▣ **Wyndham Park Lodge.** This solid Victorian house in a quiet part of town (off Castle Street) provides an excellent place to rest and a good breakfast, as well as a garden. Furnishings are in keeping with the period, with antiques and elegant patterned wallpapers and drapes, and one room has its own patio. ⊠ *51 Wyndham Rd., SP1 3AB* ☎ *01722/416517* 🖷 *01722/328851* ⊕ *www.wyndhamparklodge.co.uk* ↝ *4 rooms* ♨ *Cable TV, in-room DVD; no room phones, no a/c, no smoking* ▤ *MC, V* ¶◯¶ *BP.*

Nightlife & the Arts

★ The **Salisbury Festival** (✉ 75 New St. ☎ 01722/332241 ⊕ www.salisburyfestival.co.uk), held in May and June, has outstanding classical concerts, recitals, plays, and outdoor events. The **Salisbury Playhouse** (✉ Malthouse La. ☎ 01722/320333) presents high-caliber drama all year and is the main venue for the Salisbury Festival.

Sports

Hayball's Cycle Shop (✉ 26–30 Winchester St. ☎ 01722/411378) rents bikes for about £10 per day or £55 per week, with a £25 cash deposit.

Shopping

Ellwood Books (✉ 38 Winchester St. ☎ 01722/322975) stocks all kinds of tax-free secondhand books, including some rare first editions. **Reeve the Baker** (✉ 2 Butcher Row ☎ 01722/320367) is a great independent bakery with goodies ranging from lamb pastries to apple dumplings. **Watsons** (✉ 8–9 Queen St. ☎ 01722/320311) specializes in Aynsley and Wedgwood bone china, Waterford and Dartington glass, Royal Doulton, and fine ornaments. The buildings, dating from 1306 and 1425, have their original windows and an oak mantelpiece.

Wilton

㉑ *4 mi west of Salisbury.*

Five rivers—the Avon, the Bourne, the Nadder, the Wylye, and the Ebble—wind from Salisbury into the rich heart of Wiltshire. Following the valley of the Nadder will lead you to the ancient town of Wilton, from which the county takes its name. A market is held here every Thursday, and the Wilton Carpet Factory Shop draws visitors (Wilton is renowned for its carpets), but the main attraction is Wilton House.

★ The home of the 17th earl of Pembroke, **Wilton House** would be noteworthy if it contained no more than the magnificent 17th-century state rooms designed by Inigo Jones, Ben Jonson's stage designer and the architect of London's Banqueting House. John Webb rebuilt the house in neoclassical style after fire damaged the original Tudor mansion in 1647. In fine weather, the lordly expanse of sweeping lawns that surrounds the house, bisected by the River Avon and dotted with towering oaks and a gracious Palladian bridge, is a quintessential English scene. Wilton House contains the Single Cube Room (built as a perfect 30-foot cube) and one of the most extravagantly beautiful rooms in the history of interior decoration, the aptly named Double Cube Room. The name refers to its proportions (60 feet long by 30 feet wide and 30 feet high), evidence of Jones's classically inspired belief that beauty in architecture derives from harmony and balance. The

---

DOUBLE CUBE ROOM

Adorned with gilded furniture by William Kent, Wilton House's Double Cube was where Eisenhower prepared plans for the Normandy invasion during World War II. It has been used in many films, including *The Madness of King George* and Emma Thompson's adaptation of *Sense and Sensibility.*

room's headliner is the spectacular Van Dyck portrait of the Pembroke family. Other delights at Wilton House include old master paintings, an exhibition of 7,000 toy soldiers, and the Wareham Bears (200 dressed teddy bears). ■ TIP→ **Be sure to explore the extensive gardens; children will appreciate the large playground.** ⊠ *Off A30* ☎ *01722/746729* ⊕ *www. wiltonhouse.co.uk* ✉ *£9.75, grounds only £4.50* ⊘ *House mid-Apr.–Sept., Sun.–Fri. 10:30–5:30; grounds mid-Apr.–Sept., daily 10:30–5:30; last admission 4:30.*

Shaftesbury

22 *18 mi west of Wilton, 22 mi west of Salisbury.*

The old village of Shaftesbury—the model for the town of Shaston in Thomas Hardy's *Jude the Obscure*—lies on a ridge overlooking Black-more Vale just inside the Dorset county border. From the top of **Gold Hill,** a steep, relentlessly picturesque street lined with cottages, you can catch a sweeping view of the surrounding countryside. Although Gold Hill is something of a tourist cliché (it has even appeared in TV commercials), it's still well worth visiting.

Sherborne

23 *15 mi west of Shaftesbury.*

Once granted cathedral status, until deferring to Old Sarum in 1075, this unspoiled market town is awash with medieval buildings honed from the honey-color local stone. The focal point of the winding streets is the abbey church. Also worth visiting here are the ruins of the 12th-century Old Castle and Sherborne Castle with its grounds.

The glory of **Sherborne Abbey,** a warm, "old gold" stone church, is the delicate and graceful 15th-century fan vaulting that extends the length of the soaring nave and choir. ("I would pit Sherborne's roof against any contemporary work of the Italian Renaissance," enthused Simon Jenkins, in his *England's Thousand Best Churches.*) If you're lucky you might hear "Great Tom," one of the heaviest bells in the world, peal-ing out from the bell tower. Guided tours are offered in summer on Tues-day (10:30) and Friday (2:30), or by prior arrangement. ⊠ *Abbey Close* ☎ *01935/812452* ⊕ *www.sherborneabbey.com* ✉ *£2 suggested dona-tion, guided tour free or £3 by prior arrangement* ⊘ *Apr.–Sept., daily 8–6; Oct.–Mar., daily 8–4.*

Sherborne Castle, built by Sir Walter Raleigh in 1594, remained his home for 10 years before it passed to the custodianship of the Digby family. The interior has been remodeled in 19th-century Gothic style, and ceilings have splendid plaster moldings. After admiring the exten-sive collections of Meissen and Asian porcelain, stroll around the lake and landscaped grounds, the work of Capability Brown. The house is a half mile southeast of town. ⊠ *Off A352* ☎ *01935/813182* ⊕ *www. sherbornecastle.com* ✉ *£8, gardens only £4* ⊘ *Apr.–Oct., Tues.–Thurs., Sun., and national holiday Mon. 11–5, Sat. 2:30–5.*

Where to Stay

£ ⌂ **The Alders.** A quiet, unspoiled village 3 mi north of Sherborne contains this B&B, an old stone house with a walled garden. The lounge has an inglenook fireplace, and the bedrooms are modern and cheerfully decorated. The house displays the owner's watercolors and sleek pottery, which you can view while tasting homemade jam during breakfast at the farmhouse table. Nearby pubs provide evening meals. ✉ *Sandford Orcas DT9 4SB* ☎ *01963/220666* 🖷 *01963/220106* ⊕ *www.thealdersbb.com* ⇌ *3 rooms* ♧ *No smoking* ▭ *No credit cards* ⍾ *BP.*

Stourhead

㉔
Fodor'sChoice
★

15 mi northeast of Sherborne, 30 mi west of Salisbury.

Close to the village of Stourton lies one of Wiltshire's most breathtaking sights—Stourhead, a country-house-and-garden combination that has few parallels for beauty anywhere in Europe. Most of Stourhead was built between 1721 and 1725 by Henry the Magnificent, the wealthy banker Henry Hoare. Many rooms in the Palladian mansion contain Chinese and French porcelain, and some have furniture by Chippendale. The elegant library and floridly colored picture gallery were built for the cultural development of this exceedingly civilized family. Still, the house takes second place to the adjacent gardens designed by Hoare's son, Henry Hoare II, which are the most celebrated example of the English 18th-century taste for "natural" landscaping. Temples, grottoes, and bridges have been placed among shrubs, trees, and flowers to make the grounds look like a three-dimensional oil painting. A walk around the artificial lake (1½ mi) reveals changing vistas that conjure up the 17th-century landscapes of Claude Lorrain and Nicolas Poussin. ■ **TIP→ The best time to visit is early summer, when the massive banks of rhododendrons are in full bloom,** but the gardens are beautiful at any time of year. You can get a fine view of the estate from Alfred's Tower, a 1772 folly (a structure built for picturesque effect). In summer there are occasional concerts, sometimes accompanied by fireworks and gondoliers on the lake. A restaurant and plant shop are on the grounds. From London by train, get off at Gillingham and take a five-minute cab ride to Stourton. ✉ *Off B3092, northwest of Mere, Stourton* ☎ *01747/841152* ⊕ *www.nationaltrust.org.uk* 🖂 *£10.40, house only £6.20, gardens only £6.20* ☉ *House mid-Mar.–Oct., Fri.–Tues. 11:30–4:30 or dusk; last admission 30 mins before closing; gardens daily 9–7 or dusk.*

Where to Stay & Eat

£££ ✕⌂ **Spread Eagle Inn.** You can't stay at Stourhead, but this popular hostelry, built at the beginning of the 19th century at the entrance to the landscaped park, is the next best thing (and guests are admitted free to the house and gardens). Bedrooms are elegant and understated, with some period features. The restaurant (££) serves traditional English fare, from braised venison to chicken and tarragon pie, and there are seafood and vegetarian choices. ✉ *Northwest of Mere, Stourton BA12 6HQ* ☎ *01747/840587* 🖷 *01747/840954* ⊕ *www.spreadeagleinn.com* ⇌ *5 rooms* ♧ *Restaurant, bar; no a/c* ▭ *DC, MC, V* ⍾ *BP.*

Longleat House

★ ☺ ㉕ *6 mi north of Stourhead, 19 mi south of Bath, 27 mi northwest of Salisbury.*

Home of the marquess of Bath, Longleat House is one of southern England's most famous private estates, and possibly the most ambitiously, even eccentrically, commercialized, as evidenced by the presence of a drive-through safari park (open since 1966) with giraffes, zebras, rhinos, and lions. The blocklike Italian Renaissance building was completed in 1580 (for just over £8,000, an astronomical sum at the time) and contains outstanding tapestries, paintings, porcelain, and furniture, as well as notable period features such as the Victorian kitchens, the Elizabethan minstrels' gallery, and the great hall with its massive wooden beams. Giant antlers of the extinct Irish elk decorate the walls, while tours of the present Lord Bath's occasionally raunchy murals—described as "keyhole glimpses into my psyche," ranging from philosophical subjects to depictions of the kama sutra—can be booked separately at the front desk (free). Besides the safari park, Longleat has a butterfly garden, a miniature railway, an extensive (and fairly fiendish) hedge maze, and an adventure castle, all of which make it extremely popular, particularly in summer and during school vacations. ■ TIP➔ You can easily spend a whole day here, in which case it's best to visit the house in the morning, when tours are more relaxed, and the safari park in the afternoon. Call to confirm opening hours in winter. ⊠ *Off A362, Warminster* ☎ *01985/844400* ⊕ *www.longleat.co.uk* 🎫 *House and safari park £19, house £10, safari park £10, gardens and grounds £3* ⊙ *House Jan.–Mar., weekends and school vacations 11–3; Apr.–Sept., daily 10–5:30; Oct.–Dec., daily 11–3; guided tours only, call for times. Safari park Apr.–Oct., weekdays 10–4, weekends and school vacations 10–5. Other attractions Apr.–Oct., daily 11–5:30.*

Where to Stay & Eat

★ ££££ ✕▦ **Bishopstrow House.** This Georgian house has been converted into a luxurious but refreshingly relaxed hotel that combines antiques and fine carpets with modern amenities such as whirlpool baths and CD players. There's an airy conservatory, and the lavish, chintz-filled guest rooms overlook either the 27-acre grounds or an interior courtyard. The Mulberry restaurant creates imaginative modern European meals (£££££ fixed-price menus) with a penchant for the piquant. Bishopstrow House is 1½ mi out of town. ⊠ *Boreham Rd., Warminster BA12 9HH* ☎ *01985/212312* 🖷 *01985/216769* ⊕ *www.bishopstrow.co.uk* ↙ *32 rooms* ⸰ *Restaurant, some in-room hot tubs, golf privileges, 2 tennis courts, 2 pools (1 indoor), gym, hair salon, sauna, spa, fishing, croquet, bar, piano bar, business services, meeting rooms, helipad, some pets allowed; no a/c* ⊟ *AE, DC, MC, V* ⦿ *BP.*

EN ROUTE Four miles west of Avebury, on A4, **Cherhill Down** is a prominent hill carved with a vivid white horse and topped with a towering obelisk. It's one of a number of hillside etchings in Wiltshire, but unlike the others, this one isn't an ancient symbol—it was put there in 1780 to indicate the highest point of the downs between London and Bath. The views from the top are well worth the half-hour climb. (The best view of the horse is from A4, on the approach from Calne.)

Avebury

❷❻ *25 mi northeast of Longleat, 27 mi east of Bath, 34 mi north of Salisbury.*

★ The village of Avebury was built much later than the stone circles that brought it fame. The **Avebury Stone Circles** are one of England's most evocative prehistoric monuments—not so famous as Stonehenge, but all the more powerful for their lack of commercial exploitation. The stones were erected around 2500 BC, some 500 years after Stonehenge was started but about 500 years before that much smaller site assumed its present form. As with Stonehenge, the purpose of this stone circle has never been ascertained, although it most likely was used for similar ritual purposes. Unlike Stonehenge, however, there are no astronomical alignments at Avebury, at least none that have survived. The main site consists of a wide, circular ditch and bank, about 1,400 feet across and over half a mile around; it actually surrounds part of the village of Avebury. Entrances break the perimeter at roughly the four points of the compass, and inside stand the remains of three stone circles. The

largest one originally had 98 stones, although only 27 remain. Many stones on the site were destroyed centuries ago, especially in the 17th century when they were the target of religious fanaticism. Some were pillaged to build the thatched cottages you see flanking the fields. You can walk around the circles at any time; early morning and early evening are recommended. Be sure to visit the nearby Alexander Keiller Museum. ✉ *1 mi north of A4* ☎ *No phone* ⊕ *www.english-heritage.org.uk* 🎫 *Free* ☉ *Daily.*

In the **Alexander Keiller Museum,** finds from the Avebury area, and charts, photos, models, and home movies taken by the archaeologist Keiller himself, put the Avebury Stone Circles and the site into context. Recent revelations suggest that Keiller, responsible for the excavation of Avebury in the 1930s, may have adapted the site's layout more in the interests of presentation than authenticity. The exhibits are divided between the **Stables Gallery,** showing excavated finds, and the more child-friendly, interactive **Barn Gallery.** ✉ *1 mi north of A4* ☎ *01672/ 539250* ⊕ *www.english-heritage.org.uk* 🎫 *£4.20* ☉ *Apr.–Oct., daily 10–6; Nov.–Mar., daily 10–4.*

The Avebury monument lies at the end of **Kennett Stone Avenue,** a sort of prehistoric processional way leading to Avebury. The avenue's stones were spaced 80 feet apart, but only the half mile nearest the main monument survives intact. The lost stones are marked with concrete.

Where to Stay & Eat

£–££ ✕ **Waggon and Horses.** A 16th-century thatched building created in part with stones taken from the Avebury site, this traditional inn and pub beside the traffic circle linking A4 and A361, a two-minute drive from the prehistoric circle. Dickens mentioned the building in the *Pickwick Papers.* Excellent lunches and dinners are served beside a fire; homemade dishes include beef and Stilton pie, curries, and casseroles, or you can opt for a sandwich. In high season it's somewhat of a tourist hub. ⊠ *Beckhampton* ☎ *01672/539418* ⊟ *AE, MC, V* ⊗ *No dinner Sun.*

££ ⊡ **Manor Farm.** Views of Avebury's monoliths straggling across the field greet you from the windows of this 18th-century farmhouse right in the heart of the village. Rooms are spacious, light, and elegantly furnished, and guests have their own sitting room. The bathroom is separate, but for your exclusive use as only one room is rented at a time. Breakfast choices include Scotch pancakes with bacon, scrambled eggs with smoked salmon, and kippers. ⊠ *High St., SN8 1RF* ☎☎ *01672/539294* ⟟ *2 rooms, no bath* ⟂ *No kids under 12* ⊟ *No credit cards* ⦿ *BP.*

EN ROUTE Prehistoric relics dot the entire Avebury area; stop at the **West Kennett Long Barrow,** a chambered tomb dating from about 3250 BC, 1 mi east of Avebury on A4. As you turn right at the traffic circle onto A4, **Silbury Hill** rises on your right. This man-made mound, 130 feet high, dates from about 2500 BC and is the largest of its kind in Europe. Excavations over 200 years have provided no clue as to its original purpose, but the generally accepted notion is that it was a massive burial chamber.

Stonehenge

㉗ *26 mi south of Avebury, 8 mi north of Salisbury.*

Fodor'sChoice
★

Mysterious and ancient, Stonehenge has baffled archaeologists for centuries. One of England's most visited monuments, the circle of giant stones that sits in lonely isolation on the wide sweep of Salisbury Plain still has the capacity to fascinate and move those who view it. Sadly, though, it is now enclosed by barriers after incidents of vandalism, and amid fears that its popularity could threaten its existence. Visitors are kept on a path a short distance away from the stones, so that you can no longer walk among the giant stones or see up close the prehistoric carvings, some of which show axes and daggers. But if you visit in the early morning, when the crowds have not yet arrived, or in the evening, when the sky is heavy with scudding clouds, you can experience Stonehenge as it once was: a mystical, awe-inspiring place.

Stonehenge was begun about 3000 BC, enlarged between 2100 and 1900 BC, and altered yet again by 150 BC. It has been excavated and rearranged several times over the centuries. The medieval term "Stonehenge" means "hanging stones." Many of the huge stones that ringed the center were brought here from great distances, but it is not certain by what ancient form of transportation they were moved. The original 80 bluestones (dolerite), which made up the two internal circles, originated in the Preseli mountains, on the Atlantic coast of Wales. They may have been moved by raft over sea and river, and then dragged on rollers across country—a total journey of 130 mi as the crow flies, but closer to 240 by the practical route. Every time a reconstruction of the journey has been attempted, though, it has failed. The labor involved in quarrying, transporting, and carving these stones is astonishing, all the more so when you realize that it was accomplished about the same time that the major pyramids of Egypt were built.

Although some of the mysteries concerning the site have been solved, the reason Stonehenge was built remains unknown. It is fairly certain that it was a religious site, and that worship here involved the cycles of the sun; the alignment of the stones to point to sunrise at midsummer and sunset in midwinter makes this clear. The druids certainly had nothing to do with the construction: the monument had already been in existence for nearly 2,000 years by the time they appeared. Most historians think Stonehenge may have been a kind of neolithic computer, with a sophisticated astronomical purpose—an observatory of sorts.

A paved path for visitors skirts the stones, ensuring that you don't get very close to the monoliths. Bring a pair of binoculars to help make out the details more clearly. It pays to walk all about the site, near and far, to get that magical photo and to engage your imagination. Romantics may want to view Stonehenge at dawn or dusk, or by a full moon. Your ticket entitles you to an informative audio tour, but in general, visitor amenities at Stonehenge are limited, especially for such a major tourist attraction. ■ TIP→ **Through some tour companies and English Heritage itself, which manages the site, you can arrange access to the inner circle outside of regular hours. English Heritage requires an application and payment of £12 well in advance.** There are plans to improve the site by replacing the too-busy, too-close highway with a tunnel. A new visitor center is in the works for 2008.

Buses leave from the Salisbury bus station for Stonehenge at 11, noon, 1, and 2 (confirm times); buy an Explorer ticket on board for £6.50. There's no place to leave luggage, though. Other options are a taxi or an organized tour. Visitors coming by car from Marlborough should join A345 south for Stonehenge, turning west onto A303 at Amesbury. The monument stands near the junction with A344. ⊠ *Junction of A303 and A344/A360, near Amesbury* ☎ *0870/333–1181, 01722/343834 for information about private access outside regular hrs* ⊕ *www.english-heritage.org.uk* ☞ *£5.50* ☉ *Mid-Mar.–May and Sept.–mid-Oct., daily 9:30–6; June–Aug., daily 9–7; mid-Oct.–mid-Mar., daily 9:30–4.*

NEW FOREST TO LYME REGIS

Tucked southwest of Southampton, the New Forest was once the hunting preserve of William the Conqueror and his royal descendants. Thus protected from the deforestation that has befallen most of southern England's other forests, this wild, scenic expanse offers great possibilities for walking, riding, and biking. West of here stretches the green, hilly, and largely unspoiled county of Dorset, the setting for most of the books of Thomas Hardy, author of *Far from the Madding Crowd* and other classic Victorian-era novels. "I am convinced that it is better for a writer to know a little bit of the world remarkably well than to know a great part of the world remarkably little," he wrote, as he immortalized the towns, villages, and fields of this idyllically rural area, not least the country capital, Dorchester, an ancient agricultural center. Other places of historic interest such as Maiden Castle and the chalk-cut giant of Cerne Abbas are interspersed with bustling seaside resorts such as Weymouth. You may find Lyme Regis (associated with another writer, John Fowles) and the smaller villages scattered along the route closer to your ideal of rural England. The Jurassic coast is the place to search for fossils.

Lyndhurst

28 *26 mi southeast of Stonehenge, 18 mi southeast of Salisbury.*

Lyndhurst is famous as the capital of the New Forest. To explore the depths of this natural wonder, take A35 out of Lyndhurst (the road continues southwest to Bournemouth). To get here from Stonehenge, head south along A360 to Salisbury, then follow A36, B3079, and continue along A337 another 4 mi or so. The New Forest **Visitor Information Centre** (⊠ High St. ☎ 023/8028–2269) in the town's main car park is open daily year-round. Fans of Lewis Carroll's *Alice in Wonderland* should note that Alice Hargreaves (*née* Liddell), the inspiration for the fictional Alice, is buried in the **churchyard at Lyndhurst.**

The **New Forest** (⊕ www.thenewforest.co.uk) consists of 150 square mi of mainly open, unfenced countryside interspersed with dense woodland, a natural haven for herds of free-roaming deer, cattle, and, most famously, hardy New Forest ponies. The forest was "new" in 1079, when William the Conqueror cleared the area of farms and villages and turned it into his private hunting grounds. Although some popular spots can get crowded in summer, there are ample parking lots, picnic areas, and campgrounds. Miles of walking trails crisscross the region.

Where to Stay & Eat

★ ££££££ ╳ Chewton Glen. Once the home of Captain Frederick Marryat, author of *The Children of the New Forest,* this early-19th-century country house on extensive grounds is now a luxurious hotel that ranks among Britain's most acclaimed—and most expensive. All the rooms are decorated in rich fabrics, with an eye to the minutest detail, and the plush spa provides the latest treatments. The restaurant, the Marryat Room (£££££), is worth a pilgrimage—the fixed-price menu concentrates on classic meat and seafood dishes enlivened with contemporary elements, and there's a choice of more than 500 wines. Chewton Glen is 15 mi south of Lyndhurst. ⊠ *Christchurch Rd., New Milton BH25 6QS* ☎ *01425/275341, 800/344–5087 in U.S.* 🖷 *01425/272310, 800/398–4534 in U.S.* ⊕ *www.chewtonglen.com* 🛏 *59 rooms* ⚬ *Restaurant, cable TV, in-room data ports, 9-hole golf course, 4 tennis courts, 2 pools (1 indoor), gym, spa, croquet, business services, meeting rooms, helipad; no a/c in some rooms, no kids under 5* 🖃 *AE, DC, MC, V.*

££ ✕▥ **White Buck Inn.** This traditional forest lodge makes a welcome stop for refreshment or an overnight stay. The extensive menu relies on local fare, such as braised breast of pheasant and venison casserole. In summer you can sit in the spacious garden, where there are regular barbecues. Live Dixie jazz plays on Thursday evenings. Guest rooms vary from functional to plush chambers themed along Elizabethan or Indian lines, and all enjoy garden views. ⊠ *Bisterne Close, Burley, 7 mi west of Lyndhurst BH24 4AJ* ☎ *01425/402264* 🖷 *01425/403588* ✉ *whitebuckinn@accommodating-inns.co.uk* ➛ *7 rooms* 🖒 *Restaurant, bar* ◯ *BP* ▭ *AE, MC, V.*

£££ ▥ **Lyndhurst Park Hotel.** Perched at the edge of the New Forest, this hotel resembles a sprawling country manor house but is a modern establishment with plenty of in-room conveniences such as a trouser press. Rooms are smallish but adequate, and not too chintz-filled; you can upgrade to one with a four-poster bed. Year-round, the 17 acres of grounds, which include three ponds, are great for a stroll. The hotel frequently hosts business conferences and is used to international customers. ⊠ *High St., SO43 7NL* ☎ *023/8028–3923* 🖷 *023/8028–2127* ⊕ *www.lyndhurstparkhotel.co.uk* ➛ *59 rooms* 🖒 *Restaurant, cable TV, Wi-Fi, tennis court, pool, sauna, bar, no-smoking rooms* ▭ *AE, MC, V* ◯ *BP.*

Sports & the Outdoors

HORSEBACK RIDING The New Forest was created for riding, and there's no better way to enjoy it than on horseback. You can arrange a ride at the **Forest Park Riding Stables** (⊠ Rhinefield Rd., Brockenhurst ☎ 01590/623429 ➲ £25 for 1 hr). The **New Park Manor Stables** (⊠ New Park, Brockenhurst ☎ 01590/623919 ➲ £30 for 1 hr) gives full instruction.

WALKING The **New Forest** is fairly domesticated, and the walks it provides are not much more than easy strolls. For one such walk (about 4 mi), start from Lyndhurst and head directly south for Brockenhurst, a commuter village. The path goes through woods, pastureland, and leafy river valleys— and you may even see some New Forest ponies.

Beaulieu

➋➒ *7 mi southeast of Lyndhurst.*

☾ The unspoiled village of Beaulieu (pronounced *byoo*-lee) has three major attractions in one. **Beaulieu,** with a ruined abbey, a stately home, and an automobile museum, can satisfy different interests. In 1204 King John established **Beaulieu Abbey** for the Cistercian monks, who gave their new home its name, which means "beautiful place" in French. It was badly damaged as part of the suppression of Catholicism during the reign of Henry VIII, leaving only the cloister, the doorway, the gatehouse, and two buildings. A well-planned exhibition in one building re-creates daily life in the monastery. **Palace House** incorporates the abbey's 14th-century gatehouse and has been the home of the Montagu family since they purchased it in 1538, after the dissolution of the monasteries. In this stately home you can see drawing rooms, dining halls, and fine family portraits. The present Lord Montagu is noted for his work in establishing the **National Motor Museum,** which traces the development of motor transport from 1895 to the present. You can see more than 250 classic cars, buses, and motorcycles. Museum attractions include a monorail, audiovisual presentations, and a trip in a 1912 London bus (weekends only in winter, excluding January). ⊠ *Off B3056* ☎ *01590/ 612345* ⊕ *www.beaulieu.co.uk* ⛴ *Abbey, Palace House, and Motor Museum £15.50, joint ticket with Buckler's Hard £18.50* ⊙ *May–Sept., daily 10–6; Oct.–Apr., daily 10–5; last admission 40 mins before closing.*

Buckler's Hard

30 *2 mi south of Beaulieu.*

Among the interesting places around Beaulieu is the museum village of Buckler's Hard, a restored 18th-century hamlet of 24 brick cottages, leading down to an old shipyard on the Beaulieu River. There's a small hotel here, too. The fascinating **Maritime Museum** tells the story of Lord Nelson's favorite ship, HMS *Agamemnon,* which was built here of New Forest oak. Exhibits and model ships trace the town's shipbuilding history. Also part of the museum are four building interiors in the hamlet that re-create 18th-century village life. Easter through October, you can arrange to take a cruise on the Beaulieu River. ☎ *01590/616203* ⊕ *www. bucklershard.co.uk* ⛴ *£5.50, joint ticket with Beaulieu £18.50* ⊙ *Easter–Sept., daily 10:30–5; Oct.–Easter, daily 11–4.*

> **WORD OF MOUTH**
>
> "You will love Beaulieu . . . But also stop at Buckler's Hard, only a couple of miles outside of Beaulieu. This is the most fascinating village . . . It is where they used to build ships on the main street and slide them down to the water. Plus several of the cottages are open with furnishings . . . If you do have some time, just drive along some of the lanes in the New Forest—it is just so lovely."
>
> –Janis

Wimborne Minster

31 *7 mi northwest of Bournemouth via A341, 20 mi west of Buckler's Hard.*

The impressive minster of this quiet market town makes it seem like a miniature cathedral city. The crenellated and pinnacled twin towers of **Wimborne Minster** present an attractive patchwork of gray and reddish-brown stone. The church's Norman nave has zigzag molding interspersed with carved heads, and the Gothic chancel has tall lancet windows. ■ TIP→ **See the chained library (accessed via a spiral staircase), a survivor from the days when books were valuable enough to keep on chains.** Look out for the 14th-century astronomical clock on the inside wall of the west tower. ⊠ *High St.* ☎ *01202/884753* ⊕ *www.wimborneminster. org.uk* ⛴ *£1.50 donation requested for church, chained library free* ⊙ *Church Mar.–Dec., Mon.–Sat. 9:30–5:30, Sun. 2:30–5:30; Jan. and Feb., Mon.–Sat. 9:30–4, Sun. 2:30–4. Chained library Easter–Oct., weekdays 10:30–12:30 and 2–4; Nov.–Easter, Sat. 10–12:30.*

The **Priest's House Museum,** on the main square in a Tudor building with a garden, includes rooms furnished in period styles and a Victorian kitchen. It also has Roman and Iron Age exhibits, including a cryptic, three-faced Celtic stone head. ✉ *23 High St.* ☎ *01202/882533* 🎟 *£3* ⏲ *Apr.–Oct., Mon.–Sat. 10–4:30; also open 2 wks after Christmas.*

Kingston Lacy, a grand 17th-century house built for the Bankes family (who had lived in Corfe Castle), was altered in the 19th century by Sir Charles Barry, co-architect of the Houses of Parliament in London. The building holds a choice picture collection with works by Titian, Rubens, Van Dyck, and Velásquez, as well as the fabulous Spanish Room, lined with gilded leather and topped with an ornate Venetian ceiling. There's also a fine collection of Egyptian artifacts. Parkland with walking paths surrounds the house. ✉ *B3082, 1½ mi northwest of Wimborne Minster* ☎ *01202/883402* 🌐 *www.nationaltrust.org.uk* 🎟 *£9, park and garden only £4.50* ⏲ *House mid-Mar.–Oct., Wed.–Sun. 11–5, last admission 4. Garden and park Feb.–mid-Mar., weekends 10:30–4; mid-Mar.–Oct., daily 10:30–6; Nov. and Dec., Fri.–Sun. 10:30–4.*

Where to Eat

£££ ✕ **Primizia.** The low ceiling, tangerine walls, and tile floor lend this popular bistro an intimate feel. From the menu, which shows French and Italian influences, try the smoked salmon with mango and onion salsa or the saffron and dill risotto with king prawns and scallops. ✉ *26 Westborough* ☎ *01202/883518* ▭ *MC, V* ⏲ *Closed Sun. and Mon.*

Corfe Castle

★ ㉜ *15 mi south of Wimborne Minster.*

One of the most impressive ruins in Britain, Dorset's Corfe Castle overlooks the appealing gray limestone village of Corfe. The castle site guards a gap in the surrounding Purbeck Hills and has been fortified since at least 900. The present ruins are of the castle built between 1105, when the great central keep was erected, and the 1270s, when the outer walls and towers were built. It owes its ramshackle state to Cromwell's soldiers, who blew up the castle in 1646 during the Civil War, after Lady Bankes led its defense during a long siege. ✉ *A351* ☎ *01929/481294* 🌐 *www.nationaltrust.org.uk* 🎟 *£5* ⏲ *Mar. and Oct., daily 10–5; Apr.–Sept., daily 10–6; Nov.–Feb., daily 10–4.*

OFF THE BEATEN PATH

CLOUDS HILL – A tiny, spartan, brick-and-tile cottage served as the retreat of T. E. Lawrence (Lawrence of Arabia) before he was killed in a motorcycle accident on the road from Bovington in 1935. The house remains very much as he left it, with photos and memorabilia from the Middle East. It's particularly atmospheric on a gloomy day, as there's no electric light. ✉ *8 mi northwest of Corfe, off B3390, Wareham* ☎ *01929/405616* 🌐 *www.nationaltrust.org.uk* 🎟 *£3.50* ⏲ *Apr.–Oct., Thurs.–Sun. and national holiday Mon. noon–5 or dusk.*

Where to Stay & Eat

★ **££** ✕ **The Fox.** An age-old pub, the Fox has a fine view of Corfe Castle from its flower garden. There's an ancient well in the lounge bar and more timeworn stonework in an alcove, as well as a pre-1300 fireplace. The bar cheerfully doles out soups and sandwiches, as well as steaks and fish dishes, but things can get uncomfortably congested in summer. ⊠ *West St., Corfe* ☎ *01929/480449* ▤ *MC, V.*

££ ▥ **Castle Inn.** This thatched hotel, 10 mi west of Corfe and a five-minute walk from the sea, has a flagstone bar and other 15th-century features. Bedrooms are individually furnished, some with four-posters, and there's an extensive garden to sit in, including a rose garden. A lengthy bar menu is available daily, and on Saturday evenings the good restaurant has an à la carte menu. Satisfying walks are nearby. ⊠ *Main Rd., West Lulworth BH20 5RN* ☎ *01929/400311* ▥ *01929/400415* ⊕ *www. thecastleinn-lulworthcove.co.uk* ⤚ *15 rooms, 12 with bath* ⚭ *Restaurant, bar, some pets allowed; no a/c, no phones in some rooms* ▤ *AE, DC, MC, V* ⦿⦿ *BP.*

Dorchester

③③ *21 mi west of Corfe on A351 and A352, 43 mi southwest of Salisbury.*

In many ways Dorchester, the Casterbridge of Thomas Hardy's novel *The Mayor of Casterbridge,* is a traditional southern country town. The town owes much of its fame to its connection with Hardy, whose bronze statue looks westward from a bank on Colliton Walk. Born in a cottage in the hamlet of Higher Bockhampton, about 3 mi northeast of Dorchester, Hardy attended school in the town and was apprentice to an architect here.

Dorchester has many reminders of the Roman presence in the area. The Romans laid out the town about AD 70, and a walk along Bowling Alley Walk, West Walk, and Colliton Walk follows the approximate line of the original Roman town walls. On the north side of Colliton Park lies an excavated Roman villa with a marvelously preserved mosaic floor.

To appreciate the town's character, visit the Wednesday market in **Market Square,** where you can find handcrafted items and Dorset delicacies such as Blue Vinney cheese (which some connoisseurs prefer to Blue Stilton). Things have changed a bit since the days when, to quote Hardy, "Bees and butterflies in the cornfields at the top of the town, who desired to get to the meads at the bottom, took no circuitous route, but flew straight down High Street . . ."

The labyrinthine **Dorset County Museum** contains ancient Celtic from nearby Maiden Castle and Roman remains from town, a rural crafts gallery, and a local-history gallery. It's better known for its large collection of Hardy memorabilia. A gallery focusing on the nearby Jurassic Coast opened in 2006. ⊠ *High West St.* ☎ *01305/262735* ⊕ *www. dorsetcountymuseum.org* ▨ *£6* ⏱ *July–Sept., daily 10–5; Oct.–June, Mon.–Sat. 10–5.*

The small thatch-and-cob **Hardy's Cottage,** where the writer was born in 1840, was built by his grandfather and is little altered since that time. From here Thomas Hardy would make his daily 6-mi walk to school in Dorchester. Among other things, you can see the desk at which the

CLOSE UP

Hardy's Dorset

AMONG THIS REGION'S PROUDEST CLAIMS is its connection with Thomas Hardy (1840–1928), one of England's most celebrated novelists. If you read some of Hardy's novels before visiting Dorset—re-created by Hardy as his part-fact, part-fiction county of Wessex—you may well recognize some places immediately from his descriptions. The tranquil countryside surrounding Dorchester is lovingly described in *Far from the Madding Crowd*, and Casterbridge, in *The Mayor of Casterbridge*, stands for Dorchester itself. Any pilgrimage to Hardy's Wessex begins at the author's birthplace in Higher Bockhampton, 3 mi east of Dorchester. Salisbury makes an appearance as "Melchester" in *Jude the Obscure*. Walk in the footsteps of Jude Fawley by climbing Shaftesbury—"Shaston"—and its steeply Gold Hill, a street lined with charming cottages. Today, many of these sights seem frozen in time, and Hardy's spirit is ever present.

author completed *Far from the Madding Crowd.* ✉ *½ mi south of Blandford Rd. (A35), Higher Bockhampton* ☎ *01305/262366* ⊕ *www. nationaltrust.org.uk* 🎫 *£3* ⊗ *Apr.–Oct., Sun.–Thurs. 11–5 or dusk.*

Thomas Hardy lived in **Max Gate** from 1885 until his death in 1928. An architect by profession, Hardy designed the house, in which the dining room and the light, airy drawing room are open to the public. He wrote much of his poetry here and many of his novels, including *Tess of the d'Urbervilles* and *The Mayor of Casterbridge*. ✉ *Allington Ave., 1 mi east of Dorchester on A352* ☎ *01305/262538* ⊕ *www.nationaltrust. org.uk* 🎫 *£2.80* ⊗ *Apr.–Sept., Mon., Wed., and Sun. 2–5.*

The **Maumbury Rings** (✉ Maumbury Rd.), the remains of a Roman amphitheater on the edge of town, were built on a prehistoric site that later served as a place of execution. (Hardy's *Mayor of Casterbridge* contains a vivid evocation of the Rings.) As late as 1706, a girl was burned at the stake here.

⟳ The popular **Dinosaur Museum** has life-size models, interactive displays, and a hands-on Discovery Gallery. ✉ *Icen Way, off High East St.* ☎ *01305/269741* ⊕ *www.thedinosaurmuseum.com* 🎫 *£6* ⊗ *Apr.–Oct., daily 9:30–5:30; Nov.–Mar., daily 10–4:30.*

It's hardly what you might expect from a small county town, but the informative and well-displayed **Tutankhamun Exhibition,** in a former Catholic church, re-creates the young pharaoh's tomb and treasures in all their glory. The ticket gives you a half-price reduction to visit the small Mummies Exhibition next door, showing the process of mummification with copies of mummies. ✉ *High West St.* ☎ *01305/269571* ⊕ *www. tutankhamun-exhibition.co.uk* 🎫 *£6, Mummies Exhibition £3.80* ⊗ *Apr.–Oct., daily 9:30–5:30; Nov.–Mar., weekdays 9:30–5, weekends 10–5; last admission 30 mins before closing.*

NEED A BREAK? Drop into **Potters Café-Bistro** (⊠ 19 Durngate St. ☎ 01305/260312), occupying a 17th-century cottage, for teas, coffees, and delicious cakes and pastries, as well as sandwiches and light lunches of fish pie or tortellini. The courtyard garden is pleasant in summer.

★ After Stonehenge, **Maiden Castle** is the most important pre-Roman archaeological site in England. It's not an actual castle but an enormous, complex hill fort of stone and earth with ramparts that enclose about 45 acres. England's mysterious prehistoric inhabitants built the fort, and many centuries later it was a Celtic stronghold. In AD 43 invading Romans, under the general (later emperor) Vespasian, stormed the fort. Finds from the site are on display in the Dorset County Museum in Dorchester. To experience an uncanny silence and sense of mystery, climb Maiden Castle early in the day (access to it is unrestricted). Leave your car at the lot at the end of Maiden Castle Way, a 1½-mi lane signposted off the A354. The site is 2 mi southwest of Dorchester. ⊠ *A354.*

Fine 19th-century gardens enhance an outstanding example of 15th-century domestic architecture at **Athelhampton House and Gardens,** 5 mi east of Dorchester and 1 mi east of Puddletown. Thomas Hardy called this place Athelhall in some of his writings, referring to the legendary King Aethelstan, who had a palace on this site. The current house includes the Great Hall, with much of its original timber roof intact, the King's Room, and the Library, with oak paneling and more than 3,000 books. The 10 acres of landscaped gardens contain water features and the Great Court with its 12 giant yew pyramids. ⊠ *A35* ☎ *01305/848363* ⊕ *www.athelhampton.co.uk* ⊠ *£8* ☉ *Mar.–Oct., Sun.–Thurs. 10–5; Nov.–Feb., Sun. 10:30–dusk.*

Where to Stay & Eat

££–£££ ✕ **6 North Square.** Just behind the County Museum, this pleasant neighborhood brasserie makes an ideal stop for a relaxed lunch or evening meal. The menu may list homemade terrine for starters, and pan-fried sirloin served with blue vinny cream sauce, and sesame crusted salmon with king prawns and salsa for main courses. The atmosphere is intimate without being chi-chi, the tiled floor lending a continental air. ⊠ *6 North Sq.* ☎ *01305/267679* ▤ *MC, V* ☉ *Closed Sun.*

★ £££ ✕▥ **Yalbury Cottage.** A thatch roof and inglenook fireplaces add to the appeal of this 300-year-old cottage, 2½ mi east of Dorchester and close to Hardy's birthplace. The restaurant's three-course fixed-price menu (£32) of superior modern British and European fare might include thyme-poached quail breasts with seared foie gras, or pan-fried wild seabass with Lyonnaise potatoes and an orange butter sauce. Functional but comfortable bedrooms are available in an extension overlooking gardens or adjacent fields. ⊠ *Lower Bockhampton DT2 8PZ* ☎ *01305/ 262382* ▤ *01305/266412* ⊕ *www.yalburycottage.com* ⇥ *8 rooms* ⌂ *Restaurant, in-room DVDs, some pets allowed (fee); no a/c, no smoking* ▤ *AE, MC, V* ☉ *Closed 2 wks Jan. No lunch* ❘⊙❘ *BP.*

★ £££ ▥ **Casterbridge Hotel.** Small but full of character, this Georgian building (1790) reflects its age with period furniture and elegance. Guest rooms—one with its own patio—are individually and impeccably furnished in traditional style, and the conservatory overlooks a courtyard garden. A congenial husband-and-wife team owns and runs the hotel. ⊠ *49 High East St., DT1 1HU* ☎ *01305/264043* 🖷 *01305/260884* ⊕ *www.casterbridgehotel.co.uk* ⟟ *15 rooms* ⟐ *In-room data ports, bar; no a/c* ⊟ *AE, MC, V* ⟐ *BP.*

The Outdoors

From April through October the **Thomas Hardy Society** (⟐ Box 1438, Dorchester DT1 1YH ☎☎ 01305/251501 ⊕ www.hardysociety.org) organizes walks that follow in the steps of Hardy's novels. Readings and discussions accompany the walks, which take most of a day.

Cerne Abbas

❸❹ *6 mi north of Dorchester.*

The village of Cerne Abbas, worth a short exploration on foot, has some Tudor houses on the road beside the church. Nearby you can also see the original village stocks. Tenth-century **Cerne Abbey** is now a ruin, with little left to see except its old gateway, although the nearby Abbey House is still in use.

Cerne Abbas's main claim to fame is the colossal and unblushingly priapic **figure of a giant,** cut in chalk on a hillside overlooking the village. The 180-foot-long giant carries a huge club, and may have originated as a tribal fertility symbol long before Roman times; authorities disagree. His outlines are formed by 2-foot-wide trenches. The present giant is thought to have been carved in the chalk about AD 1200. The best place to view the figure is from the A352 itself, where you can park in any of numerous nearby turnouts.

Weymouth

❸❺ *8 mi south of Dorchester.*

Dorset's main coastal resort, Weymouth, is known for its wide, safe, sandy beaches and its royal connections. King George III took up sea bathing here for his health in 1789, setting a trend among the wealthy and fashionable people of the day. Popularity left Weymouth with many fine buildings, including the Georgian row houses lining the esplanade. Striking historical details clamor for attention: a wall on Maiden Street, for example, holds a cannonball that was embedded in it during the Civil War. Nearby, a column commemorates the launching of United States forces from Weymouth on D-Day.

Where to Eat

ff–fff ✗ **Perry's.** A busy, family-run restaurant right by the harbor, Perry's specializes in simple dishes using the best local seafood. Try the lobster or crab, or grilled fillet of turbot with leeks, new potatoes, and shellfish sauce. Meat dishes, such as roast fillet of beef, are tasty, too. ⊠ *The Harbourside, 4 Trinity Rd.* ☎ *01305/785799* ⊟ *AE, MC, V* ⟐ *No lunch Mon. and Sat.; no dinner Sun. Sept.–Easter.*

f–ff ✗ **Old Rooms.** A fisherman's pub full of maritime clutter and low beams, this popular choice has great views over the harbor. The long menu is strongest on steaks, but pastas and meat pies are other choices. There's a separate dining area, or you can mix with the locals at the bar. ⊠ 7 *Cove Row* ☎ *01305/771130* ▤ *MC, V.*

Abbotsbury

㊱ *10 mi northwest of Weymouth.*

Pretty Abbotsbury is at the western end of Chesil Beach, a 200-yard-wide, 30-foot-high bank of pebbles that decrease in size from east to west. The beach extends for 18 mi. A lagoon outside the village serves as the **Abbotsbury Swannery,** a famous breeding place for swans. Introduced by Benedictine monks as a source of meat in winter, the swans have remained for centuries, building new nests every year in the soft, moist eelgrass. ⊠ *New Barn Rd.* ☎ *01305/871858* ⊕ *www.abbotsbury-tourism.co.uk* ☑ *£7.50* ⊙ *Mid-Mar.–Sept., daily 10–6; Oct., daily 10–5; last admission 1 hr before closing.*

Where to Stay & Eat

££££ ✕🏠 **Manor Hotel.** The pedigree of this honey-color hotel and restaurant goes back more than 700 years—note its flagstone floors, oak paneling, and beamed ceilings. English and French seafood and game dishes are specialties of the restaurant (£££££); the fixed-price menu changes daily. Some of the rooms, individually decorated in pastel colors and furnished with antiques, have sea views, and Chesil Beach is a few minutes' walk away. Self-catering facilities are available. ⊠ *Beach Rd., 3 mi west of Abbotsbury, West Bexington DT2 9DF* ☎ *01308/897785* 🖷 *01308/897035* ⊕ *www.themanorhotel.com* ➱ *13 rooms* ♧ *Restaurant, playground; no a/c* ▤ *AE, MC, V* ⊠I *BP.*

Lyme Regis

㊲ *19 mi west of Abbotsbury.*

"A very strange stranger it must be, who does not see the charms of the immediate environs of Lyme, to make him wish to know it better," wrote Jane Austen in *Persuasion.* Judging from the summer crowds, most people appear to be not at all strange. The ancient, scenic town of Lyme Regis and the so-called Jurassic Coast are highlights of southwest Dorset. The crumbling seaside cliffs in this area are especially fossil rich.

Lyme Regis is famous for its curving stone breakwater, **The Cobb,** built by King Edward I in the 13th century to improve the harbor. The duke of Monmouth landed here in 1685 during his ill-fated attempt to overthrow his uncle, James II. The Cobb figured prominently in the movie *The French Lieutenant's Woman,* based on John Fowles's novel set in Lyme Regis, as well as in the film version of Jane Austen's *Persuasion.* Fowles is Lyme's most famous current resident.

☾ The small but child-friendly **Marine Aquarium** offers the usual up-close look at creatures aquatic, from conger eels to spider crabs. ⊠ *End of the Cobb* ☎ *01297/444230* ☑ *£2.50* ⊙ *Easter–Oct., daily 10–5.*

The Jurassic Coast

FOSSILS AND FOSSIL HUNTING are the lure for visitors to the coast that stretches for 95 mi between Studland Bay in the east to Exmouth (Devon) in the west. This cliff-lined coast encompasses 185 million years of the Earth's geological history, for which it has been granted World Heritage Site status. Fossils formed in the distant past are continuously being uncovered here as parts of the crumbly cliffs erode, and good examples of ammonites and dinosaur traces can be seen in museums in Dorchester and Lyme Regis. Though it is dubbed "Jurassic Coast," there are also examples of older Triassic and younger Cretacous rocks. As a rule, the older rocks can be seen in the western parts of the coast, and younger rocks form the cliffs to the east. A good path that traces the whole coast allows you to explore the area at close quarters.

Fossil hunters are free to pick and chip away at the rocks, the best stretch being within 6 mi on either side of Lyme Regis (the beach below Stonebarrow Hill, east of Charmouth, is especially fruitful). As signs along the seafront warn, the best place to find fossils is not at the rockface but on the shore. Check weather conditions and tides—collecting on a falling tide is best, and the ideal time to do it is in winter, when heavy storms are continuously uncovering new areas.

To spot the most commonly found fossils, ammonites (chambered cephalopods from the Jurassic era, related to today's nautilus), just look down hard at the shingle (large gravel) on the beach and inspect the gaps between rocks and boulders. Ammonites are usually preserved in either calcite or iron pyrite ("fools gold"); shinier, more fragile specimens may be found in aragonite. Visit the museums in Lyme to remind you what to look for: the lustrous spirals are similar in heft and size to a brass coin, most smaller than a 10p coin. Other fossils to be found include sea urchins, white oyster shells, and coiled worm tubes.

If you want to leave nothing to chance, hook up with a pro: information on guided walks is available from the tourist office and the Philpot Museum in Lyme Regis. Publications are also available for sale in the tourist offices of Lyme Regis and Dorchester; they can also tell you about coastal boat trips.

In a gabled and turreted Victorian building, the lively **Philpot Museum** contains engaging items that illustrate the town's maritime and domestic history, as well as a section on local writers and a good selection of local fossils. ⊠ *Bridge St.* ☎ *01297/443370* ⊕ *www.lymeregismuseum. co.uk* ⊡ *£2.20* ☼ *Apr.–Oct., Mon.–Sat. 10–5, Sun. 11–5; Nov.–Mar., Sat. 10–5, Sun. 11–5, also weekdays 10–5 during school holidays.*

The **Dinosaurland Fossil Museum,** in a former church, displays an excellent collection of local fossils and gives the background on regional geology and how fossils develop. Although the museum is aimed at children, most people find it informative. Ask here about guided fossil-hunting walks. The **Lyme Regis Fossil Shop** on the ground floor sells books and fascinating fossils from around the world as well as reproductions of fossils, some fashioned into jewelry or ornaments. ✉ *Coombe St.* ☎ *01297/443541* ⊕ *www.dinosaurland.co.uk* ✍ *£4* ☉ *July and Aug., daily 10–6; Sept.–June, daily 10–5.*

Where to Stay & Eat

£–££ ✕ **Bell Cliff Restaurant.** This friendly little place at the bottom of Lyme's main street makes a great spot for a light lunch or tea, although it can get noisy and cramped. Apart from teas and coffees, you can order seafood, including whitebait, plaice, and the chef's salmon fish cakes, or a gammon steak (a thick slice of cured ham) or leek and mushroom crumble. ✉ *5–6 Broad St.* ☎ *01297/442459* ▭ *MC, V* ☉ *No dinner Oct.–June.*

£££–££££ ✕▢ **Alexandra.** Magnificently sited above the Cobb, the Alexandra is a rambling, old-fashioned haven with a genteel, unhurried air. Informal lunches and teas are served in a conservatory that overlooks an expanse of lawn. The formal restaurant (£££££) has an impressive wine list to complement the fixed-price dinners, with entrées such as grilled plaice and minions of beef with glazed field mushrooms. Depending on the cost, some guest rooms have a restrained elegance and others are purely functional, although you're almost guaranteed a view over garden and sea. Bathrooms are on the small side. ✉ *Pound St., DT7 3HZ* ☎ *01297/ 442010* 🖶 *01297/443229* ⊕ *www.hotelalexandra.co.uk* ⇥ *26 rooms* ⚭ *Restaurant, bar, some pets allowed (fee); no a/c* ▭ *MC, V* ☉ *Closed late Dec.–Jan.* ⏀ *BP.*

£ ▢ **Coombe House.** Tucked away on one of the oldest lanes in Lyme (dating from the 16th century), this simple B&B has genial hosts and spacious, modern guest rooms in pastel shades. Breakfast, which includes homemade jams, is brought to your room. ✉ *41 Coombe St., DT7 3PY* ☎🖶 *01297/443849* ⊕ *www.coombe-house.co.uk* ⇥ *2 rooms* ⚭ *No a/c, no room phones, no smoking* ▭ *No credit cards* ⏀ *BP.*

Sports & the Outdoors

The 72-mi **Dorset Coast Path** (✉ South West Coast Path Association, Bowker House, Lee Mill Bridge, Ivybridge, Devon PL21 9EF ☎ 01752/ 896237 ⊕ www.swcp.org.uk) runs east from Lyme Regis to Poole, taking in the quiet bays, shingle beaches, and low chalk cliffs of the coast. Some highlights are Golden Cap, the highest point on the South Coast; the Swannery at Abbotsbury; Chesil Beach; and Lulworth Cove (between Weymouth and Corfe Castle). Villages and isolated pubs dot the route, as do many rural B&Bs.

EVEN KIDS DIG IT

In 1810 a local child named Mary Anning dug out a complete ichthyosaur near Lyme Regis (it's on display in London's Natural History Museum). Anning's obsession with Jurassic remains left her labeled locally as the "fossil woman"; throughout her life she made many valuable discoveries that were sought by museums and collectors.

3

SOUTH ESSENTIALS

Transportation

BY AIR

The small international airport at Southampton is useful for flights to the Channel Islands and some European destinations.

🛈 **Southampton International Airport** ✉ M27, Junction 5 ☎ 0870/040-0009 ⊕ www.southamptonairport.com.

BY BUS

National Express buses at London's Victoria Coach Station on Buckingham Palace Road depart every 2 hours for Portsmouth (2 hours, 15 minutes) and Winchester (2 hours). There are three buses daily to Salisbury (about 3 hours). Solent Blue and Stagecoach Hampshire Bus operate a comprehensive service in the New Forest and Winchester areas.

FARES & COSTS Wilts (Wiltshire) & Dorset Bus Co. offers both one-day Explorer and seven-day Busabout tickets; ask about the Goldrider tickets offered by Stagecoach, and Rover tickets offered by Solent Blue.

🛈 **National Express** ☎ 0870/580-8080 ⊕ www.nationalexpress.com. **Solent Blue** ☎ 023/8061-8233 ⊕ www.solentblueline.com. **Stagecoach Hampshire Bus** ☎ 0845/121-0180 ⊕ www.stagecoachbus.com. **Traveline** ☎ 0870/608-2608 ⊕ www.traveline.org.uk. **Wilts (Wiltshire) & Dorset Bus Co.** ☎ 01722/336855 ⊕ www.wdbus.co.uk.

BY CAR

The South is linked to London and other major cities by a well-developed road network, which includes M3 to Winchester (59 mi from London); A3 to Portsmouth (70 mi); and M27 from the New Forest to Portsmouth. For Salisbury, take M3 to A303, then A30. A31 connects the New Forest to Dorchester and Lyme Regis.

ROAD CONDITIONS Driving is easy in this area. In northeast Hampshire and in many parts of neighboring Wiltshire there are lanes overhung by trees and lined with thatched cottages and Georgian houses. Often these lanes begin near the exits of main highways. Salisbury Plain has long, straight roads surrounded by endless vistas; the challenge here is staying within the speed limit.

BY TRAIN

South West Trains serves the South from London's Waterloo Station. Travel times average 1 hour to Winchester, 1½ hours to Salisbury, and about 2 hours to Portsmouth. There is at least one fast train every hour on all these routes. For local information throughout the region, contact National Rail Enquiries.

CUTTING COSTS A Network card (@20), valid throughout the South and Southeast for a year, entitles you to one-third off particular fares.

FARES & SCHEDULES 🛈 **National Rail Enquiries** ☎ 0845/748-4950 ⊕ www.nationalrail.co.uk. **South West Trains** ☎ 0845/748-4950 ⊕ www.southwesttrains.co.uk.

Contacts & Resources

EMERGENCIES

🔳 **Ambulance, fire, police** ☎ 999. **Dorset County Hospital** ⊠ Williams Ave., Dorchester ☎ 01305/251150. **Queen Alexandra Hospital** ⊠ Southwick Hill Rd., Cosham, Portsmouth ☎ 023/9228-6000. **Salisbury District Hospital** ⊠ Odstock Rd., Salisbury ☎ 01722/336262.

INTERNET

Public libraries in all the cities and many of the smaller towns of the region offer free Internet access. Salisbury's tourist office also has a terminal for brief use (*see* Visitor Information, *below,* for address). Increasing numbers of hotels and B&Bs offer Internet connections, and many also provide a Wi-Fi facility.

🔳 Internet Cafés **Online Café** ⊠ 163 Elm Grove, Southsea, Portsmouth ☎ 023/9283-1106. **Salisbury Online** ⊠ 14 Endless St., above the Endless Life café, Salisbury ☎ 01722/421328 ⊕ www.salisburyonline.co.uk. **Jamie's Internet Café** ⊠ 10 Parchment St., Winchester ☎ 01962/870880 ⊕ www.jamiesinternetcafe.org.uk.

TOURS

City Sightseeing has three daily Stonehenge tours from Salisbury, April through October, costing £15 (check for availability). There are more frequent daily tours of Portsmouth from late May through September, costing £6.50. A. S. Tours arranges day tours of Stonehenge and Avebury, year-round, in six-seater minibuses. Salisbury City Guides runs daily summer (weekends in winter) walks in Salisbury. The Guild of Registered Tourist Guides maintains a directory of qualified Blue Badge guides who can meet you anywhere in the region for private tours. Local organizations such as Wessexplore can also arrange Blue Badge tours.

🔳 **A. S. Tours** ☎ 01980/862931. **City Sightseeing/Guide Friday** ☎ 01708/866000 ⊕ www.city-sightseeing.com. **Guild of Registered Tourist Guides** ☎ 020/7403-1115 ⊕ www.blue-badge.org.uk. **Salisbury City Guides** ☎ 01722/320349 ⊕ www.salisburycityguides.co.uk. **Wessexplore** ☎ 01722/326304 ⊕ www.dmac.co.uk/wessexplore.

VISITOR INFORMATION

Tourism South East can field general inquiries and put you in touch with local information centers, which are normally open Monday through Saturday 9:30 to 5:30, with reduced hours in winter.

🔳 **Tourism South East** ⊠ 40 Chamberlayne Rd., Eastleigh SO50 5JH ☎ 023/8062-5400 🖶 023/8062-0010 ⊕ www.visitsoutheastengland.com. **Avebury** ⊠ Avebury Chapel, Green St., SN8 1RE ☎ 01672/539425 ⊕ www.kennet.gov.uk. **Dorchester** ⊠ 11 Antelope Walk, DT1 1BE ☎ 01305/267992 ⊕ www.westdorset.com. **Lyme Regis** ⊠ Guildhall Cottage, Church St., DT7 3BS ☎ 01305/442138 ⊕ www.westdorset.com. **Lyndhurst** ⊠ Main Car Park, High St., SO43 7NY ☎ 023/8028-2269 ⊕ www.thenewforest.co.uk. **Portsmouth** ⊠ The Hard, PO1 3QJ ☎ 023/9282-6722 ⊕ www.visitportsmouth.co.uk ⊠ Clarence Esplanade, Southsea PO5 3PB ☎ 023/9282-6722. **Salisbury** ⊠ Fish Row, off Market Sq., SP1 1EJ ☎ 01722/334956 ⊕ www.visitsalisbury.com. **Sherborne** ⊠ 3 Tilton Ct., Digby Rd., DT9 3NL ☎ 01935/815341 ⊕ www.westdorset.com. **Weymouth** ⊠ King's Statue, The Esplanade DT4 7AN ☎ 01305/785747 ⊕ www.weymouth.gov.uk. **Winchester** ⊠ The Guildhall, Broadway, SO23 9LJ ☎ 01962/840500 ⊕ www.visitwinchester.co.uk.

The West Country

SOMERSET, DEVON, CORNWALL

WORD OF MOUTH

"The most scenic part of Devon, in my opinion, is the north coast. If you have time, don't miss the Lynmouth/Lynton area. The Valley of the Rocks has some of the best coastal views in England."
—Steve_James

"Cornwall is all about rugged scenery on the north coast; bracing Champagne-like air, beautiful gardens, and charming fishing villages on the south coast; plus Celtic history and the odd pirate."
—londonengland

"The water [in St. Ives] is a lush shade of blue, reminiscent of the Mediterranean. It is a little touristy, but for the British. Sort of like Cape Cod for New Englanders."

—socialworker

www.fodors.com/forums

Updated by
Robert
Andrews

LEAFY, NARROW COUNTRY ROADS all around the southwest lead through miles of buttercup meadows and cider-apple orchards to mellow villages of stone and thatch and heathery heights overlooking the sea. This can be one of England's most relaxing regions to visit. The secret of exploring it is to ignore the main highways and just follow the signposts—or, even better, to let yourself get lost, which won't be difficult. The village names alone are music to the ears: there's Tintinhull, St. Endellion, and Huish Episcopi—just to name a few hamlets that *haven't* been covered below.

In Somerset, Somerset, Devon, and Cornwall are the three counties that make up the long southern peninsula known as the West Country. Each has its own distinct flavor, and each comes with a regionalism that borders on patriotism. Somerset is noted for its subtly rolling green countryside; Devon's wild and dramatic moors—bare, boggy, upland heath dominated by heathers and gorse—contrast with the restfulness of its many sandy beaches and coves; and Cornwall has managed to retain a touch of its old insularity, despite the annual invasion of thousands of people lured by the Atlantic waves or the ripples of the English Channel.

Bath, among the most alluring small cities in Europe, offers up "18th-century England in all its urban glory," to use a phrase by writer Nigel Nicolson. Founded by the Romans when they discovered here the only true hot springs in England, Bath enjoyed great popularity during the 17th and 18th centuries—which also happened to be one of Britain's most creative architectural eras. Thomas Gainsborough, Lord Nelson, and Queen Victoria traveled here to sip the waters (which Charles Dickens described as tasting like "warm flatirons"), and today people come to walk in the footsteps of Jane Austen, to visit Bath Abbey and the excavated Roman baths, or shop in an elegant setting. Bristol's historic port retains a strong maritime air, and Georgian architecture and a dramatic gorge create a backdrop to what has become one of Britain's most dynamic cities. Traveling south to the cathedral city of Wells, you'll pass through the lush countryside of Somerset, best seen in a cloak of summer heat when the county's orchards give ample shade, and its old stone houses and inns welcome you with a breath of coolness. Abutting Somerset's north coast, heather-covered Exmoor was the setting for R. D. Blackmore's historical romance, *Lorna Doone*.

Devon, farther west, is famed for its wild moorland—especially Dartmoor, supposed home of the mysterious beast in Sir Arthur Conan Doyle's novel *The Hound of the Baskervilles*, and actual home of ponies and an assortment of strange tors: rocky outcroppings eroded into weird shapes. Devon's large coastal towns are as interesting for their cultural and historical appeal—many were smugglers' havens—as for their scenic beauty.

Cornwall, England's southernmost county, has a mild climate, and here you are never more than 20 mi from the sea. The county has always regarded itself as separate from the rest of Britain, and the Arthurian legends really took root in Cornwall, not least at Tintagel Castle, the legendary birthplace of Arthur. High, jagged cliffs line Cornwall's Atlantic coast—the dangerous and dramatic settings that Daphne du Maurier often wrote eloquently about—and indeed pose a menace to passing ships. The south coast, Janus-like, is filled with sunny beaches, delightful coves, and popular resorts.

Exploring the West Country

A circular tour of the West Country covers a large territory, from the stylish architecture of Bath, two hours by car from London, to the remote and rocky headlands of Devon and Cornwall to the west. Stark contrasts abound in this peninsula, and the farther west you travel, the more the sea becomes an overwhelming presence. On the whole, the northern coast is more rugged, the cliffs dropping dramatically to tiny coves and beaches, whereas the south coast shelters many more resorts and wider expanses of sand. The crowds gravitate to the south, but there are plenty of remote inlets and estuaries along this southern shore, and you don't need to go far to find a degree of seclusion.

Unless you confine yourself to a few towns—for example, Bristol, Exeter, Penzance, and Plymouth—you will be at a huge disadvantage without your own transportation. The region has a few main arteries, but you should take minor roads whenever possible, if only to see the real West Country at a leisurely pace. Rail travelers can make use of a fast service connecting the major towns, and there's also a good network of bus services.

About the Restaurants & Hotels

The more established restaurants are often completely booked on a Friday or Saturday night, so reserve well in advance; the same is true for hotels and other lodgings. Room availability can be limited on the coasts during August. Accommodations include national hotel chains, represented in all the region's principal centers, as well as ancient inns and ubiquitous bed-and-breakfast places. Many farmhouses also rent out rooms—offering tranquillity in rural surroundings—but these lodgings are often difficult to reach without a car. It's worth finding out about weekend and winter deals that many hotels offer. For information about regional food specialties, *see* the On the Menu box, *below.*

WHAT IT COSTS In pounds				
	£££££	**££££**	**£££**	**££**	**£**
RESTAURANTS	over £22	£18–£22	£13–£17	£7–£12	under £7
HOTELS	over £160	£120–£160	£90–£119	£60–£89	under £60

Restaurant prices are for a main course at dinner. Hotel prices are for two people in a standard double room in high season, including V.A.T., with no meals or, if indicated, CP (with continental breakfast), BP (Breakfast Plan, with full breakfast), or MAP (Modified American Plan, with breakfast and dinner).

Timing

In July and August, traffic chokes the roads leading into the West Country, the beaches heave with sunseekers, and the resort towns are either

TOP REASONS TO GO

A coastal walk: Pick almost any stretch of coast in Devon and Cornwall for a close encounter with the sea—raging or calm, it's always invigorating. For high, dramatic cliff scenery, choose the Exmoor coast around Lynmouth or the coast around Tintagel.

Riding or hiking on Dartmoor: Get away from it all in southern England's greatest wilderness—an empty, treeless expanse dotted with lonely, rocky outcrops called tors. Frequent organized walks are advertised at visitor centers, which also have lists of pony-trekking operations.

Roman Baths, Bath: Take a break from the town's Georgian elegance and return to its Roman days on a fascinating tour around this beautifully preserved bath complex, built around the country's only hot spring.

Seafood in Padstow: Celebrity chef Rick Stein rules the roost in this small Cornish port, and any of his establishments will strongly satisfy, though the Seafood Restaurant has the wow factor. A pre- or post-dinner stroll around the harbor, jammed with fishing boats and riotous with gulls, will allow you to soak up the spirit of this congenial town.

Tate St. Ives: There's nowhere better to absorb the local arts scene than this offshoot of London's Tate in the pretty seaside town of St. Ives. The building is half the fun—its design echoes the cylindrical gas holder that once stood here—and a marvelous rooftop café claims views over Porthmeor Beach.

A visit to Eden: It's worth the journey west for Cornwall's Eden Project alone: a wonderland of plant life, magnificently sited in a former clay pit. Two gigantic geodesic "biomes" are filled with bushes, cacti, and trees from around the world, and the elaborate outdoor plantations are equally engaging. You can spend a whole day here.

Wells Cathedral: A perfect example of medieval craftsmanship, the building is a stunning spectacle, not least for its richly sculpted west front dominating a swath of manicured lawn. Come at the end of the day when Evensong is performed to experience its lofty interior at its most evocative.

bubbling with zest or unbearably tacky, depending on your point of view. If you must visit in summer, your best option is to find a secluded hotel and make brief excursions from there. Try to avoid traveling on Saturday, when weekly rentals start and finish and the roads are jammed with vehicles; the August bank holiday (the last weekend of the month) is notorious for congested roads. Bath is particularly congested in summer, when students flock to its language schools along with many visitors. Otherwise, fall and spring are good times to escape the crowds, although the water may be too cold for swimming and there is often a strong ocean breeze. Winter has its own appeal: the Atlantic waves crash dramatically against the coast, and the austere Cornish cliffs are at their most spectacular.

The West Country

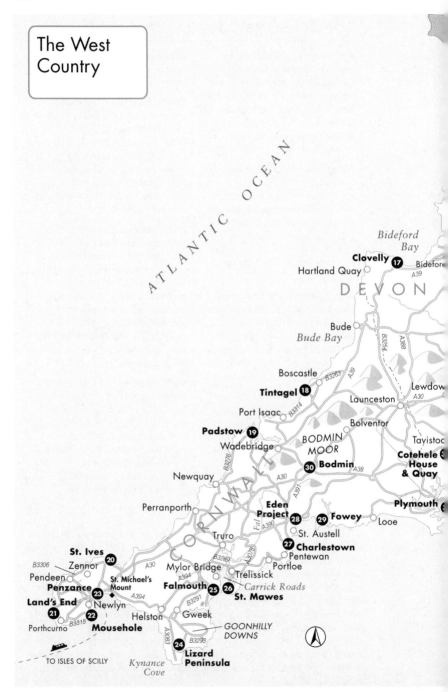

ATLANTIC OCEAN

Bideford Bay

Clovelly ⑰ Bideford

Hartland Quay

A39

D E V O N

Bude
Bude Bay

Boscastle

B3263

A39

Tintagel ⑱

B3314

Launceston

Lewdow

A30

Port Isaac

Bolventor

Padstow ⑲

Tayistoc

Wadebridge

BODMIN MOOR

Cotehele
House
& Quay

B3276

⑳ **Bodmin** A38

Newquay

A30

A391

Plymouth

Perranporth

Eden
Project ㉘

㉙ **Fowey**

A390

Looe

Truro

St. Austell

Fall

㉗ **Charlestown**

St. Ives ⑳

Pentewan

B3289

B3076

Portloe

Zennor

A30

Mylor Bridge

B3306

St. Michael's

Trelissick

Pendeen

Mount

A394

Carrick Roads

Penzance ㉓

Falmouth ㉕ ㉖

Land's End

Newlyn

A394

St. Mawes

㉑

Helston

B3291

Gweek

Porthcurno

B3315

㉒

Mousehole

A3083

GOONHILLY
DOWNS

TO ISLES OF SCILLY

㉔

Kynance
Cove

Lizard
Peninsula

GOWER
PENINSULA
Swansea
*Swansea
Bay*
WALES
M4
Newport
Bath & Lacock
1 – **10**
see detail
map
Cardiff
Bristol **11**

Bristol Channel
Chew Magna
Cheddar

Lynton/
Lynmouth **16**
Porlock
Weir
Bridgwater Bay
Minehead
EXMOOR
NATIONAL
PARK
Porlock **15** A39
14 **Dunster**
Ilfracombe
Combe
Martin
Braunton Burrows
Biosphere Reserve
B3358
Nether
Stowey
Wells **12**
Glastonbury Shepton
13 Mallet
Pilton
Barnstaple
A361
BRENDON
HILLS
B3190
B3188
QUANTOCK HILLS
S O M E R S E T
A39
A37
Dulverton
Taunton
A358
A361
◆ Sedgemoor
A303
A303
A39
Wellington
Bradford-on-Tone
A358
A303
A3088
A359
Tiverton
A361
M5
Yeovil
Exeter
39 – **43**
see detail
map
A30
Gittisham
Honiton
D O R S E T
Okehampton **36**
Drewsteignton
A30
Topsham
A3052
A376
B3174
Lyme
Regis
Bridport
Chagford **37**
Kenton
A376
A377
Sidmouth
Seaton
JURASSIC COAST
Lydford **35**
Gorge
North
Bovey
A382
A38
Budleigh
Salterton
Lyme Bay
DARTMOOR
NATIONAL
PARK
B3212
Bovey
Tracey
A380
Exmouth
Morwellham Quay **34**
3 Princetown
Yelverton
Buckfastleigh
Cockington
A379
32 Buckland
Abbey
Dartington
Dart
Torbay
Saltram
1 ◆ A38
A386
Totnes
Brixham
Yealmpton
A379
Dartmouth **38**
Kingsbridge
Slapton
A379
*Start
Bay*

English Channel

GREAT
BRITAIN

0 _____ 20 miles
0 _____ 30 km

BATH & ENVIRONS

Anyone who listens to the local speech of Bath will note the inflections that herald the closeness of England's West Country. The city, however, has strong links with the Cotswold Hills stretching north, and the Georgian architecture and mellow stone that are such a feature of Bath recall the stone mansions and cottages of that region. The hinterland of the county of Somerset has plenty of gentle, green countryside.

Bath

★ *13 mi southeast of Bristol, 115 mi west of London.*

"I really believe I shall always be talking of Bath . . . Oh! who can ever be tired of Bath," enthused Catherine Morland in Jane Austen's *Northanger Abbey,* and today thousands of people heartily agree with the sentiments expressed by the great 19th-century author. One of the delights of staying in this city, a UNESCO World Heritage Site, is being surrounded by magnificent 18th-century architecture, a lasting reminder of the vanished world described by Austen. In the 19th century Bath lost its fashionable luster and slid into a refined gentility that is still palpable. Although the 20th century saw some slight harm from World War II bombing and slightly more from urban renewal, the damage was halted before it could ruin the city's Georgian elegance.

This doesn't mean that Bath is a museum. It's lively, with good dining and shopping, excellent art galleries and museums, the remarkable excavated Roman baths, and theater, music, and other performances all year. Many people rush through Bath in a day, but there's enough to do to merit an overnight stay—or more. It does get crowded in summer; the sheer volume of sightseers may hamper your progress on a stroll. Note that parking in Bath is restricted, and any car illegally parked is likely to be ticketed and perhaps towed. ■ TIP→ **Public parking lots in the historic area fill up early, but the Park and Ride lots on the outskirts provide shuttle service into the center.**

The Romans put Bath on the map in the 1st century, when they built a temple here, in honor of the goddess Minerva, and a sophisticated network of baths to make full use of the mineral springs that gush from the earth at a constant temperature of 116°F (46.5°C). The remains of these baths are one of the city's glories. Visits by Queen Anne in 1702 and 1703 brought attention to the town, and soon 18th-century "people of quality" took it to heart. Bath became the most fashionable spa in Britain. The architect John Wood created a harmonious city, building graceful terraces (row houses), crescents (curving rows of houses), and villas of the same golden local limestone used by the Romans. His son, called John Wood the Younger, also designed notable buildings in the city. Assembly rooms, theaters, and pleasure gardens were built to entertain the rich and titled when they weren't busy attending the parties of Beau Nash (the city's master of ceremonies and chief social organizer, who helped increase Bath's popularity) and having their portraits painted by Gainsborough.

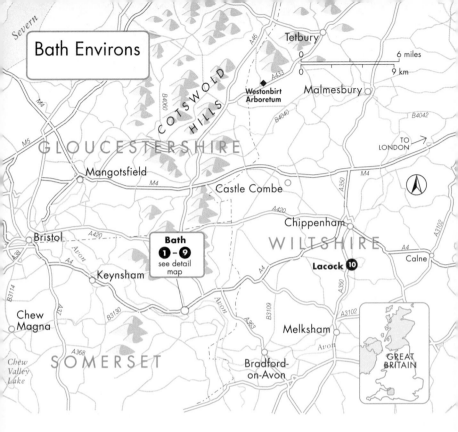

Main Attractions

2 Bath Abbey. Dominating Bath's center, this 15th-century edifice of golden, glowing stone has a splendid west front, with carved figures of angels ascending ladders on either side. Notice, too, the miter, olive tree, and crown motif, a play on the name of the current building's founder, Bishop Oliver King. More than 50 stained-glass windows fill about 80% of the building's wall space, giving the interior an impression of lightness. The abbey was built in the Perpendicular (English late-Gothic) style on the site of a Saxon abbey, and the nave and side aisles contain superb fan-vaulted ceilings. There are six services on Sunday. In the **Heritage Vaults,** accessible from outside the building (the entrance is in the abbey's south wall, off Abbey Churchyard), you can see an audiovisual presentation of the abbey's history, along with a reconstruction of the Norman cathedral that preceded it, various pieces of statuary, and a petition from 4th-century Bath, which includes what is thought to be the first mention of the word "Christian" in Britain. ⊠ *Abbey Churchyard* ☎ *01225/422462* ⊕ *www.bathabbey.org* 🖃 *Abbey £3 donation, Heritage Vaults free* ☉ *Abbey Apr.–Oct., Mon.–Sat. 9–6, Sun. 1–2:30 and 4:30–5:30; Nov.–Mar., Mon.–Sat. 9–4:30, Sun. 1–2:30. Heritage Vaults Mon.–Sat. 10–4.*

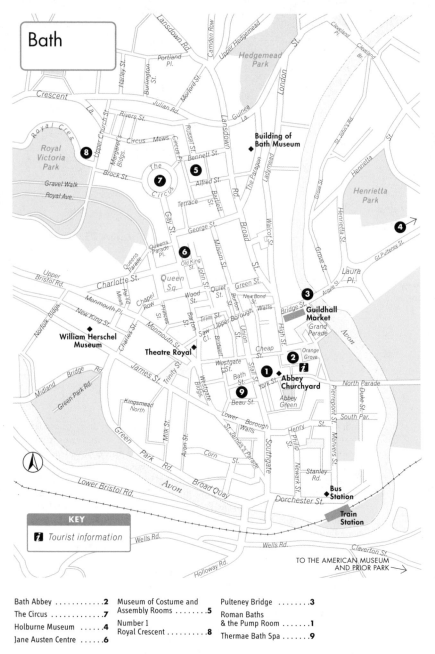

Bath

KEY

i *Tourist information*

★ ❼ **Circus.** John Wood designed the masterful Circus, a circle of curving, perfectly proportioned Georgian houses interrupted just three times for intersecting streets. Wood died shortly after work on the Circus began; his son, the younger John Wood, completed the project. Notice the carved acorns atop the houses: Wood nurtured the myth that Prince Bladud founded Bath, ostensibly with the help of an errant pig rooting for acorns (this is one of a number of variations of Bladud's story), and the architect adopted the acorn motif in a number of places. A garden fills the center of the Circus. The painter Thomas Gainsborough (1727–88) lived at No. 17 from 1760 to 1774.

★ ❹ **Holburne Museum.** One of Bath's gems, this elegant 18th-century building houses a small but superb collection of 17th- and 18th-century decorative arts, ceramics, and silverware. Highlights include paintings by Gainsborough (*The Byam Family*, on indefinite loan) and George Stubbs (*Reverend Carter Thelwall and Family*), and Rachmaninoff's Steinway piano. In its original incarnation as the Sydney Hotel, the house was one of the pivots of Bath's high society, which came to perambulate in the pleasure gardens (Sydney Gardens) that still lie behind it. One visitor was Jane Austen, whose main Bath residence was No. 4 Sydney Place, a brief stroll across the road from the museum. ⊠ *Great Pulteney St.* ☎ *01225/466669* ⊕ *www.bath.ac.uk/holburne* ☜ *£5.50* ☉ *Mid-Jan.–mid-Dec., Tues.–Sat. 10–5, Sun. and national holidays 11–5.*

❻ **Jane Austen Centre.** The one place in Bath that gives Austen any space provides a briefly diverting exhibition about the influence of the city on her writings; *Northanger Abbey* and *Persuasion* are both set primarily in the city. Displays give a pictorial introduction, and the digitally enlarged panorama of Bath in 1800 by Robert Havell helps put Austen's world in context. The cozy Georgian house, a few doors up from where the writer lived in 1805 (one of several addresses she had in Bath at different times), also includes the Austen-themed Regency Tearoom, open to the public. ■ TIP➔ You can buy tickets here for Jane Austen walking tours, which leave from the Abbey Churchyard at 11 on weekends. A tour ticket entitles you to a 20% reduction for entry to the exhibition. ⊠ *40 Gay St.* ☎ *01225/443000* ⊕ *www.janeausten.co.uk* ☜ *£5.95,* tours *£4.50* ☉ *Mar.–Oct., daily 10–5:30; Nov.–Feb., Sun.–Fri. 11–4:30, Sat 10–5:30.*

★ ❺ **Museum of Costume and Assembly Rooms.** In its role as the **Assembly Rooms,** this neoclassical building was the leading center for social life in 18th-century Bath, with a schedule of dress balls, concerts, and choral nights. Jane Austen came here often, and it was here, in the

---

JANE IN BATH

Though born and brought up in Hampshire, Jane Austen had close connections with Bath and lived here from 1801 to 1806. She was never overly fond of the place, peppering her letters with caustic comments about it (interspersed with gossip and effusions on bonnets and trimmings). Austen wrote her sister Cassandra that she left "with what happy feelings of escape." However, she is thought to have fallen in love here, and she received her only known offer of marriage while in Bath.

Ballroom, that Catherine Morland had her first, disappointing encounter with Bath's beau monde in *Northanger Abbey;* the Octagon Room was the setting for an important encounter between Anne Elliot and Captain Wentworth in *Persuasion.* Built by John Wood the Younger in 1771, the building was badly damaged by wartime bombing in 1942 but was faithfully restored. Today the Assembly Rooms house the entertaining **Museum of Costume,** displaying costumes from Jacobean times up to the present (audio guide included). Throughout the year, classical concerts are given in the Ballroom, just as they were in bygone days. ⊠ *Bennett St.* ☎ *01225/477789* ⊕ *www.museumofcostume.co.uk* ⊠ *£6.50; combined ticket with Roman Baths, valid 7 days, £13* ☉ *Mar.–Oct., daily 11–6; Nov.–Feb., daily 11–5; last admission 1 hr before closing.*

❽ **Number 1 Royal Crescent.** The majestic arc of the Royal Crescent, much used as a film location, is the crowning glory of Palladian architecture in Bath; Number 1 offers you a glimpse inside this splendor. The work of John Wood the Younger, the 30 houses fronted by 114 columns were laid out between 1767 and 1774. A house in the center is now the Royal Crescent Hotel. On the corner of Brock Street and the Royal Crescent, Number 1 Royal Crescent has been turned into a museum and furnished as it might have been at the turn of the 19th century. The museum crystallizes a view of the English class system—upstairs all is elegance, and downstairs is a kitchen display. ☎ *01225/428126* ⊕ *www.bath-preservation-trust.org.uk* ⊠ *£5* ☉ *Feb.–Oct., Tues.–Sun. and national holidays 10:30–5; Nov., Tues.–Sun. 10:30–4; last admission 30 mins before closing.*

FodorśChoice ★

❸ **Pulteney Bridge.** Florence's Ponte Vecchio inspired this 18th-century span, one of the most famous landmarks in the city and the only work of Robert Adam in Bath. It's unique in Great Britain because shops line both sides of the bridge.

❶ **Roman Baths & the Pump Room.** The hot springs have drawn people here since prehistoric times, so it's quite appropriate to begin an exploration of Bath at this excellent museum on the site of the ancient city's temple complex and primary "watering hole." Here the Roman patricians would gather to immerse themselves, drink the mineral waters, and socialize. With the departure of the Romans, the baths fell into disuse and were partially covered. When bathing again became fashionable, the site was reopened; the magnificent Georgian building now standing was erected at the end of the 18th century. During the 19th century, almost the entire Roman bath complex was rediscovered and excavated, and the museum displays relics of the temple once dedicated to Sulis Minerva. Exhibits include a mustachioed, Celtic-influenced Gorgon's head, fragments of colorful curses invoked by the Romans against some of their neighbors, and information about Roman bathing practices. The **Great Bath** is now roofless, and the statuary and pillars belong to the 19th century, but much remains from the original complex, and the steaming, somewhat murky waters are undeniably evocative. ■ TIP➡ **On August evenings, you can take torch-lighted tours of the baths.**

FodorśChoice ★

Bath's Georgian Architecture

BATH WOULDN'T BE BATH without its distinctive 18th-century Georgian architecture, much of which was conceived by antiquarian and architect John Wood the Elder (1704–54). Arriving in Bath in 1727, Wood embraced the Palladian style, made popular in Britain by Inigo Jones, and needed to look no further than the local golden limestone for building material. Influenced by nearby ancient stone circles as well as round Roman temples, he broke from convention in his design for Bath's Circus, a circle of houses broken only three times for intersecting streets. After the death of Wood the Elder, John Wood the Younger (1728–82) carried out his father's plans for the Royal Crescent, an obtuse crescent of 30 interconnected houses. Today you can stop in at No. 1 Royal Crescent for a look at one of these homes—it's like eavesdropping on the 18th century.

Adjacent to the Roman bath complex is the famed **Pump Room,** built 1792–96, a rendezvous place for members of 18th-century and 19th-century Bath society, who liked to check on the new arrivals to the city. Here Catherine Morland and Mrs. Allen "paraded up and down for an hour, looking at everybody and speaking to no one," to quote from Jane Austen's *Northanger Abbey.* Today you can take eat in the elegant space—or you can simply, for a small fee, taste the fairly vile mineral water. ✉ *Abbey Churchyard* ☎ *01225/477785* ⊕ *www.romanbaths. co.uk* ✉ *Pump Room free, Roman Baths £10, £11 in July and Aug. with audio guide; combined ticket with Museum of Costume and Assembly Rooms (valid 7 days) £13* ☉ *Mar.–June, Sept., and Oct., daily 9–6; July and Aug., daily 9 AM–10 PM; Nov.–Feb., daily 9:30–5:30; last admission 1 hr before closing.*

NEED A BREAK?

The quiet courtyard of two adjacent cafés, the **Café René and Café Parisien** (✉ 2 Shires Yard, off Broad St. ☎ 01225/447147) is handy for coffee or a lunchtime baguette. You can linger in the **Pump Room** (✉ Abbey Churchyard ☎ 01225/ 444477) for morning coffee or afternoon tea after seeing the Roman Baths.

Also Worth Seeing

American Museum and Gardens. A GreekRevival (19th-century) mansion in a majestic setting on a hill southeast of the city holds the first museum of American decorative arts to be established outside the United States. Some galleries are furnished rooms (bedrooms, parlors, and a morning room), and others contain objects—in silver, pewter, and glass, for example—dating from the 17th to 19th centuries. Several rooms are devoted to folk art, Native American culture, and quilts. The parkland includes a reproduction of George Washington's garden at Mount Vernon. ✉ *Warminster Rd. (A36), Claverton Down, 2½ mi southeast of Bath* ☎ *01225/460503* ⊕ *www.americanmuseum.org* ✉ *Museum, special exhibitions, and grounds £6.50; special exhibitions and grounds £4* ☉ *Museum: late Mar.–July, Sept., and Oct., Tues.–Sun. and national hol-*

idays noon–5; Aug., daily noon–5; late Nov.–mid-Dec., Tues.–Sun. and national holidays noon–4:30.

Building of Bath Museum. This absorbing museum in the Georgian Gothic–style Countess of Huntingdon's Chapel is an essential stop on any exploration of Bath, particularly for fans of Georgian architecture. It explains and illustrates the evolution of the city, with examples of everything from window design and wrought-iron railings to marquetry and other interior ornamentation. ⊠ *The Paragon* ☎ *01225/333895* ⊕ *www. bath-preservation-trust.org.uk* ✍ *£4* ⊙ *Mid-Feb.–Nov., Tues.–Sun. and national holidays 10:30–5. Last entry 45 mins before closing.*

❾ **Thermae Bath Spa.** The only place in Britain where you can bathe in natural hot spring water, and in an open-air rooftop location as well, this state-of-the-art complex designed by Nicholas Grimshaw consists of a Bath-stone building surrounded by a glass curtain wall. Opened (after years of delay) in 2006, the spa has four luxurious floors offering the latest spa treatments. Close by, the Cross Bath and the Hot Bath, two 18th-century thermal baths, have been brought back into use; there's also a café and shop. You can book in advance or call on the day. ⊠ *Hot Bath St.* ☎ *01225/331234* ⊕ *www.thermaebathspa.com* ✍ *£19 for 2 hrs, £29 for 4 hrs, £45 all day; extra charges for treatments* ⊙ *Daily 9 AM–10 PM; last entry at 8 PM.*

Where to Stay & Eat

Among hotel restaurants, Pimpernel's, in the Royal Crescent Hotel, is outstanding; the Olive Tree, in the Queensberry Hotel, is noteworthy.

££–££££ ✕ **Hole in the Wall.** Escape from Bath's busy-ness at this relaxed eatery serving sophisticated modern English fare in an 18th-century town house. At the bottom of a flight of stairs, the unfussy, stone-tile dining area—warmed by a generous open fire in winter—exudes calm and poise. It's the perfect environment to indulge in such dishes as grilled Devon oysters, panfried Gloucester beef, and roast partridge with braised cabbage. Cheeses come with sultana and honey bread. Pretheater meals are a good value. ⊠ *16 George St.* ☎ *01225/425242* ▤ *AE, DC, MC, V* ⊙ *No lunch Sun.*

££–£££ ✕ **Pump Room.** The 18th-century Pump Room, next to the Roman Baths, serves morning coffee, lunches of steak sandwiches or chicken and lamb dishes, and afternoon tea, often to music by a string trio. Do sample the English cheese board and homemade Bath biscuits. The Terrace Restaurant has views over the Baths and is also open occasionally for dinner (there are fixed-price menus, and reservations are essential). Be prepared to wait in line for a table during the day. ⊠ *Abbey Churchyard* ☎ *01225/444477* ▤ *AE, DC, MC, V* ⊙ *No dinner except during July, Aug., Dec., and festivals.*

££–£££ ✕ **Tilleys Bistro.** The meat and vegetarian menus of this intimate, bow-windowed eatery present an alluring selection of hot and cold dishes offered in small, medium, and large portions. Choices include French onion soup, roast lamb studded with garlic, and veal Tilleys—panfried veal stuffed with Gruyère cheese and topped with asparagus wrapped in Parma ham. Pretheater meals are available starting at 6 PM. ⊠ *3 N. Parade Passage* ☎ *01225/484200* ▤ *MC, V* ⊙ *Closed Sun.*

££ ✕ **Demuths.** This is the region's top spot for high-class vegetarian cuisine at reasonable prices. Inspiration from around the world shows in such satisfying concoctions as Keralan *thali*—coconut and vegetable curry with cauliflower *bhaji* (a mildly spiced side dish) and coriander rice—and sweet potato and *haloumi* (an eastern Mediterranean cheese with mint leaves in it) salad. The dining rooms, on two floors, are small without being crowded, and there's usually a soft jazz soundtrack. ⊠ *2 N. Parade Passage* ☎ *01225/446059* ▤ *MC, V.*

££ ✕ **Sally Lunn's.** A well-done magnet for visitors, this popular spot near Bath Abbey occupies the oldest house in Bath, dating to 1482. It's famous for the Sally Lunn bun (served here since 1680), actually a light, semisweet bread. You can choose from more than 40 sweet and savory toppings to accompany your bun, or turn it into a meal with such dishes as trencher pork (served with bread that holds the juices) with sherry and brandy sauce. Daytime diners can view the small kitchen museum in the cellar (free, 30p for nondining visitors). ⊠ *4 N. Parade Passage* ☎ *01225/461634* ▤ *MC, V* ⊙ *No dinner mid-Dec.–early Jan.*

££ ✕ **Strada.** The former home of Richard "Beau" Nash—the dictator of fashion for mid-18th-century society in Bath—and his mistress Juliana Popjoy provides an elegant setting for this outpost of a reliable chain of Italian eateries. Pizzas and pasta appear on the menu with dishes based on traditional classics, including braised lamb shank with olive oil and sage potato puree in tomato sauce. You can dine on the ground floor or in the Georgian drawing room upstairs. ⊠ *Beau Nash House, Saw Close* ☎ *01225/337753* ▤ *AE, MC, V.*

★ £££££ ✕▦ **Royal Crescent Hotel.** At the heart of the monumental Royal Crescent, this lavishly converted house is an architectural treasure, with prices to match. The furnishings are consistent with the building's period elegance, and a Palladian villa in the garden provides extra lodging. If some bedrooms are on the small side, the ample luxuries, including a pampering spa, compensate. The hotel's superb Pimpernel's restaurant (£45–£55 fixed-price dinner menus) has won consistent praise for modern British fare incorporating influences from Europe and the Far East. You can dine alfresco in summer. ⊠ *16 Royal Crescent, BA1 2LS* ☎ *01225/823333, 888/295–4710 in U.S.* 🖷 *01225/339401, 888/295–4711 in U.S.* ⊕ *www.royalcrescent.co.uk* ⇱ *31 rooms, 14 suites* ♨ *Restaurant, cable TV, in-room data ports, indoor pool, gym, sauna, spa, croquet, bar, library, meeting rooms, free parking, some pets allowed (fee)* ▤ *AE, DC, MC, V* ⊺⊙⊺ *CP.*

£££–£££££ ✕▦ **Queensberry Hotel.** Intimate and elegant, this boutique hotel in a residential street near the Circus occupies three 1772 town houses built by John Wood the Younger for the marquis of Queensberry. Renovations have preserved the Regency stucco ceilings and cornices and marble tile on the fireplaces, and each room is individually decorated in contemporary style. Four secluded, terraced gardens invite a summer aperitif. Downstairs, the semiformal, sleek, and understated Olive Tree (£££–££££) serves top-notch English and Mediterranean dishes. ⊠ *Russel St., BA1 2QF* ☎ *01225/447928* 🖷 *01225/446065* ⊕ *www.thequeensberry.co.uk* ⇱ *26 rooms, 3 suites* ♨ *Restaurant, cable TV, in-room data ports, Wi-Fi, bar, meeting rooms, free parking; no a/c* ▤ *AE, MC, V.*

FodorśChoice ★

£££–££££ ⌘ **Bath Paradise House.** Don't be put off by the 10-minute uphill walk from the center of Bath—you'll be rewarded by a wonderful prospect of the city from the upper stories of this Georgian guesthouse. Cool pastels and traditional furnishings decorate the rooms attractively, and there are open fires in winter and a lush garden for spring and summer. Rooms 3 and 5 have the best views; Nos. 11 and 12 open straight onto the garden. If the full English breakfast is too daunting, indulge in coffee and croissants in bed. ✉ *88 Holloway, BA2 4PX* ☎ *01225/317723* 🖷 *01225/482005* ⊕ *www.paradise-house.co.uk* ⇆ *11 rooms* ⌕ *Croquet, bar, free parking; no a/c, no smoking* ⊟ *AE, MC, V* ⦾| *BP.*

££–££££ ⌘ **Harington's Hotel.** It's rare to find a compact hotel in the cobblestoned heart of Bath, and this informal lodging converted from a group of Georgian town houses fits the bill nicely. The surprisingly quiet bedrooms aren't spacious, there are no views from the windows, and the parking facilities can be tricky to find, but these minuses are outweighed by the polite but friendly service and the central location. The bar serves snacks all day. Note that this three-story building has no elevator. ✉ *Queen St., BA1 1HE* ☎ *01225/461728* 🖷 *01225/444804* ⊕ *www.haringtons. co.uk* ⇆ *13 rooms* ⌕ *Cable TV, Wi-Fi, bar, parking (fee), no-smoking rooms; no a/c* ⊟ *AE, MC, V* ⦾| *BP.*

£££ ⌘ **Three Abbey Green.** A majestic sycamore tree dominates the gorgeous square, just steps away from Bath Abbey, that is home to this welcoming B&B with spacious rooms in pastel shades. Parts of the building date from 1689, but contemporary design lightens the traditional tone. The Lord Nelson room is extra big, with a four-poster, separate sitting area, and handsome fireplace; there are also family rooms. The only downsides are Bath's perennial shortage of parking space—though there are car parks nearby—and the occasional noise at night. The hosts are ready with tips for visiting the city and beyond. ✉ *3 Abbey Green, BA1 1NW* ☎ *01225/428558* 🖷 *01225/316669* ⊕ *www.threeabbeygreen.com* ⇆ *6 rooms* ⌕ *Wi-Fi; no a/c, no smoking* ⊟ *MC, V* ⦾| *BP.*

££–£££ ⌘ **Marlborough House.** A warm and informal welcome greets all who stay at this family-run Victorian establishment, close to the center of town. Each room charms with period furniture, fresh flowers, and antique beds. Leisurely breakfasts are positively encouraged; choose from home-baked muffins, scones, yogurts, pancakes, and French toast; all the food is organic, and vegans and those with special diets will find their needs amply supplied. ✉ *1 Marlborough La., BA1 2NQ* ☎ *01225/ 318175* 🖷 *01225/466127* ⊕ *www.marlborough-house.net* ⇆ *7 rooms* ⌕ *Wi-Fi, bar, some pets allowed (fee); no a/c, no smoking* ⊟ *AE, DC, MC, V* ⦾| *BP.*

£–££ ⌘ **Albany Guest House.** Homey and friendly, this Edwardian house, close to Victoria Park and the center of town, has simply furnished rooms with a floral motif. The contemporary, parchment- and plum-color attic room is the largest and best. Homemade vegetarian sausages are an option at breakfast. ✉ *24 Crescent Gardens, BA1 2 NB* ☎ *01225/313339* ⊕ *www. albanybath.co.uk* ⇆ *4 rooms, 2 with shower* ⌕ *Free parking; no a/c, no room phones, no kids under 7, no smoking* ⊟ *No credit cards* ⦾| *BP.*

Nightlife & the Arts

BARS & PUBS The small, brown and beige **Beau Bar** (✉ 34 Monmouth St. ☎ 01225/
444770), behind the Theatre Royal, serves the best cocktails in town
(it's closed Sunday). Pub aficionados will relish the friendly, unspoiled
ambience of the oak-panel **Old Green Tree** (✉ 12 Green St. ☎ 01225/
448259), a great spot for a pint.

FESTIVALS The **Bath International Music Festival** (✉ Bath Festivals Box Office, 2
★ Church St., Abbey Green ☎ 01225/463362 ⊕ www.bathfestivals.org.
uk), held for two weeks in May and June, presents concerts (classical,
jazz, and world music), dance performances, and exhibitions in and around
Bath, many in the Assembly Rooms and Bath Abbey.

The weeklong **Bath Literature Festival** (✉ Bath Festivals Box Office, 2
Church St., Abbey Green ☎ 01225/463362 ⊕ www.bathlitfest.org.uk)
in early March features readings and talks by writers, mostly in the 18th-
century Guildhall on High Street.

The **Jane Austen Festival** (☎ 01225/443000 ⊕ www.janeaustenfestival.
co.uk) celebrates the great writer with films, plays, walks, and talks during a week in late September.

THEATER The **Theatre Royal** (✉ Box Office, Saw Close ☎ 01225/448844), a magnificently restored Regency playhouse, has a year-round program that
often includes pre- or post-London tours. You have to reserve the best
seats well in advance, but you can line up for same-day standby seats
or standing room. ■ TIP➔ Check the location—sight lines can be poor.

Sports & the Outdoors

To explore the River Avon by rented punt or canoe, head for the **Bath
Boating Station** (✉ Forester Rd. ☎ 01225/312900), behind the Holburne Museum. It's open April through September.

Shopping

Bath has excellent small, family-run, and specialty shops; many close
on Sunday. The shopping district centers on Stall and Union streets (modern stores), Milsom Street (traditional stores), and Walcot Street (arts
and crafts). Leading off these main streets are alleyways and passages
lined with galleries and antiques shops.

★ **Bartlett Street Antique Centre** (✉ Bartlett St. ☎ 01225/466689) has more
than 100 showcases and stands selling every kind of antique imaginable, including silver, porcelain, and jewelry. **Beaux Arts Ceramics** (✉ 12–13
York St. ☎ 01225/464850) carries the work of prominent potters. The
covered **Guildhall Market** (✉ Entrances on High St. and Grand Parade),
open Monday through Saturday 9 to 5, is the place for everything from
jewelry and gifts to delicatessen food, secondhand books, bags, and batteries; there's a café, too. **Margaret's Buildings** (✉ Halfway between the
Circus and Royal Crescent) is a lane with gift shops and several stores
selling secondhand and antiquarian books.

Lacock

Fodor'sChoice ★

10 *3 mi south of Chippenham, 10 mi southeast of Bath.*

This lovely Wiltshire village owned by the National Trust is the victim of its own charm, its unspoiled gabled and stone-tile cottages drawing tour buses aplenty. Off-season, however, Lacock slips back into its profound slumber, the mellow stone and brick buildings little changed in 500 years and well worth a wander. Besides Lacock Abbey, there are a few antiques shops, the handsome church of St. Cyriac (built with money earned in the wool trade), a 14th-century tithe barn, and a scattering of pubs that serve bar meals in atmospheric surroundings.

Well-preserved **Lacock Abbey** reflects the fate of many religious establishments in England—a spiritual center became a home. The abbey, at the town's center, was founded in the 13th century and closed down during the dissolution of the monasteries in 1539, when its new owner, Sir William Sharington, demolished the church and converted the cloisters, sacristy, chapter house, and monastic quarters into a private dwelling. His last descendant, Mathilda Talbot, donated the property as well as Lacock itself to the National Trust in the 1940s. The abbey's grounds are also worth a wander, with a Victorian woodland garden and an 18th-century summerhouse. Harry Potter fans, take note: Lacock Abbey was used for some scenes at Hogwarts School in the film *Harry Potter and the Sorcerer's Stone*. The **Fox Talbot Museum** in a 16th-century barn at the gates of Lacock Abbey, illustrates the early history of photography with works by pioneers in the field and also exhibits contemporary artists. The museum commemorates the work of William Henry Fox Talbot (1800–77), who developed the first photographic negative at Lacock Abbey, showing an oriel window in his family home. Look for a copy of this and other results of Fox Talbot's experiments in the 1830s. ✉ *Just east of A350* ☎ *01249/730459* ⊕ *www.nationaltrust.org.uk* 🎟 *Abbey, museum, gardens, and cloisters £7.80; abbey, garden, and cloisters £6.30; museum, gardens, and cloisters £4.80; museum only (winter) £3.40* ☉ *Abbey late Mar.–Oct., Wed.–Mon. 1–5:30; museum late Feb.–Oct., daily 11–5:30; Nov.–mid-Dec. and early Jan.–mid-Feb., weekends 11–4; gardens and cloisters late-Feb.–Oct., daily 11–5:30; last admission 30 mins before closing.*

Where to Stay & Eat

£££–££££ ✕🛏 **Sign of the Angel.** An inn since the 15th century, this building measures up to expectations of comfortable antiquity—polished floors, gleaming silver, antiques, and cottage-style bedrooms (one room contains a bed that belonged to famous Victorian engineer Isambard Kingdom Brunel); some rooms are in an annex. The restaurant (££–£££) is known for its Stilton and walnut pâté, roasts, casseroles, and desserts such as meringues with clotted cream. ⊠ *6 Church St., SN15 2LB* ☎ *01249/730230* 🖷 *01249/730527* ⊕ *www.lacock.co.uk* ⤺ *11 rooms* ♨ *Restaurant, some in-room data ports, lounge, some pets allowed; no a/c* ⊟ *AE, DC, MC, V* ⊗ *Closed last wk of Dec.* ❙⊙❙ *BP.*

BRISTOL TO NORTH DEVON

From the bustling city of Bristol, your journey takes you south to the cathedral city of Wells and continues on via Glastonbury, possibly the Avalon of Arthurian legend. Proceed west along the Somerset coast into Devon, skirting the moorlands of Exmoor and tracing the northern shore via Clovelly.

Bristol

⑪ *120 mi west of London, 46 mi south of Birmingham, 13 mi northwest of Bath.*

The West Country's biggest city, Bristol has in recent years become one of the country's most vibrant centers, with a thriving cultural scene encompassing some of the best contemporary art, theater, and music. Buzzing bars, cafés, and restaurants, and a largely youthful population make it an attractive place to spend time. The city also trails a great deal of history in its wake. It can be called the "birthplace of America" with some confidence, for John Cabot and his son Sebastian sailed from the old city docks in 1497 to touch down on the North American mainland, which he claimed for the English crown. The city had been a major center since medieval times, but in the 17th and 18th centuries it became the foremost port for trade with North America. Bristol was the home of William Penn, developer of Pennsylvania, and a haven for John Wesley, whose Methodist movement played a role in colonial Georgia.

Now that the city's industries no longer rely on the docks, the historic harbor along the River Avon has been largely given over to pleasure craft. Arts and entertainment complexes, museums, stores, and restaurants fill the quayside, reflecting Bristol's fast-moving, modern face. The pubs and clubs here draw the under-25 set and make the area fairly boisterous (and best avoided) on Friday and Saturday nights.

Main Attractions

♨ **@Bristol.** The rebuilt Harbourside area has three science- and nature-theme attractions with innovative exhibits. Explore provides a "hands-on, minds-on" experience of science, and Wildwalk includes interactive natural-history exhibits and a walk through a rain forest aflutter with exotic birds and butterflies. An IMAX cinema shows mostly science-related films. Open spaces linking the sites act as a venue for live performances and multimedia activities, with shops, cafés, and restaurants nearby. ⊠ *Anchor Rd.* ☎ *0845/345–1235* ⊕ *www.at-bristol.org.uk* 🎟 *£8 for Explore @Bristol, £9 for Wildwalk, £8 for IMAX, £13–£15 for 2-attraction ticket, £20 for 3-attraction ticket* ⊗ *Weekdays 10–5, weekends and school vacations 10–6.*

NEED A BREAK? The excellent café-restaurant upstairs at the **Watershed Media Centre** (⊠ 1 Canon's Rd. ☎ 0117/927–5100) overlooks part of the harborside. Sandwiches, salads, and hot snacks are served during the day, along with coffees and cakes.

British Empire and Commonwealth Museum. This museum, in engineer Isambard Kingdom Brunel's 19th-century railway station by the modern Temple Meads train station, helps put Bristol in the context of the growth of Britain's colonial empire and the trading organization that succeeded it. It's an absorbing whirl through history and geography, with photographs, slides, and grainy film of missionaries and memsahibs. The darker side of the story of the empire is not ignored, with space devoted to slavery, the Opium Wars, and the transportation of convicts to Australia. The interactive exhibits appeal to children. ⊠ *Station Approach, Temple Meads* ☎ *0117/925–4980* ⊕ *www.empiremuseum.co.uk* ⊠ *£6.95* ☉ *Daily 10–5; last admission 4:30.*

★ **Church of St. Mary Redcliffe.** Queen Elizabeth I called the rib-vaulted, 14th-century church "the fairest in England." It was built by Bristol merchants who wanted a place in which to pray for the safe (and profitable) voyages of their ships. A chapel holds the arms and armor of Sir William Penn, father of the founder of Pennsylvania. The church is a five-minute walk from Temple Meads train station toward the docks. ⊠ *Redcliffe Way* ☎ *0117/929–1487* ⊠ *Free* ☉ *Mon.–Sat. 9–5 (until 4 in winter), Sun. 8–8.*

Clifton Suspension Bridge. In the Georgian suburb of Clifton—a sort of Bath in miniature—you can take in a monument to Victorian engineering, the 702-foot-long bridge that spans the Avon Gorge. Work began on Isambard Brunel's design in 1831, but the bridge was not completed until 1864.

★ **SS *Great Britain*.** On view in the harbor is this restored vessel, the first iron ship to cross the Atlantic. Built by the great English engineer Isambard Brunel in 1843, it remained in service until 1970, first as a transatlantic liner and ultimately as a coal storage hulk. On board, everything from the galley to the officers' quarters comes complete with sounds and smells of the time. Moored alongside is a replica of the *Matthew*, the tiny craft that carried John Cabot to North America in 1497. Your ticket admits you to the **Dockyard Museum,** which presents the history of the *Great Britain*; you can descend into the ship's dry dock for a view of the hull and propeller. ⊠ *Great Western Dockyard, Gas Ferry Rd.* ☎ *0117/926–0680* ⊕ *www.ssgreatbritain.org* ⊠ *£8.95* ☉ *Apr.–Oct., daily 10–5:30; Nov.–Mar., daily 10–4:30; last entry 1 hr before closing.*

Also Worth Seeing

New Room. Among the Dissenters from the Church of England who found a home in Bristol were John Wesley and Charles Wesley, and in 1739 they built the New Room, a meeting place that became the first Methodist chapel. Its simplicity contrasts both with the style of Anglican churches and with the modern shopping center hemming it in. Call ahead to arrange a tour that can include **Charles Wesley's House** (a 10-minute walk away), an 18th-century town house where the Wesleys lived. ⊠ *Broadmead* ☎ *0117/926–4740* ⊕ *newroombristol.org.uk* ⊠ *Free, tour of New*

Room and house £8, New Room only £4 ☉ *Mon.–Sat. and national holidays 10–4.*

Where to Stay & Eat

£££–££££ ✕ **Bell's Diner.** A local institution, this bistro in the Montpelier area occupies a converted corner shop and has polished wood floors and prints of Bristol on its pale gray walls. The inventive Mediterranean menu changes daily and includes organic and wild ingredients, as well as toothsome desserts such as prune and Armagnac soufflé. Bell's is rather hidden—take A38 (Stokes Croft) north, then turn right on Ashley Road and immediately left at Picton Street, which will lead you to York Road. ✉ *1 York Rd.* ☎ *0117/924–0357* ▭ *AE, MC, V* ☉ *Closed Sun. and Dec. 24–30. No lunch Sat. and Mon.*

£££–££££ ✕ **Juniper.** Inventive takes on traditional English cuisine, such as wild duck with braised red cabbage, are the order of the day in this cozy neighborhood restaurant with a blackboard menu that changes with the seasons. Modern art adorns the walls, and lilac tablecloths contrast with white painted brickwork. ✉ *21 Cotham Rd. S* ☎ *0117/942–1744* ▭ *AE, MC, V* ☉ *No dinner Sun., no lunch Mon.–Sat.*

£–£££ ✕ **Old India.** Bristol's former stock exchange has found a new role as a fashionable Indian eatery. All the opulent trimmings have been restored, including the mahogany paneling, rich drapes, tiled staircase, and elegant statuary. It's the perfect setting for classic Indian cuisine and innovative dishes such as *niljiri korma* (chicken breast in a mild curry sauce with rose petals) and *macchi mazadaar* (salmon with mustard seeds, coconut, curry leaves, and tamarind water). The two-course lunch and pre-theater menus are a particularly good deal. ✉ *34 St. Nicholas St.* ☎ *0117/922–1136* ▭ *MC, V* ☉ *Closed Sun.*

£ ✕ **Boston Tea Party.** Despite the name, this laid-back and vaguely eccentric place is quintessentially English, and ideal for a relaxed lunch away from the nearby rigors of the Park Street shopping scene. Good sandwiches and generous bowls of salad as well as some light hot dishes can be taken away or eaten in the backyard or the upstairs sofa salon. ✉ *75 Park St.* ☎ *0117/929–8601* ▭ *MC, V* ☉ *No dinner Sun.–Wed.*

££££ ✕▣ **Hotel du Vin.** This hip Anglo-French minichain has an ambitious outlet in the Sugar House—six former sugar-refining warehouses built in 1728 when the River Frome ran right outside the front door—close to the docklands and the city center. Rooms are crisply contemporary in style, with CD and DVD players and huge showers, but retain many original industrial features. The restaurant (£££) has an extensive wine list—visit the cellar for a private tasting session—and the menu entices with modern but robust French flavors. A good-value, fixed-price lunch is offered. ✉ *Narrow Lewins Mead, BS1 2NU* ☎ *0117/925–5577* 🖷 *0117/925–1199* ⊕ *www.hotelduvin.com* ⇌ *40 rooms* ⚒ *Restaurant, cable TV, Wi-Fi, billiards, bar, meeting rooms* ▭ *AE, DC, MC, V.*

££ ▣ **Naseby House Hotel.** On a tree-lined street in the heart of elegant Clifton, this Victorian hotel is not far from Bristol's major sights. The basement holds the plushest, most expensive bedroom, with a four-poster and a French door opening onto the garden. Period pieces fill the sitting room, and the breakfast room is also impressive. ✉ *105 Pembroke Rd., BS8*

3EF 🏨 *0117/973–7859* ⊕ *www.nasebyhousehotel.co.uk* 🛏 *14 rooms* ♨ *Some pets allowed; no a/c* ═ *MC, V* ⦿| *BP.*

Nightlife & the Arts

The **Arnolfini** (✉ 16 Narrow Quay 🕿 0117/917–2300), in a prime position on the waterfront, is one of the country's most prestigious contemporary-art venues, with a reputation for uncovering innovative yet accessible art. Admission is free. The movie theater and lively bar and bistro stay open late. The **Bristol Old Vic** (✉ King St. 🕿 0117/987–7877), the country's oldest continuously working theater, dates to 1766. Performances, from classics to new works, are staged in three spaces. **St. George's** (✉ Great George St., off Park St. 🕿 0845/402–4001), a former church built in the 18th century, serves as one of the country's leading acoustic venues for classical, jazz, and world music. Lunchtime concerts are scheduled. The **Watershed Media Centre** (✉ 1 Canon's Rd. 🕿 0117/927–5100) by the harborfront has a movie theater that shows excellent international films.

Wells

❶❷ *22 mi south of Bristol, 16 mi southwest of Bath, 132 mi west of London.*

England's smallest cathedral city, with a population of 10,000, lies at the foot of the Mendip Hills. Although it feels more like a quiet country town than a city, Wells contains one of the masterpieces of Gothic architecture, its great cathedral—the first to be built in the Early English style. The city's name refers to the underground streams that bubble up into St. Andrew's Well within the grounds of the Bishop's Palace. Springwater has run through High Street since the 15th century. Seventeenth-century buildings surround the ancient marketplace in the city center. Wells has market days on Wednesday and Saturday.

★ The great west towers of the medieval **Cathedral Church of St. Andrew,** the oldest surviving English Gothic church, can be seen for miles. Dating from the 12th century, the cathedral derives its beauty from the perfect harmony of all of its parts, the glowing colors of its original stained-glass windows, and its peaceful setting among stately trees and majestic lawns. To appreciate the elaborate west front facade, approach the building on foot from the cathedral green, accessible from Market Place through a great medieval gate called "penniless porch" (named after the beggars who once waited here to collect alms from worshippers). The cathedral's west front is twice as wide as it is high, and some 300 statues of kings and saints adorn it. Inside, vast inverted arches—known as scissor arches—were added in 1338 to stop the central tower from sinking to one side. The cathedral also has a rare and beautiful medieval clock, the second-oldest working clock in the world, consisting of the seated figure of a man called Jack Blandifer, who strikes a bell on the quarter hour while mounted knights circle in a joust. Near the clock is the entrance to the Chapter House—a small wooden door opening onto a great sweep of stairs worn down on one side by the tread of pilgrims over the centuries. Free 45-minute guided tours begin at the information desk. Tours are suspended April through October during

Quiet Hour between noon and 1 PM. A cloister restaurant serves tea, coffee, and cakes. ✉ *Cathedral Green* ☎ 01749/674483 ⊕ *www. wellscathedral.org.uk* 🎟 *£5 suggested donation* ☉ *Apr.–Sept., daily 7–7; Oct.–Mar., daily 7–6.*

NEED A BREAK? **Goodfellows Patisserie** (✉ **5 Sadler St.** ☎ **01749/673866), a little French café near the cathedral, serves exquisite cakes and pastries that complement various chocolate concoctions and excellent coffee.**

The Bishop's Eye gate leading from Market Place takes you to the magnificent, moat-ringed **Bishop's Palace,** which has most of the original 12th- and 13th-century residence. You can also see the ruins of a late-13th-century great hall. The hall lost its roof in the 16th century because Edward VI needed the lead it contained. ✉ *Market Pl.* ☎ 01749/678691 ⊕ *www.bishopspalacewells.co.uk* 🎟 *£5* ☉ *Apr.–Oct., weekdays 10:30–6, Sun. noon–6 (may also open Sat. 10:30–6); last admission at 5.*

To the north of the cathedral, the cobbled **Vicar's Close,** one of Europe's oldest streets, has terraces of handsome 14th-century houses with strange, tall chimneys. A tiny medieval chapel here is still in use.

Where to Stay & Eat

£–££ ✕ **Ask.** Part of an Italian chain of informal trattorias, this place has a marvelous location next to the cathedral and Bishop's Palace—the back window overlooks the Palace gardens. The premises are old but the large glass front admits plenty of light. Tasty pastas and pizzas dominate the menu, though the salads are worth sampling. One good option is *insalata di salmone,* a salad with mixed greens, oak-roasted salmon, red onions, cucumber, and cherry tomatoes in an orange and tarragon dressing. ✉ *Market Pl.* ☎ *01749/677681* ⊟ *AE, DC, MC, V.*

£££ ✕🏨 **The Crown.** This hotel has been a landmark in Wells since the Middle Ages, and in 1695 William Penn was arrested here for preaching without a license. A sense of the building's age remains, although most guest rooms (with the exception of four rooms with four-posters) are furnished in simple styles more modern than traditional and have whirlpool baths or full-body massage showers. The Penn Bar serves sandwiches, salads, and hot dishes. You can try the more comfortable French bistro, Anton's (££–£££), for choices such as wild boar sausages and rump of lamb. ✉ *Market Pl., BA5 2RP* ☎ *01749/673457* 🖷 *01749/679792* ⊕ *www. crownatwells.co.uk* ➳ *15 rooms* ♿ *Restaurant, bar, some pets allowed; no a/c, no room phones* ⊟ *AE, MC, V* ⍾ *BP.*

££ ✕🏨 **Ancient Gate House.** The guest rooms of the Rugantino restaurant run by Franco Rossi and his sons make a convenient base. The premises, dating to 1473, incorporate the Great West Gate and are full of character. There's an ancient stone staircase, and many rooms have four-posters. You can dine well on Italian or English dishes, made largely from local produce, in the restaurant (££–£££)—scampi with white-wine sauce is a specialty, and the fixed-price menus are appealing. Breakfast may be across the street at the White Hart. ✉ *20 Sadler St., BA5 2SE* ☎ *01749/672029* 🖷 *01749/670319* ⊕ *www.ancientgatehouse. co.uk* ➳ *9 rooms* ♿ *Restaurant, bar, some pets allowed; no a/c* ⊟ *AE, MC, V* ⍾ *BP.*

ON THE MENU

From cider to cream teas, many specialties tempt your palate in the West Country. Lamb, venison, and, in Devon and Cornwall, seafood are favored in restaurants, which have improved markedly, notably through the influence of Rick Stein's seafood-based culinary empire in Padstow, in Cornwall. In many towns the day's catch is unloaded from the harbor and transported directly to eateries. The catch varies by season, but lobster is available year-round, as is crab, stuffed into sandwiches at quayside stalls and in pubs. Seafood is celebrated at fishy frolics that include Falmouth's Oyster Festival (early October).

Somerset is the home of Britain's most famous cheese—the ubiquitous cheddar, from the Mendip Hills village. Do try to taste real farmhouse cheddar, made in the traditional barrel shape known as a truckle.

Devon's caloric cream teas consist of a pot of tea, homemade scones, and lots of thickened clotted cream and strawberry jam (clotted, or specially thickened cream, is a regional specialty and is sometimes called Devonshire cream).

Cornwall's specialty is the pasty, a pastry shell filled with chopped meat, onions, and potatoes. The pasty was devised as a handy way for miners to carry their dinner to work; today's versions are generally pale imitations of the original, though you can still find delicious home-cooked pastries if you're willing to search a little.

For liquid refreshment, try scrumpy, a homemade dry cider that is refreshing but carries a surprising kick. Look out, too, for perry, similar to cider but made from pears. English wine, similar to German wine, is made in Somerset (you may see it on local menus), and in Cornwall you can find a variant of age-old mead made from local honey.

Glastonbury

★ ⓭ *5 mi southwest of Wells, 27 mi south of Bristol, 27 mi southwest of Bath.*

A town steeped in history, myth, and legend, Glastonbury lies in the lee of Glastonbury Tor, a grassy hill rising 520 feet above the drained marshes known as the Somerset Levels. The Tor is supposedly the site of crossing ley lines (hypothetical alignments of significant places), and, in legend, Glastonbury is identified with Avalon, the paradise into which King Arthur was reborn after his death. Partly because of these associations but also because of its world-class rock-music festival, the town has acquired renown as a New Age center, mixing crystal-gazers with druids, yogis, and hippies, variously in search of Arthur, Merlin, Jesus—and even Elvis.

At the foot of **Glastonbury Tor** is **Chalice Well,** the legendary burial place of the Grail. It's a stiff climb up the Tor, but your reward is the fabulous view across the Vale of Avalon. At the top stands a ruined tower, all that remains of **St. Michael's Church,** which collapsed after a landslide in 1271.

The ruins of the great **Glastonbury Abbey,** in the center of town, are on the site where, according to legend, Joseph of Arimathea built a church in the 1st century. A monastery had certainly been erected here by the 9th century, and the site drew many pilgrims. The ruins are those of the abbey completed in 1524 and destroyed in 1539, during Henry VIII's dissolution of the monasteries. A sign south of the Lady Chapel marks the sites where Arthur and Guinevere were supposedly buried. The worthwhile visitor center has a scale model of the abbey as well as carvings and decorations salvaged from the ruins. ⊠ *Magdalene St.* ☎ *01458/832267* ⊕ *www.glastonburyabbey.com* ✆ *£4.50* ⊙ *Feb., daily 10–5; Mar., daily 9:30–5:30; Apr., May, and Sept., daily 9:30–6; June–Aug., daily 9–6; Oct., daily 9:30–5; Nov., daily 9:30–4:30; Dec. and Jan., daily 10–4:30; last admission 30 mins before closing.*

> ## TALE OF THE GRAIL
>
> According to tradition, Glastonbury was where Joseph of Arimathea brought the Holy Grail, the chalice used by Jesus at the Last Supper. Centuries later, the Grail was said to be the objective of the quests of King Arthur and the Knights of the Round Table. When monks claimed to have found the bones of Arthur and Guinevere at Glastonbury in 1191, the popular association of the town with the mythical Avalon was sealed. Arthur and Guinevere's presumed remains were lost to history after Glastonbury Abbey was plundered for its riches in 1539.

☙ The **Somerset Rural Life Museum** occupies a Victorian farmhouse and the large, 14th-century Abbey tithe barn. More than 90 feet in length, the barn once stored the one-tenth portion of the town's produce that was owed to the church. Exhibits illustrate 19th-century farming practices, and there's a cider-apple orchard nearby. Events designed for children take place most weekends during school holidays. ■ TIP→ **For a good walk, take the scenic footpath from the museum that leads up to the Tor, a half mile east.** ⊠ *Chilkwell St.* ☎ *01458/831197* ⊕ *www.somerset.gov.uk/museums* ✆ *Free* ⊙ *Apr.–Oct., Tues.–Fri. 10–5, weekends 2–6; Nov.–Mar., Tues.–Sat. 10–5.*

Where to Stay

££–££££ 🏨 **George and Pilgrims Hotel.** Pilgrims en route to Glastonbury Abbey stayed here in the 15th century. Today the ancient, stone-front hotel is equipped with modern comforts but retains its flagstone floors, wooden beams, and antique furniture; three rooms have four-posters. The rooms, newly refurbished, come in different shapes and sizes. The better ones are spacious and furnished with antiques, others are smaller, and those in the newer part of the building lack character but are cheaper. ⊠ *1 High St., BA6 9DP* ☎ *01458/831146* 🖷 *01458/832252* ⊕ *www. georgeandpilgrims.activehotels.com* ↩ *12 rooms* ☖ *Restaurant, bar, meeting rooms, some pets allowed (fee); no a/c* ⊟ *MC, V* ⊖ *BP.*

★ **£££** 🏨 **Number 3.** This elegant Georgian town house next to the abbey grounds has log fires in the winter and a terrace and walled garden for summer relaxation. Grouped around the garden, the spacious bedrooms are individually styled, with mostly pastel color schemes, traditional furniture, and drapes behind the beds. Three rooms are in the separate Garden House, and the Blue Room overlooks the abbey ruins and, through the trees, Glastonbury Tor. Generous breakfasts might include fresh fruit salad, ham and cheese, yogurt, and croissants. ⊠ *3 Magdalene St., BA6 9EW* ☎ *01458/832129* 🖨 *01458/834227* ⊕ *www. numberthree.co.uk* ⇝ *5 rooms* ♿ *No a/c, no smoking* ⦿ *CP.*

Nightlife & the Arts

Held annually a few miles away in Pilton, the **Glastonbury Festival** (☎ 01749/890470 ⊕ www.glastonburyfestivals.co.uk) is England's biggest and perhaps best rock festival. For three days over the last weekend in June, it hosts hundreds of bands—established and up-and-coming—on five stages. Pick up an issue of *New Musical Express* for the lineup. Tickets are steep—around £125—and sell out months in advance; they include entertainment, a camping area, and service facilities.

Dunster

⑭ *32 mi west of Glastonbury, 43 mi north of Exeter.*

Lying between the Somerset coast and the edge of Exmoor National Park, Dunster is a picture-book village with a broad main street. The eight-sided yarn-market building on High Street dates from 1589.

Dunster Castle, a 13th-century fortress remodeled in 1868–72, dominates the village from its site on a hill. Parkland and unusual gardens with subtropical plants surround the building, which has fine plaster ceilings and a magnificent 17th-century oak staircase. The climb to the castle from the parking lot is steep. ⊠ *Off A39* ☎ *01643/823004* ⊕ *www. nationaltrust.org.uk* 🖾 *£7.50, gardens only £4.10* ⊙ *Castle mid-Mar.–Oct., Sat.–Wed. 11–5; 1st wk Nov., Sat.–Wed. 11–4. Gardens mid-Mar.–Oct., daily 10–5; Nov.–mid-Mar., daily 11–4.*

Exmoor National Park

25 mi north of Exeter.

Less wild and forbidding than Dartmoor to its south, 267-square-mi Exmoor National Park is no less majestic for its bare heath and lofty views. The park extends right up to the coast and straddles the county border between Somerset and Devon. Some walks offer spectacular views over the Bristol Channel. Although it is interwoven with cultivated farmland and pasturage,

TAKE A HIKE

Britain's longest national trail, the awesome South West Coast Path, wraps around the coast of the peninsula for 630 mi from Minehead (near Dunster, Somerset) to South Haven Point, near Poole (Dorset). To complete the entire trail takes about 56 days. Some parts, notably the Tarka Trail section in North Devon, are open to cyclists. The **South West Coast Path Association** (⊠ Bowker House, Lee Mill Bridge, Ivybridge, PL21 9EF ☎ 01752/896237 ⊕ www.swcp.org. uk) has information about the trail. Another Web site, ⊕ **www. southwestcoastpath.com,** suggests walks as short as a few hours.

Exmoor can be desolate. Taking one of the more than 700 mi of paths and bridleways through the bracken and heather (at its best in the fall), you might glimpse the ponies and red deer for which the region is noted. ⚠ Be careful: the proximity of the coast means that mists and squalls can descend with alarming suddenness.

The national park visitor centers at Combe Martin, County Gate, Dulverton, Dunster, and Lynmouth have information and maps. The free Exmoor Visitor news sheet lists guided walks; they may have a theme (archaeology or deer, for example), and most cost £3 to £5. If you're walking on your own, check the weather, take water and a map, and tell someone where you're going. *Exmoor National Park Authority* ⊠ *Exmoor House, Dulverton TA22 9HL* ☎ *01398/323665* ⊕ *www. exmoor-nationalpark.gov.uk* 🖃 *Free.*

Porlock

🕒 *6 mi west of Dunster, 40 mi north of Exeter.*

Buried at the bottom of a valley, with the slopes of Exmoor all about, the small, unspoiled town of Porlock lies near "Doone Country," setting for R. D. Blackmore's swashbuckling saga *Lorna Doone.* This historical novel, published in 1869, is set in the late 17th century, during Monmouth's Rebellion. Porlock had already achieved a place in literary history by the late 1790s, when Samuel Taylor Coleridge declared it was a "man from Porlock" who interrupted his opium trance while the poet was composing "Kubla Khan." The 36-mi **Coleridge Way** (⊕www.exmoor-nationalpark. gov.uk) trail passes through the Quantock and Brendon hills and part of Exmoor, from Nether Stowey (site of Coleridge's farmhouse) to Porlock.

Where to Stay & Eat

£££–££££ ✕🏨 **Andrews on the Weir.** Calling itself a restaurant with rooms, this waterfront Georgian hotel is pure relaxed English country house with touches of glamour. Guest rooms have print drapes and patchwork quilts. The ambitious contemporary restaurant (£32 for two courses) takes advantage of seafood, Exmoor lamb, and duckling, and you can expect unusual desserts, such as iced parfait with banana sorbet and mocha sauce, and excellent local cheeses. ⊠ *Porlock Weir, TA24 8PB* ☎ *01643/ 863300* 🖷 *01643/863311* ⊕ *www.andrewsontheweir.co.uk* 🛏 *5 rooms* ⚬ *Restaurant, bar, some pets allowed; no a/c, no kids under 12* 🖃 *MC, V* ☉ *Closed Mon., Tues., and Jan.* ⭐️ *BP.*

Lynton & Lynmouth

🕒 *13 mi west of Porlock, 60 mi northwest of Exeter.*

A steep hill separates this pretty pair of Devonshire villages, which are linked by a cliff railway. Lynmouth, a fishing village at the bottom of the hill, crouches below 1,000-foot-high cliffs at the mouths of the East and West Lynne rivers. Lynton is higher up. To 19th-century visitors, the place evoked an Alpine scene. The grand landscape of Exmoor lies all about, with walks to local beauty spots: Watersmeet, the Valley of the Rocks, or Hollerday Hill, where rare feral goats graze.

Water and a cable system power the 862-foot **cliff railway** that connects Lynton with Lynmouth by a ride up a rocky cliff; riders get fine views over the harbor. Inaugurated in 1890, it was the gift of publisher George Newnes, who also donated Lynton's imposing Town Hall, near the top station on Lee Road. ⊠ *Lee Rd., Lynton* ☎ *01598/753908* ⊕ *www. cliffrailwaylynton.co.uk* ⌸ *£2.75 round-trip* ☉ *Mid-Feb.–mid-July and mid-Sept.–mid-Nov., daily 9–7; mid-July–mid-Sept., daily 9–9.*

Exmoor Coast Boat Cruises runs boat trips around the dramatic Devon coast from Lynmouth Harbour. A one-hour excursion takes in Lee Bay, Woody Bay, and the Valley of the Rocks. Other cruises include mackerel fishing trips (£12). ⊠ ☎ *01598/753207* ⌸ *£9* ☉ *Easter–Oct.*

Where to Stay & Eat

£££–££££ ✕▦ **Rising Sun.** A 14th-century inn and a row of thatched cottages make up this hotel with great views over the Bristol Channel. One cottage is said to have hosted the poet Percy Bysshe Shelley during his honeymoon. In the main building, corridors and creaking staircases lead to cozy rooms decorated in stylish print or solid fabrics and furnished with new pine or older wooden pieces. The traditional restaurant (*££££–£££££*) specializes in local cuisine such as Devonshire beef fillet, and there's a superb game menu December through February. ⊠ *Harbourside, Lynmouth EX35 6EG* ☎ *01598/753223* ▤ *01598/753480* ⊕ *www. risingsunlynmouth.co.uk* ⇨ *15 rooms, 1 cottage* ⌂ *Restaurant, in-room data ports, fishing, bar; no a/c, no kids under 7* ▭ *MC, V* ⏉ *BP.*

★ **££–£££** ▦ **Shelley's Hotel.** The second of Lynmouth's two hotels that claim to be Percy Bysshe Shelley's honeymoon haunt does not have such a fine location or quite as much character as the Rising Sun, but it's more spacious and modern inside. Bright rooms have big windows and good views, and the service is cheerfully efficient. Shelley and his 16-year-old bride, Harriet Westbrook, apparently left without paying their bill—although the poet later mailed £20 of the £30 owed. During his nine-week sojourn in Lynmouth, Shelley found time to write his polemical *Queen Mab.* ⊠ *8 Watersmeet Rd., Lynmouth EX35 6EP* ☎ *01598/753219* ▤ *01598/753751* ⊕ *www.shelleyshotel.co.uk* ⇨ *11 rooms* ⌂ *Restaurant, bar, no-smoking rooms; no a/c* ▭ *MC, V* ⏉ *BP.*

Clovelly

⑰ *40mi southwest of Lynton, 60 mi northwest of Exeter.*

Fodor'sChoice
★

Lovely Clovelly always seems to have the sun shining on its flower-lined cottages and stepped and cobbled streets. Alas, its beauty is well known, and day-trippers can overrun the village in summer. Perched precariously among cliffs, a steep, cobbled road—tumbling down at such an angle that it's closed to cars—leads to the toylike harbor with its 14th-century quay. The climb back has been likened to the struggles of Sisyphus, but, happily, from Easter through October a Land Rover service will (for a small fee) take you to and from the parking lot at the top. Allow about two hours (more if you stop for a drink or a meal) to take in the village. A fine 10-mi walk is a cliff-top hike along the coast from Hartland

Quay, near Clovelly, down to Lower Sharpnose Point, just above Bude.

You pay £4.75 to park and use the **Clovelly Visitor Centre** (☒ Off A39 ☏ 01237/431781 ⊕ www.clovelly. co.uk); this is the only way to enter the village if you arrive by car. The fee includes admission to a fisherman's cottage in the style of the 1930s and an exhibition about Victorian writer Charles Kingsley, who lived here as a child. All the buildings in the village are owned by the Clovelly Estate Company. People arriving by bicycle or on foot do not pay to enter. ■ TIP→ To avoid the worst crowds, visit on weekdays, preferably before or after school summer vacation. If you must visit in summer, arrive early or late in the day.

> **DONKEYS AT WORK**
>
> Donkey stables, donkey rides for kids, and abundant donkey souvenirs in Clovelly recall the days when these animals played an essential role in town life, carrying food, packages, and more up and down the village streets. Even in the 1990s, donkeys helped carry bags from the hotels. Today sledges do the work, but the animals' labor is remembered.

Where to Stay & Eat

££££ ✕☐ **Red Lion Hotel.** One of only two hotels in this coastal village, the 18th-century Red Lion sits right on the harbor. Guest rooms, some small, are decorated along a nautical theme; all have sea views. The climb up through Clovelly is perilously steep, but guests can bring cars via a back road to and from the hotel. The sophisticated restaurant (£20 and £25 fixed-price menus at dinner) specializes in seafood dishes and homemade ice creams and sorbets. ☒ *The Quay, EX39 5TF* ☏ *01237/ 431237* ☐ *01237/431044* ⊕ *www.clovelly.co.uk* ⌦ *11 rooms* ♿ *Restaurant, 2 bars; no a/c* ⊟ *AE, DC, MC, V* ⏀ *BP.*

CORNWALL
COAST & MOOR

Cornwall stretches west into the sea, with plenty of magnificent coastline to explore. One way to discover it all is to travel southwest from the cliff-top ruins of Tintagel Castle, the legendary birthplace of Arthur, along the north Cornish coast to Land's End. This predominantly cliff-lined coast, interspersed with broad expanses of sand that attract surfers, has many tempting places to stop, including Padstow (for a seafood feast) or St. Ives, a delightful artists' colony. From Land's End, the westernmost tip of Britain, known for its savage land- and seascapes and panoramic views, turn northeast, stopping in the popular seaside resort of Penzance, the harbor city of Falmouth, and a string of fishing villages including Fowey. The Channel coast is less rugged than the northern coast, with more sheltered beaches. Leave time to visit the Eden Project, with its large, surrealistic-looking conservatories in an abandoned clay pit, and to explore the boggy, heath-covered expanse of Bodmin Moor.

Tintagel

⑱ *30 mi southwest of Clovelly, 35 mi northwest of Plymouth.*

The romance of Arthurian legend thrives around Tintagel's ruined castle on the coast. Ever since the somewhat unreliable 12th-century chronicler Geoffrey of Monmouth identified Tintagel as the home of Arthur, son of Uther Pendragon and Ygrayne, devotees of the legend cycle have revered the site. In the 19th century, Alfred, Lord Tennyson described Tintagel's Arthurian connection in *The Idylls of the King*. Today the village itself has more than its share of tourist junk—including Excaliburgers. Never mind: the headland around Tintagel is splendidly scenic.

The **Old Post Office**, a 14th-century stone manor house with yard-thick walls, smoke-blackened beams, and an undulating slate-tile roof, has been restored to its Victorian appearance, when one room served as a post office. ✉ *3–4 Tintagel Centre* ☎ *01840/770024* ⊕ *www.nationaltrust.org.uk* 🖳 *£2.60* ⊙ *Late Mar.–late July and Sept., Sun.–Fri. 11–5:30; late July–Aug., daily 11–5:30; Oct., Sun.–Fri. 11–4.*

Fodor'sChoice
★
Although all that remains of the ruined cliff-top **Tintagel Castle,** legendary birthplace of King Arthur, is the outline of its walls, moats, and towers, it requires only a bit of imagination to conjure up a picture of Sir Lancelot and Sir Galahad riding out in search of the Holy Grail over the narrow causeway above the seething breakers. Archaeological evidence, however, suggests that the castle dates from much later—about 1150, when it was the stronghold of the earls of Cornwall. Long before that, Romans may have occupied the site. The earliest identified remains here are of Celtic (AD 5th-century) origin, and these may have some connection with the legendary Arthur. Legends aside, nothing can detract from the castle ruins, dramatically set off by the wild, windswept Cornish coast, on an island joined to the mainland by a narrow isthmus. (There are also traces of a Celtic monastery here.) Paths lead down to the pebble beach and a cavern known as **Merlin's Cave.** Exploring Tintagel Castle involves some arduous climbing on steep steps, but even on a summer's day, when people swarm over the battlements and a westerly Atlantic wind sweeps through Tintagel, you can feel the proximity of the distant past. ✉ *Castle Rd., ½ mi west of village* ☎ *01840/770328* ⊕ *www.english-heritage.org.uk* 🖳 *£4.30* ⊙ *Apr.–Sept., daily 10–6; Oct., daily 10–5; Nov.–Mar., daily 10–4.*

Padstow

⑲ *12 mi southwest of Tintagel.*

A small fishing port at the mouth of the Camel River, Padstow attracts attention and visitors as a center of culinary excellence, largely because of the presence here since 1975 of pioneering seafood chef Rick Stein. He has made Padstow a stop on any foodie's itinerary. Stein's empire includes two restaurants, a café, a fish-and-chips joint (gentler on the wallet), a delicatessen on South Quay, a patisserie, a cooking school (classes fill up months in advance), a gift shop, and some elegant accommodations. He's got some competition in the area, including, since spring 2006,

All About Arthur

LEGENDS CONCERNING KING ARTHUR have resonated through the centuries, enthusiastically taken up by writers and poets from 7th-century Welsh and Breton troubadours to Tennyson and Mark Twain in the 19th century, and T. H. White in the 20th century. The historical Arthur was probably a Christian Celtic chieftain battling against the heathen Saxons in the 6th century, although most of the tales surrounding him have a much later setting, thanks to the vivid but somewhat fanciful chronicles of his exploits by medieval scholars.

Places associated with Arthur and his consort Guinevere, the wizard Merlin, the knights of the Round Table, and the related legends of Tristan and Isolde (or Iseult) can be found all over Europe, but the West Country claims the closest association. Arthur was said to have had his court of Camelot at Cadbury Castle (17 mi south of Wells) and to have been buried at Glastonbury.

Cornwall in particular holds the greatest concentration of Arthurian links, notably his supposed birthplace, Tintagel, and the site of his last battle, on Bodmin Moor. However tenuous the links—and, barring the odd, somewhat ambiguous inscription, there is nothing in the way of hard evidence of Arthur's existence—the Cornish have taken the Once and Future King to their hearts, and his spirit is said to reside in the now-rare bird, the Cornish chough.

Jamie Oliver's hot new 15 Cornwall. Oliver's restaurant is south of town on B3276, right on Watergate Bay between Padstow and Newquay.

Even if seafood is not your favorite fare, Padstow is worth visiting. The cries of seagulls fill its lively harbor, a string of fine beaches lies within a short ride—including some choice strands highly prized by surfers—and two scenic walking routes await: the Saints Way across the peninsula to Fowey, and the Camel Trail, a footpath and cycling path that follows the river as far as Bodmin Moor.

Where to Stay & Eat

££££–£££££
Fodor'sChoice
★

✕🖾 **The Seafood Restaurant.** Rick Stein's flagship restaurant (££££–£££££; reservations essential), just across from where the lobster boats and trawlers unload their catches, has built its reputation on the freshest fish and high culinary artistry. The fixed-price dinners are the best option, and may include stir-fried razor clams with black beans and grilled hake with asparagus and a cream and caviar sauce. Don't want to move after your meal? Book one of the sunny, individually designed guest rooms done in clean-lined modern or plush traditional style; ask for one overlooking the harbor. ⊠ *Riverside, PL28 8BY* ☎ *01841/532700* 🖨 *01841/ 532942* ⊕ *www.rickstein.com* 🖙 *14 rooms* ♦ *Restaurant, minibars, some pets allowed (fee); no a/c* ⊟ *AE, MC, V* 🍽 *BP.*

£££££
🖾 **St. Edmund's House.** The most luxurious Rick Stein venture has a sophisticated minimalist style. Excellently equipped, the bedrooms have polished wooden floors, in-room DVD players, and French doors facing the

harbor. Booking here guarantees a dinner table at the Seafood Restaurant, where breakfast is taken, but you should reserve as far ahead as possible. ■ TIP→ **If the price here is too steep but you want to stay in Stein lodging, check out the few simple rooms above Rick Stein's Café.** ⊠ *St. Edmond's La., PL28 8BZ* ☎ *01841/532700* 🖷 *01841/532942* ⊕ *www. rickstein.com* ➴ *6 rooms* ⚲ *Minibars, cable TV, some pets allowed (fee); no a/c* ☰ *AE, MC, V* ⊙ *Closed 1 wk around Christmas* ℉❘ *BP.*

Sports & the Outdoors

BIKING   Bikes of all shapes and sizes can be rented at **Trail Bike Hire** (⊠ South Quay ☎ 01841/532594), at the start of the Camel Trail.

HIKING   The **Saints Way,** a 30-mi inland path between Padstow and the Camel Estuary on Cornwall's north coast to Fowey on the south coast, follows a Bronze Age trading route, later used by Celtic pilgrims to cross the peninsula. Several relics of such times can be seen along the way. Contact the tourist offices in Padstow or Fowey or the Cornwall Tourist Board for information.

SURFING   **Harlyn Surf School** (⊠ 23 Grenville Rd. ☎ 01841/533076) can arrange half- to five-day surfing courses.

EN ROUTE   **Newquay,** 14 mi southwest of Padstow, is the biggest, most developed resort on the north Cornwall coast. It has become Britain's surfing capital, and in summer young California-dreaming devotees can pack the wide, cliff-backed beaches. Eight miles south of Newquay and past the sandy shores of Perran Bay, **Perranporth** is another popular seaside spot. It becomes extremely busy in high season, though it's easier to escape the crowds here than in Newquay. The swells off this 3-mi stretch of beach attract swarms of surfers, and enchanting coastal walks extend along the dunes and cliffs.

St. Ives

⓴ *35 mi southwest of Padstow on A30, 10 mi north of Penzance.*

James McNeill Whistler came here to paint his landscapes, Daphne du Maurier and Virginia Woolf to write their novels. Today sand, sun, and superb art continue to attract thousands of vacationers to the fishing village of St. Ives, named after Saint Ia, a 5th-century female Irish missionary said to have arrived on a floating leaf. The town has long played host to a well-established artists' colony, and there are plenty of craftspeople, too. ■ TIP→ **Day-trippers often crowd St. Ives, so it's best to park away from the center.**

The studio and garden of Dame Barbara Hepworth (1903–75), who pioneered abstract sculpture in England, are now the **Barbara Hepworth Museum and Sculpture Garden.** London's prominent Tate gallery runs the museum. The artist lived here for 26 years. ⊠ *Trewyn Studio, Barnoon Hill* ☎ *01736/796226* ⊕ *www.tate.org.uk* 🖾 *£4.75, combined ticket with Tate St. Ives £8.75* ⊙ *Mar.–Oct., daily 10–5:30; Nov.–Feb., Tues.–Sun. and national holidays 10–4:30.*

BEACH BASICS

The beaches lining parts of the peninsula have made the West Country one of England's main family vacation destinations. Natives don't mind the water's temperature, but foreigners, especially those pampered by the warm waves of the Mediterranean, are not so eager to brave the elements. Swimming here is a bracing experience that sometimes leaves you shivering and breathless. At most resorts, red and yellow flags show the limits of safe swimming. There can be strong undertows, and beware of fast-moving tides. This region of England has the biggest concentration of winners of the Blue Flag scheme, which rewards cleanliness, water quality, easy access, and facilities. The northern coast of the peninsula has the region's best surfing beaches, and Cornwall, in particular, has a thriving surfing industry. Go ahead and give it a try: it's easy to rent equipment (including wet suits), and plenty of places offer lessons.

4

★ The spectacular **Tate St. Ives** displays the work of artists who lived and worked in St. Ives, mostly from 1925 to 1975, and has selections from the rich collection of the Tate in London. It occupies a modernist building—a fantasia of seaside deco-period architecture with a panoramic view of rippling turquoise ocean. The rooftop café is excellent, for the food and views. ⊠ *Porthmeor Beach* ☎ *01736/796226* ⊕ *www.tate.org.uk* ✉ *£5.75, combined ticket with Barbara Hepworth Museum and Sculpture Garden £8.75* ⊘ *Mar.–Oct., daily 10–5:30; Nov.–Feb., Tues.–Sun. and national holidays 10–4:30.*

NEED A BREAK?

One of Cornwall's oldest pubs (built in 1312), the harborfront **Sloop Inn** (⊠ The Wharf ☎ 01736/796584) serves simple lunches as well as evening meals in wood-beam rooms that display the work of local artists. If the weather's good, you can eat at the tables outside.

Where to Stay & Eat

£££–££££ ✕ **Porthminster Beach Café.** Unbeatable for its location alone—on the broad, golden sands of Porthminster Beach—this sleek modern eatery prepares imaginative lunches, teas, and evening meals you can savor while you take in the marvelous vista across the bay. Typical choices are Cornish crab fritters; spicy braised lamb tagine with roasted couscous, and cumin-fried almonds; and Barbary duck with seared foie gras on parsnip puree. The sister Porthgwidden Beach Café, in the Downalong area of town, has a smaller and cheaper but equally varied menu. ⊠ *Porthminster Beach* ☎ *01736/795352* ▭ *AE, MC, V* ⊘ *Closed Nov.–Easter.*

££££–£££££ ✕🏠 **Garrack Hotel.** A family-run, ivy-clad hotel with panoramic sea views from its hilltop location, the Garrack is relaxed and undemanding. Some rooms are furnished in traditional style; others are more modern. The excellent restaurant (£££–££££) specializes in local fish, including grilled or sautéed lobster, as well as Cornish lamb. Breads are made in-house, and the wine list features some Cornish vineyards. ⊠ *Burthallan La., TR26 3AA* ☎ *01736/796199* 🖷 *01736/798955* ⊕ *www.garrack.com* 🛏 *18 rooms* ⚘ *Restaurant, in-room data ports, indoor pool, gym, sauna, bar; no a/c* ☰ *AE, DC, MC, V* †⊘| *BP.*

£–££ 🖼 **Cornerways.** Everything in St. Ives seems squeezed into the tiniest

> ### SURFERS WELCOME
>
> The four-story Tate St. Ives, at the base of a cliff fronted by Porthmeor Beach, may be the only art museum with special storage space for visitors' surfboards.

of spaces, and this cottage B&B in the quiet Downalong quarter is no exception. The light, tastefully converted rooms are pleasingly simple in design, with neutral colors enlivened by modern art; the more expensive have sea views. Most rooms are named after characters in Daphne du Maurier's novels (she once stayed in one of them). Fresh local fish is offered at breakfast, and the galleries are minutes away. ⊠ *1 Bethesda Pl., TR26 1PA* ☎ *01736/796706* ⊕ *www.cornerwaysstives.com* 🛏 *6 rooms* ⚘ *No a/c, no smoking* ☰ *No credit cards* †⊘| *BP.*

Land's End

★ ❷   *10 mi southwest of St. Ives, 10 mi west of Penzance.*

The coastal road, B3306, ends at the western tip of Britain at what is, quite literally, Land's End. The sea crashes against the rocks here and lashes ships battling their way around the point. ■ TIP→ **Approach from one of the coastal footpaths for the best panoramic view.** Over the years, sightseers have caused some erosion of the paths, but new ones are constantly being built, and Cornish "hedges" (granite walls covered with turf) have been planted to prevent erosion. The scenic grandeur of Land's End remains undiminished, although the point draws crowds of people from all over the world. The Land's End Hotel here is undistinguished, though the restaurant has good views. A low-key theme park, the **Land's End Experience** (☎ *0870/458–0099*), runs a poor second to nature.

Mousehole

★ ❷   *7 mi east of Land's End, 3 mi south of Penzance.*

On B3315 between Land's End and Penzance, Mousehole (pronounced *mow*-zel, with the first syllable rhyming with "cow") merits a stop— and plenty of people do stop—to see this archetypal Cornish fishing village of tiny stone cottages. It was the home of Dolly Pentreath, supposedly the last native Cornish speaker, who died in 1777.

Penzance

❷   *3 mi north of Mousehole, 10 mi south of St. Ives.*

Superb views over Mount's Bay are one lure of this popular, unpretentious seaside resort. It's a good base for exploring the area but does get very crowded in summer. The town's isolated position has always made it vulnerable to attack from the sea. During the 16th century, Spanish raiders destroyed most of the original town, and the majority of old buildings date from as late as the 18th century. The main street is Market Jew Street, a folk mistranslation of the Cornish expression "Marghas Yow," which means "Thursday Market." Where Market Jew Street meets Causeway Head is Market House, constructed in 1837, an impressive, domed granite building that now serves as a bank.

The former main street and one of the prettiest thoroughfares in Penzance, **Chapel Street** winds down from Market House to the harbor. Its predominantly Georgian and Regency houses suddenly give way to the extraordinary **Egyptian House,** whose facade recalls ancient Egypt. Built around 1830 as a geological museum, today it houses vacation apartments. Across Chapel Street is the 17th-century **Union Hotel,** where in 1805 the death of Lord Nelson and the victory of Trafalgar were first announced from the minstrels' gallery in the assembly rooms. Near the Union Hotel on Chapel Street is one of the few remnants of old Penzance, the **Turk's Head,** an inn said to date from the 13th century.

The small collection at the **Penlee House Gallery and Museum,** in a gracious Victorian house in a park, focuses on paintings by members of the so-called Newlyn School from about 1880 to 1930. These works evoke the life of the inhabitants of nearby Newlyn, mostly fisherfolk. The museum also covers 5,000 years of West Cornwall history through archaeology, decorative arts, costume, and photography exhibits. ⊠ *Penlee Park* ☎ *01736/363625* ⊕ *www.penleehouse.org.uk* ✉ *£3, Sat. free* ☉ *May–Sept., Mon.–Sat. 10–5; Oct.–Apr., Mon.–Sat. 10:30–4:30; last admission ½ hr before closing.*

★ Rising out of Mount's Bay just off the coast, the spectacular granite and slate island of **St. Michael's Mount** is one of Cornwall's greatest natural attractions. The 14th-century castle perched at the highest point—200 feet above the sea—was built on the site of a Benedictine chapel founded by Edward the Confessor. In its time, the island has served as a church (Brittany's island abbey of Mont St. Michel was an inspiration), a fortress, and a private residence. The castle rooms you can tour include the Chevy Chase Room—a name probably associated with the Cheviot Hills or the French word *chevaux* (horses), after the hunting frieze that decorates the walls of this former monks' refectory. The battlements also offer wonderful views. Fascinating gardens surround the Mount, and many kinds of plants flourish in its microclimates. To get to the island, walk the cobbled causeway from the village of Marazion or, when the tide is in during the summer, take the ferry. There are pubs and restaurants in the village, but the island also has a café and restaurant.

■ TIP➡ Wear stout shoes for your visit to this site, which is unsuitable for anyone with mobility problems. The climb to the castle is steep. ⊠ *3 mi east of Penzance on A394, Marazion* ☎ *01736/710507* ⊕ *www. stmichaelsmount.co.uk* ✉ *Castle £6, garden £3, £1.20 for ferry each way* ☉ *Castle late Mar.–Oct., weekdays and Sun. 10:30–5.30. Garden May and June, weekdays 10–5:30; July–Oct., Thurs. and Fri. 10–5:30; last admission 4:45; Nov.–Mar., phone for hrs.*

Where to Stay & Eat

£££–££££ ✕ **Abbey Restaurant.** Sleekly modern, this restaurant has garnered enthusiastic plaudits with a short, intriguing contemporary menu that highlights fresh seafood and local meat. Starters might include pigeon and pork terrine with onion marmalade and toasted brioche, followed by such dishes as grilled lemon sole with eggplant caviar. Among the exquisite desserts are and croissant and butter pudding with apricots and pear sorbet. ✉ *Abbey St.* ☎ *01736/330680* ▭ *AE, MC, V* ⊘ *Closed Dec., Jan., and Mon.; also Tues. Feb.–May and Sept.–Nov.; Wed. in Feb. and Nov. No lunch Tues.–Thurs.*

★ **££–£££** ✕ **Admiral Benbow Inn.** One of the town's most famous inns, the 15th-century Admiral Benbow was once a smugglers' pub—look for the figure of a smuggler on the roof. Seafaring memorabilia, a brass cannon, model ships, and figureheads fill the place. In the restaurant area, decorated to resemble a ship's galley, you can dine on seafood or a steak-and-Guinness pie. ✉ *46 Chapel St.* ☎ *01736/363448* ▭ *MC, V.*

★ **£££££** 🏨 **Abbey Hotel.** Owned by former 1960s model–icon Jean Shrimpton and her husband, this small, Wedgwood-blue-colored 17th-century hotel off Chapel Street is marvelously homey. Books fill the drawing room, and antiques and chintzes decorate many of the rooms, most of which have harbor views; there's also a small, comfortable apartment. ✉ *Abbey St., TR18 4AR* ☎ *01736/366906* 📠 *01736/351163* ⊕ *www. theabbeyonline.co.uk* 🛏 *6 rooms, 1 apartment* ☖ *Dining room, some pets allowed; no a/c* ▭ *AE, MC, V* ❚◯❚ *BP.*

£–££ 🏨 **Camilla House.** This flower-bedecked Georgian house stands on a road parallel to the promenade, close to the harbor. Guest rooms are cheerfully decorated; those at the front have sea views. The owners are great sources of local information and can help with ferry crossings and flights to the Isles of Scilly. Evening meals are available on request. ✉ *12 Regent Terr., TR18 4DW* ☎ *01736/363771* ⊕ *www.camillahouse-hotel.co.uk* 🛏 *8 rooms* ☖ *Dining room, in-room data ports, Wi-Fi, bar; no a/c, no room phones, no smoking* ▭ *AE, MC, V* ❚◯❚ *BP.*

Nightlife & the Arts

★ The open-air **Minack Theatre** perches high above a beach 3 mi southeast of Land's End and about 6 mi southwest of Penzance. The slope of the cliff forms a natural amphitheater, with bench seats on the terraces and the sea as a magnificent backdrop. Different companies present plays from classic dramas to modern comedies afternoons and evenings in summer. An exhibition center tells the story of the theater's creation. ✉ *Off B3315, Porthcurno* ☎ *01736/810181* 🎫 *Exhibition center £3, performances £6 and £7.50* ⊘ *Apr.–Oct., daily 9:30–5:30; Nov.–Mar., daily 10–4. Exhibition center closed during matinees, currently May–Sept., Wed. and Fri. noon–4:30.*

Lizard Peninsula

★ **㉔** *23 mi southeast of Penzance*

The southernmost point on mainland Britain, this peninsula is a government-designated Area of Outstanding Natural Beauty. The rocky, dramatic coast is the highlight, as the interior is flat and boring. There's no coast road, unlike Land's End, so the peninsula is best explored on foot. The beaches are good. With no large town (Helston is the biggest, and is not a tourist center), it's far less busy than Land's End. The huge, eerily rotating dish antennae of the Goonhilly Satellite Communications Earth Station are visible from the road as it crosses Goonhilly Downs, the backbone of the peninsula.

A path close to the tip of the peninsula plunges down 200-foot cliffs to the tiny **Kynance Cove,** with its handful of pint-size islands. The sands here are reachable only during the 2½ hours before and after low tide. The peninsula's cliffs are made of greenish serpentine rock, interspersed with granite; souvenirs of the area are carved out of the stone.

Falmouth

25 *15 mi northeast of Kynance Cove, 12 mi south of Truro.*

The bustle of this resort town's fishing harbor, yachting center, and commercial port only adds to its charm. In the 18th century, Falmouth was the main mail-boat port for North America, and in Flushing, a village across the inlet, you can see the slate-covered houses built by prosperous mail-boat captains. A ferry service now links the two towns. On Custom House Quay, off Arwenack Street, is the King's Pipe, an oven in which seized contraband was burned.

The granite and oak-clad **National Maritime Museum Cornwall** by the harbor is an excellent place to come to grips with Cornish maritime heritage, weather lore, and navigational science. You can view the collection of 140 or so boats, examine the tools associated with Cornish boatbuilders, and study the prospect across to Flushing from the lighthouse-like Lookout, which is equipped with maps, telescopes, and binoculars. In the glass-fronted Tidal Zone below sea level, you come face-to-face with the sea itself. In summer, you can reach the museum by ferry from Falmouth's Prince of Wales Pier. ⊠ *Discovery Quay* ☎ *01326/313388* ⊕ *www.nmmc. co.uk* ☎ *£7* ☉ *Daily 10–5.*

At the end of its own peninsula stands the formidable **Pendennis Castle,** built by Henry VIII in the 1540s and improved by his daughter, Elizabeth I. You can explore the defenses developed over the centuries. In the Royal Artillery Barracks, the Key to Cornwall exhibit explores the castle's history and its connection to Cornwall and England. The castle has sweeping views over the English Channel and across the water known as Carrick Roadsto St. Mawes Castle, designed as a companion fortress to guard the roads. ⊠ *Pendennis Head* ☎ *01326/316594* ⊕ *www.english-heritage.org.uk* ☎ *£4.80* ☉ *Apr.–June and Sept., Sun.–Fri. 10–5, Sat 10–4; July and Aug., Sun.–Fri. 10–6, Sat 10–4; Oct.–Mar., daily 10–4.*

Where to Stay & Eat

★ **££–£££** ✕ **Seafood Bar.** Head down an alley off the quay to get to this restaurant with a fish tank for a window. Beyond the door is the very best local seafood, with such choices as thick crab soup, Helford River oys-

ters, or scallops from Falmouth Bay. ✉ *Quay St.* ☎ *01326/315129*
🖿 *MC, V* ⊗ *Closed Sun. and Mon. Oct.–Easter. No lunch.*

££££–£££££ 🏨 **St. Michael's Hotel.** Colorful subtropical gardens sweep down to the water at this seaside hotel in a long, low, white building overlooking Falmouth Bay. The public areas and guest rooms are sleek and contemporary, and the staff welcomes families. Treatments in the spa's four rooms are state of the art. ✉ *Stracey Rd., TR11 4NB* ☎ *01326/312707* 🖷 *01326/211772* ⊕ *www.corushotels.com* ⤳ *61 rooms, 3 suites* ♨ *2 restaurants, indoor pool, spa, gym, hot tub, sauna, bar, meeting rooms; no a/c* 🖿 *AE, MC, V* ❣️ *BP.*

St. Mawes

㉖ *16 mi east of Falmouth by road, 1½ mi east by sea, 11 mi south of Truro by ferry.*

At the tip of the Roseland Peninsula is the quiet, unspoiled village of St. Mawes, where subtropical plants thrive. The peninsula itself is a lovely backwater with old churches, a lighthouse, and good coast walking. One or two sailing and boating options are available in summer, but most companies operate from Falmouth.

The well-preserved Tudor-era **St. Mawes Castle,** outside the village, has a cloverleaf shape that makes it seemingly impregnable, yet during the Civil War, its Royalist commander surrendered without firing a shot. (In contrast, Pendennis Castle held out at this time for 23 weeks before submitting to a siege.) ✉ *A3078* ☎ *01326/ 270526* ⊕ *www.english-heritage. org.uk* 🖾 *£3.60* ⊗ *Apr.–June and Sept., Sun.–Fri. 10–5; July and Aug., Sun.–Fri. 10–6; Oct., daily 10–4; Nov.–Mar., Fri.–Mon. 10–4.*

★ North of St. Mawes on A3078 is **St. Just in Roseland,** one of the most beautiful spots in the West Country. This tiny hamlet made up of stone cottage terraces and a 13th-century church is set within a subtropical garden, often abloom with magnolias and rhododendrons on a summer's day.

WORD OF MOUTH

"We love the area around St. Mawes. You could spend your entire trip sipping cold white wine and watching all the activity in the harbor, but there are lots of things to see and do in the area. St. Just in Roseland has a very pretty church in a lovely location. Lots of fishing villages to visit." –rickmay

Where to Stay & Eat

★ **£££££** ✕🏨 **Tresanton Hotel.** It's the Cornish Riviera, Italian style: this former yachtsman's club, owned by Olga Polizzi, daughter of grand hotelier Charles Forte, makes for a luxuriously relaxed stay. Decorated in sunny whites, blues, and yellows, with terra-cotta pots on the terrace, the Tresanton seems distinctly Mediterranean, and the yacht and speedboat available in summer to guests reinforce the jet-set spirit. In the restaurant (£££££; fixed-price menu), the Italian-inspired menu includes steamed langoustine with fettuccine. The same owner has converted Endsleigh House, a country manor in Tavistock, Devon, with equal panache.

⊠ *Lower Castle Rd., TR2 5DR* ☎ *01326/270055* 🖨 *01326/270053*
⊕ *www.tresanton.com* 🛏 *27 rooms, 2 suites* ⚓ *Restaurant, boating,
fishing, bar, cinema, meeting rooms; no a/c* ▭ *AE, MC, V* ⁑ *BP.*

Charlestown

㉗ *15 mi east of Truro.*

This port was built by a local merchant in 1791 to export the huge reserves of china clay from St. Austell, 1 mi to the north, and it became
one of the ports from which 19th-century emigrants left for North
America. Charlestown has managed to avoid overdevelopment since its
heyday in the early 1800s. Its Georgian harbor often appears in period
film and television productions.

★ The sprawling, popular **Lost Gardens of Heligan** have something for all
garden lovers, as well as an intriguing history. Restored in the early 1990s
by former rock producer Tom Smit (the force behind the Eden Project)
after decades of neglect, they were begun by the Tremayne family in the
late 18th century. In Victorian times the gardens displayed exotic plants
from around the British Empire. The Jungle Garden contains surviving
plants from this era. The Italian Garden and walled Flower Gardens are
delightful, but don't overlook the extensive fruit and vegetable gardens
or Flora's Green, bordered by a ravine. It's easy to spend half a day here.
■ **TIP➜** Travel via St. Austell to avoid confusing country lanes. ⊠ *B3273, Pentewan* ☎ *0176/845100* ⊕ *www.heligan.com* 🎟 *£7.50* ☉ *Mar.–Oct.,
daily 10–6; Nov.–Feb., daily 10–5.*

Where to Stay

££ ▦ **T'Gallants.** This cheerfully refurbished Georgian house directly behind
the harbor takes its name from top gallant, one of the sails of a square-
rigged sailing ship. Ask for a south-facing room to enjoy the tranquil
morning view. The garden at the front is ideal for afternoon tea, and
bag lunches are sometimes available from the (separately run) tearoom.
⊠ *6 Charlestown Rd., PL25 3NJ* ☎ *01726/70203* ⊕ *www.t-gallants.
co.uk* 🛏 *7 rooms* ⚓ *No a/c; no smoking* ▭ *AE, MC, V* ⁑ *CP.*

Eden Project

㉘ *20 mi northeast of St Mawes, 2 mi northeast of St. Austell.*

Fodor'sChoice
★
Spectacularly set in a former china clay pit, the Eden Project presents
the world's major plant systems in microcosm. The crater contains
more than 70,000 plants, many belonging to rare or endangered species,
from three climate zones. Plants from the temperate zone are outdoors,
and those from other zones are housed in biomes—hexagonally paneled geodesic domes—that are the largest conservatories in Britain. In
one dome, olive and citrus groves mix with cacti and other plants indigenous to a warmer temperate climate. The tropical dome steams with
heat, resounds to the gushing of a waterfall, and blooms with exotic flora.
The emphasis is on conservation and ecology, but free of any moraliz-
ing. A free shuttle, the Land Train, helps the footsore, and well-informed guides provide information. An entertaining exhibition in the

visitor center gives you the lowdown on the project, and the Core, an education center, provides amusement and instruction for children. Extra attractions include open-air concerts in summer, and an ice-skating rink in winter. ■ TIP→ **To avoid the biggest crowds, visit on a Friday or Saturday, early in the morning, or after 2; you need at least half a day to see everything.** ⊠ *Bodelva, signposted off A30, A390, and A391, St. Austell* ☎*01726/811911* ⊕*www.edenproject.com* ☎*£13.80* ☼ *Apr.–Oct., daily 10–6; Nov.–Mar., daily 10–4:30; last admission 1½ hrs before closing.*

Fowey

㉙ *7 mi northeast of the Eden Project, 10 mi northeast of Charlestown.*

Nestled in the mouth of a wooded estuary, Fowey (pronounced Foy) is still very much a working china clay port as well as a focal point for the sailing fraternity. Increasingly, it's also the favored home of the rich and famous. Good and varied eating and sleeping options abound; these are most in demand during Regatta Week in mid-August and the annual Daphne du Maurier Festival in mid-May. The Bodinnick Ferry takes cars as well as foot passengers across the river for the coast road on to Looe.

WORD OF MOUTH

"We totally fell in love with Fowey . . . It was our base for visiting both the Eden Project and the Lost Gardens of Heligan. Fowey hangs on the side of a very steep hillside . . . lots of steps everywhere. There are lovely outings on the estuary and the river by boat . . . The water was crystal clear—I used to watch the fishermen pulling up their lobster pots from right below my hotel window!"

–tod

Where to Stay & Eat

££–£££ ✕ **Sam's.** You should be prepared to wait at this small and buzzing bistro with a rock-and-roll flavor. Diners squeeze onto benches and into booths to savor dishes made with local seafood, including a majestic bouillabaisse, or just a simple "Samburger." ⊠ *20 Fore St.* ☎ *01726/832273* ⌚ *Reservations not accepted* ▤ *MC, V* ☼ *Closed 2 or 3 wks in Jan. No lunch Sun.*

£££££ ▨ **Fowey Hall.** A showy Victorian edifice, all turrets, castellations, and elaborate plasterwork, this friendly, relaxed hotel with 5 acres of gardens is very family centered—despite the abundance of antiques. Guest rooms are spacious, and there are great facilities for children. You can dine in the sumptuously oak-panel Hansons or in the less formal Palm Court, which opens onto the terrace. ⊠ *Hanson Dr., PL23 1ET* ☎ *01726/ 833866* ☐ *01726/834100* ⊕ *www.foweyhallhotel.co.uk* ⇱ *20 rooms, 12 suites* ♨ *2 restaurants, cable TV with movies, in-room VCRs or DVDs, indoor pool, Ping-Pong, bar, babysitting, meeting rooms; no a/c* ▤ *AE, MC, V* ▥ *BP.*

Sports & the Outdoors

Between May and September, **Fowey River Canoe Expeditions** (⊠ 17 Passage St. ☎ 01726/833627) runs daily canoe trips up the tranquil River Fowey, the best way to observe the abundant wildlife.

Bodmin

㉚ *10 mi north of St. Austell.*

Bodmin, the county seat, was the only Cornish town recorded in the 11th-century Domesday Book, William the Conqueror's census. During World War I, the Domesday Book and the Crown Jewels were sent to Bodmin Prison for safekeeping. From the Gilbert Memorial on Beacon Hill, you can see both of Cornwall's coasts.

Fodor'sChoice
★ One of Cornwall's greatest country piles, **Lanhydrock** gives a look into the lives of the privileged rich in the 19th century. The former home of the powerful, wealthy Robartes family was originally constructed in the 17th century but was totally rebuilt after a fire in 1881. The granite exterior remains true to its original form, however, and the long picture gallery in the north wing, with its barrel-vaulted plaster ceiling depicting 24 biblical scenes, survived the devastation. A small museum in the north wing shows photographs and letters relating to the family. The house's endless pantries, sculleries, dairies, nurseries, and linen and livery cupboards bear witness to the immense amount of work involved in maintaining this lifestyle. Nine hundred acres of wooded parkland border the River Fowey, and in spring the gardens present an exquisite ensemble of magnolias, azaleas, and rhododendrons. Allow two hours to see the house and more time to stroll the grounds. ⊠ *3 mi southeast of Bodmin, signposted off A30, A38, and B3268* ☎ *01208/73320* ⊕ *www.nationaltrust.org.uk* ⊠ *£9, grounds only £5* ⊙ *House mid-Mar.–Sept., Tues.–Sun. and national holidays 11–5:30; Oct., Tues.–Sun. 11–5; garden daily 10–6; last admission 30 mins before closing.*

PLYMOUTH & DARTMOOR

Just over the border from Cornwall is Plymouth, an unprepossessing city but one with a historic old core and splendid harbor that recall a rich maritime heritage. North of Plymouth, you can explore the vast, boggy reaches of hilly Dartmoor, the setting for the Sherlock Holmes classic *The Hound of the Baskervilles*. It's a place to hike or go horseback riding away from the crowds.

Plymouth

㉛ *48 mi southwest of Exeter, 124 mi southwest of Bristol, 240 mi southwest of London.*

Devon's largest city has long been linked with England's commercial and maritime history. The Pilgrims sailed from here to the New World in the *Mayflower* in 1620. Although much of the city center was destroyed by air raids in World War II and has been rebuilt in an uninspiring style, there are worthwhile sights. A harbor tour is also a good way to see the city.

Sound Cruising Ltd (⊠ Hexton Quay, Hooe ☎ 01752/408590) runs harbor and river sightseeing trips all year; boats depart every 30 minutes in peak season from Phoenix Wharf (Tuesday through Thursday only in winter; call to check). **Tamar Cruising** (✉ Cremyll Quay, Cremyll, Torpoint ☎ 01752/822105) has harbor cruises and longer scenic trips on the Rivers Tamar and Yealm between Easter and October. Boats leave from the Mayflower Steps and Cremyll Quay.

Main Attractions

Barbican. East of the Royal Citadel is the Barbican, the oldest surviving section of Plymouth. Here, Tudor houses and warehouses rise from a maze of narrow streets leading down to the fishing docks and harbor. Many of these buildings have become antiques shops, art shops, and bookstores. It's worth a stroll.

Hoe. From the Hoe, a wide, grassy esplanade with crisscrossing walkways high above the city, you can take in a magnificent view of the inlets, bays, and harbors that make up Plymouth Sound.

★ ☾ **National Marine Aquarium.** This excellent aquarium, on a central harborside site, presents aqueous environments, from a freshwater stream to a seawater wave tank and a huge "shark theater." Not to be missed are the extensive collection of sea horses, part of an important breeding program, and the chance to walk under sharks in the Mediterranean tank. ■ TIP➜ Try to visit at shark-feeding time, which takes place three times a week. Explorocean, highlights undersea technology with demonstrations and hands-on gizmos, and there's a 3-D cinema. ✉ *Rope Walk, Coxside* ☎ *01752/600301* ⊕ *www.national-aquarium.co.uk* 🎟 *£9.50* ☾ *Apr.–Oct., daily 10–6; Nov.–Mar., daily 10–5; last admission 1 hr before closing.*

Saltram. An exquisite 18th-century home with many of its original furnishings, Saltram was built around the remains of a late Tudor mansion. Its jewel is one of Britain's grandest neoclassical rooms, a vast, double-cube salon designed by Robert Adam and adorned with paintings by Sir Joshua Reynolds, first president of the Royal Academy of Arts, who was born nearby in 1723. The Axminster carpet was created for the room. Fine plasterwork adorns many rooms, and three have their original Chinese wallpaper. Admission to the house is by timed ticket. The outstanding garden includes rare trees and shrubs. There is a restaurant in the house and a cafeteria in the Coach House. Saltram is 3½ mi east of Plymouth city center. ✉ *South of A38, Plympton* ☎ *01752/333500* ⊕ *www.nationaltrust.org.uk* 🎟 *£8, garden only £4* ☾ *House late Mar.–Oct., Sat.–Thurs. noon–4:30; last admission 3:45. Garden Mar.–Oct., Sat.–Thurs. 11–4:30; Nov.–Feb., Sat.–Thurs. 11–4.*

Also Worth Seeing

Mayflower Steps. By the harbor you can visit the Mayflower Steps, where the Pilgrims embarked in 1620; the **Mayflower Stone** marks the exact spot. They had sailed from Southampton but had to stop in Plymouth because of damage from a storm.

☾ **Plymouth Dome.** Next to Smeaton's Tower, the Dome has an exhibition that takes in exploration, battles, and the Blitz in its overview of local history; plenty of high-tech reconstructions add interest. One section covers the construction and rebuilding of Smeaton's Tower. Kids appreciate it, and it makes a great haven on a wet afternoon. ⊠ *Hoe Rd.* ☎ *01752/603300* ⊕ *www.plymouthdome.info* ⊠ *£4.75, £6.50 includes Smeaton's Tower* ☉ *Easter–Oct., daily 10–5; Nov.–Easter, Tues.–Sat. 10–4; last admission 1 hr before closing.*

Smeaton's Tower. This lighthouse, transferred here at the end of the 19th century from its original site 14 mi out to sea, provides a sweeping vista over Plymouth Sound and the city as far as Dartmoor. ⊠ *Hoe Rd.* ☎ *01752/603300* ⊕ *www.plymouthdome.info* ⊠ *£2.25, £6.50 includes Plymouth Dome* ☉ *Easter.–Oct., daily 10–4; Nov.–Easter, Tues.–Sat. 10–3.*

Where to Stay & Eat

£££–££££ ✕ **Piermasters.** Fresh seafood landed at nearby piers, notably squid, mussels, and oysters, appears high on the menu at this Barbican eatery. The decoration is basic seafront, with a tiled floor and wooden tables. There are fixed-price menus at lunch and dinner, or you can choose individual selections. ⊠ *33 Southside St.* ☎ *01752/229345* ⊟ *AE, MC, V* ☉ *Closed Sun. and 10 days over Christmas.*

££ ⌂ **Bowling Green Hotel.** Friendly and unpretentious, this Victorian house overlooks Sir Francis Drake's bowling green on Plymouth Hoe. Pine pieces and floral print fabrics decorate the guest rooms. The house is convenient for shopping and sightseeing. ⊠ *9–10 Osborne Pl., Lockyer St., PL1 2PU* ☎ *01752/209090* ▤ *01752/209092* ⊕ *www.bowlinggreenhotel. com* ⮎ *12 rooms* ♿ *In-room data ports, Wi-Fi, parking (fee); no a/c* ⊟ *MC, V* ⑩ *BP.*

Dartmoor National Park

10 mi north of Plymouth, 13 mi west of Exeter.

Even on a summer's day the scarred, brooding hills of this sprawling wilderness appear a likely haunt for such monsters as the hound of the Baskervilles, and it seems entirely fitting that Sir Arthur Conan Doyle set his Sherlock Holmes thriller in this landscape. Sometimes the wet, peaty wasteland vanishes in rain and mist, although in clear weather you can see north to Exmoor, south over the English Channel, and west far into Cornwall. Much of Dartmoor consists of open heath and moorland, unspoiled by roads—wonderful walking and horseback-riding territory but an easy place to lose your bearings. Dartmoor's earliest inhabitants left behind stone monuments and burial mounds that help you envision prehistoric man roaming these pastures. Ponies, sheep, and birds are the main animals to be seen.

Several villages scattered along the borders of this 368-square-mi reserve—one-third of which is owned by Prince Charles—make useful bases for hiking excursions. Accommodations include simple inns and some elegant havens. **Okehampton** is a main gateway, and **Chagford** is a good base for exploring North Dartmoor. Other scenic spots include **Buckland-in-the-Moor,** a hamlet with thatched-roof cottages, **Widecombe-in-the-Moor,** whose church is known as the Cathedral of the Moor, and **Grimspound,** the Bronze Age site featured in Conan Doyle's most famous tale. Transmoor Link buses connect most of Dartmoor's towns and villages. Park information centers include the main **High Moorland Visitor Centre** in Princetown and centers in Newbridge, Postbridge, and Haytor. The park also works with tourist information centers in Ivybridge, Okehampton, Tavistock, and Totnes. ✉ *High Moorland Visitor Centre, Tavistock Rd., Princetown PL20 6QF* ☎ *01822/890414* ⊕ *www.dartmoor-npa.gov.uk.*

Sports & the Outdoors

This is a great area for horseback riding; many towns have stables for guided rides. Hiking is popular, but longer hikes in the bleak, unpeopled region of Dartmoor—for example, the tors south of Okehampton—are appropriate only for the most experienced walkers. The areas around Widgery Cross, Becky Falls, and the Bovey Valley, and the short but dramatic walk along Lydford Gorge, have wide appeal, as do the many valleys around the southern edge of the moors. Guided hikes (£3–£6) are available through the park; reservations are not needed for most, but you can check with the High Moorland Visitor Centre in Princetown. Tourist information centers can help you decide what to do; another source is the **Dartmoor National Park Authority** (✉ Parke, Haytor Rd., Bovey Tracey, Newton Abbot TQ13 9JQ ☎ 01626/832093 ⊕ www.dartmoor-npa.gov.uk).

> ### STAY ON A FARM
>
> Do you plan to travel by car and want to be far from tourist resorts, traffic jams, and general hubbub? One way to experience the authentic rural life in Somerset, Devon, and Cornwall is to stay on a farm. Southwest Tourism's Web site (⊕ www.naturesouthwest.co.uk) gives details about working farms that supply accommodation—including bed-and-breakfasts and house rentals—throughout the region. Other reference points are Discover Devon (⊕ www.discoverdevon.com), for farms in Devon, and Cornish Farm Holidays (⊕ www.cornish-farms.co.uk), for Cornwall.

Buckland Abbey

32 *8 mi north of Plymouth.*

This 13th-century Cistercian monastery became the home of Sir Francis Drake in 1581. Today it is filled with mementos of Drake and the Spanish Armada and has a restaurant. From Tavistock, take A386 south to Crapstone and then head west. ✉ *Yelverton* ☎ *01822/853607* ⊕ *www.nationaltrust.org.uk* 🎫 *£7, grounds only £3.70* ☉ *Mid-Feb.–mid-Mar. and Nov., weekends 2–5; late Mar.–Oct., Fri.–Wed. 10:30–5:30; early Dec.–mid-Dec., weekends 11–5; last admission 45 mins before closing.*

Cotehele House & Quay

★ **33** *4 mi west of Buckland Abbey, 15 mi north of Plymouth.*

Just over the border in Cornwall, this was formerly a busy port on the River Tamar, but it is now usually visited for the well-preserved late-medieval manor, home of the Edgcumbe family for centuries. The house has original furniture, tapestries, embroideries, and armor, and there are impressive gardens, a restored mill, and a quay museum. A limited number of visitors are allowed per day, so arrive early and be prepared to wait. Choose a bright day, because the rooms have no electric light. Shops, a crafts gallery, and a restaurant provide other diversions. ⊠ *St. Dominick, north of Saltash, signposted off A390* ☎ *01579/352739* ⊕ *www.nationaltrust.org.uk* ✎ *£8, gardens and mill only £4.80* ☉ *House mid-Mar.–Sept., Sat.–Thurs. 11–4:30; Oct., Sat.–Thurs. 11–4. Mill mid-Mar.–June and Sept., Sat.–Thurs. 1–5:30; July and Aug., daily 1–5:30; Oct., Sat.–Thurs. 1–4:30. Gardens daily 10:30–dusk.*

Morwellham Quay

❸❹ *2 mi east of Cotehele House & Quay, 5 mi southwest of Tavistock, 18 mi north of Plymouth.*

In the 19th century, Morwellham (pronounced More-*wel*-ham) Quay was England's main copper-exporting port, and it has been carefully restored as a working museum, with quay workers and coachmen in costume, and a copper mine open to visitors. ⊠ *Off A390, on a minor road off B3257* ☎ *01822/832766, 01822/833808 recorded information* ⊕ *www.morwellham-quay.co.uk* ✎ *Apr.–Oct. £8.90, Nov.–Mar. £6* ☉ *Easter–Oct., daily 10–5:30; Nov.–Easter, daily 10–4:30; last admission 2 hrs before closing.*

Where to Stay & Eat

★ ✕⌂ **Horn of Plenty.** A "country house hotel and restaurant" is the way **££££–£££££** this establishment in a Georgian house describes itself. The restaurant (no lunch Monday) has magnificent views across the wooded, rhododendron-filled Tamar Valley. Peter Gorton's sophisticated cooking takes its inspiration from around the world; panfried sea bass with crushed Cornish new potatoes and a white-wine saffron sauce is a typical main course. There are three-course, fixed-price menus (£42), the best value being Monday's potluck menu (£25). A converted coach house and the main house contain sumptuously furnished guest rooms, many with balconies. ⊠ *3 mi west of Tavistock on A390, Gulworthy PL19 8JD* ☎⌨ *01822/832528* ⊕ *www.thehornofplenty.co.uk* ⮑ *8 rooms, 2 suites* ⌂ *Restaurant, in-room DVDs, minibars, meeting rooms, some pets allowed, no-smoking rooms; no a/c* ⊟ *AE, MC, V* ⎮⊚⎮ *BP.*

Lydford Gorge

★ **❸❺** *12 mi north of Morwellham Quay, 7 mi north of Tavistock, 9 mi east of Launceston, 24 mi north of Plymouth.*

The River Lyd has carved a spectacular 1½-mi-long chasm through the rock at Lydford Gorge, outside the pretty village of Lydford, midway between Okehampton and Tavistock on the edge of Dartmoor. Two paths follow the gorge past gurgling whirlpools and waterfalls with names such as the Devil's Cauldron and the White Lady. Sturdy footwear is recommended. Although the walk can be quite challenging, the paths can still get congested during busy periods. From Launceston, continue east along A30, following the signs. ⊠ *Off A386, Lydford* ☎ *01822/820320* ⊕ *www.nationaltrust.org.uk* ✎ *£5 Apr.–Oct., £3 mid-Feb–Mar., free*

Nov.–mid-Feb. ☉ *Apr.–Sept., daily 10–5; Oct., daily 10–4; Nov.–Mar., daily 11–3:30 (walk restricted to main waterfall).*

Where to Stay & Eat

£££–££££ ✕ **Dartmoor Inn.** Locals and visitors alike make a beeline for this 16th-century pub, a good spot for snacks such as farmhouse sausages and mashed potatoes or for something more substantial fare like a fish casserole. Fixed-price, two-course lunches and suppers are a good value during the week. The pub is at the Lydford junction. ⊠ *A386, Lydford* ☎ *01822/820221* ▤ *AE, MC, V* ☉ *Closed Mon. No dinner Sun.*

££–£££ ▥ **Castle Inn.** The heart of Lydford village, this 16th-century inn is next to Lydford Castle. Rose trellises frame its rosy brick facade, and the public rooms are snug, lamp-lighted, and full of period clutter. Vivid colors are used in the guest rooms; one room has its own roof garden. ⊠ *1 mi off A386, Lydford EX20 4BH* ☎ *01822/820241* ▦ *01822/820454* ⊕ *www.castleinnlydford.co.uk* ⇗ *9 rooms* ☖ *Restaurant, bar, some pets allowed (fee); no a/c* ▤ *AE, MC, V* ¶⊙¶ *BP.*

Sports & the Outdoors

Cholwell Stables (⊠ Mary Tavy ☎ 01822/810526) has one- or two-hour horseback rides through some of Dartmoor's wilder tracts. Riders of all abilities are escorted, and equipment is provided. The stables are about 6 mi south of Lydford; call for directions.

Okehampton

36 *8 mi northeast of Lydford Gorge, 28 mi north of Plymouth, 23 mi west of Exeter.*

This town at the confluence of the Rivers East and West Okement is a good base for exploring North Dartmoor. It has numerous pubs and cottage tearooms (giving you a chance to have a Devon cream tea), as well as a helpful tourist office. On the riverbank a mile southwest of the town center, the jagged ruins of the Norman **Okehampton Castle** occupy a verdant site with a picnic area and woodland walks. ☎ *01837/52844* ⊕ *www.english-heritage.org.uk* ☐ *£3* ☉ *Apr.–June and Sept., daily 10–5; July and Aug., daily 10–6.*

The three floors of the informative **Museum of Dartmoor Life** contain models, a working waterwheel, and photos of traditional farming methods. ⊠ *3 West St.* ☎ *01837/52295* ⊕ *www.museumofdartmoorlife.eclipse. co.uk* ▱*£2.50* ☉ *Easter–Oct., Mon.–Sat. 10:15–4:30; Nov.–Easter, Mon. and Fri. 10:15–4:30; may close for lunch.*

Sports & the Outdoors

Skaigh Stables Farm (⊠ Skaigh La., near Okehampton, Belstone ☎ 01837/ 840917, 01837/840429 evenings) arranges horseback rides by the hour, half-day, and full day from Easter through September.

Chagford

37 *9 mi southeast of Okehampton, 30 mi northeast of Plymouth.*

Chagford, once a tin-weighing station, was an area of fierce fighting between the Roundheads and the Cavaliers during the Civil War. Although officially a "town" since 1305, Chagford is more of a village, with old taverns grouped around a seasoned old church and a curious "pepper-pot" market house on the site of the old Stannary Court. With a handful of cafés and shops to browse around, it makes a convenient base from which to explore North Dartmoor.

The intriguing **Castle Drogo,** east of Chagford across A382 above the Teign Gorge, looks like a medieval fortress, complete with battlements, but construction actually took place between 1910 and 1930. Designed by Sir Edwin Lutyens for Julius Drewe, a wealthy grocer, the castle is only half finished (funds ran out). Inside, this magisterial pile combines medieval grandeur and early-20th-century comforts like the large bathrooms. ■ TIP→ **You can play croquet on the lawn and take in awesome views over Dartmoor.** Take the A30 Exeter–Okehampton road to reach the castle, which is 4 mi northeast of Chagford and 6 mi south of A30. ✉ *Drewsteignton* ☎ *01647/433306* ⊕ *www.nationaltrust.org.uk* 🎫 *£7, grounds only £4.50* ⊙ *Castle early Mar., weekends 11–4; mid-Mar.–Oct., Wed.–Mon. 11–5; early Nov., Wed.–Mon. 11–4; mid-Dec., weekends noon–4 or dusk. Grounds early Mar., weekends 10:30–4:30; mid-Mar.–Oct., daily 10:30–5:30; early Nov., daily 10:30–4:30; early Nov.–mid-Dec., Fri.–Sun. 11–4 or dusk.*

Where to Stay & Eat

★ **££££** ✕🏠 **Gidleigh Park.** One of England's foremost hotels and restaurants, lauded in poetry by Ted Hughes, occupies an enclave of landscaped gardens and streams up a lengthy, winding private drive at the edge of Dartmoor. Antiques and luxurious country-house furnishings fill the long, half-timber Tudor-style residence, and the extremely pricey contemporary French restaurant (about £75 prix-fixe; reservations essential), directed by chef Michael Caines, has been showered with culinary awards. You may see why when you dig into the roast Gressingham duckling with garlic and cabbage. The locally pumped spring water is like no other. ✉ *Gidleigh Park, TQ13 8HH* ☎ *01647/432367* 🖷 *01647/432574* ⊕ *www.gidleigh.com* 🛏 *14 rooms, 1 estate cottage* ♣ *Restaurant, putting green, tennis court, croquet, meeting rooms, helipad, some pets allowed; no a/c* ⊟ *AE, DC, MC, V* ⍟ *MAP.*

★ **£££££** 🏠 **Bovey Castle.** With the grandeur of a country estate and the facilities of a top modern hotel, Bovey Castle, built in 1906 for Viscount Hambledon, has it all. On its vast grounds, the hotel has an outstanding golf course and 24 mi of riverbank that can be used for salmon fishing. There is a resident pianist, and children have a dedicated barn filled with games. Enormous fireplaces and oak-panel rooms give a sense of early-20th-century pomp to the public rooms; bedrooms are luxurious, and even some of the bathrooms have great views across the valley. ✉ *Off B3212, North Bovey TQ13 8RE* ☎ *01647/445016* 🖷 *01647/445020* ⊕ *www.boveycastle.com* 🛏 *65 rooms* ♣ *Restaurant, 18-hole golf course, 3 tennis courts, indoor pool, lake, fishing, spa, croquet, cinema, business services, some pets allowed (fee); no a/c* ⊟ *AE, MC, V* ⍟ *BP.*

££ 🏠 **Easton Court.** Discerning travelers such as C. P. Snow, Margaret Mead, John Steinbeck, and Evelyn Waugh—who completed *Brideshead Revisited* here—made this their Dartmoor home-away-from-home. The Tudor thatched-roof house has a garden and simple but elegant cottage-style rooms in an Edwardian wing; all rooms have views over the Teign Valley. ⊠ *Easton Cross, TQ13 8JL* ☎ *01647/433469* 🖷 *01647/433654* ⊕ *www.easton.co.uk* ↶ *5 rooms* ♿ *No a/c, no kids under 10, no smoking* ⊟ *MC, V* ⏀ *BP.*

DARTMOUTH & EXETER

Sheltered by the high mass of Dartmoor to the west, the yachting center of Dartmouth, just south of the area known as the English Riviera, enjoys a mild, warm climate. To the north is Exeter, Devon's county seat, an ancient city that has retained some of its medieval character despite wartime bombing.

Dartmouth

❸ *35 mi east of Plymouth, 35 mi south of Exeter.*

An important port in the Middle Ages, Dartmouth is today a favorite haunt of yacht owners. Traces of its past include the old houses in Bayard's Cove near Lower Ferry, the 16th-century covered Butterwalk, and the two castles guarding the entrance to the River Dart. The Royal Naval College, built in 1905, dominates the town.

To make a scenic excursion, you can cross the Dart and head to **Brixham**, at the southern point of Tor Bay. It has kept much of its original charm, partly because it is still an active fishing village. Much of the catch goes straight to restaurants as far away as London. Sample fish-and-chips on the quayside, where there is a (surprisingly petite) full-scale reproduction of the vessel on which Sir Francis Drake circumnavigated the world.

Where to Stay & Eat

£££–£££££ ✕ **New Angel.** John Burton Race, TV celebrity chef, has a restaurant in this prime spot by the waterfront; it's yet another sign of the country's ongoing food revolution. The menu is British and European, with an emphasis on local fare such as Brixham turbot grilled with béarnaise sauce or roast best end of Blackawton lamb with an herb crust. Open in the mornings for coffee and croissants, this place is relaxed and family-friendly. ⊠ *2 S. Embankment* ☎ *01803/839425* 🖑 *Reservations essential* ⊟ *AE, MC, V* ⊙ *Closed Mon. No dinner Sun.*

££££–£££££ 🏨 **Royal Castle Hotel.** This hotel has truly earned the name "Royal"— several monarchs have slept here. Part of Dartmouth's historic waterfront (and consequently a hub of activity), it was built in the 17th century, reputedly of timber from wrecks of the Spanish Armada. Fireplaces and beamed ceilings are traditional features. Rooms come in different sizes and styles, but all are thoughtfully and richly furnished, with a liberal sprinkling of antiques. Number 6 has its own priest hole, a secret room used to hide Roman Catholic priests, and the pricier rooms facing the river have hot tubs. ⊠ *11 The Quay, TQ6 9PS* ☎ *01803/ 833033* 🖷 *01803/835445* ⊕ *www.royalcastle.co.uk* ↶ *25 rooms* ♿ *Restaurant, cable TV, Wi-Fi, some hot tubs, 2 bars, meeting rooms, some pets allowed; no a/c* ⊟ *AE, MC, V* ⏀ *BP.*

Two ferries cross the River Dart at Dartmouth; in summer, lines can be long, and you may want to try the inland route, heading west via A3122 to Halwell and then taking A381 north to the market town of Totnes. An attractive, relaxed approach to Dartmouth is by boat down the Dart from Totnes.

Exeter

30 mi north of Dartmouth, 48 mi northeast of Plymouth, 85 mi southwest of Bristol, 205 mi southwest of London.

Devon's county seat, Exeter, has been the capital of the region since the Romans established a fortress here 2,000 years ago. Evidence of the Roman occupation remains in the city walls. Although it was heavily bombed in 1942, Exeter retains much of its medieval character, as well as examples of the gracious architecture of the 18th and 19th centuries. The city's **Underground Passages,** which once served as conduits for freshwater, are the only medieval vaulted passages open to the public in England. At this writing the passages have closed until fall 2007 because of area redevelopment that includes the Princesshay shopping center; check with the tourist office.

Main Attractions

A LA RONDE – This 16-sided building, surely one of the most unusual houses in England, was built in 1798 by two cousins inspired by the Church of San Vitale in Ravenna, Italy. Among the 18th- and 19th-century curiosities here is an elaborate display of feathers and shells. The house is 8 mi south of Exeter. ☒ *Summer La., on A376 near Exmouth* ☎ *01395/265514* ⊕ *www.nationaltrust.org.uk* ☒ *£5* ☉ *Apr.–Oct., Sun.–Thurs. 11–5:30; last admission at 5.*

★ ③⑨ **Cathedral of St. Peter.** At the heart of Exeter, the great Gothic cathedral was begun in 1275 and completed almost a century later. Its twin towers are even older survivors of an earlier Norman cathedral. Rising from a forest of ribbed columns, the nave's 300-foot stretch of unbroken Gothic vaulting is the longest in the world. Myriad statues, tombs, and memorial plaques adorn the interior. In the minstrels' gallery, high up on the left of the nave, stands a group of carved figures singing and playing musical instruments, including bagpipes. The **Close,** a pleasant green space for relaxing, surrounds the cathedral. Don't miss the 400-year-old door to No. 10, the bishop of Crediton's house, ornately carved with angels' and lions' heads. ☒ *Cathedral Close* ☎ *01392/285983* ⊕ *www.exeter-cathedral.org.uk* ☒ *£3.50 suggested donation* ☉ *Daily 9:30–5. Free guided tours Apr.–Oct., weekdays at 11 and 2:30, Sat. at 11, Sun. at 4; July–Sept., Mon.–Sat. at 12:30.*

POWDERHAM CASTLE – Seat of the earls of Devon, this notable stately home 8 mi south of Exeter is famed for its staircase hall, a soaring fantasia of white stuccowork on a turquoise background, constructed in 1739–69. Other sumptuous rooms, adorned with family portraits by Sir Godfrey Kneller and Sir Joshua Reynolds, were used in the Merchant Ivory film *Remains of the Day.* A tower built in 1400 by Sir Philip Courtenay, ancestor of the current owners, stands in the deer park. The restau-

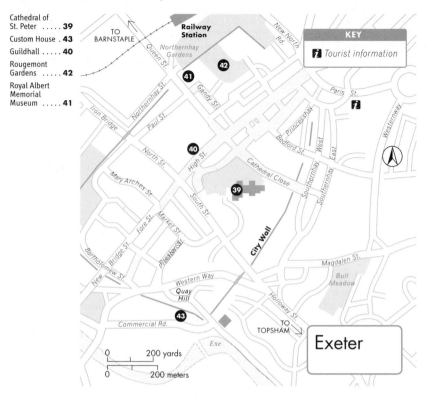

Exeter

rant serves traditional English fare, and there's a farm shop and plant center. ✉ *A379, Kenton* ☎ *01626/890243* ⊕ *www.powderham.co.uk* 🎫 *£7.45, £4.90 grounds only* ☉ *Apr.–Oct., Sun.–Fri. 10–5:30.*

41 Royal Albert Memorial Museum. This museum houses natural-history displays, superb Exeter silverware, and the work of some West Country artists. There is also an excellent international gallery and a fine archaeological section. The museum is the focus of a multiyear redevelopment plan designed to increase its appeal. ✉ *Queen St.* ☎ *01392/665858* ⊕ *www.exeter.gov.uk* 🎫 *Free* ☉ *Mon.–Sat. 10–5.*

Also Worth Seeing

43 Custom House. Exeter's historic waterfront on the River Exe was the center of the city's medieval wool industry, and the Custom House, built in 1682 on the quay, attests to the city's prosperity. Victorian warehouses flank the city's earliest surviving brick building.

40 Guildhall. Just behind the Close, this is said to be the oldest municipal building in the country still in use. The current hall, with its Renaissance portico, dates from 1330, although a guildhall has occupied this site since at least 1160. Its timber-braced roof, one of the earliest in England, dates from about 1460. ✉ *High St.* ☎ *01392/665500* 🎫 *Free* ☉ *Weekdays*

10:30–1 and 2–4, Sat. 10–noon (alternate Sat. only in winter), unless in use for a civic function.

42 Rougemont Gardens. These gardens behind the Royal Albert Memorial Museum were laid out at the end of the 18th century. The land was once part of the defensive ditch of Rougemont Castle, built in 1068 by decree of William the Conqueror. The gardens contain the original Norman gatehouse and the remains of the Roman city wall, the latter forming part of the ancient castle's outer wall; nothing else remains of the castle. ⊠ *Off Queen St.*

Where to Stay & Eat

★ **£££££** ✕ **St. Olaves.** One of the finest dining spots in the West Country, this restaurant in a Georgian house with a walled garden is part of St. Olaves Court Hotel. From the fixed-price, seasonal menus, you might try terrine of wild duck, guinea fowl, and wild mushrooms or the baked monkfish stuffed with prawns and tarragon. The bar menu is a cheaper lunchtime option. ⊠ *Mary Arches St.* ☎ *01392/217736* ▭ *MC, V.*

★ **£–££** ✕ **Herbie's.** A mellow stop for lunch or dinner, this friendly, no-frills vegetarian restaurant is ideal for unwinding over leisurely conversation. You can snack on pita bread with hummus, or tackle the carrot and cashew nut loaf or Caribbean coconut and black-pea rundown (a spicy stew). All wines and the superb ice cream are organic. ⊠ *15 North St.* ☎ *01392/258473* ▭ *MC, V* ☉ *Closed Sun. No dinner Mon.*

£–££ ✕ **Ship Inn.** Here you can lift a tankard of stout in the very rooms where Sir Francis Drake and Sir Walter Raleigh enjoyed their ale. Drake, in fact, once wrote, "Next to mine own shippe, I do most love that old 'Shippe' in Exon." The pub dishes out casual bar fare, and the upstairs restaurant serves good sausage and mashed potatoes, and baked cod with tarragon and wine. ⊠ *St. Martin's La.* ☎ *01392/272040* ▭ *MC, V.*

★ **££££–£££££** ✕▣ **Royal Clarence Hotel.** Perfectly located within the Cathedral Close, this antique establishment was acquired in 2003 by master chef Michael Caines (of Gidleigh Park fame), who has successfully transformed it into an upscale boutique hotel. The limelight rests firmly on the ultrachic restaurant (£££–££££), with its French-accented contemporary fare. A more relaxed café-bar (easier on the wallet) serves coffee, snacks, and meals all day; there's live jazz some evenings. Public areas reflect the restaurant's clean-lined, modern style, and the beautifully designed bedrooms come with state-of-the-art technology, though some are small and viewless. ⊠ *Cathedral Yard, EX1 1HD* ☎ *01392/319955 hotel, 01392/223638 restaurant* 🖷 *01392/439423* ⊕ *www.abodehotels.co.uk* ⇌ *53 rooms* ⌂ *Restaurant, 2 bars, in-room DVDs, Wi-Fi, gym, spa, meeting rooms, some pets allowed (fee); no a/c* ▭ *AE, DC, MC, V.*

£££–££££ ✕▣ **Hotel Barcelona.** This hip, classy hotel (part of the Alias mini-chain) occupies the old redbrick eye hospital, as the long corridors and big elevators testify. Bright, Gaudí-esque furnishings and ornaments from the 1930s to the 1960s give the rooms flair, and the aquamarine bathrooms with mosaic tiling are luxurious. You can find Spanish and other Mediterranean flavors in the pavilion-like bistro-restaurant, Café Paradiso. ⊠ *Magdalen St., EX2 4HY* ☎ *01392/281000* 🖷 *01392/281001* ⊕ *www.hotelbarcelona-uk.com* ⇌ *46 rooms* ⌂ *Restaurant, cable TV with*

FodorsChoice ★

movies, in-room VCRs, in-room data ports, nightclub, meeting rooms, some pets allowed (fee); no a/c ⊟ *AE, DC, MC, V.*

££ ✕▦ **White Hart.** Guests have been welcomed to this inn since the 15th century, and it is said that Oliver Cromwell stabled his horses here. Beyond the lovely cobbled entrance, the main building retains all the trappings of a period inn—beams, stone walls, courtyard—but there are also fully modern bedrooms in one wing. The hotel has a casual bar-restaurant (*£–£££*) where you can order such traditional English dishes as salmon and lamb casserole with dumplings. ⊠ *66 South St., EX1 1EE* ☎ *01392/ 279897* 🖶 *01392/250159* ⊕ *www.pubswithrooms.co.uk* ⇆ *55 rooms* ♤ *Restaurant, bar, wine bar; no a/c* ⊟ *AE, DC, MC, V* ⎮○⎮ *BP.*

Nightlife & the Arts

Among the best known of the West Country's festivals, the **Exeter Festival** (☎ 01392/265205) mixes musical and theater events each July. Some of London's best companies often stage plays at the **Northcott Theatre** (⊠ Stocker Rd. ☎ 01392/493493).

Shopping

Many of Exeter's most interesting shops are along Gandy Street, off the main High Street drag, with several good food and clothes outlets. Exeter was the silver-assay office for the West Country, and the earliest example of Exeter silver (now a museum piece) dates from 1218; Victorian pieces are still sold. The Exeter assay mark is three castles. **Bruford's of Exeter** (⊠ 17 The Guildhall Centre, Queen St. ☎ 01392/254901) stocks antique jewelry and silver.

Sports & the Outdoors

Saddles and Paddles (⊠ 4 Kings Wharf, the Quay ☎ 01392/424241) rents bikes, kayaks, and canoes and is handily placed for a 7-mi route along the scenic Exeter Canal Trail, which follows the River Exe and the Exeter Ship Canal.

WEST COUNTRY ESSENTIALS

Transportation

BY AIR

Bristol International Airport, a few miles southwest of the city on the A38, has flights to and from destinations in Britain and Europe. Continental runs a direct daily service between Bristol and New York. Plymouth has a small airport 3 mi from town. Exeter International Airport is 5 mi east of Exeter, 2 mi from the M5 motorway. Newquay Airport, 5 mi east of town, has daily flights to London Stansted and London Gatwick.

🛈 **Bristol International Airport** ⊠ Bridgwater Rd., Lulsgate, Bristol ☎ 0870/121–2747 ⊕ www.bristolairport.co.uk. **British International** ⊠ Penzance Heliport, A30, Penzance ☎ 01736/363871 ⊕ www.scillyhelicopter.co.uk. **Exeter International Airport** ⊠ M5, Junction 29, Exeter ☎ 01392/367433 ⊕ www.exeter-airport.co.uk. **Newquay Airport** ⊠ St. Mawgan, Newquay ☎ 01637/860600 ⊕ www.newquay-airport.co.uk. **Plymouth City Airport** ⊠ Crownhill, Plymouth ☎ 01752/204090 ⊕ www.plymouthairport.com.Bus Travel

National Express buses leave London's Victoria Coach Station for Bath (3½ hours), Bristol (2½ hours), Exeter (4¼ hours), Plymouth (4¾ hours), and Penzance (about 9 hours). Megabus offer a cheap, though not very comfortable, way of getting between Plymouth, Exeter, and London; you buy tickets online.

The bus company First covers the area around Bath and most of the services in North Devon, in Plymouth, and throughout Cornwall. Stagecoach Devon covers mainly South Devon. Truronian operates in West Cornwall. Ask any of these companies about money-saving one-, three-, and seven-day Explorer passes good for unlimited travel. Buses serve the main towns, but it's best to have a car if you want to explore off the beaten path. For public transportation information, contact Traveline.

4

FARES & SCHEDULES ⓕ **First** ☎ 0845/600-1420 ⊕ www.firstgroup.com. **Megabus** ☎ 0900/160-0900 ⊕ www.megabus.com. **National Express** ☎ 0870/580-8080 ⊕ www.nationalexpress. com. **Stagecoach Devon** ☎ 0870/608-2608 ⊕ www.stagecoachbus.com. **Traveline** ☎ 0870/608-2608 ⊕ www.traveline.org.uk. **Truronian** ☎ 01872/273453 ⊕ www. truronian.co.uk.

CAR TRAVEL
The fastest route from London to the West Country is via the M4 and M5 motorways, turning off for Bath (115 mi) and heading south at Bristol to Exeter, in Devon (172 mi). Allow two hours at least to drive to Bath from London, three to Exeter. Taking the M3 and A303 route is shorter and more scenic, but you may encounter delays. The main roads heading west are A30—which burrows through the center of Devon and Cornwall all the way to Land's End at the tip of Cornwall—A39 (near the northern shore of the peninsula), and A38 (near the southern shore of the peninsula, south of Dartmoor and taking in Plymouth). West of Plymouth, there are few main roads, which results in heavy traffic in summer. Still, having a car give you maximum freedom to explore rural areas.

ROAD CONDITIONS Driving can be tricky, especially as you travel farther west. Most small roads are twisting country lanes flanked by high stone walls and thick hedges that severely restrict visibility.

TRAIN TRAVEL
First Great Western and South West Trains serve the region from London's Paddington and Waterloo stations; contact National Rail Enquiries for details. Average travel time to Bath is about 90 minutes; to Exeter 2½ hours; to Plymouth, 3½ hours; and to Penzance, about 5½ hours.

CUTTING COSTS Regional Rail Rover tickets provide 8 days' unlimited travel throughout the West Country in any 15-day period, and localized Rovers cover Devon or Cornwall.
ⓕ **National Rail Enquiries** ☎ 0845/748-4950 ⊕ www.nationalrail.co.uk.

Contacts & Resources

EMERGENCIES
ⓕ **Ambulance, fire, police** ☎ 999. **Royal United Hospital** ✉ Combe Park, Bath ☎ 01225/428331. **Derriford Hospital** ✉ Derriford, Plymouth ☎ 01752/777111. **Royal Corn-**

wall Hospital (Treliske) ⊠ A390, Higher Town, Truro ☎ 01872/250000. **Royal Devon and Exeter Hospital** ⊠ Barrack Rd., Exeter ☎ 01392/411611.

INTERNET

If your hotel or B&B cannot supply an Internet connection, you'll find cafés and public libraries in all the major centers where you can get online. Broadband is widespread and Wi-Fi increasingly so.

🔢 Internet Cafés **Click Internet Café** ⊠ 13 Manvers St., Bath ☎ 01225/481008 ⊕ www. clickcafe.zen.co.uk. **Bristol Life** ⊠ 27 Baldwin St., Bristol ☎ 0117/945–9926 ⊕ www. internet-exchange.co.uk. **Exeter Central library** ⊠ Castle St., Exeter ☎ 01392/384206. **Carp Internet Café** ⊠ 32 Frankfort Gate, Plymouth ☎ 01752/221777.

TOUR OPTIONS

South West Tourism (⇨ Visitor Information) and local tourist information centers have lists of qualified guides. City Sightseeing runs 45-minute guided tours of Bath year-round. West Country Tour Guides (Blue Badge) offers walking tours around Plymouth's old town and can arrange tours throughout Devon and Cornwall.

🔢 **City Sightseeing** ☎ 01789/299123 in Stratford, 01225/330444 in Bath ⊕ www.citysightseeing.com. **West Country Tourist Guides (Blue Badge)** ☎ 01579/370224 ⊕ www. luxsoft.demon.co.uk/awctg.

VISITOR INFORMATION

Local tourist information centers are usually open Monday through Saturday 9:30 to 5:30; they are listed after the regional offices below by town. The Exeter tourist office will move to the Princesshay development in summer 2007; at this writing the address was not set, but the phone may remain the same.

🔢 **South West Tourism** ⊠ Woodwater Park, Pynes Hill, Exeter EX2 5WT ☎ 0870/442–0880 🖷 0870/442–0881 ⊕ www.visitsouthwest.co.uk. **Cornwall Tourist Board** ⊠ Pydar House, Pydar St., Truro TR1 1EA ☎ 01872/322900 🖷 01872/322895 ⊕ www. cornwalltouristboard.co.uk. **Devon Tourist Information Service** 🖅 Box 55, Barnstaple EX32 8YR 🖷 0870/608–5531, 1392/382168 from outside the U.K. ⊕ www.discoverdevon. com. **Somerset Visitor Centre** ⊠ Sedgemoor Service Station, M5 Southbound ☎ 01934/750833 🖷 01934/750646 ⊕ www.somerset.gov.uk.

Bath ⊠ Abbey Chambers, Abbey Church Yard, BA1 1LY ☎ 0906/711–2000 (calls cost 50p per minute), 0870/444–6442, 0870/420–1278 accommodation line ⊕ www.visitbath.co. uk. **Bristol** ⊠ The Annexe, Wildscreen Walk, Harbourside, BS1 5DB ☎ 0906/711–2191 50p per min, 0845/408–0474 accommodations line, 870/444–0654 from outside U.K. 🖾 Galleries Shopping Centre, Broadmead ☎ No phone ⊕ www.visitbristol.co.uk. **Exeter** ⊠ Civic Centre, Paris St., EX1 1JJ ☎ 01392/265700 ⊕ www.exeter.gov.uk. **Falmouth** ⊠ 11 Market Strand, TR11 3DF ☎ 01326/312300 ⊕ www.go-cornwall.com. **Glastonbury** ⊠ The Tribunal, 9 High St., BA6 9DP ☎ 01458/832954 ⊕ www.glastonburytic. co.uk. **Penzance** ⊠ Station Approach, TR18 2NF ☎ 01736/362207 ⊕ www.go-cornwall. com. **Plymouth** ⊠ Plymouth Mayflower, 3–5 The Barbican, PL1 2LR ☎ 01752/266030 ⊕ www.visitplymouth.co.uk. **St. Ives** ⊠ The Guildhall, Street-an-Pol, TR26 2DS ☎ 01736/796297 ⊕ www.go-cornwall.com. **Wells** ⊠ Town Hall, Market Pl., BA5 2RB ☎ 01749/672552 ⊕ www.wells-uk.com.

Oxford & the Thames Valley

5

WORD OF MOUTH

"Windsor Castle looks like a castle outside, but inside is mostly reasonably sumptuous apartments and the like. At a pinch, your sons could indulge a few military fantasies. . . . I've always found the castle a bit girly: it is, after all, where Her Maj prefers to live, and is a working royal palace."

—flanneruk

"Most folks who say Oxford is 'industrial' have not been there. Either Cambridge or Oxford is fine—wonderful in fact . . . But if you also want to visit things outside the city, Oxford is better. Blenheim Palace is just up the road and easy by local bus."

—janisj

Updated by
Christi
Daugherty

THE AREA JUST WEST OF LONDON—including the prosperous country-side of Berkshire and Oxfordshire—is called the Thames Valley for the river that winds through it on its way to the sea, a river as significant in history as the Seine or the Danube. The Thames River floods mead-ows in spring and fall and ripples past places holding significance not just for England but also the world.

Travelers to London are in luck that such rich historical treasures are within an easy day trip of the city. Anyone who wants to understand the mys-tique of the British monarchy should visit Windsor, 45 minutes from Lon-don by train and home to the medieval and massive Windsor Castle, the Queen's favorite home. Farther upstream, the quadrangles and spires of Oxford are the hallmarks of one of the world's most famous universi-ties. Within 10 mi of Oxford is the storybook village of Woodstock and Blenheim Palace, one of the grandest houses in all the land.

The railroads and motorways carrying traffic to and from London have turned much of this area into commuter territory, but you can still find timeless villages and miles of relaxing countryside. The stretches of the Thames near Marlow and Henley are lovely, with rowing clubs, piers, and sturdy waterside cottages and villas. It all conspires to make this a wonderful find, even for experienced travelers.

Exploring the Thames Valley

A great place to begin an exploration of the Thames Valley is the town of Windsor, home to the Queen's favorite palace. From there you can follow the river to Henley-on-Thames, site of the famous regatta. Next, you can head north to Oxford, and end with a visit to Blenheim Palace.

About the Restaurants

Londoners weekend here, and where they go, stellar restaurants follow. The area around Windsor and Henley claims some of Britain's best ta-bles. Simple pub food, as well as classic French cuisine, can be enjoyed in waterside settings at many restaurants beside the Thames. Reserva-tions are strongly recommended, especially on weekends.

About the Hotels

From converted country houses to refurbished Elizabethan inns, the re-gion's accommodations are rich in history and distinctive in appeal. Many hotels cultivate traditional gardens and retain a sense of the past with im-pressive collections of antiques. Book ahead, particularly in summer; you're competing for rooms with many Londoners in search of a getaway.

WHAT IT COSTS In pounds				
	££££££	££££	£££	££	£
RESTAURANTS	over £22	£18–£22	£13–£17	£7–£12	under £7
HOTELS	over £160	£120–£160	£90–£119	£60–£89	under £60

Restaurant prices are for a main course at dinner. Hotel prices are for two people in a standard double room in high season, including V.A.T., with no meals or, if in-dicated, CP (with continental breakfast), BP (Breakfast Plan, with full breakfast), or MAP (Modified American Plan, with breakfast and dinner).

TOP REASONS TO GO

Windsor Castle: The mystique of eight successive royal houses of the British monarchy permeates Windsor, where a fraction of the current Queen's vast wealth is displayed in heraldic splendor.

Oxford University: While scholars' noses are buried in their books, you get to sightsee among majestic golden-stone buildings. Be on the lookout for gargoyles around New College: the evil little creatures are wickedly creative.

Punting in Oxford: Getting out on the water is a wonderful way to experience the Thames Valley. Try your luck at using a pole to move a flat-bottom punt. You'll either proudly exhibit your strength or take a plunge into a slow-moving river. A chauffered ride, complete with Champagne, is a relaxing alternative.

Blenheim Palace: The only British historic home to be named a World Heritage Site has fine 18th-century architecture, stunning gardens, and remembrances of Winston Churchill. For a memorable treat, attend an outdoor summer concert.

Timing

High summer is lovely, but droves of visitors have the same effect on some travelers as bad weather. If crowds trouble you, but you relish a bit of sunshine, consider visiting in late spring or early fall, when the weather is not too bad, and the crowds have headed home for the school year. Book tickets and accommodations well in advance for Henley's Royal Regatta at the cusp of June and July or Ascot's Royal Meeting in mid-June. Visiting at Eton and the Oxford colleges is much more restricted during term time (generally September to late March and late April to mid-July). Avoid any driving in the London area during afternoon and morning rush hours.

WINDSOR TO HENLEY-ON-THAMES

Windsor Castle is one of the jewels of the area known as Royal Windsor, but a journey around this section of the Thames has other classic pleasures. The town of Eton holds the eponymous public school, and Ascot has its famous racecourse. The stretch of the Thames Valley around Marlow and Henley is literally the stuff of fairy tales. Walking through its fields and along its waterways, it's easy to see how it inspired Kenneth Grahame's classic 1908 children's book *The Wind in the Willows*. Whether by boat or on foot, you can discover fine wooded hills, with spacious homes, greenhouses, flower beds, and neat lawns that stretch to the water's edge.

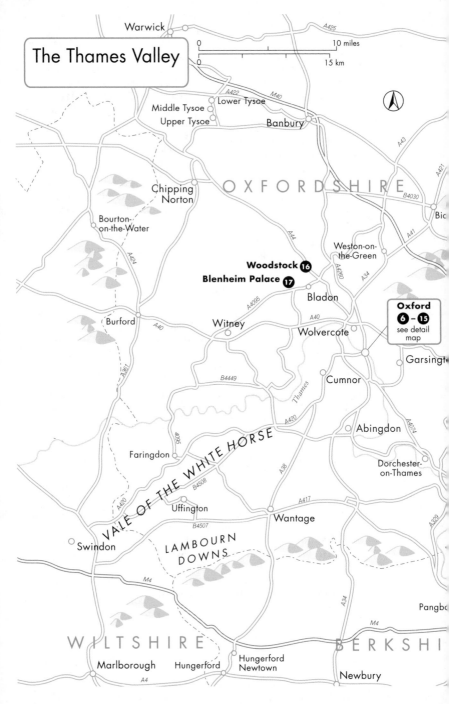

The Thames Valley

0 — 10 miles
0 — 15 km

Warwick

Middle Tysoe
Lower Tysoe
Upper Tysoe
Banbury

OXFORDSHIRE

Chipping Norton

Bourton-on-the-Water

Weston-on-the-Green

Woodstock 16
Blenheim Palace 17

Bladon

Burford

Witney

Wolvercote

Oxford 6 – 15 see detail map

Garsingt

Cumnor

Abingdon

Faringdon

VALE OF THE WHITE HORSE

Dorchester-on-Thames

Uffington

Wantage

Swindon

LAMBOURN DOWNS

Pangb

WILTSHIRE

BERKSHI

Marlborough   Hungerford   Hungerford Newtown   Newbury

Bic

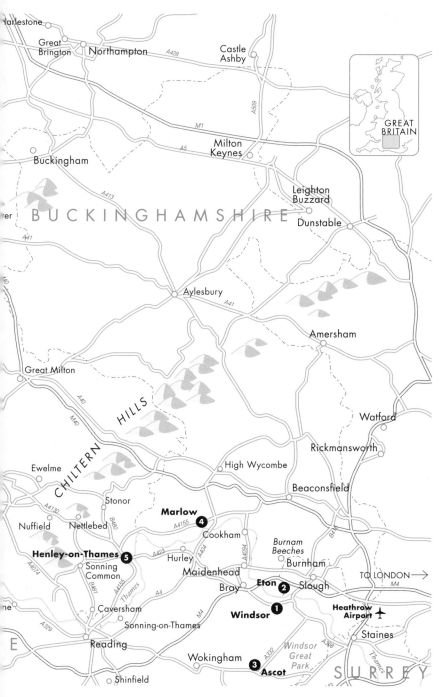

Windsor

❶ *21 mi west of London.*

Only a small part of old Windsor—the settlement that grew up around the town's famous castle in the Middle Ages—has survived. Windsor can feel overrun by tourists in the high season, but, even so, romantics will appreciate narrow, cobbled Church Lane and noble Queen Charlotte Street, opposite the castle entrance.

★ The imposing turrets and towers of **Windsor Castle** are visible for miles. From William the Conqueror to Queen Victoria, the kings and queens of England added towers and wings to the brooding structure, and it's now the largest inhabited castle in the world. Despite the multiplicity of hands involved in its design, the palace manages to have a unity of style and character. The most impressive view of Windsor Castle is from the A332 road, coming into town from the south.

William the Conqueror began work on the castle in the 11th century, and Edward III modified and extended it in the mid-1300s. One of Edward's largest contributions was the enormous and distinctive **Round Tower.** Finally, between 1824 and 1837, George IV transformed the still essentially medieval castle into the fortified royal palace you see today. Most of England's kings and queens have demonstrated their undying attachment to the castle, the only royal residence in continuous use by the Royal Family since the Middle Ages.

As you enter the castle, **Henry VIII's gateway** leads uphill into the wide castle precincts, where you are free to wander. Across from the entrance is the exquisite **St. George's Chapel** (closed Sunday). Here lie 10 of the kings of England, including Henry VI, Charles I, and Henry VIII (Jane Seymour is the only one of his six wives buried here). One of the noblest buildings in England, the chapel was built in the Perpendicular style popular in the 15th and 16th centuries, with elegant stained-glass windows, a high, vaulted ceiling, and intricately carved choir stalls. The colorful heraldic banners of the Knights of the Garter—the oldest British Order of Chivalry, founded by Edward III in 1348—hang in the choir. The ceremony in which the knights are installed as members of the order has been held here with much pageantry for more than five centuries.

Queen Elizabeth uses the castle far more than any of her predecessors did. It has become a sort of country weekend home. As such, it's a rather sleepy place most of the time. ■ TIP→ **To see it come magnificently alive, check out the Windsor Castle Changing of the Guard, which takes place at 11 AM weekdays and Saturday from April through July and on odd-numbered weekdays and Saturday from August through March.** Because the dates are changeable, it's a good idea to confirm the exact schedule before traveling to Windsor. When the Queen is in town, the guard and a regimental band parade through town to the castle gate; when she is away, a drum-and-fife band takes over.

Although a devastating fire in 1992 gutted some of the State Apartments, hardly any works of art were lost. Phenomenal repair work restored the

Grand Reception Room, the **Green and Crimson Drawing Rooms,** and the **State and Octagonal dining rooms.** A green oak hammer-beam (a short horizontal roof beam that projects from the tops of walls for support) roof looms magnificently over the 600-year-old **St. George's Hall,** where the Queen gives state banquets.

Queen Mary's Doll's House, on display to the left of the entrance to the State Apartments, is a perfect miniature Georgian palace-within-a-palace, created in 1923. Electric lights glow, the doors all have tiny little keys, and water pours from the small faucets. A miniature library holds Lilliputian-size books especially written for the young Queen by famous authors of the 1920s. *☎ 020/7766–7304 tickets, 01753/831118 recorded information ⊕ www.royalresidences.com ✉ £13.50 for Precincts, State Apartments, Gallery, St. George's Chapel (closed Sun.), Albert Memorial Chapel, and Doll's House; £7 when State Apartments are closed ☉ Mar.–Oct., daily 9:45–5:15, last admission at 4; Nov.–Feb., daily 9:45–4:15, last admission at 3.*

Just outside the castle, on St. Albans Street, the royal horses are kept in the **Royal Mews,** along with carriages, coaches, and splendid crimson and gold harnesses. The **Jubilee Garden,** created in 2002, has a stone bandstand used for concerts on summer Sunday afternoons. The garden begins at the main gates and extends to St. George's Gate on Castle Hill.

Windsor Great Park, the remains of an ancient royal hunting forest, stretches for some 8 mi (about 5,000 acres) south of Windsor Castle. Much of it is open to the public and can be seen by car or on foot, including its geographical focal points, the romantic 3-mi **Long Walk,** designed by Charles II to join castle and park, and **Virginia Water,** a 2-mi-long lake. The park contains one of Queen Victoria's most treasured residences, **Frogmore House** (☎ 020/7766–7305 ⊕ www.royalresidences.com ✉ House, gardens, and mausoleum £5.50 ☉ May and Aug., selected days only; check Web site or phone, 10–5:30). The sprawling white mansion is still a retreat for the Royal Family. Nearby, at the Royal Mausoleum at Frogmore, two famous royal couples are buried: inside, Victoria and Albert; outside, the Duke and Duchess of Windsor. It's open only a few days a year. The main horticultural delight of Windsor Great Park, the exquisite **Savill Garden** (✉ Wick La., Englefield Green, Egham ☎ 01753/847518 ⊕ www.savillgarden.co.uk ✉ £3.50–£5.50 ☉ Mar.–Oct., daily 10–6; Nov.–Feb., daily 10–4), contains a tremendous diversity of trees and shrubs.

The extensive theme park **Legoland,** 2 mi outside Windsor, does everything you could imagine with Lego building bricks. Kids can play on ingenious models and try the rides and interactive games. There's a lakeside picnic area, 150 acres of parkland, and several restaurants. *✉ Winkfield Rd. ☎ 08705/040404 ⊕ www.legoland.co.uk ✉ £23–£29 ☉ Mid-Mar.–June, Sept., and Oct., weekdays 10–5, weekends 10–6; July and Aug., daily 10–7.*

Where to Stay & Eat

Bray, a tiny village 6 mi outside Windsor, is known for its restaurants more than anything else.

★ **£££££** ✕ **Fat Duck.** One of the top restaurants in the country, this extraordinary Bray establishment packs in fans of hypercreative cuisine every night. Chef Heston Blumenthal delights in unusual taste combinations, from mango and Douglas fir sorbet to smoked bacon and egg ice cream. The fixed-price menu lists plenty of good choices, such as foie gras spiced with Szechuan peppercorn and mead, and lasagna of langoustine with pig's trotter and truffle. Lunch from Monday through Saturday, with a £50 fixed-price menu, is cheaper than the £80 per person charged at night (as is Blumenthal's Hinds Head pub just across the road). Like the food, the interior blends traditional and contemporary elements—modern art, exposed brick walls, and ancient wooden beams. ⊠ *High St., Bray-on-Thames* ☎ *01628/580333* ⊕ *www.fatduck.co.uk* ⚲ *Reservations essential* ☴ *AE, DC, MC, V* ☻ *Closed Mon. No dinner Sun.*

£££££ ✕ **Hinds Head.** Chef Heston Blumenthal also owns this traditional pub across the road, where he sells less extreme dishes to a more laid-back crowd at somewhat more reasonable prices. The atmosphere is relaxed, and the look of the place is historic, with polished wood walls, brick fireplaces, and comfortable leather chairs. The food is a brilliant modern take on traditional English cuisine, so there's oxtail and kidney pudding, and rump steak with bone-marrow sauce and triple-cooked fries. The approachable menu makes this place less intimidating than the Fat Duck, and the dress code is as casual as the mood. ⊠ *High St., Bray-on-Thames* ☎ *01628/626151* ☴ *MC, V.*

£££££ ✕ **Strok's Restaurant.** In Sir Christopher Wren's House Hotel—a mansion built in 1676 by the architect who designed St. Paul's Cathedral—Strok's offers an ever-changing continental menu and a Thames-side wooden terrace that swells with crowds in summer. Dishes may include roasted lamb with hummus and couscous, slathered in a minty yogurt sauce, or cod rice cakes sprinkled with Parmesan and lime juice. ⊠ *Thames St. at Eton Bridge* ☎ *01753/861354* ☴ *AE, DC, MC, V.*

££–£££ ✕ **Two Brewers.** Locals congregate in the two small low-ceiling rooms of this 17th-century pub. Children are not welcome, but adults will find a suitable collection of wine, espresso, and local beer, plus an excellent little menu with dishes from grilled salmon to chili and pasta. Reservations are essential on Sunday, when the pub serves a traditional roast. ⊠ *34 Park St.* ☎ *01753/855426* ☴ *AE, MC, V* ☻ *No dinner Fri.*

£££££ ✕🏨 **Cliveden.** If you've ever wondered what it would feel like to be an Edwardian grandee, splurge for a stay at this stately home, one of Britain's grandest hotels. Cliveden's opulent interior includes portraits such as Sargent's portrait of Nancy Astor (in the Great Hall), suits of armor, and a richly paneled staircase. The plush traditional bedrooms each bear the name of someone famous who has stayed here. Since people lease many of the rooms, you may feel you're in a home rather than a hotel. Waldo's (£££££), one of three restaurants, serves excellent contemporary British and French cuisine. The hotel is 10 mi north of Windsor. ⊠ *Off A404 near Maidenhead, Taplow SL6 0JF* ☎ *01628/668561* ☒ *01628/661837* ⊕ *www.clivedenhouse.co.uk* ⮑ *38 rooms, 1 cottage* ⚲ *3 restaurants, room service, in-room safes, cable TV with movies, in-room VCRs, in-room data ports, 3 tennis courts, indoor-outdoor pool, gym, hair salon, 2 outdoor hot tubs, massage, sauna, spa, steam room, boating, billiards, horseback riding, squash, lounge, library, babysitting, dry cleaning, laun-*

Fodor'sChoice ★

dry service, concierge, meeting rooms, some pets allowed, no-smoking rooms; no a/c in some rooms ⊟ *AE, DC, MC, V* ⵔⵣ *BP.*

££££ ✕⊞ **Stoke Park Club.** On a 350-acre estate 4 mi southwest of Windsor, Stoke Park can make Windsor Castle, off in the distance, seem almost humble in comparison. Architect James Wyatt perfected this version of neoclassical grandeur when he built the house for the Penn family in 1791. Antiques, paintings, and original prints decorate the elegant bedrooms. The Park Restaurant (££££) serves traditional English cuisine. *Goldfinger, Wimbledon,* and *Bridget Jones's Diary* were partly filmed here. Check ahead for special packages, which include a full English breakfast, three-course table d'hôte dinner, or both. ⊠ *Park Rd., Stoke Poges SL2 4PG* ☎ *01753/717171* 🖷 *01753/717181* ⊕ *www.stokeparkclub. com* ⵔ *21 rooms* ⵒ *2 restaurants, cable TV, in-room data ports, 27-hole golf course, 13 tennis courts, indoor pool, fitness classes, gym, hair salon, hot tub, massage, spa, steam room, fishing, croquet, squash, 2 bars, lounge, shops, meeting rooms* ⊟ *AE, DC, MC, V.*

££££ ⊞ **The Castle Hotel.** You get an exceptional view of the Changing of the Guard from this Georgian hotel, parts of which date back much further to its start in the 16th century as a coaching inn. All rooms have recently been renovated and modernized—broadband brings modern life to the historic atmosphere. In the older section guest rooms have gently tilting floors, whereas elsewhere it's smooth elegance, with tasteful fabrics in neutral tones juxtaposed against original architectural detail. The cozy lounges have beamed ceilings and plush, antique furnishings—perfect for afternoon tea. To take advantage of lower prices, book a weekend leisure break with breakfast or half board. ⊠ *High St., SL4 ILJ* ☎ *0870/400–8300* 🖷 *01753/830244* ⊕ *www.macdonaldhotels. co.uk* ⵔ *111 rooms* ⵒ *2 restaurants, room service, minibars, cable TV, some in-room broadband, bar, lounge, laundry service, meeting rooms, no-smoking rooms; no a/c in some rooms* ⊟ *AE, DC, MC, V.*

££ ⊞ **Alma Lodge.** This friendly little bed-and-breakfast in an early Victorian town house is just one of many that can be booked through the Windsor tourist office. Ornate ceilings and ornamental fireplaces are some of the house's original features, and each well-maintained room is decorated in an uncluttered Victorian style. ⊠ *58 Alma Rd., SL4 3HA* ☎🖷 *01753/862983* ⊕ *www.almalodge.co.uk* ⵔ *4 rooms* ⵒ *Some pets allowed; no a/c, no room phones, no smoking* ⊟ *MC, V* ⵔⵣ *BP.*

♻ ££ ⊞ **Langton House** This big Victorian mansion on a quiet, leafy lane in central Windsor was a residence for Queen Victoria's local governmental officials. Today it's a comfortable guesthouse with spacious rooms decorated with antiques and modern furniture. Guests have access to a small kitchen with refrigerator, toaster, microwave, and kettle. The lounge has a TV, video library, and games. This place is very child-friendly, with supplies for babies including travel cots, high chairs, and a baby monitor. ⊠ *46 Alma Rd., SL4 3HA* ☎🖷 *01753/858299* ⊕ *www.langtonhouse.co.uk* ⵔ *4 rooms* ⵒ *Cable TV, Wi-Fi, kitchen; no smoking* ⊟ *MC, V* ⵔⵣ *BP.*

Nightlife & the Arts

Windsor's **Theatre Royal** (⊠ 10th St. ☎ 01753/853888), where productions have been staged since 1910, is one of Britain's leading provincial theaters. It puts on plays and musicals year-round, including a pantomime for the six weeks after Christmas.

Eton

❷ *23 mi west of London, linked by a footbridge across the Thames to Windsor.*

Some observers may find it symbolic that almost opposite Windsor Castle—which embodies the continuity of the royal tradition—stands Eton, a school that for centuries has educated many future leaders of the country. With its single main street leading from the river to the famous school, the old-fashioned town itself is much quieter than Windsor.

★ The splendid redbrick Tudor-style buildings of **Eton College,** founded in 1440 by King Henry VI, border the north end of High Street; signs warn drivers of BOYS CROSSING. During the college semesters, the schoolboys dress in their distinctive pinstripe trousers, swallow-tailed coats, and stiff collars (top hats have not been worn by the boys since the 1940s) to walk to class, and it's all terrifically photogenic. The Gothic **Chapel** rivals St. George's at Windsor in size and magnificence, and is both impressively austere and intimate. Beyond the cloisters are the school's playing fields where, according to the duke of Wellington, the Battle of Waterloo was really won, since so many of his officers had learned discipline and strategy during their school days there. The **Museum of Eton Life** has displays on the school's history. You can also take a guided tour of the school and chapel. ⊠ *Main entrance Brewhouse Yard* ☏ *01753/ 671177* ⊕ *www.etoncollege.com* ✉ *£3.80, £4.90 with tour* ☉ *Mar.–mid- Apr., July, and Aug., daily 10:30–4:30; mid-Apr.–June and Sept., daily 2–4:30; guided tours mid-Mar.–Sept., daily at 2:15 and 3:15.*

Where to Eat

££–££££ ✕ **Gilbey's Bar & Restaurant.** Just over the bridge from Windsor, this restaurant at the center of Eton's Antiques Row serves a fine, changing menu of inspired English fare, from cod, cheddar, and chive fish cakes to lamb with black pudding and spiced cabbage. Well-priced French wines are a specialty. The conservatory is a particularly pleasant place to sit in fine weather. ⊠ *82–83 High St.* ☏ *01753/854921* ▭ *AE, DC, MC, V.*

££ ✕ **The George Inn & Eatery.** This stylish pub has stripped pine floors, wooden tables, and a menu of contemporary cuisine. You might opt for the spicy Thai beef salad or the more traditional sausage and mashed potatoes in onion gravy. The terrace is a relaxing spot for a summertime pint. ⊠ *77 High St.* ☏ *01753/861797* ▭ *AE, MC, V.*

Ascot

❸ *10 mi southwest of Runnymede, 8 mi southwest of Windsor, 28 mi south- west from London.*

The town of Ascot (pronounced *as*-cut) has for centuries been famous for horse racing and for style. Queen Anne chose to have a racecourse here, and the first race meeting took place in 1711. The impressive show of millinery for which the Royal Meeting, or Royal Ascot, is also known was immortalized in Cecil Beaton's Ascot sequence in *My Fair Lady,* in which osprey feathers and black and white silk roses transformed Eliza Doolittle into a grand lady.

Renovated in 2005, **Ascot Racecourse** (✉ A329 ☎ 01344/622211 racecourse, 01344/876876 credit-card hotline ⊕ www.ascot.co.uk) looks more gloriously upper class than ever. The races run regularly from June through December. The Royal Ascot takes place annually in June. ■ TIP→ **Tickets to all races can be purchased online and by phone. However, if you're hankering to go during the Royal Ascot, purchase your tickets well in advance.** Tickets generally go on sale in January, but call or check the Web site for details. Prices range from £7 for standing room on the heath, to £60 for seats in the stands.

Marlow

❹ *15 mi northwest of Windsor.*

Just inside the Buckinghamshire border, Marlow overflows with Thames-side prettiness. The unusual suspension bridge was built in the 1830s by William Tierney Clark, architect of the bridge linking Buda and Pest. Marlow has a number of striking old buildings, particularly the privately owned Georgian houses along Peter and West streets. In 1817 the Romantic poet Percy Bysshe Shelley stayed with friends at 67 West Street and then bought **Albion House** on the same street. His second wife, Mary, completed her Gothic novel *Frankenstein* here. **Marlow Place,** on Station Road, dates from 1721 and has been home to several princes. Marlow hosts its own miniregatta in mid-June for one day. The town is a good base from which to join the Thames Path walking trail to Henley-on-Thames. On summer weekends, tourism can often overwhelm the town.

Swan-Upping (☎ 01628/523030), a traditional event that dates back 800 years, takes place in the third week of July. By bizarre ancient laws, the Queen owns the country's swans, so each year swan-markers in skiffs start from Sunbury-on-Thames, catching the new cygnets and marking their beaks to establish ownership. The Queen's swan keeper, dressed in scarlet livery, presides over this colorful ceremony.

Where to Stay & Eat

££££ ╳ **Vanilla Pod.** Beamed ceilings and warm, vanilla-hue walls cocoon French-inspired cuisine by chef Michael Macdonald. Some of the best choices are the glazed chicken—embraced by layers of honey, coriander, and fennel—and the poached sea bass with vanilla and saffron. For dessert, indulge in the crème caramel with orange salsa and strawberry salad. The £18.50 fixed-price lunch menu offers a fantastic bargain, and the seven-course *menu gourmand* for £45 is a tour de force. ✉ *31 West St.* ☎ *01628/898101* ⌔ *Reservations essential* ▭ *AE, MC, V.*

££££–£££££ ╳▥ **Compleat Angler.** Fishing aficionados might consider this luxurious, 17th-century Thames-side inn the ideal place to stay. The name comes from Isaak Walton's 1653 masterpiece of angling advice and philosophy, which he wrote in this area. Plenty of fishy touches enhance the decor; most rooms and the Riverside Restaurant (with outstanding cooking from chef Dean Timpson ££££) have views over the Thames.

HIKING & BIKING ALONG THE THAMES

The Thames Valley is a great area to explore by foot or bike. It's not too hilly, and pubs and easily accessible lodgings dot the riverside and small towns. The Thames is almost completely free of car traffic along the Thames Path, a 180-mi national trail that traces the river from the London flood barrier to the river's source near Kemble, in the Cotswolds. The path follows towpaths from the outskirts of London, through Windsor, to Oxford and Lechlade. Good public transportation in the region makes it possible to start and stop easily anywhere along this route. In summer the walking is fine and no special gear is necessary, but in winter the path often floods—check before you head out.

The Countryside Agency has been charting and preserving Thames paths for years and offers publications about them. For maps and advice, contact the National Trails Office or the Ramblers' Association. The Chiltern Conservation Board promotes walking in the Chilterns peaks.

Biking is perhaps the best way to see the Chilterns. Routes include the 98-mi Thames Valley Cycle Route from London to Oxford, the 200-mi Oxfordshire Cycleway around the county's countryside, and the 85-mi Ridgeway Path from Uffington that follows the Chilterns; the National Trails Office has information. The 180-mi Thames Path also has plenty of biking opportunities.

CONTACTS & RESOURCES
Chiltern Conservation Board (☎ 01844/271300 ⊕ www. chilternsaonb.org). **Chiltern Way** (☎ 01494/771250 ⊕ www. chilternsociety.org.uk). **Countryside Agency** (☎ 01242/521381 ⊕ www. countryside.gov.uk ✉ London ☎ 020/7340-2900). **National Trails Office** (☎ 01865/810224 ⊕ www. nationaltrail.co.uk). **Ramblers' Association** (☎ 020/7339-8500 ⊕ www.ramblers.org.uk). **Sustrans (Thames Valley Cycle Route)** (☎ 0117/903-0504 ⊕ www. sustrans.org.uk).

A cozy conservatory serves afternoon tea. ✉ *Marlow Bridge, Bisham Rd., SL7 1RG* ☎ *0870/400-8100* 🖶 *01628/486388* ⊕ *www. compleatangler-hotel.co.uk* ➷ *61 rooms, 3 suites* ⚹ *2 restaurants, room service, minibars, cable TV with video games, boating, fishing, 2 bars, lounge, meeting rooms, some pets allowed (fee), no-smoking rooms; no a/c* ▤ *AE, DC, MC, V.*

Henley-on-Thames

⑤ *7 mi southwest of Marlow on A4155, 8 mi north of Reading, 36 mi west of central London.*

Henley's fame is based on one thing: rowing. The Henley Royal Regatta, held at the cusp of June and July on a long, straight stretch of the River Thames, has made the little riverside town famous throughout the world. Townspeople launched the Henley Regatta in 1839, initiating the

Grand Challenge Cup, the most famous of its many trophies. The best amateur oarsmen from around the globe compete in crews of eight, four, or two, or as single scullers. For many spectators, however, the social side of the event is far more important and on par with Royal Ascot and Wimbledon. Elderly oarsmen wear straw boater hats; businesspeople entertain clients and everyone admires the ladies' fashions.

The town is set in a broad valley between gentle hillsides. Henley's historic buildings, including half-timber Georgian cottages and inns (as well as one of Britain's oldest theaters, the Kenton), are all within a few minutes' walk. The river near Henley is alive with boats of every shape and size, from luxury cabin cruisers to tiny rowboats.

The 16th-century "checkerboard" tower of **St. Mary's Church** overlooks Henley's bridge on Hart Street. If the church's rector is about, ask permission to climb to the top to take in the superb views up and down the river. The adjacent **Chantry House,** built in 1420, is one of England's few remaining merchant houses from the period. It is an unspoiled example of the rare timber-frame design, with upper floors jutting out. ⊠ *Hart St.* ☎ *01491/577062* 🕮 *Free* ⊙ *Church services or by appointment.*

The handsome, riverside **River & Rowing Museum** focuses not just on the history and sport of rowing but on the Thames and the town itself. One gallery interprets the Thames and its surroundings as the river flows from its source to the ocean; another explores Henley's history and the regatta. Galleries devoted to rowing display models and actual boats, from Greek triremes to lifeboats to sleek modern rowing boats. A *Wind in the Willows* exhibit evokes the settings of the famous children's book. ⊠ *Mill Meadows* ☎ *01491/415600* ⊕ *www.rrm.co.uk* 🕮 *£6* ⊙ *May–Aug., daily 10–5:30; Sept.–Apr., daily 10–5.*

Where to Stay & Eat

££–£££ ✕ **Three Tuns Foodhouse.** What used to be a tiny pub has been redone into a delightful, antiques-filled eatery. On the menu, panfried scallops with saffron and fennel share space with chicken with thyme potatoes and Scottish chanterelle mushrooms. ⊠ *5 Market Pl.* ☎ *01491/573260* ⌂ *Reservations essential* ▤ *MC, V.*

££££ ✕▣ **Red Lion.** Ivy-draped and dignified, this redbrick 16th-century hotel overlooks the river and the town bridge. Guests have included King Charles I; Samuel Johnson, the 18th-century critic, poet, and lexicographer; and the duke of Marlborough, who used it as a base during the building of Blenheim Palace. Rooms are furnished with antiques, and some bedrooms have river views. The restaurant (*£££*) serves traditional fare such as roast pheasant or beef fillet with leek and Stilton mousse; the bar has a lighter menu. ⊠ *Hart St., RG9 2AR* ☎ *01491/572161* 🖷 *01491/410039* ⊕ *www.redlionhenley.co.uk* ⇌ *26 rooms* ⌂ *Restaurant, room service, cable TV, in-room data ports, bar, lobby lounge, babysitting, dry cleaning, laundry service, Internet room, meeting rooms; no a/c* ▤ *AE, MC, V* ⏏❶ *BP.*

£££–££££ ✕▣ **White Hart Hotel & Nettlebed Restaurant.** The focus at this modern gastro-pub with guest rooms is delectable food, prepared with fresh, local ingredients by chef-owner Chris Barber, who spent a decade as personal chef to Prince Charles. With its three-course set menu (£35) and five-course tasting menu (£55), the restaurant is pricier and more formal than the bistro, but both have the same caliber of friendly, professional staff. The soothing, light-filled guest rooms, done in olive green, gray, cream, and dark chocolate, are contemporary in style. ⊠ *A4130, Nettlebed RG9 5DD, 5 mi west of Henley-on-Thames* ☎ *01491/641245* ⊠ *01491/ 649018* ⊕ *www.whitehartnettlebed.com* ⇨ *12 rooms* ⚫ *Restaurant, room service, in-room data ports, lounge, pub, dry cleaning, laundry service, meeting rooms, no-smoking rooms; no a/c* ⊟ *AE, MC, V* ⦿ *CP.*

££££ 🏨 **Hotel du Vin.** The small British Hotel du Vin chain of boutique hotels is known for its clever use of unique buildings, and in Henley a sprawling old brick brewery became a design showplace. Bedrooms have beige carpeting and white-washed walls—everything else is black. The original brewery windows appear in unusual places, and staircases contort to fit the space. Deep bathtubs, firm beds, and a minimalist ethic make this modern hotel a pleasure. ⊠ *New St., RG9 2BP* ☎ *01491/848400* ⊕ *www.hotelduvin.com* ⇨ *43 rooms* ⚫ *Restaurant, room service, cable TV, in-room data ports, bar* ⊟ *AE, MC, V.*

££ 🏨 **Alftrudis.** This sweet Victorian house in central Henley is a real find. Its three guest rooms are neatly decorated in whites and creams, beds are comfortable, and owner Sue Lambert offers a wealth of information about the area. Book well in advance at this popular place. ⊠ *8 Norman Ave., Henley-on-Thames RG9 1SG* ☎ *01491/573099* ⊕ *www. alftrudis.co.uk* ⇨ *3 rooms* ⚫ *Cable TV, Wi-Fi* ⊟ *No credit cards* ⦿ *BP.*

Nightlife & the Arts

A floating stage and spectacular events draw a dress-code abiding crowd to the upscale **Henley Festival** (☎ 01491/843404 ⊕ www.henley-festival. co.uk) during the week after the regatta in July. Book tickets ahead.

Rowing

Henley Royal Regatta (☎ 01491/572153 ⊕ www.hrr.co.uk), a series of rowing competitions that draw participants from many countries, takes place in late June and early July each year. Large tents go up, especially along both sides of the unique straight stretch of river here known as Henley Reach (1 mi, 550 yards), and every surrounding field becomes a parking lot. The most prestigious place for spectators is the Stewards' Enclosure, but admission here is by invitation only. Fortunately, there is plenty of space on the public towpath from which to watch the early stages of the races. If you want to attend, make your plans and book a room months in advance (500,000 attend the race, including members of the Royal Family). Each day, the racing pauses twice, at noon for lunch and at 4 for tea. *See* Thames Valley Essentials, *below,* for places to rent your own boat.

OXFORD

With arguably the most famous university in the world, Oxford has been a center of learning since 1167, with only the Sorbonne preceding it. It doesn't take more than a day or two to explore its winding medieval streets, photograph its ancient, ivy-covered stone buildings (some with the "dreaming spires" described by Victorian writer Matthew Arnold), and even take a punt down one of its placid, picturesque waterways. The town center is compact and walkable, and at its heart is Oxford University. Alumni of this prestigious institution include 47 Nobel Prize winners, 25 British prime ministers (including Prime Minister Tony Blair), and 28 foreign presidents (including former U.S. President Bill Clinton), along with poets, authors, and artists such as Percy Bysshe Shelley, Oscar Wilde, and W. H. Auden. Save for its modern storefronts, the city looks much as it has for hundreds of years, in part because Adolf Hitler had vague plans to make it his European capital and so spared it from bombings.

Oxford is 55 mi northwest of London, at the junction of the Thames and Cherwell rivers. The city is more interesting and more cosmopolitan than Cambridge, and although it's also bigger, its suburbs are not remotely interesting to visitors. The interest is all at the center, where the old town curls around the grand stone buildings, good restaurants, and historic pubs. Just 8 mi northwest of the city is Blenheim Palace, one of the nation's finest stately homes.

Exploring Oxford

Oxford University is not one easily identifiable campus, but a sprawling mixture of more than 39 colleges scattered around the city center, each with its own distinctive identity and focus. Oxford students live and study at their own college, and also use the centralized resources of the over-arching university. The individual colleges are deeply competitive. Most of the grounds and magnificent dining halls and chapels are open to visitors, though the opening times (displayed at the entrance gates) vary greatly. Some colleges are open only in the afternoons during university terms. When the undergraduates are in residence, access is often restricted to the chapels and dining rooms (called halls) and sometimes the libraries, too, and you are requested to refrain from picnicking in the quadrangles. All are closed certain days during exams, usually from mid-April to late June. ■ TIP➜ **The best way to gain access is to join a walking tour led by a Blue Badge guide. These two-hour tours leave up to five times daily from the Tourist Information Centre.**

Main Attractions

 Ashmolean Museum. Britain's oldest public museum contains among its priceless collections (all university-owned) many Egyptian, Greek, and Roman artifacts uncovered during archaeological expeditions conducted by the university. Michelangelo drawings and an extraordinary statuary collection are highlights, as is the Alfred Jewel. This ancient piece features a large semiprecious stone set in gold carved with the words AELFRED MEC HEHT GEWYRCAN, which translates from old English as "Alfred ordered me to be made." The piece dates from the reign of King Alfred the Great (ruled 871–899). ✉ *Beaumont St.* ☎ *01865/278000* ⊕ *www.ashmol.ox.ac.uk* ✍ *Free* ☺ *Tues.–Sat. 10–5, Sun. noon–5.*

Balliol College. The wooden doors between the inner and outer quadrangles of Balliol (founded 1263) still bear scorch marks from 1555 and 1556, when during the reign of Mary ("Bloody Mary"), Bishops Latimer

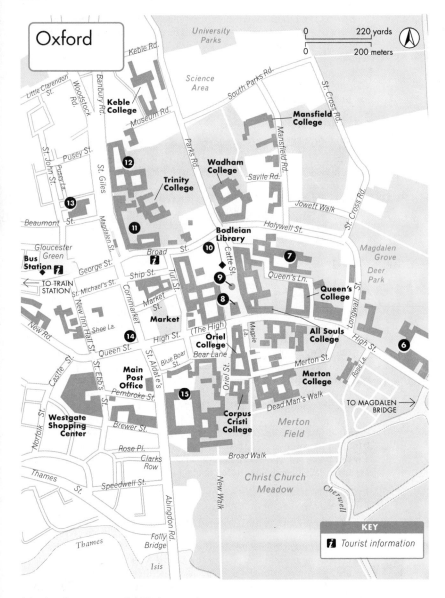

Oxford

University Parks

Science Area

Keble Rd.

Little Clarendon St.

Woodstock Rd.

Banbury Rd.

Keble College

Museum Rd.

South Parks Rd.

St. Cross Rd.

Mansfield Rd.

Mansfield College

Pusey St.

St. Giles

Parks Rd.

Wadham College

Savile Rd.

St. John St.

Pusey La.

12

Trinity College

Jowett Walk

St. Cross Rd.

Beaumont St.

13

Magdalen St.

11

Bodleian Library

Holywell St.

Magdalen Grove

Gloucester Green

Broad St.

10

Catte St.

7

Deer Park

Bus Station

George St.

Ship St.

9

Queen's Ln.

Queen's College

TO TRAIN STATION

St. Michael's St.

Turl St.

Market St.

8

New Rd.

Cornmarket

Market

(The High)

Magpie La.

All Souls College

Longwall

High St.

6

New Inn Hall St.

Shoe La.

14

High St.

Oriel College

Bear Lane

Rose La.

Castle St.

Queen St.

St. Aldate's

Blue Boar St.

Oriel St.

Merton St.

Merton College

TO MAGDALEN BRIDGE

St. Ebb's St.

Main Post Office

Pembroke St.

15

Dead Man's Walk

Norfolk St.

Westgate Shopping Center

Brewer St.

Corpus Cristi College

Merton Field

Rose Pl.

Clarks Row

Broad Walk

Cherwell

Thames St.

Speedwell St.

New Walk

Christ Church Meadow

Abingdon Rd.

Thames

Folly Bridge

Isis

0 — 220 yards
0 — 200 meters

and Ridley and Archbishop Cranmer were burned alive on huge pyres in Broad Street for their Protestant beliefs. A cross on the roadway marks the spot. The **Martyrs' Memorial** at St. Giles and Beaumont Street also commemorates the three men. ⊠ *Broad St. and St. Giles* ☎ *01865/277777* ⊕ *www.balliol.ox.ac.uk* ▣ *£1* ⊙ *Daily 2–5.*

⑮ Christ Church. Built in 1546, the college of Christ Church is referred to by its members as "The House." This is the site of Oxford's largest quadrangle, Tom Quad, named after the huge bell (6¼ tons) that hangs in the Christopher Wren–designed gate tower and rings 101 times at five past nine every evening in honor of the original number of Christ Church scholars. The vaulted, 800-year-old chapel in one corner has been Oxford's cathedral since the time of Henry VIII. The college's medieval dining hall contains portraits of many famous alumni, including John Wesley, William Penn, and 13 of Britain's prime ministers. A reproduction of this room appears in the banquet scenes at Hogwarts School in the *Harry Potter* films. Lewis Carroll was a teacher of mathematics here for many years; a shop opposite the meadows on St. Aldate's sells Alice paraphernalia. ⊠ *St. Aldate's* ☎ *01865/276150* ⊕ *www.chch.ox.ac.uk* ▣ *£4* ⊙ *Mon.–Sat. 9–5:30, Sun. 1–5:30.*

Christ Church Picture Gallery. This connoisseur's delight in Canterbury Quadrangle exhibits works by the Italian masters as well as Hals, Rubens, and Van Dyck. Drawings in the 2,000-strong collection are shown on a changing basis. ⊠ *Oriel Sq.* ☎ *01865/276172* ⊕ *www.chch.ox. ac.uk* ▣ *£3* ⊙ *Apr.–Sept., Mon.–Sat. 10:30–5, Sun. 2–5; Oct.–Mar., Mon.–Sat., 10:30–1 and 2–4:30, Sun. 2–4:30.*

★ ⑥ Magdalen College. Founded in 1458, with a handsome main quadrangle and a supremely monastic air, Magdalen (pronounced: "*maud*-lin") is one of the most impressive of Oxford's colleges and attracts its most artistic students. Alumni include such diverse people as Cardinal Wolsey, P.G. Wodehouse, Edward Gibbon, Oscar Wilde, Dudley Moore, and U.S. Supreme Court Justice David Souter. The school's large, square tower is a famous local landmark. A stroll around the Deer Park and along Addison's Walk is a good way to appreciate the place. ⊠ *High St.* ☎ *01865/276000* ⊕ *www.magd. ox.ac.uk* ▣ *£3* ⊙ *July–Sept., daily noon–6; Oct.–June, daily 1–6.*

⑦ New College. One of the university's best known and oldest colleges (dating to 1379), New College stands alongside New College Lane, known for its Italianate Bridge of Sighs. Its grounds are big and enticing, with acres of soft green grass and pristinely maintained gardens. The college buildings, in ivory stone, are partly enclosed by the medieval city wall, and feature one of the city's best displays of Gothic gar-

> **WORD OF MOUTH**
>
> "Oxford is an astoundingly beautiful place. I would simply wander, seeing as many of the college chapels and cloisters as possible. Christ Church Chapel . . . is a must-see. Magdalen College has a deer park but also something called Addison's Walk, which is an idyllic place as well."
>
> –Guy 18

goyles. Famous alumni include the actors Hugh Grant and Kate Beckinsale. ⊠ *Holywell St.* ☎ *01865/279555* ⊕ *www.new.ox.ac.uk* 🎫 *Easter–Sept. £2, Oct.–Easter free* ☉ *Easter–Sept., daily 11–5; Oct.–Easter, daily 2–5.*

★ ❾ **Radcliffe Camera and Bodleian Library.** This vast library is Oxford's most spectacular building, built in 1737–49 by James Gibbs in Italian baroque style. It's usually surrounded by crowds of tourists with digital cameras trained at its golden walls. The Camera contains part of the Bodleian Library's enormous collection, which was begun in 1602 and has grown to more than 6 million volumes. Much like the Library of Congress in the United States, it contains a copy of every book printed in Great Britain (not all are held in this building, which is the library's public face). Although only students and professors are allowed inside the Camera, the general public may step into another part of the Bodleian, the Divinity School. This superbly vaulted room dates to 1462. In the *Harry Potter* films, some interior scenes at Hogwarts School take place in the Bodleian, including the Divinity School. ⊠ *Broad St.* ☎ *01865/277224 for information on tour* ⊕ *www.bodley.ox.ac.uk* 🎫 *£4, extended tour £7* ☉ *Tours of Bodleian Mar.–Oct., weekdays at 10:30, 11:30, 2, and 3, Sat. at 10:30 and 11:30; Nov.–Feb., weekdays at 2 and 3, Sat. at 10:30 and 11:30. Children under 14 not admitted. Divinity School weekdays 9–4:45, Sat. 9–12:30.*

⓬ **St. John's College.** One of Oxford's most attractive campuses, St. John's has seven quiet quadrangles (which you first enter through a low wooden door) surrounded by elaborately carved, cloisterlike buildings. This college dates to 1555, when it was founded by a merchant named Sir Thomas White. His heart is buried in the chapel and, by tradition, students curse as they walk over it. The Canterbury Quad represented the first example of Italian Renaissance architecture in Oxford, and the Front Quad includes the buildings of the old St. Bernard's Monastary. St. John's is Tony Blair's alma mater and Oxford's wealthiest college, with an estimated endowment of half a billion dollars. ⊠ *St. Giles* ☎ *01865/277300* ⊕ *www.sjc.ox.ac.uk* ☉ *Daily 1–dusk.*

NEED A BREAK? The **Eagle and Child pub** (⊠ 49 St. Giles ☎ 01865/302925) is a favorite not only for its good ales and historical feel, but also for its literary associations. This was the meeting place of C. S. Lewis, J. R. R. Tolkien, and their circle of literary friends who called themselves the "Inklings." The pub is so close to St. John's College, and such a favorite of its students, that the college purchased it, although it remains open to the public.

❽ **University Church of St. Mary the Virgin.** Seven hundred years' worth of funeral monuments crowd this church, including the tombstone of Amy Robsart, the wife of Robert Dudley, Elizabeth I's favorite. One pillar marks the site of Thomas Cranmer's trial under Bloody Mary for his marital machinations on behalf of Henry VIII. From the top of the church's 14th-century tower, you get a panoramic view of the city's skyline with nearly every architectural style since the 11th century. The Convocation House, a part of the church accessible from Radcliffe Square, serves generous portions of warm food—cafeteria style—under the room in which the charity OxFam was founded. ⊠ *High St.* ☎ *01865/279111* ⊕ *www. university-church.ox.ac.uk* ⬚ *Church free, tower £2* ⊘ *Sept.–June, Mon.–Sat. 9–5, Sun. noon–5; July and Aug., Mon.–Sat. 9–6, Sun. noon–6; last admission to tower 30 mins before closing.*

Also Worth Seeing

⑭ Carfax Tower. Passing through Carfax, where four roads meet, you can spot this tower, all that remains of **St. Martin's Church,** where Shakespeare stood as godfather for William Davenant, who himself became a playwright. Every 15 minutes, little mechanical "quarter boys" mark the passage of time on the tower front. You can climb up the dark stairwell for a good view of the town center. ⊠ *Corner of Carfax and Cornmarket* ☎ *01865/792653* ⬚ *£1.50* ⊘ *Apr.–Oct., daily 10–5:30; Nov.–Mar., daily 10–4:30.*

⑩ Sheldonian Theatre. This fabulously ornate theater is where Oxford's impressive graduation ceremonies are held, conducted almost entirely in Latin. Dating to 1663, it was the first building designed by Sir Christopher Wren when he served as professor of astronomy. The D-shape theater has pillars, balconies, and an elaborately painted ceiling. Outside, stone pillars are topped by 18 massive stone heads, sculpted in the 1970s to replace originals destroyed by air pollution. ⊠ *Broad St.* ☎ *01865/277299* ⊕ *www.sheldon.ox.ac.uk* ⬚ *£1.50* ⊘ *Mon.–Sat. 10–12:30 and 2–4:30; mid-Nov.–Feb., closes at 3:30. Closed for 10 days at Christmas and Easter and for degree ceremonies and events.*

Where to Eat

The Old Bank and Old Parsonage hotels also have worthwhile restaurants.

★ **✕ Le Petit Blanc.** Raymond Blanc's sophisticated brasserie, a hipper
££££–£££££ cousin of Le Manoir aux Quat' Saisons in Great Milton, is the finest place to eat in Oxford. The changing menu always lists innovative, visually stunning adaptations of bourgeois French fare, sometimes with Mediterranean or Asian influences. Try the herb pancakes with mushrooms, Gruyère, and ham. The set menus here are a good value. ⊠ *71–72 Walton St.* ☎ *01865/510999* ▤ *AE, DC, V.*

££–££££ ✕ Fishers. This is widely viewed as the city's best seafood restaurant, and everything is remarkably fresh. Seafood is available grilled, fried, broiled, or resting comfortably on the half-shell. The atmosphere is bustling but relaxed; it's often fully booked. ⊠ *25–37 St. Clements St.* ☎ *01865/ 243003* ⬚ *Reservations essential* ▤ *MC, V.*

££–££££ ✕ Gee's. With its glass-and-steel framework, this former florist's shop just north of the town center makes a charming dining room. The constantly changing menu features locally raised meats and vegetables in modern versions of traditional English dishes. ⊠ *61 Banbury Rd.* ☎ *01865/553540* ▤ *AE, MC, V* ⬚ *No smoking.*

££–£££ ✕ Du Liban. From the outside this restaurant looks unassuming—it's approached up some stairs beneath a modest sign. Inside, Lebanese music swirls, the atmosphere is lively and jovial, and the students and university workers share big plates of hummus and stuffed grape leaves. After meals, diners smoke hookah pipes (which the English wonderfully call "hubbly bubblies") as bellydancers shake and shimmy between the tables. All good fun, and the food is reliably fresh and good. ⊠ *1–5 Bond St.* ☎ *01865/310066* ☰ *MC, V.*

★ **£–££** ✕ **Grand Café.** Golden-hue tiles, columns, and antique marble tables make this café both architecturally impressive and an excellent spot for a light meal or leisurely drink. Pop in for early afternoon tea, as the tasty menu lists sandwiches, salads, and tarts along with a good selection of coffee and tea. ⊠ *84 High St.* ☎ *01865/204463* ☰ *AE, DC, MC, V.*

Where to Stay

Oxford is pricey; for the cheapest lodging, contact the tourist information office for B&Bs in locals' homes.

£££££ ▦ **Le Manoir aux Quat' Saisons.** Standards are high at this 15th-century
Fodor'sChoice   stone manor house, which has luxurious rooms in occasionally over-
★   the-top styles ranging from pink rococo fantasy to chic yellow chinoiserie (most rooms have private gardens and working fireplaces, too). It has one of the country's finest kitchens (complete with cooking school; £££££), and Chef Raymond Blanc's epicurean touch shows at every turn. Decide among the innovative French creations or treat yourself to the *menu gourmand*—eight courses of haute cuisine for £95. A stroll through the hotel's herb and Japanese gardens is de rigueur. Great Milton is 12 mi east of Oxford. ⊠ *Church Rd., Great Milton OX44 7PD* ☎ *01844/ 278881* 🖷 *01844/278847* ⊕ *www.manoir.com* ➫ *32 rooms* ⌂ *Restaurant, room service, in-room safes, cable TV, in-room data ports, croquet, lounge, babysitting, dry cleaning, laundry service, concierge, meeting rooms, car rental, kennel, no-smoking rooms; no a/c in some rooms* ☰ *AE, DC, MC, V* ⊗ *CP.*

£££££ ▦ **Old Bank Hotel.** From its sleek lobby to the 20th-century British paintings on display and the modern furnishings in the guest rooms, the former Barclay's Bank has brought some style to a city that favors the traditional. Oxford's most centrally located hotel holds the contemporary Quod Bar and Grill, serving creative pastas and dishes such as duck confit. ⊠ *92–94 High St., OX1 4BN* ☎ *01865/799599* 🖷 *01865/ 799598* ⊕ *www.oxford-hotels-restaurants.co.uk* ➫ *42 rooms* ⌂ *Restaurant, room service, in-room safes, cable TV, in-room DVDs, in-room broadband, bar, lounge, babysitting, dry cleaning, laundry service, meeting room, free parking, no-smoking rooms* ☰ *AE, DC, MC, V.*

£££££ ▦ **The Randolph.** A 19th-century neo-Gothic landmark, the hotel faces both the Ashmolean and the Martyrs' Memorial. If their parents are feeling generous, undergraduates are treated to tea in the Morse Bar or dinner in the Spires Restaurant. Scenes from PBS's Inspector Morse *Mystery* series and the film *Shadowlands* were shot here. ⊠ *Beaumont St., OX1 2LN* ☎ *0870/400–8200* 🖷 *01865/791678* ⊕ *www.macdonald-hotels. co.uk* ➫ *151 rooms* ⌂ *Restaurant, room service, fans, minibars, cable TV, in-room data ports, bar, lobby lounge, laundry service, concierge, business services, Internet room, meeting rooms, parking (fee), some pets allowed (fee), no-smoking floors; no a/c* ☰ *AE, DC, MC, V.*

★ 🖼 **Old Parsonage.** This hotel, a 17th-century gabled stone house i
££££–£££££ garden next to St. Giles Church, provides a dignified escape
surrounding city center. Dark-wood paneling in the soft, red lobby anu
the guest rooms' tasteful chintzes and marble baths were completely refurbished in 2005. Memorable meals by an open fire (or in the walled
garden terrace in summer) keep people coming back. Afternoon teas with
scones and clotted cream are excellent. ☒ *1 Banbury Rd., OX2 6NN*
☎ *01865/310210* 🖨 *01865/311262* ⊕ *www.oxford-hotels-restaurants.*
co.uk 🛏 *26 rooms, 4 suites* ⚘ *Restaurant, room service, in-room safes,*
in-room broadband, bar, lobby lounge, dry cleaning, laundry service,
business services, meeting rooms, car rental, free parking, no-smoking
rooms; no a/c ⊟ *AE, DC, MC, V.*

££££ 🖼 **Malmaison Oxford Castle.** This is the place everybody's talking
about: a boutique hotel inside an artfully converted, 19th-century
prison. Much of the design remains sympathetic to the past. Rooms
are divided into the old prison wings—"A Wing" rooms are comfortable in size, "C Wing" rooms include two semicircular suites. With
its metal doors, exposed brick walls, and clever embrace of its incar-
cerating past, this hotel is not for all. You half expect guests to come
out and bang their spoons on the white metal railing if breakfast isn't
served on time. But they won't, and breakfast is always served on time.
☒ *3 Oxford Castle, OX1 1AY* ☎ *01865/248432* 🖨 *01845/365–*
4247 ⊕ *www.malmaison.com* 🛏 *86 rooms, 8 suites* ⚘ *Restaurant,*
bar, room service, cable TV, in-room broadband, in-room DVDs, Wi-
Fi, dry cleaning, laundry service, spa, business services, meeting rooms,
no-smoking rooms ⊟ *AE, MC, V* ⦿ *BP.*

£££ 🖼 **Bath Place Hotel.** Down a cobbled alleyway off Holywell Street, 17th-
century weavers' cottages have been converted into a small hotel. A number of rooms have four-poster beds; nearly all have slanting floors and
exposed beams. Some rooms have their own entrances, and others are
in the main building. There's only a breakfast room, but the adjacent
Turf Tavern serves ale and bar food. ☒ *4–5 Bath Pl., OX1 3SI* ☎ *01865/*
791812 🖨 *01865/791834* ⊕ *www.bathplace.co.uk* 🛏 *14 rooms* ⚘ *Fans,*
minibars, bar, laundry service, free parking, some pets allowed; no a/c,
no smoking ⊟ *AE, DC, MC, V* ⦿ *CP.*

££ 🖼 **Brown's Guest House.** This redbrick Victorian at the edge of central
Oxford is a good bet in a town that has precious few affordable guesthouses. Rooms are spacious and neatly decorated, with comfortable beds
(most rooms have two) and lots of light. The breakfast room is big and
homey, and the food is good and hearty. The only downside is the 15-
minute walk or a bus ride into the center. ☒ *281 Iffley Rd., OX4 4AQ*
☎ *01865/791812* 🖨 *01865/791834* ⊕ *www.brownsguesthouse.co.uk*
🛏 *8 rooms* ⚘ *Cable TV* ⊟ *No credit cards* ⦿ *BP.*

££ 🖼 **Newton Guest House.** A big, handsome Victorian mansion just a
five-minute walk from all of Oxford's action, Newton is a sprawling,
friendly place. Decent-size rooms are brightly decorated with lemony
walls and red curtains; some have original Victorian features. The breakfast menu is more varied than that of some guesthouses, with cereals
and croissants, along with the usual eggs and bacon. This is one of the

best deals in the city center, so book early. ✉ *82 Abingdon Rd., OX1 4PL* ☎ *01865/240561* 🖷 *01865/244647* ✐ *newton.house@btinternet. com* 🛏 *11 rooms* ♿ *Cable TV* ☰ *No credit cards* ❢⃝ *BP.*

££ ▥ **Victoria House Hotel.** Basic, modern rooms at a low (for Oxford) price are the draw at this no-nonsense hotel aimed at the business set. Don't expect breakfast here, but at your doorstep is a fine selection of cafés. The downstairs Mood bar attracts the trendy with its resident DJ; on weekends, clubbers use the hotel as a base. This is a lively place—if you were hoping for a quiet weekend, this is not it. ✉ *29 George St., OX1 2AY* ☎ *01865/727400* 🖷 *01865/727402* ⊕ *www.victoriahouse-hotel.co.uk* 🛏 *14 rooms* ♿ *Bar; no a/c, no smoking* ☰ *AE, DC, MC, V.*

Nightlife & the Arts

Nightlife

Nightlife in Oxford centers around student life, which in turns centers around the local pubs, though you may find a few surprises, too. **Frevd** (✉ 119 Walton St. ☎ 01865/311171), in a renovated neoclassical church, serves light meals and cocktails as well as nightly live jazz or funk. The **Kings Arms** (✉ 40 Holywell St. ☎ 01865/242369), popular with students and fairly quiet during the day, carries excellent local brews as well as inexpensive pub grub. **Raoul's** (✉ 32 Walton St. ☎ 01865/553732) is a trendy cocktail bar in the equally trendy Jericho neighborhood. The **Turf Tavern** (✉ Bath Pl. ☎ 01865/243235), off Holywell Street, includes a higgledy-piggledy collection of little rooms and outdoor space good for a quiet drink and inexpensive pub food.

The Arts

FESTIVALS & CONCERTS
The **Jacqueline Du Pre Music Building** (✉ St. Hilda's College ☎ 01865/276821), endowed with the city's best acoustics, showcases rising talent at recitals. **Music at Oxford** (☎ 01865/242865), an acclaimed series of weekend classical concerts, takes place mid-September through June in such surroundings as Christ Church Cathedral and Sir Christopher Wren's Sheldonian Theatre. **Blenheim Palace** (☎ 01993/811091, ⊕ www.blenheimpalace.com) in nearby Woodstock puts on marvelous classical and pop concerts in summer, sometimes combined with fireworks displays.

THEATERS
During term time, undergraduate productions are often given in the colleges or local halls. In summer, outdoor performances may take place in quadrangles or college gardens. Look for announcement posters. **New Theatre** (✉ George St. ☎ 0870/606–3500), Oxford's main theater, stages plays, opera, ballet, pantomime, and concerts. It's the second home of the Welsh National Opera and the Glyndebourne Touring Opera. **Old Fire Station** (✉ 40 George St. ☎ 01865/297170), an alternative theater, showcases student productions, small-scale opera, and new musicals. The **Oxford Playhouse** (✉ Beaumont St. ☎ 01865/305305) is a serious theater presenting classic and modern dramas.

Sports & the Outdoors

Biking

Bikes can be rented at **Bike Zone** (✉ 6 Market St. ☎ 01865/728877).

Punting

Fodor'sChoice
★

You may choose, like many an Oxford student, to spend a summer afternoon **punting**, while dangling your Champagne bottle in the water to keep it cool. Punts—shallow-bottomed boats that are poled slowly up the river—can be rented in several places.

From mid-March through mid-October, **Cherwell Boathouse** (✉ Bardwell Rd. ☎ 01865/515978 ⊕ www.cherwellboathouse.co.uk), a punt station and restaurant a mile north of the heart of Oxford, will rent you a boat and, if you wish, someone (usually an Oxford student) to punt it. Rentals are £10–£12 per hour; £50–£60 per day. At the foot of **Magdalen Bridge** (✉ High St. ☎ 01865/515978) you can rent a punt for £10 an hour, plus a £25 refundable deposit. At the St. Aldates Road end of Folly Bridge, **Salter's Steamers** (☎ 01865/243421 ⊕ www.salterssteamers.co.uk) rents out punts and skiffs (rowboats) for £10 per hour, £30 per half day, and £50 per day. Their chauffeured punts are £35 per hour. Three-hour jazz cruises cost £15 and include an onboard performance by the Royal Castle Jazz Band.

Spectator Sports

At the end of May, during **Oxford's Eights Week**, men and women rowers from the university's colleges compete to be "Head of the River." Because the river is too narrow for teams of eight to race side by side, the boats set off, 13 at a time, one behind another. Each boat tries to catch and bump the one in front. Spectators can watch all the way.

Oxford University Cricket Club competes against leading county teams and, each summer, the major foreign team visiting Britain. In the middle of the sprawling University Parks—itself worthy of a walk—the club's playing field is truly lovely.

Shopping

Small shops line High Street, Cornmarket, and Queen Street, and the Clarendon and Westgate centers, which lead off them, have branches of several nationally known stores. **Alice's Shop** (✉ 83 St. Aldate's ☎ 01865/723793) sells all manner of *Alice in Wonderland* paraphernalia. **Blackwell's** (✉ 48–51 Broad St. ☎ 01865/792792), family-owned and -run since 1879, stocks an excellent selection of books. The **Covered Market** (✉ Off High St.) is a good place for a cheap sandwich and a leisurely browse; the smell of pastries follows you from cobbler to jeweler to cheese-monger. **Shepherd & Woodward** (✉ 109–113 High St. ☎ 01865/249491), a traditional tailor, specializes in university gowns, ties, and scarves. The **University of Oxford Shop** (✉ 106 High St. ☎ 01865/247414), run by the university, sells authorized clothing, ceramics, and tea towels, all emblazoned with university crests.

Side Trips to Woodstock & Blenheim Palace

Woodstock

★ ⑯ *8 mi northwest of Oxford on A44.*

Handsome 17th- and 18th-century houses line the trim streets of Woodstock, at the edge of the Cotswolds. It's best known for nearby Blenheim Palace, and in the summer, tour buses clog the village's ancient streets. On a quiet fall or spring afternoon, however, Woodstock is a sublime experience: a mellowed 18th-century church and town hall mark the central square, and along its back streets you can find flower-bedecked houses and quiet lanes right out of a 19th-century etching. The public bus route No. 20 runs (usually every half hour) between Oxford to Woodstock and costs £1.90.

WHERE TO
STAY & EAT
★
££££–£££££

✕▥ **The Feathers.** Flowery, antiques-bedecked guest rooms fill this stylish hotel in the heart of town. Feathers was created from five 17th-century houses, and its elegant courtyard is favored for a summertime meal. In winter, log fires make the public rooms cozy. The seasonal menu and upscale dining room are worth the restaurant's hefty prices (££££). You might opt for lamb served with goat-cheese ravioli or seared scallops and eggplant caviar. Note when checking out that an optional 10% service charge for lodging appears on your bill. ⊠ *Market St., 0X20 1SX* ☎ *01993/812291* 🖷 *01993/813158* ⊕ *www.feathers.co.uk* ⇱ *20 rooms, 5 suites* ⚿ *Restaurant, café, room service, lounge, dry cleaning, laundry service, meeting rooms; no a/c* ▭ *AE, DC, MC, V* ⋈ *BP.*

Blenheim Palace

⑰ *8 mi northwest of Oxford via A44 to A4095.*

Fodor'sChoice
★

So grandiose is Blenheim's masonry and so breathtaking are its articulations of splendor that it was named a World Heritage Site, the only historic house in Britain to receive the honor. Built by Sir John Vanbrugh in the early 1700s, Blenheim was given by Queen Anne and the nation to General John Churchill, first duke of Marlborough. The exterior is mind-boggling, with its huge columns, enormous pediments and obelisks, all exemplars of English baroque. Inside, lavishness continues in monumental extremes. In most of the opulent rooms, great family portraits look down at sumptuous furniture, tapestries illustrating important battles, and immense pieces of silver. For some visitors, however, the most memorable room is the small, low-ceiling chamber where Winston Churchill (his father was the younger brother of the then-duke) was born in 1874; he is buried in nearby Bladon.

> **WORD OF MOUTH**
>
> "For me, Blenheim was one of those places like Versailles . . . after a point you are almost nauseous with all the ostentation. But the setting is amazing, and the exhibit on Churchill is quite fascinating . . . You could spend a whole day exploring the grounds. Depending on your schedule, while in the area you might explore Woodstock a bit. It's a fascinating village on its own."
>
> –rickmay

Sir Winston wrote that the unique beauty of Blenheim lay in its perfect adaptation of English parkland to an Italian palace. Indeed the 2,000 acres of grounds, the work of Capability Brown, 18th-century England's most gifted landscape gardener, are arguably the best example of the "cunningly natural" park in the country. Brown declared that his object at Blenheim was to "make the Thames look like a small stream compared with the winding Danube." At points he almost succeeds—the scale of these grounds must be seen to be believed.

The Pleasure Gardens, reached by a train that stops outside the main entrance to the palace, contain some child-pleasers: a butterfly house, giant hedge maze, playground, and giant chess set. The herb and lavender garden is also delightful. The train runs every 30 minutes from 11 until 5. ⊠ *Woodstock* ☎ *01993/811325* ⊕ *www.blenheimpalace.com* 🎟 *Palace, park, and gardens: mid-Feb.–mid-May and mid-Sept.–mid-Dec. £12; June–mid-Sept. £14; park and gardens only £7 or £9, depending on season* ⊙ *Palace mid-Feb.–mid-Dec., daily 10:30–4:45; park daily 9–4:45; special events, fairs, and concerts throughout year.*

EN ROUTE After taking in Blenheim Palace, stop by **Bladon,** 2 mi southeast of Woodstock on A4095 and 6 mi northwest of Oxford, to see the small, tree-lined churchyard that is the burial place of Sir Winston Churchill. His grave is all the more impressive for its simplicity.

THAMES VALLEY ESSENTIALS

Transportation

BY AIR

The Thames Valley is convenient to major airports in London (⇨ By Air *in* Essentials).

BY BUS

If you haven't rented a car, traveling by bus is the second best way to explore the Thames Valley. The Oxford Bus Company, Megabus, and the Oxford Tube offer service to Oxford several times an hour during rush hour, and hourly throughout the night. Pick-up points in London are Victoria train and bus stations, and Baker Street and Marble Arch by the Underground stops. The Oxford Bus Company also offers "The Airline," round-trip shuttle service from Oxford to Gatwick (£25) and Heathrow (£18) every half hour.

Other local bus services, such as Stagecoach, link the towns between Oxford and Henley with services to Heathrow Airport and London. Reading Buses also connect Oxford and Reading to the airports, and First of Bracknell serves the smaller towns of Berkshire. For information about buses and other forms of public transportation, contact Traveline.

CUTTING COSTS The Oxford Bus Company offers a one-day ticket (£4) and a seven-day Freedom ticket (£12), for unlimited bus travel within Oxford.

FARES &
SCHEDULES 🚹 **First** ☎ 01344/868688 ⊕ www.firstgroup.com. **Megabus** ⊕ www.megabus.co.uk. **Oxford Bus Company** ☎ 01865/785400 ⊕ www.oxfordbus.co.uk. **Reading Buses** ☎ 0118/959-4000 ⊕ www.reading-buses.co.uk. **Stagecoach Oxford Tube** ☎ 01865/772250 ⊕ www.stagecoachbus.com/oxfordshire. **Traveline** ☎ 0870/608-2608 ⊕ www.traveline.org.uk.

BY CAR

The M4 and M40 radiate west from London, bringing Oxford (56 mi) and Reading (41 mi) within an hour's drive, except during rush hour. Although the roads are good, this wealthy section of the commuter belt has heavy traffic, even on the smaller roads. Parking in towns can be a problem, too, so allow plenty of time.

BY TRAIN

Trains to Oxford (1 hour) and the region depart from London's Paddington station. Ascot (¾ hour) is easily accessible from London: trains leave Waterloo on the half hour. For timetables, call or log on to National Rail Enquiries's Web site.

🚹 **National Rail Enquiries** ☎ 0845/748-4950 ⊕ www.nationalrail.co.uk.

Contacts & Resources

EMERGENCIES

The John Radcliffe Hospital is accessible by Bus 13 from Carfax Tower in Oxford or from the A40.

🚹 **Ambulance, fire, police** ☎ 999. **John Radcliffe Hospital** ✉ Headley Way, Oxford ☎ 01865/741166. **Princess Christian's Hospital** ✉ 12 Clarence Rd., Windsor ☎ 01753/853121.

INTERNET

There are relatively few Internet cafés in this region, most in and around Oxford. Internet access is nearly impossible to find in the smaller villages. In those areas, your best bet will be your hotel or the public library.

🚹 **Internet Cafés Mices Internet Shop** ✉ 118 High St., Oxford ☎ 01865/515955. **Wired To** ✉ 138 Magdalen Rd., Oxford ☎ 01865/727770.

TOUR OPTIONS

BOAT TOURS One ideal way to see the Thames region is from the water. Water-based tours can range from 30 minutes to all day. Hobbs and Sons covers the Henley Reach and also rents boats if you want to take the active approach. Salter's Steamers runs daily steamer cruises, mid-May to mid-September from Windsor, Oxford, Abingdon, Henley, Marlow, and Reading. Thames River Cruises conducts outings from Caversham Bridge in Reading, Easter through September. French Brothers operates river trips from the Promenade in Windsor, and from Runnymede going as far as Hampton Court.

The Environment Agency's Visit Thames Web site and telephone hotline provide information about boating, fishing, and walking the Thames.

🚹 **Environment Agency Visit Thames** ☎ 0845/601-5336 ⊕ www.visitthames.com. **French Brothers** ✉ The Promenade, Windsor ☎ 01753/851900 ⊕ www.boat-trips.co.uk.

Hobbs and Sons ✉ Station Rd., Henley-on-Thames ☎ 01491/572035 ⊕ www.hobbs-of-henley.com. **Salter's Steamers** ✉ Folly Bridge, Oxford ☎ 01865/243421 ⊕ www.salterssteamers.co.uk. **Thames River Cruises** ✉ Caversham Bridge, Reading ☎ 0118/948-1088 ⊕ www.thamesrivercruise.co.uk.

BUS TOURS City Sightseeing runs guided, open-top bus tours of Windsor for £6 (daily mid-March–October, weekends only November–late December) and of Oxford for £9 (year-round).

🚩 **City Sightseeing** ☎ 01865/790522 ⊕ www.city-sightseeing.com.

WALKING TOURS Two-hour guided walking tours leave the Oxford Tourist Information Centre (⇨ Visitor Information) at 11 and 4 daily. Tickets (£6.50, £7.50 on Saturday) include admission to some colleges. Saturday tours include Christ Church. An Inspector Morse walking tour is offered at 1:30 on Saturday (£7), and ghost tours (£5.50) run June–September and October 31 on Friday and Saturday at 8 PM. The information center also sells pamphlets detailing walking tours.

Blue Badge guides provide theme walking tours (£4) of Windsor and Eton that start at the Windsor Tourist Information Centre (⇨ Visitor Information). Tours run mid-April–August on weekends at 10:30 AM. You can also purchase self-guided walking pamphlets for 50p each.

VISITOR INFORMATION

🚩 **Henley-on-Thames** ✉ King's Arms Barn, Kings Rd., RG9 2DG ☎ 01491/578034 ⊕ www.visit-henley.co.uk. **Marlow** ✉ 31 High St., SL7 1AU ☎ 01628/483597. **Oxford** ✉ 15/16 Broad St., OX1 3AS ☎ 01865/726871 ⊕ www.oxford.gov.uk. **Oxford University** ⊕ www.ox.ac.uk. **Windsor** ✉ 24 High St., SL4 1LH ☎ 01753/743900 ⊕ www.windsor.gov.uk. **Woodstock** ✉ Park St., Oxfordshire Museum, OX20 1SN ☎ 01993/813632.

The Cotswolds & Shakespeare Country

WORD OF MOUTH

"Crowds in the Cotswolds are a bit of a myth. Most visitors come in for the day—a period that lasts from 11-ish to 4:30. They congregate in half a dozen honeypots. . . . The pleasures are small ones: scenery that's best appreciated on foot, endless small villages with lived-in churches and pubs—and the world's densest concentration of gardens. Glamour and excitement we don't do here . . . Civilization is what we specialize in."
—flanneruk

Updated by
Robert
Andrews

THE ROLLING UPLANDS OF THE COTSWOLD HILLS represent the quintessence of rural England, as immortalized in countless books, paintings, and films. This blissfully unspoiled region, deservedly popular with visitors, occupies much of the county of Gloucestershire, in west-central England, with slices of neighboring Oxfordshire, Worcestershire, and Somerset. Together these make up a sweep of land stretching from Shakespeare Country in the north almost as far as the Bristol Channel in the south. On the edge of the area are two historic towns that have absorbed, rather than compromised, the flavor of the Cotswolds: Stratford-upon-Avon, with its carefully preserved Shakespeare sites and the theaters of the famed Royal Shakespeare Company, and Regency-era Cheltenham, a spa town with remarkably elegant architecture.

More than one writer has called the the Cotswolds the very soul of England. Is it the sun, or the soil? The pretty-as-a-picture villages with the perfectly clipped hedges? The mellow, centuries-old, stone-built cottages festooned with honeysuckle? Whatever the reason, this idyllic region, which from medieval times grew prosperous on the wool trade, remains a vision of rural England. Here are time-defying churches, sleepy hamlets, and ancient farmsteads so sequestered that they seem to offer everyone the thrill of personal discovery. Hidden in sheltered valleys are fabled abodes—Sudeley Castle, Stanway House, and Snowshill Manor among them. The Cotswolds can hardly claim to be undiscovered but, happily, the area's poetic appeal has a way of surviving the tour buses, crowds, and antiques shops that sometimes pierce its timeless tranquility. Here you can taste the glories of the old English village—its stone slate roofs, low-ceiling rooms, and gardens; its atmosphere is as thick as honey, and equally as sweet.

Although tourist-packed Stratford-upon-Avon veers toward becoming "Shakespeare World," it's a fascinating place, and there's more to see— castles, churches, and countryside—in this famously lovely part of Britain. Warwickshire—the county of which Stratford is the southern nexus—is a land of sleepy villages, thatch-roof cottages, and solitary farmhouses. In Warwick, the huge fortress of Warwick Castle provides a glimpse into the country's turbulent history.

Exploring the Cotswolds & Shakespeare Country

The region's major points of interest—the Cotswold Hills, Cheltenham, and Stratford-upon-Avon—are one way to organize your explorations. The Cotswold Hills, about two hours by car from London, cover some of southern England's most beautiful terrain, with which the characteristic stone cottages throughout the area are in perfect harmony. To the west of the Cotswolds lies Cheltenham, a former spa town. To the north of the Cotswolds, Stratford is surrounded by tiny villages, some with Shakespearean connections; magnificent Warwick Castle is nearby.

About the Restaurants

Good restaurants dot the Cotswolds, thanks to a steady flow of fine chefs seeking to cater to wealthy locals and waves of demanding visitors. The country's food revolution is in full evidence here. Restaurants have never had a problem with a fresh-food supply: excellent regional produce, salmon from the Rivers Severn and Wye, local lamb and pork, and pheasant, partridge, quail, and grouse in season. Also look for Gloucestershire Old Spot pork, bacon, and sausage on area menus. Perhaps surprisingly, Stratford has few restaurants serving sophisticated cuisine, though many reasonably priced bistros offer a broad choice of international fare.

About the Hotels

The hotels of this region are among Britain's most highly rated—from bed-and-breakfasts in village homes and farmhouses to luxurious country-house hotels. Many hotels present themselves as deeply traditional rural retreats, but some have opted for a sleeker, fresher style, with boldly contemporary or minimalist furnishings. B&Bs are a cheaper alternative to the fancier hotels, and most hotels offer two- and three-day packages. Stratford holds accommodations to fit every wallet, and for the most part they are well maintained—the best establishments are the older, centrally located ones, often with fine period architecture. As Stratford is *so* popular with theatergoers, book well ahead whenever possible. You should also reserve ahead if you want to visit Cheltenham in mid-March when the National Hunt Festival takes place. Keep in mind when making reservations that hotels can front on heavily trafficked roads; ask for quiet rooms.

WHAT IT COSTS In pounds				
£££££	**££££**	**£££**	**££**	**£**
RESTAURANTS over £22	£18–£22	£13–£17	£7–£12	under £7
HOTELS over £160	£120–£160	£90–£119	£60–£89	under £60

Restaurant prices are for a main course at dinner. Hotel prices are for two people in a standard double room in high season, including V.A.T., with no meals or, if indicated, CP (with continental breakfast), BP (Breakfast Plan, with full breakfast), or MAP (Modified American Plan, with breakfast and dinner).

Timing

This area contains some of England's most popular destinations, and you would do well to avoid weekends in the busier areas of the Cotswolds. During the week, even in summer, you may hardly see a soul in the more remote spots. Cheltenham is a workaday place that can absorb tour buses comfortably; Cheltenham does, however, get full at festival time and during race meetings. Note that the private properties of Hidcote Manor, Snowshill Manor, and Sudeley Castle close in winter. Hidcote Manor Garden is at its best in spring and fall. Avoid visits to Stratford and Warwick Castle on weekends and school holidays, and take in the main Shakespeare shrines in the early morning to see them at their least frenetic. If you visit Stratford during the Shakespeare Birthday Celebrations, usually on the weekend nearest to April 23, make hotel reservations as early as possible.

TOP REASONS TO GO

A drink in a Cotswold pub: The classic pubs here press all the right buttons—low wooden beams, horse brasses, inglenook fireplaces, and hanging tankards. Log fires in winter and beer gardens in summer are further enticements. Many pubs date back 300 years or more, but some have added smart dining areas. Most now offer tea and coffee, and also welcome children.

Finding the perfect village: With their golden stone cottages, Cotswold villages tend to be improbably picturesque; the hamlets of Upper and Lower Slaughter are among the most seductive. Part of the fun is to take almost any scenic lane or head for any evocatively named cluster of houses on the map.

Hidcote Manor Gardens: In a region rich with imaginative garden displays, Hidcote lays good claim to be the most eminent. Exotic shrubs from around the world and the famous "garden rooms" are the highlights of this Arts and Crafts masterpiece.

Shakespeare in Stratford: To see a play by Shakespeare in the town where he was born—and perhaps after you've visited his birthplace or other sites—is a magical experience. The Royal Shakespeare Company's productions are often outstanding.

Shopping in Cheltenham: The grand Regency terraces of Cheltenham, worth a look in themselves, make a wonderful setting for "country-chic" boutiques, antiques shops, and gift stores.

6

THE COTSWOLDS

The Thames rises among the limestone Cotswold Hills, and a more delightful cradle could not be imagined for that historic river. The Cotswolds are among the best-preserved rural districts of England, and the quiet but lovely grays and ambers of the stone buildings here are truly unsurpassed. Much has been written about the area's towns, which age has mellowed, but on closer inspection, the architecture of the villages differs little from that of villages elsewhere in England. Their distinction lies instead in the character of their surroundings: the valleys are deep and rolling, and cozy hamlets appear to drip in foliage from church tower to garden gate. Beyond the town limits, you may often discover the "high wild hills and rough uneven ways" that Shakespeare wrote about.

Over the centuries, quarries of honey-color stone have yielded building blocks for many Cotswold houses and churches and have transformed little towns into realms of gold. Nowhere else in Britain does that superb combination of church tower and gabled manor house shine so brightly, nowhere else are the hedges so perfectly clipped, nor the churchyards so peaceful. There's an elusive spirit about the Cotswolds, so make Chipping Campden, Moreton-in-Marsh, or Stow-on-the-Wold your headquarters for a few days, and wander for a while. Then ask yourself what the area is all about. Its secret seems shared by two things—

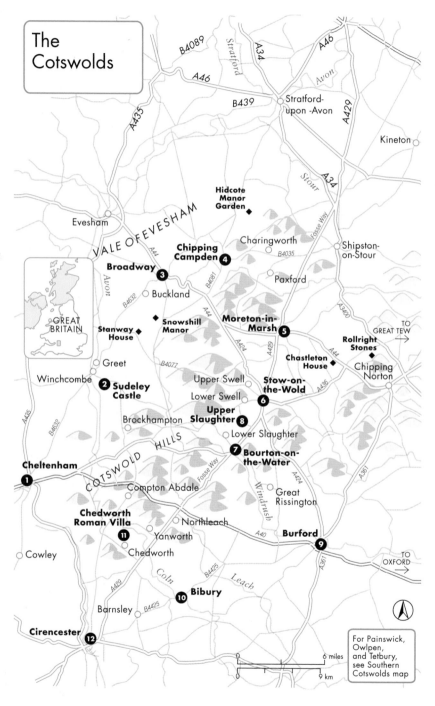

The Cotswolds

B4089
Stratford
A34
A46

A46

B439
Stratford-upon-Avon
A429

Kineton

A435

A34
Stour

Hidcote Manor Garden

Evesham

VALE OF EVESHAM

Charingworth
B4035

Shipston-on-Stour

Chipping Campden ❹

A44

Paxford

Broadway ❸

Buckland
B4632

Fosse Way

B4081

GREAT BRITAIN

Snowshill Manor

A44

Moreton-in-Marsh ❺

A3400

TO GREAT TEW →

Stanway House

A424

A429

Rollright Stones

Chastleton House

Greet

B4077

Upper Swell

Stow-on-the-Wold ❻

A44

Chipping Norton

Winchcombe

❷ **Sudeley Castle**

Lower Swell

A436

B4632

Brockhampton

Upper Slaughter ❽

Lower Slaughter

COTSWOLD HILLS

❼ **Bourton-on-the-Water**

Cheltenham ❶

Compton Abdale

Fosse Way

Windrush

Great Rissington

A361

A424

Chedworth Roman Villa ⑪

Northleach

Yanworth

A40

Burford ❾

Cowley

Chedworth

Coln

B4425

Leach

A361

TO OXFORD →

A429

❿ **Bibury**

Barnsley
B4425

Cirencester ⑫

0 ———— 6 miles
0 ———— 9 km

For Painswick, Owlpen, and Tetbury, see Southern Cotswolds map sheep and stone. The combination is not as strange as it may sound. These were once the great sheep-rearing areas of England, and during the peak of prosperity in the Middle Ages, Cotswold wool was in demand the world over. This made the local merchants rich, but many gave back to the Cotswolds by restoring old churches (the famous "wool churches" of the region) or building rows of almshouses of limestone now seasoned to a glorious golden-gray.

Begin with Cheltenham—the largest town in the area and a gateway to the Cotswolds, but slightly outside the boundaries—then move on to Sudeley Castle, Stanway House, and Snowshill Manor, among the most impressive houses of the region; the oversold village of Broadway, which has many rivals for beauty hereabouts; Chipping Campden—the Cotswold cognoscenti's favorite; and Hidcote Manor, one of the most spectacular gardens in England. Then circle back south, down through Moreton-in-Marsh, Stow-on-the-Wold, Upper Slaughter, Lower Slaughter, Bourton-on-the-Water, and end with Bibury, Tetbury, and Owlpen. This is definitely a region where it pays to go off the beaten track to take a look at that village among the trees.

6

Cheltenham

❶ *50 mi north of Bath, 13 mi east of Gloucester, 99 mi west of London.*

Although Cheltenham has acquired a reputation as snooty—the population (around 110,000) is generally well-heeled and conservative—it's also cosmopolitan. The town has excellent restaurants and bars, fashionable stores, and a thriving cultural life. Its primary claim to renown, however, is its architecture, rivaling Bath's in its Georgian elegance, with wide, tree-lined streets, crescents, and terraces with row houses, balconies, and iron railings. Like Bath, Cheltenham owes part of its fame to mineral springs. By 1740 the first spa was built, and after a visit from George III and Queen Charlotte in 1788, the town dedicated itself to idleness and enjoyment. "A polka, parson-worshipping place"—in the words of resident Lord Tennyson—Cheltenham gained its reputation for snobbishness when stiff-collared Raj majordomos returned from India to find that the springs—the only purely natural alkaline waters in England—were the most effective cure for their "tropical ailments."

Great Regency architectural set pieces—Lansdown Crescent, Pittville Spa, and the Lower Assembly Rooms, among them—were built solely to adorn the town. The Rotunda building (1826) at the top of Montpellier Walk—now a bank—contains the spa's original "pump room," in which the mineral waters were on draft. More than 30 statues adorn the storefronts of Montpellier Walk. Wander past Imperial Square, with its ironwork balconies, past the ornate Neptune's Fountain, and along the Promenade. In spring and summer, lush flower gardens enhance the town's buildings, attracting many visitors.

From the 1880s onward, Cheltenham was at the forefront of the Arts and Crafts movement, and the **Cheltenham Art Gallery and Museum** contains fine displays of William Morris textiles, furniture by Charles Voysey, and simple wood and metal pieces by Ernest Gimson. Decorative arts, such as Chinese ceramics, are well represented, and British artists, including Stanley Spencer and Vanessa Bell, make their mark in the art gallery. Other exhibits focus on local archaeology and history; one is devoted to Edward Wilson, who traveled with Robert Scott to the Antarctic on Scott's ill-fated 1912 expedition. ⊠ *Clarence St.* ☎ *01242/237431* ⊕ *www. cheltenhammuseum.org.uk* ⌑ *Free* ⊙ *Mon.–Sat. 10–5:20 (11–5:20 first Thurs. of month).*

> ### FLOWERS & FESTIVALS
>
> Parts of the town may look like something out of a Gilbert and Sullivan stage set, but Cheltenham is the site of two of England's most progressive arts festivals—the Cheltenham Festival of Literature and the town's music festival—as well as a jazz fest.

The grandest of the spa buildings remaining in town, the **Pittville Pump Room** is set amid parkland, a 20-minute walk from the town center. The classic Regency structure, built in the late 1820s, now serves mainly as a concert hall and a theatrical venue but still offers its musty mineral waters to the strong of stomach. The Pump Room may not be accessible during functions—call to check. ⊠ *E. Approach Dr., Pittville* ☎ *01242/523852* ⌑ *Free* ⊙ *Wed.–Mon. 10–4.*

Where to Stay & Eat

★
££££–£££££

✕ **Le Champignon Sauvage.** The relatively short, perfectly balanced menu at this excellent, well-established restaurant showcases contemporary French cooking. Relax in a room with cream walls and modern art as you indulge in dishes such as pressed terrine of rabbit confit followed by Cinderford lamb. Desserts, including hot fig tart, are worth the calories; you can choose among many cheeses as well. Fixed-price menus at lunch and dinner help keep the cost down. ⊠ *24 Suffolk Rd.* ☎ *01242/573449* ▭ *AE, DC, MC, V* ⊙ *Closed Sun., Mon., 3 wks in June, and 10 days in Dec. and Jan.*

££–££££

✕ **Le Petit Blanc.** In the same building as Queen's Hotel, this offshoot of renowned chef Raymond Blanc's Manoir aux Quat' Saisons in Great Milton offers French-provincial cooking in contemporary surroundings that harmonize well with the good-size Regency windows. The impressive menu takes in everything from herb pancakes with mushrooms, ham, and kirsch sauce to lemon sole meunière with new potatoes. Among the lip-smacking desserts is grilled pineapple with rum baba and piña colada sauce. ⊠ *The Promenade* ☎ *01242/266800* ▭ *AE, DC, MC, V.*

£££

✕ **The Daffodil.** Brasserie cuisine is the focus of this former cinema that preserves the heyday of 1930s elegance. Admire the art-deco trappings, sip an aperitif in the Circle Bar, and then sweep down the staircase to watch the chefs at work "on stage." Among the delightful dishes are venison marinated in gin and juniper berries. There's live jazz on Monday, when a special jazz menu is offered. ⊠ *18–20 Suffolk Parade* ☎ *01242/700055* ▭ *AE, MC, V* ⊙ *Closed Sun.*

£–££ ✕ **Boogaloos.** Choose between the brightly colored, vibrant rooms upstairs or the sofa seating in the relaxed basement for lunches of salads, baked potatoes, or more substantial fare such as shredded lamb with Thai noodles. Leave room for the homemade cakes and puddings. ⊠ *16 Regent St.* ☎ *01242/702259* ▱ *MC, V* ⊘ *No dinner.*

£££££ ▦ **Cowley Manor.** Good-bye floral prints: this Georgian mansion on 55 acres brings luxury country-house hotels into the 21st century by using modern fabrics and furniture but keeping the comfort level high enough to soothe a chic clientele. Witty sculptures and lighting complement the public rooms, bedrooms are brightly colored, and bathrooms are suitably trendy, with glass walls and large showers. Half the rooms are in the house; the rest fill a transformed stable. The spa, set into the ground, looks like a work of art. Cowley Manor is 5 mi south of Cheltenham. ⊠ *Cowley GL53 9NL* ☎ *01242/870900* ▤ *01242/870901* ⊕ *www.cowleymanor.com* ↩ *30 rooms* ⚘ *Restaurant, cable TV with movies, in-room DVDs, in-room data ports, 2 pools (1 indoor), gym, sauna, spa, steam room, billiards* ▱ *AE, DC, MC, V* ⧈ *CP.*

£££–££££ ▦ **Hotel Kandinsky.** A fashionably cool style that doesn't stint on the comfort factor makes a stay in this Georgian hotel (part of the trendy Alias minichain) a memorable experience at a fairly sensible price. Colorful rugs, huge potted plants, and the occasional touch of eccentricity offset the antiques in the guest rooms and clubby public rooms. A Mediterranean-style bistro and a hip basement nightclub are on the premises, and guests have access to a nearby pool and gym. ⊠ *Bayshill Rd., GL50 3AS* ☎ *01242/527788* ▤ *01242/226412* ⊕ *www.aliashotels.com* ↩ *48 rooms* ⚘ *Restaurant, cable TV, in-room VCRs, Wi-Fi, bar, nightclub, meeting rooms; no a/c* ▱ *AE, DC, MC, V.*

££ ▦ **Abbey Hotel.** Relaxed and family-run, this hotel in a quiet terrace near the center of town offers great value. Bedrooms are simple but stylish, decorated in subtle tones, and the breakfast area overlooks the well-stocked garden. ⊠ *14–16 Bath Parade, GL53 7HN* ☎ *01242/516053* ▤ *01242/513034* ⊕ *www.abbeyhotel-cheltenham.com* ↩ *12 rooms* ⚘ *Bar, no-smoking rooms; no a/c* ▱ *AE, MC, V* ⧈ *BP.*

Nightlife & the Arts

The grand, late Victorian **Everyman Theatre** (⊠ Regent St. ☎ 01242/572573) is an intimate venue for opera, dance, concerts, and plays. ■ **TIP→** You can often catch pre-or post-West End productions here, at a fraction of big city prices.

For information on the town's ambitious lineup of festivals, contact the **Festival Office** (⊠ Town Hall, Imperial Sq., Cheltenham GL50 1QA ☎ 01242/227979 ⊕ www.cheltenhamfestivals.co.uk). The 10-day **Festival of Literature** in October brings together world-renowned authors, actors, and critics for hundreds of readings events. Cheltenham's famous **International Festival of Music,** during the first half of July, highlights new compositions, often conducted by the composers, and classical pieces. The **International Jazz Festival,** held over five days in April and May, presents noted musicians. The **Science Festival,** which takes place over five days in June, attracts leading scientists and writers.

Sports

Important steeplechase races take place at **Cheltenham Racecourse** (✉ Prestbury Park ☎ 01242/513014), north of the town center; the Gold Cup awards crown the last day of the National Hunt Festival in mid-March.

Shopping

This is serious shopping territory. A stroll along Montpellier Walk and then along the flower-bedecked Promenade brings you to high-quality specialty stores and boutiques. A bubble-blowing Wishing Fish Clock, designed by Kit Williams, dominates the Regent Arcade, a modern shopping area behind the Promenade. General markets are held every Sunday at the Cheltenham Racecourse and every Thursday morning off Lower High Street. An indoor antiques market is open Monday through Saturday at 54 Suffolk Road; there are other antiques shops in the Suffolk area. A farmers market takes place on the Promenade on the second and fourth Friday of the month.

Cavendish House (✉ 32–48 The Promenade ☎ 01242/521300) is a high-quality department store with designer fashions. **Early Bird** (✉ 5 Suffolk Rd. ☎ 01242/233507) displays antiques, faux antiques, and enticing bric-a-brac. **Laura Ashley** (✉ 92 The Promenade ☎ 01242/580770) sells products in its distinctive, Arts and Crafts–influenced style, including clothes, handbags, and gift items. **Martin** (✉ 19 The Promenade ☎ 01242/ 522821) carries a good stock of modern jewelry.

Sudeley Castle

❷ *9 mi northeast of Cheltenham.*

One of the grand showpieces of the Cotswolds, Sudeley Castle was the home and burial place of Catherine Parr (1512–48), Henry VIII's sixth and last wife, who outlived him by one year. Here Catherine undertook, in her later years, the education of the ill-fated Lady Jane Grey and the future queen, Princess Elizabeth. Sudeley, for good reason, has been called a woman's castle. The term "castle" is misleading, for it looks more like a Tudor-era palace, with a peaceful air that belies its turbulent history. During the 17th century, Charles I took refuge here, causing Oliver Cromwell's army to besiege the castle, leaving it in ruins until the Dent-Brocklehurst family stepped in with a 19th-century renovation. The 14 acres of gardens, which include the spectacular roses of the Queen's Garden and a Tudor knot garden, are the setting for Shakespeare performances, concerts, and other events in summer. Inside the castle, however, visitors see only the West Wing, with the Long Room and temporary exhibitions that focus on such subjects as the Tudors, the Civil War, and the Victorians. The private apartments of Lord and Lady Ashcombe, where you can see paintings by Van Dyck, Rubens, Turner, and Reynolds, are viewable only on Connoisseur Tours on Wednesday and Thursday (£15, including entry to the public rooms and a guidebook). Accommodations in 13 cottages on the grounds are booked for a minimum of four-night stays. ✉ *Off B4632, Winchcombe* ☎ *01242/602308, 01242/ 604357 recorded information* ⊕ *www.sudeleycastle.co.uk* ✍ *£7.20* ☉ *Mar.–mid-Apr., May, and Sept.–mid-Oct., Sun.–Thurs. 10:30–5; mid- to late Apr., June–Aug., and late Oct., daily 10:30–5.*

Broadway

❸ *17 mi northeast of Cheltenham.*

The Cotswold town to end all Cotswold towns, Broadway has become a favorite of day-trippers. William Morris first discovered the delights of this village, and J. M. Barrie, Vaughan Williams, and Edward Elgar soon followed. Today you may want to avoid Broadway in summer, when it's clogged with cars and buses. Named for its handsome, wide main street (well worth a stroll), the village includes the renowned Lygon Arms and numerous antiques shops, tea parlors, and boutiques. Step off onto Broadway's back-roads and alleys and you can discover any number of honey-color houses and colorful gardens.

Among the attractions of **Broadway Tower Country Park,** on the outskirts of town, is its tower, an 18th-century "folly" built by the sixth earl of Coventry and later used by William Morris as a retreat. Exhibits describe the tower's past, and the view from the top takes in three counties. Peaceful countryside surrounds you on the nature trails and picnic grounds. ⊠ *Off A44* ☏ *01386/852390* ⌷ *Park free, tower £3.50* ⊙ *Tower Apr.–Oct., daily 10:30–5; Nov.–Mar., weekends 10:30–4.*

Snowshill, 3 mi south of Broadway, is one of the most unspoiled of all Cotswold villages. Snuggled beneath Oat Hill, with little room for expansion, the hamlet is centered around an old burial ground, the ★ 19th-century St. Barnabas Church, and **Snowshill Manor,** a splendid 17th-century house that brims with the collections of Charles Paget Wade, gathered between 1919 and 1956. Over the door of the house is Wade's family motto, *Nequid pereat* ("Let nothing perish"). The rooms are bursting with Tibetan scrolls, spinners' tools, ship models, Persian lamps, and bric-a-brac. The Green Room displays 26 suits of Japanese samurai armor. Children love the place. Outside, an imaginative terraced garden provides an exquisite frame for the house. ⊠ *Off A44, Snowshill* ☏ *01386/852410* ⊕ *www.nationaltrust.org. uk* ⌷ *£7.30, garden only £4* ⊙ *House: late Mar.–Oct., Wed.–Sun. noon–5. Garden: late Mar.–Oct., Wed.–Sun. 11–5:30.*

★ **Stanway House,** a perfect Cotswold manor of glowing limestone in the small village of Stanway, dates from the Jacobean era. Its triple-gabled gatehouse is a Cotswold landmark, and towering windows dominate the house's Great Hall. Divided by mullions and transoms into 60 panes, these windows are "so mellowed by time"—to quote Lady Cynthia Asquith (a former chatelaine)—"that whenever the sun shines through their amber and green glass, the effect is of a vast honeycomb." They illuminate a 22-foot-long shuffleboard table from 1620 and an 18th-century bouncing exercise machine. The other well-worn rooms are adorned with family portraits, tattered tapestries, vintage armchairs, and, at times, Lord Neidpath himself, the current owner. The partly restored baroque water garden has a fountain, built in 2004, that shoots up 300 feet; it's the tallest in Britain. On the grounds is a cricket pavilion built by J. M. Barrie, author of *Peter Pan,* who leased the house. To get to Stanway, about 5 mi south of Broadway, take B4632 south from town, turning left at B4077.

6

✉ *Off B4077, Stanway* ☎ *01386/584469* ⊕ *www.stanwayfountain. co.uk* 🖃 *House and fountain £6; fountain only £4* ☉ *House and fountain: June–Aug., Tues. and Thurs. 2–5; fountain only Sat. in July and Aug. 2–5; fountain shoots at 2:45 and 4 for 30 mins.*

Where to Stay & Eat

★ **£££££** ✕🖼 **Buckland Manor.** As an alternative to the razzmatazz of Broadway, you can splurge at this exceptional hotel 2 mi away in the idyllic hamlet of Buckland. The land was valued at £9 in the 11th-century *Domesday Book,* and the sprawling stone building dates back to Jacobean times. Public areas and guest rooms are plushly comfortable, with old pictures, fine rugs, and antiques everywhere. The gardens are well groomed and tranquil. In the baronial and expensive restaurant (jacket and tie required: £££££), you choose from a menu of traditional fare with some contemporary touches; monkfish comes with mussel soufflé, for example. ✉ *Off B4632, Buckland WR12 7LY* ☎ *01386/852626* 🖨 *01386/ 853557* ⊕ *www.bucklandmanor.co.uk* ⬚ *13 rooms* ♻ *Restaurant, cable TV, putting green, tennis court, pool, croquet, bar; no a/c, no kids under 12* ▭ *AE, DC, MC, V* ⦿⌷ *BP.*

££££–£££££ ✕🖼 **Dormy House Hotel.** Guest rooms in this converted 17th-century farmhouse overlook the Vale of Evesham from high on the Cotswolds ridge, one of the region's most celebrated vistas. Luxury rules at this establishment, where you can relax by a fireplace or in one of the bars. Traditional pieces and a mixture of brass and carved bedsteads furnish the beamed bedrooms. Noted in the region, the restaurant (£££–£££££) has a superlative wine list and specializes in contemporary fare such as Cornish sea bass with with sweet potato and marsh samphire (a fleshy saltwater plant). A more economical eating option is the beamed Barn Owl bar, a gastro-pub. The hotel is 2 mi north of Broadway. ✉ *Willersey Hill, WR12 7LF* ☎ *01386/852711* 🖨 *01386/858636* ⊕ *www. dormyhouse.co.uk* ⬚ *47 rooms* ♻ *Restaurant, café, in-room data ports, putting green, gym, sauna, steam room, billiards, croquet, 3 bars, meeting rooms, some pets allowed (fee); no a/c* ▭ *AE, DC, MC, V* ⦿⌷ *BP.*

Chipping Campden

❹ *4 mi east of Broadway, 18 mi northeast of Cheltenham.*

Undoubtedly one of the most beautiful towns in the area, Chipping Campden, with its population of about 2,500, is the Cotswolds in a microcosm—it has St. James, the region's most impressive church; frozen-in-time streets; a silk mill that was once the center of the Guild of Handicrafts; and pleasant (and not touristy) shops. One of the area's most seductive settings unfolds before you as you travel on B4081 through sublime English countryside and happen upon the town, tucked in a slight valley. North of town is lovely Hidcote Manor Gardens.

The soaring pinnacled tower of **St. James,** a prime example of a Cotswold wool church (rebuilt in the 15th century with money from wool merchants), announces the town from a distance; it's worth stepping inside to see the lofty nave. It recalls the old saying, which became popular because of the vast numbers of houses of worship in the Cotswolds, "As sure as God's in Gloucestershire." Nearby, on Church Street, is an im-

Arts & Crafts in the Cotswolds

CLOSE UP

THE ARTS AND CRAFTS MOVEMENT flourished throughout Britain in the late 19th and early 20th centuries, but the Cotswolds are most closely associated with it. The godfather of the movement was designer William Morris (1834–96), whose home for the last 25 years of his life, Kelmscott Manor in Gloucestershire, became the headquarters of the school. A lecture by Morris, "The Beauty of Life," delivered in Birmingham in 1880, included the injunction that became the guiding principle of the movement: "Have nothing in your houses which you do not know to be useful or believe to be beautiful."

Driven by the belief that the spirit of medieval arts and crafts was being degraded and destroyed by the mass production and aggressive capitalism of the Victorian era, and aided by a dedicated core of artisans, Morris revolutionized the art of house design and decoration. His work with textiles was particularly influential.

Many of Morris's followers were influenced by the Cotswold countryside, such as the designer and architect Charles Robert Ashbee, who transferred his Guild of Handicrafts from London to Chipping Campden in 1902. The village holds a permanent exhibition of pieces by the original group and those who followed in their wake. Their work can also be seen at Cheltenham's Art Gallery and Museum, and, in its original context, at Rodmarton Manor outside Tetbury (which Ashbee declared the finest application of the movement's ideals), and at Owlpen Manor. To see the Arts and Crafts ethic applied to horticulture, visit Hidcote Manor Garden, near Chipping Campden.

---

portant row of almshouses dating from King James I's reign. ⌧ *Church St.* ☎ *01386/841927* ⊕ *www.stjameschurchcampden.co.uk* ⌧ *£1 donation suggested* ☉ *Mar.–Oct., Mon.–Sat. 10–5, Sun. 2–6; Feb. and Nov., Mon.–Sat. 11–4, Sun. 2–4; Dec. and Jan., Mon.–Sat. 11–3, Sun. 2–3.*

The broad High Street, lined with stone houses and shops, follows a captivating curve; in the center, on Market Street, is the **Market Hall,** a gabled Jacobean structure built by Sir Baptiste Hycks in 1627 "for the sale of local produce."

In 1902 the Guild of Handicrafts took over the **Silk Mill,** and Arts and Crafts evangelist Charles Robert Ashbee (1863–1942) brought 150 acolytes here from London, including 50 guildsmen, to revive and practice such skills as cabinetmaking and bookbinding. The operation folded in 1920, but the refurbished building houses an exhibition and workshops, including those of a silversmith, jeweler, and stone carver. ⌧ *Sheep St.* ⌧ *Free* ☉ *Weekdays 9–5, Sat. 9–1.*

Fodor'sChoice ★ Laid out around a Cotswold manor house, **Hidcote Manor Garden** is arguably the most interesting and attractive large garden in Britain. Crowds are correspondingly large at the height of the season, but it's worthwhile anytime. A horticulturist from the United States, Major Lawrence Johnstone, created the garden in 1907 in the Arts and Crafts style. Johnstone was an imaginative gardener and widely traveled plantsman who brought back specimens from all over the world. The formal part of the garden is arranged in "rooms" without roofs, separated by hedges and often with fine topiary work and walls. Besides the variety of plants, what's impressive are the different effects created, from calm open spaces to areas packed with flowers. ■ TIP→ Look out for one of Johnson's earliest schemes, the red borders of dahlias, poppies, fuschias, lobelias, and roses; the tall hornbeam hedges; and the Bathing Pool garden, where the pool is so wide there's scarcely space to walk. The White Garden was probably the forerunner of the popular white gardens at Sissinghurst and Glyndebourne. ⊠ *Hidcote Bartrim, 4 mi northeast of Chipping Campden* ☎ *01386/ 438333* ⊕ *www.nationaltrust.org.uk* ⊠ *£7* ☉ *Late Mar.–Sept., Mon.–Wed. and weekends 10:30–6; Oct., Mon.–Wed. and weekends 10:30–5; last admission 1 hr before closing.*

Where to Stay & Eat

£££££ ✕⚅ Charingworth Manor. Views of the Cotswold countryside are limitless from this 14th-century manor-house hotel a short distance outside town. Mullioned windows and oak beams enhance the sofa-filled sitting room, and bedrooms have English floral fabrics and antique and period furniture. T. S. Eliot, a guest in the 1930s, used to enjoy walking the 50 acres of grounds. The restaurant (£38 fixed-price menu), with its low-beam ceilings, is attractive but somewhat expensive, and serves both traditional and Mediterranean-inspired dishes such as roast rump of lamb on a bean cassoulet. The hotel is 3 mi east of Chipping Campden. ⊠ *Charingworth GL55 6NS* ☎ *01386/593555* 🖷 *01386/593353* ⊕ *www.englishrosehotels.co.uk* ⮑ *23 rooms, 3 suites* ⌂ *Restaurant, in-room safes, cable TV, tennis court, indoor pool, sauna, steam room, billiards, croquet, meeting rooms; no a/c* ⊟ *AE, DC, MC, V* ⫴⦿⫴ *BP.*

£££££ ✕⚅ Cotswold House. The enduring delight of this luxury hotel in the center of Chipping Campden is the elegant harmony with which the up-to-the-minute design and fittings blend into the setting of an 18th-century Cotswold manor house. From the swirling staircase in the entrance to the guest rooms studded with contemporary art and high-tech gadgetry, it's a winning formula. The lounges invite lingering, and the patio and spacious garden offer seclusion. The formal Juliana's Restaurant (£££££; no lunch except Sunday), where there are fixed-price menus, and the livelier and cheaper Hick's Brasserie (£££–££££) offer creative takes on English and Mediterranean dishes. Hick's is open all day and is worth a stop even if you aren't staying here. The same owners run the somewhat less expensive Noel Arms Hotel; guests there have access to Cotswold House's facilities. ⊠ *The Square, GL55 6AN* ☎ *01386/ 840330* 🖷 *01386/840310* ⊕ *www.cotswoldhouse.com* ⮑ *21 rooms, 8 suites* ⌂ *2 restaurants, 2 bars, in-room data ports, Wi-Fi, cable TV, minibars; no a/c* ⊟ *AE, DC, MC, V* ⫴⦿⫴ *BP.*

££ ✕⚅ Churchill Arms. This small country gastro-pub with rooms, 1 mi southeast of Chipping Campden, makes for an intimate stay. Plain wooden tables and benches, sepia prints, a flagstone floor, and a roaring fire provide the backdrop for excellent food (££–£££). Daily specials—steamed lemon sole filled with salmon and chive mousse, and pot-roasted partridge with parsnips and red wine, for example—appear on the blackboard. Upstairs bedrooms aren't large but are nicely furnished with antiques; two are in a new wing. ⊠ *Off B4035, Paxford GL55 6XH* ☎ *01386/594000* 🖷 *01386/594005* ⊕ *www.thechurchillarms.com* ⇋ *4 rooms* ♿ *Restaurant, in-room VCRs, no-smoking rooms; no a/c* ▭ *MC, V* ⧠ *BP.*

££–£££ 🖾 **Badgers Hall.** Expect a friendly welcome at this antique B&B above a tearoom just across from the Market Hall. The spacious, spotless rooms have low, beamed ceilings and exposed stonework. Midweek guests are greeted with tea and scrumptious fresh scones on arrival, and the generous breakfast will set you up for the day. Book ahead. ⊠ *High St., GL55 6HB* ☎ *01386/840839* ⊕ *www.badgershall.com* ⇋ *2 rooms* ♿ *No smoking, no kids under 10* ▭ *No credit cards* ⧠ *BP.*

Shopping

At **Hart** (⊠ The Silk Mill, Sheep St. ☎ 01386/841100), descendants of an original member of the Guild of Handicrafts specialize in making silver items. **Martin Gotrel** (⊠ Camperdene House, High St. ☎ 01386/ 841360) crafts fine traditional and contemporary jewelry.

Moreton-in-Marsh

❺ *9 mi south of Chipping Campden, 18 mi northeast of Cheltenham, 5 mi north of Stow-on-the-Wold.*

In Moreton-in-Marsh, the houses have been built not around a central square but along a street wide enough to accommodate a market. The village has fine views across the hills. One local landmark is St. David's Church, which has a tower of honey-gold ashlar. This town of about 3,500 also possesses one of the last remaining curfew towers, dated 1633; curfew dates to the time of the Norman Conquest, when a bell was rung to "cover-fire" for the night against any invaders. From Chipping Campden, take B4081 south, then A44 south and east to reach Moreton-in-Marsh. The town has train service from London daily.

Supposed to be the largest street market in the Cotswolds, the **Tuesday market** takes over the center of the main street between 8 and 4, offering a mix of household goods, fruit and vegetables, and some arts-and-crafts stalls, gift items, and jewelry. It's no newcomer: it was chartered in 1227.

It comes as somewhat of an architectural surprise to see the blue onion domes and miniature minarets of **Sezincote,** a mellow stone house tucked into a valley near Moreton-in-Marsh. Created in the early 19th century, the house and estate were the vision of Sir Charles Cockerell, who made a fortune in the East India Company. He employed his architect brother, Samuel Pepys Cockerell, to "Indianize" the residence with Hindu and Muslim motifs. Note the peacock-tail arches surrounding the windows of the 1st floor. The exotic garden, Hindu-temple folly, and Indian-style bridge have appealed to visitors ever since the future George IV came to the estate in 1807 (and was inspired to create that Xanadu of Brighton, the Royal Pavilion). Note that children are allowed indoors only at the owners' discretion. ⊠ *Off A44* ☎ *01386/700444* 🖾 *House and grounds £6, grounds £4* ☉ *House May–July and Sept., Thurs. and Fri. 2:30–6; grounds Jan.–Nov., Thurs. and Fri. and national holidays 2–6 or dusk.*

Visiting Cotswold Gardens

PERHAPS IT'S THE SHEER BEAUTY OF THIS AREA that has inspired the creation of so many superb gardens. In 2007, the Cotswolds is celebrating the Year of the Cotswold Garden with special events, activities, and packages; check with ⊕ www.cotswolds.com or Tourist Information Centres about events and a free Garden Gate pass with special offers.

The Arts and Crafts movement in Britain transformed not only interior design but also the world of gardening; at Hidcote Manor Garden, a much-visited masterpiece of the style, hedges and walls set off vistas and surround distinct themed garden rooms. Rodmarton Manor also has a garden in this style.

In the Cotswolds, as elsewhere in England, gardens often complement a stately home and deserve as close a look as the house. At Sudeley Castle, the home of Catherine Parr (Henry VIII's last wife), for example, explore the 19th-century Queen's Garden, beloved for its roses. Britain wouldn't be Britain without a touch of eccentricity, and in the Cotswolds the garden at the Indian-style manor of Sezincote, with its temple to a Hindu god, supplies a satisfying blend of the stately and the exotic. In contrast, the 18th-century Painswick Rococo Garden, with its Gothic screen and other intriguing structures, has a pleasant intimacy. Still more different in scale and style is Westonbirt National Arboreturm, near Tetbury, with its magnificent collection of trees.

Eager to see more? The National Garden Scheme (⊕ www.ngs.org.uk) publishes annual "yellow books" that list all gardens open for individual counties and for the whole country; cost is £1 to £2 for a county, £7.99 for the whole country. Bookstores sell these, too. Also *see* Discounts & Deals *in* Essentials; depending on your itinerary, buying a pass or joining the National Trust may save you money on admissions.

Where to Stay & Eat

££ ✕ Bell Inn. The coach house of this 18th-century hostelry holds spacious but modest guest rooms, still with the original beams, and furnished with period pieces, deep carpets, and comfy sofas. The pub (££) has a courtyard and garden and prepares such dishes as trout with honey and almonds and venison sausages. In summer you can join in the obscure Cotswold game of Aunt Sally, which involves hitting a moving target with something akin to a rolling pin. ⊠ *High St., GL56 0AE* ☎ *01608/651688* ☎ *01608/652195* ✒ *5 rooms* ⚮ *Restaurant, bar, some pets allowed; no a/c, no room phones* ▤ MC, V ⦿ BP.

Stow-on-the-Wold

❻ *5 mi south of Moreton-in-Marsh, 15 mi east of Cheltenham.*

At an elevation of 800 feet, Stow is the highest town in the Cotswolds—"Stow-on-the-Wold, where the wind blows cold" is the age-old saying. Built around a wide square, Stow's imposing golden stone houses have been discreetly converted into a good number of high-quality antiques stores. The Square, as it is known, has a fascinating history. In the 18th century, Daniel Defoe wrote that more than 20,000 sheep could be sold here on a busy day; such was the press of livestock that sheep runs, known as "tures," were used to control the sheep, and these narrow streets still run off the main square. Today pubs and cafés fill the area.

Also here are St. Edward's Church and the Kings Arms Old Posting House, its wide entrance still seeming to wait for the stagecoaches that used to stop here on their way to Cheltenham. As well as being a lure for the antiques hunter, Stow is a convenient base: eight main Cotswolds roads intersect here, but all—happily—bypass the town center. The town's current population is about 2,500.

★ **Chastleton House,** one of the most complete Jacobean properties in Britain, opts for a beguilingly lived-in appearance, taking advantage of almost 400 years' worth of furniture and trappings accumulated by many generations of the single family that owned it until 1991. The house was built between 1605 and 1612 for William Jones, a wealthy wool merchant, and has an appealing authenticity: cobwebs and bric-a-brac are strewn around, wood and pewter are unpolished, upholstery uncleaned. The top floor is a glorious, barrel-vaulted long gallery, and throughout the house you can see exquisite plasterwork, paneling, and tapestries. The ornamental gardens include England's first croquet lawn (the rules of croquet were codified here in 1865) and rotund topiaries. Chastleton is 6 mi northeast of Stow, signposted off A436 between Stow and A44. ⊠ *Off A436, Moreton-in-Marsh* ☎ *01608 674355, 01494/755560 for recorded information* ⊕ *www. nationaltrust.org.uk* 🎫 *£6.50* ☉ *Apr.–Sept., Wed.–Sat. 1–5; Oct., Wed.–Sat. 1–4. Admission is by timed ticket, for which prebooking is advised.*

Where to Stay & Eat

£–££ ✕ **Queen's Head.** An excellent stopping-off spot for lunch or dinner, this pub has a courtyard out back that's perfect for a summer afternoon. The bench in front, under a climbing rose, makes a relaxing

WORD OF MOUTH

"We also fell in love with Chastleton House . . . What's interesting about the place is that they've restored it only enough to keep it from falling down, and so it has this fascinating, faded feeling like Miss Haversham's wedding banquet."   –rickmay

spot for imbibing outdoor refreshment. Besides standard pub grub, including ploughman's lunches, sandwiches, sausage and mash, and chicken pie, there are daily specials such as mushroom Stroganoff. ⊠ *The Square* ☎ *01451/830563* 🍽 *AE, MC, V* ☉ *No dinner Sun.*

££££ ✕🛏 **Royalist Hotel.** Certified as the oldest inn in the country (AD 947), this hostelry is jammed with interesting features—witches' marks on the beams, a tunnel to the church across the road—and the owners have stylishly integrated designer bedrooms and the sleek AD 947 restaurant (£34 fixed-price menu; closed Sunday and Monday). If the elegant modern English dishes here don't appeal, the adjacent Eagle and Child (££) offers a hearty brasserie-style menu from the same kitchen. ⊠ *Digbeth*

St., GL54 1BN ☎ *01451/830670* 🖨 *01451/870048* ⊕ *www.nichehotels. com* ⤳ *6 rooms, 2 suites* ⚒ *Restaurant, 2 bars, pub, meeting rooms, no-smoking rooms; no a/c* ☰ *MC, V* 🍴 *BP.*

££ 🏨 **Number Nine.** Beyond the traditional stone-and-creeper exterior of this former coaching inn are unfussy, spacious bedrooms done in soothing white and pale colors. The inglenook fireplace is a draw in winter, and wholesome breakfasts include poached fruits and specialty breads. ✉ *9 Park St., GL54 1AQ* ☎ *01451/870333* ⊕ *www.number-nine.info* ⤳ *3 rooms* ⚒ *No a/c, no room phones, no smoking* ☰ *MC, V* 🍴 *BP.*

Shopping

Stow-on-the-Wold is the leading center for antiques stores in the Cotswolds, with more than 40 dealers centered around the Square, Sheep Street, and Church Street.

Duncan Baggott Antiques (✉ Woolcomber House, Sheep St. ☎ 01451/ 830662) displays fine old English furniture, portraits and landscape paintings, and garden statuary and ornaments. Head for **Talbot Galleries** (✉ 7 Talbot Ct. ☎ 01451/832169) if you're interested in antique maps and prints. **Roger Lamb Antiques** (✉ The Sq. ☎ 01451/831371) specializes in objets d'art and small pieces of furniture from the Georgian and Regency periods, with Regency "faux bamboo," tea caddies, and antique needlework the particular fortes.

Bourton-on-the-Water

❼ *4 mi southwest of Stow-on-the-Wold, 12 mi northeast of Cheltenham.*

Bourton-on-the-Water, off A429 on the eastern edge of the Cotswold Hills, is deservedly famous as a classic Cotswold village. Like many others, it became wealthy in the Middle Ages because of wool. The little River Windrush runs through Bourton, crossed by low stone bridges; it's as pretty as it sounds. This village makes a good touring base and has a collection of quirky small museums, but in summer it can be overcrowded. A stroll through Bourton takes you past stone cottages, many converted to small stores and coffee shops.

☉ An old mill, now the **Cotswold Motor Museum and Toy Collection,** contains more than 30 vintage motor vehicles and a collection of old advertising signs (supposedly the largest in Europe), as well as two caravans (trailers) from the 1920s, ancient bicycles, and children's toys. ✉ *Sherborne St.* ☎ *01451/821255* ⊕ *www.cotswold-motor-museum.com* 🎫 *£3.50* ⊙ *Mid-Feb.–early Dec., daily 10–6.*

☉ The **Model Railway Exhibition** displays more than 40 British and Continental trains running on 500 square feet of scenic layout. There are plenty of trains, models, and toys to buy in the shop. ✉ *Box Bush, High St.* ☎ *01451/820686* ⊕ *www.bourtonmodelrailway.co.uk* 🎫 *£2.25* ⊙ *June–Sept., daily 11–5; Oct.–May, weekends 11–5 (limited opening in Jan.; call ahead).*

An outdoor reproduction of Bourton, the **Model Village** was built in 1937 to a scale of one-ninth; you can walk through it. ✉ *Old New Inn*

Antiques & Markets

CLOSE UP

THE COTSWOLDS contains one of the largest concentrations of art and antiques dealers outside London. The famous antiques shops here are, it is sometimes whispered, "temporary" storerooms for the great families of the region, filled with tole-ware, treen, faïence firedogs, toby jugs, and silhouettes, plus country furniture, Edwardiana, and ravishing 17th- to 19th-century furniture. The center of antiquing is Stow-on-the-Wold, in terms of volume of dealers. Other towns that have a number of antiques shops are Burford, Cirencester, Tetbury, and Moreton-in-Marsh. The Cotswolds have few of those "anything in this tray for £10" shops, however. For information about dealers and special events, contact the **Cotswold Antique Dealers' Association** (CADA; ✉ Broadwell House, Sheep St., Stow-

on-the-Wold GL54 1JS ☎ 01451/810407 ⊕ www.cotswolds-antiques-art.com), which represents more than 40 dealers in the area.

As across England, many towns in the region have market days, when you can purchase local produce (including special treats from Cotswold cheeses to fruit juices), crafts, and items such as clothes, books, and toys. Attending a farmers' market or a general market is a great way to mingle with the locals and perhaps find a special treasure or a tasty treat. Head for Moreton-in-Marsh on Tuesday and Cirencester on Friday and some Saturdays; tourist information offices have information on market days, or check out **Country Markets** (⊕ www.country-markets.co.uk).

☎ 01451/820467 ⊕ www.theoldnewinn.co.uk ✉ £2.75 ⊙ Apr.–Oct., daily 9–5:45; Nov.–Mar., daily 10–3:45.

Where to Stay

£££ 🏨 **The Old Manse.** Built in 1748 for the local Baptist pastor, this stone hotel is only steps away from the River Windrush. The smallish bedrooms are decorated in cream and maroon hues; one has a four-poster and a whirlpool bath, another a canopied French half-sleigh bed. Some rooms can be noisy—avoid those facing Sherborne Street if you can. Traditional English fare with a contemporary touch is served in the restaurant. There's a patio at the rear, and one at the front looking onto the river. ✉ Victoria St., GL54 2BX ☎ 01451/820082 🖷 01451/810381 ⊕ www.oldmansehotel.com ➴ 15 rooms ♿ Restaurant, bar; no a/c ▤ AE, MC, V ⧀ BP.

Shopping

The **Cotswold Perfumery** carries many perfumes that are manufactured here, and also stocks perfume bottles and jewelry. You can exercise your olfactory skills in the Perfumed Garden, part of a prebooked factory tour that takes in the laboratory, compounding room, and bottling process. ✉ Victoria St. ☎ 01451/820698 ✉ Factory tour £5 ⊙ Mon.–Sat. 9:30–5, Sun. 10:30–5.

Lower & Upper Slaughter

8 *2 mi north of Bourton-on-the-Water, 15 mi east of Cheltenham.*

Fodor'sChoice
★

To see the quieter, more typical Cotswold villages, seek out the evocatively named Lower Slaughter and Upper Slaughter (the names have nothing to do with mass murder, but come from the Saxon word *sloh,* which means "a marshy place"). Lower Slaughter is one of the "water villages," with Slaughter Brook running down the center road of the town. Little stone footbridges cross the brook, and the town's resident gaggle of geese can often be seen paddling through the sparkling water. Lower and Upper Swell are two other quiet towns to explore in the area.

Connecting the two Slaughters is **Wardens' Way** (⊕ www.cotswoldsaonb. com), a mile-long pathway that begins in Upper Slaughter at the town-center parking lot and passes stone houses, green meadows, ancient trees, and a 19th-century corn mill with a waterwheel and brick chimney. Wardens' Way continues south to Bourton-on-the-Water; the full walk from Winchcombe to Bourton is 14 mi.

Where to Stay & Eat

££££ ✕☒ **Washbourne Court.** This fine 17th-century stone building, amid 4 acres of verdant grounds beside the River Wye, has flagstone floors, beams, and open fires. The bedrooms in the main building are done in a weathered country style, whereas rooms in the converted barn and cottages are more modern. Choices in the restaurant (£££££) might include poached halibut or pork with mustard puree, followed by banana and chocolate mille-feuille. ☒ *Lower Slaughter GL54 2HS* ☎ *01451/822143* 🖷 *01451/821045* ⊕ *www.washbournecourt.co.uk* 🛏 *26 rooms, 2 suites* ♨ *Restaurant, bar; no a/c* ☰ *AE, DC, MC, V* ¶◎¶ *BP.*

Burford

9 *8 mi southeast of Bourton-on-the-Water, 18 mi north of Swindon, 18 mi west of Oxford.*

Burford's broad main street leads steeply down to a narrow bridge across the River Windrush. The village served as a stagecoach stop for centuries and has many historic inns; it is now a popular stop for tour buses and seekers of antiques. Hidden away at the end of a lane at the bottom of High Street is the splendid parish church of **St. John,** its interior a warren of arches, chapels, and shrines. The church was remodeled in the 15th century from Norman beginnings. Among the many monuments is one dedicated to

COUNTRY WALKS

Short walks thread the countryside around the historic towns and are a great way to appreciate the Cotswolds, an **Area of Outstanding National Beauty** (⊕ www. cotswoldsaonb.com). Tourist information centers carry walking maps and have information about longer trails. To branch out on your own, track the rivers on which many towns are built, following the **towpaths** that usually run along the water. The **Cotswold Way** (⊕ www. nationaltrail.co.uk), a national trail stretching about 100 mi between Bath and Chipping Campden, traces the ridge marking the edge of the Cotswolds and the Severn Valley and has incomparable views.

Henry VIII's barber, Edmund Harman, which shows four Amazonian Indians; it's said to be the first depiction of native people from the Americas in Britain. Look also for the elaborate Tanfield monument and its poignant widow's epitaph. ⊠ *Church Green* ☎ *01993/822275* 🖾 *Free, donations accepted* ⊗ *Apr.–Oct., daily 9–5; Nov.–Mar., daily 9–4.*

Where to Stay & Eat

£££   ✕🏨 **Jonathan's at the Angel.** Contemporary dishes you might see at the farmhouse-style tables of this informal brasserie (£££–££££) in a 16th-century former coaching inn include gilthead bream (a saltwater fish) with warm potato salad and saffron sauce, and venison with caramel peaches. Upstairs, the delightful guest rooms are furnished in different styles: Indian in reds and oranges, French with wooden sleigh bed, or cool-blue contemporary Italian. ⊠ *14 Witney St., OX18 4SN* ☎ *01993/ 822714* 🖨 *01993/822069* ⊕ *www.theangel-uk.com* ⇋ *3 rooms* ⌂ *Restaurant, in-room VCRs; no a/c* ▤ *MC, V* ⊗ *Closed last 2 wks of Jan. and 1st wk of Feb. Restaurant closed Mon.; no dinner Sun.* ⑩ *BP.*

££££   🏨 **Burford House.** The family photographs and memorabilia, rugs, books and toys scattered throughout this 17th-century building make it feel more like home than a hotel. The richly decorated bedrooms, filled with antiques, come with freestanding baths and power showers. If you don't stay for lunch or afternoon tea, make sure you try the homemade damson gin, maybe in one of the intimate sitting rooms or courtyard garden. There is no dinner service. ⊠ *99 High St., OX18 4QA* ☎ *01993/ 823151* 🖨 *01993/823240* ⊕ *www.burford-house.co.uk* ⇋ *8 rooms* ⌂ *Cable TV, in-room data ports, bar, lounge; no a/c* ▤ *AE, MC, V* ⑩ *BP.*

Bibury

⑩ *10 mi southwest of Burford, 6 mi northeast of Cirencester, 15 mi north of Swindon.*

The tiny town of Bibury, with a population of less than 1,000, sits idyllically beside the little River Coln on B4425; it was famed Arts and Crafts designer William Morris's choice for Britain's most beautiful village. Fine old cottages, a river meadow, and the church of St. Mary's are some of the delights here. **Arlington Row** is a famously pretty group of 17th-century weavers' cottages made of stone.

Chedworth Roman Villa

⑪ *6 mi northwest of Bibury, 9 mi north of Cirencester, 10 mi southeast of Cheltenham.*

The remains of a mile of walls is what's left of one of the largest Roman villas in England, beautifully set in a wooded valley on the eastern fringe of the Cotswolds. Thirty-two rooms, including two complete bath suites, have been identified, and the colorful mosaics are some of the most complete in England. The visitor center and museum give a detailed picture of Roman life in Britain; they may even appeal to non-fans of the period. ■ TIP→ Look carefully for the signs for the villa: from Bibury, go across A429 to Yanworth and Chedworth. The villa is also signposted from

A40. ⊠ *Yanworth* ☎ *01242/890256* ⊕ *www.nationaltrust.org.uk* ▣ *£5.50* ⊙ *Apr.–late Oct., Tues.–Sun. and national holidays 10–5; Mar., Tues.–Sun. 11–4; late Oct.–mid-Nov., Tues.–Sun. 10–4.*

Cirencester

⓬ *9 mi south of Chedworth, 14 mi southeast of Cheltenham.*

Cirencester (pronounced sirensester) has been a hub of the Cotswolds since Roman times, when it was called Corinium; the town was second only to Londinium (London) in importance. It lay at the intersection of two major Roman roads, the Fosse Way and Ermin Street (today A429 and A417). In the Middle Ages, Cirencester grew rich on wool, which funded its 15th-century parish church. Today this old market town is the area's largest, with a population of 19,000. It preserves many mellow stone buildings dating mainly from the 17th and 18th centuries, and bow-fronted shops that still have one foot in the past.

At the top of Market Place is the magnificent Gothic parish church of **St. John the Baptist,** known as the cathedral of the "woolgothic" style. Its elaborate, three-tier, three-bay south porch, the largest in England, once served as the town hall. The chantry chapels and many coats of arms bear witness to the importance of the wool merchants, benefactors of the church. A rare example of a 15th-century wineglass pulpit sits in the nave. ⊠ *Market Pl.* ☎ *01285/659317* ▣ *Free, £2 suggested donation* ⊙ *Mon.–Sat. 9:30–5 (9:30–4 in winter), Sun. 2:15–5.*

★ Not much of the Roman town remains visible, but the **Corinium Museum** displays an outstanding collection of Roman artifacts, including mosaic pavements, as well as full-scale reconstructions of local Roman interiors. Spacious galleries explore the town's history in Roman and Anglo-Saxon times and in the 18th century; they include plenty of hands-on exhibits. ⊠ *Park St.* ☎ *01285/655611* ⊕ *www.cotswold.gov.uk* ▣ *£3.70* ⊙ *Mon.–Sat. 10–5, Sun. 2–5.*

Where to Stay & Eat

£££ ✕▣ **Wild Duck Inn.** This family-run Elizabethan inn 3 mi south of Cirencester has richly decorated guest rooms with print fabrics and dark wood furniture. The mellow, deep-red dining room (££–££££) has an abundance of beams and oil portraits, and the menu is strong on fresh fish—try it in a beer batter—and such meat dishes as honey-roasted duck. Make room reservations well in advance, as the inn is popular. ⊠ *Ewen GL7 6BY* ☎ *01285/770310* ▤ *01285/770924* ⊕ *www.thewildduckinn. co.uk* ⇋ *12 rooms* ⚬ *Restaurant, some pets allowed (fee); no a/c* ▭ *AE, MC, V* ⦿| *CP.*

£ ▣ **Ivy House.** Contrary to expectations, Virginia creeper clings to this stone Victorian house, close to the center of town. The simple bedrooms have pastel colors and offer excellent value. The owners are friendly, and cyclists and walkers are welcomed. ⊠ *2 Victoria Rd., GL7 1EN* ▤▤ *01285/656626* ⊕ *www.ivyhousecotswolds.com* ⇋ *4 rooms* ⚬ *No a/c, no room phones, no smoking* ▭ *MC, V* ⦿| *BP.*

CLOSE UP

That Special Cotswold Stone

IF THERE'S ONE FEATURE of the Cotswold landscape that sums up its special flavor, it's the oolitic limestone that is the area's primary building material. This stone can be seen in everything from drystone walls (whose total length in the region is said to equal or exceed that of the Great Wall of China) to snug cottages and manor houses. Even roof tiles are fashioned from the stone, contributing to a harmonious ensemble despite the different ages of the buildings.

Malleable when first quarried, and gradually hardening with age, the stone lends itself to every use. During the late-medieval heyday of the great churches funded by wool merchants, it was used to brilliant effect in the mullions, gargoyles, and other intricate decorations on ecclesiastical

buildings. Some area quarries are still active, producing stone that is used mainly for restoration and repair purposes. The varying colors of the stone are caused by impurities in the rock. They include the honey hues of the northern reaches of the Cotswolds, and modulate to a more golden tone in the central area.

Writer and commentator J. B. Priestley, however, wrote of Cotswold stone that "the truth is that it has no color that can be described. Even when the sun is obscured and the light is cold, these walls are still faintly warm and luminous, as if they knew the trick of keeping the lost sunlight of centuries glimmering about them." Walk or drive around Cotswold villages and towns for even a day, and you will know what he meant.

Nightlife & the Arts

The **Brewery Arts Centre** (⊠ Brewery Ct. ☎ 01285/657181) includes a theater, exhibition space, and a café. It's also well known for its crafts studios and shop.

Shopping

The **Brewery Arts Centre** (⊠ Brewery Ct. ☎ 01285/657181) has studios for more than a dozen artists and craftspeople, as well as a good shop that sells their work. The **Corn Hall** (⊠ Market Pl.) is the venue for an antiques market on Thursday, Friday, and Saturday, when there's also a crafts market (unless it's the fifth Saturday in the month). Every Monday and Friday, Cirencester's central **Market Place** is packed with stalls selling a motley assortment of goods, mainly household items but some local produce and crafts, too. **Rankine Taylor Antiques** (⊠ 34 Dollar St. ☎ 01285/652529) concentrates on 17th- and 18th-century furniture, silver, pottery, and glass. **William H. Stokes** (⊠ 6–8 Dollar St. ☎ 01285/653907) specializes in oak furniture from the 16th and 17th centuries.

Painswick

13 *16 mi northwest of Cirencester, 8 mi southwest of Cheltenham, 5 mi south of Gloucester.*

This old Cotswold wool town of around 2,000 inhabitants has become a chocolate-box picture of quaintness, attracting day-trippers and tour buses. But come during the week and you can discover the place in relative tranquillity. The huddled gray stone houses and inns date from as early as the 14th century and include a notable group from the Georgian era. The churchyard of St. Mary's is renowned for its 99 yew trees (legend has it that the devil prevents the 100th from growing) planted in 1792.

The **Painswick Rococo Garden,** ½ mi north of town, has survived from the exuberant rococo period of English-garden design (1720–60). After 50 years in its original form, the 6-acre garden became overgrown with woodland. Beginning in 1984, after the rediscovery of a 1748 painting of the garden by Thomas Robins, the garden was restored. Now you can view the original architectural structures—such as the vaguely Gothic Eagle House and Exedra—and asymmetrical vistas. There's also a restaurant and a shop. ⊠ *B4073* ☎ *01452/813204* ⊕ *www. rococogarden.org.uk* 🎫 *£5* ⊙ *Mid-Jan.–Oct., daily 11–5.*

Where to Stay & Eat

££–£££   ✕⌨ **Cardynham House.** The Cotswolds are really about the art of liv-
Fodor'sChoice   ing, as this 15th to 16th-century former wool merchant's house demon-
★   strates. The stylish retreat, which retains its beamed ceilings, Jacobean staircase, and Elizabethan fireplace, has four-poster beds in all rooms but one and creative theme rooms such as the Medieval Garden, Dovecote, and Arabian Nights. One pricier room has a private pool. Downstairs, the March Hare dining room (£24.50, fixed-price menu; closed Sunday and Monday) serves delicious Thai food such as red snapper curry with coconut and lime leaves. ⊠ *The Cross, GL6 6XX* ☎ *01452/ 814006, 01452/813452 restaurant* 🖷 *01452/812321* ⊕ *www.cardynham. co.uk* 🛏 *9 rooms* ♿ *Restaurant; no a/c* ▤ *AE, MC, V* ⓞⓘ *BP.*

Owlpen

★ ⑭   *9 mi south of Painswick, 13 mi west of Cirencester.*

Prince Charles described the beauty spot of Owlpen, an off-the-beaten-path hamlet, as "the epitome of the English village." First settled in Saxon days as Olla's Pen (meaning "valley"), the village centers on a church, a Tudor manor house, and pearl-gray stone cottages, all set against a hillside. A graceful grouping of tithe barns, garden buildings, and gristmill softens the seignorial bearing of the manor house.

The triple-gabled stone **Owlpen Manor** was built between 1450 and 1616, but was restored in the 1920s by local Arts and Crafts artisans, who also created some of the furnishings. Today Nicholas and Karin Mander live here with their family. Inside are oak chests fashioned by William Morris, family portraits, Georgian doorcases, painted cloths from the Tudor and Stuart eras, and Queen Margaret's Room, said to be haunted by the spirit of Margaret of Anjou, wife of Henry VI, who visited here during the Wars of the Roses. You can also explore the terraced garden with its yew topiary, the envy of gardening masters such as Gertrude Jekyll. The Cyder Press restaurant opens at noon. ■ TIP→ **Want to linger in this idyllic place? Several cottages have been converted into guest accommodations, available for two-night or longer rentals.** ⊠ *Off B4066, near*

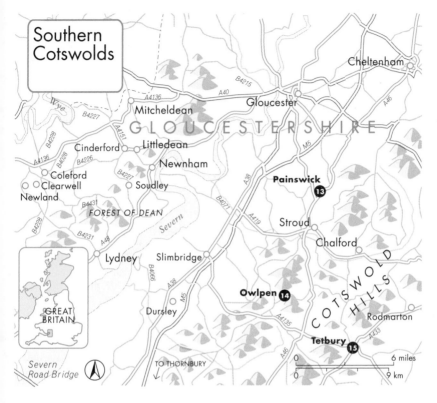

Southern Cotswolds

Uley ☎*01453/860261* ⊕*www.owlpen.com* 🏷*£5.25, gardens only £3.25* ☉ *May–Sept., Tues., Thurs., and Sun. 2–5.*

Tetbury

15 *6 mi southeast of Owlpen, 8 mi southwest of Cirencester, 12 mi south of Painswick.*

Tetbury, with about 5,300 inhabitants, claims right royal connections. Indeed, the soaring spire of the church that presides over this Elizabethan market town is within sight of Highgrove House, the Prince of Wales's abode. The town is known as one of the area's antiques centers. In the center of the village, look for the eye-catching, white-painted stone **Market House** on Market Square, dating from 1655 and built up on rows of Tuscan pillars. Various markets are held here during the week. The **Church of St. Mary** (⊠ Church St. ☎ 01666/502333), in 18th-century neo-Gothic style, has a spacious galleried interior with pews.

NEED A BREAK? **Two Toads** (⊠ 19 Church St. ☎ 01666/503696) is a relaxed spot for coffee, light lunches, and cream teas. Be sure to try the delicious pastries. The small courtyard garden is open in fine weather.

Tall gate piers and spreading trees frame the family-owned **Chavenage,** a gray Cotswold-stone Elizabethan manor house. The tour includes a room with fine tapestries, where Cromwell lodged during the Civil War, and a main hall with minstrels' gallery. ⊠ *2 mi northwest of Tetbury between B4104 and A4135* ☏ *01666/502329* ⊕ *www.chavenage.com* ▣ *£6* ⊙ *May–Sept., Thurs., Sun., and national holidays 2–5.*

One of the last English country houses constructed using traditional methods and materials, **Rodmarton Manor** (built 1909–29) is furnished with specially commissioned pieces in the Arts and Crafts style. Ernest Barnsley, a follower of William Morris, worked on the house and gardens. The notable gardens—wild, winter, sunken, and white—are divided into "rooms" bounded by hedges of holly, beech, and yew. The manor is 5 mi northeast of Tetbury. ⊠ *Off A433, Rodmarton* ☏ *01285/ 841253* ⊕ *www.rodmarton-manor.co.uk* ▣ *£7, garden only £4* ⊙ *May–Sept., Wed., Sat., and national holidays 2–5.*

★ The 600-acre **Westonbirt National Arboretum,** 3 mi southwest of Tetbury, contains one of the most extensive collections of trees and shrubs in Europe. The best times to come for color are in late spring, when the rhododendrons, azaleas, and magnolias are blooming, and in fall, when the maples come into their own. There's a gift shop, café, and restaurant. ⊠ *Off A433* ☏ *01666/880220* ⊕ *www.forestry.gov.uk* ▣ *£5 Jan. and Feb; £6.50 Mar.–Sept.; £7.50 Oct.–mid-Nov.; free mid-Nov.–Dec.* ⊙ *Daily 10–8 or dusk.*

Where to Stay & Eat

★ **£££** ✕ **Trouble House.** Simple but wonderfully tasty dishes are created at this relaxed, whitewashed pub with wooden floors, a low-beam ceiling, and fireplaces for cool days. Your order from the bar might be halibut baked in lemon slices with pumpkin and Parmesan mash, or classic cassoulet of duck confit. The pub is 2 mi northeast of Tetbury on the Cirencester Road. ⊠ *A433* ☏ *01666/502206* ▭ *AE, MC, V* ⊙ *Closed Mon. and last wk in Dec. No dinner Sun.*

£££££ ✕▣ **Calcot Manor.** Comfortable country-house furnishings with lots of greens and burgundies fill the main house and converted sandstone barns and stables of this family-friendly establishment with a luxurious spa. Guest rooms are airy and spacious; family suites have bunk beds in a separate room and refrigerators. The formal Conservatory restaurant (*£££–££££*) prepares wood-roasted meats and homemade fresh-fruit sorbets and the Gumstool Inn provides farmhouse-style fare; dinner is included in the price on weekends. The hotel is 3 mi west of town. ⊠ *A4135, GL8 8YJ* ☏ *01666/890391* ▤ *01666/890394* ⊕ *www. calcotmanor.co.uk* ⇆ *24 rooms, 6 suites* ♿ *2 restaurants, in-room data ports, tennis court, pool, gym, spa, croquet, 2 bars, meeting rooms; no a/c* ▭ *AE, DC, MC, V* ◉⃝ *BP.*

Shopping

Tetbury is home to more than 30 antiques shops, some of which are incorporated into small malls. You'll be sure to find something from **Alchemy** (⊠ Old Chapel, Long St. ☏ 01666/505281), a cornucopia of treasures from kitchenware to jewelry, and glass. **Day Antiques** (⊠ 5 New

Church St. ☎ 01666/502413) specializes in oak furniture and early pottery, metalware, and treen. **Townsend Bateson** (✉ 51A Long St. ☎ 01666/505083) displays decorative wares and some furniture.

STRATFORD-UPON-AVON & SHAKESPEARE COUNTRY

Even under the weight of busloads of visitors seeking Shakespeare, Stratford has somehow hung on to much of its ancient character and can, on a good day, still feel like an English market town. It's on the banks of the slow-flowing River Avon, just 10 mi north of the Cotswold town of Chipping Campden, close to Birmingham (37 mi to the northwest), and not far from London (102 mi to the southeast).

Take Antonio's advice (*Twelfth Night,* act 3, scene 3) and "beguile the time, and feed your knowledge with viewing the town"—or with seeing a play at the Royal Shakespeare Theatre. By the 16th century Stratford was a prosperous market town with thriving guilds and industries. Half-timber houses from this era have been preserved, and they are set off by later architecture, such as the elegant Georgian storefronts on Bridge Street, with their 18th-century porticoes and arched doorways.

This section of Warwickshire is marked by gentle hills, green fields, slow-moving, mirrorlike rivers, quiet villages, and time-burnished halls, castles (Warwick is the best example), and churches. Northwest of Warwick, reserve some time to visit Baddesley Clinton, a superb example of late-medieval domestic architecture.

Stratford-upon-Avon

10 mi north of Chipping Campden.

Around here, it doesn't take long to figure out who's the center of attention. Born in a half-timber, early-16th-century building in the center of Stratford on April 23, 1564, Shakespeare died on April 23, 1616, his 52nd birthday, in a more imposing house at New Place. Although he spent much of his life in London, the world still associates him with "Shakespeare's Avon." Here, in the years between his birth and 1587, he played as a young lad, attended grammar school, and married Anne Hathaway; and here he returned, as a prosperous man. You can see his birthplace on Henley Street; his burial place in Holy Trinity Church; Anne Hathaway's Cottage; his mother's home at Wilmcote; New Place and the neighboring Nash's House, home of Shakespeare's granddaughter.

The town is easily manageable on foot. Most sights cluster around Henley Street (off the roundabout as you come in on the A3400 Birmingham road), High Street, and Waterside, which skirts the public gardens through which the River Avon flows. Bridge Street and Sheep Street (parallel to Bridge) are Stratford's main thoroughfares and the site of most banks, shops, and eating places. The town's tourist office lies at Bridgefoot, between the canal and the river, next to Clopton Bridge— "a sumptuous new bridge and large of stone"—built in the 15th century by Sir Hugh Clopton, once lord mayor of London and one of Stratford's richest and most philanthropic residents.

The **Shakespeare Birthplace Trust** runs the main places of Shakespearean interest: Anne Hathaway's Cottage, Hall's Croft, Mary Arden's House, Nash's House and New Place, and Shakespeare's Birthplace. They have similar opening times, and you can buy a combination ticket to the three in-town properties or to all five properties, or pay separate entry fees if you want to visit only one or two. The trust hosts events by the Tudor Group, costumed interpreters who give demonstrations and talks about subjects such as how Tudor England celebrated Christmas. ☎ 01789/ 204016 ⊕ www.shakespeare.org.uk ✉ Joint ticket to 5 properties £14; joint ticket to Shakespeare's Birthplace, Hall's Croft, and Nash's House–New Place £11.

Main Attractions

★ ㉔ **Anne Hathaway's Cottage.** The most picturesque of the Shakespeare Trust properties, on the western outskirts of Stratford, was the family home of the woman Shakespeare married in 1582. The "cottage," actually a substantial Tudor farmhouse, has latticed windows and a grand thatch roof. Inside is period furniture including a rare carved Elizabethan bed; outside is a garden planted in lush Victorian style with herbs and flowers. In a nearby field the **Shakespeare Tree Garden** has 40 trees mentioned in the playwright's works, a yew maze, and sculptures with Shakespearean themes. ■ TIP→ **The best way to get here is to walk, especially in late spring when the apple trees are in blossom.** There are two main footpaths, one via Greenhill Street by the railroad bridge, the other leaving from Holy Trinity Church up Old Town and Chestnut Walk. ✉ Cottage La., Shottery ☎ 01789/204016 ⊕ www.shakespeare.org.uk ✉ £5.50, Shakespeare Trust 5-property ticket £14 ☉ Apr., May, Sept., and Oct., Mon.–Sat. 9:30–5, Sun. 10–5; June–Aug., Mon.–Sat. 9–5, Sun. 9:30–5; Nov.–Mar., Mon.–Sat. 10–4, Sun. 10:30–4; last entry 30 mins before closing.

㉒ **Hall's Croft.** One of the finest surviving Jacobean (early 17th-century) town houses, this impressive residence has a delightful walled garden. Tradition has it that Hall's Croft was the home of Shakespeare's elder daughter Susanna and her husband, Dr. John Hall, whose dispensary is on view along with the other rooms, all containing Jacobean furniture of heavy oak and some 17th-century portraits. Restoration of the house is under way, and some exhibits are being remounted. Some rooms may be closed when you visit. ✉ Old Town ☎ 01789/204016 ⊕ www. shakespeare.org.uk ✉ £3.75, Shakespeare Trust ticket for 3 in-town properties £11, 5-property ticket £14 ☉ Nov.–Mar., daily 11–4; Apr., May, Sept., and Oct., daily 11–5; June–Aug., Mon.–Sat. 9:30–5, Sun. 10–5; last entry 30 mins before closing.

㉓ **Holy Trinity Church.** The burial place of William Shakespeare, this 13th-century church sits on the banks of the Avon, with a graceful avenue of lime trees framing its entrance. Shakespeare's final resting place is in the chancel, rebuilt in 1465–91 in the late Perpendicular style. He was buried here not because he was a famed poet but because he was a lay rector of Stratford, owning a portion of the township tithes. On the north wall of

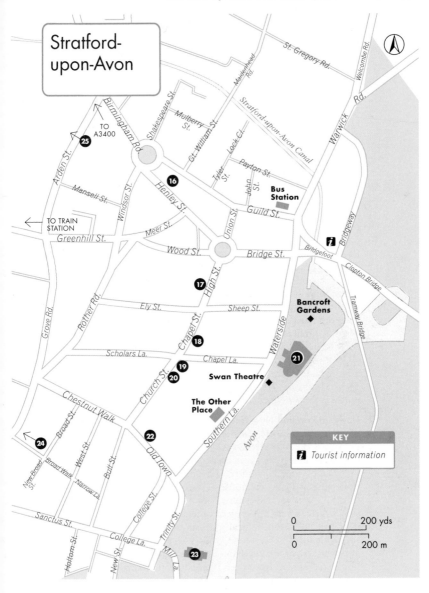

Stratford-upon-Avon

the sanctuary, over the altar steps, is the famous marble bust created by Gerard Jansen in 1623. Along with the Droeshout engraving in the First Folio, this is one of only two known contemporary portraits of Shakespeare. Rigidly stylized in the Elizabethan mode, the bust offers a more human, even humorous, perspective when viewed from the side. Also in the chancel are the graves of Shakespeare's wife, Anne; his daughter Susanna; his son-in-law, John Hall; and his granddaughter's husband, Thomas Nash. Nearby, the Parish Register is displayed, containing both Shakespeare's baptismal entry (1564) and his burial notice (1616). ⊠ *Trinity St.* ✉ *Small fee for chancel* ⊙ *Mar., Mon.–Sat. 9–5, Sun. 12:30–5; Apr.–Oct., Mon.–Sat. 8:30–6, Sun. 12:30–5; Nov.–Feb., Mon.–Sat. 9–4, Sun. 12:30–5; last admission 20 mins before closing.*

㉕ **Mary Arden's House.** A Tudor farmhouse on this bucolic site in tiny Wilmcote (3 mi northwest of Stratford) was long believed to have been the home of Mary Arden, Shakespeare's mother. In 2000, researchers discovered that it was actually the former home of Adam Palmer, and the farmhouse was renamed Palmer's Farm. However, other evidence revealed that Mary Arden lived in a modest house on the adjoining Glebe Farm, and that house has now assumed the name Mary Arden's House. The Tudor farmhouse and farm form the **Shakespeare Countryside Museum,** with crafts exhibits, a café, and a garden. Rare breeds of poultry, longhorn cows, and Cotswold sheep live on the grounds, and the museum has demonstrations of farming techniques from the last 400 years. A small falcon and owl exhibit is here, too. ⊠ *Off A3400, Wilmcote* ☎ *01789/204016, 01789/293455 information on special events* ⊕ *www.shakespeare.org.uk* ✉ *£6, Shakespeare Trust 5-property ticket £14* ⊙ *Nov.–Mar., Mon.–Sat. 10–4, Sun. 10:30–4; Sept., Oct., Apr., and May, Mon.–Sat. 10–5, Sun. 10:30–5; June–Aug., Mon.–Sat. 9:30–5, Sun. 10–5; last entry 30 mins before closing.*

⑱ **Nash's House and New Place.** This is the home of Thomas Nash, who married Shakespeare's last direct descendant, his granddaughter Elizabeth Hall. The heavily restored house has been furnished in 17th-century style, and it also contains a local museum. In the gardens (where there's an intricately laid-out Elizabethan knot garden) are the foundations of **New Place,** the house in which Shakespeare died in 1616. Built in 1483 "of brike and tymber" for a lord mayor of London, New Place was Stratford's grandest piece of real estate when Shakespeare bought it in 1597 for £60; tragically it was torn down in 1759. The man responsible for this, Reverend Francis Gastrell, had already shown his ire at the hordes of Shakespeare-related sightseers by cutting down a mulberry tree said to have been planted by the Bard himself. That act of vandalism put the townspeople into such an uproar that they stoned his house. Today a tree claimed to be a descendant of the unfortunate mulberry stands in the middle of the lawn. The **Great Garden** of New Place, beyond the knot garden, has a sculpture trail with bronze works inspired by Shakespeare's plays. ⊠ *Chapel St.* ☎ *01789/204016* ⊕ *www. shakespeare.org.uk* ✉ *£3.75, Shakespeare Trust ticket for 3 in-town properties £11, 5-property ticket £14* ⊙ *Nov.–Mar., daily 11–4; Apr., May, Sept., and Oct., daily 11–5; June–Aug., Mon.–Sat. 9:30–5, Sun. 10–5; last entry 30 mins before closing.*

㉑ **Royal Shakespeare Theatre.** The Stratford home of the Royal Shake-speare Company (RSC), amid lovely gardens along the River Avon, pres-ents some of the finest productions of Shakespeare's plays. The company has existed since 1879, established by brewer Charles Edward Flower; its original home burned down in 1926. Six years later the current building was erected. Starting in May or June 2007, the theater will close for three years. During that time there will be no tours of the original theater, and action will switch to the RSC's other theaters, including the adjacent **Swan Theatre,** the only part of the Victorian theater to survive the 1926 fire. This theater follows the lines of Shakespeare's original Globe and is one of the most exciting performing spaces in Britain. Be-side the Swan, an art gallery has theater-related exhibitions and portraits and depictions of scenes from the plays. After spring 2007, the main home of the RSC will be the temporary **Courtyard Theatre.** The the-ater is behind **The Other Place,** a modern auditorium used primarily for contemporary productions. ✉ *Waterside* ☎ *0870/609–1110 ticket hot-line, 01789/296655 information, 01789/403405 tours* 🖨 *01789/403413 box office* ⊕ *www.rsc.org.uk* 🎫 *Tour £5* ⊙ *Tour weekdays (except mati-nee days; book well in advance) 1:30 and 5:30; matinee days 5:30 and after show; Sun. noon, 1, 2, and 3. No tours when shows are being pre-pared. Gallery Mon.–Sat. 9:30–6:30, Sun. noon–4:30.*

6

NEED A BREAK? **At Cox's Yard Tea Shop** (✉ Bridgefoot ☎ 01789/404600), next to Bancroft Gar-dens in the town center, linger over tea and a scone for a relaxing break be-fore more sightseeing or a riverside walk.

⑯ **Shakespeare's Birthplace.** A half-timber house typical of its time, the play-wright's birthplace has been altered and restored since he lived here but remains a much-visited shrine. You enter through the **Shakespeare Cen-tre,** the headquarters of the Shakespeare Birthplace Trust, which is a fa-vorite with scholars, who head straight for the library; other visitors spend their time at the informative exhibition. Furnishings in the house reflect comfortable middle-class Eliza-bethan domestic life. Shakespeare's father, John, a glove maker and wool dealer, purchased the house; a reconstructed workshop shows the tools of the glover's trade. An auction notice describes the prop-erty as it was when it was offered for sale in 1847. You can also see the signatures of earlier pilgrims cut into the windowpanes, including those of Mark Twain and Charles Dickens. ✉ *Henley St.* ☎ *01789/ 204016* ⊕ *www.shakespeare.org. uk* 🎫 *£7, Shakespeare Trust ticket for 3 in-town properties £11, 5-property ticket £14* ⊙ *Nov.–Mar., Mon.–Sat. 10–4, Sun. 10:30–4; Apr. and May, Mon.–Sat. 10–5, Sun.*

> **WILL FOR SALE**
>
> In 1847 two widowed ladies were maintaining Shakespeare's birth-place in a somewhat ramshackle state. With the approach of the tercentennial of the playwright's birth, and in response to a rumor that the building was to be pur-chased by P. T. Barnum and shipped across the Atlantic, the city shelled out £3, 000 for the relic. It was tidied up and made the main attraction for the stream of Shakespeare devotees that was steadily growing into a torrent.

10:30–5; June–Aug., Mon.–Sat. 9–5, Sun. 9:30–5; Sept. and Oct., Mon.–Sat. 10–5, Sun. 10:30–5; last entry 30 mins before closing.

Also Worth Seeing

Almshouses. Immediately beyond the Guildhall on Church Street is a delightful row of timber-and-daub almshouses. These were built to accommodate the poor by the Guild of the Holy Cross in the early 15th century and still serve as housing for pensioners. ⊠ *Church St.*

⑲ Guild Chapel. This chapel is the noble centerpiece of Stratford's Guild buildings, including the Guildhall, the Grammar School, and the almshouses—all structures well known to Shakespeare. The ancient structure was rebuilt in the late Perpendicular style in the first half of the 15th century, thanks to the largesse of Stratford resident Hugh Clopton. The otherwise plain interior includes fragments of a remarkable medieval fresco of the Last Judgment. The bell, also given by Sir Hugh, still rings as it did to tell Shakespeare the time of day. ⊠ *Chapel La. at Church St.* ☎ *01789/293351* ⊠ *Free* ☉ *Daily 9–5.*

⑳ Guildhall. Dating to 1416–18, the Guildhall is occupied by **King Edward's Grammar School,** which Shakespeare probably attended as a boy; it's still used as a school. On the 1st floor is the Guildhall proper, where traveling acting companies came to perform. Many historians believe that it was after seeing the troupe known as the Earl of Leicester's Men in 1587 that Shakespeare got the acting bug and set off for London. Upstairs is the classroom in which he is reputed to have learned "little Latin and less Greek." A brass plate at its far end records the traditional position of Master Will's seat. Students use the classroom today, so visits may be made by prior arrangement only, during after-school hours or vacation time. Contact the tourist information office to schedule a visit. ⊠ *Church St.* ☎ *0870/160–7930 tourist office.*

⑰ Harvard House. This is the grand, half-timber, 16th-century home of Katherine Rogers, mother of the John Harvard who founded Harvard University in 1636. The twin-gabled facade, dating from about 1600, is one of Stratford's glories. Note the exterior beams carved with fleurs-de-lis in relief, the sculpted human faces on the corbels, and the bear and staff (symbols of the Warwick earls) on the bracket heads. Inside, the **Museum of British Pewter** displays pewter toys, tankards, and teapots, dating from Roman times to the present. ⊠ *High St.* ☎ *01789/204507* ⊕ *www.shakespeare.org.uk* ⊠ *£2.75, free if you have a 3- or 5-property ticket* ☉ *May, June, and Sept.–Nov., Fri.–Sun. 11:30–4:30; July and Aug., Thurs.–Sun. 11:30–4:30.*

Where to Eat

Stratford's restaurant scene has been more volatile than usual, perhaps because of the plans for the new theater, so call ahead.

££–££££ ✕ **Malbec.** Blending French and British styles seamlessly, this little restaurant has been stacking up the kudos since it opened a couple of years ago. Its atmosphere is laidback sophistication and its constantly changing wine list is very well chosen. The fixed price lunch (two courses for £10) is a great deal. ⊠ *6 Union St.* ☎ *01789/269106* ▤ *AE, MC, V.*

££–£££ ✕ **Lambs of Sheep Street.** Sit downstairs to appreciate the hardwood floors and oak beams of this local epicurean favorite. The modern updates of tried-and-true dishes include roast chicken with lime butter and char-grilled sausages with leek mash. Daily specials keep the menu seasonal. The two- and three-course fixed-price menus are good deals. ⊠ *12 Sheep St.* ☎ *01789/292554* ☖ *Reservations essential* ▤ *AE, MC, V.*

££–£££ ✕ **Russons.** A 16th-century building holds a quaint dining room that's a favorite with theatergoers. The fare, though reasonably priced, doesn't skimp on quality. On the daily-changing menu, chalked on a blackboard, are English specialties such as roast lamb and guinea fowl. ⊠ *8 Church St.* ☎ *01789/268822* ☖ *Reservations essential* ▤ *AE, MC, V* ⊗ *Closed Mon.*

££–£££ ✕ **The Vintner.** The imaginative, bistro-inspired menu varies each day at this café and wine bar. Shoulder of lamb is a popular main course, tapas are also popular, and a children's menu is available. To dine before curtain time, arrive early or make a reservation. The building, largely un-altered since the late 1400s, has lovely flagstone floors and oak beams. ⊠ *5 Sheep St.* ☎ *01789/297259* ▤ *AE, MC, V.*

££ ✕ **Opposition.** Pre- and post-theater meals are offered at this informal, family-style restaurant in a 16th-century building on the main dining street near the theater. The American and modern European dishes on the menu win praise from the locals. Try the roasted chicken breast with banana and basmati rice, wild mushroom pizza, or blood sausage salad. ⊠ *13 Sheep St.* ☎ *01789/269980* ▤ *MC, V.*

£–££ ✕ **Black Swan.** Known locally as the Dirty Duck, one of Stratford's most celebrated pubs has attracted actors since Garrick's days. Its little veranda overlooks the theaters and the river. You can sample English grill specialties as well as bar meals such as mussels and fries. Few people come here for the food, which is mediocre: the real attraction is the ambience and the other customers. ⊠ *Southern La.* ☎ *01789/ 297312* ▤ *AE, MC, V* ⊗ *No dinner Sun.*

Where to Stay

££££ ▦ **Alveston Manor.** This redbrick Elizabethan manor house surrounded by lawns and a terrace has ancient elements as well as a pampering spa. A few Tudor-style rooms in the main building have four-poster beds; in the rear of the hotel are most of the rooms, modern and done up in sea green and beige. Legend says the grounds were the setting for the first production of *A Midsummer Night's Dream.* The Alveston is across the river from the Royal Shakespeare Theatre. ⊠ *Clopton Bridge, CV37 7HP* ☎ *08704/008181* ☐ *01789/414095* ⊕ *www.macdonald-hotels. co.uk* ⇰ *110 rooms, 4 suites* � *Restaurant, room service, cable TV, in-room data ports, indoor pool, spa, bar, 2 lounges, dry cleaning, laundry service, meeting rooms, free parking, some pets allowed (fee), no-smoking rooms* ▤ *AE, DC, MC, V* ⦿ℇ *BP.*

★ ££££ ▦ **Shakespeare Hotel.** Built in the 1400s, this Elizabethan town house in the heart of town is a vision right out of *The Merry Wives of Windsor,* with its five gables and long, stunning, black-and-white half-timber facade. The comfortably modernized interiors have a touch of luxury; Shakespeareana and old playbills decorate in the public areas. Upstairs, rooms are named after the characters from Shakespeare's plays and the actors who have portrayed them. Hewn timbers carved with rose-and-thistle patterns decorate some rooms; all have CD players. ⊠ *Chapel St., CV37 6ER* ☎ *0870/400–8182* 🖷 *01789/415411* ⊕ *www.macdonald-hotels.co.uk* ⤶ *64 rooms, 6 suites* △ *Restaurant, room service, cable TV, bar, lounge, laundry service, meeting rooms, parking (fee), some pets allowed (fee), no-smoking rooms; no a/c* ▭ *AE, DC, MC, V.*

£££–££££ 🏨 **Stratford Victoria.** Despite its name, the Victoria is actually quite modern. It may lack the period charm of older hotels, but its up-to-date facilities, spacious rooms, and ample grounds make it a good option for those for whom Tudor beamed ceilings are nothing more than something to bump your head into. Rooms, all in dark wood with burgundy and green color schemes, come in several shapes: some have four-poster beds or accommodate four people, others are geared to business travel. Guests can use the leisure facilities, including an indoor pool, at a sister hotel, the Stratford Manor, 3 mi away. ⊠ *Arden St., CV37 6QQ* ☎ *01789/271000* 🖷 *01789/271001* ⊕ *www.marstonhotels.com* ⤶ *102 rooms* △ *Restaurant, room service, cable TV, in-room data ports, gym, hot tub, massage, bar, lounge, babysitting, laundry service, meeting rooms, broadband, free parking, no-smoking floors; no a/c* ▭ *AE, DC, MC, V* ⦿| *BP.*

★ £££ 🏨 **White Swan.** Exposed beams, low ceilings, and winding corridors make this cozy hotel a delight for those who like a little authenticity. It claims to be the oldest building in town, and the look of the exterior (circa 1450) reinforces that boast. Each room is individually decorated, and although fabrics are not luxurious, admirable effort has been made to avoid traditional chintz. Heavy antiques mix with reproductions; some rooms have fireplaces, and some have four-poster beds. Bathrooms are tucked into what little space is available. The popular pub, a traditional English boozer with ancient beams, attracts visitors and locals. ⊠ *Rother St., CV37 6NH* ☎ *01789/297022* 🖷 *01789/26877* ⊕ *www.thewhiteswanstratford.co.uk* ⤶ *41 rooms* △ *Restaurant, room service, some in-room data ports, meeting rooms, free parking; no a/c in some rooms* ▭ *MC, V* ⦿| *BP.*

> ## THE PUB'S THE THING
>
> Take a break from Shakespeare. Having a pint of ale at the White Swan, on a cool night when the fires are lit and the mood is jovial, is a true English experience. You never know which direction the conversation will turn. Or stop by another of Stratford's pubs, such as the Black Swan (also known as the Dirty Duck).

££ ⌂ **Victoria Spa Lodge.** This good-value B&B lies 1½ mi outside town, within view of the Stratford Canal. The grand, clematis-drape building dates from 1837; you can see Queen Victoria's coat of arms in two of its gables. Dark-wood and plain white furnishings decorate the lounge–breakfast room and spacious guest rooms. ✉ *Bishopton La., Bishopton, CV37 9QY* ☎ *01789/267985* 🖷 *01789/204728* ⊕ *www. victoriaspa.co.uk* ↵ *7 rooms* ⌂ *Free parking; no a/c, no room phones, no smoking* ⊟ *MC, V* ⍾ *BP.*

★ £ ⌂ **Heron Lodge.** Just a half mile outside of Stratford town center, this B&B combines budget accommodation in a family home with luxurious service. Rooms are individually decorated, and the conservatory is perfect for an afternoon cup of tea. Owners Chris and Bob Heaps are serious about breakfast, serving pancakes made from a family recipe; locally sourced ingredients—from tea to jam and sausages—appear on the menu. You can also get a top-quality English breakfast. ✉ *260 Alcester Rd., CV37 9JQ* ☎ *01789/299169* ⊕ *www.heronlodge.com* ↵ *5 rooms* ⌂ *Lounge, free parking; no a/c, no kids under 5, no smoking* ⊟ *AE, MC, V* ⍾ *BP.*

Nightlife & the Arts

Festivals

The **Stratford-upon-Avon Shakespeare Birthday Celebrations** (✉ Shakespeare Centre, Henley St., Stratford-upon-Avon, CV37 6QW ☎ 01789/415536 ⊕ www.shakespeare.org.uk) take place on and around the weekend closest to April 23 (unless Easter occurs during that time). The events, spread over four days, include a formal reception, lectures, free concerts, processions, and a special performance of a play. For tickets for the three-course birthday luncheon in the marquee on the Avon Paddock, write the Shakespeare Birthday Celebrations secretary at the address above, call, or check the Web site.

The **Mop Fair,** dating from medieval times, takes place on or around October 12, traditionally the time when laborers and apprentices from the surrounding area came to seek work. They carried implements of their trades so that prospective employers could identify them. The fair still attracts entertainers and fairground amusements.

Theater

Fodor'sChoice
★ The **Royal Shakespeare Company** (✉ Waterside, Stratford-upon-Avon, CV37 6BB ☎ 0870/609–1110 ticket hotline, 01789/296655 general information 🖷 01789/403413 ⊕ www.rsc.org.uk) performs Shakespeare plays year-round in Stratford, as well as in other venues around Britain. Stratford's Royal Shakespeare Theatre is the home of the RSC, one of the finest repertory troupes in the world and long the backbone of the country's theatrical life. Although the company's main stage will close for three years beginning in spring 2007, performances will take place at a temporary space. In September and October, visiting companies perform opera, ballet, and musicals. The Swan Theatre, behind the Royal Shakespeare Theatre, stages plays by Shakespeare contemporaries such as Christopher Marlowe and Ben Jonson. In the Other Place, the RSC performs some of its most adventurous work. Prices usually are £7 to

£45. Book ahead, as seats go fast, but day of performance (two per person to personal callers only) and returned tickets are often available. You can book tickets from London with **Ticketmaster** (☎ 0870/534–4444 ⊕ www.ticketmaster.co.uk), operating 24 hours a day. You can book tickets in the United States (a 20% surcharge applies) with **Keith Prowse** (☎ 212/398–1430 or 800/669–8687 ⊕ www.keithprowse.com).

Sports & the Outdoors

Avon Cruises (⊠ The Boatyard, Swan's Nest La. ☎🖥 01789/267073) rents boats and provides half-hour river excursions for an escape from the crowds; the company can arrange longer trips from Easter to October. **Bancroft Cruises** (⊠ Moathouse, Bridgefoot ☎ 01789/269669) runs half-hourly excursions on the river. Hourlong trips farther afield can also be scheduled.

Shopping

Chain stores and shops sell tourist junk, but this is also a good place to shop for high-quality (and high-price) silver, jewelry, and china. There's an open market (great for bargains) every Friday in the Market Place at Greenhill and Meer streets. **Antique Arms & Armour** (⊠ Poet's Arbour, Sheep St. ☎ 01789/293453) sells antique swords, sabers, and armor. The **Antique Market** (⊠ Ely St.) contains 50 stalls of jewelry, silver, linens, porcelain, and memorabilia. **B&W Thornton** (⊠ 23 Henley St. ☎ 01789/269405), above Shakespeare's Birthplace, stocks Moorcroft pottery and glass. **Chaucer Head Bookshop** (⊠ 21 Chapel St. ☎ 01789/415691) is the best of Stratford's many secondhand bookshops. The **Shakespeare Bookshop** (⊠ 39 Henley St. ☎ 01789/201820), run by the Shakespeare Birthplace, carries Elizabethan plays, Tudor history books, children's books, and general paraphernalia.

Warwick

㉖ *9 mi northeast of Stratford-upon-Avon.*

Most famous for Warwick Castle—that vision out of the feudal ages—the town of Warwick (pronounced *wa*-rick) is an interesting architectural mix of Georgian redbrick and Elizabethan half-timbering. Much of the town center has been spoiled by unattractive postwar development, but look for the 15th-century half-timber **Lord Leycester Hospital,** which has provided a home for old soldiers since the earl of Leicester dedicated it to that purpose in 1571. Within the complex are a chapel and a fine courtyard, complete with a wattle-and-daub balcony and 500-year-old gardens. Try a cream tea in the Brethren's Kitchen. *⊠ High St. ☎ 01926/491422 ⊠ £3.20 ☉ Apr.–Sept., Tues.–Sun. 10–5; Oct.–Mar., Tues.–Sun. 10–4.*

Crowded with gilded, carved, and painted tombs, the **Beauchamp Chapel** of the **Collegiate Church of St. Mary** is the essence of late-medieval and Tudor chivalry—although it was built (1443–64) to honor the somewhat-less-than-chivalrous Richard Beauchamp, who consigned Joan of Arc to the flames. Colored bosses (projecting blocks), fan tracery, and flying ribs distinguish the chapel, which holds many monuments

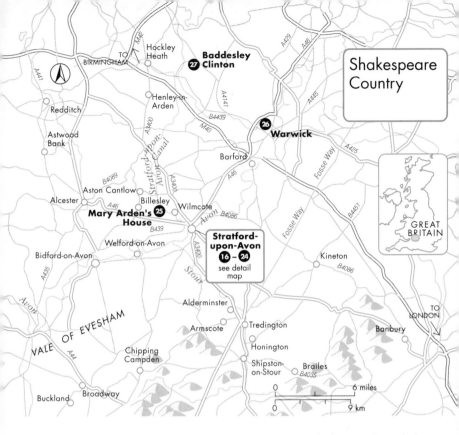

to the Beauchamps (several of whom became earl of Warwick), including Richard Beauchamp's impressive effigy in bronze and the alabaster table tomb of Thomas Beauchamp and his wife. Robert Dudley, earl of Leicester, adviser and favorite of Elizabeth I, is also buried here. There's a brass-rubbing center, and you can climb the tower in summer. It's a five-minute walk from Warwick Castle. ✉ *Church St., Old Sq.* ☎ *01926/403940* ⊕ *www.saintmaryschurch.co.uk* ✉ *Free* ⊙ *Apr.–Oct., daily 10–6; Nov.–Mar., daily 10–4:30.*

★ ℭ The vast bulk of medieval **Warwick Castle** rests on a cliff overlooking the Avon—"the fairest monument of ancient and chivalrous splendor which yet remains uninjured by time," to use the words of Sir Walter Scott. Its two soaring towers can be seen for miles: the 147-foot-high Caesar's Tower, built in 1356, and the 128-foot-high Guy's Tower, built in 1380. The towers bristle with battlements, and their irregular forms allowed defenders to shoot from numerous points. The castle's most powerful commander was Richard Neville, earl of Warwick, known during the 15th-century Wars of the Roses as the Kingmaker. Warwick Castle's monumental walls now enclose an armory with one of the best collections of medieval armor and weapons in Europe, as well as state rooms with historic furnishings and paintings by Peter Paul Rubens, Anthony van Dyck, and other old masters. Twelve rooms are devoted to an imaginative Madame Tussaud's wax exhibition, "A Royal Weekend Party—1898" (the Tussaud's Group owns the castle). Another exhibit displays the sights and sounds of a great medieval household as it prepares for an important battle. At the Mill and Engine House, you can see the turning water mill and the engines used to generate electricity early in the 20th century. Below

> **WORD OF MOUTH**
>
> "I hated the thought of Warwick Castle becoming a theme park. But [Tussaud's] made it a better visitors' experience and it isn't schlocky (well, some exhibits in the cellars tend to the tacky side). The Edwardian house party is wonderful."   –Janis

the castle, along the Avon, strutting peacocks patrol 60 acres of grounds elegantly landscaped by Capability Brown in the 18th century. ■ TIP→ **You could spend a full day exploring everything, so arrive early to beat the crowds. There are sometimes coupons on the castle's Web site for £5 off ticket prices.** Lavish medieval banquets (extra charge) and special events, including festivals, jousting tournaments, and a Christmas market, take place throughout the year, and a restaurant in the cellars serves lunch. Head to the bridge across the river to get the best view of the castle. ⊠ *Castle La. off Mill St., Warwick* ☎ *01926/495421, 08704/422000 24-hr information line* ⊕ *www.warwick-castle.co.uk* ✉ *Nov.–Feb. £13.95, Mar.–mid-July £15.95, mid-July–Oct. £17.95* ☺ *Apr.–July and Sept., daily 10–6; Aug., weekdays 10–6, weekends 10–7; Oct.–Mar., daily 10–5.*

■ NEED A BREAK?   **After a vigorous walk around the ramparts at Warwick Castle, you can drop by the cream, crimson, and golden vaulted, 14th-century Undercroft (☎ 01926/495421) for a refreshing spot of tea or a hot meal from the cafeteria.**

Where to Stay & Eat

££   ✕⊞ **Rose and Crown.** Stripped pine floorboards, red walls, big wooden tables, and solidly good food and drink set the tone at this contemporary pub (££–£££) with rooms on the town's main square. The deli board lists marinated anchovies, crayfish tails, and fruit and cheese; other options are coq au vin with sweet potato and ginger puree, and Aberdeen rump steak and chips. Bedrooms are simple but clean and modern. All in all, this is a decent value for a pint and a meal or a moderately priced room. ⊠ *30 Market Pl., CV34 4SH* ☎ *01926/411117* ⊕ *www.peachpubs. com* ⇨ *5 rooms* ⵁ *Restaurant, in-room data ports, meeting rooms; no a/c, no smoking* ⊟ *MC, V* ⦿ *CP.*

££   ⊞ **Lord Leycester Hotel.** Built in 1726, this house with an appealing central location became a hotel in 1925, and signs of age and history abound. The small, comfortably furnished rooms and even smaller bathrooms with showers are not to everyone's taste. ⊠ *17 Jury St., CV34 4EJ* ☎ *01926/491481* ☎ *01926/491561* ⊕ *www.lord-leycester.co.uk* ⇨ *49 rooms* ⵁ *2 restaurants, room service, room TVs with movies, some in-room data ports, bar, lounge, babysitting, laundry service, meeting rooms, free parking, some pets allowed (fee), no-smoking rooms; no a/c* ⊟ *AE, DC, MC, V* ⦿ *BP.*

Baddesley Clinton

★ ㉗ *6 mi northwest of Warwick, 15 mi north of Stratford-upon-Avon.*

"As you approach Baddesley Clinton, it stands before you as the perfect late medieval manor house. The entrance side of grey stone, the small, creeper-clad Queen Anne brick bridge across the moat, the gateway with a porch higher than the roof and embattled—it could not be better." So wrote the eminent architectural historian Sir Nikolaus Pevsner, and the house lives up to his praise. Set off a winding back-road, the manor retains its great fireplaces, 17th-century paneling, and three priest holes (secret chambers for Roman Catholic priests, who were hidden by sympathizers when Catholicism was banned in the 16th and 17th centuries). The café is an idyllic spot for tea and cakes. Admission to the house is by timed ticket. ■ TIP➔ **Ask about reservations for evening tours on Wednesday and Thursday; you may even be able to include dinner.** ✉ *Rising La., off A4141 near Chadwick End* ☎ *01564/783294* ⊕ *www. nationaltrust.org.uk* ⌘ *£6.80, garden only £3.40, combined ticket with Packwood House £9.80* ☉ *House Mar., Apr., and Oct., Wed.–Sun. 1:30–5; May–Sept., Wed.–Sun. 1:30–5:30. Garden Mar., Apr., and Oct., Wed.–Sun. noon–5; May–Sept., Wed.–Sun. noon–5:30; Nov.–mid-Dec., Wed.–Sun. noon–4:30.*

COTSWOLDS & SHAKESPEARE COUNTRY ESSENTIALS

Transportation

BY AIR

This area is about two hours from London; Bristol and Birmingham have the closest regional airports. Bristol's airport is 8 mi south of the city; it also has limited service from New York.

🛈 **Birmingham International Airport** ✉ A45, off Junction 6 of M42 ☎ 0870/733–5511 ⊕ www.bhx.co.uk. **Bristol International Airport** ✉ Bridgwater Rd., Lulsgate ☎ 0870/ 121–2747 ⊕ www.bristolairport.co.uk.

BY BUS

National Express serves the region from London's Victoria Coach Station. Flightlink buses run from London's Heathrow and Gatwick airports to Warwick. Megabus, a budget service that you book on the Internet, serves Cheltenham and Gloucester. Stagecoach, Castleways, and Pulhams operate local routes throughout the Stratford, Gloucestershire, and Cotswolds region. For all bus inquiries, call Traveline. Travel times vary; it can take about three hours to get to Burford or Cheltenham. Trains are faster. Although you can get around the Cotswolds by bus, service between some towns can be extremely limited, perhaps only twice a week.

Some bus routes to major Cotswold destinations are as follows (when not stated otherwise, routes are serviced by National Express buses and depart from London's Victoria Coach Station). Bourton-on-the-Water: take Pulhams buses from Cheltenham or Stow-on-the-Wold (no Sunday bus service in winter). Broadway: from Cheltenham, four Castle-ways coaches daily serve the town Monday to Saturday, and four Stage-coach coaches serve the town on Sunday. Burford (A40 turnout): Swanbrook buses leave from Cheltenham three times daily Monday to Saturday, once on Sunday; from London, change at Oxford. Chel-tenham and Cirencester: buses leave London hourly. Moreton-in-Marsh: buses depart five times daily from London, changing at Cirencester. Painswick: Stagecoach buses run from Cheltenham (hourly Monday to Saturday). Stow-on-the-Wold: Pulhams buses run six times daily (not Sunday in winter) from Moreton-in-Marsh.

FARES &
SCHEDULES
Castleways ☎ 01242/602949. **First** ☎ 0845/606-4446 ⊕ www.firstbadgerline.co.uk. **Megabus** ⊕ www.megabus.com. **National Express** ☎ 0870/580-8080 ⊕ www.nationalexpress.com. **Pulhams** ☎ 01451/820369 ⊕ www.pulhamscoaches.com. **Stage-coach** ☎ 01242/224853, 01788/535555 or 0845/600-1314 ⊕ www.stagecoachbus.com. **Swanbrook** ☎ 01452/712386 ⊕ www.swanbrook.co.uk. **Traveline** ☎ 0870/608-2608 ⊕ www.traveline.org.uk.

BY CAR

Stratford lies about 100 mi northwest of London; take M40 to Junc-tion 15. The town is 37 mi southeast of Birmingham by A435 and A46 or by M40 to Junction 15. From London, you can also take M40 and A40 to the Cotswolds. M4 is the main route west from London to south-ern Gloucestershire; expect about a two-hour drive. From Exit 20, take M5 north to Cheltenham; from Exit 15, take A419 to A429 north to the Cotswolds.

In Stratford and Cheltenham, garage your car or leave it at your hotel and forgo the stress of finding parking and negotiating one-way streets.

BY TRAIN

First Great Western, Wales and West, Virgin, Central, and Thames trains serve the region from London's Paddington Station, or, less fre-quently, from Euston. Most trains to Cheltenham (2 hours) involve a change at Swindon. A three-day or seven-day Heart of England Rover ticket is valid for unlimited travel within the region.

Four direct trains (two in the morning and two in the afternoon) from London's Paddington Station take two hours to reach Stratford; these avoid a change at Leamington Spa. Two direct trains return from Strat-ford each evening. On Sunday in winter there are no direct trains. You can travel by train *and* bus using the Shakespeare Connection Road & Rail Link from Euston Station to Coventry, then a City Sightseeing bus (⇨ Tour Options).

The Shakespeare Connection trip takes two hours, and there are four departures on weekdays—the three that would allow you to catch an evening performance in Stratford are at 9:15 AM, 10:45 AM, and 4:55 PM; Saturday departures are at 9:05 AM, 10:35 AM, and 5:05 PM; the Sun-day departure is at 9:45 AM. There's a train to London after perform-ances, usually at 11:15 PM. Schedules can change, so call to confirm times. National Rail Enquiries has further information.

Some pointers for reaching central Cotswold destinations by train follow. Broadway: train to Moreton-in-Marsh or Evesham, then bus or taxi locally to reach the town. Burford: train to Oxford, then bus from the Taylor Institute. Cirencester: train from London Paddington to Kemble (4 mi from town). Bourton-on-the-Water, Chipping Campden, and Stow-on-the-Wold: train to Moreton-in-Marsh, then local bus lines (some have minimal schedules). Moreton-in-Marsh is serviced by train from London Paddington daily. Local tourist offices have details.

FARES &
SCHEDULES   **National Rail Enquiries** ☎ 0845/748–4950 ⊕ www.nationalrail.co.uk.

Contacts & Resources

EMERGENCIES

Ambulance, fire, police ☎ 999. **Cheltenham General Hospital** ⊠ Sandford Rd. ☎ 0845/422–2222. **Stratford-upon-Avon Hospital** ⊠ Arden St., Stratford-upon-Avon ☎ 01789/205831. **Warwick Hospital** ⊠ Lakin Rd., Warwick ☎ 01926/495321.

INTERNET

Internet connections are variable in the rural Cotswolds, though full facilities are increasingly offered in the region's hotels and B&Bs; Wi-Fi may be available in some or all rooms. You'll find public Internet cafés in Cheltenham, Stratford, and Warwick. Cheltenham's Everyman Theatre has free access and a wireless facility.

Internet Cafés Smart Space Internet Café ⊠ County Bar, Everyman Theatre, Regent St., Cheltenham ☎ 01242/572573. **Stratford Leisure & Visitor Centre** ⊠ Bridgefoot, Stratford-upon-Avon ☎ 01789/268826. **The King's Head** ⊠ 39 Saltisford, Warwick ☎ 01926/775177.

TOUR OPTIONS

Based in Oxford, Cotswold Roaming is a stylish outfit offering tours of the Cotswolds (Tuesday and Saturday) in small vehicles. The full-day tour of the Cotswolds takes in Bourton-on-the-Water, Upper Slaughter and Lower Slaughter, Chipping Campden, Sudeley Castle, and Stow-on-the-Wold. Half-day tours are also offered. The pickup point is next to the Playhouse Theatre in Beaumont Street, Oxford.

The Heart of England Tourist Board (⇨ Visitor Information) arranges tours throughout the region. The tours don't include admission to the Stratford sights (most of which are within walking distance in town), so some people find the tour isn't the best value. The two-hour Shakespeare's Life in Stratford walk, led by actors, begins at 10:30 AM on Saturday October through March, Thursday and Saturday April through September, and Thursday, Saturday, and Sunday July through September. City Sightseeing runs half-day tours from Stratford-upon-Avon into the Cotswolds from Easter through September.

City Sightseeing ☎ 01789/299123 ⊕ www.city-sightseeing.com. **Cotswold Roaming** ☎ 01865/308300 ⊕ www.oxfordcity.co.uk/cotswold-roaming. **Shakespeare's Life in Stratford Walk** ☎ 01789/403405.

6

VISITOR INFORMATION

The Heart of England Tourist Board is open Monday through Thursday 9 to 5:30, Friday 9 to 5. Local tourist information centers are normally open Monday through Saturday 9:30 to 5:30, but times vary according to season. Note that Cirencester's and Stow-on-the-Wold's Web site cover the whole of the Cotswolds. The Web site ⊕ www.cotswolds.com has information from a group of tourism organizations in the area.

🚩 **The Cotswolds** ⊕ www.cotswolds.com. **Gloucestershire Cotswolds** ⊕ www.gloscotswolds.com. **Heart of England Tourism** ⊠ Larkhill Rd., Worcester WR5 2EZ ☎ 01905/761100 🖧 01905/763450 ⊕ www.visitheartofengland.com. **Shakespeare Country** ☎ 0870/160-7930 ⊕ www.shakespeare-country.co.uk. **Bourton-on-the-Water** ⊠ Victoria St., GL54 2BU ☎ 01451/820211. **Broadway** ⊠ 1 Cotswold Ct., WR12 7AA ☎ 01386/852937. **Burford** ⊠ The Brewery, Sheep St., OX18 4LP ☎ 01993/823558 ⊕ www.oxfordshirecotswolds.co.uk. **Cheltenham** ⊠ 77 Promenade, GL50 1PP ☎ 01242/522878 ⊕ www.visitcheltenham.com. **Chipping Campden** ⊠ The Old Police Station, High St., GL55 6HB ☎ 01386/841206 ⊕ www.visitchippingcampden.com. **Cirencester** ⊠ Corn Hall, Market Pl., GL7 2NW ☎ 01285/654180 ⊕ www.cotswold.gov.uk. **Moreton-in-Marsh** ⊠ High St., GL56 0AZ ☎ 01608/650881 ⊕ www.moreton-in-marsh.co.uk. **Painswick** ⊠ The Library, Stroud Rd., GL6 6UT ☎ 01452/813552. **Stow-on-the-Wold** ⊠ Hollis House, The Square, GL54 1AF ☎ 01451/831082 ⊕ www.cotswold.gov.uk. **Stratford-upon-Avon** ⊠ Bridgefoot, CV37 6GW ☎ 0870/160-7930 ⊕ www.stratford-upon-avon.co.uk. **Tetbury** ⊠ 33 Church St., GL8 8JG ☎ 01666/503552 ⊕ www.tetbury.org. **Warwick** ⊠ Court House, Jury St., CV34 4EW ☎ 01926/492212 ⊕ www.warwick-uk.co.uk.

The Northwest

MANCHESTER, LIVERPOOL & THE PEAK DISTRICT

7

WORD OF MOUTH

"In Manchester, have a look inside the glorious Town Hall, which has been used in movies as a stand-in for the Parliament in London. Walk down to the renovated Castlefield area, perhaps taking in the Museum of Science and Industry. If you fancy hedonism, trot along Canal Street, home of gay and gay-friendly crowds who like to party hard."

—Nigello

"I'd choose Chatsworth. It is among the three or four grandest houses in the United Kingdom, and it looks basically like it has for the past several centuries."

—Anglophile

Updated by
Kate Hughes

FOR THOSE LOOKING FOR THE POSTCARD ENGLAND of little villages and churches, the northwest region of England might not appear at the top of a sightseeing list. Manchester today bustles with redevelopment and youth culture, and Liverpool's upcoming stint as the European Union's Capital of Culture in 2008 is bringing exciting changes; but 200 years of smokestack industry, which abated only in the 1980s, have taken a toll on the east Lancashire landscape. The region does have some lovely scenery inland, in Derbyshire (pronounced "Darbyshire")—notably the spectacular Peak District, a huge national park at the southern end of the Pennines range, which includes the stately pile of Chatsworth and romantic Haddon Hall. You'll also find elaborately decorated half-timber buildings filling the walled city of Chester south of Liverpool. One small corner of Shropshire, Ironbridge, in the south of the region, heralded the tumultuous birth of the Industrial Revolution with the invention of the coke blast furnace and the erection of the first iron bridge in 1779.

Manchester and Liverpool were the economic engines that propelled Britain in the 18th and 19th centuries, but they suffered decline in the mid-20th century. Both cities are sloughing off the recent past and celebrating their rich industrial and maritime heritage in their excellent museums—in imposing Victorian edifices, or, in Manchester's case, in strikingly modern buildings that are a statement in themselves. The cities are now reestablished as centers of sporting and musical and excellence, and nightlife hot spots. Since 1962, the Manchester United, Everton, and Liverpool football (soccer in the United States) clubs have won everything worth winning in Britain and Europe. The Beatles launched the Mersey sound of the '60s; contemporary Manchester groups ride both British and U.S. airwaves. On the classical side of music, Manchester is also the home of Britain's oldest leading orchestra, the Hallé (founded in 1857)—just one legacy of 19th-century industrialists' investments in culture.

Exploring the Northwest

Manchester lies at the heart of a tangle of motorways in the northwest of England, about a half hour across the Pennines from Yorkshire. It's 70 mi from the southern part of the Lake District. The city spreads west toward the coast and the mouth of the River Mersey, where Liverpool is still centered on its port. The Peak District national park is less than an hour's drive southeast of Manchester, and Chester is a 40-minute drive south of Liverpool. Traveling time to Ironbridge, 55 mi south of Chester, is around 1½ hrs.

About the Restaurants

Though Manchester currently has the edge over Liverpool, dining options in both cities vary from smart café-bars offering modern British and Continental fare to excellent ethnic restaurants. Manchester has one of Britain's biggest Chinatowns, and locals also savor the 40-odd Bangladeshi, Pakistani, and Indian restaurants along Wilmslow Road in Rusholme, 1 mi south of the city center, known as Curry Mile (check out ⊕ www.rusholmecurry.co.uk). One local dish that has survived is Bakewell pudding (*never* called "tart" in these areas, as its imitations are elsewhere in England). Served with custard or cream, the pudding is the joy of Bakewell.

About the Hotels

If your trip centers on the cities of the northwest, you may want to base yourself in Manchester (which has a better choice of accommodations, though Liverpool's are improving steadily) and make Liverpool a day trip. The larger city-center hotels in both cities often markedly reduce their rates on weekends. Smaller hotels and guesthouses abound in nearby suburbs, many just a short bus ride from downtown. The Manchester Visitor Centre operates a room-booking service. Liverpool is also easily explored from Chester, which has many accommodation options.

	WHAT IT COSTS In pounds				
	£££££	**££££**	**£££**	**££**	**£**
RESTAURANTS	over £22	£18–£22	£13–£17	£7–£12	under £7
HOTELS	over £160	£120–£160	£90–£119	£60–£89	under £60

Restaurant prices are for a main course at dinner. Hotel prices are for two people in a standard double room in high season, including V.A.T., with no meals or, if indicated, CP (with continental breakfast), BP (Breakfast Plan, with full breakfast), or MAP (Modified American Plan, with breakfast and dinner).

Timing

Manchester has a reputation as one of the wettest cities in Britain, and visiting in summer won't guarantee fine weather. Nevertheless, the many indoor sights and cultural activities here and in Liverpool means that wet or cold weather shouldn't spoil a visit. Summer is the optimum time to see the Peak District, and Chatsworth and Haddon Hall are open only from spring through fall.

MANCHESTER

Manchester's center hums with the energy of cutting-edge popular music and a swank café-bar culture. The formerly grim industrial landscape has been redeveloped since the late 1980s, in part because of events as different as an IRA bombing in the city center in 1996 and the 2002 Commonwealth Games. Canals have been tidied up, cotton mills serve as loft apartments, and stylish contemporary architecture has transformed the skyline. Britain's tallest sculpture, the *B of the Bang,* at an intersection next to Manchester City Stadium, rises 184 feet in the air like a starburst of fireworks. Beetham Tower, the second-tallest building in Britain after London's Canary Wharf, opened in 2006. Bridgewater Hall and the Lowry, as well as the Imperial War Museum North, are outstanding cultural facilities. Sure, it still rains here, but the rain-soaked streets are part of the city's charm, in a bleak northern kind of way.

For most of its existence Manchester, which has a population of 2.6 million and is Britain's third-largest city, has been a thriving and prosperous place. The Romans built a fort here in AD 79 and named it Mamucium, but the city that stands today—with the imposing Town Hall, Royal Exchange, Midland Hotel, the waterways, and railway—is a product of the Industrial Revolution and the wealth it created.

It's impossible to talk about Manchester without mentioning music and football. Out of poverty and unemployment came the brash sounds of punk and the indie-record labels, and a thriving club scene. The band New Order produced a unique Mancunian sound that mixed live instruments with digital sound. The now-defunct Haçienda Club marketed New Order to the world, and Manchester became the clubbing capital of England. Joy Division, Morrissey, Stone Roses, Happy Mondays, and Oasis rose to the top of the charts. The triumphant reign of the Manchester United football club, which now faces new challenges from southern rivals Arsenal and Chelsea, has kept many eyes on Manchester.

Exploring Manchester

Manchester is compact enough that you can easily walk across the city center in 40 minutes, but buses and Metrolink trams make it easy to navigate. Deansgate and Princess Street, the main thoroughfares, run roughly north to south and west to east; the lofty terra-cotta Victorian **Town Hall** sits in the middle, close to the visitor center and the fine **Manchester Art Gallery.** Dominating the skyline at the southern end of Deansgate is Manchester's newest and highest building, Beetham Tower, which houses a Hilton Hotel and marks the beginning of the **Castlefield Urban Heritage Park,** with the Museum of Science and Industry and the canal system. Take a Metrolink tram 2 mi south for the Salford Quays dockland area, with the **Lowry** and the **Imperial War Museum;** you can spend half a day or more in this area. ■ TIP→ Shopping and nightlife offer great diversions in Manchester, but keep in mind that the museums are both excellent and free.

Main Attractions

③ Castlefield Urban Heritage Park. Site of an early Roman fort, the district of Castlefield was later the center of the city's industrial boom, which resulted in the building of Britain's first modern canal in 1764 and the world's first railway station in 1830. What had become an urban wasteland has been beautifully restored into an urban park with canal-side walks, landscaped open spaces, and refurbished warehouses. The 7-acre site contains the reconstructed gate to the Roman fort of Mamucium, the buildings of the **Museum of Science and Industry,** and several of the city's hippest bars and restaurants. ⊠ *Off Liverpool Rd., Castlefield.*

★ **Imperial War Museum North.** The thought-provoking exhibits in this striking, aluminum-clad building, which architect Daniel Libeskind described as representing three shards of an exploded globe, present the reasons for war and show its effects on society. Three Big Picture audiovisual shows envelop you in the sights and sounds of conflicts from 1914 to the present, and a storage system allows you to select trays of objects to view, including exhibits from the 2003 war in Iraq. A 100-foot viewing platform gives a bird's-eye view of the city. The museum is on the banks of the Manchester Ship Canal in Salford Quays, across the footbridge from the Lowry. It's a 10-minute walk from the Harbour

TOP REASONS TO GO

The Beatles: Whether you want to relive the Fab Four's moments of glory, visit their haunts, see their childhood homes, or just buy a Beatle pencil sharpener, a Magical Mystery Tour in Liverpool will provide it all.

Museums in Manchester and Liverpool: You don't need the excuse of rain to learn about these cities' industrial and maritime pasts, or to see the glories of English art; visit even on a sunny day. Take history lessons at the Museum of Science and Industry and the Imperial War Museum North in Manchester, and the Merseyside Maritime Museum in Liverpool. Then opt for art appreciation in the cities' galleries.

Manchester nightspots: Catch the city at night in any of its humming café-bars and pubs; strut your stuff, soak up the latest sounds, or just enjoy a good beer in a gloriously ornate Victorian pub.

Chatsworth House and Haddon Hall: Engage the past and imagine yourself as a country landowner roaming the great pile that is Chatsworth, or as a Tudor noble exercising in the intricate long gallery of the quintessentially English Haddon Hall. Each can take you a half-day—Chatsworth a day—to explore.

Ironbridge Gorge: Recall the burgeoning of England's Industrial Revolution at the complex of museums within the shadow of this graceful bridge, the first of its kind in the world.

City stop of the Metrolink tram. ✉ *Trafford Wharf Rd., Salford Quays* ☎ *0161/836–4000* ⊕ *www.iwm.org.uk* ✉ *Free* ☉ *Mar.–Oct., daily 10–6; Nov.–Feb., daily 10–5; last admission 30 mins before closing.*

The Lowry. This impressive arts center in Manchester's Salford Quays waterways occupies a dramatic modern building with a steel-gray metallic and glass exterior that reflects the light. L. S. Lowry (1887–1976) was a local artist, and one of the few who painted the industrial landscape. Galleries showcase Lowry's and other contemporary artists' work. The theater, Britain's largest outside London, presents an impressive lineup of touring companies. The nearest Metrolink tram stop is Harbour City, a 10-minute walk from the Lowry. ✉ *Pier 8, Salford Quays* ☎ *0161/876–2000* ⊕ *www.thelowry.com* ✉ *Free; prices vary for theater tickets and exhibitions; tours £3* ☉ *Building Sun. and Mon. 10–6, Tues.–Sat. 10–8, or last performance; galleries Sun.–Fri. 11–5, Sat. 10–5; tours daily 11:30, 1, and 2:30.*

★ ❷ **Manchester Art Gallery.** Behind its impressive classical portico, this splendid museum presents its collections in both a Victorian and contemporary setting. Outstanding are the vibrant paintings by the Pre-Raphaelites and their circle, exemplified by Ford Madox Brown's masterpiece *Work* and Holman Hunt's *The Hireling Shepherd*. British works from the 18th century—*Cheetah and Stag with Two Indians* by George Stubbs, for in-

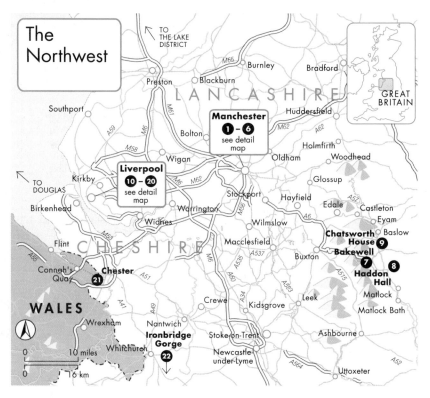

stance—and the 20th century are also well represented. The Manchester Gallery illustrates the city's contribution to art, and the 2nd-floor Craft and Design Gallery shows off the best of the decorative arts in ceramics and glass, metalwork, and furniture. ✉ *Mosely St., City Centre* ☎ *0161/235–8888* ⊕ *www.manchestergalleries.org.uk* ⌷ *Free* ⊙ *Tues.–Sun. and national holidays 10–5.*

❹ Museum of Science and Industry. The museum's five buildings, one of which is the world's oldest passenger rail station (1830), hold marvelous collections relating to the city's industrial past and present. You can walk through a reconstructed Victorian sewer, be blasted by the heat and noise of working steam engines, and see cotton looms whirring in action. The Air and Space Gallery fills a graceful cast-iron-and-glass building, constructed as a market hall in 1877. ■ TIP→ **Allow at least half a day to get the most out of all the sites, which are in the Castlefield Urban Heritage Park.** ✉ *Liverpool Rd., main entrance on Lower Byrom Rd., Castlefield* ☎ *0161/832–2244* ⊕ *www.msim.org.uk* ⌷ *Free, charges vary for special exhibitions* ⊙ *Daily 10–5.*

FodorśChoice
★

❺ PumpHouse: People's History Museum. Not everyone in 19th-century Manchester owned a cotton mill or made a fortune on the trading floor. This museum recounts powerfully the struggles of working people in

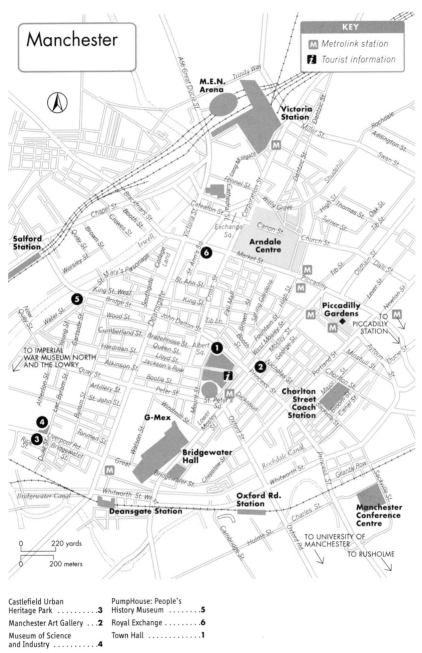

Manchester

KEY

Ⓜ *Metrolink station*

🛈 *Tourist information*

M.E.N. Arena

Victoria Station

Salford Station

Arndale Centre

Piccadilly Gardens

TO PICCADILLY STATION

Chorlton Street Coach Station

G-Mex

Bridgewater Hall

TO IMPERIAL WAR MUSEUM NORTH AND THE LOWRY

Deansgate Station

Oxford Rd. Station

Manchester Conference Centre

TO UNIVERSITY OF MANCHESTER

TO RUSHOLME

0   220 yards

0   200 meters

Castlefield Urban Heritage Park **3**	PumpHouse: People's History Museum **5**
Manchester Art Gallery ... **2**	Royal Exchange **6**
Museum of Science and Industry **4**	Town Hall **1**

the city since the Industrial Revolution. The museum tells the story of the 1819 Peterloo Massacre and has an unrivaled collection of trade-union banners, tools, toys, utensils, and photographs, all illustrating the working lives and pastimes of the city's people. ⊠ *Bridge St., City Centre* ☎ *0161/839–6061* ⊕ *www.peopleshistorymuseum.org.uk* ⊠ *Free* ☉ *Tues.–Sun. and national holidays 11–4:30.*

NEED A BREAK? The brick-vaulted, waterside **Mark Addy pub** (⊠ Stanley St., off Bridge St., City Centre ☎ 0161/832–4080) is a good spot to have a relaxing drink and sample an excellent spread of pâtés and cheeses. The pub is named for the 19th-century boatman who rescued more than 50 people from the River Irwell.

Also Worth Seeing

❻ **Royal Exchange.** Throughout its commercial heyday, this was the city's most important building—the cotton market. Built with Victorian panache in 1874, the existing structure accommodated 7,000 traders. The building was refurbished and the giant glass-dome roof restored after damage by the 1996 IRA bombing. Visit to see the lunar module–inspired Royal Exchange Theatre, to have a drink in the café, or to browse in the craft and clothes outlets in the arcade. ⊠ *St. Ann's Sq., City Centre* ☎ *0161/834–3731* ⊕ *www.royalexchange.co.uk.*

❶ **Town Hall.** Manchester's exuberant Town Hall, with its imposing 280-foot-tall clock tower, speaks volumes about the city's 19th-century sense of self-importance. Alfred Waterhouse designed the Victorian Gothic building (1867–76); extensions were added just before World War II. Over the main entrance is a statue of Roman general Agricola, who founded Mamucium in AD 79. Above him are Henry III, Elizabeth I, and St. George, the patron saint of England. Murals of the city's history, painted between 1852 and 1865 by the Pre-Raphaelite Ford Madox Brown, decorate the Great Hall, with its emblazoned hammer-beam roof. Guided tours (twice a month) include the murals, but ask at the front desk: if the rooms aren't being used, you may be allowed to wander in. ⊠ *Albert Sq., public entrance on Lloyd St., City Centre* ☎ *0161/234–5000* ⊠ *Free; guided tours £4* ☉ *Mon.–Sat. 9–4:30; not always open to public access; see tourist office in Town Hall Extension for tour information.*

Where to Eat

The city's dining scene, with everything from Indian (go to Rusholme) to modern British fare, is lively. The Manchester Food & Drink Festival, held the first two weeks of October, showcases the city's chefs and regional products with special events. The River Room at the Lowry Hotel, noted for its classic British dishes, is another excellent dining choice. The city's pubs (*see* Nightlife & the Arts, *below*) are also good for lunch or dinner.

★ ✕ **Juniper.** Chef Paul Kitchings aims to surprise and delight with his in-
££££–£££££ novative combinations of ingredients: scallops with raspberries and lamb with bees' pollen and curried mayonnaise, to name but a few. The £40 fixed-price menu offers three courses, but for £55 you can indulge in 12 bite- and small-size dishes. Gilt mirrors and large paintings decorate the restaurant's mint-green walls, and service is professional but

friendly. Altrincham, 8 mi south of Manchester, near the airport, is easily accessible by train. ✉ *21 The Downs, Altrincham* ☎ *0161/929–4008* ⌢ *Reservations essential* ⊟ *AE, MC, V* ⊗ *Closed Sun. and Mon. and 2 wks mid-Feb., 2 wks late Aug., 1 wk late Dec. No lunch Tues.–Thurs.*

★ **£££** ✕ **Market Restaurant.** Lace curtains, pretty china, and green basket-work chairs set the tone in this nicely old-fashioned, family-run restaurant. Food is up to the minute, though: you could start with a twice-baked crab soufflé, and follow with beef wrapped in bacon with Stilton butter and port-wine gravy. Leave room for a marzipan baklava with Jersey cream. Specialty beers and excellent wines fit the bill. ✉ *104 High St., Northern Quarter* ☎ *0161/834–3743* ⌢ *Reservations essential* ⊟ *AE, MC, V* ⊗ *Closed Sun.–Tues. No lunch Sat.*

£££ ✕ **Stock.** The Edwardian building that houses this buzzing Italian restaurant was once the city's stock exchange—hence its name and grand domed setting. Chef Enzo Mauro emphasizes the flavors of southern Italy on a menu that might list potato gnocchi with pumpkin and pancetta or pork fillet with rosemary and white wine; you can accompany this with a fine-quality wine. Bonuses are a good-value lunch deal, jazz on Friday, and occasional opera nights. ✉ *4 Norfolk St., City Centre* ☎ *0161/ 839–6644* ⊟ *AE, MC, V* ⊗ *Closed Sun.*

££–£££ ✕ **Le Petit Blanc.** Famed chef Raymond Blanc's upscale Manchester brasserie is faithful to its Parisian role models. Conversation buzzes in the relaxed yet elegant surroundings of the mostly white room. The menu combines the best traditions of French bourgeois cuisine with Asian and Mediterranean accents. Try the pasta with Roquefort sauce, celery, and toasted hazelnuts; finish up with banana and pecan toffee pudding with bitter chocolate and vanilla ice cream. Children are welcome and have their own menu. ✉ *55 King St., entrance on Chapel Walk, City Centre* ☎ *0161/832–1000* ⊟ *AE, MC, V.*

££–£££ ✕ **Mr. Thomas's Chophouse.** The city's oldest restaurant (1872) dishes out good old British favorites such as steak-and-kidney pudding, Cheshire gammon (ham), and corned beef hash. This hearty food is served in a Victorian-style room with a black-and-white-checked floor, brown ceilings, and dark-green tiling. The wine list is exceptional. Mr. Sam's Chophouse in Chapel Walks is just as busy and serves similar fare. ✉ *52 Cross St., City Centre* ☎ *0161/832–2245* ⊟ *AE, MC, V.*

££–£££ ✕ **Pacific.** Designed around feng-shui principles, this split-level concept restaurant fuses old and new Asian culture. The lower floor is China, the upper Thailand; each has a separate kitchen and chef. In China you can sample dim sum and à la carte dishes, with classic favorites as well as unusual delicacies such as honey-glazed eel fillets. Thailand has authentic regional cooking; try the roasted duck in red curry. ✉ *58–60 George St., City Centre* ☎ *0161/228–6668* ⊟ *AE, DC, MC, V.*

£–££ ✕ **Lal Haweli.** One of Rusholme's string of Indian restaurants, this bright and spacious establishment specializes in Nepalese offerings such as chicken sultani (with orange, pineapple, and chilies) and stir-fried Balti dishes from Pakistan, as well as tandooris and other Indian staples. The area, south of the city center, is easily accessible by bus. ✉ *68–72 Wilmslow Rd., Rusholme* ☎ *0161/248–9700* ⊟ *AE, MC, V.*

★ £–££   ✕ **Yang Sing.** One of Manchester's best Chinese restaurants, this place is popular with Chinese families, which is always a good sign. The menu of Cantonese dishes is huge, the dim sum are legendary, and there's plenty for the adventurous— ox tripe with black-bean sauce or shark's fin soup, for example. Vegetarians won't be disappointed, either. ⊠ *34 Princess St., City Centre* ☎ *0161/236–2200* ⊟ *AE, MC, V.*

> **WORD OF MOUTH**
>
> "If you like Indian food, you must go to Rusholme with its famous Curry Mile. There are also some excellent Chinese restaurants in Manchester."   –oldie

Where to Stay

£££££   🏨 **The Lowry Hotel.** The strikingly modern, ergonomic Italian design of
Fodor's Choice   this glass edifice exudes luxury and spaciousness. The clean-lined pub-
★   lic and guest rooms are washed in soothing neutral tones, enlivened by brilliant red splashes of furniture; marble bathrooms and walk-in closets enhance the bedrooms. The elegant River Room restaurant specializes in British dishes such as potted salmon, roast scallops with black pudding, and variations on a theme of strawberries. The hotel fronts the River Irwell across from the landmark Trinity Bridge designed by Santiago Calatrava. ⊠ *50 Dearman's Pl., City Centre, M3 5LH* ☎ *0161/ 827–4000* 🖷 *0161/827–4001* ⊕ *www.thelowryhotel.com* ☎ *157 rooms, 7 suites* ♻ *Restaurant, cable TV with movies, in-room DVDs, in-room broadband, in-room data ports, indoor pool, health club, hair salon, sauna, spa, steam room, bar, business services, meeting rooms, parking (fee), no-smoking floors* ⊟ *AE, DC, MC, V* ⦿I *BP.*

££££–£££££   🏨 **Arora International.** The centrally located Arora occupies one of the city's grand Victorian buildings, opposite the Manchester Art Gallery, but its design is minimalist modern. Chunky contemporary upholstered furnishings fill the public areas and guest rooms, where favored colors are beiges and muted reds and purples. Five rooms, inspired by Cliff Richard songs, contain artwork and memorabilia from Sir Cliff's own collection, and all the luxurious bathrooms have music speakers. ⊠ *18–24 Princess St., City Centre, M1 4LY* ☎ *0161/236–8999* 🖷 *0161/ 236–3222* ⊕ *www.arorainternational.com* ☎ *141 rooms* ♻ *Restaurant, in-room safes, refrigerators, cable TV, in-room broadband, Wi-Fi, gym, bar, meeting rooms* ⊟ *AE, MC, V* ⦿I *BP, EP.*

£££–£££££   🏨 **The Midland Hotel.** The Edwardian splendor of the hotel's public rooms still manages to shine through a contemporary makeover, evoking the days when this was Manchester's railroad station hotel. High tea (£16, book in advance) is still served in the grand lobby. Guest rooms, with huge photos of Manchester as bedheads, are pleasant and light, with contemporary walnut furniture and dark-purple and cream furnishings. ⊠ *Peter St., City Centre, M60 2DS* ☎ *0161/236–3333* 🖷 *0161/ 932–4100* ⊕ *www.qhotels.co.uk* ☎ *298 rooms, 14 suites* ♻ *2 restaurants, cable TV with movies, in-room safes, in-room broadband, in-room data ports, Wi-Fi, indoor pool, gym, squash court, health club, hair salon, sauna, 2 bars, lounge, business services, meeting rooms, parking (fee), some pets allowed* ⊟ *AE, DC, MC, V* ⦿I *BP.*

££££ 🏨 **The Place Apartment Hotel.** Cast-iron columns rise side by side with palm trees in this elegantly converted former cotton warehouse with loft-style apartments. It's a good alternative for people who want the convenience of a kitchen or a second bedroom. The spacious rooms, built around an atrium, still retain the original redbrick work but are fitted out in cool blues and light-wood furniture. One- and two-bedroom apartments are available. ✉ *Ducie St, Piccadilly City Centre, M1 2TP* 🕿 *0161/778–7500* 🖷 *0161/778–7507* ⊕ *www.theplacehotel.com* ⬎ *100 apartments, 8 penthouses* ⚭ *Restaurant, kitchens, cable TV, in-room DVDs, Wi-Fi, meeting rooms, parking (fee); no a/c* ⊟ *AE, DC, MC, V.*

£££–££££ 🏨 **Rossetti.** The girders, parquet flooring, and tiles of this converted Victorian textile warehouse (which used to supply floral print dresses to Queen Elizabeth II) are still here, but the feather-soft beds, Molteni furniture, and funky lights are determinedly cool. Each floor has a help-yourself breakfast bar, the café-restaurant dishes up Neapolitan pizzas, and a glitzy nightclub occupies the basement. ✉ *107 Piccadilly, City Centre, M1 2DB* 🕿 *0161/247–7744* 🖷 *0161/247–7747* ⊕ *www.aliasrossetti. com* ⬎ *56 rooms, 5 suites* ⚭ *Restaurant, in-room DVDs, in-room broadband, in-room data ports, Wi-Fi, bar, nightclub, meeting rooms, parking (fee), some pets allowed; no a/c* ⊟ *AE, MC, V* ⏁ *CP.*

££–££££ 🏨 **Jurys Inn.** A good-value outpost of the Irish-based chain, Jurys has a sleek wooden lobby and contemporary design that's light and attractive. Guest rooms are spacious, and you can use a nearby health club. The location is excellent—next to Bridgewater Hall and close to shopping on King Street and the café-bar scenes on Whitworth Street and in Castlefield. ✉ *56 Great Bridgewater St., Peter's Fields, M1 5LE* 🕿 *0161/ 953–8888* 🖷 *0161/953–9090* ⊕ *www.jurysdoyle.com* ⬎ *265 rooms* ⚭ *Restaurant, cable TV, in-room data ports, in-room broadband, Wi-Fi, bar, business services, meeting rooms, parking (fee), no-smoking floors* ⊟ *AE, DC, MC, V* ⏁ *BP.*

££ 🏨 **Castlefield Hotel.** This popular modern redbrick hotel sits near the water's edge in the Castlefield Basin. Public rooms are cheery and traditional, with patterned carpets and plain furnishings; subdued, warm tones help make the bedrooms restful. The leisure facilities and free breakfast make this a good value. ✉ *Liverpool Rd., Castlefield, M3 4JR* 🕿 *0161/832–7073* 🖷 *0161/837–3534* ⊕ *www.castlefield-hotel.co.uk* ⬎ *48 rooms* ⚭ *Restaurant, cable TV, Wi-Fi, indoor pool, health club, sauna, bar, meeting rooms, parking (fee); no a/c* ⊟ *AE, DC, MC, V* ⏁ *BP.*

£ 🏨 **The Ox.** Friendly and relaxed, this gastro-pub with rooms is a real find for those who just want the basics. Guest rooms are simple, creamy cool and modern in style. The buzz-filled restaurant, decorated with local artwork, serves modern British cuisine. Guest ales are on tap, complemented by a good selection of wines. ✉ *71 Liverpool Rd., Castlefield, M3 4NQ* 🕿 *0161/839–7740* 🖷 *0161/839–7760* ⊕ *www.theox.co.uk* ⬎ *9 rooms* ⚭ *Restaurant, bar; no a/c* ⊟ *MC, V.*

Nightlife & the Arts

Manchester vies with London as Britain's capital of youth culture but has vibrant nightlife and entertainment options for all ages. Spending time at a bar, pub, or club is definitely an essential part of any trip. For event listings, buy the *Manchester Evening News* or check out the free *Manchester Metro News* paper, usually found at tram stations.

Nightlife

The action after dark centers on the Deansgate, Northern Quarter, and Gay Village areas.

CAFÉ-BARS & PUBS **Barça** (✉ 8–9 Catalan Sq., Castlefield ☎ 0161/839–7099) is a hip canal-side bar-restaurant that has won architectural awards. **Dry Bar** (✉ 28–30 Oldham St., Northern Quarter ☎ 0161/236–9840), the original café-bar in town, is still full of young people drinking and dancing. Whether you come to see or be seen, the **Living Room** (✉ Deansgate, City Centre ☎ 0870/442–2537) is the city's top spot; a pianist plays in the early evening. **Obsidian** (✉ 18–24 Princess St., City Centre ☎ 0161/238–4348) has a huge frosted-glass bar and great cocktails. **Revolution** (✉ Arch 7, Whitworth St. W, Peter's Fields ☎ 0161/839–7558), one of the trendy bars converted from a railway arch in Deansgate Locks, is a vodka bar. **Tiger Tiger** (✉ 5–6 The Printworks, City Centre ☎ 0161/385–8080) is the place to go for a relaxed meal and to drink or dance.

★ The **Gay Village,** which came to television in the British series *Queer as Folk,* has stylish bars and cafés along the Rochdale Canal; Canal Street is its heart. The area is not only the center of Manchester's good-size gay scene but also the nightlife center for the young and trendy. The café-bar **Manto** (✉ 46 Canal St., Gay Village ☎ 0161/236–2667) draws a chic, mostly gay crowd to its split-level, postindustrial interior.

Fodor's Choice ★ **The Britons Protection** (✉ 50 Great Bridgewater St., Peter's Fields ☎ 0161/236–5895) stands out as a relaxed pub, with stained glass and cozy back rooms, a Peterloo Massacre mural, cask ales, and more than 230 whiskies and bourbons. **Peveril of the Peak** (✉ 127 Great Bridgewater St., Peter's Fields ☎ 0161/236–6364), a nifty Victorian pub with a green-tile exterior, draws a crush of locals to its tiny rooms. **Sinclair's Oyster Bar** (✉ 2 Cathedral Gates, Millennium Quarter ☎ 0161/834–0430), a half-timber pub built in the 17th century, specializes in fresh oyster dishes.

DANCE CLUBS **42nd Street** (✉ 2 Bootle St., off Deansgate, City Centre ☎ 0161/831–7108) plays retro, indie, sing-along anthems, and classic rock. **Sankey's Soap** (✉ Beehive Mill, Jersey St., Ancoats ☎ 0161/661–9668) covers anthems, drum 'n' bass breaks, beats, and hardcore.

LIVE MUSIC **Manchester Apollo** (✉ Stockport Rd., Ardwick Green ☎ 0870/401–8000) showcases acts for all musical tastes. Major rock and pop stars appear at the **Manchester Evening News Arena** (✉ 21 Hunt's Bank, Hunt's Bank ☎ 0870/190–8000). **The Roadhouse** (✉ 8 Newton St., City Centre ☎ 0161/237–9789), an intimate band venue, also hosts funk and indie nights.

The Arts

FILM The city's major center for contemporary cinema and the visual arts, the **Cornerhouse** (✉ 70 Oxford St., City Centre ☎ 0161/200–1500) has three movie screens plus galleries, a bookshop, a trendy bar, and a café.

PERFORMING-
ARTS VENUES

★ Dramatically modern **Bridgewater Hall** (⊠ Lower Mosley St., Peter's Fields ☎ 0161/907–9000) has concerts by Manchester's renowned Hallé Orchestra and hosts both classical music and a varied light-entertainment program. **The Lowry** (⊠ Pier 8, Salford Quays ☎ 0870/787–5780) contains two theaters and presents everything from musicals to dance and performance poetry. The **Opera House** (⊠ Quay St., City Centre ☎ 0870/401–6000) is a venue for West End musicals, opera, and classical ballet. The **Palace Theatre** (⊠ Oxford St., City Centre ☎ 0870/401–6000) presents large touring shows—major plays, ballet, and opera. **Royal Northern College of Music** (⊠ 124 Oxford Rd., University Quarter ☎ 0161/907–5555) hosts classical and contemporary music concerts, jazz, and opera.

THEATER **Green Room** (⊠ 54–56 Whitworth St. W, City Centre ☎ 0161/615–0500) is an alternative space for theater, poetry, dance, and performance art. **Library Theatre** (⊠ St. Peter's Sq., City Centre ☎ 0161/236–7110) in the Central Library stages classical drama, Shakespeare, chamber musicals, and new work from local playwrights. **Royal Exchange Theatre** (⊠ St. Ann's Sq., City Centre ☎ 0161/833–9833) serves as the city's main venue for innovative contemporary theater.

Football

Football (soccer in the United States) is *the* reigning passion in Manchester. Locals support the perennially unsuccessful local club, Manchester City, and glory seekers come from afar to root for Manchester United, based in neighboring Trafford. Matches for both clubs are usually sold out months in advance, but touts (scalpers, legal here) do business outside the grounds. **Manchester City** (⊠ Rowsley St., SportCity ☎ 0870/062–1894) plays at the City of Manchester Stadium. At the **Manchester City Experience** (⊠ Rowsley St., SportCity ☎ 0870/062–1894), you can see club memorabilia, visit the players' changing rooms, and go down the tunnel to pitch side. Excluding match days, there are at least five tours daily; admission is £8.25.

★ **Manchester United** (⊠ Sir Matt Busby Way, Trafford Wharf ☎ 0870/442–1968 information line, 0870/442–1999 ticket line) has home matches at Old Trafford. You can take a trip to the Theatre of Dreams at the **Manchester United Museum and Tour** (⊠ Sir Matt Busby Way, Trafford Wharf ☎ 0870/442–1994), which tells the history of the football club. The tour (not available on match days) takes you behind the scenes, into the changing rooms and players' lounge, and down the tunnel. It's open daily 9:30 to 5; admission for the museum and tour is £9.50, museum only £6. Take the tram to the Old Trafford stop and walk five minutes.

Shopping

The city is nothing if not fashion conscious; take your pick from glitzy department stores, huge retail outlets, designer shops, and idiosyncratic boutiques. Famous names are centered around Exchange Square, Deansgate and King Street; the Northern Quarter provides style for younger trendsetters.

★ **Afflecks Palace** (⊠ 52 Church St., Northern Quarter

☎ 0161/834–2039) attracts Mancunian youth with four floors of bohemian glam, ethnic crafts and jewelry, and innovative gift ideas. **Barton Arcade** (✉ 51–63 Deansgate, City Centre ☎ 0161/839–3172) has specialty shopping inside a lovely Victorian arcade.

Harvey Nichols (✉ 21 New Cathedral St., City Centre ☎ 0161/828–8888), an outpost of London's chic luxury department store, is packed with designer goods and has an excellent 2nd-floor restaurant and brasserie. The **Lowry Designer Outlet** (✉ Salford Quays ☎ 0161/848–1850), with 80 stores, has good discounts on top brands at stores such as Nike and Karen Millen.

★ The **Manchester Craft and Design Centre** (✉ 17 Oak St., Northern Quarter ☎ 0161/832–4274) houses 16 workshop–cum–retail outlets. The world's largest **Marks & Spencer** (✉ 7 Market St., City Centre ☎ 0161/831–7341) department store offers its own brand of fashion and has an excellent food department. **Oldham Street,** in the Northern Quarter, is littered with urban hip-hop boutiques and music shops. The **Royal Exchange Shopping Centre and Arcade** (✉ St. Ann's Sq., City Centre ☎ 0161/834–3731) has three floors of restaurants and specialty shops, with antiques, Belgian chocolates, teddy bears, and more, inside the former cotton market. **The Triangle** (✉ Millennium Quarter ☎ 0161/834–8961), a stylish mall in the Victorian Corn Exchange, has more than 30 stores, including independent designer shops.

CHINATOWN

The large red-and-gold Imperial Chinese Arch, erected in 1987, marks Chinatown, one of the largest Chinese communities outside London. Bordered by Portland Street, Mosley Street, Princess Street, and Charlotte Street, the area really buzzes on Sunday, when traders from all over the country stock up from the supermarkets, food stalls, herbalists, and gift shops. The many restaurants here offer excellent choices of authentic Cantonese cooking, so consider a stop here when your shopping energies run low.

THE PEAK DISTRICT

Heading southeast, away from the urban congestion of Manchester, it's not far to the southernmost contortions of the Pennine Hills. Here, about an hour from Manchester, sheltered in a great natural bowl, is Bakewell, a convenient base for exploring the 540 square mi of the Peak District, Britain's oldest—and, some say, most beautiful—national park. "Peak" is perhaps misleading; despite being a hilly area, it contains only long, flat-top rises that don't reach much higher than 2,000 feet. Yet a trip around destinations such as the grand estates of Chatsworth House and Haddon Hall involves negotiating fairly perilous country roads, each of which repays the effort with enchanting views. Outdoor activities are popular in the Peaks, particularly caving (or "potholing"), walking, and hiking. Bring all-weather clothing and waterproof shoes. The delight of the Peak District is being able to ramble for days in rugged countryside but still enjoy civilization at its finest.

Bakewell

7 *30 mi south of Manchester.*

Here, a medieval bridge crosses the winding River Wye in five graceful arches, and the 9th-century Saxon cross that stands outside the parish church reveals the town's great age. Narrow streets and houses built out of the local gray-brown stone also make Bakewell extremely appealing. Ceaseless traffic through the streets can take the shine off—though there's respite down on the quiet riverside paths. The crowds are really substantial on market day (Monday), attended by area farmers; a similarly popular traditional agricultural show takes place the first week of August. For a self-guided hourlong stroll, pick up a map at the tourist office, where the town trail begins. A small exhibition upstairs explains the landscape of the Peak District.

Where to Stay & Eat

£££ ✕ **The Prospect.** Cream and brown are the dominant colors of this intimate, wood-beam and -panel restaurant, where spacious tables, upholstered chairs, and attentive service enhance the comfort factor. If you're in the mood for tradition, opt for the Lancashire hot pot or slow-roast belly pork with parsnip mash and apple chutney. If you feel adventurous, try the chocolate torte and vodka ice cream, or the canapés and blinis that accompany the good-value fixed-price menus. ✉ *Unit 6, Theme Court, Bridge St.* ☎ *01629/810077* ▭ *AE, MC, V* ⊗ *Closed Mon. No dinner Sun.*

£-££ ✕ **The Old Original Bakewell Pudding Shop.** Given the plethora of local rivals, it takes a bold establishment to claim its Bakewell puddings as "original," but there's certainly nothing wrong with those served here, eaten hot with custard or cream. The oak-beam dining room also turns out commendable main courses of Yorkshireman (batter pudding with meat and vegetables) and steak-and-stout pie. ✉ *The Square* ☎ *01629/812193* ▭ *MC, V* ⊗ *Closes 6 PM winter, 7 PM summer.*

★
££££–£££££ ✕▭ **Fischer's.** The Fischer family bought this stately Edwardian manor primarily with their restaurant in mind. On the edge of the Chatsworth estate, rooms in the main house have fancy plasterwork ceilings, antique pine furniture, and muted colors; those in the garden annex show a more contemporary style. The formal restaurant has a more expensive menu (£60, Monday to Saturday) or a menu du jour (£30–£35, Sunday to Friday). Fish often comes with fresh pastas and delicate sauces; duck, lamb, and game receive similar care. Sunday dinner is for guests only. ✉ *Baslow Hall, Calver Rd., Baslow, DE45 1RR* ☎ *01246/583259* ▭ *01246/583818* ⊕ *www.fischers-baslowhall.co.uk* ⇗ *11*

> ### BAKEWELL PUDDING
>
> Bakewell is the source of Bakewell pudding, said to have been created inadvertently when, sometime in the 19th century, a cook at the town's Rutland Arms Hotel dropped some rich cake mixture over jam tarts and baked it. Every local bakery and tearoom claims an original recipe—it's easy to spend a gustatory afternoon tasting rival puddings.

rooms ⚐ *Restaurant, in-room data ports, bar, meeting rooms, no-smoking rooms; no a/c, no kids under 10* ⊟ *AE, DC, MC, V* ⦾ *CP.*

££ 🖾 **Haddon House Farm.** This may be a working farm, but there's nothing workaday about the fresh and imaginatively designed rooms (with themes such as Monet and Shakespeare) that the Nicholls husband-and-wife team created. The peaceful valley location, antiques, flowers, and CD players all contribute to a relaxing stay. Bathrooms have tiles hand-painted with insects and bamboo, and breakfasts are taken around the kitchen table. The location on the A6 lies between Haddon Hall and Bakewell. ⊠ *Haddon Rd., DE45 1BN* ☎ *01629/814024* 🖶 *01629/ 812759* ⊕ *www.great-place.co.uk* ⇗ *4 rooms* ⚐ *No a/c, no room phones, no kids under 5, no smoking* ⊟ *No credit cards* ⦾ *BP.*

Haddon Hall

❽ *2 mi southeast of Bakewell.*

Fodor's Choice
★

Stately house scholar Hugo Montgomery-Massingberd has called Haddon Hall, a romantic, storybook medieval manor set along the River Wye, "the *beau idéal* of the English country house." Unlike other trophy homes that are marble Palladian monuments to the grand tour, Haddon Hall remains quintessentially English in appearance, bristling with crenellations and stepped roofs and landscaped with rose gardens. The house, built mainly in the 14th century, is famous as the setting (perhaps apocryphal) for the shocking 16th-century elopement of Dorothy Vernon and Sir John Manners during a banquet; the tale became a popular Victorian-era love story. (Dorothy and Sir John are buried in Bakewell's parish church.) Constructed by generations of the Vernon family in the Middle Ages, Haddon Hall passed into the ownership of the dukes of Rutland. After the dukes moved their county seat to Belvoir Castle, little changed in the house for hundreds of years. In the early 20th century, however, the ninth duke undertook a superlative restoration. The wider world saw the hall in Franco Zeffirelli's 1996 film *Jane Eyre*; part of the 1999 *Elizabeth*, starring Cate Blanchett, was also filmed here. The virtually unfurnished house has fine plasterwork and wooden paneling, especially in the Long Gallery, and still holds some treasures, including tapestries, and a famous 1932 painting of Haddon Hall by Rex Whistler. ⊠ *A6* ☎ *01629/812855* ⊕ *www.haddonhall.co. uk* 🖾 *£7.75, parking £1* ⦾ *May–Sept., daily noon–5; Apr. and Oct., Sat.–Mon. noon–5; last admission 4.*

Chatsworth House

★ ✆ ❾ *4 mi northeast of Bakewell.*

Glorious parkland leads to Chatsworth House, ancestral home of the dukes of Devonshire and one of England's greatest country houses. The vast expanse of greenery, grazed by deer and sheep, sets off the Palladian-style elegance of "the Palace of the Peak." Originally an Elizabethan house, Chatsworth was conceived on a grand, even monumental, scale. It was altered over several generations starting in 1686, and the architecture now has a hodgepodge look, though the Palladian facade remains splendid. The house is surrounded by woods, elaborate gardens, greenhouses, rock gardens, and the most famous water cascade in the kingdom—all designed by two great landscape artists, Capability Brown and, in the 19th century, Joseph Paxton, an engineer as well as a brilliant gardener. The gravity-fed Emperor Fountain can shoot as high as 300 feet. Perennially popular with children, the farmyard area has milking demonstrations at 3, and an adventure playground. ■ TIP→ Plan on at least a half day to explore the grounds; avoid Sunday if you prefer not to be with the heaviest crowds. Do stop at the farm shop, which has terrific organic goodies. A brass band plays on Sunday afternoons in July and August.

PRIDE & CHATSWORTH

You may recognize the exterior and parkland of Chatsworth as Pemberley, home of Mr. Darcy, in the 2005 film version of *Pride and Prejudice*. It was Hollywood exaggeration to give him one of England's grandest country mansions, but no matter. The film also has some enticing views of the Peak District. Check ⊕ www.visitbritain.com or ⊕ www.visitprideandprejudice.com for more location information.

Although death duties have taken a toll on the interior grandeur, with duke after duke forced to sell off treasures to keep the place going, there is more than enough to look at. Inside are intricate carvings, Van Dyck portraits, superb furniture, and a few fabulous rooms, including the Sculpture Gallery, the library, and the Blue Drawing Room, where you can see two of the most famous portraits in Britain, Sir Joshua Reynolds's *Georgiana, Duchess of Devonshire, and Her Baby,* and John Singer Sargent's enormous *Acheson Sisters.* ✉ *Off B6012, Bakewell* ☎ *01246/582204* ⊕ *www.chatsworth-house.co.uk* 🖾 *House, gardens, and Scots rooms £12, house and gardens £9.75, gardens only £6, farmyard and adventure playground £4.50; parking £1.50* ⊙ *Mid-Mar.–mid-Dec., house daily 11–5:30, gardens daily 11–6, farmyard and adventure playground daily 10:30–5:30; last admission 1 hr before closing.*

Where to Eat

££–£££ ✕ **Devonshire Arms.** Inside this stone 18th-century coaching inn, which counts Charles Dickens as one of its many visitors, are antique settles, copper and brass, and great homemade fare. Typical dishes include deviled whitebait, steak-and-ale pie, and sausage and mash. Friday is fresh fish day, and on Sunday you can sample a Victorian breakfast (book ahead), which comes with Buck's Fizz—champagne and orange juice—and newspapers. The inn is 2 mi south of Chatsworth. ✉ *B6012, Beeley* ☎ *01629/733259* 🖃 *AE, MC, V.*

LIVERPOOL

A city lined with one of the most famous waterfronts in England, celebrated around the world as the birthplace of the Beatles, and still the place to catch that "Ferry 'Cross the Mersey," Liverpool has reversed a downturn in its fortunes with recent developments such as the Tate Liverpool and the refurbishment of Albert Dock. The naming of the city as the European Union's Capital of Culture for 2008 has accelerated plans for what Liverpool hopes will be a reinvention of itself as a center for culture and innovation. ■ TIP→ **Themed events in 2007 will focus on Liverpool's 800th birthday. Check out ⊕ www.liverpool08.com for the latest information on activities for both years.** In 2004, UNESCO named six historic areas in the city center a World Heritage Site, in recognition of the significance of its maritime and mercantile achievements.

Liverpool, on the east bank of the Mersey River estuary, at the point where it merges with the Irish Sea, developed from the 17th century through the slave trade. It became Britain's leading port for ferrying Africans to North America and for handling sugar, tobacco, rum, and cotton, which began to dominate the local economy after the abolition of the slave trade in 1807. Because of its proximity to Ireland, the city was also the first port of call for those fleeing famine, poverty, and persecution in that country. Liverpool was often the last British port of call for thousands of mostly Jewish refugees fleeing Eastern Europe.

Many of the best-known liner companies were based in Liverpool, including Cunard and White Star, whose best-known vessel, the *Titanic,* was registered in Liverpool. The city was dealt an economic blow in 1894 with the opening of the Manchester Ship Canal, which allowed traders to bypass Liverpool and head to Manchester, 35 mi east. Wartime bombing in the 1940s devastated the city's infrastructure, and rebuilding was uninspired.

As economic decline set in, Liverpool produced its most famous export—the Beatles. The group was one of hundreds that copied the rock and roll they heard from visiting American GIs and merchant seamen in the late 1950s, and one of many that played local venues such as the Cavern (demolished but since rebuilt nearby). All four Beatles were born in Liverpool, but the group's success dates from the time they left for London. Nevertheless, the city has milked the group's Liverpool connections for all they are worth, with a multitude of local attractions such as Paul McCartney's and John Lennon's childhood homes.

Despite the roughness of parts of the city, many people visit Liverpool to tour Beatles's sites, view the paintings in the renowned art galleries, watch horse racing or soccer, and learn about the city's industrial and maritime heritage at the impressive Albert Dock area.

Exploring Liverpool

Liverpool has a fairly compact center, and you can see most of the city highlights on foot. The skyline helps orientation: the Radio City tower on **Queen Square** marks the center of the city and is a stone's throw away from the '08 Place, which gives tourist information. The Liver Birds, on top of the **Royal Liver Building,** signal the waterfront and River Mersey. North of the Radio City tower lie Lime Street station and **William Brown Street,** a showcase boulevard of municipal buildings, including the outstanding **Walker Art Gallery** and **Liverpool World Museum.** The city's other museums and the **Beatles Story** are concentrated westward on the waterfront in the **Albert Dock** area, a 20-minute walk or 5-minute

bus ride away. **Hope Street,** to the east of the center, connects the city's two cathedrals, both easily recognizable on the skyline. Be prepared for building work in preparation for 2008. Allow yourself extra time if you want to visit **20 Forthlin Road** and **Mendips,** the childhood homes of Paul McCartney and John Lennon (closed in winter), as they lie outside the city center; they can be seen only on a prebooked tour.

Main Attractions

★ ⑰ **Albert Dock.** To understand the city's prosperous maritime past, head for waterfront Albert Dock, 7 acres of restored warehouses built in 1846. Named after Queen Victoria's consort, Prince Albert, the dock provided storage for silk, tea, and tobacco from the Far East until it was closed in 1972. Rescued by the Merseyside Development Corporation, the fine colonnaded brick warehouse buildings are England's largest heritage attraction, containing the **Merseyside Maritime Museum, Tate Liverpool,** and the **Beatles Story.** When weather allows, sit at an outdoor café overlooking the dock or take a boat trip through the docks and onto the river. Albert Dock is part of the area known as **Liverpool's Historic Waterfront.** ■ TIP→ Much of the pedestrian area of the Albert Dock and Waterfront area is made of cobbled stone, so be sure to wear comfortable walking shoes. ⊠ *Tourist Information Centre, Merseyside Maritime Museum,*

Waterfront ☎ *0906/680–6866 (calls cost 25p per minute)* ⊕ *www. albertdock.com* ⊙ *Information center, daily 10–5.*

⑯ **Merseyside Maritime Museum.** Part of the Albert Dock complex, the museum tells the story of the port of Liverpool using models, paintings, and original boats and equipment spread across five floors; it also has a gallery on the Battle of the Atlantic and Liverpool's role during World War II. In summer full-size vessels are on display. The Transatlantic Slavery exhibition, on the human misery engendered by the slave trade, is compelling. By late summer 2007, the museum will share space with the new International Slavery Museum. ⊠ *Albert Dock, Waterfront* ☎ *0151/478–4499* ⊕ *www.liverpoolmuseums.org.uk* 🎫 *Free* ⊙ *Daily 10–5; last admission 4.*

FodorsChoice ★

⑮ **Pier Head.** Here you can take a ferry across the River Mersey from Pierhead to Birkenhead and back. Boats leave regularly and offer fine views of the city—a journey celebrated in "Ferry 'Cross the Mersey," Gerry and the Pacemakers' 1964 hit song. It was from Pier Head that 9 million British, Irish, and other European emigrants set sail between 1830 and 1930 for new lives in the United States, Canada, Australia, and Africa. ■ TIP→ Choose a ferry (if you're short of time) or the longer 50-minute cruise with commentary ("Scousers," as locals are known, are famous for their patter); the city views are wonderful and worth the time and money. ⊠ *Pier Head Ferry Terminal, Mersey Ferries, Waterfront* ☎ *0151/330–1444* ⊕ *www. merseyferries.co.uk* 🎫 *£2.15 round-trip, cruises £4.95* ⊙ *Ferries every 30 mins weekdays 7:45–9:15 AM and 4:15–6:45 PM; cruises hrly weekdays 10–3, weekends 10–6.*

⑭ **Royal Liver Building.** Best seen from the ferry, the 322-foot-tall Royal Liver (pronounced "lie-ver") Building with its twin towers is topped by two 18-foot-high copper birds. They represent the mythical Liver Birds, the town symbol; local legend has it that if they fly away, Liverpool will cease to exist. For decades Liverpudlians looked to the Royal Liver Society for assistance—it was originally a burial club to which families paid contributions to ensure a decent send-off. ⊠ *Water St., Waterfront.*

⑱ **Tate Liverpool.** An offshoot of the London-based art galleries of the same name, the Liverpool museum, a handsome conversion of existing Albert Dock warehouses, was designed in the 1990s by the late James Stirling, one of Britain's leading 20th-century architects. Galleries display changing exhibits of challenging modern art. The excellent shop sells art books, prints, and posters, and there's a children's art-play area and a dockside café-restaurant. ⊠ *The Colonnades, Albert Dock, Waterfront* ☎ *0151/702–7400* ⊕ *www.tate.org.uk* 🎫 *Free, charge for special exhibitions* ⊙ *Tues.–Sun. and national holidays 10–5:50.*

⑫ Walker Art Gallery. With a superb display of British art and some superb Italian and Flemish works, the Walker maintains its position as one of the best British art collections outside London. Particularly notable are the unrivaled collection of paintings by 18th-century Liverpudlian equestrian artist George Stubbs, and works by J. M. W. Turner, John Constable, Sir Edwin Henry Landseer, and the Pre-Raphaelites. Modern British artists are included, too—on display is one of David Hockney's typically Californian pool scenes. Other excellent exhibits showcase china, silver, and furniture that once adorned the mansions of Liverpool's industrial barons. The Tea Room holds center stage in the airy museum lobby. ⊠ *William Brown St., City Centre* ☎ *0151/478–4199* ⊕ *www. liverpoolmuseums.org.uk* 🖃 *Free* ☉ *Daily 10–5.*

FodorsChoice
★

⑩ World Museum Liverpool. You can travel from the prehistoric to the space age through stunning displays in these state-of-the-art galleries. Ethnology, the natural and physical sciences, and archaeology all get their due on five floors. The World Cultures gallery colorfully illustrates the cosmopolitan history of the city. If the kids aren't grabbed by the monster bugs in the Bug House or afternoon shows in the Treasure House Theatre and Planetarium, they'll find plenty to do in the hands-on centers. ⊠ *William Brown St.* ☎ *0151/478–4393* ⊕ *www.worldmuseumliverpool. org.uk* 🖃 *Free* ☉ *Daily 10–5.*

On the Trail of the Beatles

★ **⑲ Beatles Story.** You can follow in the footsteps of the Fab Four at one of the more popular attractions in the Albert Dock complex. It has 18 entertaining scenes re-creating stages in their career, from the enthusiastic early days in Germany and the Cavern Club to the White Room, where "Imagine" seems to emanate from softly billowing curtains. Artifacts included are the glasses John Lennon wore when he composed "Imagine" and the blue felt bedspread used in the famous "Bed-in" in 1969. ■ TIP➜ **Avoid the crowds of July and August by visiting in the late afternoon.** You can purchase tickets online in advance, and the store has Beatles items from CDs to wallets and alarm clocks. ⊠ *Britannia Vaults, Albert Dock, Waterfront* ☎ *0151/709–1963* ⊕ *www.beatlesstory.com* 🖃 *£8.99* ☉ *Daily 10–6; last admission 1 hr before closing.*

⑬ Mathew Street. It was at the Cavern on this street that Brian Epstein, who became the Beatles' manager, first heard the group in 1961. The Cavern had opened at No. 10 as a jazz venue in 1957, but beat groups, of whom the Beatles were clearly the most talented, had taken it over. Epstein became their manager a few months after first visiting the club, and within two years the group was the most talked-about phenomenon in music. The Cavern club was demolished in 1973; it was rebuilt a few yards from the original site. At No. 5 is the Cavern Pub, opened in 1994, with Beatles memorabilia and plenty of nostalgia. ■ TIP➜ **At No. 31, check out the well-stocked Beatles Shop.**

Mendips. The august National Trust (overseers of such landmarks as Blenheim Palace) maintains the 1930s middle-class, semidetached house that was the home of John Lennon from 1946 to 1963 and is a mustsee for Beatles pilgrims. After his parents separated, John joined his aunt

Beatles Discovered . . . and Rediscovered

Brian Epstein was led to the Beatles in 1961 by a teenager who came into his record shop, NEMS (North End Music Stores) at 12–14 Whitechapel, and asked for a record by Tony Sheridan and the Beat Brothers. He couldn't find it in his catalog, but discovered that the backing band was the Beatles, a local group, playing at the nearby Cavern Club. Epstein heard the group, and the rest is history.

History lives on, though. If the Beatles Story, Mathew Street, Mendips, and 20 Forthlin Road can't sate your Beatlemania in Liverpool, consider a **Cavern City Tours** (⇨ Bus Tours *in* Northwest Essentials)

Magical Mystery Tour of the essential landmarks.

The faithful celebrate the Beatles' enduring appeal at the annual **International Beatle Week** (⊕ www.cavern-liverpool.co.uk), usually held the last week in August when what seems to be the entire city takes time out to dance, attend John and Yoko fancy-dress parties, and listen to Beatle bands from around the world. The event includes concerts, a convention, flea markets, and more. If you hold on until late 2007, Cavern City Tours plans to open the Beatle-themed **Hard Day's Night Hotel,** right on Mathew Street. Yeah, yeah, yeah!

Mimi here; she gave him his first guitar but banished him to play on the porch, saying, "The guitar's all very well, John, but you'll never make a living out of it." The house can be seen only on a tour, for which you must prebook a seat on the minibus that connects the site with Albert Dock (mornings) or Speke Hall (afternoons). ⊠ *251 Menlove Ave., Woolton* ☎ *0870/900–0256 morning tours, 0151/427–7231 afternoon tours* ⊕ *www.nationaltrust.org.uk* ⊠ *£12 includes 20 Forthlin Rd. and Speke Hall gardens* ⊙ *Late Mar.–Oct., Wed.–Sun. and national holidays; 4 departures a day, call for times.*

20 Forthlin Road. Paul McCartney lived with his family in this modest 1950s council house (a building rented from the local government), with its period-authentic windows, doors, and hedges, from 1955 to 1963; now it's a shrine for fans. A number of the Beatles' songs, including "Love Me Do" and "When I'm Sixty-Four," were written here. The house is viewable only on a tour, for which you must prebook a seat on the minibus that connects the site with Albert Dock (mornings) or Speke Hall (afternoons). ⊠ *20 Forthlin Rd., Allerton* ☎ *0870/900–0256 morning tours, 0151/427–7231 afternoon tours* ⊕ *www.nationaltrust.org* ⊠ *£12 includes Mendips and Speke Hall gardens* ⊙ *Late Mar.–Oct., Wed.–Sun. and national holidays; 4 departures a day, call for times.*

Also Worth Seeing

❷⓿ Anglican Cathedral. The largest church in northern Britain overlooks the city and the River Mersey. Built of local sandstone, the Gothic-style cathedral was begun in 1903 by architect Giles Gilbert Scott; it was finally finished in 1978. Take a look at the grand interior, view the exhibit of Victorian embroidery, and climb the 331-foot-tall tower. A refectory serves light meals and coffee. ⊠ *St. James's Mount, City Centre* ☎ *0151/*

*709–6271 ⊕ www.liverpoolcathedral.org.uk ✉ £3.50 suggested dona-
tion, tower and embroidery exhibition £4.25 ⊙ Daily 8–6. Tower
Mar.–Sept., Mon.–Sat. 11–4:30; Oct.–Feb., Mon.–Sat. 11–3:30.*

NEED A BREAK? **Prohibition Bar & Grill** (✉ 1A Bold St., City Centre ☎ 0151/707–2333) used to be a library and a gentleman's club. Now you can sink into a huge sofa for coffee or cocktails beneath the grand domed ceiling.

⑪ St. George's Hall. Built between 1839 and 1847, St. George's Hall is among the world's best Greek Revival buildings. When Queen Victoria visited Liverpool in 1851, she declared it "worthy of ancient Athens." Today the hall serves as a home for music festivals, concerts, and fairs, but it has been closed for refurbishment. The planned reopening is fall 2007; call for information. ✉ *Lime St., City Centre* ☎ *0151/225–5530.*

Where to Eat

£££–£££££ ✕ **60 Hope Street.** The combination of a ground-floor restaurant and a cheaper basement café-bar make this a popular choice for any budget. A light, polished wood floor and blue-and-cream walls help create the uncluttered backdrop for dishes that reflect a Mediterranean clime, but found only on British shores is the deep-fried jam sandwich with condensed milk ice cream. ✉ *60 Hope St., City Centre* ☎ *0151/707–6060* ▭ *AE, MC, V* ⊙ *Closed Sun. No lunch Sat. in restaurant.*

££–££££ ✕ **Blue Bar and Grill.** Expect to rub shoulders with local celebrities in this sophisticated modern restaurant and bar on the waterfront. The focal point is the beautiful Venetian crystal chandelier, a counterpoint to the original open brickwork, chunky furnishings, and plasma screens. Downstairs you can sample tapas, dim sum, and bruschetta; the fare in the upstairs gallery includes panfried goose breast and a large selection of meat and fish steaks, accompanied by different sauces. ✉ *Edward Pavilion, Albert Dock, Waterfront* ☎ *0151/709–7097* ▭ *AE, MC, V.*

££–£££ ✕ **Simply Heathcote's.** This chic contemporary restaurant, an outpost of chef Paul Heathcote's expanding empire, has a curved glass front, cherrywood furnishings, and a granite floor. The menu has a local accent—black pudding in beer batter, pork and leek sausages, bread and butter pudding—along with dishes from warmer climes. Vegetarians are well served, too. The restaurant is opposite the Royal Liver and Cunard buildings. ✉ *25 The Strand, Waterfront* ☎ *0151/236–3536* ▭ *AE, MC, V.*

£–££ ✕ **Tabac.** The warm decor and chilled-out music of this long, thin café-bar at the top of Bold Street attracts a cosmopolitan crowd. It's good for breakfasts with home-baked bread, cocktails, sandwiches, and salads, as well as daily specials such as roast chicken and cottage pie (minced beef with mashed potatoes on top). ✉ *126 Bold St., City Centre* ☎ *0151/709–9502* ▭ *MC, V.*

£ ✕ **Tate Café.** The Tate Liverpool's café-bar is a winner for daytime sustenance. There are dockside seats for warm summer days, and you can choose among the open sandwiches and salads, as well as dishes such as beef casserole with parsnip and potato chips (crisps, in Britain) and fruit cake with cheese and pear chutney. ✉ *The Colonnades, Albert Dock, Waterfront* ☎ *0151/702–7580* ▭ *MC, V* ⊙ *Closed Mon. No dinner.*

Where to Stay

With the naming of the city as the European Union's Capital of Culture in 2008, hotel options are expanding. New chains due to open in Liverpool in 2007 are the design-driven Alias and trendy Malmaison. A Hard Day's Night, a Beatles-themed hotel, may open by fall 2007.

★ **Hope Street Hotel.** Liverpool's boutique hotel, a converted carriage ware-
££££–£££££ house built in the style of a Venetian palazzo, puts the emphasis on traditional, natural materials and retains the exposed brickwork and cast-iron columns from the 1860s. A stunning oak staircase runs the height of the building. Light and elegant modern bedrooms have crisp white bed linens and custom-made walnut and cherry pieces, and benefit from floor heating. The London Carriage Works (£££££; fixed-price menus) concentrates on local and seasonal produce, used in such dishes as Suffolk lamb with buttered kale. ☒ *40 Hope St., City Centre, L1 9DA* ☎ *0151/709–3000* 🖷 *0151/709–2454* ⊕ *www.hopestreethotel.co.uk* 🛏 *41 rooms, 7 suites* ⌕ *Restaurant, cable TV, in-room DVDs, in-room broadband, in-room data ports, 2 bars, business services, meeting rooms, parking (fee); no a/c* ▭ *AE, MC, V.*

£££–££££ **Crowne Plaza Liverpool.** Many of the city's main sights are at the doorstep of this modern hotel on the waterfront next to the Royal Liver Building. A bright, bustling atrium leads to well-equipped and spacious bedrooms, done in soothing colors. Family rooms have two double beds; children under 12 stay free and even get free meals in the Plaza Brasserie. Breakfast is included in the price on weekends. ☒ *St Nicholas Place, Waterfront, L3 1QW* ☎ *0151/243–8000* 🖷 *0151/243–8111* ⊕ *www.cpliverpool.com* 🛏 *159 rooms* ⌕ *2 restaurants, room service, minibars, cable TV with movies, in-room data ports, in-room broadband, Wi-Fi, indoor pool, health club, hot tub, sauna, steam room, bar, laundry service, business services, meeting rooms, parking (fee), no-smoking rooms* ▭ *AE, DC, MC, V.*

££–£££ **Feathers Hotel.** One of a terrace of Georgian brick houses, this smart and efficient hotel close to both the city's cathedrals doesn't stint on decoration. Swags and drapes adorn the public rooms, and bedrooms have modern pine pieces and patterned fabrics in red, blue, and yellow. You can sip a drink at night in the 24-hour bar. ☒ *119–125 Mt. Pleasant, City Centre, L3 6DX* ☎ *0151/709–9655* 🖷 *0151/709–3838* ⊕ *www.feathers.uk.com* 🛏 *81 rooms* ⌕ *Restaurant, cable TV, bar, meeting rooms, parking (fee); no a/c* ▭ *AE, MC, V* ⊙ *BP.*

★ **££** **Express by Holiday Inn.** The best central accommodation in terms of value, location, and style is this offering in the upper part of the Britannia Pavilion, in a converted warehouse in the heart of the waterfront district. Management is friendly and helpful, and the rich red-and-blue decor and thick carpeting reflect the style of the chain. Try for a room with views of the dock. ☒ *Britannia Pavilion, Albert Dock, Waterfront, L3 4AD* ☎ *0151/709–1133 or 0800/434040* 🖷 *0151/709–1144* ⊕ *www.hiexpress.co.uk* 🛏 *135 rooms* ⌕ *Restaurant, cable TV with movies, in-room data ports, Wi-Fi, bar, business services, meeting room, parking (fee), some pets allowed; no a/c* ▭ *AE, MC, V* ⊙ *BP.*

£ ▣ **Liverpool Youth Hostel.** This hostel a few minutes' walk from Albert Dock really should change its name, because it offers modest hotel standards for bargain prices. The smart rooms (for two, four, or six people) are fully carpeted, with private bathrooms and heated towel rails. Guests must be members of the Youth Hostels Association; you can join on the spot (£15.50), but it's advisable to book well in advance. ✉ *Chalenor St., Waterfront, L1 8EE* ☎ *0151/709–8888* 🖷 *0151/709–0417* ⊕ *www. yha.org.uk* ⇨ *106 beds* ☖ *Cafeteria, recreation room, Internet, laundry facilities; no a/c, no room TVs* ▭ *MC, V* ⊙| *BP.*

Nightlife & the Arts

Nightlife

Baby Cream (✉ Atlantic Pavilion, Albert Dock, Waterfront ☎ 0151/702–5826), one of the city's newer bars, is a place where you can listen to weekend DJs. The ladies can pamper themselves in the glitzy black powder room. **Blue Bar** (✉ Edward Pavilion, Albert Dock, Waterfront ☎ 0151/709–7097), typical of the bars at the Albert Dock, attracts a funky, young professional crowd with its late hours, grill, and dockside seating. The **Cavern Club** (✉ 8–10 Mathew St., City Centre ☎ 0151/236–1965) draws many on the Beatles trail, who don't realize it's not the original spot—that was demolished years ago. The **Cavern Pub** (✉ 5 Mathew St., City Centre ☎ 0151/236–4041) merits a stop for nostalgia's sake; here are recorded the names of the groups and artists who *Fodor's*Choice played in the Cavern Club between 1957 and 1973. The **Philharmonic** ★ (✉ 36 Hope St., City Centre ☎ 0151/707–2837), nicest of the city-center pubs and opposite the Philharmonic Hall, is a Victorian-era extravaganza (complete with ornate toilets) decorated in colorful marble, with comfortable bar rooms and good food. **Ye Cracke** (✉ 13 Rice St., off Hope St., City Centre ☎ 0151/709–4171), one of the city's oldest pubs, was much visited by John Lennon in the 1960s.

The Arts

The well-regarded Royal Liverpool Philharmonic Orchestra plays its con-
★ cert season at **Philharmonic Hall** (✉ Hope St., City Centre ☎ 0151/709–3789). The venue also hosts contemporary music, jazz, and world concerts, and shows classic films.

Everyman Theatre (✉ 5–9 Hope St., City Centre ☎ 0151/709–4776) focuses on works by British playwrights as well as experimental productions from around the world. The **Liverpool Empire** (✉ Lime St., City Centre ☎ 0870/606–3536) presents major ballet, opera, drama, and musical performances. **Royal Court Theatre** (✉ 1 Roe St., City Centre ☎ 0151/709–4321), an art-deco building, is one of the city's most appealing sites for stand-up comedy and occasional pop and rock concerts.

Sports & the Outdoors

Horse Racing

Britain's most famous horse race, the Grand National steeplechase, has
★ been run at Liverpool's **Aintree Racecourse** (✉ Ormskirk Rd., Aintree ☎ 0151/523–2600, 0151/522–2929 booking line) almost every year since

1839. The race is held in March or April. Admission on race days is £16 (for Grand National, £12 to £73; book well in advance). The **Grand National Experience** (☎ 0151/523–2600 ☜£7 ☉ Late May–mid-Oct., Tues.–Fri. 11 and 2) includes a tour of the racecourse and admission to the visitor center; advance booking is required.

Soccer

Soccer ("football" in Great Britain) matches are played on weekends and, increasingly, weekdays. Ticket prices vary, but the cheapest seats start at about £26. Tourist offices can give you match schedules and directions to the grounds. **Liverpool** (☎ 0870/444–4949, 0870/220–2345 booking line), one of England's top clubs, plays at Anfield, 2 mi north of the city center. **Everton** (☎ 0870/442–1878, 0870/7383–7866 booking line), now reestablishing their historic competitiveness, plays at Goodison Park, about ½ mi north of Anfield.

Shopping

★ The **Beatles Shop** (✉ 31 Mathew St., City Centre ☎ 0151/236–8066) may stock the mop-top knickknack of your dreams. **Circa 1900** (✉ 11–13 Holts Arcade, India Buildings, Water St., City Centre ☎ 0151/236–1282) specializes in authentic art-nouveau and art-deco pieces, from ceramics and glass to furniture. The **Stanley Dock Sunday Market** (✉ Great Howard St. and Regent Rd., City Centre) has more than 400 stalls operating each Sunday, selling bric-a-brac, clothes, and toys from 9 to 4. The **Walker Art Gallery** (✉ William Brown St., City Centre ☎ 0151/478–4199) has a small lobby shop with high-quality glassware, ceramics, and jewelry by local designers.

CHESTER & IRONBRIDGE GORGE

Chester

㉑ *18 mi south of Liverpool.*

Cheshire is mainly a land of well-kept farms, supporting their herds of cattle, but numerous places here are steeped in history. Villages contain many fine examples of the black-and-white "magpie" type of architecture more often associated with areas to the east. The thriving center of the region is Chester.

Chester has been a prominent city since the late 1st century, when the Roman Empire expanded north to the banks of the River Dee. The original Roman town plan is still evident: the principal streets, Eastgate, Northgate, Watergate, and Bridge Street, lead out from the Cross—the site of the central area of the Roman fortress—to the four city gates, and the partly excavated remains of what is thought to have been the country's largest Roman amphitheater lie to the south of Chester's medieval castle. Since Roman times, seagoing vessels have sailed up the estuary of the Dee and anchored under the walls of Chester. The port enjoyed its most prosperous period during the 12th and 13th centuries.

History seems more tangible in Chester than in many other ancient cities. Much medieval architecture remains in the compact town center, and modern buildings have not been allowed to intrude. A negative result of this perfection is that Chester has become a favorite bus-tour destination, with gift shops, noise, and crowds.

★ Chester's unique **Rows,** which originated in the 12th and 13th centuries, are essentially double rows of stores, one at street level and the other on the 2nd floor with galleries overlooking the street. The Rows line the junction of the four streets in the old town. They have medieval crypts below them, and some reveal Roman foundations.

The city **walls,** accessible from several points, provide splendid views of the city and its surroundings. The whole circuit is 2 mi, but if your time is short, climb the steps at Newgate and walk along toward Eastgate to see the great ornamental **Eastgate Clock,** erected to commemorate Queen Victoria's Diamond Jubilee in 1897. Lots of small shops near this part of the walls sell old books, old postcards, antiques, and jewelry. Where the **Bridge of Sighs** (named after the enclosed bridge in Venice that it closely resembles) crosses the canal, descend to street level and walk up Northgate Street into Market Square.

Tradition has it that a church of some sort stood on the site of what is now **Chester Cathedral** in Roman times, but records indicate construction around AD 900. The earliest work traceable today, mainly in the north transept, is that of the 11th-century Benedictine abbey. After Henry VIII dissolved the monasteries in the 16th century, the abbey church became the cathedral church of the new diocese of Chester. The choir stalls reveal figures of people and dragons, and above is a gilded and colorful vaulted ceiling. ⊠ *St. Werburgh St., off Market Sq.* ☎ *01244/ 324756* ⊕ *www.chestercathedral.com* ✆ *£4 including audio guide* ☉ *Mon.–Sat. 9–5, Sun. 12:30–3:30.*

Chester Castle, overlooking the River Dee, lost its moats and battlements at the end of the 18th century to make way for the classical-style civil and criminal courts, jail, and barracks. The castle houses the **Cheshire Military Museum,** exhibiting uniforms, memorabilia, and some fine silver. ⊠ *Castle St.* ☎ *01244/327617* ✆ *£2* ☉ *Daily 10–4.*

Well-landscaped grounds and natural enclosures make the 80-acre
Ⓒ **Chester Zoo** one of Britain's most popular zoos, as well as the largest. Highlights include Chimpanzee Island, the jaguar enclosure, and the Islands in Danger tropical habitat. Baby animals are often on display. Eleven miles of paths wend through the zoo, and you can use the waterbus boats or the overhead train to tour the grounds. ⊠ *A41, 2 mi north of Chester* ☎ *01244/380280* ⊕ *www.chesterzoo.org* ✆ *Apr.–Oct. £13.50; Nov.–Mar. £10.50, bus £2, train £2* ☉ *Daily 10–dusk.*

Where to Stay & Eat

££–£££ ✕ **Brasserie 10/16.** Flooded with natural light from a wall of windows, this brasserie has clean, elegant lines. The Mediterranean fare is well presented, too, ranging from numerous salads to sea bass with crab and tomato risotto, and beef with horseradish mashed potatoes. Indulge yourself with the local ice creams or a trio of chocolate desserts. ⊠ *Brook-dale Pl.* ☎ *01244/322288* ⊟ *AE, MC, V.*

££–£££ ✗ **Francs.** Beyond the black-and-white half-timber exterior of this French eatery is an intimate dining area, with rustic basketwork on the walls and bentwood chairs. The menu lists choices such as fish cakes fried in a light beer batter, followed by chicken breast stuffed with garlic cheese; vegetarians might consider crepes filled with hazelnuts and leeks. Fixed-price meals are a great value, and children are welcomed with a special menu. ⊠ *14 Cuppin St.* ☎ *01244/317952* ⊟ *AE, MC, V.*

£££££ ✗▣ **Chester Grosvenor Hotel.** At this deluxe traditional hotel in a Tudor-style building downtown, handmade Italian furniture and French silk furnishings complement the English architecture. Floris toiletries, CD players, and a luxury spa are among the pampering amenities. The elegant Arkle Restaurant (named after a celebrated racehorse; closed Monday and Sunday evening and first three weeks in January; £££££) offers a fixed-price dinner as well as a daily gastronomic menu. The wine cellar has more than 600 bins. Good, hearty food is served in the brasserie (££–££££), and the intimate library serves light lunches as well as afternoon tea. Breakfast is included in the lower, weekend leisure rates. ⊠ *Eastgate St., CH1 1LT* ☎ *01244/324024* 🖷 *01244/313246* ⊕ *www.chestergrosvenor.co. uk* 🗺 *80 rooms* ♨ *2 restaurants, cable TV, in-room broadband, in-room data ports, health club, spa, Internet room, business services, meeting rooms, no-smoking rooms* ⊟ *AE, DC, MC, V.*

££££ ✗▣ **Green Bough Hotel.** Chester's leafy outskirts are the setting for this memorable small hotel a mile from the town center. Furnished with antiques, including cast-iron and carved wooden beds, and decorated with Italian fabrics and wallcoverings, the individually designed guest rooms make luxurious and soothing retreats. The Olive Tree restaurant (££££–£££££) provides top-notch contemporary British fare in intimate surroundings. Head to the rooftop garden for a relaxing drink in summer. ⊠ *60 Hoole Rd., CH2 3NL* ☎ *01244/326241* 🖷 *01244/ 326265* ⊕ *www.greenbough.co.uk* 🗺 *6 rooms, 8 suites* ♨ *Restaurant, bar, Wi-Fi, meeting room; no a/c, no kids under 11, no smoking* ⊟ *AE, DC, MC, V* ▯◯▮ *BP.*

££ ▣ **Grove Villa.** The location of this family-run B&B, a 19th-century house on the banks of the River Dee, enhances its appeal. Add antique furniture and a sense of calm, and you are guaranteed a soothing stay. Rooms are often priced at £60. ⊠ *18 The Groves, CH1 1SD* ☎ *01244/349713* ✉ *grovevilla18@btinternet.com* 🗺 *3 rooms* ♨ *No a/c, no room phones, no smoking* ⊟ *No credit cards* ▯◯▮ *BP.*

Boating

Bithell Boats (⊠ Boating Station, Souters La., The Groves ☎ 01244/325394 ⊕ www.showboatsofchester.co.uk) runs excursions on the River Dee on an excursion boat every 30 minutes daily (April through October) and hourly on weekends (November through March). Some evening cruises feature disco or live music.

Shopping

Chester has an **indoor market** in the Forum, near the Town Hall, every day except Sunday. Watergate Street hosts antiques shops, which stock anything from small ceramic pieces and clocks to furniture. **Bookland** (✉ 12 Bridge St. ☎ 01244/347323), in an ancient building with a converted 14th-century crypt, stocks travel and general-interest books.

Ironbridge Gorge

★ ㉒ *80 mi south of Liverpool, 55 mi south of Chester.*

Ironbridge Gorge is the name given to a group of villages south of Telford that were crucial in ushering in the Industrial Revolution. The Shropshire coalfields were of enormous importance to the development of the coke-smelting process, which helped make producing anything in iron much easier. The 10 component sections of the **Ironbridge Gorge Museum,** spread over 6 square mi, preserve and interpret the area's fascinating industrial history. ■ TIP➔ **Allow at least a full day to appreciate all the major sights, and perhaps to take a stroll around the famous iron bridge or hunt for Coalport china in the stores clustered near it. If you're without a vehicle, visit on a weekend or national holiday (April through October) when a shuttle bus takes you between sites.** The best starting point is the **Museum of the Gorge,** which has a good selection of literature and an audiovisual show on the gorge's history. In nearby Coalbrookdale, the **Museum of Iron** explains the production of iron and steel. You can see the blast furnace built by Abraham Darby, who developed the original coke process in 1709. Adjacent to this, the **Enginuity** exhibition is a hands-on, feet-on exploration of engineering, offering the opportunity to pull a locomotive and even "fly" a magnetic carpet. From here, drive the few miles along the river until the arches of the **Iron Bridge** come into view; it was designed by T. F. Pritchard, smelted by Darby, and erected between 1777 and 1779. This graceful arch spanning the River Severn can best be seen—and photographed or painted—from the towpath, a riverside walk edged with wildflowers and shrubs. The tollhouse on the far side houses an exhibition on the bridge's history and restoration.

A mile farther along the river is the old factory and the **Coalport China Museum** (the china is now made in Stoke-on-Trent). Exhibits show some of the factory's most beautiful wares, and craftspeople give demonstrations. Above Coalport is **Blists Hill Victorian Town,** where you can see old mines, furnaces, and a wrought-iron works. But the main draw is the re-creation of the "town" itself, with its doctor's office, bakery, grocer's, candle-maker's, sawmill, printing shop, and candy store. At the entrance you can change some money for specially minted pennies and make purchases from the shops. Shopkeepers, the bank manager, and the doctor's wife are on hand to give you advice. Craft demonstrations are scheduled in summer. ✉ *B4380, Ironbridge, Telford* ☎ *01952/884391* ⊕ *www.ironbridge.org.uk* 🎫 *Ticket to all sights £14* ⊙ *Apr.–Oct., daily 10–5; Nov.–Mar., daily 10–4.*

> **WORD OF MOUTH**
>
> "While visiting Ironbridge, don't miss the Blists Hill open-air museum, which is a re-created Victorian town, complete with shops, houses and even a working iron foundry."   –Maria H

WHERE TO STAY & EAT

£ ✕ **New Inn.** This Victorian building was moved from Walsall, 22 mi away, so that it could be part of the Blists Hill Victorian Town. It's a fully functioning pub, with gas lamps, sawdust on the floor, traditional ales, and old-fashioned lemonade and ginger beer. For an inexpensive meal, you can try a ploughman's lunch or a steak and kidney pudding from the butcher's store next door. Join in the daily sing-along around the piano at 1 and 3:30 (3 PM in winter). ✉ *Blists Hill Victorian Town* ☎ *01952/601010* 💳 *MC, V.*

★ ££ **Library House.** At one point the village's library, this small guesthouse on the hillside near the Ironbridge museums (and only a few steps from the bridge itself) has kept its attractive Victorian style while allowing for modern-day luxuries—a DVD library, for instance. Service is warm without being obtrusive. ✉ *11 Severn Bank, Ironbridge, Telford TF8 7AN* ☎ *01952/432299* 📠 *01952/433967* 🌐 *www.libraryhouse.com* *4 rooms* *Cable TV, in-room DVDs, Wi-Fi; no a/c, no room phones, no kids under 10, no smoking* 💳 *No credit cards* 🍽 *BP.*

NORTHWEST ESSENTIALS

Transportation

BY AIR

Manchester Airport, about 10 mi south of the city, is the third-largest airport in the country. About 100 airlines serve 175 international and U.K. destinations. M56 north leads directly into Manchester via the A5103. Frequent trains run from Manchester Airport to Piccadilly Railway Station (15 to 20 minutes); buses go to Piccadilly Gardens Bus Station (1 hour). A taxi from the airport to Manchester city center costs between £12 and £15. For more details, call the Greater Manchester Passenger Transport Executive (GMPTE) information line.

Liverpool John Lennon Airport, about 8 mi southeast of the city at Speke, covers inland and European destinations. There's bus service to the city center every 30 minutes; contact AirportXpress 500.

AirportXpress 500 ☎ 0870/608-2608 🌐 www.merseytravel.gov.uk. **GMPTE information line** ☎ 0161/228-7811 🌐 www.gmpte.com. **Liverpool John Lennon Airport** ✉ Off A561, Speke ☎ 0870/750-8484 🌐 www.liverpooljohnlennonairport.com. **Manchester Airport** ✉ Near Junctions 5 and 6 of M56 ☎ 0161/489-3000 🌐 www.manairport.co.uk.

BY BUS

National Express serves the region from London's Victoria Coach Station. Average travel time to Manchester or Liverpool is five hours, to Chester 5½ hours.

Chorlton Street Coach Station, a few hundred yards west of Piccadilly Railway Station in Manchester's city center, is the main bus station for regional and long-distance buses. Most local buses leave from Piccadilly Gardens Bus Station, the hub of the urban bus network. Metroshuttle operates three free circular routes around the city center; service runs every 5 to 10 minutes from 7 AM to 7 PM (Sunday 10 to 6).

In Liverpool, regional and long-distance National Express coaches use the Norton Street Coach Station, and local and cross-river buses depart from Sir Thomas Street, Queen Square, and Paradise Street.

The TransPeak service between Manchester and Derby stops at Bakewell, with departures every two hours from Manchester's Chorlton Street Bus Station.

FARES & SCHEDULES For Manchester bus information, call the GMPTE information line (⇨ By Air). For timetables and local bus (and train and ferry) service in Liverpool, call the Mersey Travel Line. For local bus information in Chester, call First; for Bakewell and the Peak District, call Traveline. The *Peak District Timetable* (60p) covers all local public transportation services and is available at area tourist offices.

🚌 **First** ☎ 01244/381461 ⊕ www.firstgroup.com. **Mersey Travel Line** ☎ 0870/608–2608 ⊕ www.merseytravel.gov.uk. **National Express** ☎ 0870/580-8080 ⊕ www.nationalexpress.com. **Traveline** ☎ 0870/608-2608 ⊕ www.traveline.org.uk.

BY CAR

Although a car is not an asset in touring the centers of Manchester, Liverpool, and Chester, it would be essential for side trips to Chatsworth, Haddon Hall in the Peak District, and Ironbridge. To reach Manchester from London, take M1 north to M6, leaving M6 at Exit 21A and joining M62 east, which becomes M602 as it enters Greater Manchester. M60 is the ring road around Manchester. Liverpool is reached by leaving M6 at the same junction, Exit 21A, and following M62 west into the city. To get to Chester from London, take M6, switching to the M56 at Exit 20A and then joining the M53 at Exit 15. If you're going to Chester from Liverpool, take the Mersey Tunnel and follow directions for M53, exiting at Junction 12. Travel time to Manchester or Liverpool from London is 3 to 3½ hours. Expect heavy traffic out of London on weekends to all destinations in the northwest. The M6 toll road, Britain's first toll motorway (£3.50, £2.50 at night), which runs between Exits 4 and 11A of the M6, provides a speedier alternative to the M6.

BY TRAIN

Virgin Trains serves the region from London's Euston Station. Direct service to Manchester and Liverpool takes three hours. Chester, with a change at Crewe, takes 2¾ hours.

There are trains between Manchester's Piccadilly Station and Liverpool's Lime Street run every half hour during the day; the trip from Manchester takes 50 minutes. The train from Chester to Liverpool's Lime Street also runs every half hour and takes 45 minutes. Call National Rail Enquiries for timetable information.

🚆 **National Rail Enquiries** ☎ 0845/748-4950 ⊕ www.nationalrail.co.uk. **Virgin Trains** ☎ 0845/722-2333 ⊕ www.virgintrains.co.uk.

BY TRAM

In Manchester, Metrolink electric tram service runs through the city center and out to the suburbs. The Eccles extension has stops for the Lowry

(Harbour City) and for the Manchester United Stadium (Old Trafford). Buy a ticket (cash only) from the platform machine before you board.
🚇 **Metrolink** ☎ 0161/205-2000 ⊕ www.metrolink.co.uk.

Contacts & Resources

EMERGENCIES
🚑 **Ambulance, fire, police** ☎ 999. **Royal Liverpool University Hospital** ✉ Prescot St., City Centre, Liverpool ☎ 0151/706-2000. **Manchester Royal Infirmary** ✉ Oxford Rd., University Quarter, Manchester ☎ 0161/276-1234.

INTERNET
Wi-Fi access is common in the public areas of larger city hotels, less so in the guest rooms. Broadband is available throughout the region. Internet cafés are thin on the ground in the cities.
🚩 **Internet Cafés Cafenet** ✉ 63 Watergate St., Chester ☎ 01244/401-116, open daily. **EasyInternet** ✉ Clayton Square Shopping Centre, City Centre, Liverpool ☎ no phone, open Monday through Saturday 10-6, Sunday 10-4. **Internet Gaming** ✉ 32 Princess St., City Centre, Manchester ☎ 0161/244-5566, open daily.

TOUR OPTIONS
BUS TOURS Cavern City Tours has a Beatles Magical Mystery Tour of Liverpool, departing from the Beatles Story, Albert Dock, daily at noon and at 2:30 on weekends (late June through late September, and some school holiday periods). The two-hour bus tour (£12) runs past Penny Lane, Strawberry Field, and other mop-top landmarks. You can also choose among specialized tours such as those that focus on John Lennon or Paul McCartney, or even hire a private guide.

A novel way to travel Liverpool is by YellowDuckmarines, amphibious vehicles from World War II. Tours run from mid-February to Christmas (£9.95 and £11.95) and leave from Albert Dock.
🚩 **Cavern City Tours** ✉ Mathew St., City Centre, Liverpool ☎ 0151/709-3285 ⊕ www. cavern-liverpool.co.uk. **YellowDuckmarines** ☎ 0151/708-7799 ⊕ www. theyellowduckmarine.co.uk.

VISITOR INFORMATION
General information about the region is available from the North West Tourist Board. Local tourist information offices are listed below by town.
🚩 **Tourist Information North West Tourism** ✉ Swan House, Swan Meadow Rd., Wigan Pier, Wigan WN3 5BB ☎ 0845/600-6040 ⊕ www.visitnorthwest.com. **Bakewell** ✉ Old Market Hall, Bridge St., DE45 1DS ☎ 01629/816558 ⊕ www.visitpeakdistrict.com. **Chester** ✉ Town Hall, Northgate St., CH1 2HJ ✉ Vicar's La., CH1 1QX ☎ 01244/402111 ⊕ www.chestertourism.com. **Liverpool,08 Place** ✉ 36-38 Whitechapel City Centre, L1 6DZ ☎ 0151/233-2008 or 0845/601-1125, 0151/709-8111 for accommodations ✉ Merseyside Maritime Museum, Albert Dock, L3 4AQ ✉ Arrival Hall, South Terminal, John Lennon Airport ☎ 0151/907-1057 ⊕ www.visitliverpool.com. **Manchester Visitor Centre** ✉ Town Hall Extension, Lloyd St., City Centre, M60 2LA ☎ 0871/222-8223 ⊕ www.visitmanchester. com ✉ International Arrivals Hall, Manchester Airport Terminal 1 ☎ 0161/436-3344 ✉ International Arrivals Hall, Manchester Airport Terminal 2 ☎ 0161/489-6412.

The Lake District

WINDERMERE, GRASMERE & KESWICK

WORD OF MOUTH

"I like the northern lakes region toward Keswick better than the more commercial Windermere area. Take your son to Beatrix Potter's Hill Top farm . . . this is the real thing. Acquire a taste for real gingerbread . . . in Grasmere. A boat cruise on a lake is fun. Also, don't miss the Castlerigg Stone Circle, near Keswick . . . the setting is perhaps the most dramatic anywhere."

—KidsToLondon

Updated by
Julius Honnor

"LET NATURE BE YOUR TEACHER . . ." Wordsworth's ideal comes true in this region of jagged mountains, waterfalls, wooded valleys, and stone-built villages. The poets Wordsworth and Coleridge, and other Englishmen and women of letters, found the Lake District an inspiring setting for their work, and visitors have followed ever since, to walk, go boating, or just relax and take in the views. In 1951 the Lake District National Park was created here from parts of the counties of Cumberland, Westmorland, and Lancashire. No mountains in Britain are finer in outline or give a greater impression of majesty; deeper and bluer lakes can be found, but none that fit so readily into the surrounding scene.

The Lake District covers an area of approximately 885 square mi and holds 16 major lakes and countless smaller stretches of water. You can cross it by car in about an hour, though that would be a shame. The mountains are not high by international standards—Scafell Pike, England's highest peak, is only 3,210 feet above sea level—but they can be tricky to climb. In spring, many of the higher summits remain snow-capped long after the weather below has turned mild.

This area can be one of Britain's most appealing reservoirs of calm, but in summer cars and tour buses often clog its narrow roads. Off-season visits can be a real treat. All those little inns and bed-and-breakfasts that turn away crowds in summer are eager for business the rest of the year (and their rates drop accordingly). It's not an easy task to avail yourself of a succession of sunny days in the Lake District—some statisticians allot to it about 250 rainy days a year—but when the sun breaks through and brightens the surfaces of the lakes, it is an away-from-it-all place to remember.

Exploring the Lake District

The Lake District is in northwest England, north of the industrial belt along the River Mersey that stretches from Liverpool to Manchester, and south of Scotland. The major gateway from the south is Kendal, and from the north, Penrith. Both are outside the park boundaries, on the M6 motorway. Main-line trains stop at Oxenholme, near Kendal, with a branch linking Oxenholme to Kendal and Windermere. The Lake District National Park breaks into two reasonably distinct sections. The southern lakes and valleys contain the park's most popular destinations, incorporating the largest body of water, Windermere, as well as most of the quintessential Lakeland towns and villages: Kendal, Bowness, Ambleside, Grasmere, Elterwater, Coniston, and Hawkshead. To the north, the landscape opens out across the bleaker fells to reveal challenging (and spectacular) walking country. Here, in the northern lakes, south of Keswick, you have the best chance to get away from the crowds.

About the Restaurants & Hotels

If the front hall has a row of muddy boots, you've probably made the right choice for a hostelry. At the best of these hotels, people eat heartily and loll about in front of fires in the evenings, sharing an almost religious dedication to the mountains. Your choices include everything from B&Bs (from the house on Main Street to farm) to small country

TOP REASONS TO GO

Take a hike: Whether it's a demanding trek up England's highest mountain, or a gentle wander around a tarn (a small mountain lake), walking is the number-one pleasure and the way to see the area at its rugged and spectacular best. Even in summer, there are fantastic opportunities to escape the crowds.

Mucking around in boats: There's nowhere better for renting a small boat or taking a cruise on a vintage boat and discovering the pleasures of bobbing around on the water. You'll get a different perspective on the mountains, too. The Coniston Boating Centre is one place to start.

Wordsworth's daffodils: The Lakes landscape has a rich literary history, in the children's books of Beatrix Potter, in the thoughtful writings of John Ruskin, and, most notably, in the poems of Wordsworth, which resonate deeper after you've seen his flowers dancing in the breeze. A stop at any of the writers' homes will enrich the experience.

Rejuvenating pints: Cumbria has some great microbreweries, and a pint of real ale in one of the region's atmospheric rural inns may never taste as good as after a long hard day up a mountain.

Sunrise at Castlerigg: The stone circle at Castlerigg, in a natural hollow ringed by peaks, is a rare reminder of the region's ancient history. Blenvathra and other mountains provides an awesome backdrop for the 38 stones. Sunrise here is magical.

8

inns to grand lakeside hotels; many hotels offer the option of paying a higher price that includes dinner as well as breakfast. Wherever you stay, book well in advance for summer visits, especially those in late July and August. In winter many accommodations close for a month or two. On weekends and in summer, it may be hard to find places willing to take bookings for a single night.

WHAT IT COSTS In pounds				
£££££	**££££**	**£££**	**££**	**£**
RESTAURANTS over £22	£18–£22	£13–£17	£7–£12	under £7
HOTELS over £160	£120–£160	£90–£119	£60–£89	under £60

Restaurant prices are for a main course at dinner. Hotel prices are for two people in a standard double room in high season, including V.A.T., with no meals or, if indicated, CP (with continental breakfast), BP (Breakfast Plan, with full breakfast), or MAP (Modified American Plan, with breakfast and dinner).

Timing

The Lake District is one of the rainiest areas in Britain, but June, July, and August hold the best hope of fine weather and are the time for all the major festivals. You will, however, be sharing the roads, hotels, trails, and lakes with thousands of other people. If you must travel at this time, turn up early at popular museums and attractions, and expect to work

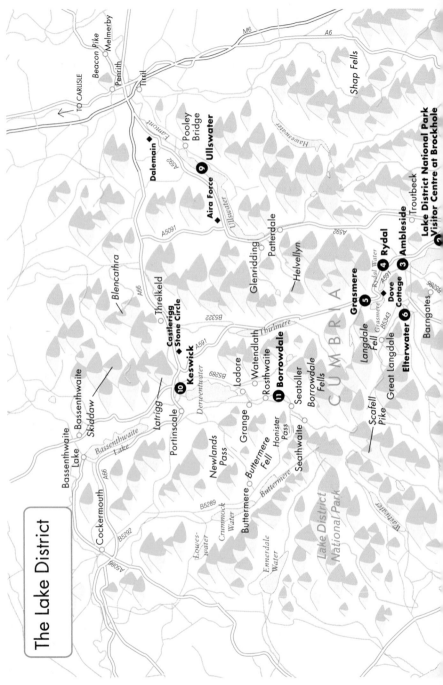

The Lake District

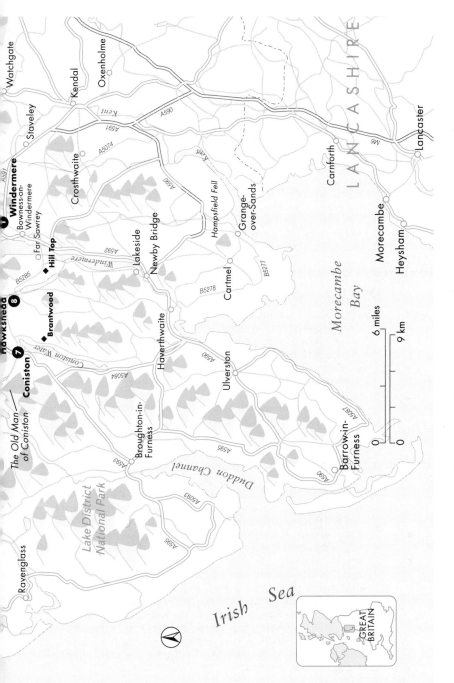

to find parking. April and May, as well as September and October, are alternatives. Later and earlier in the year there will be even more space and freedom, but many attractions close, and snow on high ground may preclude serious walking without heavy-duty equipment.

THE SOUTHERN LAKES
WINDERMERE, GRASMERE & CONISTON

Among the many attractions here are the small resort towns clustered around Windermere, England's largest lake, and the area's hideaway valleys, rugged walking centers, and monuments rich in literary associations. This is the easiest part of the Lake District to reach. An obvious route leaves the M6 motorway near Kendal and takes in Windermere, the area's natural touring center, before moving north through Ambleside and Rydal Water to Grasmere. Some of the loveliest Lakeland scenery is to be found by then turning south, through Elterwater, Hawkshead, and Coniston.

Windermere & Bowness-on-Windermere

❶ *10 mi northwest of Kendal, 80 mi north of Manchester.*

For a natural touring base for the southern half of the Lake District, you don't need to look much farther than Windermere, though it does get quite crowded in summer. The resort became popular in the Victorian era when the arrival of the railway made the remote and rugged area accessible. The day-trippers keep coming and the town has continued to flourish, despite being a mile or so from the water; the development now spreads to envelop the slate-gray lakeside village of Bowness-on-Windermere. Bowness is the more attractive, but they are so close it matters little where you stay. Bus 599, leaving every 20 minutes in summer (hourly the rest of the year) from outside Windermere train station, links the two.

★ No sights in Windermere or Bowness compete with that of **Windermere** itself. At 11 mi long, 1½ mi wide, and 200 feet deep, the lake is England's largest and stretches from Newby Bridge almost to Ambleside, filling a rocky gorge between steep, thickly wooded hills. The cold waters are superb for fishing, especially for Windermere char, a rare lake trout. In summer, steamers and pleasure craft travel the lake, and a trip across the island-studded waters, particularly the round-trip from Bowness to Ambleside or down to Lakeside, is wonderful. Although the lake's marinas and piers have some charm, you can bypass the busier stretches of shoreline (in summer they can be packed solid) by walking beyond the boathouses. Here, from among the pine trees, is a fine view across the lake. The **car ferry,** which also carries pedestrians, crosses from Ferry Nab on the Bowness side to reach Far Sawrey and the road to Hawkshead. ☎ *07860/813427* 🖃 *Car ferry £2.50 cars, 40p foot passengers* ☉ *Ferries every 30 mins Mon.–Sat. 6:50 AM–9:50 PM, Sun. 9:10 AM–9:50 PM; winter until 8:50 PM.*

The **Windermere Steamboat Centre,** right beside the lake, houses the world's finest collection of Victorian and Edwardian steam- and motor-powered yachts and launches. Displays about Windermere's nautical history include the famous names of motorboat racing on the lake. The *Dolly,* built around 1850, is one of the two oldest mechanically powered boats in the world. Among the many other vessels on view are Beatrix Potter's rowing boat and a dinghy that belonged to Arthur Ransome. ■ TIP→ For an additional £5.50, you can take a boat ride on Windermere in an antique vessel–if the weather is good. ⊠ *Rayrigg Rd., Bowness-on-Windermere* ☎ *015394/45565* ⊕ *www.steamboat.co.uk* 🎫 *£4.75* ☉ *Mid-Mar.–early Nov., daily 10–5.*

Windermere Lake Cruises (☎ 015395/31188 ⊕ www.windermere-lakecruises.co.uk) employs modern launches and vintage cruisers year-round between Ambleside, Bowness, Brockhole, and Lakeside. Ticket prices vary; a Freedom of the Lake ticket (£10.50) gives unlimited travel on any of the ferries for 24 hours.

The World of Beatrix Potter, a touristy attraction aimed at kids, interprets the author's 23 tales with three-dimensional scenes of Peter Rabbit raiding Mr. McGregor's garden, Mrs. Tiggy-Winkle in her kitchen, Jemima Puddle-duck in the woods, and more. Skip it if you can and visit Potter's former home at Hill Top and the Beatrix Potter Gallery in Hawkshead. ⊠ *The Old Laundry, Crag Brow, Bowness-on-Windermere* ☎ *015394/88444* ⊕ *www.hop-skip-jump.com* 🎫 *£6* ☉ *Easter–Sept., daily 10–5:30; Oct.–Easter, daily 10–4:30.*

In 1900, architect H. M. Baillie Scott (1865–1945) designed **Blackwell,** a quintessential Arts and Crafts house full of carved paneling and delicate plasterwork. Lakeland birds, flowers, and trees are artfully integrated into the stained glass, stonework, friezes, and wrought iron. The house showcases exhibits of works from different periods that embody Arts and Crafts ideals. Peruse the bookshop or relax in the Tea Room overlooking Windermere. ⊠ *B5360, Windermere* ☎ *015394/46139* ⊕ *www.blackwell.org.uk* 🎫 *£5.45* ☉ *Apr.–Oct., daily 10:30–5; Nov., Dec., and mid-Feb.–Mar., daily 10:30–4.*

★ ☺ The excellent **Aquarium of the Lakes,** on the quayside at the southern end of Windermere, has wildlife and waterside exhibits that focus on the region. The highlights are an underwater tunnel walk along a re-created lake bed and a re-creation of a nocturnal riverbank. You can take a boat to Lakeside from the town of Windermere or drive here. ⊠ *C5062, Lakeside* ☎ *015394/30153* ⊕ *www.aquariumofthelakes.co.uk* 🎫 *£6.25* ☉ *Apr.–Oct., daily 9–6; Nov.–Mar., daily 9–5.*

☺ The **Lakeside & Haverthwaite Railway Company** runs vintage steam trains on the 4-mi branch line between Lakeside and Haverthwaite along the lake's southern tip; you can add on a lake cruise. Departures coincide with ferry arrivals from Windermere. ☎ *015395/31594* ⊕ *www. lakesiderailway.co.uk* 🎫 *£4.90* ☉ *Apr.–Oct., daily 10:30–6.*

8

OFF THE BEATEN PATH

ORREST HEAD – To escape the traffic and have a memorable view of Windermere, set out on foot and follow the signs near the Windermere Hotel (across from the train station) to Orrest Head. The shady, uphill path winds through Elleray Wood, and after a 20-minute hike you arrive at a rocky little summit (784 feet) with a panoramic view that encompasses the Yorkshire fells, Morecambe Bay, and Troutbeck Valley.

Where to Stay & Eat

£££–££££ ✕ **Jerichos.** You can watch your meal being prepared in this stylish restaurant with an open kitchen. Choices from the modern British menu include fricassee of chicken on sage and onion mashed potatoes and sea bass on couscous. ⊠ *Birch St., Windermere* ☎ *015394/42522* ⊟ *MC, V* ⊘ *No lunch. Closed Mon., last 2 wks of Nov., and 1st wk of Dec. Also closed Sun. Jan.–Mar.*

★ **£££** ✕ **Porthole Eating House.** Superb French, Italian, and traditional English dishes have been served in this intimate, whitewashed 17th-century house for more than 30 years. Delicacies on the changing menu may include char-grilled beef with pepper sauce, and risotto of wild Lakeland mushrooms. The wine cellar stocks more than 350 vintages, or you can try a glass of Taglag, the excellent local beer. Petits fours are served with coffee. The patio is ideal for alfresco dining. ⊠ *3 Ash St., Bowness-on-Windermere* ☎ *015394/42793* ⊟ *AE, DC, MC, V* ⊘ *Closed Tues. No lunch Mon., Wed., and Sat.*

★ **££–£££** ✕ **Kwela's.** Delicious pan-African–influenced cuisine sets this restaurant apart from most of the more traditional eateries in the center of Windermere. Culinary influences on the changing menu stretch from Kenyan (roasted rack of lamb with tamarind sauce) to South African (*bobotie*—curried minced meat). The decor is stylish but refreshingly minimalist, with square wooden tables and natural colors. African-tinged jazz makes the scene even more mellow. ⊠ *4 High St., Windermere* ☎ *015394/44954* 🖷 *015394/44192* ⊟ *MC, V.*

★ **£££££** ✕🏠 **Miller Howe.** The sumptuous guest rooms in this luxurious Edwardian country-house hotel come with canopy-draped beds and binoculars that allow you to study the dazzling view across Windermere. You can relax in sitting rooms filled with fine antiques and paintings, and have afternoon tea and scones in the conservatory. The modern British restaurant (*££££–£££££*) serves sophisticated fare such as venison with onion and raisin compote. Guests have access to a health club, and the hotel arranges activities from archery to pony trekking. ⊠ *Rayrigg Rd., Bowness-on-Windermere LA23 1EY* ☎ *015394/42536* 🖷 *015394/45664* ⊕ *www.millerhowe.com* ⤶ *12 rooms, 3 suites in cottage* ⌂ *Restaurant, croquet, piano, airport shuttle, helipad, some pets allowed; no a/c, no kids under 8* ⊟ *AE, MC, V* ⧖ *MAP.*

££££–£££££ ✕🏠 **The Punch Bowl.** Under the same management as the celebrated Drunken Duck Inn, the Punch Bowl is a pleasantly modern retreat in the peaceful Lyth Valley, between Windermere and Kendal. The sleek, slate-floored bar serves fine real ales alongside a bar menu with treats (*££–£££*) such as fish pie or roast duck, whereas the bright contemporary restaurant (*£££–££££*) offers a more updated selection of locally sourced cuisine, such as Cumbrian ham with ginger. Bedrooms have oak-beam, high ceilings, with chic fabric designs and big baths—there's little Lakeland chintz here. ✉ *Off A5074, Crosthwaite, Lyth Valley LA8 8HR* ☎ *015395/68237* ⊕ *www.the-punchbowl.co.uk* ⟲ *9 rooms* ♿ *Restaurant, no-smoking rooms; no a/c* ⊟ *AE, MC, V* ⊮ *BP.*

£££ ✕▣ **The Queen's Head Hotel.** Popular with locals, this 17th-century inn north of Windermere is renowned for its innovative twist on pub food such as fried fillet of sea bass with rosti potato and sautéed beans, and for real ales (fermented twice in the cask) served from what was once an Elizabethan four-poster bed. The intimate dining rooms (£££) have oak beams, flagged floors, and roaring log fires. Guest rooms are plain (though seven have four-posters) but offer splendid views and good value. ✉ *A592, Troutbeck LA23 1PW* ☎ *015394/32174* ⊟ *015394/31938* ⊕ *www.queensheadhotel.com* ⟲ *15 rooms* ♿ *Restaurant, no-smoking rooms; no a/c, no room phones* ⊟ *MC, V* ⊮ *BP.*

££ ▣ **Boston House.** Built for railway executives in 1849, this Victorian stone house designed by Augustus Pugin, on a private drive directly above the train station, is one of Windermere's oldest buildings. The friendly owners will collect you from the station on request. One of the casual, country-style bedrooms has a four-poster. ✉ *The Terr., Windermere LA23 1AJ* ☎ *015394/43654* ⊕ *www.bostonhouse.co.uk* ⟲ *5 rooms* ♿ *No a/c, no kids under 13, no smoking* ⊟ *MC, V* ⊮ *BP.*

Sports & the Outdoors
Windermere Lake Holidays Afloat (✉ Gilly's Landing, Glebe Rd., Bowness-on-Windermere ☎ 015394/43415) rents boats, from small sailboats to large cabin cruisers and houseboats.

Shopping
The best selection of shops is at the Bowness end of Windermere, on Lake Road and around Queen's Square: clothing stores, crafts shops, and souvenir stores of all kinds. At **Lakeland Jewellers** (✉ Crag Brow, Bowness-on-Windermere ☎ 015394/42992), the local experts set semi-precious stones in necklaces and brooches. The **Lakeland Sheepskin and Leather Centre** (✉ Lake Rd., Bowness-on-Windermere ☎ 015394/44466), which also has branches in Ambleside and Keswick, stocks moderately priced leather and sheepskin goods.

Lake District National Park Visitor Centre at Brockhole

☟ ❷ *3 mi northwest of Windermere.*

Brockhole, a lakeside 19th-century mansion with 30 acres of terraced gardens sloping down to the water, serves as the park's official visitor center and has exhibits about the local ecology, flora, and fauna. It's a good stop at the start of your visit. The gardens are at their best in spring, when daffodils cover the lawns and azaleas burst into bloom. Among the park activities are lectures, guided walks, and demonstrations of traditional crafts such as drystone wall building. Some programs are geared to children, who appreciate the adventure playground here. You can also try the croquet lawn. The bookstore carries hiking guides and maps, and you can picnic here or eat at the café-restaurant. Bus 555/556 goes to the visitor center from the Windermere train station. **Windermere Lake Cruises** (☎ 015394/43360 ⊕ www.windermere-lakecruises.co.uk) runs a ferry service to the center from Ambleside. ⊠ *A591, Ambleside Rd., Windermere* ☎ *015394/46601* ⊕ *www.lake-district.gov.uk* ✉ *Free; parking £3 half day, £4 full day, £1 out of season* ☉ *Easter–Oct., daily 10–5; early–mid-Nov., weekends 10–5.*

Ambleside

❸ *5 mi north of Windermere.*

Unlike Windermere, Ambleside seems almost part of the hills and fells. Its buildings, mainly of local stone and many built in the traditional style that forgoes the use of mortar in the outer walls, blend perfectly into their setting. The small town sits at the northern end of Windermere, making it a popular center for Lake District excursions. It has a better choice of restaurants than Windermere or Bowness, and the numerous outdoor shops are handy for fell walkers. The town does, however, suffer from overcrowding in high season. Wednesday, when the local market takes place, is particularly busy.

Bridge House, a tiny 17th-century stone cottage, perches on an arched stone bridge that spans Stone Beck. This much-photographed building holds a National Trust shop and information center. ⊠ *Rydal Rd.* ☎ *015394/35599* ✉ *Free* ☉ *Easter–Oct., daily 10–5.*

Windermere Lake Cruises (☎ 015395/31188 ⊕ www.windermere-lakecruises.co.uk) has year-round service between Ambleside, Bowness, Brockhole, and Lakeside. It's a pleasant way to experience the lake.

Where to Stay & Eat

★ **£££–££££** ✕ **Glass House.** The most stylish restaurant in town occupies a converted medieval mill with a working waterwheel, adjacent to Adrian Sankey's Ambleside Glass Works. Modern British cuisine comes with a Mediterranean twist in dishes such as fillet of beef with red-wine sauce, and salmon with a tarragon crust. You can have an elegant dinner or just sip a cappuccino in the

---

LAKELAND LINGO

If someone tells you to walk along the "beck" to the "force" and then climb the "fell" to the "tarn," you've just been told to hike along the stream or river (beck) to the waterfall (force) before climbing the hill or mountain (fell) to reach a small mountain lake (tarn). Also, keep in mind that town or place names in the Lake District can be the same as the name of the lake on which the town or stands. For example, Windermere is both the lake (a "mere" is a lake, in Old English) and the town.

courtyard. There's a well-priced early evening menu weekdays from 6:30 to 7:30. Note that only "well-behaved, seated-at-all-times" children are welcome. ⊠ *Rydal Rd.* ☎ *015394/32137* ⌦ *Reservations essential* ⊟ *MC, V* ☺ *Closed Tues. and Jan.*

★ **££–££££** ✕ **Lucy's on a Plate.** This friendly café by day, restaurant by night is the perfect spot to relax, whether with mushroom stroganoff for lunch, a chocolate almond torte for afternoon tea, or grilled char for dinner by candlelight. Lucy's is famous for its puddings, and on the first Wednesday of every month a "pudding night" includes a menu of at least 30 desserts. An attached delicatessen sells high-class Cumbrian foods: sticky toffee pudding, farm cheeses, Cumberland sausage, jams, chutneys, and biscuits. Nearby Lucy 4, a wine bar and bistro, is run by the same management. ⊠ *Church St.* ☎ *015394/31191* ⊟ *MC, V.*

★ **££–£££** ▥ **The Old Vicarage.** A quiet edge of Ambleside's old center is the peaceful setting for this excellent-value B&B in a large Victorian former vicarage. Rooms are furnished in traditional English country style, with floral and print fabrics and dark wood furniture; some are well equipped for families. A log fire, great breakfasts, and a warm welcome help make this a good deal even without the pool. ⊠ *Vicarage Rd., LA22 9DH* ☎ *015394/33364* ⎙ *015394/34734* ⊕ *www.oldvicarageambleside.co. uk* ⤳ *10 rooms* ⚭ *In-room DVDs, indoor pool, sauna, lounge, piano; no a/c* ⊟ *MC, V* ▮⊙▮ *BP.*

£ ▥ **3 Cambridge Villas.** Ambleside has many inexpensive B&Bs, many clumped along Vicarage Road, but it's hard to find a more welcoming spot than this lofty Victorian house right in the center, with hosts who know a thing or two about local walks. Although space is at a premium, the rooms are pleasantly decorated with prints and wood furniture. ⊠ *Church St., LA22 9DL* ☎ *015394/32307* ⊕ *www.3cambridgevillas.co.uk* ⤳ *7 rooms, 4 with bath* ⚭ *No a/c, no room phones, no smoking* ⊟ *No credit cards* ▮⊙▮ *BP.*

Sports & the Outdoors

The fine walks in the vicinity include routes north to Rydal Mount or southeast over Wansfell to Troutbeck. Each walk will take up to a half day, there and back. Ferries from Bowness-on-Windermere dock at Ambleside's harbor, called Waterhead. ▮ **TIP→** You can rent rowboats here for an hour or two to escape the crowds and get a different view of the area.

Biketreks (⊠ 2 Milans Park ☎ 015394/31245) is a good source for bike rentals.

Rydal

❹ *1 mi northwest of Ambleside.*

The village of Rydal, on the small glacial lake called Rydal Water, is rich with Wordsworthian associations. One famous beauty spot linked with the poet is **Dora's Field,** below Rydal Mount next to the church of St. Mary's (where you can still see the poet's pew). In spring the field is awash in yellow daffodils, planted by William Wordsworth and his wife in memory of their beloved daughter Dora, who died in 1847.

If there's one poet associated with the Lake District, it is Wordsworth, who made his home at **Rydal Mount** from 1813 until his death. Wordsworth and his family moved to these grand surroundings when he was nearing the height of his career, and his descendants still live here, surrounded by his furniture, books, and portraits. You can see the study in which he worked, the family dining room, and the 4½-acre garden, laid out by the poet himself, that gave him so much pleasure. ■ TIP→ **Surrounding Rydal Mount and the areas around Dove Cottage and Grasmere are many footpaths where Wordsworth wandered. His favorite can be found on the hill past White Moss Common and the River Rothay.** Spend an hour or two walking them and you may understand why the great poet composed most of his verse in the open air. ⊠ *A591* ☎ *015394/33002* ⊕ *www. rydalmount.co.uk* ⊠ *£5, garden only £2.50* ⊙ *Mar.–Oct., daily 9:30–5; Nov.–Feb., Wed.–Mon. 10–4. Closed 3 wks in Jan.*

Grasmere

❺ *3 mi north of Rydal, 4 mi northwest of Ambleside.*

Lovely Grasmere, on a tiny, wood-fringed lake, is made up of crooked lanes in which Westmorland slate–built cottages hold shops, cafés, and galleries. The village is a focal point for literary and landscape associations because this area was the adopted heartland of the Romantic poets, notably Wordsworth and Coleridge.

Wordsworth, his wife Mary, his sister Dorothy, and four of his children are buried in the churchyard of **St. Oswald's,** which is on the River Rothay. The poet planted eight of the yew trees here. As you leave the churchyard, stop at the Gingerbread Shop, in a tiny cottage, for a special local treat.

★ William Wordsworth lived in **Dove Cottage** from 1799 to 1808, a prolific and happy time for the poet. During this time he wrote some of his most famous works, including "Ode: Intimations of Immortality" and *The Prelude;* he was also married here. Built in the early 17th century as an inn, this tiny house is beautifully preserved, with an oak-panel hall and floors of Westmorland slate. It first opened to the public in 1891 and remains as it was when Wordsworth lived here with his sister, Dorothy, and wife, Mary. Bedrooms and living areas contain much of Wordsworth's furniture and many personal belongings. Coleridge was a frequent visitor, as was Thomas De Quincey, best known for his 1822 autobiographical masterpiece *Confessions of an Opium Eater*—he moved in after the Wordsworths left. Your ticket includes admission to the **Wordsworth Museum,** which documents the poet's life and the literary contributions of Wordsworth and the Lake Poets. Besides seeing the poet's original manuscripts, you can hear his poems read aloud on headphones. Books, manuscripts, and artwork capture the spirit of the Romantic movement. The museum includes space for major art exhibitions. Afternoon tea is served at **Dove Cottage Tea Rooms and Restaurant,** also known as Villa Colombina. Opposite the tearooms, the 3°W Gallery, another Wordsworth Trust property (free; ring the bell for entry), has innovative contemporary art exhibitions. ⊠ *A591, 1 mi*

ON THE MENU

In Cumbria, which encompasses the Lake District, food is more than fuel for hiking. The area has earned a reputation for good country food using Herdwick lamb, beef, and game, as well as fish from the freshwater streams and lakes, such as salmon, Windermere char, and Borrowdale and Ullswater trout. Sold in one long strip, the thick pork-and-herb Cumberland sausage is another specialty. Local breads, cakes, pastries, and scones are scrumptious. Brown sugar, molasses, nutmeg, cinnamon, ginger, and rum—favorite ingredients in traditional cakes—were imported from the West Indies in exchange for wool and are integral to the cakes' flavor. Lyth Valley damsons (a kind of plum) have a nutty taste used in everything from beverages and desserts to cheese. Grasmere gingerbread is baked from a secret recipe, and Kendal mint cake (a candy marketed as survival food) has a home in many hikers' backpacks.

south of Grasmere ☎ *015394/35544* ⊕ *www.wordsworth.org.uk* 🎫 *£6.20* ☉ *Feb.–Dec., daily 9:30–5:30.*

Where to Stay & Eat

£££–££££   ✕ **Jumble Room Café.** This small, stone-built restaurant, dating to the 18th century, was Grasmere's first shop and is a friendly, fashionable, and colorful place, crammed with painted objets d'art. The food is an eclectic mix of international and traditional English: excellent fish-and-chips and game pie appear on the menu with Thai sweet potato ravioli. Lunches are lighter and cheaper, with good soups, and you can pop in anytime during the day for tea and cakes. ⊠ *Langdale Rd.* ☎ *015394/ 35188* ☰ *MC, V* ☉ *Closed Mon. and Tues. Easter–Nov.; Sun. eve. and Mon.–Wed. Dec.–Easter.*

★ £££££   ✕🏠 **White Moss House.** Wordsworth purchased this comfortable house, built in 1730 to overlook Rydal Water, for his son, Willie, whose family lived here until the 1930s. Pristine public areas and bedrooms are decorated with prints and traditional pieces such as the grandfather clock at the bottom of the stairs. The current hosts, the Dixons, lavish attention on guests, but the highlight of a stay is the renowned restaurant (£££££). The menu changes daily, but the five courses of contemporary English cuisine always include a soup, local meat and fish, and a choice of British cheeses. ⊠ *A591, Rydal Water LA22 9SE* ☎ *015394/35295* 🖷 *015394/35516* ⊕ *www.whitemoss.com* 🛏 *7 rooms, 1 suite* ⬠ *Restaurant, fishing, lounge; no a/c* ☰ *MC, V* ☉ *Closed Dec. and Jan.* ⫿⊙⫿ *MAP.*

★ £   🏠 **Banerigg House.** You don't have to spend a fortune to find appealing lakeside lodgings in Grasmere. This cozy, early-20th-century house, ¾ mi south of the village on A591, has unfussy, well-appointed rooms, most with lake views. Games and books fill the guest lounge. The B&B is walker-friendly, too, which means you get hiking advice from the owners, drying facilities for wet days, and a roaring fire when needed. ⊠ *Lake Rd., LA22 9PW* ☎ *015394/35204* ⊕ *www.baneriggguesthouse.*

8

co.uk ⇔ *6 rooms, 5 with bath* ⚴ *No a/c, no room phones, no room TVs, no smoking* ⊟ *No credit cards* ⦿ *BP.*

Sports & the Outdoors

The most panoramic views of lake and village are from the south, from the bare slopes of Loughrigg Terrace, reached along a signposted track on the western side of the lake. It's less than an hour's walk, though your stroll can be extended by continuing around Rydal Water, passing Rydal Mount and Dove Cottage before returning to Grasmere, a 4-mi (three-hour) walk in total.

Shopping

★ The smells wafting across the churchyard draw many people to the **Grasmere Gingerbread Shop** (⊠ Church Cottage ☎ 015394/35428). Since 1854 Sarah Nelson's gingerbread has been sold from this cramped 17th-century cottage, which was once the village school. The delicious treats, still made from a secret recipe, are available in attractive tins for the journey home or to eat right away. **The Stables** (⊠ College St. ☎ 015394/ 35453 ⊘ Closed Dec.–Easter except by appointment) antiques shop is a little Aladdin's cave piled with great books, bottles, silver candlesticks, lamps, and prints.

Elterwater

⑥ *2½ mi south of Grasmere, 4 mi west of Ambleside.*

The delightful village of Elterwater, at the eastern end of the Great Langdale Valley on B5343, is a good stop for hikers. It's barely more than a cluster of houses around a village green, but from here you can choose from a selection of excellent circular walks.

Where to Stay & Eat

£££ ✕🖼 **Britannia Inn.** At this family-owned, 500-year-old lodging in the heart of superb walking country, antiques, comfortable chairs, and prints and oil paintings furnish the cozy, beam public rooms. The smallish bedrooms are more modern in style, and two cottages with kitchens can be rented by the week. You can relax with a bar meal and Cumbrian ale on the terrace while taking in the village green and the rolling scenery beyond. The hearty traditional English food (££) is popular with locals, as are the many ales and whiskies. A nearby health club is available to guests. ⊠ *B5343, LA22 9HP* ☎ *015394/37210* 🖨 *015394/37311* ⊕ *www.britinn.net* ⇔ *9 rooms, 8 with bath* ⚴ *Restaurant, bar, lounge, some pets allowed; no a/c* ⊟ *MC, V* ⦿ *BP.*

★ **££–£££** 🖼 **Old Dungeon Ghyll Hotel.** There's no more comforting stop after a day outdoors than the Hiker's Bar of this hotel at the head of the Great Langdale Valley. The stone floor and wooden beams echo to the clatter of hikers' boots, and the roaring stove rapidly dries out wet walking gear. The old inn has provided hospitality for more than 300 years; guest rooms are done in traditional Lakeland style with patterned carpets, botanical prints, and flowered bed linens. You can include dinner in the rate. ⊠ *Off B5343, Great Langdale LA22 9JY* ☎ *015394/37272* ⊕ *www. odg.co.uk* ⇔ *13 rooms, 8 with bath* ⚴ *Restaurant, 2 bars, lounge; no a/c, no room phones, no room TVs* ⊟ *AE, MC, V* ⦿ *BP.*

Sports & the Outdoors

There are access points to Langdale Fell from several places along B5343, the main road; look for information boards at local parking places. You can also stroll up the river valley or embark on more energetic hikes to Stickle Tarn or to one of the summits of the Langdale Pikes.

Coniston

❼ *5 mi south of Elterwater.*

This small lake resort and boating center attracts climbers with the peak known as the **Old Man of Coniston** (2,635 feet); it also has sites related to John Ruskin. **Coniston Water,** the lake on which Coniston stands, came to prominence in the 1930s when Arthur Ransome made it the setting for *Swallows and Amazons,* one of a series of novels about a group of children and their adventures. The lake is about 5 mi long, a tempting stretch that drew boat and car racer Donald Campbell here in 1959 to set a water-speed record of 260 mph. He was killed when trying to beat it in 1967. His body and the wreckage of *Bluebird K7* were retrieved from the lake in 2001. Campbell is buried in St. Andrew's church in Coniston, and a stone memorial on the village green commemorates him.

The **Ruskin Museum** holds fascinating and thought-provoking manuscripts, personal items, and watercolors by John Ruskin that illuminate his thinking and influence. There is also a focus on Donald Campbell; the tailfin of his *Bluebird K7,* dragged up from Coniston Water, is here. Good local-interest exhibits include copper mining, geology, lace, and more. ⊠ *Yewdale Rd.* ☎ *015394/41164* ⊕ *www.ruskinmuseum.com* 🎟 *£3.95* ☺ *Mid-Mar.–mid-Nov., daily 10–5:30; mid-Nov.–mid-Mar., Wed.–Sun. 10:30–3:30.*

★ **Brantwood,** on the eastern shore of Coniston Water, was the cherished home of John Ruskin (1819–1900), the noted Victorian artist, writer, critic, and social reformer, after 1872. The rambling, white, 18th-century house (with Victorian alterations) is on a 250-acre estate that stretches high above the lake. Here, alongside mementos such as his mahogany desk, are Ruskin's own paintings, drawings, and books. Also on display is much of the art—he was a great connoisseur—that Ruskin collected, not least superb drawings by the landscape painter J. M. W. Turner (1775–1851). A video on Ruskin's life shows the lasting influence of his thoughts, and the **Severn Studio** has rotating art exhibitions. Ruskin himself laid out the extensive grounds with gardens and woodland walks. ■ TIP➔ It's an easy drive to Brantwood from Coniston, but it's pleasant to travel here by ferry across the lake, via either the Coniston Launch or the *Gondola,* a 19th-century steam yacht. Both depart from Coniston Pier through the summer. ⊠ *Off B5285* ☎ *015394/41396* ⊕ *www.brantwood. org.uk* 🎟 *£5.50, gardens only £3.75* ☺ *Mid-Mar.–mid-Nov., daily 11–5:30; mid-Nov.–mid-Mar., Wed.–Sun. 11–4:30.*

Coniston Launch (☎ 015394/36216 ⊕ www.conistonlaunch.co.uk) connects Coniston Pier with Ruskin's home at Brantwood, offering hourly service for most of the year (service is reduced in winter) on its wooden *Ruskin* and *Ransome* launches, which run on a solar–electric power sys-

START WALKING

You can choose gentle rambles near the most popular towns and villages or challenging hikes and climbs up some of England's most impressive peaks. Information boards at parking lots throughout the region point out the possibilities. British mountaineering began in the Lake District, with its notable hikes: the famous Old Man of Coniston, the Langdale Pikes, Scafell Pike, Skiddaw, and Helvellyn are all popular, though these require experience, energy, and proper hiking boots and clothing. The Cumbria Way (70 mi) crosses the Lake District, starting at the market town of Ulverston and finishing at Carlisle. The Coast-to-Coast Walk (190 mi) runs from St. Bees on the Irish Sea through the Lake District and across the Yorkshire Dales and the North York Moors; it ends at Robin Hood's Bay at the edge of the North Sea in Yorkshire. Guidebooks to these and other Lakeland walks are available in local bookstores— don't miss Alfred Wainwright's classic guides. For short walks, consult the tourist information centers: those at Ambleside, Grasmere, Keswick, and Windermere provide maps and advice. The other main sources of information are the Lake District National Park information centers. Several climbing organizations offer guided hikes as well as technical rock climbing.

tem. **Steam Yacht *Gondola*** (☎ 015394/41288 ⊕ www.nationaltrust.org. uk) runs the National Trust's luxurious Victorian steam yacht between Coniston Pier, Brantwood, and Park-a-Moor at the south end of Coniston Water, daily from April through October.

Where to Stay & Eat

£–££ ✕ **Jumping Jenny's.** Named after Ruskin's beloved boat, the wood-beamed tearoom at Brantwood occupies the converted coach house. It has an open log fire and mountain views, and serves morning coffee, lunch (sophisticated soups, pastas, sandwiches, and salads), and afternoon tea with tasty homemade cakes. You can sit on the terrace in warmer weather. ⊠ *Off B5285* ☎ *015394/41715* ═ *MC, V* ☺ *Closed Mon. and Tues. mid-Nov.–mid-Mar. No dinner.*

★ **££–£££** ✕▣ **Sun Hotel.** Standing at the foot of the Old Man of Coniston, this country-house hotel was built at the turn of the 20th century alongside the 16th-century coaching inn that still serves as a pub. The simply furnished guest rooms, refurbished in 2006, and conservatory restaurant have exceptional mountain views. The ancient pub (££–£££), with flagstone walls and floors and exposed beams, fills up most nights with a mix of locals and climbers. The lamb hot pot is good, and the chef prepares paella in summer: take your pick of five real ales and 36 wines. ⊠ *LA21 8HQ* ☎ *015394/41248* ☐ *015394/41219* ⊕ *www. thesunconiston.com* ▭ *10 rooms, 9 with bath* ⌂ *Restaurant, pub, some pets allowed, no-smoking rooms; no a/c* ═ *MC, V* ▢ *BP.*

★ **£** ▣ **Beech Tree Guest House.** This Victorian stone house with friendly owners and a garden is within walking distance of the town center. The individually furnished rooms, some of which look out over an ancient beech tree, are done in a country theme, and breakfast is hearty and vegetarian. There's a TV in the sitting room. ✉ *Yewdale Rd., LA21 8DX* ☎ *015394/413717* ⤳ *8 rooms, 4 with bath* ⚬ *Some pets allowed; no a/c, no room TVs, no smoking* ⊟ *No credit cards* ⧉ *BP.*

Sports & the Outdoors

Steep tracks lead up from the village to the **Old Man of Coniston.** The trail starts near the Sun Hotel and goes past an old copper mine to the peak, which you can reach in about two hours. It's one of the Lake District's most satisfying—not too arduous but high enough to feel a real sense of accomplishment and get some fantastic views (west to the sea, south to Morecambe Bay, and east to Windermere). Experienced hikers include the peak in a seven-hour circular walk from the village, also taking in the dramatic heights and ridges of Swirl How and Wetherlam.

★ **Coniston Boating Centre** (✉ Lake Rd. ☎ 015394/41366 ⊕ www.lake-district.gov.uk) is a good place to help you enjoy the water. You can rent launches, canoes, kayaks, and wooden rowboats, or even take a sailing lesson. A picnic area and café are near the center, too.

Hawkshead

❽ *3 mi east of Coniston.*

In the Vale of Esthwaite, this small market town, with a pleasing hodgepodge of tiny squares, cobbled lanes, and whitewashed houses, is perhaps the Lake District's most picturesque village. There's a good deal more history here than in most local villages, however. The Hawkshead Courthouse, just outside town, was built by the monks of Furness Abbey in the 15th century. Hawkshead later derived much wealth from the wool trade, which flourished here in the 17th and 18th centuries. As a thriving market center, it could afford to maintain the **Hawkshead Grammar School,** at which William Wordsworth was a pupil from 1779 to 1787; he carved his name on a desk inside, now on display. A house in the village (Ann Tyson's House) claims the honor of providing the young William with lodgings. The twin draws of Wordsworth and Beatrix Potter—apart from her home, Hill Top, there's a Potter gallery—conspire to make Hawkshead overcrowded throughout the year. There may be more attention in 2007, when Renée Zellweger stars in *Miss Potter,* a movie about the writer-artist's life.

⟳ The **Beatrix Potter Gallery,** in the solicitor's offices formerly used by Potter's husband, displays an annually changing selection of the artist-writer's original watercolors and drawings, as well as information on her interests as a naturalist. Potter was a conservationist and an early supporter of the National Trust. The house looks almost as it would have done in her day. Admission is by timed ticket. ✉ *Main St.* ☎ *015394/36355* ⊕*www.nationaltrust.org.uk* ⊡*£3.50* ☯ *Apr.–Oct., Sat.–Wed. 10:30–4:30.*

Hill Top was the home of children's author and illustrator Beatrix Potter (1866–1943), most famous for her *Peter Rabbit* stories. The house looks much the same as when Potter bequeathed it to the National Trust, and fans will recognize details such as the porch and garden gate, old kitchen range, Victorian dollhouse, and 17th-century four-poster bed, which were depicted in the book illustrations. ■ TIP→ Admission to this often-crowded spot is by timed ticket; you can book in advance. Try to avoid visiting on summer weekends and during school vacations. Hill Top lies 2 mi south of Hawkshead by car or foot, though you can also approach via the car ferry from Bowness-on-Windermere. ☒ *Off B5285, Near Sawrey* ☎ *015394/36269* ⊕ *www.nationaltrust.org.uk* ☒ *£5.10, gardens free when house closed* ☉ *House Easter–Oct., Sat.–Wed. 10:30–4:30; gardens and shop Easter–Oct., daily 10:30–5.*

Two miles northwest of the village (follow signs on B5285) is one of the Lake District's most celebrated beauty spots, **Tarn Hows,** a tree-lined lake. Scenic overlooks let you drink it all in, or you can take an hour to putter along the paths. A free National Trust bus runs here from Hawkshead and Coniston (Easter–October, Sunday only).

Where to Stay & Eat

£££££
Fodor'sChoice
★

✕🏠 **Drunken Duck Inn.** After four centuries, this friendly old coaching inn remains a fine place for food and lodging. Nestle into the cozy bar with oak settles and order a tasty real ale from the Duck's Barnsgate Brewery. There's an open fire, and hops hang over the bar. The two dining spaces have dark-wood furniture and hunting prints; venison with polenta and figs is typical of the modern British fare (reservations essential in restaurant; £££). Bedrooms, bright and contemporary, make use of natural materials and have wonderful views of the Langdale Pikes. The price includes afternoon tea and breakfast. The inn is 2½ mi from Ambleside and Hawkshead. ☒ *Off B5286, Barngates LA22 ONG* ☎ *015394/36347* 🖷 *015394/36781* ⊕ *www.drunkenduckinn.co.uk* ⇌ *16 rooms* ⚭ *Restaurant, pub, no-smoking rooms; no a/c* ⊟ *AE, MC, V* ⑪ *BP* ⚓ *Reservations essential.*

££
🏠 **Yewfield.** With the laid-back friendliness of a B&B but with most of the style of a fancier country-house hotel, this is a very good value for the money—especially if you can get one of the rooms with a great view across the valley from the front of the house. The 19th-century Gothic house, between Hawkshead and Tarn Hows, is on 30 acres of land. Breakfast is wholesome and vegetarian. ☒ *Hawkshead Hill, LA22 0PR* ☎ *015394/36765* 🖷 *015394/36096* ⊕ *www.yewfield.co.uk* ⇌ *6 rooms, 4 apartments* ⚭ *Lounge, library, in-room DVDs; no a/c, no kids under 9* ⊟ *MC, V* ☉ *Closed mid-Nov.–Jan.* ⑪ *BP.*

THE NORTHERN LAKES

The scenery of the northern lakes is considerably more dramatic—some would say bleaker—than much of the landscape to the south, a change that becomes apparent on your way north from Windermere. Your easiest approach is a 30-mi drive on the A6 that takes you through the wild and desolate Shap Fells, which rise to a height of 1,304 feet. This is one of the most notorious moorland crossings in the country: even in summer it's a lonely place to be, and in winter, snow on the road can be dangerous. Ullswater is possibly the grandest of all the lakes; then there's a steady route west past Keswick, south through the marvelous Borrowdale Valley.

Ullswater

○ 9 *3 mi southwest of Dalemain, 6 mi southwest of Penrith.*

Hemmed in by towering hills, Ullswater, the region's second-largest lake, draws outdoor types. Some of the finest views are from the A592 as it sticks to the lake's western shore, through the adjacent hamlets of **Glenridding** and **Patterdale** at the southern end. Lakeside strolls, tea shops, and rowboat rental all help provide the usual Lakeland experience.

Ullswater Steamers (☎ 017684/82229 ⊕ www.ullswater-steamers.co.uk) sends its oil-burning, 19th-century steamers the length of Ullswater between Glenridding and Pooley Bridge; it's a pleasant tour. The service operates 363 days a year from the pier at Glenridding.

At **Aira Force** (✉ Off A592, 5 mi north of Patterdale), a spectacular waterfall pounds under a stone bridge and through a wooded ravine to feed into Ullswater. From the parking lot (£2–£4 fee, depending on how long you stay), it's a 10-minute walk to the falls. Bring sturdy shoes in wet weather. Just above Aira Force in the woods of Gowbarrow Park is the spot where, in 1802, William Wordsworth's sister, Dorothy, observed daffodils that, as she wrote, " . . . tossed and reeled and danced and seemed as if they verily laughed with the wind that blew upon them." Two years later Wordsworth transformed his sister's words into the famous poem "I Wandered Lonely as a Cloud." And two centuries later, national park wardens patrol Gowbarrow Park in season to prevent tourists from picking the few remaining daffodils.

★ West of Ullswater's southern end, the brooding presence of **Helvellyn** (3,118 feet), one of the Lake District's most formidable mountains, recalls the region's fundamental character. It's an arduous climb to the top, especially via the challenging ridge known as Striding Edge, and the ascent shouldn't be attempted in poor weather or by inexperienced hikers. Signposted paths to the peak run from the road between Glenridding and Patterdale and pass by **Red Tarn**, at 2,356 feet the highest small mountain lake in the region.

Home of the Hasell family since 1679, **Dalemain,** 3 mi northeast of the lake, began with a 12th-century peel tower built to protect the occupants from raiding Scots, and is now a delightful hodgepodge of architectural styles. An imposing Georgian facade of local pink sandstone encompasses a medieval hall and extensions from the 16th through the 18th centuries. Inside are a magnificent oak staircase, furniture dating from the mid-17th century, a Chinese drawing room, a 16th-century fretwork room with intricate plasterwork, and many fine paintings, including masterpieces by Van Dyck. The gardens are also worth a look. ✉ A592 ☎ 01768/486450 ⊕ www.dalemain.com ✉ £6, gardens only £4 ⊙ House Apr.–Oct., Sun.–Thurs. 11–4; gardens Apr.–Oct., Sun.–Thurs. 10:30–5; Nov.–mid-Dec., Feb., and Mar., Sun.–Thurs. 11–4.

8

Where to Stay & Eat

★ £££££ ✕🏨 **Sharrow Bay.** Sublime views and exceptional service and cuisine add distinction to this country-house hotel on the shores of Ullswater. Salons with oil paintings and fringed lamp shades represent classic Lakeland style. The bedrooms are plushly opulent, although those in the Edwardian Gatehouse and in the Bank House, an Elizabethan farmhouse about 1½ mi away, are somewhat simpler. Your sophisticated dinner (reservations essential, fixed-price menu, £££££) might include roast salmon on scallop risotto or venison with sweet potato confit. Be sure to request the lake-view dining room. Stop by for afternoon tea (£17.50). ✉ *Howtown Rd., Pooley Bridge CA10 2LZ* ☎ *017684/86301* 🖷 *017684/86349* ⊕ *www.sharrowbay.co.uk* ↬ *16 rooms, 8 suites* ♨ *2 restaurants, 2 lounges, business services, some pets allowed, no-smoking rooms; no a/c in some rooms, no kids under 13* ▭ *AE, MC, V* ¶❘ *MAP.*

★ ££ ✕🏨 **Queen's Head Inn.** Once owned by the Wordsworths, this 1719 inn is a true gem. Now the home of a brewery, the traditional pub and restaurant (££–£££) is often packed with locals sampling Tirril beers as well as guest ales on tap, 40 malt whiskies, and rare domestic and imported wines. Sophisticated meals use local produce such as farmhouse cheeses and Ullswater trout, but may include more exotic dishes, such as venison with orange and port gravy. Rambling hallways lead to small, pleasant rooms with plaid bedspreads and simple wood furniture. The inn is between Ullswater and Penrith, 2½ mi northeast of the lake. ✉ *B5320, Tirril CA10 2JF* ☎ *01768/863219* 🖷 *01768/863243* ⊕ *www.queensheadinn.co.uk* ↬ *7 rooms* ♨ *Restaurant, pub; no a/c, no room phones* ▭ *MC, V* ¶❘ *BP.*

Keswick

🔟 *14 mi west of Ullswater.*

The great mountains of Skiddaw and Blencathra brood over the gray slate houses of Keswick (pronounced *kezz*-ick), on the scenic shores of Derwentwater. The town is a natural base for exploring the rounded, heather-clad Skiddaw range to the north, and the hidden valleys of Borrowdale and Buttermere (the latter reached by stunning Honister Pass) take you into the rugged heart of the Lake District. Nearby, five beautiful lakes are set among the three highest mountain ranges in England.

■ TIP→ Because traffic congestion can be horrendous in summer, and parking is difficult in the higher valleys, you may want to leave your car in Keswick. The open-top Borrowdale bus service between Keswick and Seatoller runs frequently, and the Honister Rambler minibus is perfect for walkers aiming for the high fells of the central lakes; it makes many stops from Keswick to Buttermere. The Keswick Launch service on Derwentwater links to many walks as well as the Borrowdale bus service.

★ To understand why **Derwentwater** is considered one of England's finest lakes, take a short walk from Keswick's town center to the lakeshore and follow the **Friar's Crag** path, about a 15-minute level walk from the center. This pine-tree-fringed peninsula is a favorite vantage point, with its view of the lake, the ring of mountains, and many tiny islands.

Ahead, crags line the **Jaws of Borrowdale** and overhang a mountain ravine—a scene that looks as if it emerged from a Romantic painting.

For the best lake views, take a wooden-launch cruise with **Keswick-on-Derwentwater Launch Co.** (☎ 017687/72263 ⊕ www.keswick-launch.co. uk) around Derwentwater. Between late March and November, cruises set off every hour in each direction from a dock at the shore; there is also a limited winter timetable. You can also rent a rowboat here. Buy a "hop-on, hop-off" explorer ticket and take advantage of the seven landing stages around the lake that provide access to hiking trails, such as the two-hour climb up and down Cat Bells, a celebrated lookout point on the western shore of Derwentwater.

★ A Neolithic monument about 100 feet in diameter, the **Castlerigg Stone Circle** (⊠ Off A66, 4 mi east of Keswick) lies in a brooding natural hollow called St. John's Vale, ringed by magnificent peaks and ranged by sheep. The 38 stones aren't large, but the site makes them particularly impressive. Wordsworth described them as "a dismal cirque of Druid stones upon a forlorn moor." A marked route leads to a 200-foot-long path through a pasture. You can visit during daylight, no charge.

Where to Stay & Eat

££–£££ ✕ **Morrel's.** One of the town's better eating places has cinematically themed art and wooden floors that give a contemporary edge to the refurbished bar and dining area. The relaxed restaurant prepares contemporary fare: the pork fillet is stuffed with prunes and Calvados and the duck breast comes with puy lentils and black cherries. A couple of equally stylish apartments upstairs are available for short-term rentals. ⊠ *34 Lake Rd., CA12 5DQ* ☎ *017687/72666* ▤ *MC, V* ☉ *Closed Mon.*

★ **£–££** ✕ **Square Orange Cafe.** Young locals and windblown walkers gather here for excellent teas, cordials, and some serious hot chocolate. Music is laid-back, the walls have real paintings and photos, and there are games, good pizzas, and pints of local beer for long rainy days or cold winter nights. ⊠ *20 St. Johns St.* ☎ *017687/73888* ▤ *No credit cards.*

£ ✕ **Lakeland Pedlar.** This colorful, cheerful café and bike shop serves inspired vegetarian and vegan cuisine: hearty breakfast burritos, Tex-Mex and Mediterranean food, and fun pizzas such as the Switchback, with sun-dried tomatoes, peppers, and crumbled blue cheese. You can also check out the fresh juices, espresso, and homemade cakes. Admire the fells (or the parking lot) from the outdoor tables or take food with you for the trail. ⊠ *Henderson's Yard, Bell Close* ☎ *017687/74492* ▤ *MC, V* ☉ *Closed Wed. No dinner Sept.–June.*

££££ ✕▥ **Highfield Hotel.** Slightly austere-looking and stubbornly old-fashioned, this family-run Victorian hotel overlooks the lawns of Hope Park and has lodging with great character, including turret rooms and a former chapel that holds a four-poster. The balconies of the common areas have superb valley views. The restaurant's daily-changing fixed-price menu (£££££) takes advantage of local ingredients in dishes such as roast pork with poached apricots and sea trout with sweet potatoes. No children under 8 are allowed in the restaurant. ⊠ *The Heads, CA12 5ER* ☎ *017687/72508* ▤ *017687/72508* ⊕ *www.highfieldkeswick.*

8

co.uk ⤴ *19 rooms* ⟁ *Restaurant, bar, no-smoking rooms; no a/c, no room phones* ⊟ *AE, MC, V* ⊙ *Closed mid-Nov.–Jan.* ⧖⊙⧘ *MAP.*

★ **££** ⊞ **Howe Keld.** Those in the know bypass the rows of cookie-cutter B&Bs and head here for budget TLC. The Fisher family puts you at ease in their comfortable, pretty town house–hotel. High-quality breakfasts are the big event; vegetarians do well here with fresh home-baked bread and pancakes, but there are also meaty Cumbrian fry-ups. Evening meals (on request) are a good value. ⊠ *5–7 The Heads, CA12 5ES* ☎ *017687/72417* ⊕ *www.howekeld.co.uk* ⤴ *15 rooms* ⟁ *Dining room, lounge, some pets allowed, no-smoking; no a/c, no room phones* ⊟ *No credit cards* ⊙ *Closed Jan.* ⧖⊙⧘ *BP.*

Nightlife & the Arts

The resident company at the **Theatre by the Lake** (⊠ Lake Rd. ☎ 017687/74411) presents classic and contemporary productions year-round. Touring music, opera, and dance companies also perform. The Keswick Music Society season runs from September through January, and the Words on the Water literary festival takes place in February and March.

Sports & the Outdoors

BIKING   **Keswick Mountain Bike Centre** (⊠ Southey Hill ☎ 017687/75202) rents bikes and provides information on trails; it also stocks accessories and clothing. Guided tours can be arranged with advance notice.

WATER SPORTS   **Derwentwater Marina** (⊠ Portinscale ☎ 017687/72912) offers boat rentals and instruction in canoeing, sailing, windsurfing, and rowing.

Shopping

Keswick has a good choice of bookstores, crafts shops, and wool-clothing stores tucked away in its cobbled streets, as well as excellent outdoor shops. Keswick's **market** is held Saturday. **George Fisher** (⊠ 2 Borrowdale Rd. ☎ 017687/72178), the area's largest outdoor equipment store, sells sportswear, travel books, and maps. Daily weather information is posted in the window.

EN
ROUTE
   The most scenic route from Keswick, B5289 south, runs along the eastern edge of Derwentwater, past turnoffs to natural attractions such as Ashness Bridge, the idyllic tarn of Watendlath, the Lodore Falls (best in wet weather), and the precariously balanced Bowder Stone. Farther south is the tiny village of **Grange,** a walking center at the head of Borrowdale, where there's a riverside café.

Borrowdale

❶ *7 mi south of Keswick.*

South of Keswick and its lake lies the valley of Borrowdale, whose varied landscape of green valley floor and surrounding crags has long been considered one of the region's most magnificent treasures. **Rosthwaite,** a tranquil farming village, and **Seatoller,** the southernmost settlement, are the two main centers (both are accessible by bus from Keswick), though they are little more than clusters of aged buildings surrounded by glorious countryside.

The steep **Borrowdale Fells** rise up dramatically behind Seatoller. Get out and walk whenever inspiration strikes. England's highest mountain, the 3,210-foot **Scafell Pike** (pronounced *scar*-fell) is visible from Seatoller. One route up the mountain, for experienced walkers, is from the hamlet of Seathwaite, a mile south of Seatoller.

Where to Eat

£–££ ✕ **Yew Tree Restaurant.** Two 17th-century miners' cottages make up this intimate restaurant at the foot of Honister Pass. A low-beam ceiling, open fireplace, and excellent bar serving local Hesket Newmarket Brewery beers add appeal. The menu focuses on regional ingredients: Ullswater trout, Derwentwater pike, Herdwick burgers ("herdy burgers"), and wonderful Cumbrian cheeses and sausages. ⌂ *B5289, Seatoller* ☎ *017687/77634* ▭ *D, MC, V* ☯ *Closed Mon. and 3 wks in Jan.*

£££££ ⌂ **Hazel Bank Country House.** Hikers and others appreciate the comforts of this stately, carefully restored Victorian home, which retains original elements such as the stained-glass windows. Immaculate, spacious bedrooms are done in a faux-Victorian theme, and some have four-posters and window seats. All rooms, including the sitting area, have splendid views of the Borrowdale Valley and the central Lakeland peaks. The four-course dinner for guests (included in price) focuses on local ingredients prepared with modern British flair. ⌂ *Off B5289, Rosthwaite CA12 5XB* ☎ *017687/77248* ⎙ *017687/77373* ⊕ *www.hazelbankhotel.co.uk* ⇌ *8 rooms* ♨ *Dining room, lounge, business services, Internet room; no a/c, no kids under 10, no smoking* ▭ *MC, V* ❢ *MAP.*

EN ROUTE Beyond Seatoller, B5289 turns westward through **Honister Pass** (1,176 feet) and Buttermere Fell. Boulders line the road, which is one of the most dramatic in the region; at times it channels through soaring rock canyons. The road sweeps down from the pass to the village of Buttermere, sandwiched between Buttermere (the lake) and Crummock Water at the foot of high, craggy fells.

8

LAKE DISTRICT ESSENTIALS

Transportation

BY AIR

Manchester Airport has its own rail station with direct service to Carlisle, Windermere, and Barrow-in-Furness. Manchester is 70 mi from the southern part of the Lake District.

ℹ **Manchester Airport** ⌂ Near Junctions 5 and 6 of M56 ☎ 0161/489–3000 ⊕ www.manairport.co.uk.

BY BIKE

Cycling along the numerous bicycle paths and quiet forest roads in Cumbria is pleasurable and safe. The Cumbria Cycle Way circles the county, and for local excursions guided bike tours are often available, starting at about £25 per day. Contact local tourist offices or bike-rental places for details on cycle routes.

BY BOAT & FERRY

Whether you rent a boat or take a ride on a modern launch or vintage vessels, getting out on the water is a fun (and often useful) way to see the Lake District. Check the sections on individual towns for information about additional services and boat rentals.

BY BUS

Traveline handles public transportation inquiries. National Express serves the region from London's Victoria Coach Station and from Manchester's Chorlton Street Station. Average travel time to Windermere is just over 7½ hours from London; and to Keswick, 8¼ hours. From Manchester there's one bus a day to Windermere (3½ hours); it stops in Ambleside, Grasmere, and Keswick. There's direct bus service to the Lake District from Carlisle, Lancaster, and York.

Stagecoach in Cumbria provides local service between Lakeland towns and through the valleys and high passes. Contact Traveline for an up-to-date timetable. A one-day Explorer Ticket (£6) is available on the bus and valid on all routes. Service between main tourist centers is fairly frequent on weekdays, but much reduced on weekends and bank holidays. Don't count on reaching the more remote parts of the area by bus. Off-the-beaten-track touring requires a car or strong legs.

CUTTING COSTS The YHA Shuttle Bus operates a door-to-door service for guests at eight popular hostels in the Lakes (Easter through October only). Get on and off where you like for £2 a journey, or send your luggage ahead to the next hostel if you want to walk unencumbered. The trip from Windermere station to the Windermere or Ambleside hostel is free.
🚌 **YHA Shuttle Bus** ✉ Ambleside Youth Hostel, Waterhead ☎ 015394/32304.

FARES & 🚌 **National Express** ☎ 0870/580-8080 ⊕ www.nationalexpress.com. **Traveline**
SCHEDULES ☎ 0870/608-2608 ⊕ www.traveline.org.uk.

BY CAR

A car is a good option in the Lake District to get beyond the major towns; bus service is limited. To reach the Lake District from London, take M1 north to M6, getting off either at Junction 36 and joining A590/A591 west (around the Kendal bypass to Windermere) or at Junction 40, joining A66 direct to Keswick and the northern lakes region. Travel time to Kendal is about four hours, to Keswick five to six hours. Expect heavy traffic out of London on weekends to all destinations in the Northwest; construction work also often slows progress on M6.

ROAD Roads within the region are generally very good, although many minor
CONDITIONS routes and mountain passes can be both steep and narrow. Warning signs are normally posted if snow has made a road impassable; always listen to local weather forecasts in winter before heading out. In July and August and during the long public holiday weekends, expect heavy traffic. The Lake District has plenty of parking lots, which should be used to avoid blocking narrow lanes.

BY TRAIN

For schedule information, call National Rail Enquiries. Two train companies serve the region from London's Euston Station: take a Virgin or

Northern Rail train bound for Carlisle, Edinburgh, or Glasgow and change at Oxenholme for the branch line service to Kendal and Windermere. Average travel time to Windermere (including the change) is 4½ hours. If you're heading for Keswick, you can either take the train to Windermere and continue from there by Stagecoach bus (Bus 555/556; 70 minutes), or stay on the main London–Carlisle train to Penrith Station (4 hours), from which Stagecoach buses (Bus X5) also run to Keswick (45 minutes). Direct trains from Manchester depart for Windermere five times daily (travel time 2 hours). First North Western runs a local service from Windermere and Barrow-in-Furness to Manchester Airport.

Train connections are good around the edges of the Lake District, especially on the Oxenholme–Kendal–Windermere line and the Furness and West Cumbria branch line from Lancaster to Grange-over-Sands, Ulverston, Barrow, and Ravenglass. However, these services aren't useful for getting around the central Lakeland region (you must take the bus or drive), and they are reduced, or nonexistent, on Sunday.

FARES &
SCHEDULES   **Northern Rail** ☎ 0845/600–1159 ⊕ www.northernrail.org. **National Rail Enquiries** ☎ 0845/748–4950 ⊕ www.nationalrail.co.uk. **Virgin Trains** ☎ 0845/722–2333 ⊕ www.virgintrains.co.uk.

Contacts & Resources

EMERGENCIES
Ambulance, fire, police ☎ 999. **Keswick Cottage Hospital** ✉ Croswaithe Rd., Keswick ☎ 017687/72012. **Penrith New Hospital** ✉ Bridge La., Penrith ☎ 017687/245300.

INTERNET
Internet access in the Lakes is slow and patchy. Some of the better hotels offer access but Internet cafés are all but nonexistent.
Internet Cafés Tea Too Ltd ✉ 4 Windermere Bank, Lake Rd., Windermere ☎ 015394/45657.

NATIONAL PARK
The Lake District National Park head office (and main visitor center) is at Brockhole, north of Windermere. Helpful regional national-park information centers sell books and maps, book accommodations, and provide walking advice. Call regional offices before visiting, as funding cutbacks have caused many closures.
Lake District National Park ✉ Brockhole, A591, Ambleside Rd., Windermere ☎ 015394/46601 ⊕ www.lake-district.gov.uk. **Bowness Bay** ✉ Glebe Rd., Bowness-on-Windermere ☎ 015394/42895. **Keswick** ✉ Moot Hall, Main St. ☎ 017687/72645. **Ullswater** ✉ Beckside Car Park, Glenridding ☎ 017684/82414.

TOUR OPTIONS
BUS TOURS   Mountain Goat Holidays, Lakes Supertours, and Park Tours & Travel provide minibus sightseeing tours with skilled local guides. Half- and full-day tours, which really get off the beaten track, depart from Bowness, Windermere, Ambleside, and Grasmere.
Lakes Supertours ✉ 1 High St., Windermere ☎ 015394/42751 ⊕ www.lakes-supertours.co.uk. **Mountain Goat Holidays** ✉ Victoria St., Windermere ☎ 015394/45161

8

⊕ www.lakes-pages.co.uk/goatmain.html. **Park Tours & Travel** ⊠ The Lodge, Burn-side Park, Windermere ☎ 015394/48600 ⊕ www.parktours.co.uk.

WALKING TOURS You can find walks from gentle, literary-oriented strolls to challenging ridge hikes. The Lake District National Park (⇨ National Park) or the Cumbria Tourist Board in Windermere (⇨ Visitor Information) can put you in touch with qualified guides. Blue Badge Guides can provide experts on the area. English Lakeland Ramblers organizes single-base and inn-to-inn guided tours of the Lake District from May through October. Go Higher will take you on the more challenging routes and provides technical gear and courses on mountaineering skills.

🚶 **Blue Badge Guides** ☎ 020/7403–1115 ⊕ www.blue-badge.org.uk. **English Lakeland Ramblers** ⊠ 18 Stuyvesant Oval, #1A, New York, NY 10009 ☎ 01229/587382 or 212/505–1020, 800/724–8801 in U.S. ⊕ www.ramblers.com. **Go Higher** ⊠ High Dyon Side, Distington ☎ 01946/830476 ⊕ www.gohigher.co.uk.

VISITOR INFORMATION

Cumbria Tourist Board is open Monday through Thursday 9:30 to 5:30 and Friday 9:30 to 5.

🚶 **Cumbria Tourist Board** ⊠ Ashleigh, Holly Rd., Windermere LA23 2AQ ☎ 015394/44444 ⊕ www.golakes.co.uk. **Youth Hostel Association England and Wales** ⊠ Trevelyan House, Matlock, Derbyshire, DE4 3YH ☎ 0870/870–8808 ⊕ www.yha.org.uk. **Ambleside** ⊠ Central Bldgs., Market Cross, Rydal Rd. ☎ 015394/32582. **Keswick** ⊠ Moot Hall, Market Sq. ☎ 017687/72645. **Ullswater** ⊠ Main Car Park, Glenridding ☎ 017684/82414. **Windermere** ⊠ The Gateway Centre, Victoria St. ☎ 015394/46499 ⊕ www.visiteden.co.uk.

Cambridge & East Anglia

WORD OF MOUTH

"King's College Chapel alone is worth the trip [to Cambridge] . . . It is considered the finest example of late medieval architecture in Europe. The stained-glass windows are breathtaking. And 'punting on the Cam' is a must. Some things to see in the area are the cathedral at Ely and ruins at Bury St. Edmonds."

—jrandolph

"Suffolk [has] some delightful small towns and villages, many with very big churches built with money from the wool trade. It's not very far from London but seems to be off the main tourist track. Lavenham is charming. The houses were made from unseasoned oak, with the result that they are crooked."

—MissPrism

Updated by
Julius Honnor

ONE OF THOSE BEAUTIFUL ENGLISH INCONSISTENCIES, East Anglia has no spectacular mountains or rivers to disturb the storied, quiet land. Occupying an area of southeastern England that bulges out into the North Sea, its counties of Essex, Norfolk, Suffolk, and Cambridgeshire are cut off from the central routes and pulse of the country.

Some of Britain's greatest thinkers, artists, and poets were educated at Cambridge University, one of the world's most important centers of learning and arguably the world's most attractive university town. The history of the area can also be seen in other notable constructions such as Ely Cathedral or the ruined abbey at Bury St. Edmunds.

It's easy just to visit Cambridge and move on, but delve deeper into the region and you will also be rewarded in many ways. Here the archetypal English-landscape artist John Constable painted *The Hay Wain,* a buccolic vision of Suffolk. Churches punctuate the wide vistas of fields, wetlands, and meandering waterways; at the coast, long pebbled beaches slope into the North Sea.

Exploring East Anglia

This chapters focuses on some highlights of East Anglia. For purposes of sightseeing, one central area includes the ancient university city of Cambridge, a top attraction that's easily accessible from London even as a day trip. South and east of Cambridge are the quiet towns of inland Suffolk. Farther east, it's worth getting a taste of the Suffolk Heritage Coast in towns such as Adleburgh.

About the Restaurants

In summer the coast gets so packed with people that reservations are essential at restaurants. Getting something to eat at other than regular mealtime hours is not always possible in small towns; look for cafés if you want a mid-morning or after-lunch snack.

About the Hotels

Few hotels in East Anglia have more than 100 rooms, so even the biggest hostelries offer friendly, personal service. The region is full of centuries-old, half-timber inns with rooms full of roaring fires and cozy bars. Bed-and-breakfasts are a good option in pricey Cambridge. It's always busy in Cambridge and along the coast in summer, so reserve well in advance.

WHAT IT COSTS In pounds				
	£££££	**££££**	**£££**	**££**	**£**
RESTAURANTS	over £22	£18–£22	£13–£17	£7–£12	under £7
HOTELS	over £160	£120–£160	£90–£119	£60–£89	under £60

Restaurant prices are for a main course at dinner. Hotel prices are for two people in a standard double room in high season, including V.A.T., with no meals or, if indicated, CP (with continental breakfast), BP (Breakfast Plan, with full breakfast), or MAP (Modified American Plan, with breakfast and dinner).

TOP REASONS TO GO

Cambridge: A walk though the colleges gives you a look at some grand architecture. The best views of the university's colleges and immaculate lawns (and some famous bridges), however, are from a punt on the river.

Ely Cathedral: Having stood for nearly a millennium, the region's most striking building rises high above the surrounding fens. The carved ceiling and stained glass are, quite simply, spectacular.

Constable country: In the area where Constable grew up, you can walk or row downstream from the pastel-shaded village of Dedham

straight into the setting of one of the English landscape painter's masterpieces at Flatford Mill.

Lavenham: This medieval town is the most comely of the tight-knit cluster of places that did well from the wool trade: nearby is Long Melford. Here is the region's most memorable architecture, including gnarled, timber-framed houses.

Aldeburgh: A small civilized resort with pastel-color houses and high-quality fish-and-chips, Aldeburgh really comes into its own in June, when the town's festival brings great classical music and arts to the North Sea coast.

Timing

Summer and late spring are the best times to visit. Late fall and winter can be cold, windy, and rainy, though this is England's driest region and crisp frosty days here are beautiful. During the summer "long vac" (and also over the Easter and Christmas holidays), Cambridge is empty of its students, its life and soul. To see the city in full swing, visit from October through June, although in summer there are enjoyable festivals, notably the Strawberry Fair (mid-June), and the Folk Festival and Arts Festival (both July). The world-famous Aldeburgh Festival of music and the arts takes place in June.

9

CAMBRIDGE

With the spires of its university buildings framed by towering trees and expansive meadows, its medieval streets and passages enhanced by gardens and riverbanks, the city of Cambridge is among the loveliest in England. The city predates the Roman occupation of Britain; there's confusion about exactly when the university was founded; but it does date to the 13th century. One story attributes its founding to students from Oxford, who came in search of eels—a cheap source of nourishment.

Cambridge embodies a certain genteel, intellectual, and, sometimes, anachronistically idealized image of Englishness. Think Rupert Brooke, the short-lived World War I–era poet ("There is some corner of a foreign field/That is forever England"), a Cambridgeshire lad, who called his county "The shire for Men who Understand," as well as William Wordsworth, Thackeray, Byron, Tennyson, E. M. Forster, and C. S. Lewis. The exquisite King's College choir defines the traditional English

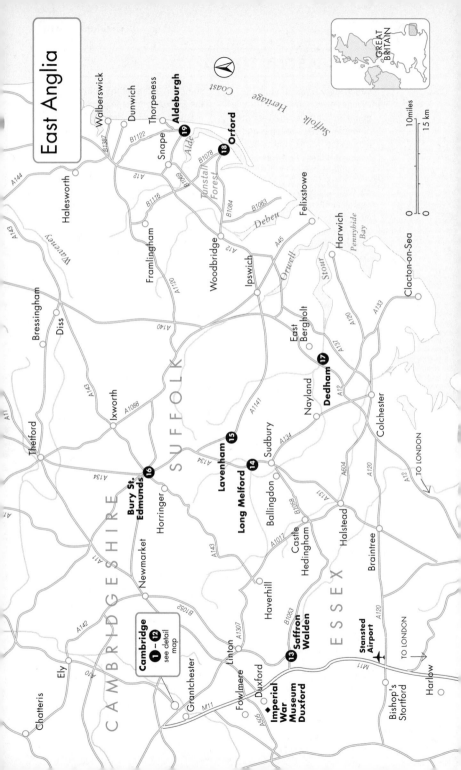

Christmas, when the *Festival of Nine Lessons and Carols* is broadcast live on Christmas Eve. On top of all this tradition and history, it remains a lively city and an extraordinary center of learning and research.

Keep in mind there is no recognizable campus: the scattered colleges *are* the university. The town reveals itself only slowly, filled with tiny gardens, ancient courtyards, imposing classic buildings, alleyways that lead past medieval churches, and wisteria-hung facades. Perhaps the best views are from the Backs, the green parkland that extends along the River Cam behind several colleges. Resulting from the larger size of the colleges and from the lack of industrialization in the city center, this broad, sweeping openness is just what distinguishes Cambridge from Oxford.

Exploring Cambridge

Exploring the city means, in large part, exploring the university. Each of the 25 oldest colleges is built around a series of courts, or quadrangles, whose velvety lawns are the envy of many a gardener. Since students and fellows (faculty) live and work in these courts, access is sometimes restricted. Visitors are not normally allowed into college buildings other than chapels, dining halls, and some libraries; some colleges charge admission for certain buildings. The university's Web site, ⊕ www.cam.ac.uk, has information about the colleges and other institutions associated with it. Public visiting hours vary from college to college, depending on the time of year, and it's best to call or to check with the city tourist office. Colleges close to visitors during the main exam time, late May to mid-June. Term time (when classes are in session) means roughly October to December, January to March, and April to June; summer term, or vacation, runs from July to September.

■ TIP➔ When the colleges are open, the best way to gain access is to join a walking tour led by an official Blue Badge guide—many areas are off-limits unless you do. The two-hour tours leave up to five times daily from the city tourist office. The other traditional view of the colleges is gained from a punt—the boats propelled by pole on the River Cam.

Main Attractions

⑩ **Christ's College.** To see the way a college has grown over the centuries you could not do better than visit here. The main gateway bears the enormous coat of arms of its patroness, Lady Margaret Beaufort, mother of Henry VII, who established the institution in 1505. It leads into a fine courtyard, with the chapel framed by an ancient magnolia. In the dining hall hang portraits of John Milton and Charles Darwin, two of the college's more famous students. You next walk past a fellows' building credited to Inigo Jones, to the spacious garden (once the haunt of Milton), and finally to a modern zigguratlike confection. ⊠ *St. Andrew's St.* ☎ *01223/334900* ⊕ *www.christs.cam.ac.uk* ☉ *Term time, except exam period, daily 9:30–dusk; out of term, daily 9:30–noon.*

⑨ **Corpus Christi College.** If you visit only one quadrangle, make it the beautiful, serene, 14th-century Old Court here. Founded in 1352, it's the longest continuously inhabited college quadrangle in Cambridge.

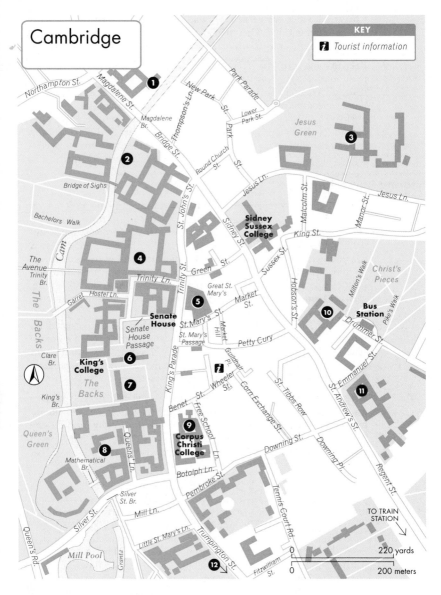

Cambridge

KEY

i Tourist information

⊠ *King's Parade* ☎ *01223/338000* ⊕ *www.corpus.cam.ac.uk* ⊠ *Free* ⊙ *Daily dawn–dusk.*

⑪ Emmanuel College. The master hand of architect Christopher Wren (1632–1723) is evident throughout much of Cambridge, particularly at Emmanuel, where he designed the chapel and colonnade. A stained-glass window in the chapel has a likeness of John Harvard, founder of Harvard University, who studied here. The college, founded in 1584, was an early center of Puritan learning; a number of the Pilgrims were Emmanuel alumni, and they remembered their alma mater in naming Cambridge, Massachusetts. ⊠ *St. Andrew's St.* ☎ *01223/334200* ⊕ *www. emma.cam.ac.uk* ⊙ *Daily 9–6, except exam period.*

★ ⑫ Fitzwilliam Museum. In a classical revival building renowned for its grand Corinthian portico, the Fitzwilliam, founded by the seventh viscount Fitzwilliam of Merrion in 1816, has one of Britain's most outstanding collections of art (including paintings by Constable, Gainsborough, the Pre-Raphaelites, and the French impressionists) and antiquities. The opulent interior displays its treasures to marvelous effect from Egyptian pieces such as inch-high figurines and painted coffins to sculptures from the Chinese Han Dynasty of the 3rd century BC. ⊠ *Trumpington St.* ☎ *01223/332900* ⊕ *www.fitzmuseum.cam.ac.uk* ⊠ *Free* ⊙ *Tues.–Sat. 10–5, Sun. noon–5; contact Cambridge Tourist Information Office for guided tours.*

❺ Great St. Mary's. Known as the "university church," Great St. Mary's has its origins in the 11th century, although the current building dates from 1478. The main reason to visit is to climb the 113-foot tower, which has a superb view over the colleges and marketplace. ⊠ *Market Hill, King's Parade* ☎ *01223/741716* ⊕ *www.ely.anglican.org/parishes/ camgsm* ⊠ *Free, tower £2* ⊙ *Mon.–Sat. 9:30–5:30, Sun. noon–5:30.*

❸ Jesus College. Unique in Cambridge, the spacious grounds of Jesus College incorporate cloisters, a remnant of the nunnery of St. Radegund, which existed on the site before the college was founded in 1496. Cloister Court exudes a quiet medieval charm, an attribute evident in the adjacent chapel, another part of the nunnery. Victorian restoration of the building includes some Pre-Raphaelite stained-glass windows and ceiling designs by William Morris. ⊠ *Jesus La.* ☎ *01223/339339* ⊕ *www. jesus.cam.ac.uk* ⊙ *Daily 8–7, except exam period.*

❼ King's College. Founded in 1441 by Henry VI, King's College's most famous landmark is its late-15th-century chapel. Other architecture of note is the neo-Gothic Porters' Lodge, facing King's Parade, which was a relatively recent addition in the 1830s, and the classical Gibbs building. ■ TIP→ **Follow the college's Back Lawn down to the river, from where the panorama of college and chapel is one of the university's most photographed views.** Past students of King's College include the novelist E. M. Forster, the economist John Maynard Keynes, and the World War I poet Rupert Brooke. ⊠ *King's Parade* ☎ *01223/331100* ⊕ *www.kings.cam.ac.uk* ⊠ *£4, includes chapel* ⊙ *Term-time, weekdays 9:30–3:30, Sat. 9:30–3:15, Sun. 1:15–2:15; out of term, Mon.–Sat. 9:30–4:30, Sun. 10–5. Times may vary; call in advance.*

★ ❻ **King's College Chapel.** Based on Sainte Chapelle, the 13th-century royal chapel in Paris, this one was constructed toward the end of the 15th century and is the final, perhaps most glorious flowering of Perpendicular Gothic in Britain. Henry VI, the king after whom the college is named, oversaw the work. This was the last period before the classical architecture of the ancient Greeks and Romans, then being rediscovered by the Italians, began to make its influence felt in northern Europe. From the outside, the most prominent features are the expanses of glass, the massive flying buttresses, and the fingerlike spires that line the length of the building. Inside, the most obvious impression is of great space—the chapel has been described as "the noblest barn in Europe"—and of light flooding in from its huge windows. The brilliantly colored bosses (carved panels at the intersections of the roof ribs) are particularly intense, although hard to see without binoculars. An exhibition in the chantries, or side chapels, explains more about the chapel's construction. Behind the altar is *The Adoration of the Magi,* an enormous painting by Peter Paul Rubens, painted for a convent in Louvain. Every Christmas Eve, a festival of carols sung by the chapel's famous choir is broadcast worldwide from here. ⊠ *King's Parade* ☎ *01223/331155* ⊕ *www.kings.cam.ac.uk* ⊡ *£4, includes college and grounds* ⊙ *Termtime, weekdays 9:30–3:30, Sat. 9:30–3:15, Sun. 1:15–2:15; out of term, Mon.–Sat. 9:30–4:30, Sun. 10–5. Times may vary; call in advance.*

❽ **Queens' College.** One of the most eye-catching colleges is Queens', named after Margaret, queen of Henry VI, and Elizabeth, queen of Edward IV. Founded in 1448, the college is tucked away on Queens' Lane, next to the wide lawns that lead down from King's College to the Backs. The secluded "cloister court" looks untouched since its completion in the 1540s. Queens' masterpiece is the **Mathematical Bridge,** the original version of which is said to have been built without any fastenings. The current bridge (1902) is securely bolted. ⊠ *Queens' La.* ☎ *01223/ 335511* ⊕ *www.quns.cam.ac.uk* ⊡ *£1.50, free Nov.–mid-Mar. and weekdays in Oct.* ⊙ *Mid-Mar.–late May, weekdays 11–3, weekends 10–4:30; late June–Sept., daily 10–4:30; Oct. weekdays 1:45–4:30, weekends 10–4:30; Nov.–mid-Mar., daily 1:45–4:30.*

❷ **St. John's College.** Two mythical beasts called "yales," with the bodies of antelopes and heads of goats, hold up the coat of arms and guard the gateway of Cambridge's second-largest college. St. John's was founded in 1511 by Henry VII's mother, Lady Margaret Beaufort. Its structures lie on two sites: from the main entrance, walk to the left through the courts to the 1831 **"Bridge of Sighs,"** whose only resemblance to its Venetian counterpart is its covering. The windowed, covered stone bridge reaches across the Cam to the mock-Gothic New Court (1825), nicknamed "the wedding cake." If you walk through to the riverbank, you can stroll along the Backs and photograph the elegant bridge. ⊠ *St. John's St.* ☎ *01223/338600* ⊕ *www.joh.cam.ac.uk* ⊡ *£2.50* ⊙ *Easter–early Nov., weekdays 10–5, Sat. 9:30–5.*

❹ **Trinity College.** Founded in 1546 by Henry VIII, Trinity replaced a 14th-century educational foundation and is the largest college in either Cambridge or Oxford, with nearly 700 undergraduates. Many of the buildings match its size, not least its 17th-century "great court." Here the massive gatehouse holds "Great Tom," a giant clock that strikes each hour with high and low notes. The college's greatest masterpiece is Christopher Wren's library, colonnaded and seemingly constructed with as much light as stone, with wood carving by the 17th-century master Grinling Gibbons. Alumni include Sir Isaac Newton, William Thackeray, and Lords George Byron, Alfred Tennyson, and Thomas Macaulay, and 31 Nobel Prize winners. Prince Charles was an undergraduate here in the late 1960s. ⊠ *St. John's St.* ☎ *01223/338400* ⊕ *www.trin.cam.ac.uk* ⊠ *£2.20, free late Oct.–mid-Mar.* ☉ *College mid-Mar.–Oct., daily 10–5, except exam period; library weekdays noon–2, Sat. in term time 10:30–12:30; hall and chapel open but hrs vary.*

Also Worth Seeing

OFF THE
BEATEN
PATH

ELY CATHEDRAL – Known affectionately as the Ship of the Fens, this can be seen for miles, towering above the flat landscape on one of the few ridges in the fens. In 1083 the Normans began work on the cathedral. In its center you see a marvel of medieval construction—the unique octagonal **Lantern Tower,** a sort of stained-glass skylight of colossal proportions, built to replace the central tower after it collapsed in 1322. The cathedral is also notable for its 248-foot-long **nave,** with its simple Norman arches and Victorian painted ceiling. Much of the decorative carving of the 14th-century **Lady Chapel** was defaced during the Reformation (mostly by knocking off the heads of the statuary), but enough tracery remains to show its original beauty. The fan-vaulted, carved ceiling remains intact, as it was too high for the iconoclasts to reach. The cathedral houses a superior Stained Glass Museum (£3.50 charge). The town of Ely itself, 16 mi north of Cambridge, fails to live up to the high expectations created by the cathedral. ⊠ *The Gallery, Ely* ☎ *01353/ 667735* ⊕ *www.cathedral.ely.anglican.org* ⊠ *£5.20, free on Sun.* ☉ *May–Oct., daily 7–7; Nov.–Apr., Mon.–Sat. 7:30–6, Sun. 7:30–5.*

OFF THE
BEATEN
PATH

IMPERIAL WAR MUSEUM DUXFORD – The buildings and grounds of this former airfield, now Europe's leading aviation museum, house a remarkable collection of more than 200 aircraft from Europe and the United States. The **Land Warfare Hall** holds tanks and other military vehicles. The **American Air Museum,** in a striking Norman Foster–designed building, contains American combat aircraft. It honors the 30,000 Americans who were killed in action flying from Britain during World War II; Duxford itself was the headquarters of the 78th Fighter Group. Check in advance for air shows (extra charge). The museum is 10 mi south of Cambridge, and a shuttle bus runs from Cambridge's Crowne Plaza hotel (Downing Street) to the Cambridge train station and Duxford. ⊠ *A505, Duxford* ☎ *01223/835000* ⊕ *duxford.iwm.org.uk* ⊠ *£13* ☉ *Mid-Mar.–Oct., daily 10–6; Nov.–mid-Mar., daily 10–4.*

❶ Magdalene College. Across Magdalene (pronounced *maud*-lin) Bridge, a cast-iron 1820 structure, lies the only one of the older colleges to be sited across the river. Magdalene Street itself is traffic-heavy, but there's relative calm inside the redbrick courts. It was a hostel for Benedictine monks for more than 100 years before the college was founded in 1542. In the second court, the college's **Pepys Library** (☎ 01223/332187

⊙ Mid-Apr.–Aug., Mon.–Sat. 11:30–12:30 and 2:30–3:30; Oct., Nov., and mid-Jan.–mid-Mar., Mon.–Sat. 2:30–3:30)—labeled *Bibliotecha Pepysiana*—contains the books and desk of the famed 17th-century diarist Samuel Pepys. ⊠ *Magdalene St.* ☎ *01223/332100* ⊕ *www.magd. cam.ac.uk* ☜ *Free* ⊙ *Daily 9–6, except exam period.*

Where to Eat

£££–£££££ ✕ **Three Horseshoes.** This early-19th-century pub-restaurant in a thatched cottage has additional dining space in the conservatory. The tempting, beautifully presented dishes focus on modern British cuisine. Some fashionable culinary accoutrements—sun-dried tomatoes, prosecco with pomegranate and campari, and provencal olives—accompany chargrilled meats or roast fish. It's 3 mi west of Cambridge, about a 10-minutes' taxi ride. ⊠ *High St., Madingley* ☎ *01954/210221* ▤ *MC, V.*

★ £££–££££ ✕ **Midsummer House.** An elegant, well-regarded restaurant beside the River Cam on the edge of Midsummer Common, the gray-brick Midsummer House has a comfortable conservatory. Fixed-price menus for lunch and dinner offer sophisticated French and Mediterranean dishes. Choices might include tender roast spring lamb or seared sea scallops. ⊠ *Midsummer Common* ☎ *01223/369299* ⊕ *www.midsummerhouse. co.uk* ⚑ *Reservations essential* ▤ *AE, MC, V* ⊙ *Closed Mon. No lunch Tues., no dinner Sun.*

££–£££ ✕ **Loch Fyne Oyster Restaurant.** Part of a small Scottish chain that harvests oysters and runs seafood restaurants, this airy, casual place across the street from the Fitzwilliam Museum is open for breakfast, lunch, and dinner. The deservedly popular oysters and other seafood—mussels, salmon, tuna, and more—are fresh and well prepared. Some good bets are the dauntingly large seafood platters. ⊠ *37 Trumpington St.* ☎ *01223/362433* ⊕ *www.lochfyne.com* ▤ *AE, MC, V.*

££ ✕ **River Bar & Kitchen.** Fashionable and stylish, this riverside eatery designed by Terence Conran focuses on contemporary food with the occasional Eastern influence, such as spicy lamb samosas with mint and cucumber dip and wonton prawns. At lunch, served between noon and 3, choose among the creative sandwiches. Dinner service begins at 6:30. ⊠ *Quayside, off Bridge St.* ☎ *01223/307030* ⚑ *Reservations essential* ▤ *AE, MC, V* ⊙ *Closed Mon. No dinner Sun.*

££ ✕ **Vaults.** Ochre and deep-red walls and metal chairs on slate floors bring a sleek, contemporary edge to the underground Vaults. The zinc-top bar with red sofas is the perfect place for lounging with a cocktail, and there is live music four nights a week. The evening menu is tapas-style: lots of small portions of an eclectic mix of international cuisine. Lunchtime menus are more traditional. ⊠ *14A Trinity St.* ☎ *01223/506090* ⚑ *Reservations essential* ▤ *AE, MC, V.*

£ ✕ **Dojo Noodle Bar.** Many highlights of Asian cuisine are represented at this trendy spot with shared tables near the river. If the different kinds of wheat, rice, or mung bean noodles aren't your thing, try a rice dish or pot stickers, tempura prawns, or chicken yakitori. ⊠ *1–2 Millers Yard, Mill La., off Trumpington St.* ☎ *01223/363471* ▤ *AE, MC, V.*

Where to Stay

There aren't many hotels downtown. For more (and cheaper) options, consider one of the numerous guesthouses on the arterial roads and in the suburbs. These start at £18 to £25 per person per night and can be booked through the tourist information center.

£££££ **Hotel Felix.** This contemporary hotel, less than 1 mi from the city center, has spacious bedrooms with clean-lined, stylish modern furnishings in neutral colors. The main part of the building is a converted Victorian mansion; today it contains some bedrooms as well as the sophisticated Graffiti restaurant and bar, serving Mediterranean food. Guests can use a health club and spa in the center of the city. ⊠ *Whitehouse La., off Huntingdon Rd., CB3 0LX* ☎ *01223/277977* ≊ *01223/277973* ⊕ *www.hotelfelix.co.uk* ⤢ *52 rooms* △ *Restaurant, room service, in-room safes, cable TV with movies, in-room data ports, lounge, babysitting, dry cleaning, laundry service, meeting rooms, free parking, some pets allowed, no-smoking rooms* ▤ *AE, DC, MC, V* ▮◯▮ *CP.*

££££–£££££ **Crowne Plaza.** In the middle of historic Cambridge, this late-20th-century building doesn't mesh well with its older neighbors but does provide the high standard of accommodation you'd expect from this chain, as well as a top-notch location. Modern amenities such as a writing desk and trouser press enhance the colorful, contemporary rooms. ⊠ *Downing St., CB2 3DT* ☎ *01223/464466* ≊ *01223/464440* ⊕ *www.cambridge.crowneplaza.com* ⤢ *198 rooms* △ *Restaurant, room service, in-room safes, minibars, cable TV with movies, in-room broadband, gym, sauna, bar, lobby lounge, pub, babysitting, dry cleaning, laundry service, concierge, business services, meeting rooms, parking (fee), no-smoking rooms* ▤ *AE, DC, MC, V.*

£££–£££££ **De Vere University Arms Hotel.** Elegant and sympathetically modernized, the 19th-century De Vere is well placed in the city center, though space is at a premium in central Cambridge: the traditionally furnished guest rooms are comfortable but not overly large. Many rooms have views of Parker's Piece, the green backing the hotel, although you pay slightly more for these; Parker's Bar also overlooks the green. The lounge serves afternoon tea by the fireplace. As for service, the quality can vary. Guests can use a health club 2 mi away. ⊠ *Regent St., CB2 1AD* ☎ *01223/351241* ≊ *01223/315256* ⊕ *www.devereonline.co.uk* ⤢ *116 rooms, 1 suite* △ *Restaurant, room service, cable TV with movies, in-room data ports, 2 bars, lounge, business services, meeting rooms, parking (fee), some pets allowed (fee)* ▤ *AE, DC, MC, V.*

£££–£££££ **Garden Moat House Hotel.** Set among the colleges in 3 acres of private grounds, this modern hotel makes the most of its peaceful riverside location. The gardens, bar, and conservatories all overlook the Cam, as do most rooms. Request a river view when you reserve. As with many chain hotels, the service and standards are high, but the architecture exhibits a brutal use of concrete and furnishings are not particularly special. Ask about lower leisure (vacation) rates, which include breakfast. ⊠ *Granta Pl. and Mill La., CB2 1RT* ☎ *01223/259988* ≊ *01223/316605* ⊕ *www.moathousehotels.com* ⤢ *117 rooms* △ *Restau-*

9

rant, room service, minibars, cable TV, Wi-Fi, indoor pool, sauna, steam room, bar, lounge, business services, meeting rooms, parking (fee), no-smoking rooms, Internet; no a/c in some rooms ⊟ *AE, DC, MC, V.*

£££–££££ ⊞ **Arundel House Hotel.** Elegantly proportioned, this Victorian hotel made up of now-connected town houses has a fine location overlooking the River Cam, with Jesus Green in the background. The comfortable bedrooms, modern in style, have locally made mahogany furniture. Rattan chairs, trailing plants, and a patio garden add a certain cachet to meals and afternoon teas in the Victorian-style conservatory. The special weekend rates are an excellent value. ⊠ *53 Chesterton Rd., CB4 3AN* ☎ *01223/367701* 🖷 *01223/367721* ⊕ *www.arundelhousehotels. co.uk* 🗹 *102 rooms* ⚲ *2 restaurants, bar, lounge, meeting rooms, free parking, no-smoking rooms; no a/c* ⊟ *AE, DC, MC, V* ⦿ *CP.*

££ ⊞ **Ashley Hotel.** Sister to the Arundel House Hotel, this pleasant smaller establishment near the center of Cambridge was converted from a private home. Rooms with double or twin beds are decent, and you can take advantage of the facilities of nearby Arundel House, where you should go to check-in. ⊠ *74 Chesterton Rd., CB4 1ER* ☎ *01223/350059* 🖷 *01223/350900* ⊕ *www.arundelhousehotels.co.uk/ashley.html* 🗹 *16 rooms* ⚲ *Free parking; no a/c, no smoking* ⊟ *AE, DC, MC, V* ⦿ *BP.*

Nightlife & the Arts

Nightlife

The city's pubs provide the mainstay of Cambridge's nightlife. The **Eagle** (⊠ Benet St. ☎ 01223/505020), first among equals, is a 16th-century coaching inn with several bars and a cobbled courtyard that's lost none of its old-time character. It's extremely busy on weekends. **Fort St. George** (⊠ Midsummer Common ☎ 01223/354327), which overlooks the university boathouses, gets the honors for riverside views. The **Free Press** (⊠ Prospect Row ☎ 01223/368337) is a small, nonsmoking, and mobile phone–free pub, attracting a student rowing clientele. The 600-year-old **Pickerel Inn** (⊠ 30 Magdalene St. ☎ 01223/355068), one of the city's oldest pubs, makes for a good stop for a soothing afternoon pint of real ale or lager and a bowl of potato wedges. Watch for the low beams.

The Arts

Cambridge supports its own symphony orchestra, and regular musical events are held in many colleges, especially those with large chapels. **King's College Chapel** (☎ 01223/331447) has evensong services Tuesday through Saturday at 5:30, Sunday at 3:30. The **Corn Exchange** (⊠ Wheeler St. ☎ 01223/357851), beautifully restored, presents concerts (classical and rock), stand-up comedy, musicals, opera, and ballet.

The newly spruced up **ADC Theatre** (⊠ Park St. ☎ 01223/503333) hosts mainly student- and fringe-theater productions, including the famous Cambridge Footlights revue, training ground for much comic talent since the 1970s. The **Arts Theatre** (⊠ 6 St. Edward's Passage ☎ 01223/5033333), the city's main repertory theater, supports a full program of theater, concerts, and events. It also has a good ground-floor bar and two restaurants, including the conservatory-style Roof Garden.

Punting on the Cam

CLOSE UP

TO PUNT IS TO MANEUVER a flat-bottom, wooden, gondolalike boat—in this case, through the shallow River Cam along the verdant Backs behind the colleges of the University of Cambridge. One benefit of this popular activity is that you get a better view of the ivy-covered walls from the water than from the front. Mastery of the sport lies in your ability to control a 15-foot pole, used to propel the punt. Collect a bottle of wine, some food, and a few friends, and you may find yourself saying things such as, "It doesn't get any better than this." One piece of advice: if your pole gets stuck, let go. You can use the smaller paddle to go back and retrieve it.

The lazier-at-heart may prefer chauffeured punting, with food supplied. Students from Cambridge may do the work, and you get a fairly informative spiel on the colleges. For a romantic evening trip, there are illuminated punts.

Sports & the Outdoors

Biking

It's fun to explore Cambridge by bike. **Geoff's Bike Hire** (✉ 65 Devonshire Rd. ☎ 01223/365629), a short walk from the railroad station, charges from £8 per day and £15 per week, or £5 for up to three hours. Advance reservations are essential in July and August. Geoff's also runs guided cycle tours of Cambridge.

Punting

You can rent punts at several places, notably at Silver Street Bridge–Mill Lane, at Magdalene Bridge, and from outside the Rat and Parrot pub on Thompson's Lane on Jesus Green. Hourly rental costs about £16 (and requires a deposit of £70). Chauffeured punting on the River Cam is also possible at most rental places. Around £12 per head is the usual rate, and your chauffeur will likely be a Cambridge student. **Scudamore's Punting Co.** (✉ Mill La. and Quayside ☎ 01223/359750) rents chauffeured and self-drive punts.

Shopping

Cambridge is a main shopping area for a wide region, and it has all the usual chain stores, many in the Grafton Centre and Lion's Yard shopping precincts. More interesting are the specialty shops found among the colleges in the center of Cambridge, especially in and around Rose Crescent and King's Parade. Bookshops are Cambridge's pride.

All Saints Garden Art & Craft Market (✉ Trinity St.) displays the wares of local artists outdoors. **Ryder & Amies** (✉ 22 King's Parade ☎ 01223/350371) carries official university wear and even straw boaters.

★ The **Bookshop** (✉ 24 Magdalene St. ☎ 01223/362457) is the best local secondhand bookshop. The **Cambridge University Press bookshop** (✉ 1

Trinity St. ☎01223/333333) stands on the oldest bookstore site in Britain. **G. David** (✉ 3 and 16 St. Edward's Passage ☎ 01223/354619), near the Arts Theatre, sells antiquarian books. **Heffer's** (✉ 20 Trinity St. ☎01223/ 568568 ✉ Children's branch, 30 Trinity St. ☎ 01223/568551) stocks many rare and imported books.

FROM SAFFRON WALDEN TO BURY ST. EDMUNDS

This central area of towns and villages within easy reach of Cambridge is testament to the amazing changeability of the English landscape. The area north of Cambridge is an eerie, flat, and apparently endless fenland, or marsh. Only a few miles south and east into Essex and Suffolk, however, all this changes to pastoral landscapes of gently undulating hills, clusters of villages, and pretty towns such as Lavenham. You'll find plenty of half-timber buildings and churches built with money from the medieval wool trade.

Saffron Walden

❸ *30 mi south of Ely, 14 mi south of Cambridge.*

Best known for its many typically East Anglian timber-frame buildings, this town owes its name to the saffron crocus fields that used to be cultivated in medieval times and processed for their dye. The common at the east end of town has a 17th-century circular earth maze, created from space left among the crocus beds. Some buildings have elaborate pargeting (decorative plasterwork), especially the walls of the former Sun Inn on Church Street, which was used by Cromwell during his campaigns. At the other end of Church Street, the tall, imposing **St. Mary the Virgin**, built between 1450 and 1525, is the largest church in Essex.

★ Palatial **Audley End House and Gardens,** a mile or so west of Saffron Walden, is a famous example of Jacobean (early-17th-century) architecture. It was once owned by Charles II, who bought it as a convenient place to break his journey on the way to the Newmarket races. Although the house was remodeled in the 18th and 19th centuries, the original Jacobean work is still on display in the magnificent Great Hall. You can walk around the park, landscaped by Capability Brown in the 18th century, and the fine Victorian gardens. ✉ *B1383* ☎ *01799/522842* ⊕ *www. english-heritage.org.uk* 🎟 *£8.95, park only £4.60* ☉ *Apr.–Sept., Wed.–Sun., park 11–6, house noon–5; Oct., park weekends 11–5, house weekends 11–4.*

Where to Stay

£ 🏨 **Archway Guesthouse.** Opposite St. Mary's, what must be one of Britain's quirkiest B&Bs embraces the early era of rock and roll by packing its public rooms with rock memorabilia and toys from the 1950s and '60s. Bedrooms are tasteful, homey, and uncluttered, and hosts Flora and Haydn Miles are personable. ✉ *Church St., CB10 1JW* ☎ *01799/ 501500* 🖶 *01799/506003* ✍ *archwayguesthouse@ntlworld.com* ➠ *7 rooms* ⚲ *No a/c, no smoking* 🚭 *No credit cards* ❏◯ *BP.*

Long Melford

⑭ *22 mi east of Saffron Walden, 14 mi south of Bury St. Edmunds.*

It's easy to see how this village got its name, especially if you walk the full length of its 2-mi-long main street, which gradually broadens to include green squares and trees and finally opens into the large triangular green on the hill. Long Melford grew rich on its wool trade in the 15th century, and the town's buildings are an appealing mix, mostly Tudor half-timber or Georgian. Many house antiques shops. Utility poles are banned to preserve the ancient look, although the parked cars down both sides of the street make this a fruitless exercise. Away from the main road, Long Melford returns to its resolutely late-medieval roots.

The largely 15th-century **Holy Trinity Church,** founded by the rich clothiers of Long Melford, stands on a hill at the north end of the village. Close up, the delicate flint flush-work (shaped flints set into a pattern) and huge Perpendicular Gothic windows that take up most of the church's walls have great impact, especially because the nave is 150 feet long. Much of the superb original stained glass remains, notably the Lily Crucifix window. The Lady Chapel has an unusual interior cloister. ⊠ *Main St.* ☎ *01787/310845* ⊕ *www.stedmundsbury.anglican.org/ longmelford* ⊗ *Daily 10–4.*

Melford Hall, distinguished from the outside by its turrets and topiaries, is an Elizabethan house with its original banqueting hall, a fair number of 18th-century additions, and pleasant gardens. Much of the porcelain and other fine pieces here come from the *Santissima Trinidad,* a ship loaded with gifts from the emperor of China and bound for Spain that was captured by one of the house's owners in the 18th century. Children's writer Beatrix Potter, who was related to the owners, visited the house often; there's a small collection of Potter memorabilia. ⊠ *Off A134* ☎ *01787/880286* ⊕ *www.nationaltrust.co.uk* 💷 *£4.70* ⊗ *Apr. and Oct., weekends 2–5:30; May–Sept., Wed.–Sun. 2–5:30.*

The birthplace and family home of Thomas Gainsborough (1727–88), **Gainsborough's House,** 2 mi south of Long Melford in Sudbury, contains many paintings and drawings by the artist and his contemporaries. Although it presents a Georgian facade, with touches of the 18th-century neo-Gothic style, the building is essentially Tudor. The walled garden has a mulberry tree planted in 1620 and a printmaking workshop. The entrance is through the café and shop on Weavers Lane. ⊠ *46 Gainsborough St., Sudbury* ☎ *01787/372958* ⊕ *www.gainsborough.org* 💷 *£3.50, free Tues. 1–5* ⊗ *Mon.–Sat. 10–5.*

Where to Stay & Eat

££££ ✕🏠 **The Bull.** The public rooms of the Bull—stone-flagged floors, bowed oak beams, and heavy antique furniture—show its long history. Throughout, the half-timber Elizabethan building is a joy, and whether you eat in the restaurant (££–£££) or the bar with its huge fireplace, service is efficient and careful. Traditional roasts mix on the menu with modern flavors, such as venison with a bitter chocolate sauce. Creature comforts and pleasant bathrooms offset the smallish size of the bedrooms, which retain their original character. ⊠ *Hall St., CO10 9JG* ☎ *01787/ 378494* 🖷 *01787/880307* ⊕ *www.thebull-hotel.com* 🔁 *23 rooms, 2 suites* ⌕ *Restaurant, bar, lounge, meeting rooms, some pets allowed, no-smoking rooms; no a/c* ⊟ *AE, DC, MC, V* ⏇ *BP.*

Lavenham

⑮ *4 mi northeast of Long Melford, 10 mi south of Bury St. Edmunds.*

Fodor'sChoice
★

Virtually unchanged since the height of its wealth in the 15th and 16th centuries, Lavenham is one of the most perfectly preserved examples of a Tudor village in England. The weavers' and wool merchants' houses occupy not just one show street but most of the town. The houses are timber frame in black oak, the main posts looking as if they could last another 400 years, though their walls are often no longer entirely perpendicular to the ground. The town has many examples of Suffolk pink buildings, in hues from pale pink to apricot, and many of these house small galleries selling paintings and crafts. The timber-frame **Guildhall of Corpus Christi** (1529), the most spectacular building in Lavenham, dominates Market Place, a square with barely a foot in the present. The guildhall is open as a museum of the medieval wool trade. ⊠ *Market Pl.* ☎ *01787/247646* ⊕ *www.nationaltrust.org.uk* 🔁 *£3.25* ☉ *Mar. and Nov., weekends 11–4; Apr., Wed.–Sun. 11–5; May–Oct., daily 11–5.*

The timber-frame **Little Hall,** a former wool merchant's house, shows the building's progress from its creation in the 14th century to its subsequent "modernization" through the 17th century and has a beautiful garden. ⊠ *Market Pl.* ☎ *01787/247179* ⊕ *www.littlehall.org.uk* 🔁 *£2.50* ☉ *Easter–Oct., Wed., Thurs., and weekends 2–5:30.*

The grand 15th-century Perpendicular **Church of St. Peter and St. Paul** (⊠ *Church St.*), set apart from the village on a hill, was built with wool money by cloth merchant Thomas Spring between 1480 and 1520. The height of its tower (141 feet) was meant to surpass those of the neighboring churches—and perhaps to impress rival towns. The rest of the church is perfectly proportioned, with intricate wood carving.

Where to Stay & Eat

££ ✕ **The Angel.** Modern British cuisine is the draw at this popular spot overlooking Lavenham's picture-book main square. The specialty of the house—home-smoked fish—earns rave reviews. You can also just sit a spell at the scrubbed pine tables to enjoy one of the local beers on tap. Eight guest rooms are available, for about £75. ⊠ *Market Sq.* ☎ *01787/ 247388* ⊟ *AE, MC, V* ⌕ *Reservations essential.*

££–££££ ✕▣ **Great House.** The town's finest "restaurant with rooms" occupies a 15th-century building on the medieval market square. Run by Régis and Martine Crépy, the dining room (££££; reservations essential) has a fixed-price menu of European fare with a French touch. From the fireplace and wood floors of the restaurant to the walled courtyard garden, dining is a pleasure. The spacious bedrooms have sloping floors, beamed ceilings, well-appointed bathrooms, and antique furnishings. Loft rooms are especially romantic. ⊠ *Market Pl., CO10 9QZ* ☎ *01787/*

Fodor'sChoice
★

247431 🖶 *01787/248007* ⊕ *www.greathouse.co.uk* ⤳ *5 rooms*
⌂ *Restaurant, bar, lounge, babysitting, some pets allowed, no-smok-*
ing rooms, Internet; no a/c ▤ *AE, MC, V* ⊙ *Closed Jan.* ⼌ BP.

★ **£££–££££** 🏠 **Lavenham Priory.** You can immerse yourself in Lavenham's Tudor history at this luxurious B&B in a sprawling house that dates in part to
the 13th century. The beamed great hall, sitting room (with TV and VCR),
and 3 acres of gardens are great places to relax, and a walled herb garden is the scene for evening drinks in warm weather. Prints and wood
furnishings fill the bedrooms; each has oak floors and ancient timbered
ceilings, and some have four-posters. Reserve well in advance. ⊠ *Water
St., CO10 9RW* ☎ *01787/247404* 🖶 *01787/248472* ⊕ *www.
lavenhampriory.co.uk* ⤳ *5 rooms, 1 suite* ⌂ *Lounge; no a/c, no room
phones, no kids under 10, no smoking* ▤ *MC, V* ⼌ BP.

Bury St. Edmunds

★ **⑯** *10 mi north of Lavenham, 28 mi east of Cambridge.*

Bury St. Edmunds owes its name, and indeed its existence, to Edmund,
the last king of East Anglia and medieval patron saint of England, who
was hacked to death by marauding Danes in 869. He was subsequently
canonized, and his shrine attracted pilgrims, settlement, and commerce.
In the 11th century the erection of a great Norman abbey (now only
ruins) confirmed the town's importance as a religious center. Robert Adam
designed the town hall in 1774. The Georgian streetscape helps make
the town one of the area's prettiest, and the nearby Greene King Westgate Brewery adds the smell of sweet hops to the air. A walk along **Angel
Hill** is a journey through the history of Bury St. Edmunds. Along one
side, the Abbey Gate, cathedral, Norman Gate Tower, and St. Mary's
church make up a continuous display of medieval architecture.

Originally three churches stood within the walls of the Abbey of St. Edmunds, but only two have survived, including **St. Mary's,** built in the 15th
century. It has a blue-and-gold embossed "wagon" (barrel-shape) roof
over the choir. ⊠ *Angel Hill at Honey Hill* ☎ *01284/706668* ⊙ *Daily
10–3; call to confirm.*

St. Edmundsbury Cathedral dates from the 15th century, but the brilliant
paint on its ceiling and the gleaming stained-glass windows are the result of 19th-century restoration by the architect Sir Gilbert Scott. Don't
miss the memorial (near the altar) to an event in 1214, when the barons
of England gathered here to take an oath to force King John to grant
the Magna Carta. The cathedral's
original Abbey Gate was destroyed
in a riot, and it was rebuilt in the
14th century with defense in
mind—you can see the arrow slits.
■ TIP➡ After your visit, stop by the Refectory, a modest café filled with locals. ⊠ *Angel Hill* ☎ *01284/
754933* ⊕ *www.stedscathedral.co.
uk* 🏷 *Free, suggested donation £3*
⊙ *Daily 7:30–6.*

> ### A HALF-PINT PUB?
>
> Pop in for a pint of the local
> Greene King ale at **The Nutshell**
> (⊠ Skinner St. ☎ 01905/764867),
> Britain's smallest pub, measuring
> just 16 feet by 7½ feet.

9

The **Abbey Ruins and Botanical Gardens** are all that remain of the Abbey of Bury St. Edmunds, which fell during Henry VIII's dissolution of the monasteries. The Benedictine abbey's enormous scale is evident in the surviving Norman Gate Tower on Angel Hill; besides this, only the fortified Abbot's Bridge over the River Lark and a few ruins remain. There are explanatory plaques amid the ruins, which are now the site of the Abbey Botanical Gardens, with roses, elegant hedges, and rare trees, including a Chinese tree of heaven planted in the 1830s. The **Bury St. Edmunds Tourist Information Centre** (⊠ 6 Angel Hill ☎ 01284/ 764667 ☉ Easter–Oct., Mon.–Sat. 9:30–5:30, Sun. 10–3; Nov.–Easter, weekdays 10–4, Sat. 10-1) has a leaflet about the ruins and can arrange a guided tour. ⊠ *Angel Hill* 🎫 *Free* ☉ *Weekdays 7:30 AM–½ hr before dusk, weekends 9 AM–dusk.*

Where to Stay & Eat

££–£££ ✕ **Maison Bleue.** This French restaurant, with the same owners as the Great House hotel in nearby Lavenham, specializes in locally caught seafood and serves some meat dishes, too. The seafood depends on the day's catch, but mussels and grilled fillets of local trout and salmon are always available, as are cheeses imported from Paris. ⊠ *30 Churchgate St.* 🎫 *01284/760623* ⌳ *Reservations essential* ▭ *AE, MC, V* ☉ *Closed Sun., Mon., Jan., and 2 wks in summer.*

★ **£££££** ✕▦ **Ickworth Hotel.** You can live like nobility in the east wing of the Italianate Ickworth House, a National Trust property 7 mi southwest of Bury St. Edmunds. The splendid public rooms have stylish 1950s and '60s furniture and striking modern art. This look extends to most bedrooms, though some still have period furnishings; all are luxe. There is no dress code and children are catered to with a free day-care room (for kids under 6) and a game center. Adults can dine in the more formal Frederick's restaurant, and the casual Café Inferno serves pizza. ⊠ *Off A143, Horringer IP29 5QE* 🎫 *01284/735350* 🖶 *01284/736300* ⊕ *www. ickworthhotel.com* ⇋ *27 rooms, 11 apartments* ⌂ *2 restaurants, room service, some kitchens, cable TV, in-room DVDs, Wi-Fi, tennis court, indoor pool, massage, spa, bicycles, croquet, horseback riding, lounge, babysitting, dry cleaning, laundry service, meeting rooms, some pets allowed, no-smoking rooms; no a/c* ▭ *AE, DC, MC, V* 🍽 *BP.*

£££–££££ ▦ **Ounce House.** Small and friendly, this Victorian B&B a three-minute walk from the abbey ruins has a great deal of charm. Print fabrics and wooden furniture furnish the stylish guest rooms. You can unwind in the antiques-filled drawing room and library, and have a drink from the honor bar. The house is close to Bury's restaurants. ⊠ *Northgate St., IP33 1HP* 🎫 *01284/761779* 🖶 *01284/768315* ⊕ *www.ouncehouse. co.uk* ⇋ *4 rooms* ⌂ *In-room data ports, bar, lounge; no a/c, no smoking* ▭ *MC, V* 🍽 *BP.*

THE SUFFOLK COAST

Constable Country, that quintessential rural landscape on the borders of Suffolk and Essex, was made famous by the early-19th-century painter John Constable. This area runs north and west of Colchester along the valley of the River Stour. The 40-mi Suffolk Heritage Coast, which wanders northward from Felixstowe up to Kessingland, is one of the most unspoiled shorelines in the country: Aldeburgh is a highlight.

Dedham

17
Fodor'sChoice
★

65 mi southeast of Cambridge, off A12 on B1029.

Dedham is the heart of Constable Country. Here, gentle hills and the cornfields of Dedham Vale, set under the district's delicate, pale skies, inspired John Constable (1776–1837) to paint some of his most celebrated canvases. He went to school in Dedham, a picture-book village that did well from the wool trade in the 15th and 16th centuries and has retained a well-off air ever since. The architecture is a mix of timber-frame medieval and Georgian. The 15th-century church looms large over handsomely sturdy, pastel-color houses. Plans are afoot to build a Constable visitor center up the Stour valley, but until then it's still possible on quiet days to imagine yourself in a Constable painting.

Two miles northeast of Dedham, off A12, the Constable trail continues in **East Bergholt,** where Constable was born in 1776. Only the stables remain of the house that was his birthplace. As well as many other views of East Bergholt, Constable painted its village church, **St. Mary's,** where his parents lie buried. It has one unusual feature—a freestanding wooden bell house in place of a tower.

From Dedham, on the banks of the River Stour, you can rent a rowboat (☉ Easter–Sept., daily 10–5, weather permitting ✉ £6 per hour ☎ 01206/ 323153), an idyllic way to travel the 2 mi downriver to **Flatford** where you can see Flatford Mill, one of the two water mills owned by Constable's father, and the subject of his most famous painting, *The Hay Wain* (1821). Near Flatford Mill is the 16th-century **Willy Lott's House** (not open to the public), which is instantly recognizable from *The Hay Wain.* Boats can also be rented in Flatford, near Bridge Cottage.

The National Trust owns Flatford Mill and the houses around it, including the thatched 16th-century **Bridge Cottage,** on the north bank of the Stour, which has a shop and a display about Constable's life. ⊠ *Off B1070, East Bergholt* ☎ *01206/298260* ⊕ *www.nationaltrust.org.uk* ✉ *Free, guided tours or audio tour £2* ☉ *Jan. and Feb., weekends 11–3:30; Mar. and Apr., Wed.–Sun. 11–5; May–Sept., daily 10–5:30; Oct., daily 11–4; Nov. and Dec., Wed.–Sun. 11–3:30. Guided tours Apr.–Oct. on days open, at 11, 1, and 2:30.*

Where to Stay & Eat

★
£££–£££££

✕ **Le Talbooth.** A longtime favorite, this sophisticated restaurant in a Tudor house idyllically set beside the River Stour has a floodlighted terrace where food and drinks are served in summer and where jazz bands play on summer Sunday nights as swans glide by. Inside, original beams, leaded-glass windows, and a brick fireplace add to the sense of age. The superb English fare at lunch and dinner may include loin of Suffolk venison, local sea bass, or whole roasted partridge. ⊠ *Gun Hill* ☎ *01206/ 323150* ⌣ *Reservations essential* 🏛 *Jacket and tie* 🔲 *AE, D, MC, V* ☉ *No dinner Sun. Nov.–June.*

9

££ ✕ **Marlborough Head.** Fine lunches, from marinated mussels to fillet of beef, are served with fine East Anglian ales at this early-18th-century pub opposite Constable's school. It gets busy during summer, so arrive early to ensure a table. ✉ *Mill La.* ☎ *01206/323250* ▭ *AE, MC, V.*

£££ ✕▣ **Milsoms.** Owned by the Milsoms of Maison Talbooth fame, this hotel and restaurant in a Victorian house reflects their high standards while providing a modern style. Room decoration is understated, with heavy natural fibers and black-and-white photos. The busy split-level restaurant (££–£££; reservations essential) specializes in updated versions of classic British fare such as shepherds pie made with roast Suffolk mutton or lamb on flageolet bean puree. In warm weather, try sitting by the pond in the garden. ✉ *Stratford Rd., CO7 6HW* ☎ *01206/322795* 🖷 *01206/323689* ⊕ *www.milsom-hotels.co.uk* ➥ *15 rooms* ♿ *Restaurant, room service, minibars, cable TV, bar, lounge, dry cleaning, laundry service, meeting rooms, no-smoking rooms; no a/c* ▭ *AE, MC, V.*

Orford

⑱ *25 mi northeast of Dedham, 80 mi east of Cambridge.*

Part of the Suffolk Heritage Coast, a 40-mi stretch that runs from Felixstowe northward to Kessingland, ancient Orford is a beautiful example of the coast's many Sites of Special Scientific Interest (legally protected nature preserves). There are numerous beaches, marshes, and broads, with an abundance of wildflowers and birds. You can reach other areas on minor roads running east off A12 north of Ipswich.

Small and squat, **Orford Castle** surveys the flatlands from atop a green mound favored by picnickers in summer. Its splendid triple-tower keep was built in 1160 as a coastal defense. Climb it for a view over what was once a thriving medieval port; the 6-mi shingle (coarse gravel) bank of Orford Ness eventually cut off direct access to the sea. ✉ *B1084* ☎ *01394/450472* ⊕ *www.english-heritage.org.uk* 🖾 *£4.30* ☼ *Apr.–Sept., daily 10–6; Oct.–Mar., Thurs.–Mon., 10–4.*

Just a boat ride beyond Orford Quay lies mysterious **Orford Ness,** Europe's biggest vegetated shingle (gravel) spit. A 5-mi-long path takes you through beaches and salt marshes to see migrating and native birds and to discover the secret past of the spit—from 1913 until the mid-1980s, it served as a military site. If you'd rather sit than walk, take the tractor-drawn trailer tour on the first Saturday of the month, July through September (reservations essential). ✉ *Orford Quay* ☎ *01394/450057* ⊕ *www.nationaltrust.org.uk* 🖾 *£6 including ferry crossing* ☼ *Apr.–June and Oct., Sat. 10–2; July–Sept., Tues.–Sat. 10–2; last ferry at 5.*

Where to Stay & Eat

££ ✕ **Butley-Orford Oysterage.** What started as a little café that sold oysters and cups of tea has become a large, bustling, no-nonsense restaurant. It still specializes in oysters and smoked salmon, as well as smoked seafood platters and seasonal fish dishes. The actual smoking takes place in the adjacent smokehouse, and products are for sale in a shop around the corner. ✉ *Market Hill* ☎ *01394/450277* ▭ *MC, V* ☼ *No dinner Sun.–Thurs. Nov.–Mar.*

★ **£££–££££** ✕▣ **Crown and Castle.** Artsy, laid-back, and genuinely friendly, this contemporary hotel in an 18th-century building near Orford Castle is a little gem. Many rooms have bathrooms with sunflower-size showerheads; ask for one of these. The garden rooms are spacious. The Trinity Bistro (££–£££), run by food writer Ruth Watson, focuses on modern British fare, including plenty of fresh fish and local Butley oysters. In warm weather, the outdoor terrace is a great place for grandstand views of Orford Castle. ⊠ *Market Hill, IP12 2LJ* ☎ *01394/450205* 🖷 *01394/450176* ⊕ *www.crownandcastle.co.uk* ⇨ *18 rooms* ⚹ *Restaurant, in-room VCRs, bar, lobby lounge, some pets allowed, no-smoking rooms; no a/c* ⊟ *MC, V* ⎮◯⎮ *BP.*

Aldeburgh

⑲ *10 mi north of Orford, 85 mi east of Cambridge.*

Aldeburgh (pronounced orl-bruh) is a quiet seaside resort, except in June during the noted Aldeburgh Festival. Its beach is backed by a promenade lined with candy-color dwellings. Twentieth-century composer Benjamin Britten lived here for some time—he was born in the busy seaside resort of Lowestoft, 30 mi to the north. Britten grew interested in the story of Aldeburgh's native son, the poet George Crabbe (1754–1832), and turned his life story into the celebrated modern opera *Peter Grimes*, a piece that captures the atmosphere of the Suffolk coast.

The **Elizabethan Moot Hall,** built of flint and timber, stood in the center of a thriving 16th-century town when first erected. Now it's just a few steps from the beach, a mute witness to the erosive powers of the North Sea. ⊠ *Market Cross, Sea Front* ☎ *01728/454666* ⊕ *www.aldeburghmuseum.org.uk* ▢ *£1* ◷ *Easter–Apr. and Oct., weekends 2:30–5; May, Sept., and Oct., daily 2:30–5; June–Aug., daily noon–5.*

Where to Stay & Eat

££–£££ ✕ **The Lighthouse.** An excellent value, this low-key brasserie relies exclusively on local produce and focuses on seafood, including oysters and Cromer crabs. All the dishes are simply but imaginatively cooked, usually with an interesting sauce that might just as easily be Italian or Asian as English. Desserts, such as the bread-and-butter pudding, are particularly good. ⊠ *77 High St.* ☎ *01728/453377* ⊟ *MC, V.*

Fodor's Choice ★

£ ✕ **The Fish and Chip Shop.** When frying time approaches, Aldeburgh's most celebrated fish-and-chip shop always has a long line, especially in summer. The Golden Galleon, along the road, is the version with seating, where you can bring wine or beer to enjoy with your succulent chips, but for the full experience you should probably join the queue here. ⊠ *137 High St.* ☎ *01728/454685* ⊟ *No credit cards.*

££££–£££££ ▣ **Brudenell.** The best rooms at this bright, stylish contemporary seaside hotel face the water. Its restaurant serves fresh, uncomplicated seafood dishes. The accommodating staff here is informal, helping guests feel more relaxed. The White Lion hotel, dating to 1563, is the Brudenell's historic sister property. ⊠ *Market Cross Pl., IP15 5BJ* ☎ *01728/452071* 🖷 *01728/454082* ⊕ *www.brudenellhotel.co.uk* ⇨ *42*

9

rooms △ Restaurant, room service, cable TV, in-room data ports, bar, lounge, some pets allowed (fee); no a/c, no smoking ➟ AE, MC, V ⦿ BP.

★ **££** ▦ **Ocean House.** Juliet and Phil Brereton are your hosts at this redbrick 1860s house practically on the beach, which is an outstanding deal for the price. Antiques and bric-a-brac decorate the public areas and bedrooms, and the two rooms with bath have views of the sea. Breakfast is hearty and home-cooked, and the warm welcome is enhanced by open fireplaces and an abundance of books and magazines. ⊠ *25 Crag Path, IP15 5BS* ☎ *01728/452094* ⤳ *6 rooms, 2 with bath △ Lounge, piano, Ping-Pong, bicycles; no a/c, no smoking* ➟ *No credit cards* ⦿ *BP.*

Nightlife & the Arts

★ East Anglia's most important arts festival, and one of the best known in Great Britain, is the **Aldeburgh Festival** (☎ 01728/687100, 01728/453543 box office ⊕ www.aldeburgh.co.uk) held during two June weeks in the small village of Snape, 5 mi west of Aldeburgh, at the Snape Maltings Concert Hall. Founded by Benjamin Britten, the festival concentrates on music but includes related exhibitions and poetry readings.

CAMBRIDGE & EAST ANGLIA ESSENTIALS

Transportation

BY AIR

For information about Stansted Airport in Essex, north of London, *see* By Air *in* Transportation *in* Essentials.

BY BUS

National Express serves the region from London's Victoria Coach Station. Average travel times: 2½ hours to Bury St. Edmunds, 2 hours to Cambridge, First buses serve parts of the region. The largest bus company is Stagecoach. Traveline can answer transportation questions.

CUTTING COSTS A FirstTourist ticket (available on the bus) from First gives a day's unlimited travel on the whole network for £9; a family pass for two parents and two children costs £20. Stagecoach sells Megarider tickets (£5) for seven days' travel within Cambridge.

FARES & SCHEDULES ▮ **First** ☎ 01603/760076 ⊕ www.firstgroup.com. **National Express** ☎ 0870/580–8080 ⊕www.nationalexpress.com. **Stagecoach** ☎01223/423554 ⊕www.stagecoachbus.com/cambridge. **Traveline** ☎ 0870/608–2608 ⊕ www.traveline.org.uk.

BY CAR

From London, Cambridge (54 mi) is off M11. At Exit 9, M11 connects with A11 to Norwich (114 mi); A14 off A11 goes to Bury St. Edmunds. A12 from London goes through east Suffolk via Colchester and Ipswich. East Anglia has few fast main roads. The principal routes are those mentioned above. Once off the A roads, traveling within the region often means taking country lanes that have many twists and turns.

BY TRAIN

The entire region is served by trains from London's Liverpool Street station; in addition, there are trains to Cambridge and Ely from King's Cross

Station. Full information on trains to East Anglia is available from National Rail Enquiries. Average travel times are one hour to Colchester and 50 to 90 minutes to Cambridge.

CUTTING COSTS An Anglia Plus Three-Day Pass costs $22 and allows unlimited travel in Norfolk, Suffolk, and part Cambridgeshire on any three days in a week.

FARES & SCHEDULES 🚩 **Anglia Plus Three-Day Pass** ☎ 0845/6007245. **National Rail Enquiries** ☎ 0845/748–4950 ⊕ www.nationalrail.co.uk.

Contacts & Resources

EMERGENCIES
🚩 **Ambulance, fire, police** ☎ 999. **Addenbrooke's Hospital** ✉ Hill's Rd., Cambridge ☎ 01223/245151.

INTERNET
An increasing number of hotels offer free Wi-Fi, and Cambridge has a good number of Internet cafés. Public libraries usually also offer Internet access.

TOUR OPTIONS
BUS TOURS City Sightseeing operates open-top bus tours of Cambridge—the Backs, the colleges, the Imperial War Museum in Duxford, and the Grafton shopping center. Tours start from Cambridge train station but can be picked up at marked bus stops throughout the city. Buy tickets from the driver, the City Sightseeing office at Cambridge train station, or the Cambridge Tourist Information Centre for £8. Tours run mid-April through September, every 15 minutes, and October to mid-April, every 20 or 30 minutes. 🚩 **City Sightseeing** ✉ Cambridge train station ☎ 01708/866000 ⊕ www.citysightseeing.com.

WALKING TOURS Qualified guides for walking tours of the major towns, including Bury St. Edmunds, Cambridge, and Ely can be booked through the respective tourist offices (⇨ Visitor Information). Those in Cambridge are particularly popular; book well in advance for tours (£8) that depart at 1:30 year-round and more frequently in summer. Ninety-minute audio tours of Lavenham are available for rental from the Lavenham Pharmacy, 99 High Street for £3.

VISITOR INFORMATION
🚩 **East of England Tourist Board** ✉ Toppesfield Hall, Market Pl., Hadleigh IP7 5DN ☎ 0870/225–4800 🖶 0870/225–4890 ⊕ www.visiteastofengland.com. **Aldeburgh** ✉ 152 High St., IP15 5AQ ☎ 01728/453637 ⊕ www.suffolkcoastal.gov.uk. **Bury St. Edmunds** ✉ 6 Angel Hill ☎ 01284/764667 ⊕ www.stedmundsbury.gov.uk. **Cambridge** ✉ Wheeler St., CB2 3QB ☎ 0871/226–8006, or 44/1223/464732 from abroad ⊕ www.visitcambridge.org. **Cambridge University** ⊕ www.cam.ac.uk. **Lavenham** ✉ Lady St. ☎ 01787/248207 ⊕ www.babergh-south-suffolk.gov.uk. **Saffron Walden** ✉ 1 Market Pl., Market Sq. ☎ 01799/510444 ⊕ www.uttlesford.gov.uk.

9

Yorkshire & the Northeast

WORD OF MOUTH

"Evensong at York Minster is beautiful, so plan around it. Go early enough that you get to sit in the Choir, where you can see (as well as hear) everything that goes on—I'm guessing that being in the queue 15–20 minutes early should be fine."

—leonberger

"Hadrian's Wall, Housesteads, and Vindolanda were the favorites of my whole family . . . The museum at Vindolanda has incredible artifacts retrieved from the Roman garrison's garbage dump. The countryside also is amazing—you can imagine that the Romans stationed there thought they were at the end of the earth!"

—Marsha

Updated by
Christi
Daugherty

A HAUNTINGLY BEAUTIFUL REGION, the north of England is known for its wide-open spaces and dramatic landscapes. In Yorkshire, the hills of the moors and dales glow pink with heather in summer, and turn black with it in winter. In the lush, green valleys known as the Yorkshire Dales, the high rainfall produces luxuriant vegetation, swift rivers, sparkling streams, and waterfalls. Throughout the area, ruined monasteries are a reminder of the turbulent past. Two of Yorkshire's biggest attractions are the result of human endeavor: the cathedral in medieval York and the sites associated with the Brontë sisters in the town of Haworth.

For many Britons the words "the Northeast" provoke a vision of somewhat bitter, near-Siberian isolation. However, the region also has small villages of remarkable charm and historic abbeys and castles that are all the more romantic for their often ruinous state. Outside of a few key sights such as Durham, with its magnificent cathedral, the Northeast is off the well-trodden tourist path. Mainly composed of the two large counties of Durham and Northumberland, it includes Hadrian's Wall. The wall marked the northern limit of the Roman Empire and stretches across prehistoric remains and moorland in this region. Much of it, remarkably, is still intact.

Yorkshire and the Northeast make up a big, diverse region, difficult to explore in a small amount of time. Those with limited time could visit York as a day trip from London; the fastest trains take just two hours. Proper exploration of the region—especially of the countryside—requires time and effort. But it's well worth it. This is the path less traveled.

Exploring Yorkshire & the Northeast

Brontë Country—basically Haworth, home of the Brontë family—is northwest of the large city of Leeds; to the north spread the hills, valleys, and villages of the Yorkshire Dales. In the center of Yorkshire, the walled city of York deserves special attention, as do its environs, from the spa town of Harrogate to magnificent Fountains Abbey to elegant Castle Howard.

10

Many people travel from the south of England to visit the historic cathedral city of Durham in the Northeast. Farther north, the city of Newcastle is the gateway to the still-impressive Roman fortifications of Hadrian's Wall, which snake through superb scenery to the west. Huge castles stud the stunning, final 40 mi of England's eastern coast, starting an hour's drive north of Newcastle.

About the Restaurants

Generally speaking, Yorkshire is not known for its cuisine, and bacon-based breakfasts and pork pies pale fairly quickly. Out in the countryside, pubs are your best bet for dining. Many offer excellent home-cooked food and locally produced meat (especially lamb) and vegetables. Roast beef dinners generally come with Yorkshire pudding, the tasty, light bread that is called a popover in the United States and Canada. It's generally served with lots of gravy. Be sure to sample local cheeses, especially Wensleydale, which has a delicate flavor and honeyed aftertaste.

In the Northeast, don't wait until 9 PM to have dinner or you can have a hard time getting a meal. Oak-smoked kippers (herring) are a regional specialty, as are the lunchtime seafood sandwiches and the stotties (large bread buns) served for afternoon tea. Try Newcastle Brown ale, whose caramel overtones have found their way even into ice cream.

About the Hotels

In Yorkshire, traditional hotels are limited primarily to major towns and cities; those in the country tend to be guesthouses. Many of the better guesthouses are at the edge of towns, but some proprietors will pick you up at the main station if you're relying on public transportation—verify before booking.

The large hotel chains don't have much of a presence in the Northeast, outside the few large cities. Instead, you can expect to find country houses converted into welcoming hotels, old coaching inns that still greet guests after 300 years, and cozy bed-and-breakfasts convenient to hiking trails.

WHAT IT COSTS In pounds				
££££	**£££**	**£££**	**££**	**£**
RESTAURANTS over £22	£18–£22	£13–£17	£7–£12	under £7
HOTELS over £160	£120–£160	£90–£120	£60–£90	under £60

Restaurant prices are for a main course at dinner. Hotel prices are for two people in a standard double room in high season, including V.A.T., with no meals or, if indicated, CP (with continental breakfast), BP (Breakfast Plan, with full breakfast), or MAP (Modified American Plan, with breakfast and dinner).

Timing

To see the heather at its lushest, visit Yorkshire in summer (and be prepared for some chilly days). York Minster makes a splendid focal point for the prestigious York Early Music Festival in early July. Spring and fall bring their own rewards: far fewer crowds and crisp, clear days, although with an increased risk of rain and fog. In the harsh winter, the tiny moorland roads become impassable, and villages can be cut off entirely. In winter, stick to York and the main towns.

The best time to see the Northeast is in summer. This ensures that the museums—and the roads—will be open, and you can take advantage of the countryside walks that are one of the region's greatest pleasures. At the end of June, Alnwick hosts its annual fair, with a costumed reenactment of a medieval fair, a market, and concerts. The Durham Regatta, England's oldest rowing event, also takes place in June.

BRONTË COUNTRY & THE YORKSHIRE DALES

The main thrust of any visit to West Yorkshire is to the gaunt hills north of the Calder Valley and south of the River Aire; a district immortalized by the mournful writings of the Brontë sisters. Haworth, an otherwise gray village, might have faded into obscurity were it not for the magnetism of the literary sisters. Every summer, thousands toil up the steep main street to visit their hometown.

TOP REASONS TO GO

York Minster: The largest Gothic cathedral in England helps make York, which retains its ancient walls and narrow streets, one of the country's most-visited towns. The building's history is told in its crypt, brilliantly converted into a museum.

Rievaulx Abbey: Heading down the tiny lane that leads to the ruins of one of the great Cistercian abbeys only serves to make it all more dramatic when the abbey's soaring arches appear out of the trees.

Castles, castles, castles: Fought over for centuries by the Scots and the English, the Northeast was one of the most heavily fortified regions in England. Some of the most spectacular castles are along the dramatic, far Northeast coast, including Dunstanburgh and Bamburgh.

Medieval Durham: A splendid Norman cathedral that dates back to the 11th century is just one of the city's charms. Take a stroll on its ancient winding streets or along the River Wear; this is a fairy-tale town hewn from stone.

Hadrian's Wall: The ancient Roman wall is a wonder for the wild countryside around it and the resiliency of its stones. Museums and surviving forts help tell the story, but nothing beats a hike along part of the Hadrian's Wall Path national trail or a ride on Hadrian's Cycleway.

The western equivalent of the North York Moors, the Yorkshire Dales are just as beautiful and nearly as wild. The word "dale" comes from the Viking word for "valley," which gives you an indication that, although the moors have steep hills, the dales are more rugged, with sharper, higher hills. These river valleys fall south and east from the Pennines. Ruined piories, narrow roads, drystone walls made without mortar, and babbling rivers make for a quintessentially English landscape, full of paths and trails to explore.

10

Haworth: Heart of Brontë Country

★ ❶ *20 mi west of Leeds.*

Whatever Haworth might have been in the past, today it is Brontë country. This old stone-built village on the edge of the Yorkshire Moors long ago gave up its own personality and allowed itself to be taken over by the doomed sisters, their mournful books, and their millions of fans. In 1820, when Anne, Emily, and Charlotte were very young, their father moved them and their other three siblings away from their old home in Bradford to Haworth. The sisters—Emily (author of *Wuthering Heights,* 1847), Charlotte (*Jane Eyre,* 1847), and Anne (*The Tenant of Wildfell Hall,* 1848) were inevitably affected by the stark, dramatic countryside around them. These days, every building they ever glanced at has been turned into a Brontë memorial, shop, or museum.

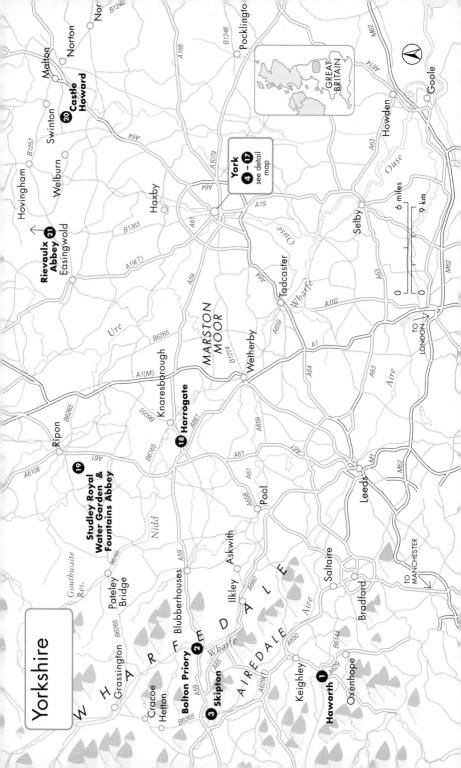

Yorkshire

GREAT BRITAIN

York 4 – 17 see detail map

18 Harrogate

19 Studley Royal Water Garden & Fountains Abbey

20 Castle Howard

21 Rievaulx Abbey

1 Haworth

2 Bolton Priory

3 Skipton

TO LONDON

TO MANCHESTER

0   6 miles
0   9 km

MARSTON MOOR

WHARFEDALE

AIREDALE

Malton
Norton
Swinton
Welburn
Hovingham
Easingwold
Haxby
Pocklington
Goole
Howden
Selby
Tadcaster
Wetherby
Pool
Leeds
Bradford
Saltaire
Keighley
Oxenhope
Ilkley
Askwith
Blubberhouses
Pateley Bridge
Grassington
Cracoe
Hetton
Knaresborough
Ripon
Gouthwaite Res.

Norton
Malton

A64
A166
B1246
B1248
B1257
B1363
A19(T)
A19
A59
A61
A64
A1(M)
B6265
B6165
B6265
A6108
A61
B6265
A59
A65
A629(T)
A650
B6144
A629
A658
A61
A659
A1
A64
A63
M62
M1
M62
A614
A162
A63
A660
Ouse
Wharfe
Ure
Nidd
Aire
Aire

To reach Haworth by bus or train, buy a Metro Day Rover for bus and rail, and take the Metro train from Leeds train station to Keighley—there are about three hourly. From Keighley, take the Keighley & Worth Valley Railway for the trip to Haworth (weekends only; £6 round-trip), or Keighley and District Bus 663, 664, or 665 (Monday–Saturday, every 20 minutes; Sunday, every ½ hour). From Bradford station, Interchange buses run every ½ hour to Keighley.

The town's **information center** has information about accommodations, maps, books on the Brontës, and inexpensive leaflets to help you find your way to such outlying *Wuthering Heights* sites as Ponden Hall (Thrushcross Grange) and Ponden Kirk (Penistone Crag). ✉ *2–4 West La.* ☎ *01535/642329* ✆ *Thurs.–Tues. 9:30–5; Wed. 10–5.*

> ## LANDSCAPE AS MUSE
>
> The rugged Yorkshire Moors helped inspire Emily Brontë's 1847 *Wuthering Heights;* if ever a work of fiction grew out of the landscape in which its author lived, it was surely this. "My sister Emily loved the moors," wrote Charlotte. "Flowers brighter than the rose bloomed in the blackest of the heath for her; out of a sullen hollow in a livid hillside her mind could make an Eden. She found in the bleak solitude many and dear delights; and not the least and best loved was liberty."

Haworth's steep, cobbled **Main Street** has changed little in outward appearance since the early 19th century, but today acts as a funnel for the people who crowd into the points of interest: the **Black Bull** pub, where the reprobate Branwell, the Brontës' only brother, drank himself into an early grave; the **post office** from which Charlotte, Emily, and Anne sent their manuscripts to their London publishers; and the **church,** with its gloomy graveyard (Charlotte and Emily are buried inside the church; Anne is buried in Scarborough).

The best of the Brontë sights in Haworth is the **Brontë Parsonage Museum.** In the somber Georgian house in which the sisters grew up, it displays original furniture (some bought by Charlotte after the success of *Jane Eyre*), portraits, and books. The Brontës moved to this simple house when the Reverend Patrick Brontë was appointed to the local church, but tragedy soon struck—his wife, Maria, and their two eldest children died within five years (done in, some scholars assert, by water wells tainted by seepage from the neighboring graveyard). The museum contains enchanting mementos of the four surviving children, including Charlotte's wedding bonnet and the sisters' spidery, youthful graffiti on the nursery wall. Branwell painted several of the portraits on display. ✉ *Church St.* ☎ *01535/ 642323* ⊕*www.bronte.info* ✆*£5* ✆*Apr.–Sept., daily 10–5:30; Oct.–Dec., Feb., and Mar., daily 11–5; last admission 30 mins before closing.*

If you have the time, you can pack a lunch and walk an hour or so along a field path, a lane, and a moorland track to the lovely, isolated waterfall that has, inevitably, been renamed the **Brontë Waterfall.** It was a favorite of the sisters, who wrote about it in poems and letters. **Top Withins,** a ruined, gloomy house on a bleak hilltop farm 3 mi from Haworth, is

10

often taken to be the inspiration for Heathcliff's gloomy mansion, Wuthering Heights. Brontë scholars say it probably isn't, but it does make an inspirational walk across the moors. There and back from Haworth is a two-hour walk. Wherever you go, wear sturdy shoes and protective clothing: if you've read *Wuthering Heights,* you have a fairly good idea of what weather can be like on the Yorkshire Moors.

☺ Haworth is on the **Keighley & Worth Valley Railway,** a gorgeous 5-mi-long branch line along which steam engines run between Keighley (3 mi north of Haworth) and Oxenhope. Kids like it even more on special days when there are family fairs en route. The **Museum of Rail Travel** (🖃 £1 ☾ Daily 11–4), at Ingrow along the line, exhibits vintage train cars. ⊠ *Railway Station, Keighley* ☎ *01535/645214, 01535/647777 for 24-hr information* ⊕ *www.kwvr.co.uk* 🖃 *£8 round-trip, £12 Day Rover ticket* ☾ *Sept.–June, weekends; July and Aug., daily; call for schedules.*

Where to Stay & Eat

££ ✕🖾 **Weavers.** Book well in advance to secure a room in this establishment converted from a number of old cottages in a fine village location. Weavers operates mainly as a restaurant (££–£££), but the few chintz-filled rooms have antique French beds and vivid bedspreads. Downstairs, the restaurant (closed Sunday night and Monday) serves traditional, organic Yorkshire fare, including smoked haddock soup and duck in brandy sauce, served with home-baked bread. ⊠ *15 West La., BD22 8DU* ☎ *01535/643822* 🖨 *01535/643822* ⊕ *www.weaversmallhotel. co.uk* 🖙 *3 rooms* ♻ *Restaurant, bar; no a/c* 🖃 *AE, DC, MC, V* ☾ *Closed 1 wk at Christmas and 1 wk in summer* 🍴 *BP.*

£ ✕🖾 **Aitches.** This intimate 19th-century stone house is close to the Brontë Parsonage on Haworth's main street. The guest rooms are modern, with pine pieces and colorful quilts and drapes. A fixed-price meal in the elegant small restaurant (££££), which is open to nonguests on Friday and Saturday only, might include pork cutlet with Stilton crumble followed by a traditional bread-and-butter pudding. ⊠ *11 West La., BD22 8DU* ☎ *01535/642501* ⊕ *www.aitches.co.uk* 🖙 *5 rooms* ♻ *Restaurant; no a/c, no room phones, no smoking* 🖃 *MC, V* 🍴 *BP.*

££ 🖾 **Old Registry.** The lovely theme guest rooms—Memories Room, Blue Heaven, Cherub Corner, and so on—in this creeper-covered Victorian house at the lower end of the main street are all individually decorated and equipped with CD players. One room has lavender-scented pillows, another has a green bed and gardening memorabilia, and there's an unusual three-poster bed in the attic room. All have large bathrooms and two have whirlpool baths. ⊠ *2–4 Main St., BD22 8DA* 🖨 *01535/646503* ⊕ *www. oldregistryhaworth.co.uk* 🖙 *10 rooms* ♻ *In-room VCR, some pets allowed; no a/c, no room phones, no smoking* 🖃 *MC, V* 🍴 *BP.*

Bolton Priory

❷ *12 mi north of Haworth, 24 mi northwest of Leeds.*

Some of the loveliest Wharfedale scenery comes into view around Bolton Priory, the ruins of an Augustinian priory, which sits on a grassy embankment inside a great curve of the River Wharfe. The priory is just a short walk or drive from the village of Bolton Abbey. You can wander through the 13th-century ruins or visit the priory church, which is still the local parish church. The duke of Devonshire owns the Bolton Abbey estate, including the ruins. Among the famous visitors enchanted by Bolton Priory were William Wordsworth and J. M. W. Turner; John Ruskin, the Victorian art critic, rated it the most beautiful of all English ruins.

Close to Bolton Priory, surrounded by woodland scenery, the River Wharfe plunges between a narrow chasm in the rocks (called the Strid) before reaching **Barden Tower,** a medieval hunting lodge. This lodge is now a ruin and can be visited just as easily as Bolton Priory, in whose grounds it stands. You can ride the scenic 4-mi **Embsay & Bolton Abbey Steam Railway** (☎ 01756/710614, 01756/795189 recorded timetable), which has a station in Bolton Abbey. ✉ *B6160, off A59* ☎ *01756/718009* ⊕ *www.boltonabbey.com* ⊠ *Free, parking £4* ⊙ *Daily 9–dusk.*

Where to Stay & Eat

££££ ✕⊡ **Devonshire Arms.** Originally an 18th-century coaching inn, and still belonging to the dukes of Devonshire, this luxurious country-house hotel is near the River Wharfe, an easy walk from Bolton Abbey. The bedrooms are tastefully decorated with antiques and family memorabilia from the family home, Chatsworth House in Derbyshire. The Burlington restaurant (£££££) has a fixed-price menu of superb traditional fare that uses game and fish from the estate. The brasserie serves modestly priced fare (££). ✉ *Bolton Abbey, Skipton BD23 6AJ* ☎ *01756/ 710441, 01756/718111 reservation line* 🖷 *01756/710564* ⊕ *www. devonshirehotels.co.uk* ⇥ *37 rooms, 3 suites* ⌂ *2 restaurants, in-room data ports, tennis court, pool, health club, sauna, fishing, 2 bars, meeting rooms, some pets allowed; no a/c* ⊟ *AE, DC, MC, V* ⦿ *BP.*

Skipton

❸ *6 mi west of Bolton Abbey, 12 mi north of Haworth, 22 mi west of Harrogate.*

Skipton in Airedale, capital of the limestone district of Craven, is a typical Dales market town with as many farmers as visitors milling in the streets. There are markets Monday, Wednesday, Friday, and Saturday, and shops selling local produce predominate.

★ **Skipton Castle,** built by the Normans in 1090 and unaltered since the Civil War (17th century), is the town's most prominent attraction and one of the best preserved of English medieval castles. After the Battle of Marston Moor during the Civil War, it remained the only Royalist stronghold in the north of England. So sturdy was the squat little fortification with its rounded battlements (in places the walls are 12 feet thick) that Oliver Cromwell ordered the roof be removed, as it had survived one bombardment after another during a three-year siege. When the castle's owner, Lady Anne Clifford, later asked if she could replace the roof, he allowed her do so, as long as it was not strong enough to withstand cannon fire. Today the buildings are still marvelously complete, and in the central courtyard, a yew tree, planted more than 300 years ago by Lady Anne herself, still flourishes. ✉ *High St.* ☎ *01756/*

10

792442 ⊕ *www.skiptoncastle.co.uk* ✉ *£5.40* ☾ *Mar.–Sept., Mon.–Sat. 10–6, Sun. noon–6; Oct.–Feb., Mon.–Sat. 10–4, Sun. noon–4.*

Where to Stay & Eat

££££–£££££ ✕▥ **Angel Inn.** Diners at the Angel clog the hidden-away hamlet of Hetton with their vehicles, such is the attraction of this locally renowned brasserie and more formal restaurant. Roasted lamb and duck are specialties (£££; reservations essential; no dinner Sunday). The ancient stone barn across the road has well-equipped guest rooms in unfussy country styles, from rustic to French. The inn is 5 mi north of Skipton. ⊠ *Off B6265, Hetton* ☎ *01756/730263* 🖷 *01756/730363* ⊕ *www. angelhetton.co.uk* ⇝ *5 rooms* ⚖ *2 restaurants, bar, in-room safes, minibars, bar; no a/c, no-smoking* ▤ *AE, DC, MC, V* ⊠⃝ *BP.*

YORK

It would be unthinkable to visit North Yorkshire without first visiting the historic cathedral city of York, and not just because of its central location. Named "Eboracum" by the Romans, York was the military capital of Roman Britain, and traces of garrison buildings survive throughout the city. After the Roman Empire collapsed in the 5th century, the Saxons built "Eoforwic" upon the ruins of a fort, but were soon defeated by Vikings (who called the town Jorvik, and used it as a base from which to subjugate the countryside). The Normans came in the 11th century and emulated the Vikings by using the town as a military base. It was during Norman times that the foundations of York Minster, the largest medieval cathedral in England, were laid.

Because York was largely a backwater during the Industrial Revolution, much of the city's medieval and 18th-century architecture has survived, making the city an architectural time capsule and a delight to explore.

Exploring York

This is a fine city for walking, especially along the walls embracing the old center; many of the narrow streets have been pedestrianized. At night some historic buildings are illuminated, too. You can get a free walking map from the tourist office in the train station; most hotels have maps in their lobbies. Tiny medieval alleys called "snickleways" provide shortcuts across the city center, but they're not on maps, so you never quite know where you'll end up; in York, this is often a pleasant surprise. July and August are the town's busiest months, when tourists choke the narrow streets and cause long lines at the popular museums and restaurants. April, May, June, and September are less crowded, although the weather is unpredictable.

The best way to explore York is to start at the Minster and head down the little medieval lane, Stonegate, which is lined with shops and leads directly to Betty's tea shop. From there you can swing right to find antiques shops, or left for more modern shops, and eventually the shopping area known as the Shambles, and the remains of the old castle.

■ TIP→ **At any point, climb the steps to the top of the city walls for some perspective on where you are in town.** The Ouse River, by the way, is more like an undeveloped canal, hidden away by buildings.

Main Attractions

★ ❺ **City walls.** York's almost 3 mi of ancient stone walls are among the best preserved in England. A walk on the narrow paved path along the top leads you through 1,900 years of history, from the time the earthen ramparts were raised by the Romans and York's Viking kings to repel raiders, to their fortification by the Normans, to their current colorful landscaping by the city council. The walls are crossed periodically by York's distinctive fortified gates or "bars": the portcullis on Monk's Bar on Goodramgate is still in working order, and Walmgate Bar in the east is the only gate in England with an intact barbican. It also has scars from the cannon balls hurled at it during the Civil War. Bootham Bar in Exhibition Square was the defensive bastion for the north road, and Micklegate Bar, in the city's southwest corner, was the monarch's entrance. For a small fee, you can explore all of these gates. To access the path and the lookout towers, find a staircase at one of the many breaks in the walls. ⊕ *www.york.gov.uk/ walls* ⬚ *Free* ☉ *Daily 8 AM–dusk.*

⟳ ❽ **Dig.** This new venture from the people behind the Jorvik Viking Centre is a great way to get young people inspired about history and archaeology. It's an ongoing archaeological dig in and beneath an old church; kids, supervised by knowledgable experts, help with the work. After your dig, record your findings and head to the lab to learn what archaeological finds discovered on the site reveal about how people lived in the past. It's an educational, fun, fascinating way to spend a couple of hours. ⬚ *St. Saviour's Church, St. Saviourgate* ☎ *01904/543403* ⊕ *www.vikingjorvik. com* ⬚ *£5.50; joint admission to Jorvik Viking Centre £11* ☉ *Apr.–Oct., daily 10–5; Nov.–Mar., daily 10–4.*

> ## WHERE ARE THE GATES?
>
> The Viking conquerors of northern England held the region for more than a century, and made York their capital. Many of the city's street names are still suffixed with the word "-gate" (Goodramgate and Micklegate, for example). "Gate" was the Viking word for "street." Adding to the confusion, the city's entrances, or gates, are called "bars," from an Old English term. As local tour guides like to say, "In York, our streets are called gates, our gates are called bars, and our bars are called pubs."

10

❶❹ **Guildhall.** The mid-15th-century guildhall, by the River Ouse, was a meeting place for the city's powerful guilds. It was also used for pageants and mystery plays (medieval dramas based on biblical stories and the lives of saints). Restoration after the damage done by World War II bombing has given it something of its erstwhile glory. The guildhall is behind the 18th-century Mansion House; you can visit it when no function is in progress. ⬚ *St. Helen's Sq.* ☎ *01904/613161* ⬚ *Free* ☉ *May–Oct., weekdays 9–5, Sat. 10–5, Sun. 2–5; Nov.–Apr., weekdays 9–5.*

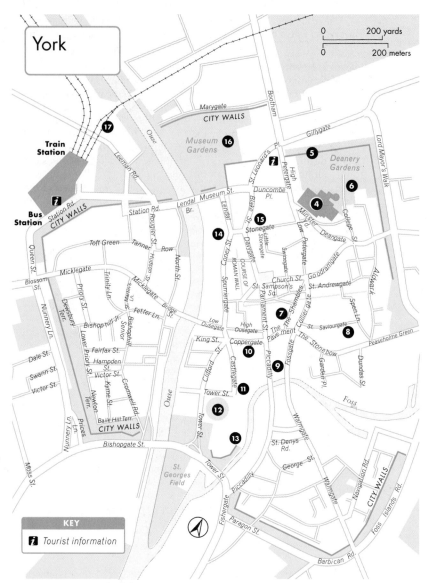

York

Castle Museum **13**
City Walls **5**
Clifford's Tower **12**
Dig **8**
Fairfax House **11**
Guildhall **14**

Jorvik Viking Centre **10**
Merchant
Adventurers' Hall **9**
National Railway
Museum **17**
The Shambles **7**

Stonegate **15**
Treasurer's House **6**
York Minster **4**
Yorkshire Museum **16**

🕐 ⑩ **Jorvik Viking Centre.** This exhibition re-creates a 10th-century Viking village. A mixture of museum and carnival ride, it requires you to "travel through time." You climb into a Disney-esque machine that propels you above straw huts and mannequins in Viking garb. Commentary is provided in 10 languages (click on the British flag to hear it in English). Kids will get a lot out of it, but adults are unlikely to learn anything new. A small collection of Viking-era artifacts is on display at the end of the ride. ✉ *Coppergate* ☎ *01904/643211, 01904/543403 advance booking* ⊕ *www.vikingjorvik.com* 🖅 *£7.75; joint admission to Dig £11* ☉ *Apr.–Oct., daily 10–5; Nov.–Mar., daily 10–4.*

🕐 ⑰ **National Railway Museum.** For train-lovers one and all: here Britain's national collection of locomotives forms part of a massive train museum. Among the exhibits are gleaming giants of the steam era, including the *Mallard*, holder of the world speed record for a steam engine (126 mph). Passenger cars used by Queen Victoria are on display, as well as the only Japanese bullet train to be seen outside Japan. You can clamber aboard the trains, some of which are started up regularly to keep the engines working. ✉ *Leeman Rd.* ☎ *01904/621261, 01904/686286 information line* ⊕ *www.nrm.org.uk* 🖅 *Free* ☉ *Daily 10–6.*

❼ **The Shambles.** York's best-preserved medieval street has half-timber stores and houses with overhangs so massive you could almost reach across the street from one 2nd-floor window to another. Once the city's street of butchers (meat hooks are still fastened outside some of the doors), today it's filled with touristy shops of scant interest to most visitors. Still, it's beautiful to walk down for the atmosphere.

> ## THE YORK EYE
>
> At the National Railway Museum, you can soar above the city on the Norwich Union Yorkshire Wheel, the observation wheel that is York's answer to the London Eye. It costs £6 for the 13-minute ride, which takes you up 175 feet for great views. It's open daily 10 to 6, and until 9 May through September. At this writing, no advance tickets were being sold, but check the museum's Web site, ⊕ www. nrm.org.uk, for an update.

⑮ **Stonegate.** This narrow, pedestrian-only street of Tudor and 18th-century storefronts and courtyards retains considerable charm. It has been in daily use for almost 2,000 years, since first being paved in Roman times. Today it's lined with jewelry stores, knickknack shops, tea shops, and ancient pubs. A passage just off Stonegate, at 52A, leads to the remnants of a 12th-century Norman stone house attached to a more recent structure. You can see the old Norman wall and window. Look out for the little red devil high up on a doorpost. Keep an eye out throughout the area for similar tiny statues that once acted as signs for businesses. The devil announced a printer's shop. ■ TIP➔ **There's another statue at the intersection of Stonegate and High Petergate, where Minerva lounges on a stack of books. She once advertised a bookseller.**

NEED A
BREAK?
At the opposite end of Stonegate from the Minster, **Betty's** (✉ 6–8 Helen's Sq., off Stonegate ☎ 01904/659142) has been a York institution since 1912. This tea-and-cakes salon in an attractive art-nouveau building is more beloved for its history and ambience than for its food, which is only so-so. Still, it's a piece of history, and a good place to take a rest. Expect to wait 10 minutes for a table.

❹ **York Minster.** Focal point of the city, this vast cathedral is the largest Gothic church in England and attracts almost as many visitors as London's Westminster Abbey. Inside, the effect created by its soaring pillars and lofty vaulted ceilings is almost overpowering. Come with binoculars if you wish to study the dazzling 128 stained-glass windows. Glowing with deep wine reds and cobalt blues, they are bested only by those in Chartres Cathedral in France. Mere statistics cannot convey the scale of the building; however, the central towers are 184 feet high, and the church is 534 feet long, 249 feet across its transepts, and 90 feet from floor to roof. Contributing to the cold, crushing splendor are the ornamentation of the 14th-century nave; the east window, one of the greatest pieces of medieval glazing in the world; the north transept's **Five Sisters** windows, five tall lancets of frosted 13th-century glass; the enormous choir screen portraying somewhat whimsical images of every king of England from William the Conqueror to Henry VI; and the imposing tracery of the **Rose Window,** commemorating the marriage of Henry VII and Elizabeth of York in 1486 (the event that ended the Wars of the Roses and began the Tudor Dynasty). Don't miss the exquisite 13th-century **Chapter House** and the **Undercroft, Treasury, and Crypt.** Finds during the latest renovation date back to Roman times, and include a Saxon child's coffin. After exploring the interior, you might take the 275 winding steps to the roof of the great **Central Tower** (strictly for those with a head for heights), not only for the close-up view of the cathedral's detailed carving but for a panorama of York and the surrounding moors. ■ TIP→ Attending Evensong here is a memorable experience. ✉ *Duncombe Pl.* ☎ *01904/557216* ⊕ *www.yorkminster. org* 🏛 *Minster £5, Undercroft, Treasury, and Crypt £3, Central Tower £3* ⊙ *Apr.–Oct., Mon.–Sat. 9–5:30, Sun. noon–3:45; Nov.–Mar., Mon.–Sat. 9:30–4:45, Sun. noon–3:45.*

*Fodor's*Choice
★

Also Worth Seeing

⓭ **Castle Museum.** A former 18th-century debtors' prison, this quirky museum of everyday items presents detailed exhibitions and re-creations, including a Victorian street complete with crafts shops and a working water mill, as well as notable domestic, costume, and arms and armor displays. One treasure is the Coppergate Helmet, a 1,200-year-old Anglo-Saxon helmet discovered during excavations of the city; it's one of only three such objects found. You can also visit the cell where Dick Turpin, the 18th-century highwayman and folk hero, spent the night before his execution. ✉ *Clifford St.* ☎ *01904/687687* ⊕ *www. yorkcastlemuseum.org.uk* 🏛 *£6.50* ⊙ *Daily 9:30–5.*

⓬ **Clifford's Tower.** Apart from the city walls, this rather sad and battered looking keep is all that remains of the old York castle. The stone tower, which sits on a grassy mound surrounded by a parking lot, dates from the mid-12th century. The Norman version that preceded it was infamously destroyed in 1190. More than 150 Jews locked themselves inside with no food or water to protect themselves from a violent mob. After several days, they were forced to choose between starvation or murder. In the end, they committed mass suicide by setting their own prison aflame. ✉ *Tower St.* ☎ *01904/646940* ⊕ *www.cliffordstower.com* 🎫 *£2.75* ⊗ *Apr.–June and Sept., daily 10–6; July and Aug., daily 9:30–7; Oct.–Mar., daily 10–4.*

★ ⑪ **Fairfax House.** This elegant Georgian (1762) town house is a museum of decorative arts. The house is beautifully decorated with period furniture, crystal chandeliers, and silk wallpaper. ✉ *Castlegate* ☎ *01904/ 655543* ⊕ *www.fairfaxhouse.co.uk* 🎫 *£4.75* ⊗ *Mon.–Thurs. and Sat. 11–5, Sun. 1:30–5; last admission 4:30; Fri., guided tours 11 and 2.*

⑨ **Merchant Adventurers' Hall.** Built between 1357 and 1368 by a wealthy medieval guild, this is the largest half-timber hall in York. Portraits, silver, and furniture are on display, and the house itself is much of the attraction. A riverfront garden lies behind the hall. On most Saturdays, antiques fairs are held inside the building. ✉ *Fossgate* ☎ *01904/ 654818* ⊕ *www.theyorkcompany.co.uk* 🎫 *£2.75* ⊗ *Apr.–Sept., Mon.–Thurs. 9–5, Fri. and Sat. 9–3:30, Sun. noon–4; Oct.–Mar., Mon.–Sat. 9–3:30; closed 1st wk in Dec.*

⑥ **Treasurer's House.** Surprises await inside this large 17th-century house, the home from 1897 to 1930 of industrialist Frank Green. With a fine eye for texture, decoration, and pattern, Green created period rooms—including a medieval great hall—as a showcase for his collection of antique furniture. Delft tiles decorate the kitchen, copies of medieval stenciling cover the vibrant Red Room, and 17th-century stump work adorns the Tapestry Room. The "ghost" cellar is shown on the guided tour. ✉ *Minster Yard* ☎ *01904/624247* ⊕ *www.nationaltrust.org.uk* 🎫 *House and garden £5; £7 with cellar tour* ⊗ *Apr.–Oct., Sat.–Thurs. 11–5; last admission 30 mins before closing.*

⑯ **Yorkshire Museum.** The natural and archaeological history of the county, including material on the Roman, Anglo-Saxon, and Viking aspects of York, is the focus of this museum. Also on display in the solid, Doric-style building is the 15th-century Middleham Jewel, a pendant gleaming with a large sapphire. The museum lies just outside the walled city, through Bootham Bar, one of York's old gates. ✉ *Museum Gardens, Museum St.* ☎ *01904/551805* ⊕ *www.yorkshiremuseum.org.uk* 🎫 *£4* ⊗ *Daily 10–5.*

Where to Eat

££–££££ ✕ **Melton's.** Once a private house, this unpretentious but excellent restaurant has local art on the walls and an open kitchen. The seasonal menus are highly imaginative with modern English and European fare, such as venison with red wine and mulled pears, and roast partridge with marscapone and grilled polenta. Melton's is a 10 minutes' walk from York Minster. ✉ *7 Scarcroft Rd.* ☎ *01904/634341* ⚑ *Reservations essential* ▤ *MC, V* ⊗ *Closed 3 wks at Christmas, and 1 wk in Aug. No lunch Mon.; no dinner Sun.*

10

★ **££–£££** ✕ **Blue Bicycle.** York's best restaurant is in a building that once served as a brothel. Downstairs are evocative walled booths and at street level is a lively room with wood floors in a candlelight glow. The menu concentrates on local beef and seafood. You can start with crab cannelloni on spinach salad, and move on to seared salmon or the fillet of Yorkshire beef on smoked-bacon mashed potatoes. The wine list is good, and the service couldn't be friendlier. ⊠ *34 Fossgate* ☎ *01904/673990* ⚘ *Reservations essential* ▭ *MC, V.*

££ ✕ **Café Concerto.** Music ephemera decorate this relaxed, intimate bistro in sight of York Minster, which prepares virtually any style of food you care to name, from Caribbean to Continental. You might choose the Cuban spiced chicken with sweet potatoes, and then homemade cake and a cappuccino. ⊠ *21 High Petergate* ☎ *01904/610478* ▭ *No credit cards.*

£ ✕ **Golden Slipper.** Although it's only a stone's throw from the busy minster, this warm and cozy place with book-lined walls resembles a country pub. Besides good homemade pies—try the pork, apple, and sage—there are stuffed baked potatoes and hot and cold sandwiches, all served until 7 PM, or 5 PM on weekends. ⊠ *20 Goodramgate* ☎ *01904/651235* ▭ *MC, V.*

Where to Stay

★ **£££££** ▦ **Middlethorpe Hall & Spa.** This splendidly restored 18th-century mansion, about 1½ mi from the city center, was the sometime home of the traveler and diarist Lady Mary Wortley Montagu (1689–1762). Antiques, paintings, and fresh flowers fill the traditionally decorated rooms, some in cottage-style accommodations around an 18th-century courtyard. The extensive grounds include a lake and a 17th-century dovecote. The Anglo–French menu of the wood-paneled restaurant changes seasonally but always has more than a hint of luxury—like the hotel itself. ⊠ *Bishopthorpe Rd., YO23 2GB* ☎ *01904/641241* ⎙ *01904/620176* ⊕ *www.middlethorpe.com* ⇄ *23 rooms, 8 suites* ⚒ *Restaurant, room TVs with movies, in-room data ports, indoor pool, gym, health club, sauna, spa, croquet, bar, laundry service, meeting rooms, free parking; no a/c, no kids under 8* ▭ *AE, MC, V* ⦿ *CP.*

££££ ▦ **Dean Court Hotel.** The clergy of York Minster, just across the way, once found accommodations at this large Victorian house. Traditionally furnished rooms with plenty of print fabrics and plump sofas have fine views overlooking the minster. The restaurant serves good English cuisine, including a hearty Yorkshire breakfast. ⊠ *Duncombe Pl., YO1 7EF* ☎ *01904/625082* ⎙ *01904/620305* ⊕ *www.bw-deancourt.co.uk* ⇄ *39 rooms* ⚒ *Restaurant, coffee shop, room service, cable TV, in-room data ports, bar, meeting rooms, parking (fee), no-smoking rooms; no a/c* ▭ *AE, DC, MC, V* ⦿ *BP.*

££££ ▦ **One3two.** This small Georgian town house manages to be plushly contemporary without sacrificing its period features. Bedrooms done in rich solid colors have teak beds and Egyptian cotton linens; the marble bathrooms have walk-in showers and deep bathtubs. You can take breakfast in the elegant, pumpkin-hue dining room, or have a champagne hamper delivered to your room. ✉ *132 The Mount, YO24 1AS* ☎ *01904/600060* 🖷 *01904/676132* ⊕ *www.one3two.co.uk* ↝ *5 rooms* ⌂ *Dining room, minibars, in-room data ports; no a/c, no smoking* ▭ *MC, V* ⦿ *BP.*

£££ 🏨 **Judge's Lodgings.** This Georgian mansion provided rooms for justices when they traveled up north from London's Inns of Court. The somewhat shabby-genteel lobby leads to the main salon—a delightful, cozy cocoon of pastels, overstuffed chairs, and gilded mirrors. The finest room in the house is the "Minster" with a sunken hot tub and a massive 7-foot four-poster (£130). ✉ *9 Lendal, YO1 2AQ* ☎ *01904/638733* 🖷 *01904/ 679947* ⊕ *www.judgeslodgings.com* ↝ *14 rooms* ⌂ *Restaurant, cable TV, bar, meeting rooms, free parking; no a/c* ▭ *AE, DC, MC, V* ⦿ *BP.*

£££ 🏨 **Mount Royale Hotel.** In a quiet country house in the upscale residential part of west York, near the racecourse, this hotel offers excellent service that is both professional and friendly. Outside near the pool, discover orange, lemon, and fig trees mingling with the sprays of flowers in the pristine English garden. Rooms are spacious and decorated simply with subtle colors; four have walk-in closets and verandas that lead to the garden. ■ TIP→ **The modern European restaurant, Sous le Mont (££–££££), is one of York's most popular; if you drive, expect to fight for parking.** This hotel is too far from the city center to walk to. ✉ *117–119 The Mount, YO24 1GU* ☎ *01904/628856, 01904/619444 for restaurant* 🖷 *01904/611171* ⊕ *www.mountroyale.co.uk* ↝ *23 rooms* ⌂ *Restaurant, room service, cable TV, pool, bar, laundry service, meeting rooms; no a/c* ▭ *AE, DC, MC, V* ⦿ *BP.*

££–£££ 🏨 **The Hazelwood.** Only 400 yards from York Minster, this tall Victorian town house stands in a peaceful cul-de-sac, away from the noise of traffic. Reds and golds dominate bedrooms furnished with rich fabrics and handsome traditional wood pieces. The memorable breakfasts include black pudding, Danish pastries, and vegetarian sausages. ✉ *24–25 Portland St., YO31 7EH* ☎ *01904/626548* 🖷 *01904/628032* ⊕ *www. thehazelwoodyork.com* ↝ *14 rooms* ⌂ *Free parking; no a/c, no room phones, no kids under 8, no smoking* ▭ *MC, V* ⦿ *BP.*

££ 🏨 **Dairy Guest House.** Victorian stained glass, pine woodwork, and intricate plaster cornices are original features of this former dairy 200 yards from the city walls. Bedrooms, done in pleasant pastels, come with books and games, and the imaginative breakfasts (served 8:30 to 9:15) can accommodate vegetarians and vegans. The flower-filled internal courtyard is lovely. ✉ *3 Scarcroft Rd., YO23 1ND* ☎ *01904/639367* ⊕ *www. dairyguesthouse.co.uk* ↝ *5 rooms* ⌂ *Some pets allowed; no a/c, no room phones, no smoking* ▭ *MC, V* ⦿ *BP.*

£–££ 🏨 **Eastons.** Two Victorian houses knocked into one, this guesthouse retains a rich sense of the era. Dark colors enhance the marble fireplaces, wood paneling, tiling, antique furniture, and big sofas. Breakfast is substantial. It's easy to find parking on the street, which is just south of the city center, 300 yards from the city walls. ✉ *88–90 Bishopthorpe Rd., YO23 1JS* ☎ *01904/626646* 🖷 *01904/626165* ⊕ *www.eastons.ws* ↝ *10 rooms* ⌂ *No a/c, no room phones, no kids under 5, no smoking* ▭ *No credit cards* ⦿ *BP.*

10

Nightlife & the Arts

Nightlife

York is full of historic pubs where you can while away an hour over a pint. The **Black Swan** (⊠ Peasholme Green ☎ 01904/686911) is the city's oldest pub, a 16th-century Tudor building. It's said to be haunted by a young girl that sits by the fireplace. The **Old White Swan** (⊠ Goodramgate ☎ 01904/540911) is vast, spreading across five medieval, half-timbered buildings on busy Goodramgate. It's known for its good pub lunches, and its ghosts—it claims to be more haunted than the Black Swan. The **Snickleway Inn** (⊠ Goodramgate ☎ 01904/656138) is in a 15th-century building with open fireplaces and a real sense of history.

The Arts

The **Early Music Festival** (☎ 01904/658338 festival office, 01904/621756 Tourist Information Centre ⊕ www.ncem.co.uk) is held each July. The **Viking Festival** (⊠ Jorvik, Coppergate ☎ 01904/543402 ⊕ www.vikingjorvik.com) takes place each February. The celebrations, including a parade and long-ship regatta, end with the Jorvik Viking Combat reenactment, when Norsemen confront their Anglo-Saxon enemies.

In a lovely 18th-century building, the **York Theatre Royal** (⊠ St. Leonard's Pl. ☎ 01904/623568) presents plays, music, poetry readings, and art.

Shopping

The new and secondhand bookstores around Petergate, Stonegate, and the Shambles are excellent. The **Minster Gate Bookshop** (⊠ 8 Minster Gate ☎ 01904/621812) sells secondhand books, old maps, and prints. **Mulberry Hall** (⊠ Stonegate ☎ 01904/620736) is a sales center for all the famous names in fine bone china and crystal. It also has a neat café. The **York Antiques Centre** (⊠ 2 Lendal ☎ 01904/641445) has 25 shops selling antiques, bric-a-brac, books, and jewelry.

YORK ENVIRONS

West and north of York, a number of sights make easy, appealing day trips from the city: the spa town of Harrogate, Studley Royal Water Garden and the ruins of Fountain Abbey, the stunning baroque Castle Howard, and magnificent Rievaulx Abbey.

Harrogate

★ ⑱ *21 mi west of York, 16 mi north of Leeds.*

During the Regency and early Victorian periods, it became fashionable for the noble and wealthy to retire to a spa to "take the waters" for relaxation. In Yorkshire the trend reached its grandest heights in Harrogate, an elegant town that flourished during the 19th century. Today the Regency buildings, parks, and spas built during that time make Harrogate an absorbing getaway. At the edge of the town center, the 200-acre grassy parkland known as the **Stray** is a riot of color in spring. The **Val-**

ley Gardens, southwest of the town center, include a boating lake, tennis courts, and a little café.

The **Royal Pump Room Museum** is in the octagonal structure built in 1842 over the original sulfur well that brought great prosperity to the town. You can still drink the evil-smelling (and nasty-tasting) spa waters here. The museum displays some equipment of spa days gone by, alongside a rather eccentric collection of fine 19th-century china, clothes, and bicycles. ⊠ *Crown Pl.* ☎ *01423/556188* ⊕ *www.harrogate.gov.uk* 🖾 *£2.80* ⊙ *Apr.–Oct., Mon.–Sat. 10–5, Sun. 2–5; Nov.–Mar., Mon.–Sat. 10–4, Sun. 2–4.*

The exotic and fully restored **Turkish Baths** (1897) allow you to experience what brought so many Victorians to Harrogate. After changing into your bathing suit, you can relax on luxurious lounge chairs in the mosaic-tile warming room. Move on to increasingly hot sauna rooms, then soak up eucalyptus mist in the steam room before braving the icy plunge pool. You can also book a massage or facial. Open hours are divided into women-only, men-only, and couples-only nights. Book in advance. ⊠ *Parliament St.* ☎ *01423/556746* ⊕ *www.harrogate.gov.uk/ turkishbaths* 🖾 *£12 per bath and sauna session, massages and treatments additional* ⊙ *Daily; call for schedules.*

Where to Eat

£ ✕ **Betty's.** The celebrated Yorkshire tearoom began life in Harrogate in the 1920s, when Swiss restaurateur Frederic Belmont brought his Alpine specialties to England. The elegant surroundings have changed little since then, and the same cakes and pastries are for sale, along with teas. A pianist plays nightly. ⊠ *1 Parliament St.* ☎ *01423/502746* ▤ *MC, V.*

Studley Royal Water Garden & Fountains Abbey

★ ⑲ *30 mi northwest of York.*

You can easily spend a day at this World Heritage Site, a 822-acre complex made up of an 18th-century water garden and deer park and the majestic ruins of medieval Fountains Abbey. Here, a neoclassical vision of an ordered universe—with lakes, spectacular water terraces, classical temples, statues, and a grotto—blends with the glories of English Gothic architecture. The abbey, on the banks of the River Skell, was founded in 1132 and completed in the early 1500s. The Cistercian monks here, called "White Monks" for the color of their robes, devoted their lives to silence, prayer, and work. Of the surviving buildings, the lay brothers' echoing refectory and dormitory impresses most; the Gothic tower was a 16th-century addition. Fountains Mill, with sections dating back to 1140, displays reconstructed mill machinery (wool was the monks' large and profitable business). The 17th-century Fountains Hall, partially built with stones taken from the abbey, has an exhibition and video display. ⊠ *Off B6265* ☎ *01765/608888* ⊕ *www. fountainsabbey.org.uk* 🖾 *£5.50* ⊙ *Mar.–Oct., daily 10–6; Feb. and Nov., daily 10–4. Free guided tours of abbey and gardens Apr.–Oct., daily at 11, 1:30, and 2:30 (June–Aug. extra tour at 3:30); water garden tour Apr.–Oct., daily at 2.*

10

The Monastic Past

THE SHEER NUMBER of once richly decorated monastic buildings here is a testament to the power of the Catholic monks of medieval Yorkshire. They became some of the richest in Europe by virtue of the international wool trade that they conducted, with the help of lay workers, from their vast religious estates. The buildings lie mostly in romantic ruins, a result of the dissolution of the monasteries during the 16th century, part of Henry VIII's struggle with the Catholic church over finances and his divorce request (the rejection of which he perceived as a calculated way to deny him a male

heir). Henry's break with Rome was made official in 1534 with the Act of Supremacy, which made him head of the Church of England. By 1540, no monasteries or abbeys remained; the king confiscated all their property, distributed the lands, and destroyed or gave away many buildings. Today the ruined abbeys at Fountains, Rievaulx, and Whitby are top attractions where you can learn about the religious and business worlds of the great monasteries, and the political machinations that destroyed them. They serve as vivid reminders of what life was like in the Middle Ages.

Castle Howard

20 *15 mi northeast of York.*

Fodor'sChoice
★

Standing serene among the Howardian Hills to the west of Malton, Castle Howard is an opulent stately home whose magnificent profile is punctuated by stone chimneys and a graceful central dome. Many people know it best as Brideshead, the home of the Flyte family in Evelyn Waugh's tale of aristocratic woe, *Brideshead Revisited,* because much of the 1981 TV series was filmed here. The house was designed for the Howard family (who still live here) by Sir John Vanbrugh (1664–1726). Amazingly, this was Vanbrugh's first building design; he went on to create Blenheim Palace, the Versailles of England.

The audacity of the great baroque house is startling, proclaiming the wealth and importance of the Howards. This was the first private residence in Britain built with a stone dome. A magnificent central hallway spanned by a hand-painted (in the 20th century) ceiling dwarfs all visitors, and there is no shortage of grandeur: vast family portraits, delicate marble fireplaces, immense and fading tapestries, huge pieces of Victorian silver on polished tables, and a great many marble busts. Outside, the stunning neoclassical landscape of carefully arranged woods, lakes, bridges, and obelisks led Horace Walpole, the 18th-century connoisseur, to comment that a pheasant at Castle Howard lives better than most dukes elsewhere. The grounds sprawl for miles, and hidden away among its hills and lakes (there's even a fanciful playground for children) are the Temple of the Four Winds and the Mausoleum, whose magnificence caused Walpole to quip that all who view it would wish to be buried alive. Hourly tours (included in the admission price) fill you in on more background and history. ⊠ *Off A64 and B1257,*

Coneysthorpe ☎ *01653/648333* ⊕ *www.castlehoward.co.uk* 🖅 *£9.50, gardens only £6.50* ⊘ *House Mar.–Oct., daily 11–6, last admission 4. Grounds daily 10–6:30 or dusk, last admission 4:30.*

Rievaulx Abbey

★ **㉑** *30 mi north of York.*

The perfect marriage of architecture and countryside, Rievaulx (pronounced ree-*voh*) Abbey has a dramatic setting; its sweeping arches soar at the precise point where a forested hillside rushes down to the River Rye. A French Cistercian sect founded this abbey in 1132, and though its monks led a life of isolation and silence, they were active in the wool business. By the end of the 13th century the abbey was massively wealthy, with hundreds of lay workers and farmland filling the valley. The evocative ruins give a good indication of how vast the abbey once was. Tiny plaques indicate where the dormitories, kitchen, chapter house, and nave once stood. Medieval mosaic tiling can still be seen here and there, and part of the symmetrical cloisters remain. The Chapter House retains the original shrine of the first abbot, William, by the entrance. By the time of Henry VIII the abbey had shrunk dramatically; only 20 or so monks lived here when the king's soldiers arrived to destroy the building in 1538. After that, the earl of Rutland owned Rievaulx, and he destroyed what was left to the best of his ability. The abbey is a 1½-hour walk northwest from Helmsley by signposted footpath, or 2 mi by vehicle. ⊠ *Off B1257* ☎ *01439/798228* ⊕ *www. english-heritage.org.uk* 🖅 *£4.20* ⊘ *Apr.–Sept., daily 10–6; Oct., daily 10–5; Nov.–Mar., Thurs.–Mon. 10–4.*

DURHAM & VICINITY

Durham, the first major town in the Northeast on the main road up from London, is by far the area's most interesting historic city. Here you get closer to the Scottish border region. Fittingly, Durham Cathedral, the greatest ecclesiastical structure of the region, has memorably been described as "half church of God, half castle 'gainst the Scot." For almost 800 years, this great cathedral was the seat of bishops who raised their own armies and ruled the turbulent northern diocese as prince–bishops with quasi-royal authority.

10

Durham

250 mi north of London, 75 mi north of York, 15 mi south of Newcastle.

The great medieval city of Durham, seat of County Durham, stands on a rocky spur, making it among the most dramatically sited cities in Britain. Despite the military advantages of its location, Durham was founded surprisingly late, probably in about the year 1000, growing up around a small Saxon church erected to house the remains of St. Cuthbert. It was the Normans, under William the Conqueror, who put Durham on the map, building the first defensive castle and beginning work on the cathedral. From here, Durham's prince–bishops, granted almost dicta-

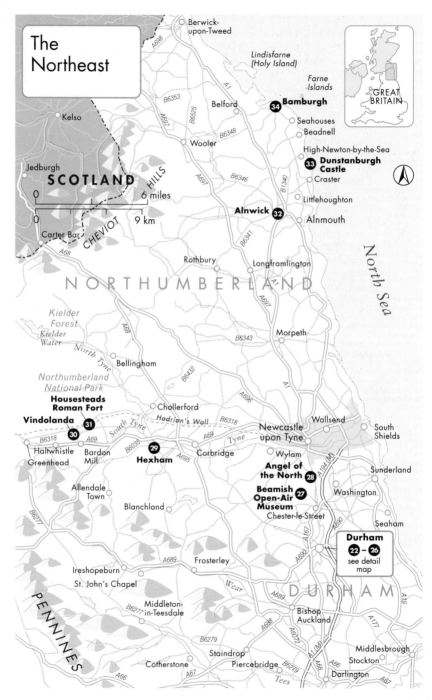

The Northeast

Berwick-upon-Tweed

A698

Lindisfarne (Holy Island)

Farne Islands

GREAT BRITAIN

B6353

Belford

Kelso

A697

B6525

B6348

Wooler

34 Bamburgh

Seahouses
Beadnell

High-Newton-by-the-Sea

Jedburgh

SCOTLAND

CHEVIOT HILLS

0   6 miles

0   9 km

A697

B6346

33 Dunstanburgh Castle

Craster

Littlehoughton

Alnwick 32

Alnmouth

Carter Bar

A68

B6341

Rothbury

Longframlington

North Sea

NORTHUMBERLAND

A1

A697

Kielder Forest
Kielder Water

A68

North Tyne

Bellingham

Morpeth

B6343

Northumberland National Park

B6432

A1

Housesteads Roman Fort

Chollerford

Hadrian's Wall

B6318

A696

Wallsend

Newcastle upon Tyne

South Shields

Vindolanda

31

30

B6318   A69

South Tyne

B6035

29

A69

Tyne

Corbridge

Haltwhistle

Bardon Mill

Hexham

A695

Wylam

Greenhead

Angel of the North 28

Sunderland

Allendale Town

Beamish Open-Air Museum 27

Washington

Blanchland

Chester-le-Street

Seaham

B6277

Durham

22 – 26
see detail map

A167

A690

Ireshopeburn

A689

Frosterley

Wear

A690

DURHAM

A19

St. John's Chapel

Bishop Auckland

A177

PENNINES

Middleton-in-Teesdale

B6277

A688

A1(M)

A68   A66

Middlesbrough
Stockton

B6279

Staindrop

Piercebridge

B6279

Tees

Darlington

A67

Cotherstone

A66

A67

Frosterley

torial local powers by William in 1072, kept a tight rein on the county, coining their own money and maintaining their own laws and courts; not until 1836 were these rights finally restored to the English Crown.

Together, the cathedral and castle, a World Heritage Site, rise high on a wooded peninsula almost entirely encircled by the River Wear (rhymes with "beer"). For centuries these two ancient structures have dominated Durham—now a thriving university town, the Northeast's equivalent to Oxford or Cambridge—and the surrounding countryside. Durham is more than its cathedral and castle, however. It's a great place to explore, with steep, narrow streets overlooked by perilously angled medieval houses and 18th-century town houses. Between 10 and 4 on Monday through Saturday, cars are charged £2 (on top of parking charges) to enter the Palace Green area. Bus 40 links parking lots and the train and bus stations with the cathedral.

㉓ Durham Castle. For almost 800 years the castle was the home of successive prince–bishops; from here, they ruled large tracts of northern England and kept the Scots at bay. Facing the cathedral across Palace Green, the castle commands a strategic position above the River Wear. It has required many renovations and repairs through the ages because of less-than-stable foundations, but it remains an impressive pile. Henry VIII first curtailed the bishops' independence, although it wasn't until the 19th century that the prince–bishops finally had their powers annulled. They abandoned the castle, turning it over to University College, one of several colleges of the University of Durham (founded 1832), the oldest in England after Oxford and Cambridge. You can visit the castle on a 45-minute guided tour. ✉ *Palace Green* ☎ *0191/334–4106* ⊕ *www.durhamcastle.com* ✏ *£5* ⊙ *Guided tours mid-Mar.–Sept., Mon.–Sat. 10–12:30 and 2–4, Sun. 10–noon and 2–4; Oct.–mid-Mar., Mon., Wed., and weekends 2–4.*

㉒ Durham Cathedral. A Norman masterpiece in the heart of the city, the
Fodor'sChoice cathedral is an amazing vision of solidity and strength, a far cry from
★ the airy lightness of later, Gothic cathedrals. Construction began in about 1090, and the main body was finished in about 1150. Durham reveals the essence of an almost entirely Norman, or Romanesque, edifice: the round arches of the nave and the deep zigzag patterns carved into them typify the heavy, gaunt style of Norman building. The technology of Durham, however, was revolutionary. This was the first European cathedral to be given a stone, rather than a wooden, roof. When you consider the means of construction available to its builders—the stones that form the ribs of the roof had to be hoisted by hand and set on a wooden structure, which was then knocked away—the achievement seems staggering.

The origins of the cathedral go back to the 10th century. In 995 monks brought to this site the remains of St. Cuthbert, which had been removed from the monastery at Lindisfarne after a Viking raid in 875. Soon the wealth attracted by Cuthbert's shrine paid for the construction of a cathedral. The bishop's throne here was claimed to be the loftiest in medieval Christendom; the miter of the bishop is the only one to be encircled by

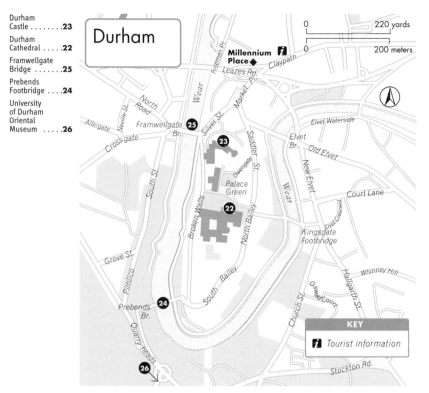

a coronet, and his coat of arms is the only one to be crossed with a sword as well as a crosier. **Cuthbert's shrine** lies surrounded by columns of local marble, with the saint's remains buried below a simple slab. An unobtrusive tomb at the west end of the cathedral, in the handsome, Moorish-influenced **Galilee Chapel,** is the final resting place of the **Venerable Bede,** an 8th-century Northumbrian monk whose contemporary account of the English people made him the country's first reliable historian. He died in Jarrow in 735, and his remains were placed here in 1020.

Upon entering the cathedral, note the 12th-century bronze **Sanctuary Knocker,** shaped like the head of a ferocious mythological beast, mounted on the massive northwestern door. By grasping the ring clenched in the animal's mouth, medieval felons could claim sanctuary; cathedral records show that 331 criminals sought this protection between 1464 and 1524. The knocker is, in fact, a reproduction. The original is kept for security reasons in the cathedral **Treasury,** along with ancient illuminated manuscripts, fragments of St. Cuthbert's oak coffin, and more church treasures well worth a look. You can view a film and an exhibit about building the cathedral, and in good weather you can climb the **tower.** There's also a restaurant and a bookstore. ⊠ *Palace Green* ☎ *0191/386–4266* ⊕ *www.durhamcathedral.co.uk* 💷 *£3.50 donation requested; Treasury £2.50, tower £2.50, guided tours £4* ☯ *Cathedral mid-June–early Sept.,* *daily 7:30 AM–8 PM; early Sept.–mid-June, Mon.–Sat. 7:30–6:15, Sun. 7:45–5. Treasury and tower Mon.–Sat. 10–4:30, Sun. 2–4:30. Choral evensong service Tues.–Sat. 5:15, Sun. 3:30. Guided tours mid-Apr.–Sept., Mon.–Sat. 11 and 2:30.*

25 Framwellgate Bridge. If you follow the far side of the Wear north from Prebends Footbridge, you can recross the river at this bridge, which dates from the 12th century. Many of the elegant town houses that line the narrow lanes back up to the cathedral now house departments of the University of Durham.

24 Prebends Footbridge. Delightful views are the reward of a short stroll along the River Wear's leafy banks, especially as you cross this footbridge, reached from the southern end of Palace Green.

26 University of Durham Oriental Museum. The museum displays fine art and craft work from all parts of Asia. The collection of Chinese ceramics is noted, and don't miss the nearby 18-acre Botanic Gardens. ⊠ *Elvet Hill, off South Rd. (A1050)* ☎ *0191/334–5694* ⊕ *www.dur.ac.uk/oriental.museum* ✍ *£1.50* ⊙ *Weekdays 10–5, weekends noon–5.*

Where to Stay & Eat

During college vacations (late March through April, July through September, and December), reasonably priced accommodations are available at the **University of Durham** (☎ 0191/334–2886 ☏ 0191/334–2892 ⊕ www.dur.ac.uk/conferences), in Durham Castle and in buildings throughout the city.

ff–fff ✕ **Bistro 21.** Relaxed and cottagey, Durham's most fashionable restaurant lies a couple of miles northwest from the center, in a superbly restored farmhouse. The eclectic and seasonal menu has such dishes as poached salmon and lamb with lemon polenta, as well as rich desserts. ⊠ *Aykley Heads* ☎ *0191/384–4354* ▭ *AE, DC, MC, V* ⊙ *Closed Sun.*

ff ✕▥ **Seven Stars Inn.** Warm oranges and tartans in the public areas enhance the coziness of this good-value early-18th-century coaching inn. The simple bedrooms are done in creamy yellows and reds and have modern pine furniture. At the restaurant (ff–fff), tuck into such dishes as rib-eye steak with black pudding and bacon or monkfish on herb mashed potatoes with saffron sauce, and finish with apple crumble or sticky toffee pudding. The inn is 2 mi south of the city and sits right on the road. ⊠ *High St. N, Shincliffe Village DH1 2NU* ☎ *0191/384–8454* ☏ *0191/386–0640* ⊕ *landmark-inns.co.uk* ⇋ *8 rooms* ⚴ *Restaurant, some pets allowed; no a/c* ▭ *MC, V* ⎆ *BP.*

fff ▥ **Swallow Three Tuns.** This cheery 16th-century inn, now part of a hotel chain, has echoes of its solid country past. Some parts retain the old oak beams and fireplaces, and a colorful modern stained-glass ceiling illumi-

> **ROW THEIR BOATS**
>
> The pretty River Wear winds through Durham, curving beneath the cathedral and castle. In mid-June each year the city hosts the prestigious Durham Regatta, Britain's oldest rowing event. Three hundred racing crews compete in events including races for single sculls and teams of eight.

10

nates other public rooms. The pastel modern bedrooms have a floral motif. Guests can use the indoor pool and health club at the nearby Swallow Royal County Hotel. Browns restaurant serves staples such as veal, steak, and salmon. ⊠ *New Elvet, DH1 3AQ* ☎ *0191/386–4326* 🖶 *0191/386–1406* ⊕ *www.swallow-hotels.com* 📨 *50 rooms* 🖧 *Restaurant, cable TV, piano bar, meeting rooms, free parking, some pets allowed; no a/c* 🖃 *AE, DC, MC, V* ⚍⦿⚍ *BP.*

★ **££** 🖼 **Georgian Town House.** Exactly as the name suggests, this friendly, family-run guesthouse, at the top of a cobbled street overlooking the cathedral and castle, makes the best of its Georgian exterior and details. Stylish modern furnishings, paintings, and stencils, evidence of the owner's hand, give all rooms a colorful individuality. Rooms at the back have the best view. ⊠ *10 Crossgate, DH1 4PS* ☎☎ *0191/386–8070* ⊕ *www. thegeorgiantownhouse.co.uk* 📨 *8 rooms* 🖧 *No-smoking rooms; no a/c* 🖃 *No credit cards* ⊙ *Closed last wk Dec.* ⚍⦿⚍ *BP.*

Nightlife & the Arts

Durham's nightlife is geared to the university set. The **Coach-and-Eight** (⊠ Bridge House, Framwellgate Bridge ☎ 0191/386–3284) can get noisy with students, but outdoor seating makes it appealing. The **Hogshead** (⊠ 58 Saddler St. ☎ 0191/386–9550) pub is a true student haunt.

Durham's **Gala Theatre** (⊠ Millennium Pl. ☎ 0191/332–4041) presents plays, concerts, and opera year-round.

Shopping

Bramwells Jewellers (⊠ 24 Elvet Bridge ☎ 0191/386–8006) has its own store specialty, a pendant copy of the gold-and-silver cross of St. Cuthbert. The food and bric-a-brac stalls in **Durham Indoor Market** (⊠ Market Pl. ☎ 0191/384–6153), a Victorian arcade, are open Monday through Saturday 9 to 5.

Beamish Open-Air Museum

㉗ *5 mi north of Durham.*

The buildings moved to this sprawling, more-than-300-acre museum village from throughout the region explore the way people in the Northeast lived and worked in the 1820s and early 1900s, the periods just before and at the peak of industrialization. A streetcar takes you around the site and to the reconstructed 1920s shopping street (called a "high street" in Britain), with a dentist's operating room, a pub, and a grocery store. On the early-20th-century farm are local Durham Shorthorn cattle and Teeswater sheep. Other attractions include a small manor house from the early 1900s, a railroad station, a coal mine, and a transportation collection; in summer a steam train makes a short run. The gift store specializes in period souvenirs and local crafts. ■ TIP➜ **Allow at least a half day if you come in summer; winter visits center on the reconstructed street, and admission prices are reduced.** ⊠ *Off A693, between Chester-le-Street and Stanley* ☎ *0191/370–4000* ⊕ *www.beamish.org.uk* 🖃 *£16 Apr.–Oct., £6 Nov.–Mar.* ⊙ *Apr.–Oct., daily 10–5; Nov.–mid-Dec. and Jan.–Mar., Tues.–Thurs. and weekends 10–4; last admission 3.*

Angel of the North

★ ㉘ *6 mi north of Beamish Open-Air Museum, 11 mi north of Durham.*

At the junction of A1(M) and A1 at Gateshead stands England's largest—and one of its most popular—sculptures, the powerful *Angel of the North.* Created by Antony Gormley in 1998, the rust-color steel sculpture is a sturdy, abstract human figure with airplane-like wings rather than arms. It stands 65 feet tall and has a horizontal wingspan of 175 feet. There's parking nearby, signposted on A167.

HADRIAN'S WALL COUNTRY

A formidable line of Roman fortifications, Hadrian's Wall was the Romans' most ambitious construction in Britain. The land through which the old wall wanders is wild and inhospitable in places, but that seems only to add to the powerful sense of history it evokes. Museums and information centers along the wall make it possible to learn as much as you want about the Roman era.

Hadrian's Wall

Fodor'sChoice
★
73 mi from Wallsend, north of Newcastle, to Bowness-on-Solway, beyond Carlisle.

Dedicated to the Roman god Terminus, the massive span of Hadrian's Wall once marked the northern frontier of the Roman Empire. Today the remnants of the wall extend 73 mi from Wallsend ("Wall's End," north of Newcastle) in the east, to Bowness-on-Solway, beyond Carlisle, in the west. The wall's completion in just four years is a good indication of Roman determination and efficiency.

At Emperor Hadrian's command, three legions of soldiers began building the wall in AD 122, in response to repeated invasions from Scotland. During the Roman era, the wall stood 15 feet high and 9 feet thick; behind it lay the vallum, a ditch about 20 feet wide and 10 feet deep. Spaced at 5-mi intervals along the wall were 3- to 5-acre forts (such as those at Housesteads), which could hold 500 to 1,000 soldiers. Every mile was marked by a thick-walled milecastle (a smaller fort that housed about 30 soldiers), and between each milecastle were two smaller turrets, each lodging four men who kept watch. For more than 250 years the Roman army used the wall to control travel and trade and to fortify Roman Britain against the barbarians to the north.

Today, the wall is a World Heritage Site, and excavating, interpreting, repairing, and generally managing the Roman remains is a Northumbrian growth industry. ■ TIP➜ **At Housesteads (the best-preserved fort) and Vindolanda, you get a good introduction to the life led by Roman soldiers on the frontier.** In summer most sites sponsor talks, Roman drama, and festivals; local tourist offices and the sites have details.

A special **Hadrian's Wall Bus** (☎ 01434/322002 ⊕ www.hadrians-wall. org) offers day passes (£6) for service between Wallsend and Carlisle,

10

stopping at Newcastle, Hexham, and the major Roman forts. The service runs daily from late May to mid-September and on Sunday throughout the year. Another bus runs daily from Wallsend to Bowness, and another from Hexham to Vindolanda (£2.45).

Sports & the Outdoors

BIKING **Hadrian's Cycleway** (⊕ www.cycleroutes.org/hadrianscycleway), between Tynemouth and Whitehaven, follows the river Tyne from the east coast until Newcastle, before chasing the entire length of Hadrian's Wall. It then continues west to the Irish Sea. Maps and guides are available at the Tourist Information Centre in Newcastle or online. **Eden's Lawn Cycle Hire** (⊠ Eden's Lawn Garage, Haltwhistle ☎ 01434/320443) rents mountain bikes for £12 per day. Bikes in the **Bike Shop** (⊠ 16–17 St. Mary's, Hexham ☎ 01434/601032) cost £15 per day.

HIKING **Hadrian's Wall Path** (☎ 01434/322022 ⊕ www.nationaltrail.co.uk/hadrianswall), a national trail completed in 2003, runs the entire 73-mi length of the wall. If you don't have time for it all, you can walk a section or take one of the less challenging circular routes, detailed in leaflets at tourist information offices along the way. One of the most scenic but also most rugged sections is the 12-mi western stretch between Sewingshields (east of Housesteads) and Greenhead.

> **FAST WALL FACTS**
>
> - No slaves were used to build the wall; it was built by skilled Roman masons with the labor of thousands of soldiers.
> - The wall was a multicultural military zone, with soldiers (and their families) coming from places such as Germany, Spain, and North Africa.
> - Only 5% of the Roman remains in the region around the wall have been excavated.

Hexham

🟢 *22 mi west of Newcastle, 31 mi northwest of Durham.*

The historic market town of Hexham makes a good base for visiting Hadrian's Wall. Just a few miles from the most significant remains, it retains enough of interest in its medieval streets to warrant a stop in its own right. First settled in the 7th century, around a Benedictine monastery, Hexham later became a byword for monastic learning, famous for its book painting, sculpture, and liturgical singing.

★ Ancient **Hexham Abbey**, a site of Christian worship for more than 1,300 years, forms one side of the town's main square. Inside, you can climb the 35 worn stone "night stairs," which once led from the main part of the abbey to the canon's dormitory, to overlook the whole ensemble. Most of the current building dates from the 12th and 13th centuries, and much of the stone, including that of the Anglo-Saxon crypt, was taken from the Roman fort at Corbridge. The interior is alive with paintings; note the portraits on the 16th-century wooden rood screen and the four panels from a 15th-century Dance of Death in the sanctuary. ⊠ *Beaumont St.* ☎ *01434/602031* ⊕ *www.hexhamabbey.org.uk* 🗺 *Re-*

quested donation £2 ☉ May–Sept., daily 9:30–7; Oct.–Apr., daily 9:30–5. Crypt daily at 11:30 and 3. No tours during services.

Where to Stay & Eat

£££–£££££ ✕⊞ **Langley Castle Hotel.** Rescued from decline by a professor from the United States in the mid-1980s, this 14th-century castle with turrets and battlements is thoroughly lavish. Bedrooms within the castle, resplendent with tapestries and four-poster beds, have deep window seats set in the 7-foot-thick walls; those in the Castle View annex are more modest. The baronial restaurant (£30 fixed-price menu) serves an excellent menu of traditional English dishes. The hotel is 6 mi west of Hexham. ✉ *Langley-on-Tyne NE47 5LU* ☎ *01434/688888* 🖷 *01434/684019* ⊕ *www.langleycastle.com* ⇖ *18 rooms* ♿ *Restaurant, in-room data ports, sauna, 2 bars, meeting rooms; no a/c* ⊟ *AE, DC, MC, V* ⦿ *BP.*

£ ⊞ **Dene House.** This peaceful, stone-built former farmhouse on 9 acres of lovely countryside has beamed ceilings and homey rooms with pine pieces and colorful quilts. Breakfasts, taken in the cozy kitchen, include homemade bread and preserves. The house is 4 mi south of Hexham; follow signs for Dye House. ✉ *B6303, Juniper, Hexham NE46 1SJ* 🖷🖷 *01434/673413* ⊕ *www.denehouse-hexham.co.uk* ⇖ *3 rooms, 1 with private bath* ♿ *Lounge; no a/c, no room phones, no room TVs, no smoking* ⊟ *AE, MC, V* ⦿ *BP.*

Vindolanda

③⓪ *4 mi west of Hexham, 41 mi northwest of Durham.*

The great garrison fort of Vindolanda holds the remains of eight successive Roman forts and civilian settlements, which have provided information about daily life in a military compound. Most of the visible remains date from the 2nd and 3rd centuries, and excavations are always under way. There's a reconstructed Roman temple, house, and shop to explore, and the museum displays rare artifacts such as writing tablets. A full-size reproduction of a section of the wall gives a sense of its massiveness. ✉ *Near Bardon Mill* ☎ *01434/344277* ⊕ *www.vindolanda.com* 🖷 *£4.95, joint ticket with Roman Army Museum £7.50* ☉ *Mid-Nov.–mid-Jan., Wed.–Sun. 10–4; mid-Feb.–Mar., Oct., and Nov., daily 10–5; Apr.–Sept., daily 10–6; call to confirm times in winter.*

In Northumberland National Park, **Once Brewed National Park Visitor Centre,** ½ mi north of Vindolanda, has informative displays about Hadrian's Wall and can advise about local walks. It's also a national tourist information center. ✉ *B6318* ☎ *01434/344396* ⊕ *www.northumberland-national-park.org.uk* 🖷 *Free* ☉ *Mid-Mar.–Nov., daily 9:30–5.*

Where to Stay & Eat

★ ££ ✕ **Milecastle Inn.** The snug traditional bar and restaurant of this remote and peaceful 17th-century pub make an excellent place to dine. Fine local meat goes into its famous pies; take your pick from rabbit, venison, wild boar, and duckling. The inn is on the north side of Haltwhistle on B6318. ✉ *Military Rd., Haltwhistle* ☎ *01434/321372* ⊟ *AE, MC, V.*

£–£££ ✕⊞ **Centre of Britain Hotel.** In a building dating in part to the 15th century, this hotel skillfully blends Scandinavian style with original features.

10

Room 3 on the 1st floor has a sauna and whirlpool bath. The restaurant's fixed-price menu (££££) includes Norwegian dishes such as sweet cured herring on rye bread as well as local pork with apricot and sage sauce. ⊠ *Main St., 3 mi east of Greenhead, Haltwhistle NE49 0BH* ☎*01434/322422* 🖷*01434/322655* ⊕*www.centre-of-britain.org.uk* ➘*9 rooms* ♨ *Restaurant, bar, laundry facilities, meeting rooms; no a/c* ⊟ *AE, DC, MC, V* ¶⊚ *BP.*

Housesteads Roman Fort

★ ❸❶ *3 mi east of Vindolanda, 38 mi northwest of Durham.*

If you have time to visit only one Hadrian's Wall site, Housesteads Roman Fort, Britain's most complete example of a Roman fort, is your best bet. It includes an interpretive center, views of long sections of the wall, the excavated 5-acre fort itself, and a museum. The steep, 10-minute walk up from the parking lot by B6318 to the site rewards the effort, especially for the sight of the wall disappearing over hills and crags into the distance. Excavations have revealed granaries, gateways, barracks, a hospital, and the commandant's house. ⊠ *B6318, 3 mi northeast of Bardon Mill* ☎ *01434/344363* ⊕ *www.english-heritage.org.uk* 🖻 *£3.80* ⊙ *Apr.–Sept., daily 10–6; Oct.–Mar., daily 10–4.*

> ### WORD OF MOUTH
>
> "Probably the most spectacular stretch of the wall is near Housesteads Roman Fort near Hexham. If you can, park at Steel Rigg and hike a bit down to the fort, then grab a bus back. There are many other Roman ruins in the vicinity. It's worth at least a day."
> –Pausanias

THE FAR NORTHEAST COAST

Before England gives way to Scotland, extraordinary medieval fortresses and monasteries line the final 40 mi of the Northeast coast. Northumbria was an enclave where the flame of learning was kept alive during Europe's Dark Ages. Castles abound, including the spectacularly sited Bamburgh and the desolate Dunstanburgh. The region also has some magnificent beaches that are far better for walking than swimming. The 3-mi walk from Seahouses to Bamburgh gives splendid views of the Farne Islands, and the 2-mi hike from Craster to Dunstanburgh Castle is unforgettable.

Alnwick

❸❷ *30 mi north of Newcastle, 46 mi north of Durham.*

Dominated by a grand castle, the little market town of Alnwick (pronounced *ann*-ick) is the best base from which to explore the dramatic coast and countryside of northern Northumberland. A weekly open-air market (every Saturday) has been held in Alnwick's cobbled **Market Place** for more than 800 years.

★ The grandly scaled **Alnwick Castle,** on the edge of the town center, is still the home of the dukes of Northumberland, whose family, the regal Percys, dominated the Northeast for centuries. Known as "the Windsor of the North," it has been remodeled several times since the first occupant, Henry de Percy, adapted the original Norman keep. Nowadays the castle is in favor as a set for films such as *Robin Hood: Prince of Thieves, Elizabeth,* and the first two Harry Potter movies (in the first, the castle grounds appear as the exterior of Hogwarts School in scenes such as the Quidditch match). In contrast with the cold, formidable exterior, the interior has all the opulence of the palatial home it still is. You see only 6 of the more than 150 rooms, but among the treasures on show are a galleried library, Meissen dinner services, niches with larger-than-life-size marble statues, and Venetian-mosaic floors. The castle's extensive gardens are the big news, however: they include a modern, 260-foot-long stepped water cascade as well as rose and ornamental gardens and a large tree house. ⊠ *Above junction of Narrowgate and Bailiffgate* ☎ *01665/510777* ⊕ *www.alnwickcastle.com, www.alnwickgarden. com* 🎫 *Castle and garden £10, castle only £8.50, garden only £5* ☻ *Castle Apr.–Oct., daily 11–5; last admission 4:15. Garden daily 10–dusk; last admission 45 mins before closing.*

Where to Stay & Eat

£££ ✕🖼 **White Swan Hotel.** The surprise feature of this comfortable, modernized, 18th-century coaching inn near the town square is that one lounge, the Olympic Suite, has been reconstructed with the paneling, stained glass, and mirrors of the *Olympic,* sister ship of the ill-fated *Titanic.* It's used as a function room, but guests can take a look. You can choose from the hearty dishes on the fixed-price menu (£20) in the Bondgate restaurant (dinner and Sunday lunch only); kipper pâté and steamed plum pudding help fill you up. ⊠ *Bondgate Within, NE66 1TD* ☎ *01665/602109* 🖨 *01665/510400* ⊕ *www.classiclodges.co.uk* ⇌ *57 rooms* ⌂ *Restaurant, bar, meeting rooms, some pets allowed; no a/c* ▭ *AE, MC, V* ⦿⦿ *BP.*

Dunstanburgh Castle

33 *7 mi north of Alnwick.*

Perched romantically on a cliff 100 feet above the shore, the ruins of Dunstanburgh Castle can be reached along a windy, mile-long coastal footpath from Craster. ■ **TIP➡ Fuel up for your walk with Craster's famous kippers (smoked and salted herring), sold around town.** Built in 1316 by the earl of Lancaster as a defense against the Scots (or perhaps as a symbol of Lancaster's deteriorating relationship with King Edward II), and later enlarged by John of Gaunt (the powerful duke of Lancaster who virtually ruled England in the late 14th century), Dunstanburgh is known to many from the popular paintings by 19th-century artist J. M. W. Turner. Several handsome sandy bays indent the coastline immediately to the north. ☎ *01665/576231* ⊕ *www.english-heritage.org.uk* 🎫 *£2.70* ☻ *Apr.–Sept., daily 10–6; Oct., daily 10–4; Nov.–Mar., Thurs.–Mon. 10–4.*

10

Bamburgh

③④ *14 mi north of Alnwick.*

Tiny Bamburgh has a splendid castle, and several beaches are a few minutes' walk away. Especially stunning when floodlighted at night, **Bamburgh Castle** dominates the coastal view for miles, set atop a great crag to the north of Seahouses and overlooking a magnificent sweep of sand backed by high dunes. It was once believed to be the legendary Joyous Garde of Sir Lancelot du Lac, one of King Arthur's fabled knights. A fortification of some kind has stood here since the 6th century, but the Norman castle was damaged during the 15th century. Much of the castle—the home of the Armstrong family since 1894—was restored during the 18th and 19th centuries, including the Victorian Great Hall, although the great Norman keep (central tower) remains intact. Exhibits include armor, porcelain, jade, furniture, and paintings. ✉ *3 mi north of Seahouses, Bamburgh* ☎ *01668/214515* ⊕ *www.bamburghcastle.com* 🎟 *£6* ⊘ *Mid-Mar.–Oct., daily 11–5; last admission 4:30.*

Where to Stay & Eat

££–£££ ✕🛏 **Lord Crewe Arms.** This cozy, stone-walled inn with oak beams is in the heart of the village, close to Bamburgh Castle. It's an ideal spot for lunch while you're touring the area. Pine furnishings decorate the simple guest rooms, but the food (££), especially seafood dishes, is excellent. ✉ *Front St., NE69 7BL* ☎ *01668/214243* 📠 *01668/214273* ⊕ *www.lordcrewe.co.uk* ⟿ *18 rooms* ⚘ *Restaurant, bar, some pets allowed; no a/c, no kids under 5* ☰ *MC, V* ⊘ *Closed Jan. and weekdays in Dec. and Feb.* ⏐◯⏐ *BP.*

YORKSHIRE & THE NORTHEAST ESSENTIALS

Transportation

BY AIR

Leeds Bradford Airport, 8 mi northwest of Leeds and about 15 mi east of Haworth, connects with domestic and European destinations. Manchester Airport, about 40 mi southwest of Leeds, is well served internationally.

Newcastle upon Tyne is the largest city in the Northeast. Newcastle Airport, 5 mi northwest of the city center, is well served for domestic destinations and major European cities. Metro trains connect the airport to the center of Newcastle, with service approximately every 8 minutes at peak times; cost is £2 one-way. The airport is about 15 minutes by car from the city center.

🛈 **Leeds Bradford International Airport** ✉ A658, Yeadon ☎ 0113/250-9696 ⊕ www. lbia.co.uk. **Manchester Airport** ✉ Near Junctions 5 and 6 of M56 ☎ 0161/489-3000 ⊕ www.manairport.co.uk. **Newcastle Airport** ✉ Off A696 ☎ 0870/122-1488 ⊕ www. newcastleairport.com.

BY BUS

National Express serves the regions from London's Victoria Coach Station. For Yorkshire, average travel times are 4¼ hours to Leeds and 6 hours to York. For the Northeast, average travel times are 6¾ hours to Durham and 7 hours to Newcastle. Connecting services to other parts of the region leave from Durham and Newcastle.

Traveline and local tourist information centers can help you discover each district's own bus company. Timetable booklets for the Yorkshire Dales and Moors are widely available, and special summer services in both national parks provide bus connections. There are local Metro buses from Leeds and Bradford into the more remote parts of the Yorkshire Dales. Other companies are Harrogate & District for services to Harrogate and Leeds, and Yorkshire Coastliner for Castle Howard and Leeds. In York, the main local bus operator is First.

CUTTING COSTS Many districts have Rover tickets; in York, the FirstWeek card (£10.50) gives a week's travel on all First bus services. With a West Yorkshire Day Rover you have a day's train and bus travel for £4.50; contact Metroline for details.

FARES & **First** ☎ 01904/883000 ⊕ www.firstgroup.com. **Harrogate & District** ☎ 01423/
SCHEDULES 566061. **Metroline** ☎ 0113/245-7676 ⊕ www.wymetro.com. **National Express** ☎ 0870/
580-8080 ⊕ www.nationalexpress.com. **Traveline** ☎ 0870/608-2608 ⊕ www.traveline.
org.uk. **Yorkshire Coastliner** ☎ 01653/692556 ⊕ www.yorkshirecoastliner.co.uk.

BY CAR

The M1, the principal route north from London, gets you to Yorkshire in about two hours, with longer travel times up into North Yorkshire. For York (193 mi), stay on M1 to Leeds (189 mi), then take A64. For the Yorkshire Dales, take M1 to Leeds, then A660 to A65 north and west to Skipton. The trans-Pennine motorway, the M62, between Liverpool and Hull, crosses the bottom of this region. North of Leeds, A1 is the major north–south road, although narrow stretches, roadwork, and heavy traffic make this slow going at times.

The most direct north–south route through the Northeast is A1, linking London and Edinburgh via Newcastle (274 mi from London; five to six hours). For Hexham and Hadrian's Wall, take the A69 west of Newcastle. For the coast, leave the A1 at Alnwick and follow the minor B1340 and B1339 for Craster and Bamburgh. A66 and A69 run east–west through the southern and middle parts of the region, respectively.

ROAD Some of the steep, narrow roads in the countryside off the main routes
CONDITIONS are difficult drives and can be perilous (or closed altogether) in winter. Main roads often closed by snowdrifts are the moorland A169 and the coast-and-moor A171. If you plan to drive in the dales or moors in winter, check the weather forecast in advance.

BY TRAIN

Great Northeastern Railways serves Yorkshire from London's King's Cross and Euston stations. Average travel times from King's Cross are 2½ hours to Leeds and 2 hours to York. There is local service from Leeds to Skipton, and from York to Harrogate. For the Northeast, average travel time to Durham and Newcastle is 3 hours. From Newcastle, there is local service north to Alnwick and to Corbridge and Hexham on the east–west line to Carlisle. All journeys take approximately ½ hour. For train travel information in the regions, call National Rail Enquiries.

CUTTING COSTS Two Regional Rover tickets for seven days' unlimited travel are available: North East (£73) and Coast and Peaks (£52.50). For the East Yorkshire area, which includes York, an unlimited travel pass valid for four days (within an eight-day period) costs £32.50.

FARES & SCHEDULES ⓘ **Great Northeastern Railways** ☎ 0845/722–5225 booking line, 44/19122–75959 from U.S. ⊕ www.gner.co.uk. **National Rail Enquiries** ☎ 0845/748–4950 ⊕ www.nationalrail.co.uk.

Contacts & Resources

DISCOUNTS & DEALS
The York Pass offers unlimited free entry to more than 30 attractions in or near the city (including Castle Howard), plus free transportation. You also get discounts on restaurants and theaters. Adult passes cost £19 (one day), £22.50 (two days), and £28.50 (three days), and can be purchased online, by phone, or at the York Tourist Information Centre.
ⓘ **York Pass** ☎ 0870/242–9988 or 01904/621756 ⊕ www.yorkpass.com.

EMERGENCIES
ⓘ **Ambulance, fire, police** ☎ 999. **York District Hospital** ⊠ Wiggington Rd., York ☎ 01904/631313. **University Hospital of North Durham** ⊠ North Rd., Durham ☎ 0191/333–2333.

INTERNET
Internet cafés are generally plentiful in cities in Yorkshire, but scarce in the countryside. Broadband is relatively rare in hotels (and virtually unheard of in guesthouses), and Wi-Fi is like gold dust. Beyond Newcastle and Durham Internet cafés are rare in the Northeast. Your best bet may be your hotel, or any good-size library. Most hotels in the region are not yet wired for broadband, much less Wi-Fi.
ⓘ Internet Cafés **Internet Exchange** ⊠ 13 Stonegate, York ☎ 01904/638808. **Reality X** ⊠ 1 Framwelgate Bridge, Durham ☎ 0191/384–5700.

NATIONAL PARKS
For information about visitor centers, walks, and guided tours, contact Yorkshire Dales National Park and North York Moors National Park.
ⓘ **Yorkshire Dales National Park** ☎ 01756/752745 ⊕ www.yorkshiredales.org.uk. **North York Moors National Park** ☎ 01439/770657 ⊕ www.moors.uk.net.

TOURS
BUS TOURS City Sightseeing runs frequent tours of York (£8.50), including stops at the minster, the Castle Museum, the Shambles, and Jorvik that allow you to get on and off the bus as you please.
ⓘ **City Sightseeing** ☎ 01904/655585 ⊕ www.citysightseeing.co.uk.

WALKING TOURS The York Association of Voluntary Guides arranges short walking tours around the city, which depart daily at 10:15; there are additional tours at 2:15 PM April through October, and at 6:45 PM July and August. The tours are free, but a gratuity is appreciated. Yorktour also schedules walks of York. Durham County Council Environment Department organizes a year-round program of guided walks, both in the town and country-side, which cost £2 to £3 per person.

🚩 **Durham County Council Environment Department** ☎ 0191/383-4144. **York Association of Voluntary Guides** ⊠ De Grey Rooms, Exhibition Sq. ☎ 01904/640780. **Yorktour** ☎ 01423/321240 ⊕ www.eddiebrowntours.com.

VISITOR INFORMATION

Local tourist information centers have varied opening hours, so call ahead. The telephone for the Haltwhistle Tourist Information Centre serves as the Hadrian's Wall Information Line.

🚩 **Hadrian's Wall Country** ⊕ www.hadrians-wall.org. **Northumbria Regional Tourist Board** ⊠ Stella House, Goldcrest Way, Newburn Riverside, Newcastle-upon-Tyne NE15 8NY ☎ 01271/336182 ⊕ www.visitnorthumbria.com. **Yorkshire Tourist Board** ⊠ 312 Tadcaster Rd., York YO2 1GS ☎ 01904/707961 ⊕ www.yorkshirevisitor.com.

Alnwick ⊠ 2 the Shambles, NE66 1TN ☎ 01665/510665 ⊕ www.alnwick.gov.uk. **Durham** ⊠ Millennium Pl., DH1 1WA ☎ 0191/384-3720 ⊕ www.durhamtourism.co.uk. **Haltwhistle** ⊠ Railway Station, NE49 9HN ☎ 01434/322002. **Harrogate** ⊠ Royal Baths, Crescent Rd., HG1 2RR ☎ 01423/537300 ⊕ www.harrogate.gov.uk. **Haworth** ⊠ 2-4 West La., BD22 8EF ☎ 01535/642329. **Hexham** ⊠ Wentworth Car Park, NE46 1QE ☎ 01434/652220 ⊕ www.hadrianswallcountry.org. **Skipton** ⊠ 35 Coach St., BD23 1LQ ☎ 01756/792809 ⊕ www.skiptononline.co.uk. **York** ⊠ De Grey Rooms, Exhibition Sq., YO1 2HB ☎ 01904/621756 ⊕ www.visityork.org ⊠ York Train Station ☎ 01904/621756.

10

Wales

WORD OF MOUTH

"For British gardens at their most splendid and beautiful, go to Bodnant Garden. . . . It takes more than one visit to appreciate the whole beauty, but in late May/early June, see the famous Laburnum Arch . . . with flowers like golden raindrops. [Nearby] is Conwy with impressive Conwy Castle."

—JC

"Okay, I'm biased seeing as I live there, but South Wales is so beautiful in the summer! . . . I'm from Swansea and we have the Gower coast . . . miles and miles of stunning coastline and beaches . . . Cardiff is near, of course, and so is Pembroke (with the castle where Henry VII was born—very historic). Tenby is a great little town, too."

—Lea_Lea

Updated by
Roger Thomas

11

WALES, KNOWN AS THE LAND OF SONG, is also a land of mountain and flood, where wild peaks challenge the sky and waterfalls thunder down steep, rocky chasms. It is a land of gray-stone castles, ruined abbeys, male-voice choirs, and a handful of cities. Pockets of the southeast and northeast were heavily industrialized in the 19th century, largely with mining and steelmaking, but long stretches of the coast and the mountainous interior remain areas of unmarred beauty. Small, self-contained Wales has three national parks (Snowdonia, including Snowdon, highest mountain in England and Wales; the Brecon Beacons; and the Pembrokeshire Coast) and five official Areas of Outstanding Natural Beauty (the Wye Valley, Gower Peninsula, Llŷn Peninsula, Isle of Anglesey, and Clwydian Range), as well as large tracts of unspoiled moor and mountain in mid-Wales, the least traveled part of the country. Riches of other sorts fill the country: medieval castles, seaside resorts, traditional market towns, the glorious Bodnant Garden and the National Botanic Garden, the stately houses of Powis and Plas Newydd, steam-powered trains running through Snowdonia and central Wales, and the cosmopolitan capital of Cardiff.

The 1941 film *How Green Was My Valley* depicted Wales as an industrial cauldron filled with coal mines. Although mining did take place in Wales, the picture was not accurate then and is certainly not accurate now, when the country has only one fully operational mine. One of the glories of visiting Wales is the drive through beautiful countryside from south to north without passing through any large towns. On such a drive, it's easy to believe that Wales has a population of about 2.9 million but is home to 5.5 million sheep. The country's 750 mi of coast consists mainly of sandy beaches, grassy headlands, cliffs, and estuaries.

The Welsh are a Celtic race. When, toward the middle of the AD first millennium, the Anglo-Saxons spread through Britain, they pushed the indigenous Celts farther back into their Welsh mountain strongholds. In fact, "Wales" comes from the Saxon word *Weallas,* which means "strangers," the name impertinently given by the new arrivals to the natives. The Welsh, however, have always called themselves *Y Cymry,* the companions. Not until the English king Edward I (1272–1307) waged a brutal campaign to conquer Wales was English supremacy established. Welsh hopes were finally crushed with the death in battle of Llywelyn ap Gruffudd, last native prince of Wales, in 1282.

Today Wales has achieved a measure of independence from its English neighbor. In a 1999 referendum, a narrow majority of the Welsh people voted for partial devolution for the country. Elections were held and the Welsh Assembly was born. Unlike the Scottish Parliament, the Welsh Assembly has no lawmaking powers, but it does have significant administrative responsibilities and considerable control over Welsh affairs. The Welsh Assembly is housed in a building on Cardiff Bay designed by the world-famous British architect Sir Richard Rogers.

The Welsh language continues to flourish. Although spoken by only a fifth of the population, it has a high profile within the country. Welsh-language schools are popular, there is a Welsh TV channel, and road signs are bilingual. Ironically, although in the 15th and 16th centuries the Tudor kings Henry VII and Henry VIII continued England's domination of the Welsh, principally by attempting to abolish the language, another Tudor monarch, Elizabeth I, ensured its survival by authorizing a Welsh translation of the Bible in 1588. Many older people say they owe their knowledge of Welsh to the Bible. You may see (and hear) Welsh throughout your travels, but everyone in Wales speaks English, too.

Exploring Wales

Wales has three main regions: south, mid, and north. The south is the most varied, for its boundaries include everything from Wales's capital city to unspoiled coastline, grassy mountains, and wooded valleys. It's a landscape of dramatic and sudden contrasts—within minutes of densely populated urban areas you can be among national parklands, moors and mountains. Mid-Wales is pure countryside, fringed on its western shores by the great arc of Cardigan Bay. Here you'll find Wales's rural heartland, an unhurried region of mountain lakes, quiet roads, hill sheep farms, and traditional market towns. North Wales is a mixture of high, rocky mountains, popular sandy beaches, and coastal hideaways. Although dominated by the rocky Snowdonia National Park, the north has a gentler, greener side along the border with England.

About the Restaurants

Today even many rural pubs are more interested in offering meals than serving pints of beer, so do consider these as a dining option. Don't overlook hotel restaurants in Wales; many, particularly those in country inns or hotels, are excellent.

About the Hotels

A 19th-century dictum, "I sleeps where I dines," still holds true in Wales, where good hotels and good restaurants often go together. Castles, country mansions, and even small railway stations are being transformed into interesting hotels and restaurants. Cozy traditional inns with low, beamed ceilings, wood paneling, and fireplaces remain Wales's pride, but they, as well as farmhouse accommodations, tend to be off the beaten track. Cardiff and Swansea have some large chain hotels, and, for luxury, Wales has a good choice of country-house hotels. An added attraction is that prices are generally lower than they are for equivalent properties in the Cotswolds, Scotland, or southeast England. A service charge may be added to the room cost; ask if it's included.

	WHAT IT COSTS In pounds sterling				
	£££££	**££££**	**£££**	**££**	**£**
RESTAURANTS	over £22	£18–£22	£13–£17	£7–£12	under £7
HOTELS	over £160	£120–£160	£90–£119	£60–£89	under £60

Restaurant prices are for a main course at dinner. Hotel prices are for two people in a standard double room in high season, including V.A.T., with no meals or, if indicated, CP (with continental breakfast), BP (Breakfast Plan, with full breakfast), or MAP (Modified American Plan, with breakfast and dinner).

TOP REASONS TO GO

Castles. Wales is the "Land of Castles." With more than 400 historic sites, it has one of the highest concentrations of castles in Europe. They range from evocative ruins of the native Welsh princes, such as Criccieth Castle, through the fairy-tale Victorian extravaganza of Castell Coch to the huge, mighty fortresses of Caernarfon and Harlech.

Cardiff old and new. The capital of Wales is young and vibrant. Compare the stately architecture of Cardiff's neoclassical Civic Centre with the futuristic form of Wales Millennium Centre, the new arts complex on lively Cardiff Bay.

Coast and mountain walks. Hike along the coast at St. David's, one of the most magical sections of the long-distance Pembrokeshire Coast Path. Or take a hike to the top of Pen-y-Fan, the highest peak in the grassy Brecon Beacons National Park.

A ride on the rails. Wales has 13 mostly narrow-gauge railways that transport you at the more leisurely pace of a bygone era along scenic routes throughout the country. The rack-and-pinion Snowdon Mountain Railway takes you to the summit of the highest mountain in England and Wales.

Pump the pedals. Brecon is great for biking. From this attractive town, country roads lead into the national park; mountain bikers can climb grassy trails and tracks up into the hills.

Timing

The weather in Wales, as in the rest of Britain, is a lottery. It can be warm in spring and cool in summer; come prepared for rain or shine. Generally speaking, southwest Wales enjoys a milder climate than elsewhere in Britain, thanks to the moderating effects of the sea. Spring and autumn can be surprisingly dry and sunny (spring may arrive very early in Pembrokeshire, in the southwest). Book ahead for major festivals such as the literary Hay Festival, Brecon Jazz, Abergavenny Food Festival, and Llangollen's International Musical Eisteddfod.

NORTH WALES
IN THE REALM OF SNOWDONIA

Wales masses all its savage splendor and fierce beauty in the north. Dominating the area is Snowdon, at 3,560 feet, the highest peak in England and Wales. It is impossible to describe the magnificence of the view from the mountain on a clear day: to the northwest the Menai Strait, Anglesey, and beyond to the Irish Sea; to the south the mountains of Merionethshire, Harlech Castle, and the Cadair Idris mountain range; and all around towering masses of wild and barren rock. If you ascend the peak by the Snowdon Mountain Railway from Llanberis, telephone from the terminus to ascertain whether Snowdon is free from mist. You lose much when clouds encircle the monster's brow, as often happens.

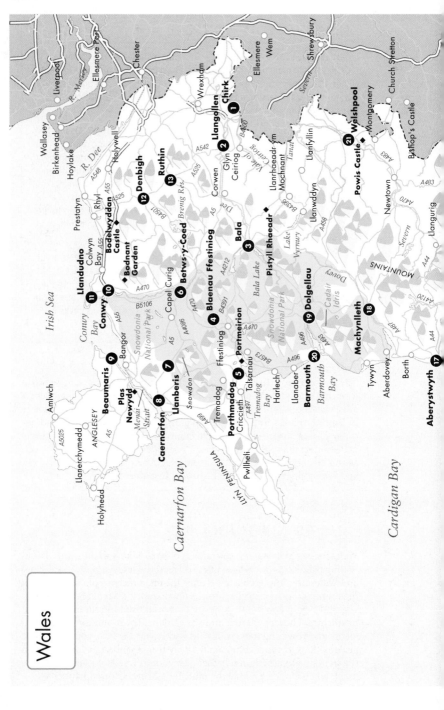

Wales

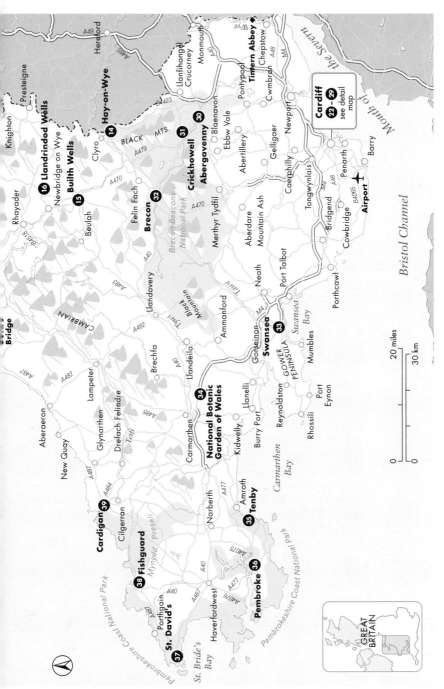

Hereford

A49

Presteigne

Knighton

14 Hay-on-Wye

16 Llandrindod Wells

Newbridge on Wye

15 Builth Wells

Clyro

BLACK MTS.

A479

31 Crickhowell

30 Abergavenny

Llanfihangel Crucorney

Monmouth

Tintern Abbey Wye

Chepstow

A48

M4

Mouth of the Severn

Cardiff **22** – **29** see detail map

Rhayader

Beulah

A518

Felin Fach

A470

32 Brecon

Brecon Beacons National Park

Blaenavon

Ebbw Vale

Aberillery

Gelligaer

Pontypool

Cwmbran

Newport

Barry

Penarth

Airport B4265

Bristol Channel

CAMBRIAN

A482

A483

Llandovery

Black Mountain

Merthyr Tydfil

Aberdare

Mountain Ash

Caerphilly

Tongwynlais

Bridgend

Cowbridge

M4

A48

Aberaeron

New Quay

A487

Lampeter

Glynarthen

Drefach Felindre

Teifi

A485

Brechfa

A40

Llandeilo

Ammanford

Neath

Port Talbot

Porthcawl

Swansea Bay

Gorseinon

33 Swansea

GOWER PENINSULA

Mumbles Bay

Reynoldston

Port Eynon

Rhossili

Cardigan **39**

Cilgerran

Fishguard **38**

Mynydd preseli

Porthgain

St. David's

37

St. Bride's Bay

Haverfordwest

A40

A487

34 National Botanic Garden of Wales

Carmarthen

Kidwelly

Llanelli

Burry Port

Carmarthen Bay

Narberth

Amroth **Tenby**

35

36 Pembroke A4075

Pembrokeshire Coast National Park

20 miles

30 km

0

GREAT BRITAIN

The peak gives its name to **Snowdonia National Park,** which extends southward all the way to Machynlleth in mid-Wales. The park consists of 840 square mi of rocky mountains, valleys clothed in oak woods, moorlands, lakes, and rivers, all guaranteeing natural beauty, and, to a lesser extent, solitude. As in other British national parks, much of the land is privately owned, so inside the park are towns, villages, and farms. The park has become a popular climbing center, and some fear that Snowdon itself is becoming worn away by the boots of too many walkers.

Along the sandy, north-facing coast, a string of seaside resorts has attracted people for well over a century. Llandudno, the dignified "Queen of the North Wales coast," was built in Victorian times as a seaside watering hole. Nearby Conwy, with its medieval castle and town walls, also deserves a look. If you prefer away-from-it-all seashore, there are two official Areas of Outstanding Beauty: the Isle of Anglesey (connected by bridge to mainland Wales), and the Llŷn Peninsula, dotted with quieter small resorts and coastal villages. Portmeirion, a mock-Italianate village, is a quite different kind of escape.

Chirk & the Ceiriog Valley

❶ *22 mi southwest of Chester, 60 mi southwest of Manchester.*

Chirk, poised on the border between England and Wales, is a handy gateway to the Ceiriog Valley, a narrowing vale that penetrates the silent, green foothills of the lofty Berwyn Mountains. The impressive medieval fortress of **Chirk Castle,** finished in its original form in 1310, has evolved into a grand home (albeit one with a medieval dungeon), complete with an 18th-century servants hall and interiors furnished in 16th- to 19th-century styles. Surrounding the castle are beautiful formal gardens and parkland. ⊠ *Off B4500* ☎ *01691/777701* ⊕ *www.nationaltrust.org. uk* ☞ *£7, garden only £4.50* ☉ *Castle mid-Mar.–June, Wed.–Sun. noon–5; July and Aug., Tues.–Sun. noon–5; Sept. and Oct., Wed.–Sun. noon–4. Garden mid-Mar.–June, Wed.–Sun. 10–6; July and Aug., Tues.–Sun. 10–6; Sept. and Oct., Wed.–Sun. 10–4.*

West of Chirk is the **Vale of Ceiriog,** nicknamed Little Switzerland. Take B4500 west 6 mi through the lovely valley to the village of Glyn Ceiriog, at the foothills of the remote Berwyn Mountains. The area attracts pony trekkers, walkers, and anglers.

Where to Stay & Eat

££–£££ ✕🏨 **Golden Pheasant.** Antiques and Victorian-style fabrics furnish this well-kept 18th-century hotel east of the village of Glyn Ceiriog. You can have a drink in the bar with its fireplace, slate floor, and beamed ceiling, or relax in deep-cushion comfort in the lounge, which overlooks the countryside. There's a three-course, fixed-price menu in the restaurant (£££££), as well as a bar menu. Specialties include Ceiriog trout and game pie. ⊠ *Off B4500, near Chirk, Glyn Ceiriog LL20 7BB* ☎ *01691/718281* ⊕ *www.goldenpheasanthotel.co.uk* 🖷 *01691/718479* ➳ *19 rooms* ⚴ *Restaurant, bar, lounge, some pets allowed (fee), no-smoking rooms; no a/c* ▭ *DC, MC, V* ⍾❶ *BP.*

£ ⊞ **Bron Heulog.** Carefully restored in period style as a guesthouse, this former home of a Victorian, liberal politician was built in 1861 and stands in 2 acres of gardens. Fireplaces, high ceilings, and an oak staircase are original elements of the large stone house. Rooms have showers. ⊠ *Waterfall Rd., off B4396, Llanrhaeadr ym Mochnant SY10 0JX* ☎ *01691/780521* ⊕ *www.kraines.enta.net* ➬ *4 rooms* ⌂ *No a/c, no room phones, no smoking* ☴ *MC, V* ⓧ *BP.*

EN ROUTE

The peat-brown water of **Pistyll Rhaeadr,** the highest waterfall in Wales, thunders down a 290-foot double cascade. To get here, take B4500 southwest from Glyn Ceiriog, and then its unnumbered continuation, to reach Llanrhaeadr ym Mochnant, in the peaceful Tanat Valley. Here, in 1588, the Bible was translated into Welsh, thus ensuring the survival of the language. Turn northwest and go 4 mi up the road to the waterfall.

Llangollen

➋ *5 mi northwest of Chirk, 23 mi southwest of Chester.*

Llangollen's setting in a deep valley carved by the River Dee gives it a typically Welsh appearance. The bridge over the Dee, a 14th-century stone structure, is named in a traditional Welsh folk song as one of the "Seven Wonders of Wales." In July the popular International Musical Eisteddfod brings crowds to town. For a particularly scenic drive in this area, head for the Horseshoe Pass.

Plas Newydd (not to be confused with the grand estate on the Isle of Anglesey with the same name) was the home from 1778 to 1828 of Lady Eleanor Butler and Sarah Ponsonby, the eccentric Ladies of Llangollen, who set up a then-scandalous single-sex household, collected curios and magnificent wood carvings, and made it into a tourist attraction even during their lifetimes. The terraced gardens have original features such as a font from an abbey. ⊠ *Hill St.* ☎ *01824/708223* 🖷 *01824/708258* ⊕ *www.llangollen.com* 🖃 *£3* ⊘ *Easter–Oct., daily 10–5.*

From the **canal wharf** (☎ 01978/860702) you can take a horse-drawn boat or a narrow boat (a slender barge) along the Llangollen Canal to ⟳ the largest navigable aqueduct in the world at Pontcysyllte. The **Llangollen Railway,** a restored standard-gauge steam line, runs for a few miles along the scenic Dee Valley. The terminus is near the town's bridge. ☎ *01978/860979, 01978/860951 recorded information* ⊕ *www.llangollen-railway. co.uk* 🖃 *£8 round-trip* ⊘ *Apr.–Oct., daily 10–5; Nov.–Mar., weekends, limited service.*

Where to Stay

£ ⊞ **Oakmere.** This sandstone Victorian residence with landscaped grounds, a few minutes' walk from Llangollen center, succeeds in preserving its period flavor. Special features include tile or polished pine floors, 19th-century furniture in walnut and mahogany, a conservatory, and spacious, high-ceiling bedrooms. There are excellent views of the valley and mountains. ⊠ *Regent St., LL20 8HS* ☎ *01978/861126* ⊕ *www. oakmere.llangollen.co.uk* ➬ *6 rooms* ⌂ *Tennis court, lounge; no a/c, no room phones, no smoking* ☴ *No credit cards* ⓧ *BP.*

All Aboard: Steam Railways

WALES IS THE BEST PLACE in Britain for narrow-gauge steam railways, many of which wind through extraordinary landscapes. The Great Little Trains of Wales (www. greatlittletrainsofwales.co.uk) operate in spring, summer, and fall through the mountains of Snowdonia and central Wales (there are also a few lines in South Wales). The ride is just part of the fun; a good deal of history is associated with the old trains and train stations, some of which served industry before they became attractions for visitors. The Ffestiniog Railway, which links two British Rail lines at the old slate town of Blaenau Ffestiniog and Porthmadog, climbs the mountainside in Snowdonia National Park around an ascending loop. Snowdonia also has Britain's only alpine-style steam-rack railway, the Snowdon Mountain Railway, where little sloping boiler engines on a rack-and-pinion track push their trains 3,000 feet up from Llanberis to the summit of Snowdon.

Nightlife & the Arts

★ The six-day **International Musical Eisteddfod** (01978/862001 www. international-eisteddfod.co.uk), held in early July, brings together amateur choirs and dancers—more than 12,000 participants in all—from all corners of the globe for a large, colorful folk-arts festival. The tradition of the *eisteddfod*, held throughout Wales, goes back to the 12th century. Originally gatherings of bards, the *eisteddfodau* of today are more like competitions or festivals.

Sports & the Outdoors

There are easy walks along the banks of the River Dee or along part of the **Offa's Dyke Path** (www.offasdyke.demon.co.uk), which passes through hills, river valleys, and lowlands. This 177-mi-long National Trail follows the line of an ancient earthen wall, still surviving in parts, which was built along the border with England in the 8th century by King Offa of Mercia to keep out Welsh raiders.

Bala

❸ *18 mi southwest of Llangollen.*

↺ The staunchly Welsh town of Bala makes a good base for exploring the eastern and southern sections of Snowdonia National Park as well as the gentler landscapes of borderland Wales. It stands at the head of Llŷn Tegid (Bala Lake), at 4 mi long the largest natural lake in Wales. This is a fine place for kayaking and windsurfing. The scenic, narrow-gauge **Bala Lake Railway** (01678/540666 01678/540535 www.bala-lake-railway.co.uk), one of the Great Little Trains of Wales, runs along the lake's southern shore. The station in Llanuwchllyn has parking.

★ To experience Wales at its wildest, you can drive over **Bwlch y Groes** (Pass of the Cross), the highest road in Wales, whose sweeping panoramas are breathtaking. To get here, take the narrow road south from Bala through Cwm Hirnant and over the mountain to Lake Vyrnwy. Turn right at the lake and drive for a mile on B4393 before heading west on the mountain road.

Where to Stay & Eat

★ ✕🄳 **Lake Vyrnwy Hotel.** Awesome views of mountain-ringed Lake Vyrnwy
££££–£££££ are just one asset of this country mansion within a 24,000-acre estate. For the ultimate sporting holiday, you can fish, bird-watch, play tennis, or take long hikes. Sailboats are also available. Leather chairs, log fires, and antiques add luxury, and the bedrooms are full of pampering touches. The sophisticated contemporary cuisine (£££££; three-course, fixed-price menu only) includes trout and duck from the reserve; partridge with saffron vegetables and a casserole of monkfish and scallops are typical dishes. ⊠ *Off B4393, Llanwddyn SY10 0LY* ☎ *01691/ 870692* 🖷 *01691/870259* ⊕ *www.lakevyrnwy.com* 🛏 *35 rooms* ♨ *Restaurant, tennis court, boating, fishing, bicycles, meeting rooms, some pets allowed (fee), kennel; no a/c* ⊟ *AE, DC, MC, V* ⍢ *BP.*

££ 🄳 **Cyfie Farm.** This refurbished, ivy-clad 17th-century farmhouse in a tranquil area close to Lake Vyrnwy has oak beams and log fireplaces. The luxurious suites, in converted barns and stables, possess all the sophistication of those in a top hotel. ⊠ *Off B4393, near Llanfyllin, Llanfihangel-yng-Ngwynfa SY22 5JE* ☎ *01691/648451* ⊕ *www. cyfiefarm.co.uk* 🛏 *3 suites* ♨ *In-room DVDs, lounge, no-smoking rooms; no a/c, no room phones* ⊟ *No credit cards* ⍢ *BP.*

Blaenau Ffestiniog

❹ *22 mi northwest of Bala, 10 mi southwest of Betws-y-Coed.*

Most of the world's roofing tiles used to come from this former "slate capital of North Wales," and commercial quarrying continues here. On the hillsides around the town is the evidence of decades of mining. The enterprises that attract attention nowadays, however, remain the old slate mines, which opened to the public in the 1970s. The Ffestiniog Railway, which begins in Porthmadog, ends in the town, near the caverns.

At the **Llechwedd Slate Caverns,** you can take two trips: a tram ride through floodlighted tunnels where Victorian working conditions have been re-created, and a ride on Britain's deepest underground railway to a mine where you can walk by an eerie underground lake. Either tour gives a good idea of the difficult working conditions the miners endured. On the surface of this popular site are a re-created Victorian village, old workshops, and slate-splitting demonstrations. ⊠ *Off A470* ☎ *01766/ 830306* ⊕ *www.llechwedd-slate-caverns.co.uk* 🎫 *Tour £8.95, grounds free* ☉ *Mar.–Sept., daily 10–5:15, Oct.–Feb., daily 10–4:15.*

Porthmadog

❺ *12 mi southwest of Blaenau Ffestiniog, 16 mi south of Caernarfon.*

The little seaside town of Porthmadog, built as a harbor to export slate from Blaenau Ffestiniog, stands at the gateway to Llŷn, an unspoiled peninsula of beaches, wildflowers, and country lanes. Its location between Snowdonia and Llŷn, as well as the good beaches nearby and the many attractions around town, makes it a lively place in summer. A mile-long embankment known as the Cob serves as the eastern approach to Porthmadog.

The oldest Welsh narrow-gauge line (founded in the early 19th century to carry slate), the **Ffestiniog Railway** runs from a quayside terminus along the Cob and continues through a wooded vale into the mountains. Its northern terminus is Blaenau Ffestiniog, where you can visit the slate caverns. ☎ 01766/516000 ⊕ www.festrail.co.uk ☞ £16.50 round-trip ⊙ Apr.–Nov., daily, plus limited winter service; call for exact times.

Fodor'sChoice   One not-to-be-missed site in North Wales is **Portmeirion,** a tiny fantasy-
★   Italianate village on a private peninsula surrounded by hills, which is said to be loosely modeled after Portofino. Begun in 1926 by architect Clough Williams-Ellis (1883–1978), the village has a hotel, restaurant, town hall, shops (selling books, gifts, and Portmeirion pottery), rental cottages, and woodland walks; beaches are nearby. Williams-Ellis called it his "light-opera approach to architecture," and the result is magical, though distinctly un-Welsh. Royalty, political figures, artists, and other celebrities have stayed here, and the cult 1967 TV series *The Prisoner* was filmed here. Portmeirion is a short trip east of Porthmadog over the Cob. ⊠ A487 ☎ 01766/770000 ⊕ www.portmeirion-village.com ☞ £6 ⊙ Daily 9:30–5:30.

North of Porthmadog is **Tremadog,** a handsome village that was the birthplace of T. E. Lawrence (1888–1935), better known as Lawrence of Arabia. In the Victorian seaside resort of **Criccieth,** a few miles west of Porthmadog on A497, a medieval castle with sweeping views crowns the headland. David Lloyd George, the prime minister of Britain from 1916 to 1922, grew up in Wales and lived here; a small museum in his childhood home honors him.

★   A wealth of legend, poetry, and song is conjured up by the 13th-century **Harlech Castle,** built by Edward I to help subdue the Welsh; it's now a UNESCO World Heritage Site. The castle, on a rocky promontory, dominates the little coastal town of Harlech, 12 mi south of Porthmadog. Its mighty ruins, visible for miles and commanding wide views, are as dramatic as its history (though you have to imagine the sea, which has since receded, edging the castle site). Harlech was occupied by Owain Glyndŵr from 1404 to 1408 during his revolt against the English. The inspiring music of Ceiriog's song *Men of Harlech* reflects the heroic defense of this castle in 1468 by Dafydd ap Eynion, who, summoned to surrender, replied: "I held a castle in France until every old woman in Wales heard of it, and I will hold a castle in Wales until every old woman in France hears of it!" Later in the 15th century the Lancastrians survived an eight-year siege during the Wars of the Roses here, and it was the last Welsh stronghold to fall in the 17th-century Civil War. ⊠ Off B4573 ☎ 01766/780552 ⊕ www.cadw.wales.gov.uk ☞ £3 ⊙ Apr., May, and Oct., daily 9:30–5; June–Sept., daily 9:30–6; Nov.–Mar., Mon.–Sat. 9:30–4, Sun. 11–4.

Where to Stay & Eat

★ **£££££** ✕🖼 **Hotel Maes-y-Neuadd.** Eight acres of gardens and parkland create a glorious setting for this luxurious country hotel in a manor house dating from the 14th century. Walls of local granite, oak-beam ceilings, and an inglenook fireplace add character; the updated bedrooms have different shapes and details but use prints and pastel fabrics. The restaurant's three-course, fixed-price menu (£££££) of Welsh, English, and French specialties uses herbs and vegetables grown in the hotel's own prolific walled garden to complement local meat, fish, and cheeses. The hotel is 3½ mi northeast of Harlech. ⊠ *Off B4573, Talsarnau LL47 6YA* ☎ *01766/780200 or 800/635–3602* 🖷 *01766/780211* ⊕ *www.neuadd. com* 🛏 *16 rooms* ⌂ *Restaurant, meeting room, some pets allowed (fee), no-smoking rooms; no a/c* ⊟ *AE, DC, MC, V* ⚍ *BP.*

> **CASTLE COUNTRY**
>
> More than 400 fortresses in Wales provide an inexhaustible supply of inspiration for any lover of history. These ancient strongholds, some of which were built by Edward I in the 13th century during his struggles with the rebellious Welsh, punctuate the landscape from south (Caerphilly) to north (Harlech, Beaumaris, Conwy), and include romantic ruins and well-preserved fortresses. To make the most of a visit, buy a guidebook or take a tour so that you can best appreciate the remains of a distant era. The great North Wales castles, such as Caernarfon, are particularly famous; four are World Heritage Sites.

★ **£££££** ✕🖼 **Hotel Portmeirion.** One of the most elegant and unusual places to stay in Wales is also supremely relaxing. Clough Williams-Ellis built his Italianate fantasy village around this waterside Victorian mansion with a library and curved, colonnaded dining room. The hotel bedrooms are comfortable and richly decorated. Accommodation is also available in cottage suites around the village and in chic, minimalistic suites in Castell Deudraeth, a castellated 19th-century house. The restaurant (£££££), which serves breakfast and has a fixed-price dinner menu, highlights local foods with a sophisticated contemporary style. ⊠ *A487, Portmeirion LL48 6ET* ☎ *01766/770000* 🖷 *01766/771331* ⊕ *www. portmeirion-village.com* 🛏 *14 rooms in main hotel, 26 rooms in cottages, 11 suites in Castell Deudraeth* ⌂ *Restaurant, cable TV, in-room VCRs, tennis court, pool, meeting rooms, some pets allowed (fee), no-smoking rooms; no a/c* ⊟ *AE, DC, MC, V* ⚍ *BP.*

★ **£££** ✕🖼 **Castle Cottage.** Close to Harlech's mighty castle, this friendly "restaurant with rooms" is a wonderful find. The emphasis is on the exceptional cuisine of chef-proprietor Glyn Roberts, who uses ingredients from salmon to Welsh lamb to create imaginative, beautifully presented contemporary dishes. There's a fixed-price dinner menu (£££££; no lunch). The hotel has three spacious modern rooms with four more in the annex, a former 16th-century pub. ⊠ *Near B4573, Harlech LL46 2YL* ☎ *01766/780479* 🖷 *01766/781251* ⊕ *www. castlecottageharlech.co.uk* 🛏 *7 rooms* ⌂ *Restaurant, in-room DVD/ VCR, no-smoking rooms; no a/c* ⊟ *MC, V* ⚍ *BP.*

£ ✕⊡ **Yr Hen Fecws.** The name of this welcoming stone restaurant and bed-and-breakfast near the quayside means "the old bakehouse." Bold modern colors blend with traditional furnishings at the bistro-style restaurant (££–£££; dinner only), which serves dishes such as fresh wild bass with ratatouille and pesto. Bedrooms have exposed slate walls, dark-wood furniture, and cheerful bed coverings. ⊠ *16 Lombard St., LL49 9AP* ☎ *01766/514625* ⊕ *www.henfecws.com* ⇨ *7 rooms* � *Restaurant; no a/c, no smoking* ▭ *MC, V* ¶○¶ *BP.*

Sports

Below Harlech Castle, on an expanse of land from which the sea has receded over the centuries, are the links of **Royal St. David's** (⊠ Harlech ☎ 01766/780361 ⊕ royalstdavids.co.uk), one of Wales's best golf courses. ■ **TIP**➔ **This stunning links course is popular, so book in advance.**

Betws-y-Coed

❻ *25 mi northeast of Porthmadog, 19 mi south of Llandudno.*

The Rivers Llugwy and Conwy meet at Betws-y-Coed, a popular resort village set among wooded hills with excellent views of Snowdonia. Busy in summer, the village has a good selection of hotels and crafts shops. The chief landmark here is the ornate iron Waterloo Bridge (1815) over the Conwy, designed by Thomas Telford (1757–1834), and the magnificent Bodnant Garden south of the town of Conwy makes a delightful excursion. On the western (A5) approach to Betws-y-Coed are the **Swallow Falls** (small admission charge), a famous North Wales beauty spot where the River Llugwy tumbles down through a wooded chasm.

Where to Stay & Eat

££–£££ ✕ **Ty Gwyn.** The restaurant in this 17th-century coaching inn overlooking Waterloo Bridge on the outskirts of Betws-y-Coed is a delight for lovers of antiques, old beams, and rustic uneven floors. Fresh local produce is used, and there are good-value bar meals and a full à la carte menu. Wild pheasant terrine and jumbo prawns sautéed with fresh garlic and chili butter are good choices on the contemporary menu. ⊠ *A5* ☎ *01690/710383* ▭ *MC, V.*

££££ ✕⊡ **Tan-y-Foel Country House.** Hidden away on a wooded hillside outside Betws-y-Coed, this quiet, contemporary hideaway has views over the Conwy Valley and Snowdonia mountain range. The vibrant hues of the stylish interior contrast with the dark stone exterior, and many bedrooms have four-posters. Chef-owner Janet Pitman, a Master Chef of Great Britain, prepares exquisite food (£££££; fixed-price menu) with French influences. ⊠ *Off A5, Capel Garmon LL26 0RE* ☎ *01690/710507* 🖷 *01690/710681* ⊕ *www.tyfhotel.co.uk* ⇨ *6 rooms* � *Restaurant, lounge; no a/c, no kids under 7, no smoking* ▭ *MC, V* ¶○¶ *BP.*

££ ⊡ **Pengwern Country House.** In Victorian times, this stone-and-slate country house on 2 acres of woodland was an artists' colony. Today the polished slate floors, beamed bedrooms, and traditional furnishings reflect the house's original charm. You can expect a warm welcome and good food (guests can arrange dinner here). The house is about a mile south of Betws-y-Coed. ⊠ *A5, Allt Dinas LL24 OHF* ⊕ *www. snowdoniaaccommodation.com* ☎🖶 *01690/710480* ⊸3 rooms ⚘ *Dining room, lounge; no a/c, no smoking* ☱ *MC, V* ⊠ *BP.*

£–££ ⌂ **Aberconwy House.** This Victorian B&B, with its garden, and flower-covered, terraced patio, has panoramic views over Betws-y-Coed and Snowdonia. Built in 1850, the house retains original features such as marble fireplaces, but has large, new windows to make the most of the setting. The modern bedrooms are a good value for the price, and the proprietors are extremely hospitable. ⊠ *Off A470, Lôn Muriau LL24 OHD* ☎ *01690/710202* 🖶 *01690/710800* ⊕ *www.aberconwy-house. co.uk* ⊸ *8 rooms* ⚘ *Lounge; no a/c, no smoking* ☱ *MC, V* ⊠ *BP.*

Llanberis

❼ *17 mi west of Betws-y-Coed, 7 mi southeast of Caernarfon.*

Llanberis, like Betws-y-Coed, is a focal point for people visiting Snowdonia National Park. The town stands beside twin lakes at the foot of the rocky **Llanberis Pass,** which cuts through the highest mountains in the park and is lined with slabs popular with rock climbers. There are hiking trails from the top of the pass, but the going can be rough for the inexperienced. Ask local advice before starting any ramble.

> **TRAINING FOR EVEREST**
>
> Lord Hunt, Sir Edmund Hillary and their team used the rock strewn slopes of Snowdonia to train for the first successful ascent of Mount Everest in 1953. The Pen-y-Gwryd Hotel, a famous climbing inn just beyond the summit of Llanberis Pass, has memorabilia from those times.

★ ☪ Llanberis's most famous attraction is the rack-and-pinion **Snowdon Mountain Railway,** with some of its track at a gradient of 1 in 5; the train terminates within 70 feet of the 3,560-foot-high summit. Snowdon, *Yr Wyddfa* in Welsh, is the highest peak south of Scotland and lies within the 840-square-mi national park. From May through September, weather permitting, trains go all the way to the summit; on a clear day, you can see as far as the Wicklow Mountains in Ireland, about 90 mi away. In 1998 the National Trust bought the mountain, ensuring its long-term protection. ☎ *0870/458–0033* ⊕ *www.snowdonrailway.co.uk* 🎫 *£21 maximum round-trip fare* ⊗ *Mar.–Oct., daily; schedule depends on customer demand.*

On Lake Padarn in the Padarn Country Park, the old Dinorwig slate quarry serves as the **National Slate Museum,** dedicated to what was an important industry here: Welsh slate roofed many a building. The museum has quarry workshops and slate-splitting demonstrations, as well as restored worker housing, all of which convey the development of the industry and the challenges faced by those who worked in it. The narrow-gauge Llanberis Lake Railway runs from here. ⊠ *A4086* ☎ *01286/ 870630* ⊕ *www.nmgw.ac.uk* 🎫 *Free* ⊗ *Easter–Oct., daily 10–5; Nov.–Easter, Sun.–Fri. 10–4.*

Caernarfon

❽ *7 mi northwest of Llanberis, 26 mi southwest of Llandudno.*

The town of Caernarfon, which has a historic pedigree as a walled medieval settlement, has nothing to rival the considerable splendor of its castle and is now overrun with tourist buses. Still, don't miss the garrison church of St. Mary, built into the city walls.

★ Standing like a warning finger, the grim, majestic mass of **Caernarfon Castle,** "that most magnificent badge of our subjection," wrote Thomas Pennant (1726–98), looms over the waters of the River Seiont. It's a UNESCO World Heritage Site. Numerous bloody encounters were witnessed by these sullen walls, erected by Edward I in 1283 as a symbol of his determination to subdue the Welsh. The castle's towers, unlike those of Edward I's other castles, are polygonal and patterned with bands of different-color stone. In 1284 the monarch thought of a scheme to steal the Welsh throne. Knowing that the Welsh chieftains would accept no foreign prince, Edward promised to designate a ruler who could speak no word of English. His long-suffering queen, Eleanor of Castile was despatched to this cold stone fortress where she gave birth to a son. Edward presented the infant to the assembled chieftains as their prince "who spoke no English, had been born on Welsh soil, and whose first words would be spoken in Welsh." The ruse worked, and on that day was created the first prince of Wales of English lineage. This tradition still holds: in July 1969, Elizabeth II presented Prince Charles to the people of Wales as their prince from this castle. In the Queen's Tower, a museum charts the history of the local regiment, the Royal Welsh Fusiliers. ✉ *Castle Hill* ☎ *01286/677617* ⊕ *www.caernarfon.com* 🏷 *£4.75* ⊙ *Apr., May, and Oct., daily 9:30–5; June–Sept., daily 9:30–6; Nov.–Mar., Mon.–Sat. 9:30–4, Sun. 11–4.*

Outside Caernarfon, the **Segontium Roman Museum** tells the story of the Roman presence in Wales; it includes material from one of Britain's most famous Roman forts. The extensive excavation site of the fort is here, too. ✉ *Beddgelert Rd. (A4085)* ☎ *01286/675625* ⊕ *www.segontium. org.uk/* 🏷 *Free* ⊙ *Tues.–Sun. 10–4:30. Museum Tues.–Sun. 12:30–4:30. Also open national holiday Mon. 10:30–4:30.*

You can take a workshop tour and short trip on a coal-fired steam locomotive at the **Welsh Highland Railway–Rheilffordd Eryri,** a narrowgauge line that operates on the route of an abandoned railway. The terminus is on the quay near Caernarfon Castle. ✉ *St. Helens Rd.* ☎ *01766/516000* ⊕ *www.festrail.co.uk* 🏷 *£16.50 round-trip* ⊙ *Apr.–Oct., daily 10–4; Nov.–Mar., limited weekend service.*

Where to Stay

££ 🏠 **Meifod Country House.** Former home of the high sheriff of Caernarfon, this opulent Victorian house has polished tile floors, wood-burning fireplaces, and bedrooms with features such as Victorian claw-foot baths and chandeliers. The atmosphere is luxurious but unpretentious, and the food (guests only) is good. The house stands in lush grounds less than 2 mi south of Caernarfon, making it a convenient base for exploring Snowdonia. ⊠ *Off A487, Bontnewydd LL55 2TY* ☏ *01286/673351* 🖷 *01286/6713256* ⊕ *www.meifodcountryhouse.co.uk* ⭐ *5 rooms* ⚴ *Dining room; no a/c, no smoking* ▭ *MC, V* ⦿ *BP.*

The Outdoors

Caernarfon Airparc operates Pleasure Flights in light aircraft over Snowdon, Anglesey, and Caernarfon; flights are 10 to 30 minutes. "Hands-on" flying lessons are offered daily (one-hour lesson £138), and there's an aviation museum (£5.50). ⊠ *Dinas Dinlle Beach Rd.* ☏ *01286/830800* 🖃 *£29–£69 per seat* ☉ *Daily 9–5.*

Beaumaris

❾ *13 mi northeast of Caernarfon.*

Elegant Beaumaris is on the Isle of Anglesey, the largest island directly off the shore of Wales and England. It's linked to the mainland by the Britannia road and rail bridge and by Thomas Telford's remarkable chain suspension bridge, built in 1826 over the Menai Strait. Though its name means "beautiful marsh," Beaumaris has become a town of pretty cottages, Georgian row houses, and bright shops. The nearest main-line train station is in Bangor, about 6 mi away on the mainland; bus service operates between the station and Beaumaris. Ferries and catamarans to Ireland leave from Holyhead, on the island's western side.

The town dates from 1295, when Edward I commenced work on impressive **Beaumaris Castle,** the last and largest link in an "iron ring" of fortifications around North Wales built to contain the Welsh. Guarding the western approach to the Menai Strait, the unfinished castle (a World Heritage Site) is solid and symmetrical, with concentric lines of fortification, arrow slits, and a moat: a superb example of medieval defensive planning. ⊠ *Castle St.* ☏ *01248/810361* ⊕ *www.cadw.wales.gov.uk* 🖃 *£3* ☉ *Apr., May, and Oct., daily 9:30–5; June–Sept., daily 9:30–6; Nov.–Mar., Mon.–Sat. 9:30–4, Sun. 11–4.*

Opposite Beaumaris Castle is the **courthouse** (☏ *01248/811691*), built in 1614. A plaque depicts one view of the legal profession: two farmers pull a cow, one by the horns, one by the tail, while a lawyer sits in the middle milking. The **Museum of Childhood Memories** is an Aladdin's cave of music boxes, magic lanterns (early optical projectors), trains, cars, toy soldiers, rocking horses, and mechanical savings banks. ⊠ *1 Castle St.* ☏ *01248/712498* 🖃 *£4* ☉ *Easter–Oct., Mon.–Sat. 10:30–5; Sun. noon–5.*

On Castle Street, the **Tudor Rose,** a house dating from 1400, is an excellent example of Tudor timberwork. To learn about the grim life of a Victorian prisoner, head to the old **gaol,** built in 1829 by Joseph Hansom (1803–82), who was also the designer of the Hansom cab. ⊠ *Steeple La.* ☏ *01248/811691* 🖃 *£1.50* ☉ *Easter–Sept., daily 10:30–5.*

The 14th-century **Church of St. Mary and St. Nicholas,** opposite the gaol in Steeple Lane, houses the stone coffin of Princess Joan, daughter of King John (1167–1216) and wife of Welsh leader Llewelyn the Great.

OFF THE BEATEN PATH

PLAS NEWYDD – Some historians rate this mansion on the Isle of Anglesey the finest house in Wales. Remodeled in the 18th century by James Wyatt (1747–1813) for the marquesses of Anglesey (who still live here), it stands on the Menai Strait about 7 mi southwest of Beaumaris (don't confuse it with the Plas Newydd at Llangollen). The interior has some fine 18th-century Gothic Revival decorations. In 1936–40 the society artist Rex Whistler (1905–44) painted the mural in the dining room. A museum commemorates the Battle of Waterloo, where the first marquess, Wellington's cavalry commander, lost his leg. The woodland walk and garden are worth exploring, and you can ask about boat trips on the strait. The views of Snowdonia are magnificent. ⊠ *Off A4080, southwest of Britannia Bridge, Llanfairpwll* ☎ *01248/714795* ⊕ *www. nationaltrust.org.uk* ⌑ *House £6, garden only £4* ⊙ *House late Mar.–early Nov., Sat.–Wed. noon–5; last admission ½ hr before closing. Garden late Mar.–early Nov., Sat.–Wed. 11–5:30.*

Nightlife & the Arts

The **Beaumaris Festival** (☎ 01248/810415) takes place annually late May through early June. The whole town is used as a site for special concerts, dance performances, and plays.

Where to Stay & Eat

£££ ✕⌂ **Ye Olde Bull's Head.** Originally a coaching inn built in 1472, this place is small and filled with history, and rooms are comfortably modern if not large. Samuel Johnson and Charles Dickens both stayed here. Eat in the stylish brasserie or the excellent oak-beam dining room (£££££; reservations essential), dating from 1617. Contemporary specialties on the fixed-price dinner menu include warm salad of pigeon breast with hazelnut oil, and the local widgeon (wild duck); seafood dishes win praise, too. ⊠ *Castle St., LL58 8AP* ☎ *01248/810329* ☎ *01248/ 811294* ⊕ *www.bullsheadinn.co.uk* ⇲ *13 rooms* ⚑ *Restaurant, bar; no a/c* ⊟ *AE, MC, V* ❑ *BP.*

★ **££** ⌂ **Cleifiog.** This cozy gem of a Georgian house overlooks the Menai Strait just a short stroll from Beaumaris Castle. Its charms include contemporary comforts, wood-panel walls, limestone floors, and a magnificent staircase dating from 1680. ⊠ *Townsend, Beaumaris LL53 7DY* ☎ *01248/811507* ⊕ *www.cleifiogbandb.co.uk* ⇲ *3 rooms* ⚑ *Lounge, in-room DVD, in-room data ports; no a/c, no room phones, no smoking* ⊟ *MC, V* ❑ *BP.*

Conwy

★ ❿ *23 mi east of Beaumaris, 48 mi northwest of Chester.*

The still-authentic medieval town of Conwy grew up around its castle on the west bank of the River Conwy. A ring of ancient but well-preserved walls, built in the 13th century to protect the English merchants who lived here, enclose the old town and add to the strong sense of history. It's well worth strolling the streets and walking on top of sections of the wall, which has 21 towers. A walk on the walls rewards with impressive views across huddled rooftops to the castle on the estuary, with mountains in the distance.

ON THE MENU

Talented chefs making use of the country's bountiful resources have put Wales firmly on the culinary map. Welsh Black beef and succulent Welsh lamb are world-renowned, and the supply of fish and seafood (including mussels and oysters) from coasts and rivers is excellent. Organic products are available to restaurants and the public from specialized companies, farm shops, and farmers' markets. Tŷ Nant Welsh springwater graces restaurant tables worldwide, and wines, such as Cariad, have won medals at French wine festivals; there's even a Welsh whisky.

Cheese making has undergone a remarkable revival. You can try traditionally named cheeses such as Llanboidy and Caws Cenarth or an extra-mature cheddar called Black Bomber. Contemporary cuisine has the buzz, but traditional dishes are worth seeking out. Cawl, for example, is a nourishing broth of lamb and vegetables, and laverbread is a distinctive-tasting pureed seaweed that's usually fried with eggs and bacon. For information on quality Welsh food, check out the Web site Wales—the True Taste (⊕ www.walesthetruetaste.com).

Fodor'sChoice
★
Of all Edward I's fortresses, **Conwy Castle,** a mighty, many-turreted stronghold built between 1283 and 1287, preserves most convincingly the spirit of medieval times. Along with Conwy's town walls, the castle is a UNESCO World Heritage Site. The eight large round towers and tall curtain wall, set on a rocky promontory, provide sweeping views of the area and the town walls. Although the castle is roofless (and floorless in places), you can read the signs, take a tour, or buy a guidebook to help you visualize the Great Hall and other chambers. Narrow stairs lead into towers such as the Chapel Tower. Conwy Castle can be approached on foot by a dramatic suspension bridge completed in 1825; engineer Thomas Telford designed the bridge with turrets to blend in with the fortress's presence. ⊠ *Castle Sq.* ☎ *01492/592358* ⊕ *www.cadw.wales.gov.uk* 🖾 *£4.50; £7 joint ticket with Plas Mawr* ⊙ *Apr., May, and Oct., daily 9:30–5; June–Sept., daily 9:30–6; Nov.–Mar., Mon.–Sat. 9:30–4, Sun. 11–4.*

What is said to be the **smallest house in Britain** (⊠ Lower Gate St. ☎ 01492/593484) is furnished in mid-Victorian Welsh style. The house, which is 6 feet wide and 10 feet high, was reputedly last occupied in 1900 by a fisherman who was more than 6 feet tall.

Plas Mawr, a jewel in the heart of Conwy, is the best-preserved Elizabethan town house in Britain. Built in 1576 by Robert Wynn (who later became both a member of Parliament and sheriff of Caernarfonshire), this richly decorated house with its ornamental plasterwork gives a unique insight into the lives of the Tudor gentry and their servants. ⊠ *High St.* ☎ *01492/580167* ⊕ *www.cadw.wales.gov.uk* 🖾 *£4.90; £7 joint ticket with Conwy Castle* ⊙ *June–Aug., Tues.–Sun. 9:30–6; Sept., Tues.–Sun. 9:30–5; Oct., Tues.–Sun. 9:30–4.*

Built in the 14th century, **Aberconwy House** is the only surviving medieval merchant's house in Conwy. Each room in the restored building reflects different eras of its long history. ⊠ *Castle St.* ☎ *01492/592246* 🎫 *£3* ⊙ *Mid-Mar.–Oct., Wed.–Mon. 11–5.*

Fodor'sChoice ★ With a reputation as the finest garden in Wales, **Bodnant Garden** remains a pilgrimage spot for horticulturists from around the world. Laid out in 1875, the 87 acres are particularly famed for rhododendrons, camellias, and magnolias. ■ TIP→ **Visit in May to see the laburnum arch that forms a huge tunnel of golden blooms.** The mountains of Snowdonia form a magnificent backdrop to the Italianate terraces, rock and rose gardens, and pinetum. The gardens are about 5 mi south of Conwy. ⊠ *Off A470, Tal-y-Cafn* ☎ *01492/650460* ⊕ *www.nationaltrust.org.uk* 🎫 *£6* ⊙ *Mid-Mar.–Oct., daily 10–5.*

Where to Stay & Eat

££–£££ ✕ **Le Gallois.** Just off the coast road 4 mi west of Conwy, this small and unpretentious restaurant is a culinary oasis. The chef-proprietor offers a changing chalkboard menu using the best local produce. Dishes like juicy scallops with a beurre blanc, Conwy crab au gratin and local lamb cooked pink with a mint and Madeira sauce are the daily fare. ⊠ *Pant yr Afon, Penmaenmawr* ☎ *01492/623820* 🍴 *MC, V* ⊙ *No lunch* ⊙ *Closed Mon. and Tues.*

£££–££££ ✕🖭 **Castle Hotel.** Sitting snugly within Conwy's medieval walls, this former coaching inn has wooden beams, old fireplaces, and plenty of antiques. Illustrious former guests include William Wordsworth, Samuel Johnson, and Charlotte Brontë. The bedrooms are smallish but plushly luxurious, with elaborate modern bathrooms. Shakespeare's restaurant (£££–££££), decorated with Victorian paintings of scenes from the Bard's plays, serves excellent modern British cuisine, such as salmon on a creamy Conwy crab risotto. Don't miss the local mussels if they're on the menu. A bar menu is also available. ⊠ *High St., LL32 8DB* ☎ *01492/582800* 🖨 *01492/582300* ⊕ *www.castlewales.co.uk* 🛏 *28 rooms* △ *Restaurant, bar, lounge, meeting rooms, some pets allowed (fee), no-smoking rooms; no a/c* 🍴 *AE, MC, V* ⊙ *BP.*

£££–££££ ✕🖭 **Sychnant Pass House.** In a peaceful location on a wooded hillside above Conwy, this hotel has all the qualities of a country house hotel but without any unnecessary formality. The enthusiastic owners, Bre and Graham Carrington-Sykes, provide a genuine welcome and good food with a set-price dinner menu (£££££). There are spacious sitting rooms with big comfortable sofas and well furnished bedrooms, some with French windows opening out on to an attractive decked terrace. The leisure facilities are excellent. ⊠ *Sychnant Pass Rd., LL32 8BJ* ☎ *01492/596868* 🖨 *01492/585486* ⊕ *www.sychnant-pass-house.co.uk* 🛏 *10 rooms* △ *Restaurant, coffee shop, indoor pool, gym, hot tub, sauna, some pets allowed, no-smoking rooms; no a/c* 🍴 *MC, V* ⊙ *BP.*

Llandudno

⓫ *3 mi north of Conwy, 50 mi northwest of Chester.*

This appealingly old-fashioned North Wales seaside resort has a wealth of well-preserved Victorian architecture and an ornate amusement pier with entertainments, shops, and places to eat. Attractively painted hotels line the wide promenade (Llandudno has the largest choice of lodging in Wales). The shopping streets behind also look the part, thanks to their original canopied walkways. Llandudno has little in the way of garish arcades, preferring to stick to its faithful cable car that climbs to the summit of the Great Orme headland above the resort. There's also an aerial cable car to the top, as well as a large, dry ski slope (with an artificial surface you can ski on year-round) and toboggan run.

Llandudno was the summer home of the family of Dr. Liddell, the Oxford don and father of the immortal Alice, inspiration for Lewis Carroll's *Alice's Adventures in Wonderland.* The book's Walrus and the Carpenter may be based on two rocks on Llandudno's West Shore near the Liddell home, which Alice possibly described to Carroll. The Alice in Wonderland connection is explored in the **Alice in Wonderland Centre,** where Alice's adventures come to life in displays of the best-known scenes from the book. Alice merchandise is for sale, too. ⊠ *3–4 Trinity Sq.* ☎ *01492/860082* ⊕ *www.wonderland.co.uk* ☎ *£2.95* ☉ *Easter–Oct., daily 10–5; Nov.–Easter, Mon.–Sat. 10–5.*

The prehistoric **Great Orme Mines** are at the summit of the Great Orme (*orme,* a Norse word meaning "sea monster"), with its views of the coast and mountains of Snowdonia. Copper was first mined here in the Bronze Age, and you can tour the ancient underground workings. ⊠ *Great Orme* ☎ *01492/870447* ⊕ *www.greatormemines.info* ☎ *£5* ☉ *Feb.–Oct., daily 10–5.*

Where to Stay & Eat

★ **£££££** ✕⛺ **Bodysgallen Hall.** Antiques, comfortable chairs by cheery fires, pictures, and polished wood distinguish one of Wales's most luxurious country-house hotels. The part 17th-, part 18th-century building is set in walled gardens 2 mi out of town. Bedrooms in the house combine elegance and practicality; seekers of privacy may prefer the cottage suites scattered around the estate and parkland. The outstanding restaurant (*£££££;* three-course, fixed-price menu at dinner) uses local ingredients in creative ways, such as beef with a wild mushroom pancake or partridge with panfried foie gras. ⊠ *Off A470, LL30 1RS* ☎ *01492/584466* 🖷 *01492/582519* ⊕ *www.bodysgallen.com* ⇆ *19 rooms, 16 cottage suites* ⅗ *Restaurant, cable TV, in-room VCRs, in-room data ports, tennis court, indoor pool, gym, sauna, spa, croquet, meeting rooms, some pets allowed, no-smoking rooms; no a/c in some rooms, no kids under 8* ⊟ *MC, V* ⍾⍾ *BP.*

£££–£££££ ✕⛺ **St. Tudno Hotel.** From the outside, one of Britain's best small seaside hotels blends unobtrusively with its neighbors, but the interior contains opulently furnished guest rooms and public areas with plenty of print fabrics and chintz. The fine contemporary cuisine (*££££*) includes dishes such as braised fillet of halibut with vanilla and Pernod velouté and saddle of hare with spicy cabbage. ⊠ *Promenade, LL30 2LP* ☎ *01492/874411* 🖷 *01492/860407* ⊕ *www.st-tudno.co.uk* ⇆ *18 rooms* ⅗ *Restaurant, in-room VCRs, in-room data ports, indoor pool, bar, some pets allowed (fee), no-smoking rooms; no a/c in some rooms* ⊟ *AE, DC, MC, V* ⍾⍾ *BP.*

££ ⬚ **Bryn Derwen Hotel.** Many hoteliers at British seaside resorts have not upgraded their accommodations and food, but this immaculate Victorian hotel exemplifies how it should be done. Fresh flowers, plush period furnishings in the public areas, and soothing, warm-hued bedrooms show the owners' attention to detail. Bryn Derwen offers truly excellent value for the price. ⊠ *34 Abbey Rd., LL30 2EE* ⊕ *www.bryn-derwen-hotel.co.uk* 🖬🖬 *01492/876804* ➥ *9 rooms* ⚓ *Dining room, lounge; no a/c, no kids under 7, no smoking* ⊟ *MC, V* ⵙ *BP.*

EN ROUTE   Inland from Rhyl, **Bodelwyddan Castle,** between Abergele and St. Asaph, is the Welsh home of London's National Portrait Gallery. Gardens, including a maze, aviary, and woodland walks, surround the Victorian castle. Galleries display Regency and Victorian portraits by artists such as John Singer Sargent, Thomas Lawrence, Dante Gabriel Rossetti, and Edwin Landseer. There are also hands-on galleries of Victorian amusements and inventions. ⊠ *Off A55, Bodelwyddan* ☎ *01745/584060* ⊕ *www.bodelwyddan-castle.co.uk* ⊠ *£5, grounds only £3* ☉ *Apr.–Sept., daily 10:30–5; Oct.–Mar., Thurs. 9:30–5, weekends 10:30–4.*

Denbigh

⑫ *25 mi southeast of Llandudno.*

This market town (market day is Wednesday) was much admired by the great English literary figure and lexicographer Dr. Samuel Johnson (1709–84). A walk along the riverbank at Lawnt (a village just south of Denbigh), which he loved, brings you to a monumental urn placed in his honor. Not that it pleased him: "It looks like an intention to bury me alive," he thundered.

Denbigh Castle, begun in 1282 as one of Edward I's ring of castles built to control the Welsh, is known as "the hollow crown" because it is not much more than a shell—though an impressive one—set on high ground, dominating the town. H. M. Stanley (1841–1904), the intrepid 19th-century journalist and explorer who found Dr. Livingstone in Africa, was born in a cottage below the castle. ☎ *01745/813385* ⊕ *www.cadw.wales.gov.uk* ⊠ *£3* ☉ *Apr.–Sept., weekdays 10–5:30, weekends 9:30–5:30.*

Ruthin

⑬ *8 mi southeast of Denbigh, 23 mi west of Chester.*

Once a stronghold of Welsh hero Owain Glyndŵr (circa 1354–1416), Ruthin is a delightful market town with elegant shops, good inns, and a fascinating architectural mix of medieval, Tudor, and Georgian buildings. The town also hosts medieval-style banquets and has a crafts complex with displays of the artisans' creations. The 17th-century **Myddleton Arms** in the town square has seven Dutch-style dormer windows, known as the "eyes of Ruthin," set into its red-tiled roof. You can tour **Ruthin Gaol,** where from 1654 to 1916 thousands of prisoners were incarcerated, and learn about prison conditions over the centuries. ⊠ *Clwyd St.* ☎ *01824/708250* ⊕ *www.ruthingaol.co.uk* ⊠ *£3* ☉ *Apr.–Oct., daily 10–5; Nov.–Mar., Tues.–Sun. 10–5.*

11

Where to Stay

£ ▦ **Eyarth Old Railway Station.** This Victorian railway station 2 mi south of Ruthin has been converted into an outstanding B&B. The modern bedrooms are spacious, with large windows looking out over the Vale of Clwyd. ⊠ *Off A525, Llanfair Dyffryn Clwyd LL15 2EE* ☏ *01824/ 703643* 🖷 *01824/707464* ⊕ *www.eyarthstation.co.uk* 🛏 *6 rooms* ⚐ *Pool, bar; no a/c* ⊟ *MC, V* ⏍ *BP.*

MID-WALES
THE HISTORIC HEARTLAND

Traditional market towns and country villages, small seaside resorts, quiet roads, and rolling landscapes filled with sheep farms, forests, and lakes make up mid-Wales, the country's green and rural heart. Because this is Wales's quietest vacation region, lodgings are scattered thinly. Outside of one or two large centers, Aberystwyth and Llandrindod Wells, accommodations are mainly country inns, small hotels, and farmhouses. This area also has some splendid country-house hotels.

Although green is the predominant color here, the landscape differs around the region. The borderlands are gentle and undulating, rising to the west into high wild mountains. Farther north, around Dolgellau, mountainous scenery becomes even more pronounced in the southern section of the Snowdonia National Park. Mountains meet the sea along Cardigan Bay, a long coastline of headlands, peaceful sandy beaches, and beautiful estuaries that has long been a refuge from the crowd. In the 19th century, Tennyson, Darwin, Shelley, and Ruskin came to this area to work and relax; today, thousands more come to delight in the numerous antiquarian bookstores of Hay-on-Wye.

Hay-on-Wye

★ ⑭ *57 mi north of Cardiff, 25 mi north of Abergavenny.*

Bookshops and a mostly ruined castle dominate this town on the border of Wales and England. Hay is a lively place, especially on Sunday, when the rest of central Wales seems to be closed down. In 1961 Richard Booth established a small secondhand and antiquarian bookshop here. Other booksellers soon got in on the act, and bookshops now fill several houses, a movie theater, shops, and a pub. At last count, there were about 40 bookstores, all in a town of only 1,300 inhabitants. It's now the largest secondhand bookselling center in the world, and priceless 14th-century manuscripts rub spines with "job lots" selling for a few pounds. Hay also has antiques and crafts centers. Things buzz in early
★ summer during the 10-day **Hay Festival** (☏ 0870/990–1299 ⊕ www. hayfestival.com), a celebration of literature that attracts famous writers from all over the world.

NEED A BREAK?

After some hard browsing, take stop off at **The Granary** (⊠ Broad St. ☎ 01497/820790), a wood-beamed former grain store by the clock tower. The chalkboard menu lists soups, lamb and spinach curry, and cheese and garlic toasties (open, toasted sandwiches).

Where to Stay & Eat

£££££ ✕▣ **Llangoed Hall.** This magnificently renovated Jacobean mansion on the banks of the River Wye, 8 mi from Hay, is owned by Sir Bernard Ashley, the husband of the late Laura Ashley, the famous Welsh fabric designer. Antiques are everywhere in the secluded country-house hotel, along with beautiful fabrics and furnishings, open fireplaces, a sweeping carved staircase, and a paneled library dating back to 1632. Bernard Ashley's personal collection of paintings adorns the walls. You can savor main courses like seared local grouse on braised red cabbage with root vegetables and pancetta sauce on the fixed-price menu. ⊠ *Llyswen, LD3 0YPL* ☎ *01874/754525* 🖷 *01874/757545* ⊕ *www.llangoedhall. com* 🗫 *23 rooms* ⚒ *Restaurant, fishing, billiards, croquet, helipad, kennel, no-smoking rooms; no a/c, no kids under 8* ☲ *AE, MC, V* ❑ *BP.*

££–£££ ✕▣ **Old Black Lion.** A 17th-century coaching inn close to Hay's center is ideal for a lunch break while you're ransacking the bookshops, or for an overnight stay in one of its country-style rooms. The oak-beamed bar serves food, and the breakfasts are especially good. The restaurant's (££–££££) sophisticated cooking has an international flavor and emphasizes local meats and produce. ⊠ *Lion St., HR3 5AD* ☎ *01497/820841* 🖷 *01497/822960* ⊕ *www.oldblacklion.co.uk* 🗫 *10 rooms* ⚒ *Restaurant, bar, lounge, no-smoking rooms; no a/c, no kids under 5* ☲ *MC, V* ❑ *BP.*

Shopping

Boz Books (⊠ 13A Castle St. ☎ 01497/821277) specializes in 19th-century novels, including first editions of Dickens. A former movie theater houses the town's largest book outpost, the **Hay Cinema Bookshop** (⊠ Castle St. ☎ 01497/820071), which stocks 200,000 volumes on subjects from art to zoology at prices from 50 pence to £5, 000.

Builth Wells

⑮ *20 mi northwest of Hay-on-Wye, 60 mi north of Cardiff.*

Builth Wells, a farming town and former spa on the banks of the River Wye, hosts Wales's biggest rural gathering. The countryside around Builth and its neighbor, Llandrindod Wells, varies considerably. Some of the land is soft and rich, with green hills and lush valleys, but close by are the wildernesses of Mynydd Eppynt and the foothills of the Cambrian Mountains, the lofty "backbone of Wales."

★ The annual **Royal Welsh Agricultural Show** (☎ 01982/553683 ⊕ www. rwas.co.uk), held in late July, is not only Wales's prime gathering of farming folk but also a colorful countryside jamboree that attracts huge crowds.

Where to Stay & Eat

★ ✕▣ **Lake Country House & Spa.** This is the place to go for total Victorian country elegance. Its 50 acres of sloping lawns and rhododendrons

££££–£££££

also contain a trout-filled lake. Comfortable and quiet, the hotel has first-class service and excellent contemporary cuisine (££££; fixed-price dinner menu) such as salmon with char-grilled eggplant and spicy couscous. Period furniture and fine fabrics decorate the large bedrooms; some have four-poster beds. The hotel is in a peaceful former spa town about 8 mi southwest of Builth. ⊠ *Llangammarch Wells LD4 4BS* ☎ *01591/620202* 🖷 *01591/620457* ⊕ *www.lakecountryhouse.co.uk* 🛏 *18 rooms* 🍴 *Restaurant, 9-hole golf course, putting green, tennis court, fishing, billiards, indoor pool, gym, hot tub, sauna, massage, croquet, bar, no-smoking rooms; no a/c* 🖃 *AE, DC, MC, V* ⏐⊙⏐ *BP.*

Llandrindod Wells

⓯ *7 mi north of Builth Wells, 67 mi north of Cardiff.*

Also known as Llandod, the old spa town of Llandrindod Wells preserves its Victorian layout and look, with turrets, cupolas, loggias, and balustrades, and greenery everywhere. On a branch-line rail route and with good bus service, Llandrindod makes a useful base for exploring the region, and the town itself is easily explored on foot. Cross over to South Crescent, passing the Glen Usk Hotel with its wrought-iron balustrade and the Victorian bandstand in the gardens opposite, and you soon reach Middleton Street, another Victorian thoroughfare. From there, head to Rock Park and the path that leads to the Pump Room. This historic building is now an alternative health center but visitors can freely "take the waters" that the Victorians found so beneficial here. On the other side of town, the lake, with its boathouse, café, and gift shop, has wooded hills on one side and a broad common on the other.

> **PLAYING DRESS-UP**
>
> During Llandrindod Wells's **Victorian Festival** (☎ 01597/823441 ⊕ www.victorianfestival.co.uk), in late August, shop assistants, hotel staff, and anyone else who cares to join in wear period costume and enjoy "old-style" entertainment.

The **Radnorshire Museum,** in Memorial Gardens, presents the spa's development from Roman times and explains some Victorian "cures" in gruesome detail. ☎ *01597/824513* 🎟 *£1* ⊙ *Apr.–Sept., Tues.–Sat. 10–5, Sun. 1–5; Oct.–Mar., Tues.–Fri. 10–4, Sat. 10–1.*

Where to Stay

££ 🏠 **Guidfa House.** Friendly hosts Tony and Anne Millan run this stylish Georgian guesthouse with a welcoming log fire and bright, individually furnished bedrooms. Cordon Bleu–trained Anne prepares dinners (for guests only) from fresh local produce; the guinea fowl with apple brandy and mushroom sauce is delicious. All in all, this is an ideal base from which to explore the countryside. ⊠ *Crossgates, near Llandrindod Wells, LD1 6RF* ☎ *01597/851241* 🖷 *01597/851875* ⊕ *www.guidfa-house.co.uk* 🛏 *6 rooms* 🍴 *Dining room; no a/c, no room phones, no kids under 10* 🖃 *MC, V* ⏐⊙⏐ *BP.*

£–££ 🏠 **Brynhir Farm.** You get a warm welcome at this immaculate, cream-washed farmhouse tucked into the hills on a 200-acre sheep and cattle farm. Country-style furnishings enhance the rooms. ✉ *Chapel Rd., Howey LD1 5PB* ☎ *01597/822425* ⊕ *www.brynhir.farm.btinternet. co.uk* ➷ *5 rooms* ♿ *Dining room; no a/c, no room phones, no smoking* ☰ *MC, V* ◯ *BP.*

EN ROUTE

From Llandrindod, take A4081/A470 to Rhayader, a good pony-trekking center and gateway town for the **Elan Valley,** Wales's Lake District. This 7-mi chain of lakes, winding between gray-green hills, was created in the 1890s by a system of dams designed to supply water to Birmingham, 73 mi to the east. From the Elan Valley, you can follow the narrow Cwmystwyth mountain road west to **Devil's Bridge,** a famous (and popular) beauty spot where three bridges set one on top of the other span a chasm over the raging River Mynach, before continuing on to Aberystwyth. (You can also take the steam-operated Vale of Rheidol Railway to this site from Aberystwyth.)

Aberystwyth

⑰ *41 mi northwest of Llandrindod Wells via A44, 118 mi northwest of Cardiff.*

Aberystwyth makes the best of several worlds as a seaside resort (complete with promenade and amusement pier) and a long-established university town that is home to the impressive National Library of Wales. It also has a small harbor and is a major shopping center for mid-Wales. More than 5,000 students expand the full-time population of 12,000. The town, midway along Cardigan Bay, came to prominence as a Victorian watering hole thanks to a curving beach set beneath a prominent headland. Aberystwyth is a good gateway for exploring mid-Wales: few towns in Wales present such varied scenery within their immediate neighborhood, from the Devil's Bridge to the green Rheidol Valley.

The massive, neoclassical **National Library of Wales,** on a hill amid the buildings of the modern University of Wales, Aberystwyth, houses notable Welsh and other Celtic literary works among its more than 4.5 million printed volumes. This self-described national treasure house also has enormous archives of maps, photographs, films, and sound recordings. ■ **TIP→ Material doesn't circulate, but the public can do research; many people pursue genealogical history here (there's a family history center).** The gallery has art shows (works may be for sale, too), and exhibitions highlight Welsh and other subjects. Films and concerts are presented in the auditorium. ✉ *Off Penglais Rd.* ☎ *01970/632800* ⊕ *www. llgc.org.uk* ☲ *Free* ◷ *Weekdays 9:30–6, Sat. 9:30–5.*

The **Ceredigion Museum,** in a flamboyant 1905 Edwardian theater, has fine collections related to folk history. Highlights include a reconstructed mud-walled cottage from 1850, exhibits from the building's music-hall past, and items illustrating the region's seafaring, lead mining, and farming history. ✉ *Terrace Rd.* ☎ *01970/633088* ⊕ *museum.ceredigion. gov.uk* ☲ *Free* ◷ *Mon.–Sat. 10–5.*

The **castle,** at the southern end of the bay near the New Promenade, was built in 1277 and rebuilt in 1282 by Edward I. It was one of several

The Language of Cymru

WELSH, THE NATIVE LANGUAGE of Wales (Cymru, in Welsh), is revered in the country, but it was not legally recognized in Britain until the 1960s. Today Welsh schoolchildren under 14 are required to take classes to learn the language, and Welsh is surviving more successfully than its Celtic cousin, Breton, which is spoken in northwestern France. Welsh may look daunting to pronounce, but it is a phonetic language; pronunciation is fairly easy once the alphabet is learned. Remember that "dd" is sounded like "th" in they, "f" sounds like "v" in save, and "ff" is the equivalent of the English "f" in forest. The "ll" sound has no English equivalent; the closest match is the "cl" sound in "close."

Terms that crop up frequently in Welsh are *bach* or *fach* (small), *craig* or *graig* (rock), *cwm* (valley; pronounced "cum"), *dyffryn* (valley), *eglwys* (church), *glyn* (glen), *llyn* (lake), *mawr* or *fawr* (great, big), *mynydd* or *fynydd* (mountain, moorland), *pentre* (village, homestead), *plas* (hall, mansion), and *pont* or *bont* (bridge).

---

strongholds to fall, in 1404, to the Welsh leader Owain Glyndŵr. Today it is a romantic ruin on a headland.

At the northern end of the beach promenade, a zigzag cliff path–nature trail at **Constitution Hill** leads to a view from the hilltop. An enjoyable way to reach the summit of Constitution Hill is by the **Aberystwyth Cliff Railway,** the longest electric cliff railway in Britain. Opened in 1896, it has been refurbished without diminishing its Victorian look. ☎ *01970/ 617642* 🎫 *£2.50 round-trip* ⊙ *Nov.–Feb., Wed.–Sun. 10–4; Mar.–Oct., daily 10–5.*

At the 430-foot summit of Constitution Hill is the **Great Aberystwyth Camera Obscura** (☎ *01970/617642*), a free modern version of a Victorian amusement: a massive 14-inch lens gives a bird's-eye view of the whole of Cardigan Bay and 26 Welsh mountain peaks.

At Aberystwyth Station you can hop on the narrow-gauge, steam-operated **Vale of Rheidol Railway** for an hour ride to the **Devil's Bridge,** where the rivers Rheidol and Mynach meet in a series of spectacular falls. Clamped between two rocky cliffs where a torrent of water pours unceasingly, this bridge well deserves its name—*Pont y Gwr Drwg,* or Bridge of the Evil One. There are actually three bridges (the oldest is 800 years old), and the walk down to the lowest bridge, "the devil's," is magnificent but strictly for the sure-footed. ✉ *Alexandra St.* ☎ *01970/625819* 🖨 *01970/623769* ⊕ *www.rheidolrailway.co.uk* 🎫 *£12.50 round-trip* ⊙ *Easter–Oct.; call for schedule.*

OFF THE BEATEN PATH

LLANERCHAERON – This late-18th-century Welsh gentry estate in the Aeron Valley, 17 mi south of Aberystwyth, near Aberaeron, is a superb example of the early work of John Nash (1752–1835). Nash was the leading architect of the Regency and the designer of Brighton's Royal Pavilion. The estate survived with few changes until the present; it is a self-contained world with stables, barns, dairy, and brewery. The walled gardens are spectacular. ⊠ *Off A482, Ciliau Aeron* ☎ *01545/570200* ⊕ *www.nationaltrust.org.uk* ⊠ *£6* ☉ *House mid-Mar.–July, Wed.–Sun. 11:30–4:30; Aug., daily 11:30–4:30; Sept. and Oct., Wed.–Sun. 11:30–4:30. Farm and garden mid-Mar.–July, Wed.–Sun. 11–5; Aug., daily 11–5; Sept. and Oct., Wed.–Sun. 11–5.*

Where to Stay & Eat

££–£££ ✕ **Gannets.** A simple, good-value bistro, Gannets specializes in hearty roasts and pies produced from locally supplied meat, fish, and game. Organically grown vegetables and a good French house wine are further draws for a university crowd. ⊠ *7 St. James's Sq.* ☎ *01970/617164* ☰ *MC, V* ☉ *Closed Sun.–Tues.*

££££ ✕▥ **Conrah Country Hotel.** Part of the appeal of this Edwardian country-house hotel on 20 acres of grounds is its air of seclusion, even though it's just 3 mi south of Aberystwyth. Traditional country furnishings and antiques decorate the house, and fresh flowers fill each room. The restaurant (*£££££*) is known for its imaginative British cuisine making use of local fish and meat. There's a three-course, prix-fixe menu at dinner. ⊠ *A487, Chancery SY23 4DF* ☎ *01970/617941* ⊟ *01970/624546* ⊕ *www.conrah.co.uk* ⟿ *14 rooms* ⌂ *Restaurant, indoor pool, sauna, croquet; no a/c, no kids under 5* ☰ *AE, DC, MC, V* ⏶⏶ *BP.*

£££–££££ ✕▥ **Harbourmaster Hotel.** A drive south on the coast road from Aberystwyth brings you to Aberaeron and the delights of this early-19th-century Georgian-style building, right on the harbor among colorfully painted structures. Modern design and strong colors dominate the public areas and bedrooms, which have wonderful harbor views. The brasserie (*££££*) produces sophisticated fare such as roasted parsnip soup and Thai monkfish red curry. ⊠ *Quay Parade, 15 mi south of Aberystwyth, Aberaeron SA46 OBT* ☎ *01545/570755* ⊟ *01545/570762* ⊕ *www.harbour-master.com* ⟿ *9 rooms* ⌂ *Restaurant, bar, some pets allowed (fee); no a/c, no kids under 5* ☰ *MC, V* ⏶⏶ *BP.*

££–£££ ✕▥ **Four Seasons.** This family-run hotel in the town center (no relation to the famous chain) is relaxed and friendly. The spacious rooms are very simply decorated. The restaurant (*££*) serves à la carte and three-course, prix-fixe menus at dinner; roast saddle of Welsh lamb is a specialty. ⊠ *50–54 Portland St., SY23 2DX* ☎ *01970/612120* ⊟ *01970/627458* ⊕ *www.fourseasonshotel.uk.com* ⟿ *16 rooms* ⌂ *Restaurant; no a/c* ☰ *AE, MC, V* ⏶⏶ *BP.*

Machynlleth

⓲ *18 mi northeast of Aberystwyth.*

Machynlleth, at the head of the beautiful Dovey Estuary, does not look like a typical Welsh country town. Its long and wide main street (Heol Maengwyn), lined with a mixed style of buildings from sober gray stone to well-proportioned Georgian, creates an atypical sense of openness and space. Machynlleth's busiest day is Wednesday, when the stalls of market traders fill the main street.

At the **Owain Glyndŵr Centre,** a small exhibition celebrates Wales's last native leader, who established a Welsh parliament at Machynlleth in the early 15th century. ⊠ *End of Heol Maengwyn* ☎ *01654/702827* 🎫 *Free* ⊙ *Easter–Sept., Mon.–Sat. 10–5.*

In a former chapel that's now a cultural and performing-arts center is the **Y Tabernacl Museum of Modern Art,** a superb gallery with permanent displays, including works by noted contemporary Welsh artist Kyffin Williams. ⊠ *Heol Penrallt* ☎ *01654/703355* ⊕ *www.momawales.org. uk* 🎫 *Free* ⊙ *Mon.–Sat. 10–4.*

☾ At the unique **Centre for Alternative Technology,** in an abandoned slate quarry in the forested hills just north of Machynlleth, a water-balanced cliff railway transports you to a futuristic, educational village equipped with all things green: alternative energy sources (solar roofs, wood-chip boilers), organic gardens, and a vegetarian café. Interactive displays present practical ideas about renewable resources, and the store is full of inspirational books and ecofriendly products. ⊠ *Off A487* ☎ *01654/ 702400* ⊕*www.cat.org.uk* 🎫*£8; lower prices in off-season* ⊙ *June–Sept., daily 10–6; Oct.–May, daily 10–4:30.*

Where to Stay & Eat

★ **£££££** ✕🏨 **Ynyshir Hall.** Idyllic gardens and grounds surround this supremely luxurious country retreat in a white-painted Georgian mansion near a wildlife reserve. Inside, the place glows: owner Rob Reen, an artist, displays his vibrant-hue work around the house. He and his wife, Joan, have decorated all surfaces in jewel-like tones. Antiques and Welsh pottery fill the public areas; the pampering guest rooms, named after artists (Hogarth, Matisse, Goya), have antique beds. The outstanding contemporary cuisine in the candlelit restaurant (£££££; fixed-price dinner menu) uses local favorites, from wild salmon and venison to farmhouse cheeses. ⊠ *Off A487, southwest of Machynlleth, Eglwysfach SY20 8TA* ☎ *01654/781209 or 800/777–6536* 🖶 *01654/781366* ⊕ *www. ynyshir-hall.co.uk* ➥ *9 rooms* ⚒ *Restaurant; no a/c, no kids under 9, no smoking* ▤ *AE, DC, MC, V* ⎩⦿⎨ *BP.*

££ ✕🏨 **Penhelig Arms.** The delightful little sailing center of Aberdovey is perched at the mouth of the Dovey Estuary, west of Machynlleth. This immaculate harborside inn has a terrace overlooking the harbor and bay, and most rooms have wonderful sea views. Meet the locals in the wood-panel Fisherman's Bar and dine in style in the fine restaurant (£££££; three-course, fixed-price dinner menu), where local seafood is a specialty. ⊠ *A493, Aberdovey LL35 0LT* ☎ *01654/767215* 🖶 *01654/767690* ⊕ *www.penheligarms.com* ➥ *15 rooms* ⚒ *Restaurant, bar, no-smoking rooms; no a/c* ▤ *MC, V* ⎩⦿⎨ *BP.*

Outdoors

The 128-mi **Glyndŵr's Way** (⊠ Tourist Office, Heol Maengwyn ☎ 01654/ 702401 ⊕ www.glyndwrsway.org.uk) walking route passes through Machynlleth before it turns east to climb above the Dovey with wonderful views north to Cadair Idris.

Dolgellau

⑲ *16 mi north of Machynlleth, 34 mi north of Aberystwyth.*

A solidly Welsh town with dark stone buildings and old coaching inns made of the local gray dolerite and slate, Dolgellau (pronounced dol-*geth*-lee) thrived with the wool trade until the mid-19th century. (Sheep are still auctioned here, but they're valued for meat rather than wool.) Prosperity left striking architecture, with buildings of different eras side by side on crooked streets that are a pre-Norman legacy. The town trail booklet, sold in the tourist office on Eldon Square, tells the story. Dolgellau, in a valley, has long been a popular base for people eager to walk the surrounding countryside. Look down the streets or above the buildings, and you'll see mountains rise up in the distance—a lovely sight.

The town became the center of the Welsh gold trade in the 19th century, when high-quality gold was discovered locally. A nugget of Dolgellau gold is used to make royal wedding rings. You can still try your luck and pan for gold in the Mawddach.

The **Museum of the Quakers,** in the town square, commemorates the area's strong links with the Quaker movement and the Quakers' emigration to the American colonies. ✉ *Eldon Sq.* ☎ *01341/422888* 💷 *Free* ☉ *Easter–Oct., daily 10–6; Nov.–Easter, Thurs.–Mon. 10–5.*

To the south of Dolgellau rises the menacing bulk of **Cadair Idris** (2,927 feet); the name means "the Chair of Idris," though no one is completely sure who Idris was—probably a warrior bard. It is said that anyone sleeping for a night on a certain part of the mountain will awaken either a poet or a madman, or not at all.

Barmouth

⑳ *10 mi west of Dolgellau.*

Barmouth, on the northern mouth of the Mawddach Estuary, is one of the few places along the Welsh coast that can be described as a full-fledged seaside resort, although it's now a bit tired. It has a 2-mi-long promenade, wide expanses of golden beach, and facilities for sea, river, and mountain-lake fishing. To appreciate the splendid location, walk along the footpath beside the railway bridge that crosses the mouth of the estuary: the bay stretches out on one side, and on the other are rugged, looming mountains and the river.

The arrival of the railroad in the 19th century made Barmouth a popular vacation spot. Alfred, Lord Tennyson was inspired to write *Crossing the Bar* by the spectacle of the Mawddach rushing to meet the sea. Charles Darwin worked on *The Origin of Species* and *The Descent of Man* in a house by the shore. Essayist and art critic John Ruskin was a frequent visitor and was trustee of the St. George's cottages built in 1871 by the Guild of St. George (Ruskin's organization, dedicated to founding agrarian communities) in 1871. Ruskin loved the walk from Barmouth up the river to Dolgellau.

Where to Stay & Eat

££££ ✕▦ **Bae Abermaw.** Perched high above the sea with panoramic views across the bay, this traditional Victorian stone house encloses a surprisingly contemporary minimalist interior. Clean lines and pale natural tones make for a relaxed atmosphere. The excellent restaurant (£££–££££) serves dishes like local panfried steak of Welsh Black fillet with dauphinoise potatoes, port-wine sauce, and baby vegetables. ⊠ *Panorama Rd., LL42 1DQ* ☎ *01341/280550* 🖷 *01341/281346* ⊕ *www. baeabermaw.com* ➥ *14 rooms* ⌂ *Restaurant, bar, lounge, meeting rooms, no-smoking rooms; no a/c* ▭ *MC, V* ⧯ *BP.*

Welshpool

㉑ *48 mi east of Barmouth, 19 mi west of Shrewsbury.*

The border town of Welshpool, "Trallwng" in Welsh, is famous as the home of Powis Castle, one of mid-Wales's greatest treasures, but it also has an appealing town center.

★ Continuously occupied since the 13th century, **Powis Castle** is one of the most opulent residential castles in Britain, with gardens that are equally renowned. Its battlements rear high on a hilltop, and Italian- and French-influenced terraced gardens surround the castle. Below gigantic yew hedges, the grounds fall steeply down to wide lawns and neat Elizabethan gardens. The interior contains many treasures: Greek vases; paintings by Thomas Gainsborough, Joshua Reynolds, and George Romney, among others; superb furniture; and the **Clive of India Museum,** with a good collection of Indian art. The tearoom is excellent. A timed-ticket system may be in effect on busy days. ⊠ *Off A483* ☎ *01938/551929* ⊕ *www. nationaltrust.org.uk* 🎫 *£9.60, gardens only £6.60* ☉ *Castle and museum Apr. and Sept., Thurs.–Mon. 1–5; July and Aug., Wed.–Mon. 1–5; Sept. and Oct., Thurs.–Mon. 1–4; Gardens Apr. and Oct., Thurs.–Mon. 11–6; July and Aug., Wed.–Sun. 11–6; Sept. and Oct., Thurs.–Sun. 11–4:30.*

The excellent **Powysland Museum,** in a converted warehouse on the banks of the Montgomery Canal, focuses on local history from the Stone Age to Victorian times. ⊠ *Canal Wharf* ☎☎ *01938/554656* 🎫 *£1* ☉ *May–Sept., Mon., Tues., Thurs., and Fri. 11–1 and 2–5, weekends 10–1 and 2–5; Oct.–Apr., Mon., Tues., Thurs., and Fri. 11–1 and 2–5, Sat. 2–5.*

SOUTH WALES
FROM CARDIFF TO CARDIGAN

The most diverse of Wales's three regions, the south covers not only the immediate region around Cardiff and the border of Wales and England, but also the southwest as far as the rugged coastline of Pembrokeshire. The very different natures of its two national parks reveals South Wales's scenic variety. The Brecon Beacons park, a short drive north of Cardiff, is an area of high, grassy mountains, lakes, and craggy limestone gorges. In contrast, the Pembrokeshire Coast National Park holds one of Europe's finest stretches of coastal natural beauty, with mile after mile of spectacular sea cliffs, beaches, headlands, and coves. Other pieces of the complicated South Wales jigsaw include traditional farmlands, cosmopolitan urban areas, rolling border country, wooded vales, and the former industrial valleys where coal was mined in huge quantities during the 19th and early 20th centuries.

Cardiff

20 mi west of the Second Severn Bridge, which carries the M4 motorway across the Severn Estuary into Wales.

Home to the Welsh Assembly and with a population of 306,000, Cardiff is financially, industrially, and commercially the most important city in Wales. It's also one of Europe's youngest and most vibrant capital cities with an appealing blend of old and brand new. Attracting increasing numbers of tourists are its handsome Civic Centre, magnificent parklands, canopied shopping arcades, and a castle with abundant Victorian verve. These traditional sights stand alongside new landmarks like the Millennium Stadium and the dazzling waterfront regeneration of the one-time coal-exporting hub of Cardiff Bay. Here a dam across the Taff and Ely rivers has created a freshwater lake edged by 8 mi of prime waterfront, an area of promenades, shops, restaurants, attractions, and exciting modern buildings like the Wales Millennium Centre.

True to the Welsh tradition of vocal excellence, Cardiff is home base for Britain's adventurous and acclaimed Welsh National Opera. Cardiff is also the sporting center of Wales and the Welsh capital of rugby football. To hear crowds singing their support for the Welsh team is a stirring experience.

Main Attractions

Cardiff Bay. Panoramic bay views, promenades, shops, restaurants, museums, and prestigious buildings make Cardiff Bay well worth a visit. The revitalized dockland, 1 mi south of the city center, can be reached by bus, train, or taxi. The **Cardiff Bay Visitor Centre** a futuristic building known locally as "the Tube" (because of its shape), tells the story of the transformation of the bay area. Next door and overlooking the bay is the timber Norwegian seamen's church where Roald Dahl (noted author whose children's books include *James and the Giant Peach* and *Charlie and the Chocolate Factory*) was baptized. It's now known as the **Norwegian Church Arts Centre** and houses a performance space, a gallery, and a café. North of the visitor center is the **National Assembly Debating Chamber,** a canopied glass structure designed by Richard Rogers that perfectly complements the neighboring modern buildings. The lively exhibition about the workings of the National Assembly, however, is across the street in the imposing Victorian building, the **Pierhead.**

★ ㉖ **Cardiff Castle.** In Bute Park, one section of the city's hundreds of acres of parkland, is an unusual historic site, with Roman, Norman, and Victorian associations. Parts of the walls are Roman, the solid keep is Norman, and the whole complex was restored and transformed into a

Victorian ego flight by the third marquess of Bute. He employed William Burges (1827–81), an architect obsessed by the Gothic period, and Burges transformed the castle into an extravaganza of medieval color and careful craftsmanship. It is the perfect expression of the anything-goes Victorian spirit, and a reflection of the fortune made by the marquess in Cardiff's booming docklands. ✉ *Bute Park* ☎ *029/2087–8100* ⊕ *www.cardiffcastle.com* ⊠ *Grounds and guided tour of castle £6.50; grounds only £3.30* ☉ *Mar.–Oct., daily 9:30–6; Nov.–Feb., daily 9:30–5; call for tour times.*

NEED A BREAK?

Café Minuet (⊠ 42 Castle Arcade ☎ 029/2034–1794 ☉ Mon.–Sat. 11–6), in the Victorian shopping arcade opposite Cardiff Castle has pale wood floors and checked tablecloths and serves tasty rustic Italian food like homemade soups, pasta, and pizzas. Service is prompt and friendly.

★ ㉔ **Castell Coch.** Perched on a hillside is the Red Castle, a turreted Victorian vision. It was built (on the site of a medieval stronghold) in the 1870s, about the time that Ludwig II of Bavaria was creating his fairy-tale castles, and it could almost be one of them. The castle was another collaboration of the third marquess of Bute and William Burges, builders of Cardiff Castle. Burges created everything—architecture, furnishings, murals—in a remarkable exercise in Victorian–Gothic whimsy. ⊠ *A470, 4 mi north of Cardiff, Tongwynlais* ☎ *029/2081–0101* ⊕ *www.cadw. wales.gov.uk* ⊠ *£3* ☉ *Apr., May, and Oct., daily 9:30–5; June–Sept., daily 9:30–6; Nov.–Mar., Mon.–Sat. 9:30–4, Sun. 11–4.*

Civic Centre. Two blocks north and east of Cardiff Castle is a well-designed complex of tree-lined avenues and Edwardian civic buildings with white Portland stone facades; Cathays Park is in the center. A Welsh dragon sits atop the domed City Hall, and inside the Marble Hall contains statues of Welsh heroes, including St. David, Henry Tudor, and Owain Glyndŵr (although he razed Cardiff in 1404). Neoclassical law courts and university campus buildings are also here. ⊠ *Bordered by North Rd. on the west and Park Pl. on the east.*

㉕ **National Museum Cardiff.** This splendid museum, next to City Hall in the Civic Centre, tells the story of Wales through its plants, rocks, archaeology, zoology, art, and industry. The Evolution of Wales gallery gives a dazzling run through Wales's existence using robotics and audiovisual effects. There's a fine collection of modern European art including the largest collection of French impressionist and postimpressionist works in the country. Allow at least half a day at the museum, and don't miss *La Parisienne* by Renoir. ⊠ *Cathays Park* ☎ *029/2039–7951* ⊕ *www. nmgw.ac.uk* ⊠ *Free* ☉ *Tues.–Sun. 10–5.*

Fodor'sChoice ★

㉘ **St. David's Centre.** South of the Civic Centre are the shopping and business areas of Cardiff. A large, modern shopping mall holds **St. David's Hall,** one of Europe's best concert halls, with outstanding acoustics. People come here for classical music, jazz, rock, ballet, and even snooker championships. Nearby is the **Cardiff International Arena,** a multipurpose center for exhibitions, concerts, and conferences.

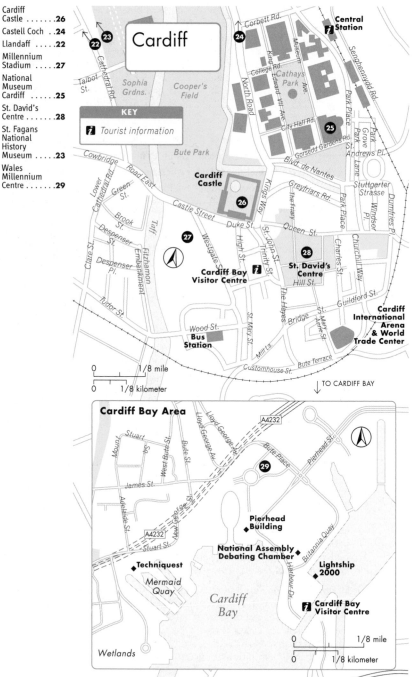

Also Worth Seeing

Caerphilly Castle. The largest and one of the most impressive fortresses in Wales was remarkable at the time of its 13th-century construction by an Anglo-Norman lord. The concentric fortification contained inner and outer defenses. More than 30 acres of grounds and a moat surrounds the castle, but Caerphilly is no longer on guard; some walls have toppled and others lean haphazardly. Exhibits in the gatehouse trace its turbulent history. The castle is 7 mi north of Cardiff. ⊠ *Access off A470–A468, Caerphilly* ☎ *029/2088–3143* ⊕ *www.cadw.wales.gov.uk* ⛁ *£3* ⊙ *Apr., May, and Oct., daily 9:30–5; June–Sept., daily 9:30–6; Nov.–Mar., Mon.–Sat. 9:30–4, Sun. 11–4.*

㉒ **Llandaff.** In a suburb that retains its village feeling, you can visit **Llandaff Cathedral,** which was repaired after serious bomb damage in World War II. The cathedral includes the work of a number of Pre-Raphaelites as well as *Christ in Majesty,* a 15-foot-tall aluminum figure by sculptor Jacob Epstein (1880–1959). To get here from Cardiff, cross the River Taff and follow Cathedral Road for about 2 mi. Guided tours available by arrangement. ☎ *029/2056–4554* ⊕ *www.llandaffcathedral.org.uk.*

㉗ **Millennium Stadium.** The modern, 72,000-seat stadium stands beside the River Taff on the site of the famous Cardiff Arms Park, the spiritual home of Welsh rugby. The stadium's retractable roof enables it to be used for concerts and special events throughout the year, as well as for rugby. On a one-hour tour you can walk the players' tunnel and see the Royal Box, dressing rooms, pitch, and broadcasting suite. ⊠ *Entrance Gate 3, Westgate St.* ☎ *029/2082–2228* ⊕ *www.millenniumstadium.com* *£5.50* ⊙ Call for times.

🦢 ㉓ **St. Fagans National History Museum.** On 100 acres of parkland and gardens, this excellent, open-air museum has farmhouses, cottages, shops, a school, chapels, St. Fagans castle (a 16th-century manor house), and terraced houses that celebrate Wales's rich rural culture and show the evolution of building styles. All but two of the structures were brought here from places around Wales. Galleries display clothing and articles from daily life. There are farming demonstrations and special events that highlight ancient rural festivals. The museum is accessible from Junction 33 on the M4. ⊠ *St. Fagans* ☎ *029/2057–3500* ⊕ *www.nmgw. ac.uk* ⛁ *Free* ⊙ *Daily 10–5.*

🦢 **Techniquest.** A large science-discovery center on the waterfront, Techniquest has 160 interactive exhibits, a planetarium, and a science theater. ⊠ *Stuart St., Cardiff Bay* ☎ *029/2047–5475* ⊕ *www.techniquest.org* ⛁ *£6.90* ⊙ *Weekdays 9:30–4:30, weekends 10:30–5.*

OFF THE BEATEN PATH

TINTERN ABBEY – When Wordsworth penned "Lines Written a Few Miles Above Tintern Abbey," he had no idea of all the people who would flock to Tintern to gaze at the abbey's substantial ruins. Remote and hauntingly beautiful as the site is, Tintern's appeal is diminished in summer because of crowds, so visit early or late in the day to best appreciate the complex stonework and tracery of the Gothic church. The abbey, 5 mi north of Chepstow and 30 mi northeast of Cardiff, is on the lush banks of the River Wye. ⊠ *A466, Tintern* ☎ *01291/689251* ⊕ *www.cadw.*

wales.gov.uk ✉ *£3.25* ⏱ *Apr., May, and Oct., daily 9:30–5; June–Sept., daily 9:30–6; Nov.–Mar., Mon.–Sat. 9:30–4, Sun. 11–4.*

㉙ **Wales Millennium Centre.** This new, huge arts complex with a curving golden steel roof and purple slate walls, is a world-class stage for full-scale ballet, opera, and musical performances. The center contains dance and recording studios, an orchestral hall, and a 1,900-seat auditorium. Seven leading Welsh cultural organizations make this their home base, including the Welsh National Opera Company and the Dance Company of Wales. There are shops, bars, and restaurants; one-hour tours are available from WMC's guides. ✉ *Cardiff Bay* ☎ *08700/402000* ⊕ *www. wmc.org.uk* ✉ *Free. Tours £5* ⏱ *Call to arrange tour.*

Where to Stay & Eat

£££££ ✕ **Armless Dragon.** It's worth the five-minute drive from the city center to eat at this comfortable restaurant with a contemporary menu that changes daily. Dishes such as Monmouthshire woodland pork with smoked bacon and creamed leeks are created from seasonal, local ingredients. There are always vegetarian options and a good-value set-dinner menu (£14). ✉ *97 Wyverne Rd.* ☎ *029/2038–2357* ⊕ *www. armlessdragon.co.uk* ⊟ *AE, MC, V* ⏱ *Closed Sun. and Mon.*

★ **£££££** ✕ **Le Gallois.** Its minimalist furnishings and varied menu help make this sophisticated restaurant, close to Sophia Gardens, one of the city's most popular. The cooking is European in style and takes advantage of local ingredients. Try the venison with poached pear, celeriac and truffle puree, claret sauce, and chocolate oil. A good-value fixed-price menu is available at lunch, and there's a fixed-price dinner menu, too. ✉ *8 Romilly Crescent* ☎ *029/2034–1264* ⊕ *www.legallois-ycymro.com* ⊟ *AE, MC, V* ⏱ *Closed Sun. and Mon.*

££–£££ ✕ **Da Venditto.** This stylish city-center restaurant specializes in pared-down, new-wave Italian cuisine with dishes like diver-caught scallops, skewered on a rosemary twig, and pancetta-wrapped monkfish with vegetable casserole. More traditional pasta dishes are also available. ✉ *7–8 Park Pl., opposite New Theatre* ☎ *029/2023–0781* ⊕ *www.vendittogroup. co.uk* ⊟ *AE, MC, V* ⏱ *Closed Sun. and Mon.*

£–££ ✕ **Harry Ramsden's.** You can dine on the (reputedly) world's most famous fish-and-chips in a chandeliered, 200-seat dining room with wonderful views across Cardiff Bay. If you like live music with your meal, call to ask for dates of gala nights and sing-along evenings. ✉ *Landsea House, Stuart St.* ☎ *029/2046–3334* ⊟ *AE, DC, MC, V.*

★ **£££££** ⌂ **St. David's Hotel and Spa.** Natural light from a glass atrium floods this stylish, up-to-the-minute luxury hotel along the waterfront. Every room, done in soothing neutral tones with sleek modern furniture, has a private balcony and views over Cardiff Bay. You can indulge in a relaxing hydrotherapy spa treatment or feast at the Tides restaurant, under the guidance of noted London chef Marco Pierre White, which specializes in modern French fare. Special promotional deals are often available. ✉ *Havannah St., CF10 6SD* ☎ *029/2045–4045* ⊟ *029/2048–7056* ⊕ *www.thestdavidshotel.com* ➲ *132 rooms* ⌂ *Restaurant, cable TV, in-room data ports, indoor pool, gym, spa, business services, meeting rooms, no-smoking rooms* ⊟ *AE, DC, MC, V.*

££–£££££   Jolyons Hotel. Every room has different antiques, design, and fabrics at this sumptuous little boutique hotel close to the Millennium Centre. All the beds are king size. The lively Bar Cwtch (which means cuddle or cubbyhole in Welsh) has sofas you can sink into and a wood-burning stove. It's a great location from which to explore all the attractions of Cardiff Bay. ⊠ *Bute Cres., Cardiff Bay, CF10 5AN* 🕾🖨 *029/2048–8775* ⊕ *www.jolyons.co.uk* 🛏 *6 rooms* ⚒ *In-room DVD, Wi-Fi, bar; no a/c, no kids, no smoking* ▭ *MC, V* ⏹ *BP.*

££   Llanerch Vineyard. The pine-furnished, country-style rooms in the farmhouse and converted outbuildings of this Vale of Glamorgan vineyard are only 15 minutes from Cardiff center, but you are deep in the green countryside here. You can walk in the surrounding vineyard and woodlands and arrange your own personal Welsh wine tasting. Take Junction 34 off M4 and follow the brown signs. ⊠ *Hensol, Pendoylan CF72 8GG* 🕾 *01443/225877* 🖨 *01443/225546* ⊕ *www.llanerchvineyard.co.uk* 🛏 *9 rooms* ⚒ *No a/c, no smoking* ▭ *MC, V* ⏹ *BP.*

£–££   Town House. Cosmopolitan in style, this immaculate guesthouse near the city center (shops and castle are a short walk away) is well known as Cardiff's best B&B. The elegant Victorian building retains many original features and has neat, well-equipped bedrooms. You can have traditional British or American breakfasts in the formal dining room. ⊠ *70 Cathedral Rd., CF1 9LL* 🕾 *029/2023–9399* 🖨 *029/2022–3214* ⊕ *www.thetownhousecardiff.co.uk* 🛏 *8 rooms* ⚒ *Lounge; no a/c, no smoking* ▭ *MC, V* ⏹ *BP.*

Nightlife & the Arts

NIGHTLIFE Cardiff's clubs and pubs support a lively nighttime scene. **Café Jazz** (⊠ 21 St. Mary St. 🕾 029/2038–7026) presents live jazz five nights a week and has TV screens in the bar and restaurant so you can view the onstage action. **Clwb Ifor Bach** (⊠ Womanby St. 🕾 029/2023–2199), a distinctively Welsh club (its name means Little Ivor's Club), has three floors of eclectic music, from funk to folk to rock.

THE ARTS The big theaters present a full program of entertainment: drama and comedy, pop and the classics. The huge **Cardiff International Arena** (⊠ Mary Ann St. 🕾 029/2022–4488) showcases artists who can draw huge crowds, from Tom Jones to Bob Dylan. **St. David's Hall** (⊠ The Hayes 🕾 029/2087–8444), a popular venue, presents the Welsh Proms in July, attracting major international orchestras and soloists, and every two years hosts the prestigious Cardiff Singer of the World competition. It also stages rock, pop, jazz, and folk events.

New Theatre (⊠ Park Pl. 🕾 029/2087–8889), a refurbished Edwardian playhouse, presents big names, including the Royal Shakespeare Company, the National Theatre, and the Northern Ballet.

Wales has one of Britain's four major opera companies, the outstanding **Welsh National Opera** (⊠ Wales Millennium Centre, Cardiff Bay 🕾 029/2063–5000 for info, 08700/402000 for tickets). The company spends most of its time touring Wales and England.

Sports

Celtic Manor (⊠ Coldra Woods, Newport ☎ 01633/410262 ⊕ www.celtic-manor.com), 12 mi northeast of Cardiff via A48, is Wales's most prestigious golf course. It will host the Ryder Cup in 2010.

Shopping

Canopied Victorian and Edwardian shopping arcades, lined with specialty stores, weave in and out of the city's modern shopping complexes. The **Cardiff Antiques Centre** (⊠ Royal Arcade ☎ 029/2039–8891), in an 1856 arcade, is a good place to buy antique jewelry. Cardiff's traditional **covered market** (⊠ The Hayes ☎ 029/2087–1214 ⊕ www.cardiff-market.co.uk) sells tempting fresh foods beneath its Victorian glass canopy. The **Learning Tree** (⊠ Morgan Arcade ☎ 029/2022–5626 ⊕ www.tweedleandpip.co.uk) is a gem of a shop selling traditional toys and funky modern ones, educational games, books, and gifts for the discerning child up to age 11.

Abergavenny

30 *28 mi north of Cardiff.*

The market town of Abergavenny, near Brecon Beacons National Park, is a popular base for walkers and hikers. The popular **Abergavenny Food Festival** (☎ 01873/851643 general information, 01873/850805 tickets ⊕ www.abergavennyfoodfestival.com), held over a weekend in September, has lectures, discussions, demonstrations, and a food market. It's another sign of the growing interest in regional Welsh food.

Ruined **Abergavenny Castle,** built early in the 11th century, has a good local museum. The castle witnessed a tragic event on Christmas in 1176: the Norman knight William de Braose invited the neighboring Welsh chieftains to a feast and, in a crude attempt to gain control of the area, had them all slaughtered as they sat at dinner. Afterward, the Welsh attacked and virtually demolished the castle. Most of what now remains dates from the 13th and 14th centuries. The castle's 19th-century hunting lodge houses the museum, with exhibits about area history from the Iron Age to the present. The re-creation of a Victorian Welsh farmhouse kitchen includes old utensils and butter molds. ⊠ *Castle Museum, Castle St.* ☎ *01873/854282* ☞ *Free* ☉ *Mar.–Oct., Mon.–Sat. 11–1 and 2–5, Sun. 2–5; Nov.–Feb., Mon.–Sat. 11–1 and 2–4.*

West of Abergavenny lie the valleys—the Rhondda is the most famous—so well described by Richard Llewellyn in his 1939 novel *How Green Was My Valley* (the basis for the 1941 film). The slag heaps of the coal mines are green now, thanks to land reclamation schemes. The area southwest of Abergavenny, around the former iron- and coal-mining town of Blaenavon, has been named a World Heritage Site by UNESCO; it

Fodor'sChoice ★ provides a fascinating glimpse into Wales's industrial past. At the **Big Pit: National Coal Museum,** ex-miners take you underground on a tour of an authentic coal mine for a look at the hard life of the South Wales miner. You can also see the pithead baths and workshops. ⊠ *Off A4043, Blaenavon* ☎ *01495/790311* ⊕ *www.nmgw.ac.uk* ☞ *Free* ☉ *Feb.–Nov., daily 9:30–5; underground tours 10–3:30.*

The **Blaenavon Ironworks,** dating from 1789, trace the entire process of iron production in that era. Well-preserved blast furnaces, a water-balance lift used to transport materials to higher ground, and a terraced row of workers' cottages show how the business operated. ✉ *A4043, Blaenavon* ☎ *01495/792615* ⊕ *www.blaenavontic.com* 🎫 *£2.50* ☉ *Apr.–Oct., daily 9:30–4:30.*

Where to Stay & Eat

£–£££ ✕ **Clytha Arms.** A converted house on the banks of the River Usk near Abergavenny serves imaginative modern food in a relaxed setting. Try the cracked whole crab seasoned with lemongrass, chili, and lime leaves. You can eat very cheaply in the bar (try the real ales) or pay a little more in the restaurant. ✉ *Off B4598, Clytha* ☎ *01873/840206* ⊕ *www.clytha-arms.com* 🖃 *AE, MC, V* ☉ *Closed Mon.*

££££ ✕▦ **Allt-yr-Ynys Country House Hotel.** This 16th-century manor house in the foothills of the Black Mountains provides a winning blend of ancient charm and present-day comfort. Stone-tiled roofs, Jacobean oak paneling, decorative plasterwork ceilings, and exposed beams recall the past, whereas the comfortable public areas, pool, and hot tub pamper modern tastes. Most of the spacious, modern bedrooms are in converted stables and outbuildings, with views over mountains and woodland. The restaurant (£££) has a reputation for excellent modern British fare; try the braised Welsh lamb with rosemary and red-currant sauce. ✉ *Off A465, 5 mi north of Abergavenny, Walterstone HR2 ODU* ☎ *01873/890307* 🖷*01873/890539* ⊕*www.allthotel.co.uk* 📭*21 rooms* ⚐ *Restaurant, indoor pool, hot tub, sauna, bar, lounge, some pets allowed (fee), no-smoking rooms; no a/c* 🖃 *AE, MC, V* ❚❶ *BP.*

Crickhowell

③① *5 mi northwest of Abergavenny.*

If you take A40 northwest out of Abergavenny, you pass Sugar Loaf mountain and come to Crickhowell, a charming town on the banks of the River Usk with little shops, an ancient bridge, and a ruined castle. **Tretower Court,** 3 mi northwest of Crickhowell, is a splendid example of a fortified medieval manor house. Nearby, and part of the site, are the ruins of a Norman castle. ✉ *A479* ☎ *01874/730279* ⊕ *www.cadw.wales.gov.uk* 🎫 *£2.50* ☉ *Apr.–Sept., daily 10–5; Mar. and Oct., daily 10–5.*

Where to Stay & Eat

££–££££ ✕▦ **Bear Hotel.** In the middle of town, this white-painted coaching inn with good food is full of character. The low-beamed bar, decorated with memorabilia from the days when stagecoaches stopped here, has a log fire in winter. Rooms in the hotel or in a modern addition in the former stable yard vary widely (some are fairly small); the most luxurious have four-poster beds and antiques. The Bear serves creative contemporary cuisine—excellent-value bar food and restaurant (££–£££) offerings such as scallops with Parma ham and venison on spinach. ✉ *A40, NP8 1BW* ☎ *01873/810408* 🖷 *01873/811696* ⊕ *www.bearhotel.co.uk* 📭 *35 rooms* ⚐ *Restaurant, bar; no a/c* 🖃 *AE, MC, V* ❚❶ *BP.*

££ ✕🖾 **Ty Croeso Hotel.** A hillside location with views over the Usk Valley adds to the appeal of this hotel (its name means "House of Welcome") in an early-19th-century grey stone building. It has comfortable rooms with print fabrics, a lounge with a log fire, and imaginative food (££–£££) with a Welsh emphasis, such as Welsh beef flamed in whisky. ⊠ *The Dardy, off B4558, NP8 1PU* 🖾🖾 *01873/810573* ⊕ *www.ty-croeso.co. uk* ⌃⊃ *8 rooms* ⌂ *Restaurant, bar, lounge; no a/c* ⊟ *AE, MC, V* 🍴 *BP.*

Brecon

32 *19 mi northwest of Abergavenny, 41 mi north of Cardiff.*

Brecon, a historic market town of narrow passageways, Georgian buildings, and pleasant riverside walks, is also the gateway to the Brecon Beacons National Park. It's particularly appealing on market days (Tuesday and Friday). You may want to purchase a hand-carved wooden love spoon similar to those on display in the Brecknock Museum.

Cavernous **Brecon Cathedral** (☎ 01874/623857 ⊕ www. breconcathedral.org.uk), with a heritage center that traces its history, stands on the hill above the middle of town. In the colonnaded Shire Hall built in 1842 is the **Brecknock Museum** (⊠ Captain's Walk ☎ 01874/624121), with its items from rural life, art exhibits, superb collection of carved love spoons, and perfectly preserved 19th-century assize court.

> ## LOVE SPOONS
>
> The rural Welsh custom of giving one's beloved a wooden spoon intricately hand-carved with symbols of love dates from the mid-17th century. Motifs include hearts, flowers, doves, intertwined vines, and chain links. These days you don't have to make the effort yourself as shops all over Wales sell the spoons as souvenirs.

The military exhibits in the **South Wales Borderers' Museum** span centuries of conflict; some relate to battles in which this regiment participated. The Zulu Room recalls the Borderers' defense of Rorke's Drift in the Anglo-Zulu war of 1879, an action dramatized in the 1964 film *Zulu*, starring Michael Caine. ⊠ *The Watton, off Bulwark* ☎ *01874/613310* ⊕ *www.rrw.org.uk* 🖾 *£3* ⊙ *Oct.–Mar., weekdays 9–5; Apr.–Sept., weekdays 9–5, weekends 10–4.*

South of Brecon, the skyline fills with mountains, and wild, windswept uplands stretch to the horizon in the Brecon Beacons National Park. The **Brecon Beacons National Park Visitor Centre** on Mynydd Illtyd, a high, grassy stretch of upland west of A470, is an excellent source of information for attractions and activities within this 519-square-mi park of hills and open moorlands. It also gives wonderful panoramic views across to Pen-y-Fan, at 2,907 feet the highest peak in South Wales. If you plan to explore Wales's high country on foot, come well equipped. Mist and rain can quickly descend, and the Beacons' summits are exposed to high winds. ⊠ *Off A470, Libanus, Brecon LD3 8ER, 5½ mi southwest of Brecon* ☎ *01874/623366* ⊕ *www.breconbeacons.org* 🖾 *Free; fee for parking* ⊙ *Daily 9:30–5; until 4:30 Nov.–Mar.*

HIKING & BIKING IN WALES

Hiking and walking are the most popular outdoor activities in Wales, and a great way to see the country. Long-distance paths include the Pembrokeshire Coast Path (which runs all along the spectacular shores of southwest Wales), the south–north Offa's Dyke Path, based on the border between England and Wales established by King Offa in the 8th century, and the Glyndŵr Way, a 128-mi-long highland route that traverses mid-Wales from the border town of Knighton via Machynlleth to Welshpool. Signposted footpaths in Wales's forested areas are short and easy to follow. Dedicated enthusiasts might prefer the wide-open spaces of the Brecon Beacons National Park or the mountains of Snowdonia.

Wales's reputation as both an on-road and off-road cycling mecca is well established. There's an amazing choice of scenic routes and terrain from challenging off-road tracks (⊕ www.mtbwales.com is for the serious cyclist) to long-distance road rides and gentle family trails; VisitWales has information to get you started.

CONTACTS & RESOURCES

Cycling Wales (⊕ www.cycling.visitwales.com). **Offa's Dyke Centre** (☎ 01547/528753 ⊕ www.offasdyke.demon.co.uk). **Pembrokeshire Coast Path** (⊕ www.nationaltrail.co.uk). **Ramblers' Association in Wales** (☎ 029/2034–3535 ⊕ www.ramblers.org.uk/wales).

Where to Stay & Eat

£ ✕ **Brecon Beacons National Park Visitor Centre Tearoom and Restaurant.** The spectacular view across the Beacons and high-quality homemade dishes make this a very popular spot. The parsnip and apple soup and the Welsh Black beef pie are among the good choices. You can indulge in a cream tea or fresh-baked cake, or just have coffee and enjoy the view. ⊠ *Off A470, Libanus, Brecon* ☎ *01874/624979* ⊕ *www.breconbeacons.org* ⊟ *MC, V* ⊗ *No dinner.*

£££–££££ ✕⊡ **Felin Fach Griffin.** Old and new blend perfectly in this modern country-style inn with old wood floors, leather sofas, and terra cotta–color stone walls hung with bright prints. Some bedrooms have four-posters. The excellent menu (£££) makes use of fresh local produce. Try the roast partridge with celeriac mash or the salmon fillet with fennel confit. ⊠ *A470, east of Brecon, Felin Fach LD3 0UB* ☎ *01874/620111* ⊟ *01874/620120* ⊕ *www.eatdrinksleep.ltd.uk* ⇆ *7 rooms* ⌂ *Restaurant, no-smoking rooms; no a/c, no room TVs* ⊟ *MC, V* ⦿ *BP.*

£–££ ⊡ **The Coach House.** This former coach house provides contemporary townhouse accommodation. The friendly Welsh speaking owners are mines of local information on where to go and what to do in the Brecon Beacons, and at the end of a hectic day's activities can offer a relaxing holistic massage. Inventive Welsh breakfasts and evening meals are served in the small stylish restaurant. ⊠ *Orchard St., LD3 8AN* ☎ *07050/691216* ⊟ *0705/691217* ⊕ *www.coachhousebrecon.co.uk* ⇆ *7 rooms* ⌂ *Restaurant, lounge, Wi-Fi, massage; no a/c, no smoking* ⊟ *MC, V* ⦿ *BP.*

£ 📷 **Felin Glais.** In the 17th century this stone building served as a barn and a home to farm animals. Now renovated and extended, it maintains its ancient character with such elements as ancient wooden beams. The spacious and comfortable bedrooms are an excellent value for the price. The owners are extremely sociable; many guests become friends. They are also enthusiastic about food (for guests only) and make good use of locally sourced produce. ⊠ *Abersycir, near Brecon, LD3 9NP* 📠 *01874/623107* ⊕ *felinglais.zookitec.com* ↩ *3 rooms* ⚲ *Dining room, refrigerators, in-room DVD/VCR, some pets allowed, no-smoking rooms; no a/c, no room phones* ☰ *No credit cards* ⎮◯⎮ *BP.*

Nightlife & the Arts

Theatr Brycheiniog (⊠ Canal Wharf 📷 01874/611622 ⊕ www. theatrbrycheiniog.co.uk), on the canal, is the town's impressive venue for the arts. It also has a gallery and waterfront bistro. Each summer, the town hosts **Brecon Jazz** (📷 01874/611622 ⊕ www.breconjazz.co. uk), an international jazz festival that attracts top performers.

Sports

Crickhowell Adventure Gear (⊠ Ship St. 📷 01874/611586), which also has a smaller shop in Crickhowell, sells outdoor gear such as clothes and climbing equipment.

Brecon is an ideal center for on- and off-road cycling. **Biped Cycles** (⊠ 4, Free St. 📠 01874/622296 ⊕ www.bipedcycles.co.uk) will rent you the right bike and equipment to take to the hills.

Swansea

③③ *36 mi southwest of Brecon, 40 mi west of Cardiff.*

Swansea, the birthplace of poet Dylan Thomas (1914–53), marks the end of the industrial region of South Wales. Despite some undistinguished post-war architecture, Wales's second-largest city (population 224,000) has a number of appealing sights, including the waterfront pedestrian Sail Bridge, which has a 300-foot-high mast. Swansea was extensively bombed during World War II, and its old dockland has reemerged as the splendid **Maritime Quarter,** a modern marina with attractive housing and shops and a seafront that commands views across the sweep of Swansea Bay.

Housed in a construction of steel, slate, and glass grafted onto an historic redbrick building, the **National Waterfront Museum's** galleries have 15 theme areas. State-of-the-art interactive technology and artifacts bring Welsh industrial and maritime history to a 21st-century audience. ⊠ *Oystermouth Rd., Maritime Quarter* 📷 *01792/638950* ⊕ *www. waterfrontmuseum.co.uk* 🎫 *Free* ☺ *Daily 10–5.*

Founded in 1841, the **Swansea Museum** contains a quirky and eclectic collection that includes an Egyptian mummy, china, local archaeological exhibits, and the intriguing Cabinet of Curiosity, which holds artifacts from Swansea's past. The museum is close to the Maritime Quarter. ⊠ *Victoria Rd.* 📷 *01792/653763* ⊕ *www.swanseaheritage. net* 🎫 *Free* ☺ *Tues.–Sun. 10–4:45.*

The **Dylan Thomas Centre,** on the banks of the Tawe close to the Maritime Quarter, is the National Literature Centre for Wales. The center houses a permanent Dylan Thomas exhibition, art gallery, restaurant and café-bookshop, and hosts literary events such as the annual Dylan Thomas Festival. The Wales Tourist Board has a leaflet for a Dylan Thomas Trail around South Wales for those interested in following in the poet's footsteps. ⊠ *Somerset Pl.* ☎ *01792/463980* ⊕ *www. dylanthomas.com* 🖾 *Free* ☉ *Daily 10–4:30.*

Swansea's modern shopping center is nothing special, but the **covered market,** part of Quadrant Shopping Centre, is the best fresh-foods market in Wales. You can buy cockles from the Penclawdd beds on the nearby Gower Peninsula, and laverbread, that unique Welsh delicacy made from seaweed, which is usually served with bacon and eggs.

The **Egypt Centre** displays a substantial collection of ancient Egyptian artifacts, such as bead necklaces from the time of Tutankhamen and the beautiful painted coffin of a Theban musician. ⊠ *Taliesin Centre, University of Wales Swansea, Singleton Park* ☎ *01792/295960* ⊕ *www. swansea.ac.uk/egypt* 🖾 *Free* ☉ *Tues.–Sat. 10–4.*

★ The 14-mi-long **Gower Peninsula,** only minutes away from Swansea's center, was the first part of Britain to be declared an area of Outstanding Natural Beauty. Its shores are a succession of sheltered sandy bays and awesome headlands. Actress Catherine Zeta-Jones was born here, in the Victorian seaside resort of Mumbles. ■ TIP→ For the area's most breathtaking views, head to Rhossili on its western tip.

Where to Stay & Eat

££–£££ ╳ **La Braseria.** This lively, welcoming spot resembles a Spanish restaurant, with its flamenco music, oak barrels, and whitewashed walls. Among the house specialties are sea bass in rock salt, roast suckling pig, and pheasant (in season). There's a good choice of 140 Spanish and French wines. ⊠ *28 Wind St.* ☎ *01792/469683* ⊕ *www.labraseria.com* ▤ *AE, MC, V* ☉ *Closed Sun.*

★ ╳🖾 **Fairyhill.** Luxuriously furnished public rooms, spacious bedrooms, **££££–£££££** and 24 acres of wooded grounds make this 18th-century country house in the western part of the scenic Gower Peninsula a restful retreat. The hotel is renowned for sophisticated cuisine and a well-chosen wine list; try the Welsh Black beef with beer-batter onions or the seared scallops with black fettucine. There's a fixed-price dinner menu (£££££). ⊠ *Off B4295, 11 mi southwest of Swansea, Reynoldston SA3 1BS* ☎ *01792/ 390139* 🖨 *01792/391358* ⊕ *www.fairyhill.net* ⇔ *8 rooms* ⚙ *Restaurant, massage, croquet, helipad; no a/c, no kids* ▤ *AE, MC, V* ⦿I *BP.*

£££–£££££ ╳🖾 **Morgans.** This old Victorian Port Authority building in the Maritime Quarter has been transformed into a strikingly modern hotel without losing any of its period features: moldings, pillars, stained glass, and wood floors. The rooms are immaculate with crisp cotton sheets and drapes of satin, silk, and suede. The stylish restaurant (£££–££££) serves dishes like seared fillet of local sea bass with buttered spinach and vanilla-bean sauce. Lighter treats at the café-bar include cockle, leek, and bacon risotto with Llanboidy cheese. ⊠ *Somerset Pl., SA1 1RR*

☎ *01792/484848* 🖷 *01792/484849* ⊕ *www.morganshotel.co.uk* 🛏 *20 rooms ♿ Restaurant, café, room service, in-room DVD, bar; no smoking ⊟ AE, MC, V.*

National Botanic Garden of Wales

★ ☕ ㉞ *20 mi northwest of Swansea, 60 mi northwest of Cardiff.*

The first modern botanic garden in Britain, opened in 2000, celebrates conservation and education. It's based at Middleton Park, a 568-acre, 18th-century estate with seven lakes, cascades, fountains, and a Japanese garden. The garden's centerpiece is the Norman Foster–designed Great Glass House, the largest single-span greenhouse in the world, which blends into the curving landforms of the Tywi Valley. The interior landscape includes a 40-foot-deep ravine, 10,000 plants from all the Mediterranean climates of the world, and the interactive Bioverse. The garden is signposted off the main road between Swansea and Carmarthen. ✉ *Off A48 or B4310, Llanarthne* ☎ *01558/667148* ⊕ *www.gardenofwales.org.uk* 🎟 *£7* ☽ *Apr.–Oct., daily 10–6; Nov.–Mar., daily 10–4:30.*

Tenby

㉟ *53 mi west of Swansea.*

Pastel-color Georgian houses cluster around a harbor in this seaside resort, where two golden sandy beaches stretch below the hotel-lined cliff top. Medieval Tenby's ancient town walls still stand, enclosing narrow streets and passageways full of shops, inns, and places to eat. From the harbor you can take a boat trip to Caldey Island and visit the monastery, where monks make perfume.

The ruins of a castle stand on a headland overlooking the sea, close to the informative **Tenby Museum and Art Gallery** (✉ Castle Hill ☎ 01834/ 842809 ⊕ www.tenbymuseum.free-online.co.uk), which recalls the town's maritime history and its growth as a fashionable resort.

The late-15th-century **Tudor Merchant's House,** in town, shows how a prosperous trader would have lived in the Tenby of old. ✉ *Quay Hill* ☎ *01834/842279* ⊕ *www.nationaltrust.org.uk* 🎟 *£2.50* ☽ *Apr.–Oct., Sun.–Fri. 11–5.*

Where to Stay

££££–£££££ 🏨 **Penally Abbey.** Built on the site of a 6th-century abbey on 5 acres of lush woodland overlooking the expanse of Camarthen Bay, this dignified 18th-century house is awash with period details. Bedrooms within the house are furnished with antiques and four-poster beds, whereas those in the adjoining St. Deiniols Lodge are light and airy with a touch of urban chic. The hotel is relaxed rather than stuffy, but service is first-class. ✉ *Off A4139, 2 mi west of Tenby, Penally SA70 7PY* ☎ *01834/ 843033* 🖷 *01834/844714* ⊕ *www.penally-abbey.com* 🛏 *17 rooms ♿ Restaurant, indoor pool, billiards; no a/c ⊟ AE, MC, V* ⅋ *BP.*

£–££ 🏨 **Ivy Bank Guest House.** This comfortable and immaculate Victorian house is just a five-minute stroll from the sea. The breakfast menu is extensive and the rooms are furnished with light flowery fabrics. ⊠ *Harding St., Tenby SA70 7ll* ☎ *01834/842311* 🖷 *01834/849053* ⊕ *www.ivybanktenby.co.uk* ⇆ *5 rooms* ⚘ *Some in-room VCRs, lounge; no smoking* ▭ *MC, V* ❙◎❙ *BP.*

Pembroke

➌➏ *13 mi west of Tenby, 13 mi south of Haverfordwest.*

In Pembroke you are entering the heart of Pembrokeshire, one of the most curious regions of Wales. All around are English names such as Deeplake, New Hedges, and Rudbaxton. Locals more often than not don't understand Welsh, and South Pembrokeshire is known as "Little England beyond Wales." History is responsible: in the 11th century, the English conquered this region with the aid of the Normans, and the English and Normans intermarried and set about building castles.

One of the most magnificent Norman fortresses is massive **Pembroke Castle,** dating from 1190. Its walls remain stout, its gatehouse mighty, and the enormous cylindrical keep proved so impregnable to cannon fire in the Civil War that Cromwell's men had to starve out its Royalist defenders. You can climb the towers and walk the walls for fine views. This was the birthplace, in 1457, of Henry Tudor, who seized the throne of England as Henry VII in 1485, and whose son Henry VIII united Wales and England in 1536. ☎ *01646/681510* ⊕ *www.pembrokecastle.co.uk* 🎫 *£3.50* ⊙ *Apr.–Sept., daily 9:30–6; Oct. and Mar., daily 10–5; Nov.–Feb., daily 10–4.*

St. David's

➌➐ *25 mi northwest of Pembroke, 16 mi west of Fishguard.*

This tiny village holds what has been described as the holiest ground in Great Britain, the Cathedral of St. David and the shrine of the patron saint of Wales, who founded a monastic community here in the 6th century. The entire area around St. David's, steeped in sanctity and history, was a place of pilgrimage for many centuries, two journeys to St. David's equaling (in spiritual value) one to Rome. Here, on the savagely beautiful coastline, edged by the Pembrokeshire Coast Path—Pembrokeshire at its unspoiled best—you can almost recapture the feeling of those days nearly 1,500 years ago, when this shrine was very nearly the sole outpost of Christianity in the British Isles. If you have a day to spare, the 6.5-mi walk along the coastal path around the St. David's headland from St. Justinian to Caerfai Bay is magnificent. ■ TIP➔ **Come in May and June to see the hedgerows and coastal path full of wild flowers.**

Unlike any other cathedral, the venerable 12th-century **St. David's Cathedral** (⊕ www.stdavidscathedral.org.uk) does not seek to dominate the surrounding countryside with its enormous mass; it is in a vast hollow. You must climb down 39 steps (called locally the Thirty-Nine Articles) to enter the cathedral. Its location helped protect the church from Viking raiders by hiding it from the view of invaders who came by sea. From the outside, purple-stoned St. David's has a simple austerity that harmonizes with the beautiful wind-swept countryside, but the interior is more intricate. Treasures include the fan vaulting in Bishop Vaughan's Chapel, the delicate carving on the choir stalls, and the oaken roof over the nave. Across the brook are the ruins of the medieval **Bishop's Palace.** ☎ *01437/720517* ⊕ *www.cadw.wales.gov.uk* ✉ *£2.50* ⊘ *Nov.–Mar., Mon.–Sat. 9:30–4, Sun. 11–4; Apr.–Oct., daily 9:30–5.*

Where to Stay & Eat

£££   ✕ **Morgan's Brasserie.** One choice sounds more delicious than the next at this classic bistro in the heart of town, which has an inventive menu based on local and organic ingredients. A blackboard lists daily specials, including Pembrokeshire-caught fish. Try the Welsh salt-marsh lamb, the Porthgain lobster with risotto, or sea bass on a bed of roasted vegetables. ✉ *20 Nun St.* ☎ *01437/720508* ⊕ *www.morgans-in-stdavids.co.uk* ▤ *MC, V.*

£££££   ✕▦ **Warpool Court Hotel.** Overlooking a stunning stretch of coastline, this hotel sits on a bluff above St. Non's Bay, near a ruined chapel. Many rooms have sea views; decorative tiles adorn public areas and some bedrooms. The building dates from the 1860s, when it housed St. David's Cathedral Choir School. The well-equipped hotel offers contemporary cuisine (*£££££;* four-course, fixed-price menu at dinner), with fish, including home-smoked salmon, as a specialty; the dining room overlooks the water. ✉ *Off Goat St., SA62 6BN* ☎ *01437/720300* 🖷 *01437/720676* ⊕ *www.warpoolcourthotel.com* ⤳ *25 rooms* ♨ *Restaurant, in-room data ports, tennis court, pool, gym, lounge; no a/c* ▤ *AE, MC, V* ❙◯❙ *BP.*

Fishguard

38   *16 mi northeast of St. David's, 26 mi north of Pembroke.*

Fishguard is a town of three parts. The ferry terminal at Goodwick across the sheltered waters of Fishguard Bay sees activity throughout the year as boats sail to Rosslare, Ireland, across the Irish Sea. Fishguard's main town stands on high ground just south of Goodwick, separating the modern port from its old harbor in the Lower Town, where gabled cottages are grouped around the quayside. The Lower Town was the setting for the 1973 film of Dylan Thomas's play *Under Milkwood,* which starred Elizabeth Taylor and Welsh actor Richard Burton.

Cardigan & the Teifi Valley

39   *18 mi northeast of Fishguard.*

The little market town of Cardigan, with its ancient bridge, was the scene of a never-allowed-to-be-forgotten victory by the Welsh over the Norman army in 1136. The town is near the mouth of the Teifi, a river that runs through a wooded valley with traditional market towns and villages. The valley also contains reminders of the area's once-flourishing woolen industry. Wales's first eisteddfod, or folk festival, took place in Cardigan Castle in 1176. The eisteddfod tradition, based on the Welsh language and arts—a sort of Welsh cultural olympics remains strong in Wales, and events large and small are held here (mainly in summer months).

Cilgerran, a village a few miles south of Cardigan, has the dramatic ruins of 13th-century **Cilgerran Castle,** which stands above a deep, wooded gorge where the River Teifi flows. ⊠ *Off A478* ☎ *01239/615136* ⊕ *www. cadw.wales.gov.uk* 🎟 *£2.50* ⊙ *Apr.–late Oct., daily 9:30–6:30; late Oct.–Mar., daily 9:30–4.*

OFF THE BEATEN PATH

NATIONAL WOOL MUSEUM – Working exhibits and displays at this museum in what was once Wales's most important wool-producing area trace the evolution of the industry. The National Textile Collection is showcased. There are also crafts workshops and a woolen mill that produces reproduction fabrics. A shop sells the best of Welsh textiles. The museum is east of Cenarth, a few miles past Newcastle Emlyn. ⊠ *Off A484, Drefach Felindre* ☎ *01559/370929* ⊕ *www.nmgw.ac.uk* 🎟 *Free* ⊙ *Apr.–Sept., daily 10–5; Oct.–Mar., Tues.–Sat. 10–5.*

Where to Stay

££ 🏨 **Wervil Grange Farm.** Enjoy the rare experience of high-quality accommodation at an immaculate Georgian farmhouse on a traditional working farm rearing sheep and Welsh Black cattle. The rooms are beautifully furnished with antiques and fine fabrics patterned in flowers and stripes. There's free fishing on the farm and easy access to beach. ⊠ *Off A487, 8 mi northeast of Cardigan, Pentregat SA44 6HW* ☎☎ *01239/654252* 🛏 *6 rooms* ⚓ *Fishing, some pets allowed; no a/c, no smoking* ⊟ *No credit cards* ⫟⫝⫟ *BP.*

WALES ESSENTIALS

Transportation

BY AIR

London's Heathrow and Gatwick airports, with their excellent door-to-door motorway links with Wales, are convenient gateways (⇨ By Air *in* Transportation *in* Essentials). Manchester Airport, which offers many international flights, is an excellent gateway for North Wales, with a journey time to the Welsh border, via M56, of less than an hour. Cardiff International Airport, a 19-mi drive from the center of Cardiff, has direct flights to European destinations and Canada, with other connecting services worldwide via Amsterdam, and flights within the British Isles to London, Stansted, Manchester, Newcastle, Glasgow, Edinburgh, Aberdeen, Cork, and Dublin. A bus service runs from the airport to Cardiff's central train and bus stations.

AIRPORTS 🗗 **Cardiff International Airport** ⊠ A4226, Rhoose ☎ 01446/711111 ⊕ www.cwlfly. com. **Manchester Airport** ⊠ Near Junctions 5 and 6 of M56 ☎ 0161/489-3000 ⊕ www. manairport.co.uk.

BY BUS

Most parts of Wales are accessible by bus. National Express serves Wales from London's Victoria Coach Station and also direct from London's Heathrow and Gatwick airports. It also has routes into Wales from many major towns and cities in England and Scotland. Average travel times from London to Wales are 3½ hours to Cardiff, 4 hours to Swansea, 5½ hours to Aberystwyth, and 4½ hours to Llandudno.

The country's regional buses make travel around Wales quite easy; Traveline Cymru has information on all services. Wales's three national parks run summer bus services. The Snowdon Sherpa runs into and around Snowdonia and links with main rail and bus services. The Pembrokeshire Coastal Bus Service operates in the Pembrokeshire Coast National Park, and the Beacons Bus serves the Brecon Beacons National Park.

FARES &
SCHEDULES
🔒 **Beacons Bus** ☎ 01873/853254 ⊕ www.breconbeacons.org. **National Express** ☎ 0870/580-8080 ⊕ www.nationalexpress.co.uk. **Pembrokeshire Coastal Bus Service** ☎ 01437/776313 ⊕ www.pembrokeshiregreenways.co.uk. **Snowdon Sherpa** ☎ 0870/608-2608 ⊕ www.snowdonia-npa.gov.uk. **Traveline Cymru** ☎ 0870/608-2608 ⊕ www.traveline-cymru.org.uk.

BY CAR
Take the M4 from London for Cardiff (151 mi), Swansea (190 mi), and South Wales. Aberystwyth (211 mi from London) and Llandrindod Wells (204 mi) in mid-Wales are well served by major roads. The A40 is also an important route through central and South Wales. From London, M1/M6 is the most direct route to North Wales. A55, the coast road from Chester in England, goes through Bangor. Mid-Wales is reached by the M54, which links with the M6/M5/M1.

ROAD
CONDITIONS
Distances in miles may not be great in Wales, but getting around takes time because there are few major highways. There is no single fast route from north to south (the mountains have discouraged that); A470 is good and scenic, and A487 runs along or near most of the coastline. Many smaller mountain roads are winding and difficult to maneuver, but they have magnificent views.

BY TRAIN
Travel time on the fast InterCity rail service from London's Paddington Station is about 2 hours to Cardiff and 3 hours to Swansea. InterCity trains also run between London's Euston Station and North Wales. Average travel times from Euston are 3¾ hours to Llandudno in North Wales (some direct trains, otherwise change at Crewe), and about 5 hours to Aberystwyth in mid-Wales (change at Birmingham).

Regional train service covers South Wales, western Wales, central Wales, the Conwy Valley, and the North Wales coast on many scenic routes, such as the Cambrian Coast Railway, running 70 mi between Aberystwyth and Pwllheli, and the Heart of Wales line, linking Swansea and Craven Arms, near Shrewsbury, 95 mi northeast.

CUTTING COSTS
For travel within Wales, ask about money-saving, unlimited-travel tickets (such as Freedom of Wales Flexi Pass, North and mid-Wales Rover, and the South Wales Flexi Rover), which include the use of bus services. Wanderer tickets are available from participating railways for unlimited travel on the narrow gauge Great Little Trains of Wales: a nine-day ticket is £55.

FARES &
SCHEDULES **Flexi Pass information** ☎ 0845/606-1660 ⊕ www.walesflexipass.co.uk. **Great Little Trains of Wales** ✉ Tallyllyn Railway, Wharf Station, Tywyn LL36 9EY ☎ 01654/710472
⊕ www.greatlittletrainsofwales.co.uk. **National Rail Enquiries** ☎ 0845/748-4950
⊕ www.nationalrail.co.uk. **Regional & Intercity Railways** ☎ 0845/748-4950 ⊕ www.
thetrainline.com. **Snowdon Mountain Railway** ✉ Llanberis, Caernarfon LL55 4TY
☎ 01286/870223 ⊕ www.snowdonrailway.co.uk.

Contacts & Resources

DISCOUNTS & DEALS

The Cadw/Welsh Historic Monuments Explorer Pass is good for unlimited admission to most of Wales's historic sites. The seven-day pass costs
£15.50 (single adult), £26 (two adults), or £32 (family ticket); the three-
day pass costs £9.50, £16.50, and £23, respectively. Passes are available at any site covered by the Cadw program. All national museums
and galleries in Wales are free.

Cadw/Welsh Historic Monuments ✉ Plas Carew, Unit 5–7, Cefn Coed, Parc Nant-
garw, Treforest CF15 7QQ ☎ 01443/336000 ⊕ www.cadw.wales.gov.uk. **National Museums and Galleries of Wales** ⊕ www.nmgw.ac.uk.

EMERGENCIES

Ambulance, fire, police ☎ 999. **Bronglais Hospital** ✉ Caradog Rd., Aberystwyth
☎ 01970/623131. **Morriston Hospital** ✉ Heol Maes Eglwys, Cwm Rhydyceirw, Swansea
☎ 01792/702222. **University Hospital of Wales** ✉ Heath Park, Cardiff ☎ 029/2074-7747.

INTERNET

Travelers without personal computers can access the Internet at Internet cafés in many towns (use ⊕ www.upmystreet.com to check locations) and in some public libraries. Tourist information offices can also
advise you. Wi-Fi hot spots exist only in the major urban centers.

Internet Cafés PC 4 You ✉ 8 Neville St., Cardiff ☎ 029/2022-0546. **Brecon Cyber
Café** ✉ 10, Lion St., Brecon ☎ 01874/624942. **Directtech.co.uk** ✉ 5 Bodhyfryd Rd.,
Llandudno ☎ 01492/872092.

NATIONAL PARKS

Brecon Beacons National Park ✉ Plas-y-Ffynnon, Cambrian Way, Brecon LD3 7HP
☎ 01874/624437 ⊕ www.breconbeacons.org. **Pembrokeshire Coast National Park**
✉ Llannion Park, Pembroke Dock SA72 6DY ☎ 0845/345-7275 ⊕ www.
pembrokeshirecoast.org.uk. **Snowdonia National Park** ✉ Penrhyndeudraeth LL48 6LF
☎ 01766/770274 ⊕ www.eryri-npa.gov.uk.

TOUR OPTIONS

BUS TOURS A good way to see Wales is by local tour bus; in summer there's a large
choice of day and half-day excursions to most parts of the country. In
major resorts and cities you should ask for details at a tourist information center or bus station.

GUIDES If you are interested in a personal guide, contact the Wales Official Tourist
Guide Association. WOTGA uses only guides recognized by the Wales
Tourist Board and will create tailor-made tours. You can book a driver-
guide or someone to accompany you as you drive.

🚶 **Wales Official Tourist Guide Association** ☎ 01633/774796 ⊕ www. walestourguides.com.

VISITOR INFORMATION

The Wales Tourist Board's Visit Wales Centre provides information and handles reservations; accommodations can also be booked online. Tourist information centers are normally open Monday through Saturday 10 to 5:30 and limited hours on Sunday, but vary by season.

🚶 **Visit Wales Centre** ✉ Box 13, Bangor LL57 4WW ☎ 08701/211251 ⊕ www.visitwales. com. **Aberystwyth** ✉ Terrace Rd. ☎ 01970/612125. **Betws-y-Coed** ✉ Royal Oak Stables ☎ 01690/710426. **Caernarfon** ✉ Oriel Pendeitsh, opposite castle entrance ☎ 01286/672232. **Cardiff** national and city information ✉ The Old Library, The Hayes ☎ 029/2022-7281 ⊕ www.visitcardiff.info. **Llandrindod Wells** ✉ Auto Palace, Temple St. ☎ 01597/822600. **Llandudno** ✉ 1-2 Chapel St. ☎ 01492/876413. **Llanfair pwllgwyngyll** ✉ Station Site, Isle of Anglesey ☎ 01248/713177. **Llangollen** ✉ Y Chapel, Castle St. ☎ 01978/860828. **Machynlleth** ✉ Owain Glyndŵr Centre ☎ 01654/702401. **Ruthin** ✉ Craft Centre, Park Rd. ☎ 01824/703992. **Swansea** ✉ Plymouth St. ☎ 01792/468321 ⊕ www.visitswanseabay.com. **Tenby** ✉ Unit 2, The Gateway Complex ☎ 01834/842402. **Welshpool** ✉ Vicarage Gardens Car Park, Church St. ☎ 01938/552043.

Edinburgh & the Lothians

WORD OF MOUTH

"If your preference is for 'less urban,' I would avoid Glasgow but do visit Edinburgh, a city which deserves the raving that everyone does about it. There is a lot of natural beauty right in and near the city such as Calton Hill and Arthur's Seat. . . . Climb the Scott Monument in Princes Street Gardens for great views."

—Daisy54

"In August, the Fringe was running at the same time as the Edinburgh International Festival. We did a lot of Fringe street venues, which were quite fun. FYI, the Book Festival was there too! The city is just plain amazing when all the venues are there. We did do the Tattoo, which was the highlight of our trip."

—Judyrem

Updated by
Shona Main
and Nick
Bruno

EDINBURGH IS TO LONDON AS POETRY IS TO PROSE, as Charlotte Brontë once wrote. One of the world's stateliest cities and proudest capitals, it is built—like Rome—on seven hills. In a skyline of sheer drama, Edinburgh Castle watches over the capital city, frowning down on Princes Street as if disapproving of its modern razzmatazz. Its ramparts still echo with gunfire each day when the traditional one-o'clock gun booms out over the city, startling unwary shoppers.

Doric, Ionic, and Corinthian pillars add a touch of neoclassical grandeur to the largely Presbyterian backdrop, and expansive gardens and greenery give Edinburgh an abundant freshness: the city council is one of the most stridently conservationist in Europe. Conspicuous from Princes Street is Arthur's Seat, a mountain of bright green and yellow furze rearing up behind the spires of the Old Town. This child-size mountain jutting 822 feet above its surroundings has steep slopes and little crags, like a miniature Highlands set down in the middle of the busy city.

Parliament & Power

Three centuries after the Union of Parliaments with England in 1707, Edinburgh is once again the seat of a Scottish parliament. A new parliament building, designed by the late Spanish architect Enric Miralles, stands adjacent to the Palace of Holyroodhouse, at the foot of the Royal Mile. Even without its own Parliament, Scotland maintained its separate legal, ecclesiastical, and educational systems. However, its desire to legislate for its own distinct needs finally was recognized with the creation of the Scottish Parliament in 1999.

Scotland now has significantly more control over its own affairs than at any time since 1707, and the 129 Members of the Scottish Parliament (MSPs), of whom 40% are women, have extensive powers in Scotland over education, health, housing, transportation, training, economic development, the environment, and agriculture. Foreign policy, defense, and fiscal policy, however, remain under the jurisdiction of the U.K. government in London.

Building the City

Towering over the city, Edinburgh Castle was actually built over the plug of an ancient volcano. Many thousands of years ago, an eastward-grinding glacier encountered the tough basalt core of the volcano and swept around it, scouring steep cliffs and leaving a trail of matter, like the tail of a comet. This material formed a ramp gently leading down from the rocky summit. On this *crag* and *tail* would grow the city of Edinburgh and its castle.

The lands that rolled down to the sea were for centuries open country, sitting between Castle Rock and the tiny community clustered by the shore that grew into Leith, Edinburgh's seaport. By the 12th century Edinburgh had become a walled town, still perched on the hill. Its shape was becoming clearer: like a fish with its head at the castle, its backbone running down the ridge, and its ribs leading briefly off on either side. The backbone gradually became the continuous thoroughfare now known as the Royal Mile, and the ribs became the closes (alleyways), some still surviving, that were the scene of many historic incidents.

TOP REASONS TO GO

Festival fever: All year-round, Edinburgh is a cultural hub with every conceivable type of art and performance, but from mid-August through early September the city is one huge festival site with the high-brow Edinburgh International Festival, the refreshingly irreverent Fringe, and the mind-expanding International Book Festival.

The Castle, the Palace, the Parliament: Visits to Edinburgh Castle, the Palace of Holyroodhouse, and the Scottish Parliament are a great way to discover not just the history of the nation but also the unique identity and pride of the Scots.

Local feasts. Edinburgh is among the best places to sample the finest, most genuine Scottish cuisine. Traditional dishes such as *cullen skink* (a rich haddock soup) and, of course, haggis are on even the most exclusive menus.

Walk among majestic buildings. Whether you stroll the ancient buildings along the Royal Mile in Old Town or explore the neoclassical grandeur of New Town, you'll appreciate the lasting legacies of the city's influence and prosperity.

A wee dram: No meal or evening in Scotland is complete without a "wee dram" of a single malt. Ask the establishment for a recommendation and hear how Scots like to talk about whisky as much as drink it.

By the early 15th century Edinburgh had become the undisputed capital of Scotland. The bitter defeat of Scotland at Flodden in 1513, when Scotland aligned itself with France against England, caused a new defensive city wall to be built. Though the castle escaped destruction, the city was burned by the English earl of Hertford under orders from King Henry VIII (1491–1547) of England. This was during a time known as the "Rough Wooing," when Henry was trying to coerce the Scots into allowing the young Mary, Queen of Scots (1542–1587) to marry his son Edward. The plan failed and Mary married Francis, the Dauphin of France. By 1561, when Mary returned from France already widowed, the guesthouse of the Abbey of Holyrood had grown to become the Palace of Holyroodhouse, replacing Edinburgh Castle as the main royal residence. Mary's legacy to the city included the destruction of most of the earliest buildings of Edinburgh Castle, held by her supporters after she was forced to flee to England, where she was eventually executed by Elizabeth I.

In the trying decades after the union with England in 1707, many influential Scots, both in Edinburgh and elsewhere, went through an identity crisis, characterized by people like the writer James Boswell (1740–95), who, though he lived with his family in Edinburgh, preferred to spend most of his time in London. Out of the 18th-century difficulties, however, grew the Scottish Enlightenment, during which educated Scots made great strides in medicine, economics, and science.

By the mid-18th century it had become the custom for wealthy Scottish landowners to spend the winter in the Old Town of Edinburgh, in town houses huddled between the high Castle Rock and the Royal Palace below. Cross-fertilized in coffeehouses and taverns, intellectual notions flourished among a people determined to remain Scottish despite their parliament's having voted to dissolve itself. One result was a campaign to expand and beautify the city, to give it a look worthy of its future nickname, the Athens of the North. Thus was the New Town of Edinburgh built, with broad streets and gracious buildings creating a harmony that even today's throbbing traffic cannot obscure.

Edinburgh Today

Today the city is the second-most important financial center in the United Kingdom, and the fifth most important in Europe. This is one of the many reasons that people from all over Britain come to live here. Not the least of the other reasons is that the city regularly is ranked near the top in "quality of life" surveys. Hand in hand with the city's academic and scientific pursuits is a rich cultural life. In October 2004 Edinburgh became UNESCO's first City of Literature, and the city is known worldwide for the Edinburgh International Festival, which attracts lovers of all the arts in August and September.

Even as Edinburgh moves through the 21st century, its tall guardian castle remains the focal point of the city and its venerable history. Take time to explore the streets—peopled by the spirits of Mary, Queen of Scots, Sir Walter Scott, and Robert Louis Stevenson—and pay your respects to the world's best-loved terrier, Greyfriars Bobby. In the evenings you can enjoy candlelit restaurants or a folk ceilidh, though you should remember that you haven't earned your porridge until you've climbed Arthur's Seat.

EXPLORING EDINBURGH & THE LOTHIANS

Numbers in the text correspond to numbers in the margin and on the Edinburgh, West Lothian & the Forth Valley, and Midlothian & East Lothian maps.

Edinburgh's Old Town has atmosphere and history, and the New Town boasts architectural heritage of the city's Enlightenment. The Princes Street Gardens roughly divide Edinburgh into two areas: the winding, congested streets of Old Town, to the south, and the orderly, Georgian architecture of New Town, to the north. Princes Street runs east–west along the north edge of the Princes Street Gardens. Explore the main thoroughfares but also don't forget to get lost among the tiny *wynds* and *closes*: old medieval alleys that connect the winding streets.

Like most cities, Edinburgh incorporates small communities within its boundaries, and many of these are as rewarding to explore as Old Town and New Town. Dean Village is close to the New Town, but it has a character all of its own. Duddingston, just southeast of Arthur's Seat, has all the feel of a country village. Then there's Corstorphine, to the west of the city center, famous for being the site of Murrayfield, Scotland's international rugby stadium. Edinburgh's port, Leith, sits on the shore of the Firth of Forth, and throbs with smart bars and restaurants.

The hills, green fields, beaches, and historic houses and castles in the countryside outside Edinburgh—Midlothian, West Lothian, and East Lothian, collectively called the Lothians—can be reached quickly by bus or car, welcome day-trip escapes from the festival crush in summer.

Old Town

Eastward of Edinburgh Castle, the historic castle esplanade becomes the street known as the Royal Mile, leading from the castle down through Old Town to the Palace of Holyroodhouse. The Mile, as it's called, is actually made up of one thoroughfare that bears, in consecutive sequence, different names—Castlehill, Lawnmarket, Parliament Square, High Street, and Canongate. The streets and passages winding into their tenements, or "lands," and crammed onto the ridge in back of the Mile really *were* Edinburgh until the 18th century saw expansions to the south and north. Everybody lived here, the richer folk on the lower floors of houses, with less well-to-do families on the middle floors—the higher up, the poorer. There are many guided tours of the area or you can walk around on your own. The latter is often a better choice in summer when tourists pack the area and large guided groups have trouble making their way through the crowds.

To give the major sights—the castle, Palace of Holyroodhouse, and Royal Museum—the time they deserve and also to see at least some of the other attractions properly, you should allow two days. Consider ending the first day with an afternoon in the Royal Museum and devoting the second afternoon to Holyroodhouse. Note that some attractions have special hours during the Edinburgh International Festival.

Main Attractions

❶ **Edinburgh Castle.** The crowning glory of the Scottish capital, Edinburgh
Fodor'sChoice Castle is popular not only because it is the symbolic heart of Scotland
★ but also because of the views from its battlements: on a clear day the vistas—stretching to the "kingdom" of Fife—are breathtaking. There's so much to see that you need at least three hours to do the site justice.

There have been fortifications here since the Picts first used it as a stronghold in the 3rd and 4th centuries AD. Anglian invaders from northern England dislodged the Picts in AD 452, and for the next 1,300 years the site saw countless battles and skirmishes.

The castle has been held over time by Scots and Englishmen, Catholics and Protestants, soldiers and royalty. In the 16th century Mary, Queen of Scots, gave birth here to the future James VI of Scotland (1566–1625), who was also to rule England as James I. In 1573 it was the last fortress to support Mary's claim as the rightful Catholic queen of Britain, causing the castle to be virtually destroyed by English artillery fire.

You enter across the **Esplanade,** the huge forecourt built in the 18th century as a parade ground; it now serves as the castle parking lot. The area comes alive with color and music each August when it is used for the

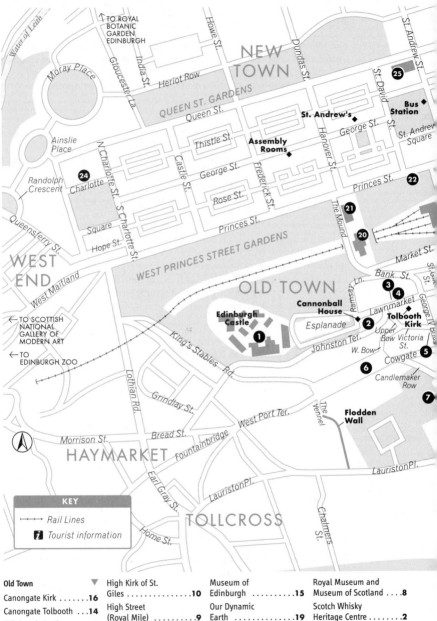

KEY

⊢—⊢—⊣ Rail Lines

🛈 Tourist information

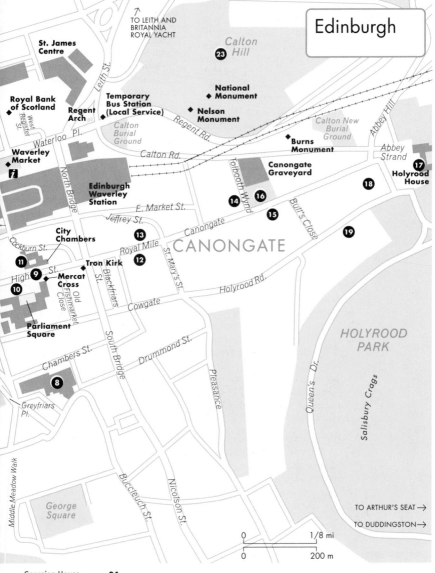

Edinburgh

St. James Centre

Royal Bank of Scotland

Regent Arch

Temporary Bus Station (Local Service)

TO LEITH AND BRITANNIA ROYAL YACHT

Calton Hill **23**

National Monument

Nelson Monument

Waterloo Pl.

Calton Burial Ground

Regent Rd.

West Register St.

Leith St.

North Bridge

Waverley Market

Calton Rd.

Calton New Burial Ground

Abbey Hill

Burns Monument

Abbey Strand

Edinburgh Waverley Station

Canongate Graveyard

Holyrood House **17**

18

Jeffrey St.

E. Market St.

14 **16**

15

Talbooth Wynd

Butt's Close

Cockburn St.

City Chambers

13

Royal Mile

Canongate

CANONGATE

19

11

High St.

9

Tron Kirk

12

St. Mary's St.

St.

10

Mercat Cross

Old Fishmarket Close

Blackfriars St.

Holyrood Rd.

Cowgate

Parliament Square

South Bridge

Drummond St.

HOLYROOD PARK

Chambers St.

8

Pleasance

Queen's Dr.

Salisbury Crags

Greyfriars Pl.

Buccleuch St.

Nicolson St.

Middle Meadow Walk

George Square

TO ARTHUR'S SEAT →

TO DUDDINGSTON →

0   1/8 mi
0   200 m

Military Tattoo, a festival of magnificently outfitted marching bands and regiments. Heading over the drawbridge and through the gatehouse, past the guards, you'll find the rough stone walls of the **Half-Moon Battery,** where the one-o'-clock gun is fired every day in an impressively anachronistic ceremony; these curving ramparts give Edinburgh Castle its distinctive appearance from miles away. Climb up through a second gateway and you come to the oldest surviving building in the complex, the tiny 11th-century **St. Margaret's Chapel,** named in honor of Saxon queen Margaret (1046–93), who had persuaded her husband, King Malcolm III (circa 1031–93), to move his court from Dunfermline to Edinburgh. Edinburgh's environs—the Lothians—were occupied by Anglian settlers with whom the queen felt more at home, or so the story goes (Dunfermline was surrounded by Celts). The **Crown Room,** a must-see, contains the "Honours of Scotland"—the crown, scepter, and sword that once graced the Scottish monarch. Upon the **Stone of Scone,** also in the Crown Room, Scottish monarchs once sat to be crowned. In the section now called **Queen Mary's Apartments,** Mary, Queen of Scots, gave birth to James VI of Scotland. The **Great Hall** displays arms and armor under an impressive vaulted, beamed ceiling. Scottish parliament meetings were conducted here until 1840. During the Napoléonic Wars in the early 19th century, the castle held French prisoners of war, whose carvings can still be seen on the vaults under the Great Hall.

> **WORD OF MOUTH**
>
> "A must, of course, when in Edinburgh is the Edinburgh Castle. If you have never been to the city before, the Castle is much more than just a castle. It is a small city in itself and you should plan on a half day to tour it all."
> —MargaretandTony
> "Take the guided tour of the castle. Even on a very windy day, it was short and a very good overview. Great history and views. Be prepared to walk up and down cobblestones." —J&G

Military features of interest include the **Scottish National War Memorial,** the **Scottish United Services Museum,** and the famous 15th-century Belgian-made cannon *Mons Meg.* This enormous piece of artillery has been silent since 1682, when it exploded while firing a salute for the duke of York; it now stands in an ancient hall behind the Half-Moon Battery. ⊠ *Off Castle Esplanade and Castlehill, Old Town* ☎ *0131/225–9846 Edinburgh Castle, 0131/226–7393 War Memorial* ⊕ *www.historic-scotland. gov.uk* ⊠ *£10.30* ☉ *Apr.–Oct., daily 9:30–6; Nov.–Mar., daily 9:30–5.*

NEED A BREAD? You can have lunch or afternoon tea overlooking panoramic views of the city at the **Redcoat Café** (⊠ Edinburgh Castle, Old Town ☎ 0131/225–9746). Baked sweets, sandwiches, soup, tea, and Starbucks coffee are all available at reasonable prices.

❾ **High Street (Royal Mile).** Some of Old Town's most impressive buildings and sights are on High Street, one of the five streets making up the Royal Mile. Also here are other, less obvious historic relics. Near Parliament

Square, look on the west side for a **heart** set in cobbles—it inspired Sir Walter Scott's novel *The Heart of Midlothian.*

Just outside Parliament House is the **Mercat Cross** (*mercat* means "market"), a great landmark of the old mercantile center, where in the early days executions were held, and where royal proclamations were—and are still—read. Across High Street from the High Kirk of St. Giles stands the **City Chambers,** now the seat of local government. Built by John Fergus, who adapted a design of John Adam in 1753, the chambers were originally known as the Royal Exchange and intended to be where merchants and lawyers could conduct business. ⊠ *Between Lawnmarket and Canongate, Old Town.*

⑩ High Kirk of St. Giles. Sometimes called St. Giles's Cathedral, this is one of the city's principal churches. There has been a church here since AD 854, although most of the present structure dates from either 1120 or 1829, when the church was restored. The tower, with its stone crown towering 161 feet above the ground, was completed between 1495 and 1500. The most elaborate feature is the **Chapel of the Order of the Thistle,** built onto the southeast corner of the church in 1911 for the exclusive use of Scotland's only chivalric order, the Most Ancient and Noble Order of the Thistle. It bears the belligerent national motto NEMO ME IMPUNE LACESSIT ("No one provokes me with impunity"). Inside the church stands a life-size statue of the Scot whose spirit still dominates the place—the great Protestant reformer and preacher John Knox. ⊠ *High St., Old Town* ☎ *0131/225–9442* ⊕ *www.stgiles.net* 🎫 *£2 suggested donation* ⊙ *May–Sept., weekdays 9–7, Sat. 9–5, Sun. 1–5; Oct.–Apr., Mon.–Sat. 9–5, Sun. 1–5.*

⑬ John Knox House. It's not certain that Scotland's severe religious reformer John Knox ever lived here, but there is evidence to show that he died here in 1572. Mementos of his life are on view inside, and the distinctive dwelling gives you a glimpse of what Old Town life was like in the 16th century. The projecting upper stories were once commonplace along the Royal Mile, darkening and further closing in the already narrow passage. Look for the initials of former owner James Mossman and his wife, carved into the stonework on the "marriage lintel." Mossman was goldsmith to Mary, Queen of Scots, and was hanged in 1573 for his allegiance to her. ⊠ *45 High St., Old Town* ☎ *0131/556–2647* ⊕ *www.scottishstorytellingcentre.co.uk* 🎫 *£3* ⊙ *Mon.–Sat. 10–6; last admission half hr before closing.*

❼ Kirk of the Greyfriars. Greyfriars Church, built circa 1620 on the site of a medieval monastery, was where the National Covenant, declaring that the Presbyterian Church in Scotland was independent of the monarch was signed in 1638. Informative panels tell the story, and there's a visitor center on-site. Be sure to search out the graveyard—one of the most evocative in Europe. Its old, tottering, elaborate tombstones mark the graves of some of Scotland's most respected heroes and despised villains. ⊠ *Greyfriars Pl., Old Town* ☎ *0131/226–5429* ⊕ *www.greyfriarskirk. com* 🎫 *Free* ⊙ *Easter–Oct., weekdays 10:30–4:30, Sat. 10:30–2:30; Nov.–Easter, Thurs. 1:30–3:30; groups by appointment.*

⏱ ⓳ Our Dynamic Earth. Using state-of-the-art technology, the 11 themed galleries at this interactive science gallery educate and entertain as they explore the wonders of the planet, from the polar regions to tropical rain forests. Geological history, from the big bang to the unknown future, is also examined. ✉ *Holyrood Rd., Holyrood* ☎ *0131/550–7800* ⊕ *www.dynamicearth.co.uk* 💷 *£8.95* ⏱ *Apr.–June, daily 10–5; July and Aug., daily 10–6; Sept. and Oct., daily 10–5; Nov.–Mar., Wed.–Sun. 10–5; last admission 1 hr before closing.*

⓱ Palace of Holyroodhouse. The setting for high drama—including at least

Fodor'sChoice one notorious murder, several major fires, and centuries of the colorful

★ life-styles of larger-than-life, power-hungry personalities—this is now Queen Elizabeth's official residence in Scotland. A doughty and impressive palace standing at the foot of the Royal Mile in a hilly public park, it is built around a graceful, lawned central court at the end of Canongate. When the queen or royal family is not in residence, you can take a guided tour; allow two hours to see everything. Many monarchs, including Charles II, Queen Victoria, and George V, have left their mark on its rooms, but it is Mary, Queen of Scots, whose spirit looms largest. For some visitors the most memorable room here is the little chamber in which David Rizzio (1533–66), secretary to Mary, Queen of Scots, met an unhappy end in 1566. Mary's second husband, Lord Darnley (Henry Stewart, 1545–65), hated Rizzio for his social-climbing ways and burst into the queen's rooms with his henchmen, dragged Rizzio into an antechamber, and stabbed him more than 50 times. Darnley himself was murdered the next year to make way for the queen's marriage to her lover, Bothwell.

The **King James Tower** is the oldest surviving section, containing the rooms of Mary, Queen of Scots, on the 2nd floor, and Lord Darnley's rooms below. Though much has been altered, there are fine fireplaces, paneling, plasterwork, tapestries, and 18th- and 19th-century furnishings throughout. At the south end of the palace front you'll find the **Royal Dining Room,** and along the south side are the **Throne Room** and other drawing rooms now used for social and ceremonial occasions.

At the back of the palace is the **King's Bedchamber.** The 150-foot-long **Great Picture Gallery,** on the north side, displays the portraits of 110 Scottish monarchs. These were commissioned by Charles II, who was eager to demonstrate his Scottish ancestry—some of the royal figures here are fictional and the likenesses of others imaginary. All the portraits were painted by a Dutch artist, Jacob De Witt, who signed a contract in 1684 with the queen's cash keeper, Hugh Wallace. The contract bound him to deliver 110 pictures within two years, for which he received an annual stipend of £120. Surely one of the more desperate scenes in the palace's history is that of the artist feverishly turning out potboiler portraits at the rate of one a week for two years.

Holyroodhouse has its origins in an Augustinian monastery founded by David I (1084–1153) in 1128. In the 15th and 16th centuries, Scottish royalty, preferring the comforts of the abbey to the drafty rooms of Edinburgh Castle, settled into Holyroodhouse, expanding and altering the buildings until the palace eventually eclipsed the monastery.

After the Union of the Crowns in 1603, when the Scottish royal court packed its bags and decamped for England, the building fell into decline. Oliver Cromwell (1599–1658), the Protestant Lord Protector of England who had conquered Scotland, ordered the palace rebuilt after a fire in 1650, but the work was poorly carried out. When the monarchy was restored with the ascension of Charles II (1630–85) to the British throne in 1660, Holyrood was rebuilt in the architectural style of Louis XIV (1638–1715), and this is the style you see today. Queen Victoria (1819–1901) and her grandson King George V (1865–1936) heralded a renewed interest in the palace: the buildings were once more refurbished and made suitable for royal residence. Behind the palace lie the open grounds and looming crags of Holyrood Park, the hunting ground of early Scottish kings.

Queen's Gallery, in a former church and school at the entrance to the palace, holds rotating exhibits from the Royal Collection. From the top of Edinburgh's minimountain, **Arthur's Seat** (822 feet), views are breathtaking. ⊠ *Abbey Strand, Holyrood, Old Town* ☎ *0131/556–1096* 📠 *0131/557–5256* ⊕ *www.royal.gov.uk* 🎟 *£8.80* ☉ *Apr.–Oct., daily 9:30–6; Nov.–Mar., daily 9:30–4:30. Last admission 1 hr before closing. Closed during royal visits.*

★ ⓫ **Real Mary King's Close.** Hidden beneath the City Chambers, this narrow, cobbled close, or lane, named after a former landowner, is said to be one of Edinburgh's most haunted sites. The close was sealed off in 1645 to quarantine residents who became sick when the bubonic plague swept through the city, and many victims were herded there to die. After the plague passed, the bodies were removed and buried, and the street was reopened. A few people returned, but they soon reported ghostly goings-on and departed, leaving the close empty for decades afterward. In 1753 city authorities built the Royal Exchange (later the City Chambers) directly over the close, sealing it off and, unwittingly, ensuring it remained intact, except for the buildings' upper stories, which were destroyed. Today you can walk among the remains of the shops and houses. People still report so-called cold spots in some rooms, ghostly visions, and eerie sounds, such as the crying of a young girl. Children under 5 are not admitted. ⊠ *Writers' Court, Old Town* ☎ *0870/243–0160* ⊕ *www.realmarykingsclose.com* 🎟 *£8* ☉ *Apr.–Oct., daily 10–9; Nov.–Mar., daily 10–4.*

❽ **Royal Museum and Museum of Scotland.** In an imposing Victorian building on Chambers Street, the Royal Museum houses an internationally renowned collection of art and artifacts relating to natural, scientific, and industrial history. Its treasures include the Lewis Chessmen, 11 intricately carved ivory chessmen found on one of the Western Isles in the 19th century. The museum's main hall, with its soaring roof and "birdcage" design, is architecturally interesting in its own right. Redevelopment between 2007 and 2011 will modernize many displays. The striking, contemporary building next door houses the Museum of Scotland, with modern displays concentrating on Scotland's own heritage. This state-of-the-art, no-expense-spared museum is full of playful models, complex reconstructions, and paraphernalia ranging from ancient Pictish articles to 21st-century cultural artifacts. ⊠ *Chambers St., Old*

Fodor'sChoice ★

Town ☎ *0131/225–4422* ⊕ *www.nms.ac.uk* ✉ *Free* ☉ *Mon. and Wed.–Sat. 10–5, Tues. 10–8, Sun. noon–5.*

NEED A BREAK? **Café Delos** (✉ Chambers St., Old Town ☎ 0131/225-7534) in the Royal Museum's main hall serves tea, coffee, cookies, cakes, and savory snacks from 10 to 4. The **Soupson Tearoom** (✉ Chambers St., Old Town ☎ 0131/225-7534), also in the museum, adds soups and salads to its offerings.

★ ⑱ **Scottish Parliament.** Scotland's somewhat controversial Parliament building is dramatically modern, with irregular curves and angles that mirror the twisting shapes of the surrounding landscape. The structure's artistry is most apparent when you step inside, where the gentle slopes, (sustainable) forest's worth of oak, polished concrete and granite, walls of glass, and subtle imagery create an understated magnificence appropriate to the modest but proud Scots. It's worth taking the 45-minute tour to see the main hall and debating chamber, a committee room, and other areas. Another option is to call well in advance to get a free ticket to view Parliament in action. Originally conceived by the late Catalan architect Enric Mirales, the design was completed by his widow, Bernadette Tagliabue, in August 2004. ✉ *Horse Wynd, Old Town* ☎ *0131/348-5200* ⊕ *www.scottish.parliament.uk* ✉ *£3.50 for tour* ☉ *Tours Nov.–Mar., daily 10:15–3:15; Apr.–Oct., weekdays 10:15–5:15, weekends 10:15–3:15; no tours when Parliament is sitting, generally Tues.–Thurs., but call or check Web site.*

Also Worth Seeing

⑯ **Canongate Kirk.** This unadorned building, built in 1688, is run by the Church of Scotland and has an interesting graveyard. Although you can find information about the graveyard in the church, local authorities actually oversee it. This is the final resting place of some notable Scots, including economist Adam Smith (1723–90), author of *The Wealth of Nations* (1776), who once lived in the nearby 17th-century Panmure House. Also buried here are Dugald Stewart (1753–1828), the leading European philosopher of his time, and the undervalued Scots poet Robert Fergusson (1750–74). Against the eastern wall of the graveyard is a bronze sculpture of the head of Mrs. Agnes McLehose, the "Clarinda" of the copious correspondence in which Robert Burns engaged while confined to his lodgings with an injured leg in 1788. The curiously literary affair ended when Burns left Edinburgh in 1788 to take up a farm tenancy and to marry Jean Armour. ✉ *Canongate, Old Town* ☎ *0131/ 556-3515* ⊕ *www.canongatekirk.com* ✉ *Free* ☉ *Daily.*

⑭ **Canongate Tolbooth.** Nearly every city and town in Scotland once had a tolbooth. Originally a customhouse where tolls were gathered, a tolbooth came to mean "town hall" and later "prison" because detention cells were in the basement. The building where Canongate's town council once met now has a museum, the **People's Story,** which focuses on the lives of "ordinary" people from the 18th century to today. Exhibits describe how Canongate once bustled with the activities of the tradespeople needed to supply life's essentials in the days before superstores. Displays include a reconstruction of a cooper's workshop and a 1940s kitchen. ✉ *163 Canongate, Old Town* ☎ *0131/529–4057* ⊕ *www. cac.org.uk* 🎫 *Free* 🕑 *Mon.–Sat. 10–5, Sun. during festival 2–5.*

⑤ George IV Bridge. It's not immediately obvious that this is in fact a bridge, as buildings are closely packed most of the way along both sides. At the corner of the bridge stands one of the most photographed sculptures in Scotland, *Greyfriars Bobby.* This statue pays tribute to the famous Skye terrier who kept vigil beside his master John Gray's grave in the Greyfriar's churchyard for 14 years after Gray died in 1858. Bobby left only for a short time each day to be fed at a nearby coffee house. The 1961 Walt Disney film *Greyfriars Bobby* tells the story, though liberties were taken with the historical details. ✉ *Between Bank St. and intersection with Candlemaker Row, Old Town.*

❸ Gladstone's Land. This narrow, six-story tenement, next to the Assembly Hall on Lawnmarket, is a survivor from the 17th century. Typical Scottish architectural features are evident on two floors, including an arcaded ground floor (even in the city center, livestock sometimes inhabited the ground floor). The house has magnificent painted ceilings and is furnished in the style of a 17th-century merchant's home. ✉ *477B Lawnmarket, Old Town* ☎ *0131/226–5856* ⊕ *www.nts.org.uk* 🎫 *£5* 🕑 *Apr.–Oct., daily 10–5; last admission at 4:30.*

❻ Grassmarket. For centuries an agricultural marketplace, Grassmarket now is the site of numerous shops, bars, and restaurants, making it a hive of activity at night. Sections of the Old Town wall can be traced on the north (castle) side by a series of steps that run steeply up from Grassmarket to Johnston Terrace above. The best-preserved section of the wall can be found by crossing to the south side and climbing the steps of the lane called the Vennel. Here, the 16th-century **Flodden Wall** comes in from the east and turns southward at Telfer's Wall, a 17th-century extension. The **cobbled cross** at the east end marks the site of the town gallows where many 17th-century Covenanters were hanged for resisting Charles I's efforts to enforce Anglican or "English" ideologies on the Scottish people. Judges were known to issue the death sentence with the words, "Let them glorify God in the Grassmarket."

⑫ Museum of Childhood. Even adults tend to enjoy this cheerfully noisy museum—a cacophony of childhood memorabilia, vintage toys, and dolls, as well as a reconstructed schoolroom, street scene, fancy-dress party, and nursery. The museum claims to have been the first in the world devoted solely to the history of childhood. It's two blocks past the North Bridge–South Bridge junction on High Street. ✉ *42 High St., Old Town* ☎ *0131/529–4142* 🖶 *0131/558–3103* ⊕ *www.cac.org.uk* 🎫 *Free* 🕑 *Mon.–Sat. 10–5, Sun. during festival 2–5.*

⑮ Museum of Edinburgh. A must-see if you're interested in the details of Old Town life, this former home, dating from 1570, is a fascinating museum of local history, displaying Scottish pottery and Edinburgh silver and glassware. ✉ *142 Canongate, Old Town* ☎ *0131/529–4143* ⊕ *www. cac.org.uk* 🎫 *Free* 🕑 *Mon.–Sat. 10–5, Sun. during festival 2–5.*

 ❷ Scotch Whisky Heritage Centre. The mysterious process that turns malted barley and springwater into one of Scotland's most important exports is revealed in this museum. Although whisky-making is not in itself packed with drama, the center manages an imaginative presentation using models and tableaux viewed while riding in low-speed barrel-cars. At one point you are inside a huge vat surrounded by bubbling sounds and malty smells. The Amber Restaurant serves lunch; you can choose among 270 Scotch whiskies. ⊠ *354 Castlehill, Old Town* ☎ *0131/220–0441* ⊕ *www.whisky-heritage.co.uk* ⊡ *£8.95* ☉ *May–Sept., daily 9:30–6:30, last tour 5:30; Oct.–Apr., daily 10–6, last tour 5.*

❹ **Writers' Museum.** Down a close off Lawnmarket is Lady Stair's House, built in 1622 and a good example of 17th-century urban architecture. Inside, the Writer's Museum evokes Scotland's literary past with such exhibits as the letters, possessions, and original manuscripts of Sir Walter Scott, Robert Louis Stevenson, and Robert Burns. The Stevenson collection is particularly strong. ⊠ *Off Lawnmarket, Old Town* ☎ *0131/ 529–4901* ⊕ *www.cac.org.uk* ⊡ *Free* ☉ *Mon.–Sat. 10–5, last admission 4:45, Sun. during festival noon–5.*

New Town

It was not until the Scottish Enlightenment, a civilizing time of expansion in the 1700s, that the city fathers decided to break away from the Royal Mile's rocky slope and create a new Edinburgh below the castle, a little to the north. This was to become the New Town, with elegant squares, classical facades, wide streets, and harmonious proportions. It wasn't just aesthetics that spurred this new development: Edinburgh's unsanitary conditions—primarily a result of overcrowded living quarters—were becoming notorious.

To help remedy this sorry state of affairs, in 1767 the city's lord provost (the Scots term for mayor), urged the town council to hold a competition to design a new district for Edinburgh. The winner was an unknown young architect named James Craig (1744–95). His plan called for a grid of three main east–west streets, balanced at either end by two grand squares. These streets survive today, though some of the buildings that line them have been altered by later development. Princes Street lies to the south, with Queen Street to the north and George Street as the axis, punctuated by St. Andrew and Charlotte squares. A map of the area reveals a geometric symmetry unusual in Britain. Even the Princes Street Gardens are balanced by the Queen Street Gardens, to the north. Princes Street was conceived as an exclusive residential address, with an open vista facing the castle. It has since been altered by the demands of business and shopping, but the vista remains.

The New Town was expanded several times after Craig's death and now covers an area about three times larger than Craig envisioned. Indeed, some of the most elegant facades came later and can be found by strolling north of the Queen Street Gardens. You can save sightseeing time by riding the free galleries bus, which connects the National Gallery of Scotland, Scottish National Portrait Gallery, Scottish National Gallery of Modern Art, and Dean Gallery daily from 11 to 5. You can board or leave the bus at any of the galleries.

Main Attractions

BRITANNIA – Moored on the waterfront at Leith, Edinburgh's port north of the city center, is the former Royal Yacht *Britannia*, launched in Scotland in 1953 and now retired to her home country. The Royal Apartments and the more functional engine room, bridge, galleys, and captain's cabin are all open to view. The land-based visitor center within the huge Ocean Terminal shopping mall has exhibits and photographs about the yacht's history. ⊠ *Ocean Terminal, Leith* ☎ *0131/555–5566* ⊕ *www.royalyachtbritannia.co.uk* ☎ *£9* ◎ *Mar.–Oct., 9:30–6; Nov.–Feb., 10–5.*

12

★ ❷❹ **Georgian House.** The National Trust for Scotland has furnished this house in period style to show the elegant domestic arrangements of an affluent family of the late 18th century. The hallway was designed to accommodate sedan chairs, in which 18th-century grandees were carried through the streets. ⊠ *7 Charlotte Sq., New Town* ☎ *0131/226–3318* ⊕ *www.nts.org.uk* ☎ *£5* ◎ *Mar., daily 11–3; Apr.–June and Sept.–Nov., daily 10–5; July and Aug., daily 10–7; Nov., daily 11–3; last admission half hr before closing.*

❷❶ **National Gallery of Scotland.** Opened to the public in 1859, the National
Fodor'sChoice Gallery presents a wide selection of paintings from the Renaissance to
★ the post-impressionist period within a grand neoclassical building designed by William Playfair. Most famous are the old-master paintings bequeathed by the duke of Sutherland, including Titian's *Three Ages of Man*. All the great names are here; works by Velázquez, El Greco, Rembrandt, Goya, Poussin, Clouet, Turner, Degas, Monet, and Van Gogh, among others, complement a fine collection of Scottish art, including Sir Henry Raeburn's *Reverend Robert Walker Skating on Duddingston Loch* and other masterworks by Ramsay, Raeburn, and Wilkie. The Weston Link connects the National Gallery of Scotland to the Royal Scottish Academy and provides expanded gallery space as well as a restaurant, bar, café, information center, and shop. The free galleries bus stops here daily on the hour from 11 to 4. ⊠ *The Mound, Old Town* ☎ *0131/624–6200 general inquiries, 0131/332–2266 recorded information* ⊕ *www.nationalgalleries.org* ☎ *Free* ◎ *Fri.–Wed. 10–5, Thurs. 10–7. Print Room, weekdays 10–12:30 and 2–4:30 by appointment.*

ROYAL BOTANIC GARDEN EDINBURGH – Britain's largest rhododendron and azalea gardens are part of the varied and comprehensive collection of plant and flower species in this 70-acre garden, just north of the city center. An impressive Chinese garden has the largest collection of wild-origin Chinese plants outside China. There is a cafeteria, plus a gift shop that sells plants and books. Take a taxi to the garden; or ride Bus 27 from Princes Street or Bus 23 from Hanover Street. To walk to the garden from the New Town, take Dundas Street, the continuation of Hanover Street, and turn left at the clock tower onto Inverleith Row (about 20 minutes). ⊠ *Inverleith Row, Inverleith* ☎ *0131/552–7171* ⊕ *www.rbge.org.uk* ☎ *Free; greenhouses £3.50* ◎ *Nov.–Feb., daily 10–4; Mar.–Sept., daily 10–7; Oct., daily, 10–6. Guided tours, Apr.–Sept., daily at 11 and 2.*

❷❷ **Scott Monument.** What appears to be a Gothic cathedral spire chopped off and planted in the east end of the Princes Street Gardens is the na-

Leith, Edinburgh's Seaport

JUST NORTH OF THE CITY, Leith sits on the south shore of the Firth of Forth and was a separate town until it merged with the city in 1920. After World War II and up until the 1980s, the declining seaport had a reputation for poverty and crime. In recent years, however, it has been revitalized with the restoration of commercial buildings as well as the construction of new luxury housing, bringing a buzz of trendiness. All of the docks have been redeveloped; the Old East and Old West docks are now the administrative headquarters of the Scottish Executive.

In earlier times, Leith was the stage for many historic happenings. In 1560 Mary of Guise, the mother of Mary, Queen of Scots, ruled Scotland from Leith; her daughter landed in Leith the following year to embark on her infamous reign. A century later, Cromwell led his troops to Leith to root out Scots's royalists. An arch of the Leith Citadel reminds all of the Scots victory. Leith also prides itself on being a "home of golf" because official rules to the game were devised in 1744, in what is today Links Park. The rolling green mounds here hide the former field and cannon sites of past battles.

It's worth exploring the lowest reaches of the Water of Leith (the river that flows through the town), an area where restaurants, shops, and pubs proliferate. The major attraction for visitors here is the former royal yacht *Britannia*, moored outside the huge Ocean Terminal shopping mall. Reach Leith by walking down Leith Street and Leith Walk, from the east end of Princes Street (20 to 30 minutes) or take Lothian Bus 22 (Britannia Ocean Drive, Leith).

---

tion's tribute to Sir Walter—a 200-foot-high monument looming over Princes Street. Built in 1844 in honor of Scotland's most famous author, Sir Walter Scott, the author of *Ivanhoe, Waverley,* and many other novels and poems, it's centered on a marble statue of Scott and his favorite dog, Maida. It's worth taking the time to explore the immediate area, Princes Street Gardens, one of the prettiest city parks in Britain. In the open-air theater, amid the park's trim flower beds, stately trees, and carefully tended lawns, brass bands occasionally play. Here, too, is the famous **monument to David Livingstone,** whose African meeting with H. M. Stanley is part of Scot-American history. ⊠ *Princes St., New Town* ☎ *0131/529–4068* ⊕ *www.cac.org.uk* ✉ *£3* ⊙ *Apr.–Sept., Mon.–Sat. 9–6, Sun. 10–6; Oct.–Mar., Mon.–Sat. 9–3, Sun. 10–3.*

OFF THE BEATEN PATH

SCOTTISH NATIONAL GALLERY OF MODERN ART – This handsome former school building on Belford Road, close to the New Town, displays paintings and sculpture, including works by Pablo Picasso, Georges Braque, Henri Matisse, and André Derain. The gallery also has an excellent restaurant in the basement. The free galleries bus stops here on the half hour. Across the street is the Dean Gallery, also part of the National Galleries of Scotland; it showcases modern art. ⊠ *Belford Rd., Dean Village* ☎ *0131/624–6200* ⊕ *www.nationalgalleries.org* ✉ *Free* ⊙ *Daily 10–5; extended hrs during festival.*

★ ㉕ **Scottish National Portrait Gallery.** A magnificent red-sandstone Gothic building dating from 1889 on Queen Street houses this must-visit institution. The gallery contains a superb Thomas Gainsborough painting and portraits by the Scottish artists Allan Ramsay (1713–84) and Sir Henry Raeburn (1756–1823), among many others. You can see portraits of classic literary figures such as Robert Burns and Sir Walter Scott, and modern portraits depict actors, sports stars, and living members of the royal family. The building's beautiful William Hole murals representing Scots from the Stone Age to the 19th century are themselves worthy of study. The free galleries bus stops here every day from 11:15 to 4:15. ⊠ *1 Queen St., New Town* ☎ *0131/624–6200* ⊕ *www. nationalgalleries.org* ✉ *Free; charge for special exhibitions* ☉ *Daily 10–5, Thurs. 10–7; extended hrs during festival.*

Also Worth Seeing

㉓ **Calton Hill.** The architectural styles represented by the extraordinary collection of monuments here include mock Gothic—the Old Observatory, for example—and neoclassical. Under the latter category falls the monument William Playfair (1789–1857) designed to honor his talented uncle, the geologist and mathematician John Playfair (1748–1819), as well as his cruciform **New Observatory.** The piece that commands the most attention, however, is the so-called **National Monument,** often referred to as "Edinburgh's [or Scotland's] Disgrace." Intended to mimic Athens's Parthenon, this monument for the dead of the Napoléonic Wars was started in 1822 to the specifications of a design by Playfair. But in 1830, only 12 columns later, money ran out, and the columned facade became a monument to high aspirations and poor fund-raising. The tallest monument on Calton Hill is the 100-foot-high **Nelson Monument,** completed in 1815 in honor of Britain's naval hero Horatio Nelson (1758–1805); you can climb its 143 steps for sweeping city views. The **Burns Monument** is the circular Corinthian temple below Regent Road. ⊠ *Bounded by Leith St. to the west and Regent Rd. to the south, Calton* ☎ *0131/556–2716* ⊕ *www.cac.org.uk* ✉ *£3 Nelson Monument* ☉ *Nelson Monument Apr.–Sept., Mon. 1–6, Tues.–Sat. 10–6; Oct.–Mar., Mon.–Sat. 10–3.*

㉑ **Royal Scottish Academy.** The William Playfair–designed Academy hosts temporary art exhibitions (Monet paintings, for example), but is also worth visiting for a look at the imposing, neoclassic architecture. The underground Weston Link connects the museum to the National Gallery of Scotland. ⊠ *The Mound, Old Town* ☎ *0131/225–6671* ⊕ *www. royalscottishacademy.org* ✉ *Free* ☉ *Mon.–Sat. 10–5, Sun. noon–5.*

WHERE TO EAT

Edinburgh has many restaurants serving sophisticated international cuisines, but you may also notice a strong emphasis on traditional style. This tends to mean the Scottish–French style that harks back to the "Auld Alliance," founded in the 13th century against the English. The Scots element is the preference for fresh and local foodstuffs; the French supply the sauces, often poured on after cooking. Restaurants tend to be

CLOSE UP

Ancestor Hunting

ARE YOU A CAMERON OR A CAMPBELL, Mackenzie or Macdonald? If so, you may be one of the more than 25 million people of Scottish descent around the world. It was the Highland clearances of the 18th and 19th century, in which tenant farmers were driven from their homes and replaced with sheep, that started the mass emigration to North America and Australia. Before or during a trip, you can do a little geneaological research or pursue your family tree more seriously.

Start at VisitScotland's Web site, ⊕ www.ancestralscotland.com, for information about clans and surnames, books, and family history societies. The site steers you to key sources, such as ⊕ www.scotlandspeople.gov.uk, the official government source of genealogical data; there's a charge for using that service.

You may want to do research at Edinburgh's **General Register Office**

for Scotland (⊠ 3 W. Register St. ☎ 0131/314–4449 for booking ⊕ www.gro-scotland.gov.uk). The fee for research here, based on how long you spend there, ranges from £10 for part of a day to £17 for a full day (a week costs £65). Space is limited, and no reservations are taken for searches of less than a day; but some places are available each day on a first-come, first-served basis.

There are plans to open the **Scotlands People Centre in Edinburgh** in late 2007 (⊕ www. scotlandspeoplehub.gov.uk); check with VisitScotland. Willing to pay for help? Companies such as **Scottish Ancestral Trail** (⊕ www.scottish-ancestral-trail.co.uk) do the research and plan a trip around your family history. Throughout Scotland, you can check bookstores for information and visit clan museums and societies.

---

small, so it's best to make reservations at the more popular ones, even on weekdays and definitely at festival time. As Edinburgh is an unusually small capital, most of the good restaurants are within walking distance of the main streets, Princes Street and the Royal Mile.

Prices

It's possible to eat well in Edinburgh without spending a fortune. Multicourse pretheater or prix-fixe options are common and almost always less expensive than ordering à la carte. Even at restaurants in the £££££ price category, you can spend under £60 for two if you order prudently. A service charge of 10% or more may be added to your bill, though this practice is not adhered to uniformly. If no charge has been added and you are satisfied with the service, a 10% tip is appropriate.

WHAT IT COSTS In pounds				
£££££	**££££**	**£££**	**££**	**£**
AT DINNER over £22	£18–£22	£13–£17	£7–£12	under £7

Prices are per person for a main course.

Old Town

FRENCH ✗ **Merchants.** This is a bustling, cheery cavern with bright scarlet walls,
££££££ mirrors, plants, and a nonstop jazz sound track, set beneath the dramatic arch of George IV Bridge. The menu ranges from simple haggis and beef to a mille-feuille of scallops and lamb chops with raspberry-and-mint sauce. Its more ambitious dishes are reminiscent of nouvelle cuisine, but Merchants really does the basics best. Prix-fixe lunches run from £10.95 to £12.95, dinners from £21.95 to £24.95. ✉ *17 Merchant St., Old Town* ☎ *0131/225–4009* ☐ *AE, DC, MC, V.*

£££–£££££ ✗ **Witchery by the Castle.** The hundreds of "witches" who were executed
Fodor'sChoice on Castlehill, just yards from where you will be seated, are the inspiration for this outstanding and atmospheric restaurant. The cavernous interior, complete with flickering candlelight, is festooned with cabalistic insignia and tarot-card characters. Gilded and painted ceilings reflect the close links between France and Scotland, as does the menu, which includes roasted quail with braised endive and scallops with spiced pork belly and carrot puree. Pre- and post-theater (5:30–6:30 and 10:30–11:30) £12.50 two-course specials are an inexpensive way to sample the exceptional cuisine. (The restaurant also offers lodging in seven sumptuous suites.) ✉ *Castlehill, Royal Mile, Old Town* ☎ *0131/225–5613* ☐ *AE, DC, MC, V.*

★ ££–£££ ✗ **Le Sept.** This charming French bistro full of light, mismatched chairs and Parisian-art posters is an Edinburgh institution. It's friendly, lively, unfussy, and famed for its crepes with adventurous fillings. The daily changing menu also lists simple staples such as delicately cooked salmon fillets and succulent lamb stew. The wine list is similarly select, and the service is always delightful. Fixed-price lunches are an unbeatable value, with three courses costing £10. ✉ *5 Hunter Sq., Old Town* ☎ *0131/225–5428* ☐ *AE, DC, MC, V.*

SCOTTISH ✗ **The Tower.** On the rooftop of the Museum of Scotland, this restau-
£££–£££££ rant offers a feast of modern aesthetics—tweed banquettes, suede chairs, glass walls—before you even get to the menu. It also has one of the finest vistas in the capital. The Tower has a high-powered ambience and a sophisticated menu with an exquisite oyster and shellfish selection, Aberdeen Angus beef, roast saddle of wild red venison, and more. The two-course pretheater (5–6:30) supper is an especially good value, but don't let the lovely Edinburgh skyline distract you from making your curtain time. ✉ *Museum of Scotland, Chambers St., Old Town* ☎ *0131/225–3003* ⌖ *Reservations essential* ☐ *AE, DC, MC, V.*

££–££££ ✗ **Doric Tavern.** Beyond the bar's grand entrance staircase is a languid bistro environment enhanced by the stripped wood floor, plain wood tables, and color scheme in subdued orange and terra cotta. The menu lists a selection of fresh fish, meat, and vegetarian dishes, plus a daily special such as roast-pigeon salad with raspberry-vinegar dressing. Prix-fixe lunch and dinner options are an excellent value. ✉ *15/16 Market St., Old Town* ☎ *0131/225–1084* ⌖ *Reservations essential* ☐ *AE, MC, V.*

££–£££ ✗ **Beehive Inn.** Some 400 years ago the Beehive was a coaching inn, and outside the pub's doors once stood the main city gallows. Bar meals and snacks are served throughout the day, downstairs or in the beer garden. Upstairs, Rafters Restaurant opens at 6 with a dinner menu; the grilled salmon steaks are a good option. The bar can be noisy, but there's usually a quieter spot to be found. You can book literary lunch and supper packages downstairs in conjunction with the McEwan's Edinburgh Literary Pub Tour, which departs from here. ⊠ *18–20 Grassmarket, Old Town* ☎ *0131/225–7171* ▤ *AE, MC, V.*

THAI
££–£££ ✕ **Thai Orchid.** The statue of a golden Buddha greets you at this stylish restaurant where each table has an orchid for its centerpiece. Rich reds and browns, a portrait of the Thai king, and the traditionally dressed staff transport you to Thailand, if only for a few hours. To start, try the *todd mun kao pode* (deep-fried corn cakes with sweet-and-sour peanut and coriander dip). Good main courses include *pla priew wan* (monkfish poached with coconut milk) or *pedt Orchid,* duck stir-fried with mango, chili, garlic, and red peppers. The sticky rice with coconut milk and mango is an unmissable dessert. ⊠ *5A Johnston Terr., Old Town* ☎ *0131/225–6633* ▤ *MC, V.*

VEGETARIAN
★ **££** ✕ **David Bann.** In the heart of the Old Town, this ultrahip vegetarian and vegan favorite attracts young locals with its light, airy, modern dining room and creative menu. Tap water comes with mint and strawberries; dishes are sizable and extremely colorful. The food is so flavorful that carnivores may forget they're eating vegetarian. Try the spinach and smoked cheese strudel and the malt-whisky pannacotta. ⊠ *56–58 St. Mary's St., Old Town* ☎ *0131/556–5888* ▤ *AE, DC, MC, V.*

New Town

CHINESE
££–£££ ✕ **Kweilin.** This pleasant family-run restaurant serves such favorites as aromatic crispy duck, and bean curd with vegetables. The lunch menu is a pricey £15 but worth it, and the special four-course dinner menus are an even better value, starting at £23 per person. Amid the traditional Chinese decor are several large paintings depicting scenes from the Kwangsi Province, of which Kweilin is the capital. ⊠ *19–21 Dundas St., New Town* ☎ *0131/557–1875* ▤ *AE, MC, V* ☯ *Closed Mon. Jan.–Nov.*

ECLECTIC
££££–£££££ ✕ **Oloroso.** In the heart of the New Town and close to the main shopping streets, this is the perfect spot for a revitalizing lunch or dinner after exploring the city. The contemporary international cooking reflects influences from Europe and Asia, service is efficient and friendly, and the bar serves some of the best cocktails in Britain. Try the roasted duck breast with braised red cabbage and apples, or the aubergine *galette* (eggplant tart) with a tomato-and-cinnamon sauce. The wine list has about 230 selections, including champagne. The dining room and roof terrace have stunning views across the Firth of Forth to the hills of Fife on one side, and the castle and city rooftops on the other. ⊠ *33 Castle St., New Town* ☎ *0131/226–7614* ▤ *AE, DC, MC, V.*

£££–££££ ✕ **The Dome.** The splendid interior of this former bank, with painted plasterwork and a central dome, provides an elegant backdrop for relaxed dining. Or you could just opt for a drink at the bar, a hot spot where sophisticates wind down after work. The toasted BLT sandwiches are almost big enough for two, but if you're ravenous the eclectic menu offers many other options: try the tortellini in a broccoli-and-blue-cheese sauce or the char-grilled chicken salad with naan bread. ☒ *14 George St., New Town* ☎ *0131/624–8624* ▭ *AE, MC, V.*

ℰℰ–ℰℰℰ ✕ **Rick's.** There's no *Casablanca* theme, and Sam doesn't play it even once, but the local office crowd makes things lively after 5 at this restaurant-bar within a hotel. The minimalist design is Manhattan-esque and ultrachic. The imaginative menu includes duck breast with pink peppercorn sauce, asparagus ravioli, and crispy salmon fillet with Asian fried rice. The bright lobby bar serves cocktails amid brash music and chrome-and-stone decor. ☒ *55A Fredrick St., New Town* ☎ *0131/ 622–7800* ▭ *AE, MC, V.*

FRENCH ✕ **Pompadour.** As might be expected of a restaurant named after the king's
★ **ℰℰℰℰ** mistress, Madame de Pompadour, the dining room here is inspired by the court of Louis XV, with subtle plasterwork and rich murals. The cuisine is also classic French, with top-quality Scottish produce completing the happiest of alliances. The extensive, well-chosen wine list complements such dishes as sea bass with crispy leeks and caviar-butter sauce, whole lobster with mustard and cheese, and loin of venison with potato pancakes. This is the place to go if you want a festive night out, and it's ideal for the formal lunch that needs lightening up. ☒ *Caledonian Hilton Hotel, Princes St., New Town* ☎ *0131/222–8777* ⌂ *Reservations essential* ▭ *AE, DC, MC, V* ☉ *Closed Sun. and Mon.*

ℰℰℰ–ℰℰℰℰ ✕ **Le Café St. Honoré.** Quintessentially Parisian in style, this restaurant reflects all that is charming about French-café dining. From the moment you enter the beautifully lit room you are transported into the decadently stylish belle epoque. A concise menu leaves more time for chat. You might start off with a warm salad of scallops, monkfish, chorizo, and pine nuts, followed by lamb confit or panfried turbot cooked with cider, green peppercorns, and prawns. ☒ *34 N.W. Thistle Street La., New Town* ☎ *0131/ 226–2211* ▭ *AE, DC, MC, V.*

ITALIAN ✕ **La Rusticana.** Hanover Street exists to delight lovers of Italian food;
ℰ–ℰℰℰ some of the best pasta and pizza restaurants compete here, but this one usually wins the day. Stronger on pasta than pizza, La Rusticana remains a good value, only marginally above average in price. A favorite of locals, it is popular for business meetings, and a generous patron of charity events. ☒ *90 Hanover St., New Town* ☎ *0131/225–2227* ☒ *25 Cockburn St., Old Town* ☎ *0131/225–2832* ▭ *AE, DC, MC, V.*

SCOTTISH ✕ **Number One.** Within the Edwardian splendor of the Balmoral Hotel,
ℰℰℰℰ–ℰℰℰℰℰ this restaurant matches its grand surroundings with a menu that highlights the best of Scottish seafood and game. Try the roulade of organic salmon with langoustine tortellini or the loin of Perthshire venison with herb crust and beetroot-and-chive *jus*. The wine list is extensive, the service impeccable. All in all, this is the kind of stylish yet unstuffy restaurant that is perfect for an intimate dinner. ☒ *Princes St., New Town* ☎ *0131/557–6727* ⌂ *Reservations essential* ▭ *AE, DC, MC, V.*

ℰℰ–ℰℰℰℰ ✕ **A Room in the Town.** At this relaxed, friendly bistro serving Scots–French fare, there's a strong emphasis on fresh local meat, with the Scottish touch accounting for slightly sweeter-than-usual sauces. You may bring your

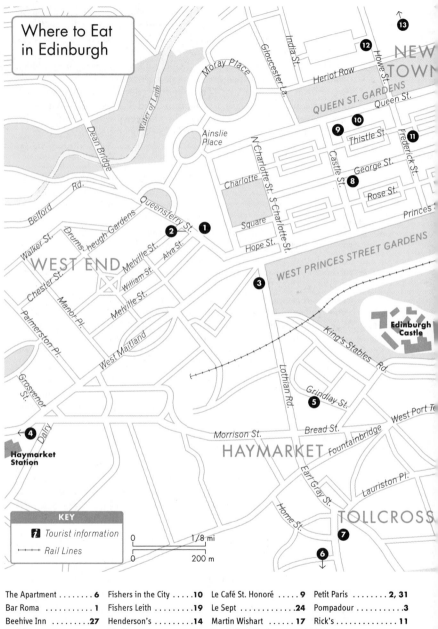

Where to Eat
in Edinburgh

KEY

i Tourist information

Rail Lines

0 ____ 1/8 mi

0 ____ 200 m

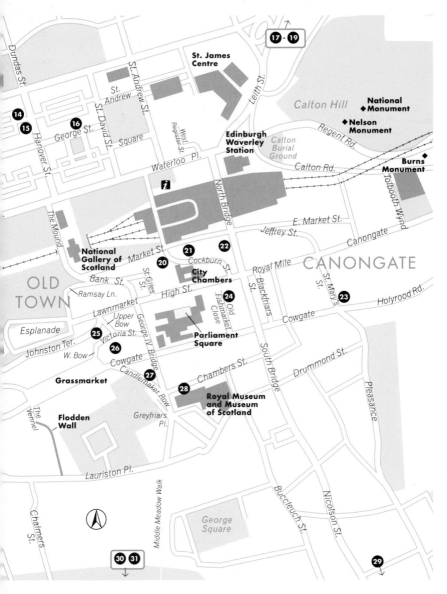

The Tower **30**
Witchery by
the Castle **26**

own bottle of wine—an excellent wineshop is just a block away—to off-set the somewhat high prices, although the restaurant serves wine, too, along with very nice brandy. Scottishly plain but Continentally cheerful thanks to bright colors and wooden fixtures, it's perfect for a sociable night out with friends. ⊠ *18 Howe St., New Town* ☎ *0131/225–8204* ⌂ *Reservations essential* ▤ *MC, V.*

VEGETARIAN
£–££

✕ **Henderson's.** This was Edinburgh's original vegetarian restaurant long before it was fashionable to serve healthful, meatless creations. The salad bar has more than a dozen different salads each day; a massive plateful costs less than £5. Tasty hot options include Moroccan stew with couscous and moussaka. Live mellow music plays six nights a week (seven during the festival). Around the corner on Thistle Street is the Bistro, from the same proprietors; it serves snacks, meals, and decadent desserts such as chocolate fondue. There's also an impressive organic wine list. ⊠ *94 Hanover St., New Town* ☎ *0131/225–2131* ▤ *AE, DC, MC, V* ⊙ *Closed Sun. except during festival.*

Haymarket

West of the Old Town and south of the West End is Haymarket, a district with its own down-to-earth character and well-worn charm. This area has many restaurants that tend to be more affordable than those in the center of town.

CHINESE
££

✕ **Jasmine.** Seafood is the specialty of this small, friendly, candlelit Cantonese restaurant, known for rapid service that deals with the constant stream of customers, even on weekdays. The subdued interior is relaxing, although tables are quite closely spaced. Delicious dishes include mixed seafood on a bed of lettuce, and mango-flavored chicken served in the shells of two half mangos. Prix-fixe lunches, starting at £6.90 for three courses, are a good value. A take-out menu is available. ⊠ *32 Grindlay St., Haymarket* ☎ *0131/229–5757* ▤ *AE, MC, V.*

SCOTTISH
££–£££

✕ **First Coast.** This attractive, laid-back bistro, just a few minutes' walk from Haymarket Station, is a favorite with locals. Hardwood floors, stone walls, soft-bude pumpkin stew and raisin couscous, panfried seabass with fennel, mustard, and ginger, and Aberdeen Angus sirloin steak with tomato-and-red-onion salad. The international wine list is as varied as the daily specials. ⊠ *99–101 Dalry Rd., Haymarket* ☎ *0131/313–4404* ▤ *MC, V.*

West End & Points West

FRENCH
££–£££

✕ **Petit Paris.** Don't be put off by the somewhat bland entrance of this lively 2nd-floor bistro; inside, it is cheerfully decorated with checked tablecloths, copper pots, and bunches of garlic. The staff is predominantly French, and the emphasis is on casual dining, local produce, and home cooking. The one-course lunch special plus coffee or tea for £5.90 is a real bargain. Try the traditional French black pudding and slow-baked rabbit with Dijon mustard sauce. ⊠ *17 Queensferry St., West End* ☎ *0131/226–1890* ⊠ *38/40 Grassmarket, Old Town* ☎ *0131/226–2442* ▤ *MC, V.*

ITALIAN ✗ **Bar Roma.** This is a genuine Italian experience, albeit in Scotland. The
££–£££ food tastes great, the place is noisy and fun, the chatty waiters are full
of energy, and the hosts are always willing to squeeze you in, no matter
how crowded the place may be. If you want to dine in peace and quiet,
avoid early evening when the office crowd warms up for a night on the
town. Specialties include ample calzone and seafood linguine. ⊠ *39A
Queensferry St., West End* ☎ *0131/226–2977* ▤ *AE, DC, MC, V.*

South Side

AFRICAN ✗ **Ndebele.** This small, friendly café—named after the tribe from South
£ Africa and Zimbabwe that has maintained the customs and language
of its Zulu ancestors—is ideally placed for a snack before a trip to the
Cameo cinema opposite. The tasty *boerewors* (South African sausage),
smoked ostrich, and the large selection of interesting sandwiches on a
choice of breads can be eaten on the spot or ordered out. Deli products,
including *biltong* (strips of cured, air-dried meat), are also for sale.
African art hangs on the wood-panel, geometric-pattern walls in bright
shades of purple and orange. ⊠ *57 Home St., Tollcross* ☎ *0131/221–
1141* ▤ *AE, MC, V.*

ECLECTIC ✗ **The Apartment.** A wacky, whirlwind affair, this popular restaurant has
££–£££ a varied, innovative menu that materializes into huge portions. Choose
from one of four menu categories: CHL (Chunky Healthy Lines), Fish
Things, Other Things, and Salad. Dishes include fabulous mussels in a
creamy sauce, North African spicy marinated-lamb patties, *merguez* (spicy
sausage) and grilled basil-wrapped goat cheese, and huge salads like *tiede*
piquant (spicy olives, potatoes, roasted peppers, and chorizo, topped with
a poached egg). ⊠ *7–13 Barclay Pl., near King's Theatre, Tollcross*
☎ *0131/228–6456* ▤ *MC, V.*

INDIAN ✗ **Kalpna.** The unremarkable facade of this vegetarian Indian restaurant,
£–££ amid an ordinary row of shops, and the low-key interior, enlivened by
Fodor'sChoice Indian prints and fabric pictures, belie the food—unlike anything you
★ are likely to encounter elsewhere in the city. *Dam aloo Kashmiri* is a
medium-spicy potato dish with a sauce made from honey, pistachios,
and almonds. *Bangan mirch masala* is spicier, with eggplant and red chili
peppers. A lunchtime buffet, perfect for the undecided, allows you to
pick and mix for only £5.50; you can do the same on Wednesday
evening for £10. ⊠ *2–3 St. Patricks Sq., South Side* ☎ *0131/667–9890*
▤ *MC, V* ☉ *Closed Sun. Jan.–Mar.*

Leith

FRENCH ✗ **Martin Wishart.** Slightly out of town but worth every penny of the taxi
★ ££££ fare, this rising culinary star woos diners with an impeccable and varied menu of beautifully presented, French-influenced dishes. Terrine of
foie gras, compote of Agen prunes, and sole Murat (glazed fillet of sole
with baby onions, artichoke, parsley, and lemon) with *pommes en cocotte* (potatoes cooked in a casserole) typify the cuisine. Reservations
are essential on weekends. ⊠ *54 The Shore, Leith* ☎ *0131/553–3557*
▤ *AE, MC, V* ☉ *Closed Sun. and Mon. No lunch Sat.*

SEAFOOD   ✕ **Skippers Bistro.** This superb seafood restaurant has a traditional,
£££–£££££   snug, cluttered interior with dark wood, shining brass, and lots of pictures and seafaring ephemera. For a starter, try the creamy fish soup.
Main dishes change daily but might include halibut, salmon, monkfish,
or sea bass in delicious sauces. Reservations are essential on weekends.
⊠ *1A Dock Pl., Leith* ☎ *0131/554–1018* ⊟ *AE, MC, V.*

££–£££££   ✕ **Fishers Leith.** Locals and visitors flock to this laid-back pub-cum-
bistro down on the waterfront, and to its sister restaurant, **Fishers in
the City,** in the New Town. The menu is the same, but Fishers Leith opened
first and is still the one with the better reputation and vibe. Bar meals
are served, although for more comfort and elegance sit in the cozy blue-
walled dining room. Seafood is the specialty—the Loch Fyne oysters are
wonderful. Watch for the daily specials: perhaps a seafood or vegetarian soup followed by North African gamba prawns as big as your hand.
Reserve ahead for the bistro. ⊠ *1 The Shore, Leith* ☎ *0131/554–5666*
⊠ *58 Thistle St., New Town* ☎ *0131/225–5109* ⊟ *AE, MC, V.*

WHERE TO STAY

The range of good hotel accommodations in Scotland's capital is expanding, both in terms of high-end and less expensive options. The inexpensive Scottish hotel, once reviled, is now at least the equal of
anything that might be found in England. Rooms are harder to find in
August and September, when the Edinburgh International Festival and
the Fringe Festival take place, so reserve at least three months in advance.
Bed-and-breakfast accommodations may be harder to find in December, January, and February, when some proprietors close for a few
weeks. Scots are trusting people—many B&B proprietors provide front-
door keys and few impose curfews.

Prices

Weekend rates in the larger hotels are always much cheaper than midweek rates, so if you want to stay in a plush hotel, come on the weekend. To save money and see how local residents live, stay in a B&B in
one of the areas away from the city center, such as Pilrig to the north,
Murrayfield to the west, or Sciennes to the south. Public buses can whisk
you to the city center in 10 to 15 minutes.

WHAT IT COSTS In pounds				
	£££££	**££££**	**£££**	**££**	**£**
FOR 2 PEOPLE	over £250	£180–£250	£120–£179	£70–£119	under £70

Prices are for two people in a standard double room in high season, usually including 17.5% V.A.T.

Old Town

£££££   🏨 **The Scotsman.** This magnificent turn-of-the-20th-century, gray-sand-
Fodor'sChoice   stone building, with a marble staircase and a fascinating history—it was
★   once the headquarters of the *Scotsman* newspaper—now houses a modern, luxurious hotel. Dark wood, earthy colors, tweeds, and contempo-

rary furnishings decorate the rooms and public spaces. North Bridge, the casual-chic brasserie, serves shellfish and grill food, and the formal Vermilion concocts beautiful presentations of Scottish–French dishes. ✉ *20 N. Bridge, Old Town, EH1 1YT* ☎ *0131/556–5565* 📠 *0131/652–3652* ⊕ *www.thescotsmanhotel.co.uk* 📑 *56 rooms, 12 suites* ⚂ *2 restaurants, cable TV, in-room data ports, indoor pool, health club, spa, bar, business services, Internet; no a/c* ▭ *AE, DC, MC, V* ◯❘ *BP.*

£££ 🏨 **Radisson SAS Edinburgh.** Although it was built in the late 1980s, this city-center hotel was designed to blend into its surroundings among the 16th-, 17th-, and 18th-century buildings on the Royal Mile. Rooms are spacious and contemporary—practical rather than luxurious. ✉ *80 High St., Royal Mile, Old Town, EH1 1TH* ☎ *0131/557–9797* 📠 *0131/557–9789* ⊕ *www.radissonsas.com* 📑 *238 rooms, 10 suites* ⚂ *Restaurant, minibars, cable TV, in-room data ports, indoor pool, health club, bar, lobby lounge, meeting rooms, parking (fee)* ▭ *AE, DC, MC, V* ◯❘ *BP.*

££–£££ 🏨 **Bank Hotel.** Each room at this small, centrally located hotel in a converted 1923 bank honors a famous Scotsman and is individually decorated with books, telescopes, and even parts of a steam engine. The massive bathrooms have enough space for antique dressing tables, and many rooms overlook the Royal Mile. This hotel is more of an experience than simply a place to rest your head, but keep in mind that there's no elevator (the building is listed) and that the hotel's entrance is through the popular Logie Baird's Bar. ✉ *1 South Bridge, Old Town, EH1 1LL* ☎ *0131/556–9940* 📠 *0131/558–1362* ⊕ *www.festival-inns.co.uk* 📑 *9 rooms* ⚂ *No a/c* ▭ *MC, V* ◯❘ *BP.*

New Town

£££££ 🏨 **Balmoral Hotel.** The attention to detail in the elegant rooms—colors
Fodor'sChoice were picked to echo the country's heathers and moors—and the sheer
★ élan that has re-created the Edwardian splendor of this grand, former railroad hotel make staying at the Balmoral a special introduction to Edinburgh. Here, below the landmark clock tower marking the east end of Princes Street, the lively buzz makes you feel as if you are at the center of city life. The hotel's main restaurant is the plush and stylish Number One, serving excellent Scottish seafood and game. If you overindulge, recuperate at the luxurious spa. ✉ *1 Princes St., on border between Old Town and New Town, EH2 2EQ* ☎ *0131/556–2414* 📠 *0131/557–3747* ⊕ *www.thebalmoralhotel.com* 📑 *188 rooms, 20 suites* ⚂ *2 restaurants, in-room data ports, indoor pool, health club, hair salon, spa, bar, meeting rooms, parking (fee)* ▭ *AE, DC, MC, V.*

££££–£££££ 🏨 **Caledonian Hilton Hotel.** "The Caley," a conspicuous block of red sandstone beyond the west end of West Princes Street Gardens, was built between 1898 and 1902 as the flagship hotel of the Caledonian Railway, and its imposing Victorian decor has been faithfully preserved. The public area has marbled green columns and an ornate stairwell with a burnished-metalwork balustrade. Rooms and corridors are exceptionally large and well appointed. ✉ *Princes St., New Town, EH1 2AB* ☎ *0131/222–8888* 📠 *0131/222–8889* ⊕ *www.hilton.co.uk* 📑 *251 rooms, 20 suites* ⚂ *3 restaurants, cable TV, in-room data ports, Wi-Fi, pool, meeting rooms, parking (fee)* ▭ *AE, DC, MC, V* ◯❘ *BP.*

★ ☶ **The Glasshouse.** Glass walls extend from the 19th-century facade of
££££–£££££ a former church, foreshadowing the daring, unique interior of Edinburgh's
chicest boutique hotel. Rooms are decorated in a minimalist style, with
soft brown and beige tones, wood, and marble. The bathrooms were
built in Denmark and shipped as intact "pods" to Britain, then fitted
into the rooms. A bedside control panel lets you control the drapes, and
the flat-screen TV swivels to face the bed or the sitting area. Floor-to-
ceiling windows overlook the New Town or the rooftop garden in back.
The hotel's halls and rooms serve as gallery space for 200 female nude
photographs by Scottish photographers Trevor and Faye Yerbury. ⊠ 2
Greenside Pl., New Town, EH1 3AA ☎ *0131/525–8200* 🖷 *0131/525–
8205* ⊕ *www.theetoncollection.com* ⮫ *65 rooms, 18 suites* ⟑ *Restaurant, room service, in-room safes, minibars, cable TV, in-room data ports,
bar, business services, meeting rooms* ⊟ *AE, MC, V.*

★ ☶ **The Howard.** Close to Drummond Place, this hotel is in a classic New
££££–£££££ Town building, elegant and superbly proportioned. Antique furniture
and original art throughout make the Howard more like a swank private club than a hotel, and you can expect the most up-to-date facilities, including butlers and Web-equipped TVs. Some of the best rooms
overlook the garden. ⊠ *34 Great King St., New Town, EH3 6QH*
☎ *0131/557–3500* 🖷 *0131/557–6515* ⊕ *www.thehoward.com* ⮫ *18
rooms, 5 suites* ⟑ *Restaurant, room service, cable TV, in-room data ports,
dry cleaning, laundry service, meeting rooms, free parking; no a/c* ⊟ *AE,
DC, MC, V* ⦿⧀ *BP.*

★ **£££** ☶ **Stuart Guest House.** A Victorian terraced house with some fine plasterwork houses this B&B, a 15-minute walk from the city center. Soft
colors and billowing curtains combine with antique and traditional-style
furniture to create an opulent interior. ⊠ *12 E. Claremont St., Canon-
mills, EH7 4JP* ☎ *0131/557–3500* 🖷 *0131/557–0563* ⊕ *www.
stuartguesthouse.com* ⮫ *5 rooms, 1 apartment* ⟑ *Wi-Fi, some pets allowed; no a/c* ⊟ *MC, V* ⦿⧀ *BP.*

££–£££ ☶ **Walton Hotel.** This B&B in a Georgian town house is a 10-minute walk
from the city center. High-ceiling, elegant rooms are furnished in an unfussy, traditional style, and there is a choice of breakfasts—traditional
Scottish, Continental, or American. Four of the rooms are on the ground
floor, and six are in the basement (all have windows). ⊠ *79 Dundas
St., New Town, EH3 6SD* ☎ *0131/556–1137* 🖷 *0131/557–8367*
⊕ *www.waltonhotel.com* ⮫ *10 rooms* ⟑ *In-room data ports, free
parking; no a/c* ⊟ *MC, V* ⦿⧀ *BP.*

££ ☶ **Ardenlee Guest House.** An exquisite Victorian-tile floor is one of many
original features at this gem of a guesthouse tucked away from the hustle and bustle of the city center. A cast-iron staircase leads to simple but
spacious rooms; some are decorated in dark blues and reds, others in
creams and terra-cotta floral prints. The walk into town is 10 minutes
(uphill), and the owner is helpful with information on sights in and around
Edinburgh. ⊠ *9 Eyre Pl., New Town, EH3 5ES* ☎ *0131/556–2838*
⊕ *www.ardenlee.co.uk* ⮫ *9 rooms, 7 with bath* ⟑ *No a/c, no room
phones* ⊟ *MC, V* ⦿⧀ *BP.*

££ ☶ **Inverleith Hotel.** Across from the Royal Botanical Gardens Edinburgh,
this renovated Victorian town house has cozy, well-lighted rooms with

velour bedspreads, dark wooden furniture, and pale-gold curtains. In winter, when the surrounding trees loose their leaves, a couple of the south-facing rooms have views of the castle. The reception doubles as a private bar for guests and sells a fine selection of malt whiskies, which you're encouraged to drink in the lounge. Several good restaurants and cafés are nearby. The hotel is a good value for the location, a 15-minute walk (uphill) into the center of town. ⊠ *5 Inverleith Terr., New Town, EH3 4NS* ☎ *0131/556–2745* ⊕ *www.inverleithhotel.co.uk* ➴ *12 rooms, 1 apartment* ⚫ *Bar, free parking; no a/c* ▭ *MC, V* ❅ *BP.*

Haymarket

££££ ☒ **Hilton Edinburgh Grosvenor Hotel.** Several converted terrace houses make up this attractive, comfortable hotel, distinguished by an elegant Victorian facade. From the moment you enter the large reception area, furnished with ample Chesterfield armchairs, you'll be pampered. The rooms are small but well decorated with tartan curtains, cream bedspreads, and dark-wood furniture. First- and 2nd-floor bedrooms have high ceilings with attractive plaster cornices. The hotel is a short walk from the West End's shopping district. ⊠ *Grosvenor St., Haymarket, EH12 5EF* ☎ *0131/226–6001* 🖷 *0131/220–2387* ⊕ *www.hilton.co.uk* ➴ *189 rooms, 3 suites* ⚫ *Restaurant, cable TV, bar, business services, meeting room; no a/c* ▭ *AE, DC, MC, V* ❅ *BP.*

★ **££–£££** ☒ **Kew House and Apartments.** The Kew's rooms and apartments are as sumptuous as a guesthouse can be without being classified a full-service hotel. Inside the elegant 1860 terraced house are unfussy rooms with light-wood modern furniture and conveniences like hair dryers, coffeemakers, and pants presses. Welcome luxuries include fresh flowers, chocolates, short-bread, and a decanter of sherry on arrival. There is also a bar for guests only. It's a 15-minute stroll to the center of town. ⊠ *1 Kew Terr., Haymarket, EH12 5JE* ☎ *0131/313–0700* 🖷 *0131/313–0747* ⊕ *www. kewhouse.com* ➴ *6 rooms, 2 apartments* ⚫ *Cable TV, some in-room broadband, Wi-Fi, bar, lounge, free parking; no a/c* ▭ *AE, DC, MC, V* ❅ *BP.*

West End & Points West

££££ ☒ **Sheraton Grand & Spa.** Beyond the reception area and sweeping grand staircase in this modern hotel are guest rooms well above average size. Many are traditionally decorated, with tartan furnishings and prints of old Edinburgh. The grandest rooms face Edinburgh Castle; if you can't book those, try the spa's rooftop pool for great city views. Three fine restaurants include the brasserie-style Terrace, overlooking the castle and Festival Square; the intimate Grill Room; and the Santini, serving Italian cuisine. The hotel bar is popular with locals, especially after work and in the evening before and after concerts at the Usher Hall. ⊠ *1 Festival Sq., Lothian Rd., West End, EH3 9SR* ☎ *0131/229–9131* 🖷 *0131/ 228–4510* ⊕ *www.sheraton.com* ➴ *260 rooms, 16 suites* ⚫ *3 restaurants, cable TV, Wi-Fi, indoor pool, gym, health club, spa, bar, meeting rooms, parking (fee)* ▭ *AE, DC, MC, V* ❅ *BP.*

££–££££ ☒ **The Bonham.** This hotel in the elegant West End carries out a successful, sophisticated flirtation with modernity that makes it stand out from its neighbors. Bold colors and contemporary Scottish art set off its late-

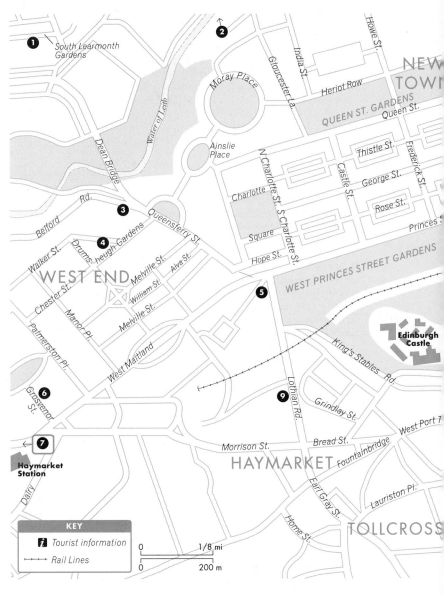

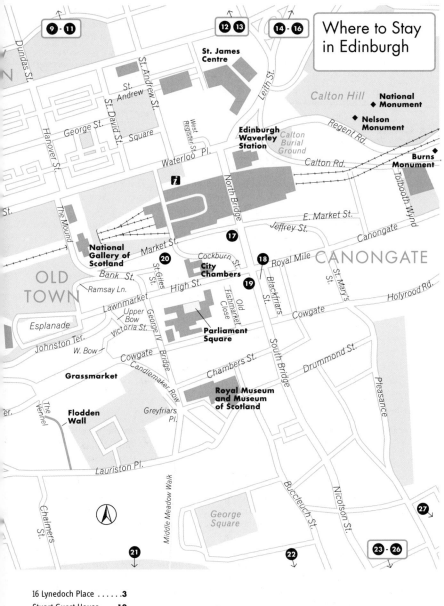

Where to Stay in Edinburgh

19th-century features and classic furniture. The good-size rooms are typical of an Edinburgh town house but offer peace and quiet without the noise often associated with this type of hotel. The chic, unadorned restaurant has oversize mirrors and a central catwalk of light; its focus is on beautifully presented contemporary cuisine. Service at the hotel is thorough, yet unobtrusive. ✉ *35 Drumsheugh Gardens, West End, EH3 7RN* ☎ *0131/226–6050* 🖷 *0131/226–6080* ⊕ *www.thebonham.com* ⮑ *48 rooms, 3 suites* ⌂ *Restaurant, cable TV, in-room data ports, business services, meeting rooms, free parking; no a/c* ▱ *AE, DC, MC, V* �
⦿|*BP.*

★ **££–££££**   ▣ **Channings.** Five Edwardian terraced town houses make up this intimate, elegant hotel in an upscale West End neighborhood just minutes from Princes Street. Beyond the clubby, oak-paneled lobby lounge are the quiet guest rooms, with restrained colors, antiques, and marble baths. North-facing rooms have great views of Fife. Channings Restaurant offers excellent value in traditional Scottish and Continental cooking. ✉ *12–16 S. Learmonth Gardens, West End, EH4 IEZ* ☎ *0131/315–2226* 🖷 *0131/332–9631* ⊕ *www.channings.co.uk* ⮑ *41 rooms, 3 suites* ⌂ *Restaurant, lobby lounge, meeting rooms; no a/c* ▱ *AE, DC, MC, V* ⦿|*BP.*

££   ▣ **16 Lynedoch Place.** Considerate hosts Andrew and Susie Hamilton (and Gertrude, the lovable dog) have opened up their beautiful Georgian terraced house as a B&B, a five-minute walk from the center of town. Rosy pinks, cool yellows, terra-cotta oranges, and floral patterns decorate the tasteful rooms. Susie goes all out for breakfast, which is served in a magnificent hunter-green dining room filled with antiques and family pictures. In a pinch, they will connect two of the guest rooms for a family. ✉ *16 Lynedoch Pl., West End, EH3 7PY* ☎ *0131/225–5507* ⊕ *www.16lynedochplace.co.uk* ⮑ *3 rooms* ⌂ *Dining room, some in-room hot tubs, cable TV, in-room data ports, library, free parking; no a/c, no room phones* ▱ *MC, V* ⦿|*BP.*

South Side

££££   ▣ **Prestonfield.** The peacocks and grazing cattle on the hotel's 20-acre grounds let you know that you've entered a different world, even though you're five minutes by car from the Royal Mile. Inside this 1687 mansion, baroque opulence reigns in the well-restored public rooms; there are plenty of antiques, rich fabrics, and gilt treasures to relax among as you sip a whisky. Guest rooms are individually decorated but mix antiques and the latest amenities, for total indulgence. The Rhubarb restaurant carries through the hedonistic note with superb Scottish fare, such as seared turbot with langoustine crushed potatoes. ✉ *Priestfield Rd., Prestonfield, EH16 5UT* ☎ *0131/225–7800* ⊕ *www.prestonfield.com* ⮑ *22 rooms, 2 suites* ⌂ *Restaurant, minibars, Wi-Fi, bar, helipad, free parking* ▱ *AE, MC, V* ⦿|*BP.*

££–£££   ▣ **Thrums Private Hotel.** Inside this detached Georgian house are small, cozy rooms decorated with antique reproductions. Breakfast is served in a large, glass-enclosed conservatory. The staff that runs the hotel is very welcoming and more than willing to advise you on what to see and do in and around Edinburgh. ✉ *14–15 Minto St., Newington, EH9 1RQ* ☎ *0131/667–5545* 🖷 *0131/667–8707* ⊕ *www.thrumshotel.com* ⮑ *15 rooms* ⌂ *Free parking; no a/c* ▱ *MC, V* ⦿|*BP.*

££ 🏠 **Ellesmere Guest House.** Rooms in this Victorian terrace house near the Bruntsfield Links have antique reproduction and modern furniture with floral bedspreads and curtains; one room has a four-poster bed. You can relax in leather wing chairs in the comfortable sitting room or take a 20-minute stroll to the Old Town. Ellesmere sits close to the King's Theatre and several good restaurants. ⊠ *11 Glengyle Terr., Bruntsfield, EH3 9LN* ☎ *0131/229–4823* 🖷 *0131/229–5285* ⊕ *www.edinburghbandb. co.uk* ⇆ *6 rooms* ⬧ *No a/c* ⊟ *No credit cards* ⫶⊙⫶ *BP.*

££ 🏠 **Teviotdale House.** The lavish Victorian interior of this 1848 town house includes canopy beds and miles of colorful, patterned fabrics. As you enter, you will be greeted by the friendly Thiebauds, your hosts. The house is a warm retreat on a tree-lined street away from but within reach of city-center bustle via a 10-minute bus ride. The hearty egg-and-sausage breakfasts are a pleasure. Note that six of the rooms have showers, but no bathtubs. ⊠ *53 Grange Loan, The Grange, EH9 2ER* ☎ *0131/667–4376* 🖷 *0131/667–4763* ⊕ *www.teviotdalehouse.com* ⇆ *7 rooms* ⬧ *Dining room; no a/c* ⊟ *AE, MC, V* ⫶⊙⫶ *BP.*

£–££ 🏠 **AmarAgua.** Deep-piled carpets, floral drapes with many swags, and well-designed furniture create restrained opulence in this Victorian town house, which is 10 minutes by bus from the city center. Rooms are themed around color combinations, and many look distinctly Asian, as the multilingual owners spent some time working in the Far East. "Carry-out" breakfasts are available for guests leaving early to catch a bus or plane. ⊠ *10 Kilmaurs Terr., Newington, EH16 5DR* ☎ *0131/667–6775* 🖷 *0131/667–7687* ⊕ *www.amaragua.co.uk* ⇆ *7 rooms* ⬧ *Internet; no a/c* ⊟ *MC, V* ⊙ *Closed Jan. and 2 wks in Oct. and Nov.* ⫶⊙⫶ *BP.*

£–££ 🏠 **Ashdene House.** On a quiet residential street, only 10 minutes from the city center by bus, sits this Edwardian house, a first-class B&B. Country-style pine furniture and vividly colored fabrics decorate the guest rooms and common areas. The owners are particularly helpful in arranging tours and evening theater entertainment, and they will recommend local restaurants. There's ample parking on the street. ⊠ *23 Fountainhall Rd., The Grange, EH9 2LN* ☎ *0131/667–6026* ⊕ *www.ashdenehouse.com* ⇆ *5 rooms* ⬧ *Free parking; no a/c, no smoking* ⊟ *MC, V* ⫶⊙⫶ *BP.*

£–££ 🏠 **Turret Guest House.** Modern furnishings in rooms with Victorian cornices, paneled doors, and high ceilings make this B&B, in a baronial town house, a nice combination of old-fashioned charm and contemporary comfort. Two of the rooms have four-poster beds. The inn is on a quiet residential street on the South Side, close to bus routes, the Commonwealth Pool, and Holyrood Park. The tempting breakfast options include omelets, sausage, haggis, waffles, pancakes, and French toast. ⊠ *8 Kilmaurs Terr., Prestonfield, EH16 5DR* ☎ *0131/667–6704* 🖷 *0131/668–1368* ⊕ *www.turretguesthouse.co.uk* ⇆ *8 rooms, 5 with bath* ⬧ *No a/c, no smoking* ⊟ *MC, V* ⫶⊙⫶ *BP.*

Leith

£££ 🏠 **Malmaison.** Once a seamen's hostel, the Malmaison, in the heart of Leith, now has stylish digs 10 minutes by bus from the city center. A dramatic black, cream, and taupe color scheme prevails in the public areas. King-size beds, CD players, and satellite TV are standard in the bedrooms, which are decorated in a bold, modern style. The French theme of the hotel, part of a small, chic British chain, is emphasized in the Café Bar and Brasserie, which serves food all day. Service may be a bit erratic. ⊠ *1 Tower Pl., Leith, EH6 7DB* ☎ *0131/468–5000* 🖷 *0131/468–5002* ⊕ *www. malmaison.com* ↝ *100 rooms, 9 suites* ♿ *Restaurant, café, cable TV, in-room data ports, gym, bar, free parking; no a/c* 🝙 *AE, DC, MC, V* ⑩ *BP.*

££ 🏠 **Ardmor House.** This low-key guesthouse combines the original features of a Victorian home with stylish contemporary furnishings. Rooms are fresh and modern, with an occasional carefully chosen antique. The friendly owners, Robin and Colin, extend a warm welcome to gay and straight travelers, and they offer a thoroughly efficient concierge service with a twist—lots of personal opinions and recommendations thrown in. Their listing of gay-friendly venues locates bars, cafés, and even saunas. ⊠ *74 Pilrig St., Leith, EH6 5AS* ☎🖷 *0131/554–4944* ⊕ *www. ardmorhouse.com* ↝ *5 rooms* ♿ *Dining room; no a/c* 🝙 *MC, V* ⑩ *BP.*

££ 🏠 **The Conifers.** This trim B&B in a red-sandstone town house north of the New Town offers simple, traditionally decorated rooms. Framed prints of old Edinburgh adorn the walls. The owner, Liz Fulton, has a wealth of knowledge about what to see and do in Edinburgh. ⊠ *56 Pilrig St., Leith, EH6 5AS* ☎ *0131/554–5162* ⊕ *www.conifersguesthouse.com* ↝ *4 rooms, 3 with bath* ♿ *No a/c, no smoking* 🝙 *No credit cards* ⑩ *BP.*

NIGHTLIFE & THE ARTS

The Arts

The jewel in Edinburgh's crown is the famed Edinburgh International Festival, which attracts the best in classical music, dance, and theater from all over the globe during three weeks from mid-August to early September. The *Scotsman* and *Herald,* Scotland's leading daily newspapers, carry listings and reviews in their arts pages every day, with special editions during the festival. Tickets are generally available from box offices in advance; in some cases they are also available from certain designated travel agents or at the door, although concerts by national orchestras often sell out long before the day of the performance. The *List* and the *Day by Day Guide,* available at the **Edinburgh and Scotland Information Centre** (⊠ 3 Princes St., East End ☎ 0131/473–3800 ⊕ www. edinburgh.org), carry the most up-to-date details about cultural events. The *List* is also available at newsstands throughout the city.

Dance

The Scottish Ballet performs at the **Festival Theatre** (⊠ 13–29 Nicolson St., Old Town ☎ 0131/529–6000) when in Edinburgh. Visiting contemporary-dance companies perform in the **Royal Lyceum** (⊠ Grindlay St., West End ☎ 0131/248–4848).

Festivals

The **Edinburgh Festival Fringe** (⊠ Edinburgh Festival Fringe Office, 180 High St., Old Town, EH1 1QS ☎ 0131/226–0026 🖷 0131/226–0016

12

⊕ www.edfringe.com) started in 1947 at the same time as the International Festival, when eight companies who were not invited to perform in the latter decided to attend anyway. Since then, the Festival Fringe has grown at about the same rate as its counterpart, making it the largest festival of its kind in the world. Its events range from the brilliant to the downright tacky. During the Fringe, Edinburgh center becomes one huge performance area, with fire eaters, jazz groups, stand-up comics, and magicians all thronging into High Street and Princes Street. Every available theater and pseudo-performance space is utilized—church halls, parks, sports fields, putting greens, and night clubs.

The **Edinburgh International Book Festival** (⊠ Charlotte Sq. Gardens, New Town ☎ 0845/373–5888 ⊕ www.edbookfest.co.uk), a two-week-long event in August, pulls together a heady mix of the biggest-selling and the most challenging authors from around the world and gets them talking about their work in a magnificent tent village. Workshops for would-be writers and children are hugely popular.

★ The **Edinburgh International Festival** (⊠ The Hub, Edinburgh Festival Centre, Castlehill, Old Town, EH1 2NE ☎ 0131/473–2020 information, 0131/473–2000 tickets ⊞ 0131/473–2003 ⊕ www.eif.co.uk) was founded in 1947 when Europe was recovering from World War II, the festival aimed to "provide a platform for the flowering of the human spirit." It was a gigantic success. Held in August, the festival has now drawn as many as 400,000 people to Edinburgh, with more than 100 acts by world-renowned music, opera, theater, and dance performers, filling all the major venues in the city. Tickets for the festival go on sale in April, and many sell out within the month. However, you may still be able to purchase tickets, which range from £6 to £60, during the festival.

The **Edinburgh International Film Festival** (⊠ Edinburgh Film Festival Office, at Filmhouse, 88 Lothian Rd., West End, EH3 9BZ ☎ 0131/228–4051 ⊞ 0131/229–5501 ⊕ www.edfilmfest.org.uk) is yet another aspect of the busy August festival logjam in Edinburgh.

The **Edinburgh International Science Festival** (Information: ⊠ Roxburgh's Court, off 323 High St., Edinburgh EH1 1PW ☎ 0131/558–7666 ⊕ www.sciencefestival.co.uk ⊠ The Hub, Castlehill, Edinburgh EH1 2NE), held around Easter each year, aims to make science accessible, interesting, but above all fun. Children's events turn science into entertainment and are especially popular.

★ The **Edinburgh Military Tattoo** (⊠ Edinburgh Military Tattoo Office, 32 Market St., Old Town, EH1 1QB ☎ 0870/755–5118 ⊞ 0131/225–8627 ⊕ www.edintattoo.co.uk) may not be art, but it is certainly Scottish culture. It's sometimes confused with the festival itself, partly because both events take place in August (though the Tattoo starts and finishes a week earlier). This celebration of martial music and skills with bands, gymnastics, and stunt motorcycle teams is set on the castle esplanade, and the dramatic backdrop augments the spectacle. Dress warmly for late-evening performances. Even if it rains, the show most definitely goes on.

The **International Jazz Festival** (✉ 29 St. Stephen St., Stockbridge, EH3 5AN ☎ 0131/225–5200 ⊕ www.edinburghjazzfestival.co.uk), held in August, attracts international top performers and brings local enthusiasts out of their living rooms and into the pubs and clubs to listen and play.

Film

The **Cameo** (✉ 38 Home St., Tollcross ☎ 0870/755–1231) has one large and two small auditoriums, which are extremely comfortable, plus a bar and late-night specials. Apart from cinema chains, Edinburgh has the excellent three-screen **Filmhouse** (✉ 88 Lothian Rd., West End ☎ 0131/228–2688 box office ⊕ www.filmhousecinema.com), the best venue for modern, foreign-language, offbeat, or simply less-commercial films.

Music

The **Festival Theatre** (✉ 13–29 Nicolson St., Old Town ☎ 0131/529–6000) hosts performances by the Scottish Ballet and the Scottish Opera. The **Playhouse** (✉ Greenside Pl., East End ☎ 0870/606–3424) leans toward popular artists and musicals. The intimate **Queen's Hall** (✉ Clerk St., Old Town ☎ 0131/668–2019) hosts small recitals. **Usher Hall** (✉ Lothian Rd., West End ☎ 0131/228–1155) is Edinburgh's grandest venue, and international performers and orchestras, including the Royal Scottish National Orchestra, perform here.

Theater

MODERN The **Theatre Workshop** (✉ 34 Hamilton Pl., Stockbridge ☎ 0131/226–5425) hosts fringe events during the Edinburgh Festival and modern, community-based theater year-round. It is wheelchair accessible. The **Traverse Theatre** (✉ 10 Cambridge St., West End ☎ 0131/228–1404) has developed a solid reputation for new, stimulating Scottish plays, performed in a specially designed flexible space.

TRADITIONAL Edinburgh has three main theaters. The **Festival Theatre** (✉ 13–29 Nicolson St., Old Town ☎ 0131/529–6000) presents opera and ballet but also the occasional excellent touring play. The **King's** (✉ 2 Leven St., Tollcross ☎ 0131/529–6000) has a program of contemporary and traditional dramatic works. The **Royal Lyceum** (✉ Grindlay St., West End ☎ 0131/248–4848) shows traditional plays and contemporary works, often transferred from or prior to their London West End showings.

The **Playhouse** (✉ Greenside Pl., East End ☎ 0870/606–3424) hosts mostly popular artists and musicals.

Nightlife

The nightlife scene in Edinburgh is vibrant—whatever you're looking for, you'll most certainly find it here, and you won't have to go far. Expect old-style pubs as well as cutting-edge bars and clubs. Live music pours out of most watering holes on weekends, particularly folk, blues, and jazz. Well-known artists perform at some of the larger venues. The *List* magazine, available at newsstands, gives locations, dates, times, and prices. Make sure you partake in at least one ceilidh (a traditional Scottish dance with music); they're fun and a good way to meet locals.

The **Edinburgh and Scotland Information Centre** (✉ 3 Princes St., East End ☎ 0845/225–5121 ⊕ www.edinburgh.org), above Waverly Market, can supply information on nightlife, especially on spots hosting dinner dances.

Bars & Pubs

Edinburgh's 400-odd pubs are a study in themselves. In the eastern and northern districts of the city you'll find some grim, inhospitable-looking places that proclaim that drinking is no laughing matter. But throughout Edinburgh many pubs have deliberately traded in their old spit-and-sawdust images for atmospheric revivals of the warm, oak-paneled, leather-chaired *howffs* of a more leisurely age. Most pubs and bars are open weekdays and Saturday from 11 AM to midnight, and from 12:30 to midnight on Sunday.

OLD TOWN   **The Canons' Gait** (✉ 232 Canongate, Old Town ☎ 0131/556–4481) sells Edinburgh's own special brew, Innis & Gunn, aged in American white-oak barrels. It also has live jazz and blues on Thursday and Saturday
★ nights. **Deacon Brodie's Pub** (✉ 435 Lawnmarket, Old Town ☎ 0131/225–6531), named for the infamous criminal who may have inspired Robert Louis Stevenson's *Strange Case of Dr. Jekyll and Mr. Hyde,* serves traditional meals and pints.

NEW TOWN   **Abbotsford** (✉ 3 Rose St., New Town ☎ 0131/225–5276) has lots of Victorian atmosphere, an ever-changing selection of five real ales, and bar lunches. **Blue Moon Café** (✉ 36 Broughton St., New Town ☎ 0131/557–0911), Edinburgh's longest running gay café, is still the best. **Café Royal Circle Bar** (✉ 19 W. Regent St., New Town ☎ 0131/556–1884) has beautiful Victorian tiled murals, oysters on the half shell, and leather booths. **80 Queen Street** (✉ 80 Queen St., New Town ☎ 0131/226–5097), with dark-wood booths, is just the place for lunch with a pint of draft beer. There is live jazz and soul on Friday and Saturday evenings.

★ **Guildford Arms** (✉ 1 W. Register St., east end of Princes St., New Town ☎ 0131/556–4312) is worth a visit for its interior alone: ornate plasterwork, cornices, friezes, and wood paneling form the backdrop for some excellent draft ales, including Orkney Dark Island. **Milne's Bar** (✉ 35 Hanover St., New Town ☎ 0131/225–6738) is known as the poets' pub because of its popularity with the Edinburgh literati. Pies and baked potatoes go well with seven real ales and varying guest beers (beers not of the house brewery). Victorian advertisements and photos of old Edinburgh give the place an old-time feel.

Standing Order (✉ 62–66 George St., New Town ☎ 0131/225–4460), in a former banking hall with a magnificent painted-plasterwork ceiling, is one of the popular and expanding J. D. Wetherspoon chain of pubs, priding itself on friendly, music-free watering holes with cheap beer—you can even lounge on leather sofas. Children are welcome. **Tonic** (✉ 34A Castle St., New Town ☎ 0131/225–6431), one of Edinburgh's reliable cocktail spots, is a stylish basement bar with bouncy stools and comfy sofas, pale wood, and chrome.

SOUTH SIDE   **Cloisters** (✉ 26 Brougham St., Tollcross ☎ 0131/221–9997) prides itself on the absence of music, gaming machines, and any other modern pub gimmicks; it specializes instead in real ales, malt whiskies, and good food, all at reasonable prices. **Leslie's Bar** (✉ 45 Ratcliffe Terr., South Side ☎ 0131/667–7205) is an unspoiled Victorian bar near the hotels and guesthouses of Newington, with a good range of traditional Scottish ales and whiskies. **Southsider** (✉ 3–7 W. Richmond St., South Side ☎ 0131/667–2003), near the antiques and junk shops of Causewayside, is popular with locals and students.

LEITH **The Cameo Bar** (✉ 23 Commercial St., Leith ☎ 0131/554–9999), a haven for the young and hip, has a backdrop of scarlet walls, art, and an open fire. **Malt and Hops** (✉ 45 The Shore, Leith ☎ 0131/555–0083), more than 260 years old, has its own cask ales and ghost, and overlooks the waterfront. **Waterline** (✉ 58 The Shore, Leith ☎ 0131/554–2425) has leather sofas to recline on, nautical charts pasted to the ceiling, and a great pub quiz every Thursday night.

Ceilidhs & Scottish Evenings

For those who feel a trip to Scotland is not complete without hearing the "Braes of Yarrow" or "Auld Robin Gray," several hotels present traditional Scottish-music evenings in the summer season. Head for the **Edinburgh Thistle Hotel** (✉ 107 Leith St., New Town ☎ 0131/556–0111) to see *Jamie's Scottish Evening,* an extravaganza of Scottish song, tartan, plaid, and bagpipes that takes place nightly. The cost is £46.50, including a four-course dinner.

Folk Clubs

You can usually find folk musicians performing in pubs throughout Edinburgh, although there's been a decline in the live-music scene because of dwindling profits and the predominance of popular theme bars.

Ensign Ewart (✉ 521 Lawnmarket, Old Town ☎ 0131/226–1928), by the castle, is a cozy, intimate pub with live folk music most nights. **Whistle Binkies Pub** (✉ South Bridge, Old Town ☎ 0131/557–5114), a friendly basement bar with great rock and folk music every night of the week, is the place for a bit of *wellie* (volume, energy).

Nightclubs

For the young and footloose, many Edinburgh dance clubs offer reduced admission and/or less expensive drinks for early revelers. Consult the *List* for special events.

The well-liked **Club Massa** (✉ 36–39 Market St., Old Town ☎ 0131/226–4224) has theme nights covering the full spectrum of musical sounds; it's open Wednesday through Sunday. The **Opal Lounge** (✉ 51A George St., New Town ☎ 0131/226–2275), a casual but stylish nightspot, evolves by a subtle change of mood and lighting from a restaurant to a club for drinks and dancing to soul or funk. **Po Na Na Souk Bar** (✉ 43B Frederick St., New Town ☎ 0131/226–2224) has a cool but cozy atmosphere, and a distinctly North African atmosphere, with its secluded booths and Bedouin furnishings. The music is a mix of funk, hip hop, R&B, house, and disco.

SPORTS & THE OUTDOORS

Golf

For the courses listed below, *SSS* indicates the "standard scratch score," or average score. VisitScotland provides a free leaflet on golf in Scotland, available from the **Edinburgh and Scotland Information Centre** (✉ 3 Princes St., East End ☎ 0131/473–3800 ⊕ www.edinburgh.org), or check online at golf.visitscotland.com.

Braids. This famous 18-hole course was founded in 1897 and laid out over several small hills 3 mi south of Edinburgh. The 9-hole course opened in 2003. ✉ *Braids Hill Rd., Braidburn* ☎ *0131/447–6666* ⚐. *Course 1: 18 holes, 5,865 yds, SSS 67. Course 2: 9 holes.*

Bruntsfield Links. Several tournaments are held each year at this noted championship course, opened in 1898 a couple miles northwest of the city. ✉ *32 Barnton Ave., Davidson's Mains* ☎ *0131/336–1479* 🖷 *0131/ 336–5538* ⚐. *18 holes, 6,407 yds, SSS 71.*

Duddingston. You'll find this public parkland course, founded in 1895, 2 mi east of the city. ✉ *Duddingston Rd. W, Duddingston* ☎ *0131/661– 7688* ⚐. *18 holes, 6,420 yds, SSS 72.*

Liberton. This public parkland course was built in 1920, 4 mi south of the city. ✉ *Kingston Grange, 297 Gilmerton Rd., Liberton* ☎ *0131/ 664–8580* 🖷 *0131/666–0853* ⚐. *18 holes, 5,412 yds, SSS 69.*

Portobello. Short and sweet, Portobello has welcomed amateur golfers since 1826. ✉ *Stanley St., Portobello, 2 mi east of city* ☎ *0131/669– 4361* ⚐. *9 holes, 2,449 yds, SSS 32.*

Rugby

At **Murrayfield Stadium** (✉ Roseburn Terr., Murrayfield ☎ 0131/346– 5000 ⊕ www.scottishrugby.org), home of the Scottish Rugby Union, Scotland's international rugby matches are played in early spring and fall. During that time of year, crowds of good-humored rugby fans from all over the world add to the sense of excitement in the city.

Running

The most convenient spot downtown for joggers is **West Princes Street Gardens,** which is separated from traffic by a 30-foot embankment. It has a ½-mi loop on asphalt paths. In **Holyrood Park,** stick to jogging on the road around the volcanic mountain for a 2¼-mi trip. For a real challenge, charge up to the summit of Arthur's Seat, or to the halfway point, the Cat's Nick.

Soccer

Like Glasgow, Edinburgh is soccer-mad, and there's an intense rivalry between the city's two professional teams. Remember, the game is called football in Britain. The **Heart of Midlothian Football Club ("Hearts")** (☎ 0131/200–7200) plays in maroon and white and is based at Tynecastle. The green-bedecked **Hibernian ("Hibs") Club** (☎ 0131/661–2159) plays its home matches at Easter Road.

SHOPPING

Shopping Districts

Despite its renown as a shopping street, **Princes Street** in the New Town may disappoint some visitors with its dull, anonymous modern architecture, average chain stores, and fast-food outlets. It is, however, one of the best spots to shop for tartans, tweeds, and knitwear, especially if your time is limited. One block north of Princes Street, **Rose Street** has many smaller specialty shops; part of the street is a pedestrian zone, so it's a pleasant place to browse. The shops on **George Street** tend to be fairly upscale. London names, such as Laura Ashley and Penhaligon's, are prominent, though some of the older independent stores continue to do good business.

The streets crossing George Street—Hanover, Frederick, and Castle—are also worth exploring. **Dundas Street,** the northern extension of Hanover Street, beyond Queen Street Gardens, has several antiques shops. **Thistle Street,** originally George Street's "back lane," or service area, has several boutiques and more antiques shops. As may be expected, many shops along the **Royal Mile** sell what may be politely or euphemistically described as tourist-ware—whiskies, tartans, and tweeds. Careful exploration, however, will reveal some worthwhile establishments. Shops here also cater to highly specialized interests and hobbies.

Close to the castle end of the Royal Mile, just off George IV Bridge, is **Victoria Street,** with specialty shops grouped in a small area. Follow the tiny West Bow to **Grassmarket** for more specialty stores. North of Princes Street, on the way to the Royal Botanic Garden Edinburgh, is **Stockbridge,** an oddball shopping area of some charm, particularly on St. Stephen Street. To get here, walk north down Frederick Street and Howe Street, away from Princes Street, then turn left onto North West Circus Place. **Stafford and William streets** form a small, upscale shopping area in a Georgian setting. Walk to the west end of Princes Street and then along its continuation, Shandwick Place, then turn right onto Stafford Street. William Street crosses Stafford halfway down.

Arcades & Shopping Centers

Like most large towns, Edinburgh has succumbed to the fashion for under-one-roof shopping. If you don't want to be distracted by wonderful views between shops—or if it's raining—try the upscale **Princes Mall** (⊠ East end of Princes St., East End), with a fast-food area, designer-label boutiques, and shops that sell Scottish woolens and tweeds, whisky, and confections. The **Ocean Terminal** (⊠ Ocean Dr., Leith) houses a large collection of shops as well as bars and eateries. Here you can also visit the former royal yacht *Britannia*. The **St. James Centre** (⊠ Princes St., East End) has Dorothy Perkins, HMV, and numerous other chain stores.

Department Stores

In contrast to other major cities, Edinburgh has few true department stores. If you plan on a morning or a whole day of wandering from department to department, trying on beautiful clothes, buying crystal or china, or stocking up on Scottish food specialties, with a break for lunch at an in-store restaurant, Jenners is your best bet.

★ **Harvey Nichols** (✉ 30–34 St. Andrew Sq., New Town ☎ 0131/524–8388)
★ is the local outpost of the high-style British chain. **Jenners** (✉ 48 Princes St., New Town ☎ 0131/225–2442) specializes in traditional china and glassware, as well as Scottish clothing (upscale tweeds and tartans). Its justly famous food hall sells shortbreads and Dundee cakes (a light fruit cake with a distinctive pattern of split almonds arranged in circles on the top), honeys, and marmalades, as well as high-quality groceries.

Specialty Shops

Antiques

Antiques dealers tend to cluster together, so it may be easiest to concentrate on one area—St. Stephen Street, Bruntsfield Place, Causewayside, or Dundas Street, for example—if you are short on time. **Courtyard Antiques** (✉ 108A Causewayside, Sciennes ☎ 0131/662–9008) stocks a mixture of high-quality antiques, toys, and militaria.

Books, Paper, Maps & Games

As a university city and cultural center, Edinburgh is endowed with excellent bookstores.

Carson Clark Gallery (✉ 181–183 Canongate, Old Town ☎ 0131/556–4710) specializes in antique maps, sea charts, and prints. **Waterstone's** (✉ 83 George St., New Town ☎ 0131/225–3436 ✉ 13–14 Princes St., East End ☎ 0131/556–3034 ✉ 128 Princes St., West End ☎ 0131/226–2666) is a large, London-based chain with a good selection of mainstream and more obscure books, as well as a consistently helpful staff.

Clothing Boutiques

Edinburgh is home to several top-quality designers—although, it must be said, probably not as many as are found in Glasgow, Scotland's fashion center—some of whom make a point of using Scottish materials in their creations.

Bill Baber (✉ 66 Grassmarket, Old Town ☎ 0131/225–3249) is one of the most imaginative of the many Scottish knitwear designers, and a long way from the conservative pastel "woolies" sold at some of the large mill shops. The **Extra Inch** (✉ 12 William St., West End ☎ 0131/226–3303) stocks a full selection of clothes in European sizes 16 (U.S. size 14) and up.

Jewelry

Hamilton and Inches (✉ 87 George St., New Town ☎ 0131/225–4898), established in 1866, is a silver- and goldsmith worth visiting not only for its modern and antique gift possibilities, but also for its late-Georgian interior, designed by David Bryce in 1834—all columns and elaborate plasterwork. **Joseph Bonnar** (✉ 72 Thistle St., New Town ☎ 0131/226–2811), tucked behind George Street, has Scotland's largest collection of antique jewelry, including 19th-century agate jewels.

Linens, Textiles & Home Furnishings

And So To Bed (✉ 30 Dundas St., New Town ☎ 0131/652–3700) has a wonderful selection of embroidered and embellished bed linens, cushion covers, and the like. **In House** (✉ 28 Howe St., New Town ☎ 0131/225–2888) sells designer furnishings and collectibles at the forefront of modern design for the home.

Outdoor Sports Gear

Tiso (✉ 123–125 Rose St., New Town ☎ 0131/225–9486 ✉ 41 Commercial St., Leith ☎ 0131/554–0804) stocks outdoor clothing, boots, and jackets ideal for hiking or camping in the Highlands or the islands.

Scottish Specialties

If you want to identify a particular tartan, several shops on Princes Street will be pleased to assist. The **Clan Tartan Centre** (✉ 70–74 Bangor Rd., Leith ☎ 0131/553–5516) has a database containing details of all known tartans, plus information on clan histories. At the **Edinburgh Old Town Weaving Company** (✉ 555 Castlehill, Old Town ☎ 0131/226–1555), you can watch and even talk to the cloth and tapestry weavers as they work, then buy the products. The company can also provide information on clan histories, and, if your name is a relatively common English or Scottish one, tell you which tartan you are entitled to wear. **Geoffrey (Tailor) Highland Crafts** (✉ 57–59 High St., Old Town ☎ 0131/557–0256) can clothe you in full Highland dress, with kilts made in its own workshops. The affiliated **21st Century Kilts** crafts stunning contemporary kilts in leather, denim, and even camouflage.

Edinburgh Crystal (✉ Eastfield, Penicuik ☎ 01968/675128), 10 mi south of the city center, is renowned the world over for its fine glass and crystal ware. Many large stores and gift shops in the city stock pieces from Edinburgh Crystal, but the largest selection is at its main premises. You can browse discontinued lines for real bargains.

SIDE TRIPS IN THE LOTHIANS

If you stand on an Edinburgh eminence—the castle ramparts, Arthur's Seat, Corstorphine Hill—you can plan a few Lothian excursions without even the aid of a map. The Lothians is the collective name given to the swath of countryside south of the Firth of Forth and surrounding Edinburgh. Many courtly and aristocratic families lived here, and the region still has the castles and mansions to prove it.

Exploration of the historic houses and castles of West Lothian and the Forth Valley, and territory north of the River Forth, can be accomplished in a full day with select stops. Stretching east to the sea and south to the Lowlands from Edinburgh, Midlothian and East Lothian are no more than one hour from Edinburgh. The inland river valleys, hills, and castles of Midlothian and East Lothian's delightful waterfronts, dunes, and golf links offer a taste of Scotland close to the capital. For many years Midlothian was off the beaten tourist path. However, the popularity of *The Da Vinci Code* has brought busloads to Rosslyn Chapel.

12

	WHAT IT COSTS In Pounds				
	£££££	**££££**	**£££**	**££**	**£**
RESTAURANTS	over £22	£18–£22	£13–£17	£7–£12	under £7
HOTELS	over £160	£120–£160	£90–£119	£60–£89	under £60

Restaurant prices are for a main course at dinner. Hotel prices are for two people in a standard double room in high season, generally including 17.5% V.A.T.

South Queensferry

7 mi west of Edinburgh.

★ ❷ This pleasant little waterside community, a former ferry port, is completely dominated by the **Forth Bridges,** dramatic structures of contrasting architecture that span the Firth of Forth at this historic crossing point. The **Forth Rail Bridge** was opened in 1890 and at the time hailed as the eighth wonder of the world, at 2,765 yards long—except on a hot summer's day when it expands by about another yard. Its neighbor is the 1,993-yard-long **Forth Road Bridge,** in operation since 1964.

Where to Eat

£–£££ ✕ **The Hawes Inn.** In his novel *Kidnapped,* Robert Louis Stevenson describes a room at this inn as "a small room, with a bed in it, and heated like an oven by a great fire of coal." The dramatic setting and history alone are well worth the trip to the inn, which is 10 mi from the city center of Edinburgh and 1 mi from Dalmeny Railway station. The open fireplaces at this 1638 pub create a sense of comfort and coziness. You'll find traditional pub fare here, such as steak pie and fish-and-chips. ✉ *Newhalls Rd.* ☎ *0131/331–1990* ▤ *AE, MC, V.*

Hopetoun House

★ ❷ *10 mi west of Edinburgh.*

The palatial premises of Hopetoun House, probably Scotland's grandest courtly seat and home of the marquesses of Linlithgow, are considered to be among the Adam family's finest designs. The enormous house was started in 1699 to the original plans of Sir William Bruce (1630–1710), then enlarged between 1721 and 1754 by William Adam (1689–1748) and his sons Robert and John. There's a notable painting collection, and the house has decorative work of the highest order, plus all the trappings to keep you entertained: a nature trail, a restaurant in the former stables, and a museum. Much of the wealth that created this sumptuous building came from the family's mining interests in the surrounding regions. ✉ *Off A904, 6 mi west of South Queensferry* ☎ *0131/331–2451* ⊕ *www.hopetounhouse.com* ✉ *£8* ☉ *Mar.–Sept., daily 10–5:30, last admission at 4:30; Oct., daily 11–4, last admission at 3:30.*

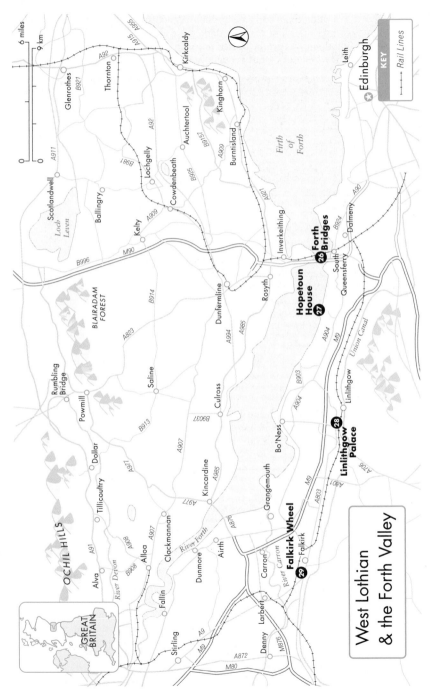

West Lothian
& the Forth Valley

Linlithgow Palace

28 *12 mi west of Edinburgh.*

On the edge of Linlithgow Loch stands the splendid ruin of Linlithgow Palace, the birthplace of Mary, Queen of Scots in 1542. Burned, perhaps accidentally, by Hanoverian troops during the last Jacobite rebellion in 1746, this impressive shell stands on a site of great antiquity, though nothing for certain survived an earlier fire in 1424. The palace gatehouse was built in the early 16th century, and the central courtyard's elaborate fountain dates from around 1535. The halls and great rooms are cold, echoing stone husks now in Historic Scotland's care. ✉ *A706, south shore of Linlithgow Loch* ☎ *01506/842896* ⊕ *www.historic-scotland.gov.uk* ⌨ *£4.50* ⊙ *Mar.–Sept., daily 9:30–6:30; Oct.–Mar., daily 9:30–4:30.*

Falkirk Wheel

★ **29** *25 mi west of Edinburgh.*

In 2002, British Waterways opened the only rotating boatlift in the world, linking two major waterways, the Forth and Clyde Canal and the Union Canal, between Edinburgh and Glasgow. Considered an engineering marvel, the wheel transports eight or more boats at a time overland from one canal to the other in about 45 minutes. The boats float into a cradle-like compartment full of water; as the wheel turns, they are transported up or down to meet the destination canal. You can board tour boats at Falkirk to ride the Wheel, or you can take a multiday barge cruise between Edinburgh and Glasgow; book in advance. At Falkirk, allow 30 minutes before your scheduled departure time to pick up your tickets and choose your boat. ✉ *Lime Rd., Tamfourhill* ☎ *01324/619888, 08700/500208 reservations* ⊕ *www. thefalkirkwheel.co.uk* ⌨ *Boat trips £8; visitor center free* ⊙ *Boat trips, Apr.–Oct., daily 9:30–5; Nov.–Mar., daily 10–3. Visitor center, Apr.–Oct., daily 9–5; Nov.–Mar. 10–5.*

Roslin

7 mi south of Edinburgh.

30 **Rosslyn Chapel** has always beckoned curious visitors intrigued by the various legends surrounding its magnificent carvings, but today it pulses with tourists as never before. Dan Brown's best-selling novel *The Da Vinci Code* has made visiting this Episcopal chapel (services continue to be held here) an imperative stop for many of its enthusiasts. Whether you are a fan of the book or not—and of the book's theory that the chapel has a secret sign that can lead you to the Holy Grail—this is a site

Fodor'sChoice
★

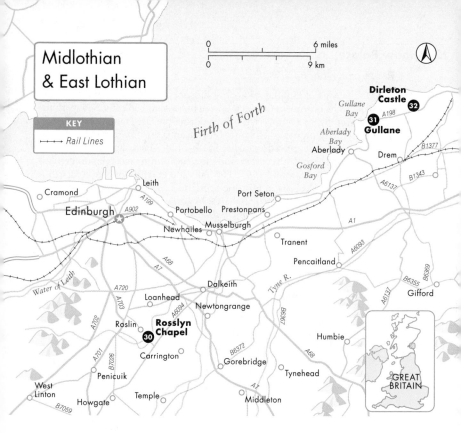

Midlothian & East Lothian

KEY

•┼──┼── Rail Lines

Firth of Forth

Gullane Bay

Dirleton Castle 32

Gullane 31 **Gullane**

Aberlady Bay

Aberlady

Drem

B1377

Gosford Bay

B1343

A6137

Cramond

Leith

Port Seton

Edinburgh

Portobello Prestonpans

Newhailes Musselburgh

Tranent

A1

A6093

B6369

Pencaitland

Tyne R.

B6355

Water of Leith

A720

Dalkeith

Gifford

A703

Loanhead

A6094

Newtongrange

B6367

A6137

B7026

Roslin

Rosslyn Chapel 30

Humbie

A702

A701

Carrington

B6372

A68

Penicuik

Gorebridge

Tynehead

West Linton

Howgate

Temple

A7

Middleton

GREAT BRITAIN

---

of immense interest. Originally conceived by Sir William Sinclair (circa 1404–80) and dedicated to St. Matthew in 1446, the chapel is outstanding for the quality and variety of the carving inside. Covering almost every square inch of stonework are human figures, animals, and plants. The meaning of these remains subject to many theories; some depict symbols from the medieval order of the Knights Templar and from Freemasonry. The chapel's design called for a cruciform structure, but only the choir and parts of the east transept walls were completed. Two bus services go to Roslin—Lothian service 15A from St. Andrew Square or Princes Street, and First service 62 from the bus station or North Bridge; check the chapel Web site, www.lothianbuses.co.uk, or www.firstgroup.com. ✉ *Roslin, Roslin is on the A701 to Penicuik/Peebles* 🕾 *0131/440–2159* ⊕ *www.rosslyn-chapel.com* 🎟 *£7* ⊙ *Mon.–Sat. 9:30–6, Sun. noon–4:45.*

Gullane

③① *15 mi northeast of Edinburgh.*

Very noticeable along this coastline are the golf courses of East Lothian, laid out wherever there is available links space. Ultrarespectable Gullane is surrounded by them, and its inhabitants are typically clad in expensive golfing sweaters. Muirfield, a course that hosts the British Open championship, is to the north of the village. Greywalls, now a hotel, was originally a private house, designed by Sir Edwin Lutyens (1869–1944). Apart from golf, you can enjoy restful summer evening strolls at Gullane's beach, well within driving distance of the village.

Where to Stay

★ **£££££** 🏨 **Greywalls.** This is the ideal hotel for a golfing vacation: comfortable, with attentive service and fine modern British cuisine that makes the most of local produce. The turn-of-the-20th-century house, designed by Sir Edwin Lutyens in the shape of a crescent and with a walled garden, is an architectural treasure. Edward VII used to stay here, as have Jack Nicklaus, Lee Trevino, Arnold Palmer, and other golfing greats. Shades of restful green predominate in the stylish fabrics from the likes of Nina Campbell, Colefax and Fowler, and Osborne and Little. A separate lodge house holds up to eight people. ✉ *Muirfield, Gullane, EH31 2EG* ☎ *01620/842144* 🖷 *01620/842241* ⊕ *www.greywalls.co.uk* ↪ *23 rooms, 1 lodge* ⚒ *Restaurant, cable TV, putting green, 2 tennis courts; no a/c* ▭ *AE, DC, MC, V* ⦿| *BP* ⊘ *Closed mid-Oct.–late-Mar.*

Golf

Muirfield. The championship course at Muirfield is one of the best-known links courses in the world, so be prepared to pay the price of fame with expensive greens fees (£120 pounds and up) and severe limitations on when you can play. This exclusivity also means you should be prepared for a degree of curtness toward visitors. A handicap certificate is required (18 or less for men, 24 or less for women). ✉ *Duncur Rd., off A198* ☎ *01620/842123* ⊕ *www.muirfield.org.uk* ⚒ *Reservations essential* ⚑ *18 holes, 6,601 yds, par 70* ⊘ *Visitors Tues. and Thurs., tee off between 8:30 and 9:50.*

Dirleton

22 mi northeast of Edinburgh.

③② In the center of this small village sits the 12th-century **Dirleton Castle,** surrounded by a high outer wall. Within the wall you'll find a 17th-century bowling green, set in the shade of yew trees and surrounded by a herbaceous flower border that blazes with color in high summer. Dirleton Castle, now in Historic Scotland's care, was occupied in 1298 by King Edward I of England as part of his campaign for the continued subjugation of the unruly Scots. ✉ *On A198, 2 mi west of North Berwick* ☎ *01620/850330* ⊕ *www.historic-scotland.gov.uk* 🎫 *£3.30* ⊘ *Apr.–Sept., daily 9:30–6; Oct.–Mar., daily 9:30–4.*

EDINBURGH & THE LOTHIANS ESSENTIALS

Transportation

BY AIR

Only a few transatlantic flights come through Edinburgh (Continental has service from Newark Liberty, near New York; Delta has service from Atlanta); you must instead fly into Glasgow, 50 mi away. Ryanair and easyJet have sparked a major price war on the Anglo-Scottish routes. They offer unbeatable, no-frills airfares on routes connecting Edinburgh Airport, Glasgow International, Prestwick Airport (30 mi south of Glasgow), and London's major airports. For more information, *see* By Air *in* Transportation *in* Essentials.

AIRPORTS Edinburgh Airport, 7 mi west of the city center, offers only a few transatlantic flights. It does, however, have air connections throughout the United Kingdom as well as with a number of European cities. Flights take off for Edinburgh Airport virtually every hour from London's Gatwick and Heathrow airports; it's usually faster and less complicated to fly through Gatwick, which has excellent rail service from London's Victoria Station.

Glasgow Airport, 50 mi west of Edinburgh, serves as the major point of entry into Scotland for transatlantic flights. Prestwick Airport, 30 mi southwest of Glasgow, after some years of eclipse by Glasgow Airport, has grown in importance, not least because of the activities of Ryanair. 🛈 **Edinburgh Airport** ☎ 0870/040-0007 ⊕ www.baa.com. **Glasgow Airport** ☎ 0870/040-0008 ⊕ www.baa.com. **Prestwick Airport** ☎ 0871/223-0700 ⊕ www.gpia.co.uk.

TRANSFERS FROM EDINBURGH AIRPORT There are no rail links to the city center, despite the fact that the airport sits between two main lines. By bus or car you can usually make it to Edinburgh in a comfortable half hour, unless you hit the morning (7:30 to 9) or evening (4 to 6) rush hours. Lothian Buses run between Edinburgh Airport and the city center every 15 minutes daily from 9 to 5 and less frequently (roughly every hour) during off-peak hours. The trip takes about 30 minutes, or about 45 minutes during rush hour. A single-fare ticket costs £3.

You can arrange for a chauffeur-driven limousine to meet your flight at Edinburgh Airport through David Grieve Chauffeur Drive for about £45 plus V.A.T. Little's Chauffeur Drive, £47 plus V.A.T. and W L Sleigh Ltd., £50 plus V.A.T.

Taxis are readily available outside the terminal. The trip takes 20 to 30 minutes to the city center, 15 minutes longer during rush hour. The fare is roughly £20. Note that airport taxis picking up fares from the terminal are any color, not the typical black cabs. 🛈 **David Grieve Chauffeur Drive** ✉ 5b Polworth Gardens, Tollcross ☎ 0131/229-8666. **Little's Chauffeur Drive** ✉ 1282 Paisley Rd. W, Paisley ☎ 0131/334-2177 ⊕ www.littles.co.uk. **W L Sleigh Ltd.** ✉ 6 Devon Pl., West End ☎ 0131/337-3171 ⊕ www.sleigh.co.uk.

TRANSFERS FROM GLASGOW AIRPORT Scottish Citylink buses leave Glasgow Airport every 15 minutes to travel to Glasgow's Buchanan Street (journey time is 25 minutes), where you can transfer to an Edinburgh bus (leaving every 20 minutes). The trip to Edinburgh takes 70 minutes and costs £9.50 round-trip and £7 one-way. A somewhat more pleasant option is to take a cab from Glasgow Airport to Glasgow's Queen Street train station (20 minutes and costs about £18) and then take the train to Waverley Station in Edinburgh. Trains leave about every 30 minutes; the trip takes 50 minutes and costs £8.10. Check times on weekends. Another, less expensive alternative is to take the bus from Glasgow Airport to Glasgow's Buchanan bus station, walk five minutes to the Queen Street train station, and catch the train to Edinburgh. Taxis from Glasgow Airport to downtown Edinburgh take about 70 minutes and cost around £95.

🄵 **Scottish Citylink** ☎ 08705/505050 ⊕ www.citylink.co.uk. **Taxis** ☎ 0141/848-4900.

BY BUS

National Express provides bus service to and from London and other major towns and cities. The main terminal, St. Andrew Square bus station, is only a couple of minutes (on foot) north of Waverley station, immediately east of St. Andrew Square. Long-distance coaches must be booked in advance from the booking office in the terminal. Edinburgh is approximately eight hours by bus from London.

Lothian Buses provides much of the service between Edinburgh and the Lothians and conducts day tours around and beyond the city. First also runs buses out of Edinburgh into the surrounding area.

🄵 **First** ☎ 0870/872-7271 ⊕ www.firstgroup.com. **Lothian Buses** ☎ 0131/555-6363 ⊕ www.lothianbuses.co.uk. **National Express** ☎ 08705/808080 ⊕ www.nationalexpress.co.uk.

BUS TRAVEL WITHIN EDINBURGH — Lothian Buses is the main operator within Edinburgh. You can buy tickets on the bus. The Bargain Day Ticket (£2.30), allowing unlimited one-day travel on the city's buses, can be purchased in advance or from the driver on any Lothian bus (exact fare is required when purchasing on a bus). The Rider Card (for which you will need a photo) is valid on all buses for seven days (Sunday through Saturday night) and costs £12; the four-week Rider costs £36.

🄵 **Lothian Buses** ✉ Waverley Bridge, Old Town ☎ 0131/555-6363 ⊕ www.lothianbuses.co.uk.

BY CAR

Downtown Edinburgh centers on Princes Street, which runs east–west and is closed to all but taxis and buses for most of its length. If you're driving from the east coast you'll come in on A1, with Meadowbank Stadium serving as a landmark. The highway bypasses the suburbs of Musselburgh and Tranent; therefore, any bottlenecks will occur close to downtown. From the Borders the approach to Princes Street is by A7/A68 through Newington. From Newington the east end of Princes Street is reached by North Bridge and South Bridge. Approaching from the southwest, you'll join the west end of Princes Street (Lothian Road) via A701 and A702; if you're coming west from Glasgow or Stirling you'll meet Princes Street from M8 or M9, respectively. A slightly more complicated approach is via M90—from Forth Road Bridge/Perth/east coast; the key road for getting downtown is Queensferry Road, which joins Charlotte Square close to the west end of Princes Street.

Driving in Edinburgh has its quirks and pitfalls, but competent drivers should not be intimidated. Metered parking in the city center is scarce and expensive, and the local traffic wardens are a feisty, alert bunch. Note that illegally parked cars are routinely towed away, and getting your car back will be expensive. After 6 PM the parking situation improves considerably, and you may manage to find a space quite near your hotel, even downtown. If you park on a yellow line or in a resident's parking bay, be prepared to move your car by 8 the following morning, when the rush hour gets under way. Parking lots are clearly signposted; overnight parking is expensive and not permitted in all lots.

Major car-rental companies have booths at the airport. Rates start at about £48 per day. If you choose to plunge yourself into Edinburgh's traffic system, take care on the first couple of traffic circles (called roundabouts) on the way into town from the airport—even experienced drivers find them challenging. By car the airport is about 7 mi west of Princes Street downtown and is clearly marked from A8. The usual route to downtown is via the suburb of Corstorphine.

BY TAXI

Taxi stands can be found throughout the downtown area. The following are the most convenient: the west end of Princes Street; South St. David Street, and North St. Andrew Street (both just off St. Andrew Square); Princes Mall; Waterloo Place; and Lauriston Place. Alternatively, hail any taxi displaying an illuminated FOR HIRE sign.

BY TRAIN

Edinburgh's main train hub, Waverley Station, is downtown, below Waverley Bridge and around the corner from the unmistakable spire of the Scott Monument. Travel time from Edinburgh to London by train is as little as 4½ hours for the fastest service.

Edinburgh's other main station is Haymarket, about four minutes (by rail) west of Waverley. Most Glasgow and other western and northern services stop here. Haymarket can be more convenient if you're staying in hotels beyond the west end of Princes Street.

First ScotRail ☎ 0845/601-5929 ⊕ www.firstgroup.com/scotrail. **National Rail Enquiries** ☎ 08457/495051 ⊕ www.nationalrail.co.uk.

Contacts & Resources

EMERGENCIES

In an emergency dial **999** for an ambulance, police or fire departments. The accident and emergency department of Edinburgh Royal Infirmary is at Lauriston Place in the city center, though the main buildings are 6 mi to the southeast in an area known as Little France.

You can find out which pharmacy is open late on a given night by looking at the notice posted on every pharmacy door. A pharmacy—or dispensing chemist, as it is called here—is easily identified by its sign, showing a green cross on a white background. Boots, a large British chain, is open weekdays from 8 AM to 9 PM, Saturday from 8 to 6, and Sunday from 10:30 to 4:30.

To retrieve lost property, try the Lothian and Borders police headquarters, open weekdays from 9 to 5. If you lose something on a public bus, contact Lothian Buses, open weekdays from 10 to 1:30.

⚕ Hospital Edinburgh Royal Infirmary ⊠ Dalkeith Rd., Little France ⊠ Accident and Emergency, Lauriston Pl., Old Town ☎ 0131/536–1000.

⚕ Late-Night Pharmacy Boots ⊠ 48 Shandwick Pl., west end of Princes St., West End ☎ 0131/225–6757.

⚕ Lost & Found Lothian and Borders police headquarters ⊠ Fettes Ave., Inverleith ☎ 0131/311–3131. **Lothian Buses** ⊠ 55 Annandale St., New Town ☎ 0131/558–8858.

INTERNET, MAIL & SHIPPING

The post office in St. James Centre is the most central and is open Monday from 9 to 5:30, Tuesday through Friday from 8:30 to 5:30, and Saturday from 8:30 to 6. There are two other main post offices in the city center. Many newsagents also sell stamps.

⌨ Internet Cafés easyInternetcafé ⊠ 58 Rose St., New Town ☎ 0131/220–3577 ⊕ www.easyinternetcafe.com. **e-corner Internet café** ⊠ 54 Blackfriars St., Old Town ☎ 0131/558–7858 ⊕ www.e-corner.co.uk. **Wired Cafe** ⊠ 1 Brougham Pl., New Town ☎ 0131/659–7820 ⊕ www.wiredcafe.info.

⌨ Post Offices City Center post offices ⊠ 40 Frederick St., New Town ☎ 0845/722–3344 ⊕ www.postoffices-dir.co.uk ⊠ St. Mary's St., Old Town ☎ 0131/556–6351. **St. James Centre** ⊠ St. Andrew Sq., East End ☎ 0845/722–3344.

TOUR OPTIONS

ORIENTATION TOURS The best way to get oriented in Edinburgh is to take a bus tour, most of which are operated by Lothian Buses. City Sightseeing open-top bus tours (£8.50) include multilingual commentary; MacTours (£8.50) are conducted in vintage open-top buses. All tours take you to the main attractions, including Edinburgh Castle, the Royal Mile, Palace of Holyroodhouse, city museums and galleries, and the Old and New towns. They depart from Waverley Bridge, and are hop-on/hop-off services, with tickets lasting 24 hours. The 60-minute Britannia Tour (£12) operates with a professional guide, and takes you from Waverly Bridge to the New Town, past Charlotte Square, art galleries, the Royal Botanic Garden Edinburgh, and Newhaven Heritage Museum, until it reaches the Royal Yacht *Britannia* moored at Leith. Tickets for all tours are available from ticket sellers on Waverley Bridge or on the buses themselves.

The money-saving Edinburgh Pass gives you bus transport (including a return ticket on the airport bus), access to more than 25 attractions, and other exclusive offers. A one-day pass costs £26; two-day pass £34, and three-day pass £40. Passes are available from the tourist information centers in Princes Street, at Edinburgh Airport, or online.

⌨ Edinburgh Pass ☎ 0131/473-3800 ⊕ www.edinburghpass.org. **Lothian Buses** ☎ 0131/555–6363 ⊕ www.edinburghtour.com.

PERSONAL GUIDES Scottish Tourist Guides can supply guides (in 19 languages) who are fully qualified and will meet clients at any point of entry into the United Kingdom or Scotland. They can also tailor tours to your interests.

⌨ Scottish Tourist Guides Contact Doreen Boyle ⊠ Old Town Jail, St. John St., Stirling FK8 1EA ☎ 01786/451953 ⊕ www.stga.co.uk.

WALKING TOURS Cadies and Witchery Tours, a fully qualified member of the Scottish Tourist Guides Association, has built a reputation for combining entertainment and historical accuracy in its lively and enthusiastic Ghosts & Gore Tour and Murder & Mystery Tour (£7.50 each), which take you through the narrow Old Town alleyways and closes, with costumed guides and other theatrical characters showing up en route. The Scottish Literary Tour Company takes you around Edinburgh's Old and New Town, with guides invoking Scottish literary characters; it also has regional tours around Scotland.

🎦 **Cadies and Witchery Tours** ⊠ 84 West Bow, Edinburgh ☎ 0131/225–6745 ⊕ www. witcherytours.com. **Scottish Literary Tour Company** ⊠ 97B West Bow, Suite 2, Edinburgh ☎ 0131/226–6665 ⊕ www.edinburghliterarypubtour.co.uk.

VISITOR INFORMATION

Several excellent city maps are available at bookstores. Particularly recommended is the *Bartholomew Edinburgh Plan,* with a scale of approximately 4 inches to 1 mi, by the long-established Edinburgh cartographic company John Bartholomew and Sons, Ltd.

The Edinburgh and Scotland Information Centre, adjacent to Waverley Station (follow the TIC signs in the station and throughout the city), offers an accommodations service (Book-A-Bed-Ahead) in addition to other services. It's open May through June and September, from Monday to Saturday 9 to 7, Sunday 10 to 5; July and August, from Monday to Saturday 9 to 8, Sunday 10 to 8; October and April, from Monday to Saturday 9 to 6, Sunday 10 to 5; November through March, from Monday to Wednesday 9 to 5, from Thursday to Saturday 9 to 6, Sunday 10 to 5.

Complete information is also available at the information desk at the Edinburgh Airport.

🎦 **Edinburgh and Scotland Information Centre** ⊠ 3 Princes St., East End ☎ 0131/ 473–3800 🖷 0131/473–3881 ⊕ www.edinburgh.org.

Glasgow

WORD OF MOUTH

"Edinburgh may be the country's capital, but Glasgow was recently rated one of the hottest cities in Europe to visit. Glasgow has much history and the best shopping. It also has the famous Glasgow School of Art (designed by Charles Rennie Mackintosh). If you want some real 'Glaswegian' flavor, go to the Barras. It is an open flea market. . . bargains galore."

—notinamerica

"I managed to see the Burrell, a really neat museum with a diverse collection and the most Degas works I have seen in one place. The Scots are absolutely lovely—I stopped for a pint and had a nice conversation. They tried to teach me how to say Burrell the right way but ended by giving up."

—wills

Updated by
Fiona Parrott

DURING THE LAST TWO DECADES of the 20th century, Glasgow under-went an urban renaissance. No longer is it a city notorious for its area seedbeds of inner-city decay; instead today's Glasgow has trendy down-town stores, a booming and diverse cultural life, stylish restaurants, and an air of confidence that makes it Scotland's most exciting city.

The city's development has been unashamedly commercial, tied up with the wealth of its manufacturers and merchants, who constructed a vast number of civic buildings throughout the 19th century. Among those who helped shape Glasgow's unique Victorian cityscape during that great period was the local-born architect Alexander "Greek" Thomson (1817–75). Side by side with the overly Victorian, Glasgow had an ar-chitectural vision of the future in the work of Charles Rennie Machin-tosh (1868–1928). The Glasgow School of Art, the Willow Tearoom, the Glasgow Herald building (now home to the Lighthouse architecture and design centre) and the churches and schools he designed point clearly to the clarity and simplicity of the best of 20th-century design.

Glasgow has always been a proud city and in the days when Britain still ruled over an empire, Glasgow pronounced itself the Second City of the Empire for it was here that Britain's great steamships, including the 80,000-ton *Queen Elizabeth,* were built. The term "Clyde-built" (from Glas-gow's River Clyde) became synonymous with good workmanship and lasting quality. Scots engineers were to be found wherever there were engines—Glaswegians built the railway locomotives that opened up the Canadian prairies, the South African veldt, the Australian plains, and the Indian subcontinent. Some of the world's greatest industrial and scientific thinkers, such as Lord Kelvin and James Watt, tested their groundbreaking theories and discoveries as young men in Glasgow.

A Brief History

Glasgow first came into prominence in Scottish history somewhere around 1,400 years ago, and typically for this rambunctious city it all had to do with an argument between a husband and wife. When the king of Strathclyde gave his wife a ring, she was rash enough to pres-ent it to an admirer. The king, having surreptitiously repossessed it, threw it into the Clyde before quizzing his wife about its disappearance. In her distress, the queen turned to her confessor, St. Mungo, for advice. He instructed her to fish in the river and—surprise—the first salmon she landed had the ring in its jaws. Glasgow's coat of arms is dominated by three salmon, one with a ring in its mouth. Not surprisingly, Mungo be-came the city's patron saint. His tomb lies in the mighty medieval cathe-dral that bears his name.

Glasgow flourished quietly during the Middle Ages. Its cathedral was the center of religious life, its university a center of serious academia. Although the city was made a burgh (i.e., granted trading rights) in 1175 by King William the Lion, its population never numbered more than a few thousand people. What changed Glasgow irrevocably was the Treaty of Union between Scotland and England, in 1707, which allowed Scot-land to trade with the essentially English colonies in America. Glasgow, with its advantageous position on Scotland's west coast, prospered. In

TOP REASONS TO GO

Inspiring architecture: The ambitious Victorians, including Alexander "Greek" Thomson, bequeathed Glasgow a solid legacy of striking buildings with artistic appeal, and architectural innovation continued into the 20th century with such buildings as Charles Rennie Mackintosh's Glasgow School of Art. Glasgow's buildings manifest the city's enduring love of grand artistic statements—just remember to look up.

Artistic treasures: Some of Britain's best museums and art galleries are in Glasgow. The Burrell Collection and the stunningly renovated Kelvingrove Art Gallery are definitely worth a visit even on a sunny day.

Retail therapy: You'll find everything from Scottish specialties to stylish fashions on the city center's hottest shopping streets, Buchanan and Sauchiehall, as well as in Princes Square. Glasgow is the biggest and most popular British retail center outside London. It's also a lot less crowded.

Great grub: Glasgow has impressive Scottish and international restaurants—Indian is a favorite cuisine—to satisfy every palate and occasion. The fresh local seafood at the Mussel Inn should not be missed; Fratelli Sarti serves authentic, mouthwatering Italian dishes; and if you're looking for a rich, hot curry go to Ashoka West End. The locals love their cafés and tearooms; check out the scene as a break from sightseeing.

Explore Burns Country: Outside the city you can witness some of the most scenic landscapes in the country, from coastlines to castles to cottages. Here you can also learn about the life and legacy of Scotland's most renowned poet, Robert Burns. Alloway and Ayr are the places to start.

came cotton, tobacco, and rum; out went various Scottish manufactured goods and clothing. The key to it all was tobacco. The prosperous merchants known as tobacco lords ran the city, and their wealth laid the foundation for the manufacturing industries of the 19th century.

As Glasgow prospered, its population grew. The "dear green place" (the literal meaning of the Gaelic *Glas Cu,* from which the name "Glasgow" purportedly derives) expanded beyond recognition, extending westward and to the south of the original medieval city, which centered around the cathedral and High Street. The 18th-century Merchant City, now largely rejuvenated, lies just to the south and east of George Square, where all but a few of the original merchants' houses remain in their original condition. As the merchants moved to quieter areas in the west of the city, the Beaux-Arts elegance of their mansions and quiet streets gave way to larger municipal buildings and commercial warehouses. During the 19th century the population grew from 80,000 to more than 1 million, and along with this enormous growth there developed a sense of exuberance and confidence that's still reflected in the city's public buildings. The City Chambers, built in 1888, are a proud statement in marble and gold sandstone, a clear symbol of the wealthy and powerful Victorian industrialists' hopes for the future.

Present & Future

Today, as always, Glasgow's eye is trained on the future. The city is Scotland's major business destination, with the Scottish Exhibition and Conference Centre serving as the hub of activity. It is also a nexus of rail routes and motorways that can deliver you in less than an hour to Edinburgh, Stirling, Loch Lomond, the Burns Country, and the Clyde coast golfing resorts. Still, Glasgow has learned to take the best of its past and adapt it for the needs of the present day. The dear green places still remain in the city-center parks; the medieval cathedral stands proud, as it has done for 800 years; the Merchant City is revived and thriving; the Victorian splendor has been cleansed of its grime; and the cultural legacy of museums and performing arts is stronger than ever.

EXPLORING GLASGOW

Glasgow's layout is hard to read in a single glance. The city center is the area roughly defined by the M8 motorway to the north and west, the River Clyde to the south, and Glasgow Cathedral and High Street to the east. The center is relatively flat and compact, making it easy to walk around Glasgow Cathedral and Provand's Lordship, High Street, and the Merchant City. In fact Glaswegians tend to walk a good deal, and the streets, most of which follow a grid plan, are designed for pedestrians. If you do get lost, just ask a local for help. Most people will be more than happy to help you find your way. The streets are also relatively safe, even at night.

The River Clyde, on which Glasgow's trade across the Atlantic developed, runs through the center of the city—literally cutting it in two and offering intriguing views of South Side buildings. In Glasgow always look up: your reward is much ornate detailing visible above eye level.

In the quieter, slightly hillier western part of the city is Glasgow University and the often forgotten bohemian side of Glasgow. Some form of transportation is required to go to either the West End or the South Side, and you should have no qualms in using Glasgow's integrated transport network of buses, subways, and trains. Information is available from Strathclyde Passenger Transport (SPT) Travel Centre. ■ TIP→ **The Discovery Ticket one-day pass (£1.90, after 9:30) is a good deal if you're traveling around.**

If you're interested in the work of architect Charles Rennie Macintosh, you might purchase a £12 **Mackintosh Trail Ticket** at major sites, visitor centers, or online from the Mackintosh Society. It includes transportation and one-day admission to many sites; www.spt.co.uk, the transit service, and the Mackintosh Society, www.crmsociety.com, have information.

Numbers in the text correspond to numbers in the margin and on the Glasgow and Ayrshire & the Clyde Valley maps.

Medieval Glasgow & the Merchant City

In this central part of the city, alongside the relatively few surviving medieval buildings, are some of the best examples of the architectural confidence and exuberance that so characterized the burgeoning Glasgow of the turn of the 20th century.

Main Attractions

② **City Chambers.** Dominating the east side of George Square, this exuberant expression of Victorian confidence, built by William Young in Italian Renaissance style, was opened by Queen Victoria (1819–1901) in 1888. Among the interior's outstanding features are the entrance hall's vaulted ceiling, the marble-and-alabaster staircases, the banqueting hall, and Venetian mosaics. The debating chamber has gleaming oak panels and fixtures. Free guided tours lasting about 45 minutes depart weekdays at 10:30 and 2:30. Note that the building is closed to all visitors during occasional civic functions. ⊠ *George Sq., City Center* ☎ *0141/ 287–2000* ⊕ *www.glasgow.gov.uk* ⊠ *Free* ☉ *Weekdays 9–4:30.*

FodorśChoice ★

① **George Square.** The focal point of Glasgow's business district is lined with an impressive collection of statues of worthies: Queen Victoria; Scotland's national poet, Robert Burns (1759–96); the inventor and developer of the steam engine, James Watt (1736–1819); Prime Minister William Gladstone (1809–98); and towering above them all, Scotland's great historical novelist, Sir Walter Scott (1771–1832). The column was intended for George III (1738–1820), after whom the square is named, but when he was found to be insane toward the end of his reign, his statue was never erected. On the square's east side stands the magnificent Italian Renaissance–style **City Chambers**; the handsome **Merchants' House** fills the corner of West George Street.

★ **③** **Glasgow Cathedral.** The most complete of Scotland's cathedrals (it would have been more complete had 19th-century vandals not pulled down its two rugged towers), this is an unusual double church, one above the other, dedicated to Glasgow's patron saint, St. Mungo. Consecrated in 1136 and completed about 300 years later, it was spared the ravages of the Reformation—which destroyed so many of Scotland's medieval churches—mainly because Glasgow's trade guilds defended it. In the lower church is the splendid crypt of St. Mungo, who was originally known as St. Kentigern (*kentigern* means "chief word,") but who was nicknamed St. Mungo (meaning "dear one") by his early followers in Glasgow. The site of the tomb has been revered since the 6th century, when St. Mungo founded a church here. ⊠ *Cathedral St., City Center* ☎ *0141/552–6891* ⊕ *www.glasgow-cathedral.com* ⊠ *Free* ☉ *Apr.–Sept., Mon.–Sat. 9:30–6, Sun. 2–5; Oct.–Mar., Mon.–Sat. 9:30–4, Sun. 2–4.*

⑩ **Glasgow Gallery of Modern Art.** One of Glasgow's boldest galleries occupies the former Royal Exchange building. The Exchange, designed by David Hamilton (1768–1843) and finished in 1829, was a meeting place for merchants and traders; later it became Stirling's Library. It incorporates the mansion built in 1780 by William Cunninghame, one of the wealthiest tobacco lords. The modern art, craft, and design collec-

13

tions contained within this handsome building include works by Scottish conceptual artists such as David Mach, and also paintings and sculptures from around the world, including Papua New Guinea, Ethiopia, and Mexico. The display scheme is designed for each floor to reflect the elements—air, fire, and water—which creates some unexpected juxtapositions and also allows for various interactive exhibits. ⊠ *Queen St., City Center* ☎ *0141/229–1996* ⊕ *www.glasgowmuseums.com* ☎ *Free* ☉ *Mon.–Wed. and Sat. 10–5, Thurs. 10–8, Fri. and Sun. 11–5.*

❺ Necropolis. A burial ground since the beginning of recorded history, the Necropolis, modeled on the famous Père-Lachaise Cemetery in Paris, contains some extraordinarily elaborate Victorian tombs. A statue of John Knox (circa 1514–72), leader of the Scottish Reformation, watches over the cemetery, which includes the tomb of 19th-century Glasgow merchant William Miller (1810–72), author of the "Wee Willie Winkie" nursery rhyme. ⊠ *Behind Glasgow Cathedral, City Center.*

❾ People's Palace. An impressive Victorian red-sandstone building dating from 1894 houses an intriguing museum dedicated to the city's social history. Included among the exhibits is one devoted to the ordinary folk of Glasgow, called the *People's Story.* Also on display are the writing desk of John McLean (1879–1923), the "Red Clydeside" political activist who came to Lenin's notice, and the famous "banana boots" worn on stage by Glasgow-born comedian Billy Connolly. Behind the museum are the well-restored Winter Gardens, a relatively sheltered spot where you can escape the often chilly winds whistling across the green. ⊠ *Glasgow Green, Glasgow Cross* ☎ *0141/271–2951* ⊕ *www.glasgow. gov.uk* ☎ *Free* ☉ *Mon.–Thurs. and Sat. 10–5, Fri. and Sun. 11–5.*

Also Worth Seeing

❼ Barras. Scotland's largest indoor market—named for the barrows, or pushcarts, formerly used by the stall holders—is a must-see for anyone addicted to searching through piles of junk for bargains. The century-old institution, open weekends only, consists of nine markets. The atmosphere is always good-humored, and you can find just about anything here. ⊠ *¼ mi east of Glasgow Cross on London Rd., Glasgow Cross* ☎ *0141/ 552–4601* ⊕ *www.glasgow-barras.com* ☎ *Free* ☉ *Weekends 10–5.*

❽ Glasgow Green. Glasgow's oldest park, on the northeast side of the River Clyde, has a long history as a favorite spot for public recreation and political demonstrations. Note the Nelson Column, erected long before London's; the McLennan Arch, originally part of the facade of the old Assembly Halls in Ingram Street; and the Templeton Business Centre, a former carpet factory built in the late 19th century in the style of the Doge's Palace in Venice. The most significant building in the park is the **People's Palace.** ⊠ *Between Greendyke St. to north and River Clyde to south, and between Green to east and Saltmarket to west, Glasgow Cross.*

⓫ The Lighthouse. Charles Rennie Mackintosh designed these former offices of the *Glasgow Herald* newspaper in 1893. Mackintosh's building now serves as a fitting setting for Scotland's **Centre for Architecture, Design and the City,** which celebrates all facets of the architectural profession. The **Mackintosh Interpretation Centre** is a great starting point for discovering more about his other buildings in the city. As you ascend the helical staircase you can take a look at Mackintosh's original designs for the building. ⊠ *11 Mitchell La., City Center* ☎ *0141/225–8414* ⊕ *www.thelighthouse.co.uk* 🖃 *£3 for Mackintosh Interpretation Centre* ☉ *Mon. and Wed.–Sat. 10:30–5, Tues. 11–5, Sun. noon–5.*

Merchant City. Among the preserved Georgian and Victorian buildings of this city-center neighborhood are many elegant designer boutiques. The **City and County buildings,** on Ingram Street, were built in 1842 to house civil servants; note the impressive arrangement of bays and Corinthian columns. To see more interesting architecture, explore the roads off Ingram Street—including Candleriggs, Wilson, and Glassford. ⊠ *Between George St. to north and Argyle St. to south, and between Buchanan St. to west and High St. to east.*

❻ Provand's Lordship. Glasgow's oldest house was built in 1471 by Bishop Andrew Muirhead as a residence for churchmen. Mary, Queen of Scots (1542–87) is said to have stayed here. After her day, however, the house fell into decline and was used as a sweets shop, a soft-drink factory, the home of the city hangman, and a junk shop. The city finally rescued it and turned it into a museum. Exhibits show the house as it might have looked in its heyday, with period rooms and a spooky recreation of the old hangman's room. ⊠ *3 Castle St., City Center* ☎ *0141/552–8819* ⊕ *www.glasgow.gov.uk* 🖃 *Free* ☉ *Mon.–Thurs. and Sat. 10–5, Fri. and Sun. 11–5.*

❹ St. Mungo Museum of Religious Life and Art. An outstanding collection of artifacts, including Celtic crosses and statuettes of Hindu gods, reflects the many religious groups that have settled throughout the centuries in Glasgow and the west of Scotland. This rich history is depicted in the stunning Sharing of Faiths Banner, which celebrates the city's many different faiths. A Zen Garden creates a peaceful setting for rest and contemplation, and elsewhere stained-glass windows include a depiction of St. Mungo himself. ⊠ *2 Castle St., City Center* ☎ *0141/553–2557* ⊕ *www.glasgowmuseums.com* 🖃 *Free* ☉ *Mon.–Thurs. and Sat. 10–5, Fri. and Sun. 11–5.*

The West End

Glasgow's West End has a stellar mix of education, culture, art, and parkland. The neighborhood is dominated by Glasgow University, founded in 1451, making it the third-oldest in Scotland, after St. Andrews and Aberdeen, and at least 130 years ahead of the University of Edinburgh. The Kelvingrove Art Gallery and Museum is one of the area's most stunning attractions.

Main Attractions

⓱ Botanic Gardens. The Royal Botanical Institute of Glasgow began to display plants here in 1842, and today the gardens include herbs, tropical plants, and a world-famous collection of orchids. The most spectacular building in the complex is the **Kibble Palace,** which reopened in October 2006 after extensive reconstruction work. Originally built in 1873, it was the conservatory of a Victorian eccentric named John Kib-

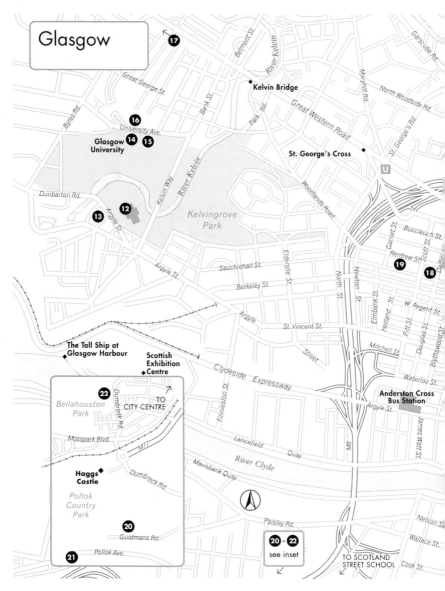

Glasgow

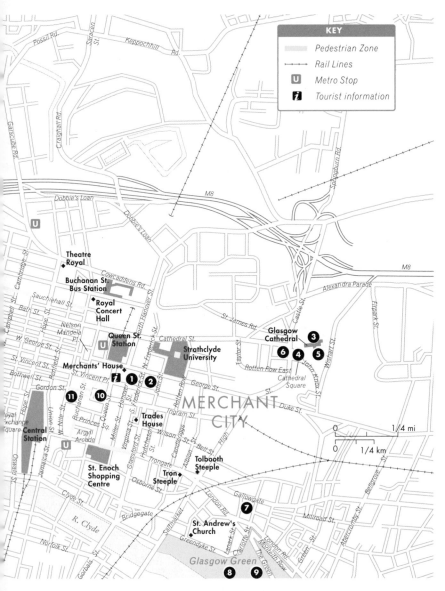

ble. Its domed, interlinked greenhouses contain tree ferns, palm trees, temperate plants, and the Tropicarium, where you can experience the lushness of a tropical rain forest. Elsewhere around the grounds are more conventional greenhouses, as well as immaculate lawns and colorful flower beds. ⊠ *Great Western Rd., West End* ☎ *0141/334–2422* ⊕ *www. glasgow.gov.uk* 🖃 *Free* ⊗ *Gardens Mar.–mid-Oct., daily 7–dusk; mid-Oct.–Feb., daily 7–4:15. Kibble Palace and other greenhouses Mar.–mid-Oct., daily 10–4:45; mid-Oct.–Feb., daily 10–4:15.*

★ ⑱ **Glasgow School of Art.** The exterior and interior, structure, furnishings, and decoration of this art-nouveau building, built between 1897 and 1909, form a unified whole, reflecting the inventive genius of Charles Rennie Mackintosh, who was only 28 years old when he won the competition for its design. Architects and designers from all over the world come to admire it, but because it's a working school of art, general access is sometimes limited. Guided tours are available; it's best to make reservations. ⊠ *167 Renfrew St., City Center* ☎ *0141/353–4526* ⊕ *www.gsa.ac.uk* 🖃 *£6.50* ⊗ *Tours Oct.–Mar., Mon.–Sat. 11 and 2; Apr.–Sept., daily 10:30, 11, 11:30, 1:30, 2, and 2:30.*

⑭ **Glasgow University.** The architecture, grounds, and great views of Glasgow all warrant a visit to the university. The Gilbert Scott Building, the university's main edifice, was built more than a century ago and is a good example of the Gothic Revival style. **Glasgow University Visitor Centre** has exhibits on the university, a coffee bar, and a gift shop and is the starting point for one-hour guided walking tours of the campus. A self-guided tour should start at the Visitor Centre and take in the East and West quadrangles, the cloisters, Professor's Square, Pearce Lodge, and the not-to-be-missed University Chapel. ⊠ *University Ave., West End* ☎ *0141/330–5511* ⊕ *www.glasgow.ac.uk* 🖃 *Free* ⊗ *May–Sept., Mon.–Sat. 9:30–5; Oct.–Apr., Mon.–Sat. 9:30–5.*

★ ⑯ **Hunterian Art Gallery.** This Glasgow University gallery houses William Hunter's (1718–83) collection of paintings (his antiquarian collection is housed in the nearby Hunterian Museum), together with prints and drawings by Tintoretto, Rembrandt, Sir Joshua Reynolds, and Auguste Rodin, as well as a major collection of paintings by James McNeill Whistler, who had a great affection for the city that bought one of his earliest paintings. Also in the gallery is a replica of **Charles Rennie Mackintosh's town house,** which once stood nearby. The rooms contain Mackintosh's distinctive art-nouveau chairs, tables, beds, and cupboards, and the walls are decorated in the equally distinctive style devised by him and his artist wife, Margaret. ⊠ *Hillhead St., West End* ☎ *0141/330–5431* ⊕ *www.hunterian.gla.ac.uk* 🖃 *Free* ⊗ *Mon.–Sat. 9:30–5.*

⑫ **Kelvingrove Art Gallery and Museum.** Following Glasgow's successful 1888 International Exhibition of Science, Art, and Industry, city officials resolved to build a museum and gallery worthy of a world-class art collection and future international exhibitions. This magnificent combination of cathedral and castle was designed in the Renaissance style and built between 1891 and 1901. J. W. Simpson and E. J. Milner Allen were the main architects; Sir George Frampton designed the cen-

Fodor's Choice
★

tral porch; and James Harrison Mackinnon designed the decorative carving on the exterior. The stunning red-sandstone edifice is an appropriate home for an art collection—including works by Botticelli, Rembrandt, and Monet—hailed as "one of the greatest civic collections in Europe." The Glasgow Room houses extraordinary works by local artists. It reopened in July 2006 after a massive renovation; today the museum has more accessible gallery space, several study centers, a theater, a visitor center, a café, and a restaurant. ⊠ *Argyle St., Kelvingrove Park, West End* ☎ *0141/287-2699* ⊕ *www.glasgowmuseums.com* 🎫 *Free* ⊙ *Mon.–Thurs., Sat. 10–5, Fri.–Sun. 11–5.*

13

☾ **Kelvingrove Park.** A peaceful retreat, the park was purchased by the city in 1852 and takes its name from the River Kelvin, which flows through it. Among the numerous statues of prominent Glaswegians is one of Lord Kelvin (1824–1907), the Scottish mathematician and physicist who pioneered a great deal of work in electricity. The park also has a massive fountain commemorating a lord provost of Glasgow from the 1850s, a duck pond, a play area and lots of exotic trees. ⊠ *Bounded roughly by Sauchiehall St., Woodlands Rd., and Kelvin Way, West End.*

Also Worth Seeing

⑲ Centre for Contemporary Arts. This arts, cinema, and performance venue is in a post-industrial-revolution Alexander Thomson building. It has a reputation for unusual visual-arts exhibitions, from paintings and sculpture to new media, and has championed a number of emerging artists, including Toby Paterson, winner of the Beck's Futures award in 2001. Simon Starling, the Scottish representative at the Venice Bienalle in 2003, has also exhibited work here. The vibrant Tempus Bar Café was created by Los Angeles–based artist Jorge Pardo. Or you can head down the street to No. 217, the Charles Rennie Mackintosh–designed Willow Tearoom. ⊠ *350 Sauchiehall St., City Center* ☎ *0141/352-4900* ⊕ *www. cca-glasgow.com* 🎫 *Free* ⊙ *Tues.–Fri. 11–6, Sat. 10–6.*

⑮ Hunterian Museum. The city's oldest museum is slated to reopen in March 2007, just in time for its bicentenary. Part of Glasgow University, the museum showcases part of the collections of William Hunter, an 18th-century Glasgow doctor who assembled a staggering quantity of valuable material. (The doctor's art treasures are housed in the nearby Hunterian Art Gallery.) The museum displays Hunter's hoards of coins, manuscripts, scientific instruments, and archaeological artifacts in a striking Gothic building. ⊠ *University Ave., West End* ☎ *0141/330-4221* ⊕ *www.hunterian.gla.ac.uk* 🎫 *Free* ⊙ *Mon.–Sat. 9:30–5.*

⓭ Museum of Transport. Here Glasgow's history of locomotive building is dramatically displayed with full-size exhibits. The collection of Clyde-built ship models is world famous. Anyone who knows what Britain was like in the 1930s will wax nostalgic at the re-created street scene from that era. ✉ *Kelvin Hall, 1 Bunhouse Rd., West End* ☎ *0141/287–2720* ✆ *Free* ⊙ *Mon.–Thurs. and Sat. 10–5, Fri. and Sun. 11–5.*

OFF THE BEATEN PATH

THE TALL SHIP AT GLASGOW HARBOUR – This maritime attraction centers around the restored tall ship the *Glenlee,* a former cargo ship originally built in Glasgow in 1896, purchased by the Spanish navy, and bought back by the Clyde Maritime Trust in 1993. The ship itself is fascinating, but take time to explore the Pumphouse Exhibition and Gallery, which has films of the restoration process and interactive exhibits. A bus (No. 100) runs every half hour from the Buchanan Street bus station. ✉ *100 Stobcross Rd., West End* ☎ *0141/222–2513* ⊕ *www.thetallship.com* ✆ *£5* ⊙ *Mar.–Oct., daily 10–5; Nov.–Feb., daily 11–4.*

The South Side: Art-Filled Parks West

Just southwest of the city center in the South Side are two of Glasgow's dear green places—Bellahouston Park and Pollok Country Park—which have important art collections: Charles Rennie Mackintosh's House for an Art Lover, the Burrell Collection, and Pollok House. Both parks are off Paisley Road, about 3 mi southwest of the city center. You can take a taxi or car, city bus, or a train from Glasgow Central Station to Pollokshaws West Station or Dumbreck. Both parks are off Paisley Road, about 3 mi southwest of the city center. You can take a taxi or car, city bus, or a train from Glasgow Central Station to Pollokshaws West Station or Dumbreck.

Main Attractions

⓴ Burrell Collection. An elegant, ultramodern building of pink-sandstone and stainless steel completed in 1983 houses thousands of items of all descriptions, from ancient Egyptian, Greek, and Roman artifacts to Chinese ceramics, bronzes, and jade. You'll also find medieval tapestries, stained-glass windows, Rodin sculptures, and exquisite French impressionist paintings—Degas's *The Rehearsal* and Sir Henry Raeburn's *Miss Macartney,* to name a few. Eccentric millionaire Sir William Burrell (1861–1958) donated the magpie collection to the city in 1944. The exterior and interior were designed with large glass walls so that the items on display could relate to their surroundings in Pollok Country Park: art and nature, supposedly in perfect harmony. You can get there via buses 45, 48, and 57 from Union Street. ✉ *2060 Pollokshaws Rd., South Side* ☎ *0141/287–2550* ✆ *Free* ⊙ *Mon.–Thurs. and Sat. 10–5, Fri. and Sun. 11–5.*

Fodor'sChoice ★

㉑ Pollok House. The classic Georgian Pollok House, dating from the mid-1700s, contains the Stirling Maxwell Collection of paintings, including works by El Greco, Murillo, Goya, Signorelli, and William Blake. Fine 18th- and early-19th-century furniture, silver, glass, and porcelain are also on display. The house has lovely gardens and looks over the White Cart River and Pollok Country Park, where, amid mature trees and abundant wildlife, the city of Glasgow's own cattle peacefully graze. Take buses 45, 47, or 57 to the Gate of Pollok County Park. ☒ *2060 Pollokshaws Rd., South Side* ☎ *0141/616–6410* ⊕ *www.nts.org.uk* ☜ *Apr.–Oct., £8; Nov.–Mar., free* ☉ *Daily 10–5.*

Also Worth Seeing

㉒ House for an Art Lover. Within Bellahouston Park is a "new" Mackintosh house: based on a competition entry Charles Rennie Mackintosh submitted to a German magazine in 1901, but which was never built in his lifetime. The building houses Glasgow School of Art's postgraduate study center and exhibits of designs for the various rooms and decorative pieces Mackintosh and his wife, Margaret, created. There's also a café and shop filled with artworks. Buses 9, 53, and 54 from Union Street will get you here. Call ahead, as the building is often closed for official functions. ☒ *Bellahouston Park, 10 Dumbreck Rd., South Side* ☎ *0141/ 353–4770* ⊕ *www.houseforanartlover.co.uk* ☜ *£3.50* ☉ *Apr.–Sept., Mon.–Wed. 10–4, Thurs.–Sun. 10–1; Oct.–Mar., weekends 10–1.*

WHERE TO EAT

The key to Glaswegian cuisine is not Glasgow. It's the flurry of international restaurants that line the streets—from late-night crepe stalls and *pakora* (Indian fried chickpea cakes) bars to elegant restaurants with worldly menus. It shouldn't be a problem getting a table at the establishment of your choice, though making reservations for a Thursday, Friday or Saturday night is still advisable.

Prices

Eating in Glasgow can be casual or lavish. For less expensive dining, consider the benefit of pretheater menus. Wine is relatively expensive in restaurants, but beer and spirits cost much the same as they would in a bar.

WHAT IT COSTS In pounds				
£££££	**££££**	**£££**	**££**	**£**
AT DINNER over £22	£18–£22	£13–£17	£7–£12	under £7

Prices are per person for a main course.

Medieval Glasgow & Merchant City

CHINESE **✕ Amber Regent.** This may not be the cheapest Chinese restaurant in
££–£££ town, but it's certainly one of the finest and most formal. For a start, the meticulously sculpted vegetables that accompany the hors d'oeuvres seem almost too artful to eat. Succulent king prawns or duck with mashed prawns in an oyster sauce readily attest to the kitchen's skill in preparing excellent Cantonese and Szechuan cuisine. Its reputation means that the restaurant can get very busy, however. For the best value, try the two- and three-course menus served between noon and 2:15. ☒ *50 W. Regent St., City Center* ☎ *0141/331–1655* ▤ *AE, DC, MC, V* ☉ *Closed Sun.*

££–£££ **✕ Loon Fung.** The pleasant, enthusiastic staff at this popular Cantonese eatery guides you through the house specials, including the famed dim sum. If you like seafood, try the deep-fried wonton with prawns, crispy stuffed crab claws, or lobster in garlic-and-cheese sauce. The first-rate three-course business lunch, available until 6:30 PM, is a bargain at £9. ⊠ *417 Sauchiehall St., City Center* ☎ *0141/332–1240* ▤ *AE, MC, V.*

CONTEMPORARY
££–££££

✕ **City Café.** This bright, contemporary restaurant, adjacent to the Scottish Exhibition and Conference Centre and the Glasgow Science Centre, possesses one of the best riverside locations in Glasgow. In good weather you can dine outside by the banks of the Clyde, and in the shadow of the mighty Finnieston Crane, the 195-foot-high hammerhead crane formerly used to load heavy cargo onto freighters. The menu dresses up traditional dishes with modern touches: roast salmon wrapped in prosciutto and served with a fennel compote, for example, or fillet of lamb with caramelized onions, broad beans, and a morel sauce. ⊠ *Finnieston Quay, City Center* ☎ *0141/227–1010* ▤ *AE, DC, MC, V.*

££–££££

✕ **Groucho Saint Jude's.** You don't have to be young and hip to dine here, but it helps. Groucho's is a fashionable spot for the young executive set after office hours. Even if this is not your crowd, don't let that stop you from tackling the extensive cocktail selection and the equally diverse menu. Away from the noisy bar, the quieter dining room serves everything from wild-mushroom risotto to grilled sirloin of Aberdeen Angus. Their two- and three-course pre- and post-theater menus are great values at £12 and £15. ⊠ *190 Bath St., City Center* ☎ *0141/352–8800* ⌕ *Reservations essential* ▤ *AE, DC, MC, V.*

CONTINENTAL
££–££££

✕ **Brasserie.** A hotel basement fitted with wooden booths provides a quiet, relaxed environment in which to appreciate a varied modern European menu. The fish cakes are a traditional favorite here, but also good are the spaghetti with mussels and clams, and the grilled rib-eye steak. Be sure to leave room for desserts such as the pineapple mille-feuille and homemade coconut sorbet. ⊠ *Malmaison Hotel, 278 W. George St., City Center* ☎ *0141/572–1001* ⌕ *Reservations essential* ▤ *AE, DC, MC, V* ☾ *No lunch Sat.*

ECLECTIC
£££–£££££

✕ **78 St. Vincent.** Originally a bank building with strikingly carved griffins on the facade, this is now a stylish restaurant where you can enjoy contemporary French-influenced Scottish cuisine. As your eyes feast on the slender Doric columns or the wall-length modern mural by Glasgow artist Donald McLean, your palate can relish the Highland venison with gin-scented *jus,* or smoked duck salad with egg, scallops, prawns, and soy-sauce dressing. The pretheater menu, served from 4 to 7, is well worth considering. ⊠ *78 St. Vincent St., City Center* ☎ *0141/ 248–7878* ▤ *AE, DC, MC, V.*

FRENCH
£££–££££

✕ **Étain.** Sir Terence Conran's glamorous establishment has been the talk of the town since it opened in 2003. A futuristic steel-and-glass elevator whisks you up to an elegant and serene dining room with tables set amid sexy metal pillars. The sophistication is reflected in Chef Geoffrey Smeddle's contemporary take on French cuisine, always using the freshest of local produce. Expect revelatory tastes in creations such as venison with a pomegranate-and-chocolate sauce or filet of sea bream with broad-bean risotto and red-pepper oil. Set aside three hours for a truly epicurean experience. A two-course set meal costs £26, and a three-course meal costs £32. ⊠ *Princes Square, Buchanan St., City Center* ☎ *0141/225–5630* ⊟ *AE, DC, MC, V* ⊘ *No dinner Sun.*

INDIAN
££–£££

✕ **Mr. Singh's India.** Three generations of an Indian family have transformed this into one of Glasgow's most popular eateries. It's a restful haven in creams and blues and plenty of beech wood, rather quirkily combined with waiters in kilts and a menu including haggis *pakora* (deep-fried haggis parcels). Meats and vegetables can be cooked in a number of different delicious sauces; try the lamb *mazadar* (hot and spicy, with Rémy Martin) or the pistachio *korma* (curried meat with onions and vegetables). ⊠ *149 Elderslie St., City Center* ☎ *0141/204–0186 or 0141/221–1452* ⊟ *AE, DC, MC, V.*

ITALIAN
££–£££

✕ **Pavarotti Trattoria.** Despite the somewhat silly name, no doubt arising from the restaurant's proximity to Scottish Opera's Theatre Royal, this is not a kitschy affair but a very good Italian restaurant. The menu changes regularly because the kitchen uses only the freshest ingredients. Consequently, the standard meat and fish dishes are unusually succulent. The lunch and pretheater set menus—£7 and £11—are an exceptionally good value. ⊠ *91 Cambridge St., City Center* ☎ *0141/332–9713* ⊟ *AE, DC, MC, V* ⊘ *No lunch Sun.*

£–££
Fodor'sChoice
★

✕ **Fratelli Sarti.** Glasgow's large Italian immigrant population is never more visible—or audible—than here. The cavernous surroundings are cluttered and the tables are pressed close together, so this is not really the place for an intimate dinner, but the food is authentic, with all of the classic dishes on an extensive menu. If you like seafood, try the wonderfully fresh and piquant pasta *vongole* (with small clams). Finish off with the light, creamy tiramisu. Note that the service can be a bit leisurely. ⊠ *121 Bath St., City Center* ☎ *0141/204–0440* ⊟ *AE, DC, MC, V.*

PAN-ASIAN
£££

✕ **Khublai Khan Barbecue.** Wild boar, ostrich, shark, and other exotic flavors feature prominently at this eclectic eatery. Odds are you'll devour the legendary Mongolian Feast, which includes an unlimited supply of barbecued meats cooked on a giant hotplate. The massive space is festooned with handwoven rugs and a huge mural of Mongolian warriors advancing threateningly. Don't worry: the service is friendly. This place is popular with groups, so it can get noisy. ⊠ *26 Candleriggs St., Merchant City* ☎ *0141/552–5646* ⊟ *AE, DC, MC, V* ⊘ *No lunch.*

RUSSIAN
★ ££–£££

✕ **Café Cossachok.** Near the Tron Theatre, this is a willfully arty place: the tables are hand-carved, the lighting is courtesy of candles, and the decor is a sea of shawls. The Russian owner pays homage to his homeland with a menu that includes delicious blintzes and trout à la Pushkin (in a thirst-rousing salty sauce). Another welcome touch is the nicely chilled selection of vodkas. There's live music on Sunday evening. This fun venue is fashionable among the fashionable, so it's best to book ahead. ⊠ *10 King St., Merchant City* ☎ *0141/553–0733* ⊟ *AE, MC, V* ⊘ *Closed Mon. No lunch Sun.*

SCOTTISH
££–£££££

✕ **City Merchant.** In Glasgow a Scottish restaurant is almost a novelty. But if you have a penchant for fresh and flavorful cuisine, this place is a joy. The secret is the kitchen's use of only local ingredients. You can

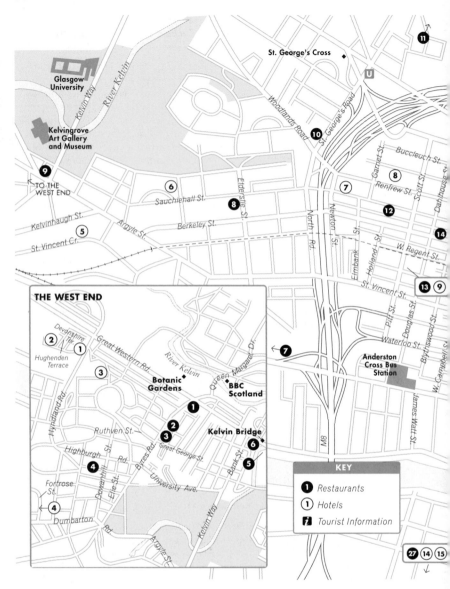

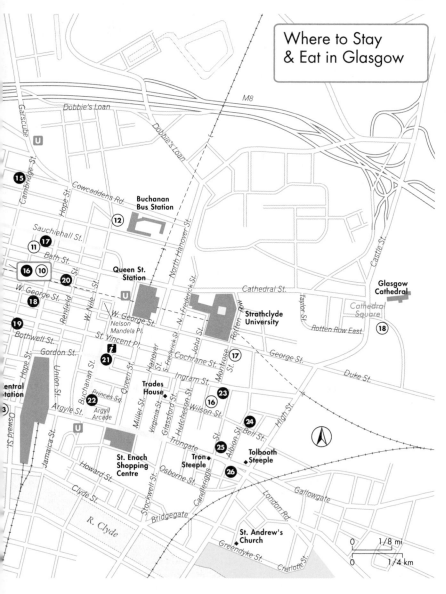

Where to Stay & Eat in Glasgow

sample the tasty cuts of venison and beef, but seafood remains the real attraction. The mussels and oysters from Loch Etive are wondrous, and the sea bass is renowned. There's a relatively inexpensive selection of wines and a wonderful cheeseboard served, as the locals like it, with oatcakes, celery, and quince. ⊠ *97–99 Candleriggs St., Merchant City* ☎ *0141/553–1577* ⊟ *AE, DC, MC, V* ⊙ *No lunch Sun.*

★ **£–£££** ✕ **Café Gandolfi.** Once the offices of a cheese market, this trendy café is now popular with the style-conscious crowd. Wooden tables and chairs crafted by Scottish artist Tim Stead are so fluidly shaped it's hard to believe they're inanimate. The café opens early for breakfast, serving croissants, eggs *en cocotte* (casserole style), and strong cups of espresso. The rest of the day the menu lists interesting soups, salads, and local specialties, all made with the finest regional produce. Don't miss the smoked venison or the finnan haddie (smoked haddock). Evenings are livened up with good beers and decent wines. The service can be a bit patchy. ⊠ *64 Albion St., Merchant City* ☎ *0141/552–6813* ⊟ *MC, V.*

£–££ ✕ **Willow Tearoom.** There are two branches of this restaurant, but the Sauchiehall Street location is the real deal. Designed by the great Charles Rennie Mackintosh in 1903 for owner Kate Cranston, the Room De Luxe (the original tearoom) is kitted out with his trademark furnishings, including high-back chairs with elegant lines and subtle curves. The tree motifs reflect the street address—*sauchie* is an old Scots word for willow. The St. Andrew's Platter is an exquisite selection of trout, salmon, and prawns. Scottish and continental breakfasts are available throughout the day, and the scrambled eggs with salmon is traditional Scots food at its finest. The in-house baker guarantees fresh scones, cakes, and pastries. ⊠ *217 Sauchiehall St., City Center* ☎ *0141/332–0521* ⊟ *MC, V* ⊙ *No dinner.*

SEAFOOD **£££–£££££** Fodor'sChoice ★ ✕ **Rogano.** The spacious art-deco interior, modeled after the style of the *Queen Mary* ocean liner—maple paneling, chrome trim, and dramatic ocean murals—is enough to recommend this restaurant. Portions are generous in the main dining area, where impeccably prepared specialties include roast rack of lamb and classic seafood dishes like seared scallops. Downstairs in the Café Rogano (£–££), the brasserie-style food is more modern and imaginative. The theater menu provides early evening and late-night bargains, and the fixed-price lunch menu is popular with locals. You can also order one of the fabulous cocktails and prop up the swank oyster bar. ⊠ *11 Exchange Pl., City Center* ☎ *0141/248–4055* ⊟ *AE, DC, MC, V.*

£–£££ Fodor'sChoice ★ ✕ **Mussel Inn.** West Coast shellfish farmers own this restaurant and feed their customers incredibly fresh, succulent oysters, scallops, and mussels. The kilo pots of mussels, beautifully steamed to order and served with any of a number of sauces, are revelatory. The surroundings and staff are unpretentious yet stylish. ⊠ *157 Hope St., City Center* ☎ *0141/572–1405* ⊕ *www.mussel-inn.com* ⊟ *AE, MC, V* ⊙ *No lunch Sun.*

West End & Environs

ECLECTIC **££–££££** ✕ **Cul De Sac.** At the end of a quiet cobbled lane, this is one of the most relaxing of Glasgow's trendy West End eateries, right on the edge of the Glasgow University campus. It's a nice alternative to the more formal restaurants in the area, and large French windows add to the friendly street-café atmosphere. The menu includes everything from affordable pasta dishes to red snapper to seared medallion of pork. ⊠ *11 Ashton La., West End* ☎ *0141/334–6688* ▭ *AE, DC, MC, V.*

INDIAN
££–£££

✕ **Killermont Polo Club.** Though not the most likely setting for an Indian restaurant, this Victorian manse on the outskirts of Glasgow's West End has the restful and romanticized atmosphere of colonial India. It specializes in the rather unique *dum pukht* cooking tradition, which for a time was held secret by the Mughal royal family. The appetizer *shammi kebab badami* consists of firm patties of minced lamb shot through with cinnamon, coriander, and almonds. The gently prepared *chandi kaliyan* main course mixes lamb with a gravy of poppy seeds, cashews, and saffron. Finish off with the gorgeous, spongy dessert, *gulab jamin.* ⊠ *2022 Maryhill Rd., West End* ☎ *0141/946–5412* ▭ *AE, DC, MC, V.*

££

✕ **Ashoka West End.** This Punjabi restaurant consistently outperforms its many competitors in quality, range, and taste. All portions are large enough to please the ravenous, but there's nothing heavy-handed about the cooking here: vegetable *samosas* (stuffed savory deep-fried pastries) are crisp and light, the selection of breads is superb, and the spicing for the lamb, chicken, and prawn dishes is fragrant. The eclectic decor— involving a bizarre mixture of plants, murals, rugs, and brass lamps— and inappropriate Western music simply emphasize Ashoka's idiosyncrasy. Reservations are a good idea on weekends. ⊠ *108 Elderslie St., West End* ☎ *0141/221–1761* ▭ *AE, MC, V* ⊗ *No lunch Sat.–Tues.*

ITALIAN
★ ££–££££

✕ **La Parmigiana.** The refreshing elegance of the surroundings is mirrored by the consistently exquisite fare at this longtime favorite. The Giovanazzis pride themselves on using the freshest of ingredients—this means you may be able to enjoy simply prepared sea bass or veal one day, guinea fowl or scallops the next. This expertise in the kitchen is reflected in the well-balanced wine list and the impeccable attentiveness of the black-jacketed *camerieri.* ⊠ *447 Great Western Rd., West End* ☎ *0141/334– 0686* ▭ *AE, DC, MC, V.*

LATIN
££–£££

✕ **Cottier's.** A converted Victorian church decorated by Glasgow artist Daniel Cottier is the unusual setting for this theater-bar-restaurant (the Arts Theatre is attached). Red walls and beamed ceilings warm the downstairs bar, where the pub grub has Tex-Mex flavors. In the restaurant try the spicy lamb cooked with coconut, lime, and cilantro, or the tuna and snapper fillets with anchovies, chili peppers, and citrus butter—two excellent choices from the South American dishes on the menu. Reservations are advised on weekends. ⊠ *93 Hyndland St., West End* ☎ *0141/357–5825* ▭ *AE, MC, V.*

MIDDLE EASTERN
£–££

✕ **Bay Tree.** This small café in the university area serves wonderful Middle Eastern food—mostly vegetarian dishes, but there are a few lamb and chicken creations as well. Egyptian *phool* (broad beans dressed with spices and herbs), Turkish *mulukia* (fried eggplant with a tomato-and-herb sauce), and *kurma* (stew with spinach, herbs, and beans) are among its delights. ⊠ *403 Great Western Rd., West End* ☎ *0141/334–5898* ▭ *No credit cards.*

13

SCOTTISH
★ **£££–££££**

✕ **Ubiquitous Chip.** Occupying a converted mews stable behind the Hillhead underground station, this restaurant is an institution among members of Glasgow's media and thespian communities. The service is friendly, and the interior very outdoorsy, with a glass roof, much greenery, and a fishpond. The menu specializes in game but has something for everyone (even vegetarian haggis); smoked salmon in Darjeeling tea is typical of the chef's clever blending of authentic Scots fare with unusual elements. For a more casual and inexpensive experience, try the brasserie and pub area upstairs (££–£££). ✉ *12 Ashton La., West End* ☎ *0141/334–5007* ▭ *AE, DC, MC, V.*

★ **££–££££**

✕ **The Brasserie at Òran Mór.** This is the more formal eatery (the other being the bistro-style Conservatory) within this handsome church-turned-cultural-center. There's lots of elegantly curved dark wood and high-backed bench seating, as well as some Alasdair Gray murals to savor. The food is equally well crafted. Expect contemporary treats using Angus beef, Gressingham duck, and sea bass. ✉ *731–735 Great Western Rd., West End* ☎ *0141/357–6226* ⌲ *Reservations essential* ▭ *AE, MC, V* ⊘ *Closed Sun. No lunch Mon., Tues., and Sat.*

VEGETARIAN
£–££

✕ **Grassroots Café.** One of Glasgow's most relaxing eateries, Grassroots serves vegetarian cooking that is wholesome, fresh, and above all, interesting. Unlike the food, which includes its specialty Thai potatoes and vegetarian chili, the interior is simple and rather plain. The list of fruit juices is exhaustive, and organic ingredients are guaranteed, including the wine. Set aside plenty of time, though, as nothing is hurried, especially for the popular weekend breakfasts. ✉ *97 St. George's Rd., West End* ☎ *0141/333–0534* ▭ *AE, MC, V.*

South Side

SCOTTISH
££

✕ **Moyra Janes.** Pull up a chair to one of the marble-topped tables in this former bank building and soak up the genteel Scots charm. This South Side favorite serves a splendid tea with mouthwatering cakes. There's a healthy dash of cosmopolitan flair to boot: alongside the all-day breakfast menu are Thai fish cakes and Italian pasta creations. ✉ *20 Kildrostan St., South Side* ☎ *0141/423–5628* ▭ *MC, V* ⊘ *Closed Sun. No dinner Mon. and Tues.*

WHERE TO STAY

Central Glasgow never really goes to sleep, so downtown hotels will be noisier than those in the leafy and genteel West End, convenient for museums and art galleries, or southern suburbs, convenient for the Burrell Collection. The flip side is that most downtown hotels are within walking distance of all the main sights, whereas you will need to make use of the (excellent) bus service if you stay in the suburbs.

Prices
Most smaller hotels and all guesthouses include breakfast in the room rate. Larger hotels usually charge extra for breakfast.

WHAT IT COSTS In pounds				
	£££££	££££	£££	££	£
FOR 2 PEOPLE	over £250	£180–£250	£120–£179	£70–£119	under £70

Hotel prices are for two people in a standard double room in high season, generally including the 17.5% V.A.T.

Medieval Glasgow & Merchant City

13

★ 🏨 **Radisson SAS.** You can't miss this eye-catching edifice behind Central Station in the city's up-and-coming financial quarter. Its glass front makes the interior, particularly the lounge, seem as though it were part of the street. Rooms are decorated in several styles—the Nordic rooms, for example, are done up in an icy shade of blue. Both restaurants—the pop-art-inspired Collage, serving Continental cuisine, and Tapaell'Ya, the tapas bar—are popular with business and artist types, as is the sleek street-level bar. ☒ *301 Argyle St., City Center, G2 8DL* ☏ *0141/204–3333* 🖷 *0141/204–3344* ⊕ *www.radissonsas.com* ➽ *250 rooms, 4 suites* ⚷ *2 restaurants, room service, in-room safes, minibars, cable TV, in-room broadband, indoor pool, gym, bar, business services, meeting rooms, convention center, parking (fee)* ⊟ *AE, DC, V* ⏀ *CP.*
££££–£££££

★ **£££–££££** 🏨 **ABode Glasgow.** Part of the stylish ABode mini-chain, this 1911 building near the boutiques of Buchanan Street has retained and embellished its best original features, like the wrought-iron elevator and gold-leaf lions, while modernizing the rooms to meet today's desire for luxury. Rooms have dramatic yet tasteful decor highlighted by leaded windows and contemporary artwork. Noted chef Michael Caines supervises the chain's restaurants: the Café Bar has a modish, international menu, and the Vibe bar downstairs is one of Glasgow's hot spots. ☒ *129 Bath St., City Center, G2 2SY* ☏ *0141/221–6789* 🖷 *0142/221–6777* ⊕ *www.abodehotels. co.uk* ➽ *60 rooms, 1 suite* ⚷ *Restaurant, room service, minibars, cable TV with movies, 2 bars* ⊟ *AE, DC, MC, V* ⏀ *CP.*

£££–££££ 🏨 **Malmaison.** This small, modern hotel, housed in a converted church, prides itself on personal service and outstanding amenities: each room has puffy down comforters and CD players. The art-deco interior employs bold colors in playful prints and geometric shapes all balanced out by traditional fabrics and furniture. The lobby's splendid staircase has a wrought-iron balustrade illustrating Napoléon's exploits (the hotel takes its name from his home). The warm Brasserie offers British–French cooking. Café Mal serves savory pasta dishes in an airy terra-cotta-hued room with iron fixtures and a spiral staircase. ☒ *278 W. George St., City Center, G2 4LL* ☏ *0141/572–1000* 🖷 *0141/572–1002* ⊕ *www.malmaison.com* ➽ *72 rooms, 8 suites* ⚷ *Restaurant, minibars, cable TV, gym, hair salon, bar, business services, meeting room* ⊟ *AE, DC, MC, V* ⏀ *CP.*

★ **££–£££** 🏨 **Langs.** This hotel's minimalist look extends from the sleek wood reception desk to the sophisticated platform beds in the bright bedrooms. The suites on the top floor come in three "flavors," ranging from "monochrome" to "pop art." Contemporary Scottish cooking is the forte of the Aurora restaurant, while the Oshi restaurant serves excellent Japanese food, including three-course pre- and post-theater meals. Japanese body treatments are available in the Oshi Spa. The downtown location puts you close to Glasgow Royal Concert Hall and the Buchanan Galleries shopping mall. ✉ *2 Port Dundas Pl., City Center, G2 3LD* ☎ *0141/333–1500* 🖷 *0141/333–5700* ⊕ *www.langshotels.co.uk* ⤳ *70 rooms, 30 suites ⌂ 2 restaurants, room service, cable TV with movies, in-room data ports, gym, massage, spa, bar, business services, meeting room, no-smoking rooms; no a/c ☰ AE, DC, MC, V* ⊧⊙⊧ *CP.*

££ 🏨 **Brunswick.** In a contemporary town house, this six-story hotel showcases quintessential Glasgow style and ambition. The rooms are done in a mostly minimalist style, but squared-off wall fixtures and occasional splashes of color make bold statements. The three-bedroom penthouse suite has a separate kitchen and a sauna. The downstairs Brutti ma Buoni (meaning "ugly but good" in Italian), has an eclectic menu, a compact but good wine list, and a selection of draught lagers. ✉ *106–108 Brunswick St., Merchant City, G1 1TF* ☎ *0141/552–0001* 🖷 *0141/552– 1551* ⊕ *www.brunswickhotel.info* ⤳ *18 rooms, 1 suite ⌂ Café, cable TV, bar; no a/c ☰ AE, MC, V* ⊧⊙⊧ *CP.*

★ £–££ 🏨 **Cathedral House Hotel.** Adjacent to Glasgow Cathedral, this Scottish Baronial–style building once served as the church's ecclesiastical headquarters—hence the name. It's suitably grand, with crow-stepped gables and towering turrets. The rooms, accessed by a spiraling stone staircase, are of varying size, but all are smartly decorated with dark-wood furnishings. The splendid restaurant and bar downstairs are very popular, but they are far enough from the rooms that the noise won't keep you up at night. A full Scottish breakfast—or a vegetarian option, if you prefer—is served in the café. ✉ *28–32 Cathedral Sq., Merchant City, G4 0XA* ☎ *0141/552–3519* 🖷 *0141/552–2444* ⊕ *www.cathedralhouse.com* ⤳ *8 rooms ⌂ Restaurant, café, bar, laundry service, free parking, no-smoking rooms ☰ AE, MC, V* ⊧⊙⊧ *BP.*

★ £ 🏨 **Bewley's.** With an emphasis on convenience and practicality, Bewley's has simple, modern appeal: no frills, just clean-cut comfort. And it's all just a stone's throw away from busy Sauchiehall Street. If the hotel doesn't have the facilities you need, the staff can often help you out: the hotel has an affiliation, for example, with a neighboring fitness center that charges hotel guests just £8 per session. Loop restaurant serves breakfast, lunch, and dinner, with specialties such as mushroom bruschetta and grilled rib-eye steak. ✉ *110 Bath St., City Center, G2 2EN* ☎ *0141/ 353–0800* 🖷 *0141/353–0900* ⊕ *www.bewleyshotels.com* ⤳ *103 rooms ⌂ Restaurant, cable TV, in-room broadband, Wi-Fi, bar; no a/c ☰ AE, DC, MC, V* ⊧⊙⊧ *CP.*

£ 🏨 **John Anderson Campus.** This University of Strathclyde's Campus Village residence has more than 500 rooms available during the summer months. These modern buildings are set within landscaped gardens near Queen Street railway station and George Square. There are rooms with one, two, or three single beds, and basic, respectable furnishings. There are five singles available for guests with mobility problems. The reception area is open 24 hours. ✉ *Weaver St., City Center, G4 0NP* ☎ *0141/553–4148* 🖷 *0141/553–4149* ⊕ *www.rescat.strath.ac.uk* ⤳ *500 rooms ⌂ Dining room, lounge, laundry facilities; no a/c, no room phones, no room TVs ☰ AE, MC, V.*

£ 🖭 **Travel Inn Metro.** This may be one of a chain of budget hotels, but its bright, metropolitan design and low prices appeal to savvy travelers. The rooms are larger than most in a 1,400-year-old city, and have nice touches like coffeemakers. Rooms facing the street can be noisy at night, so ask for one that looks out onto the graveyard, where noisemakers are highly unlikely to be found. ✉ *187 George St., Merchant City, G1 1YU* ☎ *0870/238–3320* 🖷 *0141/553–2719* ⊕ *www.premiertravelinn. com* ⬥ *239 rooms* ♨ *Restaurant, Wi-Fi, bar, meeting rooms, parking (fee), no-smoking rooms; no a/c* ⊟ *AE, MC, V.*

£ 🖭 **Victorian House.** Compared with its dramatic, bright-yellow entrance hall and reception area, the rooms in this B&B are rather plain. But its location—on a quiet residential street only a block from the Charles Rennie Mackintosh–designed Glasgow School of Art—is prime. There are plenty of restaurants and bars on nearby Sauchiehall Street, and the friendly staff is more than happy to help you choose one. ✉ *212 Renfrew St., City Center, G3 6TX* ☎ *0141/332–0129* 🖷 *0141/353–3155* ⊕ *www. thevictorian.co.uk* ⬥ *60 rooms* ♨ *Dining room; no a/c* ⊟ *MC, V* ⦿ *BP.*

West End & Environs

★   🖭 **One Devonshire Gardens.** Celebrities such as Luciano Pavarotti and Elizabeth Taylor consider this hotel, which comprises a group of Victorian
£££–£££££ houses on a sloping tree-lined street, their favorite in Glasgow. Elegance is the theme, from the sophisticated drawing room to the sumptuous guest rooms with flowing draperies and traditional mahogany furnishings; 10 of the rooms have four-poster beds. The No. 5 restaurant is equally stylish, with a menu that changes each month. Expect such delights as grilled gravlax of salmon with fennel followed by warm cherries with a chocolate brownie. Sophisticated yet unpretentious dining is also available at the Room restaurant. ✉ *1 Devonshire Gardens, West End, G12 0UX* ☎ *0141/339–2001* 🖷 *0141/337–1663* ⊕ *www.onedevonshiregardens. com* ⬥ *40 rooms* ♨ *2 restaurants, room service, cable TV, lounge, meeting room, free parking; no a/c* ⊟ *AE, DC, MC, V* ⦿ *BP.*

££ 🖭 **Town House.** A handsome old terraced house in a quiet cul-de-sac serves as a B&B. The owners are welcoming, which explains why this place thrives on repeat business. Restrained cream-and-pastel-stripe decor, stripped pine doors, and neutral fabrics complement the high ceilings, ornate plasterwork, and other original architectural features of the house. There's a comfortable sitting room with books, a coal-burning fireplace, and informative leaflets. ✉ *4 Hughenden Terr., West End, G12 9XR* ☎ *0141/357–0862* 🖷 *0141/339–9605* ⊕ *www. thetownhouseglasgow.com* ⬥ *10 rooms* ♨ *Lounge, Internet room, free parking; no a/c* ⊟ *AE, DC, MC, V* ⦿ *BP.*

£–££ 🖭 **Kirklee Hotel.** This West End B&B occupies a small and cozy Edwardian town house with home-away-from-home comforts. A bay window in the lounge overlooks a garden, and the old-fashioned morning room is adorned with embroidered settees and silk-wash wallpapers. Engravings and a library offer decorative touches that any university don would appreciate. The owners are friendly and helpful. ✉ *11 Kensington Gate, West End, G12 9LG* ☎ *0141/334–5555* 🖷 *0141/339–3828*

⊕ *www.kirkleehotel.co.uk* ⮎ *9 rooms* ⚭ *Library, Internet room; no a/c, no smoking* ⊟ *AE, DC, MC, V* ⟨O⟩ *BP.*

★ **£–££** ⊡ **Manor Park Hotel.** On a quiet street close to Victoria Park, one of Glasgow's most idyllic, this stately terraced town house combines urban spaciousness with proximity to city action. Each of the neat and airy bedrooms, even the bright attic ones, bears the name in Gaelic of a Scottish island. The friendly owners themselves are Gaelic speakers, and tartan plays its part subtly in the homey interior. ⊠ *28 Balshagray Dr., West End, G11 7DD* ☎ *0141/339–2143* 🖷 *0141/339–5842* ⊕ *www.manorparkhotel.com* ⮎ *10 rooms* ⚭ *Lounge, business services, free parking; no a/c* ⊟ *AE, MC, V* ⟨O⟩ *BP.*

£ ⊡ **Argyll Guest House.** The biggest plus at this small, cozy hotel is the friendly staff with a knack for detail. All the rooms are spacious with tasteful, Victorian-inspired furnishings. The breakfast room overlooks Kelvingrove Park, and you are welcome to have dinner at the restaurant in the guesthouse's sister hotel, the Argyll Hotel, across the street. ⊠ *966–970 Sauchiehall St., West End, G3 7TH* ☎ *0141/357–5155* 🖷 *0141/339–9469* ⊕ *www.argyllguesthouseglasgow.co.uk* ⮎ *19 rooms* ⚭ *Dining room, cable TV, bar, babysitting, laundry service; no a/c* ⊟ *AE, MC, V* ⟨O⟩ *BP.*

£ ⊡ **Number Thirty Six.** This Victorian terrace house in the West End is a 10-minute walk from the Hunterian museums and Kelvingrove Park. Each room is individually decorated, with antique furniture and colorful, sometimes crazy, paintings. The service is of the type you can get only from a family-run establishment. ⊠ *36 St. Vincent Crescent, West End, G3 8NG* ☎ *0141/248–2086* 🖷 *0141/221–1477* ⊕ *www.no36.co.uk* ⮎ *5 rooms* ⚭ *Lounge; no a/c, no TV in some rooms, no smoking* ⊟ *MC, V* ⟨O⟩ *CP.*

South Side

£££ ⊡ **Sherbrooke Castle Hotel.** Come to the Sherbrooke for a flight of Gothic fantasy. Its cavernous rooms hark back to grander times when the South Side of Glasgow was home to the immensely wealthy tobacco barons whose homes boasted turrets and towers. The spacious grounds are far from the noise and bustle of the city yet only a 10-minute drive from the city center. Like the tobacco barons, the hotel's proprietor insists on tasteful interior styling and good traditional cooking. The restaurant serves fine food, made with fresh ingredients, and prepared on the premises, including the breads. Locals flock to the busy bar. ⊠ *11 Sherbrooke Ave., Pollokshields, South Side, G41 4PG* ☎ *0141/427–4227* 🖷 *0141/427–5685* ⊕ *www.sherbrooke.co.uk* ⮎ *25 rooms* ⚭ *Restaurant, bar; no a/c* ⊟ *AE, DC, MC, V* ⟨O⟩ *BP.*

£–££ ⊡ **Ewington Hotel.** This quiet row of town houses opposite Queen's Park has an open and traditional look. Victorian-style furniture, ornately decorated bedrooms with heavy and elaborate pink-and-green floral fabrics, and an open fire in the spacious lobby all add to the relaxed, elegant character. Downtown Glasgow is only a short bus or train ride away. ⊠ *132 Queen's Dr., South Side, G42 8QW* ☎ *0141/423–1152* 🖷 *0141/422–2030* ⊕ *www.bestwestern.co.uk* ⮎ *43 rooms* ⚭ *Restaurant, bar, meeting room, free parking; no a/c* ⊟ *AE, DC, MC, V* ⟨O⟩ *BP.*

NIGHTLIFE & THE ARTS

Home to Scotland's national orchestra, and opera and dance companies, Glasgow is truly the artistic hub of the country. As for nightlife, Glasgow's mix of university students, artists, and professionals maintains a spirited pub-and-club scene.

The Arts

13

Concerts

Glasgow's **Royal Concert Hall** (⊠ 2 Sauchiehall St., City Center ☎ 0141/353–8000 ⊕ www.grch.com) has 2,500 seats and is the main venue of the Royal Scottish National Orchestra, which performs winter and spring. The **Royal Scottish Academy of Music and Drama** (⊠ 100 Renfrew St., City Center ☎ 0141/332–4101 ⊕ www.rsamd.ac.uk) is one of the main small venues for concerts, recitals, and theater productions. The **Scottish Exhibition and Conference Centre** (⊠ Finnieston, West End ☎ 0141/248–3000 ⊕ www.secc.co.uk) regularly hosts pop concerts.

Dance & Opera

Glasgow is home to the Scottish Opera and Scottish Ballet, both of which perform at the **Theatre Royal** (⊠ 282 Hope St., City Center ☎ 0141/332–9000 ⊕ www.theatreroyalglasgow.com). Visiting dance companies from many countries appear here as well.

Festivals

Celtic Connections (⊠ Glasgow Royal Concert Hall, 2 Sauchiehall St., City Center, G2 3NY ☎ 0141/353–8000 ⊕ www.celticconnections.co.uk) is an ever-expanding Celtic music festival held in the second half of January. Musicians from Africa, France, Canada, Ireland, and Scotland perform and conduct hands-on workshops on topics such as harp-making and playing. **Glasgay** (☎ 0141/552–7575 ⊕ www.glasgay.co.uk), held between late-October and mid-November, is the United Kingdom's largest multi-arts festival focusing on gay and lesbian issues. The international and Scottish line-up draws a huge audience.

Film

The **Glasgow Film Theatre** (⊠ 12 Rose St., City Center ☎ 0141/332–8128 ⊕ www.gft.org.uk), an independent public cinema, screens the best new-release films from all over the world. The **Grosvenor** (⊠ Ashton La., West End ☎ 0141/339–8444 ⊕ www.grosvenorcinema.co.uk) is a popular, compact cinema in Glasgow's West End. **UGC** (⊠ 145–159 W. Nile St., City Center ☎ 0870/907–0789), an 18-screen multilevel facility, is Glasgow's busiest movie complex. At 170 feet, it's also the world's tallest cinema building.

Theater

Tickets for theatrical performances can be purchased at theater box offices or by telephone through the booking line: **Ticket Center** (☎ 0141/287–5511).

The **Arches** (✉ 253 Argyle St., City Center ☎ 0870/240–7528 ⊕ www.thearches.co.uk) stages challenging yet accessible drama from around the world. Some of the most exciting theatrical performances take place ★ at the internationally renowned **Citizens' Theatre** (✉ 119 Gorbals St., South Side ☎ 0141/429–0022 ⊕ www.citz.co.uk), where productions, and their sets, are often of hair-raising originality. Behind the theater's striking contemporary glass facade is a glorious Victorian red-and-gilded auditorium. The **King's Theatre** (✉ 297 Bath St., City Center ☎ 0141/240–1111 ⊕ www.theambassadors.com/kings) puts on dramas, variety shows, and musicals.

The **Theatre Royal** (✉ 282 Hope St., City Center ☎ 0141/332–1133 ⊕ www.theambassadors.com) hosts performances of major dramas, including an occasional season of plays by international touring companies, as well as opera and ballet. The **Tron Theatre** (✉ 63 Trongate, Merchant City ☎ 0141/552–4267 ⊕ www.tron.co.uk) puts on Scottish and international contemporary theater.

Nightlife

Consult the biweekly magazine the *List,* available at newsstands and bookstores, and the *Scotsman, Herald,* and *Evening Times* newspapers for up-to-date performance and event listings.

Bars & Pubs

Glasgow's pubs were once known for serious drinkers who demanded few comforts. Times have changed, and many pubs have been turned into smart wine bars. Most pubs are open daily from 11 AM to 11 PM.

Many of the most popular bars are in the center of the city. **Babbity Bowster's** (✉ 16–18 Blackfriars St., Merchant City ☎ 0141/552–5055), a busy, friendly spot, serves interesting beers and good food. The classic **Drum and Monkey** (✉ 93 St. Vincent St., City Center ☎ 0141/221–6636) attracts an after-work crowd of young professionals to its friendly bar-restaurant. Local musicans play jazz on Sunday.

★ **Rogano** (✉ 11 Exchange Pl., City Center ☎ 0141/248–4055) is famous for its champagne cocktails and general air of 1920s decadence. The **Scotia Bar** (✉ 112 Stockwell St., Merchant City ☎ 0141/552–8681) serves up a taste of an authentic Glasgow pub, with some traditional folk music occasionally thrown in.

There is also a thriving scene in the West End. Despite its former austere existence as a church, the always-busy **Cottiers** (✉ Hyndland St., West End ☎ 0141/357–5825) is a famous haunt of the young. The best ★ seat is outside in the popular beer garden. The best Gaelic pub is **Uisge Beatha** (✉ 232–246 Woodlands Rd., West End ☎ 0141/564–1596). The name, pronounced *oos*-ki *bee*-ha, means "water of life" and is said to be the origin of the word "whisky." The bar serves *fraoch* (heather beer) in season and has live music on Wednesday and Sunday.

Nightclubs

As elsewhere in Britain, electronic music—from house to techno to drum and bass—is par for the course in Glasgow's dance clubs. Much of the scene revolves around Center City. **Archaos** (✉ 25 Queen St., City Center ☎ 0141/204–3189), Glasgow's most cavernous club, has three dance floors blasting house, garage, indie, R&B, soul, and hip-hop music. It's open Wednesday through Sunday from 11 PM to 4 AM. The ★ **Arches** (✉ 253 Argyle St., City Center ☎ 0901/022–0300) is one of the city's largest arts venues, but on Friday (from 11 PM to 3 AM) and Saturday (from 10:30 PM to 4 AM) it thumps with house and techno. The club welcomes big music names like Colours and Inside Out at legendary parties. A few times a month it holds dressed-up gay nights.

SPORTS & THE OUTDOORS

Golf

Several municipal courses are operated within Glasgow proper by the local authorities. Bookings are relatively inexpensive and should be made directly to the course 24 hours in advance to ensure prime tee times (courses open at 7 AM). A comprehensive list of contacts, facilities, and greens fees of the 30 or so other courses near the city is available from the tourist board.

Douglas Park. North of the city near Milngavie, Douglas Park is a long, attractive course set among birch and pine trees with masses of rhododendrons blooming in early summer. ✉ *Hillfoot, Bearsden* ☎ *0141/942–0985* ⚐ *18 holes, 5,962 yds, par 69.*

Lethamhill. The fairways of this city-owned parkland course overlook Hogganfield Loch. To get there, take the M8 north to Junction 12, and drive up the A80 about a quarter mile. ✉ *1240 Cumbernauld Rd., North City* ☎ *0141/770–6220* ⚐ *18 holes, 5,836 yds, SSS 68.*

Littlehill. Level fairways and greens make this municipal course not too difficult to play. It's on the A803 about 4 mi north of the city center. ✉ *Auchinairn Rd., North City* ☎ *0141/772–1916* ⚐ *18 holes, 6,240 yds, SSS 70.*

Sailing & Water Sports

The Firth of Clyde and Loch Lomond, about a 30-minute drive southwest and north of Glasgow, respectively, have water-sports facilities for sailing, canoeing, windsurfing, and rowing, with full equipment rental. Details are available from the tourist board.

Soccer

The city has been sports mad, especially for football (soccer), for more than 100 years, and the rivalry between its two main clubs, the Rangers and the Celtic, is legendary. Matches are held usually on Saturday in winter, and Glasgow has in total four teams playing in the Scottish Leagues. Admission prices start at about £20. Rangers wear blue and play at **Ibrox** (✉ Edmiston Dr., South Side ☎ 08706/001993 ⊕ www.rangers.co.uk). The Celtic wear white and green stripes and play in the east at **Celtic Park** (✉ 95 Kerrydale St., East End ☎ 0141/551–8653 ⊕ www.celticfc.net).

13

SHOPPING

Glasgow draws shoppers from around the country with its large department stores, designer outlets, quirky or stylish boutiques, and unique markets. Join the throngs of style-conscious and unseasonally tanned locals along Argyle, Buchanan, and Sauchiehall streets.

Arcades & Shopping Centers

The **Buchanan Galleries** (⊠ 220 Buchanan St., City Center ☎ 0141/333–9898 ⊕ www.buchanangalleries.co.uk), at the top end of Buchanan Street next to the Royal Concert Hall, is packed with high-quality shops; its magnet attraction is the John Lewis department store. By far the best shopping complex is the art nouveau **Princes Square** (⊠ 48 Buchanan St., City Center ☎ 0141/204–1685), with high-quality shops alongside pleasant cafés and a tony restaurant or two. Look particularly for the Scottish Craft Centre, which carries an outstanding collection of work created by some of the nation's best craftspeople. **St. Enoch's Shopping Centre** (⊠ 55 St. Enoch Sq., City Center ☎ 0141/204–3900) is eye-catching if not especially pleasing—it's a modern glass building that resembles an overgrown greenhouse. It houses various stores, but most could be found elsewhere.

Department Stores

Debenham's (⊠ 97 Argyle St., also accessed from St. Enoch Centre, City Center ☎ 0141/221–0088) is one of Glasgow's principal department stores, with fine china and crystal as well as women's and men's cloth-

★ ing. **Frasers** (⊠ 21–45 Buchanan St., City Center ☎ 0141/221–3880), a Glasgow institution, stocks wares that reflect the city's material aspirations—leading European designer clothes and fabrics combined with home-produced articles, such as tweeds, tartans, glass, and ceramics. The magnificent interior, set off by the grand staircase rising to various floors and balconies, is itself worth a visit.

John Lewis (⊠ Buchanan Galleries, 220 Buchanan St., City Center ☎ 0141/353–6677) is a favorite for its good-value mix of clothing and household items. **Marks & Spencer** (⊠ 2–12 Argyle St., City Center ☎ 0141/552–4546 ⊠ 172 Sauchiehall St., City Center ☎ 0141/332–6097) sells sturdy, practical clothes and accessories at moderate prices; you can also buy food items and household goods here.

Specialty Shops

Antiques & Fine Art

The **Compass Gallery** (⊠ 178 W. Regent St., City Center ☎ 0141/221–6370) hosts exhibitions focusing on abstract and expressionist art. **Cyril Gerber Fine Art** (⊠ 148 W. Regent St., City Center ☎ 0141/221–3095 or 0141/204–0276) specializes in British paintings from 1880 to the pres-

★ ent; they will ship your purchase for you, as will most galleries. **De Courcys** (⊠ 5–21 Cresswell La., West End), an antiques and crafts arcade, has quite a few shops to visit, and lots of goods, including paintings and jewelry, are regularly auctioned. It's on one of the cobblestone lanes to the rear of Byres Road.

Books & Paper

Borders (✉ 98 Buchanan St., City Center ☎ 0141/222–7700), set in a former bank building, has a particularly friendly Glasgow air and carries a wide selection of Scottish books. The **Glasgow School of Art** (✉ 167 Renfrew St., City Center ☎ 0141/353–4526) sells books, cards, jewelry, and ceramics. Students often display their work during the degree shows in June. **Papyrus** (✉ 374 Byres Rd., West End ☎ 0141/334–6514 ✉ 296–298 Sauchiehall St., City Center ☎ 0141/353–2182) carries designer cards and small gifts, as well as a good selection of books.

Clothing Boutiques

Male and female fashionistas must not miss **Cruise** (✉ 180 Ingram St., City Center ☎ 0141/572–3280), which stocks cool labels at cool prices. An eclectic array of designer clothing and accessories for women fills **Moon** (✉ 10 Ruthven La., off Byres Rd., West End ☎ 0141/339–2315). **Mr. Benn** (✉ 6 King's Ct., King St., City Center ☎ 0141/553–1936) has a funky selection of vintage clothing. **Strawberry Fields** (✉ 517 Great Western Rd., West End ☎ 0141/339–1121) sells colorful children's wear.

Food

Iain Mellis Cheesemonger (✉ 492 Great Western Rd., West End ☎ 0141/339–8998) has a seemingly endless selection of fine Scottish cheeses. **Peckham's Delicatessen** (✉ 100 Byres Rd., West End ☎ 0141/357–1454 ✉ 43 Clarence Dr., West End ☎ 0141/357–2909 ✉ Central Station, City Center ☎ 0141/248–4012 ✉ Glassford St., Merchant City ☎ 0141/553–0666) is *the* place for Continental sausages, cheeses, and anything else you'd need for a delicious picnic.

Home Furnishings & Textiles

Fancy Dans (✉ 490 Great Western Rd., West End ☎ 0141/339–0660) is crammed with stylish jewelry, stationery, and skin-care products. **Linens Fine** (✉ The Courtyard, Princes Sq., City Center ☎ 0141/248–7082) carries wonderful embroidered and embellished bed linens and other textiles. At the shop for the **National Trust for Scotland** (✉ Hutchesons' Hall, 158 Ingram St., Merchant City ☎ 0141/552–8391) many of the items for sale, such as china, giftware, textiles, toiletries, and housewares, are designed exclusively for trust properties and are often handmade.

Scottish Specialties

For high-quality gifts in Charles Rennie Mackintosh style, head to **Catherine Shaw** (✉ 24 Gordon St., City Center ☎ 0141/204–4762 ✉ 32 Argyll Arcade, City Center ☎ 0141/221–9038). **Hector Russell Kiltmakers** (✉ 110 Buchanan St., City Center ☎ 0141/221–0217) specializes in Highland outfits, wool and cashmere clothing, and women's fashions. **MacDonald MacKay Ltd.** (✉ 161 Hope St., City Center ☎ 0141/204–3930) makes, sells, and exports Highland dress and accessories.

Sports Gear

You'll find good-quality outerwear at **Tiso Sports** (✉ 129 Buchanan St., City Center ⊕ www.tiso.com ☎ 0141/248–4877), handy if you're planning some Highland walks.

SIDE TRIPS FROM GLASGOW

The jigsaw puzzle of firths and straits and interlocking islands that you see as you fly into Glasgow Airport harbors numerous tempting one-day excursion destinations. You can travel south to visit the fertile farm-lands of Ayrshire—Robert Burns country—or west to the Firth of Clyde, or southeast to the Clyde Valley, all by car or by public transportation. Palatial treasures are en route—the Marquess of Bute's Mount Stuart house on the Isle of Bute and Culzean Castle, a favored retreat for Eisenhower and Churchill that is as famous for its Robert Adam (1728–92) design as it is for its spectacular seaside setting.

The highlight of this region is Robert Burns country. As poet and hu-manist, Burns (1759–96) increases in stature. When you plunge into Burns country, remember that he is held in extreme reverence by Scots of all backgrounds. They may argue about Sir Walter Scott and Bonnie Prince Charlie, but there's no disputing the merits of the poet of "Bonnie Doon."

Paisley

㉓ *7 mi southwest of Glasgow.*

The town isn't particularly interesting, but the Abbey is worth a stop. Buses to Paisley leave from Glasgow's Buchanan Street bus station; Traveline Scotland has information.

The 12th-century Cluniac **Abbey** dominates Paisley's center. Almost completely destroyed by the English in 1307, the abbey was not totally restored until the early 20th century. It is associated with Walter Fitza-llan, the high steward of Scotland, who gave his name to the Stewart monarchs of Scotland (Stewart is a corruption of "steward"). Out-standing features include the vaulted stone roof and stained glass of the choir. Paisley Abbey is today a busy parish church; if you're visiting with a large group you should call ahead. ☎ *0141/889–7654* 💷 *Free* ☉ *Mon.–Sat. 10–3:30, Sun. services 11, 12:15, and 6:30.*

Ayrshire & the Clyde Coast

Robert Burns is Scotland's national and best-loved poet. His birthday is celebrated with speeches and dinners, feasting, and singing (Burns Suppers) on January 25, in a way in which few other countries cele-brate a poet. He was born in Alloway, beside Ayr, just an hour or so south of Glasgow, and the towns and villages where he lived and loved make for an interesting day out. Two high points of the trip, in addi-tion to the Burns connections, are Mount Stuart House, on the Isle of Bute, and south of Ayr, Culzean Castle, flagship of the National Trust for Scotland.

Ayrshire and the Clyde Coast, an hour south of Glasgow, have been a holiday area for Glaswegians for generations. Few golfers need an in-troduction to the names of Turnberry, Prestwick, or Western Gailes—all challenging links courses along this coast. There are at least 20 other courses in the area within an hour's drive.

Wemyss Bay

㉔ *31 mi west of Glasgow.*

From the old Victorian village of Wemyss Bay there's ferry service to the Isle of Bute, a favorite holiday spot for Glaswegians before air travel made it easier to go farther. The many handsome buildings, especially the station and its covered walkway between the platform and steamer pier, are a reminder of the Victorian era's grandeur and style and of the generations of visitors who used trains and ferries for their summer holidays. South of Wemyss Bay, you can look across to the Isle of Arran, another Victorian holiday favorite, and then to the island of Great Cumbrae, a weighty name for a tiny island.

Isle of Bute

㉕ *75 mi west of Glasgow.*

The Isle of Bute affords a host of relaxing walks and scenic vistas. **Rothesay,** a faded but appealing resort, is the main town. Bute's biggest draw is spectacular **Mount Stuart,** ancestral home of the marquesses of Bute, about 5 mi south of Rothesay. The massive Victorian Gothic palace, built in red sandstone, has ornate interiors, including the Marble Hall, with a star-studded vault, stained glass, arcaded galleries, and magnificent tapestries woven in Edinburgh in the early 20th century. The paintings and furniture throughout the house are equally outstanding. ⊠ *Isle of Bute* 🕾 *01700/503877* ⊕ *www.mountstuart.com* 🖃 *Gardens £3.50; house and gardens £7.50* ☉ *Gardens May–Sept., daily 10–6; house May–Sept., Sun.–Fri. 11–5, Sat. 11–1:30.*

WHERE TO STAY &
EAT
££

✕🏨 **Ardmory House Hotel.** Surrounded by colorful gardens, this small hotel in a peaceful residential area evokes a modern home-away-from-home. Muted colors decorate the plainly furnished but comfortable bedrooms. There are nice local touches, such as the fabrics woven on the island that cover the chairs. Downstairs, a cozy bar with an open fire welcomes guests. Standard pub meals such as homemade soups and pastas are on offer, while the restaurant serves more elaborate creations such as breast of duck with spiced mandarin orange and cherry mulled-wine sauce, and salmon on a nest of fettuccine and vegetables with saffron-butter sauce. ⊠ *Ardmory Rd., Ardbeg, Isle of Bute, PA20 0PG* 🕾 *01700/502346* 🖶 *01700/505596* 🛏 *5 rooms* ♨ *Restaurant, bar; no a/c, no TV in some rooms* ▭ *MC, V* ❢◻ *BP.*

Largs

㉖ *42 mi southwest of Glasgow.*

At the coastal resort of Largs, the community makes the most of the town's Viking history. This was the site in 1263 of a major battle that finally broke the power of the Vikings in Scotland, and every September a commemorative Viking Festival is held. **Vikingar!** tells the story of the Viking influence in Scotland by way of film, tableaux, and displays. ⊠ *Barrfields, Greenock Rd.* 🕾 *01475/689777* ⊕ *www.vikingar.co.uk* 🖃 *£4.10* ☉ *Apr.–Sept., daily 10:30–5:30, Sat. 12:30–3:30; Oct. and Mar., daily 10:30–3:30; Nov.–Feb., weekends 10:30–3:30.*

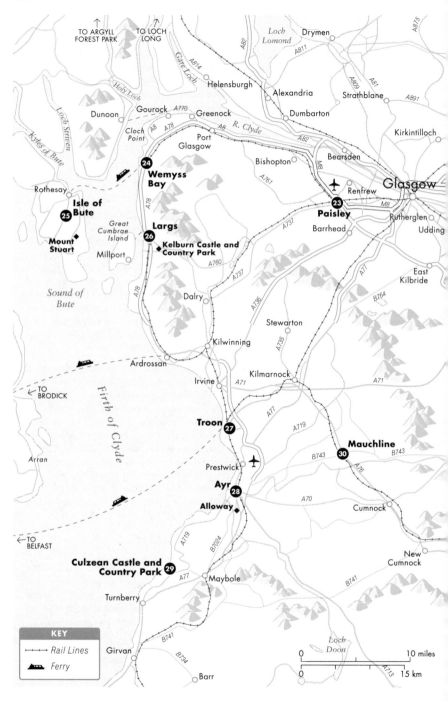

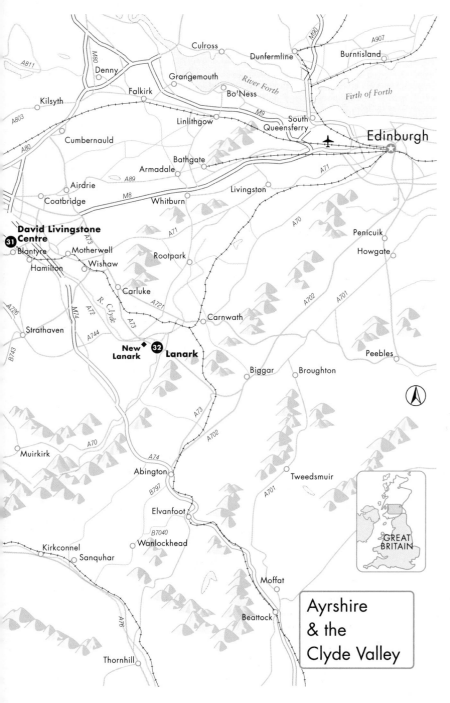

Ayrshire
& the
Clyde Valley

GREAT
BRITAIN

Just south of Largs is **Kelburn Castle and Country Park,** the historic estate of the earl of Glasgow. There are walks and trails through the mature woodlands, including the mazelike Secret Forest, which leads deep into the thickets. There are many surprises along the way for kids, including the Crocodile Swamp, the Gingerbread House, and mysterious Castle with No Entrance. The adventure center and commando-assault course wear out even the most overexcited of children. The excellent riding school provides year-round activities including paddock rides, hacks around the grounds, jumps in the arena, and lessons for all ages and abilities. ⊠ *Fairlie, Ayrshire* ☎ *01475/568685* ⊕ *www. kelburncountrycentre.com* ⊠ *Grounds and castle £6.50* ⊙ *Grounds Easter–Oct., daily 10–6; Nov.–Easter, daily 11–5. Castle July–Sept., daily tours at 1:30, 2:45, and 4.*

Troon

27 *28 mi south of Glasgow.*

The small coastal town of Troon is famous for its international golf course, Royal Troon. You can easily see why golf is popular here: at times, the whole 60-mi-long Ayrshire coast seems one endless course.

WHERE TO
STAY & EAT
★ ££–£££££ ✕ **MacCallums Oyster Bar.** The main ingredients at MacCallums come straight from the sea, and the menu varies depending on the day's catch. You can usually count on lobster in garlic butter; seared scallops; or grilled langoustines. Excellent light white wines match the freshness of the food. Solid wooden tables and other simple furniture add a rustic touch to the dining room. Hidden among the boatyards and customs buildings of Troon Harbour, this top-class restaurant is easy to miss, but you can find it next to the Seacat Ferry Terminal. ⊠ *The Harbour* ☎ *01292/ 319339* ⊟ *DC, MC, V* ⊙ *Closed Sun. evening and Mon.*

GOLF **Royal Troon.** This famous spot for golf was founded in 1878 and has two 18-hole courses: the Old, or Championship, Course and the Portland Course. Access for nonmembers is limited between May and mid-October to Monday, Tuesday, and Thursday only; day tickets cost £200 and include two rounds, morning coffee, and a buffet lunch. ⊠ *Craigend Rd.* ☎ *01292/311555* ⊕ *www.royaltroon.co.uk* ⅄ *Old Course: 18 holes, 7,150 yds, SSS 74. Portland Course: 18 holes, 6,289 yds, SSS 70.*

★ **Western Gailes.** Known as the finest natural links course in Scotland, Western Gailes is entirely nature-made, and the greens are kept in truly magnificent condition. This is the final qualifying course when the British Open is held at Troon or Turnberry. Tom Watson lists the par-5 sixth as one of his favorite holes. The course is a few miles north of Troon. ⊠ *Gailes, Irvine* ☎ *01294/311357* ⊕ *www.westerngailes.com* ⅄ *18 holes, 6,700 yds, par 71* ⊠ *Mon., Wed., Fri. £100 per round, £150 per day (lunch included); Sun. afternoon £110 per round* ⊙ *Mon., Wed., Fri., and Sun. afternoon.*

Ayr

28 *34 mi south of Glasgow.*

The commercial port of Ayr is Ayrshire's chief town, a peaceful and elegant place with an air of prosperity and some good shops. Robert Burns was baptized in the Auld Kirk (Old Church) here and wrote a humorous poem about the Twa Brigs (Two Bridges) that cross the river nearby. He described Ayr as a town unsurpassed "for honest men and bonny lasses."

If you're on the Robert Burns trail, head for **Alloway,** on B7024 in Ayr's southern suburbs. A number of sights here are part of the **Burns National Heritage Park** (www.burnsheritagepark.com). In Alloway, among the middle-class residences, you'll find the one-room thatched **Burns Cottage,** where Scotland's national poet was born in 1759 and which his father built. To his fellow Scots he's more than a great lyric bard; he's the champion of the underdog, the lover of noble causes, the hater of pomposity and cant, the prophet of social justice. A **museum** next to the cottage contains an original manuscript of "Auld Lang Syne" and other important Burns manuscripts and aritfacts. ⊠ *Murdoch's Lone, Alloway* ☎ *01292/441215* ⊕ *www.robertburns.org* ▣ *£4; £5 ticket includes admission to Tam o' Shanter Experience and Burns Monument* ☉ *Apr.–Sept., daily 9:30–5:30; Oct.–Mar., daily 10–5.*

Find out all about Burns at the **Tam o' Shanter Experience.** Here you can enjoy a 10-minute audiovisual journey through his life and times, then watch as one of Burns's most famous poems, "Tam o' Shanter," is brought to life on a three-screen theatrical set. It's down the road from Burns Cottage and around the corner from Alloway's ruined church. ⊠ *Murdoch's Lone, Alloway* 01292/443700 ⊕ www.robertburns.org ▣ *£2; £5 ticket includes Burns Cottage and Burns Monument* ☉ *Apr.–Sept., daily 10–5:30; Oct.–Mar., daily 10–5.*

Auld Kirk Alloway is where Tam o' Shanter, in Burns's eponymous poem, unluckily passed a witches' revel—with Old Nick himself playing the bagpipes—on his way home from a night of drinking. Tam, in flight from the witches, managed to cross the **Brig o' Doon** (*brig* is Scots for *bridge*) just in time. His gray mare, Meg, lost her tail to the closest witch. (Any resident of Ayr will tell you that witches cannot cross running water.)

The **Burns Monument** overlooks the Brig o' Doon. ☎ *No phone* ⊕ *www.robertburns.org* ▣ *£2; £5 ticket includes Burns Cottage and Tam o' Shanter Experience* ☉ *Apr.–Sept., daily 9:30–5; Nov.–Mar., daily 10–4.*

WHERE TO EAT
★ **££–££££** ✕ **Fouter's Bistro.** Fouter's is in a long and narrow cellar, yet its white walls and decorative stenciling create a sense of airiness. The cuisine is also light and skillful—no heavy sauces here. Try the roast Ayrshire lamb with pan juices, red wine, and mint, or sample the "Taste of Scotland" appetizer—smoked salmon, trout, and other goodies. This is modern Scottish and French cooking at its best. ⊠ *2A Academy St.* ☎ *01292/261391* ⊕ *www.fouters.co.uk* ▤ *DC, MC, V* ☉ *Closed Sun. and Mon.*

GOLF **Prestwick.** Tom Morris was involved in designing this challenging Ayrshire coastal links course, which saw the birth of the British Open Championship in 1860. Prestwick, about 5 mi north of Ayr, has excellent, fast rail links with Glasgow. ⊠ *2 Links Rd., Prestwick* ☎ *01292/477404* ⊕ *www.prestwickgc.co.uk* ▨ *18 holes, 6,544 yds, par 71* ▣ *Weekdays £105 per round, £160 per day; Sun. £135 per round* ☉ *Sun.–Fri.*

Culzean Castle & Country Park

★ **㉙** *50 mi south of Glasgow.*

The dramatic cliff-top Culzean (pronounced ku-*lain*) Castle and Country Park is the National Trust for Scotland's most popular property, yet it remains unspoiled. Robert Adam designed the neoclassical mansion, complete with a walled garden, in 1777. In addition to its marvelous interiors, it contains the National Guest Flat, donated by the people of Scotland in appreciation of General Eisenhower's (1890–1969) services during World War II. As president he stayed here once or twice, and his relatives still do so occasionally. Between visits it's used by the National Trust for official entertaining. The rooms on the approach to this apartment evoke the atmosphere of World War II: mementos of Glenn Miller (1904–44), Winston Churchill (1874–1965), and other personalities of the era all help create a suitably 1940s mood. Culzean's perpendicular sea cliff affords views across the Firth of Clyde to Arran and the Irish coast. Not a stone's throw away, it seems, the pinnacle of Ailsa Craig rears from midchannel. There are guided tours of the castle from July to September at 11 and 3 and from October to June at 3. ☎ *01655/884400* ⊕ *www.nts.org.uk* ✉ *Park £8; park and castle £12* ☉ *Park, daily 9:30–sunset; castle, Mar.–Oct., daily 10:30–5, last admission at 4:30.*

> **WORD OF MOUTH**
>
> "There is plenty to fill your time in Ayrshire. . . including some of the Robert Burns sites. Culzean is great because it isn't just the castle (which is fabulous) but also a country park, adventure playground, cafés, etc." —janis

GOLF   **Turnberry.** The Ailsa Course at Turnberry is perhaps the most famous links course in Scotland. Right on the seashore, the course is open to the elements, and the ninth hole requires you to hit the ball over the open sea. The British Open was staged here in 1977, 1986, and 1994. A second course, the Kintyre, is more compact than the Ailsa, with tricky sloped greens. Five of the holes have sea views, the rest are more inland. The town of Turnberry is about 5 mi south of Culzean Castle; the Westin Turnberry Resort provides luxurious accommodations. ✉ *Turnberry Hotel, Golf Courses and Spa, Turnberry* ☎ *01655/331000* ⊕ *www. turnberry.co.uk* ⚐ *Ailsa Course: 18 holes, 6,976 yds, SSS 72. Kintyre Course: 18 holes, 6,853 yds, SSS 72* ⚑ *Ailsa Course: weekdays £125 per round for hotel guests, £180 per round for nonguests; weekends £150 per round for hotel guests, £190 per round for nonguests. Kintyre Course: daily £105 per round for hotel guests, £120 per round for nonguests* ☉ *Daily.*

Mauchline

㉚ *26 mi south of Glasgow.*

Mauchline has strong connections with Robert Burns. There's a **Burns House** here and four of his daughters are buried in the churchyard. **Poosie Nansie's Pub**, where Burns used to drink, is still serving pints today. The village is also famous for making curling stones.

Ayrshire & the Clyde Coast Essentials

BY BUS

From Glasgow, take the bus to Largs; Ardrossan for Arran; Ayr for the Burns Heritage Trail; and Troon, Prestwick, and Ayr to play golf. Bus companies also operate one-day guided excursions; for details contact the tourist information center in Glasgow, Strathclyde Passenger Transport (SPT) Travel Centre. Traveline Scotland has a very helpful Web site.

🚌 **Traveline Scotland** ☎ 0870/608-2608 ⊕ www.travelinescotland.com. **SPT Travel Centre** ⊠ Buchanan Bus Station, Killermont St. ☎ 0141/333-3708 ⊕ www.spt.co.uk.

BY CAR

Begin your trip from Glasgow westbound on the M8, signposted for Glasgow Airport and Greenock. Join the A8 and follow it from Greenock to Gourock and around the coast past the Cloch Lighthouse. Head south on the A78 to the old Victorian village of Wemyss Bay and take the ferry over to Bute to see Mount Stuart (leave your car behind: a bus service takes you to the house from the ferry). Then continue down the A78 through Largs, Troon, and on to Ayr and Alloway. Head to Culzean Castle, then return to Ayr and turn eastward on the B743 and then head north on A76. Glasgow is only a half hour away on the fast A77.

BY TRAIN

You can travel via train to Largs; Ayr for the Burns Heritage Trail; and Troon, Prestwick, and Ayr to play golf.

🚌 **National Rail** ☎ 0845/748-4950 ⊕ www.nationalrail.co.uk.

VISITOR INFORMATION

All of the visitor centers in the area can provide you with brochures on the Burns Heritage Trail.

🚌 **Ayr** ⊠ 22 The Sandgate ☎ 01292/678100. **Largs** ⊠ Promenade ☎ 01292/678100. **Rothesay** ⊠ The Winter Gardens, Rothesay, Isle of Bute ☎ 01292/678100.

Clyde Valley

The River Clyde is (or certainly was) famous for its shipbuilding and heavy industries, yet its upper reaches flow through some of Scotland's most fertile farmlands, rich with tomato crops. It's an interesting area, with ancient castles as well as museums that tell the story of manufacturing and mining prosperity.

Blantyre

8 mi southeast of Glasgow.

 In the not-very-pretty town of Blantyre, look for signs to the **David Livingstone Centre,** a park area around the tiny (tenement) apartment where the great explorer of Africa (1813–73) was born. Displays tell of his journeys, of his meeting with Stanley ("Dr. Livingstone, I presume"), of Africa, and of the area's industrial heritage. In winter it's a good idea to call ahead. ⊠ *165 Station Rd.* ☎ *01698/823140* ⊕ *www.nts.org.uk* 💷 *£5* ⊙ *Apr.–Sept., Mon.–Sat. 10–5, Sun. 12:30–5; Oct.–Mar., Mon.–Sat. 10:30–4, Sun. 12:30–4.*

Bothwell Castle, with its well-preserved walls, dates to the 13th century and stands above the River Clyde. It's close to the David Livingstone Centre. ✉ *Uddingston* ☎ *01698/816894* 🎫 *£3* ⊙ *Apr.–Sept., daily 9:30–6.30; Oct.–Mar., Mon.–Wed. and Sat. 9:30–4.30, Sun. 2–4.30, Thurs. 9:30–noon.*

Lanark

③②   *19 mi southeast of Glasgow.*

★   Set in pleasing, rolling countryside, Lanark is a typical old Scottish town. It's now most often associated with its unique neighbor **New Lanark,** a World Heritage Site that was home to a social experiment—a model community with well-designed workers' homes, a school, and public buildings. The River Clyde powers its way through a beautiful wooded gorge, and its waters were harnessed to drive textile mill machinery before the end of the 18th century.

After many changes of fortune the mills eventually closed and were converted into a hotel and private residential properties. As a result, residents have moved in and New Lanark has maintained its unique environment, where those leading normal everyday lives mix easily with the tourists. One of the mills has been converted into an **interpretive center,** which tells the story of this brave social experiment. Upstream, the Clyde flows through some of the finest river scenery anywhere in Lowland Scotland, with woods and spectacular waterfalls.

To get here, take the train from Glasgow Central Station to Lanark; for details call National Rail, or check out the timetable online. If you drive, take the A724 east out of Glasgow, south of the river through Rutherglen; then travel on the A72 past Chatelherault toward Lanark. Before reaching Lanark, follow the signs down a long winding hill, to New Lanark. Return to Glasgow the quick way by joining the M74 from the A744 west of Lanark (the Strathaven road). ☎ *01555/665876* ⊕ *www.newlanark.org* 🎫 *£5.95* ⊙ *Daily 11–5.*

WHERE TO STAY   🏨 **New Lanark Mill Hotel.** Housed in a converted cotton mill at the 18th-
££   century model village of New Lanark, this hotel is decorated in a spare, understated style that allows the impressive architecture of barrel-vaulted ceilings and elegant Georgian windows to speak for itself. Right next to the river in the heart of the village, the hotel has all the attractions—visitor center, shops, Falls of Clyde Wildlife Reserve—at its doorstep. ✉ *New Lanark, ML11 9DB* ☎ *01555/667200* 🖶 *01555/ 667222* ⊕ *www.newlanark.org* 🛏 *38 rooms, 8 cottages* ♿ *Restaurant; no a/c* ▭ *AE, DC, MC, V* ⋈ *BP.*

GLASGOW ESSENTIALS

Transportation

BY AIR

Glasgow Airport is about 7 mi west of the city center on the M8 to Greenock. The airport serves international and domestic flights, and most major European carriers have frequent and convenient connections (some via airports in England) to many cities on the continent. Local Scottish connections can be made to Aberdeen, Barra, Benbecula, Campbeltown, Inverness, Islay, Kirkwall, Shetland (Sumburgh), Stornoway, and Tiree.

Prestwick Airport, on the Ayrshire coast about 30 mi southwest of Glasgow and for some years eclipsed by Glasgow Airport, has grown in importance, not least because of lower airfares from Ryanair.

Ryanair and easyJet have sparked a major price war on the Anglo-Scottish routes (e.g., between London and Glasgow). Ryanair offers rock-bottom air fares between Prestwick and London's Stansted Airport. Budget-minded easyJet has similar services from Glasgow to Stansted and Luton, respectively. *See* the Essentials section at the end of this book for more information.

🛈 **Glasgow Airport** ☎ 0141/887–1111 ⊕ www.baa.co.uk. **Prestwick Airport** ☎ 01292/511006 ⊕ www.gpia.co.uk.

TRANSFERS **From Glasgow Airport:** Although there's a railway station about 2 mi from Glasgow Airport (Paisley Gilmour Street), most people travel to the city center by bus or taxi. It takes about 20 minutes, slightly longer at rush hour. Metered taxis are available outside domestic arrivals. The fare should be £15 to £18.

Express buses run from Glasgow Airport (outside departures lobby) to near the Central railway station, to Queen Street railway station, and to the Buchanan Street bus station. There's a service every 15 minutes throughout the day. The fare is £3.30 on both Scottish Citylink and Fairline buses.

The drive from Glasgow Airport into the city center is normally quite easy, even if you're used to driving on the right. The M8 motorway runs beside the airport (Junction 29) and takes you straight into the Glasgow city center.

From Prestwick Airport: An hourly coach service makes trips to Glasgow but takes much longer than the train. There's a rapid half-hourly train service (hourly on Sunday) direct from the terminal building to Glasgow Central. Strathclyde Passenger Transport and ScotRail offer an Air-Train discount ticket that allows you to travel for 50% of the standard rail fare. Just show a valid airline ticket (boarding cards are not accepted), for a flight to or from Prestwick Airport when you purchase your rail ticket from a booking office or conductor.

By car the city center is reached via the fast A77 in about 40 minutes (longer in rush hour). Metered taxi cabs are available at the airport. The fare to Glasgow is about £40.

BY BUS

Glasgow's bus station is on Buchanan Street at Argyle Street, not far from Central Station. The main intercity operators are National Express and Scottish Citylink, which serve numerous towns and cities in Scotland, Wales, and England. Buchanan Street is close to the underground station of the same name and to the Queen Street station. Traveline Scotland can provide information on schedules and fares.

⌂ Buchanan Street bus station ☎ 0141/333-3708. **National Express** ☎ 0870/580-8080 ⊕ www.nationalexpress.co.uk. **Scottish Citylink** ☎ 0870/505050 ⊕ www.citylink.co.uk. **Traveline Scotland** ☎ 0870/608-2608 ⊕ www.travelinescotland.com.

WITHIN
GLASGOW

Bus service is reliable within Glasgow, and connections are convenient from buses to trains and the underground. Note that buses require exact fare, which varies by the destination, though it's usually around £1.

The many bus companies cooperate with the underground and ScotRail to produce the Family Day Tripper Ticket (£15 for two adults), which gets you around the whole area, from Loch Lomond to Ayrshire. The tickets are a good value and are available from Strathclyde Passenger Transport Travel Centre and at main railway and bus stations.

⌂ Strathclyde Passenger Transport Travel Centre ✉ St. Enoch Sq., City Center ☎ 0870/608-2608 ⊕ www.spt.co.uk.

BY CAR

If you come to Glasgow from England and the south of Scotland, you'll probably approach the city from the M6, M74, and A74. The city center is clearly marked from these roads. From Edinburgh the M8 leads to the city center and is the route that cuts straight across the city center and into which all other roads feed. From the north either the A82 from Fort William or the A/M80 from Stirling also feed into the M8 in the Glasgow city center. From then on you only have to know your exit: Exit 16 serves the northern part of the city center, Exit 17/18 leads to the northwest and Great Western Road, and Exit 18/19 takes you to the hotels of Sauchiehall Street, and the Scottish Exhibition and Conference Centre.

BY SUBWAY

Glasgow is the only city in Scotland that has a subway (or underground, as it's called here). The system was built at the end of the 19th century and takes the simple form of two circular routes, one going clockwise and the other counterclockwise. The bright orange paint and circular routes of the trains, gave it the nickname the "Clockwork Orange."

Flat fares (£1) and the Discovery Ticket one-day pass (£1.90, after 9:30) are available. Trains run regularly from Monday through Saturday from early morning to late evening, with a limited Sunday service, and connect the city center with the West End (for the university) and the city south of the River Clyde. Look for the orange U signs marking the 15 stations. Further information is available from Strathclyde Passenger Transport Travel Centre.

⌂ Strathclyde Passenger Transport Travel Centre ✉ St. Enoch Sq., City Center ☎ 0870/608-2608 ⊕ www.spt.co.uk.

BY TAXI

You'll find metered taxis (usually black and of the London sedan type) at stands all over the city center. Most have radio dispatch. Some have also been adapted to take wheelchairs. You can hail a cab on the street if its FOR HIRE sign is illuminated. A typical ride from the city center to the West End or the South Side costs around £6.

🔝 **Glasgow Taxis** ☎ 0141/429-7070 ⊕ www.glasgowtaxisltd.co.uk.

BY TRAIN

Glasgow has two main rail stations: Central and Queen Street. Central is the arrival and departure point for trains from London's Euston station (five hours). It also serves other cities in the northwest of England and towns and ports in the southwest of Scotland. Queen Street station has frequent connections to Edinburgh (50 minutes) and serves the north of Scotland. For details contact National Rail.

A regular bus service links the Queen Street and Central stations. Both are close to stations on the Glasgow underground. At Queen Street go to Buchanan Street, and at Central go to St. Enoch. City taxis are available at both stations.

🔝 **Greater Glasgow and Clyde Valley Tourist Board** ✉ 11 George Sq., near Queen Street station, City Center ☎ 0141/204-4400 ⊕ www.seeglasgow.com. **National Rail** ☎ 0870/748-4950 ⊕ www.nationalrail.co.uk. **Strathclyde Passenger Transport Travel Centre** ✉ St. Enoch Sq., City Center ☎ 0870/608-2608 ⊕ www.spt.co.uk.

Contacts & Resources

EMERGENCIES

In case of any emergency, dial **999** to reach an ambulance or the police or fire departments (no coins are needed for emergency calls from public phones). Note that pharmacies generally operate on a rotating basis for late-night opening; hours are posted in storefront windows. Munro Pharmacy is open daily 9 to 9.

🔝 **Dentists Glasgow Dental Hospital** ✉ 378 Sauchiehall St., City Center ☎ 0141/211-9600 weekdays 9-3.

🔝 **Hospitals Glasgow Royal Infirmary** ✉ Castle St., near cathedral, City Center ☎ 0141/211-4000. **Glasgow Western Infirmary** ✉ Dumbarton Rd., near university, West End ☎ 0141/211-2000. **Southern General Hospital** ✉ 1345 Govan Rd., south side of Clyde Tunnel, South Side ☎ 0141/201-1100. **Stobhill Hospital** ✉ 133 Balornock Rd., near Royal Infirmary and Bishopriggs, North City ☎ 0141/201-3000.

🔝 **Pharmacy Munro Pharmacy** ✉ 693 Great Western Rd., West End ☎ 0141/339-0012.

INTERNET, MAIL & SHIPPING

The main post office is at St. Vincent Street; there smaller post offices around the city. As for Internet access, you can find it everywhere—in a variety of cafés, hotels, even some of the larger and B&B's. Most access points offer broadband and Wi-Fi.

🔝 **Internet Cafés easyInternet Cafe** ✉ 57-61 St. Vincent St., Glasgow ☎ 0141/222-2365. **Icafe** ✉ 223 Great Western Rd., Glasgow ☎ 0141/572-0786. **Yeeha Internet** ✉ 48 West George St., Glasgow ☎ 0141/332-6543.

🔝 **Post Office Main post office** ✉ St. Vincent St., City Center ☎ 0845/722-3344.

TOUR OPTIONS

You can purchase a £12 **Mackintosh Trail Ticket** at major sites, visitor centers, or online from the Mackintosh Society; www.spt.co.uk (the transit service) and the Charles Rennie Mackintosh Society, www.crmsociety. com, have information.

BOAT TOURS   Cruises are available on Loch Lomond and to the islands in the Firth of Clyde; contact the Greater Glasgow and Clyde Valley Tourist Board for details. Contact the *Waverley* paddle steamer from June through August, and Clyde Marine Cruises from May through September.
🚩 **Clyde Marine Cruises** ✉ Victoria Harbour, Greenock ☎ 01475/721281 ⊕ www. clyde-marine.co.uk. **Greater Glasgow and Clyde Valley Tourist Board** ✉ 11 George Sq., near Queen Street station, City Center ☎ 0141/204-4400 ⊕ www.seeglasgow. com. **Waverley** ✉ 36 Anderston Quay ☎ 0845/1304647.

BUS TOURS   City Sightseeing bus tours leave daily from the west side of George Square. The Greater Glasgow and Clyde Valley Tourist Board can give further information and arrange reservations. Details of longer tours northward to the Highlands and islands can be obtained from the tourist board or Strathclyde Passenger Transport Travel Centre.

Classic Coaches operates restored coaches from the 1950s, '60s, and '70s on tours to the north and west and to the islands. The following Glasgow companies run regular bus tours around the region: Scotguide Tours, Southern Coaches, and Weirs Tourlink.
🚩 **Greater Glasgow and Clyde Valley Tourist Board** ✉ 11 George Sq., near Queen Street station, City Center ☎ 0141/204-4400 ⊕ www.seeglasgow.com. **Southern Coaches** ✉ Barshagra Garage, Lochlibo Rd. ☎ 0800/298-1655. **Strathclyde Passenger Transport Travel Centre** ✉ St. Enoch Sq., City Center ☎ 0870/608-2608 ⊕ www. spt.co.uk. **Weirs Tourlink** ✉ 145 Dlasetter Ave. ☎ 0141/944-6688.

PRIVATE GUIDES   Little's Chauffeur Drive arranges personally tailored car-and-driver tours, both locally and throughout Scotland. The Scottish Tourist Guides Association also provides a private-guide service. Taxi firms offer city tours. If you allow the driver to follow a set route, the cost is £16 per hour for up to five people. If you wish the driver to follow your own route, the charge will be £16 an hour or the reading on the meter, whichever is greater. You can book tours in advance and be picked up and dropped off wherever you like. Contact Glasgow Taxis.
🚩 **Glasgow Taxis** ☎ 0141/429-7070 ⊕ www.glasgowtaxisltd.co.uk. **Little's Chauffeur Drive** ✉ 1282 Paisley Rd. W, South Side ☎ 0141/883-2111 ⊕ www.littles.co.uk. **Scottish Tourist Guides Association** ☎🖷 01786/451-953 ⊕ www.stga.co.uk.

WALKING TOURS   The Greater Glasgow and Clyde Valley Tourist Board can provide information on special walks on a given day. Glasgow Walking organizes specialized tours of the city's architectural treasures. For spine-chilling tales about the city accompanied by costumed characters like Mary, Queen of Scots, contact Mercat Glasgow.
🚩 **Glasgow Walking Tour** ☎ 01620/825722 ⊕ www.glasgowarchitecture.co.uk/glasgow_walking_tours.htm. **Greater Glasgow and Clyde Valley Tourist Board** ✉ 11 George Sq., near Queen Street station, City Center ☎ 0141/204-4400 ⊕ www.seeglasgow. com. **Mercat Glasgow** ☎ 0141/586-5378 ⊕ www.mercat-glasgow.co.uk.

VISITOR INFORMATION

The Greater Glasgow and Clyde Valley Tourist Board provides information and has an accommodations-booking service, a bureau de change, a Western Union money-transfer service, city bus tours, guided walks, boat trips, and coach tours around Scotland. Books, maps, and souvenirs are also available. The office is open September through June, from Monday to Saturday 9 to 6, and July through August, from Monday to Saturday 9 to 8, Sunday 10 to 6. The tourist board's branch office at the airport is open from Monday to Saturday 7:30 to 5, Sunday 8 to 3:30 (Sunday 7:30 to 5, April through September).

🚹 **Greater Glasgow and Clyde Valley Tourist Board** ⊠ 11 George Sq., near Queen St. station, City Center ☎ 0141/204–4400 🖷 0141/221–3524 ⊕ www.seeglasgow.com. **Lanark** ⊠ Horsemarket, Ladyacre Rd. ☎ 01555/661661.

13

The Borders & the Southwest

DUMFRIES & GALLOWAY,
SIR WALTER SCOTT COUNTRY

WORD OF MOUTH

"If you want fine countryside, quaint towns, and romantic ruined abbeys, look at Melrose, Jedburgh, and Dryburgh, three abbeys within a few miles of each other. Melrose and Jedburgh are in neat small towns, Melrose a bit nicer than Jedburgh, and Dryburgh is on the River Tweed in a wild setting—because of its setting, it is the most romantic of the three. All three are in the gorgeous Borders area with a rolling pastoral setting."

—PalQ

"Check out the remote Hermitage Castle, where Bothwell lay wounded and Mary, Queen of Scots made a daring 40-mile round-trip ride to visit him from Jedburgh, all in one day. Of course it took us only an hour by car."

—TuckH

Updated by
Fiona Parrott

IF YOU ARE COMING TO SCOTLAND by road or rail from England, you'll first encounter either the Borders area or the Southwest, also known as Dumfries and Galloway, depending on the route you take. Although there are no checkpoints or customs posts, you will begin to notice all the idiosyncrasies that distinguish Scotland—like its myriad names for things—just as soon as you pass the first Scottish signs by the main roads heading north.

Many people rush through this area, stop in Edinburgh or Glasgow, and then plunge northward to the Highlands, thus missing portions of Scotland that are as beautiful and historically important as elsewhere. The Borders and the Southwest have more stately homes, fortified castles, and medieval monastic houses than anywhere else in Scotland. If you take the time to explore, you'll see that there's more to Scotland than brooding lochs and glens.

14

The Borders region embraces the whole 90-mi course of one of Scotland's greatest rivers, the Tweed, and its tributaries. Passing mill chimneys, peel towers (small fortified towers), ruined abbeys, stately homes, and woodlands luxuriant with game birds, the rivers flow in a series of fast-rushing torrents and dark serpentine pools through the history of two nations. For at different times, parts of the region have been in English hands, just as slices of northern England (Berwick-upon-Tweed, for example) have been in Scottish hands.

All the main routes from London to Edinburgh traverse the Borders region, whose hinterland of undulating pastures, woods, and valleys is enclosed within three lonely groups of hills: the Cheviots, the Moorfoots, and the Lammermuirs. Innumerable hamlets and towns dot the land, giving valley slopes a lived-in look, yet the total population is still relatively sparse. Sheep outnumber human beings by 14 to 1—which is just as Sir Walter Scott, the region's most famous resident, would have wanted it. His pseudo-baronial home at Abbotsford is the most visited of Scottish literary landmarks.

To the west is the region of Dumfries and Galloway, on the shores of the Solway Firth. It might appear to be an extension of the Borders, but the Southwest has a history and milieu all its own. Inland, the earth rises toward high hills, forest, and bleak but captivating moorland, whereas nearer the coast are pretty farmlands, small villages, and unassuming towns. The shoreline is washed by the North Atlantic Drift (Scotland's answer to the Gulf Stream), and first-time visitors are always surprised to see palm trees and exotic plants thriving in gardens and parks along the coast.

Exploring the Borders & the Southwest

The Borders region is characterized by upland moors and hills, with fertile, farmed, and forested river valleys. Borders towns cluster around and between two great rivers—the Tweed and its tributary, the Teviot. These are mostly textile towns with plenty of personality—Borders folk are sure of their own identity and are fiercely partisan toward their own native towns.

Dumfries and Galloway, especially inland, shares the upland characteristics and, if anything, has a slightly wilder air—the highest hill in Dumfries and Galloway is the Merrick, at 2,765 feet. Easygoing and peaceful, towns in this region are usually very attractive, with wide streets and colorful frontages.

The best way to explore the region is to get off the main, and often crowded, arterial roads—the A1, A697, A68, A76, A7, M74/A74, and A75—and onto the little back roads (allow extra time to drive these). You may occasionally be delayed by a herd of cows, but this is often far more pleasant than, for example, tussling on the A75 with heavy-goods vehicles rushing to make the Irish ferries.

About the Restaurants & Hotels
From top-quality, full-service hotels to quaint 18th-century drovers' inns to cozy bed-and-breakfasts, the Borders has plenty of lodging options. Most good restaurants in the region tend to be within hotels rather than independent establishments. Lodging in Dumfries and Galloway may be a little less expensive than in the Borders. There are farmhouse B&Bs, where mornings start with hearty, extra-fresh breakfasts. Many of these B&Bs are *working* farms, where early-morning activity and the presence of animals are an inescapable part of the scene.

WHAT IT COSTS In pounds				
£££££	**££££**	**£££**	**££**	**£**
RESTAURANTS over £22	£18–£22	£13–£17	£7–£12	under £7
HOTELS over £160	£120–£160	£90–£119	£60–£89	under £60

Restaurant prices are for a main course at dinner. Hotel prices are for two people in a standard double room in high season, generally including the 17.5% V.A.T.

Timing
Because many properties are privately owned and shut down from early autumn until early April, the area is less well suited to off-season touring than some other parts of Scotland. The region does look magnificent in autumn, however, especially along the wooded river valleys of the Borders. Late spring is the time to see the rhododendrons in the gardens of Dumfries and Galloway.

THE BORDERS

Although the Borders has many attractions, it is most famous for being the home base for Sir Walter Scott (1771–1832), the early-19th-century poet, novelist, and creator of *Ivanhoe,* who single-handedly transformed Scotland's image from that of a land of brutal savages to one of romantic and stirring deeds and magnificent landscapes.

A visit to at least one of the region's four great ruined abbeys makes the quintessential Borders experience. The monks in these striking, long-abandoned religious orders were the first to work the fleeces of their sheep flocks, thus laying the groundwork for what is still the area's main manufacturing industry.

TOP REASONS TO GO

Ancient abbeys: The region's four famous ruined abbeys—Melrose, Dryburgh, Jedburgh, and Kelso—reveal a long history of struggle and conflict. Vestiges of intricately carved capitals, decorative gargoyles, and painstakingly exquisite tracery reveal a flicker of the abbeys' former brilliance.

Country biking: Away from busy roads like the A68, A7, and A1, the Borders area is ideal for bicycling. In the Southwest, too, once you're off the beaten track, you'll discover quiet roads and country lanes that beg to be explored. There are bike-rental shops in many towns, including Peebles, Dumfries, and Castle Douglas.

Stately homes and castles: Transport yourself back to a time of real extravagance. Paxton and Manderston Houses hold well-preserved treasures from different eras, and you can sip ale on the grounds of 12th-century Traquair House. Splendid Floors Castle, a highlight of the Borders, is the largest inhabited castle in Scotland.

Scott's Scotland: In this part of the country there are enough monuments and sites dedicated to Sir Walter Scott to make his life and works a theme of your visit. Don't miss the epic Abbotsford House, Smailhom Tower, Dryburgh Abbey and Scott's View.

Sweaters and sweets: The Borders is well known for its knitwear industry, and mill shops are abundant. Throughout the region also look for the specialty peppermint or fruit-flavor boiled sweets (hard candies), tablet (a sugary caramel-like candy), and fudges. Many villages have small craft shops that sell locally made pottery, jewelry, and ornaments, so you won't go home empty-handed.

Borders folk take great pride in the region's fame as Scotland's main woolen-goods manufacturing area. To this day the residents possess a marked determination to defend their towns and communities. Changing times have allowed them to reposition their priorities: instead of guarding against southern raiders, they now concentrate on maintaining a fiercely competitive rugby team for the popular intertown rugby matches.

Borders communities have also reestablished their identities through the gatherings known as the Common Ridings. Long ago it was essential that each town be able to defend its area, and over the centuries this need became formalized in mounted gatherings to "ride the marches," or patrol the boundaries. (You are welcome to watch and enjoy the excitement of clattering hooves and banners proudly displayed, but this is essentially a time for native Borderers.) The Common Ridings possess much more authenticity and historic significance than the concocted Highland Games, so often taken to be the essence of Scotland. The little town of Selkirk claims its Common Riding is the largest mounted gathering anywhere in Europe.

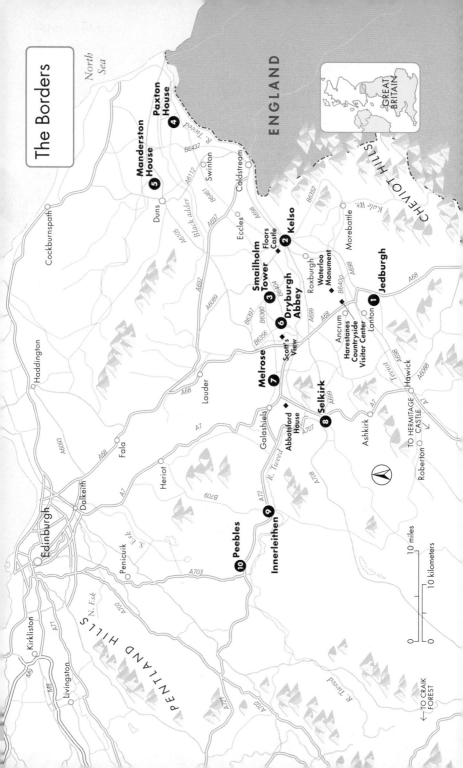

The Borders

North Sea

ENGLAND

GREAT BRITAIN

CHEVIOT HILLS

Cockburnspath

Paxton House **4**

Manderston House **5**

Duns

Black adder

Swinton

Coldstream

Eccles

Kelso **2**

Floors Castle

Smailholm Tower **3**

Dryburgh Abbey **6**

Roxburgh

Waterloo Monument

Scott's View

Morebattle

Kale Wr.

Jedburgh **1**

Lonton

Ancrum

Harestanes Countryside Visitor Center

Melrose **7**

Selkirk **8**

Galashiels

Abbotsford House

Ashkirk

Hawick

TO HERMITAGE CASTLE

Roberton

Haddington

Lauder

Fala

Heriot

Dalkeith

Edinburgh

Peniquik

Innerleithen **9**

Peebles **10**

R. Tweed

PENTLAND HILLS

N. Esk

S. Esk

Kirkliston

Livingston

TO CRAIK FOREST

R. Tweed

10 miles

10 kilometers

Jedburgh

❶ *50 mi south of Edinburgh, 95 mi southeast of Glasgow.*

The town of Jedburgh (*-burgh* is always pronounced *burra* in Scots) was for centuries the first major Scottish target of invading English armies. In more peaceful times it developed textile mills, most of which have since languished. The large landscaped area around the town's tourist information center was once a mill but now provides an encampment for the armies of modern tourists. The past still clings to this little town, however. The ruined abbey dominates the skyline and remains a reminder of the formerly strong, governing role of the Borders abbeys.

★ **Jedburgh Abbey,** the most impressive of the Borders abbeys, was nearly destroyed by the English earl of Hertford's forces in 1544–45, during the destructive time known as the Rough Wooing. This was English king Henry VIII's (1491–1547) armed attempt to persuade the Scots that it was a good idea to unite the kingdoms by the marriage of his young son to the infant Mary, Queen of Scots (1542–87); the Scots disagreed and sent Mary to France instead. The full story is explained in vivid detail at the **Jedburgh Abbey Visitor Centre,** which also provides information on interpreting the ruins. Ground patterns and foundations are all that remain of the once-powerful religious complex. ⊠ *High St.* ☎ *01835/863925* ⊕ *www.historic-scotland.gov.uk* 🎫 *£4.50* ⊙ *Apr.–Sept., daily 9:30–6:30; Oct.–Mar., daily 9:30–4:30.*

The **Mary, Queen of Scots House,** a *bastel* (from the French *bastille*), was the fortified town house in which, as the story goes, Mary stayed before embarking on her famous 20-mi ride to visit her wounded lover, the earl of Bothwell (circa 1535–78), at Hermitage Castle. Interpretative displays relate the tale and illustrate other episodes in her life. Some of her possessions are also on display, as well as tapestries and furniture of the period. ⊠ *Queen St.* ☎ *01835/863331* 🎫 *£3* ⊙ *Mon.–Sat. 10–4:30, Sun. 11–4:30.*

☾ The **Harestanes Countryside Visitor Centre,** in a former farmhouse 3 mi (5 km) north of Jedburgh, conveys life in the Scottish Borders with changing art exhibitions and interpretive displays on the natural history of the region. Crafts such as woodworking and tile-making are taught at the center, and finished projects are often on display. There's a gift shop and tearoom, and outside are paths for countryside walks, plus the biggest children's play area in the Borders. The quiet roads are suitable for bicycle excursions. ⊠ *Close to the junction of the A68 and B6400* ☎ *01835/830306* 🎫 *Free* ⊙ *Apr.–Oct., daily 10–5.*

OFF THE
BEATEN
PATH

HERMITAGE CASTLE – To appreciate the famous 20-mi ride of Mary, Queen of Scots, to visit her wounded lover, the earl of Bothwell, travel southwest from Jedburgh to this, the most complete remaining example of the bare and grim medieval border castles, full of gloom and foreboding. Restored in the early 19th century, it was built in the 14th century to guard what was at the time one of the important routes from England into Scotland. The original owner, Lord Soulis, notorious for diabolical excess, was captured by the local populace, which wrapped him in lead and boiled him in a cauldron—or so the tale goes. ⊠ *On an unclassified road 2 mi*

14

(3 km) west of B6399, about 15 mi south of Hawick near Liddesdale ☎ *01387/376222* ⊕ *www.historic-scotland.gov.uk* ⊡ *£3* ⊙ *Apr.–Sept., daily 9:30–6:30; last admission half hr before closing.*

Where to Stay & Eat

★ **££–£££** ✕ **Cross Keys.** This traditional pub, a national treasure, specializes in local ingredients, from fish to game. A splendid array of Scottish beers—real ale, as it is known here—is served. This is the quintessential village inn, right down to the green outside the front door. ⊠ *The Green, Ancrum TD8 6XH, 3 mi northeast of Jedburgh* ☎ *01835/830344* ⊕ *www. ancrumcrosskeys.co.uk* ⊟ *DC, MC, V.*

£–££ ▥ **Spinney Guest House.** A converted farm cottage, this B&B offers simple but carefully decorated rooms. Additionally, there are two one-bedroom wood cabins (perfect for couples who like privacy), and a two-bedroom cabin where three people can sleep comfortably. Each cabin has a kitchenette and a small patio. The common room in the main house has several welcoming armchairs. ⊠ *Langlee, off A68, Jedburgh TD8 6PB* ☎ *01835/863525* ▤ *01835/864883* ⊕ *www.thespinney-jedburgh. co.uk* ⊅ *3 rooms, 3 cabins* ⚭ *Dining room, some kitchenettes, some microwaves, some refrigerators, lounge; no a/c, no room phones* ⊟ *MC, V* ⊙ *Closed Dec.–Feb.* ⦿ *BP.*

£ ▥ **Hundalee House.** This B&B in an 18th-century manor has richly decorated Victorian-style rooms with four-poster beds, fireplaces, and modern facilities. Fifteen acres of gardens and woods surround the house, and there are splendid views across to the English border at Carter Bar and to the Cheviot hills in the southeast. ⊠ *Off A68, 1 mi south of Jedburgh, TD8 6PA* ☎ *01835/863011* ⊕ *www.accommodation-scotland. org* ⊅ *4 rooms* ⚭ *Dining room, lounge; no a/c, no room phones* ⊟ *No credit cards* ⊙ *Closed Nov.–Mar.* ⦿ *BP.*

Biking&

Christopher Rainbow Tandem & Bike Hire (⊠ 8 Timpendean Cottages ☎ 01835/830326 or 07799/525123) rents tandem bikes, mountain bikes, and touring bikes. It's ideally placed for exploring the four Borders abbeys, Tweed, and Borderloop cycleways. The company provides tour itineraries, as well as luggage forwarding. It's on the A698, near the junction with the A68, between Jedburgh and Ancrum.

Kelso

❷ *12 mi northeast of Jedburgh.*

One of the most charming Borders burghs, Kelso is often described as having a Continental flavor—some people think it resembles a Belgian market town. The town has a broad, paved Market Square and fine examples of Georgian and Victorian Scots town architecture.

Kelso Abbey is the least intact ruin of the four great Borders abbeys—just a bleak fragment of what was once the largest of the group. It was here in 1460 that the nine-year-old James III was crowned king of Scotland. On a main invasion route, the abbey was burned three times in the 1540s alone, on the last occasion by the English earl of Hertford's forces in 1545, when the 100 men and 12 monks of the garrison were butchered and the structure all but destroyed. ⊠ *Bridge St.* ☎ *0131/668–8800* ⊕ *www.historic-scotland.gov.uk* ⊠ *Free* ⊙ *24 hrs.*

Fodor's Choice ★ Just on the outskirts of Kelso stands the palatial **Floors Castle,** the largest inhabited castle in Scotland. The ancestral home of the dukes of Roxburghe, Floors is an architectural extravagance bristling with peppermill turrets and towers. It stands on the "floors," or flat terrain, on the banks of the River Tweed opposite the barely visible ruins of Roxburghe Castle. The enormous home was built in 1721 by William Adam (1689–1748) and modified by William Playfair (1789–1857), who added the turrets and towers in the 1840s. A holly tree in the deer park marks the place where King James II of Scotland (1430–60) was killed by a cannon that "brak in the shooting." ⊠ *A6089* ☎ *01573/223333* ⊕ *www.floorscastle.com* ⊠ *Grounds £3, castle and grounds £6* ⊙ *Apr.–Oct., daily 10–4:30; last admission half hr before closing.*

14

Where to Stay & Eat

★ **£££–££££** ✕🖭 **Ednam House Hotel.** People return again and again to this large, stately hotel on the banks of the River Tweed, close to Kelso's grand abbey and old Market Square. The main hall, part of the original 1761 home, welcomes you with deep-seated armchairs, paintings, and an open fire. The restaurant's three windowed walls overlook the garden and river, and its Scottish fare includes fresh local vegetables, smoked wild salmon, Borders beef, Highland venison, and homemade traditional puddings. ⊠ *Bridge St., Kelso, TD5 7HT* ☎ *01573/224168* 🖷 *01573/226319* ⊕ *www.ednamhouse.com* ⤙ *32 rooms* ⚬ *Restaurant, golf privileges, fishing, horseback riding, 2 bars; no a/c* ▭ *MC, V* ⊙ *Closed late Dec. and early Jan.* ⦿ *BP.*

★ **££–£££** ✕🖭 **Edenwater House.** This handsome stone house overlooks Edenwater, a trout stream that runs into the River Tweed. Four well-appointed guest rooms afford superb views of the river and two of the Cheviot hills. The inn is filled with antiques and serves what some connoisseurs regard as the best food in the Borders. Roast saddle of hare with foie gras and filet of monkfish crusted with basil and coriander in beurre blanc are two of the dishes you might find on the menu. The restaurant is open Friday and Saturday for nonguests, too, and offers a £30 three-course dinner. Children under 10 are not admitted to the restaurant. ⊠ *Off the B6461, Ednam, TD5 7QL* ☎ *01573/224070* 🖷 *01573/226615* ⊕ *www.edenwaterhouse.co.uk* ⤙ *4 rooms* ⚬ *Restaurant, fishing, lounge, Internet room; no a/c, no room phones* ▭ *MC, V* ⊙ *Closed Sun.–Wed. and Jan. 1–14* ⦿ *BP.*

Smailholm Tower

❸ *8 mi northwest of Kelso.*

This characteristic Borders structure stands uncompromisingly on top of a barren, rocky ridge in the hills south of Mellerstain. Built solely for defense, the 16th-century peel's stones are unadorned. If you let your imagination wander in this windy spot, you can almost see the flapping pennants and rising dust of an advancing raiding party and hear the anxious securing of doors and bolts. Sir Walter Scott found this spot inspiring. His grandfather lived at nearby Sandyknowe Farm (not open to the public), and the young Scott visited the tower often during his childhood. A museum here displays costumed figures and tapestries relating to Scott's Borders folk ballads. ✉ *Off B6404* ☎ *01573/460365* ⊕ *www. historic-scotland.gov.uk* 🎫 *£3* ⊘ *Apr.–Sept., daily 9:30–6:30; Oct., Sat.–Wed. 9:30–4:30; Nov.–Mar., weekends 9:30–4:30; last admission half hr before closing.*

Paxton House

❹ *19 mi northeast of Kelso.*

Stately Paxton House is a comely Palladian mansion designed in 1758 by James and John Adam, with interiors designed by their brother Robert. There is Chippendale and Trotter furniture, and the splendid Regency picture gallery, an outstation of the National Galleries of Scotland, has a magnificent collection of paintings. The garden is delightful, with a squirrel hide and a restored boathouse containing a museum of salmon fishing. The adjacent crafts shop and tearoom are open daily 9 to 5. ✉ *Paxton, 15 mi northeast of Coldstream, take A6112 and B6461* ☎ *01289/ 386291* ⊕ *www.paxtonhouse.com* 🎫 *Joint ticket for house and garden, £6; garden only, £3* ⊘ *Apr.–Oct., daily 11–5; last tour at 4:15.*

Manderston House

❺ *16 mi northeast of Kelso.*

Manderston House is a good example of the grand, no-expense-spared Edwardian country house. The family that built it made its fortune selling herring to Russia. A Georgian house from the 1790s was completely rebuilt from 1903 to 1905 to the specifications of John Kinross. The silver-plated staircase was modeled after the one in the Petit Trianon, at Versailles. Look for the collection of late-19th- and early-20th-century cookie tins. There's much to see downstairs in the kitchens, and outside, among other buildings, is the octagonal, one-of-a-kind marble dairy where lunch, dinner, or afternoon tea can be arranged for groups. You can reach the house by traveling northeast from Coldstream along the A6112 to Duns, then taking the A6105 east. ✉ *Off A6105* ☎ *01361/ 882636* 🖷 *01361/882010* ⊕ *www.manderston.co.uk* 🎫 *Grounds £3.50, house and grounds £7* ⊘ *House mid-May–Sept., Thurs. and Sun.1:30–5; grounds mid-May–Sept., Thurs. and Sun. 11:30–dusk.*

Dryburgh Abbey

★ ❻ *10 mi west of Kelso.*

The final resting place of Sir Walter Scott and his wife, and the most peaceful and secluded of the Borders abbeys, Dryburgh Abbey sits on gentle parkland in a loop of the Tweed. The abbey suffered from English raids until, like Melrose, it was abandoned in 1544. The style is transitional, a mingling of rounded Romanesque and pointed early English. The north transept, where the Haig and Scott families lie buried, is lofty and pillared, and once formed part of the abbey church. ✉ *On B6404,*

off A68 ☎ *01835/822381* ⊕ *www.historic-scotland.gov.uk* ✉ *£4*
🕙 *Apr.–Sept., daily 9:30–6:30; Oct.–Mar., daily 9:30–4:30.*

OFF THE
BEATEN
PATH

SCOTT'S VIEW – There's no escaping Sir Walter in this part of the country: 3 mi north of Dryburgh on the B6356 is possibly the most photographed rural view in the south of Scotland. The sinuous curve of the River Tweed and the gentle landscape unfolding to the triple peaks of the Eildons and then rolling out into shadows beyond are certainly worth seeking. You arrive at this peerless vista, where Scott often came to meditate, by taking the B6356 north from Dryburgh. A poignant tale is told about the horses of Scott's funeral cortege: on their way to Dryburgh Abbey they stopped here out of habit as they had so often in the past.

Where to Stay & Eat

£££–££££ ✕🏨 **Dryburgh Abbey Hotel.** Mature woodlands and verdant lawns surround this imposing, 19th-century mansion, which is adjacent to the abbey ruins on a sweeping bend of the River Tweed. Throughout the hotel you'll feel a sense of quiet and peace in keeping with the location. The rooms are large and sumptuous, with canopy beds and lace-trimmed curtains. The restaurant specializes in traditional Scottish fare such as roasted lamb or belly of pork. ✉ *Off B6404, St. Boswells, TD6 0RQ* ☎ *01835/822261* 🖨 *01835/823945* ⊕ *www.dryburgh.co.uk* 🛏 *36 rooms, 2 suites* ♿ *Restaurant, golf privileges, pool, fishing; no a/c* ▤ *AE, MC, V* ⫶◉⫶ *BP.*

Melrose

❼ *8 mi west of Dryburgh Abbey.*

Though it is small, there is nevertheless a bustle about Melrose, the perfect example of a prosperous Scottish market town and one of the loveliest in the Borders. It is set round a square lined with 18th- and 19th-century buildings housing myriad small shops and cafés. Despite its proximity to the much larger town of Galashiels (5 mi to the northwest, and still active with textile mills and knitwear shops), Melrose has rejected industrialization. You'll likely hear local residents greet each other by first name in the square.

★ Just off the square, down Abbey Street, sit the ruins of **Melrose Abbey,** one of the four Borders abbeys. "If thou would'st view fair Melrose aright, go visit it in the pale moonlight," wrote Scott in *The Lay of the Last Minstrel,* and so many of his fans took the advice literally that a sleepless custodian begged him to rewrite the lines. Today the abbey is still impressive: a red-sandstone shell with slender windows, delicate tracery, and carved capitals, all carefully maintained. Among the carvings high on the roof is one of a bagpipe-playing pig. An audio tour is included in the admission price. ✉ *Abbey St.* ☎ *01896/822562* ⊕ *www. historic-scotland.gov.uk* ✉ *£4.50* 🕙 *Apr.–Sept., daily 9:30–6:30; Oct.–Mar., daily 9:30–4:30; last entry half hr before closing.*

In 1811 Sir Walter Scott, already an established writer, bought a farm on this site named Cartleyhole, which was a euphemism for the real name, Clartyhole (*clarty* is Scots for "muddy" or "dirty"). The name was surely not romantic enough for Scott, who renamed the property **Abbotsford House** after a ford in the nearby Tweed used by the abbot of Melrose. Scott even-

Fodor'sChoice
★

The World of Sir Walter Scott

SIR WALTER SCOTT (1771-1832) was probably Scottish tourism's best propagandist. Thanks to his fervid "Romantik" imagination, his long narrative poems—such as *The Lady of the Lake*—and a long string of historical novels, including *Ivanhoe, Waverley, Rob Roy, Redgauntlet,* and *The Heart of Midlothian,* the world fell in love with the image of heroic Scotland. Scott wrote of Scotland as a place of Highland wilderness and clan romance, shaping outsiders' perceptions of Scotland in a way that to an extent survives even today.

Scott was born in College Wynd, Edinburgh. A lawyer by training, he was an assiduous collector of old ballads and tales. *The Lay of the Last Minstrel,* a romantic poem published in 1805, brought him fame. In 1811 Scott bought the house that was to become Abbotsford, his Borders mansion near Melrose.

Scott started on his series of Waverley novels in 1814, at first anonymously, and by 1820 had produced *Waverley, Guy Mannering, The Antiquary, Tales of My Landlord* (three series), and *Rob Roy.* Many of his verse narratives and novels focused on real-life settings, in particular the Trossachs, northwest of Stirling, an area that rapidly became, and still remains, popular with visitors.

Apart from his writing, Scott is also remembered for rediscovering the Honours of Scotland—the crown, scepter, and sword of state of the Scottish monarchs—in 1819. These symbols had languished at the bottom of a chest in Edinburgh Castle since 1707, when Scotland lost its independence. Today they are on display in the castle.

tually had the house entirely rebuilt in the Scots baronial style. The result was called "the most incongruous pile that gentlemanly modernism ever devised" by art critic John Ruskin. That was Mr. Ruskin's idiosyncratic take; most people have found this to be one of the most fetching of all Scottish abodes. A gently seedy mansion chock-full of Scottish curios, paintings, and mounted deer heads, it seems an appropriate domicile for a man of such an extraordinarily romantic imagination. It's worth visiting just to feel the atmosphere that the most successful writer of his day created and to see the condition in which he wrote, driving himself to pay off his endless debts. To Abbotsford came most of the famous poets and thinkers of Scott's day, including Wordsworth and Washington Irving. With some 9,000 volumes in the library, Abbotsford is the repository for the writer's collection of Scottish memorabilia and historic artifacts. Scott died here in 1832, and the house is today owned by his descendants. It's 2 mi west of Melrose. ⊠ *B6360, Galashiels* ☎ *01896/752043* ⊕ *www.scottsabbotsford.co.uk* 🎟 *£5* ⊗ *Late Mar.–May and Oct., Mon.–Sat. 9:30–5; June–Sept., daily 9:30–5.*

🗘 **Thirlestane Castle** is a large, turreted, and castellated house, part of which was built in the 13th century and part in the 16th century. It looks for all the world like a French château, and it brims with history. The former home of the Duke of Lauderdale (1616–82), one of Charles II's advisers, Thirlestane is said to be haunted by the duke's ghost. Exquisite 17th-century plaster ceilings and rich collections of paintings, porcelain, and furniture fill the rooms. In the nursery, children are invited to play with Victorian-style toys and to dress up in masks and costumes. Guided tours are available 11 to 2. ⊠ *Off A68, Lauder, 9 mi north of Melrose* ☎ *01578/722430* ⊕ *www.thirlestanecastle.co.uk* ⊠ *Grounds £3, castle and grounds £7* ⊗ *Mid-Apr.–June and Sept., Sun., Wed., Thurs. 10–3; July and Aug., Sun.–Thurs. 10–3.*

Where to Stay & Eat

££–£££ ✕ **Hoebridge Inn.** Whitewashed walls, oak-beamed ceilings, and an open
Fodor'sChoice fire welcome you into this converted 19th-century bobbin mill. The cui-
★ sine is a blend of British and Mediterranean styles with occasional Asian influences. You might have lamb served with rosemary mashed potatoes and red-currant sauce or panfried tiger prawns with chili and lime syrup, accompanied by a salad of bean sprouts and *mangetout* (peas in their edible pods). The inn lies in Gattonside, next to Melrose but a 2-mi drive along the B6360, thanks to the intervention of the Tweed; you can also reach the inn by a footbridge from the town. ⊠ *Off B360, Gattonside* ☎ *01896/823082* ⊕ *www.thehoebridgeinn.com* ☰ *MC, V* ⊗ *Closed Sun. evenings and Mon.*

££–£££ ✕⊞ **Burts Hotel.** This charming whitewashed building dating from the 18th century sits in the center of Melrose. Floral pastels fill the rooms and public areas. The bar is particularly welcoming, with a cheerful open fire and a wide selection of fine malt whiskies; it is ideal for a quiet dram before or after a meal. The vast restaurant has high-back upholstered chairs and white-linen tablecloths. Lamb with apple sauce and lentils or chicken breast with truffle foam are typical entrées on the prix-fixe, multicourse menu costing £32. Fishing can be arranged. ⊠ *Market Sq., TD6 9PL* ☎ *01896/822285* ⊠ *01896/822870* ⊕ *www.burtshotel.co.uk* ⊅ *20 rooms* ⚲ *Restaurant, fishing, bar; no a/c* ☰ *AE, MC, V* ⦿❘ *BP.*

The Arts

The Wynd Theatre (⊠ 3 Buccleuch St. ☎ 01896/823854) has a monthly program of four nights of drama from national touring companies, two concerts of folk, blues, jazz, or oratorio from touring national and international companies, plus classic films on two Fridays. There's also an art gallery highlighting top contemporary Scottish artists, plus a bar and nearby parking. Tickets cost £5 to £10 for performances or £5 for films.

Selkirk

➑ *7 mi south of Melrose.*

Selkirk is a hilly outpost with a smattering of antiques shops and an assortment of bakers selling the Selkirk Bannock (fruited sweet bread-cake) and other cakes. Sir Walter Scott was sheriff (judge) of Selkirkshire from 1800 until his death in 1832, and his statue stands in Market Place. **Sir Walter Scott's Courtroom,** where he presided, contains a display examining Scott's life, his writings, and his time on the bench, and it includes an audiovisual presentation. ⊠ *Market Pl.* ☎ *01750/20096* ⊠ *Free*

🕐 *Apr. and Sept., weekdays 10–4, Sat. 10–2; May–Aug., weekdays 10–4, weekends 2–4; Oct., Mon.–Sat. 1–4.*

Halliwell's House Museum, tucked off the main square in Selkirk, was once an ironmonger's shop, which is now re-created downstairs. Upstairs, an exhibit tells the town's tale, with useful background information on the Common Ridings. ✉ *Market Pl.* ☎ *01750/20096* 💷 *Free* 🕐 *Apr.–June and Sept., Mon.–Sat. 10–5, Sun. 10–noon; July and Aug., Mon.–Sat. 10–5, Sun. 10–1; Oct., Mon.–Sat. 10–4, Sun. 10–noon.*

The **Lochcarron of Scotland Cashmere and Wool Centre** houses a museum where you can learn about the manufacture of tartans and tweeds. ✉ *Waverley Mill, Rodgers Rd.* ☎ *01750/726000* ⊕ *www.lochcarron. com* 💷 *Free; tour £2.50* 🕐 *June–Sept., Mon.–Sat. 9–5, Sun. noon–5; Oct.–May, Mon.–Sat. 9–5. Guided tours Mon.–Thurs. at 9:30, 11:30, 1:30, and 2:30; Fri. at 10:30 and 11:30.*

Innerleithen

⑨ *15 mi northwest of Selkirk.*

🕐 The main reason to come to Innerleithen is to see **Robert Smail's Printing Works.** The fully operational, restored print shop with a reconstructed waterwheel fascinates adults and older children, who can try their hand at old-fashioned typesetting. ✉ *7–9 High St.* ☎ *01896/830206* 💷 *£5* 🕐 *Easter and June–Sept., Mon. and Thurs.–Sat. noon–5, Sun. 1–5; last admission at 4:15.*

Fodor'sChoice
★

Near the town of Innerleithen stands **Traquair House,** said to be the oldest continually occupied house in Scotland. Inside you are free to discover secret stairways, a maze, more than 3,000 books, and a bed used by Mary, Queen of Scots, in 1566. Ale is still brewed in the 18th-century brew house here, and it comes highly recommended. You may even spend the night, if you wish. ✉ *B709, Traquair, 1 mi from Innerleithen* ☎ *01896/830323* 🖷 *01896/830639* ⊕ *www.traquair.co.uk* 💷 *Grounds £3.50, house and grounds £6.20* 🕐 *Easter–May and Sept., daily noon–5; June–Aug., daily 10:30–5; Oct., daily 11–4; Nov., weekends noon–4; last admission half hr before closing.*

Where to Stay

££££ 🏨 **Traquair House.** To stay in one of the guest rooms in the 12th-century part of Traquair House is to experience a slice of Scottish history. Each spacious room is individually decorated with antiques and canopied beds. During your stay you may explore those parts of the house that are open to the public, or walk in the parkland and gardens. In the 18th-century lower drawing room you can savor a glass

> **WORD OF MOUTH**
>
> "Traquair House, while not a castle, is a very large manor house still inhabited by the Maxwell-Stuarts and very interesting. There are relics of Mary, Queen of Scots on display, including her crucifix. A working brewery turns out excellent beer."   –Underhill

of the house ale before an open fire. Dinner can be arranged. ⊠ *B709, Traquair, EH44 6PW* ☎ *01896/830323* 🖷 *01896/830639* ⊕ *www. traquair.co.uk* ⌐ *3 rooms* ⌂ *Dining room; no a/c* ⊟ *MC, V* ⍗⌐ *BP.*

Peebles

🔟 *6 mi west of Innerleithen.*

Thanks to its excellent though pricey shopping, Peebles gives the impression of catering primarily to leisured country gentlefolk. Architecturally the town is nothing out of the ordinary, just a very pleasant burgh. Don't miss the splendid dolphins ornamenting the bridge crossing the River Tweed.

Neidpath Castle, a 15-minute walk upstream along the banks of the Tweed, perches artistically above a bend in the river. It comes into view as you approach through the tall trees. The castle is a medieval structure remodeled in the 17th century, with dungeons hewn from solid rock. You can return on the opposite riverbank after crossing an old railroad viaduct. ⊠ *Off A72* ☎ *01721/720333* 🖷 *£3* ☉ *July–early Sept., Mon.–Sat. 10:30–5, Sun. 12:30–5; last admission half hr before closing.*

Where to Stay & Eat

£££££ ╳🖬 **Peebles Hydro.** Not only does the Hydro have something for everyone, but it has it in abundance: pony rides, a putting green, and a giant chess and checkers game are just a few of the diversions. The elegant Edwardian building stands on 30 acres of land, and you are welcome to explore every inch. The public areas and most rooms have lofty ceilings and elegant, antique-reproduction furnishings. The restaurant has a Scottish menu that includes local salmon, lamb, and beef. ⊠ *Innerleithen Rd., EH45 8LX* ☎ *01721/720602* 🖷 *01721/722999* ⊕ *www. peebleshotelhydro.com* ⌐ *132 rooms* ⌂ *Restaurant, cable TV, putting green, tennis court, pool, gym, hair salon, hot tub, sauna, steam room, fishing, bicycles, badminton, billiards, horseback riding, bar, recreation room, babysitting, children's programs (ages infant–16), playground, laundry service; no a/c* ⊟ *AE, DC, MC, V* ⍗⌐ *BP.*

FodorsChoice ★

★ **£££–££££** ╳🖬 **Cringletie House.** With medieval-style turrets and crow-step gables, this small-scale, peaceful retreat manages to be fancy *and* homey, Victorian (it was built in the 1860s), and modern (flat-screen TVs). A British-country-house style predominates. Some of the individually decorated bedrooms have fireplaces and four-posters, and all overlook the 28-acre grounds. From the drawing room there are views over the valley. A walled garden grows produce used in the excellent restaurant, which draws locals for Scottish fare such as boned quail stuffed with trompette mushrooms, and loin of deer from the neighboring estate. The afternoon tea, served in the conservatory, is especially recommended. ⊠ *Edinburgh Rd., off A703, EH45 8PL* ☎ *01721/725750* 🖷 *01721/730244* ⊕ *www. cringletie.com* ⌐ *14 rooms* ⌂ *Restaurant, cable TV, in-room data ports, putting green, tennis court, fishing, croquet, lounge, babysitting, some pets allowed; no a/c* ⊟ *AE, MC, V* ⍗⌐ *BP.*

14

Shopping

Be prepared for temptations at every turn as you browse the shops on High Street and in the courts and side streets leading off it. The German-born and Swiss-trained watchmaker Jurgen Tubbecke sells his handcrafted chronometers at the **Clockmaker** (⊠ 3 High St. ☎ 01721/723599). **Head to Toe** (⊠ 43 High St. ☎ 01721/722752) stocks natural beauty products, handmade pine furniture, and handsome linens—from patchwork quilts to silk flowers. Among the many jewelers on High Street is **Keith Walter** (⊠ 28 High St. ☎ 01721/720650), a gold- and silversmith who makes items on the premises. He also stocks jewelry made by other local designers. If you need a rest after a heavy day of shopping, repair to the **Simply Delicious** (⊠ 56 High St. ☎ 01721/720630), a gift store with a coffee shop upstairs overlooking bustling High Street. There are also cooking and garden departments.

DUMFRIES & GALLOWAY

Galloway covers the southwestern portion of Scotland, west of the main town of Dumfries. Here a gentle coastline gives way to farmland and then breezy uplands that gradually merge with coniferous forests. Use caution when negotiating the A75—you are liable to find aggressive trucks bearing down on you as these commercial vehicles race for the ferries at Stranraer and Cairnryan. Trucks notwithstanding, once you are off the main roads, Dumfries and Galloway offer some of the most pleasant drives in Scotland—though the occasional herd of cows on the way to be milked is a potential hazard.

Gretna Green

⓫ *10 mi north of Carlisle, 87 mi south of Glasgow, 92 mi southwest of Edinburgh.*

Gretna Green is, quite simply, an embarrassment to native Scots. What else can you say about a place that advertises "amusing joke weddings," as does one of the visitor centers here? These strange goings-on are tied to the reputation this community developed as a refuge for runaway couples from England, who once came north to take advantage of Scotland's more lenient marriage laws. This was the first place they reached on crossing the border. At one time anyone could perform a legal marriage in Scotland, and the village blacksmith (known as the "anvil priest") did the honors in Gretna Green. The blacksmith's shop is still standing, and today it contains a collection of blacksmithing tools, including the anvil over which many weddings were conducted.

Golf

Powfoot. A pleasant mix of links and parkland holes (nine of each) and views south over the Solway Firth to distract you make this lesser-known British Championship course a pleasure to play. The course is 7 mi west of Gretna Green, and greens fees are £33 to £55. ⊠ *Powfoot Golf Club, Cummertrees, Annan* ☎ *01461/700276* ⊕ *www.powfootgolfclub. com* ⚑ *18 holes, 6,266 yds, SSS 71* ☉ *Weekdays and Sun. after 1.*

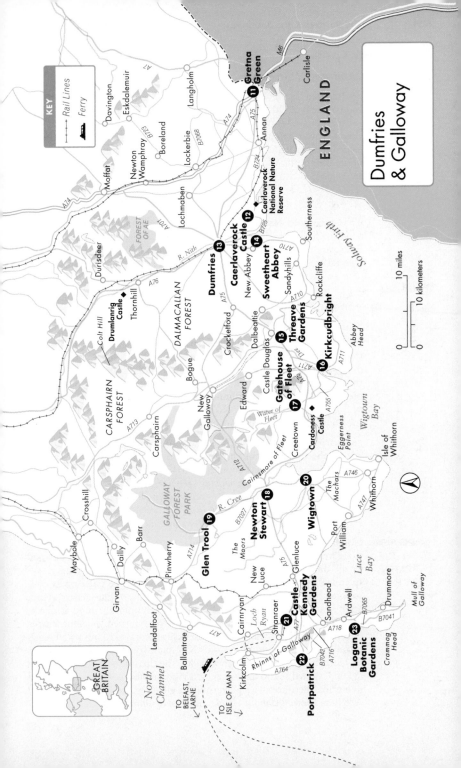

Dumfries & Galloway

KEY
- Rail Lines
- Ferry

ENGLAND

Carlisle

11 Gretna Green

Davington
Eskdalemuir
Langholm
Moffat
Newton Wamphray
Boreland
Lockerbie
Annan
Durisdeer
Lochmaben
Thornhill
Drumlanrig Castle
Colt Hill
12 Caerlaverock National Nature Reserve
13 Dumfries
14 Caerlaverock Castle
New Abbey
14 Sweetheart Abbey
Southerness
Sandyhills
Rockcliffe
Crockefford
Dalbeattie
15 Threave Gardens
16 Kirkcudbright
Abbey Head
Bogue
Castle Douglas
Edward
New Galloway
17 Gatehouse of Fleet
Cardoness Castle
Creetown
Water of Fleet
Eggerness Point
Isle of Whithorn
Carsphairn
CARSPHAIRN FOREST
DALMACALLAN FOREST
FOREST OF AE
Crosshill
Barr
Cairnsmore of Fleet
GALLOWAY FOREST PARK
18 Newton Stewart
20 Wigtown
The Machars
Whithorn
Maybole
Dailly
Pinwherry
19 Glen Trool
The Moors
New Luce
Glenluce
Port William
Luce Bay
Girvan
Lendalfoot
Ballantrae
Crosshill
Cairnryan
Loch Ryan
Stranraer
21 Castle Kennedy Gardens
Sandhead
Ardwell
Drummore
Mull of Galloway
Crammag Head
23 Logan Botanic Gardens
22 Portpatrick
Kirkcolm
Rhinns of Galloway
North Channel
TO BELFAST, LARNE
TO ISLE OF MAN

GREAT BRITAIN

Solway Firth
Wigtown Bay

10 miles
10 kilometers
0

Caerlaverock Castle

⑫ *26 mi west of Gretna Green.*

Fodor's Choice
★

The moated Caerlaverock Castle overlooks a nature reserve on a coastal loop of the B725. Built in a triangular design unique to Britain, this 13th-century moated fortress has solid-sandstone masonry and an imposing double-tower gatehouse. King Edward I of England (1239–1307) besieged the castle in 1300, when his forces occupied much of Scotland at the start of the Wars of Independence. The castle suffered many times in Anglo-Scottish skirmishes, as the video presentation attests. ⊠ *Off B725* ☎ *01387/770244* ⊕ *www.historic-scotland.gov.uk* ⊡ *£4.50* ⊙ *Apr.–Sept., daily 9:30–6:30; Oct.–Mar., daily 9:30–4:30.*

The **Caerlaverock National Nature Reserve** lets you observe wintering wild-fowl, including various species of geese, ducks, swans, and raptors. There are free guided walks throughout the year. ⊠ *Off B725, east of Caerlaverock Castle* ☎ *01387/770275* ⊡ *Free* ⊙ *Daily 24 hrs.*

Dumfries

⑬ *8 mi north of Caerlaverock Castle, 76 mi south of Glasgow, 81 mi southwest of Edinburgh.*

Author J. M. Barrie (1860–1937) spent his childhood in Dumfries, and the garden of Moat Brae House is said to have inspired his boyish dreams in *Peter Pan*. The River Nith meanders through Dumfries, and the pedestrians-only town center makes wandering and shopping a pleasure. The town also contains the Globe Inn, a favorite *howff* (pub) of Scotland's national poet Robert Burns (1759–96), as well as one of the houses he lived in and his mausoleum.

Not surprisingly, in view of its close association to the poet, Dumfries has a **Robert Burns Centre,** housed in a sturdy former mill overlooking the river. The center has an audiovisual program and an extensive exhibit on the life of the poet. During the Dumfries Festival, held late May through early June, films are screened in the theater. ⊠ *Mill Rd.* ☎ *01387/264808 or 01387/263666* ⊡ *Free; £1.60 for audiovisual show* ⊙ *Apr.–Sept., Mon.–Sat. 10–8, Sun. 2–5.*

OFF THE BEATEN PATH

DRUMLANRIG CASTLE – This spectacular estate is as close as Scotland gets to the treasure houses of England—which is not surprising, since it's owned by the dukes of Buccleuch, one of the wealthiest British peerages. Resplendent with romantic turrets, this pink-sandstone palace was constructed between 1679 and 1691 by the first duke of Queensbury, who, after nearly bankrupting himself building the place, found it disappointing on his first overnight stay and never returned. The Buccleuchs inherited the palace and soon filled the richly decorated rooms with French furniture from the period of Louis XIV, family portraits, and paintings by Holbein, Rembrandt, and Murillo. The theft of a da Vinci painting in 2003, valued at £30 million, means visits are now conducted by guided tour only. There are also a playground, a gift shop, and a tearoom. ⊠ *Off A76 near Thornhill, about 18 mi northwest of Dumfries* ☎ *01848/600283*

⊕ *www.buccleuch.com* ⬛ *Park £4, castle and park £7* ☉ *May and June, Sat.–Thurs. noon–4; July and Aug., daily noon–4.*

The Arts

Gracefield Arts Centre (✉ 28 Edinburgh Rd. ☎ 01387/262084) has galleries with constantly changing exhibits. The **Dumfries and Galloway Arts Festival** (☎ 01387/260447 ⊕ www.dgartsfestival.org.uk) is usually held at the end of May at several venues throughout the region.

Biking

Cycles can be rented from **G&G Cycle Centre** (✉ 10–12 Academy St. ☎ 01387/259483). The staff gives advice on where to ride.

Shopping

Dumfries is the main shopping center for the region, with all the big-name chain stores as well as specialty shops. **Greyfriars Crafts** (✉ 56 Buccleuch St. ☎ 01387/264050) sells mainly Scottish goods, including glass, ceramics, and jewelry. For a souvenir that's easy to pack, try **David Hastings** (✉ Maryng, Shieldhill, near Amisfield ☎ 01387/710451), with more than 100,000 old postcards and postal history items. The store is open weekdays 10 to 3 or by appointment. The shop is in a house called Maryng in a group of houses called Shieldhill.

New Abbey

7 mi south of Dumfries, 83 mi south of Glasgow, 88 mi southwest of Edinburgh.

At the center of the village of New Abbey is the red-tinted and roofless **⑭ Sweetheart Abbey.** The odd name is a translation of the abbey's previous name, St. Mary of the Dolce Coeur. The abbey was founded in 1273 by the Lady of Galloway, Devorgilla (1210–90), in memory of her husband, John Balliol (?–1269), who was buried in Bardard Castle in England. It is said Devorgilla had his heart embalmed and placed in a tiny casket that she carried everywhere. After she died, Devorgilla was laid to rest before the High Altar of Sweetheart Abbey with the casket resting on her breast. The couple's son, also named John (1249–1315), was the puppet king installed in Scotland by Edward of England when the latter claimed sovereignty over Scotland. After John's appointment the Scots gave him a scathing nickname that would stay with him for the rest of his life: Toom Tabard (Empty Shirt). ✉ *A710 at New Abbey* ☎ *01387/850397* ⬛ *£2.50* ☉ *Apr.–Sept., daily 9:30–6:30; Oct.–Mar., Sat.–Wed. 9:30–4:30.*

Castle Douglas

6 mi west of Dalbeattie.

★ ⑮ The main reason to come to this pleasant town is to visit **Threave Gardens.** The National Trust for Scotland cares for several garden properties, including the sloping parkland around the mansion house of Threave. This horticultural undertaking demands the employment of many gardeners—and it is at Threave that the gardeners train, thus ensuring there is always some fresh development or experimental planting here.

You can stop by the restaurant and visitor center as well. ✉ *South of A75, 1 mi west of Castle Douglas* ☎ *01556/502575* ⊕ *www.nts.org. uk* ✉ *Gardens £5, house and gardens £9* ⊙ *Gardens and estate daily 9:30–sunset; visitor center Feb., Mar., Nov., and Dec., daily 10–4; Apr.–Oct., daily 9:30–5:30.*

Threave Castle, not to be confused with the mansion in Threave Gardens, was an early home of the Black Douglases, who were the earls of Niths-dale and lords of Galloway. The castle was dismantled in the religious wars of the mid-17th century, though enough of it remains to have housed prisoners from the Napoléonic Wars of the 19th century. It's a few minutes from Castle Douglas by car and is signposted from the main road. To get there, you must leave your car in a farmyard and walk the rest of the way. Make your way down to the reeds by the river on an occasionally muddy path. At the edge of the river you can then ring a bell, and, rather romantically, a boatman will come to ferry you across to the great stone tower looming from a marshy island in the river. ✉ *North of A75, 3 mi west of Castle Douglas* ☎ *07711/223101* ✉ *£3.50, includes ferry* ⊙ *Apr.–Sept., daily 9:30–6:30.*

Sports & the Outdoors

BIKING You can rent bicycles from **Castle Douglas Cycle Centre** (✉ Church St. ☎ 01556/504542).

BOATING The **Galloway Sailing Centre** (✉ Loch Ken ☎ 01644/420626) rents dinghies, kayaks, and canoes. It also offers sailing, windsurfing, canoeing, mountain biking, archery, and rock-climbing courses.

Shopping

It's well worth the short drive north from Castle Douglas (A75 then B794) to visit **Benny Gillies Books, Maps and Prints** (✉ 31–33 Victoria St., Kirkpatrick Durham ☎ 01556/650412 ⊕ www.bennygillies.co.uk). The shop has an outstanding selection of secondhand and antiquarian Scottish books, hand-colored antique maps, and prints depicting areas throughout Scotland.

Galloway Gems (✉ 130–132 King St. ☎ 01556/503254) sells mineral specimens, polished stone slices, and a range of Celtic- and Nordic-inspired jewelry. The **Posthorn** (✉ 26–30 St. Andrew St. ☎ 01556/502531) is renowned for its display of figurines by Border Fine Art as well as Scotland's biggest display of Moorcroft glazed and enamel pottery.

Kirkcudbright

16 *11 mi southwest of Castle Douglas, 103 mi south of Glasgow, 109 mi southwest of Edinburgh.*

Kirkcudbright (pronounced "Kirk-*coo*-bray"), on an estuary of the River Dee, is an 18th-century town of Georgian and Victorian houses, some of them washed in pastel shades and roofed with the blue slates of the district. A fishing town, since the early 20th century it has also been known as a haven for artistic types, and its L-shape main street is full of crafts and antiques shops. The **Tolbooth Arts Centre,** in the old tolbooth, gives a history of the town's artists' colony and its leaders, E. A.

Hornel, Jessie King, and Charles Oppenheimer. Some of their paintings are on display, as are works by modern artists and craftspeople. ⊠ *High St.* ☎ *01557/331556* ⌨ *Free* ⊙ *Oct.–Apr., Mon.–Sat. 11–4; May, June, and Sept., Mon.–Sat. 11–5, Sun. 2–5; July and Aug., Mon.–Sat. 10–6, Sun. 2–5.*

14

The 18th-century **Broughton House** was once the home of the artist E. A. Hornel, one of the "Glasgow Boys" of the late 19th century. Many of his paintings hang in the house, which is furnished in period style and contains an extensive library specializing in local history. There's also a Japanese garden. ⊠ *12 High St.* ☎ *01557/330437* ⊕ *www.nts.org. uk* ⌨ *£5* ⊙ *Easter–June and Sept. and Oct., daily noon–5; July and Aug., daily 10–5.*

Conspicuous in the town center are the stone walls of **MacLellan's Castle,** a once-elaborate castellated mansion dating from the 16th century. You can walk around the interior, though the rooms are bare. There are lovely views over the town from the windows. ⊠ *Off High St.* ☎ *01557/ 331856* ⌨ *£2.50* ⊙ *Apr.–Sept., daily 9:30–6:30.*

Stuffed with local paraphernalia, the delightfully old-fashioned **Stewartry Museum** allows you to putter and absorb as much or as little as takes your interest in the display cases. ⊠ *St. Mary St.* ☎ *01557/331643* ⌨ *Free* ⊙ *Oct.–Apr., Mon.–Sat. 11–4; May–Sept., Mon.–Sat. 10–6, Sun. 2–5.*

Gatehouse of Fleet

⓱ *9 mi west of Kirkcudbright, 108 mi southwest of Glasgow, 114 mi southwest of Edinburgh.*

A peaceful, pleasant backwoods sort of place, Gatehouse of Fleet has a castle guarding its southern approach. **Cardoness Castle** is a typical Scottish tower house, severe and uncompromising. The 15th-century structure once was the home of the McCullochs of Galloway, then the Gordons—two of the area's important and occasionally infamous families. ⊠ *A75, 1 mi southwest of Gatehouse of Fleet* ☎ *01557/814427* ⊕ *www.historic-scotland.gov.uk* ⌨ *£3* ⊙ *Apr.–Sept., daily 9:30–6:30; Oct., Sat.–Wed. 9:30–4:30; Nov.–Mar., weekends 9:30–4:30.*

The **Mill on the Fleet** is a converted mill in which you can learn the history behind this small town's involvement in the cotton industry. Arts and crafts are exhibited, and the tearoom serves light lunches and delicious home-baked goods. ⊠ *High St.* ☎ *01557/814774* ⌨ *£2.75* ⊙ *Easter–Oct., daily 10:30–5.*

Where to Stay

£££–£££££ ▥ **Cally Palace.** Many of the public rooms in this Georgian hotel, built in 1763 as a private mansion, retain their original grandeur, with elaborate plaster ceilings and marble fireplaces. The bedrooms are individually decorated and well equipped with plush robes and a complimentary bottle of sherry. Surrounding the house are 150 acres of parkland, with gardens, a loch, and a golf course. In the restaurant, local ingredients star in such dishes as seared medallions of venison. The staff is exceptionally friendly and prepared to spoil you. ⊠ *Off A75, DG7 2DL* ☎ *01557/814341* 🖹 *01557/814522* ⊕ *www.mcmillanhotels.co.uk* ➪ *56 rooms* ⌂ *Restaurant, cable TV, 18-hole golf course, putting green, tennis court, pool, hot tub, sauna, bicycles, billiards, croquet, bar; no a/c in some rooms* ⊟ *AE, MC, V* ⊘ *Closed Jan. and Feb.* ⊺◯⊺ *MAP.*

£ 🖾 **High Auchenlarie Farmhouse.** You are sure to get a hearty breakfast at this 300-year-old working cattle ranch—sausage, bacon, eggs, and grilled tomatoes are on the menu, although lighter options are also available. Set high on a hillside overlooking Wigtown Bay, the B&B provides tremendous views—on a clear day you can see all the way to the Isle of Man. The rooms have solid-wood furniture that adds to the country feel. ⊠ *DG7 2HB* ☎ *01557/840231* ➪ *3 rooms* ⌂ *Dining room; no a/c, no room phones* ⊟ *No credit cards* ⊘ *Closed Nov.–Feb.* ⊺◯⊺ *BP.*

Newton Stewart

⓲ *20 mi west of Gatehouse of Fleet, 89 mi southwest of Glasgow, 108 mi southwest of Edinburgh.*

The bustling town of Newton Stewart makes a good touring base for the western region of Galloway. The A712 heading northeast from town takes you to the **Galloway Forest Park,** where you can walk or bicycle along the paths. At the Clatteringshaws Visitor Centre there are exhibits about the region's wildlife and a reconstruction of an Iron Age dwelling. ⊠ *A712, 7 mi northeast of Newton Stewart* ☎ *01671/402420* ⊕ *www.cast.org.uk/clatteringshaws.htm* 🖺 *Free* ⊘ *Apr.–Sept., daily 10:30–5; Oct., daily 10:30–4:30.*

Birders may prefer the **Wood of Cree Nature Reserve,** owned and managed by the Royal Society for the Protection of Birds. To get there, take the minor road that travels north from Newton Stewart alongside the River Cree east of the A714. The entrance is next to a small parking area at the side of the road. In the reserve you can see such species as the redstart, pied flycatcher, and wood warbler. ⊠ *4 mi north of Newton Stewart* ☎ *01671/402861* 🖺 *Donations accepted* ⊘ *Daily 24 hrs.*

Glen Trool

★ ⓳ *12 mi north of Newton Stewart, 77 mi southwest of Glasgow, 96 mi southwest of Edinburgh.*

Glen Trool is one of Scotland's best-kept secrets. With high purple-and-green hilltops shorn rock-bare by glaciers, and with a dark, winding loch and thickets of birch trees sounding with birdcalls, the setting almost looks more highland than the real Highlands. Note **Bruce's Stone,** just above the parking lot, marking the site where in 1307 Scotland's champion Robert the Bruce (King Robert I, 1274–1329) won his first victory in the Scottish Wars of Independence. To get here, follow the A714 north and turn right at the signpost for Glen Trool. This road leads you toward the hills that have thus far been the backdrop for the woodlands. Watch for another sign for Glen Trool. Follow this little road through increasingly wild woodland scenery to its terminus at a parking lot. Only after you have left the car and climbed for a few minutes onto a heathery knoll does the full, rugged panorama become apparent. ⊠ *Bargrennan* ☎ *01671/840302* ◷ *Mar.–Sept., daily 10–5; Oct., weekdays 10:30–4, weekends 10–4:30* ◩ *Free.*

EN ROUTE
The **Machars** is the name given to the triangular promontory south of Newton Stewart. This is an area of pretty rolling farmlands, yellow-gorse hedgerows, rich grazing for dairy cattle, and stony prehistoric sites. Most of the glossy, green expanse is used for dairy farming. Fields are bordered by dry *stane dykes* (dry walling) of sharp-edge stones, and small hills and hummocks give the area its characteristic frozen-wave look, a reminder of the glacial activity that shaped the landscape.

14

Wigtown

❷⓿ *8 mi south of Newton Stewart, 96 mi southwest of Glasgow, 114 mi southwest of Edinburgh.*

More than 20 bookshops, mostly antiquarian, specialized and secondhand stores, have sprung up on the brightly painted main street of Wigtown, voted Scotland's national book town. In an area of grassy marshland near the muddy shores of Wigtown Bay there's a monument to the Wigtown Martyrs, two women who were tied to a stake and left to drown in the incoming tide in 1685, during Covenanting times. Dumfries and Galloway's history is inextricably linked with the ferocity of the so-called Killing Times (roughly 1650–99), when the Covenanters were persecuted for their belief that there should be no bishops in the Church of Scotland, and that the king should not be head of the church.

The 10-day **Wigtown Literary Festival** (☎ 01988/403222 ⊕ www.wigtownbooktown.co.uk), held in late September, has readings, performances, and other events around town. The **Bookshop** (⊠ 17 N. Main St. ☎ 01988/402499), one of the country's largest secondhand bookstores, offers temptingly full shelves.

Wigtown's **Bladnoch Distillery** is Scotland's southernmost malt whisky producer. It has a visitor center and a gift shop, and tours are available. ⊠ *Wigtown* ☎ *01988/402605 or 01988/402235* ⊕ *www.bladnoch. co.uk* ◩ *Free; tours £1* ◷ *Easter–June and Sept. and Oct., weekdays and holidays 9–5; July and Aug., weekdays 9–5, Sat. 11–5, Sun. noon–5.*

Stranraer

23 mi west of Wigtown, 89 mi southwest of Glasgow via A77, 133 mi southwest of Edinburgh.

Stranraer is also the main ferry port to Northern Ireland—if you happen to make a purchase in one of its shops, you may wind up with some euro coins from Ireland in your change.

★ ㉑ The **Castle Kennedy Gardens** surround the shell of the original Castle Kennedy, which was burned in 1716. The current 14th earl of Stair lives on the grounds in Lochinch Castle, built in 1864 (not open to the public). Parks scattered around the property were built by the second earl of Stair in 1733. The earl was a field marshal and used his soldiers to help with the heavy work of constructing banks, ponds, and other major landscape features. When the rhododendrons are in bloom, the effect is kaleidoscopic. There's also a pleasant tearoom. ⊠ *North of A75, 3 mi east of Stranraer* ☎ *01776/702024* ⊕ *www.castlekennedygardens. co.uk* 🖅 *£4* ⊙ *Easter–Sept., daily 10–5.*

Portpatrick

㉒ *8 mi southwest of Stranraer, 97 mi southwest of Glasgow, 143 mi southwest of Edinburgh.*

The holiday town of Portpatrick lies across the Rhinns of Galloway from Stranraer. Once an Irish ferry port, Portpatrick's harbor eventually proved too small for larger vessels. Today the village is the starting point for Scotland's longest official long-distance footpath, the **Southern Upland Way,** which runs a switchback course for 212 mi to Cockburnspath, on the east side of the Borders. The path begins on the cliffs just north of the town and follows the coastline for 1½ mi before turning inland. Just south of Portpatrick are the lichen-yellow ruins of 16th-century **Dunskey Castle,** accessible from a cliff-top path off the B7042.

★ ㉓ The spectacular **Logan Botanic Gardens,** one of the National Botanic Gardens of Scotland, are a must-see for garden lovers. Displayed here are plants that enjoy the prevailing mild climate, especially tree ferns, cabbage palms, and other southern-hemisphere exotica. ⊠ *Off B7065 at Port Logan* ☎ *01776/860231* 🖅 *£3.50* ⊙ *Mar. and Oct., daily 10–5; May–Sept., daily 10–6.*

To visit the southern tip of the Rhinns of Galloway, called the **Mull of Galloway,** follow the B7065/B7041 until you run out of land. The cliffs and seascapes are rugged, and there is a lighthouse and a bird reserve.

BORDERS & THE SOUTHWEST ESSENTIALS

Transportation

BY AIR

The nearest Scottish airports are at Edinburgh, Glasgow, and Prestwick (outside of Glasgow).

BY BOAT & FERRY

P&O European Ferries runs a service from Larne, in Northern Ireland, to Cairnryan, near Stranraer, several times daily. The crossing takes 1 hour on the "Superstar Express" service, 1¾ hours on other services. Stena Line operates a ferry service between Stranraer and Belfast.
🎵 P&O European Ferries ☎ 0870/242777 ⊕ wwwpoirishsea.com. **Stena Line** ☎ 08705/707070 ⊕ www.stenaline.com.

BY BUS

If you're approaching from the south, contact Scottish Citylink or National Express. For bus links from Edinburgh and Glasgow contact First or Stagecoach Western. Stagecoach Western serves towns and villages in Dumfries and Galloway.

🚌 **First** ☎ 0870/872-7271 ⊕ www.firstbus.co.uk. **National Express** ☎ 08705/808080 ⊕ www.nationalexpress.com. **Scottish Citylink** ☎ 08705/505050 ⊕ www.citylink.co. uk. **Stagecoach Western** ☎ 01387/253496 in Dumfries, 01563/525192 in Kilmarnock, 01776/ 704484 in Stranraer ⊕ www.stagecoachbus.com.

BY CAR

The main route into both the Borders and Galloway from the south is the M6, which becomes the M74 at the border. Or you can take the scenic and leisurely A7 northeastward through Hawick toward Edinburgh or the A75 and other parallel routes westward into Dumfries and Galloway and to the ferry ports of Stranraer and Cairnryan.

There are, however, several other routes: starting from the east, the A1 brings you from the English city of Newcastle to the border in about an hour. The A1 has the added attraction of Berwick-Upon-Tweed, on the English side of the border, but traffic on the route is heavy. Moving west, the A697, which leaves the A1 north of Morpeth (in England) and crosses the border at Coldstream, is a leisurely back-road option. The A68 is probably the most scenic route to Scotland: after climbing to Carter Bar, it reveals a view of the Borders hills and windy skies before dropping into the ancient town of Jedburgh. If you're driving on narrow country roads, allow plenty of time even though distances aren't long.

BY TRAIN

There is no train service in the Borders, apart from the Edinburgh–London King's Cross line. Trains stop at Berwick-Upon-Tweed, just south of the border. First Edinburgh has a bus service linking Hawick, Selkirk, and Galashiels with rail services at Carlisle, Edinburgh, and Berwick.

There is only limited service in the Southwest. Trains from London's Euston to Glasgow stop at Carlisle, just south of the border, and some also stop at Lockerbie. There are direct trains from Carlisle to Dumfries and the Nith Valley, stopping at Gretna Green and Annan. From Glasgow, there are services to Stranraer, the Nith Valley, and Dumfries.

🚆 **First Edinburgh** ☎ 0131/663-9233 or 0870/608-2608 ⊕ www.firstgroup.com. **National Rail** ☎ 08457/484950 ⊕ www.nationalrail.co.uk.

Contacts & Resources

EMERGENCIES

Dial **999** for an ambulance, the police, or the fire department (no coins are needed for emergency calls from public telephone booths). All towns in the region have at least one pharmacy. Pharmacies are not found in rural areas, where general practitioners often dispense medicine. The police will provide assistance in locating a pharmacist in an emergency.

INTERNET

Unless your hotel or B&B offers access, the best places for checking e-mail in this region are public libraries. They're free, and if you call in advance you can book a computer ahead of time.

📶 Internet Cafés @ CyberCafe ⊠ 8-10 Devonshire St., Carlisle ☎ 01228/512308 ⊕ www.atcybercafe.co.uk. Ewart Library ⊠ Catherine St., Dumfries ☎ 01387/253820 ⊕ www.ewart.org. Lochside Library ⊠ Lochside Rd., Dumfries ☎ 01387/268751 ⊕ www.dgcommunity.net.

SPORTS & THE OUTDOORS

FISHING The *Scottish Borders Angling Guide* is the best way to find your way around the many Borders waterways. *Fishing in Dumfries and Galloway* covers the Southwest. The tourist boards for Dumfries and Galloway and the Borders carry these and other publications, as well as a comprehensive information pack.

GOLF There are more than 30 courses in Dumfries and Galloway and 21 in the Borders. The Freedom of the Fairways Pass (five-day pass, £95; three-day pass, £69) allows play on all 21 Borders courses and is available from the Scottish Borders Tourist Board. The Gateway to Golf Pass (10-round pass, £100; 6-round pass, £80) is accepted by all clubs in Dumfries and Galloway.

TOUR OPTIONS

Tours of the region are primarily conducted by Edinburgh- and Glasgow-based companies. James French runs coach tours in the summer. Margot McMurdo arranges custom-tailored, chauffeur-driven tours, and golf and fishing packages. Her "Splendour of Scott Country" tour covers the Borders area.

📶 James French ⊠ French's Garage, Coldingham ☎ 01890/771283 ⊕ www. jamesfrenchandson.com. Margot McMurdo ⊠ Tweedview Farmhouse, Oliver Farm, Tweedsmuir ☎🖨 01899/880207 ⊕ www.aboutscotland.com/tour/guide/margot.html.

VISITOR INFORMATION

The Scottish Borders Tourist Board has offices in Jedburgh and Peebles, and the Dumfries and Galloway Tourist Board can be found in Dumfries and Stranraer. Seasonal information centers are at Castle Douglas, Gatehouse of Fleet, Gretna Green, Hawick, Kelso, Kirkcudbright, Melrose, Newton Stewart, and Selkirk.

📶 Dumfries and Galloway Tourist Board ⊠ 64 Whitesands, Dumfries DG1 2RS ☎ 01387/253862 ⊠ 26 Harbour St., Stranraer DG9 7RA ☎ 01776/702595 ⊕ www. dumfriesandgalloway.co.uk. Scottish Borders Tourist Board ⊠ Murray's Green, Jedburgh TD8 6BE ☎ 0870/608-0404 ⊠ High St. Peebles, EH45 8AG ☎ 0870/608-0404 ⊕ www.scot-borders.co.uk.

The Central Highlands, Fife & Angus

WORD OF MOUTH

"If you want to visit places with links to Wallace and Rob Roy . . . forget everything you saw in the films with Mel Gibson and Liam Neeson. . . . The National Wallace Monument on a hill near Stirling can be seen from miles away. . . . For Rob Roy you're looking at the Trossachs, easily accessible from Stirling . . . [and] his grave at Balquhidder."
—Craigellachie

"We visited both Glamis and Falkland castles and LOVED both. However, we were completely taken with Falkland Palace and the grounds. Either way, though, you can't go wrong!"
—Ani

Updated by
Shona Main
and Nick
Bruno

STAND ON STIRLING CASTLE ROCK TO SURVEY the whole Central Highlands region, and you will see Scotland coast to coast. This is where Scotland draws in her waist, from the Clyde in the west to the Forth in the east. You can judge just how near the area is to the well-populated Midland Valley by looking out from the ramparts of Edinburgh Castle: the Highland hills, which meander around the Trossachs region and above Callander, are clearly visible.

The Romantic poets, especially William Wordsworth (1770–1850), sang the praises of the Trossachs, but it was Sir Walter Scott (1771–1832) who definitively put this area on the tourist map by setting his 1810 dramatic verse narrative, *The Lady of the Lake,* in the landscape of the Trossach hills. Scott's verse was an immediate and huge success, and visitors flooded in to trace the events of the poem across the region. The poem mentions every little bridge and farmhouse and is still the most comprehensive guide to the area.

Just as the Trossachs have long attracted those with discriminating tastes, so has Loch Lomond, Scotland's largest loch in terms of surface area. The hard rocks to the north confine it there to a long thin ribbon, and the more yielding Lowlands allow it to spread out and assume a softer, wider form. Here the Lowlands' fields and lush hedgerows quickly give way to dark woods and crags—just a half hour's drive north from Glasgow. So beloved is the area, in fact, that 720 square mi of it were designated part of Scotland's first national park, Loch Lomond and the Trossachs National Park, in 2002.

The Highland boundary fault runs through Loch Lomond, close to Callander, to the northeast above Perth, and into the old county of Angus. Within the region the physical contrast between Lowland and Highland is quite pronounced. Remember that even though the Central Highlands are easily accessible from Edinburgh and Glasgow, there is still much high, rough country in the region. But if the glens and lochs prove to be too lonely or intimidating, it's only a short journey to the softer and less harsh Lowlands.

To the east of the Central Highlands, bordering the North Sea, are Fife and Angus, with breezy cliff-top walks, fishing villages, and open beaches. These areas sandwich Scotland's fourth-largest—and often overlooked—city, Dundee. Scotland's east coast has only light rainfall throughout the year; northeastern Fife, in particular, may claim the record for the most sunshine and the least rainfall in Scotland, which all adds to the enjoyment when you're touring the East Neuk (*neuk,* pronounced nyook, is Scots for corner) or exploring the cobbled lanes of the famous golf center of St. Andrews.

Fife proudly styles itself as a "kingdom," and its long history—which really began when the Romans went home in the 4th century and the Picts moved in—lends some substance to the boast. From medieval times its earls were first among Scottish nobility and crowned the country's kings. For many people, however, the most historic event in the region was the birth of golf. Legend has it that this occured in St. Andrews during the 15th century, an ancient university town by the sea. The Royal

TOP REASONS TO GO

The home of golf. St. Andrews is where the great, the good, and the enthusiastic tee off on the world's most famous links, the Old Course. The area claims another world-famous green, with Gleneagles in the lusher and more undulating Perthshire.

Exploring Loch Lomond. You can see the sparkling waters of Scotland's largest loch by car, by boat, or on foot. A popular option is the network of cycle tracks that creep over Loch Lomond and the Trossachs National Park, offering every conceivable terrain. The Scottish weather ensures a little bit of every season, too.

Historic castles and palaces. Choosing among some of Scotland's most splendid fortresses and mansions is a challenge. Among the highlights are Stirling Castle, with its palace built by James V and its surrounding Old Town; Scone

Palace, near Perth, a residence displaying grand aristocratic acquisitions; and beautiful Glamis Castle in Angus, which connects British royalty from Macbeth to the late Princess Margaret.

Bag a monroe, or just a picnic spot. The way to experience the Central Highlands is to head out on foot. The fit and well-kitted-out can bag a monroe (hills over 3,000 feet that are named after the mountaineer that listed them); the woodland paths and gentle rambles of the Trossachs will stir even the sedentary.

Maritime history. The wee fishing villages of the East Neuk, the polar exploration ship RRS *Discovery* in Dundee, and the Signal Tower of Arbroath: seafaring and the exploitation of the sea's resources are written large in the history books of Fife and Angus, making the area a must for salty dogs.

15

& Ancient Golf Club, the ruling body of the game worldwide, still has its headquarters here.

Not surprisingly, fishing and seafaring have also played a role in the history of the East Neuk coastal region. From the 16th through the 19th centuries, a large population lived and worked in the small ports and harbors that form a continuous chain around Fife's coast. North, across the Firth of Tay, lies the region of Angus, whose particular charm is its variety: in addition to its seacoast towns and pleasant Lowland market centers, there's also a hinterland of lonely rounded hills with long glens running into the typical Grampian Highland scenery beyond. Striking out from Dundee, you can make a number of day trips to uplands or seacoast.

Exploring the Central Highlands, Fife & Angus

The main towns of Stirling and Perth serve as roadway hubs for the Central Highlands, making both places natural starting points for touring. Stirling itself is worth covering in some detail on foot. The Trossachs are a short distance from Stirling, all easily covered in a loop. You can get to Loch Lomond from either Glasgow or Stirling. The main road up the west bank (A82) is not recommended for leisurely touring, as the traffic is heavy and it's not a relaxing drive. Do use this road, however, if you are on your way to Oban, Kintyre, or Argyll. Loch Lomond is best seen from one of two cul-de-sac roads: by way of Drymen at the south end, up to Rowardennan, or if you are pressed for time, west from Aberfoyle to reach Loch Lomond near its northern end, at Inversnaid. Getting around Perthshire is made interesting by the A9, a fast main artery. Exercise caution while driving the A9 itself, however; there have been many auto accidents in this area.

Fife lies south of the River Tay and north of the Firth of Forth, stretching far up the Forth Valley (which is west and a little north of Edinburgh), with St. Andrews on its eastern coast. Northwest of Fife and across the Firth of Tay, the city of Dundee and its rural hinterland, Angus, stretch still farther north and west toward the foothills of the Grampian Mountains.

About the Restaurants

Regional country delicacies—loch trout, river salmon, lamb, and venison—appear regularly on even modest menus in Fife, Angus, and Central Highlands restaurants. As you would expect, there's a particular emphasis on seafood in the coastal towns, with East Neuk lobster served in St. Andrews and the unforgettable Arborath smokie (lightly smoked haddock) a favorite in villages such as Auchmithie. Affluent St. Andrews supports some stylish hotel restaurants as well as cafés and bistros that serve the student population.

About the Hotels

In Stirling and Callander, as well as in the small towns and villages throughout the region, you'll find a selection of accommodations out of all proportion to the size of the communities (industrial towns are the exceptions). These attest to the popularity of the area. Many country-house inns around the region are a match for the grand hotels in comfort, while adding a personal touch to the service. If you're staying in Fife, the obvious base is St. Andrews, with ample accommodation; Dundee is a good port to drop anchor in for day trips around Angus.

WHAT IT COSTS In Pounds				
£££££	**££££**	**£££**	**££**	**£**
RESTAURANTS over £22	£18–£22	£13–£17	£7–£12	under £7
HOTELS over £160	£120–£160	£90–£119	£60–£89	under £60

Restaurant prices are for a main course at dinner. Hotel prices are for two people in a standard double room in high season and generally include the 17.5% V.A.T.

Timing

The Trossachs and Loch Lomond are always crowded in high summer, so the area makes a good choice for off-season touring. Make reservations in advance if you travel in summer; weekends can be particularly busy. Fife and Angus are never swamped with tourists, but St. Andrews buzzes with golfers in summer. The golf business lingers until the Dunhill Cup in October. Across the region fall colors make for spectacular touring, and winter brings dramatic Highland light.

STIRLING

26 mi northeast of Glasgow, 36 mi northwest of Edinburgh.

Stirling is one of Britain's great historic towns. In some ways, the city is a little Edinburgh with similar "crag-and-tail" foundations and a royal half-mile street leading to the castle. Built on a steep-sided plug of rock, the castle dominates the landscape, and its esplanade affords views of the surrounding valley plain of the River Forth. Stirling's strategic position, commanding the lowest bridge on the Forth, was appreciated by the Stewart kings, and they spent a lot of time at its castle—a fact that, together with the relics of freedom fighters in the neighborhood, has led some Scottish nationalists to declare that Stirling, not Edinburgh, should really be the capital city.

The historic part of town is tightly nestled around the castle—everything is within easy walking distance. An impressive proportion of the Old Town walls remain and can be seen from Dumbarton Road, as soon as you step outside the tourist information center. You can either take a taxi or walk—if you're feeling energetic—out to Bannockburn Heritage Centre or the National Wallace Monument, on the town's outskirts.

Main Attractions

★ ❻ **Bannockburn Heritage Centre.** In 1298, the year after William Wallace's victory, Robert the Bruce (1274–1329) materialized as Scotland's champion, and the final bloody phase of the Wars of Independence began. Bruce's rise resulted from the uncertainties and timidity of the great lords of Scotland (ever unsure of which way to jump and whether to bow to England's demands). This tale is recounted at the Bannockburn Heritage Centre, hidden among the sprawl of housing and commercial development on the southern edge of Stirling. This was the site of the famed Battle of Bannockburn in 1314. In Bruce's day the Forth had a shelved and partly wooded floodplain. So he cunningly chose this site, noting the boggy ground on the lower reaches in which the heavy horses of the English would founder. The events of this time have been re-created within the center by means of an audiovisual presentation, models and costumed figures, and an arresting mural depicting the battle in detail. ⊠ *Off A80* ☎ *01786/ 812664* ⊕ *www.nts.org.uk* ⊡ *£10* ⊘ *Site daily. Heritage Centre Apr.–Oct., daily 10–5:30; Feb., Mar., and Nov.–mid-Dec., daily 10:30–4.*

❼ **National Wallace Monument.** It was near Old Stirling Bridge that the Scottish freedom fighter William Wallace (circa 1270–1305) and a ragged army of Scots won a major victory in 1297. The movie *Braveheart,* directed by and starring Mel Gibson, was based on Wallace's life. A more accurate version of events is told in an exhibition and audiovisual presentation at this pencil-thin museum on the Abbey Craig. Up close, this Victorian shrine to William Wallace, built between 1856 and 1869, becomes less slim and soaring, revealing itself to be a substantial square tower with a creepy spiral stairway. To reach the monument, follow the Bridge of Allan signs (A9) northward, crossing the River Forth by

15

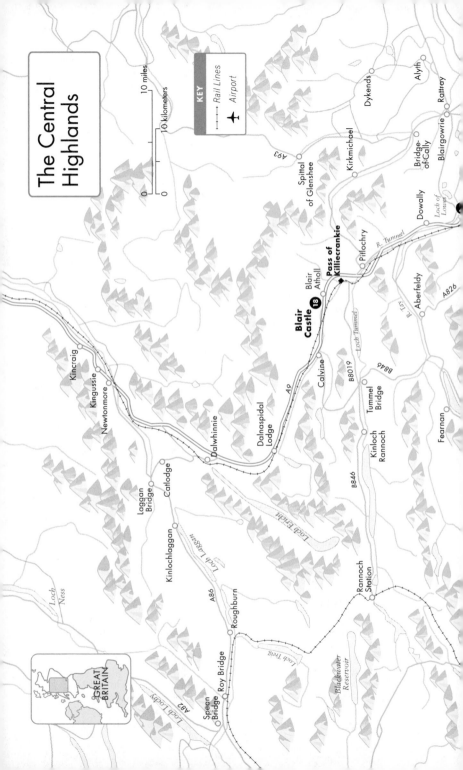

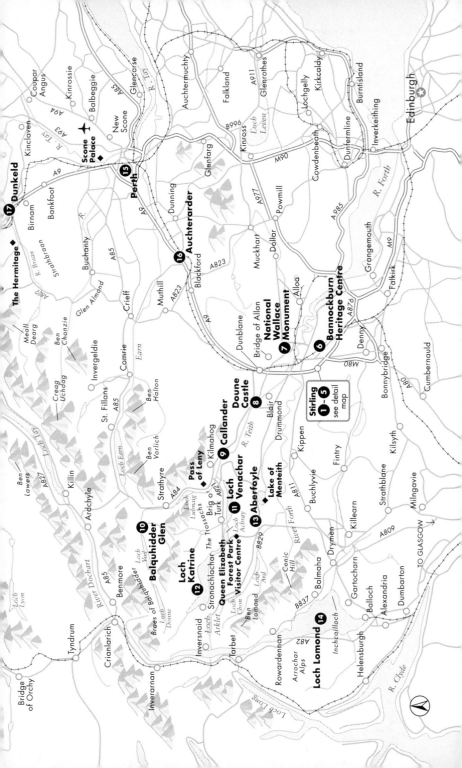

Robert Stephenson's (1772–1850) New Bridge of 1832, next to the historic old one. The National Wallace Monument is signposted at the next traffic circle. ⊠ *Abbey Craig* ☎ *01786/472140* ⊕ *www. nationalwallacemonument.com* ☞ *£6.50* ⊙ *Mar.–May and Oct., daily 10–5; June, daily 10–6; July and Aug., daily 9:30–6:30; Sept., daily 9:30–6; Nov.–Feb. daily 10:30–4.*

🖐 **④** **Old Town Jail.** The original town jail, now restored, has living exhibitions about life in a 19th-century Scottish prison. Furnished cells, models, and staff—dressed as prisoners, wardens, and prison reformers—bring the gruesome prison regime to life. From October through March, these living-history performances take place only on weekends. ⊠ *Access from St. John's St.* ☎ *01786/450050* ⊕ *www.oldtownjail.com* ☞ *£5; £5.95 with an actor as guide* ⊙ *Apr.–Sept., daily 9:30–6; Oct. and Mar., daily 9:30–5; Nov.–Feb., daily 9:30–4; last admission 1 hr before closing.*

① **Stirling Castle.** Its magnificent strategic position made Stirling Castle the

Fodor'sChoice   grandest prize in the Scots Wars of Independence in the late 13th and

★   early 14th centuries, and perhaps the most important single fortress in Scotland. The Battle of Bannockburn in 1314 was fought within sight of its walls, and the victory by Robert the Bruce yielded both the castle and freedom from English subjugation for almost four centuries. The daughter of King Robert I (Robert the Bruce), Marjory, married Walter Fitzallan, the high steward of Scotland. Their descendants included the Stewart dynasty of Scottish monarchs (Mary, Queen of Scots, was a Stewart, though she preferred the French spelling, *Stuart*). The Stewarts were responsible for many of the works that survive within the castle walls today.

You'll enter the castle through its outer defenses, which consist of a great curtain wall and batteries from 1708, built to bulwark earlier defenses by the main gatehouse. From this lower square the most conspicuous feature is the **Palace,** built by King James V (1512–42) between 1538 and 1542. The decorative figures festooning the ornately worked outer walls show the influence of French masons. Work is under way to recreate the furnishings and tapestries of the Palace during the reign of James V and his French queen, Mary of Guise. This will transform the empty rooms into the richly adorned living quarters of the kings and queens of Scotland. Overlooking the upper courtyard is the **Great Hall,** built by King James IV (1473–1513) in 1503. Before the Union of Parliaments in 1707, when the Scottish aristocracy sold out to England, this building had been used as one of the seats of the Scottish Parliament. After 1707 it sank into decline, becoming a riding school, then a barracks. It has since been restored to its original splendor.

Among the later works built for regiments stationed here, the **King's Old Building** stands out; it is a 19th-century baronial revival on the site of an earlier building. The oldest building on the site is the **Mint,** or **Coonzie Hoose,** perhaps dating as far back as the 14th century. Views from the **Nether Bailey,** the westernmost section of the ramparts, give you an appreciation of the castle's strategic location. ⊠ *Castlehill* ☎ *01786/450000* ⊕ *www.historic-scotland.gov.uk* ☑ *£8.50, including admission to Argyll's Lodging* ☉ *Apr.–Sept., daily 9:30–6; Oct.–Mar., daily 9:30–5.*

Also Worth Seeing

➋ **Argyll's Lodging.** A nobleman's town house built in three phases from the 16th century onward, this building is actually older than the name it bears—that of Archibald, the ninth earl of Argyll (1629–85), who bought it in 1666. It was for many years a military hospital, then a youth hostel. It has now been refurbished to show how the nobility lived in 17th-century Stirling. Specially commissioned reproduction furniture and fittings are based on the original inventory of the house's contents at that time. ⊠ *Castle Wynd* ☎ *01786/431319* ⊕ *www.historic-scotland. gov.uk* ☑ *£3.30; £8 with admission to Stirling Castle* ☉ *Apr.–Sept., daily 9:30–5:30; Oct.–Mar., daily 9:30–4:30.*

➎ **Back Walk.** The upper Back Walk, a gentle but relentless uphill path that eventually leads to the castle, will take you along the outside of the city's walls, past a watchtower and the grimly named Hangman's entry, carved out of the great whinstone boulders that once marked the outer defenses of the town. Walking it is a good way to understand the city. One of several access areas is off Dumbarton Road, opposite the tourist information center. Also near the information center, on Corn Exchange Road, is a modern statue of Robert MacGregor (1671–1734), better known as Rob Roy, notorious cattle dealer and drover, part-time thief and outlaw, Jacobite (most of the time), and hero of Sir Walter Scott's namesake novel (1818). Rob is practically inescapable if you visit Callander and the Trossachs, where he had his home. ⊠ *Runs from Dumbarton Rd. to Castle Rock.*

❸ **Church of the Holy Rude.** The nave of this handsome church survives from the 15th century, and a portion of the original medieval timber roof can also be seen. This is the only Scottish church still in use to have witnessed the coronation of a Scottish monarch—James VI (1566–1625) in 1567. ⊠ *Top of St. John's St.*

Where to Stay & Eat

£££ ✕ **Hermann's Brasserie.** Run by Austrian Hermann and his Glaswegian wife, the brasserie makes an arresting marriage of culture and food. The Black-Watch-tartan carpet and alpine murals are as well matched as the *cullen skink* (an archetypal Scottish soup of fish and potato) and Wiener schnitzel. ⊠ *58 Broad St.* ☎ *01786/450632* ▭ *AE, MC, V.*

££–£££ ✕ **The Riverhouse.** Right at the foot of Stirling Castle, this restaurant sits by its own tranquil loch and is built in the style of a Scottish *crannog* (ancient loch dwelling). Popular with both families and couples, local produce dominates the menu, yet the food reflects Eastern and Mediterranean influences. Try the curried Scottish lamb with lime yogurt. ⊠ *Greig St.* ☎ *01786/465577* ▭ *AE, MC, V.*

★ **£££–££££** ✕🏨 **Stirling Highland Hotel.** The attractive 1854 building this hotel occupies was once the Old High School, and many original architectural features remain, including the fully working observatory on the roof. Furnishings are old-fashioned, with solid wood, tartan, florals, and low-key, neutral color schemes. The modern-Scottish Scholars Restaurant (£££££, fixed-price menu) offers outstanding seafood, game, and Aberdeen Angus beef. ⊠ *Spittal St., FK8 1DU* ☎ *01786/272727* 🖷 *01786/272829* ⊕ *www.paramount-hotels.co.uk* ⇒ *96 rooms* ◇ *Restaurant, in-room data ports, pool, health club, sauna, bar, some pets allowed (fee); no a/c* ▭ *AE, DC, MC, V* ⊙ *BP.*

£ 🏨 **Castlecroft.** Tucked beneath Stirling Castle, this warm and comfortable modern house is well situated for sightseeing in the Old Town, and it overlooks fine views of the Trossachs and Grampian mountains to the north. ⊠ *Ballengeich Rd., FK8 1TN* ☎ *01786/474933* 🖷 *01786/466716* ⊕ *www.castlecroft-uk.com* ⇒ *6 rooms* ◇ *Lounge, no-smoking rooms; no a/c, no room phones* ▭ *MC, V* ⊙ *BP.*

£ 🏨 **Kilronan House.** Situated in Bridge of Allan close to the Wallace Monument and many shops and restaurants, this granite B&B offers quality accommodation and good value for the money. High ceilings and other details recall the house's genteel Victorian origins, and the well-tended gardens are a pleasant place to relax. ⊠ *15 Kenilworth Rd., FK9 4DU* ☎ *01786/831054* ⊕ *www.kilronan.co.uk* ⇒ *2 rooms* ◇ *Lounge; no a/c, no room phones, no room TVs, no smoking* ▭ *No credit cards* ⊙ *BP.*

The Arts

The **Macrobert Arts Centre** (⊠ Stirling University ☎ 01786/466666 ⊕ www.macrobert.stir.ac.uk) has a theater, art gallery, and studio with programs that range from films to pantomime.

Shopping

House of Henderson (⊠ 6–8 Friars St. ☎ 01786/473681), a Highland outfitter, sells tartans, woolens, and accessories and offers a made-to-measure kilt service. **Village Glass** (⊠ 11 Henderson St. ☎ 01786/832137) sells original glassware handblown on the premises.

South of Stirling, at Larbert (and signposted off the A9), is **Barbara Davidson's pottery studio** (⊠ Muirhall Farm ☎ 01324/554430), run by one of the best-known potters in Scotland, in an 18th-century farm setting. It's open from Monday to Saturday, 10 to 5. You can make an appointment to paint a pot, which will be glazed, fired, and mailed to you; and in July and August you can even try throwing your own pot.

THE TROSSACHS & LOCH LOMOND

Immortalized by Wordsworth and Sir Walter Scott, the Trossachs (the name means "bristly country") may contain some of Scotland's loveliest forest, hills, and glens, well justifying its designation as the country's first national park. This popular area is easily accessible from Glasgow, Stirling, and Edinburgh. The Trossachs has a very peculiar charm, for it combines the wildness of the Highlands with the prolific vegetation of an old Lowland forest. Its open ground is a dense mat of bracken and heather, and its woodland is of silver birch, dwarf oak, and hazel—trees that fasten their roots into the crevices of rocks and stop short on the very brink of lochs. The most colorful season is fall, particularly October, a lovely time when most visitors have departed and the hares, deer, and game birds have taken over.

Doune Castle

★ ❽ *9 mi northwest of Stirling.*

The Highland-edge community of Doune was once a center for pistol making. No self-respecting Highland chief's attire was complete without a prestigious and ornate pair of pistols. Today Doune is more widely known for one of the best-preserved medieval castles in Scotland. It's also a place of pilgrimage for fans of Monty Python's *Holy Grail,* which was filmed here. Doune Castle looks like an early castle is supposed to look: grim and high-walled, with echoing, drafty stone vaults. Construction of the fortress began in the early 15th century on a now-peaceful riverside tract. The best place to photograph this squat, walled fort is from the bridge, a little way upstream, west on A84. Be sure to climb up to the curtain-wall walk for good views. The castle is signposted to the left as you enter the town from the Dunblane road. ⊠ *Off A84* ☎ *01786/841742* ⊕ *www.historic-scotland.gov.uk* 💷 *£3.50* ☉ *Apr.–Sept., daily 9:30–6; Oct.–Mar., Sat.–Wed. 9:30–4.*

Callander

❾ *8 mi northwest of Doune.*

A traditional Highland-edge resort, Callander bustles throughout the year, even during off-peak times, simply because it is a gateway to Highland scenery, and Loch Lomond and the Trossachs National Park. As a result, there's plenty of window-shopping here, plus nightlife in pubs and a good selection of accommodations.

Callander's **Rob Roy and Trossachs Visitor Centre** provides another encounter with the overly romanticized "tartan Robin Hood," Rob Roy MacGregor. A man of great physical strength and courageous energy, MacGregor is known as a defender of the downtrodden and scourge of authorities. He was, in fact, a medieval throwback, a cattle thief, an embezzler of lairds' rents, and the operator of a vicious protection racket among poor farmers. You can learn more about his high jinks from the high-tech account in the modern visitor center. Hollywood paid homage to this local folk legend with the 1995 film *Rob Roy*, starring actors Liam Neeson and Jessica Lange. The visitor center also provides information about the national park. ✉ *Ancaster Sq.* ☏ *01877/330342* ⊕ *www.robroyvisitorcentre.com* ✉ *£3.85* ☉ *July and Aug., daily 9–6; Mar.–June and Sept.–Dec., daily 10–5; Jan. and Feb., daily 11–4.*

Ⓒ The **Hamilton Toy Collection** is one of the most extensive in Britain. Both kids and adults can spend hours amidst every conceivable toy from the Victorian age until the 1970s: teddy bears, porcelain dolls, toy soldiers, Matchbox cars, Thunderbirds memorabilia, and a wonderful selection of model railways. ✉ *111 Main St.* ☏ *01877/330004* ✉ *£2* ☉ *Apr.–Oct., Tues.–Sun. 11–4:30.*

A walk is signposted from the east end of the main street to the **Bracklinn Falls,** over whose lip Sir Walter Scott once rode a pony to win a bet. It's a 1½-mi walk through the woods up to the **Callander Crags,** with views of the Lowlands as far as the Pentland Hills behind Edinburgh. The walk begins at the west end of the main street.

Where to Stay & Eat

££££–£££££ ✕🖼 **Roman Camp.** This former hunting lodge, dating to 1625, has 20 acres of gardens with river frontage, yet it's within easy walking distance of Callander's town center. The antiques-filled sitting rooms and library are more reminiscent of a stately family home than a hotel. The restaurant (£££££, fixed-price menu) has a good reputation for its salmon, trout, and other seafood, all cooked in an imaginative, modern Scottish style. Also delicious is the fillet of Scotch beef with an herb-potato scone and wild-mushroom mousseline. ✉ *Main St., Callander, Perthshire, FK17 8BG* ☏ *01877/330003* 🖷 *01877/331533* ⊕ *www.roman-camp-hotel.co.uk* 🛏 *11 rooms, 3 suites* ♨ *Restaurant, fishing, bar, lounge, library; no a/c* ☰ *AE, DC, MC, V* ⦿| *BP.*

Sports & the Outdoors

BICYCLING **Wheels/Trossachs Backpackers** (✉ Invertrossachs Rd. ☏ 01877/331100 ⊕ www.scottish-cycling.co.uk) is a friendly firm that can help you find the best mountain bike routes around the Trossachs and offers hostel accommodation for cyclists (£15 for a dorm bed).

GOLF **Callander golf course,** designed by Tom Morris in 1890, has fine views and a tricky moorland layout. Keep between the trees on the 15th hole and you may end up with a hole-in-one. ⊠ *Aveland Rd.* ☎ *01877/330090* ⚑ *18 holes, 5,151 yds, par 66.*

Shopping

The **Edinburgh Woollen Mill Group** operates three mill shops in and near Callander. All the stores have a vast selection of woolens on display, including luxurious cashmere and striking tartan throws, and will provide overseas mailing and tax-free shopping. *Callander Woollen Mill:* ⊠ *12–18 Main St.* ☎ *01877/330612* ⊠ *Kilmahog Woollen Mill:* ⊠ *North of town at Trossachs Turning* ☎ *01877/330268* ⊠ *Trossachs Woollen Mill:* ⊠ *North of town at Trossachs Turning* ☎ *01877/330178.*

15

Balquhidder Glen

🔟 *12 mi north of Callander.*

A 20-minute drive from Callander, through the Pass of Leny and beyond Strathyre, is Balquhidder Glen (pronounced *bal*-whidd-*er*), a typical Highland glen that runs westward. The flat-bottom profile was formed by prehistoric glaciers, and Forestry Commission plantings have replaced much of the natural woodlands above. You may notice a boarded-up look of some of the area's houses, many of which are second homes for affluent residents of the south. The glen is also where Loch Voil and Loch Doune spread out, adding to the stunning vistas. This area is often known as the Braes (Slopes) of Balquhidder and was once the home of the MacLarens and the MacGregors. **Rob Roy MacGregor's** grave is signposted beside Balquhidder village. The site of his house, now a private farm, is beyond the parking lot at the end of the road up the glen. The glen has no through road, though there is a right-of-way (on foot) from the churchyard where Rob Roy is buried, through the plantings in Kirkton Glen and then on to open windy grasslands and a blue *lochan* (little lake). This path eventually drops into the next valley, Glen Dochart, and rejoins the A84.

Where to Stay & Eat

£££–£££££ ╳🏨 **Monachyle Mhor.** Set in 2,000 acres of forests and moorland, this
Fodor'sChoice beautiful Highland lodge has magnificent views across lochs Voil and
★ Doine. The hotel offers complimentary salmon and trout fishing. The rooms eschew the traditional look, embracing clean lines and modish luxury, like plush animal print throws. The bright and airy restaurant (£££££, fixed-price menu) serves expertly prepared and presented contemporary food that shows the chef's lightness of touch: try the cream of celeriac, apple, and lime soup, or wild sea bass with new season's pea risotto. ⊠ *Balquhidder, FK19 8PQ* ☎ *01877/384622* 🖷 *01877/384305*

⊕ *www.monachylemhor.com* ⇆ *9 rooms, 2 suites* ⚭ *Restaurant, Wi-Fi, boating, fishing; no a/c* ▭ *MC, V* ⦿ *BP.*

The Trossachs

10 mi west of Callander.

The Trossachs are almost a Scottish visual cliché. With harmonious scenery of hill, loch, and wooded slopes, they have been a popular touring region since the late 18th century, at the dawn of the age of the Romantic poets. Influenced by the writings of Sir Walter Scott, early visitors who strayed into the Highlands from the central belt of Scotland admired this as the first "wild" part of Scotland they encountered. Perhaps because the Trossachs represent the very essence of what the Highlands are supposed to be, the whole of this area, including Loch Lomond, is now protected as a national park, Scotland's first. Here you'll find birch and pine forests, vistas down lochs where the woods creep right to the water's edge, and, in the background, peaks that rise high enough to be called mountains, though they're not as high as those to the north and west.

⑪ The A821 runs west together with the first and gentlest of the Trossachs lochs, **Loch Venachar.** A sturdy gray-stone building, with a small dam at the Callander end, controls the water that feeds into the River Teith (and, hence, into the Forth). A few minutes after it passes Loch Venachar the A821 becomes muffled in woodlands and twists gradually down to the village of **Brig o' Turk.** (*Turk* is Gaelic for the Scots *tuirc,* meaning wild boar, a species that has been extinct in this region since about the 16th century.) ⊠ *On A821.*

Loch Achray, stretching west of Brig o' Turk, dutifully fulfills expectations of what a verdant Trossachs loch should be: small, green, reedy meadows backed by dark plantations, rhododendron thickets, and lumpy hills, thickly covered with heather.

★ ⑫ At the end of Loch Achray, a side road turns right into a narrow pass, leading to **Loch Katrine,** the heart of the Trossachs. Sir Walter Scott traveled here in the early 19th century and was inspired to write *The Lady of the Lake.* At that time, the road here was narrow and almost hidden by the overhanging crags and mossy oaks and birches. Today it ends at a slightly anticlimactic parking lot with a shop, café, and visitor center. To see the finest of the Trossachs lochs properly, you must—even for just a few minutes—walk a bit farther along the level, paved road beyond the parking lot (open only to Strathclyde Water Board vehicles). Loch Katrine's water is taken by aqueduct and tunnel to Glasgow—a Victorian feat of engineering that has ensured the purity of the supply to Scotland's largest city for more than 100 years. The steamer **SS *Sir Walter Scott*** (☎ 01877/376316 ⛴ £7.25 morning, £6.25 afternoon) embarks on cruises of Loch Katrine during summer, leaving from Trossachs Pier. Take the cruise if time permits, as the shores of Katrine remain undeveloped and scenic. ⊠ *Off A821* ☎ *01877/376316* ⊗ *Visitor center, Apr.–late-Oct., daily 9–5; Cruises, May–Oct., Thurs.–Tues. 11, 1:45, and 3:15 Wed. 1:45 and 3:15.*

Aberfoyle

⑬ *11 mi south of Loch Katrine, in the Trossachs.*

Aberfoyle has numerous souvenir shops and an attraction that appeals mainly to children. The **Scottish Wool Centre** tells the story of Scottish wool "from the sheep's back to your back." You can see live specimens of the main breeds in the sheep amphitheater and try your hand at spinning in the textile display area. In the Border collie training area, dogs in training to assist shepherds practice herding ducks. The shop stocks a huge selection of woolen garments and knitwear. ⊠ *Off Main St.* ☎ *01877/ 382850* ▣ *Demonstrations Mar.–Oct. £2.50* ☉ *Apr.–Oct., daily 9:30–5.30; Nov., Dec., Feb., and Mar., daily 10–5; Jan., daily 10–4:30.*

The tiny island of **Inchmahome**, on the Lake of Menteith, was a place of refuge in 1547 for the young Mary, Queen of Scots. A ferry takes passengers from the lake's pier to the island (£2.80, April–September): if the boat is not there when you arrive at the pier, turn the board so that the white side faces the island and the boat will come and collect you. ⊠ *Off A81, 4 mi east of Aberfoyle.*

15

Where to Stay & Eat

££££ ✕▦ **Macdonald Forest Hills Hotel.** A traditional-Scottish-country-house theme pervades this hotel, from the rambling white building itself to the wood-paneled lounges, log fires, and numerous sporting activities. More than 20 acres of gardens and grounds surround the building, which sits on a grassy hillside overlooking Loch Ard. Chintz drapes and reproduction antiques fill the bedrooms. The restaurant (£££££, fixed-price menu) has tartan decor that makes an appropriate backdrop for nicely prepared Scottish game, salmon, beef, and lamb. ⊠ *Kinlochard, FK8 3TL* ☎ *01877/387277* 🖨 *01877/387307* ⊕ *www.foresthills-hotel.co. uk* �'c *56 rooms* △ *2 restaurants, tennis court, indoor pool, gym, sauna, boating, fishing, bicycles, horseback riding, children's programs (ages 5–12); no a/c, no kids under 5* ⊟ *AE, DC, MC, V* ❑ *BP.*

Sports & the Outdoors

BICYCLING **Trossachs Cycle Hire** (⊠ Trossachs Holiday Park ☎ 01877/382614 ⊕ www. trossachsholidays.co.uk) rents out bicycles from March through October (£12–£20 per day) and will provide advice on what routes to take.

WALKING The long-distance walkers' route, the **West Highland Way,** which runs 95 mi from Glasgow to Fort William, follows the bank of Loch Lomond at Inversnaid, which you can reach from the B829. A brief stroll up the path is pleasant, particularly if you're visiting during the spring, when birdsong fills the oak-tree canopy.

Loch Lomond

⑭ *14 mi west of Aberfoyle, 34 mi west of Callander.*

The upper portion of Loch Lomond, Scotland's largest loch in terms of surface area, is a sparkling ribbon of water snaking into the hills. Toward the south, the more yielding Lowlands allow the loch to spread out. Wooded islands, some of which can be visited, rise up though this portion of the loch. This geographic line is indicative of the Highland boundary fault, which runs through Loch Lomond and the hills.

Before starting your exploration of the loch, take time to visit **Loch Lomond Shores** at Balloch on the southern tip of the loch. A castlelike structure here contains the **Loch Lomond and the Trossachs National Park Gateway Centre,** your introduction to Scotland's first national park. A film about the area is shown, and there are shops, restaurants, slipways, and beaches. ⊠ *Off A82, near Balloch* ☎ *01389/722199* ⊕ *www. lochlomondshores.com* ☾ *Weekdays 11–5, weekends 11–6.*

At the little settlement of **Balmaha,** the versatile recreational role filled by Loch Lomond is clear: cruising craft are at the ready, hikers appear out of woodlands on the West Highland Way, and day-trippers stroll at the loch's edge. The heavily wooded offshore islands look alluringly close. One of the best ways to explore them is by taking a cruise or renting a boat. ⊠ *On B837.*

The island of **Inchcailloch** (*inch* comes from *innis,* Gaelic for island), just offshore, can be explored in an hour or two. Pleasant pathways thread through oak woods planted in the 18th century, when the bark was used by the tanning industry. ⊠ *On B837.*

Loch Lomond is seldom more than a narrow field's length away from the B837 as the road runs northwest to the town of **Rowardennan.** Where the drivable road ends, in a parking lot crunchy with pinecones, you can ramble along one of the marked loch-side footpaths or make your way toward Ben Lomond, 3½ mi away. ⊠ *End of B837.*

Where to Stay & Eat

★ **£££** ✕ **Méson del Lago.** In the warmer months, you can sit on the *terraza,* watch the sun sparkle on the water, listen to the breeze rustle through the palm trees, and almost believe you are on the Mediterranean. The fresh and arresting flavors of the authentic tapas add to the illusion, which is perhaps broken only by the concentration of Glaswegian accents. ⊠ *Lomond Shores* ☎ *01389/753834* ▭ *MC, V.*

£££££ ✕▥ **Cameron House.** This beautifully located hotel offers country-club facilities on the shores of Loch Lomond. Pastel shades and antique reproductions decorate the bedrooms. The elegant Georgian Room serves excellent Scottish-French cuisine, such as lamb roasted in garlic and fennel, with a mille feuille of wild mushrooms. The Marina Restaurant and Bar on the water's edge is informal but stylish and has an open kitchen with a wood-burning oven, perfect for pizzas. ⊠ *Loch Lomond, Alexandria, Dunbartonshire, G83 8QZ* ☎ *01389/755565* ▤ *01389/759522* ⊕ *www.devereonline.co.uk/cameronhouse* ⇗ *96 rooms, 7 suites* ♨ *3 restaurants, cable TV, 9-hole golf course, 2 tennis courts, 2 pools, health club, hair salon, hot tub, sauna, steam room, fishing, croquet, squash, bar, children's programs (ages 5–12); no a/c* ▭ *AE, DC, MC, V* ⏐❍⏐ *BP.*

Sports & the Outdoors

BOAT TOURS   **MacFarlane and Son** (⊠ *Boatyard, Balmaha, Loch Lomond* ☎ *01360/ 870214*) runs cruises on Loch Lomond and rents rowboats and small powerboats to those who prefer to do their own exploring. From Tarbet, on the western shore, **Cruise Loch Lomond** (✉ Boatyard, Tarbet ☎ 01301/702356 ⊕ www.cruiselochlomondltd.com) runs tours all year.

HIKING Walking is by far the most popular activity in the **Loch Lomond and the Trossachs National Park** (⊕ www.lochlomond-trossachs.org). There are near-endless possibilities: from carefree meanders on well-kept paths to exhilarating weeklong hikes—like the West Highland way—over vast expanses of mountains, seashore, moors, and forests. You can see and feel the geological variations and enjoy an abundance of Scottish flora and fauna—not to mention the likelihood of experiencing all four seasons in one day! To find out more about the different types of walks call the local tourist information center or visit the National Park's Web site for maps and detailed information.

Shopping
At **Thistle Bagpipe Works** (✉ Luss, Dunbartonshire ☎ 01436/860250), on the western shore of Loch Lomond, you can commission your own made-to-order set of bagpipes. You can also order a complete Highland outfit, including kilt and jacket.

15

PERTHSHIRE

The town of Perth serves a wide rural hinterland and has a well-off air, making it one of Scotland's most interesting shopping towns outside of Edinburgh and Glasgow. Perth's rural hinterland is grand in several senses. On the Highland edge, prosperous-looking farms are scattered across heavily wooded countryside, and even larger properties are screened by trees and parkland. All this changes as the mountain barrier is penetrated, giving rise to grouse moors and open, hilly areas.

Perth

🚸 *36 mi northeast of Stirling, 43 mi north of Edinburgh, 61 mi northeast of Glasgow.*

Although the town of Perth has an ancient history dating to the Dark Ages, it has been rebuilt and recast innumerable times, and sadly, no trace remains of the pre-Reformation monasteries that once dominated the skyline. In fact, modern Perth has swept much of its colorful history under a grid of busy streets. It can make a good stop on the way to the Highlands. Nearby Scone Palace is its chief attraction.

Perth has long been a focal point in Scottish history, and several critical events took place here, including the assassination of King James I of Scotland (1394–1437) and John Knox's (1514–72) preaching in St. John's Kirk in 1559. Later, the 17th-century religious wars in Scotland saw the town occupied, first by the marquis of Montrose (1612–50), then later by Oliver Cromwell's (1599–1658) forces. The Jacobites also occupied the town in the 1715 and 1745 rebellions.

On the North Inch of Perth, look for Balhousie Castle and the **Regimental Museum of the Black Watch.** Some will tell you the Black Watch was a Scottish regiment whose name is a reference to the color of its tartan. An equally plausible explanation, however, is that the regiment was established to keep an undercover watch on rebellious Jacobites. *Black* is the Gaelic word *dubh*, meaning, in this case, "hidden" or "covert," used in the same sense as the word *blackmail*. A wide range of uniforms, weaponry, and marching banners are displayed. The castle is closed on the last Saturday in June. ✉ *Facing North Inch Park, entrance from Hay St.* ☎ *0131/310–8530* ⊕ *www.theblackwatch.co.uk* 🎟 *Free* 🕙 *May–Sept., Mon.–Sat. 10–4; Oct.–Apr., weekdays 10–3:30.*

The Round House, with its magnificent and newly restored dome and rotunda, contains the **Fergusson Gallery,** displaying a selection of 6,000 works—paintings, drawings, and prints—by the Scottish artist J. D. Fergusson (1874–1961). ✉ *Marshall Pl.* ☎ *01738/441944* 🎟 *Free* 🕙 *Mon.–Sat. 10–5.*

🅲 **Scone Palace** (pronounced *skoon*) is much more cheerful and vibrant than
Fodor'sChoice Perth's other castles. The palace is the current residence of the earl of
★ Mansfield but is open to visitors. Although it incorporates various earlier works, the palace today has mainly a 19th-century theme, with mock castellations that were fashionable at the time. There's plenty to see if you're interested in the acquisitions of an aristocratic Scottish family: magnificent porcelain, furniture, ivory, clocks, and 16th-century needlework. A coffee shop, restaurant, gift shop, and play area are on-site, and the extensive grounds have a pine plantation. The palace has its own mausoleum nearby, on the site of a long-gone abbey on **Moot Hill,** the ancient coronation place of the Scottish kings. To be crowned, they sat on the Stone of Scone, which was seized in 1296 by Edward I of England, Scotland's greatest enemy, and placed in the coronation chair at Westminster Abbey, in London. It was returned to Scotland in November 1996 and is now on view in Edinburgh Castle. Some Scots hint darkly that Edward was fooled by a substitution and that the real stone is hidden, waiting for Scotland to regain its independence. ✉ *Braemar Rd.* ☎ *01738/552300* ⊕ *www.scone-palace.co.uk* 🎟 *£7.20* 🕙 *Apr.–Oct., daily 9:30–5:30; last admission at 5.*

Where to Stay & Eat

£££–££££ ✕🖾 **Parklands.** This top-quality hotel, a stylish Georgian town house overlooking lush woodland, is perhaps best known for its restaurant, Acanthus Restaurant and Colourist Bistro (£££££), serving Scottish fish, game, and beef. A sense of elegance permeates the low-key, contemporary interior. ✉ *2 St. Leonard's Bank, PH2 8EB* ☎ *01738/622451* 🖨 *01738/622046* ⊕ *www.theparklandshotel.com* 🛏 *14 rooms* ⚄ *2 restaurants; no a/c* ⊟ *AE, DC, MC, V* 🍽 *BP.*

★ **££** ✕🖾 **Sunbank House Hotel.** A lesson in traditional style, this early-Victorian gray-stone mansion in a fine residential area near Perth's Branklyn Gardens provides solid, unpretentious comforts along with great views over the River Tay and the city. The restaurant (£££££) serves imaginatively prepared, Continental-style (with Italian overtones), prix-fixe dinners and specializes in locally raised meats and game. ⊠ *50 Dundee Rd., PH2 7BA* ☎ *01738/624882* 🖷 *01738/442515* ⊕ *www.sunbankhouse.com* 🛏 *9 rooms* ⅏ *Restaurant, lounge, no-smoking rooms; no a/c* ⊟ *MC, V* ⦿*| BP.*

Nightlife & the Arts

The new Horsecross development brings together all of Perth's cultural facilities. The Victorian **Perth Repertory Theatre** (⊠ 185 High St. ☎ 0845/6126324) stages plays and musicals. **Perth Concert Hall** (⊠ King Edward St. ☎ 0845/6126324) hosts musical performances of all types.

Shopping

Some Perth stores sell Scottish freshwater pearls from the River Tay in delicate settings, some of which take their theme from Scottish flowers. Make your choice at **Cairncross Ltd., Goldsmiths** (⊠ 18 St. John's St. ☎ 01738/624367), where you can also admire a display of some of the more unusual shapes and colors of pearls. **C & C Proudfoot** (⊠ 104 South St. ☎01738/632483) sells a comprehensive selection of sheepskins, leather jackets, rugs, slippers, and handbags.

Auchterarder

16 *13 mi southwest of Perth.*

Famous for the Gleneagles Hotel and nearby golf courses, Auchterarder also has a flock of tiny antiques shops to amuse Gleneagles's golf widows and widowers.

Where to Stay & Eat

£££££
Fodor's Choice
★

✕⛶ **Gleneagles Hotel.** One of Britain's most famous hotels, Gleneagles is the very essence of modern grandeur. Like a vast, secret palace, it stands hidden in breathtaking countryside amid world-famous golf courses. For the most celebrated Scottish dining experience, enjoy Andrew Fairlie's signature dishes of lobster smoked over whiskey barrels, and black truffle gnocchi. Recreation facilities are nearly endless: four restaurants, a shopping arcade, a spa, the Gleneagles Equestrian Centre, the Falconry Centre, and more, all of which make a stay here a luxurious and unforgettable experience. ⊠ *Auchterarder, PH3 1NF, near Perth* ☎ *01764/662231* 🖷 *01764/662134* ⊕ *www.gleneagles.com* 🛏 *216 rooms, 13 suites* ⅏ *4 restaurants, room service, minibars, cable TV, Web TV, 9-hole golf course, 3 18-hole golf courses, 5 tennis courts, pro shop, 2 indoor pools, gym, hot tub, outdoor hot tub, sauna, spa, steam room, fishing, bicycles, horseback riding, squash, children's programs (ages 4–10), concierge; no a/c* ⊟ *AE, DC, MC, V* ⦿*| BP.*

Dunkeld

17 *14 mi north of Perth.*

Thomas Telford's sturdy river bridge of 1809 carries the road into the town of Dunkeld. Here, the National Trust for Scotland not only cares for grand mansions and wildlands but also actively restores smaller properties. The effects of its Little Houses project can be seen in the square off the main street, opposite the fish-and-chips shop. All the houses on the square were rebuilt after the 1689 defeat of the Jacobite army here, which occurred after its early victory in the Battle of Killiecrankie.

Across the Tay from Dunkeld lies the village of Birnam. The wood on Birnam Hill, which overlooks the village, is where Macbeth met the three witches who foretold and sealed his fate. Altogether less spooky is the **Beatrix Potter Garden,** which celebrates the life and work of this much loved children's writer who spent her childhood holidays in the area. An enchanting garden walk allows you to peep into the homes of Peter Rabbit and Mrs. Tiggywinkle, and there is an exhibition and a shop selling books and toys. ⊠ *Birnam, by Dunkeld* ☎ *01350/727674* ☉ *Garden, daily dawn–dusk; exhibition and shop, Mon.–Sat. 10–4, Sun. 2–4.*

★ On the outskirts of Dunkeld, **The Hermitage** is a woodland walk that follows the River Braan. In the 18th century, the dukes of Atholl constructed two follies (a fantasy building) here, **Ossian's cave** and the awesome **Ossian's Hall,** above a spectacular—and noisy—waterfall. You'll also be in the presence of Britain's tallest tree, a Douglas Fir measuring 214 feet. ⊠ *1 mi west of Dunkeld on A9.*

Shopping
At the **Jeremy Law of Scotland's Highland Horn and Deerskin Centre** (⊠ City Hall, Atholl St. ☎ 01350/727569), you can purchase stag antlers and cow horns shaped into walking sticks, cutlery, and tableware. Deerskin shoes and moccasins, small leather goods made from deerskin, and a specialty malt-whisky collection of more than 200 different malts are also sold.

Blair Castle

⑱ *25 mi north of Dunkeld.*

Fodor'sChoice
★

Thanks to its historic contents and war-torn past, Blair Castle is one of Scotland's most highly rated sights. The turreted white castle was home to successive dukes of Atholl and their families, the Murrays, until the death of the 10th duke. One of the castle's fascinating details is a preserved piece of floor still bearing marks of the red-hot shot fired through the roof during the 1745 Jacobite rebellion—the last occasion in Scottish history that a castle was besieged. The castle holds not only military artifacts—historically, the duke was allowed to keep a private army, the Atholl Highlanders—but also a collection of furniture and paintings. Outside is a Victorian walled garden. ⊠ *From Dunkeld, take A9 to Blair Atholl and follow signs* ☎ *01796/481207* ⊕ *www.blair-castle. co.uk* ⊠ *£7.20* ☉ *Apr.–Oct., daily 9:30–5; last admission at 4.*

Shopping
The **House of Bruar** (⊠ A9, just north of Blair Atholl ☎ 01796/483236) is an Aladdin's cave for shopaholics who love top-quality Scottish clothing, blown glass, and Scottish sweets and condiments. Take a walk up the path that crosses the Bruar Falls, accessed at the back of the shopping complex. There are two bridges with waterfalls, pools, rock formations, and indigenous trees at either side.

FIFE & ANGUS

East of Perth is Fife, known for St. Andrews, a town that has more to offer than fabulous golf. Also here are East Neuk seaside villages such as Crail, with unusual Dutch-influenced architecture. Angus, north of Fife, contains the city of Dundee and more rural attractions.

St. Andrews

19 *52 mi northeast of Edinburgh, 83 mi northeast of Glasgow.*

St. Andrews is unlike any other Scottish town. Once Scotland's most powerful ecclesiastical center as well as the seat of the country's oldest university and then, much later, the very symbol and spiritual home of golf, the town has a comfortable, well-groomed air, sitting almost smugly apart from the rest of Scotland. This air of superiority has received a huge boost from Prince William's presence as a student here (he graduated in 2005), which has also led to a record number of foreign students enrolling at the university.

The town's modern claim to fame is mainly its status as the home of golf. Forget that Scottish kings were crowned here, or that John Knox preached here, or that Reformation reformers were burned at the stake here. Thousands flock to St. Andrews to play at the Old Course, home of the Royal & Ancient Club, but nongolfers can find much to do in the city's medieval streets.

St. Andrews Cathedral is today only a ruined, poignant fragment of what was formerly the largest and most magnificent church in Scotland. Work on it began in 1160, and after several set backs it was finally consecrated in 1318. The church was subsequently damaged by fire and repaired, but fell into decay during the Reformation. Only ruined gables, parts of the nave's south wall, and other fragments survive. The on-site museum helps you interpret the remains and gives a sense of what the cathedral must once have been like. The cathedral is near St. Rule's Tower, which has great views of the town. ✉ *Off Pends Rd.* ☎ *01334/472563* ⊕ *www.historic-scotland.gov.uk* ✑ *£3.50 includes admission to St. Rule's Tower; £6 includes admission to St Andrews Castle* ☉ *Apr.–Sept., daily 9:30–6; Oct.–Mar., daily 9:30–4.*

On the shore north of the cathedral stands **St. Andrews Castle,** which was begun at the end of the 13th century. Although now a ruin, the remains include a rare example of a cold and gruesome bottle-shape dungeon, in which many prisoners spent their last hours. Even more atmospheric is the castle's mine and countermine. The former was a tunnel dug by besieging forces in the 16th century; the latter, a tunnel dug by castle defenders in order to

WORD OF MOUTH
"In St. Andrews, the castle is well worth a visit, and I would try to get a tour from the university admissions office. This would cover much of the town's important history and fill you in on lots of interesting traditions. A day along the Fife coastal route would also be worthwhile."   –ashields

15

meet and wage battle below ground. You can stoop and crawl into this narrow passageway—an eerie experience, despite the addition of electric light. The visitor center has a good audiovisual presentation on the castle's history. ⊠ *North Castle St.* ☎ *01334/477196* ⊕ *www.historic-scotland.gov.uk* 🎫 *£4.50 includes admission to St. Rule's Tower; £6 includes admission to St. Andrews Cathedral* ☉ *Apr.–Sept., daily 9:30–6; Oct.–Mar., daily 9:30–4.*

The **Royal & Ancient Golf Club of St. Andrews,** the ruling house of golf worldwide, is the spiritual home of all who play or follow the game. Its clubhouse on the dunes—a dignified building open to members only—is adjacent to the famous Old Course. The town of St. Andrews prospers on golf, golf schools, and golf equipment (the manufacture of golf balls has been a local industry for more than 100 years), and the greatest golfers in the world play on the Old Course. As to the game and its origins on the Royal & Ancient's course, golf was perhaps originally played with a piece of driftwood, a shore pebble, and a convenient rabbit hole on the sandy, coastal turf. Citizens of St. Andrews were playing golf on the town links as far back as the 15th century. Rich golfers, instead of gathering on the links favored by the common people, formed themselves into clubs. Founded as the Society of St. Andrews Golfers in 1754, the Royal & Ancient Golf Club of St. Andrews took its current name in 1834. ⊠ *The Scores* ☎ *01334/460000* 🖷 *01334/460001* ⊕ *www.randa.org.*

The **British Golf Museum** explores the centuries-old relationship between St. Andrews and golf and displays golf memorabilia from the 18th century to the 21st century. It's just opposite the Royal & Ancient Golf Club. ⊠ *Bruce Embankment* ☎ *01334/460046* ⊕ *www.britishgolfmuseum. co.uk* 🎫 *£5* ☉ *Mar.–Oct., Mon.–Sat. 9:30–5:30; Sun. 10–5; Nov.–Feb., Mon.–Sat. 10–4.*

St. Andrews is the site of Scotland's oldest university. Founded in 1411, the **University of St. Andrews** now consists of two stately old colleges in the middle of town and some modern buildings on the outskirts. A third, weatherworn college, originally built in 1512, has become a girls' school. The handsome university buildings can be explored on guided walks, sometimes led by students clad in scarlet gowns. ☎ *01334/462245* ⊕ *www. st-andrews.ac.uk* 🎫 *Tours, £4* ☉ *Tours: June–Aug., weekdays 11 and 2:30.*

Where to Stay & Eat

★ **£££** ✕ **The Seafood Restaurant.** This glass-walled building is perched on the banks of the West Sands. Formerly the site of an open-air theater, the kitchen, visible to all diners, creates a sense of drama all its own. The food is adventurous without being flashy: start with lobster in a mango and chili sauce, then move on to the wild sea bass served with roasted fennel. ⊠ *Bruce Embankment* ☎ *01334/479475* ▭ *AE, MC, V.*

£–££ ✕ **Westport.** In summer while the students are away, it can be easy to forget that St. Andrews is a university town, but this place seems vibrant and youthful year-round. If you want to drink and graze, have a snack at the bar; for something more substantial, such as rib-eye steak with root-vegetable fries or oyster and pea risotto, a table at the restaurant in the back is worth the wait. ⊠ *170 South St.* ☎ *01334/473186* ▭ *AE, MC, V.*

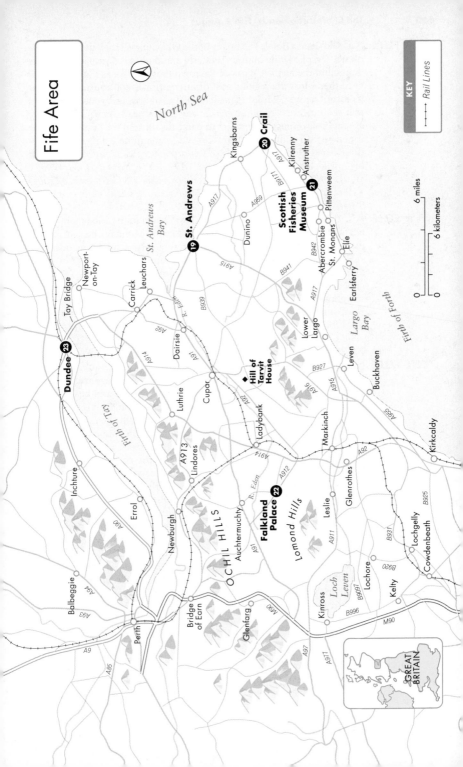

Fife Area

North Sea

KEY

Rail Lines

6 miles

6 kilometers

St. Andrews Bay

Firth of Forth

Largo Bay

Firth of Tay

OCHIL HILLS

Lomond Hills

Loch Leven

GREAT BRITAIN

19 St. Andrews

20 Crail

21 Scottish Fisheries Museum

22 Falkland Palace

23 Dundee

Kingsbarns

Kilrenny

Anstruther

Pittenweem

Abercrombie

St. Monans

Elie

Earlsferry

Dunino

Newport-on-Tay

Tay Bridge

Carrick

Leuchars

Dairsie

Luthrie

Cupar

Hill of Tarvit House

Lower Largo

Leven

Buckhaven

Kirkcaldy

Ladybank

Markinch

Glenrothes

Leslie

Lindores

Newburgh

Inchture

Errol

Balbeggie

Perth

Bridge of Earn

Glenfarg

Auchtermuchty

Kinross

Lochore

Kelly

Cowdenbeath

Lochgelly

R. Eden

R. Tay

A917

A919

A959

A917

A915

B9131

B9171

B942

B941

A917

B927

A916

A915

A92

A91

A92

A913

A914

A912

A911

B931

B920

B925

B996

B9097

M90

A90

A94

A93

A9

A85

A94

A85

A90

A92

A91

B939

££££££ ╳▢ **Old Course Hotel.** The image of the Old Course Hotel defines St. Andrews. Despite being built in 1968, the building is so sympathetic to the dunes and the historic parts of the town that it looks as if it has always been there. It is the regular host of international golf tournaments, but its location and facilities make it appeal to almost everyone. The staff's ability to meet every whim makes any stay a heady experience. There are multiple dining choices, but to make the most of the luxury here, opt for an aperitif in the Sands Bar followed by an intimate dinner in the top-floor Road Hole Grill, which serves sophisticated Scottish cuisine and has a wine list that goes on forever. ✉ *A91, KY16 9SP* ☎ *01334/474371* 🖷 *01334/477668* ⊕ *www.oldcoursehotel.co.uk* ⇥ *114 rooms, 32 suites* ♧ *2 restaurants, minibars, cable TV, indoor pool, health club, hair salon, 3 bars, shop, Internet; no a/c* ▤ *AE, MC, V* ¶⊙¶ *BP.*

★ ££££££ ╳▢ **The Peat Inn.** This popular inn is best known for its outstanding modern Scottish-style restaurant (closed Sunday and Monday), considered one of the finest in the country. Mouthwatering entrées might include roast scallops with pea puree, or medallions of monkfish and lobster with artichoke hearts in a lobster sauce. Save room for desserts such as the rich chocolate pot with rosemary. A detached building houses the bright, contemporary two-room suites. make reservations well in advance. ✉ *Jct. B940 and B941, 6 mi southwest of St. Andrews* ◁ *Cupar, Fife, KY15 5LH* ☎ *01334/840206* 🖷 *01334/840530* ⊕ *www.thepeatinn.co.uk* ⇥ *8 suites* ♧ *Restaurant, bar, free parking; no a/c* ▤ *AE, MC, V* ¶⊙¶ *CP.*

★ ££££–££££££ ╳▢ **St. Andrews Bay Golf Resort & Spa.** Just 2 mi from St. Andrews, this baronial hotel has spectacular views of the bay and superb golf. The rooms eschew swags and frills, opting instead for simple elegance. Look for thoughtful touches like luxurious linens on the beds and heated floors in the ample bathrooms. The restaurants are excellent: the crimson-walled Esperante offers a inventive menu that draws from the flavors of Tuscany, while the more casual Squire serves Scottish country-style dishes such as rump of lamb with a pea and mint puree. Golfers will find inspiration in the velvety fairways of two cliff-top courses, especially the Torrance Course: 7,037 breathtaking yards designed by the great Scottish player Sam Torrance. ✉ *St. Andrews Bay, KY16 8PN* ☎ *01334/ 837000* 🖷 *01334/471115* ⊕ *www.standrewsbay.com* ⇥ *192 rooms, 17 suites* ♧ *3 restaurants, room service, in-room safes, minibars, cable TV, in-room DVDs, in-room data ports, 2 golf courses, pool, health club, hot tub, sauna, spa, 3 bars, laundry service, business services, meeting rooms, convention center* ▤ *AE, DC, MC, V* ¶⊙¶ *BP.*

££ ▢ **Aslar Guest House.** Inside this terraced town house dating from 1865 you'll find large rooms decorated with antique and reproduction furniture. One room has a four-poster bed, another a fireplace. St. Andrews's historic center is within walking distance. ✉ *120 North St., KY16 9AF* ☎ *01334/473460* 🖷 *01334/477540* ⊕ *www.aslar.com* ⇥ *6 rooms* ♧ *Cable TV, lounge, Internet; no a/c, no room phones* ▤ *MC, V* ¶⊙¶ *BP.*

Nightlife & the Arts

THEATER The **Byre Theatre** (✉ Abbey St. ☎ 01334/475000 ⊕ www.byretheatre.com) commissions and produces new works. Experimental and youth theater, small-scale operatic performances, contemporary dance, and Sunday night jazz (in the foyer) are also on the bill. There's an excellent café-bar.

Golf

One 9-hole and five 18-hole courses are open to visitors. For information about availability—there's usually a waiting list, which varies according to the time of year—contact **St. Andrews Links Trust** (⊠ Pilmour House, St. Andrews KY16 9SF ☎ 01334/466666 ⊕ www.standrews. org.uk). Greens fees range from £80 to £115 for a round on the Old Course and from £22 to £55 for a round on the five other courses.

Balgove Course. Redesigned and reopened in 1993, Balgove is a beginner-friendly course at which you can turn up and tee off without prior reservation. *⚑ 9 holes, 1,520 yds, par 30.*

Eden Course. The inland and aptly named Eden, designed in 1914 by Harry S. Colt, has an easy charm compared to the other St. Andrews Links courses. *⚑ 18 holes, 6,162 yds, par 70.*

Jubilee Course. This windswept course, opened in 1897, offers quite a challenge even for experienced golfers. *⚑ 18 holes, 6,805 yds, par 72.*

★ **New Course.** Not exactly new—it opened in 1895—the New Course is rather overshadowed by the Old Course, but it has a firm following of golfers who appreciate the loop design. *⚑ 18 holes, 6,604 yds, par 71.*

Old Course. Believed to be the oldest golf course in the world, the Old Course was first played in the 15th century. Each year, more than 44,000 rounds are teed off, and no doubt most get stuck in one of its 112 bunkers. A handicap certificate is required. *⚑ 18 holes, 6,566 yds, par 72.*

Strathtyrum Course. Those with a high handicap will enjoy a toddle around this course, opened in 1993, without the worry or embarrassment of holding up more experienced golfers. *⚑ 18 holes, 5,094 yds, par 69.*

Shopping

Renton Oriental Rugs (⊠ 72 South St. ☎ 01334/476334) is the best place in the region, if not in all Scotland, to buy rugs and carpets of all colors, patterns, and sizes. Many of those on display are antiques. The **St. Andrews Pottery Shop** (⊠ Church Sq., between South St. and Market St. ☎ 01334/477744) sells decorative domestic stoneware, porcelain, ceramics, enamel jewelry, and terra-cotta pots.

Crail

❷⓿ *10 mi south of St. Andrews via A917.*

Fodor'sChoice
★

The oldest and most aristocratic of East Neuk burghs, Crail is where many fish merchants retired and built cottages. The town landmark is a picturesque Dutch-influenced town house, or *tolbooth*, which contains the oldest bell in Fife, cast in Holland in 1520. As you head into East Neuk from this tiny port, look about for tolbooths, market crosses, and merchant houses and their little *doocots* (dovecotes, where pigeons were kept)—typical picturesque touches of this region. Full details on the heritage of the region can be found in the **Crail Museum & Heritage Center.** ⊠ 62–64 Marketgate ☎ 01333/450869 ⤷ *Free* ☉ *Easter and June–Sept., Mon.–Sat. 10–1 and 2–5, Sun. 2–5; after Easter–end of May, weekends and holidays 2–5.*

Anstruther

4 mi southwest of Crail via A917.

㉑ Anstruther, locally called Ainster, has a lovely waterfront with a few shops brightly festooned with children's pails and shovels, a gesture to summer vacationers. Facing Anstruther harbor is the **Scottish Fisheries Museum**, in a colorful cluster of buildings, the earliest of which dates from the 16th century. The museum illustrates the life of Scottish fisherfolk through documents, artifacts, model ships, paintings, and tableaux. These displays, complete with the reek of tarred rope and net, have been known to induce nostalgic tears in not a few old deckhands. There are also floating exhibits at the quayside. ⊠ *Anstruther Harbor* ☎ *01333/310628* ⊕ *www.scotfishmuseum.org* 🖃 *£4.50* ⊙ *Apr.–Oct., Mon.–Sat. 10–5:30, Sun. 11–5; Nov.–Mar., Mon.–Sat. 10–4:15, Sun. noon–4:15; last admission 45 mins before closing.*

Falkland

20 mi west of St. Andrews.

㉒

★ One of the loveliest communities in Scotland, Falkland is a royal burgh of twisting streets and crooked stone houses. **Falkland Palace,** a former hunting lodge of the Stuart monarchs, dominates the town. The castle is one of the earliest examples in Britain of the French Renaissance style. Overlooking the main street is the palace's most impressive feature— the walls and chambers on its south side, all rich with Renaissance buttresses and stone medallions, built by French masons in the 1530s for King James V (1512–42). He died here, and the palace was a favorite resort of his daughter, Mary, Queen of Scots (1542–87). The gardens behind the palace contain a rare survivor: a royal tennis court—not at all like its modern counterpart—built in 1539. In the beautiful gardens, overlooked by the palace turret windows, you may easily imagine yourself back at the solemn hour when James on his deathbed pronounced the doom of the house of Stuart: "It cam' wi' a lass and it'll gang wi a lass." ⊠ *Main St.* ☎ *01337/857397* ⊕ *www.nts.org.uk* 🖃 *Gardens and palace £10* ⊙ *Mar.–Oct., Mon.–Sat. 10–6, Sun. 1–5.*

Dundee

㉓ *14 mi northwest of St. Andrews, 58 mi north of Edinburgh, 79 mi northeast of Glasgow.*

The small, industrial city of Dundee sits near the mouth of the River Tay, surrounded by the farms and glens of rural Angus and the coastal grassy banks and golf courses of northeastern Fife. Dundee has a large student population, a lively music and nightlife scene, smart restaurants, and several historical and nautical sights. The popular comic strips *The Beano* and *The Dandy* were first published here in the 1930s, so statues depicting Desperate Dan, Dawg, and a catapult-wielding Minnie the Minx, were erected in the City Square.

★ ☾ Between a 17th-century mansion and a cathedral, this strikingly modern building houses one of Britain's most exciting artistic venues, **Dundee Contemporary Arts.** Its galleries specialize in the best works of both Scottish and international artists. There are children's workshops and meet-the-artist events throughout the year. There are also two movie theaters showing mainly independent, revival, and children's films, a craft shop, and a buzzing café-bar called Jute that's open until midnight. ✉ *152 Nethergate* ☎ *01382/909252* ⊕ *www.dca.org.uk* ✍ *Free* ☉ *Tues., Wed., Fri., Sat. 10:30–5:30, Thurs. 10:30–8:30, Sun. noon–5.*

☾ Dundee's urban renewal program—its determination to shake off its industrial past—was motivated in part by the arrival of the RRS (Royal Research Ship) *Discovery,* the vessel used by Captain Robert Scott (1868–1912) on his polar explorations. The steamer was originally built and launched in Dundee; now it's a permanent resident. An onboard exhibition allows you to sample life as it was aboard the intrepid ship. One popular exhibit lets you experience life in Antarctica hands-on and heads-in—you'll feel the temperature and the wind chill as if you were there. ✉ *Discovery Quay* ☎ *01382/201245* ⊕ *www.rrsdiscovery. com* ✍ *£8.65; £10.95 with Verdant Works* ☉ *Apr.–Oct., Mon.–Sat. 10–5, Sun. 11–6; Nov.–Mar., Mon.–Sat. 10–5, Sun. 11–5.*

Where to Stay & Eat

£–££ ✕ **Het Theatercafe.** At the lively Rep Theatre, you have a choice of the café-bar upstairs, which serves light fare and good coffee, or the restaurant downstairs. The international dishes include chicken *satay* (grilled meat on skewers) and Cajun chicken or fish cakes. Theater posters of past productions and stills of actors decorate the walls. ✉ *Tay Sq.* ☎ *01382/206699* ⊕ *www.het-theatercafe.co.uk* ⊟ *MC, V* ☉ *Closed Sun.*

£££ ✕⊡ **Apex City Quay.** This contemporary quayside hotel has sleek, Scandinavian-style rooms with easy chairs, satiny pillows, and CD/DVD players to help you unwind. To relax further, or to exercise, head for the Japanese spa and fitness center. The restaurant and brasserie, both with views of the harbor, have globally influenced menus. There are numerous variations of simple Italian and Asian dishes, as well as perfectly cooked steaks. ✉ *1 W. Victoria Dock Rd., DD1 3JP* ☎ *01382/202404* ⊟ *01382/201401* ⊕ *www.apexhotels.com* ⚬ *145 rooms, 8 suites* ⚬ *2 restaurants, cable TV, in-room DVDs, in-room data ports, indoor pool, health club, spa, lounge, business services, meeting rooms, free parking; no a/c* ⊟ *MC, V* ⦿ *CP.*

Nightlife & the Arts

The **Dundee Repertory Theatre** (✉ Tay Sq. ☎ 01382/223530) is home to the nationally respected Dundee Rep Ensemble as well as Scotland's preeminent contemporary-dance group, Scottish Dance Theatre. Popular with locals, the restaurant and bar welcome late night comedy shows and jazz bands.

The **Speedwell Bar** (✉ 165–168 Perth Rd. ☎ 01382/667783), called Mennie's by the locals, is in a mahogany-paneled building brimming with Dundonian character. It's renowned for superb cask beers.

15

Arbroath

㉔ *15 mi north of Dundee via A92.*

You'll find traditional boatbuilding in the fishing town of Arbroath. It also has several small curers and processors, and shops sell the town's most famous delicacy, "Arbroath smokies"—whole haddock gutted and lightly smoked.

Arbroath Abbey, founded in 1178, is an unmistakable presence in the town center; it seems to straddle whole streets, as if the town were simply ignoring the red-stone ruin in its midst. Surviving today are remains of the church, as well as one of the most complete examples in existence of an abbot's residence. From here in 1320 a passionate plea was sent by King Robert the Bruce (1274–1329) and the Scottish Church to Pope John XXII (circa 1245–1334) in far-off Rome. The pope had until then sided with the English kings, who adamantly refused to acknowledge Scottish independence. The Declaration of Arbroath stated firmly, "For as long as but a hundred of us remain alive, never will we on any conditions be brought under English rule. It is in truth not for glory, nor riches, nor honours that we are fighting, but for freedom—for that alone, which no honest man gives up but with life itself." Some historians describe this plea, originally drafted in Latin, as the single most important document in Scottish history. The pope advised English king Edward II (1284–1327) to make peace, but warfare was to break out along the border from time to time for the next 200 years. The excellent visitor center recounts this history in well-planned displays. ⊠ *Arbroath town center* ☎ *01241/878756* ⊕ *www.historic-scotland.gov. uk* ⊠ *£4* ☽ *Apr.–Sept., daily 9:30–6; Oct.–Mar., daily 9:30–4.*

Arbroath was the base for the construction of the Bell Rock lighthouse on a treacherous, barely exposed rock in the early 19th century. A signal tower was built to facilitate communication with the builders working far from shore. That structure now houses the **Signal Tower Museum,** which tells the story of the lighthouse, built by Robert Stevenson (1772–1850) in 1811. The museum also houses a collection of items related to the history of the town, its customs, and the local fishing industry. ⊠ *Ladyloan, west of harbor* ☎ *01241/875598* ⊕ *www.angus. gov.uk* ⊠ *Free* ☽ *Sept.–June, Mon.–Sat. 10–5; July and Aug., Mon.–Sat. 10–5, Sun. 2–5.*

Where to Eat

£–££ ✕ **But 'n' Ben.** A few miles along the coast, this restaurant offers a taste of quality Scottish home cooking, including smoked fish pâté and lemon drizzle cake, all at reasonable prices. After lunch, stroll down to the Auchmithie's lovely, shingle beach. ⊠ *Auchmithie, North of Arbroath, 3 mi east of A92* ☎ *01241/877223* ▭ *MC, V* ☽ *Closed Tues.*

Kirriemuir

㉕ *17 mi west of Arbroath.*

Kirriemuir stands at the heart of Angus's red-sandstone countryside and was the birthplace of the writer J. M. Barrie (1860–1937), best known

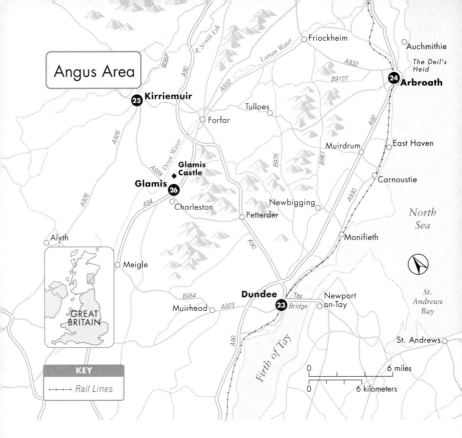

abroad as the author of *Peter Pan*. **J. M. Barrie's Birthplace** has the upper
floors furnished as they might have been in Barrie's time, complete with
manuscripts and personal mementos. The outside washhouse is said to
have been Barrie's first theater. Next door, at 11 Brechin Road, is an
exhibition about the author. A ticket includes admission to Camera Obscura, which affords magnificent views of the surrounding area on a clear
day. ⊠ *9 Brechin Rd.* ☎ *01575/572646* ⊕ *www.nts.org.uk* ✉ *£10, includes Camera Obscura* ☉ *Apr.–Oct., Mon.–Sat. 11–5, Sun. 1–5.*

Glamis

26 *6 mi south of Kirriemuir via A928.*

Fodor'sChoice **Glamis Castle**, one of Scotland's best-known and most beautiful castles,
★ connects Britain's royalty through 10 centuries, from Macbeth ("Thane
of Glamis") to the late Princess Margaret—born here in 1930 in the ancestral home of her mother—the first royal princess born in Scotland
in 300 years. The property of the earls of Strathmore and Kinghorne
since 1372, the castle was largely reconstructed in the late 17th century;
the original keep, which is much older, is still intact. One of the most
famous rooms in the castle is Duncan's Hall, the legendary setting for
Shakespeare's *Macbeth*. Guided tours allow you to see fine collections

of china, tapestries, and furniture. Also on the premises are several shops, a produce stall, and a restaurant. ⊠ *A94, 1 mi north of Glamis* ☎ *01307/840393* ⊕ *www.strathmore-estates.co.uk* ⊠ *Grounds £3.70, Castle £7.30* ⊙ *Mar.–Oct., daily 10–6; Nov. and Dec., daily noon–4.*

CENTRAL HIGHLANDS, FIFE & ANGUS ESSENTIALS

Transportation

BY AIR

The Central Highlands can be reached easily from the Edinburgh, Dundee, and Glasgow airports by train, car, or bus. Dundee Airport is off the A85, 2 mi west of the city center. ScotAirways operates a popular direct flight to Dundee from London City Airport. The Tay estuary and its two bridges makes for a stunning view during take off or landing.

🚩 **ScotAirways** ☎ 0870/6060707 ⊕ www.scotairways.com.

BY BUS

A good network of buses connects the Central Highlands, Fife, and Angus with Edinburgh and Glasgow. For information, contact Scottish Citylink or National Express. Scottish Citylink operates hourly service to Dundee from both Glasgow and Edinburgh. First Ltd. serves the area around Stirling, and Stagecoach Fife Buses serves Fife and St. Andrews. Strathtay Scottish operates across Fife's and Angus's smaller towns and villages. Traveline is a service that helps you plan all public transportation journeys.

🚩 **Bus Information First Ltd.** ⊠ Goosecroft Rd. bus station, Stirling ☎ 08708/727271. **National Express** ☎ 08705/808080 ⊕ www.nationalexpress.com. **Scottish Citylink** ☎ 08705/505050 ⊕ www.citylink.co.uk. **Stagecoach Fife Buses** ☎ 01592/261461 ⊕ www.stagecoachbus.com. **Stagecoach Perth** ⊠ Ruthvenfield Rd., Inveralmond Industrial Estate, Perth ☎ 01738/629339 ⊕ www.stagecoachbus.com.

Strathtay Scottish ☎ 01382/228345. **Travel Dundee** ☎ 08706/082608 ⊕ www. traveldundee.co.uk. **Traveline Scotland** ☎ 08706/082608 ⊕ www.travelinescotland.com.

BY CAR

You'll find easy access to the area from the central belt of Scotland via the motorways. The M9 runs within sight of the walls of Stirling Castle, and Perth, Dundee, and St. Andrews can be reached via the M90 over the Forth Bridge from Edinburgh. Local tourist information centers can give you information on two signed touring routes are useful: the Perthshire Tourist Route, and the Deeside Tourist Route, with a spectacular journey via Blairgowrie and Glenshee to Deeside and Aberdeen. If you're coming from Fife, you can use the A91 and the A914 and then cross the Tay Bridge to reach Dundee, though the quickest way is to use the fast-paced, less-scenic M90/A90. Travel time from Edinburgh to Dundee is about one hour, from Edinburgh to St. Andrews, 1½ hours.

Fife is easy to get around—although it can be difficult to find a place to park in St. Andrews. Most roads are quiet and uncongested. The most interesting sights are in the east, which is served by a network of cross-country roads. Angus is likewise an easy region to explore because it's serviced by a fast main road, the A90, plus the A92, a gentler road; rural roads run between the Grampians and the A90.

BY TRAIN

The Central Highlands are linked to Edinburgh and Glasgow by rail. First Scotrail operates the Glasgow to Aberdeen service, which stops at Stirling, Gleneagles, Perth, Dundee, Arboroath, and Montrose. From Perth you can travel to Dunkeld, Pitlochry, and Blair Atholl, and onward to Inverness. From Edinburgh you can travel direct to Stirling or through Fife to Dundee and onward to Aberdeen. Several Savers ticket options are available, although in some cases on the ScotRail system, discount fares must be purchased before your arrival in the United Kingdom. Contact National Rail or ScotRail for details.

🚺 **First ScotRail** ☎ 08457/484950 ⊕ www.firstgroup.com/scotrail. **National Rail Enquiries** ☎ 08457/484950 ⊕ www.nationalrail.co.uk.

Contacts & Resources

EMERGENCIES

Dial ☎ **999** in case of an emergency to reach an ambulance, or the fire or police departments. Late-night pharmacies are not found outside the larger cities. In the larger centers, such as Stirling, Perth, St. Andrews and Dundee, pharmacies use a rotating system for off-hours and Sunday prescription service: your hotel will have details.

🚺 **Hospitals Ninewells** ⊠ Ninewells Ave., Dundee ☎ 01382/660111. **Perth Royal Infirmary** ⊠ Taymount Terr., Perth ☎ 01738/623311. **Stirling Royal Infirmary** ⊠ Livilands Gate, Stirling ☎ 01786/434000.

INTERNET

🚺 **Gigabytes Internet Access Point** ⊠ 5 St. Paul's Sq., Perth ☎ 01738/451580 ⊕ www.gig-at-bytes.com. **Networx Internet Cafe** ⊠ 68 Murray Pl., Stirling ☎ 01786/471122.

TOURING OPTIONS

Fishers Tours has bus tours year-round both within and outside the region. Lochs and Glens operates bus tours of Scotland year-round. Heritage Golf Tours Scotland specializes in golf vacations that include hotel and car rental and course reservations. Links Golf St. Andrews tailors tours to individual requirements.

🚺 **Bus Tours Fishers Tours** ⊠ 16 West Port, Dundee ☎ 01382/227290 ⊕ www.fisherstours.co.uk. **Lochs and Glens** ⊠ Gartocharn, West Dunbartonshire ☎ 01389/713713 ⊕ www.lochsandglens.com.

🚺 **Golf Tours Heritage Golf Tours Scotland** ⊠ Swilken House, 21 Loch Dr., Helensburgh, G84 8PY ☎ 01436/674630 ⊕ www.golftours-scotland.co.uk. **Links Golf St. Andrews** ⊠ 7 Pilmour Links, St. Andrews, KY16 9JG ☎ 01334/478639 ⊕ www.linksgolfstandrews.com.

VISITOR INFORMATION

In the Central Highlands, the Auchterader, Dunkeld, Loch Lomond & the Trossachs, Perth, and Stirling tourist offices are open year-round. Seasonal tourist information centers are open (generally from April to October) in Aberfoyle, Balloch, Callander, and other towns. In Fife and Angus, the Arbroath, Dundee, and St. Andrews tourist offices are open year-round. Smaller tourist information centers operate seasonally in towns including Crail and Kirriemuir. You can contact them at www.visitscotland.com.

🚩 **Arbroath** ⊠ Market Pl., Arbroath DD11 1HR ☎ 01241/872609. **Auchterarder** ⊠ 90 High St. ☎ 01764/663450 ⊕ www.perthshire.co.uk. **Dundee** ⊠ 21 Castle St., Dundee DD1 3AA ☎ 01382/527527 ⊕ www.angusanddundee.co.uk. **Dunkeld** ⊠ The Cross ☎ 01350/727688 ⊕ www.perthshire.co.uk. **Loch Lomond & the Trossachs National Park Gateway Centre** ⊠ Loch Lomond Shores, near Balloch ☎ 01389/722199 or 0845/345-4978 ⊕ www.lochlomond-trossachs.org. **Perth** ⊠ Lower City Mills, W. Mill St. ☎ 01738/450600 ⊕ www.perthshire.co.uk. **St. Andrews** ⊠ 70 Market St., St. Andrews KY16 9NU ☎ 01334/472021 ⊕ www.standrews.com. **Stirling** ⊠ 41 Dumbarton Rd. ☎ 08707/200620 ⊠ Royal Burgh of Stirling Visitor Centre, Castle Esplanade ☎ 08707/200622 ⊕ www.visitscottishheartlands.org.

Aberdeen & the Northeast

CASTLE COUNTRY, THE MALT WHISKY TRAIL

WORD OF MOUTH

"We drove on up through Braemar and Balmoral and along the Dee. By now we were well off the beaten path, on a B road. We stopped at Kildrummy Castle—a ruin not far from Huntly and a nice contrast to elegant, inhabited Scone. We were the only ones there and had a great time running around exploring the ruins. Did we mention that it had been a marvelous, sunny day to this point?"

ms_go—

"I suggest doing the Glenlivet tour. One of our trip highlights was the drive through the Glenlivet Estate via Tomintoul (from the south) to the distillery. The scenery was beautiful, and we saw pheasants, deer, and shaggy Highland cattle. The tour was fantastic as well."

—bettyk

Updated by
Shona Main
and Nick
Bruno

HERE, IN THIS GRANITE SHOULDER of Grampian, are Royal Deeside, the countryside that Queen Victoria made her own; the Castle Country route, where fortresses stand hard against the hills; and the Malt Whisky Trail, where peaty streams embrace the country's greatest concentration of distilleries. The region's gateway is the city of Aberdeen, constructed of granite and now aglitter with new wealth and new blood drawn together by North Sea oil.

Because of its isolation, Aberdeen has historically been a fairly autonomous place. Even now it's perceived by many U.K. inhabitants as lying almost out of reach in the Northeast. In reality, it's only 90 minutes' flying time from London or a little more than two hours by car from Edinburgh. Its magnificent, confident 18th- and early-19th-century city center amply rewards exploration.

Some credit Sir Walter Scott with having opened up Scotland for tourism through his poems and novels. Others say General Wade did it when he built the Highland roads. But it was probably Queen Victoria who gave Scottish tourism its real momentum when, in 1842, she first came to Scotland and when, in 1847—on orders of a doctor, who thought the relatively dry climate of upper Deeside would suit her—she bought Balmoral. At first sight she described it as "a pretty little castle in the old Scottish style." The pretty little castle was knocked down to make room for a much grander house in full-flown Scottish baronial style, designed, in fact, by her husband, Prince Albert. Before long the entire Deeside and the region north were dotted with handsome country houses and mock-baronial châteaux. The locals, bless 'em, took it all in stride. To this day, the hundreds who line the road when the queen and her family arrive for services at the family's parish church at Crathie are invariably visitors to Deeside.

Balmoral is merely the most famous castle in the area. A Castle Trail leads you to such fortresses as the ruined medieval Kildrummy Castle, which once controlled the strategic routes through the valley of the River Don. Grand mansions such as Haddo House, with its symmetrical facade and elegant interior, surrender any defensive role entirely and instead make statements about their owner's status.

South of Elgin and Banff, the glens embrace Scotland's greatest concentration of malt-whisky distilleries. With so many in Morayshire, where the distilling is centered in the valley of the River Spey and its tributaries, there's now a Whisky Trail. Follow it to experience a surprising wealth of flavors, considering that whisky is made of three basic ingredients.

The Northeast's chief attraction lies in the gradual transition from high mountain plateau—by a series of gentle steps through hill, forest, and farmland—to the Moray Firth and North Sea coast, where the word "unadulterated" is redefined. Here you'll find some of the United Kingdom's most perfect wild shorelines, both sandy and sheer cliff. The Grampian Mountains, to the west, contain some of the highest

TOP REASONS TO GO

Castle Trail: Some 75 fairy-tale castles, all built between the 15th and 19th centuries, tell stories of clan power and feudal wealth. They range from crumbled ruins overgrown with gorse, such as Dunnotar, to still-grand piles like Balmoral that brim with priceless antiques and art. Some choices ones are on the Castle Trail (⊕ www.agtb.org/castletrail.htm).

Malt Whisky Trail: Whisky connoisseurs know this area as the home of the Malt Whiskey Trail. Tour the distilleries and learn how the sweet single malts such as Glenfiddich are crafted. At the Speyside Cooperage in Craigellachie, see how whisky barrels are made.

An awe-inspiring landscape: Between dark, brooding Lochnagar,

the undulating plains of Banffshire, and the gold-fringed coastline of Cullen, a different kind of beauty is always over the hill or around the bend in the road.

Charming fishing villages: The Northeast was built on the fishing industry, and scores of picturesque fishing villages, such as Cullen and Findochty, have beautiful harbors and eateries that serve the day's catch.

Fine food: The heather-clad hills and lush grasslands make for well-fed animals and the juiciest cuts of meat in Scotland. It is beyond the main drags, such as at the Old Monastery in Findochty and Minmore House in Glenlivet, where the prodigious produce of the Northeast speaks for itself.

16

ground in the nation, in the area of the Cairngorms. In recognition of this area's very special nature, Cairngorms National Park (Scotland's second, after Loch Lomand and the Trossachs National Park) was created in 2003.

Exploring Aberdeen & the Northeast

Once you have spent time in Aberdeen, you may be inclined to venture west into Deeside, with its royal connections and looming mountain backdrop, and then pass over the hills into the Castle Country to the north. You might head farther west to touch on Speyside and the Whisky Trail, before meandering back east and south along the pristine coastline at Scotland's northeasternmost tip.

About the Restaurants & Hotels

The Northeast has some splendid country hotels with log fires and old Victorian furnishings, where you can also be sure of eating well. Many hotels in Aberdeen offer competitive rates on weekends. Partly in response to the demands of spendthrift workers in the oil industry, restaurants have cropped up all over Aberdeen, and the quality of the food improves yearly.

WHAT IT COSTS In Pounds				
£££££	**££££**	**£££**	**££**	**£**
RESTAURANTS over £22	£18–£22	£13–£17	£7–£12	under £7
HOTELS over £160	£120–£160	£90–£119	£60–£89	under £60

Restaurant prices are for a main course at dinner. Hotel prices are for two people in a standard double room in high season, generally including the 17.5% V.A.T.

Timing

Because the National Trust for Scotland tends to close its properties in winter, many of the Northeast's castles are not suitable for off-season travel, though you can always see them from the outside. Duff House and some of the distilleries are open much of the year, but May to August are probably the best times to visit.

ABERDEEN

In the 18th century, local granite quarrying produced a durable silver stone that would be used boldly in the glittering blocks, spires, columns, and parapets of Victorian-era Aberdonian structures. The city remains one of the United Kingdom's most distinctive, although some would say it depends on the weather and the brightness of the day. The mica chips embedded in the rock look like a million mirrors in the sunshine. In rain and heavy clouds, however, their sparkle is snuffed out.

The North Sea has always been important to Aberdeen. In the 1850s the city was famed for its sleek, fast clippers that sailed to India for cargoes of tea. In the late 1960s the course of Aberdeen's history was unequivocally altered when oil and gas were discovered offshore, sparking rapid growth and further industrialization.

Aberdeen centers on Union Street, with its many fine survivors of the Victorian and Edwardian streetscape. Marischal College, dating from the late 16th century, has many grand buildings that are worth exploring in a half- or full day. Old Aberdeen is very much a separate area of the city, north of the modern center and clustered around St. Machar's Cathedral and the many fine buildings of the University of Aberdeen. You can take a bus to the area and spend a few hours exploring.

Main Attractions

❶ Aberdeen Art Gallery. The museum contains diverse paintings, prints and drawings, sculpture, porcelain, costumes, and much else—from 18th-century art to major contemporary works by Lucien Freud and Henry Moore. Local marble has been used in interior walls, pillars, and the central fountain, designed by the acclaimed British sculptor Barbara Hepworth. The museum also hosts frequent temporary exhibitions and has a good café. ⊠ *Schoolhill* ☎ *01224/523700* ⊕ *www.aagm.co.uk* ✉ *Free* ⊙ *Mon.–Sat. 10–5, Sun. 2–5.*

★ ❺ King's College. Founded in 1494, King's College is now part of the University of Aberdeen. Its **chapel,** which was built around 1500, has an unmistakable flying (or crown) spire. That it has survived at all was be-

The Scots Tongue

"MUCH," SAID DOCTOR JOHNSON, "may be made of a Scotchman if he be caught young." This quote sums up, even today, the attitude of some English people—confident in their English, the language of parliament and much of the media—to the Scots language. The Scots have long been made to feel uncomfortable about their mother tongue, and until the 1970s (and in some private schools, even today) they were actively encouraged to ape the dialect of the Thames Valley ("standard English") in order to "get on" in life.

The Scots language (that is, Lowland Scots, not Gaelic) was a northern form of Middle English and in its day was the language used in the court and in literature. It borrowed from Scandinavian, Dutch, French, and Gaelic. After a series of historical blows—such as the decamping of the Scottish court to England after 1603 and the printing of the King James Bible in English but not in Scots—it declined as a literary or official language. It survives in various forms but is virtually an underground language, spoken at home, in shops, and on the playground, the farm, and the quayside among ordinary folk, especially in its heartland, in the Northeast. You may even find yourself exporting a few useful words, such as *dreich* (gloomy), *glaikit* (acting and looking foolish), or *dinna fash* (don't worry), all of which are much more expressive than their English equivalents.

Some Scottish words are used and understood across the entire country (and world), such as *wee* (small), *aye* (yes), *lassie* (girl), and *bonny* (pretty). Regional variations are evident even in the simplest of greetings. When you meet someone in the Borders, *Whit fettle?* (What state are you in?) or *Hou ye lestin?* (How are you lasting?) may throw you for a loop; elsewhere you could hear *Hou's yer dous?* (How are your pigeons?). If a group of Scots take a fancy to you at the pub, you may be asked to *Come intil the body o the kirk*, and if all goes well, your departure may be met with *haste ye back* (return soon).

Scottish Gaelic, an entirely different language, is still spoken across the Highlands and Hebrides. There's also a large Gaelic-speaking population in Glasgow as a result of the Celtic diaspora—islanders migrating to Glasgow in search of jobs in the 19th century. Sizable populations in Canada, and smaller groups in New Zealand, Australia, and the United States bring the number of Gaelic speakers to roughly 60,000 worldwide. Speakers of Gaelic in Scotland were once persecuted, after the failure of the 18th-century Jacobite rebellions. Official persecution has now turned to guilt-tinged support.

One of the joys of Scottish television is watching Gaelic news programs to see how the ancient language copes with such topics as nuclear energy, the Internet, and the latest band to hit the charts. A number of Gaelic words have been absorbed into English: *banshee* (a wailing female spirit), *galore* (plenty), *slob* (a slovenly person), and *brat* (a spoiled or unruly child).

To experience Gaelic language and culture in all its unfettered glory, you can attend the Royal National Mod—a competition-based festival with speeches, drama, and music, all in Gaelic—which is held in a different location every year.

16

cause of the zeal of the principal, who defended his church against the destructive fanaticism that swept through Scotland during the Reformation, when the building was less than a century old. Today the renovated chapel plays an important role in university life. The tall oak screen that separates the nave from the choir, the ribbed wooden ceiling, and the stalls constitute the finest medieval wood carvings found anywhere in Scotland. The **King's College Centre** will tell you more about the university. ⊠ *High St.* ☎ *01224/272660* ⊕ *www.abdn.ac.uk/kcc* ⊙ *Weekdays 9:30–5, Sat. 11–4.*

★ ❹ **Marischal College.** Founded in 1593 by the Earl Marischal (the earls Marischal held hereditary office as keepers of the king's mares), Marischal College was a Protestant alternative to the Catholic King's College in Old Aberdeen. The two joined to form the University of Aberdeen in 1860. The original university building has undergone extensive renovations, and the current facade was built in 1891. The spectacularly ornate work is set off by the gilded flags, and this turn-of-the-20th-century creation is still the world's second-largest granite building. Only El Escorial, outside Madrid, is larger. The main part of the building, no longer needed by the university, is at present the subject of various plans, one of which would turn it into a hotel. The fascinating main galleries of the **Marischal Museum** hold two exhibits: the Encyclopaedia of the North East displays artifacts and photographs relating to the region's heritage; Collecting the World explores what local collectors gathered on their world travels and displays Egyptian and 19th-century ethnographic material. ⊠ *Broad St.* ☎ *01224/274301* ⊕ *www.abdn. ac.uk* ⊠ *Free* ⊙ *Museum weekdays 10–5, Sun. 2–5.*

★ ℭ ❸ **Provost Ross's House.** Dating from 1593 with a striking modern extension, this building holds the excellent **Aberdeen Maritime Museum,** which tells the story of the city's involvement with the sea, from early inshore fisheries to tea clippers and the North Sea oil boom. It's a fascinating place for kids, with its ship models, paintings, and equipment associated with the fishing, shipbuilding, and oil and gas industries. ⊠ *Ship Row* ☎ *01224/337700* ⊕ *www.aagm.co.uk* ⊠ *Free* ⊙ *Mon.–Sat. 10–5, Sun. noon–3.*

❻ **St. Machar's Cathedral.** It is said that St. Machar was sent by St. Columba to build a church on a grassy platform near the sea, where a river flowed in the shape of a shepherd's crook. This spot fit the bill. Although it was founded in AD 580, most of the existing building dates from the 15th and 16th centuries. The central tower collapsed in 1688, reducing the building to half its original length. The nave is thought to have been rebuilt in red sandstone in 1370, but the final renovation was completed in granite by the middle of the 15th century. Along with the nave ceiling, the twin octagonal spires were finished in time to take a battering in the Reformation, when the barons of the Mearns stripped the lead off the roof of St. Machar's and stole the bells. The cathedral suffered further mistreatment—including the removal of stone by Oliver Cromwell's English garrison in the 1650s—until it was fully restored in the 19th century. ⊠ *Chanonry* ☎ *01224/485988* ⊙ *Daily 9–5.*

Aberdeen

River Don

Don St.

Beach Esplanade

Seaton Park

King St.

Don St.

0 ____ 1/4 mile

0 ____ 1/4 kilometer

Tillydrone Rd.

Tillydrone Ave.

Chanonry

OLD ABERDEEN

Seaton Pl. E.

Kings

Portal

Don St.

Dunbar St.

St. Machar's Dr.

School Rd.

Links

High St.

School Dr.

Golf

Powis Cresent

Bedford Rd.

College Bounds

University Rd.

King St.

Regent Walk

Linksfield Stadium

Linksfield Rd.

Golf Rd.

Course

Sunnyside

Bedford Pl.

Sunnybank Rd.

Orchard St.

Pittodrie Pl.

Spital

Pittodrie St.

Elmbank Ter.

Froghall Ter.

King St.

Merkland Rd.

Powis Pl.

Kings Cr.

Park Rd.

George St.

Causeway End

Nelson St.

Seaforth Rd.

Urquhart Rd.

Hutcheon St.

George St.

W. North St.

King St.

Park Rd.

Constitution St.

Skene Sq.

Maberly St.

Galowgate

Beach Blvd.

Rosemount Pl.

John St.

St. Andrew

Cotton St.

Rosemount Viaduct

His Majesty's Theatre

Schoolhill

Upper Kirkgate

Broad St.

Castle St.

Justice St.

Mitler St.

Union Ter.

Union St.

Ship Row

Marischal St.

Regent Quay

Guild St.

S. College St.

Railway Station

Bus Station

Market St.

Upper Dock

Victoria Dock

Blaikies Quay

Commercial Quay

Albert Basin

Also Worth Seeing

② **Provost Skene's House.** Now a museum portraying civic life, the house has restored, furnished period rooms and a painted chapel. Steeply gabled and built from rubble, it dates in part from 1545. The house was originally a mayor's domestic dwelling (provost is Scottish for "mayor"). Its costume gallery displays colorful exhibitions of fashions from different centuries. ⊠ *Guestrow off Broad St.* ☎ *01224/641086* ⊕ *www. aagm.co.uk* ⊡ *Free* ⊙ *Mon.–Sat. 10–5, Sun. 1–4.*

OFF THE BEATEN PATH

DUNNOTTAR CASTLE – For an afternoon trip out from Aberdeen, it's hard to beat this magnificent cliff-top castle, which straddles a headland overlooking Stonehaven, 15 mi south of Aberdeen. Building began in the 14th century, when Sir William Keith, Marischal of Scotland (keeper of the king's mares and one of the king's right-hand men), decided to build a tower house to demonstrate his power. Subsequent generations added on to the structure over the centuries, and important visitors included Mary, Queen of Scots. The castle is most famous for holding out for eight months against Oliver Cromwell's army in 1651–52, and thereby saving the Scottish crown jewels, which had been stored here for safekeeping. Reach the castle via the A90; take the Stonehaven turnoff and follow the signs. Wear sensible shoes to investigate the ruins. ⊠ *Stonehaven* ☎ *01569/762173* ⊡ *£4* ⊙ *Easter–Oct., Mon.–Sat. 9–6, Sun. 2–5; Nov.–Easter, Fri.–Mon. 9–sunset.*

Where to Stay & Eat

££££
Fodor's Choice
★

✕ **Silver Darling.** Huge windows overlook the harbor at this quayside favorite, one of Aberdeen's most acclaimed restaurants. It specializes, as its name suggests, in fish (a silver darling is a herring). Try the ravioli with langoustine, mushrooms, samphire, and vanilla or the macadamia nut–crusted North Sea halibut with a spicy lemongrass-and-coconut emulsion. Stark white tablecloths add a hint of sophistication; tasteful flowers throw in a dash of color. ⊠ *Pocra Quay, Footdee* ☎ *01224/576229* ⌂ *Reservations essential* ⊟ *AE, DC, MC, V* ⊙ *Closed Sun. No lunch Sat.*

££–£££
✕ **Lascala Ristorante.** Glowing blues and reds and abundant plants set the scene at this classic Italian eatery. Veal and fish are prominent on the menu, and the daily specials make the most of fresh produce. Reserve ahead, as the restaurant can get busy. ⊠ *51 Huntly St.* ☎ *01224/626566* ⊟ *AE, DC, MC, V* ⊙ *Closed Mon. No lunch.*

★ **££**
✕ **Blue Moon.** Devoid of the usual posters of the Taj Mahal, Aberdeen's favorite Indian restaurant is refreshingly light and modern. Soothing shades of blue defy the fieriness of the curries. The menu is simple: you pick the type of curry you prefer, then the main ingredient. There's a choice of prawn, chicken, lamb, vegetables, or Quorn—a low-fat meat substitute popular amongst British vegetarians. There is a second location on Alford Lane. ⊠ *11 Holburn St.* ☎ *01224/589977 or 01224/589988* ⊠ *1 Alford La.* ☎ *01224/593000* ⊟ *MC, V.*

£–££
✕ **Ashvale.** Ask anyone about this place and the response will probably be overwhelmingly positive. Fish-and-chips are undoubtedly the specialty here, but the menu extends to steaks, chicken, and vegetarian dishes. Attempt the "Whale"—a gigantic 1-pound fillet of battered cod—and

you'll be rewarded with a free dessert. Prices are a little more inflated than the modest surroundings suggest, but you're paying for the tremendous food and reputation rather than the ambience. ⊠ *42–48 Great Western Rd.* ☎ *01224/596981* ⊟ *AE, MC, V.*

££££–£££££
Fodor'sChoice
★
✕🖃 **Marcliffe at Pitfodels.** This spacious country-house hotel situated on 11 wooded acres combines old and new to impressive effect. Some of the individually decorated rooms have reproduction antique furnishings, whereas others are more modern. The restaurant (££££) serves the freshest local seafood and top-quality Aberdeen Angus beef, and you can choose from more than 400 wines to go with your meal. Since it opened in 1993, this faux château has hosted such dignitaries as Prince Charles, Prime Minister Tony Blair, the Sultan of Brunei, and actor Charlton Heston. ⊠ *N. Deeside Rd., Pitfodels, AB15 9YA* ☎ *01224/ 861000* 🖷 *01224/868860* ⊕ *www.marcliffe.com* ⟿ *37 rooms, 2 suites* ♦ *Restaurant, room service, minibars, cable TV, bar, laundry service, no-smoking rooms; no a/c* ⊟ *AE, DC, MC, V* ⦿| *BP.*

£££££
🖃 **Thistle Aberdeen Caledonian Hotel.** This large downtown hotel, generally considered the best in the city, offers pleasant views over the city gardens. The generously sized rooms are decorated with dark-wood furniture and chintz drapes and bedcovers. The restaurant serves tasty dishes from a menu best described as modern Mediterranean, and the more casual café has curries, burgers, and pizzas at reasonable prices. Ask about special weekend deals that include dinner and breakfast. ⊠ *10–14 Union Terr., AB10 1WE* ☎ *0870/333–9151* 🖷 *0870/333–9251* ⊕ *www. thistlehotels.com* ⟿ *73 rooms, 4 suites* ♦ *Restaurant, café, in-room data ports, bar, no-smoking rooms; no a/c* ⊟ *AE, DC, MC, V* ⦿| *BP.*

£££–££££
🖃 **Atholl Hotel.** With its many turrets and gables, this granite hotel recalls a bygone era. It is in the middle of a leafy residential area to the west of the city. Rooms are done in rich, dark colors; if space is more important than a view, opt for a room on the 1st floor. The restaurant prepares such traditional Scottish dishes as lamb cutlets and roasted rib of beef. ⊠ *54 Kings Gate, AB15 4YN* ☎ *01224/323505* 🖷 *01224/321555* ⊕ *www.atholl-aberdeen.com* ⟿ *35 rooms* ♦ *Restaurant, cable TV, in-room broadband, bar, laundry service, no-smoking rooms; no a/c* ⊟ *AE, DC, MC, V* ⦿| *BP.*

££
🖃 **The Jays Guest House.** Alice Jennings or her husband George will greet you at the front door of this cozy granite home. The warmth and friendliness of your hosts, who are pleased to recommend local restaurants or help plan trips out of town, will make your stay memorable. The spacious rooms are impeccably clean. Breakfasts may include scrumptious oatcakes, savory omelets, or your own special request. ⊠ *422 King St., AB24 3BR* ☎ *01224/638295* 🖷 *01224/638360* ⊕ *www.jaysguesthouse. co.uk* ⟿ *10 rooms* ♦ *Dining room, cable TV, Wi-Fi, Internet room, no-smoking rooms; no a/c, no room phones* ⊟ *MC, V* ⦿| *BP.*

Nightlife & the Arts

Aberdeen has a fairly lively nightlife scene revolving around pubs and clubs. Theaters, concert halls, arts centers, and cinemas are also well represented. The principal newspapers—the *Press and Journal* and the

Evening Express—and *Aberdeen Leopard* magazine can fill you in on what's going on anywhere in the Northeast. Aberdeen's tourist information center has a monthly publication with an events calendar.

The Arts

Aberdeen is a rich city, both financially and culturally. August sees the world-renowned **Aberdeen International Youth Festival** (box office ⊠ Music Hall, Union St. ☎01224/213800), which attracts youth orchestras, choirs, dance troupes, and theater companies from many countries. During the festival some companies take their productions to other venues in the Northeast.

ARTS CENTERS **Aberdeen Arts Centre** (⊠ 33 King St. ☎ 01224/635208 ⊕ www. aberdeenartscentre.org.uk) hosts experimental plays, poetry readings, and exhibitions by local and Scottish artists. The **Lemon Tree** (⊠ 5 W. North St. ☎ 01224/642230) has an innovative and international program of dance, stand-up comedy, puppet theater, and folk, jazz, and rock-and-roll music. **Peacock Visual Arts** (⊠ 21 Castle St. ☎ 01224/639539) displays photographic, video, and slide exhibits of contemporary art and architecture.

CONCERT HALLS The Edwardian **His Majesty's Theatre** (⊠ Rosemount Viaduct ☎ 01224/641122) hosts performances on par with those in some of the world's biggest cities. It is a regular venue for musicals and operas, as well as classical and modern dance. The **Music Hall** (⊠ Union St. ☎ 01224/641122) presents seasonal programs of concerts by the Scottish National Orchestra, the Scottish Chamber Orchestra, and other major groups. Events also include folk concerts, crafts fairs, and exhibitions.

FILM **The Belmont** (⊠ 49 Belmont St. ☎ 01224/343536) screens independent and classic films. **UGC Cinemas** (⊠ Queen's Link Leisure Park, Links Rd. ☎ 0871/200–2000) shows recent releases.

Nightlife

With a greater club-to-clubber ratio than either Edinburgh or Glasgow, loud music and dancing dominate a night out in Aberdeen. There are also plenty of pubs and pool halls for those with two left feet. Pubs close at midnight on weekdays and 1 AM on weekends; clubs go until 2 or 3 AM.

BARS & PUBS Union Street is lined with bars of all sorts. **Archibald Simpson** (⊠ 5 Castle St. ☎ 01224/621365) has cheap drinks and a typical pub menu, so patrons range from families who stop by for a meal early in the evening to groups of young people guzzling drinks before heading to the clubs. Drawing a slightly older crowd, the traditional **Old Blackfriars** (⊠ 52 Castle St. ☎01224/581922) enjoys a nice location at the end of Union Street. The lighting is dim and the big fireplace warms things up on a chilly evening. This cask ale pub has a great selection—Belhaven St Andrews Ale and Caledonian 80 top the list.

Dating from 1850, **The Prince of Wales** (⊠ 7 St. Nicholas La. ☎ 01224/640597) has retained its paneled walls and wooden tables. Here you can belly up to the longest bar in Aberdeen. Good-quality food and reasonable prices draw lunchtime crowds. **Soul** (⊠ 333 Union St. ☎01224/

211150), in a converted church, has private booths with stained-glass windows and ecclesiastical furnishings. The eclectic menu includes everything from chicken satay and mussels. It's the most interesting of the Union Street hangouts.

DANCE CLUBS People tend to dress up a bit to go clubbing, and jeans or sneakers might get you turned away at the door. Clubs are open until 2 AM during the week and until 3 AM on Friday and Saturday nights.

The Moroccan-style **Kef** (✉ 9 Belmont St. ☎ 01224/648000) entices those who'd prefer to lounge on floor cushions and sip cocktails than work up a sweat on the dance floor. **Ministry** (✉ 16 Dee St. ☎ 01224/594585) one of the few permanent fixtures in the city's volatile club scene, hosts theme nights for collegiate crowds.

MUSIC CLUBS The **Lemon Tree** (✉ 5 W. North St. ☎ 01224/642230), with a wide-ranging music program, is the main rock venue and stages frequent jazz concerts.

Sports & the Outdoors

Biking

Alpine Bikes (✉ 64–70 Holburn St. ☎ 01224/211455) rents mountain bikes and will give you advice on good routes.

Golf

Greens fees range from £14 to £80 per round at the golf courses in and around Aberdeen. Make reservations at least 24 hours in advance. Some private courses restrict tee times for visiting golfers to certain days or hours during the week, so be sure to check that the course you wish to play is open when you want to play it.

Murcar. Sea views and a variety of terrain are the highlights of this course, founded in 1909, but it is most famous for its 7th hole, which course designer Archibald Simpson considered to be one of his finest. The clubhouse is undergoing refurbishment in early 2006. ✉ *Bridge of Don* ☎ *01224/704354* ⚐ *18 holes, 6,314 yds, SSS 72.*

Royal Aberdeen Golf Club, Balgownie. This old club, founded in 1780, is the archetypal Scottish links course: long and testing over uneven ground, with the frequently added hazard of a sea breeze. Prickly gorse is inclined to close in and form an additional hurdle. The two courses are tucked behind the rough, grassy sand dunes, and there are surprisingly few views of the sea. A handicap certificate (the limit is 24) or letter of introduction is required. It's a bit costly at £40 to £95 per round; Silverburn is less expensive. ✉ *Links Rd., Bridge of Don* ☎ *01224/702571* ⊕ *www.royalaberdeengolf.com* ⚐ *Reservations essential* ⚐ *Balgownie: 18 holes, 6,415 yds, par 70; Silverburn: 18 holes, 4,021 yds, SSS 61* ☉ *Balgownie: tee off weekdays 10–11:30 and 2–3:30; weekends after 3:30; Silverburn: daily.*

Westhill. This parkland course, founded in 1977, overlooks Royal Deeside. It is the most inexpensive in the area, charging £14 to £25 per day. ✉ *Westhill Heights* ☎ *01224/740159* ⚐ *18 holes, 5,849 yds, SSS 69.*

16

Shopping

You'll find most of the large national department stores in the Bon Accord, St. Nicholas, and Trinity shopping malls or along Union Street.

There are clusters of small specialty shops in the Chapel Street–Thistle Street area at the west end of Union Street. At the **Aberdeen Family History Society Shop** (⊠ 158–164 King St. ☎ 01224/646323) you can browse through publications related to local history and genealogical research. For a small fee the Aberdeen & North East Family History Society will undertake some research on your behalf. For Scottish kilts, tartans, crests, and other traditionally Scottish clothes, a good place to start is **Alex Scott & Co** (⊠ 43 SchoolHill ☎ 01224/643924). **Colin Wood** (⊠ 25 Rose St. ☎ 01224/643019) is the place to go for small antiques, prints, and regional maps. **Nova** (⊠ 18–20 Chapel St. ☎ 01224/641270), where the locals go for gifts, stocks Scottish silver jewelry. You'll also find major U.K. brand names, such as Neal's Yard, Dartington Glass, and Crabtree and Evelyn.

ROYAL DEESIDE & CASTLE COUNTRY

Deeside, the valley running west from Aberdeen down which the River Dee flows, earned its "royal" appellation when discovered by Queen Victoria. To this day, where royalty goes, lesser aristocracy and freshly minted millionaires follow. It's still the aspiration of many to own a grand shooting estate in Deeside. In a sense this yearning is understandable because piney hill slope, purple moor, and blue river intermingle tastefully here. Royal Deeside's gradual scenic change adds a growing sense of excitement as you travel deeper into the Grampians.

There are castles along the Dee as well as to the north in Castle Country, a region that also illustrates the gradual geological change in the Northeast: uplands lapped by a tide of farms. All the Donside and Deeside castles are picturesquely sited, with most fitted out with tall slender turrets, winding stairs, and crooked chambers that epitomize Scottish baronial style. All have tales of ghosts and bloodshed, siege and torture. Many were tidied up and "domesticated" during the 19th century. Although best toured by car, much of this area is accessible either by public transportation or on tours from Aberdeen.

Crathes Castle

 16 mi west of Aberdeen.

Crathes Castle was once the home of the Burnett family. Keepers of the Forest of Drum for generations, the family acquired lands here by marriage and later built a castle, completed in 1596. The National Trust for Scotland cares for the castle and the grand gardens, with their calculated symmetry and clipped yew hedges. Make sure to sample the tasty home baking in the tearoom. ⊠ *Off A93, 3½ mi east of Banchory* ☎ *01330/844525* ⊕ *www.nts.org.uk* 🖅 *Castle £10; garden £10; castle and garden £10* ⊙ *Castle Apr.–Sept., daily 10–5:30; Oct., daily 10–4:30; Nov.–Mar., Thurs.–Sun. 10:30–3:45.*

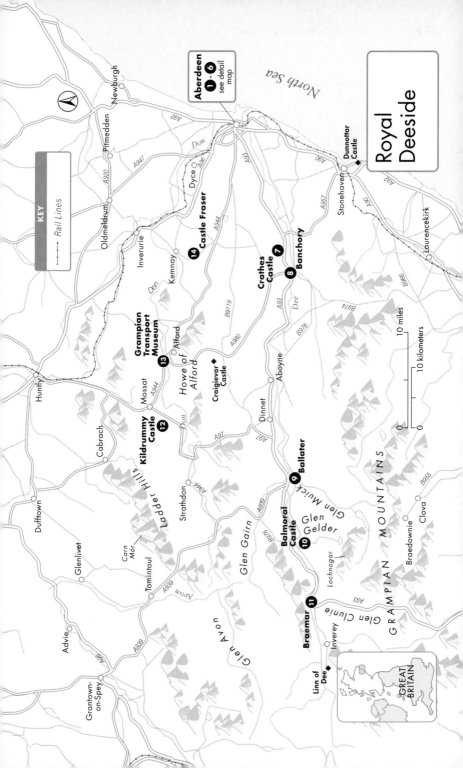

Banchory

❽ *3 mi west of Crathes Castle, 19 mi west of Aberdeen via A93.*

Banchory is an immaculate town filled with pinkish granite buildings. It's usually bustling with ice-cream-eating strollers, out on a day trip from Aberdeen. If you visit in autumn and have time to spare, drive for a mile along the B974 south of Banchory to the **Brig o'Feuch** (pronounced fyooch, the *ch* as in loch). The area around this bridge is very pleasant: salmon leap in season, and the fall colors and foaming waters make for an attractive scene.

Where to Stay & Eat

££££ ╳▥ **Banchory Lodge.** With the River Dee flowing a few yards beyond the garden, tranquil Banchory Lodge is an ideal spot for anglers. The house was built in the 17th century and it retains its period charm. Rooms are individually decorated, though all have bold color schemes and tartan or floral fabrics. The restaurant (££–£££) serves Scottish cuisine with French overtones; try the pork grilled with Stilton cheese or the smoked hake in a creamy white-wine sauce. ⊠ *Dee St. Banchory, AB31 5HS* ☎ *01330/822625* 🖷 *01330/825019* ⊕ *www.banchorylodge.co.uk* ⇆ *22 rooms* ♿ *Restaurant, fishing, bicycles, bar, lounge; no a/c* ⊟ *AE, DC, MC, V* ⦿ *BP.*

Ballater

❾ *43 mi west of Aberdeen.*

The handsome holiday resort of Ballater, once noted for the curative properties of its local well, has profited from the proximity of the royals, nearby at Balmoral. You might be amused by the array of BY ROYAL APPOINTMENT signs proudly hanging from many of its various shops (even monarchs need bakers and butchers). Take time to stroll around this well-laid-out community. The railway station houses the tourist information center and a display on the glories of the Great North of Scotland branch railway line, closed in the 1960s along with so many others in this country.

 As long as you have your own car, you can capture the feel of the eastern Highlands yet still be close to town. Start your expedition into

> **WORD OF MOUTH**
>
> "Ballater is a convenient base for Royal Deeside/Balmoral/Braemar, Aberdeen, the Castle Trail, and even over to the Whisky Trail/Dufftown."   –janisj

Glen Muick (Gaelic for pig, pronounced mick) by crossing the River Dee and turning upriver on the south side, shortly after the road forks. The native red deer are quite common throughout the Scottish Highlands, but the flat valley floor here is one of the very best places to see them. Beyond the lower glen, the prospect opens to reveal not only grazing herds but also fine views of the battlement of cliffs edging the mountain called Lochnagar.

Where to Stay & Eat

£££–££££ ✕🖻 **Raemoir House Hotel.** With portions dating from the 16th to 19th centuries, this baronial former home evokes the past but offers today's comforts. Guest rooms—a number of which have four-poster beds—have a genteel period charm and large, modern bathrooms. The restaurant (£££££; fixed-price menu), in an oval ballroom, has a solid reputation based upon exquisite Scottish fare created with seasonal local produce. And the morning room, despite its name, is the perfect place to nurse a wee nip of whisky before bed. You can take some lovely walks on the estate's 3,500 acres of hillock and woodland. ⊠ *Off A980, Raemoir, AB31 4ED* ☎ *01330/824884* 🖷 *01330 822171* ⊕ *www.raemoir.com* ⤴ *17 rooms, 3 suites* ⚬ *Restaurant, lounge; no a/c* ☱ *AE, DC, MC, V* ⦿| *BP.*

£££–££££ 🖻 **Hilton Craigendarroch Hotel.** This magnificent country-house hotel, just outside Ballater on a hillside overlooking the River Dee, manages to keep everyone happy. Choose between a luxurious room in the main house and a private, less-expensive pine lodge set among the trees. Fitted with every kind of labor-saving appliance, the lodges are perfect for families. The hotel's restaurants include the Oaks, for modern Scottish food, and the Club House brasserie, for lighter fare. ⊠ *Braemar Rd., AB35 5XA* ☎ *013397/55858* 🖷 *013397/55447* ⊕ *www.hilton.com* ⤴ *39 rooms, 6 suites* ⚬ *2 restaurants, room service, some in-room hot tubs, some kitchens, some microwaves, some refrigerators, cable TV, tennis court, 2 pools, wading pool, gym, hair salon, hot tub, sauna, billiards, squash, 2 bars, babysitting, laundry facilities, laundry service, business services, some pets allowed, no-smoking rooms; no a/c* ☱ *AE, DC, MC, V.*

Golf

Ballater. The mountains of Royal Deeside surround this course laid out along the sandy flats of the River Dee. Ideal for a relaxing round of golf, the course makes maximum use of the fine setting between river and woods. The club, originally opened in 1906, has a holiday atmosphere, and the shops and pleasant walks in nearby Ballater make this a good place for nongolfing partners. Reservations are advised; cost is £23–£38. ⊠ *Victoria Rd.* ☎ *013397/55567* ⊕ *www.ballatergolfclub.co.uk* ⛳ *18 holes, 6,112 yds, par 70.*

Shopping

For a low-cost gift you could always see what's being boiled up at **Dee Valley Confectioners** (⊠ Station Sq. ☎ 013397/55499). The **McEwan Gallery** (⊠ On A939, 1 mi west of Ballater ☎ 013397/55429) displays fine paintings, watercolors, prints, and books (many with a Scottish or golf theme) in an unusual house built by the Swiss artist Rudolphe Christen in 1902.

Balmoral Castle

➓ *7 mi west of Ballater.*

The enormous parking lot is indicative of the popularity of Balmoral Castle, one of Queen Elizabeth II's favorite family retreats. Balmoral is a Victorian fantasy, designed, in fact, for Queen Victoria (1819–1901) by her consort, Prince Albert (1819–61) in 1855. "It seems like a dream to be here in our dear Highland Home again," Queen Victoria wrote. "Every year my heart becomes more fixed in this dear Paradise." Balmoral's visiting hours depend on whether the royals are in residence. In truth, there are more interesting and historic buildings to explore, as the only part of the castle on view is the ballroom, with an exhibition of royal artifacts. The Carriage Hall has displays of commemorative china, carriages, and native wildlife. Perhaps it's just as well that most of the house is closed to the public, for Balmoral suffers from a bad rash of tartanitis. Thanks to Victoria and Albert, stags' heads abounded, the bagpipes wailed incessantly, and the garish Stuart tartan was used for every item of furnishings, from carpets to chair covers. A more somber Duff tartan, black and green to blend with the environment, was later adopted, and from the brief glimpse you may get of Balmoral's interior, it's clear that royal taste is now more restrained. Queen Elizabeth II, however, follows her predecessors' routine in spending a holiday of about six weeks in Deeside, usually from mid-August to the end of September. During this time Balmoral is closed to visitors.

Victoria loved Balmoral more for its setting than its house, so be sure to take in its pleasant gardens. Year by year Victoria and Albert added to the estate, taking over neighboring houses, securing the forest and moorland around it, and developing deer stalking and grouse shooting here. In consequence, Balmoral is now a large property, as the grounds run 12 mi along the Deeside road. Its privacy is protected by belts of pinewood, and the only view of the castle from the A93 is a partial one, from a point near Inver, 2 mi west of the gates. But there's an excellent bird's-eye view of it from an old military road, now the A939, which climbs out of Crathie, northbound for Cockbridge and the Don Valley. This view embraces the summit of Lochnagar, in whose *corries* (hollows) the snow lies year-round. Around and about Balmoral are some notable spots—Cairn O'Mount, Cambus O'May, and the Cairngorms from the Linn of Dee—and some of them may be seen on pony-trekking expeditions, which use Balmoral stalking ponies and go around the grounds and estate. When the royals are in residence, even the grounds are closed to the public. ⊠ *A93* ☎ *013397/42534* ⊕ *www.balmoralcastle. com* ☜ *£6* ⊗ *Apr.–July, daily 10–5; last admission 1 hr before closing.*

EN ROUTE As you continue west into Highland scenery, pine-framed glimpses appear of the "steep frowning glories of dark Lochnagar," as it was described by the poet Lord Byron (1788–1824). Lochnagar (3,786 feet) was made known to an audience wider than hill walkers by the Prince of Wales, who published a children's story, *The Old Man of Lochnagar*.

Braemar

⑪ *17 mi west of Ballater, 60 mi west of Aberdeen, 51 mi north of Perth via A93.*

The village of Braemar is associated with the Braemar Highland Gathering, held every September. Although there are many such gatherings celebrated throughout Scotland, this one is distinguished by the presence of the royal family. Competitions and events include hammer throwing, caber tossing, running races, Highland dancing, and bagpipe playing. You can find out more at the **Braemar Highland Heritage Centre,** in a converted stable block in the middle of town. It tells the history of the village with displays and a film, and it also has a gift shop. ✉ *The Mews, Mar Rd.* ☎ *013397/41944* 🎟 *Free* ☉ *Apr.–Sept., daily 9–6; Oct., daily 9–5; Nov.–Mar., daily 10–noon and 1–5.*

Braemar is dominated by **Braemar Castle** on its outskirts. The castle dates from the 17th century, although its defensive walls, in the shape of a pointed star, came later. At Braemar (the *braes,* or slopes, of the district of Mar) the standard, or rebel flag, was first raised at the start of the spectacularly unsuccessful Jacobite Rebellion of 1715. At the time of this writing, the castle was closed to the public; check ahead. ✉ *A93* ☎ *013397/41219* ⊕ *www.braemarcastle.co.uk.*

OFF THE BEATEN PATH

LINN OF DEE – Although the main A93 slinks off to the south from Braemar, a little unmarked road will take you farther west into the hilly heartland. In fact, even if you do not have your own car, you can still explore this area by catching the post bus that leaves from the Braemar post office once a day. The road offers views over the winding River Dee and the blue hills before passing through the tiny hamlet of Inverey and crossing a bridge at the Linn of Dee. *Linn* is a Scots word meaning "rocky narrows," and the river's gash here is deep and roaring. Park beyond the bridge and walk back to admire the sylvan setting.

16

Where to Stay

£ 🏨 **Callater Lodge.** The owners of this superior B&B, a Victorian-era granite house with pleasant grounds, extend a warm welcome to those seeking a comfortable place to rest in the center of the village. The rooms are homey and modern, and the lounge and well-stocked library, both with fireplaces, are pleasant spots to while away the hours. You can easily walk to number of places to dine. ✉ *9 Glenshee Rd., AB35 5YQ* ☎ *013397/41275* 🖨 *013397/41345* ⊕ *www.hotel-braemar.co.uk* ⇆ *6 rooms* ⚭ *Bar, library; no a/c* ☰ *AE, DC, MC, V* ☉ *Closed Nov. and Dec.* ¶⊙¶ *BP.*

Golf

Braemar Golf Course. This tricky 18-hole course, founded in 1902, is laden with foaming waters. Erratic duffers take note: the compassionate course managers have installed, near the water, poles with little nets on the end for those occasional shots that may go awry. The cost for a round is £14 during the week, £17 on weekends. ✉ *Cluny Bank Rd.* ☎ *013397/41618* ⚑ *18 holes, 4,916 yds, SSS 64.*

Kildrummy Castle

★ ⑫ *23 mi north of Ballater.*

Kildrummy Castle is significant because of its age—it dates to the 13th century—and because it has ties to the mainstream medieval traditions of European castle building. It shares features with Harlech and Caernarfon, in Wales, as well as with Château de Coucy, near Laon, France. Kildrummy underwent several expansions at the hands of England's King Edward I (1239–1307); the castle was back in Scottish hands in 1306, when it was besieged by King Edward I's son. The defenders were betrayed by Osbarn the Smith, who was promised a large amount of gold by the English forces. They gave it to him after the castle fell, pouring its molten down his throat, or so the ghoulish story goes. Kildrummy's prominence ended after the collapse of the 1715 Jacobite uprising. It had been the rebel headquarters and was consequently dismantled. ⊠ *A97* ☎ *01975/571331* ⊕ *www.historic-scotland.gov.uk* ▦ *£3* ⊙ *Apr.–Sept., daily 9:30–6:30; last entry half hr before closing.*

Kildrummy Castle Gardens, behind the castle and with a separate entrance from the main road, are built in what was the original quarry for the castle. This sheltered bowl within the woodlands has a broad range of shrubs and alpine plants and a notable water garden. ⊠ *A97* ☎ *019755/ 71203 or 019755/71277* ⊕ *www.kildrummy-castle-gardens.co.uk* ▦ *£3* ⊙ *Apr.–Oct., daily 10–5; call to confirm opening times late in season.*

Where to Stay & Eat

★
££££–£££££
✕▦ **Kildrummy Castle Hotel.** A grand late-Victorian country house, this elegant lodging offers a peaceful stay and attentive service. Hand-carved oak paneling, elaborate plasterwork, and gentle color schemes create a serene environment, enhanced by the views of nearby Kildrummy Castle Gardens. The Scottish cuisine served in the excellent restaurant (*£££–££££*) uses local game as well as seafood. ⊠ *A97, Kildrummy, AB33 8RA, by Alford, Aberdeenshire* ☎ *019755/71288* 🖷 *019755/71345* ⊕ *www.kildrummycastlehotel.co.uk* ⮑ *16 rooms* ♤ *Restaurant, fishing, bar, laundry service, some pets allowed, no-smoking rooms; no a/c* ▤ *MC, V* ⊙ *Closed Jan.* ⦿ *BP.*

Alford

9 mi east of Kildrummy, 28 mi west of Aberdeen.

A plain and sturdy settlement in the Howe (Hollow) of Alford, this town gives those who have grown somewhat weary of castle hopping a break:
⑬ it has a museum instead. The **Grampian Transport Museum** specializes in road-based means of locomotion, backed up by an archives and library. One of its more unusual exhibits is the *Craigievar Express*, a steam-driven creation invented by the local postman to deliver mail more efficiently. ⊠ *Alford* ☎ *019755/62292* ⊕ *www.gtm.org.uk* ▦ *£5.20* ⊙ *Apr.–Sept., daily 10–5; Oct., daily 10–4.*

Craigievar Castle is much as the stonemasons left it in 1626, with its pepper-pot turrets and towers. It was built in relatively peaceful times by William Forbes, a successful merchant. The castle is closed for repairs and the reopening date is uncertain; but the impressive facade is certainly worth a look. ⊠ *A 980, 5 mi south of Alford* ☎ *013398/83635* ⊕ *www.nts.org.uk.*

Castle Fraser

⑭ *8 mi southeast of Alford.*

The massive Castle Fraser, southeast of Alford, is the largest of the castles of Mar. Although it shows a variety of styles reflecting the taste of its owners from the 15th through the 19th centuries, its design is typical of the cavalcade of castles that exist here in the Northeast, and for good reason, as this—along with many other of the region's castles, including Midmar, Craigievar, Crathes, and Glenbuchat—was designed by a family of master masons called Bell. The walled garden includes a 19th-century knot garden, with colorful flowerbeds, box hedging, gravel paths, and splendid herbaceous borders. Have lunch in the tearoom or the picnic area. ✉ *8 mi southeast of Alford off A944* ☎ *01330/833463* ⊕ *www.nts.org.uk* 🎫 *£10* ⊙ *Castle Easter–June and Sept., weekends and Tues.–Thurs. noon–5; July and Aug., daily 11–5; grounds daily 8–sunset; last admission 45 mins before closing.*

THE NORTHEAST & THE MALT WHISKY TRAIL

This route starts inland, traveling toward Speyside—the valley, or strath, of the River Spey—famed for its whisky distilleries, which it promotes in yet another signposted trail. Distilling scotch is not an intrinsically spectacular process. It involves pure water, malted barley, and sometimes peat smoke, then a lot of bubbling and fermentation, all of which cause a number of odd smells. The result is a prestigious product with a fascinating range of flavors that you either enjoy immensely or not at all.

16

Instead of assiduously following the Malt Whisky Trail, just dip into it and blend it with some other aspects of the lower end of Speyside—the county of Moray. Whisky notwithstanding, Moray's scenic qualities, low rainfall, and other reassuring weather statistics are also worth remembering. The suggested route then allows you to sample the northeastern seaboard, including some of the best but least-known coastal scenery in Scotland.

Dufftown

★ ⑮ *54 mi from Aberdeen via A96 and A920, turn west at Huntly.*

Many make **Glenfiddich Distillery,** a half mile north of Dufftown, their first stop on the Malt Whisky Trail. The independent company of William Grant and Sons Limited was the first to realize the tourist potential of the distilling process. The company began offering tours and subsequently built an entertaining visitor center. The audiovisual show and displays are as worthwhile as the tour (£15), and the traditional stone-walled premises with the typical pagoda-roof malting buildings are pleasant. You don't have to like whisky to come away feeling you've learned something about a leading Scottish export. ✉ *North of Dufftown on A941* ☎ *01340/820373* ⊕ *www.glenfiddich.com* 🎫 *Free* ⊙ *Easter–mid-Oct., Mon.–Sat. 9:30–4:30, Sun. noon–4:30; mid-Oct.–Easter, weekdays 9:30–4:30.*

On a mound just above the Glenfiddich Distillery is a grim, gray,

> **WORD OF MOUTH**
>
> "We took the Glenfiddich tour, and were fascinated by their extraordinary commitment to detail and quality control. I still like the Macallan whisky better, but you could definitely do worse for a tour." —mr_go

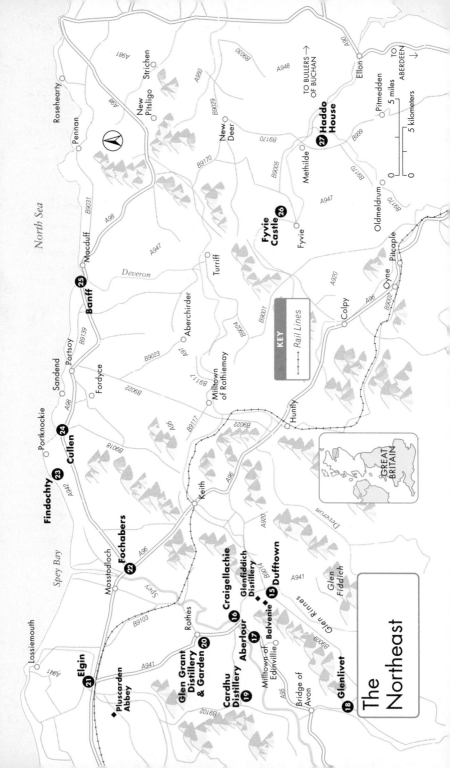

The Northeast

KEY

→+ Rail Lines

North Sea

TO BULLERS
OF BUCHAN →

TO
ABERDEEN →

GREAT
BRITAIN

0   5 miles

0   5 kilometers

and squat curtain-walled castle, **Balvenie.** This fortress, which dates from the 13th century, once commanded the glens and passes toward Speyside and Elgin. ✉ *Dufftown* ☎ *01340/820121* 🎫 *£3* ⊙ *Apr.–Sept., daily 9:30–6:30; last entry half hr before closing.*

Mortlach Church, set in a hollow by the Dullan Water, is thought to be one of Scotland's oldest Christian sites, perhaps founded by St. Moluag, a contemporary of St. Columba, as early as AD 566. Note the weathered Pictish cross in the churchyard and the even older stone under cover in the vestibule, with a strange Pictish elephantlike beast carved on it. Though much of the church was rebuilt after 1876, some early work survives, including three lancet windows from the 13th century and a leper's squint (a hole extended to the outside of the church so that lepers could hear the service but be kept away from other people).

Craigellachie

⑯ *4 mi northwest of Dufftown via A941.*

Renowned as an angling resort, Craigellachie, like so many Speyside settlements, is sometimes enveloped in the malty reek of the local industry. Just before the village you'll notice the huge **Speyside Cooperage and Visitor Centre,** a major stop on the Malt Whisky Trail. Inside you can watch craftspeople make and repair oak barrels used in the local whisky industry. ✉ *Dufftown Rd.* ☎ *01340/871108* ⊕ *www.speysidecooperage. co.uk* 🎫 *£3.10* ⊙ *Weekdays 9:30–4.*

Aberlour

⑰ *2 mi southwest of Craigellachie via A95.*

Aberlour, often listed as Charlestown of Aberlour on maps, is a handsome little burgh, essentially Victorian in style, though actually founded in 1812 by the local landowner. The names of the noted local whisky stills are Cragganmore, Aberlour, and **Glenfarclas,** just west of town. Tour guides tell the story of Glenfarclas and the Grant family, and tours end with tastings in the Ship Room, the intact lounge of an ocean liner called the *Empress of Australia.* ☎ *01807/500257* ⊕ *www.glenfarclas.co.uk* 🎫 *£3.50* ⊙ *Apr.–May, weekdays 10–5, June–Sept., Mon.–Sat. 10–4; Oct.–Mar., weekdays 10–4.*

Where to Eat

£ ✕ **Old Pantry.** This pleasant corner restaurant, overlooking Aberlour's tree-shaded central square, serves everything from a cup of coffee with a sticky cake to a three-course spread of soup, roast meat, and traditional pudding. ✉ *The Sq.* ☎ *01340/871617* 💳 *MC, V.*

Glenlivet

★ **⑱** *10 mi southwest of Aberlour via A95 and B9008.*

Glenlivet is a very small village with a very famous distillery by the same name. Founded in 1824 by George Smith, today Glenlivet Distillery produces one of the best-known 12-year-old single malts in the world.

Take the free distillery tour for a chance to see inside the huge bonded warehouse where the whisky steeps in oak casks. The River Livet runs through the glen and past the distillery in an area renowned for its birdlife. There is a coffee shop on the premises. ☒ *Glenlivet, Ballindalloch* ☎ *01340/821720* ⊕ *www.glenlivet.com* ☒ *Free* ☉ *Apr.–Oct., Mon.–Sat. 10–4, Sun. 12:30–4.*

Where to Stay & Eat

★ **££–£££** ✕🏠 **Minmore House.** With the distinctive feel of a private home, the Minmore House has faded chintz in the drawing room (where afternoon tea is served) and a paneled library. An eclectic mix of antique furnishings decorate the guest rooms. The restaurant (*£££££*) serves a prix-fixe dinner of exceptional contemporary Scottish cuisine that may include Aberdeen Angus beef. After dinner, enjoy one of more than 100 malt whiskies in the library bar. The Speyside Way long-distance footpath passes below the house, and the area is famous for bird-watching. ☒ *Glenlivet, Ballindalloch, Banffshire, AB37 9DB* ☎ *01807/590378* 🖷 *01807/ 590472* ⊕ *www.minmorehousehotel.com* ☜ *10 rooms* ⚷ *Restaurant, bar, library, some pets allowed (fee); no a/c, no room TVs, no kids under 7* ☰ *AE, MC, V* ☉ *Closed Feb.* ⍟ *BP.*

EN ROUTE

From Glenlivet, make your way back to Bridge of Avon, and turn right (north) onto the A95 toward Aberlour. When you reach Marypark, turn west onto a minor road, signed Knockando, which takes you over the river Spey. Once across the river, turn north onto the B9102 and within a few minutes you will arrive at Cardhu, another Malt Whisky Trail stop.

Cardhu Distillery

⑲ *10 mi north of Glenlivet via B9008, A95, and B9102.*

Cardhu Distillery was established by John and Helen Cumming in 1811, though officially they founded it in 1824, after distilling was made legal by the Excise Act of 1823. Today its product lies at the heart of Johnnie Walker Blends. Guided tours take you to the mashing, fermenting, and distilling halls. You may even taste the remarkably smooth single malt before it gets near any blending vats. ☒ *Knockando* ☎ *01340/ 872555* ☒ *£4* ☉ *Dec.–Feb., weekdays 11–3; Mar.–June, Oct., and Nov., weekdays 9:30–4:30; July–Sept., Mon.–Sat. 9:30–4:30, Sun. 11–4; last tour 1 hr before closing.*

Glen Grant Distillery & Garden

⑳ *12 mi northeast of Cardhu via B9102 and A941.*

James Grant founded the distillery in 1840 when he was only 25, and it was the first in the country to be electrically powered. Glen Grant will come as a welcome relief to less-than-enthusiastic companions of dedicated Malt Whisky Trail followers, because in addition to the distillery there is a large and beautiful garden. The gardens are planted and tended as Major Grant planned them, with orchards and woodland walks, log bridges over waterfalls, a magnificent lily pond, and azaleas and rhododendrons in profusion. Now owned by Chivas Regal, Glen Grant produces a distinctive pale-gold, clear whisky, with an almost floral or fruity

CLOSE UP

Whisky, the Water of Life

CONJURED FROM AN INNOCUOUS MIX of malted barley, water, and yeast, malt whisky is for many synonymous with Scotland. Clans produced whisky for hundreds of years before it emerged as Scotland's national drink and major export. Today those centuries of expertise result in a sublimely subtle drink with many different layers of flavor. Each distillery produces a malt with—to the expert—instantly identifiable, predominant notes peculiarly its own.

There are two types of whisky: malt and grain. Malt whisky, generally acknowledged to have a more sophisticated bouquet and flavor, is made with malted barley—barley that is soaked in water until the grains germinate and then dried to halt the germination, all of which adds extra flavor and a touch of sweetness to the brew. Grain whisky also contains malted barley, but with the addition of unmalted barley and maize. Blended whiskies, which make up many of the leading brands, usually balance malt and grain whisky distillations; deluxe blends contain a higher percentage of malts. Blends that contain several malt whiskies are called "vatted malts." Whisky connoisseurs often prefer to taste the single malts: the unblended whisky from a single distillery. In simple terms, malt whiskies may be classified into "eastern" and "western" in style, with the whisky made in the east of Scotland, for example in Speyside, being lighter and sweeter than the products of the western isles, which often have a taste of peat smoke or even iodine.

The production process is, by comparison, relatively straightforward: just malt your barley, mash it, ferment it and distill it, then mature to perfection. To find out the details, join a distillery tour, and be rewarded with a dram.

16

---

finish, using peculiarly tall stills and special purifiers. ✉ *A941, Rothes* ☎ *01542/783318* ⊕ *www.chivas.com* 🖃 *£4* ⊙ *Apr.–Oct., Mon.–Sat. 10–4, Sun. 12:30–4.*

Elgin

㉑ *10 mi north of Rothes via A941, 69 mi northwest of Aberdeen, 41 mi east of Inverness via A96.*

As the center of the fertile Laigh (low-lying lands) of Moray, Elgin has been of local importance for centuries. Like Aberdeen, it's self-support-ing and previously remote, sheltered by great hills to the south and lying between two major rivers, the Spey and the Findhorn. Beginning in the 13th century, Elgin became an important religious center, a cathedral city with a walled town growing up around the cathedral and adjacent to the original settlement. Left in peace for at least some of its history, Elgin prospered, and by the early 18th century it became a mini-Edin-burgh of the north and a place where country gentlemen spent their win-ters. It even echoed Edinburgh in carrying out wide-scale reconstruction in the early part of the 18th century: much of the old town was swept away in a wave of rebuilding, giving Elgin the fine neoclassical buildings that survive today.

★ Cooper Park contains a magnificent ruin, the **Elgin Cathedral,** consecrated in 1224. Its eventful story included devastation by fire: a 1390 act of retaliation by Alexander Stewart (circa 1343–1405), the Wolf of Badenoch. The illegitimate-son-turned-bandit of King David II (1324–71) had sought revenge for his excommunication by the bishop of Moray. The cathedral was rebuilt but finally fell into disuse after the Reformation in 1560. By 1567 the highest authority in the land, the regent earl of Moray, had stripped the lead from the roof to pay for his army. Thus ended the career of the religious seat known as the Lamp of the North. Some traces of the cathedral settlement survive—the gateway Pann's Port and the Bishop's Palace—although they've been drastically altered. Cooper Park is a five-minute walk northeast of Elgin Museum, across the bypass road. ☎ *01343/547171* ⊕ *www.historic-scotland.gov.uk* ✉ *£4* ⊙ *Apr.–Sept., daily 9:30–6:30; Oct.–Mar., Sat.–Wed. 9:30–4:30: last admission half hr before closing.*

Where to Stay & Eat

££££–£££££ ✕▦ **Mansion House Hotel.** The crenellated tower is the first thing you are likely to see as you drive up to this 19th-century baronial mansion. The handsome building is set amid woodland on a flawless green lawn overlooking the River Lossie. The rooms are individually decorated; all are pleasant and comfortable. The restaurant (£££££) serves fine Scottish cuisine, such as loin of venison roasted with juniper berries. ✉ *The Haugh, IV30 1AW* ☎ *01343/548811* 🖷 *01343/547916* ⊕ *www. mansionhousehotel.co.uk* ⤴ *23 rooms* ♨ *Restaurant, room service, cable TV, pool, gym, hair salon, massage, sauna, bar; no a/c* ☰*AE, MC, V* ⊙❙*BP.*

Shopping

Gordon and MacPhail (✉ 58–60 South St. ☎ 01343/545110), an outstanding delicatessen and wine merchant, also stocks rare malt whiskies. This is a good place to shop for gifts for those foodies among your friends. **Johnstons of Elgin** (✉ Newmill ☎ 01343/554099) is a woolen mill with a worldwide reputation for its luxury fabrics, especially cashmere. The bold color range is particularly appealing. The large shop stocks not only the firm's own products but also top-quality Scottish crafts and giftware. There's also a coffee shop on the premises.

Fochabers

㉒ *9 mi east of Elgin.*

Just before reaching the center of Fochabers, you'll see the works of a major local employer, Baxters of Fochabers. From Tokyo to New York, upmarket stores stock the company's soups, jams, chutneys, and other gourmet products—all of which are made here, close to the River Spey. The **Baxters Highland Village** presents a video, *Baxters Experience,* about the history of the business, plus interactive exhibits and cooking demonstrations. You can have a look in a re-creation of the Baxters' first grocery shop, a real shop that stocks Baxters' goods, and a shop called the Best of Scotland, specializing all kinds of Scottish products. A restaurant serves up an assortment of delectables. ✉ *1 mi west of Fochabers* *on A96* ☎ *01343/820666* ⊕ *www.baxters.com* ✉ *Free* ☉ *Jan.–Mar., daily 10–5; Apr.–Dec., daily 9–5:30.*

Once over the Spey Bridge and past the cricket ground (a very unusual sight in Scotland), you'll find the symmetrical, 18th-century Fochabers village square lined with antiques dealers. Through one of these shops, Pringle Antiques, you can enter the **Fochabers Folk Museum,** a converted church that has a fine collection of items relating to past life in the village and surrounding area. Exhibits include carts and carriages, farm implements, and Victorian toys. ⊠ *Behind Pringle Antiques* ☎ *01343/ 821204* ✉ *Free* ☉ *Easter–Oct., daily 9:30–1 and 2–5.*

Whisky lovers should take the A96 a few minutes southwest from Fochabers to see the **Strathisla Distillery.** Strathisla Distillery was built in 1786 and now produces the main component of the Chivas Regal blend. Guided tours take you through the mash house, tun room, and still house, ending with a tasting session. ⊠ *Seafield Ave., Keith* ☎ *01542/783044* ⊕ *www.chivas.com* ✉ *£5* ☉ *Apr.–Oct., Mon.–Sat. 10–4, Sun. 12:30–4.*

Shopping

Antiques (Fochabers) (⊠ Hadlow House, The Sq. ☎ 01343/820838) carries quirky old kitchenware, stripped pine, china, pictures, jewelry, and antique furniture. **Art and Antiques** (⊠ 33–35 High St. ☎ 01343/829104) combines an unusual mix of original art by the owners with ceramic, glassware, and small pieces of furniture. **Pringle Antiques** (⊠ High St. ☎ 01343/820362) is a good place to shop for small furniture, pottery, glassware, silver, and jewelry. At **the Quaich** (⊠ 85 High St. ☎ 01343/ 820981) you can stock up on cards and small gifts, then sit with a cup of tea and a home-baked snack.

Findochty

❷❸ *10 mi east of Fochabers on A942.*

The residents of Findochty (pronounced *Finech-ty*) are known for their fastidiousness and creativity in painting their houses, taking the art of house painting to a new level. Some residents even paint the mortar between the stonework a different color from the exterior. The harbor, with many colorful small sailing boats tied up to the quay, has a faint echo of the Mediterranean about it. A 15-minute stroll about the older part of the village will take you past several blocks of painted homes.

Where to Eat

★ **££££** ✕ **Old Monastery.** On a broad, wooded slope set back from the coast near Buckie, with westward views as far as the hills of Wester Ross, sits the Old Monastery, once a Victorian religious establishment. The monastic theme carries through to the restrained interior of the Cloisters Bar and the Chapel Restaurant, where the cream-painted walls are hand stenciled in shades of terra cotta and green. Local specialties—fresh fish, venison, and Aberdeen Angus beef—make up the Scottish prix-fixe menu. The restaurant is on an unclassified road off the A98. Follow signs to Drybridge, but instead of turning into the village, continue up the hill for 1½ mi. ⊠ *Drybridge, Buckie* ☎ *01542/832660* ▭ *AE, MC, V* ☉ *Closed Mon. and Tues. No dinner Sun.*

EN
ROUTE

Driving east you'll pass a string of salty little fishing villages. They paint a colorful scene with their gabled houses and fishing nets set out to dry amid the rocky shoreline.

Cullen

★ ㉔   *3 mi east of Findochty.*

This beautiful old fishing town sits between a monumental railway viaduct and a dramatic stretch of white sands. Bowfiddle Rock pierces the beach, and its harbor provides a sheltered spot for swimming, sunning yourself or just staring out tosea. The 18th-century town above, with its Georgian square, has specialty shops—antiques and gift stores, butchers, an ironmonger, a baker, a pharmacy, and a locally famous ice-cream shop among them—as well as several hotels and cafés.

Where to Stay & Eat

££–£££   ✕🏨 **The Seafield Hotel.** A former coaching inn built in 1822, this hotel has retained its high standards. Deep, rich colors prevail, and comfort and friendliness are key. The restaurant (£££), with its golden walls and tartan carpet, has an extensive à la carte Scottish menu that includes seafood, game, beef, and lamb and a stock of more than 200 malt whiskies. ⊠ *Seafield St., Cullen, AB56 4SG* ☎ *01542/840791* 📠 *01542/ 840736* ⊕ *www.theseafieldarms.co.uk* ⤴ *21 rooms* ⚖ *Restaurant, room service, bar, laundry service, no-smoking rooms, Internet; no a/c* ▭ *AE, MC, V* ❙❉❙ *BP.*

Banff

㉕   *36 mi east of Elgin, 47 mi north of Aberdeen.*

Midway along the northeast coast, overlooking Moray Firth and the estuary of the River Deveron, Banff is a fishing town of considerable elegance that feels as though it's a million miles from tartan-clad Scotland. Part Georgian, like Edinburgh's New Town, and part 16th-century small burgh, like Culross, Banff is an exemplary east-coast salty town, with a tiny harbor and fine architecture. It's also within easy reach of plenty of unspoiled coastline—cliff and rock to the east, at Gardenstown (known as Gamrie) and Pennan, or beautiful little sandy beaches westward toward Sandend and Cullen.

The jewel in Banff's crown is the grand mansion of **Duff House,** a splendid William Adam–designed (1689–1748) baroque mansion that has been restored as an outstation of the National Galleries of Scotland. Many fine paintings are displayed in rooms furnished to reflect the days when the house was occupied by the dukes of Fife. A good tearoom and a shop are found in the basement. ⊠ *Off A98* ☎ *01261/818181* ⊕ *www. duffhouse.com* 📷 *£5.50* ☉ *Apr.–Oct., daily 11–5; Nov.–Mar., Thurs.–Sun. 11–4.*

Golf

Banff, Duff House Royal Golf Club. Just moments away from the sea, this club combines a coastal course with a parkland setting. It lies only minutes from Banff center, within the parkland grounds of Duff House, a country-house art gallery. The club has inherited the ancient traditions of seaside play (golf records here go back to the 17th century). Mature trees and gentle slopes create a pleasant playing environment. Cost is £25 to £74, depending on day and season. ✉ *The Barnyards* ☎ *01261/ 812075* ⊕ *www.theduffhouseroyalgolfclub.co.uk* ⌂ *Reservations essential* ⌕ *18 holes, 6,161 yds, par 70.*

Fyvie Castle

❷⁶ *18 mi south of Banff.*

In an area rife with castles, Fyvie Castle stands out as the most complex. Five great towers built by five successive powerful families turned a 13th-century foursquare castle into an opulent Edwardian statement of wealth. There are some superb paintings on view, including 12 Raeburns, as well as sumptuous interiors and many walks on the castle grounds. It is rumored that a former lady of the house, Lillia Drummond, was starved to death by her husband, who entombed her body inside the walls of a secret room. In the 1920s when the bones were disrupted during renovations, such terrible misfortune followed that they were quickly returned and the room sealed off. Her name is carved into the windowsill of the Drummond Room. ✉ *Off A947 between Oldmeldrum and Turriff* ☎ *01651/891266* ⊕ *www.nts.org.uk* ✉ *£10* ☉ *Castle Easter–June and Sept., Sat.–Wed., noon–5; July and Aug., daily 11–5; grounds daily 9:30–dusk; last admission 45 mins before closing.*

Haddo House

★ ❷⁷ *12 mi southeast of Fyvie Castle.*

Created as the home of the Gordon family, earls and marquesses of Aberdeen, Haddo House—designed by William Adam—is now cared for by the National Trust for Scotland. Built in 1732, the elegant mansion has a light and graceful Georgian design, with curving wings on either side of a harmonious, symmetrical facade. The interior is late-Victorian ornate, filled with magnificent paintings (including works by Pompeo Batoni and Sir Thomas Lawrence) and plenty of objets d'art. Pre-Raphaelite stained-glass windows by Sir Edward Burne-Jones grace the chapel. Outside is a terrace garden with a fountain, and few yards farther is Haddo Country Park, which has walking trails leading to memorials about the Gordon family. ✉ *Off B999, 8 mi northwest of Ellon* ☎ *01651/851440* ⊕ *www.nts.org.uk* ✉ *£10* ☉ *House Easter, May, June, and Sept., weekends 11–4:30; July and Aug., daily 11–4:30; garden year-round, daily 9:30–6.*

ABERDEEN & THE NORTHEAST ESSENTIALS

Transportation

BY AIR
Aberdeen is easy to reach from other parts of the United Kingdom, as well as Europe. British Airways, bmi/British Midland, easyJet, and KLM U.K. provide service between Aberdeen and most major U.K. airports.

🛪 **bmi/British Midland** ☎ 0870/607-0555 ⊕ www.flybmi.com. **British Airways** ☎ 0870/850-9850 ⊕ www.ba.com. **easyJet** ☎ 0871/244-2366 ⊕ www.easyjet.com. **KLM U.K.** ☎ 0870/507-4074 ⊕ www.klmuk.com. **SAS** (Scandinavian Airlines) ☎ 0870/6072-7727 ⊕ www.scandinavian.net.

AIRPORTS   Aberdeen Airport—serving both international and domestic flights—is in Dyce, 7 mi west of the city center on the A96 (Inverness).
🛪 **Aberdeen Airport** ☎ 0870/040-0006 ⊕ www.baa.co.uk.

AIRPORT   First Aberdeen Bus 27 operates between the airport terminal and Union
TRANSFERS   Street in the center of Aberdeen. Buses (£1.50) run frequently at peak times, less often at midday and in the evening; the journey time is approximately 40 minutes. The drive to the center of Aberdeen is easy via the A96 (which can be busy during rush hour).

Dyce is on First ScotRail's Inverness–Aberdeen route. The rail station is a short taxi ride from the terminal building. The ride takes 12 minutes, and trains run approximately every two hours. If you intend to visit the western region first, you can travel northwest, from Aberdeen, by rail, direct to Elgin via Inverurie, Insch, Huntly, and Keith.
🛪 **First Aberdeen** ☎ 01224/650000 ⊕ www.firstaberdeen.co.uk. **First ScotRail** ☎ 08457/484950 ⊕ www.firstgroup.com/scotrail.

BY BUS
Long-distance buses run to and from most parts of Scotland, England, and Wales. Contact National Express for bus connections with English towns. Contact Scottish Citylink for bus connections with Scottish towns.

First Aberdeen operates services within the city of Aberdeen. Timetables are available from the tourist information center at St. Nicholas House.
🛪 **First Aberdeen** ☎ 01224/650000 ⊕ www.firstaberdeen.co.uk. **National Express** ☎ 08705/808080 ⊕ www.nationalexpress.com. **Scottish Citylink** ☎ 08705/505050 ⊕ www.citylink.co.uk.

BY CAR
You can travel from Glasgow and Edinburgh to Aberdeen on a continuous stretch of the A90/M90, a fairly scenic route that runs up Strathmore, with a fine hill view to the west. The coastal route, the A92, is a more leisurely alternative, with its interesting resorts and fishing villages. The most scenic route, however, is the A93 from Perth, north to Blairgowrie and into Glen Shee. The A93 then goes over the Cairnwell Pass, the highest main road in the United Kingdom. (This route isn't recommended in winter, when snow can make driving difficult.)

Aberdeen is a compact city with good signage. Its center is Union Street, the main thoroughfare running east–west, which tends to get crowded with traffic. Anderson Drive is an efficient ring road on the city's west side; be extra careful on its many traffic circles. It's best to leave your car in one of the parking garages (arrive early to get a space) and walk around, or use the convenient park-and-ride stop at the Bridge of Don, north of the city. Street maps are available from the tourist information center, newsdealers, and booksellers.

Around the northeast roads are generally not busy, but speeding and erratic driving can be a problem on the main A roads. The rural side roads are a pleasure to drive.

BY TAXI

You'll find taxi stands throughout the center of Aberdeen: along Union Street, at the railway station at Guild Street, at Back Wynd, and at Regent Quay. The taxis have meters and are mostly black, though some are beige, maroon, or white.

BY TRAIN

You can reach Aberdeen directly from Edinburgh (2½ hours), Glasgow (3 hours), and Inverness (2½ hours). Get a First ScotRail timetable for full details. There are also London–Aberdeen routes that go through Edinburgh and the east-coast main line.

🚆 Train Information **First ScotRail** ☎ 0845/601-5929 ⊕ www.firstgroup.com/scotrail.

Contacts & Resources

EMERGENCIES

Dial ☎ **999** in case of an emergency to reach an ambulance, or the fire, coast guard, or police departments (no coins are needed for emergency calls made from public phone booths). For a doctor or dentist, consult your hotel receptionist, B&B proprietor, or the yellow pages.

There's a lost-property office at the Grampian Police headquarters.

Notices on pharmacy doors will guide you to the nearest open pharmacy at any given time. Anderson Pharmacy (open Monday through Saturday, 9 to 4) and Boots the Chemists Ltd. (open weekdays 8:30 to 5, Saturday 8:30 to 6, Sunday 11 to 5:30), both in Aberdeen, keep longer hours than most.

🚆 Emergency Contact **Grampian Police** ⊠ Force Headquarters, Queen St., Aberdeen ☎ 0845/600-5700.

🚆 Hospitals **Aberdeen Royal Infirmary** ⊠ Accident and Emergency Department, Foresterhill, Aberdeen ☎ 01224/681818. **Dr. Gray's Hospital, Elgin** ⊠ Accident and Emergency Department, at end of High St. on A96 ☎ 01343/543131.

🚆 Late-Night Pharmacies **Anderson Pharmacy** ⊠ 34 Holburn St., Aberdeen ☎ 01224/587148. **Boots the Chemists Ltd** ⊠ Bon Accord Centre, George St., Aberdeen ☎ 01224/626080.

INTERNET

🚆 Internet Cafés **Café-LAN** ⊠ 11 Market St., Aberdeen ☎ 01224/593054 ⊕ www.cafe-lan.com. **Easy Internet Cafe** ⊠ 434 Union St., Aberdeen ☎ 01224/658899 ⊕ www.easyinternetcafe.com.

TOUR OPTIONS

BUS TOURS First Bus conducts city tours, available on most days between July and mid-September. Grampian Coaches offers daily tours encompassing the Castle Trail, Malt Whisky Trail, and Royal Deeside (£12 to £14).

🚆 **First Bus** ☎ 01224/650000 ⊕ www.firstgroup.com. **Grampian Coaches** ☎ 01224/650024 ⊕ www.firstgroup.com/grampian.

16

PRIVATE GUIDES The Scottish Tourist Guides Association can supply experienced personal guides, including foreign-language-speaking guides if necessary.

🎵 **Scottish Tourist Guides Association** ✉ The Old Town Jail, St. John's St., Stirling FK8 1EA ☎ 01786/447784 ⊕ www.stga.co.uk.

VISITOR INFORMATION

The tourist information center in Aberdeen has a currency exchange and supplies information on all of Scotland's Northeast. There are also year-round tourist information offices in Braemar and Elgin.

🎵 Tourist Information **Aberdeen** ✉ 23 Union St. ☎ 01224/288828 ⊕ www. castlesandwhisky.com. **Ballater** ✉ The Old Royal Station, Station Sq. ☎ 013397/55306. **Braemar** ✉ The Mews, Mar Rd. ☎ 013397/41600 ⊕ www.braemarscotland.co.uk. **Elgin** ✉ 17 High St. ☎ 01343/542666.

Argyll & the Isles

WORD OF MOUTH

"Iona was the most beautiful place I have ever been (I've lived and traveled extensively in Europe and Africa). Besides the historical artifacts from the development of Christianity there, it was such a deeply spiritual place—from the brilliant flowers among the ruins to the seascape to the little tea room near the convent. I had the most profound sensation of return and peace there."

—lilybart

"Duart Castle is really charming. It is still family owned/lived in (as are many Scottish castles), and they are doing a good job of creating a lovely tourist experience without getting 'touristy'."

—Janis

Updated by
Fiona Parrott

DIVIDED IN TWO by the long peninsula of Kintyre, western Scotland is characterized by a complicated, splintered seaboard. The west is an aesthetic delight, though it does catch those moist (yes, that's a euphemism) Atlantic weather systems. But the occasional wet foray is a small price to pay for the glittering freshness of oak woods and bracken-covered hillsides and for the bright interplay of sea, loch, and rugged green peninsula. Only a few decades ago the Clyde estuary was a coastal playground for people living in Glasgow and along Clydeside: their annual holiday was a steamer trip to any one of a number of resorts, known as going *doon the watter.*

Some impressive castles gaze out over this luxuriant landscape. Ruined Dunstaffnage and Kilchurn castles once guarded the western seaboard; turreted Inveraray Castle and magnificent Brodick, on the Isle of Arran, now guard their own historic interiors, with hundreds of antiques and portraits. The Kilmartin area has stone circles, carved stones, and burial mounds from the Bronze Age and earlier, taking imaginative travelers thousands of years back in time. Gardens are another Argyll specialty thanks to the temperate west-coast climate—Crarae Gardens, south of Inveraray, invites you down winding paths through plantings of magnolias and azaleas that reach their colorful peaks in late spring.

Western Scotland's tiny islands are essentially microcosms of Scotland: each has its jagged cliffs or tongues of rock, its smiling sands and fertile pastures, its grim and ghostly fortress, and its tale of clan outrage or mythical beast. The pace of life is gentle out here, and the roads narrow and tortuous. Arran is the place for hill walking on Goat Fell, the mountain that gives the island its distinctive profile. On Islay you can hunt down peaty, iodine-scented malt whisky. Mull has yet more castles, a short stretch of narrow-gauge railway, and the pretty port of Tobermory, with its brightly painted houses. Iona (just off Mull's western tip) is famous as an early seat of Christianity in Scotland and the burial place of Scottish kings in the Dark Ages. You could spend all your time touring these larger islands, but plenty of small islands are just as lovely, and they're blissfully uncrowded.

Exploring Argyll & the Isles

With long sea lochs carved into its hilly, wooded interior, Argyll is a beguiling interweaving of water and land. The Kintyre Peninsula stretches between the islands of the Firth of Clyde (including Arran) and the islands of the Inner Hebrides. Loch Fyne tends to get in the way of a breezy mainland tour: it's a long haul around the end of this fjordlike sea loch to Inveraray. Ferry services allow all kinds of interisland tours and can shorten mainland trips as well.

About the Restaurants

This part of Scotland has a few restaurants of distinction, and local ingredients are high in quality: the seafood, fresh from the sparkling lochs and sea, could hardly be better. Beef, lamb, and game are also common. In rural districts it's prudent to choose a hotel or guesthouse that serves a decent evening meal as well as breakfast.

TOP REASONS TO GO

Whisky, whisky, whisky: This part of Scotland is whisky country. Take the "whisky walk" in Port Ellen, on the Isle of Islay; it's a leisurely 3-mi stroll passing Ardbeg, Laphroaig and Lagavulin distilleries. Here the whiskies share the distinct flavors of peat, seaweed, and iodine. Arran, Oban, and Jura also have their own unique distilleries.

Seaside biking: Oban and Arran are two great cycling destinations. Biking along the coast provides breathtaking scenery; just keep in mind it rains a lot in this part of the country, so bring rain gear.

Iona and its abbey: Maybe it's the remoteness—especially if you explore beyond the abbey—that adds to the almost mystical sense of history here, but a visit to this early center of Scottish Christianity is a magical experience. This was also the burial place of Scottish kings until the 11th century.

Fantastic fishing and golf: The largest skate in Britain are found in the waters off the isle of Mull. There are 20 coastal settlements suited to sea angling where charter-boat companies offer trips. If it's loch and river sites you're after, there are 50 for game fishing that yield salmon, trout, and other fish. Prefer to tee off? Western Scotland has about two dozen golf courses, notably some fine coastal links. Machrihanish, near Campbeltown, is the best known.

Glorious gardens: Plants flourish in the mild Gulf Stream that brushes against this broken, western coastline. For vivid flowers, trees, birds, and butterflies, visit Crarae Gardens, southwest of Inveraray. The Achamore House Gardens on the Isle of Gigha is another colorful extravaganza.

17

About the Hotels

Accommodations in Argyll and on the isles range from châteaulike hotels to modest inns. Many traditional provincial hotels and small coastal resorts have been equipped with modern conveniences yet retain their personalized service and historic charm. Apart from these, however, your choices are limited; the best overnight option is usually a simple guest house offering bed, breakfast, and an evening meal.

WHAT IT COSTS In Pounds				
£££££	**££££**	**£££**	**££**	**£**
RESTAURANTS over £22	£18–£22	£13–£17	£7–£12	under £7
HOTELS over £160	£120–£160	£90–£119	£60–£89	under £60

Restaurant prices are for a main course at dinner. Hotel prices are for two people in a standard double room in high season, generally including the 17.5% V.A.T.

Timing

This part of the mainland is close enough to Glasgow that it's convenient to reach year-round. You can take advantage of quiet roads and

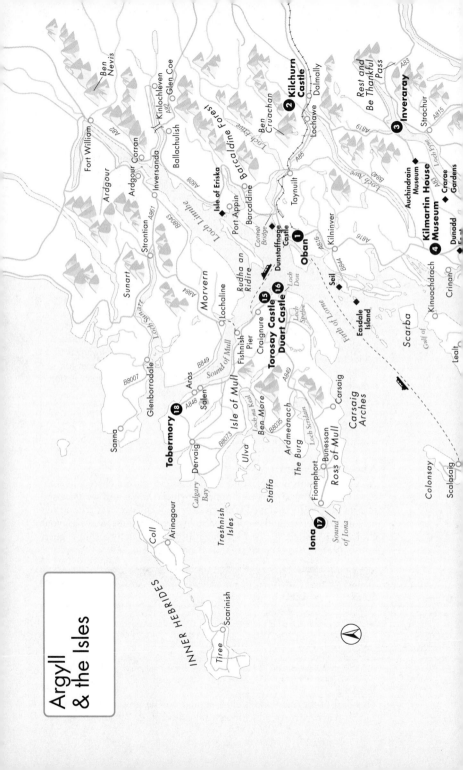

Argyll & the Isles

INNER HEBRIDES

Ben Nevis

Fort William

Ardgour

Ardgour Corran

Kinlochleven

Glen Coe

Inversanda

Ballachulish

A82

Sunart

Strontian

Loch Sunart

Morvern

Lochaline

Glenborrodale

Sanna

Aros

Salen

Dervaig

Calgary Bay

Tobermory 18

Treshnish Isles

Arinagour

Coll

Tiree

Scarinish

Ulva

Staffa

Ben More

The Burg

Isle of Mull

Fishnish Pier

Craignure

Fionnphort

Bunessan

Ross of Mull

Ardmeanach

Iona 17

Sound of Iona

Loch Linnhe

Barcaldine Forest

Isle of Eriska

Port Appin

Barcaldine

Connel Bridge

Rudha an Ridire

Sound of Mull

Torosay Castle 15

Duart Castle

16

Loch Don

Loch Spelve

Carsaig

Carsaig Arches

Loch na Keal

Loch Scridain

Ben Cruachan

Kilchurn Castle 2

Lochawe

Dalmally

Taynuilt

Dunstaffnage Castle 1

Oban

Kilninver

Seil

Esdale Island

Firth of Lorne

Scarba

Gulf of Corryvreckan

Lealt

Rest and Be Thankful Pass

A83

Inveraray 3

Strachur

Loch Fyne

Auchindrain Museum

Kilmartin Museum 4

Crarae Gardens

Dunadd

Kinuachdrach

Crinan

Colonsay

Scalasaig

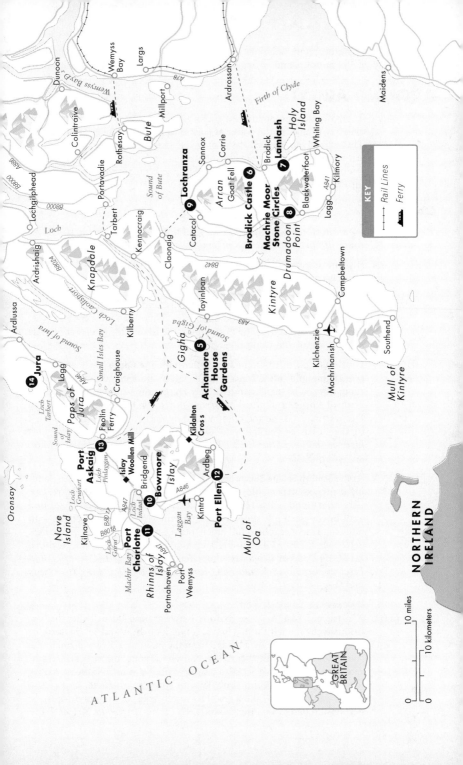

plentiful accommodations in early spring and late autumn. In winter short daylight hours and strong winds can make island stays rather bleak.

AROUND ARGYLL

Topographical grandeur and rocky shores are what make Argyll special. Try to take to the water at least once, even if your time is limited. The sea and the sea lochs have played a vital role in the history of western Scotland since the time of the war galleys of the clans. Oban is the major ferry gateway and transport hub, with a main road leading south into Kintyre.

Oban

❶ *96 mi northwest of Glasgow, 125 mi northwest of Edinburgh, 50 mi south of Fort William, 118 mi southwest of Inverness.*

It's almost impossible to avoid Oban when touring the west. Luckily it has a waterfront with some character and serves as a launch point for several ferry excursions. A traditional Scottish resort town, Oban has *ceilidhs* (song, music, and dance festivals) and tartan kitsch as well as late-night revelry in pubs and hotel bars. There's an inescapable sense, however, that just over the horizon, on the islands or down Kintyre, lie more peaceful and traditional environs.

Four miles north of Oban stands **Dunstaffnage Castle**, once an important stronghold of the MacDougall clan in the 13th century. From the ramparts you have outstanding views across the **Sound of Mull** and the **Firth of Lorne,** a nautical crossroads of sorts, once watched over by Dunstaffnage Castle and commanded by the galleys (*birlinn* in Gaelic) of the Lords of the Isles. ✉ *Off A85* ☎ *01631/562465* ⊕ *www. historic-scotland.gov.uk* ✉ *£3* ☉ *Apr.–Sept., daily 9:30–6; Oct.–Mar., Sat.–Wed. 9:30–4.*

☙ At the **Scottish Sealife Sanctuary** kids, as well as adults, love the outstanding display of marine life, including shoals of herring, sharks, rays, catfish, otters, and seals. There's even a children's adventure playground and, of course, a gift shop. The restaurant serves morning coffee with homemade scones, plus a full lunch menu, and afternoon tea. To get here drive north from Oban for 10 mi on A828. ✉ *Barcaldine, Connel* ☎ *01631/720386* ⊕ *www.sealsanctuary.co.uk* ✉ *£10.50* ☉ *Jan.–mid-Feb., weekends 10–4; mid-Feb.–June and Sept.–Dec., daily 10–4; July and Aug., daily 10–5.*

Where to Stay & Eat

££££££ ✕🏨 **Isle of Eriska.** A severe, baronial-style granite facade belies the luxurious welcome within this hotel, set on its own island 10 mi north of Oban and accessible by a bridge from the mainland. Every detail in the spacious rooms has been carefully chosen for your comfort. The restaurant serves innovative Scottish cuisine made with local ingredients: try the scallop and zucchini timbale with lobster, artichoke, and champagne butter sauce. Take a stroll to watch seals and otters offshore or herons and badgers on the grounds. ✉ *Ledaig, by Oban, Argyll, PA37*

1SD ☎ 01631/720371 ⊟ 01631/720531 ⊕ *www.eriska-hotel.co.uk* ⇔ *24 rooms △ Restaurant, 6-hole golf course, tennis court, pool, health club; no a/c* ⊟ *AE, MC, V* ⊘ *Closed Jan.* ⫶⦿⫶ *MAP.*

£££–££££ ⊡ **Manor House Hotel.** On the coast near Oban, this 1780 stone house, once the home of the duke of Argyll, has wonderful sea views. The public areas are furnished with antiques, the bedrooms with lovely reproductions. The restaurant serves a five-course prix-fixe meal of Scottish and French dishes, including lots of local seafood and game in season, complemented by a carefully selected wine list. The house is within walking distance of the center of the city and the bus, train, and ferry terminals. ⊠ *Gallanach Rd., Oban, Argyll, PA34 4LS* ☎ *01631/562087* ⊟ *01631/563053* ⊕ *www.manorhouseoban.com* ⇔ *11 rooms △ Restaurant, bar, lounge; no a/c, no kids under 12* ⊟ *AE, MC, V* ⫶⦿⫶ *MAP.*

££ ⊡ **Kilchrenan House.** A fully refurbished Victorian-era stone house, this bed-and-breakfast is a few minutes' walk from the town center. Comfortable rooms, many with antique furnishings, overlook the sea and the islands. ⊠ *Corran Esplanade, Oban, Argyll, PA34 5AQ* ☎ *01631/562663* ⊕ *www.kilchrenanhouse.co.uk* ⇔ *10 rooms △ Dining room, lounge; no a/c* ⊟ *MC, V* ⊘ *Closed Dec. and Jan.* ⫶⦿⫶ *BP.*

★ £ ⊡ **Dungrianach.** Meaning "the sunny house on the hill," Dungrianach is a late-Victorian house set high in a wooded area with superb views of the islands. Although it feels quite isolated, it's only a few minutes' walk from the center of town and the ferry piers. Antique and reproduction furniture fill the guest rooms. ⊠ *Pulpit Hill, Oban, Argyll, PA34 4LU* ☎ *01631/562840* ⊕ *www.dungrianach.com* ⇔ *2 rooms △ Dining room, lounge; no a/c, no room phones* ⊟ *No credit cards* ⊘ *Closed Oct.–Mar.* ⫶⦿⫶ *BP.*

Sports & the Outdoors

BIKING You can rent bicycles from **Oban Cycles** (⊠ 29 Lochside St. ☎ 01631/566996), whose shopkeepers will give you advice on waterside routes to take as far out as Ganavan Bay and Dunstaffnage Castle.

FISHING **The Gannet** (⊠ 3 Kiel Croft, Benderloch ☎ 01631/720262 ⊕ www.fishntrip.co.uk), a charter-fishing company run by Adrian Lauder, offers sea-angling trips for £460 a day. Fishing parties are limited to 10 people (8 for skate-fishing).

Lochawe

18 mi east of Oban.

Lochawe is a loch-side community squeezed between the broad shoulder of Ben Cruachan and Loch Awe itself. The road gets busy in peak season, filled with people trying to find parking near Lochawe Station.

★ ➋ **Kilchurn Castle,** a ruined fortress at the east end of the loch, was built in the 15th century by Sir Colin Campbell (d. 1493) of Glenorchy, and rebuilt in the 17th century. Airy vantage points amid the towers have fine panoramas of the surrounding highlands and loch. It's only accessible by boat from the pier. ⊠ *1 mi northeast of Lochawe on A85* ☎ *01866/833333* ⊕ *www.historic-scotland.gov.uk* ⇔ *Free* ⊘ *Daily 24 hrs.*

The **Duncan Ban Macintyre Monument** was erected in honor of this Gaelic poet (1724–1812), sometimes referred to as the Robert Burns of the Highlands. The view from here is one of the finest in Argyll, taking in Ben Cruachan and the other peaks nearby, as well as Loch Awe and its scattering of islands. To find the monument from Dalmally, just east of Loch Awe, follow an old road running southwest toward the banks of Loch Awe—you'll see the round, granite structure from the road's highest point, often called Monument Hill.

Inveraray

★ ❸ *21 mi south of Lochawe, 61 mi north of Glasgow, 29 mi west of Loch Lomond.*

On the approaches to Inveraray, note the ornate 18th-century bridgework that carries the road along the loch side. This is your first sign that Inveraray is not just a jumble of houses; in fact, much of it was designed as a planned town for the third duke of Argyll in the mid-18th century. The current seat of the Campbell duke is **Inveraray Castle,** a smart, grayish-green turreted stone house with a self-satisfied air, visible through trees from the town itself. Like the town, the castle was built around 1743. Tours of the interior convey the history of the powerful Campbell family. ⊠ *Off A83* ☎ *01499/302203* ⊕ *www.inveraray-castle. com* ▢ *£6.30* ⊗ *Apr.–May and Oct., Mon.–Thurs. and Sat. 10–1 and 2–5:45, Sun. 1–5:45; June–Sept., Mon.–Sat. 10–5:45, Sun. 1–5:45.*

The **Inveraray Jail** houses realistic courtroom scenes, carefully re-created cells, and other paraphernalia that give you a glimpse of life behind bars in Victorian times—and today. The site includes a Scottish crafts shop. ⊠ *Inveraray* ☎ *01499/302381* ⊕ *www.inverarayjail.co.uk* ▢ *£6.25* ⊗ *Apr.–Oct., daily 9:30–6; Nov.–Mar., daily 10–5; last admission 1 hr before closing.*

Ardkinglas Woodland Garden has one of Britain's finest collections of conifers, set off by rhododendron blossoms in early summer. You'll find it around the head of Loch Fyne, about 4 mi east of Inveraray. ⊠ *A83, Cairndow* ☎ *01499/600261* ⊕ *www.ardkinglas.com* ▢ *£3* ⊗ *Daily dawn–dusk.*

★ Step back a few centuries at the open-air **Auchindrain Museum,** a rare surviving example of an 18th-century communal tenancy farm. The old bracken-thatch and iron-roof buildings, about 20 in all, give you a feel for early farming life in the Highlands, and the interpretation center explains it all. Among the furnished buildings are cottages, longhouses, and barns. It's 5 mi south of Inveraray. ⊠ *A83* ☎ *01499/500235* ⊕ *www.auchindrainmuseum.org.uk* ▢ *£4.50* ⊗ *Apr.–Sept., daily 10–5.*

★ Well worth a visit for plant lovers are the **Crarae Gardens,** where magnolias, azaleas, and rhododendrons flourish in the moist, lush environment. The flowers and trees attract several different species of birds and butterflies. The gardens are 10 mi southwest of Inverary. ⊠ *Off A83* ☎ *01546/886614* ⊕ *www.nts.org.uk* ▢ *£5* ⊗ *Gardens daily 9:30–6 or dusk; visitor center Apr.–Sept., 10–5.*

Where to Stay & Eat

££–££££ ✕🖼 **The George Hotel.** This 18th-century former coaching inn has been
Fodor'sChoice run by the Clark family for six generations, and the warmth of the wel-
★ come reflects the benefit of continuity. Roaring log fires invite repose in
the common rooms, and antiques and oil paintings in the rooms make
you feel as though you were in another, slower-paced era. Locals fill the
restaurant (££) to sample the excellent food, such as king scallop and bacon
kebabs with lemon basil and shallots. ⊠ *Main St. E, Inveraray, Argyll,
PA32 8TT* ☎ *01499/302111* 🖨 *01499/302098* ⊕ *www.thegeorgehotel.
co.uk* ⤶ *15 rooms* ⌂ *Restaurant, 2 bars; no a/c* ▭ *MC, V* ⍟❙ *BP.*

Crinan

32 mi south of Inverary.

Crinan is synonymous with its canal, the reason for this tiny community's existence and its mainstay. The narrow road beside the Crinan
Hotel bustles with yachting types waiting to pass through the locks, bringing a surprisingly cosmopolitan feel to such an out-of-the-way corner
of Scotland.

★ ❹ For an exceptional encounter with early Scottish history, visit the **Kilmartin House Museum**, about 8 mi north of Crinan. The museum explores
the stone circles and avenues, burial mounds, and carved stones dating
from the Bronze Age and earlier that are scattered thickly around this
neighborhood. Nearby **Dunadd Fort**, a rocky hump rising out of the level
ground between Crinan and Kilmartin, was once the capital of the early
kingdom of Dalriada, founded by the first wave of Scots who migrated
from Ireland around AD 500. Clamber up the rock to see a basin, a foot-
print, and an outline of a boar carved on the smooth upper face of the
knoll. ⊠ *At Kilmartin, on A816* ☎ *01546/510278* ⊕ *www.kilmartin.
org* 🎟 *£4.60* ◷ *Daily 10–5:30.*

**OFF THE
BEATEN
PATH**

CASTLE SWEEN – The oldest stone castle on the Scottish mainland, dating from the 12th century, sits on a rocky bit of coast about 12 mi south
of Crinan. You can reach it by an unclassified road from Crinan that
grants outstanding views of the Paps of Jura (the mountains on Jura),
across the sound. There are some deserted white-sand beaches here.

Where to Stay & Eat

★ **££** ✕🖼 **Allt-Na-Craig.** This large stone Victorian house was once the home
of *Wind in the Willows* author Kenneth Graham. The house is set in
lovely gardens overlooking Loch Fyne on the edge of the village. Nearby
is the yacht-filled eastern basin of the Crinan Canal. Charlotte Nicol's
food is well worth a stay. ⊠ *2 mi south of Lochgilphead, Ardrishaig,
PA30 8EP* ☎ *01546/603245* ⊕ *www.allt-na-craig.co.uk* ⤶ *5 rooms,
1 cottage* ⌂ *Restaurant; no a/c* ▭ *MC, V* ⍟❙ *BP.*

Kintyre Peninsula

75 mi (to Campbeltown) south of Inverary.

Rivers and streams crisscross this long, narrow strip of green pasture-
lands and hills stretching south from Lochgilphead.

17

The **Isle of Gigha,** barely 5 mi long, is sheltered in a frost-free, sea-warmed climate between Kintyre and Islay. The island was long favored by British aristocrats as a summer destination. One relic of the Isle of Gigha's aristocratic legacy is the **Achamore House Gardens,** which produce lush shrubberies with spectacular azalea displays in late spring. For a nimble day trip, take the 20-minute ferry to Gigha from Tayinloan and walk right over to the gardens. You may not want to take your car, as the walk is fairly easy. ☎ *01583/505390* ⊕ *www.isle-of-gigha.co.uk* ⌨ *Gardens £2; ferry £4.50 per person plus £15.80 per car* ☉ *Gardens daily dawn–dusk. Ferry Mon.–Sat. 9–5, Sun. 11, 2, and 3.*

Golf

Machrihanish. Many enthusiasts discuss this course in hushed tones—it's a kind of out-of-the-way golfers' Shangri-la. It was laid out in 1876 by Tom Morris on the links around the sandy Machrihanish Bay. The drive off the first tee is across the beach to reach the green—an intimidating start to a memorable series of individual holes. If you're short on time, consider flying from Glasgow to nearby Campbeltown, the last town on the long peninsula of Kintyre. ⊠ *Machrihanish, near Campbeltown* ☎ *01586/810277* ⊕ *www.machgolf.com* ⚑ *Reservations essential* ⚐ *18 holes, 6,225 yds, par 70* ⌨ *Weekdays and Sun. £35 per round, £55 per day; Sat. £45 per round, £65 per day* ☉ *Daily.*

ARRAN

Many Scots, especially those from Glasgow and the west, are well disposed toward Arran, as it reminds them of unhurried childhood holidays. Called "Scotland in Miniature" by the tourist board, Arran really does have it all: mountains, glens, beaches, waterfalls, standing stone circles, Viking forts, castles, and a malt-whisky distillery, one of more than 40 illegal stills that hid in the remote glens of 18th-century Arran.

To get to Arran, take the ferry from Ardrossan, on the mainland. (It's also possible to take the ferry from Claonaig on the Kintyre Peninsula in summer.) You'll see a number of fellow travelers wearing hiking boots: they're ready for the delights of Goat Fell, the impressive peak (2,868 feet) that gives Arran one of the most distinctive profiles of any island in Scotland. As the ferry approaches Brodick, you'll see Goat Fell's cone. Arran's southern half is less mountainous; the Highland Boundary Fault crosses just to the north of Brodick Bay. Exploring the island is easy, as the A841 road neatly circles it.

Brodick

1 hr by ferry from Ardrossan.

The largest township on Arran, Brodick is really a village, its frontage lined by a number of Victorian hotels, set spaciously back from a promenade and beach. Arran's biggest cultural draw is **Brodick Castle,** on the north side of Brodick Bay. The red-sandstone structure, parts of which date back to the 13th century, is cosseted by trees and parkland and several rooms are open to the public. The castle's furniture, paintings, and silver are opulent in their own right—try counting the number of deer heads on the hall walls—but the real attraction is the garden, where brilliantly colored rhododendrons bloom, particularly in late spring and early summer. There are many unusual varieties of azalea, though the ordinary yellow kind is unmatched for its scent: your first encounter with these is like hitting a wall of perfume. Save time to visit the Servants' Hall, where an excellent restaurant serves morning coffee (with hot scones), a full lunch menu that changes daily,

> **WORD OF MOUTH**
>
> "Regarding Isle of Arran, no lochs but one lake (Tanna). Arran really is Scotland in miniature and IMO certainly worth several days. There is a reasonable bus service to most of the villages. The drive from Brodick to Lochranza is one of my favorites. There are also a lot of hiking/biking opportunities. It's easily accessible from Edinburgh and Glasgow."   –historytraveler

and afternoon teas with home-baked goods. ⊠ *1 mi north of Brodick Pier* ☎ *01770/302202* ⊕ *www.nts.org.uk* ⊠ *Gardens £4; castle and gardens £10* ☉ *Castle and gardens Easter–Oct., daily 11–4:30; restaurant Easter–Oct., daily 10–4.30, Nov. and Dec., Fri.–Sun. 10–3:30.*

Where to Stay & Eat

££–£££ ✕ **The Brodick Bar.** Local beef, lamb, and game, plus the most succulent scallops you'll ever taste, are what keeps the locals (and visitors) coming back to this casual, friendly, small-town pub and restaurant. ⊠ *Alma Rd., Brodick* ☎ *01770/302169* ▭ *MC, V.*

£–££ ⊡ **Glencloy Farmhouse.** This 19th-century sandstone house is surrounded by colorful gardens and nestled in a peaceful valley. Brodick and views of the hills and sea are a few minutes' walk away. Breakfast is a treat, with organic eggs, homemade jam, and fresh-baked bread and muffins. ⊠ *Brodick, Isle of Arran, KA26 8DA* ☎ *01770/302251* ⤶ *5 rooms, 2 with bath* ⌂ *Dining room; no a/c, no room phones* ▭ *MC, V* ⏇ *BP.*

Shopping

Arran's shops are well stocked with locally produced goods. The Home Farm is a popular shopping area with several shops and a small restaurant. The **Duchess Court Shops** (⊠ The Home Farm ☎ 01770/302831) include Bear Necessities, with everything bearly; the Nature Shop, with nature-oriented books and gifts; and Arran Aromatics, one of Scotland's top makers of toiletries. **The Island Cheese Company** (⊠ The Home Farm ☎ 01770/302788), stocks Arran blue cheese among other handmade Scottish cheeses.

Lamlash

❼ *4 mi south of Brodick.*

With views offshore to Holy Island, now a Buddhist retreat, Lamlash has a breezy seaside-holiday atmosphere. To reach the highest point accessible by car, go through the village and turn right beside the bridge onto Ross Road, which climbs steeply from a thickly planted valley, **Glen Scorrodale,** and yields fine views of Lamlash Bay. From Lamlash you can explore the southern part of Arran: 10 mi southwest is the little community of **Lagg**, sitting peacefully by the banks of the Kilmory Water, and **Whiting Bay** has a waterfront string of hotels.

Where to Stay & Eat

★ ££ ✕⌂ **Lagg Hotel.** Arran's oldest inn is an 18th-century lodge with fireplaces in the common rooms and gardens that meander down to the river. Each room is quiet and bright, if a little flowery, and many overlook the riverside flower beds or woodland. Simple home cooking in the restaurant (££) and friendly locals in the bar add up to a fine evening. The inn is 8 mi west of Whiting Bay. ☒ *Kilmory, Isle of Arran, KA278PQ* ☎ *01770/870255* 🖷 *01770/870250* ⊕ *www.lagghotel.com* ⮌ *13 rooms* △ *Restaurant, 2 bars; no a/c, no smoking* ▭ *MC, V* ⏐◯⏐ *BP.*

Biking
You can rent bicycles at **Whiting Bay Cycle Hire** (☒ Elim, Silverhill, Whiting Bay ☎ 01770/700382), open May through September.

Machrie

11 mi north of Lagg.

The area surrounding Machrie, home to a popular beach, is littered with prehistoric sites: chambered cairns, hut circles, and standing stones dating from the Bronze Age. From Machrie, a well-surfaced track takes you

★ ❽ to a grassy moor by a ruined farm, where you can see the **Machrie Moor Stone Circles:** small, rounded granite-boulder circles and much taller, eerie red-sandstone monoliths. Out on the bare moor, the lost and lonely stones are very evocative, well worth a walk to see if you like the feeling of solitude. The stones are about a mile outside of Machrie; just follow the HISTORIC SCOTLAND sign pointing the way.

Horseback Riding
Even novices can enjoy a guided ride on a mount from **Cairnhouse Riding Centre** (☒ On A84, 2 mi south of Machrie ☎ 01770/860466). The stables are in Blackwaterfoot.

Shopping
The **Old Byre Showroom** (☒ On A841, 2 mi north of Machrie ☎ 01770/840227) sells sheepskin goods, hand-knit sweaters, designer knitwear, leather goods, and rugs. The store is at Auchencar Farm.

Lochranza

❾ *14 mi north of Brodick.*

North of Brodick is Lochranza, a community sheltered by the Bay of Loch Ranza, which spills into the flat-bottom glacial glen. The village is set off by a picturesque ruin, **Lochranza Castle**, set on a low sand spit. This is said to have been the landing place of Robert the Bruce when he returned from Rathlin Island in 1307 to start the campaign that won Scotland's independence. A sign indicates where you can pick up the key to get in. ☒ *Off A841* ☎ *0131/668–8800* ⊕ *www.historic-scotland.gov.uk* ⮌ *Free* ☽ *Apr.–Sept., daily 9:30–6; Oct.–Mar., Mon.–Sat. 9:30–4, Sun. 2–4.*

ISLAY & JURA

Islay has a character distinct from that of the rest of the islands that make up the Hebrides. In contrast to areas where most residents live on crofts (small plots generally worked by people in their spare time), Islay's western half in particular has large self-sustaining farms. Many of the island's best beaches, wildlife preserves, and historical sites are also on its western half, whereas the southeast is mainly an extension of Jura's inhospitable quartzite hills. Islay is particularly known for its birds, including the rare chough (a crow with red legs and beak) and, in winter, its barnacle geese. Several distilleries produce delectable malt whiskies. A peaty taste characterizes the island's malt whiskies, which are available in local pubs, off-license shops, and distillery shops. Though not all have shops, most distilleries welcome visitors by appointment; some charge a small fee for a tour, which you can redeem against a purchase of whisky.

Although it's possible to meet an Islay native in a local pub, such an event is statistically less likely on Jura, with its one road, one distillery, one hotel, and six sporting estates. In fact, you have a better chance of bumping into one of the island's red deer, which outnumber the human population by at least 20 to 1. The island has a much more rugged look than Islay, with its profiles of the Paps of Jura, a hill range at its most impressive when basking in the rays of a west-coast sunset.

17

Bowmore

❿ *11 mi north of Port Ellen on Islay.*

Compact Bowmore is about the same size (population 1,000) as Port Ellen, but it works slightly better as a base for touring because it's central to Islay's main routes. Sharing its name with the whisky made in the distillery by the shore, Bowmore is a tidy town, its grid pattern having been laid out in 1768 by the local landowner Daniel Campbell, of Shawfield. Main Street stretches from the pier head to the commanding parish church, built in 1767 in an unusual circular design—so the devil could not hide in a corner.

★ The **Islay Woollen Mill,** set in a wooded hollow by the river, has a fascinating array of working machinery; the proud owner will take you around. The shop here sells high-quality products that were woven onsite. Beyond the usual tweed, there's a distinctive selection of hats, caps, and clothing made from the mill's own cloth. All the tartans and tweeds worn in the film *Braveheart* were woven here. The mill is 3 mi north of Bowmore via A846; follow signs for Port Askaig. Look for the sign for the mill on the main road about a mile east beyond the tiny community of Bridgend. ⊠ *Off A846* ☎ *01496/810563* ⊕ *www.islaywoollenmill. co.uk* 🖾 *Free* 🕑 *Mon.–Sat. 10–5.*

Where to Stay & Eat

£££–££££ ✕🏨 **Harbour Inn.** The cheerfully noisy bar is frequented by off-duty distillery workers who are happy to rub elbows with travelers and exchange island gossip. The superb restaurant (££) serves morning coffee, lunch, and dinner. Menus highlight local lobster, crab, prawns, and island lamb and beef. The bedrooms are bright and contemporary, with simple wood or velvet-upholstered furniture. ⊠ *The Square, Bowmore, Islay, PA43 7JR* ☎ *01496/810330* 🖷 *01496/810990* ⊕ *www.harbour-inn.com* ⇨ *7 rooms* ᗒ *Restaurant, lounge; no a/c* ☰ MC, V ⦿ BP.

Shopping

You can purchase whisky and take a tour at **Bowmore Distillery** (⊠ School St. ☎ 01496/810671). The facility was founded 1779.

Port Charlotte

⓫ *11 mi west of Bowmore via A846/A847, on Islay.*

Above the road on the north side in a converted *kirk* (church) is the **Museum of Islay Life,** a haphazard but authentic and informative display of times past. ⊠ *A847* ☎ *01496/850358* 🖃 *£2* ⊗ *Apr.–Oct., Mon.–Sat. 10–5, Sun. 2–5.*

Port Ellen

⓬ *11 mi south of Bowmore on Islay.*

The sturdy community of Port Ellen was founded in the 1820s, and much of its architecture dates from the following decades. It has a harbor, a few shops, and a handful of inns. The road traveling east from Port Ellen for 3 mi passes three top distilleries and makes a very pleasant afternoon's "whisky walk." Tours are free at all three distilleries, but you must call ahead for an appointment. **Ardbeg Distillery** (☎ 01496/302244) is the farthest from Port Ellen. It closed in 1981, but whisky aficionados cheered when the malt flowed again in 1997. **Laphroaig Distillery** (☎ 01496/302418) is a little less than a mile from Port Ellen toward Ardberg. The whisky it produces is one of the most distinctive in the Western Isles, with a tangy, peaty seaweed-and-iodine flavor. **Lagavulin Distillery** (☎ 01496/302400) has the whisky with the strongest iodine scent of all the island malts.

About 8 mi northeast of Port Ellen is one of the highlights of Scotland's Celtic heritage. After passing through a pleasantly rolling, partly wooded landscape, take a narrow road (it's signposted KILDALTON CROSS) from Ardbeg. This leads to a ruined chapel with surrounding kirkyard, in which ★ stands the finest carved cross anywhere in Scotland: the 8th-century **Kildalton Cross.** Carved from a single slab of epidiorite rock, the ringed cross is encrusted on both sides with elaborate designs in the style of the Iona school. The surrounding grave slabs date as far back as the 12th and 13th centuries. ⊕ *www.historic-scotland.gov.uk.*

Port Askaig

⓭ *3 mi northeast of Loch Finlaggan via A846, on Islay.*

Serving as the ferry port for Jura, Port Askaig is a mere cluster of cottages. Uphill, just outside the village, a side road travels along the coast, giving impressive views of Jura on the way. At road's end, the **Bunnahabhain Distillery** (☎ 01496/840646) sits on the shore. It was established in 1881. You can also purchase whisky at the **Caol Ila Distillery** (☎ 01496/ 840207), which filled its first bottle in 1846.

Where to Stay & Eat

££ ╳⊞ **Port Askaig Hotel.** The hotel grounds extend all the way to the shore at this modern roadside inn overlooking the Sound of Islay and the island of Jura. Accommodations are comfortable without being luxurious, and the traditional Scottish food (£) is well prepared, using homegrown produce. ⊠ *Port Askaig, Isle of Islay, Argyll, PA46 7RD* ☎ *01496/840245* ☎ *01496/840295* ⊕ *www.portaskaig.co.uk* ➳ *8 rooms, 6 with bath* ⌂ *Restaurant, 2 bars; no a/c, no room phones* ⊟ *MC, V* ⫽⊙⫽ *BP.*

Jura

⓮ *5 mins by ferry from Port Askaig.*

The rugged, mountainous landscape of the island of Jura, home to only 200 people, looms immediately east of Port Askaig. Having crossed the Sound of Islay from Port Askaig, you will find it easy to choose which road to take—Jura has only one, starting at Feolin, the ferry pier. Apart from the initial stretch it's all single-lane. The A846 starts off below one of the many raised beaches, then climbs across moorland, providing scenic views across the Sound of Jura. The ruined Claig Castle, on an island just offshore, was built by the Lords of the Isles to control the sound.

Beyond the farm buildings of Ardfin, and Jura House (with gardens that are occasionally open to the public), the road turns northward across open moorland with scattered forestry blocks and the faint evidence, in the shape of parallel ridges, of the original inhabitants' "lazy beds," or narrow fields separated by furrows to drain away the excess water. The original settlements were cleared with the other parts of the Highlands when the island became more of a sheep pasture and deer forest. The community of Craighouse has the island's only distillery, the **Isle of Jura Distillery** (⊠ A846 ☎ 01496/820240), producing malt whisky since 1810. Phone ahead to reserve your place on a tour.

The settlement of **Kinuachdrach** once served as a crossing point to Scarba and the mainland. To get to Kinuachdrach after crossing the river at Lealt, follow the track beyond the surface road for 5 mi. The coastal footpath to Corryvreckan lies beyond, over the bare moors. This area has two enticements: the first, for fans of George Orwell (1903–50), is the house of **Barnhill** (not open to the public), where the author wrote *1984*; the second, for wilderness enthusiasts, is the whirlpool of the **Gulf of Corryvreckan** and the unspoiled coastal scenery.

Where to Stay & Eat

££ ╳⊞ **Jura Hotel.** In spite of its monopoly, this hotel set in pleasant gardens can be relied on for high-quality accommodations. Rooms are simple and a bit old-fashioned. The restaurant serves good, satisfying food prepared with local ingredients. ⊠ *Craighouse, Isle of Jura, PA60 7XU* ☎ *01496/820243* ☎ *01496/820249* ⊕ *www.jurahotel.co.uk* ➳ *20 rooms, 11 with bath* ⌂ *Restaurant, bar, lounge; no a/c, no room phones, no room TVs* ⊟ *AE, DC, MC, V* ⫽⊙⫽ *BP.*

17

IONA & THE ISLE OF MULL

Though Mull certainly has an indigenous population, the island is often called the Officers' Mess because of its popularity with retired military personnel. Across from the Ross of Mull is the island of Iona, cradle of Scottish Christianity and ancient burial site of the kings of Scotland.

Craignure

40-min ferry crossing from Oban, 15-min ferry crossing to Fishnish (5 mi northwest of Craignure) from Lochaline.

Craignure, little more than a pier and some houses, is close to the Isle of Mull's two best-known castles, Torosay and Duart. Reservations for the year-round ferries that travel from Oban to Craignure are advisable in summer. The ferry from Lochaline to Fishnish, just northwest of Craignure, does not accept reservations and does not run on Sunday.

★ ⑮ A trip to **Torosay Castle** can include the novelty of steam-and-diesel service on a narrow-gauge railway, which takes 20 minutes to run from the pier at Craignure to the grounds of Torosay (about ½ mi). Scottish baronial in style, the turreted mid-19th-century castle has a friendly air. You are free to wander round the principal rooms, which include the front hall dominated by a collection of red deer stag antlers. The castle's gardens are home to blue poppies and many other rare plants. ⊠ *Off A849, about 1 mi southeast of Craignure* ☎ *01680/812421* 🖷 *01680/ 812470* ⊕ *www.torosay.com* ✉ *Train £3; gardens £4.50; castle and gardens £5.50* ◷ *Castle: Easter–Oct., daily 10:30–5:30; last admission at 5. Gardens: Easter–Oct., daily 9–7; Nov.–Easter, daily dawn–dusk.*

⑯ The 13th-century **Duart Castle** was ruined by the Campbells in 1691. Since it served as the ancient seat of the Macleans, it was purchased and restored by Sir Fitzroy Maclean in 1911. Inside, one display depicts the wreck of the *Swan*, a Cromwellian vessel sunk offshore in 1653 and excavated in the 1990s by marine archaeologists. Outside you can visit nearby **Millennium Wood**, planted with groups of Mull's indigenous trees. If you're an enthusiastic hiker you can walk 4 mi along the shore from Torosay to Duart Castle; if you have less energy, you can drive the 3 mi from Craignure. To reach Duart by car, take the A849 and turn left around the shore of Duart Bay. ⊠ *3 mi southeast of Craignure* ☎ *01680/ 812309* ⊕ *www.duartcastle.com* ✉ *£4.50* ◷ *Apr., Sun.–Thurs., 11–4; May–mid-Oct., daily 10:30–5:50.*

Where to Stay & Eat

££ ✕🖭 **Craignure Inn.** This 18th-century whitewashed drover's inn, a short walk from the ferry pier, has a lively bar that often hosts local musicians. Hearty, home-cooked meals (£–££) include staples such as shepherd's pie and fish-and-chips. The rooms are warm and snug, with polished-wood furniture, exposed beams, and views of the Sound of Mull. ⊠ *Craignure, Isle of Mull, Argyll, PA65 6AY* ☎ *01680/812305* ⊕ *www.craignure-inn.co.uk* ↪ *3 rooms* ♧ *Restaurant, bar; no a/c* ⊟ *MC, V* ⑩ *BP.*

EN ROUTE

Between Craignure and Fionnphort at the end of the Ross of Mull, the double-lane road narrows as it heads southwest. Inland, the stepped-rock faces in Glen More reach their highest point in Ben More. Stay on the A849 for a pleasant drive the length of the Ross of Mull, a wide promontory with scattered settlements. The A849 continues through the village of Bunessan and eventually ends in a long parking lot opposite the houses of Fionnphort. The vast parking spaces is a testament to the popularity of the nearby island of Iona, which does not allow cars. Ferry service is frequent in summer.

Iona

Fodor'sChoice ★

5 mins by ferry from Fionnphort, which is 36 mi west of Craignure.

No less a travel writer than Dr. Samuel Johnson (1709–84) wrote, "We were now treading that illustrious Island which was once the luminary of the Caledonian regions." The fiery and argumentative Irish monk Columba (circa 521–97) chose Iona for the site of a monastery in 563 because it was the first landing place from which he could *not* see Ireland. Christianity had been brought to Scotland (Galloway) by St. Ninian (circa 360–432) in 397, but until St. Columba's church was founded, the word had not spread widely among the ancient northerners, the Picts. As the most important Christian site in the land, Iona was the burial place of the kings of Scotland until the 11th century, so many kings, 48 of them Scottish (others were Pictish and Celtic), are interred here, not to mention princes and bishops. The tombstones that are still visible are near the abbey. Many carved slabs also commemorate clan chiefs.

Beyond the ancient cloisters, the island's most delightful aspect is its almost mystical tranquillity—enhanced by the fact that most visitors make only the short walk from the ferry pier to the abbey (by way of the nunnery), rather than press on to the island's farther reaches.

Iona Abbey survived repeated Norse sackings but finally fell into disuse around the time of the Reformation. Restoration work began at the turn of the 20th century. In 1938 the **Iona Community** (☎ 01681/700404 ⊕ www.iona.org.uk), an ecumenical religious group, was founded. It was involved in rebuilding the abbey and now offers multiday programs at several buildings on the island. Today the restored buildings, including the abbey, serve as a spiritual center under the jurisdiction of the Church of Scotland. Guided tours, run by the Iona Community, are every half hour in summer and on demand in winter. ☎ *01681/700793 ⊕ www.historic-scotland.gov.uk ☑ £4 ☉ Apr.–Sept., daily 9:30–6; Oct.–Mar., daily 9:30–4.*

Where to Stay & Eat

££–££££ ✕🏠 **St. Columba Hotel.** An 1846 former manse, St. Columba stands next to the cathedral about ¼ mi from the ferry pier. All front rooms have glorious views across the Sound of Iona to Mull. Chefs in the restaurant (£££) serve exceptional three-course meals using organic ingredients. ⌧ *Isle of Iona, Argyll, PA76 6SL* ☎ *01681/700304* 🖨 *01681/ 700688 ⊕ www.stcolumba-hotel.co.uk 🛏 27 rooms ⚐ Restaurant, lounge; no a/c, no room TVs ☉ Closed mid-Oct.–Easter ⊟ MC, V ⟟⦶ BP.*

Shopping

Iona has a few pleasant surprises for shoppers, the biggest of which is the **Old Printing Press Bookshop** (⊠ Beside St. Columba Hotel ☎ 01681/700699), an excellent antiquarian bookstore.

Tobermory

⑱ *22 mi northwest of Craignure on the Isle of Mull.*

Founded as a fishing station, Tobermory gradually declined, hastened by the arrival of railroad service in Oban. Still, the brightly painted crescent of 18th-century buildings around the harbor—now a popular mooring for yacht captains—gives Tobermory an adorably Mediterranean look. It's a popular vacation destination for Scots.

Where to Stay & Eat

££–£££ ✕▦ **The Tobermory Hotel.** Made up of a row of former fishermen's cottages, this lodging sits on Tobermory's waterfront. Most rooms have views of the bay. Some have nice touches like four-poster beds. Using local produce, the restaurant (££–£££) prepares traditional dishes with a twist: for example, the spiced-salmon fillet is served over a haddock-and-prawn roll and topped with lemon-and-coriander cream, and the Angus-beef casserole is accompanied by a cheese trencher and crusty bread. ⊠ *Tobermory, Isle of Mull, Argyll, PA75 6NT* ☎ *01688/302091* 🖷 *01688/302254* ⊕ *www.thetobermoryhotel.com* ⤴ *16 rooms* ⌂ *Restaurant, bar, lounge; no a/c* ⊟ *MC, V* ⦿ *BP.*

££ ▦ **Fairways Lodge.** Between the third and fourth fairways of the local golf course, this modern bungalow has a breathtaking view out over Tobermory Bay. Rooms are prettily furnished with antique and reproduction items. You can walk into town in a few minutes, though it's a bit of a steep climb back. ⊠ *Tobermory, Isle of Mull, Argyll, PA75 6PS* 🖷🖷 *01688/302792* ⊕ *www.fairwaysmull.com* ⤴ *5 rooms* ⌂ *Dining room, golf privileges, lounge; no a/c* ⊟ *MC, V* ⦿ *BP.*

ARGYLL & THE ISLES ESSENTIALS

Transportation

BY AIR

British Airways Express flies from Glasgow to Campbeltown (on the Kintyre Peninsula) and the island of Islay.

🛪 **British Airways Express** ☎ 0870/8509850 ⊕ www.ba.com. **Campbeltown Airport** ☎ 01586/553797 ⊕ www.hial.co.uk. **Islay Airport** ☎ 01496/302361 ⊕ www.hial.co.uk.

BY BOAT & FERRY

Caledonian MacBrayne (CalMac) operates car-ferry service to and from the main islands. An Island Hopscotch ticket reduces the cost of island-hopping. Western Ferries operates between Dunoon and Gourock.

🛥 **Caledonian MacBrayne** ⊠ Ferry Terminal, Gourock ☎ 01475/650100 ⊕ www.calmac.co.uk. **Western Ferries** ⊠ Hunter's Quay, Dunoon ☎ 01369/704452 ⊕ www.western-ferries.co.uk.

BY BUS

Scottish Citylink runs daily bus service from Glasgow's Buchanan Street station to the mid-Argyll region and Kintyre. The other companies listed below provide local service within the region.

🚌 **Alex Dunuachie** ⊠ Jura ☎ 01496/820314. **B. Mundell Ltd** ⊠ Islay ☎ 01496/840273. **Bowmans Coaches** ⊠ Mull ☎ 01680/812313 ⊕ www.bowmanscoaches.co.uk. **Oban & District Buses** ⊠ Oban and Lorne ☎ 01631/570500. **Scottish Citylink** ☎ 08705/505050 ⊕ www.citylink.co.uk. **Stagecoach Western Buses** ⊠ Arran ☎ 0870/6082608. **West Coast Motor Service** ⊠ Mid-Argyll and Kintyre ☎ 01586/552319 ⊕ www.westcoastmotors.co.uk.

BY CAR

Negotiating this area is easy except in July and August, when the roads around Oban may be congested. There are some single-lane roads, especially on the east side of the Kintyre Peninsula and on the islands.

You'll probably have to board a ferry at some point; all ferries take cars as well as pedestrians. The A85 takes you to Oban, the main ferry terminal for Mull. The A83 rounds Loch Fyne and heads down Kintyre to Kennacraig, the terminal for Islay. Farther down the A83 is Tayinloan, the ferry port for Gigha. You can reach Brodick on Arran by ferry from Ardrossan, on the Clyde coast (A8/A78 from Glasgow), or, in summer, you can travel to Lochranza from Claonaig on the Kintyre Peninsula.

BY TRAIN

Oban and Ardrossan are the main rail stations. For information call First ScotRail. All trains connect with ferries. A narrow-gauge railway takes ferry passengers from the pier head at Craignure (Mull) to Torosay Castle, a distance of about half a mile.

🚆 **First ScotRail** ☎ 08457/484950 ⊕ www.firstgroup.com/scotrail.

Contacts & Resources

EMERGENCIES

Dial **999** in case of an emergency to reach an ambulance, coast guard, or the fire or police departments (no coins are needed for emergency calls made from public phone booths). Lorne and Islands District General Hospital has an emergency room.

🏥 **Hospital Lorne and Islands District General Hospital** ⊠ Glengallen Rd., Oban ☎ 01631/567500.

INTERNET

Beyond the main hubs of Brodick and Oban, finding access in this part of the country isn't easy. Some of the larger hotels may provide you with the service but those are few and far between. The best places to go are public libraries and tourist centers—and they're free.

🌐 Internet Access **Oban Tourist Information Centre** ⊠ Argyll Sq., Oban ☎ 01631/563122 ⊕ www.oban.org.uk. **Oban Library** ⊠ 77 Albany St., Oban ☎ 01631/571444 ⊕ www.argyll-bute.gov.uk. **Auchrannie Spa Resort** ⊠ Brodick, Isle of Arran ☎ 01770/302234.

TOUR OPTIONS

BOAT TOURS Gordon Grant Tours leads an excursion to Mull and Iona. From Taynuilt, near Oban, boat trips are available from Loch Etive Cruises. Sea Life Surveys offers four- and six-hour whale-watching and wildlife day trips from Tobermory, on the Isle of Mull. Turas Mara runs daily excursions in summer from Oban and Mull to Iona and specializes in wildlife tours.

Gordon Grant Tours ✉ Waterfront, Railway Pier, Oban ☎ 01631/562842. **Loch Etive Cruises** ✉ Taynuilt ☎ 01866/822430. **Sea Life Surveys** ✉ Torrbreac, Dervaig, Mull ⊕ www.sealifesurveys.co.uk ☎ 01688/400223. **Turas Mara** ✉ Penmore Mill, Dervaig, Mull ☎☎ 01688/400242.

BUS TOURS Many of the bus companies listed in Bus Travel (⇨ *above*) arrange sightseeing tours. Bowmans Tours runs trips from Oban to Mull and Iona between March and October.

Bowmans Tours ✉ Scallastle Farm, Craignure, Mull ☎ 01680/812313 🖷 01631/563221 ⊕ www.bowmanstours.co.uk.

VISITOR INFORMATION

The tourist offices in Lochgilphead, at the northern trip of Knapdate, north of the Kintyre Peninsula, and Tobermory (Mull) are open April through October only; the rest are open year-round. For information on the region, visit www.visitscottishheartlands.com.

Bowmore, Islay ✉ The Sq. ☎ 08707/200617. **Brodick, Arran** ✉ The Pier ☎ 01770/302140 🖷 01770/302395 ⊕ www.ayrshire-arran.com. **Craignure, Mull** ✉ The Pierhead ☎ 08707/200610. **Dunoon** ✉ 7 Alexandra Parade ☎ 08707/20062. **Inveraray** ✉ Front St. ☎ 08707/200616. **Lochgilphead** ✉ Lochnell St. ☎ 08707/200618. **Oban** ✉ Argyll Sq. ☎ 08707/200630. **Tobermory, Mull** ✉ Main St. ☎ 08707/200625.

The Great Glen, Northern Highlands & Skye

WORD OF MOUTH

"Adding a day in Inverness does not necesarily mean spending it in Inverness. Logically, Inverness can be a home base for the amazing amount of sight-seeing around that area. Another recommendation: HIKING around the Fort William area will provide you the opportunity to combine castles, historical sites, and walking."

—Viajero2

"Skye—that's another story. Go there! It's gorgeous. Great small towns, interesting pottery, hiking, moun-tains, misty vistas, castles, going out in a small boat looking at the seals."

—adrienne

Updated by
Nick Bruno
and Shona
Main

THE ANCIENT RIFT VALLEY of the Great Glen is a dramatic feature on the map of Scotland, giving the impression that the top half of the country has slid southwest. This expansive wilderness contains the highest mountain in the United Kingdom, Ben Nevis (4,406 feet). To the west and the far north lies the atmospheric, sparsely populated territory of the true "Caledonia stern and wild": the land of Highland clans, red deer, golden eagles, Celtic mists, and legends. This is where you'll find Eilean Donan, the most romantic of Scottish castles; the land's end at John o'Groats; Destitution Road, which cuts through desolate moor studded with eerie peaks; and Skye, the mysterious island famed for its lush southern shores and jagged Cuillin crags farther north.

Nature lovers are drawn to the landscape's vivid purple and emerald moorland, its forests and astonishingly varied wildlife (mountain hares, red deer, golden eagles, ospreys). Something more otherworldly and fantastical also draws the curious. In 1933, during a quiet news week, the editor of an Inverness paper decided to run a story about a strange sighting of something splashing about in Loch Ness. More than 70 years later, the dubious Loch Ness phenomenon lives on. Impressive and historic castles are also on the agenda in the Great Glen; perhaps one of the best known is Urquhart Castle, a favorite haunt of Nessie-watchers. To the east of Inverness are two top-of-the-list castles that are still inhabited: Cawdor Castle and Brodie Castle.

Inverness may be officially a city now, but it feels like a Lowland town. South of Inverness, in Speyside, the River Spey draws anglers from around the world, and connoisseurs of *uisge beatha* follow the Malt Whisky Trail. Fort William, without a monster on its doorstep, makes do with Ben Nevis and the Road to the Isles, a title sometimes applied to the breathtaking scenic route to Mallaig.

The old counties of Ross and Cromarty (sometimes called Easter and Wester Ross), Sutherland, and Caithness constitute the most northern portion of mainland Scotland. Much of Sutherland and Wester Ross are made up of Lewisian gneiss, the oldest rocks in Britain, scoured and hollowed by glacial action into numerous lochs. On top of this rolling, wet moorland landscape sit strangely shaped, quartzite-capped sandstone mountains, eroded and pinnacled. Take a walk here, and the Ice Age doesn't seem so far away. Many place-names in this region reflect its early links with Scandinavia. Sutherland was once the southernmost land belonging to the Vikings. Cape Wrath got its name from the Viking word *hvarth* (turning point), and Laxford, Suilven, and dozens of other names in the area have Norse rather than Gaelic derivations.

Exploring the Great Glen, Northern Highlands & Skye

One classic route originates in Fort William and heads to Mallaig, taking in the unique qualities of the birch-knoll and blue-island West Highland views. Another possible route centers on Inverness, moving east into Speyside, then west down the Great Glen. It was here that the rash adventurer Prince Charles Edward Stuart (1720–88) arrived for the final Jacobite Rebellion of 1745–46, and it was from here that he departed after the last battle. From Inverness, the gateway to the Northern Highlands,

TOP REASONS TO GO

Awesome landscapes. Perhaps the most dramatic scenery in Scotland can be found in the Northern Highlands and Skye. Skye's landscapes range from the lush, tree-lined road leading to Sleat to the ragged outline of the Cuillin Hills. For untamed wilderness in the far north, Durness and Cape Wrath cannot be matched. Look for wildlife in the wilderness, too: you may see red deer in the woods, grouse on the moors, or seals around the seaside lochs.

Hiking the mountains and glens. Scotland is renowned for its hill walking. Some of the best routes are around Glen Nevis, Glencoe, and on Ben Nevis, the highest mountain in Great Britain. If you head for the hills, you should be fit and properly outfitted. Cairngorm National Park, southeast of Inverness, is another option.

The Isle of Skye. The best known of the Inner Hebrides islands has it all: mountains and 350 miles of rocky coastline, good food and hotels, an atmospheric castle, and some appealing towns—plus links to the story of Bonnie Prince Charlie.

The Malt Whisky Trail. Benromach, in Forres, is the smallest distillery in Moray, while Dallas Dhu, where whisky is no longer in production, is preserved as a museum. You can strike out from here to nearby distilleries covered in Chapter 16.

Castle country. You can take your pick: Cawdor Castle, east of Inverness, is still lived in by the family and has true character; Eilean Donan, near Skye, is set on an islet and epitomizes the enduring romance of Scotland's castles.

roads fan out like the spokes of a wheel to join the coastal route around the rim of mainland Scotland. Ferry services to the islands are generally very reliable, weather permitting. Inverness has an airport with direct links to London, Edinburgh, and Glasgow, and you can reach destinations such as the fishing town of Ullapool in an hour by car from Inverness.

About the Restaurants & Hotels

Inverness, Fort William, and Aviemore have plenty of hotels, B&Bs, cafés, and restaurants in all price ranges. Outside of the towns, a wealth of country-house hotels and charming inns serve superb meals; Skye has a number of these. Most country-house inns serve hearty seafood and meat-and-potatoes meals. You should have no trouble finding a room for a night; however, the area is quite busy in peak season.

WHAT IT COSTS In Pounds				
	££££	£££	££	£
	£££££	**££££**	**£££**	**££**	**£**
RESTAURANTS	over £22	£18–£22	£13–£17	£7–£12	under £7
HOTELS	over £160	£120–£160	£90–£119	£60–£89	under £60

Restaurant prices are for a main course at dinner. Hotel prices are for two people in a standard double room in high season, generally including the 17.5% V.A.T.

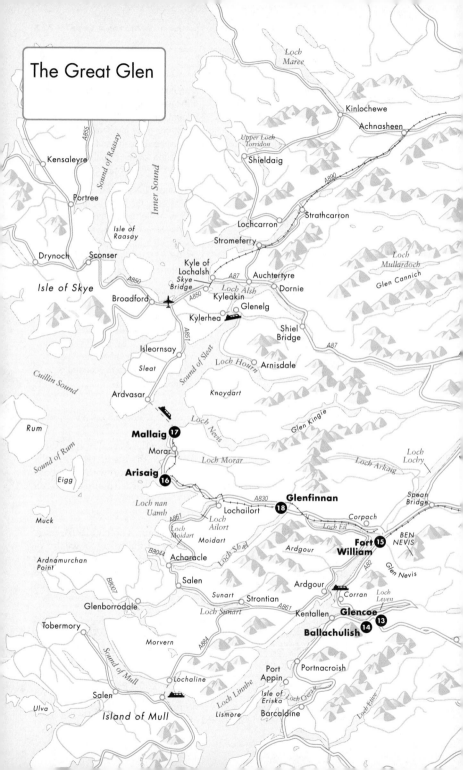

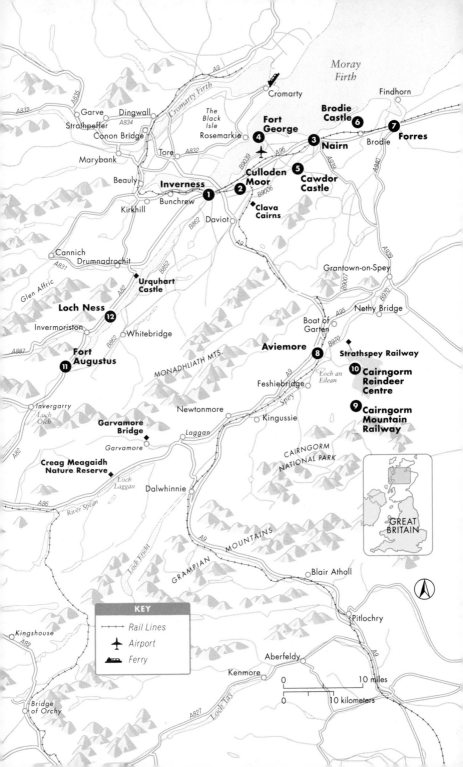

Timing

This is a spring and autumn kind of area—summer contends with pesky biting midges (they are fierce; bring insect repellant), and winter brings raw chill. However, in summer, if the weather is settled, it can be very pleasant in the far west, perhaps on the Road to the Isles, toward Mallaig. In the Northern Highlands, the earlier in the spring or later in the autumn you go, the greater the chances of your encountering the elements in their extreme form, and the fewer attractions and accommodations you will find open; even tourist-friendly Skye closes down almost completely by the end of October.

SPEYSIDE & LOCH NESS

Because Jacobite tales are interwoven with landmarks throughout this entire area, you should first learn something about this thorny but colorful period of Scottish history in which the Jacobites tried to restore the exiled Stuarts to the British monarchy. One of the best places to do this is at Culloden, just east of Inverness, where a major battle ended in final, catastrophic defeat for the Jacobites. Inverness itself is not really a town in which to linger, unless you need to do some shopping. Other areas to concentrate on are the inner Moray Firth moving down into Speyside, before moving west into the Great Glen. Loch Ness is just one of the attractions hereabouts.

Inverness

❶ *176 mi north of Glasgow, 109 mi northwest of Aberdeen, 161 mi northwest of Edinburgh.*

Inverness has tourist-friendly amenities and shops aplenty including a well-equipped visitor center. Throughout its past, the town was burned and ravaged by the restive Highland clans competing for dominance in the region, so little remains to be seen of its past. Only a decorative wall panel here and a fragment of tower there remain amid the 19th-century developments and modern shopping facilities. Nevertheless, Inverness makes a good base for exploring the northern end of the Great Glen.

One of Inverness's few historic landmarks is the **castle** (the local Sheriff Court), nestled above the river. The current structure is Victorian, built after a former fort was blown up by the Jacobites in the 1745 campaign. The excellent, although small, **Inverness Museum and Art Gallery** (⊠ Castle Wynd ☎01463/237114 ⊕ www.invernessmuseum.com) covers archaeology, art, local history, and the natural environment in its lively displays.

Where to Stay & Eat

★ ££££ ✕🏠 **Glenmoriston Town House.** If you are looking for excellent fishing, this stylish hotel has exclusive rights to a stretch of the River Nairn. Many of the nicely appointed rooms have wonderful river views. The sophisticated restaurant, Abstract, is one of the best in the region. Its French-influenced cuisine, which includes dishes such as roasted scallops on a pea puree and sea bream with an oyster-and-citrus tartar, has garnered numerous awards. The bar is arguably the most sophisticated-looking place in town to sample a malt or two—indeed there are nearly 200 to choose from and a decent cocktail list to boot. ✉ *Ness Bank, IV2 4SF* ☎ *01463/223777* 🖷 *01463/712378* ⊕ *www.glenmoristontownhouse. com* 🛏 *30 rooms* ♻ *2 restaurants, room service, cable TV, in-room data ports, lounge, laundry service, Internet; no a/c* ☰ *AE, DC, MC, V* ⧆ *BP.*

££ 🏠 **Ballifeary House.** The particularly helpful proprietors at this well-maintained bed-and-breakfast, in a pretty 19th-century villa, offer high standards of comfort and service. Rooms and common areas are decorated with Victorian-style furnishings. It's a short stroll from your room to several good restaurants in downtown Inverness. ✉ *10 Ballifeary Rd., IV3 5PJ* ☎ *01463/235572* 🖷 *01463/717583* ⊕ *www.ballifearyhousehotel.co. uk* 🛏 *6 rooms* ♻ *Dining room, lounge; no a/c, no room phones, no kids under 15, no smoking* ☰ *MC, V* ⧆ *BP.*

££ 🏠 **The Lodge at Daviot Mains.** Built in Highland-lodge style, this B&B is filled
Fodor'sChoice with the comforts of home. Rooms are tastefully decorated with carpets
★ and plush, Victorian-style furnishings. The master bedroom has a four-poster canopy bed and bay windows. The dining room, for guests only and by advance booking, serves traditional Scottish cooking; you might find wild salmon on the menu. The Lodge at Daviot Mains is 5 mi south of Inverness on the A9. ✉ *Daviot Mains, Inverness, IV2 5ER* ☎ *01463/772215* 🖷 *01463/772099* ⊕ *www.thelodgeatdaviotmains.co.uk* 🛏 *6 rooms* ♻ *Dining room, in-room data ports; no a/c, no smoking* ☰ *MC, V* ⧆ *BP.*

££ 🏠 **Moyness House.** Scottish author Neil M. Gunn (1891–1973), known for short stories and novels that evoke images of the Highlands, such as *Morning Tide, Highland River,* and *Butcher's Broom,* once lived in this lovely Victorian villa. Just past the well-trimmed hedges is a quiet residential street a few minutes' walk from downtown Inverness. Careful decorative touches grace each colorful room. The friendly owners provide excellent service and sound sightseeing advice. ✉ *6 Bruce Gardens, Inverness, IV3 5EN* ☎ *01463/233836* ⊕ *www.moyness.co.uk* 🛏 *7 rooms* ♻ *Lounge; no a/c, no smoking* ☰ *AE, MC, V* ⧆ *BP.*

£–££ 🏠 **Atholdene House.** This family-run stone villa dating from 1879 extends a warm welcome with a roaring fire, parlor games, and drinks in the common room. Rooms are simply decorated, with a mix of contemporary and antique furnishings. Downtown Inverness is a short walk away. ✉ *20 Southside Rd., IV2 3BG* ☎ *01463/233565* 🖷 *01463/729101* ⊕ *www.atholdenehouse.com* 🛏 *11 rooms, 2 with shared bath* ♻ *Lounge, Internet; no a/c, no room phones, no smoking* ☰ *MC, V* ⧆ *BP, CP.*

Nightlife & the Arts

BARS & LOUNGES **Blackfriars Pub** (✉ Academy St. ☎ 01463/233881) prides itself on its cask-
★ conditioned ales. You can enjoy one to the accompaniment of regular live entertainment, including *ceilidhs* (a mix of country dancing, music, and song; pronounced *kay*-lees) and poetry readings.

THEATER & The **Eden Court Theatre** (✉ Bishops Rd. ☎ 01463/234234) showcases
CABARET drama, but the varied program includes movies and music. There's also an art gallery and an excellent café.

Golf

Inverness Golf Club, established in 1883, welcomes visitors to its parkland course 1 mi from downtown. ✉ *Culcabock Rd.* ☎ *01463/ 239882* ⊕ *www.invernessgolfclub.co.uk* ⛳ *18 holes, 6,256 yds, par 69.*

Shopping

The most interesting goods are to be found in the specialty outlets in and around town. Don't miss the atmospheric indoor **Victorian Market** (✉ Academy St.), built in 1870, which houses more than 40 privately owned specialty shops.

CLOTHING **Duncan Chisholm and Sons** (✉ 47–51 Castle St. ☎ 01463/234599 ⊕ www. kilts.co.uk) specializes in Highland dress and tartans. Mail-order and made-to-measure services are available.

LOCAL **Highland Wineries** (✉ Moniack Castle, Kirkhill ☎ 01463/831283) creates
SPECIALTIES wines from Scottish ingredients, such as birch sap, and also makes jams, marmalade, and other preserves. Midway between Inverness and Nairn on the A96 is **Taste of Moray** (✉ Gollanfield ☎ 01667/462340). It merits a stop for its restaurant alone, but make sure to stroll through the food hall, which stocks a huge selection of Scottish, and especially Morayshire, produce. There's an excellent selection of gift items and household wares.

Culloden Moor

❷ *5 mi east of Inverness via B9006.*

Culloden Moor was the scene of the last major battle fought on British soil. Here, on a cold April day in 1746, the outnumbered Jacobite forces of Bonnie Prince Charlie were destroyed by the superior firepower of George II's army. The victorious commander, the duke of Cumberland (George II's son), earned the name of "Butcher" Cumberland for the bloody reprisals carried out by his men on Highland families. The duke's army killed more than 1,000 soldiers. The National Trust for Scotland has re-created a slightly eerie version of the battlefield as it looked in 1746. The uneasy silence of the open moor overshadows the merry clatter from the visitor center's coffee shop and the tinkle of cash registers. Plans are under way for a new visitor center, with a possible completion date later in 2007. ✉ B9006 ☎ 01463/790607 ⊕ *www.nts.org. uk* 🖾 *£5* ⊙ *Visitor center Feb., Nov., and Dec., daily 11–4; Mar., daily 10–4; Apr.–Oct., daily 9–6; last entry half hr before closing.*

Nairn

❸ *12 mi east of Culloden Moor, 17 mi east of Inverness via B9006/B9091, 92 mi west of Aberdeen.*

Although Nairn has the air of a Lowland town, it's actually part of the Highlands. A once-prosperous fishing village, Nairn has something of a split personality. King James VI (1566–1625) once boasted of a town so large the residents in either end spoke different languages. This was a reference to Nairn, whose fisherfolk, living by the sea, spoke Lowland Scots, whereas its uptown farmers and crofters spoke Gaelic.

Nairn's historic flavor has been preserved at the **Nairn Museum,** in a handsome Georgian building. Exhibits emphasize artifacts, photographs, and model boats relating to Nairn's fishing past. A genealogy service is also offered. ✉ *Viewfield House, Viewfield Dr.* ☎ *01667/456791* 🖾 *£2.50* ⊙ *Apr.–Oct., Mon.–Sat. 10–4:30; Nov., Sat. 10–4:30, Sun. 2–4:30.*

Where to Stay & Eat

★ **£££££** ✕⊡ **Boath House.** The stunning 1820s manor house is surrounded by 20 manicured acres. Its spacious rooms have handsome 19th-century furniture and contemporary Scottish art. Should you find yourself in need of some rest and relaxation, an Aveda spa awaits you on the lower level. The restaurant's chef uses local produce, seasonal game, and fresh fish and seafood straight off the boat. ⊠ *Auldearn, near Nairn, IV12 5TE* ☎ *01667/454896* 🖨 *01667/455469* ⊕ *www.boath-house.com* 🛏 *5 rooms, 1 cottage* ⌂ *Restaurant, spa, Internet; no a/c* ▭ *AE, MC, V* ⦿ *BP.*

Golf

Nairn Golf Club, founded in 1887, hosted the 1999 Walker Cup on its Championship Course, a traditional Scottish coastal golf links with what are claimed to be the finest greens in Scotland. Book well in advance. ⊠ *Seabank Rd.* ☎ *01667/453208* ⊕ *www.nairngolfclub.co.uk* 🏌 *18 holes, 6,721 yds, par 79.*

Fort George

★ ❹ *10 mi west of Nairn.*

After the battle at Culloden, the nervous government in London ordered the construction of a large fort on a promontory reaching into the Moray Firth: Fort George was started in 1748. It's perhaps the best-preserved 18th-century military fortification in Europe. A visitor center and tableaux portray the 18th-century Scottish soldier's way of life, as does the **Regimental Museum of the Queen's Own Highlanders.** ⊠ *Ardersier* ☎ *01667/460232* ⊕ *www.historic-scotland.gov.uk* 🎟 *£6.50* ☉ *Apr.–Sept., daily 9:30–6:30; Oct.–Mar., daily 9:30–4:30; last admission 45 mins before closing.*

18

Cawdor Castle

🕯 ❺ *5 mi southwest of Nairn.*

★

Shakespeare's (1564–1616) Macbeth was Thane of Cawdor, but the sense of history that exists here is more than fictional. Cawdor is a lived-in castle, not an abandoned, decaying structure, and it's especially intriguing because of this. The earliest part of the castle is the 14th-century central tower; the rooms contain family portraits and paraphernalia reflecting 600 years of history. Outside the castle walls are sheltered gardens and woodland walks. There's lots of creepy stories and fantastic tales amid the dank dungeons and drawbridges. ⊠ *Cawdor, off B9090, 5 mi southwest of Nairn* ☎ *01667/404401* ⊕ *www. cawdorcastle.com* 🎟 *Grounds £3.70; castle £7* ☉ *May–mid-Oct., daily 10–5.*

> **WORD OF MOUTH**
>
> "At Cawdor Castle, as we started talking to each other about the drawbridge, a beautiful and elegant woman who had entered in front of us turned and explained how the drawbridge worked. We thanked her and she continued on her way. When we were looking at some photos in the castle, we realized that the woman was Lady Cawdor!"   –theatrelover

Brodie Castle

★ ❻   *8 mi east of Nairn.*

The original medieval castle here was rebuilt and extended in the 17th and 19th centuries. Fine examples of late-17th-century plasterwork are preserved in the Dining Room and Blue Sitting Room; an impressive library and a superb collection of pictures extend into the 20th century. Brodie Castle is in the care of the National Trust for Scotland. ✉ *Off A96, Brodie, by Nairn* 📞 *01309/641371* ⊕ *www.nts.org.uk* ✑ *Grounds £1; castle £8* ⊘ *Grounds daily 9:30–sunset; castle, Apr., July, and Aug., daily noon–4; May–July and Sept., Sun.–Thurs. noon–4.*

Forres

❼   *10 mi east of Nairn via A96.*

The burgh of Forres is a Scottish medieval town with a handsome tolbooth (the former courthouse and prison) as its centerpiece. Forres is a key point on the Malt Whisky Trail; Benromach Distillery is part of the trail. **Dallas Dhu Historic Distillery,** a port of call on the Malt Whisky Trail, was the last distillery built in the 19th century and is open to visitors. ✉ *Mannachie Rd.* 📞 *01309/676548* ⊕ *www.maltwhiskytrail.com* ✑ *£4.50* ⊘ *Apr.–Sept., daily 9:30–6:30; Oct.–Mar., Sat.–Wed. 9:30–4:30.*

At the eastern end of town, don't miss **Sueno's Stone,** a soaring Pictish pillar of stone carved with ranks of cavalry, foot soldiers, and dying victims.

Aviemore

❽   *6 mi southwest of Boat of Garten via B970, 30 mi south of Forres.*

Once a quiet junction on the Highland Railway, Aviemore now has all the brashness and concrete boxiness of a year-round holiday resort. The area is useful as a walking base, but you must be dressed properly and carry emergency safety gear for high-level excursions onto the near-arctic plateau.

★   For skiing and rugged hiking follow the B970 to **Cairngorm National Park.** Past Loch Morlich at the high parking lots on the exposed shoulders of the Cairngorm Mountains are dozens of trails for hiking and cycling. The park is especially popular with birding enthusiasts, as it is the best place to see the Scottish crossbill, the only bird unique to Britain. ✉ *Aviemore* 📞 *01479/873535* ⊕ *www.cairngorms.co.uk.*

❾   The **CairnGorm Mountain Railway,** a funicular railway to the top of Cairn Gorm (the mountain that gives its name to the Cairngorms), operates both during and after the ski season and affords extensive views. At the top is a visitor center and restaurant. Be forewarned: it can get very cold above 3,000 feet, and weather conditions can change rapidly, even in the middle of summer. Prebooking is recommended. ✉ *Off B9152* 📞 *01479/861336* ⊕ *www.cairngormmountain.com* ✑ *£8.75* ⊘ *Daily 10–4:30.*

 ❿ On the high slopes of the Cairngorms, you may see the reindeer herd that was introduced here in the 1950s. Inquire at the **Cairngorm Reindeer Centre,** by Loch Morlich, about accompanying the herders on their daily rounds. ✉ *Loch Morlich, Glen More Forest Park* ☎ *01479/861228* ⊕ *www.rendeer-company.demon.co.uk* ⊠ *£9* ◷ *Feb.–Dec., daily 10–5.*

The place that best sums up Speyside's piney ambience is probably a nature reserve called **Loch an Eilean** (signs guide you there from Aviemore). On the **Rothiemurchus Estate** (☎ 01479/810858 ⊕ www.rothiemurchus. net), a converted cottage beside Loch an Eilan serves as a visitor center. The estate also offers several diversions, including stalking, fly-fishing, off-road driving, and clay-pigeon shooting.

Six mi northeast of Aviemore is the peaceful village of Boat of Garten, where the scent of pine trees mingles with an equally evocative smell—that of steam trains. It is the terminus of the **Strathspey Steam Railway** (☎ 01479/810725 ⊕ www.strathspeyrailway.co.uk), and the oily scent of smoke and steam hangs faintly in the air near the authentically preserved train station.

Where to Stay & Eat

£££–££££ ✕⊡ **The Cross.** Meals are superb and the wine list extensive at this "restaurant with rooms." The fixed-price dinner, which could be fillet of local venison with port and red currants or pike mousse with a prawn sauce, is included in the price of your room, though you can dine here even if you are not an overnight guest. Bedrooms—all with king- or queen-size beds—are individually decorated and may have a balcony, canopy bed, or antique dressing table. ✉ *Tweed Mill Brae, Ardbroilach, PH21 1LB* ☎ *01540/661166* 🖶 *01540/661080* ⊕ *www.thecross.co.uk* ⇨ *8 rooms* ♨ *Restaurant; no a/c* ⊟ *AE, MC, V* ◷ *Hotel closed Jan. No dinner Sun. and Mon.* †◎† *BP, MAP.*

Fort Augustus, Caledonian Canal & Loch Ness

45 mi west of Aviemore.

Traveling north up the Great Glen takes you parallel to Loch Lochy (on the eastern shore) and over the Caledonian Canal at Laggan Locks. From this beautiful spot, which offers stunning vistas of lochs, mountains, and glens in all directions, you can look back on the impressive profile of Ben Nevis. The best place to see the locks of the Caledonian Canal in action is at **Fort Augustus**, at the southern tip of Loch Ness. The canal, which links the lochs of the Great Glen—Loch Lochy, Loch Oich, and Loch Ness—owes its origins to a combination of military as well as political pressures that emerged at the time of the Napoleonic Wars with France. The great Scottish engineer Thomas Telford (1757–1834) surveyed the route in 1803. The canal, which took 19 years to complete, has 29 locks and 42 gates. The **Caledonian Canal Heritage Centre** (✉ Ardchattan House, Canalside, Fort Augustus ☎ 01320/366493), in a converted lockkeeper's cottage, gives the canal's history.

From the B862, just east of Fort Augustus, you'll get your first good long view of **Loch Ness,** which has a greater volume of water than any other Scottish loch, a maximum depth of more than 800 feet, and its own monster—at least according to popular myth. Early travelers who passed this way included English lexicographer Dr. Samuel Johnson (1709–84) and his guide and biographer, James Boswell (1740–95),

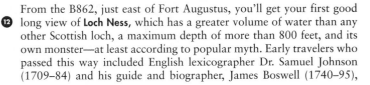

who were on their way to the Hebrides in 1783. A more leisurely alternative to the fast-moving traffic on the busy A82 to Inverness, and one that combines monster-watching with peaceful road touring, is to take the B862 from Fort Augustus and follow the east bank of Loch Ness; join the B852 just beyond Whitebridge and take the opportunity to view the waterfalls at Foyers. The B862 runs around the end of Loch Ness, then climbs into moorland and forestry plantation.

If you're in search of the infamous beast Nessie, head to Drumnadrochit, 21 mi north of Fort Augustus: here you'll find **Loch Ness 2000,** a visitor center that explores the facts and the fakes, the photographs, the unexplained sonar contacts, and the sincere testimony of eyewitnesses. All that's really known is that Loch Ness's huge volume of water has a warming effect on the local weather, making the lake conducive to mirages in still, warm conditions. You can book cruises on the loch here, too. ⊠ *Off A82* ☎ *01456/450573 or 01456/450218* ⊕ *www.loch-ness-scotland.com* ⊡ *£5.95* ☉ *Easter–May, daily 9:30–5; June and Sept., daily 9–6; July and Aug., daily 9–8; Oct., daily 9:30–5:30; Nov.–Easter, daily 10–3:30; last admission half hr before closing.*

Urquhart Castle, near Drumnadrochit, is a favorite Loch Ness monster–watching spot. This weary fortress stands on a promontory overlooking the loch, as it has since the Middle Ages. The castle was begun in the 13th century and was destroyed before the end of the 17th century to prevent its use by the Jacobites. A visitor center gives an idea of what life was like here in medieval times. ⊠ *2 mi southeast of Drumnadrochit on A82* ☎ *01456/450551* ⊕ *www.historic-scotland.gov.uk* ⊡ *£6.50* ☉ *Apr.–Oct., daily 9:30–5:45; Oct.–Apr., daily 9:30–3:45; last admission 45 mins before closing.*

TOWARD THE SMALL ISLES

Fort William may not be the most pretty of towns, but it's got enough attractions to fill a few rainy hours. Strike west toward the coast if the weather looks clear: On a sunny day the Small Isles—Rum, Eigg, Canna, and Muck—look as blue as the sea and sky together. From here you can also visit Skye via the ferry at Mallaig, or take a day cruise from Arisaig to the Small Isles. South of Fort William, Ballachulish and Glencoe are within easy striking distance and worth the trip.

Glencoe

★ **⑬** *92 mi north of Glasgow, 44 mi northwest of Edinburgh.*

Glencoe, where great craggy buttresses loom ominously over the road, has a special place in the folk memory of Scotland: it was the site of an infamous massacre in 1692, still remembered in the Highlands for the treachery with which soldiers of the Campbell clan, acting as a government militia, treated their hosts, the MacDonalds. According to Highland code, in his own home a clansman should give shelter even to his sworn enemy. In the face of bitter weather, the Campbells were accepted as guests by the MacDonalds. Apparently acting on orders from the British government, the Campbells turned on their hosts, committing murder "under trust." The National Trust for Scotland's **Visitor Center** at Glencoe (at the west end of the glen) tells the story of the MacDonald massacre and also has an excellent display on mountaineering. ☎ 01855/811307 ⊕ www.nts.org.uk ⌨ £5 ☉ Mar.–Sept., daily 9:30–5:30; Oct.–Nov., daily 10–5; Dec.–Feb., Thurs.–Sun. 10–4.

Ballachulish

⓮ 1 mi west of Glencoe, 15 mi south of Fort William, 39 mi north of Oban.

Ballachulish, once a slate-quarrying community, serves as a gateway to the western approaches to Glencoe (though there is a Glencoe village as well).

Where to Stay & Eat

£££££ ✕ Airds Hotel. This former ferry inn, dating to the 17th century, has some of the finest views in all of Scotland. Quilted bedspreads and family mementos make you feel at home. The staff is happy to arrange fishing trips and the restaurant serves Scottish cuisine, including venison and grouse. ⊠ Port Appin, Argyll, PA38 4DF ☎ 01631/730236 �🖶 01631/730535 ⊕ www.airds-hotel.com ⇆ 11 rooms, 1 suite, cottage ⚙ Restaurant, fishing, bicycles, lounge, Internet; no a/c ⊟ MC, V ⦿ MAP.

££££–£££££   ✕ Ballachulish House. In a building from 1640, this intimate country-house
Fodor$Choice   hotel nestles near the shore of Loch Linnhe. The Georgian-style bedrooms
★   have luxurious Egyptian linens; some have four-poster beds. The pretty golf course that surrounds the hotel has fine greens and majestic mountain scenery, but the restaurant is what makes the hotel outstanding. Expect sophisticated Scottish fare, including house-smoked Gressingham duck. ⊠ Ballachulish, PH49 4JX ☎ 01855/811266 �🖶 01855/811498 ⊕ www.ballachulishhouse.com ⇆ 8 rooms ⚙ Restaurant, 9-hole golf course, lounge; no room TVs, no kids under 10 ⊟ AE, MC, V ⦿ BP.

Fort William

⓯ 15 mi north of Ballachulish, 69 mi southwest of Inverness, 108 mi northwest of Glasgow, 138 mi northwest of Edinburgh.

As its name suggests, Fort William originated as a military outpost, first established by Oliver Cromwell's General Monk in 1655 and refortified by George I (1660–1727) in 1715 to help combat an uprising by the turbulent Jacobite clans. It remains the southern gateway to the Great Glen and the far west, and it's a bustling, tourist-oriented place.

The **West Highland Museum**, in the town center, explores the history of Prince Charles Edward Stuart and the 1745 Rebellion. Included in the museum's folk exhibits are a tartan display and a collection of Jacobite relics. ⊠ Cameron Sq. ☎ 01397/702169 ⊕ www.westhighlandmuseum. org.uk ⌨ £3 ☉ June, Mon.–Sat. 10–5; July and Aug., Mon.–Sat. 10–5, Sun. 2–5; Oct.–May, Mon.–Sat. 10–4.

Great Britain's highest mountain, the 4,406-foot **Ben Nevis**, looms over Fort William less than 4 mi from Loch Linnhe, an inlet of the sea. A trek to its summit is a rewarding experience, but you should be fit and well prepared—food and water, map and compass, first-aid kit, whis-

18

tle, hat, gloves, and warm clothing (yes, even in summer) for starters. Ask for advice at the local tourist office.

Where to Stay & Eat

★ **££–£££** ✕ **Crannog Seafood Restaurant.** With its reputation for quality and simplicity, this seafood restaurant has single-handedly transformed the local dining scene. The sight of a fishing boat drawing up on the shores of Loch Linnhe to take its catch straight to the kitchen says it all about the freshness of the fish. From the window seats you can watch the sun setting on the far side of the loch. ✉ *The Waterfront at The Underwater Centre* ☎ *01397/705589* ▭ *MC, V.*

£££££ ✕▢ **Inverlochy Castle Hotel.** A red-granite Victorian mansion, Inverlochy Castle stands on 50 acres of woodlands in the shadow of Ben Nevis. Dating from 1863, the hotel retains all the splendor of its period, with a fine fresco ceiling and a Great Hall. The bedrooms are plush and comfortable. An excellent restaurant serves local specialties including roe deer and Isle of Skye crab. ✉ *Torlundy, PH33 6SN, 3 mi northeast of Fort William on A82* ☎ *01397/702177* ▤ *01397/702953* ⊕ *www. inverlochycastlehotel.com* ⬐ *14 rooms, 3 suites* ⚲ *Restaurant, tennis court, fishing, billiards, croquet, library, Internet; no a/c* ▭ *AE, MC, V* ☉ *Closed Jan. and Feb.* ▯ *BP.*

££–£££ ▢ **The Grange.** A delightful, white-frosted confection of a Victorian villa stands in pretty gardens a 10-minute walk from downtown. Interesting antiques, fresh flowers, log fires, and views of Loch Linnhe await you here. ✉ *Grange Rd., Fort William, PH33 6JF* ☎ *01397/ 705516* ▤ *01397/701595* ⊕ *www.thegrange-scotland.co.uk* ⬐ *4 rooms* ⚲ *Lounge; no a/c, no room phones, no kids under 12* ▭ *MC, V* ☉ *Closed Oct.–Mar.* ▯ *BP.*

Sports & the Outdoors

BICYCLING For a thrilling ride down Ben Nevis, take the gondola up to the beginning of the **Nevis Range Mountain Bike Track** (open from May to September, weather permitting) and then shoot off on a 2,000-foot descent. Rent mountain and road bikes from **Off Beat Bikes** (✉ 117 High St. ☎ 01397/ 704008 ⊕ www.offbeatbikes.co.uk).

GOLF The **Fort William Golf Course** has spectacular views of Ben Nevis and ★ welcomes visitors. ✉ *Torlundy, Fort William* ☎ *01397/704464* ⚑ *18 holes, 5900 yds, par 68.*

HIKING This area—especially around Glen Nevis, Glencoe, and Ben Nevis—is very popular with hikers. **Ben Nevis** is a large and dangerous mountain, where snow can fall on the summit plateau any time of the year. For in-depth info and maps, go to the Fort William information center and Nevisport.

For a walk in **Glen Nevis,** drive north from Fort William on the A82 toward Fort Augustus. Turn right up the unclassified road signposted Glen Nevis. Drive about 6 mi, past a youth hostel and a campground, and cross the River Nevis over the bridge at Achriabhach (Lower Falls). Notice the southern flanks of Ben Nevis rising to the east and the Mamores mountains to the west. Park at a parking lot about 2½ mi from the bridge. Starting here, a footpath leads to waterfalls and a steel-cabled bridge (1 mi), and then to Steall, a ruined croft beside a stream (a good picnic place).

You can continue up the glen for some distance. Watch your step going through the tree-lined gorge. The return route is back the way you came.

Shopping

★ The majority of shops here are along the busy High Street. **Nevisport** (⊠ High St. ☎ 01397/704921) has been selling outdoor supplies, maps, and travel books for more than 30 years from its flagship store. The **Scottish Crafts and Whisky Centre** (⊠ 135–139 High St. ☎ 01397/704406) has lots of crafts and souvenirs, as well as homemade chocolates and a vast range of malt whiskies, including miniatures and limited-edition bottlings.

Arisaig

⑯ *22 mi west of Fort William.*

Considering its small size, Arisaig, gateway to the **Small Isles,** offers a surprising choice of high-quality options for dining and lodging. To the north of Arisaig, the road cuts across a headland to reach a stretch of coastline where silver sands glitter with the mica in the local rock; clear water, blue sky, and white sand lend a tropical flavor to the beaches—when the sun is shining.

From Arisaig try to visit a couple of the Small Isles: **Rum, Eigg, Muck,** and **Canna,** each tiny and with few or no inhabitants. Rum serves as a wildlife reserve. **Arisaig Marine Ltd.** (⌁ Arisaig Harbour, Arisaig, Inverness-shire PH39 4NH ☎ 01687/450224 ⊕ www.arisaig.co.uk) runs a boat service from the harbor at Arisaig to the islands at Easter and from May to September, daily at 11.

Where to Stay & Eat

£££ ✕⌷ **Arisaig Hotel.** A former coaching inn built in 1720, this hotel close to the water has magnificent views of the Small Isles. The inn has retained its provinciality with simple furnishings, and its restaurant (££–£££) is renowned for its home cooking. High-quality local ingredients are used to good advantage: lobster, langoustines, and crayfish are specialties, as are "proper" puddings, such as fruit crumbles. ⊠ *Arisaig, PH39 4NH* ☎ *01687/ 450210* ⊟ *01687/450310* ⊕ *www.arisaighotel.co.uk* ➪*13 rooms* ⌂*Restaurant, 2 bars, lounge, recreation room, shop; no a/c* ⊟ *MC, V* ⍟*BP.*

Mallaig

⑰ *8 mi north of Arisaig, 44 mi northwest of Fort William.*

After the approach along the coast, the workaday fishing port of Mallaig itself is anticlimactic. This is the departure point for the southern ferry connection to the Isle of Skye. Mallaig is also the starting point for day cruises up the Sound of Sleat, which separates Skye from the mainland. The sound offers views into the rugged Knoydart region and its long, fjordlike sea lochs, Lochs Nevis and Hourn. For year-round cruises to

★ Loch Nevis, Inverie, and Tarbet, contact **Bruce Watt Sea Cruises** (⊠ Western Isles Guest House, East Bay, Mallaig, PH41 4QG ☎ 01687/462320).

A small, unnamed side road just south of Mallaig leads east to **Loch Morar,** the deepest of all the Scottish lochs (more than 1,000 feet); the next deepest point is miles out into the Atlantic, beyond the continental shelf. The

Bonnie Prince Charlie

HIS LIFE BECAME THE STUFF OF LEGENDS. Charles Edward Louis John Casimir Silvester Maria Stuart, better known as Bonnie Prince Charlie, was born in Rome in 1720. The grandson of ousted King James II of England, Scotland, and Ireland (King James VII of Scotland) and son of James Stuart, he was the focus of Jacobite hopes to reclaim the throne of Scotland.

In 1745 Charles led a Scottish uprising to restore his father to the throne. He sailed to the Outer Hebrides with only a few men but with promised support from France. When that support failed to arrive, he sought help from the Jacobite supporters, many from the Highland clans, who were faithful to his family. With 6,000 men behind him, Charles saw victory in Prestonpans and Falkirk, but the tide turned when he lied to his men about additional Jacobite troops waiting south of the border. When these fictitious troops did not materialize, his army retreated to Culloden where, on April 16, 1746, they were massacred.

Charles escaped to the Isle of Benbecula where he met and fell in love with Flora MacDonald. After James had hidden there for a week, Flora dressed him as her maid and brought him to sympathizers on the Isle of Skye. They helped him escape to France.

Scotland endured harsh reprisals from the government after the rebellion. As for Charles, he spent the rest of his life in drunken exile, taking the title count of Albany. In 1772 he married Princess Louise of Stolberg-Gedern, only to separate from her eight years later. He died a broken man in Rome in 1788.

—by Fiona G. Parrott

loch is said to have its own resident monster, Morag, who undoubtedly gets less recognition than his famous cousin Nessie.

Glenfinnan

⑱ *26 mi southeast of Mallaig.*

Glenfinnan has much to offer if you're interested in Scottish history. Here the National Trust for Scotland has capitalized on the romance surrounding the story of the Jacobites and their intention of returning a Stuart monarch and the Roman Catholic religion to a country that had become staunchly Protestant. In Glenfinnan in 1745, the clans joined forces and rallied to Prince Charles Edward Stuart's cause.

The raising of the prince's standard is commemorated by the **Glenfinnan Monument,** an unusual tower on the banks of Loch Shiel; the story of his campaign is told in the nearby visitor center. Note that the figure at the top of the monument is of a Highlander, not the prince. The view down Loch Shiel from the Glenfinnan Monument is one of the most photographed in Scotland. ⊠ *A830* ☎ *01397/722250* ⊕ *www.nts.org.uk* 🎫 *£3* ⊗ *Monument year-round, daily 24 hrs.; visitor center Apr.–June, Sept., and Oct., daily 10–5; July and Aug., daily 9:30–5:30.*

As impressive as the Glenfinnan Monument (especially if you've tired of the Jacobite "Will He No Come Back Again" sentiment) is the curving railway viaduct that stretches across the green slopes behind the monument. The **Glenfinnan Viaduct,** 21 spans and 1,248 feet long made an appearance in the *Harry Potter* films.

The most relaxing way to take in the landscape of birch- and bracken-covered wild slopes is by rail. The best ride is on the **Jacobite Steam Train** (☎ 01463/239026 ⊕ www.westcoastrailway.co.uk), which runs between July and September.

Where to Stay & Eat

★ **££–££££** ╳⊞ **Glenfinnan House.** This high-ceilinged hotel was built in the 18th century by Alexander MacDonald VII of Glenaladale, who was wounded fighting for Bonnie Prince Charlie. There are few remnants of its early years, as it was transformed into an even grander mansion in the mid-19th century. Today you'll discover the dark-wood interiors from this period in the tastefully serene guest rooms. From many of the rooms there are stunning lochside views of Ben Nevis. Scottish fare with a contemporary twist is served in the stately dining room. ⊠ *Glenfinnan, PH37 4LT* ☎⊞ *01397/722235* ⊕*www.glenfinnanhouse.com* ⇆*13 rooms* ⌂*Restaurant, bar, lounge, recreation room; no a/c, no room TVs* ⊟ *MC, V* ⭑⊙⭑ *BP.*

THE NORTHERN LANDSCAPES

Wester Ross and Sutherland have some of the most distinctive mountain profiles in all of Scotland. The essence of Caithness, the area at the top of Scotland, is space, big skies, and distant blue hills beyond endless rolling moors. There's a surprising amount to see and do on the east coast beyond Inverness.

18

Ullapool

⓳ *50 mi northwest of Inverness, 238 mi north of Glasgow.*

By the shores of salty Loch Broom, Ullapool was founded in 1788 as a fishing station to exploit the local herring stocks. The town comes to life when the ferry to Lewis in the Outer Hebrides arrives and departs. Ullapool is an ideal base for hiking and taking wildlife and nature cruises. In the **Ullapool Museum,** films, photographs, and audiovisual displays tell the story of the area from the ice age to modern times. ⊠ *7–8 W. Argyle St.* ☎⊞ *01854/612987* ☑*£3* ⊙ *Apr.–Oct., Mon.–Sat. 10–5.*

Where to Stay & Eat

★ **£££–££££** ╳⊞ **Ceilidh Place.** You can borrow one of the many books scattered throughout this comfortable house and while away the hours enjoying the views of the bay. The inn's restaurant (£££) specializes in seafood and vegetarian food, and *Ceilidhs* (country dancing, music, and song; pronounced *kay*-lees) and other events are held frequently during summer. The bunkhouse across the road is an inexpensive alternative. ⊠ *W. Argyle St., IV26 2TY* ☎ *01854/612103* 🖶 *01854/613773* ⊕ *www. theceilidhplace.com* ⇆ *24 rooms, 10 with bath* ⌂ *Restaurant; no a/c, no phones in some rooms, no room TVs* ⊟ *AE, DC, MC, V* ⭑⊙⭑ *BP.*

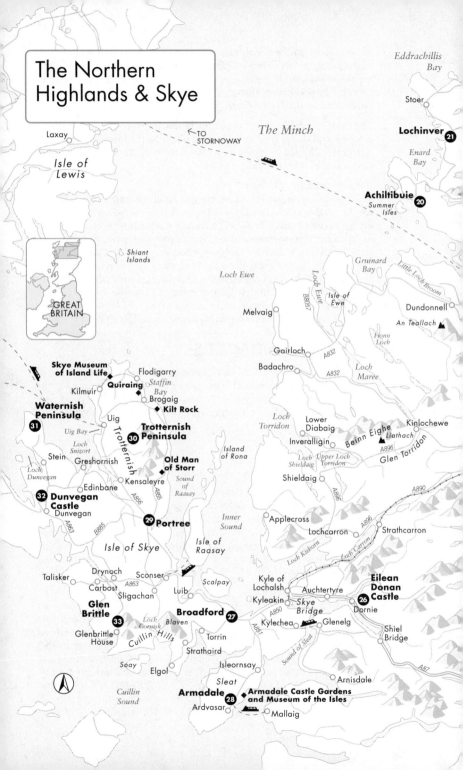

The Northern Highlands & Skye

Laxay

Isle of Lewis

Shiant Islands

GREAT BRITAIN

Skye Museum of Island Life

Flodigarry

Kilmuir

Quiraing

Staffin Bay

Brogaig

♦ Kilt Rock

Waternish Peninsula 31

Uig

Uig Bay

Loch Snizort

Trotternish Peninsula 30

Trotternish

Stein

Greshornish

Old Man of Storr ♦

Loch Dunvegan

Edinbane

Kensaleyre

Dunvegan Castle 32

Dunvegan

Island of Rona

Sound of Raasay

Portree 29

Inner Sound

Isle of Skye

Isle of Raasay

Talisker

Drynoch

Sconser

Carbost

A863

Scalpay

Glen Brittle

Sligachan

Luib

Glenbrittle House

Loch Coruisk

Blaven

Broadford 27

Cuillin Hills

Torrin

Soay

Strathaird

Elgol

Isleornsay

Sleat

Cuillin Sound

Armadale 28

Ardvasar

Armadale Castle Gardens and Museum of the Isles ♦

Mallaig

← TO STORNOWAY

The Minch

Eddrachillis Bay

Stoer

Lochinver 21

Enard Bay

Achiltibuie 20

Summer Isles

Loch Ewe

Gruinard Bay

Little Loch Broom

B8057

Isle of Ewe

Dundonnell

Melvaig

An Teallach ▲

Fionn Loch

Gairloch

A832

Loch Maree

Badachro

A832

Kinlochewe

Lower Diabaig

Beinn Eighe

Liathach ▲

A896

Glen Torridon

Loch Torridon

Inveralligin

Upper Loch Torridon

Loch Shieldaig

Shieldaig

A890

Applecross

A896

Lochcarron

Strathcarron

Loch Kishorn

Loch Carron

Loch Carron

Kyle of Lochalsh

Auchtertyre

Eilean Donan Castle 26

Kyleakin

Skye Bridge

Dornie

Kylerhea

Glenelg

Shiel Bridge

Sound of Sleat

Arnisdale

A87

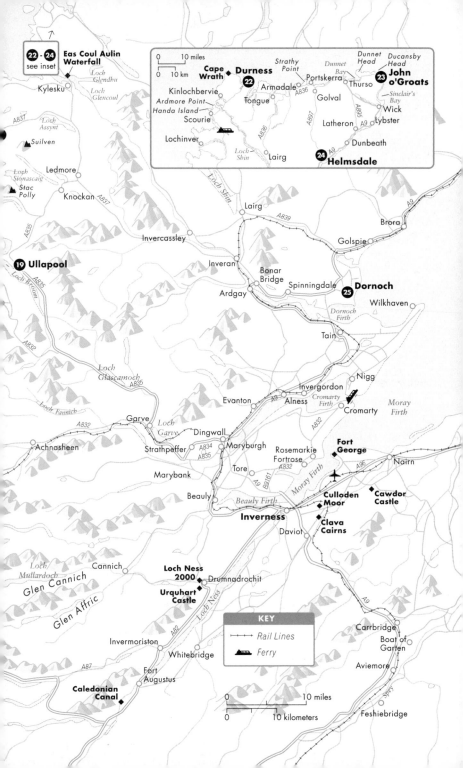

| EN
| ROUTE

Drive north of Ullapool into **Coigach and Assynt,** along Destitution Road and you'll enter an atmospheric landscape where mysterious-looking peaks with Norse names like Stac Polly and Suilven rear out of the bleak, hummocky moors.

Achiltibuie

20 *25 mi northwest of Ullapool.*

Achiltibuie is a crofting (tenant farming) community set in magnificent mountain and coastal scenery. Offshore are the attractive **Summer Isles,** whose history dates back to Viking raids. Cruises from Ullapool visit the largest and only inhabited island, Tanera Mhor, where you can buy special Summer Isle stamps—Tanera Mhor is the only Scottish island to have a private postal service.

At the **Achiltibuie Smokehouse,** Summer Isles Foods smokes all sorts of fish—salmon, haddock, eel, and trout—which can be purchased in the small shop; mail order is also available. ⊠ *Altandhu* ☏ *01854/622353* ⊕ *www.summerislesfoods.com* ☉ *Easter–mid-Oct., weekdays 9:30–5.*

The **Hydroponicum** produces luscious fruit and vegetables year-round. You can sample the produce in the Lilypond Cafe and pick up goodies in the shop. ⊠ *Achiltibuie* ☏ *01854/622202* ⊕ *www.thehydroponicum. com* 🎫 *£5.50 for guided tour* ☉ *Apr.–Sept., daily 10–6; Oct., weekdays 11:30–3.*

Lochinver

21 *18 mi north of Achiltibuie via unclassified road, 38 mi north of Ullapool via A835/A837.*

Lochinver is a bustling shoreside community of whitewashed cottages, with a busy harbor used by the west coast fishing fleet, and a few dining and lodging options. The road to the town from the south winds through a wild landscape of birch trees and heather, with some outstanding sea views. Behind the town the mountain Suilven rises abruptly. This unusual monolith is best seen from across the water, however. Take the cul-de-sac, **Baddidarroch Road,** for the finest photo opportunity.

Bold souls spending time at Lochinver may enjoy the interesting single-lane B869 **Drumbeg Loop** to the north of Lochinver—it has several challenging hairpin turns along with breathtaking views. (The junction is on the north side of the River Inver bridge on the outskirts of the village, signposted as STOER and CLASHNESSIE.) Just beyond the scattered community of Stoer, a road leads west to **Stoer Point Lighthouse.** If you're an energetic walker, you can hike across the short turf and heather along the cliff top for fine views east toward the profiles of the northwest mountains. There's also a red-sandstone sea stack: the **Old Man of Stoer.** This makes a pleasant excursion on a long summer evening. If you stay on the Drumbeg section, there's a particularly tricky hairpin turn in a steep dip, which may force you to take your eyes off the fine view of Quinag, yet another of Sutherland's shapely mountains.

Where to Stay & Eat

££££ ✕⌨ **Inver Lodge Hotel.** On a hillside above Lochinver, this modern hotel has stunning views of the sea from all its bedrooms. Floral fabrics and traditional mahogany furniture decorate the smart guest rooms. The restaurant (£££££) makes the most of fresh, local seafood on its Scottish menu; try the lobster, straight from the sea the day you dine. Anglers feel especially at home here, with three salmon rivers and many trout lochs within easy reach. ⌂ *Iolaire Rd., Sutherland, IV27 4LU* ☎ *01571/844496* 🖷 *01571/844395* ⊕ *www.inverlodge.com* ⛟ *20 rooms* ⌂ *Restaurant, room service, sauna, fishing, recreation room; no a/c, no kids under 10* ▭ *AE, DC, MC, V* ⊗ *Closed Nov.–Easter* ⋔⦿ *BP.*

£ ⌨ **Polcraig Guest House.** This quiet detached house with views toward Lochinver Bay has high-quality accommodations. Rooms in this B&B are pretty and uncluttered with pine furniture, floral prints, and a green, blue, or pink color scheme. ⌂ *Lochinver, Sutherland, IV27 4LD* ☎🖷 *01571/844429* ✎ *cathelmac@aol.com* ⛟ *5 rooms* ⌂ *No-smoking rooms; no a/c, no room phones* ▭ *No credit cards* ⋔⦿ *BP.*

Durness

㉒ *55 mi north of Lochinver.*

The sudden patches of green at Durness, on the north coast, are caused by the richer limestone outcrops among the acid moorlands. The limestone's most spectacular feature is **Smoo Cave,** a cave system hollowed out of the limestone by water action. Access is via a steep cliff path. Boat tours run daily from April through September; reservations are advised. The seasonal **tourist information center** (⌂ Durine, Durness IV27 4PN ☎ 01971/511259) has information on this and other local attractions.

Artisans sell pottery, leatherwork, weaving, paintings, and more from their studios at **Balnakeil Craft Village** (☎ 01971/511777). The village, on an unnamed road but clearly signed from Durness, is open April through October.

If you've made it this far north, you'll probably want to go all the way to **Cape Wrath,** at the northwest tip of Scotland. You can't drive your own vehicle. May through September, a small boat (☎ 01971/511376) ferries people across the Kyle of Durness, a sea inlet, from Keoldale; a minibus (☎ 01971/511287) will then take you to the lighthouse. The highest mainland cliffs in Scotland, including **Clo Mor,** at 920 feet, lie between the Kyle and Cape Wrath.

John o'Groats

㉓ *90 mi east of Durness via A836.*

The windswept little outpost of John o'Groats is usually taken to be the most northern community on the Scottish mainland, though that is not strictly accurate, as an exploration of the little network of roads between Dunnet Head and John o'Groats will confirm. Head east to **Duncansby Head** for spectacular views of cliffs and sea stacks by the lighthouse—

18

and puffins, too. Wick, a good-size town 17 mi south of John o'Groats, is also worth seeing if you've made it this far north.

The Arts

The **Lyth Arts Centre** (✉ Lyth, 4 mi off A9 ☎ 01955/641270), between Wick and John o'Groats, is in an old country school. From April through November each year, it hosts performances by professional touring music and theater companies, as well as exhibitions of contemporary fine art.

Cruising

John o'Groats Ferries (☎ 01955/611353 ⊕ www.jogferry.co.uk) operates wildlife cruises (as well as trips to Orkney) from John o'Groats Harbor. The 1½-hour trip takes you past spectacular cliff scenery and bird life into the Pentland Firth, to Duncansby Stacks, and to the island of Stroma. Cruises cost £14 and are available daily from mid-June through August, at 2:30.

Helmsdale

㉔ *53 mi south of John o'Groats.*

The **Timespan Heritage Centre,** a thought-provoking mix of displays, artifacts, and audiovisual materials, portrays the history of the area from the Stone Age to the 1869 gold rush in the Strath of Kildonan. The complex also includes a café and an art gallery. ✉ *Helmsdale* ☎ *01431/821327* ⊕ *www.timespan.org.uk* 🎫 *£4* ⊙ *Easter–Oct., Mon.–Sat. 10–5, Sun. 2–5; last admission 1 hr before closing.*

Dornoch

㉕ *10 mi south of Golspie, 40 mi north of Inverness.*

A town of sandstone houses, tiny rose-filled gardens, and a 13th-century cathedral with stunning traditional and modern stained-glass windows, Dornoch is well worth a visit. It is noted for its links. You may hear it referred to as the St. Andrews of the North. Royal Dornoch is the jewel in its crown, praised by the world's top golfers.

Where to Stay & Eat

★ ✕▦ **Dornoch Castle Hotel.** A genuine late-15th-century castle that once £££–££££ sheltered the bishops of Caithness, this hotel blends the quite old and the more modern. Bedrooms wear pastel stripes and floral fabrics. This is not a luxury hotel, but it's clean and comfortable, with well-cooked Scottish food in the restaurant (£££–££££): try the roast haunch of venison with juniper-and-cranberry sauce. ✉ *Dornoch, Sutherland, IV25 3SD* ☎ *01862/810216* 🖷 *01862/810981* ⊕ *www.dornochcastlehotel. com* 🛏 *22 rooms, 2 suites* ⚭ *Restaurant, room service; no a/c* ▭ *AE, MC, V* ⑩ *BP.*

££ ▦ **Highfield House.** On its own grounds on the edge of town, this B&B has accommodations in a modern family home. Rooms are light and airy, with pastel colors and natural-wood furnishings. ✉ *Evelix Rd., IV25 3HR* ☎ *01862/810909* 🖷 *01862/811605* ⊕ *www.highfieldhouse.co. uk* 🛏 *3 rooms* ⚭ *Dining room; no a/c, no room phones, no kids under 12, no smoking* ▭ *No credit cards* ⑩ *BP.*

Golf

Were it not for its remote northern location, **Royal Dornoch** would undoubtedly be a candidate for the British Open Championship. It's a superb, breezy, and challenging links course. ⊠ *Golf Rd., Dornoch* ☎ *01862/810219* ⚑ *18 holes, 6,200 yds, par 70.*

SKYE, THE MISTY ISLAND

Skye ranks near the top of most visitors' priority lists: the romance of Prince Charles Edward Stuart (1720–88), known as Bonnie Prince Charlie, combined with the misty Cuillin Hills and their proximity to the mainland all contribute to its popularity. Today Skye remains mysterious and mountainous, an island of sunsets that linger brilliantly until late at night and of beautiful, soft mists. Much photographed are the old crofts, some of which are still inhabited, with their thick stone walls and thatch roofs. Much written about is the story known as the Adventure—the history of the "prince in the heather" and pretender to the British throne, Bonnie Prince Charlie. After defeat at Culloden, Bonnie Prince Charlie wandered over the Highlands, eventually getting to Skye and then back to the mainland.

To reach Skye, you can cross over the bridge spanning the narrow channel of Kyle Akin, between Kyle of Lochalsh and Kyleakin, or take the (more romantic) ferry options between Mallaig and Armadale or between Glenelg and Kylerea. You can tour comfortably around the island in two or three days. Orientation is easy: follow the only roads around the loops on the northern part of the island and enjoy the road running the length of the Sleat Peninsula in southern Skye, taking the loop roads that exit to the north and south as you please. There are some stretches of single-lane road, but none poses a problem.

Kyle of Lochalsh

55 mi west of Inverness, 120 mi northwest of Glasgow.

This little town is the mainland gateway to Skye. Time used to mean nothing in this part of Scotland—so many other things were of greater importance. But the area has seen great changes as the Skye Bridge has transformed not only travel to Skye but the very seascape itself. The nost notable attraction here is Eilean Donan Castle, 8 mi to the east in Dornie.

Guarding the confluence of lochs Long, Alsh, and Duich stands that most ❷❻ picturesque of all Scottish castles, **Eilean Donan Castle,** perched on an islet
Fodor'sChoice connected to the mainland by a stone-arched bridge. Dating from the 14th
★ century, this romantic icon has massive stone walls, timber ceilings, and winding stairs. Empty and neglected for years after being bombarded by frigates of the Royal Navy during an abortive Spanish-Jacobite landing in 1719, it was almost entirely rebuilt from a ruin in the early 20th century. The castle has appeared in many travel brochures and movies. ⊠ *Off A97, Dornie* ☎ *01599/555202* ⊕ *www.eileandonancastle.com* ⊡ *£5* ☉ *Apr.–Oct., daily 10–5:30.*

Broadford

27 *8 mi west of Kyle of Lochalsh via Skye Bridge.*

One of the larger of Skye's settlements, Broadford lies along the shore of Broadford Bay, which has on occasion welcomed whales to its sheltered waters.

OFF THE BEATEN PATH

THE ROAD TO ELGOL – The B8083 leads from Broadford to one of the finest views in Scotland. This road passes through **Strath Suardal** and little **Loch Cill Chriosd** (Kilchrist) by a ruined church. Skye marble, with its attractive green veining, was produced from the marble quarry at **Torrin.** You can appreciate breathtaking views of the mountain **Bla Bheinn** (*Blaven*) as the A881 continues to Elgol. For even better views, take a boat trip on the **Bella Jane** (⊠ Elgol Jetty ☎ 0800/731–3089 ⊕ www.bellajane.co.uk) from Elgol jetty toward Loch Coruisk; you'll be able to land and walk up to the loch itself, as well as see seals during your boat trip. The boat excursion is available from April through October. (round-trip tickets start at £18).

Bicycling

If you want to explore the nearby countryside, **Fairwinds Bicycle Hire** (⊠ Fairwinds, Elgol Rd. ☎ 01471/822270) rents bicycles year-round.

Shopping

Craft Encounters (⊠ A850 ☎ 01471/822754) stocks local crafts, including pottery and jewelry.

Armadale

28 *17 mi south of Broadford, 43 mi south of Portree, 5 mi (ferry crossing) west of Mallaig.*

Rolling moorlands, scattered with rivers and lochans, give way to enchanting hidden coves and scattered waterside communities here in **Sleat,** the southernmost part of Skye. Sleat well rewards a day or two spent exploring its side roads and its many craft outlets, including Harlequin Knitwear off A851. For most visitors, Armadale is the first town to visit.

The popular **Armadale Castle Gardens and the Museum of the Isles,** including the Clan Donald Centre, tell the story of the MacDonalds and their proud title—the Lords of the Isles—with the help of an excellent audiovisual presentation. In the 15th century the clan was powerful enough to threaten the authority of the Stuart monarchs of Scotland. There are extensive gardens and nature trails, plus a gift shop, restaurant, and library. They also have high-quality accommodations in seven cottages. ⊠ *½ mi north of Armadale Pier* ☎ *01471/844305 or 01471/844275* ⊕ *www.clandonald.com* ⊡ *£5* ⊙ *Apr.–Oct., daily 9:30–5:30, last entry 30 mins before closing.*

Where to Stay & Eat

£££££ ✕⊡ **Kinloch Lodge.** This country-house hotel is run with flair by Lord and Lady Macdonald. Bookcases filled with interesting volumes and family photographs fill the warm, restful lounges, and the elegant bedrooms are furnished with antiques and chintz fabrics. Expect fabulous

CLOSE UP

Clans & Tartans

WHATEVER THE ORIGINS OF THE CLANS—some with Norman roots, intermarried into Celtic society; some of Norse origin, the product of Viking raids on Scotland; others traceable to the monastic system; yet others possibly descended from Pictish tribes—by the 13th century the clan system was at the heart of Gaelic tribal culture. By the 15th century the clan chiefs of the Scottish Highlands were a threat even to the authority of the Stewart monarchs.

The word *clann* means "family" or "children" in Gaelic, and it was the custom for clan chiefs to board out their sons among nearby families, a practice that helped to bond the clan unit and create strong allegiances: the chief became "father" of the tribe and was owed loyalty by lesser chiefs and ordinary clansmen.

The clan chiefs' need for strong men-at-arms, fast-running messengers, and bards for entertainment and the preservation of clan genealogy was the probable origin of the Highland Games, still celebrated in many Highland communities each year, and which are an otherwise rather inexplicable mix of sports, music, and dance.

Gradually, by the 18th century, increasing knowledge of Lowland agricultural improvements, and better roads into the Highlands that improved communication of ideas and "southern" ways, began to weaken the clan system. After Bonnie Prince Charlie's defeat at Culloden in 1746, many chiefs lost their lands, tartan was banned, and clan culture withered.

Tartan's own origins as a part of the clan system are disputed; the Gaelic word for striped cloth is *breacan*—piebald or spotted—so even the word itself is not Highland. However, in the days before mass manufacture, when cloth was locally spun, woven, and dyed using plant derivatives, each neighborhood would have different dyestuffs—bilberry, iris, bramble, water lily—and therefore different colors available. In this way, particular colors and patterns of the local weavers could become associated with an area and therefore clan, but were not in any sense a clan's "own by exclusive right."

It took the influence of Sir Walter Scott, with his romantic view of Highland history, to create the "modern myth" of clans and tartan. Sir Walter engineered George IV's visit to Scotland in 1822, which turned into a tartan extravaganza. The idea of one tartan or group of tartans "belonging" to one particular clan was created at this time, with new patterns and color ways dreamed up and "assigned" to particular clans. Queen Victoria and Prince Albert reinforced the tartan culture later in the century.

It is considered "proper" in some circles to wear the "right" tartan, that is, that of your clan. You may be able to find a clan connection with the expertise such as that available at **Scotland's Clan Tartan Centre** (⊠ 70–74 Bangor Rd., Leith, Edinburgh ☎ 0131/553–5161).

18

fare; Lady Macdonald runs renowned cooking courses. ⊠ *Off A851, Sleat, Isle of Skye, IV43 8QY* ☎ *01471/833214* 🖷 *01471/833277* ⊕ *www.kinloch-lodge.co.uk* 🛏 *16 rooms* ⚖ *Restaurant, fishing, 2 lounges, helipad; no a/c* ⊟ *AE, MC, V* ⦿⦿ *MAP.*

Shopping

Ragamuffin (⊠ Armadale Pier ☎ 01471/844217) specializes in designer knitwear and clothing.

Portree

㉙ *43 mi north of Armadale.*

Portree, the population center of the island, is a pleasant place clustered around a small and sheltered bay. It makes a good touring base and has a number of crafts shops. On the outskirts of town is **Tigh na Coille: The Aros Experience** (*Tigh na Coille* is Gaelic for "house of the forest," and *Aros* means "home" or "homestead"), which provides an excellent account of Skye's often turbulent history. You'll find a gift shop, restaurant, and theater. Forest walks can be enjoyed in the surrounding woodlands. ⊠ *Viewfield Rd.* ☎ *01478/613649* ⊕ *www.aros.co.uk* 🖾 *£3 for taped guide* ☉ *Daily 10–5.*

Where to Stay & Eat

££££–£££££ ✕🖃 **Cuillin Hills Hotel.** Just outside Portree, this gabled hotel has rooms with views over Portree Bay toward the Cuillins. Bold floral patterns enliven the bedrooms. The seafood dishes in the restaurant (£££££) are especially good: try the local prawns, lobster, or scallops, or the glazed ham carved from the bone. ⊠ *Isle of Skye, IV51 9QU* ☎ *01478/ 612003* 🖷 *01478/613092* ⊕ *www.cuillinhills-hotel-skye.co.uk* 🛏 *27 rooms* ⚖ *Restaurant, cable TV, bar; no a/c* ⊟ *AE, MC, V* ⦿⦿ *BP.*

££–£££ ✕🖃 **Rosedale Hotel.** Converted 19th-century buildings right on the harbor house modern accommodations—rooms are done in pastels and florals—and a restaurant serving delicious Scottish cooking. The menu (££££) might include breast of duck with cranberries and parsnip puree, or pasta rolls with smoked haddock and lemon butter. Ask for a room at the front for harbor views. ⊠ *The Harbour, IV51 9DB* ☎ *01478/613131* 🖷 *01478/612531* ⊕ *www.rosedalehotelskye.co.uk* 🛏 *19 rooms* ⚖ *Restaurant, bar, lounge; no a/c* ⊟ *MC, V* ☉ *Closed Dec.–Mar.* ⦿⦿ *BP.*

Shopping

An Tuireann Arts Centre (⊠ Struan Rd. ☎ 01478/613306) is a showcase for locally made crafts and is a good place to look for unusual gifts.

Trotternish Peninsula

㉚ *16 mi north of Portree via A855.*

As A855, the main road, goes north from Portree, cliffs rise to the left, the remnants of ancient lava flow. In some places the hardened lava has created spectacular features, including a curious pinnacle called the **Old Man of Storr.** The A855 travels past neat white croft houses and forestry plantings to **Kilt Rock.** Everyone on the Skye tour circuit stops here to peep over the cliffs (there is a safe viewing platform) for a look at the geology of the cliff edge: columns of two types (and colors) of rock create a folded, pleated effect, just like a kilt.

The spectacular **Quiraing** dominates the horizon 5 mi past Kilt Rock. For a closer view of the strange pinnacles and rock forms, make a left onto a small road at Brogaig by Staffin Bay. There's a parking lot near the point where this road breaches the ever-present cliff line; you walk back toward the Quiraing itself, where the rock formations and cliffs are most dramatic. The trail is on uneven, stony ground, and it's a steep scramble up to the rock formations. In ages past, stolen cattle were hidden deep within the Quiraing's rocky jaws.

The main A855 reaches around the top end of Trotternish, to the **Skye Museum of Island Life** at Kilmuir, where you can see the old crofting ways brought to life. Flora Macdonald, helpmate of Bonnie Prince Charlie, is buried nearby. ⊠ *Kilmuir* ☎ *01470/552206* ⊕ *www.skyemuseum. co.uk* ⌨ *£1.75* ⊙ *Easter–Oct., daily 9–5:30, call for winter hrs.*

Where to Stay & Eat

£££–£££££ ✕⌂ **Flodigarry Country House Hotel.** Close links with Flora Macdonald, Prince Charles Edward Stuart's helpmate, are not the least of the attractions at this country-house hotel. Yes, you can actually have a room in Flora's own cottage, adjacent to the hotel, where six of her children were born. The main hotel is a bit grander, and serves excellent seafood in the restaurant (£££££). ⊠ *Staffin, Isle of Skye, IV51 9HZ* ☎ *01470/ 552203* 🖷 *01470/552301* ⊕ *www.flodigarry.co.uk* ⌁ *18 rooms* ⌂ *Restaurant, bar; no a/c, no room TVs* ▭ *MC, V* ⍫ *BP.*

Waternish Peninsula

❸ *20 mi northwest of Portree via A850.*

The northwest corner of Skye has scattered crofting communities, magnificent coastal views, and a few good restaurants well worth the trip in themselves. In the Hallin area look westward for an islet-scattered sea loch with small cliffs rising from the water. Just above the village of Stein, on the left side of the road, is a restored and inhabited "black house"—a thatched cottage blackened over time because a hole in its roof stood in for a chimney.

Stoneware pottery is fired in a wood-fired kiln at the **Edinbane Pottery Workshop and Gallery,** in southern Waternish. You can watch the potters work, then buy from the showroom. ⊠ *Edinbane* ☎ *01470/582234* ⊕ *www.edinbane-pottery.co.uk* ⊙ *Easter–Oct., daily 9–6; Nov.–Easter, weekdays 9–6.*

Where to Stay & Eat

★ ✕ **Loch Bay Seafood Restaurant.** On the waterfront in the village of Stein
£££–£££££ stands this distinctive black-and-white restaurant. It's where the island's top chefs relax on their nights off, so you know the food must be good. The seafood is freshly caught and simply prepared. ⊠ *Near fishing jetty, Stein* ☎ *01470/592235* ▭ *MC, V* ⊙ *Closed Nov.–Easter and weekends except Sat. July–Oct.*

18

£££–££££ ✕🏠 **Greshornish House.** Greshornish is a quirky hotel with spacious, if rather eclectically furnished, public rooms and bedrooms. The hotel's best feature is its restaurant, where mahogany tables are laid with damask, crystal, and candelabras. Menu highlights include scallops poached in white wine with flakes of smoked haddock and cream, and local lobster. ⊠ *Greshornish, Isle of Skye, IV51 9PN* ☎ *01470/582266* 🖷 *01470/582345* ⊕ *www.greshornishhotel.co. uk* ⟿ *9 rooms* ♿ *Restaurant, tennis court, fishing, croquet; no a/c* ☰ *AE, MC, V* ⏨ *MAP.*

Dunvegan Castle

㉜ *22 mi west of Portree.*

In a commanding position above a sea loch, Dunvegan Castle has been the seat of the chiefs of Clan MacLeod for more than 700 years. Though the structure has been greatly changed over the centuries, a gloomy ambience prevails, and there's plenty of family history on display, notably the Fairy Flag—a silk banner, thought to be originally from Rhodes or Syria and believed to have magically saved the clan from danger. Make time to visit the gardens, with their water garden and falls, fern house, a walled garden, and various viewing points. Dunvegan Sea Cruises runs a boat trip from the castle to the nearby seal colony for £6 per person. ⊠ *At junction of A850 and A863, Dunvegan* ☎ *01470/521206* ⊕ *www. dunvegancastle.com* 🖷 *Garden £5; castle and garden £7* ⏱ *Mid-Mar.–Oct., daily 10–5; Nov.–mid-Mar., daily 11–4; last entry 30 mins before closing.*

Where to Stay & Eat

£££££ ✕🏠 **Three Chimneys Restaurant with Rooms.** One of Skye's top-notch
Fodor's Choice restaurants, Shirley and Eddie Spear's shoreside cottage might be small
★ on space, but it's big on flavor: fresh local seafood, beef, lamb, and game are transformed into dishes such as prawn and lobster bisque, or grilled loin of lamb with honey-roasted root vegetables and sherried button-mushroom sauce. Skye soft fruits—raspberries, strawberries, black currants—may follow for dessert. Adjacent to the restaurant are luxury accommodations in a courtyard wing, with magnificent sea views from all the rooms. ⊠ *B884, Colbost, by Dunvegan, Isle of Skye, IV55 8ZT* ☎ *01470/511258* 🖷 *01470/511358* ⊕ *www.threechimneys.co.uk* ⟿ *6 rooms* ♿ *Cable TV, in-room DVDs; no a/c* ☰ *AE, MC, V* ⏱ *No lunch Sun.* ⏨ *BP.*

££ 🏠 **Roskhill House.** A 19th-century croft house that once housed the local post office in its dining room, this pretty white hotel feels like a home away from home. Bold colors decorate the bedrooms, and the lounge is filled with books and games. Stone walls, stick-back chairs, and a scarlet carpet lend the dining room a publike air. In the morning, a full Scottish breakfast, including vegetarian options, is served. ⊠ *Roskhill, by Dunvegan, Isle of Skye, IV55 8ZD* ☎ *01470/521317* ⊕ *www. roskhillhouse.co.uk* ⟿ *4 rooms* ♿ *Dining room; no a/c, no room phones, no room TVs* ☰ *MC, V* ⏨ *BP.*

Glen Brittle

★ ㉝ *28 mi southeast of Glendale.*

You can safely enjoy spectacular mountain scenery in Glen Brittle, with some fine views of the Cuillin Ridge (which is not for the casual walker, as there are many steep and dangerous cliff faces). Glen Brittle extends off the A863/B8009 on the west side of the island.

GREAT GLEN, NORTHERN HIGHLANDS & SKYE ESSENTIALS

Transportation

BY AIR

Inverness Airport has flights from London, Edinburgh, and Glasgow. Domestic flights covering the Highlands and islands are operated by British Airways, Servisair, easyJet, and Eastern Airways. Fort William has bus and train connections with Glasgow, so Glasgow Airport can be an appropriate access point.

🛈 **British Airways** ☎ 08457/733377 ⊕ www.britishairways.com. **easyJet** ☎ 0870/600-0000 ⊕ www.easyjet.com. **Eastern Airways** ☎ 08703/669100 ⊕ www.easternairways.com. **Servisair** ☎ 01667/464040 ⊕ www.servisair.com.

🛈 **Glasgow Airport** ☎ 0870/0400008 ⊕ www.glasgowairport.com. **Inverness Airport** ✉ Dalcross ☎ 01667/462445 ⊕ www.hial.co.uk.

BY BUS

Megabus (a budget service that you must book online) and Scottish Citylink and National Express run buses to and around the region. There is limited service available within the Great Glen area. Highland Country Buses operates buses down the Great Glen and around Fort William. A number of postbus services, which also deliver mail, travel to the remotest corners. Highland Country Buses provide bus service in the Highlands area.

🛈 **Highland Country Buses** ✉ Fort William Bus Station, Ardgour Rd., Fort William ☎ 01397/702373. **Inverness Coach Station** ✉ off Academy St., Inverness ☎ 01463/233371. **Megabus** ☎ 01738/639095 ⊕ www.megabus.com. **National Express** ☎ 08705/808080 ⊕ www.nationalexpress.co.uk. **Royal Mail Post Buses** ✉ 7 Strothers La., Inverness, IV1 1AA ☎ 0845/7740740 ⊕ www.royalmail.com/postbus. **Scottish Citylink** ☎ 08705/505050 ⊕ www.citylink.co.uk.

BY CAR

The fast A9 brings you to Inverness in roughly three hours from Glasgow or Edinburgh. Because of the infrequent bus services and sparse railway stations, a car is definitely the best way to explore this region. In the Great Glen and Speyside, A82 and A9 are major roads, but there are many smaller ones. In many areas, twisting, winding single-lane roads demand driving dexterity. Local rules of the road require that when two cars meet, whichever driver reaches a passing place first must stop in it or opposite it and allow the oncoming car to continue. Never park in

18

passing places; these sections of the road can also allow traffic behind you to pass. In sparsely populated areas, distances between gas stations can be considerable.

BY TRAIN

There are connections from London to Inverness and Fort William (including overnight sleeper service), as well as reliable links from Glasgow and Edinburgh. The scenic West Highland line links Fort William to Mallaig; steam trains are a bonus in the summer months. There's a train service between Glasgow (Queen Street) and Inverness, via Aviemore, which gives access to the heart of Speyside. From Inverness there is service north to Thurso and Wick. The main railway stations on the west coast include Oban and Kyle of Lochalsh (for Skye).

National Rail ☎ 08457/484950 ⊕ www.nationalrail.co.uk. **First ScotRail** ☎ 08457/484950 ⊕ www.firstgroup.com/scotrail.

Contacts & Resources

EMERGENCIES

In case of any emergency, dial **999** for an ambulance, the police, the coast guard, or the fire department (no coins are needed for emergency calls from phone booths). Pharmacies are not common away from the larger towns, and doctors often dispense medicines in rural areas. In an emergency, the police will assist you in locating a pharmacist.

Hospitals Belford Hospital ⊠ Belford Rd., Fort William ☎ 01397/702481. **Raigmore Hospital** ⊠ Old Perth Rd., Inverness ☎ 01463/704000. **Town and County Hospital** ⊠ Cawdor Rd., Nairn ☎ 01667/452101.

INTERNET

Many hotels have Internet access, and Inverness and Fort William have Internet cafés; also check public libraries.

Internet Cafés One World ⊠ 123 High St., Fort William ☎ 01397/702673. **Clanlan** ⊠ 29 Castle St., Inverness ☎ 01463/237608.

TOUR OPTIONS

BOAT TOURS Several small firms run cruises along the spectacular west-coast seaboard. Contact the local tourist information center for details about local operators.

VISITOR INFORMATION

Aviemore, Fort William, Inverness, Portree, Stornoway, and Tarbert have year-round tourist offices. Other tourist centers, open seasonally, include those at Ballachulish, Fort Augustus, Grantown-on-Spey, Kingussie, Mallaig, Nairn, Dunvegan, Durness, Ullapool, Broadford, Helmsdale, John o'Groats, and Kyle of Lochalsh. A regional Web site for the Highlands, www.visithighlands.com, covers this whole area.

Aviemore ⊠ Grampian Rd. ☎ 01479/810363. **Dornoch** ⊠ The Square, Dornoch, IV25 3SD ☎ 01862/810555. **Dunvegan** ⊠ 2 Lochside, Dunvegan, Isle of Skye, IV55 8WB ☎ 01470/521581. **Durness** ⊠ Sango, IV27 4PZ ☎ 01971/511259. **Fort William** ⊠ Cameron Centre, Cameron Sq. ☎ 01397/703781. **Inverness** ⊠ Castle Wynd ☎ 01463/234353 ⊕ www.inverness-scotland.com. **Portree** ⊠ Bayfield House, Bayfield Rd., Portree, Isle of Skye, IV51 9EL ☎ 01478/612137. **Ullapool** ⊠ Argyll St., Ullapool, IV26 2UR ☎ 01854/612135.

UNDERSTANDING
GREAT BRITAIN

BOOKS & MOVIES

CHRONOLOGY

BOOKS & MOVIES

Books

Many writers' names have become inextricably linked with the regions in which they set their books or plays. Hardy's Wessex, Daphne Du Maurier's Cornwall, Wordsworth's Lake District, Shakespeare's Arden, and Brontë Country are now evocative catchphrases, treasured by local tourist boards. However hackneyed the tags may be, you *can* still get a heightened insight about an area through the eyes of authors of genius, even though they may have written a century or more ago. Here are a few works that may provide you with an understanding of their authors' loved territory.

Thomas Hardy's novels *The Mayor of Casterbridge, Tess of the d'Urbervilles,* and *Far from the Madding Crowd* (and indeed almost everything he wrote) are solidly based on his Wessex (Dorset) homeland. Daphne Du Maurier had a deep love of Cornwall from her childhood; *Frenchman's Creek, Jamaica Inn,* and *The King's General* all capture the county's Celtic mood. The wildness of Exmoor in Devon is captured in the historical novel *Lorna Doone* by R. D. Blackmore. The Brontë sisters' *Wuthering Heights, The Tenant of Wildfell Hall,* and *Jane Eyre* breathe the sharp air of the moors around the writers' Haworth home. William Wordsworth, who was born at Cockermouth in the Lake District, depicts the area's rugged beauty in many of his poems, especially the *Lyrical Ballads.*

Virginia Woolf's visits to Vita Sackville-West at her ancestral home of Knole, in Sevenoaks, inspired the novel *Orlando.* The stately home is now a National Trust property. The country around Bateman's, near Burwash in East Sussex, the home where Rudyard Kipling lived for more than 30 years, was the inspiration for *Puck of Pook's Hill* and *Rewards and Fairies.* American writer Henry James lived at Lamb House in Rye, also in East Sussex, as did E. F. Benson, whose delicious Lucia novels take place in a thinly disguised version of the town. Bateman's and Lamb House are National Trust buildings.

A highly irreverent and very funny version of academic life, *Porterhouse Blue,* by Tom Sharpe, will guarantee that you look at Oxford and Cambridge with a totally different eye. John Fowles's *The French Lieutenant's Woman,* largely set in Lyme Regis, is full of local color about Dorset.

The late James Herriot's veterinary surgeon books, among them *All Creatures Great and Small,* give evocative accounts of life in the Yorkshire dales during much of the 20th century; the books were made into popular television shows. For a perceptive account of life in the English countryside, try Ronald Blythe's well-regarded *Akenfield: Portrait of an English Village.*

Mysteries are almost a way of life in Britain, partly because many of the best English mystery writers set their plots in their home territories. Modern whodunits by P. D. James and Ruth Rendell convey a fine sense of place, and Ellis Peters's Brother Cadfael stories re-create life in medieval Shrewsbury with a wealth of telling detail. Colin Dexter's Inspector Morse mysteries capture the flavor of Oxford's town and gown. There are also always the villages, vicarages, and scandals of Agatha Christie's "Miss Marple" books.

The fans of Arthurian legends can turn to some excellent, imaginative novels that not only tell the stories but also give fine descriptions of the British countryside. Among them are *Sword at Sunset,* by Rosemary Sutcliffe, *The Once and Future King,* by T. H. White, and the four Merlin novels by Mary Stewart; *The Crystal Cave, The Hollow Hills, The Last Enchantment,* and *The Wicked Day.* Edward Rutherfurd's historical novels *Sarum, London,* and *The Forest* deal with British history with a grand sweep from the prehistoric past to the present.

An animal's close-to-the-earth viewpoint can reveal all kinds of countryside insights about Britain. *Watership Down,* a runaway best-seller about rabbits, was written by Richard Adam in the early '70s. *The Wind in the Willows,* by Kenneth Grahame, gives a vivid impression of the Thames Valley almost 100 years ago, which still holds largely true today. Devon, the northern part in particular, is the setting of Henry Williamson's *Tarka the Otter,* a beloved nature story published in the 1920s; many paths in the region are signposted as part of the Tarka Trail.

Those interested in writers and the surroundings that influenced their works should look at *A Literary Guide to London,* by Ed Glinert, and *The Oxford Literary Guide to the British Isles,* edited by Dorothy Eagle and Hilary Carnell (now out of print). One author currently in vogue is Jane Austen: Janeites will want to read Maggie Lane's *Jane Austen's World* and Nigel Nicolson's wonderful *World of Jane Austen.* For a vast portrait of everyone's favorite English author, dig into Peter Ackroyd's *Dickens.*

Good background books on English history are *The Oxford Illustrated History of Britain,* edited by Kenneth O. Morgan, and *The Story of England,* by Christopher Hibbert. *The Isles,* a history by Norman Davies, challenges conventional Anglocentric assumptions. *The English: A Portrait of a People,* by Jeremy Paxman, examines the concept of Englishness in a changing world. *The London Encyclopaedia,* by Ben Weinreb and Christopher Hibbert, now out of print, is invaluable as a source of information on the capital. Simon Schama's three-volume *History of Britain,* with handsome color illustrations, was written to accompany the BBC–History Channel television series. Peter Ackroyd's illustrated nonfiction *London: A Biography* captures the city's energy and its quirks from prehistory to the present. Jan Morris's *The Matter of Wales* is a notable introduction to the country.

Scottish history is both extensive and absorbing. The most accessible book on the subject to date, Tom Devine's *The Scottish Nation,* examines the last three centuries from the Act of Union to the reestablishment of the Scottish Parliament. Another pivotal historical book is Neal Ascherson's *Stone Voices: The Search for Scotland,* in which archaeology, geology, myth, and travel combine to create an impressive image of Scotland as a nation.

The finest book on Britain's stately homes is Nigel Nicolson's *Great Houses of Britain,* written for the National Trust (now out of print). Also spectacular are the picture books *Great Houses of Britain and Wales* and *Great Houses of Scotland,* by Hugh Montgomery-Massingberd. *The Buildings of England* and *The Buildings of Scotland,* written by Nikolaus Pevsner but much updated since his death, are part of a multivolume series, organized by county, which sets out to chronicle in detail every building of any importance. Pevsner's *Best Buildings of Britain* is a grand anthology with lush photographs. New Pevsner Architectural Guides continue to be published. For the golden era of Georgian architecture, check out John Summerson's definitive *Architecture in Britain 1530–1830.* Simon Jenkins's *England's Thousand Best Churches,* with photographs, describes parish churches (not cathedrals) large and small. The same author's delightful *England's Thousand Best Houses,* also illustrated with photographs, has pithy descriptions (and star ratings) of small and large houses open to the public. Mark Girouard has written several books that are incomparable for their behind-the-scenes perspective on art and architecture: *Life in the English Country House* focuses on houses over the centuries, and *The Victorian Country House* addresses the lifestyles of the rich and famous of the 19th century. For the ultimate look at English villages, see *The Most*

Beautiful Villages of England, by James Bentley, with ravishing photographs by Hugh Palmer.

There are many delightful travel books about Britain, including Susan Allen Toth's *England for All Seasons* and *My Love Affair with England.* Bill Bryson's *Notes from a Small Island,* published in 1996, is perennially popular, though it is dating a bit. Few of today's authors have managed to top the wit and perception of Henry James's magisterial *English Hours.* As for "the flower of cities all," *London Perceived* is a classic text by the noted literary critic V. S. Pritchett, and John Russell's *London* is a superlative text written by a particularly eloquent art historian.

Movies

From *Wuthering Heights* to *Jane Eyre,* great classics of literature have been rendered into great classics of film. It's surprising to learn, however, how many of them were creations of Hollywood and not the British film industry (which had its heyday from the 1940s to the 1960s). From Laurence Olivier to Kenneth Branagh, noted director-actors have cross-pollinated the cinema in Britain and the United States.

Films have also produced another phenomenon: they can motivate travelers to visit specific locations and sights in a favorite film. VisitBritain (www.visitbritain. com) has recognized this by including a movies section on its Web site that identifies key locations and producing "movie maps" with the locations for certain films such as the Harry Potter series. Another Web site, www.filmlondon.org.uk, has a section about recent movies filmed in the city. For more information on movies filmed in Scotland, you can buy *The Pocket Scottish Movie Book* by Brian Pendreigh, or you can visit the Scotland the Movie Guide Web site (⊕ www. scotlandthemovie.com).

A survey can begin with the dramas of Shakespeare: Olivier gave the world a memorable *Othello* and *Hamlet,* Orson Welles a moody *Macbeth,* Branagh gave

up mod versions of *Hamlet* and *Much Ado About Nothing.* Leonardo DiCaprio graced Australian Baz Luhrmann's contemporary version of *Romeo and Juliet.* Going behind the scenes, so to speak, Tom Stoppard created the Oscar winner *Shakespeare in Love.* Charles Dickens has also provided the foundation for film favorites: David Lean's immortal *Great Expectations,* George Cukor's *David Copperfield,* and *A Christmas Carol,* with Alastair Sim as Scrooge, top this list, which continues to grow with additions such as Douglas McGrath's *Nicholas Nickleby.*

McGrath's *Emma,* starring Gwyneth Paltrow, and Ang Lee's *Sense and Sensibility,* starring Emma Thompson and Kate Winslet, are just two of the recent film versions of Jane Austen's works. Keira Knightley plays Elizabeth Bennet in the latest *Pride and Prejudice* (2005). *Pandaemonium,* about the youthful Wordsworth and Coleridge, is fanciful but has great Lake District scenery and some insight into the poets' early work.

Harry Potter and the Sorcerer's Stone (in Britain, *Harry Potter and the Philosopher's Stone*), based on the wildly popular children's books by J. K. Rowling, was filmed in many British locations, including London, Gloucester, the Cotswolds, Northumbria, and Yorkshire. The film attracted such attention that the British Tourist Authority created a Harry Potter map, "Discovering the Magic of Britain," as a guide to the film sites and places of related interest. The second movie, *Harry Potter and the Chamber of Secrets,* used some of the same settings as the first. *Harry Potter and the Prisoner of Azkaban* and *Harry Potter and the Goblet of Fire* have followed suit.

The *Da Vinci Code,* the adaptation of Dan Brown's bestselling novel, includes scenes filmed in Britain, including Rosslyn Chapel near Edinburgh. Lincoln Cathedral stands in for Westminster Abbey, though. (*Fodor's Guide to the Da Vinci Code* fills you in on the novel's settings.)

Of the film versions of Agatha Christie's books, one is especially treasured: *Murder, She Said,* which starred the inimitable Margaret Rutherford. With its quiet English village setting, harpsichord score, and the dotty Miss Marple as portrayed by Rutherford, this must be the most English of all Christie films.

Lovers of opulence, spectacle, and history have many choices—in particular, Robert Bolt's version of Sir Thomas More's life and death, *A Man for All Seasons.* His *Lady Caroline Lamb* is surely the most beautiful historical film ever made. Richard Harris made a stirring Lord Protector in *Cromwell,* and the miniseries on Queen Elizabeth I, starring Glenda Jackson, is a great BBC addition to videos. Elizabeth's adversary came to breathless life in Vanessa Redgrave's rendition of *Mary, Queen of Scots,* certainly one of her finest performances. More recent and a chilling performance of tortuous times is Cate Blanchett as *Elizabeth.* The 2004 movie *Arthur,* with Clive Owen and Keira Knightley, gives a new spin to Arthurian tales. *Miss Potter,* a 2007 release, explores the life of the beloved children's book writer and illustrator Beatrix Potter, who had a home in the Lake District; Renée Zellweger plays the lead.

The quintessential "kilt movies" are *Rob Roy* (1995), with Liam Neeson and Jessica Lange—shot at and around Glen Nevis and Glencoe, the gardens of Drummond Castle, and Crichton Castle—and Mel Gibson's *Braveheart* (1995), the story of Scotland's first freedom fighter, Sir William Wallace (circa 1270–1305), which also uses the spectacular craggy scenery of Glen Nevis. Both films are great on atmosphere though not so hot on accurate historical detail; they do give a fine preview of Scotland's varied scenery. *Highlander* (1986), with Christopher Lambert and Sean Connery, also uses the spectacular crags of Glencoe, along with the prototypical Scottish castle Eilean Donan—almost a visual cliché in Scottish terms. It's not a kilt film, but *The Queen,* which deals with Queen Elizabeth and the Royal Family after the death of Princess Diana in 1997, has magnificent scenes of Scotland—not at filmed at Balmoral but at Culzean Castle and other places.

Musicals? Near the top of anyone's list are four films set in England—three of them in Hollywood's England—that rank among the greatest musicals of all time: Walt Disney's *Mary Poppins,* George Cukor's *My Fair Lady,* Sir Carol Reed's Oscar-winner *Oliver!,* and—yeah, yeah, yeah!—the Beatles' *A Hard Day's Night,* a British production.

If you're seeking a look at contemporary Britain, you might view *My Beautiful Laundrette,* about Asians in London; *Secrets and Lies,* about a dysfunctional London family; or *Trainspotting,* about Edinburgh's dark side. Manchester's rocking music scene from the 1970s to early 1990s is the subject of the well-named *24 Hour Party People.* You might lighten up with *The Full Monty,* about six former steelworkers in Sheffield who become strippers, or one of numerous romantic comedies: *Notting Hill,* with Julia Roberts and Hugh Grant; Hugh Grant again in *Four Weddings and a Funeral;* Gwyneth Paltrow in *Sliding Doors;* and Renée Zellweger (and Hugh Grant, again) in *Bridget Jones's Diary* and *Bridget Jones: The Edge of Reason.* Grant is also good in *About a Boy,* the film version of Nick Hornby's book about a cynical Londoner who learns about commitment. *Calendar Girls,* filmed in rural Yorkshire, follows the true story of middle-aged women who raise money for charity with an (almost) bare-all calendar.

Quintessentially British are some comedies of the 1950s and 1960s: Alec Guinness's *Kind Hearts and Coronets,* Peter Sellers's *The Mouse That Roared,* and Tony Richardson's Oscar-winner and cinematic style-setter, *Tom Jones,* starring Albert Finney, are best bets. In 2001 American director Robert Altman took a biting look at the British class system in *Gosford Park,* a country-house murder mystery set in the 1930s that stars mostly British actors, including Jeremy Northam and Maggie Smith. A more staid, upstairs-downstairs look at the class system is the film of the novel *The Remains of the Day*, featuring Anthony Hopkins as the stalwart butler, with Emma Thompson. Today some people's visions of turn-of-the-last-century England have been captured by the Merchant and Ivory films, notably their *Howard's End*, which won many awards.

CHRONOLOGY

3000 BC   First building of Stonehenge (later building 2100–1900 BC)

54 BC–AD 43   Julius Caesar's exploratory invasion of England. Romans conquer England, led by Emperor Claudius

60   Boudicca, a native British queen, razes the first Roman London (Londinium)

122–27   Emperor Hadrian completes the Roman conquest and builds a wall across the north to keep back the Scottish Picts

300–50   Height of Roman colonization, administered from such towns as Verulamium (St. Albans), Colchester, Lincoln, and York

410   Roman rule of Britain ends, after waves of invasion by Jutes, Angles, and Saxons

ca. 490   Possible period for the legendary King Arthur, who may have led resistance to Anglo-Saxon invaders; in 500 the Battle of Badon is fought

550–700   Seven Anglo-Saxon kingdoms emerge—Essex, Wessex, Sussex, Kent, Anglia, Mercia, and Northumbria—to become the core of English social and political organization for centuries

563   St. Columba, an Irish monk, founds monastery on the Scottish island of Iona; begins to convert Picts and Scots to Christianity

597   St. Augustine arrives in Canterbury to Christianize Britain

871–99   Alfred the Great, king of Wessex, unifies the English against Viking invaders, who are then confined to the northeast

1040   Edward the Confessor moves his court to Westminster and founds Westminster Abbey

1066   William, duke of Normandy, invades, defeats King Harold at the Battle of Hastings, and is crowned William I at Westminster in December

1086   Domesday Book completed, a survey of all taxpayers in England, drawn up to assist administration of the realm

1167   Oxford University founded

1170   Thomas à Becket murdered in Canterbury; his shrine becomes center for international pilgrimage

1189   Richard the Lionhearted embarks on the Third Crusade

1209   Cambridge University founded

1215   King John forced to sign Magna Carta at Runnymede. It promulgates basic principles of English law: no taxation except through Parliament, trial by jury, and property guarantees

1272–1307   Reign of Edward I, a great legislator; in 1282–83 he conquers Wales and reinforces his rule with a chain of massive castles

1337–1453 Edward III claims the French throne, starting the Hundred Years War. In spite of dramatic English victories—1346 at Crécy, 1356 at Poitiers, 1415 at Agincourt—the long war of attrition ends with the French driving the English out from everywhere but Calais, which finally falls in 1558

1348–49 The Black Death (bubonic plague) reduces the population of Britain from around 4¼ million to around 2½ million; decades of social unrest follow

1399 Henry Bolingbroke (Henry IV) deposes and murders his cousin Richard II; beginning of the rivalry between houses of York and Lancaster

1402–10 The Welsh, led by Owain Glendŵr, rebel against English rule

1455–85 The Wars of the Roses; the York-Lancaster struggle erupts into civil war

1477 William Caxton prints first book in England

1485 Henry Tudor (Henry VII) defeats Richard III at the Battle of Bosworth and founds the Tudor dynasty; he suppresses private armies, develops administrative efficiency and royal absolutism

1530s Under Henry VIII the Reformation takes hold; he dissolves the monasteries and finally demolishes medieval England, replacing it with a restructured society. The land goes to wealthy merchant families, creating new gentry

1555 During the reign of papal supporter Mary I (reigned 1553–58), Protestant bishops Ridley and Latimer are burned in Oxford; in 1556 Archbishop Cranmer is burned

1558–1603 Reign of Elizabeth I: Protestantism reestablished; Drake, Raleigh, and other freebooters establish English claims in the West Indies and North America

1568 Mary, Queen of Scots, flees to England; in 1587 she is executed

1588 Spanish Armada fails to invade England

1603 James VI of Scotland, son of Mary, Queen of Scots and Lord Darnley, becomes James I of England

1605 Guy Fawkes and friends plot to blow up Parliament

1611 King James Authorized Version of the Bible published

1620 Pilgrims sail from Plymouth on the *Mayflower* and settle in what becomes New England

1629 Charles I dissolves Parliament, decides to rule alone

1642–49 Civil War between the Royalists and Parliamentarians (Cavaliers and Roundheads); the Parliamentarians win

1649 Charles I executed; England is a republic

1653 Oliver Cromwell becomes Lord Protector, establishing England's only dictatorship

1660 The Restoration: Charles II restored to the throne; accepts limits to royal power

1666 The Great Fire: London burns for three days; its medieval center is destroyed

1689 Accession of William III (of Orange) and his wife, Mary II, as joint monarchs; royal power further limited

1700s Under the first four Georges, the Industrial Revolution develops and with it Britain's domination of world trade

1707 Union of English and Scots parliaments under Queen Anne

1714 The German Hanoverians succeed to the throne; George I's deficiency in English leads to the establishment of a council of ministers, the beginning of the cabinet system of government

1715, Two Jacobite rebellions fail to restore the House of Stuart to the
1745–46 throne; in 1746 Charles Edward Stuart (Bonnie Prince Charlie) is decisively defeated at Culloden Moor in Scotland

1756–63 Seven Years' War; Britain wins colonial supremacy from the French in Canada and India

1775–83 Britain loses the American colonies that become the United States

1795–1815 Britain and its allies defeat France in the Napoléonic Wars; in 1805, Admiral Lord Nelson is killed at Trafalgar; in 1815, Battle of Waterloo is fought

1801 Union with Ireland

1811–20 Prince Regent rules during his father's (George III) madness, the Regency period

1825 The Stockton to Darlington railway, the world's first passenger line with regular service, is established

1832 The Reform Bill extends the franchise, limiting the power of the great landowners

1834 Parliament outlaws slavery

1837–1901 During the long reign of Victoria, Britain becomes the world's richest country, and the British Empire reaches its height; railways, canals, and telegraph lines draw Britain into one vast manufacturing net

1851 The Great Exhibition, Prince Albert's brainchild, is held in the Crystal Palace, Hyde Park

1861 Prince Albert dies from typhoid fever at 42

1887 Victoria celebrates her Golden Jubilee; in 1901 she dies, marking the end of an era

1914–18 World War I: fighting against Germany, Britain loses a whole generation, with 750, 000 men killed in trench warfare alone; enormous debts and inept diplomacy in the postwar years undermine Britain's position as a world power

1919 Ireland declares independence from England; bloody Black-and-Tan struggle is one result

1936 Edward VIII abdicates to marry American divorcée Wallis Simpson

1939–45 World War II: Britain declares war on Germany when Germany invades Poland in September 1939. London badly damaged during the Blitz, September '40–May '41; Britain's economy shattered

1945 Labour wins a landslide victory; stays in power for six years, transforming Britain into a welfare state

1952 Queen Elizabeth II accedes to the throne

1973 Britain joins the European Economic Community after referendum

1975 Britain begins to pump North Sea oil

1981 Marriage of Prince Charles and Lady Diana Spencer

1982 Falklands regained in war with Argentina

1987 Conservatives under Margaret Thatcher win a third term in office

1990 John Major takes over as prime minister

1991 The Persian Gulf War

1992 Great Britain and European countries join to form one European Community (EC), whose name changed to European Union in 1993

1994 The Channel Tunnel opens a direct rail link between Britain and Europe

1996 The Prince and Princess of Wales receive a divorce.

1997 New Labour" comes to power, with Tony Blair as prime minister. Diana, Princess of Wales, dies at 36 in a car crash in Paris. She is buried at Althorp in Northamptonshire

1999 London welcomes the new century on December 31, with the gala opening of the Millennium Dome in Greenwich

2001 The Millennium Dome closes, its future uncertain. Prime Minister Tony Blair is elected to a second term

2002 Queen Elizabeth celebrates her Golden Jubilee. Queen Elizabeth (the Queen Mother) and Princess Margaret die. Euro coins and notes enter circulation as the currency of 12 European Union nations, but Britain continues to ponder adopting the euro

2003 Britain joins U.S. and coalition forces in invading Iraq; Saddam Hussein is overthrown, and he is captured before the end of the year

2005 Prince Charles and Camilla Parker Bowles wed in a civil ceremony in April. The ban on the traditional sport of fox hunting with hounds is put into effect. Tony Blair is elected to a historic third term as prime minister. London wins the bid for the 2012 Olympics in July; the same week, terrorists explode bombs in three tube stops and on one bus.

Great Britain Essentials

PLANNING TOOLS, EXPERT INSIGHT,
GREAT CONTACTS

There are planners, and there are those who fly by the seat of their pants. We happily place ourselves among the planners. Our writers and editors try to anticipate all the issues you may face before and during any journey, and then they do their research. This section is the product of their efforts. Use it to get excited about your trip to Great Britain, to inform your travel planning, or to guide you on the road should the seat of your pants start to feel threadbare.

GETTING STARTED

We're really proud of our Web site: Fodors.com is a great place to begin any journey. Scan Travel Wire for suggested itineraries, travel deals, restaurant and hotel openings, and other up-to-the-minute info. Check out Booking to research prices and book plane tickets, hotel rooms, rental cars, and vacation packages. Head to Talk for on-the-ground pointers from travelers who frequent our message boards. You can also link to loads of other travel-related resources.

▌ RESOURCES

ONLINE TRAVEL TOOLS

VisitBritain's U.S. Web site, ⊕ www.visitbritain.com/usa, focuses on information most helpful to Britain-bound U.S. travelers, from practical information to money-saving deals. Also useful are the official Web sites ⊕ www.enjoyengland.com, ⊕ www.visitscotland.com, and ⊕ www.visitwales.com. The official London Web site for visitors is ⊕ www.visitlondon.com. Some of the Web sites listed below discuss money-saving passes for historic sites and gardens; match them to your itinerary to see if they are worthwhile.

ALL ABOUT GREAT BRITAIN

Historic Sites British Monarchy ⊕ www.royal.gov.uk has an official Web site. **English Heritage** ⊕ www.english-heritage.org.uk cares for historic properites; look into discount passes sold at properties on online. **Great Britain Heritage Pass** ⊕ www.gbheritagepass.com, created by VisitBritain, offers free entry to more than 600 attractions; buy it online. **Historic Scotland** ⊕ www.historic-scotland.gov.uk cares for more than 300 properties. **I-UK** ⊕ www.i-uk.com is run by the government's Foreign and Commonwealth. **National Gardens Scheme** ⊕ www.ngs.org.uk opens private gardens to the public. **National Trust** ⊕ www.nationaltrust.org.uk offers information about castles and stately homes; check about membership and dis-count passes sold before your trip. **National Trust for Scotland** ⊕ www.nts.org.uk is responsible for historic buildings in Scotland; membership may save you money. **Royal Oak Foundation** ⊕ www.royal-oak.org is the U.S. affiliate of the National Trust; membership can save you money. **24 Hour Museum** ⊕ www.24hourmuseum.org.uk is packed with information about museums.

Currency Conversion Google ⊕ www.google.com does currency conversion. Just type in the amount you want to convert and an explanation of how you want it converted (e.g., "14 Swiss francs in dollars"), and then voilà. **Oanda.com** ⊕ www.oanda.com also allows you to print out a handy table with the current day's conversion rates. **XE.com** ⊕ www.xe.com is a good currency conversion Web site.

Safety Transportation Security Administration (TSA) ⊕ www.tsa.gov.

Time Zones Timeanddate.com ⊕ www.timeanddate.com/worldclock can help you figure out the correct time anywhere in the world.

Weather Accuweather.com ⊕ www.accuweather.com is an independent weather-forecasting service with especially good coverage of hurricanes. **Weather.com** ⊕ www.weather.com is the Web site for the Weather Channel.

Other Resources CIA World Factbook ⊕ www.odci.gov/cia/publications/factbook/index.html has profiles of every country in the world. It's a good source if you need some quick facts and figures.

VISITOR INFORMATION

Contacts at Home VisitBritain ✉ 551 5th Ave., 7th fl., New York, NY 10176 ☎ 212/986-2200 or 800/462-2748 ⊕ www.visitbritain.com/usa ✉ 625 N. Michigan Ave., Suite 1510, Chicago, IL 60611 ☎ 800/462-2748.

In London Britain and London Visitor Centre ✉ 1 Regent St., Piccadilly Circus, SW1Y 4NX ☎ No phone ⊕ www.visitbritain.com. **London Visitor Centre** ✉ Arrivals Hall, Waterloo International Terminal, Waterloo Rd. ☎ No phone ⊕ www.visitlondon.com.

▌ THINGS TO CONSIDER

GOVERNMENT ADVISORIES

As different countries have different world views, look at travel advisories from a range of governments to get more of a sense of what's going on out there. And be sure to parse the language carefully. For example, a warning to "avoid all travel" carries more weight than one urging you to "avoid nonessential travel," and both are much stronger than a plea to "exercise caution." A U.S. government travel warning is more permanent (though not necessarily more serious) than a so-called public announcement, which carries an expiration date.

The U.S. Department of State's Web site has more than just travel warnings and advisories. The consular information sheets issued for every country have general safety tips, entry requirements (though be sure to verify these with the country's embassy), and other useful details.

■ TIP➔ **If you're a U.S. citizen traveling abroad, consider registering online with the State Department (https://travelregistration.state.gov/ibrs/), so the government will know to look for you should a crisis occur in the country you're visiting.**

General Information & Warnings **Australian Department of Foreign Affairs & Trade** ⊕ www.smarttraveller.gov.au. **Consular Affairs Bureau of Canada** ⊕ www.voyage.gc.ca. **U.K. Foreign & Commonwealth Office** ⊕ www.fco.gov.uk/travel. **U.S. Department of State** ⊕ www.travel.state.gov.

GEAR

Britain can be cool, damp, and overcast, even in summer. You'll want a heavy coat for winter and a lightweight coat or warm jacket for summer. There's no time of year when a raincoat or umbrella won't come in handy. For the cities, pack as you would for an American city: coats and ties for expensive restaurants and nightspots, casual clothes elsewhere. Jeans

are popular in Britain and are perfectly acceptable for sightseeing and informal dining. Casual blazers are popular here with men. For women, ordinary street dress is acceptable everywhere. Pack insect repellent if you're hiking; midges (biting insects) are particularly annoying in Scotland in summer.

For sightseeing, pack a pair of binoculars to help you look at painted ceilings. If you plan to stay in budget hotels, take your own soap. Many do not provide soap, and some give guests only one tiny bar per room.

SHIPPING LUGGAGE AHEAD

Imagine globetrotting with only a carry-on in tow. Shipping your luggage in advance via an air-freight service is a great way to cut down on backaches, hassles, and stress—especially if your packing list includes strollers, car-seats, etc. There are some things to be aware of, though. First, research carry-on restrictions; if you absolutely need something that's isn't practical to ship and isn't allowed in carry-ons, this strategy isn't for you. Second, plan to send your bags several days in advance to U.S. destinations and as much as two weeks in advance to some international destinations. Third, plan to spend some money: it will cost least $100 to send a small piece of luggage, a golf bag, or a pair of skis to a domestic destination, much more to places overseas. Some people use Federal Express to ship their bags, but this can cost even more than air-freight services. All these services insure your bag (for most, the limit is $1,000, but you should

PACKING 101

Why do some people travel with a convoy of huge suitcases yet never have a thing to wear? How do others pack a duffle with a week's worth of outfits *and* supplies for every contingency? We realize that packing is a matter of style, but there's a lot to be said for traveling light. These tips help fight the battle of the bulging bag.

MAKE A LIST. In a recent Fodor's survey, 29% of respondents said they make lists (and often pack) a week before a trip. You can use your list to pack and to repack at the end of your trip. It can also serve as record of the contents of your suitcase—in case it disappears in transit.

THINK IT THROUGH. What's the weather like? Is this a business trip? A cruise? Going abroad? In some places dress may be more or less conservative than you're used to. As you create your itinerary, note outfits next to each activity (don't forget accessories).

EDIT YOUR WARDROBE. Plan to wear everything twice (better yet, thrice) and to do laundry along the way. Stick to one basic look—urban chic, sporty casual, etc. Build around one or two neutrals and an accent (e.g., black, white, and olive green). Women can freshen looks by changing scarves or jewelry. For a week's trip, you can look smashing with three bottoms, four or five tops, a sweater, and a jacket.

BE PRACTICAL. Put comfortable shoes atop your list. (Did we need to say this?) Pack lightweight, wrinkle-resistent, compact, washable items. (Or this?) Stack and roll clothes, so they'll wrinkle less. Unless you're on a guided tour or a cruise, select luggage you can readily carry. Porters, like good butlers, are hard to find these days.

CHECK WEIGHT AND SIZE LIMITATIONS. In the United States you may be charged extra for checked bags weighing more than 50 pounds. Abroad some airlines don't allow you to check bags over 60 to 70 pounds, or they charge outrageous fees for every excess pound—or bag. Carry-on size limitations can be stringent, too.

CHECK CARRY-ON RESTRICTIONS. Research restrictions with the TSA. Rules vary abroad, so check them with your airline if you're traveling overseas on a foreign carrier. Consider packing all but essentials (travel documents, prescription meds, wallet) in checked luggage. This leads to a "pack only what you can afford to lose" approach that might help you streamline.

RETHINK VALUABLES. On U.S. flights, airlines are liable for only about $2,800 per person for bags. On international flights, the liability limit is around $635 per bag. But items like computers, cameras, and jewelry aren't covered, and as gadgetry can go on and off the list of carry-on no-no's, you can't count on keeping things safe by keeping them close. Although comprehensive travel policies may cover luggage, the liability limit is often a pittance. Your home-owner's policy may cover you sufficiently when you travel—or not.

LOCK IT UP. If you must pack valuables, use TSA-approved locks (about $10) that can be unlocked by all U.S. security personnel.

TAG IT. Always tag your luggage; use your business address if you don't want people to know your home address. Put the same information (and a copy of your itinerary) inside your luggage, too.

REPORT PROBLEMS IMMEDIATELY. If your bags—or things in them—are damaged or go astray, file a written claim with your airline *before leaving the airport.* If the airline is at fault, it may give you money for essentials until your luggage arrives. Most lost bags are found within 48 hours, so alert the airline to your whereabouts for two or three days. If your bag was opened for security reasons in the States and something is missing, file a claim with the TSA.

verify that amount); you can, however, purchase additional insurance for about $1 per $100 of value.

Luggage Concierge ☎ 800/288-9818 ⊕ www.luggageconcierge.com. **Luggage Express** ☎ 866/744-7224 ⊕ www.usxpluggageexpress.com. **Luggage Free** ☎ 800/361-6871 ⊕ www.luggagefree.com. **Sports Express** ☎ 800/357-4174 ⊕ www.sportsexpress.com specializes in shipping golf clubs and other sports equipment. **Virtual Bellhop** ☎ 877/235-5467 ⊕ www.virtualbellhop.com.

PASSPORTS & VISAS

U.S. citizens need only a valid passport to enter Great Britain for stays of up to six months. Travelers should be prepared to show sufficient funds to support and accommodate themselves while in Britain (credit cards will usually suffice for this) and to show a return or onward ticket. Health certificates are not required.

PASSPORTS

We're always surprised at how few Americans have passports—only 25% at this writing. This number is expected to grow in coming years, when it becomes impossible to re-enter the United States from trips to neighboring Canada or Mexico without one. Remember this: A passport verifies both your identity and nationality—a great reason to have one.

U.S. passports are valid for 10 years. You must apply in person if you're getting a passport for the first time; if your previous passport was lost, stolen, or damaged; or if your previous passport has expired and was issued more than 15 years ago or when you were under 16. All children under 18 must appear in person to apply for or renew a passport. Both parents must accompany any child under 14 (or send a notarized statement with their permission) and provide proof of their relationship to the child.

■ TIP→ Before your trip, make two copies of your passport's data page (one for someone at home and another for you to carry separately). Or scan the page and e-mail it to someone at home and/or yourself.

There are 13 regional passport offices, as well as 7,000 passport acceptance facilities in post offices, public libraries, and other governmental offices. If you're renewing a passport, you can do so by mail. Forms are available at passport acceptance facilities and online.

The cost to apply for a new passport is $97 for adults, $82 for children under 16; renewals are $67. Allow six weeks for processing, both for first-time passports and renewals. For an expediting fee of $60 you can reduce this time to about two weeks. If your trip is less than two weeks away, you can get a passport even more rapidly by going to a passport office with the necessary documentation. Private expediters can get things done in as little as 48 hours, but charge hefty fees for their services.

VISAS

U.S. citizens are not required to obtain a visa prior to traveling in Great Britain for stays of less than six months.

U.S. Passport Information U.S. Department of State ☎ 877/487-2778 ⊕ http://travel.state.gov/passport.

U.S. Passport & Visa Expediters A. Briggs Passport & Visa Expeditors ☎ 800/806-0581 or 202/464-3000 ⊕ www.abriggs.com. **American Passport Express** ☎ 800/455-5166 or 603/559-9888 ⊕ www.americanpassport.com. **Passport Express** ☎ 800/362-8196 or 401/272-4612 ⊕ www.passportexpress.com. **Travel Document Systems** ☎ 800/874-5100 or 202/638-3800 ⊕ www.traveldocs.com. **Travel the World Visas** ☎ 866/886-8472 or 301/495-7700 ⊕ www.world-visa.com.

SHOTS & MEDICATIONS

No special shots are required or suggested for Britain.

■ TIP→ If you travel a lot internationally—particularly to developing nations—refer to the CDC's *Health Information for International Travel* (aka Traveler's Health Yellow Book).

Trip Insurance Resources

INSURANCE COMPARISON SITES		
Insure My Trip.com		www.insuremytrip.com.
Square Mouth.com		www.quotetravelinsurance.com.
COMPREHENSIVE TRAVEL INSURERS		
Access America	866/807-3982	www.accessamerica.com.
CSA Travel Protection	800/873-9855	www.csatravelprotection.com.
HTH Worldwide	610/254-8700 or 888/243-2358	www.hthworldwide.com.
Travelex Insurance	888/457-4602	www.travelex-insurance.com.
Travel Guard International	715/345-0505 or 800/826-4919	www.travelguard.com.
Travel Insured International	800/243-3174	www.travelinsured.com.
MEDICAL-ONLY INSURERS		
International Medical Group	800/628-4664	www.imglobal.com.
International SOS	215/942-8000 or 713/521-7611	www.internationalsos.com.
Wallach & Company	800/237-6615 or 504/687-3166	www.wallach.com.

Info from it is posted on the CDC Web site (www.cdc.gov/travel/yb), or you can buy a copy from your local bookstore for $24.95. Health Warnings **National Centers for Disease Control & Prevention** (CDC) ☎ 877/394-8747 international travelers' health line ⊕ www.cdc.gov/travel. **World Health Organization** (WHO) ⊕ www.who.int.

TRIP INSURANCE

We believe that comprehensive trip insurance is especially valuable if you're booking a very expensive or complicated trip (particularly to an isolated region) or if you're booking far in advance.

Comprehensive travel policies typically cover trip-cancellation and interruption, letting you cancel or cut your trip short because of a personal emergency, illness, or, in some cases, acts of terrorism in your destination. Such policies also cover evacuation and medical care. Some also cover you for trip delays because of bad weather or mechanical problems as well as for lost or delayed baggage. Another type of coverage to look for is financial default—that is, when your trip is disrupted because a tour operator, airline, or cruise line goes out of business. Generally you must buy this when you book your trip or shortly thereafter, and it's only available to you if your operator isn't on a list of excluded companies.

If you're going abroad, consider buying medical-only coverage at the very least. Neither Medicare nor some private insurers cover medical expenses anywhere outside of the United States besides Mexico and Canada (including time aboard a cruise ship, even if it leaves from a U.S. port). Medical-only policies typically reimburse you for medical care (excluding that related to pre-existing conditions) and hospitalization abroad, and provide for evacuation.

Expect comprehensive travel insurance policies to cost about 4% to 7% of the total price of your trip (it's more like 12% if you're over age 70). A medical-only policy may or may not be cheaper than a comprehensive policy. Always read the fine print of your policy to make sure that you are covered for the risks that are of most concern to you. Compare several policies to make sure you're getting the best price and range of coverage available.

In Britain, National Health Service hospitals give free, 24-hour treatment in Accident and Emergency sections, although delays can be an hour or more.

BOOKING YOUR TRIP

Unless your cousin is a travel agent, you're probably among the millions of people who make most of their travel arrangements online. But have you ever wondered just what the differences are between an online travel agent (a Web site through which you make reservations instead of going directly to the airline, hotel, or car-rental company), a discounter (a firm that does a high volume of business with a hotel chain or airline and accordingly gets good prices), a wholesaler (one that makes cheap reservations in bulk and then re-sells them to people like you), and an aggregator (one that compares all the offerings so you don't have to)? Is it truly better to book directly on an airline or hotel Web site? And when does a real live travel agent come in handy?

Booking engines like Expedia, Travelocity, and Orbitz are actually travel agents, albeit high-volume, online ones. And airline travel packagers like American Airlines Vacations and Virgin Vacations—well, they're travel agents, too. But they may still not work with all the world's hotels.

An aggregator site will search many sites and pull the best prices for airfares, hotels, and rental cars from them. Most aggregators compare the major travel-booking sites such as Expedia, Travelocity, and Orbitz; some also look at airline Web sites, though rarely the sites of smaller budget airlines. Some aggregators also compare other travel products, including complex packages—a good thing, as you can sometimes get the best overall deal by booking an air-and-hotel package.

▌ ONLINE

You really have to shop around. A travel wholesaler such as Hotels.com or Hotel-Club.net can be a source of good rates, as can discounters such as Hotwire or Priceline, particularly if you can bid for your hotel room or airfare. Indeed, such sites sometimes have deals that are unavailable elsewhere. They do, however, tend to work only with hotel chains (which makes them just plain useless for getting hotel reservations outside of major cities) or big airlines (so that often leaves out upstarts like jetBlue and some foreign carriers like Air India). Also, with discounters and wholesalers you must generally prepay, and everything is nonrefundable. And before you fork over the dough, be sure to check the terms and conditions, so you know what a given company will do for you if there's a problem and what you'll have to deal with on your own.

▌ TIP→ To be absolutely sure everything was processed correctly, confirm reservations made through online travel agents, discounters, and wholesalers directly with your hotel before leaving home.

▌ WITH A TRAVEL AGENT

If you use an agent—brick-and-mortar or virtual—you'll pay a fee for the service. And know that the service you get from some online agents isn't comprehensive. For example Expedia and Travelocity don't search for prices on budget airlines like jetBlue, Southwest, or small foreign carriers. That said, some agents (online or not) *do* have access to fares that are difficult to find otherwise, and the savings can more than make up for any surcharge.

A knowledgeable brick-and-mortar travel agent can be a godsend if you're booking a cruise, a package trip that's not available to you directly, an air pass, or a complicated itinerary including several overseas flights. What's more, travel agents that specialize in a destination may have exclusive access to certain deals and insider information on things such as charter flights. Agents who specialize in types of travelers (senior citizens, gays and lesbians, naturists) or types of trips (cruises, luxury travel, safaris) can also be invaluable.

A top-notch agent planning your trip to Russia will make sure you get the correct

Online Booking Resources

AGGREGATORS		
Kayak	www.kayak.com	looks at cruises and vacation packages.
Mobissimo	www.mobissimo.com.	
Qixo	www.qixo.com	compares cruises, vacation packages, and even travel insurance.
Sidestep	www.sidestep.com	compares vacation packages and lists travel deals.
Travelgrove	www.travelgrove.com	compares cruises and vacation packages.
BOOKING ENGINES		
Cheap Tickets	www.cheaptickets.com	discounter.
Expedia	www.expedia.com	large online agency that charges a booking fee for airline tickets.
Hotwire	www.hotwire.com	discounter.
lastminute.com	www.lastminute.com	specializes in last-minute travel; the main site is for the U.K., but it has a link to a U.S. site.
Luxury Link	www.luxurylink.com	has auctions (surprisingly good deals) as well as offers on the high-end side of travel.
Onetravel.com	www.onetravel.com	discounter for hotels, car rentals, airfares, and packages.
Orbitz	www.orbitz.com	charges a booking fee for airline tickets, but gives a clear breakdown of fees and taxes before you book.
Priceline.com	www.priceline.com	discounter that also allows bidding.
Travel.com	www.travel.com	allows you to compare its rates with those of other booking engines.
Travelocity	www.travelocity.com	charges a booking fee for airline tickets, but promises good problem resolution.
ONLINE ACCOMMODATIONS		
Hotelbook.com	www.hotelbook.com	focuses on independent hotels worldwide.
Hotel Club	www.hotelclub.net	good for major cities worldwide.
Hotels.com	www.hotels.com	big Expedia-owned wholesaler that offers rooms in hotels all over the world.
Quikbook	www.quikbook.com	offers "pay when you stay" reservations that allow you to settle your bill when you check out, not when you book.
OTHER RESOURCES		
Bidding For Travel	www.biddingfortravel.com	a good place to figure out what you can get and for how much before you start bidding on, say, Priceline.

visa application and complete it on time; the one booking your cruise may get you a cabin upgrade or arrange to have bottle of champagne chilling in your cabin when you embark. And complain about the surcharges all you like, but when things don't work out the way you'd hoped, it's nice to have an agent to put things right.

■ TIP→ Remember that Expedia, Travelocity, and Orbitz are travel agents, not just booking engines. To resolve any problems with a reservation made through these companies, contact them first.

If you opt not to use a travel agent, Great Britain is an easy destination to plan without one. Booking flights, making hotel reservations, and even buying theater tickets are all things that can be done online or by telephone. Reviews of hotels and restaurants by fellow travelers are also readily available.

Agent Resources **American Society of Travel Agents** ☎ 703/739-2782 ⊕ www. travelsense.org.

▌ ACCOMMODATIONS

Hotels, bed-and-breakfasts, or small country houses—there's a style and price to suit most travelers. The lodgings listed are the cream of the crop in each price category. Wherever you stay, make reservations well in advance: Great Britain is popular.

Properties are assigned price categories based on a range that includes the cost of the least expensive standard double room in high season (excluding holidays) and the most expensive. Lodgings are indicated in the text by ⊞. Properties indicated by ✕⊞ are lodging establishments whose restaurants warrant a special trip. Price-category information is given in each chapter. Unless otherwise noted, all lodgings listed have a private bathroom, air-conditioning, a room phone, and a television.

We always list the facilities that are available—but we don't specify whether they cost extra: when pricing accommodations, always ask what's included and what costs extra. Throughout Britain, lodging prices

10 WAYS TO SAVE 🏨

1. Join "frequent guest" programs. You may get preferential treatment in room choice and/or upgrades in your favorite chains.

2. Call direct. You can sometimes get a better price if you call a hotel's local toll-free number (if available) rather than a central reservations number.

3. Check online. Check hotel Web sites, as not all chains are represented on all travel sites.

4. Look for specials. Always inquire about packages and corporate rates.

5. Look for price guarantees. For overseas trips, look for guaranteed rates. With your rate locked in you won't pay more, even if the price goes up in the local currency.

6. Look for weekend deals at business hotels. High-end chains catering to business travelers are often busy only on weekdays; to fill rooms they often drop rates dramatically on weekends.

7. Ask about taxes. Verify whether local hotel taxes are included in quoted rates. In some places taxes can add 20% or more to your bill.

8. Read the fine print. Watch for add-ons, including resort fees, energy surcharges, and "convenience" fees for such things as unlimited local phone service you won't use or a free newspaper in a language you can't read.

9. Know when to go. If your destination's high season is December through April and you're trying to book, say, in late April, you might save money by changing your dates by a week or two. Ask when rates go down, though: if your dates straddle peak and non-peak seasons, a property may still charge peak-season rates for the entire stay.

10. Weigh your options (we can't say this enough). Weigh transportation times and costs against the savings of staying in a hotel that's cheaper because it's out of the way.

Online Booking Resorces

CONTACTS

The Apartment Service	020/8944-1444 020/8944-6744	www.apartmentservice.com.
At Home Abroad	212/421-9165	www.athomeabroadinc.com.
Barclay International Group	516/364-0064 or 800/845-6636	www.barclayweb.com.
English Country Cottages	0870/781100	www.english-country-cottages.co.uk, from studio apartments to castles.
Hometours International	865/690-8484	thor.he.net/~hometour.
In the English Manner	01559/371600	www.english-manner.co.uk
American agent	213/629-1811 or 800/422-0799,	apartments and cottages.
Interhome	954/791-8282 or 800/882-6864	www.interhome.us.
National Trust	0870/458-4422	www.nationaltrustcottages.co.uk, houses and cottages.
Suzanne B. Cohen & Associates	207/622-0743	www.villaeurope.com.
Vacation Home Rentals Worldwide	201/767-9393 or 800/633-3284	www.vhrww.com.
Villas International	415/499-9490 or 800/221-2260	www.villasintl.com.

often include breakfast of some kind, but this is generally not the case in London.

Most hotels and other lodgings require you to give your credit-card details before they will confirm your reservation. If you don't feel comfortable e-mailing this information, ask if you can fax it (some places even prefer faxes). However you book, get confirmation in writing and have a copy of it handy when you check in.

Be sure you understand the hotel's cancellation policy. Some places allow you to cancel without any kind of penalty—even if you prepaid to secure a discounted rate—if you cancel at least 24 hours in advance. Others require you to cancel a week in advance or penalize you the cost of one night. Small inns and B&Bs are most likely to require you to cancel far in advance. Most hotels allow children under a certain age to stay in their parents' room at no extra charge, but others charge for them as extra adults; find out the cutoff age for discounts.

■ TIP→ Assume that hotels operate on the European Plan (**EP**, no meals) unless we specify

that they use the Breakfast Plan (**BP**, with full breakfast), Continental Plan (**CP**, Continental breakfast), Full American Plan (**FAP**, all meals), Modified American Plan (**MAP**, breakfast and dinner) or are all-inclusive (**AI**, all meals and most activities).

APARTMENT & HOUSE RENTALS

For a home base that is roomy enough for a family and comes with cooking facilities, consider renting furnished "flats" (the word for apartments in Great Britain) or a house. These can save you money, especially if you're traveling with a group, and provide more privacy than a hotel or a B&B. If you're interested in home exchange but don't feel like sharing, some home-exchange directories list rentals as well. If you deal directly with local agents, get a recommendation from someone who has used the company. Unlike with hotels, there's no accredited system for apartment-rental standards. The London Where to Stay section *in* Chapter 1 also has information about rentals. The National Trust rents historic cottages in rural locations by the week at often reasonable prices.

Also *see* Cottages *and* Historic Buildings.

BED & BREAKFASTS

A special British tradition, and the backbone of budget travel, B&Bs are usually in a family home. They vary in style and grace, but these days most have private bathrooms. They range from the ordinary to the truly elegant. Guesthouses are a slightly larger and sometimes more luxurious version of the same thing.

Tourist Information Centres around the country can help you find and book a B&B, even on the day you arrive. Bed & Breakfast (GB) reservation service offers rooms in a range of prices and has discounts for families and off-peak reductions. It represents tourist board–accredited places in London, across the country, and in France. Wolsey Lodges, a consortium of more than 180 private homes mostly in Britain, includes many luxurious country homes and some more modest houses; some are historic. Guests are encouraged to dine with their hosts at least one night of their stay. For reservation services in London, *see* the Where to Stay section *in* Chapter 1.

Reservation Services Bed & Breakfast.com ☎ 512/322-2710 or 800/462-2632 ⊕ www. bedandbreakfast.com also sends out an online newsletter. **Bed & Breakfast (GB)** ☎ 800/454-8704, 0871/781-0834 in U.K. ⊕ www.bedbreak.com. **Bulldog Club** ☎ 877/727-3004 in U.S. ⊕ www.bulldogclub.com. **Host & Guest Service** ☎ 020/7385-9922 in U.K. ⊕ www.host-guest.co.uk. **Wolsey Lodges** ☎ 01473/822058, 01473/827500 for brochure ⊕ www.wolseylodges.com.

COTTAGES

Cottages and houses are available for weekly rental in all areas of the country. These vary from quaint older homes to brand-new buildings in scenic surroundings. For families and large groups, they offer the best value-for-money accommodations, but because they are often in isolated locations, a car is vital. Lists of rental properties are available free of charge from VisitBritain (⊕ www.visitbritain.com). Some National Trust properties have cottages available on the estates of stately homes. Luxury Cottages Direct deals exclusively in four- and five-star properties. You may find discounts of up to 50% on rentals during the off-season (October through March).

Luxury Cottages Direct ☎ 029/2021-2491 ⊕ www.luxury-cottages.co.uk. **National Trust** ☎ 0870/458-4422 ⊕ www.nationaltrust cottages.co.uk. **Rural Retreats** ☎ 01386/701177 ⊕ www.ruralretreats.co.uk.

FARMHOUSES

Farmhouses have become increasingly popular in recent years; their special appeal is the rustic, rural experience. Consider this option only if you are touring by car. Prices are generally very reasonable. Ask VisitBritain (⊕ www.visitbritain.com) for the booklet "Stay on a Farm," contact Farm Stay UK, or check the Web sites for regional tourist boards given at the end of each chapter. Scottish Farmhouse Holidays specializes in Scotland.

Farm Stay UK ☎ 024/7669-6909 📠 024/7669-6630 ⊕ www.farmstayuk.co.uk. **Scottish Farmhouse Holidays** ☎ 01890/751830 ⊕ www.scotfarmhols.co.uk.

HISTORIC BUILDINGS

Want to spend your vacation in a Gothic banqueting house, an old lighthouse, a seaside castle, or maybe in an apartment at Hampton Court Palace? Several organizations, such as the Landmark Trust, National Trust (⇨ Cottages, *above*), and Vivat Trust have specially adapted historic buildings to rent. Celtic Castles represents castles and castle hotels in several countries including Britain. Rural Retreats renovates historic buildings including lighthouses around Britain. Stately Holiday Homes has rentals in houses and cottages in historic or rural settings. Most are self-catering (meaning that they include kitchens).

Celtic Castles ☎ 870/050-3232 ⊕ www. celticcastles.com. **Landmark Trust** ☎ 01628/825925 ⊕ www.landmarktrust.org.uk. **Portmeirion Cottages** ☎ 01766/770000 ⊕ www.

portmeirion-village.com. **Rural Retreats**
☎ 01386/701177 ⊕ www.ruralretreats.co.uk.
Stately Holiday Homes ☎ 01638/674756
⊕ www.statelyholidayhomes.co.uk. **Vivat
Trust** ☎ 020/7336-8825 from U.S., 0845/
090-0194 from U.K. ⊕ www.vivat.org.uk.

HOME EXCHANGES

With a direct home exchange you stay in
someone else's home while they stay in
yours. Some outfits also deal with vacation homes, so you're not actually staying
in someone's full-time residence, just their
vacant weekend place.

Exchange Clubs Home Exchange.com
☎ 800/877-8723 ⊕ www.homeexchange.
com; $59.95 for a 1-year online listing.
HomeLink International ☎ 800/638-3841
⊕ www.homelink.org; $80 yearly for Web-
only membership; $125 includes Web access
and two catalogs. **Intervac U.S.** ☎ 800/756-
4663 ⊕ www.intervacus.com; $78.88 for
Web-only membership; $126 includes Web
access and a catalog.

HOSTELS

Although the decor may be basic, some
hostels in Great Britain are in extraordinary locations, and others are simply beautiful. Hostels offer bare-bones lodging at
low, low prices—often in shared dorm
rooms with shared baths—to people of all
ages, though the primary market is young
travelers, especially students. Most hostels
serve breakfast; dinner and/or shared cooking facilities may also be available. In
some hostels you aren't allowed to be in

your room during the day, and there may
be a curfew at night. Nevertheless, hostels
provide a sense of community, with public rooms where travelers often gather to
share stories. Many hostels are affiliated
with Hostelling International (HI), an umbrella group of hostel associations with
some 4,500 member properties in more
than 70 countries. Other hostels are completely independent and may be nothing
more than a really cheap hotel.

Membership in any HI association, open
to travelers of all ages, allows you to stay
in HI-affiliated hostels at member rates.
One-year membership is about $28 for
adults; hostels charge about $10–$30 per
night. Members have priority if the hostel is full; they're also eligible for discounts
around the world, even on rail and bus
travel in some countries.

Hostelling International–USA ☎ 301/495-
1240 ⊕ www.hiusa.org. **YHA England and
Wales** ☎ 0870/870-8808, 0870/770-8868, or
0162/959-2600 ⊕ www.yha.org.uk.

HOTELS

Britain is a popular vacation destination,
so be sure to reserve hotel rooms weeks
(months for London) in advance. The
country has everything from budget chain
hotels to luxurious retreats in converted
country houses. In many towns and cities
you will find old inns that are former
coaching inns, which served travelers as
they journeyed around the country in
horse-drawn carriages and stagecoaches.
Most hotels have rooms with "en suite"
bathrooms—as private bathrooms are
called—although some older ones may
have only washbasins; in this case, showers and bathtubs (and toilets) are usually
just down the hall. When you book a
room in the mid-to-lower price categories,
it's best to confirm your request for a
room with en suite facilities. Especially in
London, rooms and bathrooms may be
smaller than what you find in the United
States. Tourist Information Centres will reserve rooms for you, usually for a small
fee. A great many hotels offer special week-

WORD OF MOUTH

Did the resort look as good in real life as it
did in the photos? Did you sleep like a baby,
or were the walls paper thin? Did you get
your money's worth? Rate hotels and write
your own reviews in Travel Ratings or start
a discussion about your favorite places in
Travel Talk on www.fodors.com. Your comments might even appear in our books. Yes,
you, too, can be a correspondent!

end and off-season bargain packages. All hotels listed have private bath unless otherwise noted.

Hotels in Britain are graded from one to five stars, and guesthouses, inns, and B&Bs are graded from one to five diamonds by VisitBritain in association with the Automobile Association (AA) and the Royal Automobile Association (RAC). Basically, the more stars or diamonds a property has, the more facilities it has, and the facilities will be of a higher standard. A property with one star or diamond has the minimum necessary for a night's sleep and won't include any extras such as minibars, a concierge, or on-site dining. At the top of the scale, five-star properties will have luxurious decor, a broad range of facilities such as a swimming pool and health club, and a highly trained staff. VisitScotland and VisitWales also have a grading system of from one to five stars, based on quality and comfort.

Chains such as Premier Travel Inn offer low rates and reliable rooms, and are usually close to major sights and cities. At this writing VisitLondon.com, London's official Web site, was offering a lowest-price guarantee on hotel rooms. LondonTown.com's London Visitor Information Centre provides free maps, tourist information, and last-minute hotel bookings in the city, with savings of up to 50%. Its kiosk in Leicester Square is open daily 8 AM–11 PM. Lastminute.com offers deals on hotel rooms all over the United Kingdom. Hotel rates in major cities tend to be cheapest on weekends, while rural hotels are cheapest on weeknights. Early December and most of January have the lowest occupancy rates, so hotels offer cheaper rooms at these times.

Local Resources **Lastminute.com** ⊕ www.lastminute.com. **Premier Travel Inn** ☎ 0870/242–8000, 1582/567890 outside the U.K. ⊕ www.premiertravelinn.co.uk. **London-Town.com's London Visitor Information Centre** ⊠ Leicester Sq. ☎ 020/7292–2333 ⊕ www.londontown.com. **VisitLondon** ⊕ www.visitlondon.com.

■ AIRLINE TICKETS

Most domestic airline tickets are electronic; international tickets may be either electronic or paper. With an e-ticket the only thing you receive is an e-mailed receipt citing your itinerary and reservation and ticket numbers. The greatest advantage of an e-ticket is that if you lose your receipt, you can simply print out another copy or ask the airline to do it for you at check-in. You usually pay a surcharge (up to $50) to get a paper ticket, if you can get one at all. The sole advantage of a paper ticket is that it may be easier to endorse over to another airline if your flight is canceled and the airline with which you booked can't accommodate you on another flight.

■ TIP→ Discount air passes that let you travel economically in a country or region must often be purchased before you leave home. In some cases you can only get them through a travel agent.

■ RENTAL CARS

When you reserve a car, ask about cancellation penalties, taxes, drop-off charges (if you're planning to pick up the car in one city and leave it in another), and surcharges (for being under or over a certain age, for additional drivers, or for driving across state or country borders or beyond a specific distance from your point of rental). All these things can add substantially to your costs. Request car seats and extras such as GPS when you book.

Rates are sometimes—but not always—better if you book in advance or reserve through a rental agency's Web site. There are other reasons to book ahead, though: for popular destinations, during busy times of the year, or to ensure that you get certain types of cars (vans, SUVs, exotic sports cars).

■ TIP→ Make sure that a confirmed reservation guarantees you a car. Agencies sometimes overbook, particularly for busy weekends and holiday periods.

In Great Britain your own driver's license is acceptable. However, you may choose to get an International Driving Permit (IDP), which can be used only in conjunction with a valid driver's license and which translates your license into 10 languages. Check the AAA Web site for more info as well as for IDPs ($10) themselves. These permits are universally recognized, and having one in your wallet may save you a problem with the local authorities. Companies may not rent cars to people who are under 23 or over 75.

Rental rates vary widely, beginning at £25 ($48) a day and £160 ($300) a week for a midsized car, usually with manual transmission. Air-conditioning and unlimited mileage generally come with larger automatic transmission cars. As in the United States, prices are higher at times of heaviest use—summer and holidays. Car seats for children usually cost about £20 ($36) extra. Adding one extra driver is usually included in the original rental price.

CAR-RENTAL INSURANCE

Everyone who rents a car wonders whether the insurance that the rental companies offer is worth the expense. No one—including us—has a simple answer. It all depends on how much regular insurance you have, how comfortable you are with risk, and whether or not money is an issue.

If you own a car, your personal auto insurance may cover a rental to some degree, though not all policies protect you abroad; always read your policy's fine print. If you don't have auto insurance, then seriously consider buying the collision- or loss-damage waiver (CDW or LDW) from the car-rental company, which eliminates your liability for damage to the car. Some credit cards offer CDW coverage, but it's usually supplemental to your own insurance and rarely covers SUVs, minivans, luxury models, and the like. If your coverage is secondary, you may still be liable for loss-of-use costs from the car-rental company. But no credit-card insurance is valid unless you use that card for *all* transactions, from reserving to paying the final bill. All companies exclude car rental in some countries, so be sure to find out about the destination to which you are traveling.

■ TIP→ Diners Club offers primary CDW coverage on all rentals reserved and paid for with the card. This means that Diners Club's company—not your own car insurance—pays in case of an accident. It *doesn't* mean your car-insurance company won't raise your rates once it discovers you had an accident.

Some countries require you to purchase CDW coverage or require car-rental companies to include it in quoted rates. Ask your rental company about issues like these in your destination. In most cases it's cheaper to add a supplemental CDW plan to your comprehensive travel-insurance policy (⇨ Trip Insurance *under* Things to Consider *in* Getting Started, *above*) than to purchase it from a rental company. That said, you don't want to pay for a supplement if you're required to buy insurance from the rental company.

■ TIP→ You can decline the insurance from the rental company and purchase it through a third-party provider such as Travel Guard (www.travelguard.com)–$9 per day for $35,000 of coverage. That's sometimes just under half the price of the CDW offered by some car-rental companies.

▌ TRAIN PASSES

If you plan to travel a lot by train in Great Britain, consider purchasing a BritRail Pass, which gives unlimited travel over the entire British rail network and can save you money. But be aware that if you don't plan to cover many miles, you may come out ahead by buying individual tickets. You must buy your BritRail Pass before you leave home. They are available from most travel agents or from ACP Rail International, DER, or Rail Europe; check their Web sites for complete details. Note that EurailPasses are not honored in Britain and that the rates listed here are subject to change.

BritRail passes come in two basic varieties. The Classic pass allows travel on consecutive days, and the FlexiPass allows a number of travel days within a set period of time. The cost (in U.S. dollars) of a BritRail Consecutive Pass adult ticket for 8 days is $311 standard and $469 first-class; for 15 days, $469 standard and $702 first-class; for 22 days, $592 and $891; and for a month, $702 and $1,054. The cost of a BritRail FlexiPass adult ticket for 4 days' travel in two months is $275 standard and $409 first-class; for 8 days' travel in two months, $399 standard and $598 first-class; and for 15 days' travel in two months, $604 standard and $901 first-class. Prices drop by about 25% for off-peak travel passes between October and March. Passes for students, seniors, and ages 16 to 25 are discounted, too.

For shorter journeys, try the London Plus Pass. This is an excellent deal, offering four days of first-class travel spread over eight days for $176. Two and seven days of travel are other options.

The England Flexipass, England Consecutive Pass, BritRail Pass Plus Ireland, Scottish Freedom, and Freedom of Wales pass are other options, and you can purchase a Eurostar ticket for Paris or Brussels in conjunction with a BritRail Pass.

Many travelers assume that rail passes guarantee them seats or sleeping accommodations on the trains they wish to ride. Not so. You need to book seats ahead

Car Rental Resources

AUTOMOBILE ASSOCIATIONS		
U.S.: American Automobile Association (AAA)	315/797-5000	www.aaa.com; most contact with the organization is through state and regional members.
National Automobile Club	650/294-7000	www.thenac.com; membership is open to California residents only.
Local Agencies Dimple Car Hire	020/8205-1200 020/7243-4408	www.dimple-selfdrive.co.uk.
Easy Car	0906/333-3333, 60p per minute within U.K.	www.easycar.com.
Europcar	020/259-1600	www.europcar.com.
MAJOR AGENCIES		
Alamo	800/462-5266	www.alamo.com.
Avis	800/230-4898	www.avis.com.
Budget	800/527-0700	www.budget.com.
Hertz	800/654-3131	www.hertz.com.
National Car Rental	800/227-7368	www.nationalcar.com.
WHOLESALERS		
Auto Europe	888/223-5555	www.autoeurope.com.
Europe by Car	212/581-3040 in New York or 800/223-1516	www.europebycar.com.
Eurovacations	877/471-3876	www.eurovacations.com.
Kemwel	877/820-0668	www.kemwel.com.

even if you are using a rail pass, especially on trains that may be crowded, particularly in summer on popular routes.

There are also some discount passes for travel within regions; individual chapters in this book have information, or you can contact National Rail Enquiries. You can purchase these when you're in Britain.

Discount Passes ACP Rail International
☎ 866/938-7245 ⊕ www.acpmarketing.net.
DER Travel Services ☎ 800/782-2424
🖷 800/782-2424 for information, 800/860-9944 for brochures ⊕ www.der.com. **National Rail Enquiries** ☎ 0845/748-4950 ⊕ www.nationalrail.co.uk **Rail Europe** ☎ 877/257-2887 ⊕ www.raileurope.com ☎ 416/482-1777 or 800/361-7245 🖷 0870/584-8848.

▌VACATION PACKAGES

Packages *are not* guided excursions. Packages combine airfare, accommodations, and perhaps a rental car or other extras (theater tickets, guided excursions, boat trips, reserved entry to popular museums, transit passes), but they let you do your own thing. During busy periods packages may be your only option, as flights and rooms may be sold out otherwise. Packages will definitely save you time. They can also save you money, particularly in peak seasons, but—and this is a really big "but"—you should price each part of the package separately to be sure. And be aware that prices advertised on Web sites and in newspapers rarely include service charges or taxes, which can up your costs by hundreds of dollars.

■ TIP➔ Some packages and cruises are sold only through travel agents. Don't always assume that you can get the best deal by booking everything yourself.

Each year consumers are stranded or lose their money when packagers—even large ones with excellent reputations—go out of business. How can you protect yourself? First, always pay with a credit card; if you have a problem, your credit-card company may help you resolve it. Second, buy trip insurance that covers default. Third,

choose a company that belongs to the United States Tour Operators Association, whose members must set aside funds to cover defaults. Finally, choose a company that also participates in the Tour Operator Program of the American Society of Travel Agents (ASTA), which will act as mediator in any disputes. You can also check on the tour operator's reputation among travelers by posting an inquiry on one of the Fodors.com forums.

Organizations American Society of Travel Agents (ASTA) ☎ 703/739-2782 or 800/965-2782 ⊕ www.astanet.com. **United States Tour Operators Association** (USTOA) ☎ 212/599-6599 ⊕ www.ustoa.com.

■ TIP➔ Local tourism boards can provide information about lesser-known and small-niche operators that sell packages to only a few destinations.

▌GUIDED TOURS

Guided tours are a good option when you don't want to do it all yourself. You travel along with a group (sometimes large, sometimes small), stay in prebooked hotels, eat with your fellow travelers (the cost of meals sometimes included in the price of your tour, sometimes not), and follow a schedule. But not all guided tours are an if-it's-Tuesday-this-must-be-Belgium experience. A knowledgeable guide can take you places that you might never discover on your own, and you may be pushed to see more than you would have otherwise. Tours aren't for everyone, but they can be just the thing for trips to places where making travel arrangements is difficult or time-consuming (particularly when you don't speak the language). Whenever you book a guided tour, find out what's included and what isn't. A "land-only" tour includes all your travel (by bus, in most cases) in the destination, but not necessarily your flights to and from or even within it. Also, in most cases prices in tour brochures don't include fees and taxes. And remember that you'll be expected to tip your guide (in cash) at the end of the tour.

TRANSPORTATION

▌ BY AIR

Flying time to London is about 6½ hours from New York, 7½ hours from Chicago, 9½ hours from Dallas, and 10 hours from Los Angeles. If you're flying to Europe from Great Britain, plan to arrive at the airport two hours in advance.

Airlines & Airports Airline and Airport Links.com ⊕ www.airlineandairportlinks. com has links to many of the world's airlines and airports.

Airline Security Issues Transportation Security Administration ⊕ www.tsa.gov has answers for almost every question that might come up.

AIRPORTS

Most international flights to London arrive at either Heathrow Airport (LHR), 15 mi west of London, or at Gatwick Airport (LGW), 27 mi south of the capital. Most flights from the United States go to Heathrow, with Terminals 3 and 4 handling transatlantic flights (British Airways uses Terminal 4). Gatwick is London's second gateway, serving 21 U.S. destinations. A third, newer airport, Stansted (STN), is 35 mi northeast of the city. It handles mainly European and domestic traffic. Luton Airport (LLA), 30 mi north of the city, serves British and European destinations. Luton is the hub for the low-cost easyJet airline. Manchester (MAN) in northwest England handles some bmi/ British Midland flights from the United States. Birmingham (BHX), in the Midlands, handles mainly European and British flights as well as flights from Chicago, Denver, Newark, New York, and Orlando. Bristol (BRS) has limited service from New York, as does Newcastle (NCL).

Almost all international flights to Scotland arrive at Glasgow Airport; Continental has service from New York to Edinburgh. For information about those airports and transfers to Glasgow and Edinburgh, *see* the Essentials sections at the end of Chap-

ters 12 and 13.

The British destinations served by different carriers can change, so check online.

Heathrow and Gatwick are enormous and can seem like shopping malls where planes just happen to land. Heathrow in particular may tempt shoppers, with designer boutiques, jewelry stores, Harrods outlets, and enough perfume to scent half the world. Gatwick's shopping options are slightly less overwhelming, but can easily while away a few hours of flight delay. Both airports have bars and pubs, and other dining options. In 2006, Yotel was opening pod hotels in Heathrow and Gatwick with cabin-size rooms to be booked by four-hour blocks or overnight. By comparison, other airports, including Manchester, Birmingham, and London's Luton and Stansted, have much more limited shopping and dining options; a delay of a few hours may seem like years.

Airport Information Birmingham Airport ☎ 0870/733-5511 ⊕ www.bhx.com. **Heathrow Airport** ☎ 0870/000-0123 ⊕ www.baa.co.uk/heathrow. **Gatwick Airport** ☎ 0870/000-2468 ⊕ www.baa.co.uk/ gatwick. **Luton Airport** ☎ 01582/405100 ⊕ www.london-luton.co.uk. **Manchester Airport** ☎ 0161/489-3000 ⊕ www.manairport. co.uk. **Stansted Airport** ☎ 0870/000-0303 ⊕ www.baa.co.uk/stansted.

GROUND TRANSPORTATION

See London Essentials *in* Chapter 1 for information on transportation between London and the airport. Essentials sections in other chapters cover ground transportation from other cities.

TRANSFERS BETWEEN AIRPORTS

See London Essentials *in* Chapter 1 for information on transportation between the London airports.

FLIGHTS

British Airways is the national flag carrier and offers mostly nonstop flights from 18

FLYING 101

Flying may not be as carefree as it once was, but there are some things you can do to make your trip smoother.

MINIMIZE THE TIME SPENT STANDING IN LINE. Buy an e-ticket, check in at an electronic kiosk, or–even better–check in on your airline's Web site before leaving home. Pack light and limit carry-on items to only the essentials.

ARRIVE WHEN YOU NEED TO. Research your airline's policy. It's usually at least an hour before domestic flights and two to three hours before international flights. But airlines at some busy airports have more stringent requirements. Check the TSA Web site for estimated security waiting times at major airports.

GET TO THE GATE. If you aren't at the gate at least 10 minutes before your flight is scheduled to take off (sometimes earlier), you won't be allowed to board.

DOUBLE-CHECK YOUR FLIGHT TIMES. Do this especially if you reserved far in advance. Schedules change, and alerts may not reach you.

DON'T GO HUNGRY. Ask whether your airline offers anything to eat; even when it does, be prepared to pay.

GET THE SEAT YOU WANT. Often, you can pick a seat when you buy your ticket on an airline Web site. But it's not guaranteed; the airline could change the plane after you book, so double-check. You can also select a seat if you check in electronically. Avoid seats on the aisle directly across from the lavatories. Frequent fliers say those are even worse than back-row seats that don't recline.

GOT KIDS? GET INFO. Ask the airline about its children's menus, activities, and fares. Sometimes infants and toddlers fly free if they sit on a parent's lap, and older children fly for half price in their own seats. Also inquire about policies involving car

seats; having one may limit seating options. Also ask about seat-belt extenders for car seats. And note that you can't count on a flight attendant to produce an extender; you may have to ask for one when you board.

CHECK YOUR SCHEDULING. Don't buy a ticket if there's less than an hour between connecting flights. Although schedules are padded, if anything goes wrong you might miss your connection. If you're traveling to an important function, depart a day early.

BRING PAPER. Even when using an e-ticket, always carry a hard copy of your receipt; you may need it to get your boarding pass, which most airports require to get past security.

COMPLAIN AT THE AIRPORT. If your baggage goes astray or your flight goes awry, complain before leaving the airport. Most carriers require this.

BEWARE OF OVERBOOKED FLIGHTS. If a flight is oversold, the gate agent will usually ask for volunteers and offer some sort of compensation for taking a different flight. If you're bumped from a flight *involuntarily*, the airline must give you some kind of compensation if an alternate flight can't be found within one hour.

KNOW YOUR RIGHTS. If your flight is delayed because of something within the airline's control (bad weather doesn't count), the airline must get you to your destination on the same day, even if they have to book you on another airline and in an upgraded class. Read the Contract of Carriage, which is usually buried on the airline's Web site.

BE PREPARED. The Boy Scout motto is especially important if you're traveling during a stormy season. To quickly adjust your plans, program a few numbers into your cell: your airline, an airport hotel or two, your destination hotel, your car service, and/or your travel agent.

U.S. cities to Heathrow and Gatwick airports outside London, along with flights to Manchester and Birmingham. It offers myriad add-on options that help bring down ticket costs. In addition, it has a vast program of discount airfare-hotel packages. Britain-based Virgin Atlantic is a strong competitor in terms of packages. London is a very popular destination, so many U.S. carriers have flights and packages there, too.

Because Great Britain is such a small country, internal air travel is much less important than it is in the United States. For trips of less than 200 mi, the train is often quicker, with rail stations more centrally located. Flying tends to cost more, but for longer trips—for example, between London and Glasgow or Edinburgh—or where a sea crossing is involved, to places such as the Scottish islands, air travel has a considerable time advantage.

If you intend to fly to Scotland from London, take advantage of the current fare wars on internal routes—notably between London's four airports and Glasgow–Edinburgh. Among the cheapest are Ryanair between London Stansted (with its excellent rail links from London's Liverpool Street Station) and Glasgow Prestwick; easyJet offers bargain fares from London Luton/Gatwick/Stansted (all with good rail links from central London) to Glasgow, Edinburgh, Aberdeen, and Inverness. Even British Airways now offers competitive fares on some flights.

British Airways operates shuttle services between Heathrow or Gatwick and Manchester. Passengers can simply turn up and get a flight (usually hourly) without booking. bmi/British Midland operates from Heathrow to Leeds and Manchester, as well as to Washington, D.C., Chicago, Las Vegas, and major cities in eastern Canada; it also serves Chicago, Las Vegas, and Toronto from Manchester.

Low-cost airlines such as easyJet, bmi baby, and Ryanair offer flights within the United Kingdom as well as to cities in Ireland and continental Europe. Prices are low, but these airlines usually use satellite cities and fly out of smaller British airports such as Stansted and Luton (both near London). On the opposite end of the price spectrum, Maxjet and Eos offer more expensive service (between premium economy and business class) for travelers willing to pay for more comfortable flights.

To & from Great Britain Aer Lingus ☎ 800/474-7424, 0845/084-4444 in London ⊕ www.aerlingus.com to Heathrow, Gatwick. **American Airlines** ☎ 800/433-7300, 020/7365-0777 in London ⊕ www.aa.com to Heathrow, Gatwick, Manchester, Newcastle. **bmi/British Midland** ☎ 800/788-0555, 020/8745-7321 in London ⊕ www.flybmi.com. **British Airways** ☎ 800/247-9297, 0845/773-3377 in London ⊕ www.britishairways.com to Heathrow, Gatwick. **Delta** ☎ 800/241-4141, 0800/414767 in London ⊕ www.delta.com to Gatwick. **Eos** ☎ 888/357-3677, 0800/019-6468 in London ⊕ www.eosairlines.com from New York to London Stansted. **Maxjet** ☎ 888/435-9629, 0800/023-4300 in London ⊕ www.maxjet.com from Washington and New York to London Stansted. **Northwest Airlines** ☎ 800/225-2525, 0870/507-4074 in London ⊕ www.nwa.com to Gatwick. **United** ☎ 800/538-2929, 0845/844-4777 in London ⊕ www.ual.com to Heathrow. **US Airways** ☎ 800/622-1015, 0845/600-3300 in London ⊕ www.usairways.com to Gatwick. **Virgin Atlantic** ☎ 800/862-8621, 01293/747-747 in London ⊕ www.virgin-atlantic.com to Heathrow, Gatwick.

Within Great Britain & to Europe bmi baby ☎ 0870/264-2229 in London ⊕ www.bmibaby.com. **easyJet** ☎ 0870/600-0000 in London ⊕ www.easyjet.com. **Ryanair** ☎ 0870/246-0000 in London ⊕ www.ryanair.com.

▌ BY BOAT

Ferries, hovercraft, and Seacats (a kind of ferry) travel regular routes to France, Spain, Ireland, and Scandinavia.

Hoverspeed provides fast travel to France and Belgium. P&O runs ferries between

Belgium, Great Britain, Ireland, France, the Netherlands, and Spain. DFDS Seaways covers Denmark, Holland, Germany, Norway, Poland, and Sweden. Stena Line serves Ireland and the Netherlands.

For fares and schedules, contact ferry companies directly. Travelers checks (in pounds), cash, and major credit cards are accepted for payments. Prices vary; booking early ensures cheaper fares, but also ask about special deals. The Ferry Information Service can help with questions about routes and overviews of ferry companies. Seaview is a comprehensive online ferry- and cruise-booking portal for Great Britain and Continental Europe.

For information about ferry travel between the Scottish mainland and various islands, *see* the Essentials sections *in* the pertinent chapter.

DFDS Seaways ☎ 01255/240240 or 0870/533-3000 ⊕ www.dfdsseaways.co.uk. **Ferry Information Service** ☎ 020/7436-2449 ⊕ www.ferryinformationservice.co.uk. **Hoverspeed** ☎ 0870/240-8070 ⊕ www.hoverspeed.com. **P&O Irish Sea** ☎ 0870/242-4777 ⊕ www.poirishsea.com. **P&O North Sea** ☎ 0870/129-6002 ⊕ www.ponsf.com. **P&O Portsmouth** ☎ 0870/242-4999 ⊕ www.poportsmouth.com. **P&O Stena Line** ☎ 0870/600-0600 ⊕ www.posl.com. **Seaview** ⊕ www.seaview.co.uk. **Stena Line** ☎ 0870/570-7070 ⊕ www.stenaline.co.uk.

▌BY BUS

Britain has a comprehensive bus (short-haul) and coach (the British term for long-distance buses) network that offers an inexpensive way of seeing the country. National Express is the major coach operator, and Victoria Coach Station in London is the hub of the National Express network, serving around 1,200 destinations within Great Britain and, via Eurolines, continental Europe. Tickets (payable by most major credit cards; reservations are advisable) and information are available from any of the company's 2,500 agents nationwide, including offices at London's Heathrow and Gatwick airport coach stations. Green Line is the next-largest national service; although it serves fewer destinations, airports and major tourist towns are covered. In Scotland, Scottish Citylink runs a similar operation.

A newcomer on the bus travel scene, Megabus has been packing in budget travelers, with special cross-country fares for as little as £1 per person. Its double-decker buses serve cities across Britain. Though relatively new, it has been giving National Express a run for its money with rock-bottom fares, new buses, and a cheerful attitude. Megabus does not accommodate wheelchairs, and the company strictly limits luggage to one checked piece per person, and one piece of hand luggage. In London, the company's buses depart from the Green Line bus stand at Victoria Station.

Coach tickets can be as low as half the price of a train ticket, and buses are just as comfortable as trains. However, most bus services take twice as long as trains. Nearly all bus services have a no-smoking policy, and National Express has onboard refreshments and toilets. There is only one class of service.

Double-decker buses make up many of the extensive networks of local bus services, run by private companies. Check with the local bus station or tourist information center for bus schedules. Most companies offer day or week Explorer or Rover unlimited-travel tickets, and those in popular tourist areas invariably operate special scenic tours in summer. The top deck of a stately double-decker bus is a great place from which to view the countryside.

CUTTING COSTS

National Express offers discount Brit Explorer passes to non-British passport holders. The passes start at £79 for 7 days of travel, and must be bought in person at a Brit Explorer shop—these are scattered around the country including locations at Heathrow Airport and Victoria Station in London. A Discount Coach Card for students, 16–25, and over-50, which costs

£10 and is good for one year, qualifies you for 20% to 30% discounts off many fares. Most companies offer a discount for children under 15. Scottish Citylink offers an Explorer pass in different permutations for travel during three consecutive days, any five days out of ten, or any eight days out of sixteen. Available from Scottish Citylink offices, they cost £39–£85.

Apex tickets (cheap advance-purchase tickets) save money on standard fares, and traveling midweek is cheaper than over weekends and at holiday periods. Tourist Trail Passes, sold by National Express, offer great savings if you plan to tour Britain; they can be bought in advance. Prices run from £49 for 2 days of unlimited travel within 3 days to £205 for 15 days of unlimited travel within two months.

FARES & SCHEDULES

You can find schedules online, pick them up from tourist information offices, or get them by phone from the various bus companies. Fares vary based on how close to the time of travel you book—Megabus tickets, for example, are cheaper if ordered in advance online—so contact the individual companies either online or by phone for ticket prices.

PAYING

Tickets for National Express can be bought from the Victoria, Heathrow, or Gatwick coach stations, or by phone with a credit card, or via the National Express Web site, or from most British travel agencies. Tickets for Megabus must be purchased online in advance, or by phone (avoid this, as the surcharge is at least 60p per minute). Surcharges for tickets bought online in advance rarely rise above £5.

Most companies will accept MasterCard and Visa for advance purchases, but cash only if you're purchasing your tickets on the bus on the day of travel.

RESERVATIONS

There are no surcharges for booking in advance; in fact, it's a much better idea, as busy routes and times can book up quickly.

With most bus companies (National Express, Megabus, Green Line), if you pay in advance your receipt can be e-mailed to you, and your name is placed on a list given to the bus driver, who then checks you off when you arrive. This makes it easy for international travelers who cannot have their tickets mailed to them.

Bus Information Green Line ☎ 0870/608-7261 ⊕ www.greenline.co.uk. **Megabus** ☎ 0900/160-0900 ⊕ www.megabus.com, 60p per minute for calls from landlines in U.K. **National Express** ☎ 0870/580-8080 ⊕ www.nationalexpress.com. **Scottish Citylink** ☎ 08705/505050 ⊕ www.citylink. co.uk. **Victoria Coach Station** ☎ 020/7730-3466 for station, 020/7730-3499 for booking ⊕ www.tfl.gov.uk/vcs.

▋ BY CAR

With about 60 million inhabitants in a country the size of California, and a road system designed in part for horse-drawn carriages, Britain can be a challenging place in which to drive. That's even without considering that people drive on the left side of the road, and the gear shift is on the wrong side entirely. In major cities such as London, Liverpool, Manchester, Glasgow, and Edinburgh, it's best to rely on the comprehensive public transportation network. All those cities suffer from traffic congestion, and learning to drive within their borders is an art.

Outside the cities, a car can be very handy. Many sights are not easily reached without one—castles, for example, are rarely connected to any public transportation system. Small villages might have only one or two buses a day pass through them. If it's the deep countryside you want to see, and you don't feel like doing it on a package tour, consider driving. Away from the towns and cities you can find miles of small, little-used roads and lanes where driving can be a real pleasure. Driving between the tall hedgerows is a truly British experience that you're likely to find as exhilarating as it is (occasionally) scary. Just drive slowly when you need to, watch other drivers, and ignore the impatient honking of the locals. In a few hours, you may well be speeding along like a native.

GASOLINE

Gasoline is called petrol in Britain and is sold by the liter. The price you see posted at a petrol station is the price of a liter, and there are about four liters in a U.S. gallon. Petrol is becoming increasingly expensive; it was more than 90p ($1.60) per liter at press time. This means gas costs the equivalent of close to $7 a gallon. Supermarket pumps just outside the city centers frequently offer the best prices. Unleaded petrol is predominant, denoted by green stickers on fuel pumps and pump lines. Premium and super premium are the two varieties, and most cars run on regular premium. Diesel is prevalent; be sure not to use it by mistake. Along busy motorways, most large stations are open 24 hours a day, seven days a week. In rural areas, hours can vary. Most service stations accept major credit cards, and most are self-service.

PARKING

Parking regulations are strictly enforced everywhere, so look out for signs that display the rules where you're thinking of parking. If there are no signs on a street, it's free to park there. However, be sure there are no signs; many streets have centralized "pay and display" machines, in which you deposit the required money and get a ticket allowing you to park for a set period of time. You display that ticket in your front windshield. In London, parking meters are insatiable—£1 doesn't buy you 15 minutes—and some permit only a two-hour stay. Prices are considerably lower elsewhere, and in small towns you can usually find free parking, or lots that charge a nominal fee, such as £1 a day. In town centers, your best bet is usually to park in a public car lot. Square blue street signs with a white "P" in the center direct you to the nearest lot.

If you park on the street, follow these basic rules: do not park within 15 yards of an intersection. Do not park on double yellow lines or in bus lanes. Park as close to the curb as possible—Britain's narrow streets leave little room for cars to park. On "Red Routes"—busy roads with red lines painted on the street—you cannot park or even stop to let a passenger out of the car.

ROAD CONDITIONS

There's a very good network of highways (motorways) and divided highways (dual carriageways) throughout most of Britain, although in more remote areas (including parts of Wales and Scotland), where unclassified roads join village to village and are little more than glorified agricultural cart tracks, travel is noticeably slower. Motorways (with the prefix *M*), shown in blue on most maps and road signs, are mainly two or three lanes in each direction. Other fast major roads (with the prefix *A*) are shown on maps in green and red. Sections of fast dual carriageway (with black-edged, thick outlines on maps) have both traffic lights and traffic circles, and right turns are sometimes permitted. Turnoffs are often marked by highway numbers, rather than place names, so know the road numbers.

The vast network of lesser roads, for the most part old coach and turnpike roads, might make your trip take twice the time but show you twice as much. Minor roads drawn in yellow or white, the former prefixed by *B*, the latter unlettered and unnumbered, are the ancient lanes and byways, a superb way of discovering the real Britain. Some of these (the white roads, in the main) are pothole-filled switchbacks, littered with blind corners and barely wide enough for one car. Should you take one of these, be prepared to reverse into a passing place if you meet an oncoming car or tractor.

ROAD MAPS

You should purchase maps and atlases in advance from bookstores, or buy them in Britain. Good planning maps are available from Britain's Automobile Association or the Royal Automobile Club. The excellent Ordnance Survey or Collins maps, available from newsstands and bookstores in Britain, cost about £5 for a paper foldout to £7 for a spiral-bound paperback.

In the U.K. **Automobile Association** ☎ 0870/600-0371 ⊕ www.theaa.co.uk. **Royal Automobile Club** ☎ 0800/731-1104 ⊕ www. rac.co.uk.

ROADSIDE EMERGENCIES

If your car breaks down, position the red hazard triangle (which should be in the trunk, or "boot" as it is called) a few paces away from the rear of the car. Leave the hazard warning lights on. On major highways, emergency roadside telephone booths are positioned within walking-distance intervals. Contact your car-rental company (there should be an emergency assistance phone number on the car's paperwork) or call the police for help. You can also call the British Automobile Association toll-free. You can join and receive assistance from the AA on the spot, but the charge (around £75) is higher than a simple membership fee. If you are a member of the AAA (American Automobile Association) or another association, check your membership details before you travel; reciprocal agreements may give you free roadside aid.

Emergency Services **Ambulance, fire, police** ☎ 999. **Automobile Association** ☎ 0800/ 085-2721 ⊕ www.theaa.co.uk.

RULES OF THE ROAD

The most important thing you can do while driving here is to remember to drive on the left. You may find it's easier than you expected, as the steering and mirrors on U.K. cars are designed for driving on the left. You use the side mirrors much more when driving this way, and if you have a standard transmission car, you have to shift gears with your left hand. Left-handed people will be in their element, but righties will have to work a bit. Study your map before leaving the rental car lot, and give yourself plenty of time to adjust. The use of seat belts is obligatory in the front and back seats.

It is illegal to talk on a hand-held cell phone while driving.

If you plan to drive in Britain, pick up a copy of the official Highway Code (£1.50) at a service station, newsstand, or bookstore.

Speed limits are complicated, and there are speed cameras everywhere. Watch your speedometer. The speed limit (shown on circular red signs) is generally 30 mph in towns, 60 mph on two-lane highways, and 70 mph on motorways. At traffic circles (called "roundabouts"), you turn clockwise; you will see signs before the roundabout that indicate where each exiting road is headed. As cars enter the circle, they must yield to those already in the circle. If you're taking an exit all the way around the circle, stay to the center until just before your own exit. If your exit is the first one off the roundabout, stay to the outside and signal that you're taking the first turnoff.

Pedestrians have the right-of-way on "zebra" crossings (black-and-white-stripe crosswalks between two orange-flashing globe lights). If there's a person waiting to cross the street, treat the crossing like a stop sign. The curb on each side of the zebra crossing has zigzag markings. It is illegal to park within zigzag areas or to pass another vehicle at a zebra crossing. At other crossings, pedestrians must yield to traffic, but they do have the right-of-way over traffic turning left—if they dare.

Drunk-driving laws are strictly enforced. The legal limit is 80 milligrams of alcohol, which means roughly two units of alcohol—two glasses of wine, one pint of beer, or one glass of whisky.

▌ BY TRAIN

Operated by private companies, the train system in Britain is extensive and useful, though less than ideal. Some trains are old, and virtually all lines suffer from delays, schedule changes, and occasional crippling strikes. Worst of all, you can pay quite a lot for all of that. Work is under way to improve the situation, but resolution is years away. All major cities and even most small towns are served by trains, and despite the difficulties, rail travel is the most pleasant way to cover long distances. On long-distance runs, some rail lines have buffet cars; on others, you can purchase snacks from a mobile snack cart.

CLASSES

Most rail lines have first-class and second-class cars. In virtually all cases, second class is perfectly comfortable. First class generally has superior seating and tables—but in many cases the only difference between first and second class is the size of the seats, which are marginally larger in first. First class usually costs two to three times the cost of second class, though, so it's usually not worth the cost. However, first class is also usually quieter and less crowded, which can be priceless. Check with National Rail Enquiries for details.

CUTTING COSTS

Whenever possible, purchase your tickets at least two weeks in advance of your journey. Ticket prices are set on a sliding scale. The closer to the time of the journey, the more expensive the tickets. Even a reservation 24 hours in advance can provide a discount. Look into cheap day returns if you plan to travel a round-trip in one day. A single ticket from London to Cardiff, in Wales, can cost you £22 if you purchase it two weeks in advance, or more than £100 if you purchase it on the day you want to travel. Ticket prices are also more expensive during rush hour—so plan to travel after 9:30 AM, and before 4:30 PM or after 6:30 PM.

National Rail Enquiries has information about rail passes such as Rovers, which save you money on individual railroads. Purchasing a BritRail Pass before you leave home may also save you money. *See* Train Passes in Booking Your Trip, *above.*

FARES & SCHEDULES

The best way to find out which train to take, which station to catch it at, and what times trains travel to your destination is to call National Rail Enquiries. This free service covers all the country's rail lines.

If you want more information, the monthly *OAG Rail Guide* (about £7 and available from WH Smith branches and most larger main line rail stations) covers all national rail services and Eurostar, as well as buses, ferries, and rail-based tourist facilities. You can find timetables of rail services in Britain and some ferry services in the *Thomas Cook European Timetable*, issued monthly and available at travel agents and some bookstores in the United States.

PAYING

Cash and credit cards are accepted by all train ticket offices, and over the phone.

RESERVATIONS

Reserving your ticket in advance is always recommended; it will help you save money.

CHANNEL TUNNEL

Short of flying, taking the Channel Tunnel is the fastest way to cross the English Channel: 35 minutes from Folkestone to Calais, 60 minutes from motorway to motorway, or 2 hours and 15 minutes from London's St. Pancras Station to Paris's Gare du Nord. The Belgian border is just a short drive northeast of Calais. High-speed Eurostar trains use the same tunnels to connect London's St. Pancras Station directly with Midi Station in Brussels in around 2 hours. If purchased in advance, round-trip tickets from London to Belgium or France cost around £125.

Channel Tunnel Car Transport Eurotunnel ☏ 0870/535-3535 in the U.K., 070/223210 in Belgium, 03-21-00-61-00 in France ⊕ www. eurotunnel.com. **French Motorail/Rail Europe** ☏ 0870/241-5415 ⊕ www.raileurope.co. uk/frenchmotorail.

Channel Tunnel Passenger Service Eurostar ☏ 0870/518-6186, in the U.K. ⊕ www. eurostar.co.uk. **Rail Europe** ☏ 888/382-7245 in the U.S., 0870/584-8848 in the U.K. inquiries and credit-card bookings ⊕ www. raileurope.com.

Other Information National Rail Enquiries ☏ 0845/748-4950, 020/7278-5240 outside Britain ⊕ www.nationalrail.co.uk.

ON THE GROUND

▌ COMMUNICATIONS

INTERNET

Getting online in British cities isn't difficult: public Internet stations and Internet cafés, some open 24 hours, are becoming more and more common. Even coffee shops may have access points. Prices differ from place to place, so spend some time to find the best deal. Wi-Fi hotspots are often within high-end hotels, major airports and train stations, and Internet cafés. More hotels are upgrading their Internet services and offering ISDN and Wi-Fi. If you use a hotel's in-room modem line, always check modem rates before plugging in. Out in the countryside, your options may well be fewer. You can always check a town's public library if you can't find other access.

If you're traveling with a laptop, carry a spare battery and adapter. If you are going to use dial-up, get a telephone cord that's compatible with a British phone jack; these are widely available in Britain at airports and electronics stores. Never plug your computer into any socket before asking about surge protection. Some hotels do not have built-in current stabilizers, and extreme electrical fluctuations and surges can short your adapter or even destroy your computer. Before connecting your computer to a phone line, you may want to test the line as well. IBM sells an invaluable pen-size modem tester that plugs into a telephone jack to check whether the line is safe to use.

Cybercafes ⊕ www.cybercafes.com lists over 4,000 Internet cafés worldwide.

PHONES

The good news is that you can now make a direct-dial telephone call from virtually any point on earth. The bad news? You can't always do so cheaply. Calling from a hotel is almost always the most expensive option; hotels usually add huge surcharges to all calls, particularly international ones. In some countries you can phone from call centers or even the post office. Calling cards usually keep costs to a minimum, but only if you purchase them locally. And then there are mobile phones (⇨ *below*), which are sometimes more prevalent—particularly in the developing world—than land lines; as expensive as mobile phone calls can be, they are still usually a much cheaper option than calling from your hotel.

British Telecom runs the telephone service in Great Britain and is generally reliable. All calls (including local calls) made within the United Kingdom are charged according to the time of day. The standard rate applies weekdays 8 AM to 6 PM; a cheaper rate is in effect weekdays 6 PM to 8 AM and all day on weekends, when it's even cheaper. A local call before 6 PM costs 15p for three minutes; this doubles to 30p for the same from a pay phone. A daytime call to the United States will cost 24p a minute on a regular phone (weekends are cheaper), 80p on a pay phone.

A word of warning: 0870 numbers are *not* toll-free numbers in Britain; numbers beginning with this or the 0900 (premium rate) prefix cost extra to call. The amount varies—and is usually relatively small when dialed from within the country—but can be excessive when dialed from outside Britain.

The country code for Great Britain is 44. When dialing a British number from abroad, drop the initial 0 from the local area code. For example, let's say you're calling Buckingham Palace—020/7839–1377—from the United States. First, dial 011 (the international access code), then 44 (Great Britain's country code), then 20 (London's center city code—without its initial 0), then the remainder of the telephone number.

CALLING WITHIN BRITAIN

For long-distance calls within Britain, dial the area code (which usually begins with

LOCAL DO'S & TABOOS

Generally speaking, British people are soft-spoken, reserved, and ruthlessly polite. The spontaneity and outspokenness common in the United States can seem jarring in juxtaposition to their often quiet coolness. They also don't smile as much as North Americans, but there is a general consensus in Britain that this tendency to smile is one of the better things about "Yanks," as they call Americans, usually with some affection. Politeness and etiquette are still more ingrained in Britain than in the United States, and being on your best behavior when dealing with locals is always welcome.

Anti-Americanism is an issue throughout much of Europe, and it is possible, albeit unlikely, that Americans might encounter unkind comments about their nationality or government. You may be asked piercing questions about your own political beliefs. There is no right or wrong way to handle this, but do remember that these are sensitive times, and try not to take offense. Be polite and friendly, but if you don't want to talk about politics, say so and then walk away.

If you're visiting a family home, a simple bouquet of flowers is a welcome gift. If you're invited for a meal, bringing a bottle of wine is appropriate, if you wish, as is some candy for the children. In London and other urban centers, European-style kisses on one or two cheeks when meeting a woman friend are common. Elsewhere in the country, a warm handshake is the norm.

Punctuality is of prime importance, so call ahead if you anticipate a late arrival. Spouses do not generally attend business dinners, unless invited. If you invite someone to dine, it's usually assumed that you will pick up the tab. However, if you are the visitor, your host may insist on paying.

The British express gratitude more readily and frequently than Americans or Canadians. When buying a newspaper, for example, they may say "thank you" at least four times: When the shopkeeper takes the items, when he or she takes the money, when change is given, and when the item is bagged and handed to the customer. In most other countries, one "thank you" might cover all of that. Paradoxically, the country is known for service with a scowl—the person working the counter when you buy that newspaper might not say "thank you" once. Poor service is a constant subject of conversation among English residents of major cities, but in the countryside it's virtually unheard of. The person working the store counter might well talk your ear off. Expect to encounter both experiences.

01, except in London), followed by the telephone number. The area code prefix is used only when you are dialing from outside the region. In provincial areas, the dialing codes for nearby towns are often posted in the phone booth. You do not need to dial the area code if you are making a call within the same area code.

Cell phones are very popular, but there are three types of pay phones: those that accept (a) only coins, (b) only British Telecom (BT) phone cards, or (c) BT phone cards and credit cards. The coin-operated phones are of the push-button variety; their workings vary, but there are usually instructions on each unit. Most take 10p, 20p, 50p, and £1 coins. Insert the coins *before* dialing (minimum charge is 20p). If you hear a repeated single tone after dialing, the line is busy; a continual tone means the number is unobtainable (or that you have dialed the wrong—or no—prefix). The indicator panel shows how much money is left; add more whenever you like. If there is no answer, replace the receiver and your money will be returned.

To call the U.K. operator, dial 100. For directory inquiries (information), dial 118500.

CALLING OUTSIDE BRITAIN

For direct overseas dialing from Britain, dial 00, then the country code, area code, and number. For the international operator, credit card, or collect calls, dial 155; for international directory assistance, dial 118505.

The country code for the United States is 1.

Access Codes **AT&T Direct** In the U.K., there are AT&T access numbers to dial the U.S. using three different phone types: ☎ 0500/890011 Cable & Wireless, 0800/890011 British Telecom, 0800/013–0011 AT&T. **MCI World-Phone** ☎ 0800/279–5088 in the U.K. for the U.S. via MCI. **Sprint International Access** ☎ 0800/890877.

CALLING CARDS

Public card phones operate with British Telecom (BT) chip cards that you can buy from post offices or newsstands. They are ideal for longer calls; are composed of units of 20p; and come in values of £3, £5, £10, and £20. To use a card phone, lift the receiver, insert your card, and dial the number. An indicator panel shows the number of units used. At the end of your call, the card will be returned. Where credit cards are taken, slide the card through, as indicated. Beware of buying cards that require you to dial a free phone number; some of these are not legitimate. It's better to get a BT card.

MOBILE PHONES

If you have a multiband phone (some countries use different frequencies than what's used in the United States) and your service provider uses the world-standard GSM network (as do T-Mobile, Cingular, and Verizon), you can probably use your phone abroad. Roaming fees can be steep, however: 99¢ a minute is considered reasonable. And overseas you normally pay the toll charges for incoming calls. It's almost always cheaper to send a text message than

to make a call, since text messages have a very low set fee (often less than 5¢).

If you just want to make local calls, consider buying a new SIM card (note that your provider may have to unlock your phone for you to use a different SIM card) and a prepaid service plan in the destination. You'll then have a local number and can make local calls at local rates. If your trip is extensive, you could also simply buy a new cell phone in your destination, as the initial cost will be offset over time.

■ **TIP** ➔ If you travel internationally frequently, save one of your old mobile phones or buy a cheap one on the Internet; ask your cell phone company to unlock it for you, and take it with you as a travel phone, buying a new SIM card with pay-as-you-go service in each destination.

Rental cell phones are available in cities and towns; check the rate schedule before you rent a cell phone and start to calling. Another option in Britain is to rent a phone through your car-rental company.

Cellular Abroad ☎ 800/287–5072 ⊕ www.cellularabroad.com rents and sells GMS phones and sells SIM cards that work in many countries.

Mobal ☎ 888/888–9162 ⊕ www.mobalrental.com rents mobiles and sells GSM phones (starting at $49) that will operate in 140 countries. Per-call rates vary throughout the world.

Planet Fone ☎ 888/988–4777 ⊕ www.planetfone.com rents cell phones, but the per-minute rates are expensive.

■ CUSTOMS & DUTIES

You're always allowed to bring goods of a certain value back home without having to pay any duty or import tax. But there's a limit on the amount of tobacco and liquor you can bring back duty-free, and some countries have separate limits for perfumes; for exact figures, check with your customs department. The values of so-called "duty-free" goods are included in these amounts. When you shop abroad, save all your receipts, as customs inspectors may ask to see them as well as the items you purchased. If the total value of your goods is more than the duty-free limit, you'll have to pay a tax (most often a flat percentage) on the value of everything beyond that limit.

Fresh meats, plants and vegetables, controlled drugs, and firearms and ammunition may not be brought into the United Kingdom. Pets from the United States or Canada with the proper documentation may be brought into the country without quarantine under the U.K. Pet Travel Scheme (PETS). The process takes about six months to complete and involves detailed steps.

You will face no customs formalities if you enter Scotland or Wales from any other part of the United Kingdom.

Information in Britain HM Customs and Excise ☎ 0208/929–0152, 0845/010–9000 advice service ⊕ www.hmce.gov.uk. **Pet Travel Scheme** ☎ 0870/241–1710 ⊕ www.defra.gov.uk/animalh/quarantine/index.htm.

U.S. Information U.S. Customs and Border Protection ⊕ www.cbp.gov.

▌ EATING OUT

The stereotypical notion of English meals as parades of roast beef, overcooked vegetables, and stodgy puddings (desserts) is gradually being replaced—particularly in London and other major cities—with a more contemporary picture of the country as hot foodie territory. From trendy gastro-pubs to the see-and-be-seen dining shrines, Britain is shedding its tired image and becoming known for a global palate.

The restaurants reviewed in this book are the cream of the crop in each price category. Properties indicated by ✕⌂ are lodging establishments whose restaurants warrant a special trip. Price-category information is given in each chapter. In general, restaurant prices are high. If you're watching your budget, seek out pubs and ethnic restaurants, which offer excellent food at reasonable prices.

CUTTING COSTS

Eating out in Britain's big cities in particular can be an expensive affair, but you can do it cheaply. Try local cafés, often called workers' cafés, where heaping plates of British comfort food (bacon sandwiches and stuffed baked potatoes, for example) are served. Fast-food outlets also offer cheap meals for those on a budget. Britain has plenty of the big names in fast food, as well as smaller places selling sandwiches, fish and chips, burgers, falafel, kebabs, and the like. Check out curry houses; Indian food is very popular throughout the country. Marks & Spencer, Sainsbury's, Tesco, Waitrose, and Budgens are chain supermarkets with outlets throughout the country. They're good choices for groceries, sandwiches, or picnic fixings.

MEALS & MEALTIMES

Cafés serving the traditional English breakfast of eggs, bacon, beans, half a grilled tomato, and strong tea are often the cheapest—and most authentic—places for breakfast. For lighter morning fare (or for real brewed coffee), try the continental-style sandwich bars and coffee shops offering croissants and other pastries.

At lunch, you can grab a sandwich between sights, pop into the local pub, or sit down in a restaurant. Dinner, too, has no set rules, but a three-course meal is standard in most mid-range or high-end restaurants. In cities pre- or post-theater menus, offering two or three courses for a set price, are usually a good value. Note that most pubs do not have any waitstaff and that you are expected to go to the bar, order a beverage and your meal, and inform them of your table number. Also, in cities, many pubs do not serve food after 3 PM, so they're usually a better lunch option than dinner.

On Sunday, for pure Englishness, a traditional roast beef, pork or lamb dinner still tops the list. Its typical accompaniment is Yorkshire pudding—a savory soufflé-like batter of eggs, milk, and flour oven-baked until crisp, then topped with a rich, dark gravy. Shepherd's pie, a classic pub dish, is made with diced or minced lamb and a mashed potato topping, and "bangers and mash" are English sausages with mashed potatoes and onion gravy. In the pubs, you'll also find a ploughman's lunch—crusty bread, English cheese (perhaps cheddar, blue Stilton, crumbly Cheshire, or smooth red Leicester), and pickles. And there's also fish-and-chips, usually made from cod or haddock deep-fried in a crispy batter and served with thick french fries. Take time for afternoon tea—whether with scones (with cream and jam, called a "cream tea") and pastries or just a hot cup of Assam or some other fancy tea, it's still a civilized respite.

You can eat your way around the country seeking out regional specialties. Every region has its own cheese, beer, cake, and candy—from the crumbly, sharp cheeses of the Yorkshire and Derbyshire dales to the hard cheddars of Somerset, the creamy goats' rounds in Wales, and the nutty Cornish yarg. In Devon and Cornwall, look for tooth-tingling fudge and toffee made with clotted cream.

Breakfast is generally served between 7:30 and 9, lunch between noon and 2, dinner or supper between 7:30 and 9:30, sometimes earlier, seldom later except in large cities. These days tea is rarely a proper meal anymore (it was once served between 4:30 at 6), and tea shops are often open all day in touristy areas (they're not found at all in non-touristy places). So you can have a cup and pastry or sandwich whenever you feel you need it. Sunday roasts at pubs last from 11 AM or noon to 3 or 4 PM.

As of 2007, there will be no smoking in pubs, clubs, and restaurants throughout Britain.

Unless otherwise noted, the restaurants listed in this guide are open daily for lunch and dinner.

PAYING

Credit cards are widely accepted in restaurants, but not in pubs, which generally still require cash (although a growing minority are taking plastic). Be sure that you don't double pay a service charge. Many restaurants exclude service charges from the printed menu (which the law obliges them to display outside), then add 10% to 15% to the check, or else stamp SERVICE NOT INCLUDED along the bottom, in which case you should add the 10% to 15% yourself. Just don't pay twice for service—some restaurateurs have been known to add service, but leave the total on the credit-card slip blank. Larger establishments generally accept major credit cards; pubs, small cafés, or ethnic restaurants may be cash-only.

For guidelines on tipping *see* Tipping *below.*

PUBS

A common misconception among visitors to Britain is that pubs are bars. This is not exactly true. Pubs are also gathering places, conversation zones, even restaurants. In many pubs, alcohol is almost an afterthought. Pubs are, generally speaking, where people go to meet their friends and catch up on one another's lives. In small towns, pubs act almost as town halls. Many people in a pub drink soft drinks, tea, or coffee, rather than beer, and hard liquor is usually in short supply. Even if you don't drink alcohol, go to a pub and have an orange juice or a soda, relax and meet the locals. Traditionally pub hours are 11–11, with last orders called about 20 minutes before closing time, but laws have been relaxed recently. Some pubs now stay open until midnight or 1 AM.

Most pubs tend to be child-friendly, but others have restricted hours for children. If a pub serves food, it will generally allow children in during the day with adults. Some pubs are more strict than others, though, and will not admit anyone younger than 18. Some will allow children in during the day, but only until 6 PM. If you're in doubt, ask the bartender. However, that's usually not necessary, since family friendly pubs tend to be packed with kids, parents and all of their accoutrements, so you can just use your common sense. Some even have children's play areas with jungle gyms and toys.

RESERVATIONS & DRESS

Regardless of where you are, it's a good idea to make a reservation if you can. We only mention them specifically when reservations are essential (there's no other way you'll ever get a table) or when they are not accepted. For popular restaurants, book as far ahead as you can (often 30 days), and reconfirm as soon as you arrive. (Large parties should always call ahead to check the reservations policy.) We mention dress only when men are required to wear a jacket or a jacket and tie.

Online reservation services make it easy to book a table before you even leave home. OpenTable covers most states, including 20 major cities, and has limited listings in Canada, Mexico, the United Kingdom, and elsewhere. DinnerBroker has restaurants throughout the United States as well as a few in Canada. Toptable handles restaurants mostly in London and Great Britain.

OpenTable ⊕ www.opentable.com. **Dinner-Broker** ⊕ www.dinnerbroker.com. **Toptable** ⊕ www.toptable.co.uk.

WINES, BEER & SPIRITS

Although hundreds of varieties of beer are brewed around the country, the traditional brew is known as bitter and is not carbonated; it's usually served at room temperature. Fizzy American-style beer is called lager. There are also plenty of other potations: stouts like Guinness and Murphy's are thick, pitch-black brews you'll either love or hate; ciders, made from apples, are an alcoholic drink in Britain (Bulmer's and Strongbow are the names to remember); shandies are a mix of lager and lemon soda; and black-and-tans are a blend of lager and stout named for the distinctive uniforms worn by early-20th-century British troops. Real ales, which have a natural second fermentation in the cask, have a shorter shelf life (so many are brewed locally) but special flavor. Generally the selection and quality of cocktails is higher in a wine bar or café than in a pub. The legal drinking age is 18.

You can order Scotland's most famous beverage—whisky (here, most definitely spelled without an *e*)—at any pub in Scotland. All pubs serve any number of single-malt and blended whiskies.

▌ ELECTRICITY

The electrical current in Great Britain is 240 volts (in line with the rest of Europe), 50 cycles alternating current (AC); wall outlets take three-pin plugs, and shaver sockets take two round, oversize prongs. Blackouts and brownouts are rare and are usually fixed in a few hours. For converters, adapters, and advice, contact the British Airways Travel Shop.

Consider making a small investment in a universal adapter, which has several types of plugs in one lightweight, compact unit. Most laptops and mobile phone chargers are dual voltage (i.e., they operate equally well on 110 and 220 volts), so require only an adapter. These days the same is true of small appliances such as hair dryers. Always check labels and manufacturer instructions to be sure. Don't use 110-volt outlets marked FOR SHAVERS ONLY for high-wattage appliances such as hair-dryers.

British Airways Travel Shop ⊠ 213 Piccadilly, London W1J 9HQ ☎ 0845/606-0747. **Steve Kropla's Help for World Traveler's** ⊕ www.kropla.com has information on electrical and

---

WORD OF MOUTH

Was the service stellar or not up to snuff? Did the food give you shivers of delight or leave you cold? Did the prices and portions make you happy or sad? Rate restaurants and write your own reviews in Travel Ratings or start a discussion about your favorite places in Travel Talk on www.fodors.com. Your comments might even appear in our books. Yes, you, too, can be a correspondent!

telephone plugs around the world. **Walkabout Travel Gear** ⊕ www.walkabouttravelgear.com has a good coverage of electricity under "adapters."

▌ EMERGENCIES

If you need to report an emergency, dial 999 for police, fire, or ambulance. Be prepared to give the telephone number you're calling from. National Health Service hospitals give free, 24-hour treatment in Accident and Emergency sections, although delays can be an hour or more. Prescriptions are valid only if made out by doctors registered in the U.K. For additional information, *see* the Essentials sections at the end of each chapter.

Foreign Embassies American Embassy ✉ 24 Grosvenor Sq., London W1 ☎ 020/7499–9000 ⊕ www.usembassy.org.uk; for passports, go to the **U.S. Passport Unit** ✉ 55 Upper Brook St., London W1 ☎ 020/7499–9000.

General Emergency Contacts Ambulance, fire, police ☎ 999.

▌ HEALTH

SPECIFIC ISSUES IN GREAT BRITAIN

If you take prescription drugs, keep a supply in your carry-on luggage and make a list of all your prescriptions to keep on file at home while you are abroad. You will not be able to renew a U.S. prescription at a pharmacy in Britain. Prescriptions are accepted only if issued by a U.K.-registered physician.

If you are traveling in the Scottish Highlands and islands in summer, pack some midge repellent and antihistamine cream to reduce swelling: the Highland midge is a force to be reckoned with.

▌ HOURS OF OPERATION

Most banks are open weekdays from 9:30 until 3:30 or 4:30. Some have Thursday evening hours, and a few are open Saturday morning. Many offices are open week-

days 9:30–5:30. *See* Mail, *below* below for post-office hours.

Most gas stations (called petrol stations) in major cities and towns and on busy motorways are open seven days, 24 hours. In small towns or out in the countryside and off the motorways, hours vary considerably but are usually daily 8 AM to 8 PM.

The major national museums and galleries are open daily from 9 until 6, including lunchtime, but have shorter hours on Sunday. Regional museums are usually closed Monday and have shorter hours in winter. In London, many museums are open late one evening a week, usually Wednesday or Thursday.

British pharmacies are called chemists. Independent chemist shops are generally open Monday through Saturday 9:30 to 5:30, although in larger cities some stay open until 10 PM; local newspapers list which pharmacies are open late. In London, the leading chain drugstore, Boots, is open until 6; the Oxford Street and Piccadilly Circus branches are open daily, and until 8 PM Thursday.

Usual business hours are Monday through Saturday 9 to 5:30, Sunday noon to 4. Outside the main centers, most shops close at 1 PM once a week, often Wednesday or Thursday. In small villages, many also close for lunch and do not open on Sunday at all. In large cities—especially London—department stores stay open late (usually until 7:30 or 8) one night a week, usually Thursday. On national holidays, most stores are closed, and over the Christmas holidays, most restaurants are closed as well (⇨ Holidays, *below*).

HOLIDAYS

Holidays are January 1, New Year's Day; Good Friday and Easter Monday; May Day (first Monday in May); spring and summer bank holidays (last Monday in May and August, respectively); December 25, Christmas Day; and December 26, Boxing Day (day after Christmas). If any of these holidays falls on a weekend, then the holiday is observed on the following Monday. During the Christmas holidays, many restaurants, as well as museums and other attractions, may close for at least a week—call to verify hours. Book hotels for Christmas travel well in advance, and check whether the hotel restaurant will be open.

Scots take the take after New Year's as a holiday, to nurse the residual effects of Hogmanay, as New Year's Eve is known there. Easter Monday is not a holiday in Scotland.

▌MAIL

Stamps may be bought from post offices (open weekdays 9 to 5:30, Saturday 9 to noon), from stamp machines outside post offices, and from news dealers' stores and newsstands. Mailboxes, known as post or letter boxes, are painted bright red; large tubular ones are set on the edge of sidewalks, and smaller boxes are set into post-office walls. Allow seven days for a letter to reach the United States by airmail. Surface mail service can take up to four or five weeks. The useful Royal Mail Web site has information on everything from buying stamps to finding a post office.

Airmail letters up to 10 grams to North America cost 47p; postcards, 42p. Letters within Britain are 30p for first-class, 20p for second-class. Always check rates before sending mail, because they are subject to change.

If you're uncertain where you'll be staying, arrange to have your mail sent to American Express. The service is free to cardholders and traveler's check holders; all others pay a small fee. You can also collect letters at any main or sub post office throughout Britain, so mail can reach you while you are traveling. Ask the sender to mark the envelope POSTE RESTANTE or TO BE CALLED FOR. The letter must be marked with the recipient's full name (as it appears on your passport), and you'll need your passport or another official form of identification for collection.

Royal Mail ⊕ www.royalmail.com.

SHIPPING PACKAGES

Most department stores and retail outlets can arrange to ship your goods back home. You should check your insurance for coverage of possible damage. If you want to ship goods yourself, use an overnight postal service, such as Federal Express, DHL, or Parcelforce. Shipping to the United States can take anywhere from overnight to a month, depending on how much you pay.

Contact the services listed below for information about the nearest office or package drop-off point.

Express Services DHL ☎ 0870/110-0300 ⊕ www.dhl.co.uk. **Federal Express** ☎ 0800/ 123800 ⊕ www.fedex.com. **Parcelforce** ☎ 0870/850-1150 ⊕ www.parcelforce.co.uk.

▌MONEY

Prices in Britain are generally high, largely because the exchange rate is so unfavorable for other currencies, particularly the U.S. dollar. Prices are higher in London than elsewhere in the country, to the point where "London prices" is used as a warning in rural areas (as in "You wouldn't want to go there, they charge London prices"). A cup of coffee will run from 60p to £3, depending on where you buy it; a pint of beer is about £2.25 in the countryside and £3 in a city, and a ham sandwich costs £2.25–£3.50. A short taxi ride averages £8.

Prices throughout this guide are given for adults. Substantially reduced fees are almost always available for children, students, and senior citizens.

▌ TIP➡ Banks never have every foreign currency on hand, and it may take as long as a week to order. If you're planning to exchange funds before leaving home, don't wait till the last minute.

ATMS & BANKS

Your own bank will probably charge a fee for using ATMs abroad; the foreign bank you use may also charge a fee. Nevertheless, you'll usually get a better rate of exchange at an ATM than you will at a currency-exchange office or even when changing money in a bank. And extracting funds as you need them is a safer option than carrying around a large amount of cash.

Make sure before leaving home that your credit and debit cards have been programmed for ATM use abroad—ATMs in Britain accept PINs of four or fewer digits only; if your PIN is longer, ask about changing it. If you know your PIN as a word, learn the numerical equivalent, since most keypads in Britain show numbers only, not letters. Most ATMs are on both the Cirrus and Plus networks.

ATMs are widely available throughout Britain and are the easiest way to get pounds. Look for them at most mainstreet banks, at large supermarkets, such as Sainsbury's and Tesco's, some tube stops in London, and many rail stations. Major banks include Barclays, HSBC, and NatWest.

CREDIT CARDS

Credit cards are widely accepted throughout Britain, but they are not accepted at all establishments, and some places require a minimum expenditure. If you plan to pay with a card in a small hotel, store, or restaurant, make your intentions known early on. The Discover card is not accepted in Britain.

Throughout this guide, the following abbreviations are used: **AE,** American Express; **DC,** Diners Club; **MC,** MasterCard; and **V,** Visa.

It's a good idea to inform your credit-card company before you travel, especially if you're going abroad and don't travel internationally very often. Otherwise, the credit-card company might put a hold on your card owing to unusual activity—not a good thing halfway through your trip. Record all your credit-card numbers—as well as the phone numbers to call if your cards are lost or stolen—in a safe place, so you're prepared should something go wrong. Both MasterCard and Visa have general numbers you can call

(collect if you're abroad) if your card is lost, but you're better off calling the number of your issuing bank, since MasterCard and Visa usually just transfer you to your bank; your bank's number is usually printed on your card.

If you plan to use your credit card for cash advances, you'll need to apply for a PIN at least two weeks before your trip. Although it's usually cheaper (and safer) to use a credit card abroad for large purchases (so you can cancel payments or be reimbursed if there's a problem), note that some credit-card companies *and* the banks that issue them add substantial percentages to all foreign transactions, whether they're in a foreign currency or not. Check on these fees before leaving home, so there won't be any surprises when you get the bill.

▨ TIP➔ **Before you charge something, ask the merchant whether or not he or she plans to do a dynamic currency conversion (DCC). In such a transaction the credit-card *processor* (shop, restaurant, or hotel, not Visa or MasterCard) converts the currency and charges you in dollars. In most cases you'll pay the merchant a 3% fee for this service in addition to any credit-card company and issuing-bank foreign-transaction surcharges.**

Dynamic currency conversion programs are becoming increasingly widespread. Merchants who participate in them are supposed to ask whether you want to be charged in dollars or the local currency, but they don't always do so. And even if they do offer you a choice, they may well avoid mentioning the additional surcharges. The good news is that you *do* have a choice. And if this practice really gets your goat, you can avoid it entirely thanks to American Express; with its cards, DCC simply isn't an option.

Reporting Lost Cards American Express ☎ 800/992-3404 in the U.S. or 336/393-1111 collect from abroad ⊕ www.americanexpress. com. **Diners Club** ☎ 800/234-6377 in the U.S. or 303/799-1504 collect from abroad ⊕ www.dinersclub.com. **MasterCard** ☎ 800/ 622-7747 in the U.S. or 636/722-7111 collect from abroad ⊕ www.mastercard.com. **Visa**

☎ 800/847-2911 in the U.S. or 410/581-9994 collect from abroad ⊕ www.visa.com.

CURRENCY & EXCHANGE

The unit of currency in Britain is the pound sterling (£), divided into 100 pence (p). The bills (called notes in Britain) are 50, 20, 10, and 5 pounds. Scotland and the Channel Islands have their own bills, and the Channel Islands their own coins, too. Scottish bills are accepted in the rest of Britain, but you cannot use Channel Islands currency outside the islands. Coins are £2, £1, 50p, 20p, 10p, 5p, 2p, and 1p.

At the time of this writing, the exchange rate was about U.S. $1.96 to the pound.

British post offices exchange currency with no fee, and at decent rates.

WORST-CASE SCENARIO

All your money and credit cards have just been stolen. In these days of real-time transactions, this isn't a predicament that should destroy your vacation. First, report the theft of the credit cards. Then get any traveler's checks you were carrying replaced. This can usually be done almost immediately, provided that you kept a record of the serial numbers separate from the checks themselves. If you bank at a large international bank like Citibank or HSBC, go to the closest branch; if you know your account number, chances are you can get a new ATM card and withdraw money right away. **Western Union** (☎ 800/325-6000 ⊕ www.westernunion. com) sends money almost anywhere. Have someone back home order a transfer online, over the phone, or at one of the company's offices, which is the cheapest option. The U.S. State Department's **Overseas Citizens Services** (☎ 202/647-5225) can wire money to any U.S. consulate or embassy abroad for a fee of $30. Just have someone back home wire money or send a money order or cashier's check to the state department, which will then disburse the funds as soon as the next working day after it receives them.

■ TIP→ Even if a currency-exchange booth has a sign promising no commission, rest assured that there's some kind of huge, hidden fee. (Oh . . . that's right. The sign didn't say no *fee*.) And as for rates, you're almost always better off getting foreign currency at an ATM or exchanging money at a bank.

TRAVELER'S CHECKS & CARDS

Some consider this the currency of the cave man, and it's true that fewer establishments accept traveler's checks these days. Nevertheless, they're a cheap and secure way to carry extra money, particularly on trips to urban areas. Both Citibank (under the Visa brand) and American Express issue traveler's checks in the United States, but Amex is better known and more widely accepted; you can also avoid hefty surcharges by cashing Amex checks at Amex offices. Whatever you do, keep track of all the serial numbers in case the checks are lost or stolen.

Taking traveler's checks to Britain can be more trouble than not; they are not accepted in many establishments. It's a better idea to use an ATM card to get cash. Remember to buy the traveler's checks in British pounds if you do buy them.

American Express now offers a stored-value card called a Travelers Cheque Card, which you can use wherever American Express credit cards are accepted, including ATMs. The card can carry a minimum of $300 and a maximum of $2,700, and it's a very safe way to carry your funds. Although you can get replacement funds in 24 hours if your card is lost or stolen, it doesn't really strike us as a very good deal. In addition to a high initial cost ($14.95 to set up the card, plus $5 each time you "reload"), you still have to pay a 2% fee for each purchase in a foreign currency (similar to that of any credit card). Further, each time you use the card in an ATM you pay a transaction fee of $2.50 on top of the 2% transaction fee for the conversion—add it all up and it can be considerably more than you would pay when simply using your own ATM card.

Regular traveler's checks are just as secure and cost less.

American Express ☎ 888/412-6945 in the U.S., 801/945-9450 collect outside of the U.S. to add value or speak to customer service ⊕ www.americanexpress.com.

▌ RESTROOMS

Public restrooms are sparse in Britain. Most big cities maintain public facilities that are clean and modern. If there is an attendant, which is rare, you are expected to pay admission (usually 30p). Rail stations and department stores have public restrooms that occasionally charge a small fee, usually 20p. Most pubs, restaurants, and even fast-food chains reserve their bathrooms for customer use only. Hotels and museums are usually a good place to find clean, free facilities. Some upscale London establishments have attendants who expect a small tip—about £1. On the road, gas-station facilities are usually clean and free.

Find a Loo The Bathroom Diaries ⊕ www. thebathroomdiaries.com is flush with unsanitized info on restrooms the world over—each one located, reviewed, and rated.

▌ SAFETY

Britain has a low incidence of violent crime. However, petty crime is on the rise, and tourists can be the target, although this problem is limited almost exclusively to city centers such as London and Liverpool.

When in a city center, if you're paying at a shop or a restaurant, never put your wallet down or let your bag out of your hand. When sitting on a chair in a public place, keep your purse on your lap. Always use the bag hooks in public toilet stalls instead of putting your bag on the floor where it may be snatched.

Don't wear expensive jewelry or watches, as they are easily lifted. Store your passport in the hotel safe; use your driver's license for identification. Don't leave anything in your car—take valuables with you and put everything else, even a coat, out of sight in your trunk.

Over the years there have been terrorist incidents in Britain and Northern Ireland, and although U.S. citizens are not targeted, some have been injured. In July 2005, a few days after London won the bid for the 2012 Olympics, bombs exploded in three tube (subway) stations and on one bus. Bomb threats are taken seriously. Don't leave any bags unattended, as they may be viewed as a security risk and taken away by the authorities. If you see any unattended bags on the train or tube, find a worker and report it. Never hesitate to get off of a tube, train, or bus if you feel unsafe or uncomfortable.

Women are unlikely to be harassed, but the usual precautions apply—be vigilant if walking alone at night and avoid dimly lighted or deserted areas. Avoid unlicensed minicabs.

Although scams do occur in Britain, they are not pervasive. Do, however, watch out for pickpockets, particularly in London and other large cities. They often work in pairs, with one distracting you in some way (asking for directions or bumping into you) while the other takes your valuables. Always take a licensed black taxi or call a car service (sometimes called minicabs) recommended by your hotel. Passengers have been robbed or overcharged by unlicensed drivers in fake cabs. Avoid using minicab services offered by drivers on the street. In most cases, they will drive an indirect route and overcharge you. Always buy theater tickets from a reputable dealer. If you are driving in from a British port, beware of thieves posing as fake customs officials. The thieves stop travelers after they have followed them away from the port. Then they flag them down and "confiscate illegal goods."

When withdrawing cash from an ATM, be sure to cover the number pad with one hand while inputting your PIN. Also, if you're getting money out of an ATM, beware of someone bumping into you to distract you. If anybody claims you've dropped money while getting cash from a machine, ignore him or her. This is a common distraction scam for a pickpocket. You may want to use ATMs inside banks rather than those outside them. In London, scams are most common at ATMs on Oxford Street and around Piccadilly Circus.

■ TIP→ Distribute your cash, credit cards, I.D.s, and other valuables between a deep front pocket, an inside jacket or vest pocket, and a hidden money pouch. Don't reach for the money pouch once you're in public.

■ SPORTS & THE OUTDOORS

In addition to the associations listed below, VisitBritain and local Tourist Information Centres can recommend places to enjoy your favorite sport.

BIKING

Bikes are banned from freeways and most divided highways or main trunk roads, but on side roads and country lanes, the bike is one of the best ways to explore Britain. The National Cycle Network covers about 7,000 mi of cycling and walking routes. Cyclists can legally use public bridleways—green, unsurfaced tracks reserved for horses, walkers, and cyclists. Some former railway lines have become popular bike paths, too. Bikes, from racing to mountain, are usually available for rental, and prices vary by area, anywhere from £3 to £5 an hour to £7–£20 for a full day. A deposit of £25 or more is often required.

Sustrans (a nonprofit organization concerned with sustainable transportation) and the Cyclists' Touring Club (CTC, a national organization) can provide route guides and information on cycling in England. Call tourist information offices for lists of local rental outlets.

Cyclists' Touring Club ☎ 0870/873-0060 ⊕ www.ctc.org.uk. **Landranger by Ordnance Survey** ☎ 08456/050505 ⊕ www. ordnancesurvey.co.uk. **National Cycle Network (Sustrans)** ☎ 0117/926-8893 ⊕ www.

sustrans.org.uk. **Stanfords** ⊠ 12–14 Long Acre, London WC2E 9LP ☎ 020/7836-1321 ⊕ www.stanfords.co.uk.

BOATING

Boating can be a leisurely way to explore the countryside. For boat-rental operators along Britain's several hundred miles of historic canals and waterways, contact the Association of Pleasure Craft Operators or Waterway Holidays UK. British Waterways has maps and other information. Waterway Holidays UK arranges boat accommodations of all kinds, from traditional narrow boats (small, slender barges) to motorboats and sailboats.

Association of Pleasure Craft Operators ☎ 01952/813572. **British Waterways** ☎ 01923/201120 ⊕ www.waterscape.com. **Waterway Holidays UK** ☎ 0870/241-5956 ⊕ www.waterwayholidaysuk.com.

GOLF

Originally invented in Scotland, golf is a beloved pastime all over Britain. Some courses take advantage of spectacular natural settings, from the ocean to mountain backdrops. Most courses are reserved for club members and adhere to strict rules of protocol and dress. However, many famous courses can be used by visiting golfers if they reserve well in advance. Package tours with companies such as Golf International and Owenoak International Golf Travel allow visitors into usually exclusive clubs. VisitBritain has a "Golf in Britain" map and brochure that covers 147 courses; VisitScotland has ample information on its Web site. For further information on courses, fees, and locations, try the Web sites UK Golf Guide and Golfcourses.org. **Golf Courses** ⊕ www.golfcourses.org. **Golf International** ☎ 212/986-9176, 800/833-1389 in U.S. ⊕ www.golfinternational.com. **Owenoak International Golf Travel** ☎ 203/854-9000, 800/426-4498 in U.S. ⊕ www.owenoak.com. **UK Golf Guide** ⊕ www.uk-golfguide.com.

WALKING

Walking and hiking, from the slowest ramble to a mountainside climb requiring technical equipment, are enormously popular in Britain. Chapters in this book contain information about a number of long-distance paths; www.nationaltrail.co.uk has information about stunning National Trails. The Ramblers' Association publishes a magazine and a yearbook full of resources, and a list of B&Bs within 2 mi of selected long-distance footpaths. **Countryside Commission** ☎ 01242/521381 ⊕ www.countryside.gov.uk and www.nationaltrail.co.uk. **Long Distance Walkers Association** ☎ 01753/866685 ⊕ www.ldwa.org.uk. **The Ramblers' Association** ☎ 020/7339-8500 ⊕ www.ramblers.org.uk.

▌ TAXES

An airport departure tax of £20 (£10 for travel within U.K. and EU countries) per person is included in the price of your ticket.

The British sales tax (V.A.T., Value Added Tax) is 17.5%. The tax is almost always included in quoted prices in shops, hotels, and restaurants. The most common exception is at high-end hotels, where prices often exclude V.A.T. Be sure to verify whether the room price includes V.A.T. Outside of hotels and rental car agencies, which have specific additional taxes, there is no other sales tax in Britain.

Most travelers can get a V.A.T. refund by either the Retail Export or the more cumbersome Direct Export method. Refunds apply for V.A.T. only on goods being taken out of Britain, and purchases must exceed a minimum limit (check with the store—generally £50–£100). Many large stores provide V.A.T.-refund services, but only if you request them; they will handle the paperwork. For the Retail Export method, you must ask the store to complete Form V.A.T. 407 (you must have identification—passports are best), to be given to customs at your last port of departure. Have the form stamped like any customs form by

customs officials when you leave the country or, if you're visiting several European Union countries, when you leave the EU. Be ready to show customs officials what you've bought; budget extra time at the airport for this. After you're through passport control, take the form to a refund-service counter for an on-the-spot refund (if the retailer has an agreement with the firm running the counter; ask the store when you make your purchase), or mail it back to the store or a refund service from the airport or after you arrive home. The refund will be forwarded to you in about eight weeks, minus a service charge, either in the form of a credit to your charge card or as a British check, which American banks charge you to convert.

With the Direct Export method, the goods are mailed directly to your home; you must have a Form V.A.T. 407 certified by customs, police, or a notary public when you get home and then sent back to the store, which will refund your money. For inquiries, call the local Customs & Excise office listed in the telephone directory. Remember, V.A.T. refunds can't be processed after you arrive back home.

A service also processes refunds for most shops. You receive the total refund stated on the form. Global Refund is a Europe-wide service with 225,000 affiliated stores and more than 700 refund counters at major airports and border crossings. Its refund form, called a Tax Free Check, is the most common across the European continent. The service issues refunds in the form of cash, check, or credit-card adjustment. **V.A.T. Refunds Global Refund** ☎ 800/566-9828 ⊕ www.globalrefund.com. **Her Majesty's Customs & Excise office** ☎ 0845/010-9000 within U.K., 208/929-0152 from outside U.K. ⊕ http://customs.hmrc.gov.uk.

▌ TIME

Britain sets its clocks by Greenwich Mean Time, five hours ahead of the U.S. East Coast. British summer time generally coincides with American daylight savings time adjustments.

EFFECTIVE COMPLAINING

Things don't always go right when you're traveling, and when you encounter a problem or service that isn't up to snuff, you should complain. But there are good and bad ways to do so.

TAKE A DEEP BREATH. This is always a good strategy, especially when you are aggravated about something. Just inhale, and exhale, and remember that you're on vacation.

COMPLAIN IN PERSON WHEN IT'S SERIOUS. In a hotel, serious problems are usually better dealt with in person, at the front desk; if it's something quick, you can phone.

COMPLAIN EARLY RATHER THAN LATE. Whenever you don't get what you paid for (the type of hotel room you booked or the airline seat you pre-reserved) or when it's something timely (the people next door are making too much noise), try to resolve the problem sooner rather than later.

BE WILLING TO ESCALATE, BUT DON'T BE HASTY. Try to deal with the person at the front desk of your hotel or with your waiter in a restaurant before asking to speak to a supervisor or manager.

SAY WHAT YOU WANT, AND BE REASONABLE. When things fall apart, be clear about what kind of compensation you expect. Don't leave it to the hotel or restaurant or airline to suggest what they're willing to do for you. That said, the compensation you request must be in line with the problem.

CHOOSE YOUR BATTLES. You're more likely to get what you want if you limit your complaints to one or two specific things that really matter rather than a litany of wrongs.

DON'T BE OBNOXIOUS. There's nothing that will stop your progress dead in its tracks as readily as an insistent "Don't you know who I am?" or "So what are you going to do about it?"

NICE COUNTS. This doesn't mean you shouldn't be clear that you are displeased. Passive isn't good, either.

DO IT IN WRITING. If you discover a billing error or some other problem after the fact, write a concise letter to the appropriate customer-service representative.

▌ TIPPING

Some restaurants, bars, and most hotels add a service charge of 10%–15% to the bill. In this case, you are not obliged to tip extra. If no service charge is indicated, add 10% to 15% to your total bill. Beware when signing credit-card slips that you fill in the correct total; some restaurants leave the gratuity entry empty even when they have levied a service charge. There's no need to tip at clubs (it's acceptable at posher establishments, though) unless you're being served at your table. Taxi drivers should also get 10%–15%. If you get help from a hotel concierge, a tip of £2 (£5 or more for a major service) is appropriate. You are not expected to tip theater or cinema ushers, elevator operators, or bartenders in pubs. Hairdressers and barbers should receive 10%–15%.

INDEX

PHOTO CREDITS

NOTES

NOTES

NOTES

ABOUT OUR WRITERS

Longtime contributor Robert Andrews loves warm beer and soggy moors, but hates shopping malls and the sort of weather when you're not sure if it's raining—all of which he found in abundance while updating the South, West Country, and Cotswolds & Shakespeare Country chapters. He writes and revises other guidebooks and has penned his own guide to Devon and Cornwall.

A native New Yorker, Ferne Arfin has been living in London for more than 20 years. A contributor to the *Sunday Telegraph* and Fodor's Travel Wire, she updated London Shopping—perfect work for a Chelsea shophound.

Nick Bruno is a freelance writer, photographer, and English-Italian translator living in Dundee. He contributes to many publications, including *Moon Metro*, AA Guides, and *Time Out*. He worked with Shona Main on Scotland chapters that covered territory from Edinburgh to the Isle of Skye.

Texan by birth and Anglophile at heart, Christi Daugherty now lives in London, where she works as a freelance writer and editor. Her Fodor's territory included Where to Stay in London, as well as chapters on areas from the Southeast to Yorkshire. She has written and edited guidebooks to several cities.

Londoner Adam Gold is passionate about dispensing advice on where to grab a glorious pub lunch. Fittingly, he updated London Nightlife and the Pubs sections of the London chapter. He writes and edits for national newspapers and magazines.

Julius Honnor lives in London, but his Fodor's beat included rural spots in the Lake District and East Anglia, where he made many great discoveries. His work for other guidebooks has taken him to Italy and other places around the globe.

Writer and editor Kate Hughes acquired a liking for the big city when she studied classical literature in Liverpool. Having since indulged her penchant for the country and landed gentry by getting a master's in garden history, she feels qualified to pass judgment on matters both urban and rural. She is responsible for the Northwest chapter.

Shona Main, who lives in Dundee, writes about travel, culture, and social affairs for such publications as the *Press and Journal*, the *Herald*, and the *Sunday Post Magazine*. When she's not keeping tabs on Scotland's busy arts, shopping, and dining scenes, she travels to Italy. Her territory extended from Edinburgh to the Northern Highlands.

Fiona G. Parrott comes from California but has lived in Scotland since 1999. A freelance writer, she contributes to magazines on both sides of the Atlantic. When she's not spending time with her Scottish husband and son, or writing and traveling, she's teaching at Glasgow and Strathclyde universities. She updated the Glasgow, Borders & the Southwest, and Argyll & the Isles chapters.

Always hoping to entertain—and surprise—his readers, Fodor's contributor Roger Thomas spends almost every minute tracking down the latest and the best of Wales. He has to: he's editor of *A View of Wales* magazine.

A Londoner born and bred, Alex Wijeratna updated the London Where to Eat section. With his English/Sri Lankan roots, Alex knows that the real flavor of London is found in its ethnic diversity. He has written for newspapers including the *Daily Mail* and the *Times*.